CONTEMPORARY
advertising
and Integrated Marketing Communications

CONTEMPORARY
advertising
and Integrated Marketing Communications

sixteenth edition

William F. Arens
Michael F. Weigold

CONTEMPORARY ADVERTISING, SIXTEENTH EDITION

1 2 3 4 5 6 7 8 9 LWI 24 23 22 21 20

ISBN 978-1-260-25930-8 (bound edition)
MHID 1-260-25930-7 (bound edition)
ISBN 978-1-264-02071-3 (loose-leaf edition)
MHID 1-264-02071-6 (loose-leaf edition)

Portfolio Manager: *Meredith Fossel*
Senior Product Developer: *Anne Leung*
Marketing Manager: *Nicole Young*
Senior Project Manager, Core Content: *Kathryn D. Wright*
Senior Project Manager, Assessment Content: *Keri Johnson*
Project Manager, Media Content: *Karen Jozefowicz*
Senior Buyer: *Laura Fuller*
Senior Designer: *Debra Kubiak*
Senior Content Licensing Specialists: *Ann Marie Jannette and Jacob Sullivan*
Cover Image: *McGraw-Hill Education*
Compositor: *Aptara®, Inc.*

Library of Congress Cataloging-in-Publication Data

Names: Arens, William F., author. | Weigold, Michael F., 1958- author.
Title: Contemporary advertising and integrated marketing communications /
    William F. Arens, Michael F. Weigold.
Description: Sixteenth edition. | New York, NY : McGraw-Hill Education,
    [2021] | Includes index.
Identifiers: LCCN 2019041920 (print) | LCCN 2019041921 (ebook) | ISBN
    9781260259308 (hardcover) | ISBN 9781264020713 (spiral bound) | ISBN
    9781260735352 (ebook) | ISBN 9781260735413 (ebook other)
Subjects: LCSH: Advertising.
Classification: LCC HF5821 .B62 2021 (print) | LCC HF5821 (ebook) | DDC
    659.1—dc23
LC record available at https://lccn.loc.gov/2019041920
LC ebook record available at https://lccn.loc.gov/2019041921

To Debbie

My partner in everything
MFW

the preface

What's New?

Quite a lot. The 16th edition of *Contemporary Advertising and Integrated Marketing Communications* represents a larger overhaul than executed for many recent editions. The rate of change in the advertising and IMC world has accelerated, and the book's changes are meant to keep pace.

We provide a chapter-by-chapter breakdown of what is new for our returning adopters later in this introduction. But here we introduce our biggest changes to the book: the addition of significantly more information about digital media throughout the text and the fuller realization of the book itself as a digital product, incorporating McGraw-Hill's latest digital learning technologies such as SmartBook and Connect.

Two editions ago we introduced a social media chapter. With hindsight, it is clear that changes in the industry and in consumer behavior justify that decision. By one estimate there are over 3 billion active social media users in the world, a penetration of 42 percent of the global population. Even with saturation in North America (88% penetration) and Europe (94%), billions of people living in Africa, Central and Eastern Asia, and South America will be joining social communities over the next five years. In response, the CMO Survey conducted by Deloitte, Duke's Fuqua School of Business, and the American Marketing Association suggests that the portion of marketing budgets spent on social (currently 9.8%) will nearly double in the next five years.

There have been other big changes since the last edition, perhaps none bigger than the growing attention to consumer privacy and data protection. After disclosures about the collection, without consent, of millions of Facebook users' personal information by Cambridge Analytica, Congress and the American people reached what some have called a watershed moment. The incident and its aftermath are included in the book's opening vignette.

Another important change to this edition is the expansion of each chapter's coverage of ethics to a broader focus on ethics, diversity, and inclusion. Advertising has made strides in diversifying both its ranks and its messages, in part because America's marketplaces and work spaces are more diverse than ever. Even so, much work remains for an industry that has not always led on the issue. My hope is that a deeper focus on diversity will reinforce valuing and practicing inclusion as an important learning outcome of your course.

Digital disruption continues to roil industries that include cable companies, newspapers and magazines, film and television production studios, broadcast networks, and advertising agencies. Cable, a major disrupter in an earlier time, is now in decline, and pay services such as Hulu and Netflix are standard ways that consumers watch "TV." The fact that many streaming services are advertising-free poses a new challenge for marketers who've long been able to count on network and cable television's power and reach.

One "victim" of disruption has been traditional production methods in print, audio, and video. William Arens created a uniquely elegant chapter that focused on production techniques used for decades in traditional media. This focus was unique among IMC texts and distinguished the book in an important way from its competitors. However, digital production methods have largely reduced or even eliminated traditional methods. As a result, Chapter 12 from the 15th edition, titled *Print, Electronic, and Digital Media Production,* has been eliminated. Instead, information on production is now included in the relevant media chapters. With this change, the text returns to a total of 18 chapters, its length prior to the introduction of the social media chapter.

Texts are part of the digital disruption too. Backed by McGraw-Hill's Connect and SmartBook technologies, instructors can do more than introduce and reinforce the concepts of IMC. Rather, with these platforms, instructors can help students gain mastery of what they are learning through application. Created by the authors of the text, Connect and SmartBook bring advertising and IMC practice alive and help ensure retention of learning objectives from the text. Instructors can assign activities that include case studies, video cases, and concept reinforcement. The experience is completely customizable, so that instructors can use as much or as little of the Connect content as they wish, or even create their own content for application of unique lecture material. The exercises can be done strictly for student study or used for online homework, quizzes, exams, or projects.

Best of all, both technologies scale easily to the size of your class. As an instructor who regularly teaches advertising and IMC to over 200 students a semester, I love that Connect and SmartBook can scale to provide an engaging experience for large classes.

As always, I want to know what you think. Drop me a line about what you like and don't like at mweigold@gmail.com; I'd love to hear from you. Advice from adopters has been influential in every revision, none more than this one. Also follow my advertising and IMC teaching blog on twitter: @MichaelWeigold7

The Audience for This Book

Those of us who teach advertising and IMC know that students find them to be fascinating. The majority of your students have never known a world without likes, tweets, posts, filters, and stories—and not just as consumers, but as creators. It is not a stretch to say that no generation has ever been more media-savvy, nor more active in creating media content.

That makes the study of IMC and advertising more important today than ever before. The study of IMC gives students, regardless of their major field of study, an understanding of the tools they use today and will use in the future. It teaches them to think and plan strategically; gather and analyze research data; compute and evaluate alternative courses of action; cooperate with others in developing creative solutions; analyze competitive proposals; understand why people behave the way they do; express themselves and their ideas with clarity and simplicity; defend their point of view with others; appreciate and assess the quality of different creative endeavors; and use powerful ideas to speak with knowledge, confidence, and conviction.

In addition, students of advertising and IMC gain several specific benefits. The study of IMC can help students to

- Appreciate the diversity of audiences and the value of listening and understanding before communicating.
- Understand the real economic, social, and cultural roles of advertising and, conversely, the impact of a society's values on advertising.
- Realize how advertising supports news and entertainment and relates to the whole field of communications.
- Appreciate the global effect of IMC on business, industry, and national economies.
- Comprehend the strategic function of IMC within the broader context of business and marketing.
- Evaluate and even apply the impressive artistic creativity and technical expertise required in IMC.
- Discover what people in advertising and related disciplines do, how they do it, and what the career opportunities in these fields now offer.

Student-Oriented Features for the Twenty-First Century

Our mission in *Contemporary Advertising and Integrated Marketing Communications* continues to be presenting advertising as it is actually practiced. Now, in the 16th edition, our purpose remains the same. We also believe advertising and IMC should be taught in an intelligible manner and lively style relevant to students in higher education.

Award-Winning Graphic Design

Design thinking is being embraced by companies all over the world because it affects every aspect of how we live, work, and interact. For a text on creating messages designed to persuade and inform, beautiful design helps do more than teach—it inspires. The open, airy look of the text continues to contribute to learning by making the text material colorful, inviting, and accessible to students. Throughout the book, chapter overviews, chapter learning objectives, and key terms printed in boldface type all work together to make the material as reader-friendly as possible.

Chapter-Opening Vignettes

To capture and hold student interest, each chapter begins with a story. Many of the vignettes have been updated for this edition. Wherever possible, the opening story is then woven throughout the chapter to demonstrate how textbook concepts actually come to life in real-world situations. For example, throughout Chapter 1, we examine how privacy concerns roiled digital media companies and led to significant changes in privacy laws. In Chapter 4, the story of McDonald's advertising is complemented with numerous examples that range from global to local. In Chapter 7 we examine the actual media plan of an organization dedicated to addressing the lives of people living with HIV. And in Chapter 15 we look at how the popular game Fortnite is linking people and brands together in new, engaging ways. The integration continues in Connect, where the opening vignettes are featured in many video cases.

Extensive Illustration Program

The best way to teach is to set a good example. So each of the 18 chapters features beautiful full-color illustrations of recent award-winning ads, commercials, and campaigns that demonstrate the best in the business. *Contemporary Advertising and Integrated Marketing Communications* is one of the most heavily illustrated textbooks on the market, with all the major media represented—print, electronic, digital, social, and out-of-home—in a balanced manner. The author carefully selected each example and illustration for both their quality and their relevance to your students. Nearly half of the ads are new to this edition.

Furthermore, we feature a mix of local, national, and international ads from both business-to-business and consumer campaigns. In-depth captions tell the stories behind many of the ads and explain how the ads demonstrate the concepts discussed in the text.

The book is liberally illustrated with models, charts, graphs, and tables. Some of these encapsulate useful information on advertising concepts or the advertising industry. Others depict the processes employed in account management, research, account planning, media planning, and creative thinking.

Full-Color Portfolios

In addition to the individual print ads and actual frames from TV commercials, the book contains several multipage portfolios of outstanding creative work. These include "Strategic Use of the Creative Mix," "Outstanding Magazine Ads," "Advertising on the Internet," "Corporate Advertising," and others. Accompanying captions and questions tie the ads to topics germane to the chapter in which they appear.

Ad Lab

Active participation enhances learning, so Ad Labs play a significant role in virtually every chapter. These unique sidebars to the world of advertising introduce students to topics of current interest or controversy and then involve them in the subject by posing questions that stimulate critical thinking. Some of the many topics presented in Ad Labs include government regulation, bottom-up marketing, creativity, the psychological impact of color, advertising on the internet, "green" advertising, sales promotion, and direct-response advertising.

Ethics, Diversity, and Inclusion

As noted earlier, the chapter by chapter box on ethics has been expanded in this edition to include a focus on diversity and inclusion. In *every* chapter of the book, we introduce a current issue—to focus attention on the most critical social questions facing marketers today. These include programs available to your students that are designed to make the industry more diverse (Chapter 1), the story of the first female CEO of a company listed on the New York Stock Exchange (Chapter 2), how the 4A's is leading on making agency workplaces safe and collaborative in the #metoo era (Chapter 4), how the Association of Minority Market Research Professionals is helping improve the diversity of research samples (Chapter 7), and many more.

My IMC Campaign

For instructors who offer students semester-long projects as a way of getting their hands dirty, we've included this valuable resource. In each chapter, students receive practical advice on developing a real campaign, culminating with tips on developing a plans book and a client presentation.

My IMC Campaign is a chapter-by-chapter guide for students enrolled in classes that involve semester-long campaign projects. From our conversations with dozens of professors, we know that semester-long projects are a major component of many advertising and IMC courses. These projects help students gain their first experience with the practice of marketing communications. We applaud instructors who make the effort to offer their students this opportunity, and we are proud to provide a chapter-by-chapter project guide.

The My IMC Campaign feature offers students practical advice for developing their projects. The advice ranges from frameworks for developing creative strategy, media plans, and situation analyses, to practical tips on using collaborative software, developing presentations, and working in teams. We believe professors who incorporate experiential learning in their classes will find this new feature greatly assists their efforts to give students real-world experience in advertising.

People behind the Ads

Behind the thousands of ads we see and hear are real human beings—the writers, designers, programmers, executives, and media specialists. In the final analysis, the marketing communications industry is more than a collection of concepts, processes, and activities. It is an industry of people, some of the smartest, most creative, and most interesting people in the world. Your students will meet some of the most interesting right here, many offering insights provided uniquely for this text. The feature presents students contemporary practitioners who are already industry legends (Bogusky, Steele), enduring legends (Bernbach, Gallup, Lasker), and new leaders changing the industry every day. New to this edition are the inspiring stories of Dayana Falcon, Sales Marketing Manager for Disney Advertising, and Tria Chingcuangco, Director of Strategy and Planning at PowerPhyl Media.

Additional Learning Aids

Each chapter concludes with a summary followed by questions for review and discussion. These pedagogical aids help students review chapter contents and assimilate what they have learned. Throughout the text, key ideas and terms are highlighted with boldface type and defined when introduced. The definitions of all these terms are collected at the end of the book in a thorough and extensive glossary.

The Advertising Experience Exercises

True to the text's agency approach, the 16th edition of *Contemporary Advertising and Integrated Marketing Communications* continues hands-on application exercises that place students in the advertisers' shoes to help them see how advertising is done in the real world. Effective as outside assignments or in-class discussion starters, the Advertising Experience allows students to effectively apply their knowledge of each chapter.

Many exercises also require students to access the web and perform research on questions relevant to the chapter topic.

This edition continues our commitment to our IMC core. The need to consider advertising within an IMC framework is no longer debated in either industry or academia. The focus on the message receiver, as compared to the message creator, has improved the practice of marketing communications. While advertising remains an important part of the book, we give greater coverage to other promotional elements. You will find that in choosing between the words *advertising* versus *IMC,* we emphasize the former when the practices we describe are largely those of advertising agencies. When practices are used across broader or more integrated messaging platforms, we use *IMC.*

For the Professor: The 16th Edition Has Been Thoroughly Revised

Our continuing goal has been to bring clarity to the often-murky subject of advertising. Our method has been to personally involve students as much as possible in the practical experiences of advertising, while simultaneously giving them a clear understanding of advertising's dynamic role in both marketing management and the human communication process. In the pursuit of this objective, we have included significant modifications and improvements in the 16th edition of *Contemporary Advertising and Integrated Marketing Communications*.

Current and Concise

As with every new edition, our first effort was to update all statistics and tables and to document the most recent academic and professional source material to give *Contemporary Advertising and Integrated Marketing Communications* the most current and relevant compendium of academic and trade citations in the field. We've referenced important recent research on topics ranging from the effects of advertising and sales promotion on brand building to relationship marketing, integrated communications, and internet advertising. And, where appropriate, we've redesigned the building-block models that facilitate student comprehension of the often-complex processes involved in human communication, consumer behavior, marketing research, and IMC.

In our last edition we introduced a new, simpler organization scheme for the chapters. Part One, which covers Chapters 1–4, is titled "What Are Advertising and Integrated Marketing Communications?" The focus of these chapters is to introduce students to the practice of advertising and to the role advertising plays in the United States and the world. In Part Two, "Planning the Campaign," covering Chapters 5–10, we present detailed information about research and the development of strategy for markets, media, and creative. Finally, Part Three, "Executing and Evaluating the Campaign," explains how the strategic decisions of a campaign are realized in the creation of copy and art and decisions about IMC platforms, including major media. This part of the book covers Chapters 11–18. The book concludes with an epilogue, "Repositioning a Brand." Original author Bill Arens' choice of MasterCard as the subject of the book's epilogue is another testament to his genius. For nearly 30 years the "Priceless" campaign has epitomized the big idea. "Priceless" continues to epitomize the promise of MasterCard as 2019 begins. When Bill selected the campaign, he wanted to show how IMC done right means choosing the right idea and adapting it to the times. Now, many years after he made that decision, the campaign still reinforces that idea.

As always, we have prudently governed the length of the text material. The illustrations, graphics, sidebar information, and overall design are all aimed at keeping the text open, airy, and inviting while sharpening *clarity*—the hallmark of *Contemporary Advertising and Integrated Marketing Communications*.

Compared to the true length of other comprehensive course books, *Contemporary Advertising and Integrated Marketing Communications* is one of the most concise texts in the field. In this edition, the inclusion of many new topics and concepts has not come at the price of expanding the text.

Fresh, Contemporary, Relevant Examples

For the 16th edition, we added many new, real-world examples, selected for their currency and their relevance to students. Likewise, many of the chapter-opening stories are new, such as the advertising success stories of M&M's, Amazon, Fortnite, and Corona. Others document marketing or communication misfires such as the Lance Armstrong fiasco. All of the full-color portfolios have been updated, expanded, or replaced with more recent examples, and all of the Ad Labs and Ethics, Diversity, and Inclusions have been updated and edited for currency and accuracy.

Global Orientation Integrated Throughout

In light of the increasing globalization of business, we introduce the subject of global advertising early in the book in Chapter 4, "The Scope of Advertising: From Local to Global." All the international data have been extensively revised and updated to reflect the increased importance of advertising in the new economic and marketing realities of Asia, especially China; Europe; and Latin America.

CASE STUDY: Epilogue: Repositioning a Brand

So that students can see how many of the principles taught in the text come together in the real world, we have included an updated Epilogue, immediately following Chapter 18, on the complete story behind the highly successful "Priceless" branding campaign for MasterCard, created by McCann Worldwide in New York. We are greatly indebted to both McCann and MasterCard for authorizing us to share the details of this fascinating, student-relevant campaign and for the tremendous assistance they gave us in the creation of the Epilogue.

Local and Business-to-Business Advertising Coverage

Throughout the book, *Contemporary Advertising and Integrated Marketing Communications* addresses the needs of both small and large consumer and business-to-business advertisers with its many examples, case histories, Ad Labs, and advertisements. Moreover, this is one of the few texts to devote adequate attention to the needs of the small retail advertiser by discussing how local advertisers can integrate their marketing communications.

Highlights of This Revision

Each chapter of *Contemporary Advertising and Integrated Marketing Communications* has been thoroughly updated to reflect the most recent trends, facts, and statistics available. We have created several new chapter-opening vignettes for this edition and have rewritten significant portions of the remaining vignettes to ensure they are up-to-date and current. As with previous editions, many of these vignettes are referenced within their corresponding chapters and in chapter-concluding review questions.

Chapter 1, "Advertising and IMC Today"

A new opening vignette introduces the issue of digital marketing and privacy concerns, including the GDPR, European legislation that offers consumers significantly more privacy protection. The discussion of concept and practice of IMC is updated throughout. The definition of relationship marketing for LO1-4 is updated to the current one used by the AMA. The discussion of lifetime customer value has been expanded to make this concept clearer for students. The practice of IMC by Disney offers concrete examples that show how every consumer touchpoint with the company is carefully managed. The new Ethics, Diversity, and Inclusion (EDI) box is introduced and two important industry-sponsored programs for students are described. The Portfolio Review is thoroughly updated to illustrate how ads communicate.

Chapter 2, "The Big Picture: The Functions of Advertising and Its Evolution"

The chapter's title has changed to better represent the learning objectives. This chapter has long featured Coke as a way to illustrate the history of advertising. The opening vignette has been updated to the present. We've continued to emphasize the importance of branding early in the text and expanded on our earlier discussion. Students now learn how a brand vision is created, understand how companies develop and maintain a brand personality, and read vision statements of some of the world's most famous brands. The EDI box features Mary Wells Lawrence, an advertising legend and one of the earliest women to lead a major advertising agency. The My IMC Campaign box has been updated to ensure students learn about the latest tools for staying connected and working together.

Chapter 3, "The Big Picture: Economic, Ethical, and Regulatory Aspects"

The chapter is slightly retitled to include the word "Ethical." The opener is updated to include the latest information about Lance Armstrong, Michael Vick, and Tiger Woods and their difficulties following scandals. The ethical dilemmas that arise from advertising are placed squarely in the context of its economic functions. The four assumptions of market economics have been expanded and made more accessible to students. Nike's dominance of Adidas in the U.S. market and the success of Apple's iPhone are presented to show how advertising stimulates competition. Nike's attention-grabbing ad featuring Colin Kaepernick is presented to frame the discussion of advertising's effect on our values. The Kaepernick ad is then the focus of the EDI box later in the chapter. The discussion of cigarettes in the "regulatory issues" section now includes additional information on e-cigarettes and the FDA. The privacy section is updated and a new section on "protecting consumer data" has been added to acknowledge the costs of data breaches. The National Advertising Review Council changed its name to the Advertising Self-Regulatory Council (ASRC), a change acknowledged in the chapter. ASRC groups, including CARU, ERSP, and IBA, are introduced and described.

Chapter 4, "The Scope of Advertising: From Local to Global"

The chapter updates the McDonald's vignette and more information about McDonald's global IMC campaigns are included. Ad Lab 4-B updates all statistics regarding the ad industry. The 4A's "Enlightened Workplace Certification Program" is the subject of the chapter's EDI box, replacing the focus on account reviews from the 15th edition. Nancy Hill is no longer the CEO of the 4A's, so the People behind the Ads (PBTA) feature introduces students to Marla Kaplowitz, the current CEO.

Chapter 5, "Marketing and Consumer Behavior: The Foundations of IMC"

Examples are updated throughout the chapter. The ELM and the discussion of the role of habit in psychological processes has been expanded and made more accessible to students. The revised EDI box assesses the halting progress in agency diversity.

Chapter 6, "Market Segmentation and the Marketing Mix: Determinants of Campaign Strategy"

We've retained the spectacular "The man your man could smell like" campaign for Old Spice and referenced its lessons more often throughout the chapter. Ad Lab 6–B focuses on a new brand, Amazon, currently the most highly valued company in the world. Exhibit 6-13 shows that differentiation often fails to translate into brand success, at least when the differentiations leave consumers unimpressed.

Demographics discussion in the chapter contains significantly more material on Millennials and Hispanics.

Chapter 7, "Research: Gathering Information for IMC Planning"

All statistics for companies and research expenditures have been updated. The use of exploratory research in storytelling is explained and linked to the Budweiser opening vignette. New Google research tools, including Think Insights and Google Keyword, are introduced. The new EDI box discusses how strides are being made to ensure the ethnic diversity of samples used in marketing research.

Chapter 8, "Marketing and IMC Planning"

The opening vignette featuring Mountain Dew has been thoroughly revised and updated for this edition. The section on a marketing plan's mission statement has been expanded and now includes mission statements from several global brands. The discussion of how brands select target markets is illustrated through the example of the Jaguar I-Pace. Ernest Martin's seven approaches to developing a positioning strategy are now more broadly defined and supplemented with examples. Our text's "eighth" strategy is associated with the Blue Ocean strategy developed by W. Chan Kim and Renee Mauborgne. Marketing tactics are now illustrated through the clever GoPro campaign to encourage brand users to post their videos. The use of mobile payment systems in tracking user behavior is described under planning. The Portfolio Review is updated with new, fresh executions by IKEA, Adidas, and Faber Castel.

Chapter 9, "Planning Media Strategy: Disseminating the Message"

The chapter is thoroughly revised in collaboration with Jordan Alpert, assistant professor in the Department of Advertising at the University of Florida. A former postdoctoral fellow in cancer prevention and control in the Department of Health Behavior and Policy at Virginia Commonwealth University School of Medicine, Jordan has nine years of industry experience, including stops as marketing communications manager at About.com, senior account executive at IMC2, account executive at Sharpe Partners, junior account executive at TMP Worldwide, and assistant media planner at Universal McCann.

The chapter updates include new information about the HIV.gov campaign and shows how media planning helps in this important cause. The text has been substantially revised throughout. Ad Lab 9–A gives students the chance to apply what they've learned to a fictitious but realistic media buy. The EDI box discusses groups often ignored in media plans, including LGBT consumers. Information on programmatic buying is expanded. The PBTA individual for the chapter is now Tria Cingcuangco, Director, Strategy & Planning at PowerPhyl Media.

Chapter 10, "Creative Strategy and the Creative Process"

The chapter expands on the information versus transformational distinction and shows how the former concept is fundamental in search ads. Target and the retailer's great ads remain the focus of the chapter, but added attention is given to the brand's product concept and media choices. The chapter's definition of creativity is expanded through insights from Lee Odden, David Meerman Scott, Seth Godin, and Daniel Pink. The EDI box, which still focuses on the use of sex in ads, now explicitly references the #metoo movement and its impact on responsible messages.

Chapter 11, "Creative Execution: Art and Copy"

Information on production has been added by consolidating material from the now deleted Chapter 12, "Print, Electronic, and Digital Media Production." Tips for writing great copy from Demian Farnworth at Copyblogger are included in My IMC Campaign. The discussion of typography from the deleted chapter can now be found in this chapter. The EDI box addresses the need for copywriters to be sensitive to the power of words to hurt people, even when the intent of the ad is humor. On a more inspiring note, Procter & Gamble's "Like a Girl" campaign is applauded for reframing hurtful words into words of empowerment for women. The material on major categories of production techniques (Live Action, Animation, and Special Effects) has been eliminated as these categories are too restrictive in the age of digital production. The section on writing copy for digital media has been updated and revised. The focus of the PBTA box, Alex Bogusky, returned to the advertising industry in 2018.

Chapter 12, "Advertising in Print Media"

The opener of this chapter, which was Chapter 13 in the last edition, is updated. Sadly, the story for newspapers has not improved. Native advertising is introduced as a concept in the "Using Magazines in the Creative Mix" section and is the feature of Ad Lab 12-B. The Portfolio Review is completely updated with new, fresh ads. The EDI box is updated to focus more specifically on elderly consumers and to reflect current legislation on sweepstakes. The auditing firm for print is now named the Alliance for Audited Media, a change noted in the chapter.

Chapter 13, "Using Electronic Media: Television and Radio"

A new opening vignette describes how M&M's has developed a strong brand through the creative use of television spots. The chapter highlights the many transformations affecting TV and radio, especially from digital media and streaming services. The recent decline of cable is noted. The My IMC Campaign 13-A includes streaming video as an option for TV and podcasts as an option for radio. The section on DTV has been replaced by a focus on streaming video. The EDI box that focuses on children and teens as an audience for TV spots has been completely rewritten. Ad Lab 13-A continues a focus on ratings but has also been completely updated to reflect the current issues in measuring audiences in the digital age. Product placement is now discussed in this chapter, where it logically belongs. Ad Lab 13-C, which focuses on measuring radio, has been updated to reflect audiences across audio options. Content from the deleted Chapter 12 on production of radio and TV is now in the final section of the chapter.

Chapter 14, "Using Digital Interactive Media"

Our opener focuses on the new giant in digital advertising—Amazon—and shows how it is using strategies from legacy and digital companies to thrive. Spending on digital media now exceeds that on TV, which is noted. In general, "internet" companies are now referred to as digital media. The latest Pew Internet & American Project Life Study's findings are included throughout the chapter. The disruptive potential of 5G technology is discussed. The section on "Measuring the Digital Audience" has been completely rewritten and updated, with highlights on privacy and data security. The emergence of Comscore as a challenger to Nielsen in measuring digital audiences is explained. A significantly revised

EDI box updates data privacy issues to the present. Most of the Portfolio Review ads are new. The "Other Interactive Media" section introduces voice-controlled devices like the Amazon Echo as an advertising medium.

Chapter 15, "Social Media"

The new opener focuses on online gaming craze Fortnite and demonstrates the social nature of online gaming. The remainder of the chapter is significantly revised to reflect the dramatic changes in the use of social media that have occurred over the past few years. The EDI box highlights the impact of social media on bullying, especially of teenagers, and raises questions about the role that social media platforms should play in protecting users. The ways social media have transformed business, especially local businesses, is highlighted. The PBTA feature on Mark Zuckerberg is updated to reflect the recent travails of Facebook.

Chapter 16, "Using Out-of-Home, Exhibitive, and Supplementary Media"

The new opener highlights Corona's creative and socially responsible campaign for World Ocean Day. OOH statistics and uses are updated throughout. The Portfolio Review is updated with new, creative executions. Geotargeting and geofencing are introduced and their uses are explained.

Chapter 17, "Relationship Building: Direct Marketing, Personal Selling, and Sales Promotion"

A new PBTA features an interview with Disney executive Dayana Falcon. The opener, which has long focused on Geico, now features the sponsorship opportunities available at Disney theme parks. The EDI box focuses on advertising issues related to marketing to elderly Americans.

Chapter 18, "Relationship Building: Public Relations, Sponsorship, and Corporate Advertising"

The Netflix vignette focused on Reed Hasting's proactive response to a potential crisis is updated to show the success of the streaming giant.

Uses for This Text

Contemporary Advertising and Integrated Marketing Communications was written for undergraduate students in liberal arts, journalism, mass communication, and business schools. However, because of its practical, hands-on approach, depth of coverage, and marketing management emphasis, it is also widely used in independent schools, university extension courses, and courses on advertising management. The wealth of award-winning advertisements also makes it a resource guide to the best work in the field for students in art and graphic design courses and for professionals in the field.

Many of the stories, materials, and techniques included in this text come from the authors' personal experiences in marketing communications and in higher education. Others come from the experiences of friends and colleagues in the business. We believe this book will be a valuable resource guide, not only in the study of advertising but later in the practice of it as well. In all cases, we hope readers will experience the feel and the humanness of the advertising world—whether they intend to become professionals in the business, to work with practitioners, or simply to become more sophisticated consumers.

Our goal with each new edition is to produce a finer book. We think instructors and students alike will approve of many of the changes we've made to this one. We would love to hear from you—what you like, what you don't, what we should look to add in the future. E-mail Mike Weigold at mweigold@gmail.com.

Michael F. Weigold

our thanks

We are grateful to all of the individuals who serve as the focus of our People Behind the Ads feature. I am especially grateful to Dayana Falcon, Alex Bogusky, Tria Chingcuangco, Cliff Marks, Samantha Avivi, John Posey, Jon Steel, and Joe Zubi for the time and energy that they spent sharing their thoughts about their advertising and marketing careers.

Modern texts are integrated learning tools, and this one is no exception. The Connect exercises that accompany the book offer students a chance to apply what they've learned, assess their level of understanding, and integrate concepts and practices. I am immensely grateful to the amazing team of scholars below who reviewed this material and made it significantly better.

- Susan Westcott Alessandri, Suffolk University
- Sheila Baiers, Kalamazoo Valley Community College
- Steven W. Rayburn, Texas State University
- Lisa M. Sciulli, Indiana University of Pennsylvania
- Amanda Stoecklein, State Fair Community College
- Corliss Thornton, Georgia State University
- Gary B. Wilcox, University of Texas at Austin

This edition benefited from the abilities and efforts of some great people at McGraw-Hill. Kelly I. Pekelder and Anne Leung served as the Product Developers of the text and always worked to make the product better. Both are a delight to work with. The book benefited greatly from their skills. I am also grateful to our Portfolio Manager Meredith Fossel, Marketing Manager Nicole Young, and our Senior Project Managers Kathryn Wright and Keri Johnson. Thanks are also due to our wonderful photo researcher Ann Marie Jannette.

I am appreciative of my department chair, Tom Kelleher, and of my wonderful colleagues in the Department of Advertising at the University of Florida for their support and encouragement and for making Florida a special place to work. Go Gators!

William Arens created a special text, and it is my great honor to extend his legacy. His son Chris and I collaborated over several editions, and Chris's warm personality and professional insights continue to make this book better than it would be otherwise. Jordan Alpert brought his talent and experience to the Media Planning chapter and ensured the continued currency of this important topic for IMC students.

Finally, thanks to Debbie Treise for her support, encouragement, and love.

M. F. W.

You're in the driver's seat.

Want to build your own course? No problem. Prefer to use our turnkey, prebuilt course? Easy. Want to make changes throughout the semester? Sure. And you'll save time with Connect's auto-grading too.

65%
Less Time Grading

Laptop: McGraw-Hill; Woman/dog: George Doyle/Getty Images

They'll thank you for it.

Adaptive study resources like SmartBook® 2.0 help your students be better prepared in less time. You can transform your class time from dull definitions to dynamic debates. Find out more about the powerful personalized learning experience available in SmartBook 2.0 at **www.mheducation.com/highered/connect/smartbook**

Make it simple, make it affordable.

Connect makes it easy with seamless integration using any of the major Learning Management Systems—Blackboard®, Canvas, and D2L, among others—to let you organize your course in one convenient location. Give your students access to digital materials at a discount with our inclusive access program. Ask your McGraw-Hill representative for more information.

Padlock: Jobalou/Getty Images

Solutions for your challenges.

A product isn't a solution. Real solutions are affordable, reliable, and come with training and ongoing support when you need it and how you want it. Our Customer Experience Group can also help you troubleshoot tech problems—although Connect's 99% uptime means you might not need to call them. See for yourself at **status.mheducation.com**

Checkmark: Jobalou/Getty Images

FOR STUDENTS

Effective, efficient studying.

Connect helps you be more productive with your study time and get better grades using tools like SmartBook 2.0, which highlights key concepts and creates a personalized study plan. Connect sets you up for success, so you walk into class with confidence and walk out with better grades.

Study anytime, anywhere.

Download the free ReadAnywhere app and access your online eBook or SmartBook 2.0 assignments when it's convenient, even if you're offline. And since the app automatically syncs with your eBook and SmartBook 2.0 assignments in Connect, all of your work is available every time you open it. Find out more at **www.mheducation.com/readanywhere**

> *"I really liked this app—it made it easy to study when you don't have your text-book in front of you."*
>
> - Jordan Cunningham, Eastern Washington University

Calendar: owattaphotos/Getty Images

No surprises.

The Connect Calendar and Reports tools keep you on track with the work you need to get done and your assignment scores. Life gets busy; Connect tools help you keep learning through it all.

Learning for everyone.

McGraw-Hill works directly with Accessibility Services Departments and faculty to meet the learning needs of all students. Please contact your Accessibility Services office and ask them to email accessibility@mheducation.com, or visit **www.mheducation.com/about/accessibility** for more information.

Tegrity: Lectures 24/7

Tegrity in Connect is a tool that makes class time available 24/7 by automatically capturing every lecture. With a simple one-click start-and-stop process, you capture all computer screens and corresponding audio in a format that is easy to search, frame by frame. Students can replay any part of any class with easy-to-use, browser-based viewing on a PC, Mac, iPod, or other mobile device.

Educators know that the more students can see, hear, and experience class resources, the better they learn. In fact, studies prove it. Tegrity's unique search feature helps students efficiently find what they need, when they need it, across an entire semester of class recordings. Help turn your students' study time into learning moments immediately supported by your lecture. With Tegrity, you also increase intent listening and class participation by easing students' concerns about note-taking. Using Tegrity in Connect will make it more likely you will see students' faces, not the tops of their heads.

Test Builder in Connect

Available within Connect, Test Builder is a cloud-based tool that enables instructors to format tests that can be printed or administered within a LMS. Test Builder offers a modern, streamlined interface for easy content configuration that matches course needs, without requiring a download.

Test Builder allows you to:

- access all test bank content from a particular title.
- easily pinpoint the most relevant content through robust filtering options.
- manipulate the order of questions or scramble questions and/or answers.
- pin questions to a specific location within a test.
- determine your preferred treatment of algorithmic questions.
- choose the layout and spacing.
- add instructions and configure default settings.

Test Builder provides a secure interface for better protection of content and allows for just-in-time updates to flow directly into assessments.

contents in brief

detailed contents

Part Two   Planning the Campaign

AD LAB 5–A
The Context of Choice: How a Product's
Perceived Value Varies by the Products It
Is Compared With 160

MY IMC CAMPAIGN 5–A
Understanding What Consumers Look
for in a Product 165

ETHICS, DIVERSITY & INCLUSION
Helping an Industry Look Like America 169

AD LAB 5–B
Applying Consumer Behavior Principles
to Ad Making 173

PEOPLE BEHIND THE ADS
Jon Steel: Advertising Legend 174

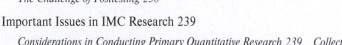

Part Three   Executing and Evaluating the Campaign

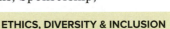

CONTEMPORARY
advertising
and Integrated Marketing Communications

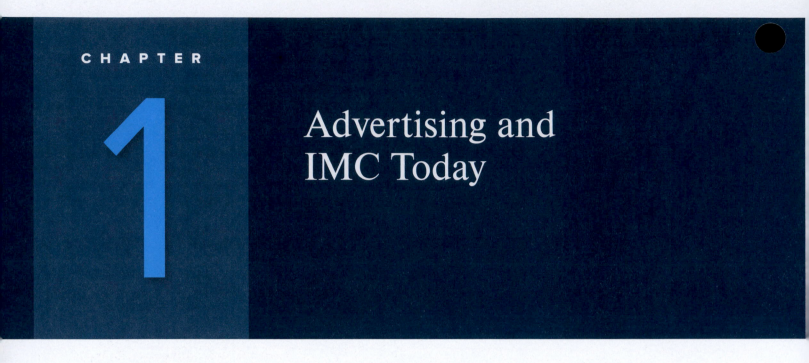

CHAPTER

1

Advertising and IMC Today

LEARNING OBJECTIVES

This chapter introduces you to several important themes and concepts, including advertising, integrated marketing communications (IMC), marketing, and relationship marketing. It also describes how advertising functions as a special kind of communication, one that is of great value in a company's marketing strategy.

After studying this chapter, you will be able to:

LO1-1   Define integrated marketing communications.

LO1-2   Clarify what advertising is and how it differs from other kinds of marketing communications.

LO1-3   Describe the human communication process and compare it with how advertising communicates.

LO1-4   Offer reasons why companies want relationships with their customers and show how IMC helps them to develop such relationships.

LO1-5   Define marketing and identify the four elements of marketing strategy.

LO1-6   Illustrate IMC's role in marketing strategy.

LO1-7   Identify important categories under promotion: the communication element of strategy

maxkabakov/iStock/Getty Images

For most of advertising's history, its value to companies was its utility in helping consumers discover and learn about brands. While advertising still plays that role, the biggest change of the past 20 years is this: Advertising now helps brands learn about consumers. ■ This change has shifted billions of marketing dollars away from legacy media, such as newspapers, to digital media, especially Google and Facebook. Companies that advertise through these digital giants easily uncover a wealth of information about prospects and customers. In turn, the sophisticated use of data analytics helps ensure that subsequent advertising efforts are more precise, more accountable, and more powerful. ■ The flip side is that consumers are not always happy that advertisers know so much about them. You may be surprised to learn what almost any company can find about you, according to Bernard Marr,[1] a writer for *Forbes* and other publications:

1. Your search history (Google, or your other search engine) and your browsing history (your internet service provider, even in "incognito" mode).

2. Your age and gender (Google).

3. The quality of your relationship (Facebook, based on algorithms that analyze your posts).

4. Where you've traveled (from your phone). Also, how fast you were traveling and the locations of your home and work.

5. Where your pet lives (from geolocation data associated with pictures taken on your phone when the pictures appear in Instagram).

6. What you purchase (credit card issuers, who share the information to determine your creditworthiness).

7. Your favorite food items at the supermarket (based on coupons and loyalty programs).

8. Whether you are pregnant, even if you haven't told anyone (Target).[2]

9. The videos you watch (YouTube, which is owned by Google).

10. Everything you've ever asked Siri, Cortana, or Alexa (Apple, Microsoft, and Amazon, respectively).

11. What your kid sister says to Barbie (Mattel, based on the "Hello Barbie" talking doll).[3]

12. Whether you are likely to commit a crime, or be a victim of one (Chicago Police Department and others using computer-based "Heat Lists").[4]

13. When and where you drive (your auto insurance company if it is Progressive and you use Snapshot to get lower rates) and whether you are running red lights or stop signs, even when no one is around (your local municipality using cameras that photograph your license plates).

14. How religious, smart, happy, and emotionally stable you are. And your political and sexual orientations, as well as your alcohol and drug use (Facebook analysis of your "likes").[5]

Even this list is just the tip of the iceberg. Perhaps it is obvious that Google can track your e-mail (if you use Gmail), your searches, your destinations (Google maps), and your appointments (Google calendar), but did you realize that Google is getting pretty good at predicting when you will die? Pretty good as in close to 95 percent accurate at predicting the deaths of hospitalized patients.[6] ■ Unsettling? Many think so. So perhaps it is not surprising that two of the biggest IMC events as the 2010s draw to a close are related to consumer privacy. ■ The first was the passage of a law by the European Union called the General Data Protection Regulation, or GDPR for short. The law took effect in the summer of 2018, and while the legislation is European, its impact affects virtually every major internet company. The law is intended to make it easy for consumers to discover what companies know about them and to require consent before such information is collected in the first place. Big web companies

responded quickly to the changes. Google no longer analyzes e-mails to serve specific ads, and Facebook claimed it would create a dashboard for users to regulate what information they share. Other companies, including ad-server Drawbridge, announced they would no longer do business in the EU.[7] ■ The other major event was the improper sharing of data by Facebook with a political advisory company called Cambridge Analytica. According to Facebook, the data of nearly 87 million users were shared. CEO Mark Zuckerberg quickly found himself testifying before congressional panels about the specific event and the company's privacy practices. In the aftermath, Facebook took several immediate steps that included denying some information to third-party apps, limiting the time certain data are kept at the site, and making it easier for users to see what information about them is being shared.[8] In perhaps its most controversial move, the company began a reputation rating system for users, scored from zero to one. Those with a bad reputation will, inevitably, find little of their content shared. One problem? Users can't discover the rating that Facebook assigned them.[9] ■ What do these events mean for online privacy? It is not clear. Perhaps they represent a new era of consumerism in which online privacy will become more important. Or perhaps these are just minor bumps on the road to increasingly easy information access about everyone. One thing is certain: The enormous amounts of data big internet companies keep is central to their business models. This ensures that while Google and Facebook will work hard to mollify consumers, and Congress, they have little incentive to delete what they know about us. Or to stop learning more.

Look around. If your TV or radio is on, if you've sorted through your mail, or if you've checked in on Instagram, it is likely that you've just seen a brand. In fact, you've probably been exposed to many brand messages today.

Brand messages seem to be everywhere because marketers spend lots of money trying to reach you. Every year, expenditures on advertising alone amount to hundreds of dollars for every man, woman, and child living in the United States. Perhaps you think that the money spent trying to reach you is largely wasted. When was the last time, after all, that you bought something just because it was advertised? Answering that question can be difficult because many things influence your buying decisions. And you may not always be aware of them.

One way to demonstrate how brand messages, or, more broadly, **marketing communications,** work, and at the same time introduce some important concepts, is to tell a story about an ordinary person, perhaps someone like you. The story is about a woman who sees an ad and ultimately buys a product. As you read, think about all the factors that influence her decision. In addition, try to identify which influences conform to your definition of "advertising," and which do not.

> Sharon, a college student, decides it is finally time to buy some clothes. Normally she would head to the mall, but an ad in her Facebook feed announcing a clothing store grand opening catches her attention. The ad features photos of women Sharon's age wearing attractive jackets, hats, sweaters, and cotton jeans. Connecting the pictures and running through the company's logo are two thin, bright green lines. The store is called Green Threads.
>
> The ad says that Green Threads clothing is made exclusively from natural materials and that all of their products are "workshop free." Sharon isn't quite sure what that means, but it calls to mind an article she once read describing terrible conditions at the factory of one of her favorite mall brands. She had decided never to buy that brand again.
>
> Grabbing her bike Sharon sets off for the store. On arrival she notices a sturdy bike rack near the attractive, naturally lit entrance. How thoughtful, she thinks (it bothers her that so many retailers cater only to drivers). Inside she spots clothes in the darker colors and the natural fabrics that she loves. Sharon selects a pair of jeans and a beautiful sweater and considers whether she should buy them.
>
> The clothes list for at least 20 percent over their mall equivalents. Sharon asks a clerk whether the store ever runs sales. He smiles and shakes his head no. To reduce excess inventory, he explains, Green Threads donates unsold clothes to local charities. Sensing Sharon's concern about the prices, he hands her a pamphlet titled "Our Philosophy" and encourages her to learn more about the company's business practices. He admits that Green Threads clothes are not the cheapest available, but points out that all the store's products are made from natural fibers and stitched in the U.S. The cotton used in the clothes is grown organically and all wool comes from farms that treat livestock humanely.
>
> Sharon is not sure what to do. She is impressed with Green Threads' corporate philosophy and she loves the clothes. But she also hates spending extra money. After going back and forth she finally decides to buy the jeans and the sweater.
>
> Over the next few months Sharon concludes that she made the right choice. Her friends compliment her when she wears her sweater and she believes that wearing Green Threads clothes helps others see that she supports socially responsible companies. Eventually she posts a positive online review of the store. She's happy to see other five-star reviews there as well. She also sees that some of the reviews are not as positive and that these most often complain about high prices.
>
> Soon Sharon is receiving e-mails from Green Threads announcing new arrivals at the store. She also notices that Green Threads display ads appear much more frequently in her Facebook feed. She much prefers the social media posts to a paper catalog, thinking it is one less thing for her to recycle. After a few weeks, Sharon decides to check out the new spring line of clothes arriving at the store.

What happened between Sharon's first exposure to the ad and her purchase? In this case, a Facebook ad helped make Sharon *aware* of Green Threads and allowed her to *comprehend* what the store offered and how it differed from its competition. The ad also sparked a series of events that ultimately resulted in a purchase. But the ad wasn't the sole, or even the most important, reason that Sharon became a customer. Much of what she learned about Green Threads came from other sources—for example, her reaction to the look and feel of the store, her initial impressions of the clothing, the helpful sales clerk, and the corporate brochure. Even the thoughtfully placed bike rack helped Sharon form a positive impression of the company.

Sharon's story helps to illustrate a central idea of this book: Companies do not create ads or other promotional messages in isolation. Instead, they strive to make sure that every experience a customer has with the company reinforces core ideas about who they are and what their products are like. Such evidence can come in advertising messages, but from a broader perspective, it comes from every consumer experience with the company. When a company strategically plans, coordinates, and integrates messages that target important audiences about its products or brands, it is practicing **integrated marketing communications,** or **IMC.**

My IMC Campaign 1-A
Overview

Welcome to My IMC Campaign, an important feature of this text. My IMC Campaign should be useful in any of the following situations:

- Your instructor has asked you and others in your class to work on part or all of a marketing campaign, either individually or in groups.

- You are doing an internship and want practical advice on how to help your company advertise.

- You would like to apply the concepts and ideas that you are reading about in this book to the real world.

Instructors approach advertising projects differently. Some assign students to create ads for a real product, although you never actually contact the company that makes the product. Some assign a fictional brand in a real product category. Perhaps your instructor has secured a real client, such as a small local business or firm. You may even have to find a client yourself by making inquiries in your community. Finally, your instructor may ask you to help a charity or nonprofit with its advertising. In all of these instances, the good news is that developing a campaign follows a similar path. And the My IMC Campaign feature is designed to help you do it well.

Let's begin with a definition. An IMC campaign involves the creation and placement of strategic messages that are unified by an underlying theme or core message. The messages are intended to help promote a brand, product, service, organization, or idea. They are aimed at a group called a target audience, individuals or organizations important to the advertiser. Campaigns have specific objectives, such as increasing product awareness or persuading people to try a service or donate money to a cause. The messages appear in various media, such as Facebook, radio, or billboards. Even if you do not do all of these activities, your understanding of the concepts introduced in this text will be much deeper and richer to the extent you have a chance to apply them.

As what you have read so far suggests, in an effective IMC campaign there is a great deal of planning that occurs before messages are developed. So, while you may be itching to create ads for your client, you have lots of work to do first. Think about your favorite ad that is running right now. It is successful because the people who created it thought carefully about the audiences that are important to reach, the media that can effectively reach them, and the objectives that are crucial to success. On a much smaller scale and with far fewer resources, you face similar challenges. My IMC Campaign is designed to help you in that quest.

In subsequent chapters, you will develop a deeper understanding of your brand or client, create a plan for marketing and advertising activities, conduct research so that you can better understand your target audience, formulate media strategy, and design effective advertisements. Finally, you'll find out how to implement evaluation programs to test whether your ads have been successful. By the end of the semester, you may not be a top advertising professional, but you'll have some real experience in the art and science of IMC.

The My IMC Campaign topics are listed below. You may find it useful or necessary to jump around as you develop your own campaign.

1. Overview
2. Tools for Teamwork
3. Your Assignment
4. Understanding Your Client; Creating Local Advertising; Agency Review; Ways to Be a Better Client
5. Understanding What Consumers Look for in a Product
6. Segmenting the Audience
7. Research; Methods for Pretesting; Methods for Posttesting; Developing an Effective Questionnaire
8. Developing the Situation Analysis; Developing IMC Objectives; Ways to Set IMC Budgets
9. Developing Media Objectives and Strategies
10. The Creative Brief
11. Product Facts for Creatives; Creating Great Headlines and Copy; Design Principles; Writing Effective Copy; Creating Effective Radio Commercials; Creating Effective TV Commercials
12. Producing Ads
13. The Pros and Cons of Magazine Advertising; The Pros and Cons of Newspaper Advertising; Planning and Evaluating Print Media
14. Planning and Buying TV and Radio; The Pros and Cons of Broadcast TV Advertising; The Pros and Cons of Cable TV Advertising; The Pros and Cons of Radio Advertising
15. Using Interactive Media
16. Using Social Media
17. Using Out-of-Home, Exhibitive, and Supplementary Media
18. Developing a Plans Book
19. Corporate Blogging; The Client Presentation

How did IMC factor in Sharon's purchase decision? Recall that she was conflicted about buying clothes at Green Threads because they were pricey. Cost was a serious consideration for Sharon because she is on a limited budget. But the information Sharon learned that day helped create a *conviction* that Green Threads was a company with both great clothes and a socially responsible way of doing business. That unique combination of attributes helped Sharon decide that, even at a higher price, Green Threads clothes

In relationship marketing and IMC, companies don't just advertise to customers, they listen too. This ad from Wells Fargo is meant to show the company is responsive to consumer concerns about its banking practices.

Source: Wells Fargo

were more desirable to her than clothes sold at the mall. No other retailer offered her both important qualities. The uniqueness of the offerings at Green Threads led Sharon to form a *desire* to buy from the store. And, after thinking carefully about her clothes budget, she took *action* and made a purchase.

Why do companies practice IMC? Because IMC helps companies adopt a consumer-centric, rather than marketer-centric, perspective when they create brand messages. And in today's marketing environment, nothing is more important than understanding and effectively communicating with consumers. Another reason companies use an IMC perspective is that consumers learn about brands from far more sources than just advertising. Smart companies try to think carefully about all of the ways consumers experience their brands. In some cases, advertising may play a crucial role in engaging and persuading consumers. In others, it may play a smaller role, or even none at all. Companies that practice IMC evaluate the strategic importance of advertising within the context of all possible ways they can communicate.

What Is Advertising?

Now that you know what IMC is, let's focus on an important element in many IMC campaigns: advertising. Many of the most vivid and memorable IMC messages you encounter are advertisements. But not all. Information about brands can appear in many forms—commercials, websites, and text messages—or in the form of product placements in TV shows, coupons, sales letters, event sponsorships, telemarketing calls, or e-mails. You may refer to them all as "advertising." But the correct term for such an assortment of tools is **marketing communications.** Advertising is just one type of marketing communications.

So what is advertising and how does it differ from other kinds of marketing messages?

At the beginning of the 20th century, Albert Lasker, often regarded as the father of modern advertising (see People behind the Ads: Albert Lasker and Claude Hopkins later in this chapter), defined it as "salesmanship in print, driven by a reason why."[10] But that was before the advent of radio, television, or the web. The nature and scope of the business world, and advertising, were limited in Lasker's time. As media technologies have changed, so have the concept and practice of advertising.

Images of advertising sometimes reflect the functions that it serves a person in his or her professional life. Journalists, for example, might define it as a communication, public relations, or persuasion process; businesspeople see it as a marketing process; economists and sociologists tend to focus on its economic, societal, or ethical significance. And some consumers might define it simply as a nuisance. Interestingly, scholars and professionals also disagree somewhat about how to define advertising, as scholars Jef Richards and

Companies use ads to differentiate their brands from those of competitors. But guided by an IMC philosophy, ads are just one part of an overall message strategy. Progressive finds a humorous way to remind consumers of its iconic spokesperson "Flo" by encouraging people to dress like her on Halloween. When people do so, it turns parties into yet another way of encountering and developing attitudes about the Progressive brand.

Source: Progressive Casualty Insurance Company

Catharine Curran discovered in a research study intended to find agreement about a definition. Their multi-wave panel study suggested the following definition comes closest to a consensus of experts:

> **Advertising** is a paid, mediated form of communication from an identifiable source, designed to persuade the receiver to take some action, now or in the future.[11]

Let's take a closer look at this definition. Advertising is, first, a form of *communication*, often defined as a process through which meaning is exchanged between individuals using a system of symbols, signs, or behavior. It differs from other forms in that advertising is a very *structured* form of applied communication, employing both verbal and nonverbal elements, *composed* to fill specific space and time formats determined by the sponsor.

Second, advertising is directed to groups of people, usually referred to as audiences, rather than to individuals. These people could be **consumers,** who buy products like cars, phones, or food for their personal use. Or they might be businesspeople, who buy fleets of trucks or thousands of computers for commercial or government use.

Third, the costs of advertising are paid by sponsors. GM, Walmart, Starbucks, and your local fitness salon pay Facebook or a local radio or TV station to carry the ads you read, see, and hear. A few sponsors don't have to pay for their ads. The American Red Cross, United Way, and American Cancer Society are among the many charitable organizations whose **public service messages** are carried at no charge because of their nonprofit status.

Fourth, most advertising is intended to be *persuasive*—to encourage audiences to take action, such as buying something, or at least to make people more favorably disposed toward a product, service, or idea. A few ads, such as legal announcements, are intended merely to inform, not to persuade.

In addition to promoting tangible **goods** such as oranges, oatmeal, and olive oil, advertising helps publicize the intangible **services** of banks, beauty salons, bike repair shops, and breweries. Advertising is also used to advocate a wide variety of **ideas,** whether economic, political, religious, or social. In this book, the term **product** is used to include goods, services, and ideas.

Fifth, an ad *identifies* its sponsor. Typically, sponsors want to be identified, or why pay to advertise? An important difference between advertising and *public relations* is that many PR activities (e.g., publicity) aren't openly sponsored. We'll discuss the differences between advertising and other forms of marketing communications later in this chapter.

Finally, advertising reaches people through a channel of communication referred to as a **medium.** An advertising medium is any nonpersonal means used to present an ad to a large audience. Advertising media include radio, television , newspapers, websites, social media, search engines, video games, billboards, and so on. When you tell somebody how much you like a product, that's sometimes called *word-of-mouth (WOM)* advertising. Although WOM is a communication medium, it has not generally been considered an advertising medium. However, the popularity of social media, such as Facebook and Twitter, is forcing advertisers to reconsider this belief. In fact, social media is an ideal platform for advertisers to encourage digital WOM, as when people share their favorite brands and ads or provide ratings of their experiences at restaurants and hotels.

Historically, advertisers used the traditional **mass media** (the plural of *medium*) to deliver their messages. But modern technology enables advertising to reach people efficiently through a variety of *addressable media* (e.g., direct mail) and *digital media* (like the web). Advertisers also use an increasing variety of *nontraditional media* such as shopping carts, blimps, and billboards to find their audience. A thorough understanding of the strengths, weaknesses, and capabilities of different media is important, and this text devotes several chapters to the subject.

Now that you better understand the types of messages that do and do not qualify as advertising, let's focus more deeply on two important dimensions of modern advertising: engagement and integration. First, contemporary advertising focuses less on making a single sale and more on helping companies foster relationships with consumers and other stakeholders. This was a key theme developed in the vignette that opened this chapter. In other words, modern advertising is less about informing consumers and more about engaging them and building relationships. Second, today's advertising is strategically created to complement other marketing communications efforts, such as public relations, sales promotions, product placements, and direct sales. This may seem obvious, but it was not always so. Decades ago ad campaigns were developed without much thinking about other marketing efforts. Today it is best to think of effective advertising as one tool among many that can be artfully used in integrated marketing communications efforts.

In the next section of this chapter, we'll flesh out a bit more about advertising by examining it as a form of communication. Then, we consider the strategic element of advertising by showing the importance marketers place on building relationships and practicing integrated marketing communication. Looking ahead to the other chapters in Part One, we will trace the evolution of IMC from its earliest practice, delve more deeply into the role of marketing messages in a market economy, review the most important regulatory and legal considerations practitioners must keep in mind, and consider the scope of advertising from local to global. Finally, we will consider the audiences for advertising messages.

Communication: What Makes Advertising Unique

LO 1-3

First and foremost, advertising is communication—a special kind of communication. McCann Worldgroup, the ad agency for MasterCard, claims that advertising is "truth well told." This means that ethical advertisers and the agencies they employ work together to discover the best methods possible to tell their story truthfully and creatively. To succeed, they must understand the advertising communication process, which derives from the basic human communication process.

The Human Communication Process

Success in life depends on our ability to inform others or persuade them to do something (or stop doing something). The first scholars to study human communication formulated a model like the one in Exhibit 1-1. The process begins when one party, called the **source,** formulates an idea, **encodes** it as a **message,** and sends it via some **channel** to another party, called the **receiver.** The receiver must **decode** the message in order to understand it. To respond, the receiver formulates a new idea, encodes it, and then sends the new message back through some channel. A message that acknowledges or responds to the original message constitutes **feedback,** which also affects the encoding of a new message.[12] And, of course, all this takes place in an environment characterized by **noise**—the cacophony of many other distractions.

Applying this model to advertising, the source is the sponsor, the message is the ad, the channel is the medium, the receiver is the consumer or prospect, and the noise is the din of competing messages, including other ads. But this model oversimplifies the

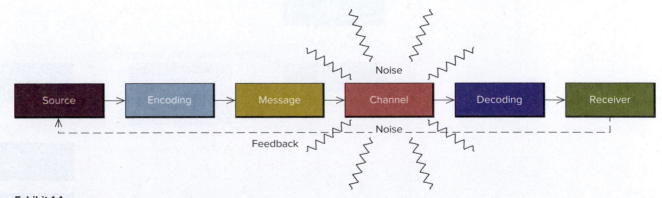

Exhibit 1-1
The traditional human communication process.

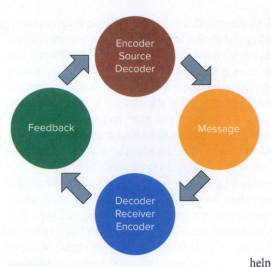

Exhibit 1-2
The interactive model of communication.

Applying the Communication Process to Advertising

process that occurs in advertising or other sponsored marketing communications. It doesn't take into account either the structure or the creativity inherent in composing the advertising message. We need to consider some of the many complexities involved, especially with the advent of *interactive media,* which let consumers participate in the communication by extracting the information they need, manipulating what they see, and responding in real time. The realization that much contemporary communication, especially in marketing, is better characterized as dialogue has led many scholars to revise the communication model to reflect interactivity, as depicted in Exhibit 1-2.

Exhibit 1-2 presents an interactive model of communication. In this model, no single entity operates as a source or receiver. Instead, two or more entities serve both roles in an ongoing process. This model better represents marketers' understanding of their relationships with consumers today. Marketers no longer dominate the exchange of messages. Rather, they are engaged in a conversation with consumers who send their own messages, both to the marketer and to other consumers. The interactive model helps remind companies that they do not have as much control over messages as the traditional model seems to suggest. It also reminds companies that the reputation of brands is not just a function of what the company says, but what consumers and others say as well.

Communications scholar Barbara Stern proposes a more sophisticated communication model, one that views advertising as *composed commercial text* rather than informal speech. The Stern model helps remind us that in advertising, sources, messages, and receivers have multiple dimensions. Some of these dimensions exist in the real world; others exist on a different level of reality—a virtual world within the text of the advertising message itself.

Source Dimensions: The Sponsor, the Author, and the Persona

In oral communication, the source is typically one person talking to another person or a group. But in advertising, identifying the source of a message is not so simple. Certainly the real-world **sponsor,** that is, the company that is advertising a product or idea, is legally responsible for the communication and has a message to communicate to actual consumers. But as the Stern model in Exhibit 1-3 shows, the path from sponsor to consumer can be long and circuitous. To begin with, the sponsor does not usually produce the message. That is the typical role of the sponsor's ad agency. So the **author** of the communication is actually a creative team at an ad agency. Commissioned by the sponsor to create the advertising message, these people exist in the real world but are unknown to the reader or viewer.

Exhibit 1-3
The Stern model of the advertising communication process.

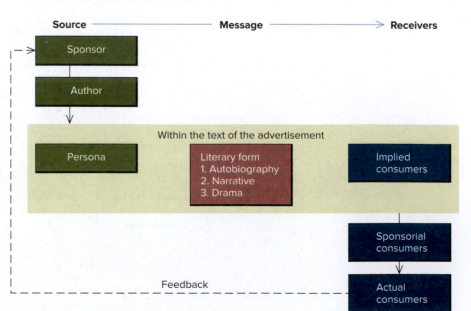

At the same time, *within the text* of the ad is a real or imaginary spokesperson (a **persona**) who lends some voice or tone to the ad. To the consumer, this persona, who represents the sponsor, is the source of the within-text message. But the persona's discourse is composed and crafted by the ad's authors solely for the purposes of the text; it is not a part of real life. It exists only in the virtual world of the ad. As an example, the Garnier ad shown in Ad Lab 1-A presents a living person, a woman whose daily stresses cause people to see her as older at night than when she first wakes. Although her experiences seem spontaneous, the entire "day" has been planned by ad agency creatives. (See Ad Lab 1-A, "Advertising as a Literary Form.")

Message Dimensions: Autobiography, Narrative, and Drama

Advertising messages may also be multidimensional. As artful imitations of life, they typically use one or a blend of three literary forms: autobiography, narrative, or drama. In **autobiographical messages,** "I" tell a story about myself to "you," the audience eavesdropping on my personal experience. Other ads use **narrative messages** in which a third-person persona tells a story about others to an imagined audience. Finally, in the **drama message,** the characters act out events as though in a play. The audience is an invisible observer of the actions in the ad.

The creators of ads make important decisions about what kind of persona and which literary form to use to express the message. Key considerations are the emotions, attitudes, and motives that drive customers in their target audience. Words and visuals are placed in the structured format most suitable to the medium selected for delivering the message. The format may be a dramatic 30-second TV commercial; an autobiographical, full-page, black-and-white magazine ad; a colorful, narrative brochure; or a multipage website that employs a variety of message styles. In all cases, though, the message exists only within the text of the ad. Doing all this effectively requires great skill, but it's this creativity that distinguishes advertising from all other forms of communication.

Receiver Dimensions: Implied, Sponsorial, and Actual Consumers

The receivers of advertising are also multidimensional. First, *within the text,* every ad or commercial presumes an audience. These **implied consumers,** who are addressed by the ad's persona, are not real. They are imagined by the ad's creators to be ideal consumers who accept uncritically the arguments made by the ad. These are the people imagined by the copywriter as he or she composes the words that will appear on paper or in electronic or digital form. They are, in effect, part of the ad's drama.

When we move outside the text of the ad, though, the first audience is, in fact, a group of decision makers at the sponsor or advertiser. These **sponsorial consumers** are the gatekeepers who decide if the ad will run or not. So, before an ad ever gets a chance to persuade a real consumer, the ad's authors must first persuade the sponsor's executives and managers who pay for the campaign and must approve it.

The **actual consumers**—equivalent to the receiver in oral communications—are people in the real world who make up the ad's target audience. They are the people to whom the sponsor's message is ultimately directed. But they will get to see, hear, or read it only with the sponsor's approval.[13]

Actual consumers do not usually think or behave the same as the implied consumer or even the sponsorial consumer. Thus, the advertiser (and the creative team) must be concerned about how the actual consumer will decode, or interpret, the message. The last thing an advertiser wants is to be misunderstood.

Unfortunately, message interpretation is only partially determined by the words and symbols in the ad. The medium used has an effect as well. As Marshall McLuhan said, "The medium is the message." Communications professionals are very interested in how different media affect the way people receive and interpret promotional messages.

These four ads show how advertising messages typically come in one or a blend of three literary forms: autobiography, narrative, or drama.

Autobiography tells its story from a first-person point of view and may often use the word *I*. In the L'Oreal ad (autobiography), a woman is followed throughout her busy day, demonstrating the toll that life's stresses take on youthful beauty. The narrative form typically uses a third-person voice, which often exudes a well-informed, authoritative quality to tell the reader about the product. In the next example, a narrator describes the heroic efforts to save a white lion in desperate need of treatment for his deteriorating teeth. The video, and the treatment, is sponsored by Fixodent. The drama form uses the style of theater to create or perform a scene, so the reader receives the message by implication rather than by direct telling. The ad for Wilkenson Sword blades depicts a sensual "battle" between two sultry characters.

Two other key elements are the persona, which usually represents the advertiser, and the implied consumer. Sometimes a character may represent the implied consumer. The persona may be a trade character, such as the Pillsbury Doughboy, or a real person, such as Eminem, shown below in the Brisk Iced Tea ad. A logo may even be a form of persona. Ads may also employ a number of literary forms simultaneously.

1. Autobiography.
Source: L'Oréal International

2. Narrative.
Source: Procter & Gamble

3. Drama.
Source: Wilkinson Sword

4. Mixture of literary forms and elements.
Source: PepsiCo Inc.

The characteristics of the receivers are also very important, and in Chapter 5, we'll see how attitudes, perceptions, personality, self-concept, and culture are important influences that affect the way people receive and respond to messages.

Finally, the sponsor's messages must vie with hundreds of competing commercial and noncommercial messages every day. They are referred to as **noise.** So the sender doesn't know *how* the message is received, or even *if* it's received, until a consumer acknowledges it.

Feedback and Interactivity

That's why feedback is so important. It completes the cycle, verifying that the message was received. Feedback employs a sender-message-receiver pattern, except that it is directed from the receiver back to the source.

In advertising, feedback takes many forms: redeemed coupons, website visits, phone inquiries, visits to a store, tweets, Facebook posts, increased sales, responses to a survey, or e-mail inquiries. Dramatically low responses to an ad indicate a break in the communication process. Questions arise: Is the product wrong for the market? Is the message unclear? Have the right media been chosen? Without feedback, these questions cannot be answered.

Long gone are the days when audiences could be considered passive receivers of impersonal mass messages. They are active decision makers who control what communications they receive and choose the information they want about a particular product. Social media allow for instantaneous, real-time feedback on the same channel used by the message sender. The increased opportunities for feedback mean companies can develop richer, deeper relationships with consumers today as compared with earlier times. This is a fundamental change for advertisers, and we explore this topic more deeply in the section to follow.

LO 1-4

IMC and Relationship Marketing

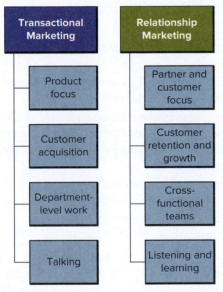

Exhibit 1-4
A comparison of transactional and relationship marketing. Adapted from Kotler and Keller.[17]

As companies have become less advertising-centric and more IMC-centric, they've shifted their focus from a focus on sales to a concern with building relationships with consumers. This shift has rich implications for brand messages.

A market-driven firm's overriding purpose is to profitably create happy, loyal customers. Customers, not products, are the lifeblood of the business. This realization has created a trend away from simple *transactional marketing* to **relationship marketing**[14]— defined by the American Marketing Association as marketing "with the conscious aim to develop and manage long-term and/or trusting relationships with customers, distributors, suppliers, or other parties in the marketing environment."[15] As can be seen in Exhibit 1-4, the shift from a transactional to a relationship focus has broad implications for the goals of marketing and the focus of advertising and IMC. None of these changes is more significant than the elevation of listening as a corporate value. Consider these examples: In response to a consumer campaign to eliminate plastic straws in England, McDonald's converted theirs to paper ones; adidas responded to consumer wishes for sustainability by creating over a million running shoes using garbage collected from ocean water.[16]

Consumers can choose many different products and services. As a result, the customer relationship—in which a sale is only the beginning—is the key strategic resource of the successful modern business. Companies that commit to relationship marketing are generally trying to accomplish three things: (1) identify, satisfy, retain, and maximize the value of profitable customers; (2) strategically manage the contacts between the customer and the company to ensure their effectiveness; and (3) develop a full and useful view of the customer by acquiring data.

The Importance of Relationships

To succeed, companies focus on managing loyalty among carefully chosen customers and **stakeholders** (employees, centers of influence, stockholders, the financial community, and the press). This is important for a number of reasons:

1. *The cost of lost customers.* Great marketing will not win back a customer lost from shoddy products or poor service. The real profit lost is the **lifetime customer value (LTCV)** to a firm. Brad Sugars, writing for *Entrepreneur,* argues that LTCV can be expressed quantitatively using the following formula: (Average Value of a Sale) × (Number of Repeat Transactions) × (Average Retention Time in Months or Years for a Typical Customer). LTCV gives a company a clearer picture of how much it should spend on marketing efforts to recruit new customers and retain existing ones.[18] It also makes clear the cost of marketing or product failures, as negative word of mouth can have a terrible snowballing effect. And if one lost customer influences only one other customer not to patronize the business, the LTCV loss doubles. With the pervasiveness of social media, this is more important today than ever before.

2. *The cost of acquiring new customers.* Defensive marketing, which attempts to retain loyal customers, typically costs less than offensive marketing, which seeks new

customers, because it isn't easy to lure satisfied customers away from competitors.[19] In fact, it costs five to eight times as much in marketing, advertising, and promotion to acquire a new customer as it does to keep an existing one.

3. *The value of loyal customers.* Repeat customers keep a company profitable even in tough economic times.[20] Retention is enormously profitable because acquiring new customers is almost five times as expensive as retaining old ones. In addition, long-term customers are less sensitive to the marketing efforts of other companies.[21] The bottom line is a company that makes a small increase in customer retention may be rewarded with big profits in return.[22]

For all of these reasons, a company's first market should always be its current customers. Many marketers commit resources to *postsale* activities, making customer retention their first line of defense. They have discovered the primary benefit of focusing on relationships: increased retention and optimized lifetime customer value.[23]

Levels of Relationships

Most business is conducted with repeat customers. This places a premium on customer retention. Retention can be achieved by offering special benefits to loyal customers, effectively rewarding and thanking them for business, and providing an incentive for a continued relationship in the future. CVS, a national pharmacy company, successfully retains its customers with a variety of rewards programs. The more a customer spends, the more CVS offers savings and coupons.

Source: CVS.

It is neither profitable nor realistic for every company to invest heavily in deep customer relations. Marketing experts Kotler and Armstrong distinguish five levels of relationships that can develop between a company and its stakeholders, depending on their mutual needs:

- *Basic transactional relationship.* The company sells the product but does not follow up in any way (McDonald's).
- *Reactive relationship.* The company (or salesperson) sells the product and encourages customers to call if they encounter any problems (Men's Wearhouse).
- *Accountable relationship.* The salesperson phones customers shortly after the sale to check whether the product meets the expectations and asks for product improvement suggestions and any specific disappointments. This information helps the company continuously improve its offering (Acura dealers).
- *Proactive relationship.* The salesperson or company contacts customers from time to time with suggestions about improved product use or helpful new products (Verizon).
- *Partnership.* The company works continuously with customers (and other stakeholders) to discover ways to deliver better value (financial planner).[24]

How should a company choose the type of relationship to earn with its stakeholders? It can be a difficult question. Different stakeholders require different types of relationships. The relationship a company seeks with a customer is different from the one it seeks with its suppliers. Additionally, some companies deal with significant overlap in stakeholder roles. An employee may also be a customer and a stockholder.

The number of stakeholders is also important. The more there are, the more difficult it is to develop an extensive personal relationship with each. Some customers may prefer a transactional relationship.[25] Most people wouldn't want a phone call from a store-label soft drink company. But Mtn Dew believes its customers *do* want a relationship with the brand. As a result, the company has encouraged users to design new flavors and bottle designs. This is because of the potential for **interactive customer relationships,** which makes it easy for companies and customers to communicate in digital media. In such relationships, companies encourage consumers to "feel like they're a part of your brand in a unique way."[26]

Mtn Dew also places a great deal of emphasis on creating a "Dew-x-perience" for its customers. For example, it employs a variety of hip-hop and Latin recording artists in various "street marketing" efforts to distribute bottles of Dew. It also sponsors extreme athletes and appears at sporting events such as the Gravity Games and ESPN's X Games with vans full of merchandise and giveaways.[27]

A company must also consider its profit margins. High-profit product or service categories make deeper, personal relationships more important (see Exhibit 1-5). Low profit margins imply a marketer should pursue basic transactional relationships augmented by brand-image advertising.[28]

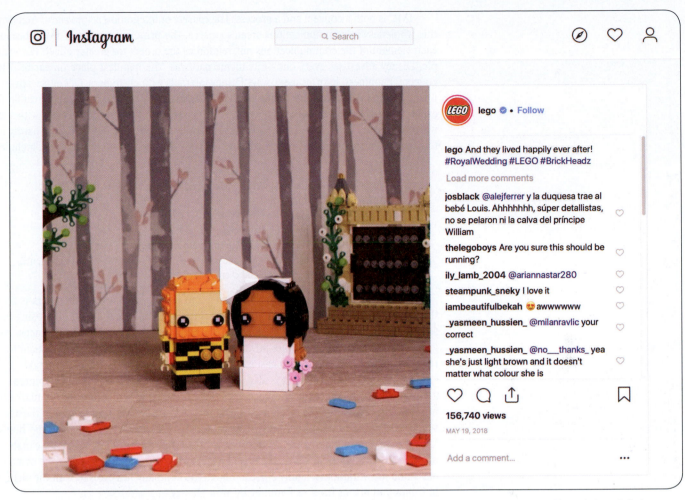

LEGO, like many contemporary brands, stays close to its customers through regular and creative use of social media. This ad cleverly helps to celebrate Harry and Meghan's royal wedding. How does the use of social media change the relationship between a brand like LEGO, and its consumers?

Source: Instagram/Lego Group.

No matter how a company builds relationships with stakeholders, the strategic use of IMC is vital. Is the company committed to a basic transactional relationship? Then the practice of IMC can guide the company as it evaluates the efficient and careful use of media. Is the company committed to a deeper relationship? Then it will be prepared to spend large amounts of money to support, engage, and satisfy stakeholders.

Exhibit 1-5
Relationship levels as a function of profit margin and number of customers.

	Profit margins		
	High	Medium	Low
Many	Accountable	Reactive	Basic
Medium	Proactive	Accountable	Basic
Few	Partnership	Accountable	Reactive

Number of customers

IMC is both a concept and a process. The *concept* of integration is *wholeness*. Achieving this wholeness in communications creates *synergy*—the principal benefit of IMC—because each element of the communications mix reinforces the others for greater effect. For example, Disney advertises every one of its theme parks as "the happiest place on earth." That concept, happiness, informs many ways Disney interacts with customers. Of course, advertising messages emphasize colorful Disney characters, luxury hotels, fun rides, and great family experiences. But the happy experience at a Disney park also involves interactions with staff, who are referred to as cast members. These interactions, as suggested by IMC, are hardly left to chance. The company's service guidelines, cleverly linked to its famous Dwarfs, include:

1. Be *Happy* . . . make eye contact and smile!
2. Be like *Sneezy* . . . greet and welcome each and every guest. Spread the spirit of Hospitality . . . It's contagious!
3. Don't be *Bashful* . . . seek out Guest contact.
4. Be like *Doc* . . . provide immediate service recovery.
5. Don't be *Grumpy* . . . always display appropriate body language at all times.
6. Be like *Sleepy* . . . create DREAMS and preserve the "MAGICAL" Guest experience.
7. Don't be *Dopey* . . . thank each and every Guest![29]

Disney messaging through its advertising and its guidance to cast members is more than merely consistent; it's reinforcing. Cast members see the ads too, and advertising messages can motivate them to ensure guests experience Disney parks as happy places. And guests perceive the ads in a more powerful way when the messages encourage them to reflect on happy interactions with cast members from previous visits. This is synergy.

While IMC is a concept, it is also, as Tom Duncan, an IMC scholar, has pointed out, a *process* in which communication becomes the driving, integrating force in the marketing mix and throughout the organization. Consumers are part of that process too. In the age of social media, brand marketers must "assess their IMC capability and understand how to leverage the consumer's voice."[30] In other words, for IMC to retain value, its capability must be fluid rather than static. Here too Disney is a great example. Even as the company has stood for wholesome, family entertainment, the company has evolved with the changes in values and norms from its founding by Walt Disney.

The Evolution of the IMC Concept

Glen Nowak and Joe Phelps, advertising professors from the Universities of Georgia and Alabama, argue that IMC developed as a consequence of several important trends, including escalating media costs, splintering consumer markets, and skepticism about traditional mass media advertising. These have led marketers to question the wisdom of creating walls between disciplines such as public relations, direct-response advertising, and sales promotion.[31]

The IMC approach, according to Nowak and Phelps, focuses on four related tactics: (1) less emphasis on advertising relative to other promotional tools, (2) heavier reliance on targeted messages and on reaching smaller segments, (3) increased use of consumer data, and (4) changed expectations for marketing communications suppliers.

Although IMC is considered crucial to any contemporary marketing effort, it has proven surprisingly difficult to define. Nowak and Phelps noted that IMC is used by some to mean *"one voice"* (i.e., ensuring all elements of the marketing mix converge on a single idea), by others to mean *integrated communications* (that advertising can and should achieve both action and awareness objectives simultaneously), and by still others to mean *coordinated marketing communications* (ensuring the various marketing mix elements such as advertising direct-response, sales promotions, and the like, work together).[32]

One scholar's review suggests that a complete definition would include four elements: first, that IMC refers both to a concept (or idea) and process (a sequence of steps); second that IMC draws on management skill at strategic planning; third, that IMC, as compared with traditional promotional approaches, places greater emphasis on audiences, channels, and results; and finally that IMC represents a broadened view of brand promotion. He concludes that IMC is best defined as "the concept and process of strategically managing audience-focused, channel-centered, and results-driven brand communication programs over time."[33]

The marketing of luxury products such as Lexus is also guided by IMC principles. Consumers receive messages about such brands from many sources, including advertising, dealerships, and the popular press. Preserving the value of the Lexus brand thus requires careful attention to all consumer "touch points."

Source: Toyota Motor Corporation

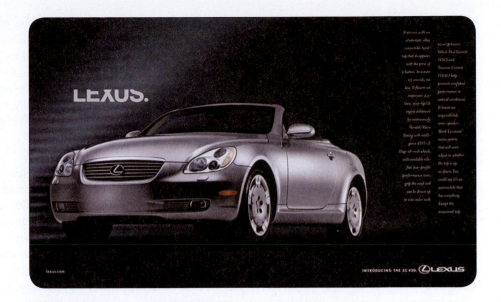

How the Customer Sees Marketing Communications

Clearly, to understand IMC, we have to look through the customer's eyes. Customers develop perceptions of the company or brand through a variety of sources: news reports, word of mouth, gossip, experts' opinions, financial reports, websites, blogs, and even the CEO's personality.

All these communications or brand contacts, sponsored or not, create an *integrated product* in the consumer's mind.[34] In other words, customers automatically integrate all the brand-related messages that they encounter. The way they integrate those messages determines their perception of the company. IMC gives companies a better opportunity to manage or influence those perceptions and create a superior relationship with those stakeholders.

The Four Sources of Brand Messages

To influence customers' perceptions, marketers must understand one of the basic premises of IMC: that *everything we do (and don't do) sends a message.* That is to say, every corporate activity has a message component. Duncan and Moriarty describe four sources of company/ brand-related messages stakeholders receive: *planned, product, service,* and *unplanned.* Each of these influences a stakeholder's relationship decision, so marketers must know where these messages originate, what effect they have, and the costs to influence them.

1. *Planned messages.* These are the traditional promotional messages—advertising, sales promotion, personal selling, merchandising materials, publicity releases, event sponsorships. These often have the *least* impact because they are seen as self-serving. Planned messages should be coordinated to work toward a predetermined set of communications objectives.

2. *Product messages.* In IMC theory, every element of the marketing mix sends a message. Messages from the product, price, or distribution elements are typically referred to as *product* (or *inferred*) *messages.* For example, customers and other stakeholders receive one product message from a $25,000 Rolex watch and a different one from a $30 Timex. Product messages also include packaging, which communicates about the product through the use of color, type, imagery, design, layout, and materials.

   Product messages have great impact. When a product performs well, it reinforces the purchase decision. However, a gap between the product's performance and advertised promises creates violated expectations.

3. *Service messages.* Employee interactions also send messages to customers. In many organizations, customer service people are supervised by operations, not marketing. Yet the service messages they send have greater marketing impact than the planned

messages. With IMC, marketing people work with operations to minimize negative messages and maximize positive ones.

4. *Unplanned messages.* Companies have little control over the unplanned messages that emanate from employee gossip, unsought news stories, comments by the trade or competitors, word-of-mouth rumors, or major disasters. Unplanned messages may affect customers' attitudes dramatically, but they can sometimes be anticipated and influenced, especially by managers experienced in public relations.[35]

The Integration Triangle

The integration triangle developed by Duncan and Moriarty is a simple illustration of how perceptions are created from the various brand message sources (see Exhibit 1-6). Planned messages are *say* messages—what companies say about themselves. In the story of Sharon and Green Threads, the Facebook ad was an example of this. Product and service messages are *do* messages because they represent what a company does. The bike rack, socially aware business practices, and helpful clerk were examples of this in the Green Threads story. Unplanned messages are *confirm* messages because that's what others say and confirm (or not) about what the company says and does. The positive posts on Google and any positive (or negative) news articles that Sharon might encounter about Green Threads are examples of this. Constructive integration occurs when a brand does what its maker says it will do and then others confirm that it delivers on its promises.[36]

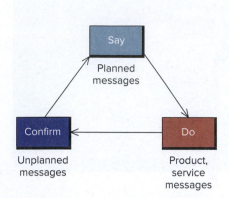

Exhibit 1-6
The integration triangle.

The Dimensions of IMC

To maximize the synergy benefits of IMC, Duncan suggests three priorities for an organization's integration process. It should first ensure consistent positioning, then facilitate purposeful interactivity between the company and its customers or other stakeholders, and finally actively incorporate a socially responsible mission in its relationships with its stakeholders.

As Duncan's IMC model shows in Exhibit 1-6, the cross-functional planning and monitoring of IMC activities result in an enhanced relationship with customers and other stakeholders, which leads to stakeholder loyalty and ultimately to greater brand equity.

The interest in IMC is global.[37] Large American-based companies such as McDonald's, IBM, and General Motors use IMC in campaigns throughout the globe, and foreign-based firms such as BMW, Lenovo, Samsung, and Sony practice IMC in their marketing efforts, including those aimed at U.S. consumers. IMC helps each of these firms maximize its resources and link communications activities directly to organizational goals and the resulting bottom line.[38]

While this text deals with most major facets of IMC and brand messages, advertising frequently has a central role. Why? Because advertising is typically the element of marketing communications over which a company has greatest control. As such, it remains an important component of almost every great IMC campaign. And it is likely to remain so for the foreseeable future.

Marketing: Determining the Type of IMC Message to Use

We now consider the marketing dimension of IMC because that's what defines IMC's role in business. Every business performs a number of diverse activities, typically classified into three broad functional divisions:

- Operations (production/manufacturing)
- Finance/administration
- Marketing

Of all the business functions, marketing is the only one whose primary role is to bring in revenue. Without revenue, of course, a company cannot recover its initial investment, pay its employees, grow, or earn a profit. So marketing is very important.

What Is Marketing?

Over the years, the concept of marketing has evolved based on the supply of and demand for products. Because we need to understand marketing as it relates to IMC, we define the term as follows:

Marketing is the activity, set of institutions, and processes for creating, communicating, delivering, and exchanging offerings that have value for customers, clients, partners, and society at large.[39]

Companies that exist to make a profit are not the only organizations that use marketing principles. Charities also apply these ideas in their quest to increase donations. The "crack" in the pavement is part of an unusual outdoor ad in San Francisco that reminds city residents of how important the Red Cross would be in an earthquake.

Source: American Red Cross

Marketing is a **process**—a sequence of actions or methods—aimed at satisfying customer needs profitably. This process includes developing products, pricing them strategically, making them available to customers through a distribution network, and promoting them through sales and advertising activities. A company's ultimate goal of the marketing process is to profitably exchange products or services with customers who need or want them. And the role of advertising is to inform, persuade, and remind groups of customers, or markets, about the need-satisfying value of the company's goods and services. Even nonprofit organizations use the marketing process to develop and promote services that will satisfy their constituents' needs.

Advertising and the Marketing Process

Companies and organizations use many different types of advertising, depending on their particular marketing strategy. The marketing strategy will determine who the targets of advertising should be, where ads should appear, what media should be used, and what advertising should accomplish. (Exhibit 1-7 shows some of the ways advertising can be classified, based on these strategic marketing elements.) These criteria will also determine what different advertising skills are required.

By Target Audience	By Geographic Area	By Purpose	By Medium
Consumer advertising: Aimed at people who buy the product for their own or someone else's use.	*Local (retail) advertising:* Advertising by businesses whose customers come from only one city or local trading area.	*Product advertising:* Promotes the sale of products and services.	*Print advertising:* Newspapers, magazines.
Business advertising: Aimed at people who buy or specify products and services for use in business.	*Regional advertising:* Advertising for products sold in one area or region but not the entire country.	*Nonproduct (corporate or institutional) advertising:* Promotes the organization's mission or philosophy rather than a specific product.	*Broadcast (electronic) advertising:* Radio, TV.
• *Trade:* Aimed at wholesalers and retailers of products and services who buy for resale to their customers.	*National advertising:* Advertising aimed at customers in several regions of the country.	*Commercial advertising:* Promotes products, services, or ideas with the expectation of making a profit.	*Out-of-home advertising:* Outdoor, transit.
• *Professional:* Aimed at people licensed under a code of ethics or set of professional standards.	*International advertising:* Advertising directed at foreign markets.	*Noncommercial advertising:* Sponsored by or for a charitable or nonprofit institution, civic group, or religious or political organization.	*Direct-mail advertising:* Advertising sent through the Postal Service and by e-mail.
• *Agricultural:* Aimed at people in farming or agribusiness.		*Action advertising:* Attempts to stimulate immediate action by the reader.	*Interactive advertising:* Web, social media, mobile, etc.
		Awareness advertising: Attempts to build the image of a product or familiarity with the product's name and package.	

Exhibit 1-7
The classifications of advertising.

Ethics, Diversity & Inclusion

Programs for Advertising Students

Many U.S. industries have struggled to ensure that career opportunities are available to all people. The advertising industry is no exception. In addition, advertising has a special role in cultural understanding of diversity because of its power and prominence. Many see ads as a mirror of society, or even a powerful creator of social norms and values. But how can ads represent the diversity of people from all walks of life if the people who create those ads come from the majority culture only?

The Ethics, Diversity & Inclusion portion of each chapter will explore this important dimension and demonstrate how the advertising industry has, and has not, met its social responsibility towards people from all backgrounds. Even today full inclusion remains a work in progress.

The good news is that the advertising world knows it must do a better job of diversifying its ranks. If you are a student of advertising, there are two important programs that you should know about. These programs represent concerted efforts by the industry to attract the very best talent.

The American Association of Advertising Agencies, better known as the 4A's, sponsors a fantastic internship program known as MAIP (Multicultural Advertising Internship Program). If you have an interest in working in an agency, or learning more about agency life, the MAIP is a great opportunity. Students can choose a specific advertising area of focus (media, creative, public relations, etc.) and work in a variety of locations around the U.S. Applications are normally due in October, and interns are notified of their selection in February. To apply, visit https://maip.aaaa.org/application/.

A second great program is offered by the American Advertising Federation, or AAF. It is called the Most Promising Multicultural Students program. The MPMS offers students an opportunity to meet with high-power professionals in New York for several days of networking and coaching. Your school must have an AAF dues-paying chapter to be eligible. These applications are also due in October. You can find out more about this program at www.aaf.org/AAFMemberR/Awards_and_Events/Awards/Most_Promising_Multicultural_Students/Eligibility.aspx.

If you meet the criteria for these programs, my advice to you is go for it. Past participants routinely rave about their experiences in both programs. Why not help your career and help change the world?

Identifying Target Markets and Target Audiences

A firm's marketing activities are always aimed at a particular segment of the population—its **target market.** Likewise, advertising is aimed at a particular group called the **target audience.** When we see an ad that doesn't appeal to us, it may be because the ad is not aimed at any of the groups we belong to. For example, a TV commercial for denture cream isn't meant to appeal to teens. They're not part of either the target market or the target audience. There are two main types of target markets, *consumers* and *businesses.*

Consumer Markets

Most ads you encounter fall under the broad category of **consumer advertising.** Usually sponsored by the producer (or manufacturer) of the product or service, these ads are typically directed at **consumers,** people who buy the product for their own or someone else's personal use. One example is **retail advertising,** advertising sponsored by retail stores and businesses. Consumer advertising also includes noncommercial *public service announcements (PSAs)* from organizations such as the American Cancer Society or the Partnership for a Drug-Free America.

To create messages that are persuasive, advertising professionals try to understand how people act and think—and why they buy, what they buy. This area of study is the province of *consumer behavior,* our focus in Chapter 5. The better an advertiser understands the buying behavior of people, the better it can bring its products into the collective consciousness of prospective customers.

This ad for Nivea helps to identify the target audience and convey a "personality" of the brand. The images, copy, layout, and placement of the ad are designed to attract and resonate with the company's target audiences.

Source: Beiersdorf AG

Industrial/Business Markets

Companies use **business advertising** to reach people who buy or specify goods and services for business use. It tends to appear in specialized business publications or professional journals, in direct-mail pieces sent

Trade advertising is aimed not at consumers but at people who buy or influence business purchases. This website encourages businesses to consider using tough Corning glass for packaging their products.

Source: Corning Incorporated

to businesses, or in trade shows. Because business advertising (also called **business-to-business, or B2B, advertising**) rarely uses consumer mass media, it is typically invisible to consumers. However, some business-to-business ads, by firms such as FedEx, do appear on TV and in consumer magazines.

In addition to general business advertising, there are three specialized types of business advertising: trade, professional, and agricultural. Companies aim **trade advertising** at resellers (wholesalers, dealers, and retailers) to obtain greater distribution of their products. For example, Sunkist places trade advertising in publications such as *California Grocer* to develop more grocery outlets and to increase sales to existing outlets.

Advertising aimed at teachers, accountants, doctors, dentists, architects, engineers, lawyers, and the like is called **professional advertising** and typically appears in official publications of professional societies (such as the *Archives of Ophthalmology*). Professional advertising has three objectives: to convince professionals (people with specialized training who work under a code of ethics) to recommend or prescribe a specific product or service to their clients, to buy brands of equipment and supplies for use in their work, or to use the product personally.

Companies use **agricultural (or farm) advertising** to promote products and services used in agriculture to farmers and others employed in agribusiness. FMC Corp., a large agricultural chemical company, for example, might advertise its plant nutrition products to growers using *California Farmer* magazine. Agricultural advertising typically shows farmers how the advertised product will increase efficiency, reduce risks, and widen profit margins.

Professional advertising targets audiences in fields such as accounting, medicine, and education. Law firms are the intended target of this ad from Wells & Drew Companies.

Source: Wells & Drew Companies, Jacksonville, FL

Business customers tend to be very knowledgeable and sophisticated, and they may require extensive technical information before making the purchase decision. So people who work in business-to-business advertising often require more specialized product knowledge and experience than their consumer advertising colleagues.

Implementing Marketing Strategy

LO 1-6

After selecting a target market for its products, a firm designs a strategy to serve that market profitably. As we'll discuss in Chapter 6, marketing strategy is the particular blend, or *mix,* of strategic elements over which the marketer has control: product concept, pricing, distribution, and communication. For ease of memory, marketers often refer to these elements as the 4Ps: product, price, place, and promotion. Each of these elements also influences the type of message used.

Product: Features and Benefits

Products have multiple features and solve a variety of problems. Advertising typically focuses on those features (product or brand components) or benefits (problems the brand can solve or ways the brand can provide desired rewards) of greatest relevance to the target audience. Consider automobiles. All have tires, a steering wheel, and windshields, and all will get you from one location to another. However a Prius, with its hybrid engine, will do so in an environmentally friendly way. A BMW Z4 will draw admiring looks from others. And a Ford F150 will complement an outdoor lifestyle. Part of the way we know these things is because advertising messages remind us why a brand is special.

Price: Strategies for Emphasizing Value

Consumers view value as the ratio of a brand's quality to its price. If two brands are priced similarly, the one higher in quality is the better value. If two brands are equal in quality, the one with the lower price is the better value. The implications for advertising strategy are straightforward. Some products (Suave personal care brands, No-Ad lotions) are publicized using **price advertising,** in which an ad claims the product is equal in quality to competing brands but sells at a lower cost. Other goods and services, which do not attempt to compete on price, emphasize product quality. **Image advertising,** which creates a perception of a company or a personality for a brand, is rarely explicit about price. Apple's iPods and Macs generally sell for more than competing brands, so Apple emphasizes how "cool" its technologies are and almost never mentions price. **Sale advertising** is used most often by retailers, dealers, and shops to call attention to a recent drop in the price of a brand or service. Such advertising allows retailers to match competitor price drops, move inventory, or increase retail traffic. However, when a brand is frequently put on sale, consumers may believe it is not worth its regular price. For this reason, some manufacturers prohibit retailers from discounting their products.

Place: The Distribution Element

The third element of marketing strategy, place (or, more accurately, distribution), also affects the type of advertising used. Global marketers such as Coca-Cola, Toyota, and IBM may use **global advertising,** in which messages are consistent in ads placed around the world. Other firms may promote their products in foreign markets with **international advertising,** which may contain different messages and even be created locally in each geographic market. The field of international marketing is so important that we discuss global advertising issues in every chapter of this book.

Companies that market in several regions of the United States and use the major mass media are called *national advertisers,* and their promotion is called **national advertising.** Some companies sell in only one part of the country or in two or three states. They use **regional advertising,** placing their ads in local media or regional editions of national media. Finally, businesses and retailers that sell within one small trading area typically use **local advertising** placed in local media or direct mail. We'll explore this topic further in Chapter 4.

Promotion: The Communication Element

The final element of marketing strategy is communication. As we mentioned at the beginning of this chapter, advertising is just one of the tools in the marketing communications tool kit. **Marketing communications** typically refers to all the *planned messages* that companies and organizations create and disseminate to support their marketing objectives. In addition to advertising, major marketing communication tools include *personal selling, sales promotion, public relations activities,* and *collateral materials.* The extent to which an organization uses any or all of these tools again depends on its marketing needs, objectives, and strategy.

Each marketing communication tool offers particular opportunities and benefits to the marketer. **Personal selling,** for example, in which salespeople deal directly with customers either face-to-face or via telemarketing, offers the flexibility possible only through human interaction. Personal selling is ideal for conveying information, giving demonstrations, and consummating the sale (or exchange), especially on high-ticket items such as cars, real estate, and furniture as well as most business-to-business products. The drawback to personal selling is its high cost, so companies that emphasize personal selling in their marketing mix often spend a lower percentage of sales on advertising than other firms. We'll discuss personal selling in greater detail in Chapter 17.

As a marketing communications tool, advertising enables marketers to reach more prospects at lower cost than a salesperson could ever do. Further, the creativity inherent in advertising allows the marketer to create an image or personality, full of symbolic meaning and benefits, for the company's brand. No salesperson can do this. However, advertising does suffer from credibility gaps, a topic we'll discuss in Chapter 3.

Advertising can be used to satisfy a variety of sponsor objectives. Some advertising is meant to help generate profits for the advertiser; some is sponsored by nonprofit groups. Some ads try to spur the target audience to immediate action; others, to create awareness or understanding of the advertiser's offering.

To promote their goods and services, companies use **product advertising.** To sell ideas, though, organizations use **nonproduct advertising.** An ExxonMobil ad that touts a new gasoline additive as a way of encouraging consumers to fuel up at an ExxonMobil service station is a product ad. But an ExxonMobil ad promoting the company's mission or philosophy (e.g., how the company develops new technologies to conserve energy and protect the environment) is called *nonproduct, corporate,* or *institutional advertising.* Why do companies communicate their good works or activities to consumers? We'll answer that question in Chapter 18.

Global companies must advertise not only in their home country but also overseas to cover the distribution element of their marketing strategies. This ad for Kentucky Fried Chicken targets consumers through a purely illustrative advertisement, overcoming any language barriers.

Vincent Thian/AP Images

(continued on page 28)

Great advertising is both timeless and contemporary. This Portfolio Review presents some of the best recent work by agencies around the world. Examine the ads as you would both as a consumer and as an advertising professional. Train your eye to notice how art, copy, and color make ads grab the attention of consumers. Don't be afraid to critique the ads as well. Given your understanding of the target audience and the brand, what approach would you have taken?

Social media regularly features some of the best advertising created today. At the top, Eggo's social media team engages with the popular Netflix show *Stranger Things* after Eleven reveals it is her favorite food. At the right, Reese Witherspoon responds on Instagram to a call to help storm victims in Puerto Rico by sharing an awkward adolescent pic. And Wholesome Culture, a company dedicated to meatless diets, creates a new take on an old message (see top left of next page).

(top) Source: Twitter/Kellogg NA Co.; (bottom) Source: Twitter/Reese Witherspoon

Greenpeace created a fake whale carcass that was left on beaches without warning to visitors. It helped illustrate the toll of thoughtless disposal of plastics on our oceans.

How hot and spicy is KFC? This ad, part of a broader campaign, uses a metaphor to make a point that words can't.

Can a highlighter be interesting? Stabilo shows that it can when it helps highlight overlooked women in U.S. history.

Source: STABILO International GmbH .

Alvogen markets pharmaceutical products in Greenland, which has strict regulations on the text that can be used to promote health products. The challenge was accepted by its ad agency, which created beautiful and informative images to inform consumers.

Source: Alvogen

Promoting flame-broiled burgers by showing actual photos of Burger King franchises burning is edgy. But that's exactly what makes this campaign interesting and irresistible.

Source: Burger King Corporation

In Ireland mobile phone blackout areas are called "black spots." To promote its broad wireless coverage, Irish company eir swapped every black dot in an issue of the *Daily Mail Magazine* with colored ones. Hard to miss that one!

Source: eir

People BEHIND the Ads

**Albert Lasker and Claude Hopkins:
Advertising Legends**

(left) Everett Collection Historical/Alamy Stock Photo; (right) Source: Claude Hopkins

Albert Lasker didn't start out wanting an advertising career at all. His dream was to become a great newspaper reporter. One of eight children, Lasker began writing a weekly newsletter at 12 and working for his hometown paper while still in high school.

In his teens, he set his sights on New York, home of the country's biggest dailies. But, as he later recalled, there was just one problem:

My father had a dread of my becoming a newspaperman, because in those days (and this is no exaggeration) almost every newspaperman was a heavy drinker. . . . I was very devoted to my father, and he proposed instead that I go to a

firm in what he considered a kindred field—Lord & Thomas in Chicago, an advertising agency.[40]

Just 19 when he arrived in Chicago, Lasker was given only menial office tasks around the agency. His plan was to stay for a short while and then eventually move on to become a reporter. But a gambling loss equivalent to nearly his entire annual salary dashed those prospects. In an early display of his persuasive abilities, Lasker convinced agency owner Thomas to cover his debt in exchange for a portion of his weekly pay.

If he proved to be a poor gambler, Lasker quickly showed other talents. He convinced his bosses to "temporarily" assign him a sales territory vacated by a departing employee and soon brought in thousands of dollars more business each month than the man he replaced. Reflecting on his predecessor, Lasker later wrote: "He was a fine man, but he wasn't a 'closer.'"[41]

"So far as I know, no ordinary human being has ever resisted Albert Lasker," Claude Hopkins once observed.[42] Lasker's persuasive talents were rooted in his gifts as both a leader and a visionary. Impressing everyone he worked with, Lasker was quickly promoted through the agency ranks. He was still in his early twenties when he bought Lord & Thomas and began creating the first true "modern" ad agency.

Lasker's assumption as leader at Lord & Thomas corresponded with a change in what ad agencies did for clients. Once considered

(continued from page 23)

Similarly, while commercial advertising seeks profits, **noncommercial advertising** is used around the world by governments and nonprofit organizations to seek donations, volunteer support, or changes in consumer behavior.

Some ads are intended to bring about immediate action by the reader; others have a longer-term goal. The objectives of **awareness advertising,** for example, are to create an image for a product and to position it competitively with the goal of getting readers or viewers to select the brand the next time they shop.

A direct-mail ad, on the other hand, exemplifies **action (or direct-response) advertising** because it seeks an immediate, direct response from the reader. Most ads on TV and radio are awareness ads, but some are a mixture of awareness and action. For example, a 60-second TV commercial may devote the first 50 seconds to image building and the last 10 to a toll-free phone number for immediate information.

Sales promotion is a communication tool that offers special incentives to motivate people to act right away. The incentives may be coupons, free samples, contests, or rebates on the purchase price. By offering added value, sales promotion accelerates sales. So it is a very effective tool. It is often used in conjunction with advertising—to promote the promotion. However, like personal selling, it is very expensive; it suffers from other drawbacks as well, as we'll discuss in Chapter 10. While ad agencies create and place media advertising, most sales promotion efforts are created by firms that specialize in that field.

to be media brokers, agencies were just beginning to provide creative services for advertisers. Lasker embraced this change and Lord & Thomas soon became famous for its creative work. This was due in no small part to Lasker's willingness to pay top dollar for talent and for his lifelong fascination with "how advertising works." It was his interest in the latter that led to one of Lasker's two most famous hires, John E. Kennedy. Kennedy, a former Canadian police officer, was toiling in relative anonymity as a freelance copywriter when, as legend has it, he sat at a bar beneath the famous ad agency and wrote on a piece of paper:

> I am in the saloon downstairs. I can tell you what advertising is. I know you don't know. It will mean much to me to have you know what it is and it will mean much to you. If you wish to know what advertising is, send the word "yes" down by the bell boy. Signed—John E. Kennedy[43]

Lasker, intrigued, invited Kennedy up. Like many in his day, Lasker believed that advertising was best thought of as a kind of news. But Kennedy's deceptively simple idea was that advertising was "salesmanship in print." This philosophy helped shape and define the work produced by Lord & Thomas for many years and proved influential not only with Lasker, but with generations of advertising professionals such as Rosser Reeves, Claude Hopkins, John Orr Young (cofounder of Young & Rubicam), and David Ogilvy.

While the salesmanship-in-print notion was Kennedy's, the man who put the idea into practice was Kennedy's successor, Claude Hopkins. Hopkins believed advertising had one function: selling. A man of amazing energy, curiosity, and talent, Hopkins believed that there were basic principles that could be discovered through repeated testing and that these principles would guarantee success. Hopkins even claimed these principles were understood and he set them out in a book, *Scientific Advertising*.

As we will see in Chapter 2, later generations of advertising professionals such as Bill Bernbach eventually rejected the idea that advertising is a science, and few today would call it that. Thus, many of the "principles" that Hopkins described now appear quaint and simplistic.

But if Hopkins was wrong about some things, he was remarkably prescient about others. For example, he believed that agency people should develop a deep understanding of the product and the consumer. He also understood the value of research both before and after a campaign (he especially liked the use of coupons as a way of gauging advertising effectiveness, foreshadowing the popularity of direct-response advertising today). Finally, Hopkins advocated finding a "preemptive claim" for each brand, an attribute that could be used to distinguish the brand from its competitors. One famous example was Hopkins's claim for Schlitz that the brand's bottles were "washed with live steam." The fact that all beer bottles were sterilized with steam did nothing to diminish, in the minds of consumers, the association of Schlitz with purity, cleanliness, and safety. Hopkins eventually became one of the ad industry's highest paid talents, earning a six-figure salary.

The Lord & Thomas agency endured after Lasker and Hopkins ended their careers, eventually becoming Foote, Cone, & Belding, now part of the Interpublic empire. And while Albert Lasker never did become a reporter, he lived a rich, full life. In his retirement, he donated much of his wealth to charities. Especially noteworthy was his creation of the Albert and Mary Lasker Foundation, named for the executive and his wife. The foundation has helped fund and reward groundbreaking clinical and basic medical research since 1945 (www.laskerfoundation.org).

Public relations (PR) is an umbrella process—much like marketing—responsible for managing the firm's relationships with its various *publics*. These publics may include customers but are not limited to them. Public relations is also concerned with employees, stockholders, vendors and suppliers, government regulators, interest groups, and the press. So PR is much larger than just a tool of marketing communications. However, as part of their marketing mix, marketers use a number of **public relations activities** because they are so good at creating awareness and credibility for the firm at relatively low cost. These activities (often referred to as **marketing public relations [MPR]**) include publicity, press agentry, sponsorships, special events, and a special kind of advertising called **public relations advertising,** which uses the structured, sponsored format of media advertising to accomplish public relations goals. While PR is closely aligned with advertising, it requires very different skills and is usually performed by professionals in PR firms rather than ad agency people. However, advertising people need to understand how important PR activities are, so we'll discuss the topic in some detail in Chapter 18.

Companies use a wide variety of promotional tools other than media advertising to communicate information about themselves and their brands. These **collateral materials** include flyers, brochures, catalogs, posters, sales kits, product specification sheets, instruction booklets, and so on. These materials may be very inexpensive or frightfully costly. But because they contribute so much information to customers and prospects, they are very important to both closing sales and reinforcing prior sales decisions. The people who produce collateral materials may work for the company's advertising agency, but often they work for outside graphic design firms, packaging specialists, and independent film and video producers.

Additional Benefits of Integrated Marketing Communications

In recent years, as new media have proliferated and the cost of competition has intensified, sophisticated marketers have searched for new ways to get more bang (and accountability) from their marketing communications buck. The result has been a growing understanding on the part of corporate management that (1) the efficiencies of mass media advertising are not what they used to be; (2) consumers are more sophisticated, cynical, and distrusting than ever before; (3) tremendous gaps exist between what companies say in their advertising and what they actually do; and (4) in the long run, nourishing good customer relationships is far more important than making simple exchanges.[44] As we've emphasized in this chapter, this has led to a growing movement toward integrating all the messages created by an advertiser's various communication agencies and sent out by various departments within the company to achieve consistency. IMC is not only an important marketing trend, it is *the* business imperative for the 21st century.

While the name, and some would say the practice, of IMC is a somewhat new development, dating to the end of the 20th century, it can be argued that IMC is in fact a continuation of the kind of strategic thinking that evolved with the growth and sophistication of advertising. To see that more clearly, the next chapter presents an overview of the development of advertising, illustrated through the history of Coca-Cola.

Chapter Summary

Advertising is a paid, mediated form of communication from an identifiable source, designed to persuade the receiver to take some action, now or in the future. To maximize advertising effectiveness, most companies work to ensure that their advertisements complement other messaging efforts. This practice is called integrated marketing communications, or IMC.

Advertising is a type of communication, similar in some ways to ordinary communication, but different as well. Ordinary human communication begins when a source formulates an idea, encodes it as a message, and sends it via some channel or medium to a receiver. The receiver must decode the message in order to understand it. To respond, the receiver formulates a new idea, encodes that concept, and then sends a new message back through some channel. A message generated in response to the original message is feedback. In advertising, the communication process is complex because of the multidimensional nature of the source, the message, and the recipient. Traditionally, advertising has been a one-way process, but interactive technologies offer companies feedback in real time and a wealth of consumer data. This feedback is vital to modern marketing.

Advertising is an important tool for companies that practice IMC, the concept and process of strategically managing and coordinating the messages that consumers receive about brands. Practiced well, IMC creates synergies among various channels of communications. It is also fundamentally important for companies for guiding how they engage stakeholders (which includes consumers, but also other groups including employees and the public) and build credible relationships with them.

Marketing's primary role is to attract revenues. The targets of a firm's marketing will determine the targets of its advertising. Marketers address two major types of audiences with their advertising: consumers and businesses. Within each of these categories, though, are special forms of advertising, such as retail, trade, professional, and agricultural.

A firm's marketing mix—or strategy—establishes the type of advertising needed and the skills required to implement it. The marketing mix includes those elements over which the marketer has control: product, price, distribution, and communication. Depending on the product marketed, the advertiser may use packaged-goods advertising, professional services advertising, or some other type such as high-tech advertising. Likewise, the firm's pricing strategy will determine if it should use sale advertising.

The distribution strategy dictates the firm's use of local, regional, national, or international advertising. The communication element determines the mix of marketing communications tools to be used. These include advertising, personal selling, sales promotion, public relations activities, and collateral materials.

To achieve consistency in all the organization's messages, sophisticated companies seek to integrate their marketing communications with all other corporate activities through a process called integrated marketing communications.

Important Terms

action advertising, *28*

actual consumers, *11*

advertising, *8*

agricultural (farm) advertising, *21*

author, *10*

autobiographical messages, *11*

awareness advertising, *28*

business advertising, *20*

business-to-business (B2B) advertising, *21*

channel, *9*

collateral materials, *29*

consumer advertising, *20*

consumers, *8, 20*

decode, *9*

direct-response advertising, *28*

drama message, *11*

encode, *9*

feedback, *9*

global advertising, *22*

goods, *8*

ideas, *8*

image advertising, *22*

implied consumers, *11*

integrated marketing communications (IMC), *5*

interactive customer relationships, *14*

international advertising, *22*

lifetime customer value (LTCV), *13*

local advertising, *22*

marketing, *18*

marketing communications, *4, 7, 23*

marketing public relations (MPR), *29*

mass media, *8*

medium, *8*

message, *9*

narrative messages, *11*

national advertising, *22*

noise, *9, 12*

noncommercial advertising, *28*

nonproduct advertising, *23*

persona, *11*

personal selling, *23*

price advertising, *22*

process, *19*

product, *8*

product advertising, *23*

professional advertising, *21*

public relations (PR), *29*

public relations activities, *29*

public relations advertising, *29*

public service messages, *8*

receiver, *9*

regional advertising, *20*

relationship marketing, *13*

retail advertising, *22*

sale advertising, *22*

sales promotion, *28*

services, *8*

source, *9*

sponsor, *10*

sponsorial consumers, *11*

stakeholders, *13*

target audience, *20*

target market, *20*

trade advertising, *21*

Review Questions

1. What is advertising and how does it differ from other marketing communications techniques?

2. In the marketing communications process, what are the various dimensions of the source, the message, and the receiver?

3. Why do many companies practice IMC and what benefits does it afford companies that practice it well?

4. What kinds of relationships do brands have with consumers and what factors determine which type of relationship is appropriate?

5. What are the advantages of the interactive communications model over the traditional one? How has the growth of interactive communications improved the practice of IMC?

6. With whom else besides consumers do brands seek to develop relationships?

7. What are the two broad categories of target markets?

8. In addition to consumer advertising, what specific form of business advertising would a pharmaceutical company be likely to employ?

9. What are the four elements that comprise a company's marketing strategy (or marketing mix) and how do they affect the type of advertising a company uses?

10. What is the purpose of awareness advertising?

11. What important marketing activities fall under the heading of "promotions"?

The Advertising Experience

1. **Brand Relationships**

   This chapter has emphasized building relationships as an important objective for IMC. Think about your favorite brands. Do you feel as though you have a "relationship" with any? What do the companies that support these brands do to ensure you are happy in the relationship? How does this relationship affect your response to new product offerings from these companies? How and when do you communicate to others your positive feelings or excitement about the brand?

2. **Role of Advertising**

   In Chapter 1, you learned about the standard definition of advertising and the various roles and forms that advertising can take. Browse through the following websites and discuss what type of advertising each uses and what the purpose of the advertising is:

   a.   American Cancer Society: www.cancer.org

   b.   Amazon: www.amazon.com

   c.   Nike: www.nike.com

d.   Ford: www.ford.com
e.   McDonald's: www.mcdonalds.com
f.   MINI: www.MINIUSA.com
g.   United Parcel Service: www.ups.com

3. Literary Forms in Television Ads

Watch three television or YouTube ads and examine them for literary form. Do they take the form of autobiography, narrative, or drama? For each ad, discuss why you think its creator chose this particular form over another.

4. Dealing with Unwanted Brand Messages

Reread the brief account of Sharon and her discovery of a new clothing store. Imagine a news reporter interviews a former

employee of Green Threads who falsely accuses the company of disposing of waste in an environmentally unsafe fashion. What are some ways that the retailer could deal with this unwanted claim? Do any of these ways of responding to the information, even if it is false, carry their own risks?

5. The Double-Edged Sword of Communication Feedback

The feedback that many companies seek from customers has a flip side, consumer privacy concerns. This is explored in the chapter opening. How much privacy should consumers expect? When does a company go too far in obtaining information about its prospects and customers? What will it mean for digital marketers if legislation restricts their access to consumer information?

End Notes

1.   Bernard Marr, "21 Scary Things Big Data Knows About You," *Forbes*, March 8, 2016, www.forbes.com/sites/bernardmarr/2016/03/08/21-scary-things-big-data-knows-about-you/#50606a586e7d.

2.   Charles Duhigg, "How Companies Learn Your Secrets," *New York Times Magazine*, February 16, 2012, www.nytimes.com/2012/02/19/magazine/shopping-habits.html?pagewanted=all&_r=1.

3.   Bernard Marr, "Barbie Wants to Chat with Your Child—But Is Big Data Listening In?" *Forbes*, December 17, 2015, www.forbes.com/sites/bernardmarr/2015/12/17/barbie-wants-to-chat-with-your-child-but-is-big-data-listening-in/#177abe8f2978.

4.   Upturn, "Predictive Policing: From Neighborhoods to Individuals," *in Civil Rights, Big Data, and Our Algorithmic Future*, 2014, https://bigdata.fairness.io/predictive-policing/.

5.   Bernard Marr, "How Facebook 'Likes' Reveal Your Intimate Secrets," LinkedIn, June 13, 2013, www.linkedin.com/pulse/20130613061334-64875646-how-facebook-likes-reveal-your-intimate-secrets/.

6.   Anthony Cuthbertson, "Google AI Can Predict When People Will Die with '95 Percent Accuracy,'" *Independent*, June 19, 2018, www.independent.co.uk/life-style/gadgets-and-tech/news/google-ai-predict-when-die-death-date-medical-brain-deep-mind-a8405826.html.

7.   Nitasha Tiku, "Europe's New Privacy Law Will Change the Web, and More," *Wired*, March 19, 2018, www.wired.com/story/europes-new-privacy-law-will-change-the-web-and-more/.

8.   "Facebook Scandal Hit 87 Million Users," *BBC News*, April 4, 2018, www.bbc.com/news/technology-43649018.

9.   Sean Keach, "Social Score: Facebook Has TRUST Ratings for Users—but It Won't Tell You Your Score," *The Sun*, August 21, 2018, www.thesun.co.uk/tech/7067261/facebook-trust-rating-score-check/.

10. Stephen R. Fox, *The Mirror Makers: A History of American Advertising and Its Creators* (Urbana, IL: University of Illinois Press, 1997).

11. Jef I. Richards and Catharine M. Curran, "Oracles on 'Advertising': Searching for a Definition," *Journal of Advertising* 31 (2002), pp. 63–77.

12. Claude Elwood Shannon and Warren Weaver, *The Mathematical Theory of Communication* (Urbana, IL: University of Illinois Press, 1971).

13. Barbara B. Stern, "A Revised Communication Model for Advertising: Multiple Dimensions of the Source, the Message, and the Recipient," *Journal of Advertising*, June 1994, pp. 5–15.

14. Lisa Nirell, *The Mindful Marketer* (London: Palgrave Macmillan, 2014); Larry Weber and Lisa L. Henderson, *The Digital Marketer* (Hoboken, NJ: John Wiley & Sons, 2014).

15. American Marketing Association, "Relationship Marketing," 2017, www.ama.org/resources/Pages/Dictionary.aspx?dLetter=R.

16. Gemma Joyce, "Five Times Customers Asked for Change and Brands Actually Delivered It," *Brandwatch*, July 12, 2018, www.brandwatch.com/blog/5-times-customer-change/

17. Philip Kotler and Kevin Lane Keller, *Marketing Management* (New York: Pearson, 2011).

18. Brad Sugars, "How to Calculate the Lifetime Value of a Customer," *Entrepreneur*, August 8, 2012, www.entrepreneur.com/article/224153.

19. Rolph Anderson, Srinivasan Swaminathan, and Rajiv Mehta, "Prospering in Tough Economic Times through Loyal Customers," *International Journal of Management and Economics* 41 (2014), pp. 76–91.

20. D. Van den Poel and B. Larivière, "Customer Attrition Analysis for Financial Services Using Proportional Hazard Models," *European Journal of Operational Research* 157 (2004), pp. 196–217.

21. Philip Kotler and Kevin Lane Keller, *Marketing Management* (New York, NY: Pearson, 2011).

22. Philip Kotler and Gary Armstrong, *Principles of Marketing* (Englewood Cliffs, NJ: Prentice Hall, 2014).

23. Jessica Tsai, "Are You Smarter Than a Neuromarketer?" *Customer Relationship Management*, January 2010, pp. 19–20.

24. Philip Kotler and Gary Armstrong, *Principles of Marketing*, (Englewood Cliffs, NJ: Prentice Hall, 2014).

25. Philip Kotler and Gary Armstrong, *Principles of Marketing*, (Englewood Cliffs, NJ: Prentice Hall, 2014).

26. E. J. Shultz, "Mtn Dew Plans Big Spending Boost behind Kickstart, Diet Dew," *Advertising Age*, January 21, 2014, http://adage.com/article/news/mtn-dew-plans-big-spending-boost-kickstart-diet-dew/291192/.

27. E. J. Shultz, "Mtn Dew Plans Big Spending Boost behind Kickstart, Diet Dew," *Advertising Age*, January 21, 2014, http://adage.com/article/news/mtn-dew-plans-big-spending-boost-kickstart-diet-dew/291192/.

28. Jerry G. Kliatchko, "Revisiting the IMC Construct: A Revised Definition and Four Pillars," *International Journal of Advertising* 27 (2008), pp. 133–60.

29. "Disney's Four Keys to a Great Guest Experience," *Disney at Work*, 2019, *http://disneyatwork.com/disneys-four-keys-to-a-great-guest-experience/*.

30. Sandra Luxton, Mike Reid, and Felix Mavondo, "Integrated Marketing Communication Capability and Brand Performance," *Journal of Advertising* 44 (2015), pp. 37–46.

31. Glen Nowak and Joseph Phelps, "Conceptualizing the Integrated Marketing Communications Phenomenon: An Examination of Its Impact on Advertising Practices and Its Implications for Advertising Research," *Journal of Current Issues and Research in Advertising*, Spring 1994, pp. 49–66.

32. Glen Nowak and Joseph Phelps, "Conceptualizing the Integrated Marketing Communications Phenomenon: An Examination of Its Impact on Advertising Practices and Its Implications for Advertising Research," *Journal of Current Issues and Research in Advertising*, Spring 1994, pp. 49–66.

33. Jerry Kliatchko, "Revisiting the IMC Construct: A Revised Definition and Four Pillars," *International Journal of Advertising* 27 (2008), pp. 133–60.

34. Charles R. Taylor, "Integrated Marketing Communications in 2010 and Beyond," *International Journal of Advertising* 29 (2010), p. 161–64.

35. Thomas R. Duncan and Sandra E. Moriarty, *Driving Brand Value: Using Integrated Marketing to Manage Stakeholder Relationships* (New York: McGraw-Hill, 1997).

36. Thomas R. Duncan and Sandra E. Moriarty, *Driving Brand Value: Using Integrated Marketing to Manage Stakeholder Relationships* (New York: McGraw-Hill, 1997).

37. Jerry G. Kliatchko and Don E. Shultz, "Twenty Years of IMC: A Study of CEO and CMO Perspectives in the Asia-Pacific Region," *International Journal of Advertising* 33 (2014), pp. 373–90, *www.academia.edu/7295960/Twenty_Years_of_IMC*.

38. Sandra Luxton, Mike Reid, and Felix Mavondo, "Integrated Marketing Communication Capability and Brand Performance," *Journal of Advertising* 44 (2014), pp. 37–46.

39. "Definition of Marketing," American Marketing Association (approved July 2013), *www.ama.org/the-definition-of-marketing/*.

40. Albert Davis Lasker, "The Personal Reminiscences of Albert Lasker," *American Heritage* 6, no. 1 (December 1954).

41. Albert Davis Lasker, "The Personal Reminiscences of Albert Lasker, *American Heritage* 6, no. 1 (December 1954).

42. Claude C. Hopkins, *My Life in Advertising* (New York: Harper & Bros., 1927; repr. The Editorium, LLC, 2009).

43. Dr. Robert C. Worstell, Claude C. Hopkins, John E. Kennedy, and Albert D. Lasker, *Scientific Advertising Origins*, Lulu.com (2014).

44. MMC Learning, Integrated Marketing Communications. *http://multimediamarketing.com/mkc/marketingcommunications/*

CHAPTER

2

The Big Picture: The Functions of Advertising and Its Evolution

---

LEARNING OBJECTIVES

Advertising and IMC play important roles in the national and global economies. But they evolved relatively recently in human history. Why did advertising develop, and why is it so important in modern life? To help answer these questions, this chapter introduces the principles of free-market economics, the functions and effects of advertising in a free economy, the evolution of advertising as an economic tool, and advertising's overall impact on society. You will gain an understanding of why the practice of advertising began, how it changed, why it will continue to evolve, and why it is an important part of a market economy.

After studying this chapter, you will be able to:

LO2-1   Discuss the functions advertising performs in free markets.

LO2-2   Identify milestones in the history of advertising.

LO2-3   Discuss how the role of advertising has changed over time.

LO2-4   Offer evidence for the importance of branding, including descriptions of the benefits that strong brands offer companies.

LO2-5   Delineate the impact of advertising on society yesterday, today, and tomorrow.

(both) Source: The Coca-Cola Company

John Pemberton's original recipe included coca leaves and kola nuts, stimulants meant to relieve headaches. The storied traces of cocaine are long gone from the Coca-Cola formula, but today's logo is still based on the heading of the original recipe.[1] Like the swirls of the logo, urban legend and myth surround the world's most valuable brand. Although the company cultivates the mystique, especially by guarding the "secret formula," Coke's advertising has been nothing but charming and positive from the start. ■ In 1886, Pemberton sold his new remedy for five cents a glass in an Atlanta drugstore. The first Coca-Cola advertisement appeared in the *Atlanta Journal* that same month. ■ But Pemberton was an inventor, not a marketer, and the company was still quite small when in 1892 Asa Candler purchased rights to the beverage from Pemberton's family for $2,300. ■ Candler incorporated the Coca-Cola Company and gave birth to the brand. He aggressively attracted customers with novel promotions, including handing out coupons for free samples. Candler also placed ads in the new media of the era, on wall murals and on fixtures in

stores, such as calendars, clocks, and soda fountains. ■ In 1906, agency head William D'Arcy convinced Candler to start a newspaper advertising campaign. From the start, Coke advertising associated the brand with appealing images, from fresh-faced young women to Santa Claus. D'Arcy believed that "Coca-Cola advertising should create scenes that drew people in and made them a part of the pleasant interludes of everyday life."[2] Ads of the 1920s and 1930s showed people enjoying Coke during activities such as boating that many aspired to—perhaps realistically during the boom years but wistfully during the Depression. ■ D'Arcy handled the Coke account until 1956, when the agency faltered in the face of a new medium, television. It gracefully passed the account to fresh talent McCann-Erickson, but not without commemorating its 50-year relationship with Coca-Cola in a *Wall Street Journal* ad. ■ McCann-Erickson's Coke campaigns of the 1950s, 1960s, and 1970s hooked into the popular culture spreading through TV by featuring performers and their music. For some of the most memorable spots in TV history, see

Portfolio Review: The Modern History of Advertising in this chapter. ■ Coke's success has been extraordinary, but not without missteps. Coke experimented with a new recipe and in 1985 pulled out all the stops to introduce New Coke. The public's reaction to New Coke was negative and immediate: Some people began hoarding Old Coke, while others lobbied the company and prepared to sue. Coke realized that it was the brand—not its taste—that customers were loyal to. As Coca-Cola's president noted in a later press conference, "All the time and money and skill poured into consumer research on the new Coca-Cola could not measure or reveal the deep and abiding emotional attachment to original Coca-Cola. . . . Some cynics will say we planned the whole thing. The truth is we are not that dumb and we are not that smart."[3] The company pulled the plug on New Coke and returned to its old formula. ■ Coca-Cola recovered market share with the help of the seven-year "Always Coca-Cola" advertising campaign. The Creative Edge agency contributed a whimsical series of computer-generated TV spots, bringing Coke advertising into the digital age and showing simple, Coke-worthy moments in the lives of animated polar bears. ■ At the start of the new millennium, critics suggested that Coca-Cola advertising was adrift. Investors wanted the company to divert more energy into the growing sports drink sector instead: "Why pump money into marketing for a slowing brand when you should be coming up with a better Powerade or Dasani?" asked one major shareholder.[4] ■ Why indeed? Through 120 years of cultural change, new technologies, and market trends, the Coca-Cola Company's careful stewardship of the brand's value has made Coke not only the world's best-selling carbonated beverage but also the world's most venerable brand. ■ As of 2020, Coke is still setting the pace for IMC. From customizable bottles to throw-back Santa ads, Coke finds ways to link its brands to deep, heartfelt emotions. The result is continued marketing dominance. Coke has held a nearly 43 percent share of U.S. soft drink volume for over a decade. It owns an even more impressive 48 percent share of the global market. Coke succeeds at IMC not because it is the most innovative or edgy marketer. It succeeds because it understands its brand, its customers, and the deep relationship between the two.

The Functions of Advertising

LO 2-1

Advertising performs a variety of functions and, when executed correctly, its effects may be dramatic. To see how this works, let's go back to the beginnings of Coca-Cola, when druggist John Pemberton was still mixing the syrup in his lab. (For a chronology of the evolution of the Coca-Cola brand and and company, see Exhibit 2-1.)

Pemberton's business partner and bookkeeper, Frank Robinson, suggested the name "Coca-Cola" to identify the two main flavors and because he thought that "the two Cs would look well in advertising."[5] Robinson wrote down the name in his flowing script, creating the logo that is now instantly recognizable around the world. Later, a distinctive bottle shape became standard throughout the company. The proprietary curvy bottle helped customers differentiate Coca-Cola from other drinks. The creation of the Coca-Cola logo and contour bottle illustrates one of the most basic functions of **branding** as well as advertising: *to identify products and their source and to differentiate them from others.* (The functions and effects discussed here are listed in Exhibit 2-2.)

When Pemberton first began selling Coca-Cola at Jacobs' Pharmacy, he needed to let people know what it was—although we associate the word *cola* with a cold, dark, sparkling beverage, the people of Atlanta didn't automatically make the same connection. Therefore, Pemberton and Robinson added the suggestion *drink* before *Coca-Cola* on the signs that they had painted and placed in front of the drugstore.[6] Ads in the *Atlanta Journal* let readers know why they should drink it (because it is "delicious, exhilarating, refreshing, and invigorating"), how much it cost, and where they could get it. This demonstrates another basic function of advertising: *to communicate information about the product, its features, and its location of sale.*

1880s and 1890s		1900s and 1910s	
1884	John Pemberton develops "Pemberton's French Wine Coca," an alcoholic headache remedy.	**1901**	Candler begins the first free drink coupon campaign.
1885	Prohibition laws are passed in Atlanta; Pemberton reformulates his drink into a nonalcoholic version and calls it "Coca-Cola."	**1906**	D'Arcy creates a newspaper ad campaign for Coca-Cola.
		1906	The first international syrup plant opens in Havana, Cuba.
1886	Coca-Cola goes on sale in an Atlanta drugstore.	**1911**	Coca-Cola's advertising budget reaches $1 million.
1887	A dying Pemberton sells stakes in his company to four businessmen.	**1912**	Copycat colas abound.
		1915	The "contour" Coke bottle is designed and becomes the standard.
1888	Asa Candler secures sole rights to make and sell Coca-Cola.	**1916**	Candler resigns from Coca-Cola and is elected mayor of Atlanta.
1894	Coca-Cola is first sold in bottles.	**1919**	Coca-Cola introduces the six-pack to encourage buying enough to take home.

1920s and 1930s		1940s, 1950s, and 1960s	
1923	Robert Woodruff becomes company president.	**1941**	After years of battling the short form, the company begins to use the word "Coke" in ads.
1928	More people drink Coca-Cola from bottles than from the fountain.	**1942**	Coca-Cola avoids sugar rationing by supplying the army with Coke.
1928	Coca-Cola sponsors the Olympic Games in Amsterdam.	**1943**	General Eisenhower sends a telegram asking for 10 Coca-Cola bottling plants to be set up in war zones.
1930	Bottlers go door-to-door installing Coke-branded bottle openers in homes.	**1950**	Coke is the first product to appear on the cover of *Time* magazine.
1931	Haddon Sundblom's classic Santa Claus appears in Coca-Cola ads.	**1955**	Coca-Cola introduces family-size bottles.
1935	Coin-operated vending machines become widely available.	**1964**	First pop-tab cans introduced.

1970s and 1980s		1990s and 2000s	
1971	Coca-Cola teaches the world to sing with the "hilltop" TV spot.	**1993**	Polar bears appear in ads as part of the "Always Coca-Cola" campaign. Advertising annual spending reaches $1 billion.
1978	The People's Republic of China allows Coca-Cola, and no other drink company, to operate in the country.	**2002**	Coca-Cola begins high-visibility sponsorship of *American Idol*.
1982	Diet Coke is born.	**2005**	Coke Zero, sweetened with aspartame, is developed and marketed.
1985	New Coke is released with much fanfare in April but is rejected by consumers.	**2011**	Coke introduces special white cans to partner with the World Wildlife Fund and protect polar bears.
1985	Classic Coke returns to the shelves in July, sweetened entirely with high-fructose corn syrup.	**2014**	Coke sparks controversy with "It's beautiful" Super Bowl ad.
1985	Astronauts use a special "space can" to drink Coca-Cola aboard the shuttle.	**2018**	Coke unites all of its namesake beverages, Coca-Cola, Coke Zero, and Coca-Cola Life, under a single trademark. The change is shared with consumers during a 60-second Super Bowl spot.

Exhibit 2-1
Coca-Cola chronology: The story of Coke and its parent company.

Exhibit 2-2
Functions and effects of advertising as a marketing tool.

- To identify products and differentiate them from others.
- To communicate information about the product, its features, and its place of sale.
- To induce consumers to try new products and to suggest reuse.
- To stimulate the distribution of a product.
- To increase product use.
- To build value, brand preference, and loyalty.
- To lower the overall cost of sales.

After Asa Candler gained control of the Coca-Cola Company, he began to develop the drink's market on a grander scale. He mailed thousands of coupons for free drinks to Atlanta residents. Thousands more were handed out on the street and inserted in magazines. To cover the costs of the samples, the company gave free syrup to the soda fountains that offered the beverage. The free sample campaign accompanied Coca-Cola's introduction in new markets. This campaign illustrates another function of advertising: *to induce consumers to try new products and to suggest reuse.*

Through the early part of the 20th century, Coca-Cola wasn't the dominant force we know today. Competitors such as Pepsi and the now-defunct Moxie cut into Coca-Cola's market share. Outside forces also threatened the entire industry; sugar rationing during wartimes was especially damaging. Prior to the entry of the United States in World War II, Coca-Cola executives persuaded the government to give Coke to troops to boost their morale. To accomplish this, the D'Arcy advertising agency gathered endorsements from U.S. officers in training camps to support Coke's bid to become an official military supplier—and therefore to be exempt from rationing. The War Department agreed to the plan, and Coca-Cola borrowed $5.5 million to establish 64 bottling plants near the front lines. The risky investment had great returns. Surveys found returning vets preferred Coke by eight to one over Pepsi.[7] Coca-Cola masterfully blended patriotism with another of the most important functions of advertising: *to increase product use.*

As soft drinks became a staple in convenience stores, restaurants, and homes throughout the United States, Coca-Cola began campaigns outside the country. The first international bottling plants were established in Canada, Cuba, and Panama in 1906; today, the company bottles Coke in more than 200 countries. Coca-Cola franchise bottlers around the world can tweak the recipe to match local tastes by altering the amount of sweetener they add to the base syrup. Bottlers and distributors also supplement the company's advertising with their own promotions and event sponsorships–from a community clean-up day in Armenia to a major film festival in South Korea. Through various activities, Coca-Cola has succeeded in accomplishing yet another function of advertising: *to stimulate the distribution of a product*–in this case, on a global level.

In a free-market economy, when one company starts to make significant profits, other companies immediately jump in to compete. Over the years, to battle the constant competitive threat, Coca-Cola has funded ongoing marketing communications campaigns to accomplish yet another function of advertising: *to build value, brand preference, and loyalty.* Although the taste test wars of the 1980s showed that many people liked the taste of Pepsi better than that of Coke, such blind preference has never knocked Coca-Cola out of the top spot. A century of consistently upbeat messages has made its mark. Coca-Cola advertising, such as its current campaign, "The Wonder of Us," has always promoted a common voice and a common theme: Coca-Cola makes life's relaxing moments even better.

For more than 120 years, the Coca-Cola Company has used a variety of media to communicate this message to diverse audiences. Why? To achieve the most significant function of advertising: *to lower the overall cost of sales.* For the cost of reaching just one prospect through personal selling, companies can reach thousands of people through media advertising. The average cost to make a face-to-face field sales call is about $170. Multiply that $170 by the more than 15 million people who watch a network TV show, and the cost comes to a staggering cost of $2.55 billion. However, for only $500,000, Coca-Cola can buy a 30-second TV commercial during a top-rated show and reach the same 15 million people. Through television, advertisers can talk to a thousand prospects for about $30–less than 20 percent of what it costs to talk to a single prospect through personal selling.[8]

Now, considering this brief synopsis of Coca-Cola history, how does Coke's advertising fit with the basic assumptions of a free-market economy? Has Coke's advertising helped make the soft drink available to more people at lower cost? Has it informed them about where they can buy Coke and why they should drink it? Has the freedom to advertise and has Coke's success spurred competition from other companies? What externalities might have had a positive or negative impact on the Coca-Cola Company's efforts to market its beverages?

The marketers of Coca Cola have harnessed the power of advertising to tell an amazing story, a story that has left a powerful idea in the minds of hundreds of millions of consumers. At the center of each of those stories is the brand. In fact, many IMC activities are devoted to branding. Consider each of these pairings: retailer–Nordstrom's; energy drink–Red Bull; digital assistant–Amazon Echo; wireless service–Verizon. In each case, a generic product category is paired with a strong brand in that category. To the extent that you found yourself having a clearer, stronger, and more positive response to the brand than to a generic example from the category, you've experienced the power of branding.

We elaborate on the importance of branding, and demonstrate how it is accomplished, later in this chapter. But first we review the history of advertising in North America. How did an industry that did not even exist 200 years ago become such a powerful force in modern life? Why is it so important today? And how has it evolved to meet the needs of marketers and consumers over the decades?

The Evolution of Advertising

LO 2-2

Thousands of years ago, people spent most of their time meeting basic survival needs: food, clothing, shelter. They lived in small, isolated communities where artisans and farmers bartered products and services. Distribution was limited to how far vendors could walk and "advertising" to how loud they could shout. Because goods weren't produced in great quantity, there was no need for advertising to stimulate mass purchases. There were also no mass media available for possible advertisers to use. Nevertheless, archaeologists have found evidence of messages meant to encourage trade among the Babylonians dating back as far as 3000 BC.

This bronze plate advertises a tailor's shop in ancient China and is considered one of the oldest ad messages still available.

Historic Collection/Alamy Stock Photo

Early Advertising

Civilizations began emerging approximately 5,000 years ago as people mastered agriculture. A stable food supply meant people could settle, and soon cities began forming in Europe, Asia, and South America. Trade among cities led to the development of merchant classes and markets.

There was very little advertising at this time. Why? First, most people made what they used themselves. People's lives were devoted to farming, raising livestock, and hard labor. Mass media were nonexistent. There were no easy ways to move goods and services long distances. The emergence of advertising as an industry would have to wait for the appearance of machinery, wealth, population growth, mechanized transportation, and mass media.

During this **preindustrial age,** several important events contributed to the eventual development of modern advertising. The Chinese invented paper, and Europe had its first paper mill by 1275. Around 1439, Johannes Gutenberg invented the movable-type printing press in Germany. The press was not only the most important development in the history of advertising, and indeed communication, but it also revolutionized the way people lived and worked.

The introduction of printing allowed information to be established, substantiated, recorded, and transported. People no longer had to rely on their memories. Movable letters provided the flexibility to print in local dialects. The slow hand transcription of monks and scholars gave way to more rapid volume printing by a less select group. Some entrepreneurs bought printing presses, mounted them in wagons, and traveled from town to town selling printing. This new technology made possible the early instances of advertising—posters, handbills, and signs—and, eventually, the first mass medium—the newspaper.

In 1472, the first ad in English appeared: a handbill tacked on church doors in London announcing a prayer book for sale. Two hundred years later, the first newspaper ad was published, offering a reward for the return of 12 stolen horses. Soon newspapers carried ads for coffee, chocolate, tea, real estate, and medicines, and even personal ads. These early ads were still directed to a very limited number of people: the customers of the coffeehouses where most newspapers were read.

By the early 1700s, the world's population stood at about 600 million people, and some cities were big enough to support larger volumes of advertising. Samuel Johnson, a famous English literary figure, observed in 1758 that advertisements were now so numerous they were "negligently perused," and it had become necessary to gain attention "by magnificence of promise." This was the beginning of *puffery* in advertising.

In the colonies, the *Boston Newsletter* began carrying ads in 1704. About 25 years later, Benjamin Franklin, the father of advertising art, made ads more readable by using large headlines and considerable white space. In fact, Franklin was the first American known to use illustrations in ads.

In the mid-1700s, the Industrial Revolution began in England, and by the early 1800s, it had reached North America. Machinery began to replace animal power. By using machines to mass-produce goods with uniform quality, large companies increased their productivity. It now costs people less to buy a product than to make it themselves. As people left the farm to work in the city, mass urban markets began to emerge, further fueling market development and the growth of advertising.

The Industrial Age and the Birth of Ad Agencies

The **industrial age** started during the second half of the 19th century and lasted well into the 20th. As we have seen, ads were created prior to the industrial age, but it was not until this period that it can be said that an advertising industry existed anywhere in the world. It was a period marked by tremendous growth and maturation of the country's industrial

An early form of advertising. Until the advent of public schooling, most people couldn't read—so signs featured symbols of the goods or services for sale, such as the chair on this cabinetmaker's sign in Williamsburg, Virginia.

Pat & Chuck Blackley/Alamy Stock Photo

(continued on page 44)

:: The Modern History of Advertising

While advertising is thousands of years old, it has come into its own only in the last 100 years, thanks to a growing population hungry for goods and services and a rapidly changing technology that could make these products available.

If we look back at the ad campaigns of 30, 50, 70, and even 100 years ago, we get a fascinating indication of how life was lived back then, and we can also see how the development of modern advertising parallels the development of our own standard of living. As British writer and diplomat Norman Douglas said in 1917, "You can tell the ideals of a nation by its advertisements."[9]

•   Study the array of historical ads in this Portfolio Review and consider how well each relates to the seven functions and effects of advertising discussed in this chapter.

Coca-Cola was first served at a small pharmacy in Atlanta in 1886. Coca-Cola's inventor, John S. Pemberton, placed an ad in the *Atlanta Journal* proclaiming that the soft drink was "delicious and refreshing."
Source: Library of Congress Prints and Photographs, LC-USZ62-39705

This full-color ad from the 1920s would have been considered very modern at the time of publication. Then as now, Coke combines a contemporary image with a timeless message.

The Image Works Archives/The Image Works

Appearing in publications across the country, this 1930s print ad for Coca-Cola was one of the first to incorporate Santa Claus. Interestingly, it was not until the mid-19th century that Santa Claus began to be portrayed in this rotund, jolly manner, and in fact, artists working for Coca-Cola played a major role in popularizing the Santa Claus we know today.

Source: The Coca-Cola Company

Coke ushered in the 1980s with a famous commercial featuring all-pro defensive lineman "Mean" Joe Greene. The commercial debut was featured during the 1980 Super Bowl. A young fan shares his coke with the NFL's "meanest" player, who responds with a smile and a souvenir for the boy. The influential ad inspired parodies, including a 2009 Coke Super Bowl spot starring Troy Polamalu and a 2012 ad for Downy featuring Greene and Amy Sedaris.

(all) Source: The Coca-Cola Company

Do polar bears and penguins really get along? Because they live on different continents, we may never really know. However, Coca-Cola's playful depiction of polar bears and penguins sharing a Coke as an ice-breaker is another great example of how Coca-Cola continues to build value, brand preference, and loyalty with its advertisements.

(all) Source: The Coca-Cola Company

Coke's "Arctic Explorer," which ran in 2011 and 2012, illustrated the plight of real polar bears. Do you think that Coca-Cola's decision to issue the beverage in all-white cans helped consumers to associate with and relate to the plight of the polar bears?

Source: The Coca-Cola Company

Actor Gillian Jacobs, known for her roles on TV shows *Community* and *Love,* encourages Diet Coke drinkers to do what they want. "It's delicious," she says, and "It makes me feel good. Life is short. If you want to live in a yurt, yurt it up." Website MarketWatch suggests that "the campaign appears to be attempting to strike a rebellious, tongue-in-cheek tone."

(all) Source: The Coca-Cola Company

It wasn't until 1729 that Ben Franklin, innovator of advertising art, made ads more readable by using larger headlines, changing fonts, and adding art. This 1767 ad announces the availability of Stage-Waggons to carry passengers from Powles Hook Ferry to Philadelphia.

Source: *Pennsylvania Gazette*, April 24, 1766

(continued from page 39)

base. As U.S. industry met the basic needs of much of the population, commodity markets became saturated. Fresh mass markets then developed for the new, inexpensive brands of consumer luxury and convenience goods called **consumer packaged goods.**

By the mid-1800s, the world's population had doubled to 1.2 billion. Producers needed mass consumption to match the high levels of manufactured goods. Fortunately, breakthroughs in bulk transportation—the railroad and steamship—facilitated distribution of products beyond the manufacturer's local market. But with the need for mass consumption came the increasing need for mass-marketing techniques to inform consumers of the availability of products.

During the 1800s, manufacturers were principally concerned with production. The burden of marketing fell on wholesalers, who used advertising primarily as an information vehicle. Ads appeared in publications called *price currents* that informed retailers about the sources of supply and shipping schedules for commodities. Montgomery Ward and Sears Roebuck produced the earliest catalogs, bringing a wide variety of products to new, rural markets. Only a few innovative manufacturers (mostly of patent medicines, soaps, tobacco products, and canned foods) foresaw the usefulness of mass media advertising to stimulate consumer demand.

The American *profession* of advertising began when Volney B. Palmer set up business in Philadelphia in 1841. Palmer was essentially a mediator, buying large volumes of discounted newspaper advertising space and reselling to advertisers at a profit. The advertisers usually prepared the ads themselves.

In 1869, Francis Ayer formed an ad agency in Philadelphia and named it after his father. N. W. Ayer & Sons was the first agency to charge a commission based on the "net cost of space" and the first to conduct a formal market survey. Ayer became the first ad agency to operate as agencies do today—planning, creating, and executing complete ad campaigns in exchange for media-paid commissions or fees from advertisers. In 1892, Ayer set up a copy department and hired the first full-time agency copywriter.

The telegraph, telephone, typewriter, phonograph, and, later, motion pictures all let people communicate as never before. With the development of the nationwide railroad system, the United States entered a period of spectacular economic growth. In 1896, when the federal government inaugurated rural-free mail delivery, direct-mail advertising and mail-order selling flourished. Manufacturers now had an ever-increasing variety of products to sell and a new way to deliver their advertisements and products to the public.

With the advent of public schooling, the nation reached an unparalleled 90 percent literacy rate. Manufacturers gained a large reading public that could understand print ads. The United States thus entered the 20th century as a great industrial state with a national marketing system propelled by advertising. With the end of World War I, the modern period in advertising emerged.

During the 19th century, wholesalers controlled the marketing process because they distributed the manufacturers' unbranded commodity products. When those markets became saturated, though, the wholesalers started playing one manufacturer off against another. This hurt manufacturers' profits dramatically, so they started looking for ways to wrest back control. The manufacturers changed their focus from a *production* orientation to a *marketing* orientation. They dedicated themselves to new product development, strengthened their own sales forces, packaged and branded their products, and engaged in heavy national brand advertising. Early brands included Wrigley's spearmint gum, Coca-Cola, Jell-O, Kellogg's corn flakes, and Campbell's soup.

In the 1920s, the era of salesmanship had arrived and its bible was *Scientific Advertising,* written by the legendary copywriter Claude Hopkins at Albert Lasker's agency, Lord & Thomas (see People behind the Ads at the end of this chapter). Published in 1923, it claimed that "Advertising has reached the status of a science. It is based on fixed principles." Hopkins outlawed humor, style, literary flair, and anything that might detract from his basic copy strategy of a preemptive product claim repeated boldly and often.[10]

Ethics, Diversity & Inclusion

Mary Wells Lawrence

Susan Wood/Getty Images

What's the name of the first female CEO of a company listed in the New York Stock Exchange? The answer is Mary Wells Lawrence, an advertising trailblazer who helped found the Wells Rich Greene agency. Mary Wells' accomplishments include some of the most iconic ads of the 1960s and 70s for Alka Seltzer ("Plop, Plop, fizz fizz" and "I can't believe I ate the whole thing"), I ♡ NY, Ford ("Quality is job 1"), and Sure deodorant ("Raise your hand if you're Sure"). Like the character Peggy Olson on *Mad Men,* Wells entered advertising with too much talent to be ignored, even in a sexist industry. In turn, she helped open doors for the many talented women in advertising today.

Mary Wells was born in 1928 and is, at the time of this writing, still alive in her 90s. She studied at the Carnegie Institute of Technology before writing copy for a department store. After a move to New York, she became an ad manager for Macy's, then a copywriter for McCann Erickson, Coke's lead agency. Still a young talent, Wells began drawing attention from industry leaders. Bill Bernbach helped recruit Wells to join the hottest agency in America at that time, Doyle Dane Bernbach. She spent seven years learning from Bernbach, one of the greatest creatives in the history of advertising (see People Behind the Ads: William Bernbach at the end of this chapter).

When Wells finally left DDB, a former colleague, Jack Tinker, convinced her to create a campaign for Braniff Airways. The effort, accompanied by the slogan "The End of the Plain Plane," helped turn around the struggling airline. Showing that she understood IMC before the term had ever been created, Wells' campaign extended to all aspects of the passenger experience, including redesigned crew uniforms and bright new plane colors.

Mary Wells was now a national figure and ready to strike out on her own. But as a woman in the 1960s, finding support for the idea was difficult. Her firm, Jack Tinker and Partners, valued her work and talent. They even promised to make her a president of the company. But as Wells recounts in her book, *A Life in Advertising:*

> Instead, when we met he offered to pay me as if I were the president, to give me the authority of the president, but he said he could not give me the title of president, because he was certain that would limit the exciting growth of Jack Tinker & Partners. "It is not my fault, Mary—the world is not ready for women presidents. . . ." He was shocked at the blazing fury that came over me, the war he saw in my eyes. I left him sitting in my office talking to himself.

Instead, she founded her own shop, Wells Rich Greene, in 1966. The agency attracted top clients, including Procter & Gamble, Sheraton Hotels, and, of course, Braniff. As CEO, Wells described her management style this way, "My way of running an agency was as if it were a motion-picture company with a lot of productions happening at one time; I was the director, sometimes the star. The people I hired were the cast of characters, and I was Elia Kazan, Mike Nichols, or Robert Altman—whatever it took to make them as good as they could possibly be."

In 1969, the highest-paid person working in advertising was said to be Mary Wells. She continued in her role until 1990, when, at age 62, she stepped away from agency life. But Wells was hardly finished changing the world. In 2008, she helped launch wowOwow, a website for and created by women. Its founders and contributors included Whoopi Goldberg, Peggy Noonan, Marlo Thomas, and Lily Tomlin.

When the *New York Times* tracked down Mary Wells in 2012, she reflected on the excitement of her life in the advertising world. Ambition, noted Wells, is nothing to be ashamed of, "You can't just be you. You have to double yourself. You have to read books on subjects you know nothing about. You have to travel to places you never thought of traveling. You have to meet every kind of person and endlessly stretch what you know."

And perhaps thinking about the changes she helped usher into the ad world, she noted, "There were and are so many talented women in the advertising business, and the real wonder is why they aren't all running worldwide agencies of their own. I'm looking into that."

Sources: Ginia Bellafante, "A Pioneer in a Mad Men's World," *New York Times,* June 8, 2012; Mary Wells Lawrence, *A Big Life in Advertising* (New York: Touchstone, 2003).

This full page of advertising from an 1894 *Scientific American* (*www.scientificamerican.com*) *is historically telling. The ads feature unbranded commodities such as soap, paper, paint, or services. Advertising focused on persuading consumers to prefer specific brands was still decades away.*

Source: *Scientific American*

Radio was born at about the same time and rapidly became a powerful new advertising medium. World and national news now arrived direct from the scene, and a whole new array of family entertainment—music, drama, and sports—became possible. Suddenly, national advertisers could quickly reach huge audiences. In fact, the first radio shows were produced by their sponsors' ad agencies.

On October 29, 1929, the stock market crashed, the Great Depression began, and advertising expenditures plummeted. In the face of declining sales and corporate budget cutting, the advertising industry needed to improve its effectiveness. It turned to research. Daniel Starch, A. C. Nielsen, and George Gallup founded research groups to study consumer attitudes and preferences. By providing information on public opinion, the performance of ad messages, and sales of advertised products, these companies started the marketing research industry.

During this period, each brand sought to convince the public of its own special qualities. Wheaties was the "Breakfast of Champions" not because of its ingredients but because of its advertising. Manufacturers followed this strategy of *product differentiation* vigorously, seeking to portray their brands as different from and better than the competition by offering consumers quality, variety, and convenience.

The Depression ended in 1941 with America's involvement in World War II. The ad industry did its part in aiding the war effort, as demonstrated in the ad shown at the top left of the next page.

The Golden Age of Advertising

The postwar period from 1946 through the 1970s is sometimes referred to as advertising's "Golden Age." This is because the introduction of television helped make the advertising industry a focus of great attention, which led to both acclaim and criticism.

Postwar prosperity of the late 1940s and early 1950s seemed to many to create a culture in which consumers tried to climb the social ladder by buying more and more modern products. A creative revolution ensued in which ads focused on product features that implied social acceptance, style, luxury, and success. Giants in the field emerged—people such as Leo Burnett, David Ogilvy, and Bill Bernbach, who built their agencies from scratch and forever changed the way advertising was planned and created.[11]

Rosser Reeves of the Ted Bates Agency introduced the idea that every ad must point out the product's USP *(unique selling proposition)*—features that differentiate it from competitive products. The USP was a logical extension of the Lasker and Hopkins "reason why" credo.

But as more and more imitative products showed up in the marketplace, all offering quality, variety, and convenience, the effectiveness of this strategy wore out. Companies turned to a new mantra: **market segmentation,** a process by which marketers searched for unique groups of people whose needs could be addressed through more specialized products. The image era of the 1960s was thus the natural culmination of the creative revolution. Advertising's emphasis shifted from product features to brand image or brand personality as advertisers sought to align their brands with particularly profitable market segments. Cadillac, for example, became the worldwide image of luxury, the consummate symbol of success.

Just as me-too product features killed the product differentiation era, me-too images eventually killed the market segmentation era. With increased competition, a new kind of advertising strategy evolved in the 1970s, in which competitors' strengths became just as important as the advertiser's. Jack Trout and Al Ries insisted that what really mattered was how the brand ranked against the competition in the consumer's mind—how it was positioned.

Advertisers and agencies pitched in to do their part during World War II. Shortages of many basic consumer goods reduced ad expenditures during the war.

Source: Henry McAlear, U.S. Army, Recruiting Publicity Bureau

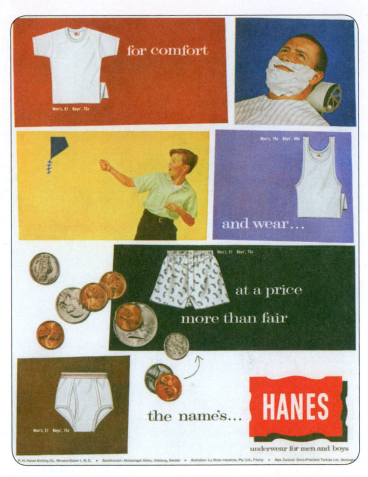

By the middle of the 20th century, advertisers knew it was important to tell consumers why they should prefer a particular brand over its competitors. This 1958 ad for Hanes gives consumers several benefits to think about.

Source: Hanesbrands Inc.

Positioning strategy proved to be an effective way to separate a particular brand from its competitors by associating that brand with a particular set of customer needs that ranked high on the consumer's priority list. Thus, it became a more effective way to use product differentiation and market segmentation. The most famous American ads of the positioning era were Volkswagen ("Think small"), Avis ("We're only no. 2"), and 7UP ("The uncola"). Product failures of the period, such as Life Savers gum and RCA computers, were blamed on flawed positioning.

Product differentiation, market segmentation, and positioning are all important strategies to understand, and you'll learn more about them in Chapter 6.

While this was all going on in the United States, across the Atlantic, a new generation of advertising professionals had graduated from the training grounds of Procter & Gamble (P&G) and Colgate-Palmolive and were now teaching their clients the secrets of mass marketing. Lagging somewhat behind their U.S. counterparts due to the economic ravages of World War II, European marketers discovered the USP and the one-page strategic brief, or summary statement, that P&G had popularized to bring focus to ad campaigns. Immediately following the war, French advertising pioneer Marcel Bleustein-Blanchet waged a frustrating battle to introduce U.S. research techniques to his country; a decade or two later, in-depth attitude and behavioral research was all the rage.[12] Because commercial TV was not yet as big as in the United States, European advertisers divided their media money between newspapers and outdoor media, along with a healthy dose of cinema advertising. Germany, the Netherlands, and Scandinavia wouldn't get commercial TV for another decade.[13]

Doyle Dane Bernbach's "Think small" ad for Volkswagen was named the greatest ad of all time by Advertising Age. *These clever, simple, and elegant ads from the same campaign offer further proof of the brilliance of William Bernbach's creative talent. Learn more about Bernbach in People behind the Ads at the end of the chapter.* (both) Source: Volkswagen of America, Inc.

Demarketing is used to dampen demand for products, especially those that create unwanted costs for society. This public service message created for France's ANPAA (National Association for Prevention of Alcoholism and Addiction) uses the metaphor of a fish hook and the tagline: "It's your choice to keep off the hook" to convey the dangerous addictive qualities of alcohol. Source: National Association for Prevention of Alcoholism and Addiction

In the 1970s, though, the European Common Market already offered untapped opportunities. Following the American example, agencies and clients began to think multinationally to gain economies of scale. But it was not easy. While physically close, the countries of Europe were still separated by a chasm of cultural diversity that made the use of single Europe-wide campaigns nearly impossible.[14]

The Postindustrial Age

Beginning around 1980, the **postindustrial age** has been a period of cataclysmic change. Citizens became increasingly aware of the sensitive environment in which we live and alarmed by our dependence on vital natural resources. Acute energy shortages of the 1970s and 1980s introduced a new marketing term, **demarketing.** Producers of energy and energy-consuming goods used advertising to *slow* the demand for their products. Ads asked people to refrain from operating washers and dryers during the day when the demand for electricity peaked. In time, demarketing became a more aggressive strategic tool for advertisers to use against competitors, political opponents, and social problems. The California Department of Health Services, for example, is one of many organizations today that actively seek to demarket the use of tobacco.

Then, following a period of unprecedented boom in the West and bust in the East, the Berlin Wall and the Iron Curtain came tumbling down. This finally ended the Cold War. Newly freed nations in the former Warsaw Pact states offered millions of under-served consumers. To expand globally, big multinational companies and their advertising agencies went on a binge, buying other big companies and creating a new word in the financial lexicon: *megamerger.*

My IMC Campaign 2-A

Tools for Teamwork

Advertising agencies look for at least three qualities in the people they hire: talent, a great work ethic, and the ability to work well with others. If you are working on your campaign in a group, you'll find those qualities—especially the third—to be important as well.

Your campaign assignment may be the first time you've worked on a group project. If so, you'll discover that working in a team is very different from doing a project on your own.

First, you will need to coordinate everything that you do. That means each person must create schedules that accommodate not only his or her own obligations, but also those of the group. Second, you will be sharing work. Tools that help you share documents, calendars, and other files will help you produce better work and do it faster. Third, you should consider the importance of leadership in a group. Your group will usually perform better if someone is formally appointed as leader, at least in the sense of organizing meetings, maintaining a calendar, and keeping track of what has to be done. Finally, everyone is accountable. Talk to your professor about whether he or she expects peer evaluations or some other means to assess differences in group member effort and performance.

Many internet tools are now available to help improve the coordination of teams. Best of all, they are free. The ones I prefer are those created by Google because they are easy to use, powerful, and integrated (both with each other and with mobile devices). If you would prefer not to use a Google product, I've tried to find equivalents where possible.

Staying Connected

E-mail, of course, remains an essential tool. You may have a university e-mail account, but these can be problematic because (1) your inbox space is limited, (2) spam filters in these accounts are often very aggressive (too much useful mail is moved to the spam folder), and (3) they lack many useful tools for organizing and labeling your mail. Tech site Hubspot recommends Gmail (www.gmail.com) for teams. It is an excellent free mail service that you will most likely never fill up (which means you never have to delete e-mails and your inbox never gets too full). You can use "labels" to quickly identify mail from people in your group. And with "contacts" you can set up groups of e-mail addresses to message easily and quickly. Use "tasks" to create a to-do list right in your e-mail list. These programs also work well with many mobile devices. Microsoft and Zoho offer quality alternatives (https://blog.hubspot.com/marketing/free-email-accounts)

Creating Documents

If you already own Microsoft Office, you have a strong suite of tools for collaboration in the cloud (www.office.com/). Alternatively, if the Google ecosystem is best for you, then Google docs (http://docs.google.com) is a free suite of simple yet powerful document creation tools that includes a word processor, a spreadsheet program, and a presentation creator. You can share some or all of the documents you create with others and edit them simultaneously. So if a group member is working on a creative brief, he or she can share it immediately with everyone else for edits and comments. If you would prefer a non-Google solution, Techradar recommends LibreOffice as a powerful, Microsoft-compatible suite of programs that is free to use (www.techradar.com/news/the-best-free-office-software).

Staying Organized

Many people find that calendars and to-do lists are essential. Google has an excellent calendar program (www.google.com/calendar) that everyone in the team can edit. You can also sync the calendar with many mobile devices. As I indicated before, Google's "task" program is built into Gmail.

Conducting Research

Powerful tools for doing research are also available for free on the web. For secondary research purposes, it is great to have a program that allows you to copy and store documents, web pages, photos, charts, and other kinds of information. A powerful and popular program is Evernote (www.evernote.com). Your group may also find itself collecting primary data. If you need to administer a survey, consider a useful component of Google docs called "forms." With forms, you can easily create a web-based survey and have your data set up in a Google spreadsheet as it comes in. A non-Google program that does the same thing is SurveyMonkey (www.surveymonkey.com).

Working Well and Staying Accountable

Learning to adapt to group projects is not easy for everyone. Knowing what to expect and developing the skills to work well with others are essential. For guidance, consider these thoughts from experts:

- MIT: http://hrweb.mit.edu/learning-development/learning-topics/teams/articles/basics
- *Psychology Today:* www.psychologytoday.com/us/blog/cutting-edge-leadership/201301/characteristics-good-work-team-members

If you volunteer to be a team leader (or are appointed one), some helpful tips can be found here:

- Qualities of a great team leader: http://smallbusiness.chron.com/10-effective-qualities-team-leader-23281.html
- Roselind Torres on new leadership styles: www.ted.com/talks/roselinde_torres_what_it_takes_to_be_a_great_leader/discussion

If you are doing peer evaluations in your class, your professor will likely have a form that you should use. These types of forms can be found throughout the web. Some examples include these:

- www.lapresenter.com/coopevalpacket.pdf
- www.northwestern.edu/searle/docs/History%20and%20Philosphy%20Self%20and%20Peer%20Evaulation.pdf

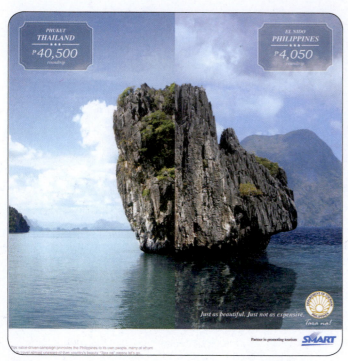

This ad for the Department of Tourism, Philippines is considered comparative advertising because it makes claims about both the sponsoring brand and a competitor.

Source: The Philippine Department of Tourism

By now European and Asian advertising had caught up with the United States. TV was the hot medium, and agencies focused on growth, acquisitions, and superior creative executions. For several years, Young & Rubicam in New York and Dentsu in Japan alternated as the largest advertising agency in the world. Two brothers in London, Charles and Maurice Saatchi, started acquiring agencies globally. In rapid succession, a number of high-profile U.S. agencies disappeared under the Saatchi & Saatchi umbrella—big companies such as Ted Bates Worldwide and Dancer, Fitzgerald, Sample. Saatchi & Saatchi was suddenly the largest agency in the world. More buyouts followed as the big agencies from Europe, the United States, and Japan emulated the merger mania of their huge multinational clients. Names of agency founders disappeared from the doors, replaced by initials and acronyms: WPP Group, RSCG, TBWA, FCA, DDB Needham, and FCB, to mention just a few.

The European agencies fueled their growth by establishing huge bulk-media-buying conglomerates, although their now-sophisticated clients stopped looking to the agencies for research and marketing advice. Rather, they expected extraordinary creative executions to give their brands an edge, and the agencies delivered. Awards at the Cannes International Advertising Festival disclosed the blossoming of creative advertising from Spain and confirmed the creative leadership of the British, who were only slightly ahead of the French.[15]

Two related economic factors characterized the marketing world of this period: (1) the aging of traditional products, with a corresponding growth in competition, and (2) the growing affluence and sophistication of the consuming public, led by the huge baby boomer generation.[16]

The most important factor was competition, intensified by lower trade barriers and growing international trade. As high profits lured imitators into the marketplace, each offering the most attractive product features at lower cost, consumers benefited from more choices, higher quality, and lower prices.

On the demand side, newly affluent consumers concerned themselves more with the quality of their lives. With their basic commodity needs already met, baby boomers were interested in saving time and money to spend on leisure-time activities or on products, services, and social causes that represented their aspirations.

As the 1990s unfolded, the traditional advertising industry found itself threatened on all sides and suffering from overpopulation.[17] Clients demanded better results from their promotional dollars; small, imaginative, upstart agencies competed for (and won) some big accounts that had never been available to them; TV viewers appeared immune to conventional commercials; and media options based on new technologies promised to reinvent advertising. In three short years, the advertising agency business lost more than 13,500 jobs. Major clients such as Coca-Cola defected from Madison Avenue, giving various portions of their business to specialists in small, regional creative shops and media-buying services. But the setback went far beyond the agency business. Throughout the media world, newspapers, magazines, and TV networks all lost advertising dollars.[18]

By the mid-1990s, U.S. marketers began shifting dollars back from sales promotion to advertising to rebuild value in their brands. In 1994, ad budgets surged ahead by 8.1 percent to $150 billion nationally. And throughout the rest of the 1990s, ad spending increased about 7 percent every year until the year 2000, when U.S. advertisers spent $247.5 billion, a whopping 11.3 percent increase over the previous year.[19] Consumers began discovering the benefits of "going online," as personal computers became commonplace. Advertisers, enthralled with the potential of the internet, began exploring ways to take advantage of this new medium.

But then the bubble burst. In 2001, the combination of a mild recession, a stock market decline, and the bust of the dot-coms contributed to a record decline in advertising activity. On September 11 of that year, terrorists attacked the United States, and suddenly all marketing and advertising seemed to stop—not just in North America but also around the world.[20] The end result: Spending in the United States declined 6.5 percent to $231 billion, and overseas spending dropped 8.6 percent to $210 billion.[21]

A year later, though, the economy seemed to be turning around and marketers were again starting to spend money on advertising. By 2005, U.S. advertising expenditures had reached $264 billion, more than completely recovering from the 2001 decline.[22] But the old days were gone for good. Technology, evolving lifestyles, new fears over security, and the rising cost of reaching consumers had changed the advertising business forever. Two developments from the early 2000s were little noticed then, but in time would shake up the marketing world. Larry Page and Sergey Brin, two Stanford grad students, developed AdWords, an advertising program for their search engine, Google, that eventually generated billions in profits. And Mark Zuckerberg dropped out of Harvard, headed west, and named his new social media company Facebook. By tapping into a strong consumer desire to connect with others, Zuckerberg created what may well be the greatest word-of-mouth marketing platform in history. The internet had created an electronic frontier—what Tom Cuniff, VP/creative director at Lord, Dentsu & Partners, calls "the second creative revolution."[23]

The Global Interactive Age: Looking at the 21st Century

LO 2-3

By the start of the new millennium, the rest of the world had in many respects caught up to North America, thanks to improved economic conditions and a desire for expansion. Recent estimates of worldwide advertising expenditures exceed $600 billion per year.[24] The importance of advertising in individual countries depends on the country's level of development and national attitude toward promotion. Typically, advertising expenditures are higher in countries with higher personal incomes. As Exhibit 2-3 shows, the top 5 global marketers are based in different countries.

Although the Communist countries once condemned advertising as an evil of capitalism, eastern European countries now encourage private enterprise and realize the benefits of advertising. And the United States now looks elsewhere to find its biggest economic rival. Some estimates suggest the Chinese economy, which is growing at more than 10 percent a year, will surpass that of America in the near future. Indeed, by some measures it already has.[25]

Widespread availability of cable TV and satellite receivers allows viewers to watch channels devoted to single types of programming, such as news, home shopping, sports, or comedy. This shift transformed television from the most widespread of mass media to a more specialized, "narrowcasting" medium. Small companies and product marketers that appeal to a limited clientele use TV to reach audiences with unique interests.

But increasingly, consumers are cutting their cables to watch TV via the web on such popular services as Netflix, Hulu, and Amazon Prime. This trend has proven so strong that as of 2015, both HBO and Showtime, which have operated as premium cable channels since their inceptions, have made their services available outside of cable to internet viewers.[26]

Exhibit 2-3
Top Global Marketers

2017	Marketer	Headquarters	WW Spend (billions)
1.	Samsung Electronics	South Korea	$ 1.2
2.	Procter & Gamble Co.	U.S.A	10.5
3.	L'Oreal	France	8.6
4.	Unilever	U.K./Netherlands	8.5
5.	Nestlé	Switzerland	7.2

Source: Ad Age Data Center: Worlds Largest Advertisers

AD Lab 2–A

What Kills Bugs Dead?

Successful marketing communications sometimes take on a life of their own. Over the years, advertising agencies have created many successful product slogans for their clients, which have become part of our popular culture. Here are some of the most famous. Test your knowledge and see how many advertisers you can identify.

1. "Think different."
2. "_____ kills bugs dead."
3. "Don't leave home without it."
4. "Diamonds are forever."
5. "Good to the last drop."
6. "Just Do It."
7. "When it rains, it pours."
8. "We bring good things to life."
9. "M'm! M'm! Good!"
10. "Let your fingers do the walking."

Answers

5. Maxwell House Coffee
4. DeBeers
3. American Express
2. Raid
1. Apple

10. Yellow Pages
9. Campbell Soup Co.
8. General Electric (GE)
7. Morton Salt
6. Nike

Laboratory Applications

1. Now that you know a little about slogans, create one for yourself personally or for your (real or imagined) company. Which qualities and characteristics do you want your slogan to highlight? Share your slogan with your classmates and gauge their reactions.

2. Business cards serve a higher purpose than simply providing information for a Rolodex. They are mini-advertisements. Create a business card for yourself using your slogan.

Internet Exercise

1. Need help getting started on your slogan assignment? Adslogans.com has step-by-step instructions that lead you through the process (www.adslogans.co.uk/general/students.html). For more ideas, look at slogans and ad campaigns past and present at www.adflip.com.

Modern advertisers understand that ads should explain a brand benefit in a clear, compelling, and creative way. Amundsen's agency, Ogilvy & Mather, Ukraine, uses a clever metaphor to demonstrate why "six times distilled" is worth purchasing in a vodka.

Source: Amundsen Premium Vodka

In September of 2008, the global economy began an economic slowdown. Many companies, faced with declining sales and lower revenue, cut back on advertising expenditures.

Particularly hard hit was the newspaper industry. Through late 2011, newspapers saw 20 consecutive quarters of ad revenue decline, and the total decline through 2012 was 48.8 percent.[27] Even worse, as the U.S. economy slowly improved heading into 2015, newspaper advertising revenue has failed to recover.

In truth, despite strong government intervention on behalf of banks, insurers, and auto manufacturers, and despite scattered "occupy" protests around the country, capitalism is likely to remain the greatest influence on markets in the United States. By 2015, the U.S. economy was growing again, but at a very slow rate.

Advertising has come a long way from the simple sign on the bootmaker's shop. Today it is a powerful influence that announces the availability and location of products, describes their quality and value, imbues brands with personality, and simultaneously defines the personalities of the people who buy them while entertaining us. More than a reflection of society and its desires, advertising can start and end fads, trends, and credos—sometimes all by itself.

The endless search for competitive advantage and efficiency has made advertising's journey in the last 100-plus years fascinating. Now companies are realizing that their most important asset is not capital equipment, or research capability, or their line of products. In the global marketplace, their most important asset is their customer and the relationship

New technology has meant new media, manifested largely in the internet. This has opened new avenues of exposure for advertisers. This site for Coke shows that beautiful layout and design are not confined to the traditional medium of print.

Source: The Coca-Cola Company

they have with that person or organization. Protecting that asset is the marketing imperative for the 21st century. In an effort to do a better job of *relationship marketing,* companies understand that they must be consistent in both what they say and what they do. It's not enough to produce outstanding advertising anymore. They must integrate all their marketing communications with everything else they do, too. That's what *integrated marketing communications* really means.

How Advertising Turns Products into Brands

The history of Coca-Cola provides a useful introduction to a powerful marketing idea: branding. In a world where consumers have many options for quenching their thirst, the Coca-Cola brand suggests that only one ice cold, sweet, fizzy, delicious choice is the best. That so many people agree suggests the power of branding. One estimate of the value of that brand in 2018 estimated it was $80 billion.[28]

But what is a **brand**? Scott M. Davis and Michael Dunn define the concept as follows:

> Promises made to customers . . . based on multiple experiences over time . . . delivered with a consistently high level of quality and value . . . that are perceived to be unparalleled relative to the competition, . . . ultimately resulting in deep, trust-based relationships . . . , which in turn, [garner] great amounts of loyalty and profits over time.[29]

Let's unpack this definition to highlight the following important elements: A brand is a promise about a product. It allows consumers to reasonably expect that a particular product will do something valuable or desirable, and that this will happen each time the consumer chooses the product. Your next hamburger at McDonald's will taste like your last. Your next Toyota Camry will offer reliability and comfort at a reasonable price.

Brands aspire to create more than just a set of expectations among users. Great brands inspire loyalty, emotion, and admiration. Some who prefer Coke do not accept that other cola brands are just as good. Instead, they believe that Coke is the best. Strong brands successfully forge relationships with their users that can seem more like fandom than mere expectation. For example, when Apple introduces a new product, such as the Apple Watch, millions will buy one sight unseen. Apple has earned their trust, and they believe the product will be exciting and desirable.

Finally, because brands are unique and consistently deliver desired benefits, companies can charge more. Any consumer can find cheaper substitutes for Coke and Apple products. But the cheaper alternatives are not attractive to loyal users because of the value they attach to the Coke and Apple brands. Although they are more expensive, Coke and Apple are seen by loyal users to be better values than cheaper alternatives. Their additional quality is worth the price.

Why Do Companies Brand Their Products?

One of the foremost experts on branding, David Aaker, argues that brands are company assets.[30] He notes that the value of a brand to a company is significant. The brands Apple, Google, and IBM are worth over $40 billion to their companies, and brands like Jack Daniel's and Burberry are worth over 50 percent of their companies' total value.

As a result, smart companies allocate money in support of their brands. Advertising and IMC activities are included in the branding efforts of many firms, but branding is accomplished through a broader set of customer experiences. For example, Starbucks invests in the quality of its outlets and brewing equipment, Ritz Carlton allocates large budgets to training its employees,[31] Samsung spends more than most companies on the packaging of its technologies, and L.L.Bean and Lands' End offer unconditional money-back guarantees on every purchase.

Given the importance of brands today, it is worth recalling that early ads from the 19th century did not focus on brands. Instead, advertising featured the generic products of manufacturers—the companies that made textiles, or equipment, or canned goods. This began to change as marketers observed the success of several notable brands, such as Coca-Cola and Ivory soap. These brands demonstrated to marketers just how valuable branding activities could be. The financial worth of most modern consumer-focused companies is directly related to the strength of their brands.

Among the more specific benefits provided to a company by strong brands are these:

1. They allow companies to charge more for their products.
2. They afford protection against price wars.
3. They make it more likely a new product will succeed.
4. They afford leverage in negotiating with channel partners.
5. They make companies more attractive to co-branding partners.
6. They help companies more effectively deal with a brand crisis.
7. They help companies recruit top talent.
8. They garner consumer loyalty.[32]

Each of these benefits has been enjoyed by Coca-Cola over its long history. For example, item 6 in the list suggests that strong brands help companies deal with a crisis. Coke experienced such a crisis when it introduced New Coke. Loyal Coke drinkers rejected the brand's reformulation, but quickly forgave the company when it brought back the old formula. Or consider item 3. When Coke introduced Diet Coke, the brand extension was an immediate hit.

Creating a Brand Vision

A **brand vision**, according to Aaker, is "an articulated description of the aspirational image for the brand; what you want the brand to stand for in the eyes of customers and other relevant groups."[33] When the brand vision is effective, it differentiates the brand from competitors and helps to inspire great advertising and marketing ideas. In 2010, Mercedes Benz adopted the tagline "The best or nothing." The tagline fit with a vision that no other car equals the quality or driving experience of a Mercedes. Joachim Schmidt, head of sales for the company, explained the thinking behind the vision: "Our customers expect nothing less than technological leadership. For us, that means we want to deliver the very best in all areas—be that in research and development, production, sales, service and aftermarket business or in purchasing."[34]

Creating a brand vision starts from consideration of the environment in which the brand competes: its customers, competitors, capabilities, challenges, and opportunities. Next, Aaker recommends identifying all aspirational associations for the brand and grouping them into lists. The list should include things like product attributes, consumer benefits, brand personality, and so forth. Finally, those concepts that matter most to customers receive final consideration for the vision. Done properly, such an analysis can yield visions as powerful as those listed below:

- Amazon: *To be Earth's most customer-centric company where people can find and discover anything they want to buy online*
- Casper: *Great sleep, made simple*
- Coca-Cola: *To refresh the world in mind, body and spirit. To inspire moments of optimism and happiness through our brands and actions. To create value and make a difference.*
- Google: *Google's mission is to organize the world's information and make it universally accessible and useful.*
- IKEA: *At IKEA our vision is to create a better everyday life for the many people.*
- Patagonia: *Build the best product, cause no unnecessary harm, use business to inspire and implement solutions to the environmental crisis*
- Starbucks: *To inspire and nurture the human spirit—one person, one cup and one neighborhood at a time.*
- Twitter: *To give everyone the power to create and share ideas and information instantly, without barriers.*

These powerful brand visions inspire customers and company employees alike. From an IMC perspective, they allow companies to make decisions about new products, innovations, marketing programs, and corporate policy. Brand visions are big enough to endure but flexible enough to adapt with changing times. Walt Disney opened his first theme park, Disneyland, in 1955 in Anaheim, California. Over a half century later, parks serve guests in Orlando, Paris, Shanghai, Tokyo, and Hong Kong. Disney did not live to see the openings of the resorts that were built after Disneyland, but his vision endured and lives in each of them today: *"We create happiness by providing the best in entertainment for people of all ages everywhere."*

The Brand Personality

In addition to their brand visions, many companies adopt a brand personality. The brand personality can be quite different from the vision. Consider that Progressive Insurance uses the following vision: "to reduce the human trauma and economic costs associated with automobile accidents. We do this by providing our customers with services designed to help them get their lives back in order again as quickly as possible."[35] As with all great brand visions, this one is aspirational. But the brand personality is reflected in the Progressive spokesperson Flo. Flo, portrayed by actress Stephanie Courtney, is "so goshdarned perky she makes Kelly Ripa look like Amy Winehouse," wrote one blogger.[36] Flo is a somewhat geeky, very retro, high-energy, super-friendly cashier at Progressive. While Flo's personality seems independent of Progressive's ambitious vision, she is very effective. Why? According to one observer, "She's a tangible person and personality in an increasingly virtual world—as real as the shopkeeper you never have to deal with anymore, because you buy everything on Amazon."[37]

As a brand personality, Flo does not contradict the Progressive Insurance vision. Rather, she serves to address an important element of the vision, one especially important to the company's marketing efforts. Progressive uses Flo to make clear to consumers that buying insurance from Progressive is easy and simple.

Not every brand personality is reflected as an actual person, such as Flo. Google's personality is exemplified by the simplicity and elegance of its website and products. Shoppers think of Walmart for large selection and cheap prices. Target might have a smaller selection and be a bit more expensive, but it is also fun and has a sense of style. Kia uses animated hamsters to give its Soul a fun, young, relevant personality. Brand observer Brendan Butler lists several other examples of personality types and the brands that exemplify them, including purist (Dove, Disney, and *Sesame Street*), pioneer (Jeep, Discovery Channel), and rebel (Harley Davidson and Red Bull).[38]

The brand vision and brand personality are important to the individuals who work to communicate about the brand because brand messages are reflections of both. As the creator of cool technologies, Apple relies on young, energetic advertisements. Walmart, reflecting the family values of founder Sam Walton, is not interested in being edgy or unusual in its advertising messages; it prefers an honest, friendly message.

As a student of advertising and IMC, you will find this book to be a resource for you as you learn to tell brand stories. But what story? IMC is how the story is shared, but the story itself is found in the brand or the company. The challenge of advertising effectively when a brand vision or personality is vague, weak, or inconsistent is significant. Good advertising can inform people about almost anything. However, great advertising can only be created for strong, clear, strategically defined brands.

The Broader Impact of Advertising on Society and Ethics

Advertising has been a major factor in improving the standard of living in the United States and around the world. By publicizing the material, social, and cultural opportunities of a free enterprise society, advertising has encouraged increased productivity by both management and labor.

With just a small amount of money, for instance, you can buy a car. It may be secondhand, but advertising lets you know it's available. If you earn more money, you can buy a new car or one with more luxury features. You can also make a statement about yourself as an individual with your purchase. As it does for many products, advertising has created a personality for each automobile model on the market, in part by informing you of the options, benefits, performance, looks, and styles available to buy. You, as a free individual, can select the brand that best matches your needs and aspirations.

Ads are not just used to sell products. They are also used to promote ideas and causes. This website for the American Heart Association encourages people to "go red" to help fight heart disease in women.

Source: American Heart Association, Inc.

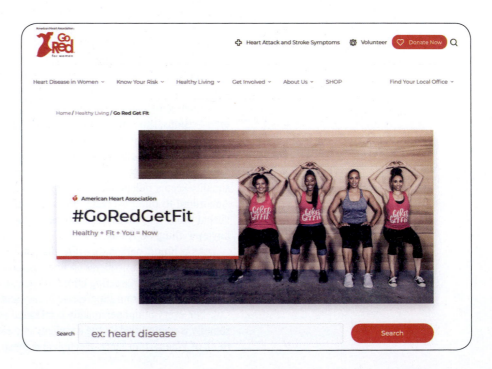

The Ad Council works with agency talent to tackle difficult social issues and causes. Promoting tolerance and LGBT acceptance has been a major focus for the organization in recent years.

Source: Ad Council

Advertising serves other social needs besides stimulating sales. Free media are not really "free"; newspapers must pay for paper, ink, and energy, and radio stations require equipment, buildings, and towers. All media organizations must pay salaries and benefits for reporters, engineers, and management. Facebook, Google, magazines, radio and television networks and stations, and many websites receive their primary income from advertising. This facilitates freedom of the press and promotes the availability of more complete information.

Some advertising organizations also foster growth and understanding of important social issues and causes through public service. The Red Cross, United Way, and other noncommercial organizations receive continuous financial support and volunteer assistance due in large part to the power of advertising.

However, advertising is certainly not without its shortcomings. Since its beginnings, the profession has struggled with issues of honesty and ethics. Consumers suffered for years from unsubstantiated product claims, especially for patent medicines and health devices. The simmering resentment finally boiled over into a full-blown consumer movement, which led to government regulation and ultimately to industry efforts at self-regulation.

In 1906, Congress responded to public outrage over unethical drug ads by passing the Pure Food and Drug Act to protect the public's health and control drug advertising. In 1914, it passed the Federal Trade Commission Act to protect the public from unfair business practices, including misleading and deceptive advertising.

By the early part of the 20th century, industry leaders began to form groups to improve advertising effectiveness and promote professionalism. The focus of these vigilance committees was safeguarding the integrity of the industry. The Association of National Advertisers (ANA), the American Advertising Federation (AAF), and the Better Business Bureau (BBB) are outgrowths of those early groups. These organizations are the result of

People BEHIND the Ads

Bettmann/Getty Images

Apple's famous campaign of the early 1980s asked consumers to "Think different." The ads used icons such as Einstein, Gandhi, and Picasso. They should have included Bill Bernbach.

The modern stereotype is that ad agencies are unconventional places populated with quirky visionaries. But that notion would have surprised professionals in the early 1960s. Back then agencies tended to be every bit as corporate as their clients. The stars were the account executives, not the creative directors. The agencies of that earlier age preferred safe, cautious campaigns developed through careful testing.

Through the 1950s, creativity carried little currency. After all, Claude Hopkins had dismissed the role of creativity by declaring that "scientific principles" were the key to effective advertising. Hopkins famously opened his book *Scientific Advertising* by noting:

The causes and effects [of advertising] have been analyzed until they are well understood. The correct methods of procedure have been proved and established. We know what is most effective, and we act on basic laws.[39]

But by 1959, a creative revolution was brewing, led by the founder and creative leader of an upstart New York agency, Doyle Dane Bernbach (DDB). Contradicting Hopkins's claim that advertising was a science, Bernbach wrote: "I don't want academicians. I don't want scientists. I don't want people who do the right things. I want people who do inspiring things. . . . Let us blaze new trails."[40]

There is little doubt that by the end of the 1950s, advertising was ready for a revolution. Every ad looked like every other—bright colors, smiling, upper-class families, all showcasing the latest Detroit offering. The car itself would be bigger, faster, longer, and more elaborate than last year's model. The copy would go on about new luxuries, comforts, and technologies. The ad would almost scream "American Dream" to consumers enjoying the postwar boom. Why stand out? Why take a risk?

Then came Bernbach. DDB's car client was a new German import: Volkswagen. The agency's unenviable task: market the decidedly unsexy "people's car" imported from a country against whom America had just concluded a world war. And the brand was everything Detroit's offerings were not: tiny, unusual, and humble.

Yet almost overnight Volkswagen entered the collective consciousness of American consumers. DDB placed it there by creating brilliant, even outrageous, "anti-advertising," that looked like nothing Americans had ever seen. Instead of bright colors, outdoor scenes, and smiling families, DDB's ads were black and white, stark, and simple. Audacious, punchy

Source: DDB Worldwide Communications Group Inc

a fundamental truth: The biggest opponents of unethical advertisers are advertisers who embrace ethical and truthful communication practices.

In the 1970s, a new American consumer movement grew out of the widespread disillusionment following the Kennedy assassination, the Vietnam War, the Watergate scandals, and the sudden shortage of vital natural resources—all communicated instantly to the world via new satellite technology. These issues fostered cynicism and distrust of the establishment and tradition and gave rise to a new twist in moral consciousness. On the one hand, people justified their personal irresponsibility and self-indulgence in the name of self-fulfillment. On the other, they attacked corporate America's quest for self-fulfillment (profits) in the name of social accountability.

Today, corporate America has generally cleaned up many of the inequities in advertising. But now attention has shifted to more subtle problems of inclusion and diversity in the industry and in ads, puffery, advertising to children, advertising legal but unhealthy products, concerns about wealth inequality and climate change, and other concerns regarding advertisers' ethics and social responsibilities.

In short, advertising has had a pronounced effect on society as well as the economy. It has also fostered a host of social attitudes and laws that have dramatically affected advertising itself. Inevitably, because of its prominence, advertising is at the heart of many controversies. And because of its importance, it attracts the attention of regulators. We'll take a closer look at these issues in Chapter 3.

headlines encouraged people to reconsider everything they usually considered when buying a car. "Think small," read one, putting a tiny photo of the car in the top left portion of the ad. "Lemon," read another. A headline that seemed to insult the brand? Outrageous. Until consumers, hooked by something so different and original, were drawn into the body copy. There they discovered that the lemon in question had been pulled from the assembly line because of stringent quality controls.

Bernbach wrote copy that encouraged consumers to reject groupthink, the mass society, and the idea that everyone should be like everyone else. The appeals were simple, straightforward, clean, and specific. For those tiring of the "keep up with your neighbors" treadmill, Bernbach wrote the manual for stepping off. One Volkswagen ad from 1963 showed readers "How to do a Volkswagen ad." "Speak to the reader," the copy noted, "Don't shout. He can hear you. Especially if you talk sense."

Bernbach's efforts for other clients were just as smart, unusual, and fresh. Ads for Levy's bread featured people of many ethnicities enjoying the product. The message: "You don't have to be Jewish" to like rye bread. Ads for Avis acknowledged it was the number two car company in the United States. Why not choose number one? Because the people at Avis "work harder." Unstated, but just as clear, was the notion that employees at industry leader Hertz took customers for granted.

The culture at DDB was a reflection of Bernbach himself. Thomas Frank notes that Bernbach "was an ideologue of disorder, an untiring propagandist for the business value of the principles of modern art."[41] Front and center was his insistence that agency culture respect creative talent. Copywriter Phyllis Robinson recalled it this way, "we just felt very free, as if we had broken our shackles, gotten out of jail, and were free to work the way we wanted to work."[42]

The new culture fostered by Bernbach also extended to the relationship of client and agency. In the old days, agencies knuckled under if a client demanded advertising be done a certain way. DDB clients were expected to respect the agency's ideas. If they didn't, Bernbach was prepared to walk.

DDB and Bernbach took the advertising business by storm. Founded in 1949, the agency rocketed from obscurity to international prominence in a mere 10 years. Soon every ad agency was playing catch-up by trying to transform its own culture.

Source: DDB Worldwide Communications Group Inc

Bernbach passed away in 1982 after a fabled career, but his legacy is intact. *Harper's Magazine,* noting his passing, wrote that Bernbach had made "a greater impact on American culture than any of the distinguished writers and artists" appearing in the magazine during its 133 years. And when *Advertising Age* published a top-100 list of the greatest advertising campaigns (https://adage.com/article/special-report-the-advertising-century/ad-age-advertising-century-top-100-advertising-campaigns/140150) and individuals (https://adage.com/article/special-report-the-advertising-century/ad-age-advertising-century-top-100-people/140153) of the 20th century, the number one spots went to DDB's Volkswagen ads and Bill Bernbach.

Chapter Summary

Advertising has a number of functions and effects in a free economy. It identifies and differentiates products; communicates information about them; induces nonusers to try products and users to repurchase them; stimulates products' distribution; increases product use; builds value, brand preference, and loyalty; and lowers the overall cost of sales.

Advertising is a relatively recent development in human history. In ancient times when most people could not read or write, there was little need for advertising. As the world expanded, urban populations soared, and manufacturing and communication technologies developed, so too did advertising. Print was the first major technology to affect advertising; digital technologies are the most recent.

The industrial age brought changing economies and increased competition and thus marked the emergence of advertising as an industry. Since World War II, advertisers have used a variety of strategies, such as product differentiation, market segmentation, and positioning, to differentiate their products. Recently, the advertising industry experienced a period of retrenchment and reevaluation, but the future offers new opportunities for advertisers and agencies that can harness the

interactive revolution and develop deep relationships with their customers. Economic hardships in 2008 and 2009 led to cutbacks in ad budgets, but smart companies continue to advertise and will emerge with gains in market share.

Among the most important marketing developments of the past 100 years has been the recognition of the power of brands. Brands, guided by brand visions, offer important benefits to consumers and are critical economic assets to the companies that manage them. Brands provide the stories that advertising and IMC professionals use to create great campaigns.

As a social force, advertising has helped improve the standard of living in the United States and around the world. Advertising makes us aware of the availability of products, imbues products with personality, and enables us to communicate information about ourselves through the products we buy. Through its financial support, advertising also fosters the free press and the growth of many nonprofit organizations.

However, advertising has also been severely criticized over the years for its lack of honesty and ethics. This has given rise to numerous consumer movements and laws that regulate the practice of advertising.

Important Terms

brand, *53*

brand vision, *54*

branding, *36*

consumer packaged goods, *44*

demarketing, *48*

industrial age, *39*

market segmentation, *46*

positioning strategy, *47*

postindustrial age, *48*

preindustrial age, *39*

Review Questions

1. What are the four fundamental assumptions of free-market economics?
2. What are the primary functions of advertising in a free economy?
3. What has had the greatest impact on the way advertising has evolved?
4. How does advertising lower the cost of sales?
5. How would you differentiate the advertising used in the industrializing age and the industrial age?
6. What has been the most important influence on advertising in the postindustrial age?
7. What are three examples of companies or organizations that use a demarketing strategy?
8. What companies can you think of that are engaged in marketing warfare?
9. As a consumer, are you likely to save money buying at a store that doesn't advertise? Explain.
10. What effects do you believe advertising has had on society in general? Explain.

The Advertising Experience

1. **Ad Action: Demarketing**

   Identify a social problem at your school that has had an effect on you or your community. Then create a print demarketing advertisement that addresses this problem. The ad should have a visual element as well as a slogan. What incentive have you created for your audience to change? Why do you think the incentive will resonate with people who see your ad?

2. **Economic Perspectives of Advertising**

   Visit the website that follows for a reading on the economics of advertising. After studying it, do you believe advertising primarily promotes monopoly or does it foster many buyers and sellers? Support your argument with points from the article:

   a. "Advertising," The Library of Economics and Liberty: *The Concise Encyclopedia of Economics*—an interesting primer by Prof. George Bittlingmayer, University of Kansas: www.econlib.org/library/Enc/Advertising.html

3. **Advertising History**

   Visit the following websites to see what else you can learn about the early advertising efforts of companies here and abroad. Can you find some early ads for Kodak? Coca-Cola? Sunkist? Who are some of the other major advertisers listed? What specific characteristics in art and copy styles do you notice that make these ads different from advertising today?

   a. "The Emergence of Advertising in America" section of the John W. Hartman Center for Sales, Advertising, and Marketing History at Duke University: http://scriptorium.lib.duke.edu/eaa

   b. Archives of the History of Advertising Trust: www.hatads.org.uk/

   c. History Matters: http://historymatters.gmu.edu/mse/ads/amadv.html

   d. The Museum of Broadcast Communications (Chicago): www.museum.tv/

   e. Nineteenth-century advertising in *Harper's Weekly* magazine: http://advertising.harpweek.com

   f. USATVADS (a large—more than 1 million examples—pay-site collection of American television commercials): www.usatvads.net

   g. Advertising, marketing, and commercial imagery collections of the National Museum of American History at the Smithsonian: http://americanhistory.si.edu/collections/subjects/advertising

4. Volkswagen's advertising from the early 1960s was clearly quite different from that of its competitors—perhaps because of its decision to pair copywriters with art directors, a partnership that is now all but standard in the advertising industry. But did other automakers sit up and take notice? Find some examples of American auto advertising in the years since that could potentially have been influenced by DDB's VW work.

5. Some Coca-Cola investors want the company to spend more on advertising products in growing categories, such as sports drinks, and less on trying to revive consumer interest in full-calorie soft drinks. How would you respond to these shareholders?

6. After stirring up consumers' emotions and shaking their faith in the company by introducing New Coke, company executives have been treading somewhat lightly for the last 20 years. Do you think their efforts to conserve and protect the brand have stifled the creativity of Coca-Cola advertising? Why or why not?

End Notes

1. "Barbara Mikkelson, "Cocaine-Cola," *Urban Legends Reference Pages: Coca-Cola,* May 2, 1999, *www.snopes.com/cokelore/cocaine.asp*.

2. Quoted in Frederick Allen, *Secret Formula: The Inside Story of How Coca-Cola Became the Best-Known Brand in the World* (New York: Harper Collins Publishers Pty, 1994), p. 76; U.S.

Library of Congress American Memory Collection, "Highlights in the History of Coca-Cola Television Advertising," updated November 29, 2000, *http://memory.loc.gov/ammem/ccmphtml/colahist.html#darcy*.

3. Donald Keough, quoted in Blair Matthews, "Coca-Cola's Big Mistake: New Coke 20 Years Later," *Soda Pop Dreams Magazine,* Spring 2005, *www.pww.on.ca/36_newcoke.htm*; Barbara Mikkelson, "Knew Coke," *Urban Legends Reference Pages: Coca-Cola,* May 2, 1999, *www.snopes.com/cokelore/snewcoke.asp*.

4. Marc Inboden, quoted in "Ads Aim to Put Fizz Back in Coke," *Tulsa World,* April 2, 2006, p. E3.

5. Quoted in "The Chronicle of Coca-Cola: Birth of a Refreshing Idea," *Coca-Cola Journey,* January 1, 2012, *www.coca-colacompany.com/stories/the-chronicle-of-coca-cola-birth-of-a-refreshing-idea*; Coca-Cola Heritage Timeline, *www.coca-colacompany.com/coca-cola-music/timeline*; Barbara Mikkelson, "Design Err Shape," *Urban Legends Reference Pages: Coca-Cola,* May 2, 1999, *www.snopes.com/cokelore/bottle.asp*.

6. "The Chronicle of Coca-Cola: Birth of a Refreshing Idea," *Coca-Cola Journey,* January 1, 2012, *www.coca-colacompany.com/stories/the-chronicle-of-coca-cola-birth-of-a-refreshing-idea*; Jack Hayes, "Dr. John S. Pemberton (inventor of Coca-Cola)," *Nation's Restaurant News,* February 1996, pp. 120–21, Library of Congress American Memory Project, *http://rs6.loc.gov/ammem/ccmphtml/colainvnt.html*.

7. Frederick Allen, *Secret Formula: How Brilliant Marketing and Relentless Salesmanship Made Coca-Cola the Best-Known Product in the World* (New York: HarperCollins, 1994), cited in Eleanor Jones and Florian Ritzmann, "Coca-Cola Goes to War: Coca-Cola at Home," *http://xroads.virginia.edu/~class/coke/coke.html*; Pat Watters, *Coca-Cola: An Illustrated History* (New York: Doubleday, 1978), cited in Eleanor Jones and Florian Ritzmann, "Coca-Cola Goes to War: Coca-Cola at Home," *http://xroads.virginia.edu/~class/coke/coke.html*.

8. "Sales Call Costs," *The Controller's Report,* January 2001, p. 9; Claire Atkinson, "Cost of 'American Idol' Finale Spot Hits $1.3 Million," *Advertising Age* (online), April 17, 2006.

9. Norman Douglas, *South Wind* (London: Martin Secker, 1917; repr. Hard Press, 2006).

10. William O'Barr, address to the Council on Advertising History, Duke University, March 12, 1993, reported in *Advertising in America: Using Its Past, Enriching Its Future* (Washington, DC: Center for Advertising History of the National Museum of American History, 1994), p. 6.

11. Leonard L. Bartlett, "Three Giants—Leo Burnett, David Ogilvy, William Bernbach: An Exploration of the Impact of the Founders' Written Communications on the Destinies of Their Advertising Agencies," paper presented to the annual meeting of the Association for Education in Journalism and Mass Communication, Kansas City, August 13, 1993.

12. Marcel Bleustein-Blanchet, *La Rage de Convaincre* (Paris: Editions Robert Laffont, 1970), pp. 307–10, 375; Jean-Marc Schwarz, "A Brief History of Ad Time," *Adweek,* February 14, 1994, p. 46.

13. Jean-Marc Schwarz, "A Brief History of Ad Time," *Adweek,* February 14, 1994, p. 46.

14. Jean-Marc Schwarz, "A Brief History of Ad Time," *Adweek,* February 14, 1994, p. 46.

15. Jean-Marc Schwarz, "A Brief History of Ad Time," *Adweek,* February 14, 1994, p. 46.

16. Lester C. Thurow, "The Post-Industrial Era is Over," *New York Times,* September 4, 1989, pp. 27.

17. William F. Arens and Jack J. Whidden, "La Publicité aux Etats-Unis: Les Symptômes et les Stratégies d'une Industrie Surpeuplée," *L'Industrie de la Publicité au Québec* (Montreal: Le Publicité Club de Montréal, 1992), pp. 383–84.

18. Warren Berger, "Chaos on Madison Avenue," *Los Angeles Times Magazine,* June 5, 1994, pp. 12, 14.

19. Bob Coen, "Bob Coen's Insider's Report," December 2002, McCann-Erickson WorldGroup, *www.universalmccann.com/ourview.html*.

20. Judann Pollock, "Marketing Put on Hold," *Advertising Age,* September 17, 2001, pp. 1, 25.

21. Bob Coen, "Bob Coen's Insider's Report," December 2002, McCann-Erickson WorldGroup, *www.universalmccann.com/ourview.html*.

22. R. Craig Endicott, "Interactive Marketing & Media Fact Pack 2006," *Advertising Age,* April 17, 2006, p. 10.

23. Tom Cuniff, "The Second Creative Revolution," *Advertising Age,* December 6, 1993, p. 22.

24. "US, China, Japan, Germany and the UK Lead as the Top Five Ad Markets," *eMarketer,* December 10, 2014, *www.emarketer.com/Article/Advertisers-Will-Spend-Nearly-600-Billion-Worldwide-2015/1011691*.

25. Matt Schiavenza, "China Economy Surpasses US in Purchasing Power, But Americans Don't Need to Worry," *International Business Times,* October 8, 2014, *www.ibtimes.com/china-economy-surpasses-us-purchasing-power-americans-dont-need-worry-1701804*.

26. Jason Abbruzzese, "Showtime Planning Standalone Internet Offering," *Mashable,* November 5, 2014, *mashable.com/2014/11/05/showtime-internet-offering/*.

27. Newspaper Association of America, "Trends and Numbers," updated May 25, 2012, *www.naa.org/Trends-and-Numbers/Advertising-Expenditures/Quarterly-All-Categories.aspx*.

28. "Coca-Cola's Brand Value from 2006 to 2019 (in billion U.S. dollars)," *Statista, www.statista.com/statistics/326065/coca-cola-brand-value/*.

29. Scott M. Davis and Michael Dunn, *Building the Brand-Driven Business* (San Francisco: Jossey-Bass, 2002), p. 15.

30. David Aaker, *Aaker on Branding: 20 Principles That Drive Success* (New York: Morgan James Publishing, 2014).

31. "Training the Talented the Ritz Carlton Way," *American Management Assocation,* January 24, 2019, *www.amanet.org/training/articles/training-the-talented-the-ritz-carlton-way.aspx*.

32. Scott M. Davis and Michael Dunn, *Building the Brand-Driven Business* (San Francisco: Wiley, 2002), pp. 17–18.

33. David Aaker, *Aaker on Branding: 20 Principles That Drive Success* (New York: Morgan James Publishing, 2014).

34. "Mercedes-Benz Has New Global Slogan: The Best or Nothing," *Autotrader, www.autotrader.com/car-news/mercedes-benz-has-new-global-slogan-best-or-nothin-67400*.

35. Progressive Casualty Insurance Company, "Core Values," 2019.

36. Aaron Parsley, "5 Things to Know About TV's Progressive Insurance Lady," *People Magazine,* September 2, 2009, *https://people.com/tv/5-things-to-know-about-tvs-progressive-insurance-lady/*.

36. Nicole LaPorte, "Flo the Progressive Lady, Stephanie Courtney, Interview," *Daily Beast,* May 30, 2010, *www.thedailybeast.com/flo-the-progressive-lady-stephanie-courtney-interview*.

38. Brendan Butler, "12 Examples of Brand Personality to Inspire You," *Career Addict,* August 18, 2017, *www.careeraddict.com/12-examples-of-brand-personality-to-inspire-you*.

39. Claude Hopkins, *Scientific Advertising* (1923; repr. Cosimo, Inc., 2007).

40. Bill Bernbach, Letter dated May 15, 1947, cited in "Let Us Blaze New Trails," *Letters of Note,* June 24, 2013, *www.lettersofnote.com/2013/06/let-us-blaze-new-trails.html?m=1*.

41. Thomas Frank, *The Conquest of Cool: Business Culture, Counterculture, and the Rise of Hip Consumerism* (Chicago: University of Chicago Press, 1998).

42. Keith Reinhard, "DDB's Four Freedoms," Innova DDB Ghana, March 24, 2016, *https://innovaddb.wordpress.com/2016/03/24/ddbs-four-freedoms/*.

CHAPTER

3

The Big Picture: Economic, Ethical, and Regulatory Aspects

LEARNING OBJECTIVES

To identify and explain the economic, social, ethical, and legal issues advertisers must consider. The basic economic principles that guide advertising also have social and legal effects. These effects may lead governments to take corrective measures. Society determines what is offensive, excessive, and irresponsible; governments determine what is deceptive and unfair. To be law-abiding, ethical, socially responsible, and economically effective, advertisers must understand and address these issues.

After studying this chapter, you will be able to:

LO3-1   Relate advertising activities to the workings of a free-market economy.

LO3-2   Identify and give examples of the two main types of social criticisms of advertising.

LO3-3   Explain the difference between social responsibility and ethics in advertising.

LO3-4   Describe how governments regulate advertising here and abroad.

LO3-5   Discuss regulatory issues that affect U.S. advertisers and commercial speech.

LO3-6   Classify ways that federal agencies regulate advertising to protect both consumers and competitors.

LO3-7   Define the roles state and local governments play in advertising regulation.

LO3-8   List the ways that private organizations help reduce fraudulent and deceptive advertising.

Source: Outside Magazine

Would you be more likely to buy a watch brand if you knew that Jeff Gordon wears it? What if it was the preferred brand of Maria Sharapova or Leonardo DiCaprio? Swiss luxury watchmaker TagHeuer must think so because it pays these stars to appear in ads. And shoe company Nike spends millions on endorsement contracts. The company has long partnered with Michael Jordan and has exclusive deals with many other athletes, including Chris Paul and Serena Williams. The athletes agree to wear Nike clothes and use Nike gear during competitions. Many also appear in Nike ads. ■ Are celebrity endorsements worth the big bucks that TagHeuer and Nike spend on them? Business professors Jagdish Agrawal and Wagner Kamakura argue that celebrities help make ads believable, enhance ad recall, increase brand recognition, and ultimately influence consumers to choose an endorsed brand.[1] So it should be no surprise that as many as one of five TV commercials features someone famous. ■ Former world champion cyclist Lance Armstrong made tens of millions of dollars from endorsements and in return helped companies like Nike become dominant global brands. So has

elite golfer Tiger Woods. Woods has said that "if you are given a chance to be a role model, I think you should always take it because you can influence a person's life in a positive light, and that's what I want to do. That's what it's all about." ■ Unfortunately, as virtually everyone knows, both Amstrong and Woods went through embarrassing public scandals. The resulting furors were more than personal tragedies for these men. Millions of people were distressed by the upsetting news about their heroes. And the companies that made Tiger and Lance highly paid endorsers were each faced with a public relations disaster. ■ It happens all the time. The long list of famous individuals who have lost endorsement deals because of controversy includes Madonna (Pepsi), Ludacris (Pepsi), Jose Canseco (California Egg Commission), Kobe Bryant (McDonald's), Mary Kate Olsen (milk), Eminem (Ford), and Kate Moss (Chanel). ■ The dilemma for companies that sponsor celebrities was highlighted in a series of events that led Nike to stop its sponsorship of Atlanta Falcons quarterback Michael Vick after he confessed to criminal activities that included cruelty to animals. Nike signed a major sponsorship deal with Vick as a rookie in the NFL. When news broke that the quarterback was being investigated for acts involving animal cruelty, the company faced a quandary. The quarterback initially argued that the illegal acts were done by associates. No matter how implausible that claim might have seemed, many believed that Vick was entitled to a presumption of innocence before trial. Nike had to determine whether to drop its support of Vick before his day in court or stand by the athlete. As the experiences of Kobe Bryant and the Duke lacrosse team made clear, being accused of a crime is not the same as being guilty. Nike decided to suspend sales of Vick's product lines shortly after the story broke. But it did not break its endorsement contract until Vick admitted guilt. The marketing community generally applauded this approach as one that acknowledged both the seriousness of the crime and Vick's right to a presumption of innocence before trial. ■ Companies increasingly understand that they take a risk when they associate their brands too closely with a single endorser. Jeremy Mullman, writing for *Advertising Age,* says that Nike has been recently moving toward an "ensemble approach" to endorsements. Translation: Nike uses a pool of athletes to promote its wares rather than one big star. Risk to the brand is reduced, therefore, should any of the athletes stumble. Under Armour, a Nike competitor, uses a similar approach. A company VP notes that Under Armour doesn't "let any one person get bigger than the brand."[2] ■ Lessons? Tiger Woods, Lance Armstrong, and Michael Vick earned big endorsement contracts because of the things they do as athletes. And yet, for all three, the journey from endorsement superstar to marketing disaster happened with lightning speed. For brands, the lesson is caution in aligning a product's image too closely with real and potentially flawed human beings. ■ As for Woods, Armstrong, and Vick, life goes on. *Outside* magazine took a gamble and decided to play on Lance Armstrong's flaws by using him to promote a clip online called "How to Fix a Flat Tire." More recently Armstrong started a podcast called "The Move." Vick returned to football and Woods to golf, although neither was able to recover his earlier successes. All seemed contrite regarding their "sins." What could make such adored individuals do such foolish things? Maybe the question is really how does the uncritical adoration we offer celebrities and stars become a catalyst for the very behaviors that we ultimately find so disappointing.

This chapter also focuses most specifically on the advertising dimension of IMC. While other kinds of promotional messages are relevant to the themes we develop here, advertising is most often associated with offenses that attract attention from critics and regulators alike.

The Many Controversies about Advertising

Advertising may be the most visible of business activities. By making bold claims about their brands, companies risk public criticism if their advertising offends or if their products don't measure up. But this is exactly why defenders of advertising say advertised products are safer—a company tries harder to fulfill its promises when its name and reputation are on the line.

Beyond the impact of any single ad, the practice of advertising is both applauded and criticized for its influence on the economy and on society. For years, critics have associated advertising with a wide range of sins—some real, some imagined.

John O'Toole, former chair of Foote, Cone & Belding and president of the American Association of Advertising Agencies, believed that many critics attack advertising because it *isn't something else.* Advertising isn't journalism, education, or entertainment—although it can perform the functions of all three. Our definition of advertising emphasizes that ads are meant to be persuasive, to tell one side of a story. They are not intended to be a neutral perspective on a brand or service. As a form of communication, advertising shares certain characteristics with journalism, education, and entertainment, but it shouldn't be judged by

Views of offensiveness vary a great deal. This ad for Shoebaloo created by agency Kessels Kramer entitled "Amputee" uses a model with a disability to get its message across. Does this ad make you feel uncomfortable? Or is it empowering?

Source: Shoebaloo Advertisement by KesselsKramer

Citaat uit brief van Lianda aan fotografe

00 Ik zelf ben altijd erg geïnteresseerd geweest in de modellenwereld.
Het was, zoals voor vele meisjes, ook voor mij een grote droom.
Ik schrijf 'was', omdat die droom voor mij in duigen viel op 19 december 1995 toen ik werd aangereden door een vrachtwagen en daarbij mijn rechterbeen verloor. Ik ben de periode na het ongeluk heel positief geweest, omdat er nog zoveel dingen mogelijk zijn, maar modellenwerk had ik uit mijn hoofd gezet".

lianda

uit Zeeland

their standards. Sponsors advertise because they hope it will help them sell some product, service, or idea.[3]

Notwithstanding O'Toole's defense, many controversies still swirl around the whole field of advertising. Some focus on advertising's *economic* role. For example, how does advertising affect the value of products? Does it cause higher prices? Does it promote competition or discourage it? How does advertising affect overall consumer demand? What effect does it have on consumer choice and on the overall business cycle?

Other controversies focus on the *societal* effects of advertising. For instance, does advertising make us more materialistic? Does it tempt people into buying things they don't need? Does it affect people subliminally in ways they can't control? (For more on this topic, see the Ethics, Diversity & Inclusion box in Chapter 8.) Does it corrupt the art and culture of our society? Does advertising debase our language? How much do advertisers know about us and how safe is our privacy?

From these economic and social controversies, questions arise concerning where to locate responsibility for advertising. How much latitude should marketers have in the kinds of products they promote and how they advertise them? And what about consumers? Do they have some responsibility in the process? Finally, what is the proper role of government? What laws should we have to protect consumers? And what laws go too far and violate the marketer's freedom of speech?

People differ, sometimes strongly, in their answers to such questions. But the process of raising the issues and considering them in a thoughtful way helps advertisers better understand the effects of their messages. It also helps government better evaluate the tradeoffs of commercial speech policies. And it will help you develop your own set of principles and moral compass as a consumer of advertising, and perhaps one day, as a creator of it. This chapter addresses some of the major questions and criticisms about advertising, both the pros and the cons, and delves into the regulatory methods used to remedy and minimize advertisers' abuses.

As will be shown later in this chapter, the underlying principle of free-market economics is that society is best served by empowering people to make their own decisions and act as free agents. This fundamentally utilitarian framework, derived from the idea that society should promote behaviors that foster the greatest good for the most people, offers a system of economic activity—capitalism—that has raised living standards better than any other economic system in history. This is why the wealthiest societies around the world practice free-enterprise economics.

By using this framework for our discussion of advertising controversies, we have a basis for understanding how advertising may contribute to, or detract from, the basic goal of free enterprise: "the most good for the most people."

Economics: How Advertising Functions in Free Markets

Advertising is most fundamentally intended to serve an economic function. Understanding that function is important for considering the benefits, and the harms, that supporters and critics attach to advertising.

Principles of Free-Market Economics

In the United States and in some other countries of the world, a market economy determines what and how much is produced and consumed. Harvard economist N. Gregory Mankiw defines a market economy as one in which "Firms decide whom to hire and what to make. Households decide . . . what to buy with their incomes. These firms and households interact in the marketplace, where prices and self-interest guide their decisions."[4] Such an economy is characterized by four assumptions:

1. *Self-interest.* People and firms pursue their self-interested goals. Whether it is a nicer house, a faster car, or a Harvard education, people always want more—for less. Marketers are also self-interested. They want to generate profits and grow their businesses. Marketers succeed, and consumers benefit, when they offer brands or products that are desirable and affordable. In free economies, marketers must compete with other marketers for consumer business. This open competition between self-interested sellers marketing to self-interested buyers leads to greater product availability at more competitive prices.

2. *Complete information.* The assumption suggests that buyers know the prices offered by sellers, forcing marketers to keep prices low enough to create demand. Buyers make better decisions when they have more information about the products from which they can choose. Sellers can also more efficiently find consumers of their goods by providing information about what they sell. When information suggests a brand is more valuable than those with which it competes, its seller can charge more.

3. *Many buyers and sellers.* Having many sellers ensures that if one does not meet customer needs, another will capitalize on the situation by producing a better product or a less expensive version of an existing product. Similarly, a wide range of buyers ensures that sellers can find customers interested in unique products if they can be offered at a fair price.

4. *Absence of externalities (social costs).* Sometimes the sale or consumption of products may benefit or harm people who are not involved in the transaction. For example, in March 2009, India's Tata Group introduced the world's cheapest car, Nano, which retailed for just $2,000. This gave millions of poor Indians access to affordable transportation. But by increasing the numbers of people who drive automobiles, the Tata may increase health problems and accelerate climate change through increases in air pollution and carbon emissions. In such cases, governments may use taxation and/or regulation to compensate for or minimize harms from the externalities.

These assumptions describe an *ideal* economy, not one that actually exists. For example, you almost never have complete information about products that you buy. But the assumption tells us that the more information you have about a product before you buy it, the more satisfied you will probably be with your purchase. Free-market economists believe that the closer an economy comes to satisfying the four assumptions, the better for everyone.

Given these assumptions, what is the role of advertising in a free economy? We consider that question next.

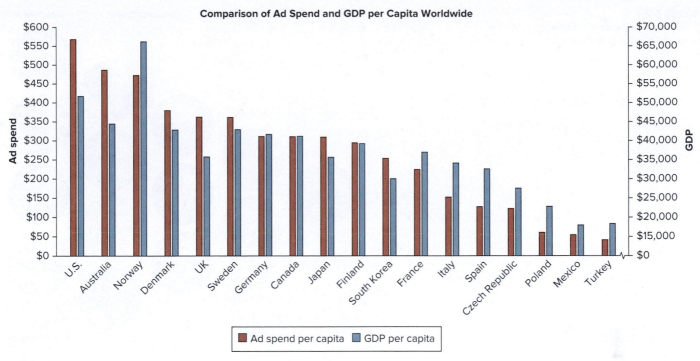

Exhibit 3-1

Advertising spending per capita (excluding direct mail) worldwide is correlated with GDP per capita.

The Economic Impact of Advertising

Advertising expenditures historically average between 1 and 2 percent of the U.S. gross domestic product (GDP).[5] In relation to the total U.S. economy, this percentage is small. In 2018 advertisers spent an average of $670 on every man, woman, and child living in the U.S. By comparison, spending is only $414 per capita in the UK and a mere $6.26 per capita in India. And, as illustrated in Exhibit 3-1, worldwide there is a positive relationship between per capita spending on advertising and personal wealth.[6]

The economic effect of advertising is like the break shot in billiards or pool. The moment a company begins to advertise, it sets off a chain reaction of economic events, as shown in Exhibit 3-2. The extent of the chain reaction, although hard to predict, is related to the force of the shot and the economic environment in which it occurred. Let's consider the economic questions we posed earlier.

Effect on the Value of Products

Why do most people prefer Coca-Cola to some other cola? Why do some people prefer iPods to an unadvertised brand? Are the advertised products functionally better? Not necessarily. Advertising has given these brands *added value.*

Some believe that a product's *image,* created in part by advertising and promotion, is *an inherent feature of the product itself.*[7] While an ad may not address a product's quality directly, the positive image conveyed by advertising implies quality. By simply making the product better known, advertising can make the product more desirable. In this way, advertising adds value to the brand.[8] That's why people pay more for Bufferin than an unadvertised brand displayed right next to it—even though all buffered aspirin, by law, are (referring to all types) functionally the same.

Advertising also adds value to a brand by educating customers about new uses for a product. Kleenex was originally advertised as a makeup remover, later as a disposable handkerchief. AT&T first promoted the telephone as a necessity and later as a convenience. Apple ads for the iPhone regularly explain how apps give the device greater functionality.

In a free-market system, consumers can choose the qualities they want in products they buy. For example, a car buyer who considers low price to be important can buy an economy car. If status and luxury are important, he or she can buy an SUV or a sports car, and if environmental concerns are paramount, a hybrid. Many of our wants are emotional,

Exhibit 3-2
The economic effect of advertising is like the opening break shot in billiards.

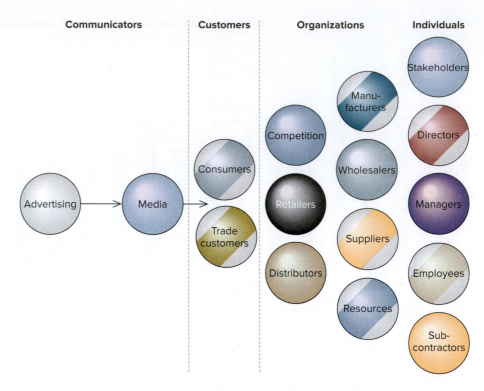

social, or psychological rather than functional. One way we communicate who we are (or want to be) is through the products we purchase and display. By associating the product with some desirable image, advertising offers people the opportunity to satisfy those symbolic wants and needs. So, for example, buying a hybrid car is not just a way to help protect the environment; it is also a way to show others that being environmentally friendly is important to how you see yourself.

In terms of our economic framework, by adding value to products, advertising helps both the consumer and the advertiser. It also contributes to the number of sellers. That increases competition, which also serves the consumer's self-interest.

Effect on Prices

If advertising adds value to products, it follows that advertising also increases prices, right? And if companies stopped advertising, products would cost less, right? Not necessarily. Economists have argued about the impact of advertising on prices and in some cases still disagree.

Some advertised products do cost more than unadvertised products, but the opposite is also true. Both the Federal Trade Commission and the Supreme Court have ruled that, by encouraging competition, advertising has the effect of keeping prices down. That again serves the consumer's self-interest.

Sweeping statements about advertising's positive or negative effect on prices are almost always simplistic. We can make some important points, though:

■ As a cost of doing business, advertising is paid for by the consumer. In most product categories, though, the amount spent on advertising is trivial compared with the total cost of the product. One estimate suggests that advertising costs as a percentage of sales range from nearly 10 percent for packaged goods to just 0.4 percent for retailer Walmart.[9]

■ Advertising is one element of the mass distribution system that enables many manufacturers to engage in mass production, which lowers the unit cost of products. These savings can then be passed on to consumers in the form of lower prices. In this indirect way, advertising helps lower prices.

■ In industries subject to government price regulation (agriculture, utilities), advertising has had no effect on prices. When the government deregulated many of these industries in an effort to restore free-market competition, advertising has affected price—usually downward, but not always.

Does advertising lead to higher prices? Economists believe that in many cases ads can actually contribute to lower prices for products. This ad for Southwest Airlines is designed to attract price-sensitive consumers to the savings they can get.

Source: Southwest Airlines Co.

■ Price is a prominent element in many retail ads, which tends to hold down prices. On the other hand, national manufacturers use advertising to stress features that make their brands better; in these cases advertising may support higher prices. As we noted in Chapter 2, companies advertise to support their brands in an effort to become more profitable.

Effect on Competition

Some believe advertising restricts competition because small companies can't compete with the immense advertising budgets of large firms. Conversely, small firms often rely on advertising to inform consumers about their brands' unique benefits. If new brands could not be promoted, how would consumers learn about choices that might better serve their needs and wants? Nike is the largest athletic shoe company in the world and has a dominant market share (nearly 36 percent as of 2017) in the United States compared to adidas (6.3 percent). But Nike was founded in 1974, many years after adidas (1949). Despite its longer history and early lead, adidas could not prevent Nike from overtaking it in the athletic shoe business, and advertising and IMC were a big driver of Nike's growth.

Intense competition can reduce the number of businesses in an industry. However, some of the firms eliminated by competition may be those that served customers least effectively. In other cases, competition is reduced because of mergers and acquisitions (big companies working in their own self-interest).

High costs may inhibit the entry of new competitors in industries that spend heavily on advertising. In some markets, the original brands probably benefit greatly from this barrier. However, the investments needed for plants, machinery, and labor are of far greater significance. These are typically the real barriers to entry, not advertising.

Advertising by big companies often has only a limited effect on small businesses because a single advertiser is rarely large enough to dominate the whole country. Regional oil companies, for example, compete very successfully with national oil companies on the local level. In fact, the freedom to advertise encourages more sellers to enter the market. And we've all seen nonadvertised store labels compete very effectively with nationally advertised brands on the same grocery shelves.

Effect on Consumer Demand

The question of advertising's effect on total consumer demand is complex. Many studies show that promotional activity affects aggregate consumption, but they disagree as to the extent. Social and economic forces, including technological advances, the population's educational level, increases in population and income, and changes in lifestyle, are more significant. For example, the demand for LCD TVs and smartphones expanded at a tremendous rate, thanks in part to advertising but more to favorable market conditions. At the same time, advertising hasn't reversed declining sales of retailers, carbonated beverages, or newspapers.

In Chapter 6 we'll see that marketing promotions can help get new products off the ground by giving more people more complete information, thereby stimulating **primary demand**—demand for the entire product class. In declining markets, when the only information people want is price information, advertising can influence **selective demand**—demand for a particular brand. But the only effect it will have on primary demand is to slow the rate of decline. In growing markets, advertisers generally compete for shares of that growth. In mature, static, or declining markets, they compete for each other's shares—*conquest sales.*

The famous "Got Milk" campaign promoted primary rather than selective demand because the goal of the campaign was to have consumers drink more milk, not a particular brand of milk. The "Got Milk?" campaign created by agency Goodby Silverstein & Partners for the California Milk Processor Board was around for over 20 years, and its memorable two-word slogan is undoubtedly one of the most famous taglines in advertising history.

Source: The California Milk Advisory Board

Effect on Consumer Choice

The best way for a manufacturer to beat the competition is to make a unique product. For example, look at the long list of car models, sizes, colors, and features designed to attract different buyers. It is not uncommon for the typical grocery store to carry more than 100 different brands of breakfast cereals—something for everybody.

Do people really need so many choices? The freedom to advertise encourages businesses to create new brands and improve old ones. When one brand reaches market dominance, smaller brands may disappear for a time. But the moment a better product comes along and is advertised skillfully, the dominant brand loses out to the newer, better product. Once again, the freedom to advertise promotes the existence of more sellers, and that gives consumers wider choices.

Effect on the Business Cycle

The relationship between advertising and a nation's gross domestic product has long been debated. A country's gross domestic product, or GDP, is a measure of the market value of all goods and services produced by that country during a fixed period of time, usually one year. It has been called "the world's most powerful statistical indicator of national development and progress."[10] John Kenneth Galbraith, a perennial critic of advertising, concedes that by helping maintain consumer demand (encouraging more buyers), advertising helps sustain employment and economic growth.[11]

Consumer demand is considered a pillar of a strong economy by some economists. When President Obama championed a billion-dollar stimulus act in 2008, his purpose was to create demand by putting more money in consumers' pockets. The failure of the stimulus to restore strong growth in the economy was due, in part, to its failure to create demand. Instead of purchasing products or services, many consumers used the money to pay off debt or increase savings. However, consumer demand began rising again after 2010 and has continued an upward trend to the present, as shown in Exhibit 3.3.

Exhibit 3.3

U.S. Consumer Demand

Sources: "U.S. Consumer Spending," *Trading Economics*, TradingEconomics.com; U.S Bureau of Economic Analysis.

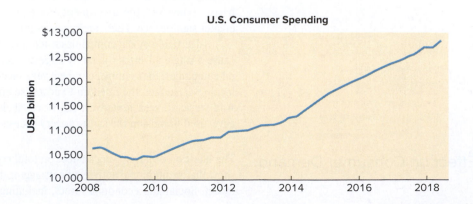

U.S. Consumer Spending

Historically, in hard economic times, companies cut promotional expenditures. That may help short-term profits, but some studies show that businesses that continue to advertise during a recession are better able to protect, and even build, market share.[12] However, if everybody just keeps advertising, it is unlikely that the recessionary cycle will turn around. We conclude that when business cycles are up, advertising contributes to the increase. When business cycles are down, advertising may act as a stabilizing force by encouraging more buyers to buy. During recessions, or times of low consumer demand, even when companies are not cutting marketing dollars, they try to spend their IMC budgets more efficiently (i.e., on less expensive promotional tools) and they look for ways to measure the return on investment (ROI) of their marketing spending.

The Abundance Principle: The Economic Impact of Advertising in Perspective

To individual businesses such as Quaker Oats, the local car dealer, or the convenience store on the corner, advertising pays back more than it costs. If advertising didn't pay, no one would use it. And the various news and entertainment media that depend on advertising for financial support would go out of business.

To the economy as a whole, the importance of advertising may best be demonstrated by the *abundance principle.* It states that in an economy that produces more goods and services than can be consumed, advertising serves two important purposes: It keeps consumers informed of their alternatives *(complete information),* and it allows companies to compete more effectively for consumer dollars *(self-interest).* This competition generally results in more and better products at lower prices.

Advertising stimulates competition *(many buyers and sellers).* In countries where consumers have more income to spend after their physical needs are satisfied, advertising also stimulates innovation and new products. However, no amount of advertising can achieve long-term acceptance for products that do not meet consumer approval. Despite massive advertising expenditures, fewer than a dozen of the 50 best-known cars developed in the 20th century are still sold today. Or to take a more recent example, advertising expenditures on 3-D TV sets failed to create consumer demand.

Conversely, nearly 8 out of 10 Americans own a smartphone, first introduced by Apple in 2007. To introduce its phone, Apple used clever ads, including one featuring clips of famous stars picking up a phone and saying, "hello." The product was an immediate hit. Great advertising, combined with a great product, created demand that accounts for nearly $500 billion in global sales each year.[13] Apple's innovation caught the attention of other tech companies, and today competition among manufacturers such as Apple and Samsung is fierce. This competition has meant that smartphones in 2020 are leagues better than the original models. Consider that the original iPhone had a 320×480 pixel TFT display, while the iPhone 11 carries a $2,688 \times 1,242$ pixel OLED display. The newer model takes better pictures and features stronger screens, faster processors, and more memory.

(all) Source: Apple, Inc.

Advertising stimulates a healthy economy by creating consumers who are more informed, better educated, and more demanding. It also, by design, draws enormous attention to itself. Ads invite people to think about the specific products they are promoting, and, in addition, to reflect on the impact of the advertising industry itself. So it is not surprising that the advertising industry has drawn a good deal of social criticism and legal regulation, the subject of our next sections.

The Social Impact of Advertising

LO 3-2

Because it's so visible, advertising is frequently criticized, both for what it is and for what it isn't. Many of the criticisms focus on the *style* of advertising, saying it's deceptive or manipulative. Collectively we might refer to these as **short-term manipulative criticisms.** Other criticisms focus on the *social or environmental impact* of advertising. These are **long-term macro criticisms.**[14] A short-term criticism is one that suggests that a particular ad has harmed a particular consumer at a specific point in time. Long-term criticisms are ones that deal with the broad impact of many ads on many people over long periods of time.

In our discussion of the economic impact of advertising, we focused primarily on the first two principles of free-market economics: self-interest and many buyers and sellers. The social aspect of advertising typically involves the last two principles: *complete information* and *absence of externalities.* We can examine many issues from these two perspectives. Some of the most important are deception and manipulation in advertising, the effect of advertising on our value system, commercial clutter, stereotypes, and offensiveness.

Deception in Advertising

A common short-term criticism of advertising is that it is often deceptive. The good news for most consumers is that false factual claims are illegal (see Ad Lab 3–A below for ways ad claims can be false). According to the FTC, "[w]hen consumers see or hear an advertisement, whether it's on the Internet, radio or television, or anywhere else, federal law says that ad must be truthful, not misleading, and, when appropriate, backed by scientific evidence."[15]

But concepts of truth and falsity can be, as you might expect, murky, and this can diminish advertising's credibility. The late scholar Ivan Preston noted that anything that detracts from the satisfaction of a transaction between buyers and sellers ultimately hurts both parties.[16] If a brand does not live up to its claims, dissatisfaction occurs—and in the long term that is as harmful to the advertiser as to the buyer.

This chainsaw doesn't literally have small warriors marching along the blade, of course. Consumers recognize that this is exaggeration, or puffery. Puffery may not be believable at a literal level. But bragging of this sort can serve as a metaphor for the benefits the brand is promoting. What benefits do you think STIHL is promoting for its chainsaw in this ad?
Source: STIHL Inc.

The EDSEL LOOK is here to stay
—it has the new ideas next year's cars are copying!

Despite extensive advertising efforts, some products, like the Edsel automobile, will fail simply because they do not meet the expectations of customers at that particular time. Many of the best-known cars developed in the 20th century are no longer sold today.

Pictorial Press Ltd/Alamy Stock Photo

For advertising to be effective, it must have credibility with consumers. So deception not only detracts from the complete information principle of free enterprise but also risks being self-defeating. Because, as noted above, deception in advertising is illegal, Preston sought to bring attention to puffery, claims featured in many ads that can best be thought of as nonspecific boasts. Preston thought that such meaningless (but legal) claims are sometimes taken literally and therefore become deceptive. More specifically, **puffery** refers to exaggerated, subjective claims that can't be proven true or false, such as "America's favorite pasta," "Finger lickin' good," or "Taste the rainbow" (can you identify the brands that use these slogans?).

Under current advertising law, the only ads that can be considered deceptive are those that are *factually false* or convey a false impression and therefore have the potential to deceive or mislead reasonable people.[17] Puffery is excluded from this requirement because it is assumed that reasonable people don't believe it. Preston points out that because advertisers regularly use puffery and nonproduct facts when advertising, they must think consumers *do* believe it. **Nonproduct facts** are not about the brand but about the consumer or the social context in which the consumer uses the brand. An example is "Pepsi. The choice of a new generation."

Even when ads are not deceptive, they rarely tell the whole story about a brand. They tell part of the story, generally a part favorable to the advertiser. People expect advertisers to be proud of their products and probably don't mind if they puff a little. But when advertisers cross the line between simply giving their point of view and creating false expectations, people begin to object. Papa John's Pizza no doubt thought it was just puffing when it advertised "Better ingredients. Better pizza." Pizza Hut saw it differently, though, and sued Papa John's for deceptive advertising. A U.S. district judge agreed and awarded Pizza Hut close to half a million dollars in damages. The judge then ordered Papa John's to stop using its "Better ingredients" slogan.[18] This decision was later overturned on appeal, but the case still goes to show that there are limits on what an advertiser can safely puff.[19]

Preston believed these kinds of problems could be avoided if marketers improved the kind of information they give in their advertising. He thought that advertisers should have a reasonable basis for any claims they make, whether those claims are facts about the product, nonfacts such as "Coke is it," or nonproduct facts.[20] This, he thought, would contribute positively to our free-market system. Ad Lab 3–A lists some other common deceptive practices.

The Effect of Advertising on Our Value System

This Nike ad featuring former NFL quarterback Colin Kaepernick uses nonproduct facts to appeal to its viewers. Kaepernick created controversy by kneeling during the National Anthem, resulting in both praise and criticism. Who do you think this ad is trying to appeal to?

Source: Nike, Inc.

A long-term argument, often voiced by consumer advocates, is that advertising degrades people's value systems by promoting a materialistic way of life. Advertising, they say, encourages us to buy more cars, more DVDs, more clothing, and more junk we don't need. It is destroying the essence of our "citizen democracy," replacing it with a selfish consumer democracy.[21]

Critics claim advertising manipulates us into buying things by playing on our emotions and promising greater status, social acceptance, and sex appeal. It causes people to take up harmful habits, makes impoverished kids buy $300 sneakers, and tempts ordinary people to buy useless products to emulate celebrity endorsers.[22] Advertising, say its detractors, is so powerful that consumers are helpless to defend themselves against it.

Certainly there's no question that advertisers spend millions trying to convince people their products will make them sexier, healthier, and more successful. The volume of advertising seems to suggest that every problem can be solved by a purchase.

However, this argument exaggerates the power of advertising. In fact, most Americans express a healthy skepticism toward it. One study showed that only 17 percent of U.S. consumers see advertising as a source of information to help them decide what to buy.[23] Perhaps that's why more advertised products fail than succeed in the marketplace.

Even if we assume that most people can willingly accept or reject an advertising message, they are still not getting the whole picture. After all, advertising is supported by marketers who want to sell their products, but nobody markets the opposite stance of

AD Lab 3–A

Unfair and Deceptive Practices in Advertising

The courts have held that these acts constitute unfair or deceptive trade practices and are therefore illegal.

False Promises

Making an advertising promise that cannot be kept, such as "restores youth" or "prevents cancer." When Listerine claimed to prevent or reduce the impact of colds and sore throats, the FTC banned the campaign and required the company to run millions of dollars' worth of corrective ads.

Incomplete Description

Stating some but not all of a product's contents, such as advertising a "solid oak" desk without mentioning that only the top is solid oak and the rest is pine.

False and Misleading Comparisons

Making false comparisons, either explicitly or by implication, such as "Like Tylenol, Advil doesn't upset my stomach." That implies that Advil is equal in avoiding stomach upset, though in truth Tylenol is better. To some people, Advil's claim might even suggest that Tylenol upsets the stomach, which is also false.

Bait-and-Switch Offers

Advertising an item at an unusually low price to bring people into the store and then "switching" them to a higher-priced model by claiming that the advertised product is out of stock or poorly made.

Visual Distortions and False Demonstrations

Using trick photography or computer manipulation to enhance a product's appearance—for example, a TV commercial for a "giant steak" dinner special showing the steak on a miniature plate that makes it look extra large. In one classic case, General Motors and its window supplier, Libby Owens-Ford, rigged a demonstration to show how clear their windows were. The GM cars were photographed with the windows down, the competitor's car with the windows up—and Vaseline smeared on them.

False Testimonials

Implying that a product has the endorsement of a celebrity or an authority who is not a bona fide user, or implying that endorsers have a certain expertise that in fact they don't.

Partial Disclosure

Stating certain facts about the advertised product but omitting other material information. An example is claiming, "Kraft's Singles processed cheese slices are made from five ounces of milk," which gives Singles more calcium than the imitators' without mentioning that processing loses about two ounces of the milk.

Small-Print Qualifications

Making a statement in large print, such as Beneficial's "Instant Tax Refund," only to qualify or retract it in obscure, small, or unreadable type elsewhere in the ad: "If you qualify for one of our loans." To the FTC, if readers don't see the qualification, it's not there.

Laboratory Applications

1. Describe some examples of deception you have seen in advertising.
2. Who is affected by unfair or deceptive advertising practices and what remedies are available to them?

---

why we don't need to or shouldn't buy a particular product at all. In this sense, consumers don't have *complete information*. This is an important issue of *externalities* because the aggregate activities of the nation's advertisers affect many people outside the immediate marketing transaction and create an unexpected cost to society.

The Proliferation of Advertising

One of the most common long-term complaints about advertising is that there's just too much of it. In the United States, the average person may be exposed to 500 to 1,000 commercial messages a day. With so many products competing for attention, advertisers themselves worry about the impact of excessive advertising. According to Nielsen, ad clutter is still on the rise. In 2005, the amount of nonprogram time on network TV—which includes advertising, public service announcements, and program promotions—ranged from about 16 minutes per hour during prime time to nearly 21 minutes per hour in daytime, a day part that is particularly important to advertisers.[24] And the situation is even worse on some cable networks: Spike TV experimented with commercial breaks lasting as long as 10 minutes.[25] The networks add to the problem by jamming every possible moment with promotions for their shows. Too much advertising creates an externality not only for consumers (nuisance) but also for the advertisers themselves—the more commercials that hit

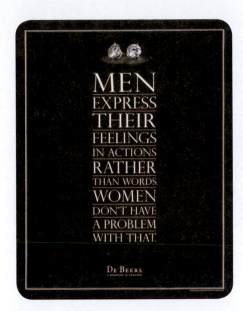

The use of stereotypes is considered unethical by many, even when done in a light-hearted way. Is this attempt by De Beers Diamonds to capitalize on gender stereotypes funny? Or is it offensive?

Source: De Beers Diamond Jewellers US Inc.

The Use of Stereotypes in Advertising

the consumer's brain, the less effective any single one can be. Some of the rise in digital and social media IMC expenditures can be traced to marketer dissatisfaction with clutter in traditional media.

Commercial radio is just as cluttered as TV. Conscious of the negative effects of ad clutter, Clear Channel—the largest radio group in the United States, with over 1,200 stations—introduced the "Less Is More" program. Reduced inventory allowed Clear Channel to raise the price of its scarcer spots.[26] The Federal Communications Commission, which in years past regulated advertising on all broadcast television, now focuses primarily on limiting ads in TV programming aimed at children 12 and under—advertising may not exceed 10.5 minutes per hour on weekends and 12 minutes per hour on weekdays.[27]

Clutter is not so evident in other countries. In the European Union, for example, TV broadcasters can carry no more than 12 minutes of commercials per hour.[28]

In North America we should be so lucky. During election periods, the clutter problem gets worse, seriously devaluing an advertiser's commercial. In 2004, an unexpectedly large number of political ads ran on television in Ohio, a crucial swing state in the presidential election. Ad spending exceeded $20 million, an estimated increase of 50 percent from the previous presidential campaign, and three out of four commercials that aired one weekend were for political candidates.[29] In 2008, another presidential election year, political ad spending set a record of $2.8 billion. That was easily eclipsed by the $4.2 billion spent in 2010, a year without a presidential contest and the $6 billion spent in 2012.[30] The final tab for the 2016 election cycle, headed by Donald Trump's contest with Hilary Clinton? Over $6.5 billion.[31]

Advertising has long been criticized for insensitivity to minorities, women, immigrants, the disabled, the elderly, and other groups.[32] This long-term argument also addresses externalities because advertising affects the nature of our culture and environment, even when we do not want it. This is ironic because marketing and advertising practitioners are supposed to be professional students of the communication process and consumer behavior. But, in fact, they sometimes lose touch with the very people they're trying to reach.

In recent years, national advertisers have become more sensitive to the concerns of minorities and women. Latinos, African Americans, Asians, Native Americans, and others are now usually portrayed with sensitivity in ads, not only because of pressure from watchdog groups, but also because it's just good business; these consumers represent sizable target markets. Marilyn Kern-Foxworth, a professor and expert on minorities in advertising, believes that positive role portrayal in some mainstream ads has raised the self-esteem of African American youth.[33] As we'll see in Chapter 4, this positive trend has accelerated with the emergence of many ad agencies that specialize in reaching minority markets.

The image of women is also changing from their historic depiction as either homemakers or sex objects. This may be partially due to the growing number of women in executive positions with both advertisers and agencies. Stanford professor Debra Meyerson says, "the glass ceiling definitely exists, but at the same time, there are an increasing number of women who are breaking through it."[34] In 2007, about 59 percent of all women were in the workforce, with more than 48 million in managerial and professional careers.[35] Advertisers want to reach, not offend, this sizable market of upwardly mobile consumers. Some agencies now retain feminist consultants to review ads that may risk offending women.[36] In 2003, Ann Fudge shattered the glass ceiling when she was named chair and CEO of Young and Rubicam and became the first African American woman to head a major U.S. advertising agency. *Forbes* named Fudge one of the 100 most powerful women in America in 2004. And in 2007, Nancy Hill became the first female head of the American Association of Advertising Agencies (AAAA) (see People behind the Ads in Chapter 4). The days when sexist practitioners like Don Draper, the central character of AMC's *Mad Men,* defined the culture of ad agencies are now far in the past.

Advertising may sometimes perpetuate stereotypes, but it can also help dispel them. In this PSA from The Shelter Pet Project, people who believe animals end up in shelters because of behavioral problems are shown that pets may often end up there through no fault of their own.
Source: Shelter Pet Project

However, problems still exist, especially in local and regional advertising and in certain product categories such as beer and sports promotions. Many advertisers are just not sensitive to the externalities that their ads can create, and some may perpetuate male and female stereotypes without even realizing it.

Of course, avoiding negative stereotypes is not the same as embracing cultural diversity. Research evidence suggests that many Americans value their ethnic identities and prefer brands that speak to them. This in turn has led agencies to see the value of diversifying their own ranks to better understand and communicate with their clients' consumers[37] (see Ethics, Diversity & Inclusion," in Chapter 5).

With tightening markets, advertisers must double their efforts to maintain or expand market share. One way is to expand into minority communities, which have enormous buying power and are growing at a faster rate than the rest of the population. The ad for Bounty Paper Towels targeted at the Spanish community and the ad for Quaker Oats targeted at the African American community are good examples of efforts to expand the market share of these two popular brands.

(Bounty) Source: The Advertising Archives; (Quaker) Source: Pepsi Cola Company

Offensiveness in Advertising

Phil Knight, cofounder of Nike, Inc., has said, "It doesn't matter how many people hate your brand as long as enough people love it." In this ad for Antonio Federici Ice Cream, a heavily pregnant nun is featured with the tagline "immaculately conceived . . . ice cream is our religion." Do you agree with Knight's statement? Would this ad make more consumers love or hate the Federici brand?

Photoshot/Newscom

The Social Impact of Advertising in Perspective

Offensiveness is a short-term style argument that also speaks to externalities. Parents are sometimes upset by ads that embrace provocative or sexual themes, especially when the advertiser targets children or teens. Prominent targets of parental ire include Calvin Klein and Abercrombie & Fitch.[38]

Taste, of course, is highly subjective: What is bad taste to some is perfectly acceptable to others. And tastes change. What is considered offensive today may not be so tomorrow. People were outraged when the first ad for underarm deodorant appeared in a 1927 *Ladies Home Journal;* today no one questions such ads. Yet, even with the AIDS epidemic, many broadcast networks still do not air condom commercials during the day; instead, the "Make a Difference" condom campaign was placed in prime time. Networks known to run condom ads include Fox, MTV, Comedy Central, BET, CNN, TNT, USA, TBS, and NBC (after 10 p.m.).[39]

Taste is also geographic. A shockingly bloody ad for a small surfwear company in Sydney, Australia, showed a gutted shark lying on a dock. Protruding from its cut-open belly were a human skeleton and an intact pair of surfer shorts. The tagline: "Tough clothes by Kadu—Triple stitched. Strongest materials available. Homegrown and sewn."[40]

While we might consider that ad quite offensive in North America, it won the Grand Prix at the International Advertising Festival in Cannes. In Australia it received wide media coverage because two surfers were killed by sharks while it was running. Rather than pulling the ad out of respect, the company reveled in its timeliness, and local surfers responded favorably.[41] But roles were reversed with a global campaign to increase Australian tourism that ran in 2006. The campaign tagline, "Where the bloody hell are you?," was viewed as quaint in America, where the term "bloody" is uncontroversial. In Australia and England, where the adjective is considered strong language, consumers and critics complained.

Today, grooming, fashion, and personal hygiene products often use partial nudity in their ads. Where nudity is relevant to the product, people are less likely to regard it as obscene or offensive—except when the advertising targets kids. In Europe, nudity in commercials is commonplace.[42]

Some consumers get so offended by both advertising and TV programming that they boycott sponsors' products. Of course, they also have the option to just change the channel. Both of these are effective strategies for consumers because, ultimately, the marketplace has veto power. If ads don't pull in the audience, the campaign will falter and die.

Marketing professionals earnestly believe in the benefits that advertising brings to society. Advertising, they say, encourages the development and speeds the acceptance of new products and technologies. It fosters employment. It gives consumers and business customers a wider variety of choices. By encouraging mass production, it helps keep prices down. And it stimulates healthy competition between producers, which benefits all buyers.[43] Advertising, they point out, also promotes a higher standard of living; it pays for most of our news media and subsidizes the arts; it supports freedom of the press; and it provides a means to disseminate public information about important health and social issues.

Critics of advertising might disagree with many of these points. Some argue that rather than supporting a free press, advertising actually creates an externality that interferes with it. The media, they say, pander to national advertisers to attract ad dollars. In the process, they modify their editorial content to suit their corporate benefactors and shirk their responsibility of presenting news in the public interest.[44]

A balanced perspective might suggest that while advertising may legitimately be criticized for offering less-than-complete information and, in some instances, for creating unwanted externalities, it should also be applauded when it contributes to economic growth and consumer prosperity. In most cases, by being a rich information source (albeit not a complete one), advertising contributes to the existence of many buyers and sellers and, therefore, to the goals of both consumers and marketers. Moreover, while advertising is biased, it is broadly recognized as such by its intended targets. It offers consumers information they are not likely to get anywhere else. And for many, it is a legitimate form of speech in societies that value diverse viewpoints. And while advertisers have been known to pressure news outlets for favorable coverage, there is no easy way for media groups to replace the income advertising provides. Where their interests collide, it is ultimately a news organization's job to determine whether they will serve advertisers or their audience.

Social Responsibility and Advertising Ethics

LO 3-3

When advertising violates one of the basic economic assumptions we've described, some corrective action is needed. As we'll discuss in the next section, laws determine what advertisers can and cannot do, but they also allow a significant amount of leeway. That's where ethics and social responsibility come into play. An advertiser can act unethically or irresponsibly without breaking any laws. If laws did not prevent vodka brands from sponsoring shows aimed at children, that would not mean it was ethical or responsible to do so. As Ivan Preston says, ethics begin where the law ends.[45]

Being **ethical** means doing what is morally right in a given situation. **Social responsibility** means doing what society views as best for the welfare of people in general or for a specific community of people. Together, ethics and social responsibility can be seen as the obligation of advertisers to society, even when there is no legal obligation.

Without advertising, public service organizations would be unable to reach a mass audience to educate people about important health and social issues. Here, the Ad Council promotes awareness of diversity.
Source: The Advertising Council

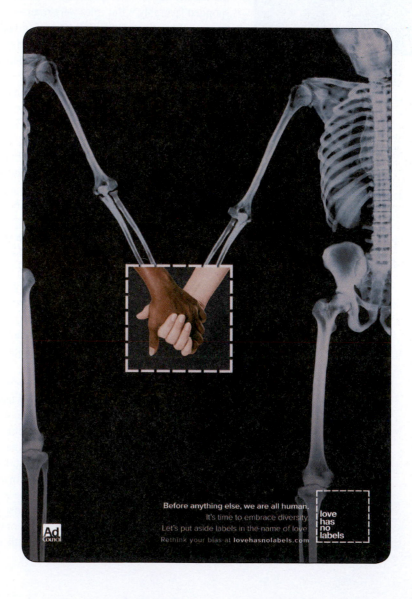

Advertisers' Social Responsibility

The foundation of any human society is peaceful and respectful relationships among its members. Without harmony, societies collapse. So institutions have some responsibility for helping maintain social harmony through proper stewardship of individuals and groups, honesty and integrity in relationships, adherence to accepted ethical standards, willingness to assist various segments of the society, and respect for the privacy of others.

Advertising plays an important role in developed countries. It influences a society's stability and growth. It helps secure large armies, creates entertainment events attracting hundreds of thousands of fans, and often affects the outcome of political elections. Such power places a burden of responsibility on those who sponsor, buy, create, produce, and sell advertising to maintain ethical standards that support the society and contribute to the economic system.

In most countries, for example, the advertising industry is part of a large business community. Like any good neighbor, it has responsibilities: to keep its property clean, participate in civic events, support local enterprises, and improve the community. U.S. advertising professionals have met these challenges by forming local advertising clubs, the American Advertising Federation (AAF), the American Association of Advertising Agencies (AAAA), and the Ad Council. These organizations provide thousands of hours and millions of dollars' worth of pro bono (free) work to charitable organizations and public agencies. They also provide scholarships and internships, contributions that serve the whole of society. As we discuss later, they even regulate themselves fairly effectively.

Advertisers such as AT&T, IBM, and Honda commit significant dollars to supporting the arts, education, and various charitable causes as well as their local Better Business Bureaus and Chambers of Commerce. Still, advertisers are regularly chided when they fail the social responsibility litmus test. Concerned citizens, consumer advocates, and special-interest groups pressure advertisers when they perceive the public's welfare is at risk. The earliest "green advertising" campaigns, for instance, exemplified a blatant effort by some advertisers to cash in on consumers' desire for a cleaner environment. Some promoted nebulous product qualities, such as "environmental friendliness," that had no basis in fact. Finally, when the state attorneys general got together and defined relevant terms for use in green advertising, marketers cleaned up their act.

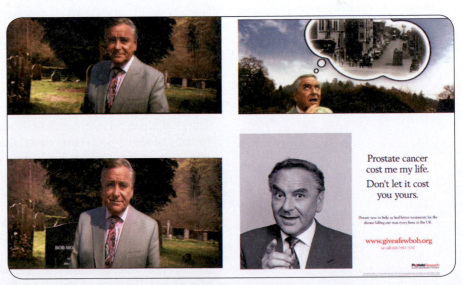

This award-winning ad, called "Give a few Bob," featured British TV celebrity Bob Monkhouse talking about the dangers of prostate cancer. Monkhouse died from the disease four years before the commercial was made. Using computer effects, the ad agency that produced the spot created an ad in which Monkhouse jokes about his own death. Effective or creepy? Or both?

(all) Source: The Communications Agency for the Prostate Cancer Research Foundation and the Monkhouse Family

Ethics, Diversity, & Inclusion

Colin Kaepernick and Nike

Former NFL quarterback Colin Kaepernick was drafted by the San Francisco 49ers in the 2011 draft. The second-round pick began his career, like many rookies, on the bench. But when the 49ers starting quarterback was injured, Kaepernick stepped in and eventually led the team to the 2012 Super Bowl. Although San Francisco lost the big game, Kaepernick continued as a starter and the 49ers went to the playoffs for three more seasons. By 2016, Kaepernick's style of play, which relied heavily on his mobility and speed, became less effective, perhaps due to age and the toll of NFL hits. He lost his starting job but remained with the team as a backup.

During the 2016 NFL preseason, Kaepernick ignited a national controversy by remaining seated on the bench during the playing of the National Anthem. He explained his actions by saying, "I am not going to stand up to show pride in a flag for a country that oppresses black people and people of color. To me, this is bigger than football and it would be selfish on my part to look the other way. There are bodies in the street and people getting paid leave and getting away with murder."[46]

For the final preseason game of 2016 Kaepernick choose to kneel as a form of protest rather than stay seated, explaining he wished to show more respect for armed service members. He continued his protest throughout the season and inspired others, including a number of NFL players, to do the same.

After opting out of his contract, Kaepernick found himself unemployed and without a team. The athlete maintains he is being blackballed and has sued the NFL. Conversely, a couple of NFL teams, including the Ravens and Broncos, have indicated they've made offers and blame the quarterback for rejecting them.

In 2018 Nike celebrated the 30th anniversary of its memorable "Just Do It" slogan by featuring Kaepernick as one athlete in a series of memorable images. The quarterback's face is shown in closeup, along with the headline "Believe in something. Even if it means sacrificing everything." The athlete is reported to be receiving a multi-million-dollar payday for the campaign.

Nike and Kaepernick already had a sponsorship deal in place extending to the football player's rookie season. The new ad extends the deal and also includes a line of clothing and shoes. Some of the money in the deal will be donated to Kaepernick's nonprofit group.

Responses to the campaign have been divided. Opinion has, in many instances, also broken down across demographic

Ethics of Advertising

Philosophies of ethics span the centuries since Socrates. We can hardly do them justice here. But for practical purposes, let's consider three levels of ethical responsibility and apply them to advertising.

On one level, ethics comprise two interrelated components: the traditional actions taken by people in a society or community, which are customs, and the philosophical rules that society establishes to justify past actions and decree future actions, which are principles. Customs and principles create the primary rules of ethical behavior in the society and enable us to measure how far an individual or company (or advertiser) strays from the norm.

Every individual also faces a second set of ethical issues: the attitudes, feelings, and beliefs that add up to a personal value system. When these two systems conflict, should the individual act on personal beliefs or on the obligation to serve society? For example, non-smoking ad agency people may create ads for a tobacco client. At the first societal level of ethics there is some conflict: Smoking has been a custom in the United States for centuries and is not illegal today. However, the U.S. Surgeon General has declared that smoking is a national health problem (harming innocent people violates an important principle). This conflict at the first ethical level passes the responsibility for decision making to the second, individual level. Recognizing this, many agencies give their employees considerable latitude regarding whether they work on a tobacco (or alcohol) account.

When the group or individuals cannot resolve an ethical dilemma, they must redefine the issue in dispute. Thus, the third level of ethics concerns singular ethical concepts such as good, bad, right, wrong, duty, integrity, and truth. Are these concepts absolute, universal, and binding? Or are they relative, dependent on situations and consequences? A person's moral and ethical philosophy, influenced by religion, society, and individual values, will determine his or her answer (see Exhibit 3-4).

lines, including race and age, with African Americans and younger Americans generally offering support. Initial suggestions that the campaign would risk Nike profits were dissipated when the company reported sales increases of over 30 percent following the appearance of the ads. One commentator noted that over two-thirds of Nike consumers are under 35, making the company's association with Kaepernick less risky than it might seem.

Many have praised Kaepernick's courage in the face of harsh criticism, including comments from U.S. President Donald Trump, who tweeted that anthem protesters should be fired. Among the athlete's supporters is *GQ* magazine, which named him a 2017 "Citizen of the Year," and Amnesty International, which awarded him a "Ambassador of Conscience" honor. Others believe Kaepernick's actions and rhetoric insult first responders, the flag, and the sacrifices of men and women in the armed forces.

The controversy is all the more interesting because Nike provides uniforms for every NFL team. The league itself seems flummoxed about how to handle the issue. On the one hand, it collaborates with its players in growing the league's audiences and profits, but on the other hand, it is sensitive to the large numbers of people offended by the protest. As of 2018 league ratings have dropped for two years in a row, although it is unclear how much this is due to player demonstrations.

Questions

1. What is your opinion of Colin Kaepernick's anthem protests? Has the athlete chosen an effective way to raise issues of race in the U.S.? Why or why not?

2. Consider the position you adopted in Question 1 and present arguments for the other side. In other words, if you defended Kaepernick's means of protesting, present the arguments of those who find them offensive and disrespectful. If you oppose Kaepernick's behaviors, explain why so many have supported the athlete and called him courageous. You need not change your mind, but try to gain a better understanding of why the issue has aroused such passions.

Let's say, for example, the copywriter for a cigarette ad is a smoker, and he writes copy that implies that smoking is a favorable behavior. But the ad's art director, a nonsmoker, complains that the ad is unethical because the copy conflicts with the truth that smoking is unsafe. At this point they reach the third ethical level, and a more senior person, such as the creative director, may step in and lead a discussion aimed at clarifying the agency's ethical policy regarding the promotion of cigarettes.

As we mentioned before, ethics is such an important topic that we address those issues that pertain to advertising in Ethics, Diversity & Inclusion sidebars in each chapter. The Ethics box here examines the controversies surrounding former NFL quarterback Colin Kaepernick's National Anthem protests and his subsequent participation in ads for Nike.

Exhibit 3-4
Levels of ethical responsibility.

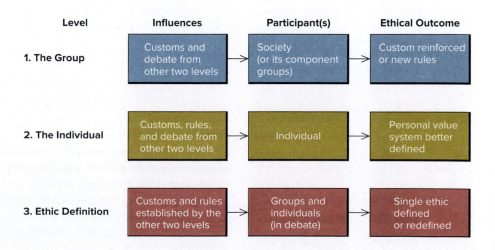

Level	Influences	Participant(s)	Ethical Outcome
1. The Group	Customs and debate from other two levels	Society (or its component groups)	Custom reinforced or new rules
2. The Individual	Customs, rules, and debate from other two levels	Individual	Personal value system better defined
3. Ethic Definition	Customs and rules established by the other two levels	Groups and individuals (in debate)	Single ethic defined or redefined

My IMC Campaign 3-A

Your Assignment

You will be working on an advertising/IMC campaign, or part of one, this semester. Few things are more important for you when preparing for a semester-long project than understanding the final product that is expected of you. It is only when you know what is expected at the end that you can plan what happens in between.

What You May Be Working On

Different classes have different projects, but it is likely that you will work on one or more of the following for a brand, service, or firm:

- A campaign audit.
- A research report.
- A marketing or IMC plan, including a SWOT analysis.
- An advertising or IMC budget.
- A media plan.
- A creative brief or creative platform.
- A plans book.

Below we explain each of these in turn and give you guidance about where you can find information in this text and on the Internet.

Campaign Audit

Many classes begin by having teams audit the plans books from prior semesters. This accomplishes several things. First, it gives you an idea about what you will be doing all semester. Second, it introduces you to the importance of seeing how research, strategy, planning, budgeting, and creativity all flow together. If you don't have access to the work of other students, why not look over the work of the very best? Visit the Effie Award website www.effie.org/, where you can find great ads and a lot of background information about the campaigns.

Research Report

You may be asked to conduct formative research for the brand. This may include secondary research, useful for gathering information for your IMC plan; qualitative primary research, in which you conduct a focus group or series of in-depth interviews; and quantitative research, in which you administer a survey. You'll find a lot of information in Chapter 7 about these activities. Your university likely has a web page devoted to secondary marketing research. A useful collection of market research resources can also be found here: http://blog.hubspot.com/marketing/market-research-tools-resources.

Marketing or IMC Plan

Many classes require that you create a marketing or IMC plan. We've included lots of information in this text to help. Be sure to read Chapter 8 carefully, as it is your guide to the art and science of planning. Then, to make things more concrete, use the appendices of the book to create an outline for your plan. Your instructor may have his or her own outline; if so, use that.

Media Plan

A media plan shows the specific allocations of the budget to different media and promotional activities. It will also specify what vehicles will be used for the campaign, as well as when and how often the ads will run. You will most likely want to use a spreadsheet to show the calendar. We have a sample media plan in Chapter 9.

The Creative Brief

The creative brief is a fairly short document that is used to inform and guide the people who create the ads. It contains information that has been distilled from some of the documents that we've just reviewed, such as the IMC plan. There are as many different outlines for creative briefs as there are ad agencies, but in many instances the differences are superficial. Chapter 11 gives some suggestions for a creative brief and shows you the elements of message strategy. For examples of creative briefs, visit the following sites:

- SmileyCat blog (for a brief written for a web campaign): www.smileycat.com/miaow/archives/000226.php
- Hubspot blog: https://blog.hubspot.com/agency/create-compelling-creative-brief

The Plans Book

If you are doing a plans book, it means you are doing almost everything we've reviewed to this point. A typical plans book will include research findings, an IMC plan, a creative brief, media plans, and, in many cases, mock-ups of real ads. But it puts these things together in a seamless, integrated way, so that the reader has a clear understanding of the entire arc of a planned campaign. In many plans books there will also be a section on campaign evaluation (ways of assessing the campaign).

Most advertisers today strive to maintain ethical standards and practice socially responsible advertising. Once a free-swinging, unchecked business, advertising is today a closely scrutinized and heavily regulated profession. Advertising's past shortcomings have created layers of laws, regulations, and regulatory bodies. Consumer groups, governments, special-interest groups, and even other advertisers now review, control, and modify advertising in order to create more *complete information* and reduce the impact of unwanted *externalities*.

For an institution as prominent and influential as advertising, society believes that self-regulation is not enough. As a result, there are many laws governing what advertisers can and cannot do. These laws are passed by legislatures, enforced by the executive branch, and interpreted by the judiciary. This system is repeated at the state and local levels.

On the national level, the president, cabinet departments, and various federal commissions are responsible for executing the laws passed by Congress. On the state level, governors, attorneys general, and state departments administer laws. Locally, mayors, city managers, city attorneys, and police chiefs enforce the laws passed by city councils.

Similarly, local laws are interpreted by municipal courts, while the superior courts and state supreme courts interpret state laws. Federal laws are interpreted by federal district courts and the U.S. Supreme Court. Every day, advertisers from the local copy shop to international soft drink marketers have to deal with the actions and decisions of all these branches of government. We'll discuss shortly some of the most important issues that concern U.S. regulators.

Government Restraints on International Advertisers

LO 3-4

The campaigns of global advertisers often use similar themes and even the same ads across frontiers. Other governments often regulate advertising more extensively than either the United States or Canada. And while Europe has moved toward uniformity in marketing activities, the laws governing advertising remain largely national.[47] So advertisers need to keep up with the changing legal environments of the countries in which they advertise.

Europe and the United States have very different perspectives on privacy protection, with Europeans generally favoring stricter controls. As examples, Europeans must give permission for collection of personal data, and they have the right to review any data that are collected. Such data cannot be shared between companies unless consumers give permission they may do so. Work e-mail is off limits to employers, and retailers may not request a shopper's telephone number at checkout.[48] European courts have ruled people have a "right to be forgotten," mandating that Google eliminate search results for an individual who requests that this information be destroyed.[49]

Many countries prohibit puffery. In Germany, for example, advertisers may use only scientifically provable superlatives. McCann-Erickson once had to retranslate the old Coca-Cola slogan, "Refreshes you best," because it implied a leadership position that was unprovable. The agency substituted "Refreshes you right."[50]

Many European countries also ban coupons, premiums, free tie-in offers, and the like. Companies may advertise price cuts only during "official sales periods," and advertisers often need government approval before publishing a sale ad. Across Europe, advertising on television must be clearly recognizable and kept separate from other programming.[51]

In Singapore, the state-owned broadcasting company yanked a Qantas Airline spot after the Ministry of Information and the Arts criticized the ad's "harmful values." The spot had used the line "last of the big spenders," which the ministry felt encouraged reckless spending by consumers (see Ad Lab 3–B).[52]

With the rapid growth of China's economy and the growth of a prosperous middle class, the country has faced new challenges in regulating advertising. A draft of new regulations were issued by China's National People's Congress that regulate ads for specific products (i.e., tobacco, pharmaceuticals) and provide clarity about penalties for false advertising, the use of paid spokespeople, and government supervision of advertising.[53] But regulations may still only be rough guides to the rules that advertisers must follow, as the Communist Party remains firmly in control and social media censorship is strictly enforced.[54]

In international advertising, the only way to navigate this morass of potential legal problems is to retain firms that specialize in advertising law.

AD Lab 3–B

The Importance of Good Legal Counsel in Advertising

For many years, Jack Russell had dreamed of this opportunity—opening a members-only club for young people who were not yet old enough to drink. He could already taste the success that was about to be his—money, fame, and fortune were all within his reach. He took every avenue possible to promote the new, exclusive club. He ran ads in local entertainment magazines and community newspapers. Local rock radio stations, though, were the mainstay—shouting out the good news for kids all over town, complete with a phone number and address for sending in their charter membership fees. Jack's wonderful idea was about to take flight. But then the local district attorney ripped the magic carpet out from underneath him. You see, Jack Russell was selling memberships to a club that had not opened yet. In fact, he hadn't even signed the lease on the proposed premises. To the DA, it smelled of scam. He figured Jack was taking money from kids for something that didn't exist. The DA charged him with false advertising—and fraud. When Jack answered his ringing doorbell, two uniformed officers were standing there. They handcuffed him, gave him a ride downtown, and threw him in jail. If Jack had just passed his ads by a communications lawyer, he could have avoided a very embarrassing and expensive nightmare. And he'd be a free man.

Ethical and legal problems with advertising seem to pop up constantly. Not only government officials but also competitors and consumer rights groups scrutinize ads carefully—either for their own self-interest or to protect the rights of consumers. As a result, every agency and advertiser needs to have a strong understanding of the laws that govern advertising. They also need to retain the services of a good law firm that specializes in advertising and communication law.

One such firm is Reed Smith's Advertising, Technology, and Media Group. With 77 communications law specialists spread among its 18 offices, Reed Smith is well situated to counsel advertisers throughout the United States, the United Kingdom, and Europe. Its clients come from all levels of the industry—from blue chip advertisers (such as Merck, Pfizer, Sony, and Lancôme) to ad agencies (such as Worldwide Partners, Inc.) to advertising associations (such as the Association of National Advertisers and the Advertising Research Foundation).

Reed Smith routinely provides its clients with a wide array of services: checking advertising copy for legal acceptability; reviewing conventional and online promotional concepts involving sweepstakes, games, and contests; researching comparative advertising and copyright violations; and representing clients before federal and state regulatory bodies and courts. The firm also helps clients in their relationships with the media, internet service providers, talent, and performers' unions.

The chair of the firm's advertising, technology, and media group, Douglas J. Wood, is the author of *Please Be Ad-Vised* (ANA, 2004), a comprehensive reference written for advertising and marketing professionals.

Reed Smith also publishes a free e-mail newsletter and a sophisticated website, both under the name of *AdLaw by Request*, which provide clients and prospects with summaries and analyses of new and proposed legislation affecting advertising. The website (www.adlawbyrequest.com) offers a wide array of regularly updated resources, including downloadable contract forms, sample legal documents, and articles on the legal complexities of all types of advertising and marketing communications.

Laboratory Applications

1. Go to adlawbyrequest.com and explore the website. Click on "In the Courts" in the topics listed on the right side of the page and read about current advertising-related legal cases. Pick one that interests you, read it, and then write a brief report including the title of the case, the names of the parties involved, the issues at stake, and a summary of the decision that was handed down if there has been a judgment.

2. Click "Regulatory—United States" in the topics listed on the right side of the page. Summarize one of the posts concerning the actions of a federal regulatory agency (such as the FTC, FCC, FDA, etc.). Then visit the website of the agency to find out more about its mission. In your opinion, how well does the action of the federal agency described in the post fit with its mission?

3. What ethical, social, or legal issues do you think will be addressed in the next 10 years relative to advertising and the internet?

Current Regulatory Issues Affecting U.S. Advertisers

Freedom of Commercial Speech

LO 3-5

Both federal and state courts have made a number of significant rulings pertaining to advertising issues. The most important of these concern First Amendment rights and privacy rights. We'll discuss each of these, paying special attention to the controversy surrounding tobacco advertising as well as the sensitive issue of advertising to children.

The Supreme Court historically distinguishes between "speech" and "commercial speech" (speech that promotes a commercial transaction). The Court first ruled on the issue of whether commercial speech is protected by the First Amendment in a 1942 case, *Valentine v. Chrestensen*. Chrestensen wanted to distribute handbills in New York for his business. When told to stop by the police, who were enforcing an anti-littering ordinance, Chrestensen turned to the courts to argue he had a right to advertise. After several appeals brought the case before the Supreme Court, the news for advertisers was not good. The justices ruled that government was free to regulate "purely commercial advertising," implying that whatever forms of speech the First Amendment protected, advertising was not among them.[55] While the *Valentine* decision concluded there was no constitutionally guaranteed protection for commercial speech, court rulings ever since have suggested otherwise.

The trend started in 1976 when the Supreme Court held in *Virginia State Board of Pharmacy v. Virginia Citizens Consumer Council* that truthful ads enjoy protection under the First Amendment as commercial speech.[56] The next year the Court declared that bans by state bar associations on attorney advertising also violated the First Amendment. Now, a third of all lawyers advertise, and a few states even permit client testimonials.

In 1980, the Court used *Central Hudson Gas v. Public Service Commission* to offer guidance about when commercial speech can be regulated. The four-pronged *Central Hudson* test includes the following parts:

1. *Does the commercial speech at issue concern a lawful activity?* The ad in question must be for a legal product and must be free of misleading claims.
2. *Will the restriction of commercial speech serve the asserted government interest substantially?* The government must prove that the restriction on speech will go a long way toward solving an important problem.
3. *Does the regulation directly advance the government interest asserted?* The government must establish conclusively that cessation of commercial speech would be effective in remedying the problem that government is trying to address.
4. *Is the restriction no more than necessary to further the interest asserted?* The government should show that there are no other means to accomplish the same end without restricting free speech.[57]

In 1982, the Supreme Court upheld an FTC order allowing physicians and dentists to advertise. Since then, advertising for medical and dental services has skyrocketed.

In 2011, a Supreme Court ruling had important implications for commercial speech. The case *Sorrell v. IMS Health Inc.* concerned data mining. In this case, the Court invalidated a state law that made the practice illegal, at least for drug companies. Many saw this as a broader protection for commercial speech than the one outlined in the *Central Hudson* case. Decide for yourself by rereading the test proposed in the *Central Hudson* case, and then applying it to the facts in *Sorrell v. IMS Health Inc.*[58] Do you agree, as some have written, that this is a big win for commercial speech?[59]

The issue of freedom of commercial speech is far from settled. Allowing greater freedom of commercial speech enhances the "government interests" of many buyers and sellers and complete information. But critics contend that advertising regulations can help reduce externalities related to controversial or unhealthy products.

The Tobacco Advertising Controversy

While all 50 states permit adults to legally use tobacco products, smoking causes diseases that kill or disable more than half a million people annually and cost taxpayers billions of dollars every year in health costs—a major externality. To recover these costs, a majority of states' attorneys general sued the tobacco industry. In 1998, they reached a historic settlement that imposed limits on brand-name promotion at events with young attendees, banned the use of cartoon characters (like Joe Camel) in cigarette ads, and created a fund of over $200 billion to be used by the various signatory states. Much of that money was in fact used to reimburse the various law firms that the states had hired to negotiate the settlement.[60] Today, state budgets rely heavily on the revenues obtained in the suit.[61]

For businesspeople who believe that commercial speech should be afforded protection under the First Amendment, the tobacco case is ominous. Many people are antismoking, anti-alchohol, antipornography, or antigun. But free speech advocates have First Amendment concerns about efforts to abridge speech, whether it's for any political, social, or religious idea or a legal, commercial product. They warn that this limitation of freedom

Few products arouse greater concern about the effects of advertising than tobacco products. Tobacco is legal in every state but is governed by stringent restrictions on marketing. This ad for Blu e-cigarettes tries to distance its product from traditional cigarettes. Although e-cigs contain a variety of ingredients, including nicotine, they do not have tobacco. What advertising restrictions, if any, should apply to them?

Source: blu Electronic Cigarettes

of commercial speech threatens every legal business in America, especially because restrictions on the freedom to advertise often give a huge, monopolistic advantage to those big brands that are already the category leaders.[62]

The most recent controversy surrounding "cigarettes" is the marketing of e-cigarettes. According to the FDA, e-cigarettes are "battery-operated products designed to deliver nicotine, flavor, and other chemicals" by turning water and additives into a vapor.[63] While e-cigs do not have tobacco, they do contain nicotine. Are e-cigarettes a dangerous gateway for teens on the path to tobacco use, or a healthier alternative to tobacco products? While the debate over the health threat from e-cigs has yet to be settled, some have argued that over-restrictive advertising for e-cigarettes may actually result in poorer health outcomes for society. How? Writing in *The Washington Post,* Jonathan H. Adler notes that new FDA restrictions mean that "straightforward factual claims—even claims that do no more than repeat public statements made by the FDA—are prohibited." Such claims might include information letting consumers know that e-cigs, while possibly dangerous, are still much safer than tobacco.[64]

The Issue of Advertising to Children

Advertising to children presents different challenges. Kids aren't sophisticated consumers. Their conceptions of self, time, and money are immature. Their ability to understand the consequences of some of their choices and behaviors is not as informed or sophisticated as that of an adult. This makes it likely that child-oriented advertising can lead to false beliefs or unrealistic product expectations.

While most children and parents are joint consumers, more children are becoming sole decision makers. To protect them, and their parents, most agree that advertisers should not intentionally deceive children. The central issue is how far advertisers should go to ensure that children are not misled by ads.

To promote responsible children's advertising and to respond to public concerns, the Better Business Bureau (BBB) National Programs, Inc. established the **Children's Advertising Review Unit (CARU).** CARU advises advertisers and agencies and also offers informational material for children, parents, and educators. For more than 20 years, CARU's *Self-Regulatory Guidelines for Children's Advertising* has guided marketers in the development of child-directed advertising for all traditional media. In 2009 CARU revised its guidelines, at least partially in response to requests from the FTC and the Department of Health and Human Services. The revisions dealt with new standards for food advertised to children on TV, to food packaging, and to guidelines for marketing via online video games and product placements.

The basic activity of CARU is the review and evaluation of child-directed advertising in all media. When children's advertising is found to be misleading, inaccurate, or inconsistent with the *Guidelines,* CARU seeks changes through voluntary cooperation of the advertisers.[65] For an overview of the basic principles underlying CARU's *Guidelines,* see www.asrcreviews .org/wp-content/uploads/2012/04/Self-Regulatory-Program-for-Childrens-Advertising-Revised-2014-.pdf.

Many countries are stricter than the United States with respect to advertising to children. Sweden and Norway, for example, do not permit any television commercials that target children under 12, and no advertisements at all are allowed during children's programs. Germany and Holland prohibit sponsorship of children's shows, and the Flemish region of Belgium permits no ads five minutes before or after any programs for children. While the highest level of advertising to children is in Australia (an average of 34 ads per hour), that country allows no ads on programs aimed at preschool children.[66]

In the area of television advertising, the government and consumer groups play an important role at both the national and international levels to ensure that adequate consumer protection for children is maintained and strengthened where necessary. For more on child-oriented TV advertising, see the Ethics, Diversity & Inclusion feature in Chapter 6.

Consumer Privacy

The second major regulatory issue facing advertisers is privacy. As you read in the first chapter of this text, the increased use of wireless devices, mobile phones, and the Internet, all of which can be used for advertising, has put the issue of **privacy rights** in the news. The issue deals with people's right to protect their personal information. Privacy is an ethical issue as well as a legal one. It's also a practical issue: Prospective customers who are tracked, subjected to marketing calls, or find their inboxes filled with spam aren't likely to buy the offending company's products.

Internet users worry about people they don't know, and even businesses they do know, getting personal information about them. And their concern is not without reason. Many websites create profiles of their visitors to get data such as e-mail addresses, clothing sizes, or favorite books. Some sites also track users' surfing habits, usually without their knowledge, to better target ads for products.

To create these user profiles, web advertisers store files called **cookies,** on consumer hard drives, that keep a log of internet activities, allowing sites to track customers' web-surfing habits. The cookies are created when consumers first visit a site or use some feature like a personalized news service or a shopping cart.

Because internet users access online content on a variety of devices, including phones, tablets, smart TVs, etc., advertisers have turned to new technologies for tracking their behaviors, including methods for obtaining real-time location data from phones.[67] Other privacy worries center on the data collected by giant web companies like Facebook and Google. For example, the search-engine giant's business model focuses on using data that consumers, willingly or not, share during search, while using e-mail, posting photos, texting friends, or scanning Google Maps. These data are helpful for serving targeted ads, but also raise concerns about what happens to the information and to what purposes it is put.[68]

Internet companies argue that such tracking is not personal; it's typically performed anonymously and helps them customize content to match users' interests. However, DoubleClick, a leading provider of marketing tools for web advertisers, direct marketers, and web publishers, has acquired Abacus Direct, a direct-mail company with an extensive offline database of retail and catalog purchasers. This enables DoubleClick to combine online profiles with offline names, addresses, demographic information, and purchasing data.[69] In turn, DoubleClick is a subsidiary of the largest web advertiser, Google. This means that Google has potential access to an enormous amount of information about web users. Companies like Apple and Facebook do as well.

Advertisers would be wise to take consumer privacy concerns seriously. A Pew opinion survey from 2015 found over 9 out of 10 respondents believe that "being in control of who can get information about them is important." A similar majority indicate that "controlling what information is collected about them is important."[70]

Fortunately, consumers are not completely helpless. They can disable the cookies on their computers. But this may limit their access because some websites *require* that cookies be accepted. Internet surfers also have the option to "opt in." This feature allows users to set the terms under which they give personal information. Also available is the "opt-out" feature, which allows sites to continuously gather information about visitors unless they specifically inform the site not to by clicking on a button.

Responding to consumer concerns, the Federal Trade Commission, together with the Network Advertising Initiative (an organization comprised of leading Internet advertising networks, including AdKnowledge, 24/7, Ad Force, and DoubleClick), has created a framework for self-regulation of online profiling. The Fair Information Practice Principles consist of five core elements:

- *Notice,* which requires that the website clearly post its privacy policy.
- *Choice,* which relates to consumers' level of control over being profiled and how their information is used.
- *Access,* the ability for consumers to access information collected about them and make amendments to it.
- *Security,* which requires that network advertisers make reasonable efforts to protect the data they collect from loss, misuse, or improper access.
- *Enforcement,* a requirement that all industry members subject themselves to monitoring by an independent third party to ensure compliance with the Fair Information Practice Principles.[71]

Naturally, internet companies would prefer to avoid government intervention and the layers of laws and regulations that would bring. So it's in everybody's interest for self-regulation to work.

Protecting Consumer Data

Consumer privacy is not just about what reputable companies do with data. It is also about protecting data that companies collect about consumers from those who would steal it. Recent events suggest that people have a good deal to worry about when it comes to ensuring the information they provide companies is shielded from foreign states and criminal organizations.

As can be seen in Exhibit 3.5, a staggering number of people have been affected by data breaches. The largest of these, a hacking of Yahoo accounts by "a state-sponsored actor," affected nearly 3 billion people.

Exhibit 3.5

Data breaches of the 21st century.

Source: Data from Taylor Armerding, "The 18 Biggest Data Breaches of the 21st Century," *CSO*, December 20, 2018, www.csoonline.com/article/2130877/the-biggest-data-breaches-of-the-21st-century.html.

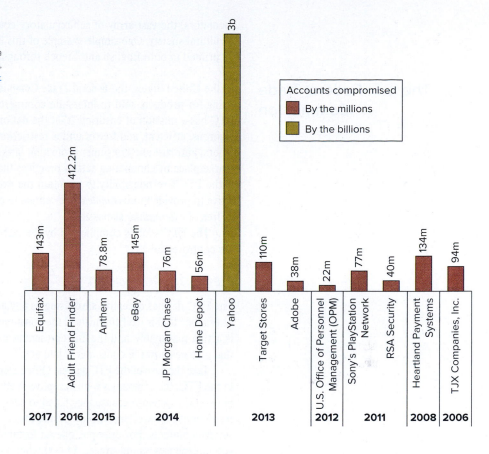

In "smaller" incidents, hundreds of millions experienced privacy compromises from hacks at Adult Friend Finder, eBay, Target Stores, Uber, Verisign, Home Depot, Adobe, and Sony Playstation. The biggest bank in the United States, JP Morgan Chase, could not protect its customers from data theft in 2014, nor could one of the nation's largest credit bureaus, Equifax. Even the Office of Personnel Management, a bureaucracy of the U.S. government entrusted with keeping personal records of tens of millions of current and former employees, could not prevent Chinese hackers from accessing its sensitive records. Worse, although the breach happened in 2012, it was not uncovered for two years.

The issue of data security is a complicated one, as companies struggle to protect their customers and employees. The response has been piecemeal, with states often taking the lead. At the beginning of 2018, every U.S. state had laws in place requiring companies to notify consumers if their information has been hacked.[72] But reporting breaches is different from preventing them, and there is every indication that the pace of attempted theft is rising.[73] The challenge for industry and government is to keep pace with evolving technologies, both for protecting and compromising data, while credibly offering consumers assurance it is safe to store data online.

Government Regulation of Advertising in North America

The U.S. government controls advertisers through laws, regulations, and judicial interpretations. Among the many federal agencies and departments that regulate advertising are the Federal Trade Commission, the Food and Drug Administration, the Federal Communications Commission, the Patent and Trademark Office, and the Library of Congress. Because their jurisdictions often overlap, advertisers may sometimes have difficulty complying with their regulations.

Canada has a similar maze of federal regulators. But the Canadian legal situation is considerably more complex than the United States' due to the separate (but often concurrent) jurisdictions of federal and provincial governments, the broad powers of government regulators, the vast array of self-regulatory codes, and the complexity of a bilingual and bicultural society. One simple example of this is the fact that all packages and labels must be printed in both English and French throughout Canada.[74]

The U.S. Federal Trade Commission

In the United States, the **Federal Trade Commission (FTC)** is the major regulator of advertising for products sold in interstate commerce. Established by an act of Congress, the FTC has a mission of ensuring "that the nation's markets function competitively, and are vigorous, efficient, and free of undue restrictions."[75] The commission enforces a variety of federal antitrust and consumer protection laws and works to enhance the operation of the marketplace by eliminating acts or practices that are deceptive or unfair. In other words, it is the FTC's responsibility to maintain the existence of *many sellers* in the marketplace, strive to provide more *complete information* to consumers, and keep the marketing process as free of *externalities* as possible.

The FTC's job is complicated by the fact that the definitions of *deceptive* and *unfair* are controversial.

Defining Deception

The FTC defines **deceptive advertising** as any ad that contains a representation, omission, or practice that is likely to mislead the consumer. The misled consumer should be one who is acting reasonably, and the misrepresentation should be material, that is, it must be one that changes how the consumer would act.[76]

Take the case of the FTC against Office Depot, Buy.com, and Value America. According to the FTC, the companies were deceptive in advertising "free" and "low-cost" personal computer (PC) systems because they failed to adequately disclose the true costs and important restrictions on the offers. The low cost of the computers was contingent on long-term internet service contracts. For example, one ad featured a computer for $269. But the purchaser's actual expenses would exceed $1,000 when taking into account the cost of the required three-year internet service contract.

Without admitting any wrongdoing, the companies all signed consent agreements, agreeing to disclose the information prominently in the future to help consumers easily determine the real costs of such deals.[77]

The FTC is a powerful regulator. The commission cracked down on Exxon and ordered a groundbreaking educational campaign to inform consumers that the right octane for most cars is regular octane, not the more expensive premium grade. The FTC also looks at environmental claims such as biodegradable, degradable, photodegradable, and recyclable. To avoid confusing terminology, the FTC and the Environmental Protection Agency (EPA) worked jointly with attorneys general from many states to develop uniform national guidelines for environmental marketing claims.

Defining Unfairness

According to FTC policy, ads that are not technically deceptive may still be considered unfair to consumers. **Unfair advertising** occurs when a consumer is "unjustifiably injured" or there is a "violation of public policy" (such as other government statutes). In other words, unfair advertising is due to the inadequacy of *complete information* or some other *externality*. For example, practices considered unfair are claims made without prior substantiation, claims that exploit vulnerable groups such as children and the elderly, and cases where the consumer cannot make a valid choice because the advertiser omits important information about the product or about competing products mentioned in the ad.[78]

In one case, the FTC found that an automaker's failure to warn of a safety problem was not deceptive but was unfair. Advertising organizations have argued that the word *unfair* lacks a clear meaning. They have lobbied Congress to eliminate the FTC's power to prosecute on unfairness grounds, and Congress did pass a compromise bill requiring the FTC to show that (1) an alleged unfair practice involves substantial, unavoidable injury to

In Canada, all packages and labels must be printed in both English and French, and most major companies also run their ads in both languages.

Roberto Machado Noa/LightRocket/Getty Images

consumers; (2) the injury is not reasonably avoidable by consumers themselves; and (3) the injury is not outweighed by benefits to consumers or competition.[79] This legislation resulted in the FTC becoming more restricted in its effort to regulate unfairness.[80]

Comparative Advertising

Advertisers use **comparative advertising** to claim superiority to competitors in some aspect. In the United States, such ads are legal (and encouraged by the FTC) so long as the comparison is truthful. In fact, the FTC cracked down on the Arizona Automobile Dealers Association for restricting truthful, nondeceptive comparative price advertising among its members.[81]

In 1994, the AADA's 199 members constituted 99 percent of the new automobile and truck dealers in Arizona. The FTC challenged the association's Standards for Advertising Motor Vehicles, which, among other things, prohibited members from advertising that prices are equal to or lower than a competitor's, or are the lowest; that the advertiser will match or beat any price; or that the advertiser will offer compensation if it cannot offer an equal or lower price.

These prohibitions, according to the FTC, unreasonably restrained competition among the member dealers and injured consumers by depriving them of truthful information concerning the prices and financing available for new cars and trucks.

The 1988 Trademark Law Revision Act closed a loophole in the Lanham Act, which governed comparison ads but did not mention misrepresenting another company's product. Under current law, any advertiser that misrepresents its own or another firm's goods, services, or activities is vulnerable to a civil action.

In addition to being truthful, comparative ads must compare some objectively measurable characteristic. And great scrutiny must be given to the substantiation. Given the potential for sizable damages—up to millions of dollars—for faulty comparative advertising, the greatest care must be exercised in this area.[82]

Investigating Suspected Violations

If it receives complaints from consumers, competitors, or its own staff members who monitor ads in various media, the FTC may decide to investigate an advertiser. The agency has broad powers to pursue suspected violators and demand information from

This ad for SmartWater relates to several interesting issues in advertising. From a legal perspective, federal law requires that celebrity endorsers actually use the product. From a creative perspective, this ad demonstrates that sexual appeal can indeed be used to market water.

Source: Glaceau SmartWater

them. Typically, the FTC looks for three kinds of information: *substantiation, endorsements,* and *affirmative disclosures.*

If a suspected violator cites survey findings or scientific studies, the FTC may ask for **substantiation.** Advertisers are expected to have supporting data before running an ad, although the FTC sometimes allows postclaim evidence. The FTC does not solicit substantiation for ads it is not investigating.

The FTC also scrutinizes ads that contain questionable **endorsements** or **testimonials.** If a noncelebrity endorser is paid, the ad must disclose this on-screen.[83] The endorsers may not make claims the advertiser can't substantiate. Further, celebrity endorsers must actually use the product or service (if portrayed), and they can be held personally liable if they misrepresent it.[84]

Advertisers must make **affirmative disclosure** of their product's limitations or deficiencies: for example, EPA mileage ratings for cars, pesticide warnings, and statements that saccharin may be hazardous to one's health.

Remedies for Unfair or Deceptive Advertising

When the FTC determines that an ad is deceptive or unfair, it may take three courses of action: negotiate with the advertiser for a consent decree, issue a cease-and-desist order, and/or require corrective advertising.

A **consent decree** is a document the advertiser signs agreeing to stop the objectionable advertising without admitting any wrongdoing. Before signing, the advertiser can negotiate specific directives with the FTC that will govern future advertising claims.

If an advertiser won't sign a consent decree, the FTC may issue a **cease-and-desist order** prohibiting further use of the ad. Before the order is final, it is heard by an administrative law judge. Most advertisers sign the consent decree after the hearing and agree, without admitting guilt, to halt the advertising. Advertisers that violate either a consent decree or a cease-and-desist order can be fined up to $11,000 per showing of the offending ad.

The FTC may also require **corrective advertising** for some period of time to explain and correct offending ads. In 1999, the FTC ruled that pharmaceutical giant Novartis advertised without substantiation that its Doan's Pills brand was more effective against back pain than its rivals. Because the deceptive advertising had gone on for more than nine years, the FTC ordered Novartis to run $8 million worth of corrective advertising. The advertising was to include this statement: "Although Doan's is an effective pain reliever, there is no evidence that Doan's is more effective than other pain relievers for back pain." The FTC also ordered Novartis to place the statement on Doan's packaging for a year.[85]

To help advertisers avoid such expense, the FTC will review advertising before it runs and give "advance clearance" in an advisory opinion. It also publishes *Industry Guides and Trade Regulation Rules,* which gives advertisers, agencies, and the media ongoing information about FTC regulations.

In Canada, the laws are even tougher and the consequences stiffer. It's an offense for any public promotion to be "false or misleading in a material respect." It is not necessary that anyone be misled by the representation, only that it be false. An *offense* is a crime. If convicted, an advertiser or agency executive could go to jail, pay a fine, or both.[86]

The Food and Drug Administration (FDA)

A division of the Department of Health and Human Services, the **Food and Drug Administration (FDA)** enforces the Federal Food, Drug, and Cosmetic Act and several other health laws. The agency monitors the manufacture, import, transport, storage, and sale of over $1 trillion worth of products annually, which accounts for about 9 cents of every dollar spent annually by American consumers.[87] And it does so at a cost to taxpayers of about $3 per person.[88]

It's the FDA's job to see that the food we eat is safe, the cosmetics we use won't hurt us, and the medicines and therapeutic devices we buy are safe and effective. With authority over the labeling, packaging, and branding of packaged foods and therapeutic devices, the FDA

revolution® (selamectin)

Topical Parasiticide For Dogs and Cats

CAUTION:
U.S. Federal law restricts this drug to use by or on the order of a licensed veterinarian.

INDICATIONS:
Revolution kills adult fleas and prevents flea eggs from hatching for one month and is indicated for the prevention and control of flea infestations (*Ctenocephalides felis*), prevention of heartworm disease caused by *Dirofilaria immitis*, and the treatment and control of ear mite (*Otodectes cynotis*) infestations in dogs and cats. Revolution also is indicated for the treatment and control of sarcoptic mange (*Sarcoptes scabiei*) and for the control of tick (*Dermacentor variabilis*) infestations in dogs, and the treatment of intestinal hookworm (*Ancylostoma tubaeforme*) and roundworm (*Toxocara cati*) infections in cats. Revolution is recommended for use in dogs and cats six weeks of age and older.

WARNINGS:
Not for human use. Keep out of the reach of children.
May be irritating to skin and eyes. Wash hands after use and wash off any product in contact with the skin immediately with soap and water. If contact with eyes occurs, then flush eyes copiously with water. In case of ingestion by a human, contact a physician immediately. The material safety data sheet (MSDS) provides more detailed occupational safety information. For a copy of the MSDS or to report adverse reactions attributable to exposure to this product, call 1-800-366-5288.

Flammable—Keep away from heat, sparks, open flames or other sources of ignition.

PRECAUTIONS:
Use with caution in sick, debilitated or underweight animals (see SAFETY).
Prior to administration of Revolution, dogs should be tested for existing heartworm infections. At the discretion of the veterinarian, infected dogs should be treated to remove adult heartworms. Revolution is not effective against adult *D. immitis* and, while the number of circulating microfilariae may decrease following treatment, Revolution is not effective for microfilariae clearance.

Hypersensitivity reactions have not been observed in dogs with patent heartworm infections administered three times the recommended dose of Revolution. Higher doses were not tested.

ADVERSE REACTIONS:
Following treatment with Revolution, transient localized alopecia with or without inflammation at or near the site of application was observed in approximately 1% of 691 treated cats. Other signs observed rarely (≤0.5% of 1743 treated cats and dogs) included vomiting, loose stool or diarrhea with or without blood, anorexia, lethargy, salivation, tachypnea, and muscle tremors.

DOSAGE:
The recommended minimum dose is 2.7 mg selamectin per pound (6 mg/kg) of body weight.

Administer the entire contents of a single dose tube of Revolution topically in accordance with label directions. (See ADMINISTRATION for the recommended treatment intervals.)

For cats over 15 lbs use the appropriate combination of tubes.

For dogs over 85 lbs use the appropriate combination of tubes.
Recommended for use in animals 6 weeks of age and older.

ADMINISTRATION:
Firmly depress the cap to puncture the seal on the Revolution tube; then remove the cap to administer the product.

Part the hair on the back of the animal at the base of the neck in front of the shoulder blades until the skin is visible. Place the tip of the tube on the skin and squeeze the tube to empty its entire contents directly onto the skin in one spot. Do not massage the product into the skin. Due to alcohol content, do not apply to broken skin. Avoid contact between the product and fingers. Do not apply when the hair coat is wet. Bathing or shampooing the animal 2 or more hours after treatment will not reduce the effectiveness of Revolution. Stiff hair, clumping of hair, hair discoloration, or a slight powdery residue may be observed at the treatment site in some animals. These effects are temporary and do not affect the safety or effectiveness of the product. Discard empty tubes in your ordinary household refuse.

Flea Control in Dogs and Cats
For the prevention and control of flea infestations, Revolution should be administered at monthly intervals throughout the flea season, starting one month before fleas become active. In controlled laboratory studies >98% of fleas were killed within 36 hours. Results of clinical field studies using Revolution monthly demonstrated >90% control of flea infestations within 30 days of the first dose. Dogs and cats treated with Revolution, including those with pre-existing flea allergy dermatitis, showed improvement in clinical signs associated with fleas as a direct result of eliminating the fleas from the animals and their environment.

If the dog or cat is already infested with fleas when the first dose of Revolution is administered, adult fleas on the animal are killed and no viable fleas hatch from eggs after the first administration. However, an environmental infestation of fleas may persist for a short time after beginning treatment with Revolution because of the emergence of adult fleas from pupae.

Heartworm Prevention in Dogs and Cats
For the prevention of heartworm disease, Revolution must be administered on a monthly basis. Revolution may be administered year-round or at least within one month after the animal's first exposure to mosquitoes and monthly thereafter until the end of the mosquito season. The final dose must be given within one month after the last exposure to mosquitoes. If a dose is missed and a monthly interval between dosing is exceeded then immediate administration of Revolution and resumption of monthly dosing will minimize the opportunity for the development of adult heartworms. When replacing another heartworm preventive product in a heartworm disease prevention program, the first dose of Revolution must be given within a month of the last dose of the former medication.

At the discretion of the veterinarian, cats ≥6 months of age may be tested to determine the presence of existing heartworm infections before beginning treatment with Revolution. Cats already infected with adult heartworms can safely be given Revolution monthly to prevent further infections.

Ear Mite Treatment in Dogs and Cats
For the treatment of ear mite (*O. cynotis*) infestations in dogs and cats, Revolution should be administered once as a single topical dose. A second monthly dose may be required in some dogs. Monthly use of Revolution will control any subsequent ear mite infestations. In the clinical field trials ears were not cleaned, and many animals still had debris in their ears after the second dose. Cleansing of the infested ears is recommended to remove the debris.

Sarcoptic Mange Treatment in Dogs
For the treatment of sarcoptic mange (*S. scabiei*) in dogs, Revolution should be administered once as a single topical dose. A second monthly dose may be required in some dogs. Because of the difficulty in finding sarcoptic mange mites on skin scrapings, effectiveness assessments also were based on resolution of clinical signs. Resolution of the pruritus associated with the mite infestations was observed in approximately 50% of the dogs 30 days after the first treatment and in approximately 90% of the dogs 30 days after the second monthly treatment.

Tick Control in Dogs
For the control of tick (*Dermacentor variabilis*) infestations in dogs, Revolution should be administered on a monthly basis. In heavy tick infestations, complete efficacy may not be achieved after the first dose. In these cases, one additional dose may be administered two weeks after the previous dose, with monthly dosing continued thereafter.

Nematode Treatment in Cats
For the treatment of intestinal hookworm (*A. tubaeforme*) and roundworm (*T. cati*) infections, Revolution should be applied once as a single topical dose.

NADA 141-152, Approved by FDA.

 Animal Health
Exton, PA 19341, USA
Div. of Pfizer Inc
NY, NY 10017

www.revolutionpet.com

To provide consumers with more complete information, the U.S. Food and Drug Administration regulates the content of pharmaceutical ads. It used to require that advertisers include all the information from the product insert in its ads. This necessitated lengthy commercials with miniscule copy. In 1997, the rule was changed allowing pharmaceutical companies to advertise on TV and radio as long as they mentioned any important side effects and directed consumers to other sources for further information, such as their magazine ads or their websites. Notice how this magazine ad for Revolution (www.revolutionpet.com) complies with the FDA's disclosure requirements.

(all) Source: Zoetis, Inc.

strives to give consumers *complete information* by ensuring that products are labeled truthfully with the information people need to use them properly. The FDA requires manufacturers to disclose all ingredients on product labels, in in-store product advertising, and in product literature. The label must accurately state the weight or volume of the contents. Labels on therapeutic devices must give clear instructions for use. The FDA can require warning statements on packages of hazardous products. It regulates "cents off" and other promotions on package labels and has jurisdiction over the use of words such as *giant* or *family* to describe package sizes.

When consumer-oriented drug ads became common in the mid-1980s, the FDA ruled that any ad for a brand-name drug must include all the information in the package insert.[89] That meant advertisers had to run lengthy commercials or use minuscule type in print ads. In 1997, the FDA changed that rule, allowing pharmaceutical companies to advertise their drugs on broadcast media as long as they mentioned any important possible side effects and directed people to their print ads, their internet sites, or consumers' own doctors for more information.[90] With that ruling, prescription drug advertising soared on television and radio, tripling over the next five years. It's estimated that in 2005, pharmaceutical companies spent some $4 billion in direct-to-consumer advertising.[91] Although the FDA is responsible for ensuring that these ads are fair and accurate, the agency is so understaffed that many questionable and, unfortunately, deceptive or misleading ads do get through. However, any time the FDA has sent a letter to marketers citing false advertising claims, the companies have stopped running the misleading ads.[92]

The **Nutritional Labeling and Education Act (NLEA)** gives the FDA additional muscle by setting stringent legal definitions for terms such as *fresh, light, low fat,* and *reduced calories.* It also sets standard serving sizes and requires labels to show food value for one serving alongside the total recommended daily value as established by the National Research Council.[93]

The first time the FDA took severe action against a prominent marketer over a labeling dispute, it seized 2,400 cases of Procter & Gamble's Citrus Hill Fresh Choice orange juice. Fresh Choice was made from concentrate, not fresh-squeezed juice as P&G claimed.[94] Due to increased FDA scrutiny, many advertisers are now more cautious about their health and nutritional claims.

The Federal Communications Commission (FCC)

The seven-member **Federal Communications Commission (FCC)** is an independent federal agency with jurisdiction over the radio, television, telephone, satellite, internet, and cable TV industries. The FCC is responsible for protecting the public interest and encouraging competition. Its control over broadcast advertising is actually *indirect,* stemming from its authority to license broadcasters (or take away their licenses). The FCC stringently controls the airing of obscenity and profanity, and it can restrict both the products advertised and the content of ads. For example, the FCC required stations to run commercials about the harmful effects of smoking even before Congress banned cigarette advertising on TV and radio.

In the 1980s, the FCC decided there were enough buyers and sellers that marketplace forces could adequately control broadcast media, so it deregulated both radio and TV stations. The FCC no longer limits commercial time or requires stations to maintain detailed program and commercial logs. However, stations still keep records of commercial broadcasts to assure advertisers they ran.

The 1992 Cable Television Consumer Protection and Competition Act gave the FCC additional teeth. It placed new controls on the cable TV industry to encourage a more service-oriented attitude and to improve the balance between rates and escalating ad revenues.[95] The FCC can set subscriber rates for cable TV, so subscription revenues should slow while advertising rates rise.

In addition to protecting consumers' interests, the FCC and other government entities can also attempt to regulate to promote the common good. In 2004, for example, the FCC revised its rules to further limit children's exposure to advertising while watching child-oriented TV. More types of ads are now counted toward the maximum 10.5 minutes of nonprogram time per hour on weekends (12 minutes per hour on weekdays). Spots that pointed kids to interactive websites featuring a show's characters—and selling products and services associated with the characters—were especially on the hot seat. Activist groups applauded and most networks just groaned, but NBC and Disney filed suit in 2005. A federal court of appeals ordered the FCC to open a review of the revised rules.[96]

The Patent and Trademark Office and the Library of Congress

A basic role of government is to promote and protect the economic well-being *(self-interest)* of its citizens. One way the U.S. government does this is by promoting "the Progress of Science and useful Arts, by securing for limited Times to Authors and Inventors the exclusive Right to their respective Writings and Discoveries"—in other words, by registering and protecting their **intellectual property.**[97]

Through the issuance of **patents,** the government provides incentives to invent, invest in, and disclose new technology worldwide. By registering trademarks and copyrights, the government helps businesses protect their investments, promote their goods and services, and safeguard consumers against confusion and deception in the marketplace *(complete information).*

A trademark such as Coca-Cola, AT&T, or Levi's is a valuable asset. According to the Lanham Trade-Mark Act (1946), a **trademark** is "any word, name, symbol, or device or any combination thereof adopted and used by a manufacturer or merchant to identify his goods and distinguish them from those manufactured or sold by others."[98]

Coca-Cola's trademark varies from country to country. But the overall look is retained through use of similar letterforms and style, even with different alphabets.
dominika zarzycka/Shutterstock

Patents and trademarks are registered with and protected by the **U.S. Patent and Trademark Office,** part of the Department of Commerce. Ownership of a trademark may be designated in advertising or on a label, package, or letterhead by the word *Registered,* the symbol ®, or the symbol ™. If someone persists in using a trademark owned by another or confusingly similar to another's mark, the trademark owner can ask for a court order and sue for trademark infringement.

The Library of Congress protects all copyrighted material, including advertising, in the United States. A **copyright** is a form of protection provided to the authors of "original works of authorship," including literary, dramatic, musical, artistic, and certain other "intellectual works."[99] A copyright issued to an advertiser grants the exclusive right to print, publish, or reproduce the protected ad for the life of the copyright owner plus 50 years. An ad can be copyrighted only if it contains original copy or illustrations. An idea cannot be copyrighted; nor can slogans, short phrases, and familiar symbols and designs (although the latter may be trademarkable).

Copyright is indicated by the word *Copyright,* the abbreviation *Copr.,* or the symbol © followed by the year of first publication and the name of the advertiser or copyright owner.

State and Local Regulation

Advertisers are also subject to state or local laws. Since the U.S. federal deregulation trend of the 1980s, state and local governments have taken a far more active role.

Regulation by State Governments

State legislation governing advertising is often based on the truth-in-advertising model statute developed in 1911 by *Printer's Ink,* for many years the major trade publication of the industry. The statute holds that any maker of an ad found to contain "untrue, deceptive, or misleading" material is guilty of a misdemeanor. Today most states enforce laws patterned after this statute.

All states also have "little FTC acts," consumer protection laws that govern unfair and deceptive business practices. States can investigate and prosecute cases, and individual consumers can bring civil suits against businesses. To increase their clout, some states team up on legal actions—for example, to challenge deceptive ad promotions in the airline, rental car, and food-making industries. As one observer pointed out, "Many of the food manufacturers could litigate some of the smaller states into the ground, but they might not be willing to fight it out against 10 states simultaneously."[100]

Different states have different regulations governing what can be advertised. Some states prohibit advertising for certain types of wine and liquor, and most states restrict the use of federal and state flags in advertising.

This can present a major problem to national marketers. And, in some cases, it actually hurts consumers. For example, many companies trying to conduct environmentally responsible marketing programs feel stymied by the different state laws governing packaging materials and recycling.[101] In the tobacco case discussed earlier, numerous state attorneys general acting together proved a formidable foe for the giant tobacco industry. In the end, facing the prospect of an infinite number of lawsuits from individual states and even municipalities, the industry buckled under, agreeing to settle and pay hundreds of billions of dollars.[102]

Regulation by Local Governments

Many cities and counties also have consumer protection agencies to enforce laws regulating local advertising practices. The chief function of these agencies is to protect local consumers against unfair and misleading practices by area merchants.

In one year alone, the Orange County, California, district attorney's office received more than 1,200 complaint letters from consumers about everything from dishonest mechanics and phony sale ads to a taco stand that skimped on the beef in its "macho" burrito.[103] In a case against Los Angeles–based Closet Factory, Inc., the DA collected $40,000 in fines to settle a false advertising suit. The company was charged with running newspaper ads that gave consumers a false sense of urgency regarding "sales" that actually never end. This type of advertising, known as a *continuous sale,* violates the state's Business and Professions Code. It also advertises a false percentage off the regular price. Because the sale is never really over, the sale price becomes the regular price.[104]

Nongovernment Regulation

LO 3-8

Nongovernment organizations also issue advertising guidelines (see Exhibit 3-6). In fact, advertisers face considerable regulation by business-monitoring organizations, related trade associations, the media, consumer groups, and advertising agencies themselves.

Exhibit 3-6
American Association of Advertising Agencies' policy statement and guidelines for comparative advertising.

The Board of Directors of the American Association of Advertising Agencies recognizes that when used truthfully and fairly, comparative advertising provides the consumer with needed and useful information.

However, extreme caution should be exercised. The use of comparative advertising, by its very nature, can distort facts and, by implication, convey to the consumer information that misrepresents the truth.

Therefore, the Board believes that comparative advertising should follow certain guidelines:

1. The intent and connotation of the ad should be to inform and never to discredit or unfairly attack competitors, competing products, or services.
2. When a competitive product is named, it should be one that exists in the marketplace as significant competition.
3. The competition should be fairly and properly identified but never in a manner or tone of voice that degrades the competitive product or service.
4. The advertising should compare related or similar properties or ingredients of the product, dimension to dimension, feature to feature.
5. The identification should be for honest comparison purposes and not simply to upgrade by association.
6. If a competitive test is conducted, it should be done by an objective testing source, preferably an independent one, so that there will be no doubt as to the veracity of the test.
7. In all cases the test should be supportive of all claims made in the advertising that are based on the test.
8. The advertising should never use partial results or stress insignificant differences to cause the consumer to draw an improper conclusion.
9. The property being compared should be significant in terms of value or usefulness of the product to the consumer.
10. Comparatives delivered through the use of testimonials should not imply that the testimonial is more than one individual's thought unless that individual represents a sample of the majority viewpoint.

The Better Business Bureau (BBB)

The largest of the U.S. business-monitoring organizations is the **Better Business Bureau (BBB),** established in 1916. Funded by dues from more than 100,000 member companies, it operates primarily at the local level to protect consumers against fraudulent and deceptive advertising and sales practices. When local bureaus contact violators and ask them to revise their advertising, most comply.

The BBB's files on violators are open to the public. Records of violators that do not comply are sent to appropriate government agencies for further action. The BBB often works with local law enforcement agencies to prosecute advertisers guilty of fraud and misrepresentation. Each year, the BBB investigates thousands of ads for possible violations of truth and accuracy.

The Council of Better Business Bureaus is the parent organization of the Better Business Bureau and a sponsoring member of the National Advertising Review Council. One of its functions is to help new industries develop standards for ethical and responsible advertising. The Code of Advertising of the Council of Better Business Bureaus (the BBB Code) has been called the most important self-regulation of advertising.[105] The BBB Code is only a few pages long, but it is supplemented by a monthly publication called *Do's and Don'ts in Advertising Copy,* which provides information about advertising regulations and recent court and administrative rulings that affect advertising.[106] Since 1983, the National Advertising Division of the Council of Better Business Bureaus has published guidelines for advertising to children, a particularly sensitive area.

The Advertising Self-Regulatory Council (ASRC)

The **Advertising Self-Regulatory Council (ASRC)** was established in 1971 as the National Advertising Review Council by the Council of Better Business Bureaus, the American Association of Advertising Agencies, the American Advertising Federation, and the Association of National Advertisers. Its primary purpose is to promote and enforce standards of truth, accuracy, taste, morality, and social responsibility in advertising.

ASRC is one of the most comprehensive and effective mechanisms for regulating American advertising. A U.S. district court judge noted in a 1985 case that its "speed, informality, and modest cost," as well as its expertise, give the organization special advantages over the court system in resolving advertising disputes.[107]

ASRC Operating Arms

The ASRC has several operating arms, including the **National Advertising Division (NAD)** of the Council of Better Business Bureaus and the **National Advertising Review Board (NARB).** The NAD monitors advertising practices and reviews complaints about advertising from consumers and consumer groups, brand competitors, local Better Business Bureaus, trade associations, and others. The appeals board for NAD decisions is the NARB, which consists of a chairperson and 70 volunteer members (40 national advertisers, 20 agency representatives, and 10 laypeople).[108]

The NAD–NARB Review Process

To encourage consumers to register complaints, the NAD itself runs ads that include a complaint form. Most target untruthfulness or inaccuracy.

When the NAD finds a valid complaint, it contacts the advertiser and requests that any claims be substantiated. If substantiation is inadequate, the NAD requests modification or discontinuance of the claims.

The case of a leather flight jacket shows how well the NAD process works. Neil Cooper LLC manufactures a leather jacket. In its print ads it claims that its A-2 leather flight jackets are the "official battle gear of U.S. Air Force Pilots." Avirex, Ltd., a competing company, complained to the NAD because it manufactures the A-2 jacket currently being purchased by the Department of Defense and worn by U.S. pilots, not Neil Cooper. Neil Cooper explained that, while it was not the current supplier, many pilots preferred its jacket. Notwithstanding, the NAD sided with Avirex and recommended that Neil Cooper make clear that it is selling

To help consumers make informed decisions, scientists at the Good Housekeeping Research Institute evaluate products before they are accepted for publication in Good Housekeeping magazine as well as for the Good Housekeeping Seal. This gives consumers a trustworthy, authoritative voice to listen to when making purchasing decisions.

Source: Hearst Communications, Inc.

a reproduction of an authentic A-2 flight jacket. Neil Cooper agreed.[109]

If the NAD and an advertiser reach an impasse, either party can request a review by an NARB panel (consisting of three advertisers, one agency representative, and one layperson). The panel's decision is binding. If an advertiser refuses to comply with the panel's decision (which has never yet occurred), the NARB will refer the matter to an appropriate government body.

The ASRC also sets policies for the Children's Advertising Review Unit (CARU), the Electronic Retailing Self-Regulation Program (ERSP), and the Online Interest-Based Accountability Program (IBA). CARU "evaluates child-directed advertising and promotional material in all media to advance truthfulness, accuracy and consistency with its Self-Regulatory Program. . . ."[110] The ERSP assists with inquiries or disputes about the accuracy of claims communicated in direct-response ads. The IBA, according to the ASRC, "regulates online behavioral advertising (OBA) across the Internet"[111] by ensuring companies follow seven principles for online marketing. These principles include education, transparency, consumer control, data security, material changes, sensitive data, and accountability.[112]

Regulation by the Media

Almost all media review ads and reject those they regard as objectionable, even if they aren't deceptive. Many people think the media are more effective regulators than the government.

Internet

Key players in the self-regulation of internet advertising include the IAB (Interactive Advertising Bureau) and the AAAA (American Association of Advertising Agencies). The groups in 2009 issued guidelines for digital ads in the form of seven principles: education (advertisers should educate consumers about how online advertising works), transparency (advertisers should clearly disclose data collection and use practices), consumer control (consumers should be able to choose whether and what data are collected and shared), data security (information that is collected should be safe), material changes (advertisers should obtain consent from consumers before changing their privacy policies), sensitive data (some data, such as data about children, prescriptions, medical records, etc.) merit special treatment, and accountability (online advertisers should work together to ensure firms follow the principles). The IAB has indicated that the Direct Marketing Association and the Council of Better Business Bureaus have formulated similar guidelines for digital ads.[113]

Television

Of all media, the TV networks conduct the strictest review. Advertisers must submit commercials intended for a network or affiliated station to its *broadcast standards* department. Many commercials (in script or storyboard form) are returned with suggestions for changes or greater substantiation. Ads are rejected outright if they violate network policies. (See Ad Lab 3–C.)

The major U.S. broadcast networks base their policies on the original National Association of Broadcasters Television Code. But network policies vary enough that it's difficult to prepare universally acceptable commercials. Cable networks and local stations tend to be much less stringent. Most observers would agree that in recent years, with increased competition from cable networks, broadcast networks have relaxed their standards considerably, for both content and commercials.

AD Lab 3–C

Editorial or Advertising: It's Adversarial

Pick up a glossy magazine such as *Vogue, Esquire,* or *Sports Illustrated* and you'll find it loaded with ads for cars, liquor, and cigarettes. Advertising agencies like buying space in these upscale publications as long as nothing in the publication directly offends their clients. Agencies are very protective of their clients, so they're careful about where their ads are placed. If an ad runs alongside a story that might reflect badly on the client's product or, even worse, might offend the client's customers, the ad agency will either pull the ad or request that the article be dropped. Moreover, agencies and their clients want to be warned ahead of time when a controversial story will appear. Increasingly, this is becoming a sore point with magazine editors and is creating an ethical stir in the industry. Editors see it as an assault on their independence and integrity. Advertisers see it as their responsibility to sponsor content suitable for, and not offensive to, their customers.

On the other hand, a survey sponsored by the Newspaper Advertising Association and the American Society of Magazine Editors discovered that newspaper ads actually meet consumer expectations better than the quality of news coverage. Consumers told the survey they believe newspaper ads are useful and relevant, saving them both time and money by allowing them to comparison shop at home. As a result, newspaper editors are now looking at expanding their partnerships with advertisers.

"I think we need to have advertising and editorial work more closely together to produce a paper, especially since advertising has this solid local franchise," said *Washington Post* research chief Sharon P. Warden.

In the world of print media, publishers are the businesspeople who worry about the bottom line, and editors worry about editorial content and journalistic integrity. Often their interests collide. To interest more advertisers, magazine publishers now create whole sections, sometime entire issues, devoted to *advertorials*—pages of commercial copy dressed up as news stories. Often it's difficult to differentiate between actual editorial copy and advertising text. *Sports Illustrated (SI)* publishes an annual special issue called *Golf Plus,* figuring that the 500,000-plus copies will generate higher interest from advertisers such as Foot Joy and Titleist golf balls.

Maxim Publications is one of a few remaining publications that separate the editorial and business sides of publications. Even so, advertisers with *Maxim* exert influence over the content that surrounds their ads by reminding editors of revenue loss if certain material is published. *Ms* magazine solved the conflict by going ad-free in 1990.

Print is not the only medium that falls under editorial scrutiny. Radio and TV are also constantly monitored for content. Some advertisers buying time on radio stations that air syndicated personalities such as Rush Limbaugh specify "NO RUSH." Because of the show's controversial content, they simply refuse to allow their ads

to be placed there. Except for the news, television is taped in advance. Many advertisers can review episodes prior to airing and decide to pull the ads if necessary. (See Chapters 15 through 18 for more information on media buying.)

One Michigan homemaker was angered by sexual innuendoes on Fox's TV sitcom *Married . . . with Children.* So she persuaded Procter & Gamble and other leading advertisers not to buy time on the show. Similarly, many blue-chip advertisers shunned the police drama *NYPD Blue* on ABC because of scenes with partial nudity and blunt language—until it did too well in the ratings for them to ignore. During the coming-out episode of *Ellen* in 1997, many advertisers such as Chrysler pulled their spots. The spots, however, were quickly replaced by other sponsors eager to be part of a show that was expected to reach an unusually large audience.

"With TV, it's a case of supply and demand, and right now the demand for commercial time exceeds the supply," said Kevin Goldman, a former advertising columnist for *The Wall Street Journal.*

However, the case is not the same for magazines. "Magazines are different because there's a finite number of advertisers that want in on a particular book. If Chrysler pulls out of an issue, the pool of advertisers that might take its place is shallow," explained Goldman.

Moreover, magazines (especially new specialty magazines) increasingly tailor their editorial focus to reach niche audiences or a particular demographic. This narrows their options for ad dollars to those marketers targeting the same groups—in effect, giving greater influence to fewer advertisers.

Years ago, the American Society of Magazine Editors (ASME) drew up guidelines on how magazines should distinguish advertising from regular editorial pages. The ASME created a three-paragraph "Standard for Editorial Independence" following a few episodes in which editors left magazines as a result of apparent interference from their corporate employers. The standard states, "Editors need the maximum possible protection from untoward commercial or extra-journalistic pressures. The chief editor of any magazine must have final authority over the editorial content, words and pictures, that appear in the publication."

Laboratory Applications

When is it OK for an advertiser to give its "editorial" view in a publication or on a show? Provide data to support your answers to the following questions:

1. To what degree, if at all, should an advertiser exercise control over placement of its ads or content of the publication?

2. What effect, if any, could advertorials have on national problems such as age discrimination, racism, sexism, and teenage pregnancy? Be specific.

Radio

The U.S. radio networks, unlike TV networks, supply only a small percentage of their affiliates' programming, so they have little or no say in what their affiliates advertise. A radio station is also less likely to return a script or tape for changes. Some stations, such as KLBJ in Austin, Texas, look mainly at whether the advertising is illegal, unethical, or immoral.[114] They don't want spots to offend listeners or detract from the rest of the programming.

Every radio station typically has its own unwritten guidelines. KDWB, a Minneapolis-St. Paul station with a large teenage audience, turned down a psychic who wanted to buy advertising time.[115] KSDO in San Diego, a station with a business and information format, won't air commercials for X-rated movies or topless bars.[116] SiriusXM, or satellite radio, tends to use standards related to its individual channels. Listeners are likely to hear very different spots on the Catholic Channel than they will on Howard Stern's program.

Magazines

National magazines monitor all advertising, especially by new advertisers and for new products. Newer publications eager to sell space may not be so vigilant, but established magazines, such as *Time* and *Newsweek,* are highly scrupulous. Many magazines will not accept advertising for certain types of products. The *New Yorker* won't run discount retail store advertising or ads for feminine hygiene or self-medication products. *Reader's Digest* won't accept tobacco ads.

Some magazines test every product before accepting the advertising. *Good Housekeeping* rejects ads if its tests don't substantiate the advertiser's claims. Products that pass are allowed to feature the Good Housekeeping "Seal of Approval."

Newspapers

Newspapers also monitor and review advertising. Larger newspapers have clearance staffs who read every ad submitted; most smaller newspapers rely on the advertising manager, sales personnel, or proofreaders.

Most papers have their own acceptability guidelines, ranging from one page for small local papers to more than 50 pages for large dailies such as the *Los Angeles Times.* Some codes are quite specific. The *Detroit Free Press* won't accept classified ads containing such words as *affair* or *swinger.* Some newspapers require advertisers that claim "the lowest price in town" to include a promise to meet or beat any price readers find elsewhere within 30 days.

One problem advertisers face is that newspapers' codes are far from uniform. Handgun ads may be prohibited by one newspaper, accepted by another if the guns are antique, and permitted by a third so long as the guns aren't automatic. In addition, newspapers regularly revise their policies.

Regulation by Consumer Groups

Starting in the 1960s, the consumer movement became increasingly active in fighting fraudulent and deceptive advertising. Consumers demanded that products perform as advertised and that more product information be provided for people to compare and make better buying decisions. The consumer movement gave rise to **consumerism,** social action dramatizing the rights of the buying public. It is clear now that the U.S. consumer can influence advertising practices dramatically.

Today, advertisers and agencies pay more attention to product claims, especially those related to energy use and the nutritional value of processed foods. Consumerism fostered the growth of consumer advocacy groups and regulatory agencies and promoted more consumer research by advertisers, agencies, and the media in an effort to learn what consumers want—and how to provide it. Investment in public goodwill pays off in improved consumer relations and sales.

Consumer Information Networks

Organizations such as the Consumer Federation of America (CFA), the National Council of Senior Citizens, the National Consumer League, and the National Stigma Clearinghouse exchange and disseminate information among members. These **consumer information networks** help develop state, regional, and local consumer organizations and work with national, regional, county, and municipal consumer groups.

Consumer interests also are served by private, nonprofit testing organizations such as Consumers Union, Consumers' Research, and Underwriters Laboratories.

Consumer Advocates

Consumer advocate groups investigate advertising complaints received from the public and those that grow out of their own research. If a complaint is warranted, they ask the advertiser to halt the objectionable ad or practice. If the advertiser does not comply, they release publicity or criticism about the offense to the media and submit complaints with substantiating evidence to appropriate government agencies for further action. In some instances, they file a lawsuit to obtain a cease-and-desist order, a fine, or other penalty against the violator.

Today, with so many special-interest advocacy groups, even the most sensitive advertisers feel challenged. To attract attention, advertising must be creative and stand out from competing noise. Yet advertisers fear attention from politically correct activists (the "PC police"). Calvin Klein ads were attacked by the Boycott Anorexic Marketing group. A Nike ad starring Porky Pig was protested by the National Stuttering Project in San Francisco. An animated public service spot from Aetna Insurance drew complaints from a witches' rights group.[117]

When the protests start flying, the ads usually get pulled. Steve Hayden, chair of BBDO Los Angeles, believes it would be possible to get any spot pulled with "about five letters that appear on the right stationery."[118] As Shelly Garcia noted in *Adweek,* "The way things are these days, nothing motivates middle managers like the need to avoid attention." She lamented the fact that "there are fewer and fewer opportunities to have any fun in advertising."[119]

Self-Regulation by Advertisers

Advertisers also regulate themselves. Most large advertisers gather strong data to substantiate their claims. They maintain careful systems of advertising review to ensure that ads meet both their own standards and industry, media, and legal requirements. Many advertisers try to promote their social responsibility by tying in with a local charity or educational organization.

Many industries maintain advertising codes that companies agree to follow. These codes also establish a basis for complaints. However, industry advertising codes are only as effective as the enforcement powers of the individual trade associations. And because enforcement may conflict with antitrust laws, trade associations usually use peer pressure rather than hearings or penalties.

Self-Regulation by Ad Agencies and Associations

Most ad agencies monitor their own practices. Professional advertising associations also oversee members' activities to prevent problems that might trigger government intervention. Advertising publications report issues and court actions to educate agencies and advertisers and warn them about possible legal infractions.

Advertising Agencies

Although advertisers supply information about their products or services to their agencies, the agencies must research and verify product claims and comparative product data before using them in advertising. The media may require such documentation before accepting the advertising, and substantiation may be needed if government or consumer agencies challenge the claims.

Agencies can be held legally liable for fraudulent or misleading advertising claims. For this reason, most major advertising agencies have in-house legal counsel and regularly submit their ads for review. If any aspect of the advertising is challenged, the agency asks its client to review the advertising and either confirm claims as truthful or replace unverified material.

People BEHIND the Ads

Edward Boyd: Advertising Legend

Courtesy of The Family of Edward Boyd

now it's Pepsi-for those who think young
You see the change—today people are putting more into their leisure, finding more ways to enjoy life. This is thinking young. And this is the life for Pepsi —light, bracing, clean-tasting Pepsi. Think young. Say "Pepsi, please!"

Source: Pepsi Cola Company

You probably think that there is too much advertising directed at people like you. That can be annoying. But imagine a world in which ads never seem to be directed to you. For African American consumers, that description was not far from the mark until well into the 20th century.

Today, of course, companies spend hundreds of millions of dollars on marketing activities that target blacks, Hispanics, and other ethnic groups. But it was not always so. For most of our country's history, long after the elimination of slavery, blacks encountered many barriers, legal and cultural, to full participation in American life. The most obvious of these barriers were the Jim Crow laws of the South that mandated public separation of the races. But even outside the South, blacks were often denied opportunities taken for granted by whites. From corporate boardrooms to professional sports, only white males were allowed to compete.

The year 1947 proved a watershed for change in both sports and boardrooms. Most famously, it was the year that Jackie Robinson broke the color barrier to become the first black regular in big league baseball. Less well known, but in many ways just as importantly, it was the year that Ed Boyd was hired to improve

Pepsi's marketing efforts with black Americans. Donald M. Kendall, former chair and CEO at Pepsi, noted, "Jackie Robinson may have made more headlines, but what Ed did— integrating the managerial ranks of corporate America—was equally groundbreaking."

Boyd was a 33-year-old executive at the National Urban League in New York City when he and a small group of black salesmen were hired by Pepsi CEO Walter S. Mack. Mack wanted to increase sales to the country's 14 million African Americans. Boyd and his team were given the charge of figuring out how to do it. Mack had actually had the idea as early at 1940, when he hired the first black executive at Pepsi, Herman T. Smith, and two young black interns. However, World War II put Mack's plans on hold.

By 1947 he was ready to try again, and Boyd's group was given relatively free reign to design the campaign. Their challenge was not easy. Very few ads at that time targeted blacks, and those that did were often demeaning. Boyd noted, "We'd been caricatured and stereotyped," and he set out to change that.

The team decided to create advertising that represented blacks as "normal Americans." For example, one series of ads offered consumers profiles of 20 great black achievers, including Ralph Bunche, the 1950 winner of the Nobel Peace Prize. Another ad featured students at black colleges. Still other ads showed black middle-class families in grocery stores buying Pepsi. The common theme: Blacks shared the American Dream too, and their business was important.

Of course, the reality of America in the late 1940s was nowhere near as perfect as the view depicted in Pepsi's ads. As Boyd and his black sales team traveled around the United States, they regularly encountered discrimination. The group rode on segregated trains and stayed in black-only hotels. They even faced insults and discrimination from co-workers at Pepsi. At one point the men received threats from the Ku Klux Klan.

Advertising Associations

Several associations monitor industrywide advertising practices. The **American Association of Advertising Agencies (AAAA)**, an association of the largest advertising agencies throughout the United States, controls agency practices by denying membership to any agency judged unethical. The AAAA *Standards of Practice and Creative Code* set advertising principles for member agencies.

The **American Advertising Federation (AAF)** helped establish the FTC, and its early vigilance committees were the forerunners of the Better Business Bureau. The AAF

Source: Pepsi Cola Company

But they persevered. In just a few short years, Boyd and his team produced results that exceeded Mack's expectations for increasing sales of Pepsi to blacks. But helping the brand increase its market share is really just part of the story. Stephanie Capparell, a *Wall Street Journal* reporter who wrote a book about Boyd's history-making team, recounts:

> On their way to nudging their country to a better place, the sales team helped define niche marketing some thirty years before it became a widespread business strategy. They gave formal talks to white drivers and salesmen about their role in the company, thereby instigating some of the earliest formalized diversity training. They also helped to instill in African Americans a unique sense of brand loyalty—to products produced by companies with a commitment to social progress as much as to product quality.

When Walter Mack retired from Pepsi in 1950, support for Boyd and his group gradually eroded. He finally left the company in 1951. In the decades that followed, Boyd lived a full, rich, and active life, working in ad agencies, for CARE, as a consultant, and even as a farmer. But memory of his history-making achievements at Pepsi faded until the publication of Capparell's book in 2006.

On April 30, 2007, Boyd passed away, depriving the world of one of its great civil rights pioneers. Through his tireless and frequently underappreciated efforts to bring black consumers into the mainstream of American life, Boyd made history. He was practicing ethnic target marketing years before the business world would embrace such a strategy. He fundamentally altered the image that white Americans had of their black fellow citizens. And he taught corporations an important lesson on the value of embracing diversity, both within the corporate ranks and in choosing customers to serve. Ed Boyd lived a life dedicated to fighting for justice and equality. It is a measure of how much our nation has changed from Boyd's time at Pepsi that just days after his passing, Barack Obama formally announced his own history-making candidacy for president.

Source: Stephanie Capparell, *The Real Pepsi Challenge: The Inspirational Story of Breaking the Color Barrier in American Business* (Simon and Schuster, Inc., 2008), p. xi.

Advertising Principles of American Business, adopted in 1984, define standards for truthful and responsible advertising. Since then, the trade association has established the Principles and Practices for Advertising Ethics (see Exhibit 3-7). Because most local advertising clubs belong to the AAF, it is instrumental in influencing agencies and advertisers to abide by these principles.

The **Association of National Advertisers (ANA)** is comprised of 370 major manufacturing and service companies that are clients of member agencies of the AAAA. These companies, pledged to uphold the ANA code of advertising ethics, work with the ANA through a joint Committee for Improvement of Advertising Content.

Exhibit 3-7
Principles and Practices for Advertising Ethics by the American Advertising Federation (AAF).

1. Advertising, public relations, marketing communications, news, and editorial all share a common objective of truth and high ethical standards in serving the public.
2. Advertising, public relations, and all marketing communications professionals have an obligation to exercise the highest personal ethics in the creation and dissemination of commercial information to consumers.
3. Advertisers should clearly distinguish advertising, public relations, and corporate communications from news and editorial content and entertainment, both online and offline.
4. Advertisers should clearly disclose all material conditions, such as payment or receipt of a free product, affecting endorsements in social and traditional channels, as well as the identity of endorsers, all in the interest of full disclosure and transparency.
5. Advertisers should treat consumers fairly based on the nature of the audience to whom the ads are directed and the nature of the product or service advertised.
6. Advertisers should never compromise consumer's personal privacy in marketing communications, and their choices as to whether to participate in providing their information should be transparent and easily made.
7. Advertisers should follow federal, state, and local advertising laws, and cooperate with industry self-regulatory programs for the resolution of advertising practices.
8. Advertisers and their agencies, and online and offline media, should discuss privately potential ethical concerns, and members of the team creating ads should be given permission to express internally their ethical concerns.

Source: Institute for Advertising Ethics, "Principles and Practices for Advertising Ethics," Reprinted with permission of the American Advertising Federation.

The Ethical and Legal Aspects of Advertising in Perspective

Unquestionably, advertising offers considerable benefits to marketers and consumers alike. However, there's also no disputing that advertising has been and still is too often misused. As former *Adweek* editor Andrew Jaffe said, the industry should do all it can to "raise its standards and try to drive out that which is misleading, untruthful, or downright tasteless and irresponsible." Otherwise, he warned, the pressure to regulate even more will become overwhelming.[120]

Advertising apologists point out that of all the advertising reviewed by the Federal Trade Commission in a typical year, 97 percent is found to be satisfactory.[121] In the end, advertisers and consumers need to work together to ensure that advertising is used intelligently, ethically, and responsibly for the benefit of all.

Chapter Summary

As one of the most visible activities of business, advertising is both lauded and criticized for the role it plays in selling products and influencing society. Some controversy surrounds advertising's role in the economy. To debate advertising's economic effects, we employ the four basic assumptions of free enterprise economics: self-interest, many buyers and sellers, complete information, and absence of externalities.

The economic impact of advertising can be likened to the opening shot in billiards—a chain reaction that affects the company as well as its competitors, customers, and the business community. On a broader scale, advertising is often considered the trigger on a country's mass distribution system, enabling manufacturers to produce the products people want in high volume, at low prices, with standardized quality. People may argue, though, about how advertising adds value to products, affects prices, encourages or discourages competition, promotes consumer demand, narrows or widens consumer choice, and affects business cycles.

Although controversy surrounds some of these economic issues, few dispute the abundance principle: In an economy that produces more goods and services than can be consumed, advertising gives consumers more complete information about the choices available to them, encourages more sellers to compete effectively, and thereby serves the self-interest of both consumers and marketers.

Social criticisms of advertising may be short-term manipulative arguments or long-term macro arguments. While the economic aspect of advertising focuses on the free enterprise principles of self-interest and many buyers and sellers, the social aspect typically involves the concepts of complete information and externalities.

Critics say advertising is deceptive; it manipulates people into buying unneeded products, it makes our society too materialistic, and there's just too much of it. Further, they say, advertising perpetuates stereotypes, and all too frequently, it is offensive and in bad taste.

Proponents admit that advertising is sometimes misused. However, they point out that despite its problems, advertising offers many social benefits. It encourages the development of new products and speeds their acceptance. It fosters employment, gives consumers and businesses a wider variety of product choices, and helps keep prices down by encouraging mass production. It stimulates healthy competition among companies and raises the overall standard of living. Moreover, sophisticated marketers know the best way to sell their products is to appeal to genuine consumer needs and be honest in their advertising claims.

In short, while advertising can be criticized for giving less than complete information and for creating some unwanted externalities, it also contributes to the free enterprise system by encouraging many buyers and sellers to participate in the process, thereby serving the self-interest of all.

Under growing pressure from consumers, special-interest groups, and government regulation, advertisers have developed higher standards of ethical conduct and social responsibility. Advertisers confront three levels of ethical consideration: the primary rules of ethical behavior in society, their personal value systems, and their personal philosophies of singular ethical concepts.

The federal and state courts are involved in several advertising issues, including First Amendment protection of commercial speech and infringements on the right to privacy. Advertising is regulated by federal, state, and local government agencies, business-monitoring organizations, the media, consumer groups, and the advertising industry itself. All of these groups encourage advertisers to give more complete information to consumers and eliminate any externalities in the process.

Advertisers face a myriad of regulations at several levels: international, national, statewide, and local. At the national level in the U.S., the Federal Trade Commission, the major federal regulator of advertising in the United States, is responsible for protecting consumers and competitors from deceptive and unfair business practices. If the FTC finds an ad deceptive or unfair, it may issue a cease-and-desist order or require corrective advertising.

The Food and Drug Administration (FDA) monitors advertising for food and drugs and regulates product labels and packaging. The Federal Communications Commission (FCC) has jurisdiction over the radio and TV industries, although deregulation has severely limited its control over advertising in these media. The Patent and Trademark Office governs ownership of U.S. trademarks, trade names, house marks, and similar distinctive features of companies and brands. The Library of Congress registers and protects copyrighted materials.

Nongovernment regulators include the Council of Better Business Bureaus and its National Advertising Division. The NAD, the most effective U.S. nongovernmental regulatory body, investigates complaints from consumers, brand competitors, or local Better Business Bureaus and suggests corrective measures. Advertisers that refuse to comply are referred to the National Advertising Review Board (NARB), which may uphold, modify, or reverse the NAD's findings.

Other sources of regulation include the codes and policies of the print media and broadcast media. Consumer organizations and advocates also control advertising by investigating and filing complaints against advertisers and by providing information to consumers. Finally, advertisers and agencies regulate themselves.

Important Terms

Advertising Self-Regulatory Council (ASRC), *97*

affirmative disclosure, *92*

American Advertising Federation (AAF), *102*

American Association of Advertising Agencies (AAAA), *102*

Association of National Advertisers (ANA), *103*

Better Business Bureau (BBB), *97*

cease-and-desist order, *92*

Children's Advertising Review Unit (CARU), *87*

comparative advertising, *91*

consent decree, *92*

consumer advocates, *101*

consumer information networks, *101*

consumerism, *100*

cookies, *87*

copyright, *95*

corrective advertising, *92*

deceptive advertising, *90*

endorsements, *92*

ethical, *78*

Federal Communications Commission (FCC), *94*

Federal Trade Commission (FTC), *90*

Food and Drug Administration (FDA), *92*

intellectual property, *94*

long-term macro citicisms, *72*

National Advertising Division (NAD), *97*

National Advertising Review Board (NARB), *97*

nonproduct facts, *73*

Nutritional Labeling and Education Act (NLEA), *94*

patent, *94*

primary demand, *70*

privacy rights, *87*

puffery, *73*

selective demand, *70*

short-term manipulative citicisms, *72*

social responsibility, *78*

substantiation, *92*

testimonials, *92*

trademark, *94*

unfair advertising, *90*

U.S. Patent and Trademark Office, *95*

Review Questions

1. What role does advertising play in our economic system?
2. What are the two types of social criticisms of advertising and what are specific examples that can illustrate them?
3. What is puffery? Give some examples. When does puffery cross the line to deception?
4. Does advertising affect people's values? In what ways? Does it affect everyone equally or some more than others?
5. What is the difference between an advertiser's ethics and its social responsibility? What are ways in which advertisers can act that are both ethical and responsible, while still ensuring they provide the best products at competitive prices?
6. How does government regulation of advertising in the United States differ from regulation in many foreign countries?
7. How does commercial speech differ from political speech? Do you think advertisers should have the same First Amendment rights as everyone else? Explain your response.
8. What is the role of the FTC in advertising? Do you think this role should be expanded or restricted?
9. How has the pervasiveness of the Internet and digital advertising and retailing affected advertisers? What risks do consumers take buying things on the web?
10. How well do advertisers regulate themselves? In what areas do you think advertisers have done well, and where should they clean up their act?

The Advertising Experience

1. **Ad Action: "I Know It When I See It"**

   Where is the socially accepted line between "erotic suggestiveness" and "explicit sexuality" in advertising? Describe three hypothetical ads: one that is safely suggestive, one that is as suggestive as it is acceptable (say, for a prime-time network TV spot or national newsmagazine), and one that is just over the line of explicitness. Compare your responses with those of others in your study group. How and why do you think your answers differ? What roles might your ages or social backgrounds play in these differences?

2. **Regulation of Advertising**

   The FTC's Division of Advertising Practices protects consumers from deceptive and unsubstantiated advertising. Review what you have learned by exploring the policies and guides available on the division's website (www.ftc.gov/about-ftc/bureaus-offices/bureau-consumer-protection/our-divisions/division-advertising-practices). Then answer the following:

   a. Give a general description of what the FTC considers to be deceptive and unfair advertising.

   b. Describe the requirements for substantiating advertising and the process advertisers and their agencies must undergo to do so.

   c. Choose another topic covered on the site and discuss its relevance and importance to the advertising industry.

   Be sure to check out the following sites related to the regulation of the advertising industry:

   - Council of Better Business Bureau's National Advertising Division (NAD): https://bbbprograms.org/programs/nad/
   - Consumers International: www.consumersinternational.org

3. **Responding to Critical Commentary**

   Go to the following website that hosts critical commentary by Duke University professor William O'Barr on advertising and marketing. Using what you have learned in Chapters 1, 2, and 3, analyze several of the examples of unethical ads. What are the criticisms such ads have provoked? Does the criticism involve long-term macro arguments or short-term manipulative arguments?

   - Advertising and Society Review: Ethics and Advertising: http://muse.jhu.edu/article/221968

4. Review Nike's campaign with Colin Kaepernick and try to lay out the arguments for and against the company's partnership with the former player. What do you think are the ethical issues surrounding the campaign? What are the social responsibility issues? Finally, what are the business issues? If the campaign results in a surge of shoe sales, does that mean it was the right thing to do? If it results in a sales decline, does that mean it was the wrong thing to do?

5. Some believe that Lance Armstrong has been "rehabilitated," in the sense that he's paid for his transgressions. What are the varying perspectives that you can identify about whether he should receive lucrative sponsorship dollars, given his behaviors? Can you identify potential sponsors that would make different decisions about paying Armstrong for his endorsement?

6. Benetton and Abercrombie & Fitch get free publicity when their advertising campaigns draw protests. At what point does controversy become a negative externality rather than a positive boost? What might be some signs that a campaign has gone too far?

End Notes

1. Jagdish Agrawal and Wagner A. Kamakura, "The Economic Worth of Celebrity Endorsers," *Journal of Marketing* 59 (2005), pp. 56–63.
2. Jeremy Mullen, "Reducing the Risk of Vick-timization," *Advertising Age,* July 23, 2007, *https://adage.com/article/news/reducing-risk-vick-timization/119451.*
3. John O'Toole, *The Trouble with Advertising* (New York: Times Books, 1985), pp. 7–14.
4. N. Gregory Mankiw, *Principles of Economics* (Boston: Cengage, 2014), p. 10.
5. Eric Chemi, "Advertising's Century of Flat-Line Growth," *Bloomberg Business*, March 3, 2014, *www.bloomberg.com/bw/articles/2014-03-03/advertisings-century-of-flat-line-growth.*
6. "Average Ad Spending per Capita," *Marketing Charts,* June 12, 2015, *www.marketingcharts.com/traditional/average-ad-spending-per-capita-us-tops-list-51916/attachment/strategyanalytics-average-ad-spend-per-capita-in-2014-mar2015/.*
7. Ernest Dichter, *Handbook of Consumer Motivations* (New York: McGraw-Hill, 1964), pp. 6, 422–31.
8. Richard E. Kihlstrom and Michael H. Riordan, "Advertising as a Signal," *Journal of Political Economy*, June 1984, pp. 427–50.
9. Steve McKee, "What Should You Spend on Advertising?," *Bloomberg Businessweek,* February 10, 2009, *www.businessweek.com/smallbiz/content/feb2009/sb20090210_165498.htm.*
10. Philipp Lepenies, *The Power of a Single Number: A Political History of GDP* (New York: Columbia University Press, 2016).
11. John Kenneth Galbraith, "Economics and Advertising: Exercise in Denial," *Advertising Age,* November 9, 1988, pp. 80–84.
12. Fabiana Giacomotti, "European Marketers Keep Up Ad Budgets," *Adweek,* January 24, 1994, pp. 16–17.
13. "Smartphone Sales Value Worldwide from 2013 to 2017," *Statista, www.statista.com/statistics/412145/global-smartphone-sales-value-global-region/.*
14. Michael Schudson, *Advertising, The Uneasy Persuasion: Its Dubious Impact on American Society* (New York: Basic Books, 1984).
15. "Truth in Advertising," Federal Trade Commission, *www.ftc.gov/news-events/media-resources/truth-advertising.*
16. Ivan Preston, "A New Conception of Deceptiveness," paper presented to the Advertising Division of the Association for Education in Journalism and Mass Communication, August 12, 1993.
17. Ivan Preston, "A New Conception of Deceptiveness," paper presented to the Advertising Division of the Association for Education in Journalism and Mass Communication, August 12, 1993.
18. "Pizza Hut Files Suit Against Pizza Rival," *Advertising Age,* August 13, 1998; "Papa John's Ordered to Move 'Better' Slogan," *Advertising Age,* January 5, 2000, *http://adage.com.*

19. Barry Newman, "An Ad Professor Huffs Against Puffs, but It's a Quixotic Enterprise," *The Wall Street Journal,* January 24, 2003, pp. A1, A9.

20. Ivan Preston, *The Tangled Web They Weave* (Madison: University of Wisconsin Press, 1994), pp. 185–98.

21. Andrew Jaffe, "Advertiser, Regulate Thyself," *Adweek,* August 2, 1993, p. 38.

22. Andrew Jaffe, "Advertiser, Regulate Thyself," *Adweek,* August 2, 1993, p. 38.

23. Ivan Preston, *The Tangled Web They Weave* (Madison: University of Wisconsin Press, 1994), p. 164.

24. Kevin Downey, "TV Ad Clutter Worsens, and Buyers Grouse," *Media Life,* February 15, 2002, *www.medialifemagazine.com.*

25. Brian Steinberg, "Spike's Supersized Ad Breaks Buck TV's Clutter-Busting Trend," *Ad Age Media News,* September 13, 2010.

26. Sean Leahy, "Encouraging Words for Less Is More," *Media Life,* July 20, 2005, *www.medialifemagazine.com/News2005/ jul05/jul18/3_wed/news2wednesday.html.*

27. "Children's Educational Television: Commercial Time Limitations," *FCC Guide,* November 6, 2017, *www.fcc.gov/guides/ childrens-educational-television.*

28. Europa, "TV without Frontiers: Commission Proposes Modernised Rules for Digital Era TV and TV-Like Services," press release, December 13, 2005, *http://europa.eu.int/rapid/ pressReleasesAction.do?reference=IP/05/1573.*

29. Cliff Peale and Gregory Korte, "Drowning in TV Political Ads?" *Cincinnati Enquirer,* October 30, 2004, *www.enquirer.com/ editions/2004/10/30/loc_elexads.html.*

30. Steve McClellan, "Political Ad Spend to Soar," *Adweek,* August 23, 2010.

31. Christopher Ingraham, "Somebody just put a price tag on the 2016 election. It's a doozy," *Washington Post,* April 14, 2017, *www.washingtonpost.com/news/wonk/wp/2017/04/14/ somebody-just-put-a-price-tag-on-the-2016-election-its-a-doozy/?utm_term=.727fb333aae1*

32. Shelly Garcia, "What's Wrong with Being Politically Correct?" *Adweek,* November 15, 1993, p. 62.

33. Adrienne Ward, "What Role Do Ads Play in Racial Tension?" *Advertising Age,* August 10, 1992, pp. 1, 35.

34. Joy Dietrich, "Women Reach High," *Advertising Age International,* January 1, 2000, quoted in Genaro C. Armas, "Women Gaining in Workplace," *Advocate,* Baton Rouge, LA, April 24, 2000 (retrieved from Lexis-Nexis Academic Universe); Associated Press, "Glass Ceiling Cracking as Women Make Gains; Women Taking More Executive Posts, but Income Gap Still Wide," Deseret News, April 24, 2000.

35. U.S. Census Bureau, *Statistical Abstract of the United States,* 2007, *www.census.gov.*

36. John B. Ford and Michael S. La Tour, "Differing Reactions to Female Role Portrayals in Advertising," *Journal of Advertising Research,* September/October 1993, pp. 43–52.

37. Gavin O'Malley, "Marketers Advised to Target Ethnic Preferences," *Online Media Daily,* November 29, 2011.

38. "Revealing Abercrombie Catalog Sparks a Boycott," *Cincinnati Enquirer,* June 26, 2001, *www.enquirer.com/editions/2001/06/26/ tem_revealing.htm.*

39. "Intimacy Ads Gain Prime-Time Permission," *Drug Store News,* September 26, 2005, p. 70.

40. Laurel Wentz, "Cheaply Made Gore Scores," *Advertising Age,* July 4, 1994, *https://adage.com/article/news/cheaply-made-gore-scores/91121.*

41. Laurel Wentz, "Cheaply Made Gore Scores," *Advertising Age,* July 4, 1994, *https://adage.com/article/news/cheaply-made-gore-scores/91121.*

42. William M. O'Barr, "Sex and Advertising," *Advertising & Society Review* 12, no. 2 (2011), *http://muse.jhu.edu/journals/advertising_ and_society_review/v012/12.2.o-barr.html.*

43. John E. Calfee, *Fear of Persuasion: A New Perspective on Advertising and Regulation,* p. 96 (Agora Association, 1997).

44. Robert W. McChesney, *The Political Economy of Media: Enduring Issues, Emerging Dilemmas* (New York: Monthly Review Press, 2008).

45. Ivan Preston, *The Tangled Web They Weave* (Madison: University of Wisconsin Press, 1994), pp. 94, 127–31.

46. Steve Wyche, "Colin Kaepernick Explains Why He Sat during National Anthem," NFL Productions LLC, August 28, 2016, *www.nfl.com/news/story/0ap3000000691077/article/colin-kaepernick-explains-why-he-sat-during-national-anthem.*

47. James Maxeiner and Peter Schotthoffer, eds., *Advertising Law in Europe and North America* (Deventer, The Netherlands: Kluwer Law and Taxation Publishers, 1992), p. v; Rein Rijkens, *European Advertising Strategies* (London: Cassell, 1992), pp. 201–202.

48. Bob Sullivan, "'La Difference' Is Stark in EU, U.S. Privacy Laws," *NBCNews.com,* October 19, 2006, *www.nbcnews.com/ id/15221111/ns/technology_and_science-privacy_lost/t/ladifference-stark-eu-us-privacy-laws/#.VYFJfs9VhBc.*

49. Jo Best, "Google Has to Apply 'Right to Be Forgotten' Everywhere, Says France," *ZDNet,* June 15, 2015, *www.zdnet .com/article-google-has-to-apply-right-to-be-forgotteneverywhere-says-france/.*

50. Karly Preslmayer, "Austria," *in Advertising Law in Europe and North America,* ed. James Maxeiner and Peter Schotthoffer (Deventer, The Netherlands: Kluwer Law and Taxation Publishers, 1992).

51. Peter Schotthoffer, "European Community," in *Advertising Law in Europe and North America,* ed. James Maxeiner and Peter Schotthoffer (Deventer, The Netherlands: Kluwer Law and Taxation Publishers, 1992), p. 89.

52. "Last Minute News: Singapore Condemns Ads with Harmful Values," *Advertising Age,* August 29, 1994, p. 42.

53. Steven Elsinga, "New Advertising Law Expected in China," *China Briefing,* March 4, 2015, *www.china-briefing.com/ news/2015/03/04/new-advertising-lawexpected.html.*

54. Ad Age Staff, "The Golden Rules of Operating in China," *Advertising Age,* April 23, 2012, *http://adage.com/china/article/ china-news/the-golden-rules-of-operating-in-china/234257/.*

55. *Valentine, Police Commissioner of the City of New York v. Chrestensen,* 316 U.S. 52 (1942).

56. James R. Maxeiner, "United States," in *Advertising Law in Europe and North America,* ed. James Maxeiner and Peter Schotthoffer (Deventer, The Netherlands: Kluwer Law and Taxation Publishers, 1992), p. 321; see also *Virginia State Board of Pharmacy v. Virginia Citizens Consumer Council,* 425 U.S. 748 (1976).

57. *See Central Hudson Gas & Electric Corp. v. Public Service Commission of New York,* 447 U.S. 557 (1980).

58. 564 U.S. 552 (2011).

59. Steven W. Colford, "Big Win for Commercial Speech," *Advertising Age,* March 29, 1993, pp. 1, 47.

60. "Tobacco Settlement Agreement at a Glance," *National Association of Attorneys General, www.naag.org.*

61. Joy Johnson Wilson, "Summary of the Attorneys General Master Tobacco Settlement Agreement," March 1999, *http:// academic.udayton.edu/health/syllabi/tobacco/summary.htm.*

62. John Malmo, "Restricting Commercial Speech Isn't Justifiable," *The Commercial Appeal* (Memphis, TN), July 5, 1999, p. B3; John Malmo, "Banning Tobacco Ads Spells Monopoly," *The Commercial Appeal* (Memphis, TN), August 9, 1999, p. B4 (retrieved from ProQuest).

63. U.S. Food and Drug Administration, "Electronic Cigarettes (e-Cigarettes), *www.fda.gov/NewsEvents/PublicHealthFocus/ucm172906.htm*.

64. Monte Morin, "Jury Is Out on Health Effects of E-Cigarettes," *Los Angeles Times,* January 16, 2014, *http://articles.latimes.com/2014/jan/16/science/la-sci-e-cigarettes-science-20140117*; Jonathan H. Adler, "Why FDA Regulations Limiting E-Cigarette Marketing May Cost Lives and Violate the Constitution," *The Washington Post,* December 12, 2017, *www.washingtonpost.com/news/volokh-conspiracy/wp/2017/12/12/why-fda-regulations-limiting-e-cigarette-marketing-may-cost-lives-and-violate-the-constitution/?utm_term=.5de5ca6c39cd*

65. Children's Advertising Review Unit, Council of Better Business Bureaus, Inc., "Self-Regulatory Program for Children's Advertising," 2008, *www.caru.org/guidelines*.

66. Sue Dibb, Kelly Haggart, Lucy Harris, and Alina Tugend, *A Spoonful of Sugar: Television Food Advertising Aimed at Children: An International Comparative Survey* (London: Consumers International, Programme for Developed Economies, 1996).

67. Richard Qiu, "Beyond the Cookie: Digital Advertising and Privacy in the Cross-Screen Age," *The Guardian,* September 25, 2013, *www.theguardian.com/media-network/media-network-blog/2013/sep/25/cookiedigital-advertising-privacy-screens*.

68. Simon Hill, "Google Photos: Should You Be Worried About Privacy?" *Android Authority,* June 16, 2015, *www.androidauthority.com/google-photosworried-privacy-616339/*.

69. Mark Sakalosky, "DoubleClick's Double Edge," *ClickZ,* September 3, 2002.

70. Mary Madden, "Privacy and Cybersecurity: Key Findings from Pew Research," *Pew Research Center,* January 16, 2015, *www.pewresearch.org/key-datapoints/privacy/*; Mary Madden and Rainie Lee, "Americans' Attitudes About Privacy, Security and Surveillance," *Pew Research Center,* May 20, 2015, *www.pewinternet.org/2015/05/20/americans-attitudes-about-privacy-security-and-surveillance/*.

71. *www.ftc.gov/news-events/press-releases/2000/07/federal-trade-commission-issues-report-online-profiling*.

72. Ieuan Jolly, "Data Protection in the United States: Overview," *Thomson Reuters Practical Law,* October 1, 2018, *https://content.next.westlaw.com/Document/I02064fbd1cb611e38578f7ccc38dcbee/View/FullText.html?contextData=(sc.Default)&transitionType=Default&firstPage=true&bhcp=1*.

73. Herb Weisbaum, "Data Breaches Happening at Record Pace, Report Finds," *NBC News,* July 24, 2017, *www.nbcnews.com/business/consumer/data-breaches-happening-record-pace-report-finds-n785881*.

74. Eric Gross and Susan Vogt, "Canada," in *Advertising Law in Europe and North America,* ed. James Maxeiner and Peter Schotthoffer (Deventer, The Netherlands: Kluwer Law and Taxation Publishers, 1992), pp. 39, 41.

75. Federal Trade Commission, "Vision, Mission, and Goals," 1997.

76. Minette E. Drumwright, "Ethical Issues in Advertising and Sales Promotion," in *Ethics in Marketing,* ed. N. Craig Smith and John A. Quelch (Burr Ridge, IL: Irwin, 1993), p. 610.

77. Ann Carrns, "FTC Settles with Office Depot, Buy.com, Value America over 'Low Cost' PC Ads," *The Wall Street Journal,* June 30, 2000, p. B4.

78. Dean Keith Fueroghne, *But the People in Legal Said . . .* (Burr Ridge, IL: Professional, 1989), p. 14.

79. Christy Fisher, "How Congress Broke Unfair Ad Impasse," *Advertising Age,* August 22, 1994, p. 34.

80. "Editorial: A Fair FTC Pact?" *Advertising Age,* March 21, 1994, p. 22.

81. Federal Trade Commission, "Arizona Trade Association Agrees to Settle FTC Charges It Urged Members to Restrain Competitive Advertising," news release, February 25, 1994, *www.ftc.gov/opa/predawn/F95/azautodealers.htm*.

82. W. Thomas Hofstetter and Frederick T. Davis, "Comparative advertising in courts: Outline of briefs," *Antitrust Law Journal,* 49, no. 2 (1980).

83. "Crackdown on Testimonials," *The Wall Street Journal,* July 13, 1993, p. B7.

84. Minette E. Drumwright, "Ethical Issues in Advertising and Sales Promotion," in *Ethics in Marketing,* ed. N. Craig Smith and John A. Quelch (Burr Ridge, IL: Irwin, 1993), pp. 615–16.

85. Ira Teinowitz, "Doan's Decision Sets Precedent for Corrective Ads," *Advertising Age,* September 4, 2000, p. 57; Federal Trade Commission, "Doan's Pills Must Run Corrective Advertising: FTC Ads Claiming Doan's Is Superior in Treating Back Pain Were Unsubstantiated," press release, May 27, 1999.

86. Eric Gross and Susan Vogt, "Canada," in *Advertising Law in Europe and North America,* ed. James Maxeiner and Peter Schotthoffer (Deventer, The Netherlands: Kluwer Law and Taxation Publishers, 1992), pp. 50, 67.

87. U.S. Census Bureau, *www.census.gov*; U.S. Food and Drug Administration, *www.fda.gov*.

88. U.S. Food and Drug Administration, *www.fda.gov*.

89. "The Growing Brouhaha over Drug Advertisements," *The New York Times,* May 14, 1989, p. F8.

90. U.S. Food and Drug Administration, "FDA to Review Standards for All Direct-to-Consumer Rx Drug Promotion," news release, August 8, 1997.

91. Jean Grow, "'Your Life Is Waiting!': Symbolic Meanings in Direct-to-Consumer Antidepressant Advertising," *Journal of Communication Inquiry,* April 2006, pp. 163–88.

92. "FDA Seeks Rx for Drug Ads; New Policy Delays Process," *Newsday* (Nassau and Suffolk edition), December 5, 2002.

93. Steven W. Colford, "Labels Lose the Fat," *Advertising Age,* June 10, 1991, pp. 3, 54; Steven W. Colford and Julie Liesse, "FDA Label Plans under Attack," *Advertising Age,* February 24, 1992, pp. 1, 50; John E. Calfee, "FDA's Ugly Package: Proposed Label Rules Call for Vast Changes," *Advertising Age,* March 16, 1992, p. 25; Pauline M. Ippolito and Alan D. Mathios, "New Food Labeling Regulations and the Flow of Nutrition Information to Consumers," *Journal of Public Policy & Marketing,* Fall 1993, pp. 188–205.

94. John Carey, "The FDA Is Swinging a Sufficiently Large Two-by-Four," *BusinessWeek,* May 27, 1991, p. 44; Steven W. Colford, "FDA Getting Tougher: Seizure of Citrus Hill Is Signal to Marketers," *Advertising Age,* April 29, 1991, pp. 1, 53.

95. Joe Mandese, "Regulation," *Advertising Age,* November 30, 1992, p. 23.

96. Todd Shields, "Viacom Battles FCC Kids' Ad Rules," *Media-Week,* October 10, 2005, *www.mediaweek.com/mw/news/recent_display.jsp?vnu_content_id=1001263021*.

97. U.S. Const., art. I, § 8.

98. Lanham Trademark Act of 1946, Pub. L. No. 79-489, § 1127, 60 Stat. 427.

99. U.S. Copyright Office, Library of Congress, 1997.

100. Wayne E. Green, "Lawyers Give Deceptive Trade-Statutes New Day in Court, Wider Interpretations," *The Wall Street Journal,* January 24, 1990, p. B1.

101. Howard Schlossberg, "Marketers Say State Laws Hurt Their 'Green' Efforts," *Marketing News,* November 11, 1991, pp. 8–9.

102. Frank Phillips, "Mass. in Court to Defend Curbs on Tobacco Ads," *Boston Globe,* April 7, 2000, p. A1; Gaylord Shaw, "Smoking Ads a Smoldering Issue: High Court May Review

City's Ban on Tobacco Displays," *Newsday* (Long Island, NY), March 18, 2000, p. A31.

103. E. J. Gong, "Fraud Complaints on the Rise, Reports D.A.," *Los Angeles Times,* February 13, 1994, p. B1.

104. Orange County District Attorney, "Closet Factory to Pay Penalty for Misleading Advertising," press release, June 24, 2002.

105. James Maxeiner, "United States," in *Advertising Law in Europe and North America,* ed. James Maxeiner and Peter Schotthoffer (Deventer, The Netherlands: Kluwer Law and Taxation Publishers, 1992), p. 321.

106. James Maxeiner, "United States," in *Advertising Law in Europe and North America,* ed. James Maxeiner and Peter Schotthoffer (Deventer, The Netherlands: Kluwer Law and Taxation Publishers, 1992), p. 321.

107. Felix H. Kent, "Control of Ads by Private Sector," *New York Law Journal,* December 27, 1985, reprinted *in Legal and Business Aspects of the Advertising Industry,* ed. Felix H. Kent and Elhanan C. Stone (1986), pp. 20–79.

108. "ASRC Snapshot," *ASRC, www.asrcreviews.org/about-us/.*

109. Better Business Bureau, "NAD Pilots Successful Resolution between Neil Cooper and Avirex," news release, August 11, 2000, *www.nadreview.org/casereports.asp.*

110. "About US—CARU," *ASRC, www.asrcreviews.org/category/caru/about_caru/*; Advertising Self-Regulatory Council, Children's Advertising Review Unit, Washington, DC, 2012.

111. "About Us—Accountability," *ASRC, www.asrcreviews.org/category/ap/about-the-accountability-program/.*

112. "About the Self-Regulatory Principles for Online Behavioral Advertising," *Self-Regulatory Principles Overview,* July 2009, *www.aboutads.info/obaprinciples.*

113. IAB et al., "Self-Regulatory Principles for Online Behavioral Advertising," July 2009, *www.aboutads.info/resource/download/seven-principles-07-01-09.pdf.*

114. Public Relations Department, KLBJ, Austin, TX, 1991.

115. Public Relations Department, KDWB, Minneapolis/St. Paul, MN, 1991.

116. Public Relations Department, KSDO, San Diego, CA, 1991.

117. Kevin Goldman, "From Witches to Anorexics, Critical Eyes Scrutinize Ads for Political Correctness," *The Wall Street Journal,* May 19, 1994, p. B1.

118. Shelly Garcia, "What's Wrong with Being Politically Correct?" *Adweek,* November 15, 1993, p. 62.

119. Shelly Garcia, "What's Wrong with Being Politically Correct?" *Adweek,* November 15, 1993, p. 62.

120. Andrew Jaffe, "Advertiser, Regulate Thyself," *Adweek,* August 2, 1993, p. 38.

121. Federal Trade Commission, 1991.

4

The Scope of Advertising: From Local to Global

LEARNING OBJECTIVES

To introduce the people and groups that sponsor, create, produce, and transmit advertisements here and abroad. Advertising people may serve in a variety of roles. This chapter discusses the basic tasks of both the client and the advertising agency, the roles of suppliers and the media, the ways agencies acquire clients and are compensated, and the overall relationship between the agency and the client.

After studying this chapter, you will be able to:

LO4-1 Identify the various groups in the advertising business and explain their relationships with one another.

LO4-2 Describe what advertisers do and detail the organizational structures they use to manage advertising both here and abroad.

LO4-3 Classify the types of advertising agencies.

LO4-4 Account for the range of tasks people perform in an ad agency and an in-house advertising department.

LO4-5 Discuss how agencies attract new clients and how they make money.

LO4-6 Explain the stages in the agency–client relationship.

LO4-7 List the factors that affect the client–agency relationship.

LO4-8 Indicate how suppliers and the media help advertisers and agencies.

Large Coffee. 1,50 €.   i'm lovin' it

Source: McDonald's

Thomas Friedman once wrote that "No two countries that both had McDonald's had fought a war against each other since each got its McDonald's." Friedman's point was really not about McDonald's per se, but rather that economic development and international trade reduce conflict. Still, who can rule out the possibility that international harmony correlates with the availability of Happy Meals? ■ The foods you can get at McDonald's are similar to those sold in thousands of competing restaurants and chains. Its menu item ingredients—ground beef, potatoes, and, more recently, salads and yogurt—are widely available. And indeed, there are plenty of competitors out there. But none is so successful. What is McDonald's secret? ■ One could start with the company's dedication to offering value: a tasty, affordable meal served quickly. Add the relentless focus on quality, such as ensuring that meals are freshly prepared and cooked properly and that the restaurants are clean, attractive, and comfortable. ■ But it's hard to avoid the conclusion that integrated marketing communications (IMC) is part of the equation as well. Throughout its history,

McDonald's has invested heavily in marketing, both in the United States and around the world. And that investment has paid dividends by helping make the McDonald's brand one of the most valuable in the world. ■ The slogans are part of advertising lore. "You deserve a break today." "Two all beef patties, special sauce, lettuce, cheese, pickles, onions, on a sesame seed bun." "Have you had your break today?" And, of course, the current global campaign, "I'm lovin' it!" A good example of the far-reaching success of this campaign is depicted in the ad above from Finland, featuring a beautiful McDonald's coffee seascape. ■ Behind the deceptive simplicity of McDonald's ads lies a well-honed IMC strategy that reinforces a core message about the brand, promotes the company's key food offerings, and helps remind audiences that McDonald's is a fun place to get a fast, delicious meal. ■ McDonald's is a global brand, with franchises in over 100 countries. Customers entering a McDonald's franchise can always expect to encounter the Golden Arches, a menu of American food items, and fast, friendly service. Employees will be found dressed in colorful, clean uniforms. The unified brand message is also reinforced with advertising. McDonald's current campaign runs globally, so in dozens of countries customers hear the familiar, "BA DA BA BA BA," followed by "I'm lovin' it." ■ But the global campaign is just one aspect of McDonald's marketing communications efforts. It also customizes its offerings and its advertising to suit local preferences. McDonald's does not serve pork in predominantly Muslim countries (and it refers to hamburgers as "beefburgers"). In countries where beef is not a big part of the regular diet (such as India), the company offers the McVeggie sandwich along with many chicken options. Local soft drink brands are available in Scotland and Brazil and beer is available in Belgium. ■ This willingness to suit local tastes while remaining true to the brand is also reflected in the company's advertising. McDonald's allocates a substantial portion of its advertising budget to cooperative efforts with franchises.

Franchise groups make their own decisions about hiring ad agencies and campaign themes. ■ Even at the national level, McDonald's often runs several campaigns simultaneously. For example, alongside the "I'm lovin it" ads, the company runs ads promoting specific menu items, such as its premium salad offerings. The advertiser also runs ads designed to increase restaurant traffic at a particular time of day, such as breakfast or dinner. Other spots target carefully selected markets, such as Hispanics, African Americans, or working moms. ■ To help with so many different objectives, the company works with a variety of agencies. For example, Burrell has helped with advertising directed at African Americans, and Tribal DDB is the company's U.S. digital agency. ■ It may be true that anyone can make a hamburger. But building one of the world's most iconic global brands is a rare feat. McDonald's success is built on a smart business model and flawless execution. But it is also built on great IMC.

This chapter focuses on the advertising component of IMC, for several reasons. First, advertising agencies remain major players in the creation of IMC campaigns, and advertising typically represents a substantial portion of the IMC budget of firms from small to large. Second, a solid understanding of client–agency relationships in this chapter will serve as a good foundation for understanding how advertising agencies relate to other IMC agencies. Finally, an examination of the advertiser–agency relationship helps set the stage for our later examination in this text of media.

When a business, nonprofit, or individual uses advertising to market a product, service, or idea, that entity is frequently called an advertiser. In other chapters we've avoided using the term "advertiser" to better remind you that marketers have a broader communications toolbox than just paid advertising. So elsewhere we use the term "marketer" or "company." But in this chapter we'll view the marketer as a person or organization that has chosen advertising to reach its target audience, and in doing so we'll refer to the marketer as an advertiser.

The Advertising Industry

The simplicity and focus of McDonald's ads hide the great complexity of what happens behind the scenes. This chapter will help you see this as it introduces you to the people who work in the advertising industry.

The Organizations in Advertising

The advertising business has evolved into four distinct groups. Two of the most important ones are the *marketers (or advertisers)* and the *agencies*. Advertisers (clients) are the companies—like McDonald's, Coca-Cola, or the local shoe store—that pay to advertise themselves and their products. Advertisers range in size from small independent businesses to huge multinational firms, and in type from service organizations to industrial manufacturers to local charities and political action committees. *Advertising agencies* specialize in helping advertisers plan, create, and prepare ad campaigns and other promotional materials.

A third group, *suppliers,* includes the photographers, illustrators, printers, digital service bureaus, color film separators, video production houses, web developers, programmers, and others who assist both advertisers and agencies in preparing advertising materials. Suppliers also include consultants, research firms, and professional services that work with both advertisers and agencies. The fourth group, *media,* sells time (on radio and TV) and space (in print, outdoor, or digital media) to carry the advertiser's message to the target audience.

The People in Advertising

When most people think of advertising, they imagine the agency copywriters and art directors. But the majority of people in advertising are employed by advertisers. Most companies have an advertising department, even if it's just one person. Many other people work for the suppliers and the media. They're in advertising, too.

The fact is, advertising is a very broad field that employs a wide variety of people in sales, research, management, accounting, computer science, and law, as well as specialists in the communication arts—artists, writers, photographers, musicians, performers, and cinematographers.

In this chapter, we'll see what all these people do. In the process, you'll get a good understanding of how the business operates both in the United States and abroad.

Advertisers (the Clients)

LO 4-2

While most companies have some sort of advertising department, its importance depends on the company's size and industry, the size of the advertising program, the role advertising plays in the company's marketing mix, and, most of all, the involvement of top management.

To get a sense of the diversity of companies that advertise, we'll look first at local advertisers to see how they operate. Then we'll examine regional and national advertisers. Finally, we'll look at the companies that market their products globally.

Local Advertising: Where the Action Is

There are about 19,000 American firms with 500 or more employees. But there are more than 5 million that employ fewer than 20, according to the Census Bureau.[1] The vast majority of these small firms are local. Local businesses use IMC to grow, flourish, and fulfill the dreams of their owners and workers. Let's see how one small business, Rubio's, used IMC to grow from a small start-up to a strong regional food chain. Not long after graduating from San Diego State, Ralph Rubio opened his first Mexican restaurant. He offered an unusual specialty: fish tacos—lightly battered and fried whitefish served in soft-shelled corn tortillas with white sauce, salsa, cabbage, and a wedge of lime. At the time, very few other Mexican eateries offered fish tacos, and none featured them. So Rubio found fish tacos hard to sell, even with his secret batter recipe (which he'd gotten from a street vendor in

San Felipe, Mexico). The first month's sales at the restaurant averaged only $163 a day.

Rubio started using small newspaper ads with coupons to lure courageous customers. It worked. As business picked up, he expanded his advertising to radio and TV, targeting his market further with ads on Hispanic stations (whose listeners knew what fish tacos were). And he went after younger, venturesome customers aged 18 to 34 by advertising at local movie theaters. Business picked up some more. Rubio soon opened another restaurant, and then another.

With each new opening, Rubio distributed direct-mail flyers in the area and took free samples to nearby stores. Working with an artist, he created a cartoon character named Pesky Pescado based on the fish taco. He purchased a 15-foot inflatable Pesky to display at his restaurants. Employee T-shirts sported Pesky's picture, and Rubio sold Pesky T-shirts and sweatshirts to enthusiastic patrons. He also offered bumper stickers and antenna balls to add some fun

Local advertisers such as Rubio's Coastal Grill (www.rubios.com) must find ways to differentiate their products from the competition—and then create awareness through advertising. Rubio's website touts its use of fresh ingredients and sustainable seafood, which sets it apart from other restaurants.

Source: Rubio's Restaurants, Inc.

My IMC Campaign 4-A

Understanding Your Client

Obtaining a clear understanding of what your client wants from you and what you are prepared to do for your client is essential for a mutually satisfying relationship. From your end it is vital that you be clear about the finished product. In many classes this might be a plans book, which contains research, an advertising plan, a media plan, and even some creative. In other classes you might not provide all of that. In either case, make sure your client knows what to expect. If previous classes have done campaign work for other clients, you might wish to show your client that work.

As important as it is that your client understand you, it is equally crucial that you understand your client's expectations. Recognize that some clients may not have a clear set of expectations at first; these may in fact evolve over time. Even in this instance, asking the right questions can get your clients thinking about what they hope advertising will do for them.

Below you will find some questions that might prove useful for getting to know your client better. Dr. Debbie Treise, who regularly teaches advertising campaigns at the University of Florida, uses this form. Sending it to the client in advance of a meeting can make your first interaction more useful and informative.

1. Provide a complete description of your product/service:
   What is its current positioning against competitors?
   What is the brand personality as you perceive it?
   Does it need changing?
   Are there seasonal trends for your product?
   Would you be willing to share annual sales trend information?
2. Do you have information on your company to share? Your mission statement? How would you describe the culture of your organization?
3. Do you have a definite target market in mind? Are you targeting consumers, groups, businesses, or some combination?
4. Is the market local? Regional? National? International?
5. Would you be willing to share:
   Information on your competition?
   Information on your market?
   Information on market trends? Legal trends?
   Advertising that your competition has used?
   Previous advertising efforts you have undertaken?
6. What is the time period of this campaign? Do you have definite start and stop dates in mind?
7. What is the budget?
8. Do you have any specifications on the budget breakdown in terms of promotion versus advertising? Any other specifications?
9. What are your marketing objectives for this campaign?
10. Please list your advertising/communications objectives for this campaign (i.e., to increase knowledge, change attitudes, elicit a specific behavior).
11. Are there media that you would like us to be sure to consider?
12. Are there media that you would prefer we not recommend?
13. Do you have a current, active website? If so, what is its primary purpose? Who accesses it?
14. Do you have any specifications on creative executions? Are you looking to continue current efforts or to come up with something completely different?
15. Are there any current clients/consumers that we could contact?
16. Are there potential clients/customers that we could contact?
17. Who should we contact when we have questions? What is the best time to contact this person? How does he or she prefer to be contacted (e-mail, phone, fax)?

to his promotions. To further integrate his activities, Rubio took an active part in community affairs, including tie-ins with a blood bank, a literacy program, and fund-raising activities for both a Tijuana medical clinic and a local university's athletic program.

As the popularity of the fish taco grew, so did Rubio's revenues, doubling every year for the first five years. He trademarked the phrase "Rubio's, Home of the Fish Taco," and a local restaurant critic, commenting on things San Diegans couldn't do without, called fish tacos "the food San Diegans would miss the most." After 19 years, Rubio had over 200 restaurants in six states. Together they produced more than $188 million in annual sales and helped Rubio's serve more than 50 million fish tacos.[2]

Every year, advertisers spend billions of dollars in the United States. Almost half of that is spent on **local advertising,** ads placed by local businesses in a particular city or county targeting customers in their geographic area.

Local advertising is sometimes called *retail advertising* because retail stores account for so much of it. But retail advertising isn't always local; Sears and JCPenney advertise

Issue-oriented organizations such as Mom's Demand Action use advertising to advance their perspectives. This ad shows a disturbing image to make a powerful point about gun laws.

Source: Everytown for Gun Safety Action Fund

nationally. And many businesses besides retail stores use local advertising: banks, real estate developers, movie theaters, auto mechanics, plumbers, radio and TV stations, funeral homes, museums, and local politicians, to name a few. McDonald's franchises engage in local advertising too. Because many franchises are locally owned and operated, they are good examples of small businesses that use advertising to achieve marketing objectives.

Local advertising is critically important because most consumer sales are made (or lost) locally. McDonald's may spend billions advertising nationwide, but if its franchises don't make a strong effort locally, those dollars are wasted. When it comes to making the sale and dealing with customers, local advertising is where the action is—where relationships often start and truly develop.

Types of Local Advertisers

There are four main types of local advertisers:

1. Dealers or local franchisees of national companies (McDonald's, Ford dealers, Kinko's, H&R Block).
2. Stores that sell a variety of branded merchandise, usually on a nonexclusive basis (convenience, grocery, and department stores).
3. Specialty businesses and services (banks, insurance brokers, restaurants, music stores, shoe repair shops, remodeling contractors, florists, hair salons, attorneys, accountants).
4. Governmental and nonprofit organizations (municipalities, utility companies, universities, charities, arts organizations, political candidates).

A small, local business—for example, a hardware, clothing, or electronics store—may have just one person in charge of advertising. That person, the **advertising manager,** performs the administrative, planning, budgeting, and coordinating functions. He or she may lay out ads, write copy, and select the media. A manager with some artistic talent may even design the ads and produce them on a desktop computer.

Chain stores often maintain a completely staffed advertising department to handle production, media placement, and marketing support services. The department needs artists, copywriters, and production specialists. The department head usually reports to a vice president or marketing manager, as shown in Exhibit 4-1.

Types of Local Advertising

Ads that are placed in local media are product, institutional, or classified advertising. Each serves a different purpose.

Product Advertising   **Product advertising** promotes a specific product or service and stimulates short-term action while building awareness of the business. When a McDonald's franchise promotes its premium salads, it is engaging in product advertising. Local advertisers use three major types of product ads: regular price-line, sale, and clearance.

Regular price-line advertising informs consumers about services or merchandise offered at regular prices. An accounting firm might use regular price-line advertising to promote its accounting and tax services.

To stimulate sales of particular merchandise or increase store traffic, local merchants often use **sale advertising,** placing items on sale and offering two-for-one specials or other deals. Local advertisers use

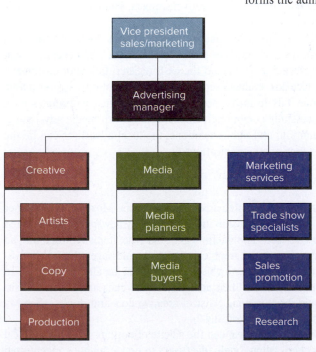

Exhibit 4-1
Typical department structure for small advertisers with high volumes of work, such as grocery store chains.

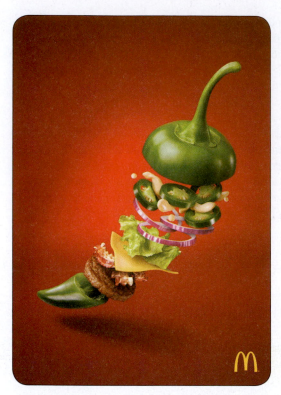

In this campaign McDonald's uses advertising to focus on one of its special menu items, the Jalapeno Burger.

Source: McDonald's

clearance advertising (a special form of sale advertising) to make room for new product lines or new models and to get rid of slow-moving lines, floor samples, broken or distressed merchandise, or out-of-season items. Companies going out of business also use clearance advertising.

Institutional Advertising   **Institutional advertising** attempts to create a favorable long-term perception of the business as a whole, not just of a particular product or service. A McDonald's franchise using an ad to let consumers know it uses beef and produce from local farms is a good example of this type. Many types of businesses use institutional advertising to promote an *idea* about the company and build long-term goodwill. It makes the public aware of what the business stands for and attempts to build reputation and image. An institutional ad might focus on convenient hours, a new credit policy, store expansion, or company philosophy.

Although readership is often lower, effective institutional ads build a favorable image for the business, attract new customers, and encourage customer loyalty. They also help companies to deepen relationships within the community that the business serves.

Classified Advertising   Advertisers use **classified advertising** in the newspaper for many reasons: to locate and recruit new employees, offer services (such as those of an employment agency or business opportunity broker), or sell or lease merchandise (such as cars, real estate, and office equipment). Many McDonald's franchises use classifieds to recruit new employees.

Local Advertisers: Where IMC Began

When Ralph Rubio built his restaurant business, his promotional activities involved a lot more than just running ads. In fact, he did everything he could to develop a *relationship* with his customers and to promote a good word-of-mouth reputation. That meant using publicity, sales promotion, and direct response as well as media advertising—all integrated with consistently good food, reasonable prices, and excellent service. This combination constitutes **integrated marketing communications (IMC)**—joining together in a consistent manner everything that communicates with customers. Thanks to IMC, Rubio's fish taco became a local staple.

Local advertisers and the local agencies that serve them are not stuck with the traditional national view that advertising means "ads placed in the media." By necessity, local advertisers wear many hats every day. They tend the cash register, talk with customers, prepare mailers, write and place ads, evaluate suppliers' trade promotions, answer phone inquiries, spruce up the office, talk to media people, and coordinate the graphics for a seasonal promotion. By successfully combining personal selling with media advertising, direct marketing, sales promotion, and public relations, the local advertiser can be the consummate integrator of marketing communications.[3]

Creating Local Advertising

For many years, local advertisers had limited advertising options. Most relied on either newspapers or radio, with some local television in the mix. Many newspaper ads featured what professionals would call a *schlock* approach—heavy bold type, items crowded into ad space, loud headlines, and unsophisticated graphic design. If the message is honest, consistent, and effective and meets the advertiser's objectives, that may be all that matters. To direct and control the creative aspects of their ads and commercials and ensure consistency, local advertisers should develop a checklist of creative do's and don'ts. (See My IMC Campaign 4–B, "Creating Local Advertising.")

In recent years, digital media have expanded the palette of options available for local advertisers. Google and Facebook allow small advertisers to create highly concentrated and efficient campaigns. And "deal-of-the-day" sites such as Groupon allow local advertisers to run sale advertising in e-mails received by thousands of local customers. Smart local

My IMC Campaign 4-B

Creating Local Advertising

Is your client a local business or service? Use these time-tested practices to guide your thinking about how local advertising can help.

- *Digital is local too.* Local media aren't just newspapers and radio. Facebook and Google offer advertisers an effective way to tailor campaigns to local audiences.

- *Stand out from the competition.* Make your ads easily recognizable. Ads with unusual art, layout, and typefaces have higher readership. Make the ads distinctive, but keep their appearance consistent.

- *Use a simple layout.* The layout should carry the reader's eye through the message easily and in proper sequence from headline to illustration to explanatory copy to price to store name. Avoid too many typefaces.

- *Use a dominant element.* A large picture or headline ensures quick visibility. Photos of real people and action pictures win more readership, as do photos of local people or places. Color attracts more readers.

- *Stress the benefits.* Present the emotional reason to buy or the tangible performance element customers seek.

- *Make the headline count.* Use a compelling headline to feature the main benefit.

- *Watch your language.* Make your writing style active, lively, and involving. Make the readers feel they already own the product. Avoid negativism and profanity.

- *Make the copy complete.* Emphasize the benefits most appealing to customers.

- *Make your visual powerful and eye-catching.* Focus on the benefit. The main visual is often more important than the headline. Photos work better than artwork.

- *Specify branded merchandise.* If the item is a known brand, say so.

- *Include related items.* Make two sales instead of one by offering related items along with a featured one.

- *Urge readers to buy now.* Ask for the sale. Stimulate prompt action by using "limited supply" or "this week only."

- *Don't forget the business name and address.* Check every ad to be certain the business name, address, phone number, and hours are included.

- *Don't be too clever.* Many people distrust or misunderstand cleverness.

- *Don't use unusual or difficult words.* Everyone understands simple language. Use it.

- *Don't generalize.* Be specific. Shoppers want all the facts before they buy.

- *Don't make excessive claims.* Advertisers lose customers when they make claims they can't back up.

- *Plan ad size carefully.* Attention usually increases with size.

- *Consider your target customers.* People notice ads more if they are directed at their own gender or age group.

- *Use tie-ins* with local or special news events.

business owners can use Instagram and blogs to emphasize their ties to the community and the ways that the business supports local concerns.

Finding big ideas for local ad campaigns can be extremely difficult. Some advertisers look to the merchandise for ideas; others look to the customer. An important goal for local advertisers is to achieve a consistent, distinctive look that makes their ads both appealing and identifiable. We discuss the creative process in depth in Chapters 10 and 11.

Local advertisers can turn to a number of sources for creative help, including reps from the local media, local ad agencies, freelancers and consultants, creative boutiques, syndicated art services, and the *cooperative advertising programs* of wholesalers, manufacturers, and trade associations. McDonald's offers its franchises considerable help in designing ads and promotional materials.

Cooperative Advertising

As a service to their distributors and dealers, and to ensure proper reproduction of their products, wholesalers, manufacturers, and trade associations often provide local advertisers with ready-made advertising materials and cooperative advertising programs where the costs are shared.

AD Lab 4–A

The Co-op Marriage

On the surface, cooperative advertising seems like a great arrangement for retailers. A manufacturer supplies advertising materials (saving the retailer production costs) and pays a percentage of the media cost. The retailer drops in the store's logo, arranges for the ad to run, and collects the co-op dollars from the manufacturer. The small retail business can stretch its ad budget and associate its business with a nationally advertised product. The retailer receives professionally prepared ads and acquires greater leverage with the local media that carry the co-op ads.

But as with any marriage, there is give and take.

A retailer may have to sell a lot of merchandise to qualify for significant co-op funds. More often, the retailer and manufacturer have different advertising objectives and different ideas about how the ads should be executed.

The manufacturer often wants total control. The manufacturer expects co-op ads to tie in with its national advertising promotions. It wants the right product advertised at the right time. Manufacturers prepare guideline pamphlets specifying when and where the ads should appear, what form they should take, and what uses of the name and logo are not allowed.

Retailers have their own ideas about which products to advertise when. They're more concerned with daily volume and with projecting an image of value and variety. An appliance store might prefer to advertise inexpensive TVs even though the manufacturer wants to emphasize its top-of-the-line models.

Manufacturers worry that retailers will place the product in a cluttered, ugly ad or next to inferior products; that the ad will run in inappropriate publications; and that it will not run at the best time. Retailers counter that they know the local market better. In short, manufacturers think they don't have enough control; retailers think they have too much.

A retailer contemplating co-op funds should consider the following questions:

- What requirements must be met in order for ads to qualify for co-op money?
- What percentage is paid by each party?
- When can ads be run?
- What media can be used?
- Are there special provisions for message content?
- What documentation is required for reimbursement?
- How does each party benefit?
- Do cooperative ads obscure the retailer's image?

Laboratory Applications

1. Look through a daily paper in your city. Identify two ads that can qualify as co-op. Do the ads fit both the store's image and the manufacturer's image? Explain.

2. A store may develop its own ad and drop in the manufacturer's logo, or it may take an ad created by the manufacturer and simply add the store's location. Which do your two ads do?

There are two key purposes for **cooperative (co-op) advertising:** to build the manufacturer's brand image and to help its distributors, dealers, or retailers make more sales.[4] Every year, national manufacturers give their local retailers millions for co-op projects. Whereas co-op spending favored newspapers years ago, budgets today increasingly favor digital, mobile, and social media.[5] To take one example, Ford Motor Co. requires that it's local dealers spend a quarter of their co-op dollars on digital.[6]

In **vertical cooperative advertising,** the manufacturer provides the complete ad and shares the cost of the advertising time or space. The local newspaper sets the name and address of the local advertiser, or the radio station adds a tagline with the advertiser's name, address, and phone number. Bridgestone makes vertical co-op advertising even more customizable for its retailers. It developed templates for newspaper ads, flyers, and point-of-sale (POS) materials that retail managers can download and edit to fit their needs. After only a few minutes of training, dealers without any graphic design expertise can create local advertising that looks as polished as national advertising.[7] (See Ad Lab 4–A for the pros and cons of co-op advertising.)

With **horizontal cooperative advertising,** firms in the same business (real estate agents, insurance agents, pharmacies, car dealers, or travel agents) or in the same part of town advertise jointly. Competing auto dealers, for example, might pool their dollars to advertise their common retail area as the "Mile of Cars."

Regional and National Advertisers

Regional advertisers operate in one part of the country—in one or several states—and market exclusively within that region. Examples include regional grocery and department store

Exhibit 4-2

Ten biggest brands as measured by total U.S. measured-media spending in 2017

2017 Rank	Brand	2017 Total U.S. Ad Spend ($billion)	Headquarters
1	Comcast Corp.	$5.7	Philadelphia
2	Procter & Gamble	4.4	Cincinnati
3	AT&T	3.5	Dallas
4	Amazon	3.4	Seattle
5	General Motors	3.2	Detroit
6	Verizon	2.6	New York
7	Ford Motor Co.	2.5	Dearborn, MI
8	Charter Comm	2.4	Stamford, CT
9	Alphabet (Google)	2.4	Mountain View, CA
10	Samsung	2.4	Suwon, S. Korea

Source: "200 Leading National Advertisers 2018 Fact Pack," *Ad Age*, Crain Communications Inc.

chains, governmental bodies (such as state lotteries), franchise groups (such as the Southern California Honda dealers), telephone companies (such as SBC), and statewide or multi-state banks (like Bank of America).

Other companies sell in several regions or throughout the country and are called **national advertisers.** These include consumer packaged-goods manufacturers (such as Procter & Gamble and Johnson & Johnson), national airlines (Delta, American), media and entertainment companies (Disney, Time Warner), electronics manufacturers (Apple, Hewlett-Packard), all the auto companies, and restaurant chains like McDonald's. These firms make up the membership of the **Association of National Advertisers (ANA)** and comprise the largest advertisers in the country (see Exhibit 4-2).

How National and Local Advertisers Differ

The basic principles of advertising are the same in both local and national advertising. However, local advertisers have special challenges stemming from the day-to-day realities of running a small business. As a result, local and national advertisers differ in terms of focus, time orientation, and resources (see Exhibit 4-3).

Focus   National companies are concerned about building their brands, so their advertising tends to focus on the competitive features of one brand over another, especially in conquest sales situations. Local merchants or dealers often carry hundreds of different brands or numerous models of an exclusive brand, so they focus on attracting customers to a particular **point**—their place of business. That's why local car dealers typically advertise their dealerships rather than the make of car. And local grocers often promote only those brands for which they receive co-op advertising or trade allowances from the national manufacturer.

In every product category, big companies battle for market share against a few competitors, and every share point is worth millions of dollars. Local advertisers compete with many companies, so their focus is on gross sales or volume: 60 cars a month, five new insurance policies a week, 55 oil changes a day.

National advertisers plan *strategically* to launch, build, and sustain brands. Local advertisers think *tactically.* Will a new $15,000 sign bring more people into the store? Should we stay open on Labor Day? Can we attract more lunchtime customers by reducing our prices or by offering free refills on soft drinks?

The relationship with the customer may be the greatest difference between national and local advertisers. National advertisers' marketing executives rarely see retail customers; instead, they traditionally think in terms of large groups of people—segments, niches, target markets—with various geographic, demographic, or psychographic descriptions. They design their strategies and campaigns to appeal to these large groups.

	National	Local
Focus	Brand Market share Strategies Markets	Point Volume, gross sales Tactics Customers
Time	Long-term campaigns	Short-term ads
Resources	$5–$10 million+ Many specialists	Less than $1 million A few generalists

Exhibit 4-3

Differences between local and national advertisers.

McDonald's encourages their franchises to craft campaigns to suit local markets. In the ad shown above, McDonald's franchises tout the benefits of joining the company for a career.

Source: McDonald's

But local advertisers deal with individual customers every day. They also interact with customers in nonbusiness ways; they may be neighbors, friends, or schoolmates. The local advertiser gets feedback every day—on the company's advertising, prices, product performance, employee service, store decor, and the new sign out front. The national marketer gets occasional feedback—from surveys and from customer complaint lines.

Time Orientation   National and local advertisers also have different time orientations. National companies think long term. They develop five-year strategic plans and budget for annual advertising campaigns. Local advertisers worry that this week's ad in the *Pennysaver* didn't *pull* (a term rarely used by national marketers) as well as last week's; a New York advertiser may have months to develop a network TV campaign; the coffeehouse downtown may have to churn out a new newspaper ad every week to reach its local customers.

Resources   Finally, national advertisers have more resources available—both money and people. A local advertiser that spends $100,000 a year has a relatively large budget. A national advertiser needs to spend at least $5 million a year just to get started. (Procter & Gamble, the largest U.S. advertiser, spends close to $5 billion annually.)[8]

The national advertiser has an army of specialists dedicated to the successful marketing of its brands. The local advertiser may have a small staff or just one person—the owner—to market the business. So the local entrepreneur has to know more about every facet of marketing communications.

How Large Companies Manage Their Advertising

In large companies, many people are involved in advertising. Company owners and top corporate executives make key advertising decisions; sales and marketing personnel often assist in the creative process, help choose the ad agency, and evaluate proposed ad programs; artists and writers produce ads, brochures, and other materials; product engineers and designers give input to the creative process and provide information about competitive products;

Advertising can help make sales promotions more effective, especially when they are teamed with a summer movie blockbuster, Minions. *In this screenshot, McDonald's offers its customers a chance to win prizes, including a trip to Universal Studios Orlando, when they buy select food items that have the Minions game piece on them.*

Source: McDonald's

administrators evaluate the cost of ad campaigns and help plan budgets; and clerical staff members coordinate various promotional activities, including advertising.

A large company's advertising department may employ many people and be headed by an advertising manager who reports to a marketing director or marketing services manager. The exact department structure depends on many variables. Most large advertisers tend to use some mix of two basic management structures: *centralized* and *decentralized.*

Centralized Organization   Companies are concerned with cost efficiency and continuity in their communications programs. Thus, many embrace the **centralized advertising department** because it gives the greatest *control* and offers both *efficiency* and *continuity* across divisional boundaries. In centralized departments, an advertising manager typically reports to a marketing vice president. In addition, companies may organize the department in any of five ways:

- By product or brand.
- By subfunction of advertising (copy, art, print production, media buying).
- By end user (consumer advertising, trade advertising).

- By media (radio, TV, digital, out-of-home).
- By geography (southwestern U.S. advertising, European advertising).

The consumer goods giant General Mills, for example, is one of the nation's largest advertisers. It operates a vast marketing services department with some 350 employees and spends more than $894 million annually on advertising alone, along with millions more on other promotional activities.[9]

General Mills's Marketing Services is really many departments within a department. Its centralized structure enables it to administer, plan, and coordinate the promotion of more than 100 brands. It also supervises five outside ad agencies and operates its own in-house agency for new or smaller brands.[10]

Organized around functional specialties (market research, media, graphics), Marketing Services helps General Mills's brand managers consolidate many of their expenditures for maximum efficiency. The media department, for example, prepares all media plans for the marketing divisions. The production and art department designs the packages for all brands and the graphics for the company's in-house agency. From one spot, Marketing Services handles a wide variety of brands efficiently and effectively (see Exhibit 4-4).

Decentralized Organization   As companies become larger, diversify their product lines, acquire subsidiaries, and establish divisions in different regions or countries, a centralized advertising department can become impractical.

In a **decentralized system,** the company sets up separate ad departments for different divisions, subsidiaries, regions, brands, or other groups. The general manager of each division or brand is responsible for that group's advertising.

For large companies with many divisions, decentralized advertising offers flexibility. Campaigns and media schedules can be adjusted faster. New approaches and creative ideas can be introduced more easily, and sales results can be measured independently of other divisions. In effect, each division is its own marketing department, with the advertising manager reporting to the division head (see Exhibit 4-5).

A drawback, though, is that decentralized departments often concentrate on their own budgets, problems, and promotions rather than the good of the whole company. Across divisions, ads typically lack uniformity, diminishing the power of repetitive corporate advertising. Rivalry among brand managers may even escalate into unhealthy competition.

Transnational Advertisers

Companies advertising abroad typically face markets with different value systems, environments, and languages. Their customers have different purchasing abilities, habits, and motivations. Media customary to U.S. and Canadian advertisers may be unavailable or ineffective. The companies will therefore likely need different advertising strategies. But

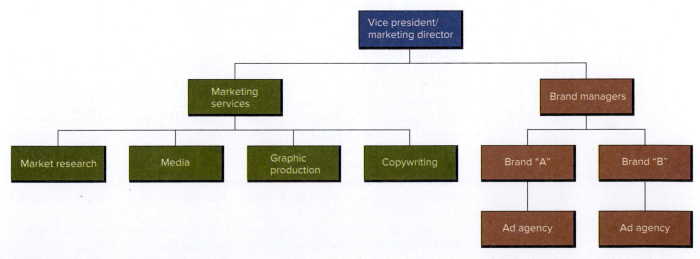

Exhibit 4-4
General Mills has a centralized advertising department like this model.

Exhibit 4-5
In a decentralized system, each division is its own marketing department.

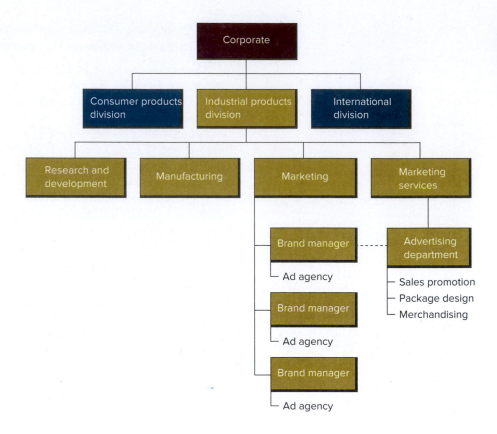

they face a more basic problem: How should they manage and produce the advertising? Should their U.S. agency or in-house advertising department do it? Should they use a foreign agency or set up a local advertising department?

As advertisers enter international markets, they may start by simply exporting their existing products. At first, the home office controls all foreign marketing and advertising. Everything is centralized. Then, as companies get more involved in foreign markets, they may form joint ventures or invest in foreign facilities. Advertisers typically view such operations as foreign marketing divisions and use a decentralized **international structure,** in which the divisions are responsible for their own product lines, marketing operations, and profits, and create customized advertising for each market.[11]

Procter & Gamble, for example, is a nearly 200-year-old company with annual sales of $83 billion. It sells more than 300 consumer brands to more than 5 billion consumers in 140 countries. These brands include such market leaders as Tide, Ivory soap, Pampers, Folgers, Pringles, and Crest.[12]

P&G is one of the biggest and most influential consumer advertisers in the world; its expenditures in the United States alone exceed $4.9 billion annually. But more than half its sales come from abroad.[13] Each overseas division is set up almost like a separate company with its own research and development department, manufacturing plant, advertising department, sales force, and finance and accounting staff. Every brand within a division has a **brand manager** who oversees a brand group and directs his or her own ad agency to create the brand's media advertising. Brand managers work under a marketing manager, who reports to a *category manager.*[14]

Each division also has an advertising department to help coordinate sales promotion and merchandising programs across brands. The corporate advertising department provides statistical information and guidance.

While the brand manager's primary goal is to use advertising and promotion to build market share, the category manager focuses on sharpening overall strategy and building profits.[15] In recent years, P&G has streamlined the system by eliminating extra layers of management and redundant facilities. This ensures that each brand has the single-minded drive needed for success and gives more authority to brand managers.[16]

As companies continue to grow and prosper around the world, they may invest directly in many countries. True **multinational corporations** strive for full, integrated participation in world markets.[17] Foreign sales often grow faster than domestic sales. Multinationals such as Exxon and IBM earn about 50 percent of their sales abroad. Typically, the top 25 U.S. multinational corporations earn more than 40 percent of their revenues and two-thirds of their profits overseas.[18]

A multinational usually exerts strong centralized control over all its marketing activities. Multinational firms such as Microsoft get strong direction and coordination from headquarters and have a standardized product line and marketing structure.

Multinationals that use a *standardized approach* to marketing and advertising in all countries are **global marketers,** and they create global brands. They assume that the way the product is used and the needs it satisfies are universal.[19] Estée Lauder, for example, markets its cosmetics globally. In 2018, supermodel Grace Elizabeth became the latest in a long line of international stars to promote the company's products. Estée Lauder's Pleasures is the world's fourth largest fragrance brand.[20] Global advertisers include Coca-Cola, British Airways, British Petroleum, FedEx, and, of course, McDonald's.[21]

Companies must research extensively before attempting a global advertising strategy. So much depends on the product and where they try to sell it. A "no" answer to any of the following questions means the attempt will probably fail:

1. *Has each country's market for the product developed in the same way?* A Ford is a Ford in most markets. On the other hand, many Europeans use clotheslines, so they don't need fabric softeners for dryers.
2. *Are the targets similar in different nations?* Chinese consumers like PCs and Microsoft Windows. The same is true in Europe and the United States. But when Chinese web users search the internet, they prefer BAIDU, a home-grown search engine, to Google.
3. *Do consumers share the same wants and needs?* Breakfast in Brazil is usually a cup of coffee. Kellogg's corn flakes won't be served the same way there as in the United States, where people commonly eat cereal for breakfast.[22]

According to J. Walter Thompson, the secret to success in global advertising is knowing how to tap into basic human emotions and uncover universal appeals that don't depend solely on language.[23] Sports competition has broad appeal around the world, which is one reason McDonald's has been an Olympics sponsor.

Ultimately, the advertising direction a company takes depends on many variables: breadth of product line, quality of management, ability to repeat marketing strategies across countries, costs, and the decision to operate internationally, multinationally, or globally. Every organization operates in a slightly different environment. This alters the search for an *ideal structure* into a search for a *suitable structure*.[24] Most companies blend aspects of centralized and decentralized structures to fit their own needs.

Humor is an important ingredient in McDonald's global messages. Messages like this one resonate in a variety of cultures. In this ad, created by DDB Finland, McDonald's humorosly promotes its real milkshakes by depicting a cow jumping on a trampoline.

Source: McDonald's

The Advertising Agency

The Role of the Advertising Agency

Why does a company such as McDonald's hire an advertising agency in the first place? Couldn't it save money by hiring its own staff and creating its own ads? How does Leo Burnett win such a large account? Must an agency's accounts be that big for it to make money? This section sheds some light on these issues and gives a clearer understanding of what agencies do and why so many advertisers use agencies.

The American Association of Advertising Agencies (AAAA) defines an **advertising agency** as an independent organization of creative people and businesspeople who specialize in developing and preparing marketing and advertising plans, advertisements, and other

AD Lab 4–B

How Big Is the Agency Business?

Advertising today is a significant worldwide business with a strong presence in the United States. In 2015 there were more than 13,000 U.S. agencies employing more than 183,000 people. Agency employment grew steadily after the recession of 2008 but beginning in 2017 actually declined. Why? The growth of digital advertising, which is frequently done by companies themselves or consultancies.

1. Agencies need fewer people than businesses in many other industries: Nearly half of all firms employ fewer than 10 people. Small agencies can be satisfying workplaces. But what if you want to work for a big power player? Visit the websites of some of the top 10 U.S. agencies (see below) and jot down your impressions.

2. What are the advantages and disadvantages of working in advertising? Visit these agency blogs and news sites to find out about life inside an ad agency.
   - FCB Exchange: www.fcbexchange.com/
   - The Richards Group: https://richards.com/social/
   - Wieden+Kennedy: www.wk.com/news/
   - Wunderman Thompson (formerly JWT): www.jwt.com/en/news
   - Ocean Media: www.oceanmediainc.com/#!news
   - Sukle: sukle.com/blog/
   - Ogilvy: www.ogilvy.com/
   - Waggener Edstrom: www.we-worldwide.com/blog

World's Top 5 Agency Companies

2017 Rank	Network, Parent / Selected Units	Headquarters	2017 Worldwide Revenue (billions)
1	WPP	London	$19.7
2	Omnicom Group	New York	15.3
3	Publicis Group	Paris	10.9
4	Interpublic Group	New York	7.9
5	Dentsu	Tokyo	7.8

World's Top 5 Agencies

2017 Rank	Agency	WW Revenue (billions)
1	Dentsu	$2.3
2	BBDO WW	2.0
3	DDB WW	1.7
4	TWBA WW	1.4
5	McCann	1.4

All data from "World's Largest Agency Companies," *Advertising Age Datacenter Agency Report 2018*, Crain Communications Inc.

promotional tools. The agency also purchases advertising space and time in various media on behalf of different advertisers, or sellers (its clients), to find customers for their goods and services.[25]

This definition offers clues to why so many advertisers hire ad agencies. First, an agency like Leo Burnett is *independent*. The agency isn't owned by the advertiser, the media, or the suppliers, so it can bring an outside, objective viewpoint to the advertiser's business—a state the advertiser can never attain.

Second, like all full service agencies, Leo Burnett employs a combination of *businesspeople* and *creative people,* including administrators, accountants, marketing executives, researchers, market and media analysts, writers, and artists. They have day-to-day contact with outside professional suppliers who create illustrations, take photos, retouch art, shoot commercials, record sound, and print brochures.

The agency provides yet another service by researching, negotiating, arranging, and contracting for commercial space and time with the various print, electronic, and digital media. Because of its *media expertise,* Leo Burnett saves its clients time and money.

Agencies don't work for the media or the suppliers. Their moral, ethical, financial, and legal obligation is to their clients. Just as a well-run business seeks professional help from attorneys, accountants, bankers, or management specialists, advertisers use agencies out of *self-interest* because the agencies can create more effective advertising and select more effective media than the advertisers can themselves. Today, almost all sizable advertisers rely on an ad agency for expert, objective counsel, and unique creative skills—to be the "guardian of their brands."[26] Ad Lab 4–B gives a snapshot of advertising agencies in the United States.

Finally, a good agency serves its clients' needs because of its daily exposure to a broad spectrum of marketing situations and problems both here and abroad. As technology has enabled companies to work across borders with relative ease, the advertising business has boomed worldwide. All the large U.S. agencies, for example, maintain offices in many foreign countries.

Types of Agencies

Advertising agencies are typically classified by their geographic scope, range of services, and the type of business they handle.

Local Agencies

Many communities have reputable small ad agencies that offer expert assistance to local advertisers. A competent **local agency** can help

- Analyze the local advertiser's business and the product or service being sold.
- Evaluate the markets for the business, including channels of distribution.
- Evaluate the advertiser's competitive position and offer strategic options.
- Evaluate media alternatives and offer rational recommendations.
- Devise an integrated communications plan and implement it with consistency and creativity.
- Save the advertiser valuable time by taking over media interviewing, analysis, checking, billing, and bookkeeping.
- Assist in other aspects of advertising and promotion by implementing sales contests, publicity, grand openings, and other activities.

Unfortunately, local advertisers use ad agencies less extensively than national advertisers. Many advertisers simply don't spend enough money on advertising to warrant hiring an agency. And some large agencies don't accept local advertisers because their budgets are too low to support the agency's overhead.

Regional and National Agencies

Every major city has numerous agencies that can produce and place the quality of advertising suitable for national campaigns. **Regional** and **national agencies** typically participate in a regional trade group such as the Western States Advertising Agency Association (WSAAA). The *Standard Directory of Advertising Agencies* (the Red Book) lists these agencies geographically, so they're easy to find.

International Agencies

The largest national agencies are also **international agencies.** That is, they have offices or affiliates in major communication centers around the world and can help their clients market internationally or globally as the case may be. Likewise, many foreign-based agencies have offices and affiliates in the United States. For example, the largest advertising agency organization in the world today, WPP Group, is based in London. But it owns several of the top agencies in the United States, such as Ogilvy & Mather and Grey Worldwide.

Full-Service Agencies

The modern **full-service advertising agency** supplies both advertising and nonadvertising services in all areas of communications and promotion. *Advertising services* include

Leo Burnett is one of many McDonald's ad agencies. Visit the agency's website at www.leoburnett.com *to see examples of its work for McDonald's and other clients.*

Source: Leo Burnett Worldwide

planning, creating, and producing ads; performing research; and selecting media. *Nonadvertising functions* run the gamut from packaging to public relations to producing sales promotion materials, annual reports, and trade show exhibits. In keeping with IMC, many of the largest agencies today are in the forefront of *interactive media.*[27]

Full-service agencies may specialize in certain kinds of clients. Most, though, can be classified as either *general consumer agencies* or *business-to-business agencies.*

General Consumer Agencies   A **general consumer agency** represents the widest variety of accounts, but it concentrates on *consumer accounts*—companies that make goods purchased chiefly by consumers (soaps, cereals, cars, pet foods, toiletries). Some ads are placed in consumer media (TV, radio, magazines, and so on) that pay a *commission* to the agency. General agencies often derive much of their income from these commissions.

General agencies include the international superagency groups headquartered in communication capitals such as New York, London, Paris, and Tokyo, as well as many other large firms in New York, Chicago, Los Angeles, Minneapolis, Montreal, and Toronto. A few of the better-known names in North America are McCann, Ogilvy, Wieden & Kennedy, Goodby, Silverstein & Partners, Giant Spoon, Anomaly, and Cossette Communications-Marketing (Canada). But general agencies also include the thousands of smaller *entrepreneurial agencies* located in every major city across the country (Crispin Porter + Bogusky, Miami; Rubin/Postaer, Los Angeles; Fallon Worldwide, Minneapolis).

Profit margins in entrepreneurial agencies are often slimmer, but these shops are often more responsive to the smaller clients they serve. They offer the hands-on involvement of the firm's principals, and their work is frequently startling in its creativity. For these very reasons, many large agencies are spinning off smaller subsidiaries. Gotham, Inc., for example, is a hot creative shop in New York that was spun off by the Interpublic Group to do work for a variety of clients its bigger sister agencies couldn't serve.[28] Some entrepreneurial agencies, such as Zubi Advertising in Coral Cables, Florida, carve a niche for themselves by serving particular market segments.

Business-to-Business Agencies   A **business-to-business agency** represents clients that market products to other businesses. Examples are electronic components for computer manufacturers, equipment used in oil and gas refineries, and MRI equipment for radiology. High-tech advertising requires some technical knowledge and the ability to translate that knowledge into precise, as well as persuasive, communications.

Most business-to-business advertising is placed in trade magazines or other business publications. These media are commissionable, but their circulation is smaller, so their rates are far lower than those of consumer media. Because commissions usually don't cover the cost of the agency's services, business agencies typically charge their clients service fees. They can be expensive, especially for small advertisers, but failure to obtain a business agency's expertise may carry an even higher price in lost marketing opportunities.

Business and industrial agencies may be large international firms such as MacLaren/Lintas in Toronto or HCM/New York, or smaller firms experienced in areas such as recruitment, biomedical, or electronics advertising.

Specialized Service Agencies

Many agencies assist their clients with a variety of limited services. In the early 1990s the trend toward specialization blossomed, giving impetus to many of the small agency-type groups called *creative boutiques* and other specialty businesses such as *media-buying services* and *interactive agencies.*

Burrell Communications handles ads for national clients, including Toyota and Tide, that develop campaigns aimed at African American consumers. To see examples of the agency's work, visit www.burrell.com.

(top) Source: Toyota Motor Sales, U.S.A., Inc.; (bottom) Source: Procter & Gamble

McDonald's uses the creative ideas of its partner agencies to come up with clever executions for its ads. The company worked with its ad agency in Hong Kong and asked local children to answer the question, "if you could build the McDonald's of your dreams—what would it look like?" The result was a McDonald's themed restaurant designed solely by kids and selling only Happy Meals.

Source: McDonald's

Creative Boutiques   Some talented artists—such as graphic designers and copywriters—set up their own creative services, or **creative boutiques.** They work for advertisers and occasionally subcontract to ad agencies. Their mission is to develop exciting creative concepts and produce fresh, distinctive advertising messages. In the 1990s, Creative Artists Agency (CAA), a Hollywood talent agency, caused a stir on Madison Avenue (the collective term for New York agencies) by taking on the role of a creative boutique, using its pool of actors, directors, and cinematographers to create commercials for Coca-Cola. McCann-Erickson Worldwide remained Coke's *agency of record,* but the majority of the creative work came from CAA. Since that time, Coke has allowed numerous other smaller shops to work on its account. At one point, Coke employed more than 20 different agencies, and the company continues to use the multiagency approach.[29]

Advertising effectiveness depends on originality in concept, design, and writing. However, while boutiques may be economical, they usually don't provide the research, marketing, sales expertise, or deep customer service that full-service agencies offer. Thus, boutiques tend to be limited to the role of creative suppliers.

Media-Buying Services   Some years ago, a few experienced agency media people started setting up organizations to purchase and package radio and TV time. The largest **media-buying service** (or *media agency*) is Starcom Mediavest. Based in Chicago, it is owned by the Publicis Group, has offices around the world, and places more than $25 billion worth of advertising annually for a wide variety of clients.[30]

Media time and space are perishable. So radio and TV stations presell as much time as possible and discount their rates for large buys. The media-buying service negotiates a special discount and then sells the time or space to agencies or advertisers.

Media-buying firms provide customers (both clients and agencies) with a detailed analysis of the media buy. Once the media package is sold, the buying service orders spots, verifies performance, sees that stations "make good" for any missed spots, and even pays the media bills. Compensation methods vary. Some services charge a set fee; others get a percentage of what they save the client.

Media agencies have experienced so much growth in the last decade that they have become major players on the advertising stage. We'll discuss them in greater detail in Chapter 9.

Interactive Agencies   With the stunning growth of the Internet and the heightened interest in integrated marketing communications has come a new breed of specialist—the **interactive agency.** Avenue A/Razorfish and Digitas are just two of the many firms that specialize in designing web pages and creating fun, involving, information-rich, online advertising.[31] When McDonald's introduced a digital game in its Happy Meals titled "Fairies and Dragons," its advertising partner was Fuel Industries.

Other specialists, such as *direct-response* and *sales promotion agencies,* are also growing in response to client demands for greater expertise and accountability. In the IMC era, it is rare that a large company relies on an advertising agency alone for its branding efforts.

What People in an Agency Do

LO 4-4

The American Association of Advertising Agencies (AAAA) is the national trade association of the advertising agency business and the industry's spokesperson with government, media, and the public (see the box People behind the Ads: Marla Kaplowitz later in this chapter). Its approximately 450 agency members, representing a wide spectrum of small, medium, and large agencies, place 80 percent of all national advertising handled by agencies in the United States.[32]

McDonald's uses two-way message channels to share information with customers and respond to their needs. The "Our Food, Your Questions" site is a great example of this. By addressing customer concerns in a proactive way, McDonald's helps protect its brand and build customer loyalty.

Source: McDonald's

The AAAA Service Standards explain that an agency's purpose is to interpret to the public, or to desired segments of the public, information about a legally marketed product or service. How does an agency do this? First, it studies the client's product to determine its strengths and weaknesses. Next, it analyzes the product's present and potential makers. Then, using its knowledge of distribution channels and available media, the agency formulates a plan to carry the advertiser's message to consumers, wholesalers, dealers, or contractors. Finally, the agency writes, designs, and produces ads; contracts for media space and time; verifies media insertions; and bills for services and media used.

The agency also works with the client's marketing staff to enhance the advertising's effect through package design, sales research and training, and production of sales literature and displays. To understand these functions, consider the people who were involved, directly or indirectly, in the creation, production, and supervision of the McDonald's campaign created by Leo Burnett.

Account Management

The **account executives (AEs)** at Leo Burnett are the liaisons between the agency and the client. Large agencies typically have many account executives, who report to **management (or account) supervisors.** They in turn report to the agency's director of account (or client) services.

Account executives are in the middle of the fray; they are responsible for formulating and executing advertising plans (discussed in Chapter 8), mustering the agency's services, and representing the client's point of view to the agency. McDonald's account executive has to be well versed in the extraordinary range of media and demonstrate how her agency's creative work satisfies both her client's marketing needs and the market's product needs. Characteristically, an AE must be able to see things from all points of view. He or she must be enterprising, courageous, and demanding, but also tactful, artistic and articulate, meticulous, forgiving, perceptive, ethical, and discreet. And what's more, an AE must always deliver the work on time and within budget.

flavor that's in perfect harmony

See how we fine tune
our oatmeal

FRUIT & MAPLE OATMEAL

Filled with notes of fresh apples, plump raisins, juicy cranberries and brown sugar, Fruit and Maple Oatmeal is pitch-perfect in every way. See what happens when wholesome meets delicious – your taste buds will sing! Available all day. Also available without brown sugar. At participating McDonald's.

Some McDonald's advertising is devoted to specific menu items. These ads give existing customers a reason to visit the restaurant chain more often and may attract new customers who are unaware of the variety of offerings at McDonald's. By promoting their Fruit & Maple Oatmeal, do you think McDonald's is attracting a broader base of health-conscious customers who would normally not visit McDonald's?

Source: McDonald's

Research and Account Planning

Agency creatives (artists and copywriters) require a wealth of product, market, and competitive information because, at its core, advertising is based on information. Therefore, before creating any advertising, agencies research the uses and advantages of the product, analyze current and potential customers, and try to determine what will influence them to buy. After the ads are placed, agencies use more research to investigate how the campaign fared. Chapter 7 discusses some of the many types of research ad agencies conduct.

Account planning is a hybrid discipline that uses research to bridge the gap between account management and creatives. The account planner defends the consumer's point of view and the creative strategy in the debate between the agency's creative team and the client.

Account planners study consumer needs and desires through surveys and focus groups, but primarily through personal interviews. They help the creative team translate its findings into imaginative, successful campaigns. Not attached to either account management or creative, the account planner balances both elements to make sure the research is reflected in the ads.[33]

Through good account planning, Del Rivero Messiano DDB, McDonald's Hispanic agency, developed a unique and award-winning spot targeted to Spanish-language consumers. The commercial features a young man who dreams he is playing an ancient Aztec game, *juego de pelotas*. A key element of the spot is the Spanish word "sueño," which means both *dream* and *sleep*. Although his alarm clock rouses him from the wonderful dream, he can hit the snooze button and return to his fantasy because he knows he can pick up a fast breakfast at McDonald's.

By putting the consumer, rather than the advertiser, at the center of the process, account planning changes the task from simply creating an advertisement to nurturing a relationship between consumer and brand. That requires understanding, intuition, and insight. When performed properly, planning provides that mystical leap into the future—the brilliant, simplifying perspective that lights the way for the client and the creatives. For more on one of the greatest planners of all time, see People behind the Ads: Jon Steel in Chapter 5.

Creative Concepts

Most ads rely heavily on **copy,** the words that make up the headline and message. The people who create these words, called **copywriters,** must condense all that can be said about a product into a few pertinent, succinct points.

Ads also use nonverbal communication. That is the purview of the **art directors,** graphic designers, and production artists, who determine how the verbal and visual symbols will fit together. (The creative process is discussed in Chapters 10 and 11.) The agency's copywriters and artists work as a creative team under a **creative director.** Each team is usually assigned a particular client's business.

One award-winning ad for McDonald's focuses on the Ronald McDonald House charity. Titled "First Step," the ad tells the story of a young toddler whose medical care was made more affordable by the organization. The beautiful spot was developed by an experienced DDB Chicago team, including creative director Bill Cimino, copywriter Geoff McCartney, and art director Gordon West.

Advertising Production: Print and Broadcast

Once an ad is designed, written, and approved by the client, it is turned over to the agency's print production manager or broadcast producers.

For print ads, the production department buys type, photos, illustrations, and other components and works with printers, engravers, and other suppliers. For a broadcast commercial, production people work from an approved script or storyboard. They use actors, camera operators, and production specialists (studios, directors, editors) to produce a commercial. The "First Step" commercial described earlier was directed by a famous commercial director named Joe Pytka and was filmed at Pytka's studio.

But production work is not limited to just ads and commercials. Dealer kits and direct mailings are just two examples of other types of media that may be created as part of a campaign.

Media Planning and Buying

Ad agencies provide many media services for their clients: research, negotiating, scheduling, buying, and verifying. Media planning is critical because the only way advertisers can communicate is through some medium. We discuss media extensively in Chapters 9 and 12 through 17, but for now it's important to understand the changes over the last decade that have made the media function so important.

With the fragmentation of audiences from the explosion of new media options, media planning and buying is no simple task. Today, many more media vehicles are available for advertisers to consider, as the traditional major media offer smaller audiences than before—at higher prices. Add to this the trend toward IMC and relationship marketing, and the media task takes on added significance. This has fueled the growth of media specialty companies and simultaneously recast agency media directors as the new rising stars in the advertising business.

Tight budgets demand ingenious thinking, tough negotiating, and careful attention to details. In an age of specialization, what advertisers really need are exceptional generalists who understand how advertising works in coordination with other marketing communication tools and can come up with creative media solutions to tough marketing problems. Many products owe their success more to creative media buying than to clever ads.

Traffic Management

One of the greatest sins in an ad agency is a missed deadline. If an agency misses a deadline for a monthly magazine, for example, the agency will have to wait another month before it can run the ad, much to the client's displeasure.

The agency traffic department coordinates all phases of production and makes sure everything is completed before client and/or media deadlines. Traffic is often the first stop for recent college graduates and an excellent place to learn about agency operations.

Additional Services

The growth of IMC has caused some agencies to employ specialists who provide services besides advertising. Larger agencies often have a fully staffed **sales promotion department** to produce nonadvertising creative material. Or, depending on the nature and needs of their clients, they may employ public relations people and direct marketing specialists, web page designers, home economics experts, or package designers.

Agency Administration

In small agencies, administrative functions may be handled by the firm's principals. Large agencies often have departments for accounting, human resources, data processing, purchasing, financial analysis, legal issues, and insurance.

How Agencies Are Structured

An ad agency organizes its functions, operations, and personnel according to the types of accounts it serves, its size, and its geographic scope.

In small agencies (annual billings of less than $20 million), each employee may wear many hats. The owner usually supervises daily business operations, client services, and new business development. Account executives generally handle day-to-day client contact. AEs may also do some creative work, such as writing copy. Artwork may be produced by

Exhibit 4-6
Typical advertising agency organization.

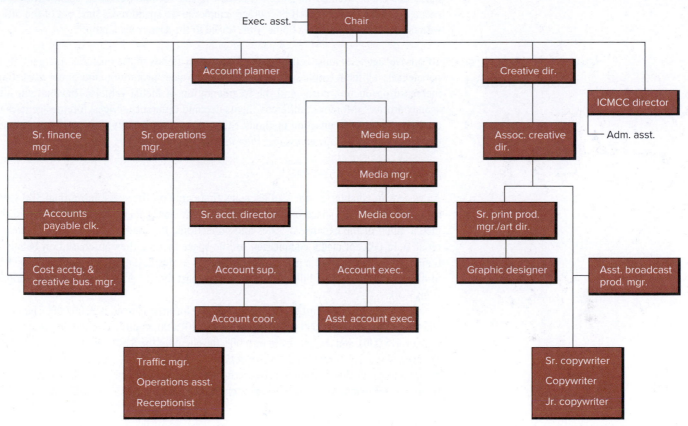

The 2019 rate card from People *magazine. The cards are used by agency media planners to estimate costs for running campaigns in print.*
Source: Meredith Corporation

an art director or purchased from an independent studio or freelance designer. Most small agencies have production and traffic departments or an employee who fulfills these functions. They may have a media buyer, but in very small agencies, account executives also purchase media time and space. Exhibit 4-6 shows how a typical advertising agency is organized.

Medium and large agencies are usually structured in a *departmental* or *group system.* In the **departmental system,** the agency organizes its various functions—account services, creative services, marketing services, and administration—into separate departments.

In the **group system,** the agency is divided into a number of "little" agencies or groups. Each group may serve one large account or, in some cases, three or four smaller ones. An account supervisor heads each group's staff of account executives, copywriters, art directors, a media director, and any other necessary specialists. A very large agency may have dozens of groups with separate production and traffic units.

To deal with the economic pressures, many agencies have looked for ways to reorganize. TBWA\Chiat\Day in Venice, California, credits its laid-back office design with encouraging creativity throughout the agency. Based on an idealized city, the layout by architect Clive Wilkinson features open workstations clustered into communities and arranged around public gathering places. The idea is to free employees to roam and interact. A black surfboard displays the skull and crossbones of the self-proclaimed "pirates of the industry."[34]

In Chicago, Leo Burnett, which was traditionally highly centralized, restructured itself into numerous client-oriented mini-agencies, each meant to function as an agency within an agency.[35] And in France, Y&R encourages employees to spend more time out of the office with clients and to work from home while linked to the agency via laptop.[36]

How Agencies Are Compensated

LO 4-5

To survive, agencies must make a profit. But recent trends in the business—mergers of superagencies, shifts in emphasis from advertising to sales promotion and direct marketing, increased production costs, and the fragmentation of media vehicles—have all cut into agency profits.[37] Moreover, different clients demand different services, forcing agencies to develop various compensation methods. Still, there are really only three ways for agencies to make money: *media commissions, markups,* and *fees* or *retainers.*

Media Commissions

As we saw in Chapter 2, when ad agencies first came on the scene more than 100 years ago, they were really space brokers, or reps, for the newspapers. Because they saved the media much of the expense of sales and collections, the media allowed the agencies to retain a 15 percent **media commission** on the space or time they purchased on behalf of their clients. That started a tradition that endures to this day, although agencies have had to discover other ways of billing clients over the past few decades. Let's see how commissions work.

Say a national rate-card price for a full-page color magazine ad is $100,000. The magazine bills the agency $85,000 (the cost of the ad, $100,000, minus a commission discount of 15%, or $15,000), and the agency in turn bills the client for the $100,000. For large accounts, the agency typically provides extensive services (creative, media, accounting, and account management) for this commission. With dwindling profits, though, and clients negotiating smaller commissions, many agencies now charge a fee for services that used to be free.[38]

Markups

In the process of creating an ad, the agency normally buys a variety of services or materials from outside suppliers—for example, software, photos, postage, and illustrations. The agency pays the supplier's charge and then adds a **markup** to the client's bill, typically 17.65 percent of the invoice (which becomes 15 percent of the new total).

For example, a markup of 17.65 percent on an $8,500 photography bill yields $1,500 in net revenue. When billing the client, the agency adds the $1,500 to the $8,500 for a new total of $10,000. When the client pays the bill, the agency keeps the $1,500 (15 percent of the total)—which, not coincidentally, is the standard commission agencies normally receive.

$$\$8,500 \times 17.65\% = \$1,500$$
$$\$8,500 + \$1,500 = \$10,000$$
$$\$10,000 \times 15\% = \$1,500$$

Some media—local newspapers, for example—allow a commission on the higher rates they charge national advertisers but not on the lower rates they charge local advertisers. So, to get their commission, local agencies have to use the markup formula above.

Today many agencies find that the markup doesn't cover their costs of handling the work, so they're increasing their markups to 20 or 25 percent. While this helps, agency profits are still under pressure, forcing many agencies to adopt a fee system in place of, or in addition to, commissions and markups.

Fees

Clients today expect agencies to solve problems rather than just place ads, so fees are becoming more common. In fact, very few national advertisers still rely on the 15 percent commission system. An equal number now use some fee-based system. The rest use some reduced commission or incentive system.[39]

Ethics, Diversity & Inclusion

Enlightened Workplace Certification Program

How can agencies foster a workplace that does more than eliminate discrimination, but go beyond to foster "cultures of inclusion, equity, creative dialogue and social transformation"? For the 4A's, the answer to that question is the Enlightened Workplace Certification Program.

According to 4A's President Marla Kaplowitz, "For participating agencies, this program signals to employees, clients and potential talent that guidelines and best practices have been put in place. This is an investment in a holistic approach for agencies to create safe, trusting, empowering and collaborative environments where all can thrive."[40]

How does it work? Agencies will be provided with self-evaluation tools for ferreting out problems. Members of each office, department, or team participate in a workshop that encourages conversations about race, gender, power, and influence. Then, benchmarks and standards for behaviors/actions are used to ensure individuals are supported and abuses are identified and investigated. Finally, organizations that meet the standards are recognized with a certification.

According to Digiday, the program is driven "mostly by the current conversation around sexual harassment." The goal, according to the publication, is "to support agencies to eliminate, among other things, bullying and intimidation in the workplace."[41]

Who are these bullies? According to one agency employee, it is the creatives who've accumulated the most trophies. "You're trying to make sure your ideas win and that you're attached to a winning piece of business," she said. "So people can get aggressive, especially those at big agencies with those big personalities."[42]

The 4A's has offered workshops around the country, including the following cities: New York, Chicago, Dallas, Los Angeles, and San Francisco.

The response so far from agencies has been positive.

According to Keesha Jean-Baptiste, 4A's SVP of talent engagement and inclusion, "Since announcing the 4A's Enlightened Workplace Certification in February, we've received interest from more than 100 agencies. It's a testament to the fact that there is real appetite for change and a huge sign that agencies are willing to do the work."[43]

There are two pricing methods in the fee system. With the **fee–commission combination,** the agency charges a basic monthly fee for all its services to the client and retains any media commissions earned. In the **straight-fee or retainer method,** agencies charge for all their services, either by the hour or by the month, and credit any media commissions earned to the client.

Accountability is a major issue in client–agency relationships. With a new type of agency compensation, the **incentive system,** the agency earns more if the campaign attains specific, agreed-upon goals. DDB Needham, for example, offers its clients a "guaranteed results" program. If a campaign meets or exceeds agreed-upon marketing objectives, the agency earns more; if it falls short, the agency earns less. Kraft General Foods rewards its agencies based on their performance. An A grade gets an extra 3 percent commission; C grades are put on review.[44]

The In-House Agency

Some companies set up a wholly owned **in-house agency** (or *house agency*) to save money and tighten control over their advertising. The in-house agency may do all the work of an independent full-service agency, including creative tasks, production, media placement, publicity, and sales promotion.

Advertisers with in-house agencies hope to save money by cutting overhead, keeping the media commission, and avoiding markups on outside purchases. Small, local advertisers in particular seek this goal.

Advertisers also expect more attention from their house agencies, which know the company's products and markets better and can focus all their resources to meet its deadlines. Management is often more involved in the advertising when it's done by company people, especially in "single-business" companies. And some in-house advertising is outstanding, especially in the fashion field. But usually companies sacrifice more than they gain. In-house flexibility is often won at the expense of creativity. Outside agencies typically offer greater experience, versatility, and talent. In-house agencies have difficulty attracting and keeping the best creative people, who tend to prefer the variety and challenge offered by independent agencies.

The biggest problem for in-house agencies is loss of objectivity. In the shadow of internal politics, linear-thinking policymakers, and harangues from management, ads may become insipid contemplations of corporate navels rather than relevant messages to customers. In advertising, that's the kiss of death.

The Client–Agency Relationship

How Agencies Get Clients

Many factors affect the success of a company's advertising program, but one of the most important is the relationship between the advertiser and its agency.

To succeed, advertising agencies need clients. New clients come from personal contact with top management, referrals from satisfied clients or advertising consultants, publicity on recent successful campaigns, trade advertising, direct-mail solicitation, or the agency's general reputation.[45] The three most successful ways to develop new business are having clients who strongly champion the agency, having superior presentation skills, and cultivating a personal relationship with a network of top executives.

Referrals

Most good agencies get clients by referral—from existing clients, friends, review consultants, or even other agencies. The head of one company asks another who's doing her ads, and the next week the agency gets a call. If a prospective client presents a conflict of interest with an existing client, the agency may decline the business and refer the prospect to another agency.[46]

Independent *agency review consultants* often help arrange marriages between agencies and clients. In fact, independent advisers are now involved in most important account shuffles on Madison Avenue.[47]

Sales reps for media and suppliers frequently refer local advertisers to an agency they know. So it's important for agencies to maintain cordial relations with the media, suppliers, other agencies, and, of course, their existing clients.

While much of McDonald's advertising is instantly recognizable, this campaign shows the company is sometimes prepared to produce edgier ads and often needs assistance to get the job done right. In the ad campaign "I See Fries," consumers were encouraged to see McDonald's fries in everyday objects and to share a picture using a special Fry Finding Filter in Meitu, a photo-sharing app in China. The "I See Fries" ad was actually a collaboration among various McDonald's agencies: Tribal Worldwide Shanghai, DDB Group Sydney, and DDB Asia Pacific. Having multiple McDonald's agencies work together highlights the importance of good relationships. The ad proved successful when more than 674,000 customers shared "I See Fries" photos.

Source: McDonald's

Presentations

An advertiser may ask an agency to make a presentation—anything from a simple discussion of the agency's philosophy, experience, personnel, and track record to a full-blown audiovisual presentation of a proposed campaign. Successful agencies, therefore, need excellent presenters.

Some advertisers ask for or imply that they want a **speculative presentation,** meaning they want to see what the agency will do before they sign on. But most agencies prefer to build their presentations around the work they've already done, to demonstrate their capabilities without giving away ideas for a new campaign. Invariably, the larger the client, the bigger the presentation.

The presentation process also allows the agency and the advertiser to get to know each other before they agree to work together. Advertising is a people business, so human qualities—integrity, mutual regard, trust, and communication—play an important role.

Networking and Community Relations

Agencies frequently find that the best source of new business is people their employees know in the community. Some agencies work pro bono (for free) for charities or nonprofit organizations such as the American Indian College Fund. Matt Freeman, the young CEO of Tribal DDB, volunteers his time on behalf of the Ad Council and The Hunger Site. Leo Burnett partners with GlobalGiving, an organization that matches needs with donors.

Agencies may help local politicians (a controversial practice in some areas) or contribute to the arts, education, religion, or the community. Some agencies sponsor seminars; others assist ad clubs or other professional organizations. All these activities help an agency gain visibility and respect in its community.

Soliciting and Advertising for New Business

Lesser-known agencies must take a more aggressive approach. An agency may solicit new business by advertising, writing letters, making cold calls, or even having a viral video on YouTube. An agency principal usually solicits new business, but staffers help prepare presentations.

Today, more agencies are advertising themselves. Many agencies submit their best ads to competitions around the world to win awards and gain publicity and professional respect for their creative excellence.[48]

Stages in the Client–Agency Relationship

Just as people and products have life cycles, so do relationships. In the advertising business, the life cycle of the agency–client relationship passes through four distinct stages: *prerelationship, development, maintenance,* and *termination.*[49]

The Prerelationship Stage

The **prerelationship stage** occurs before an agency and client officially do business. They may know each other by reputation, by previous ads, or through social contact. Initial perceptions usually determine whether an agency is invited to pitch the account. Through the presentation process, the agency tries to give the best impression it can because it is selling and the client is buying (the My IMC Campaign 4-C segment titled "Agency Review" offers guidelines for selecting an agency).

The Development Stage

Once the agency is appointed, the **development stage** begins. During this honeymoon period, the agency and the client are at the peak of their optimism and eager to develop a mutually profitable relationship. Expectations are at their highest, and both sides are most forgiving. During development, the rules of the relationship are established. The respective roles get set quickly, the true personalities of all the players come out, and the agency creates its first work. At this point, the agency's output is eagerly awaited and then judged very thoroughly. The agency also discovers how receptive the client is to new ideas, how easy the client's staff is to work with, and how well the client pays its bills. During the development stage, the first problems in the relationship also occur.

The Maintenance Stage

The year-in, year-out, day-to-day working relationship is called the **maintenance stage.** When successful, it may go on for many years. McDonald's and Leo Burnett have partnered since 1981. Other long-lasting relationships include Unilever–JWT, ExxonMobil–McCann-Erickson, and Hammermill Papers–BBDO Worldwide, all more than 80 years. Unfortunately, the average client–agency relationship is much shorter—usually five to six years.

The Termination Stage

At some point, an irreconcilable difference may occur, and the relationship reaches the **termination stage.** Perhaps the agency has acquired a competing account, or the agency's creative work doesn't seem to be working. Often one party or the other simply decides it is time to move on.

During the nervous 1990s, several long-standing client–agency relationships were terminated. After 75 years, AT&T replaced Ayer as the company's lead agency on its

My IMC Campaign 4-C

Agency Review

What will your client look for in your agency team? This agency review should give you an idea. To use this scale, an advertiser would rate each agency on a scale from 1 (strongly negative) to 10 (strongly positive). Use the "Creative Abilities" qualities below for this chapter's AdForum exercise.

General Information

_____ Size compatible with our needs.

_____ Strength of management.

_____ Financial stability.

_____ Compatibility with other clients.

_____ Range of services.

_____ Cost of services; billing policies.

Marketing Information

_____ Ability to offer marketing counsel.

_____ Understanding of the markets we serve.

_____ Experience dealing in our market.

_____ Success record; case histories.

Creative Abilities

_____ Well-thought-out creativity; relevance to strategy.

_____ Art strength.

_____ Copy strength.

_____ Overall creative quality.

_____ Effectiveness compared to work of competitors.

Production

_____ Faithfulness to creative concept and execution.

_____ Diligence to schedules and budgets.

_____ Ability to control outside services.

Media

_____ Existence and soundness of media research.

_____ Effective and efficient media strategy.

_____ Ability to achieve objectives within budget.

_____ Strength at negotiating and executing schedules.

Personality

_____ Overall personality, philosophy, or position.

_____ Compatibility with client staff and management.

_____ Willingness to assign top people to account.

_____ Ability to articulate rationale behind work.

References

_____ Rating by current clients.

_____ Rating by past clients.

_____ Rating by media and financial sources.

$200 million consumer long-distance account, splitting the business between Y&R and FCB, both in New York.[50] Seagram fired DDB Needham from its $40 million Chivas Regal account after a 32-year marriage. And Anheuser-Busch dropped a bombshell on D'Arcy Masius Benton & Bowles when it pulled the Budweiser account after 79 years.[51] Both Ayer and D'Arcy have since disappeared from the agency landscape.

The way a termination is handled will affect both sides for a long time and is an important factor in whether the two ever get back together. After losing the Apple Computer account in 1986, TBWA\Chiat\Day gave Madison Avenue a lesson in class by placing a full-page ad thanking Apple for their many years together. In 1997, the account came back.[52]

Factors Affecting the Client–Agency Relationship

LO 4-7

Many forces influence the client/agency relationship. Generally, they can be grouped into the four Cs: *chemistry, communication, conduct,* and *changes.*

The most critical factor is the personal *chemistry* between the client's and the agency's staff. A very nasty (and public) breakup of a partnership between Walmart and Draft FCB boiled down to differences in the cultures of the two firms.[53]

Poor *communication,* a problem often cited by both agencies and advertisers, leads to misunderstandings about objectives, strategies, roles, and expectations—and to poor advertising. Constant, open communication and an explicit agreement on mutual contribution for mutual gain are key to a good relationship.[54]

Dissatisfaction with agency *conduct,* or performance, is the most commonly cited reason for agency switches in every country.[55] The service the agency gave two years ago may

My IMC Campaign 4-D

Ways to Be a Better Client

These are some ideas your client may wish to keep in mind as it thinks about working with you.

Relationships

- *Cultivate honesty.* Be truthful in your meetings and in your ads.
- *Be enthusiastic.* When you like the ads, let the agency know.
- *Be frank when you don't like the advertising.* Always cite a reason when turning down an idea.
- *Be human.* React like a person, not a corporation. Laugh at funny ads even if they don't work.
- *Be willing to admit you're unsure.* Don't be pressured. Let your agency know when you need time.
- *Allow the agency to feel responsible.* Tell the agency what you feel is wrong, not how to fix it.
- *Care about being a client.* Creative people work best for clients they like.

Management

- *Don't insulate your top managers from creative people.* Agency creatives work best when objectives come from the top, not filtered through layers.
- *Set objectives.* For timely and quality service from your agency, establish and openly share your marketing objectives.
- *Switch people, not agencies.* When problems arise, agencies often prefer to bring in fresh talent rather than lose you as a client.
- *Be sure the agency makes a profit on your account.* Demanding more services from your agency than fees or commissions can cover hurts relationships.

Production

- *Avoid nitpicking last-minute changes.* Perfection is important, but waiting until the last moment to make minor changes can damage the client–agency relationship. Agencies see such behavior as indecisive and/or arrogant and lose respect for the client.
- *Be aware of the cost of changes (both time and money).* The cost of making major changes at the production stage may be five times greater than in the earlier stages.
- *Don't change concepts during the production stage.* Late changes can inadvertently alter product positioning and image.

Media

- *Understand the economics (and economies) of media.* Be prepared to deal with costs per thousand (CPMs), costs per ratings point (CPP), and other key elements of media planning and buying so that you can evaluate and appreciate your agency's media strategy.
- *Understand the importance of lead time.* Early buys can eliminate late fees, earn discounts, make you eligible for special promotions, strengthen your agency's buying position, and reduce anxiety.
- *Avoid interfering with the agency's media relationship.* The stronger your agency's buying position, the greater the discounts available to you. Refrain from cutting deals with media reps directly and plan media use well in advance.
- *Avoid media arrogance ("they need us").* Some media will deal with clients, and some won't. Misinterpret this relationship and you may either pay more than you should or be too late to get into a medium you need.
- *Avoid insularity.* Be willing to let your mind travel beyond your immediate environment and lifestyle.
- *Suggest work sessions.* Set up informal give-and-take sessions with creatives and strategists.
- *Keep the creative people involved in your business.* Agency creatives do their best work for you when they're in tune with the ups and downs of your business.

Research

- *Share information.* Pool information to create new and bigger opportunities.
- *Involve the agency in research projects.* An agency's creative talent gets its best ideas from knowledge of your environment.

Creative

- *Learn the fine art of conducting the creative meeting.* Deal with the important issues first: strategy, consumer benefits, and reasons why.
- *Look for the big idea.* Concentrate on positioning strategy and brand personality. Don't allow a single ad—no matter how brilliant—to change the positioning or personality of the product.
- *Insist on creative discipline.* The creative process stimulates concepts and actions. Discipline helps keep focus on those that count the most.
- *Don't be afraid to ask for great advertising.* Agencies prefer the high road, but as the client you must be willing to accompany them. If the agency slips, be strong and ask it to try again.

not be valued by the client in the same way today.[56] Or perhaps the agency doesn't understand the client's marketing problems. And clients change, too. Does the client give the agency timely, accurate information? Does it appreciate good work, or does it treat the agency like a vendor?[57] (For more on how clients hold up their end of the relationship, see the My IMC Campaign 4-D segment, "Ways to Be a Better Client.")

Changes occur in every relationship. Unfortunately, some of them damage the agency-client partnership. The client's market position or policies may change, or new management may arrive. Agencies may lose key staff people. Client conflicts may arise if one agency buys another that handles competing accounts. Legally, an ad agency cannot represent a client's competition without the client's consent.[58] Saatchi & Saatchi was forced to resign Helene Curtis under pressure from Saatchi's biggest client, Procter & Gamble.[59]

Perhaps the best way to improve understanding between clients and agencies would be to have staff members change places for a while. A Foote, Cone & Belding account executive did just that with great success, filling in temporarily as marketing manager at Levi's Jeans for Women. It gave her a whole new perspective on her agency job and the daily challenges her client was facing.[60]

The Suppliers in Advertising

LO **4-8**

Spend a few weeks inside an ad agency, and you are likely to see many different vendors making presentations about the special services they can provide. These service providers are called **suppliers.** Without their services, it would be impossible to produce the billions of dollars' worth of advertising placed every year.

Although we can't mention them all, important suppliers include *art studios and web design houses, printers, engravers, film and video production houses,* and *research companies.*

Art Studios and Web Designers

Art studios design and produce artwork and illustrations for advertisements. They may supplement the work of an agency's art department or even take its place for small agencies. Art studios are usually small organizations with as few as three or four employees. Some, though, are large enough to employ several art directors, graphic designers, layout artists, production artists, and sales reps.

Most studios are owned and managed by a graphic designer or illustrator. He or she calls on agencies and advertising managers to sell the studio's services, takes projects back to the office to be produced, and then delivers them for the client's approval. The work is time-consuming and requires organization and management skills as well as a core competency in art direction and computer graphics.

Similar to art studios, **web design houses** employ specialists who understand the intricacies of web-based technologies and can design ads and web pages that are both effective and cost efficient.

Printers and Related Specialists

The printers who produce brochures, stationery, business cards, sales promotion materials, and point-of-purchase displays are vital to the advertising business. Ranging from small instant-print shops to large offset operations, **printers** employ or contract with highly trained specialists who prepare artwork for reproduction, operate digital scanning machines to make color separations and plates, operate presses and collating machines, and run binderies.

Film and Video Houses

Few agencies have in-house TV production capabilities. Small agencies often work with local TV stations to produce commercials. But the large agencies normally work with **independent production houses** that specialize in film or video production or both.

Research Companies

Advertisers are concerned about the attitudes of their customers, the size of potential markets, and the acceptability of their products. Agencies want to know what advertising approaches to use, which concepts communicate most efficiently, and how effective past campaigns have been.

The media are concerned with the reading and viewing habits of their audiences, the desired markets of their advertiser customers, and public perceptions toward their own particular medium.

Research, therefore, is closely allied to advertising and is an important tool for marketing professionals. But most firms do not maintain a fully staffed research department.

Most marketers work with web design houses that understand both the intricacies of programming languages and the various elements of good web design. The McDonald's website provides rich content and a high degree of interactivity. As shown in these screenshots, among the many offerings on the website, customers can browse the history of McDonald's, learn about promotions and special offers, and even build their own meal and determine its nutritional value.

(all) Source: McDonald's

Instead, they use **independent research companies** or consultants. Research firms come in all sizes and specialties, and they employ statisticians, field interviewers, and computer programmers, as well as analysts with degrees in psychology, sociology, and marketing. We discuss research in Chapter 7.

The Media of Advertising

The *medium* that carries the advertiser's message is the vital connection between the company that manufactures a product or offers a service and the customer who may wish to buy it. Although the plural term **media** commonly describes channels of mass

Exhibit 4-7
Spending across media categories 2007–2017.
Source: AdAge Datacenter, "Share of U.S. Ad Spending by Medium," *AdAge Marketing Fact Pack 2018* (Crain Communications Inc.).

Ad Spending by Medium 2021 (estimated)			Ad Spending by Medium 2007		
Rank	Name	Spending (percentage)	Rank	Name	Spending (percentage)
1	Internet	48.2%	1	TV	33.0%
2	TV	28.8	2	Newspaper	28.0
3	Radio	7.8	3	Magazine	14.5
4	Newspaper	5.0	4	Radio	11.9
5	Out of home	4.9	5	Internet	8.2

communication such as television, radio, newspapers, and magazines, it also refers to other communications vehicles such as direct mail, out-of-home media (transit, billboards, etc.), specialized media (aerial/blimps, inflatables), specialty advertising items (imprinted coffee mugs, balloons), and new communication technologies such as digital media, interactive TV, and satellite networks. (Exhibit 4-7 shows ad spending by medium for 2021 (estimated) and 2007.)

It's important to understand the various media, their role in the advertising business, and the significance of current media trends. For a person seeking a career in advertising, the media may offer the first door to employment, and for many they have provided great financial rewards.

We classify advertising media into seven major categories: *print, electronic, digital interactive, social media, out-of-home, direct response,* and *other media.* Due to recent media trends, there is some overlap. We shall mention these in passing, along with a brief description of each major category.

Print Media

The term **print media** refers to any commercially published, printed medium—such as newspapers and magazines—that sells advertising space to a variety of advertisers. In the United States in 2014, there were 1,331 daily newspapers and more than 900 weekly newspapers and shoppers' guides.[61] Most are local. However, some national newspapers such as *USA Today, The Wall Street Journal, Barron's,* and trade publications such as *Electronic News* and *Supermarket News* have become quite successful. Once strictly a local newspaper, *The New York Times* is now distributed to nearly half a million readers nationwide.[62]

Magazines, on the other hand, have long been national, and some periodicals, such as *Elle,* publish editions in many countries. For over a decade, though, the trend has been toward localization and specialization.

As of 2017, 7,176 magazines were published in the United States.[63] These include national consumer publications such as *Time* and *National Geographic;* national trade publications such as *Progressive Grocer* and *Marketing News;* local city magazines such as *Palm Springs Life* and *Chicago;* regional consumer magazines such as *Sunset;* and local or regional trade or farm publications such as *California Farmer.*

Print media also include directories; school or church newspapers and yearbooks; and programs used at sporting events and theatrical performances. As we shall see in Chapter 12, the vast array of newspapers and magazines makes it possible for both consumer and business advertisers to pinpoint the delivery of their messages to highly select target markets in a variety of fields or geographic locations.

Electronic Media

The **electronic media** of radio and television used to be called the broadcast media. But with the advent of cable TV, many programs are now transmitted electronically through wires rather than broadcast through the air.

The big four television networks—NBC, CBS, ABC, and Fox—reach in excess of 97 percent of all households. Each accomplishes this through partnerships with over 200 affiliate stations.[64] Cable television reaches additional tens of millions of people and features popular channels like USA, the Disney Channel, and ESPN. And despite the advent of new digital technologies, 14,000 radio stations continue to prosper across the United States. We discuss electronic media in more detail in Chapter 13.

Digital Interactive Media

Free Fly Apparel leverages the power of social media, an attractive image, and a memorable, compelling benefit to show how advertising is practiced today. The ad shows that even smaller companies can effectively and efficiently reach national audiences using the right medium.

Source: Facebook/Free Fly Apparel

Digital interactive media allow the audience to participate actively and immediately. The internet offers tiny companies with scant resources instant access to customers worldwide.

As we shall see in Chapters 14 and 15, this presents a challenge to advertisers and agencies to learn new forms of creativity. They have to deal with a whole new environment for their ads. It's an environment where customers may spend 20 minutes or more, not just 30 seconds, and where advertising is a dialogue, not a monologue.[65]

Technology and competition for viewers have led to tremendous audience fragmentation. Running a spot on network TV used to cover the majority of a market. Now ad budgets must be bigger to encompass many media. Wherever elusive customers hide, new media forms emerge to seek them out. But for the big, mass-market advertiser, this represents an enormous financial burden.

Social Media

In previous editions we've categorized sites such as Facebook, Twitter, YouTube, LinkedIn, and others as digital interactive media. However, these unique web destinations are so important that they deserve their own category. **Social media** is a term for sites where the prime motivation for audience consumption is audience-created content. This content, from friends, family, business associates, acquaintances, celebrities, and others, is highly credible, immediate, and persuasive. Needless to say, advertisers want to participate in social media exchanges. And they are finding more and more ways to do just that. Chapter 15 focuses exclusively on social media.

Out-of-Home Media

The major categories of out-of-home media are *outdoor advertising* and *transit advertising*. In the United States, most **outdoor advertising** (billboard) companies are local firms, but most of their revenue comes from national advertisers such as liquor and airline companies. **Transit advertising** (bus, taxi, and subway advertising) is an effective and inexpensive medium to reach the public while they're in the retail neighborhood. Out-of-home media also include posters in bus shelters and train stations, billboards in airport terminals, stadium scoreboards, flying banners and lights, skywriting, and kiosk posters. We go into greater detail about these media options in Chapter 16.

McDonald's not only uses out-of-home advertising, it does so in a creative way.

Courtesy of Outdoor Advertising Association of America

Direct Response

The purpose of much IMC is to create an enduring, positive perception of a brand or company. But some efforts are meant to have a much faster, more immediate impact. These messages are designed to induce a consumer to buy right now, or to take some other desired action. Direct-response advertising is designed to generate an immediate response. For example, when companies mail or e-mail their advertising directly to prospective customers without using one of the commercial media forms, it's called **direct-mail advertising.** The ad may be a simple sales letter, or it may be a complex package with coupons, brochures, samples, or other devices designed to stimulate a response. Direct mail using the Postal Service ("snail mail") is the most expensive medium on a cost-per-exposure basis, but it is also the most effective because marketers can target customers directly without competition from other advertisers. We discuss direct mail in Chapter 17.

People BEHIND the Ads

Marla Kaplowitz, CEO, American Association of Advertising Agencies

Monica Schipper/Getty Images

The 4A's is the national trade association for marketing communications companies, including many of the largest agencies, as well as numerous small and mid-sized agencies across the United States. The agencies that the AAAA serves employ more than 65,000 people and place the vast majority of all national advertising.

In 2008, to broad acclaim, the organization named Nancy Hill its first-ever female CEO. After 91 years, many thought it was certainly time. When Hill finally chose to step down in 2017, the 4A's turned to another talented woman, Marla Kaplowitz. Kaplowitz was selected after an extensive search that included over 70 candidates.

Kaplowitz cut her teeth in many agency roles. Her start came at DMB&B and then Ammirati Puris Lintas. Next she joined Procter & Gamble's media agency Mediavest. Finally, in 2011 she accepted a position as CEO of MEC North America.

Agency work is just a part of how Kaplowitz prepared for her current role. She also serves on the boards of the Trustworthy Accountability Group, the Ad Council, and the Digital Advertising Alliance.

Kaplowitz leads a group facing numerous challenges. Agencies face financial squeezes from big clients, increased calls for accountability, technological changes that include programmatic media buying and selling, and the emergence of consultancies, organizations that advise clients on the quality of their agencies. What follows are some of Kaplowitz's thoughts on ensuring a strong future for advertising agencies.

On what is special about the 4A's "The creativity. Not just the creative, but the creativity. We needed to make sure we could continue to help empower agencies in their quest for business and in their relationships with marketers to bring that insightful creativity [that] drives commerce and influences culture."[66]

On cultural sensitivity in advertising "[T]here needs to be a deeper understanding of what it means to think about people of all backgrounds. Whether you're talking about race, ethnicity, gender, age, nationality—all those things come together, and you have to be aware of that in the messages that are being put out there and you have to be responsible."[67]

On the client of the future "What is the responsibility of marketers to really understand the intersection of data and creativity and technology and connecting with consumers and how you deliver that in those brand experiences?"[68]

On building bridges "Agencies need to once again be valued for the partnership that they deliver and the work because it's about growing their business. My goal is to make sure that I work and partner closely with the ANA (Association of National Advertisers) and (ANA President) Bob Liodice and hope to be very connected to them moving forward."[69]

On making the industry more diverse "Although the 4A's has discussed and created programs focused on diversity issues in the industry, we have not done enough for our members to address inclusion in the workplace. It's time for action, so we are creating a series of playbooks and tools—guides to really help our members." One new initiative, she said, is an "enlightened workplace certification."[70]

Other Media

Technology has spawned a host of new advertising media that can confound even the most knowledgeable media planner and buyer. Advertising appears on digital home hubs such as Amazon's Echo. Computers dial telephones and deliver messages by simulating speech or playing a prerecorded message. Computers can also put callers on hold and play prerecorded sales messages until a customer service rep answers. Business presentations are copied to DVDs that are mailed to prospective customers. As progress continues, so will the proliferation of new media and the opportunities for those seeking careers (or fortunes) in the media.

Media around the World

Many U.S. advertising people get used to foreign styles of advertising faster than they get used to foreign media. In the United States, if you want to promote a soft drink as a youthful, fun refresher, you use TV. In some parts of Europe, Asia, South America, and Africa you may not be able to. Around the world, most broadcast media are owned and controlled

This ad for McDonald's helps celebrate an Islamic observance. Sensitivity to the infinite diversity of worldwide cultures and beliefs is important for a global advertiser's success.

Source: McDonald's

by the government, and many governments do not allow commercial advertising on radio or television. In Egypt, Coke removed its iconic name from bottles and replaced it with names of famous cities. The campaign represented a unique twist on the soft drink manufacturer's global "share a Coke" campaign and was a rousing success.[71]

Where countries do allow TV advertising, TV ownership is high, cutting across the spectrum of income groups. In less developed countries, though, TV sets may be found only among upper-income groups. This means advertisers may need a different media mix in foreign markets.

Virtually every country has access to radio, television, newspapers, magazines, outdoor media, and direct mail. However, the legalities of different media forms vary from country to country. Generally, the media available to the international advertiser can be categorized as either *international* or *foreign media,* depending on the audience they serve.

International Media

In the past, **international media**–which serve several countries, usually without any change in content–have been limited to newspapers and magazines. Several large American publishers such as Time, McGraw-Hill, and Scientific American circulate international editions of their magazines abroad. Usually written in English, they tend to be read by well-educated, upper-income consumers and are therefore good vehicles for advertising high-end, brand-name products. *Reader's Digest,* on the other hand, is distributed to 126 foreign countries and printed in the local language of each. Today, television is also a viable international medium. And we are beginning to see the emergence of commercial *global media vehicles,* such as CNN.

Foreign Media

Advertisers use **foreign media**–the local media of each country–for large campaigns targeted to consumers or businesses within a single country. Because foreign media cater to their own national audience, advertisers must produce their ads in the language of each country. In countries such as Belgium and Switzerland, with more than one official language, ads are produced in each language.

Unlike the United States, most countries have strong national newspapers that are a good medium for national campaigns. Advertisers also get broad penetration of lower-income markets through radio, which enjoys almost universal ownership. And cinema advertising is a viable alternative to TV in markets with low TV penetration or restricted use of commercial TV.

Chapter Summary

The advertising business is made up of four main groups: advertisers (clients), agencies, suppliers, and media. It employs a wide range of artists and businesspeople, sales reps and engineers, top executives, and clerical personnel.

Advertisers can be classified based on their geographic activities as local, regional, national, and transnational. Local advertising is placed by businesses in a particular city or county and aimed at customers in the same geographic area. It is important because most sales are made or lost in the local arena.

There are three types of local advertising: product, institutional, and classified. Product advertising can be further divided into regular price-line advertising, sale advertising, and clearance advertising. Institutional advertising creates a long-term perception of the business as a whole by positioning it within the competitive framework. Classified advertising is used to recruit new employees, offer services, and sell or lease new or used merchandise.

Local advertisers are the consummate integrators of marketing communications. Successful local advertisers wear many hats every day, and many of their daily activities help advertise the business. Building relationships is a key element.

Local advertisers can get creative assistance from local ad agencies, media, freelancers and consultants, creative boutiques, syndicated art services, and desktop publishers. Wholesalers, manufacturers, and trade groups often help with cooperative advertising.

Regional advertisers operate in one or several states and market exclusively within that region. National advertisers operate in several regions or throughout the country and comprise the largest advertisers.

Local and national advertisers differ in focus, time orientation, and resources. National advertisers focus on brand building, share of market, grand strategies, and market groups. Local advertisers focus on daily traffic, gross sales or volume, tactical solutions, and the individual customers they see every day. National advertisers have a long-term perspective, local advertisers a short-term one. National advertisers also have more money and more employees.

A large company's advertising department may be centralized or decentralized. Each structure has advantages and disadvantages. The centralized organization is the most typical and may be structured by product, subfunction of advertising, end user, or geography. Decentralized departments are typical of large, far-flung organizations with numerous divisions, subsidiaries, products, countries, regions, and/or brands.

Transnational advertisers face unique challenges. Their markets have a different value system, environment, and language with customers of different purchasing abilities, habits, and motivations. Media customary in the United States may be unavailable or ineffective. Companies therefore often need different advertising strategies. To manage their advertising, transnational advertisers use an international, multinational, or global marketing structure.

Ad agencies are independent organizations of creative people and businesspeople who specialize in developing and preparing advertising plans, ads, and other promotional tools on behalf of their clients.

Like their clients, ad agencies may be local, regional, national, or international in scope. Agencies can be classified by the range of services they offer and the types of business they handle. The two basic types are full-service agencies and specialized service agencies, such as creative boutiques, media-buying services, and interactive agencies. Agencies may specialize in either consumer or business-to-business accounts. The people who work in agencies may be involved in account management, research, account planning, creative services, production, traffic, media, new business, administration, or a host of other activities.

Agencies may be organized into departments of functional specialties or into groups that work as teams on various accounts. Agencies charge fees or retainers, receive commissions from the media, or mark up outside purchases made for their clients.

Some advertisers develop in-house agencies to save money by keeping agency commissions for themselves. However, they risk losing objectivity and creativity.

Most agencies get clients through referrals, publicity on successful campaigns, advertising, personal solicitation, or networking. The client–agency relationship goes through four stages: prerelationship, development, maintenance, and termination. Numerous factors affect the relationship, including chemistry, communication, conduct, and changes.

The suppliers in advertising are all the people and organizations that assist in the business. Examples are art studios and web designers, printers, photoengravers, film and video houses, talent agencies, research firms, and consultants.

The media of advertising include the traditional mass media of print, electronic, and out-of-home as well as more specialized channels such as direct response, digital interactive media, social media, and specialty advertising.

Print media include magazines and newspapers as well as directories, Yellow Pages, school yearbooks, and special event programs. Electronic media include radio, TV, and cable TV. Out-of-home refers to billboard and transit advertising. Direct-mail advertising is the most expensive medium on a cost-per-exposure basis but also typically is the most effective at generating inquiries or responses. Interactive media let customers participate, turning advertising from a monologue to a dialogue.

In foreign markets, advertisers are faced with different media mixes, different legal constraints, and different economies of advertising.

Important Terms

Review Questions

1. What roles do the major organizations involved in the advertising business perform?

2. What are the differences between a local advertiser and a national advertiser?

3. What services might a modern full-service advertising agency offer a large business-to-business advertiser?

4. What are the most important things an advertiser should consider when selecting an agency?

5. How does an agency make money? What is the best way to compensate an agency? Explain your answer.

6. If you owned an ad agency, what would you do to attract new business? Be specific.

7. What are the advantages and disadvantages of an in-house agency?

8. What are the major influences on the client–agency relationship? What can clients and agencies do to maintain a good relationship?

9. What is meant by the term *interactive media?* Give some examples.

10. If you were planning to advertise your brand of computers in Europe, would you likely use foreign or international media? Why?

The Advertising Experience

1. **Advertising Agencies**

   Ad agencies often specialize in a particular type of business or focus on a special market and/or consumer. Visit the websites for the following agencies:

   - 9th Wonder: www.9thwonder.com
   - BBDO: www.bbdo.com
   - Crispin Porter Bogusky: www.cpbgroup.com
   - Dept: www.deptagency.com/en-ie/
   - DDB Worldwide Communications Group Inc.: www.ddb.com
   - Fallon: www.fallon.com
   - Foote, Cone & Belding: www.fcb.com
   - JWT: www.jwt.com
   - Leo Burnett: www.leoburnett.com
   - McCann Worldgroup: www.mccann.com
   - Muse Communications: www.museusa.com
   - Ogilvy: www.ogilvy.com
   - RPA: www.rpa.com
   - Saatchi & Saatchi: www.saatchi.com
   - TBWA\Chiat\Day: www.tbwachiat.com
   - Y+R: www.yr.com

   Answer the following questions for each:

   a. What is the focus of the agency's work (e.g., consumer, business-to-business, ethnic, general market)?

   b. What are the scope and size of the agency's business? Who make up its clientele?

   c. What is the agency's mission statement or philosophy? How does that affect its client base?

   d. What is the agency's positioning (e.g., creative-driven, strategy [account]-driven, media-driven)?

   e. What is your overall impression of the agency and its work?

1. **Agencies and Clients (Advertisers)**

   The advertising industry is truly vast, and advertisers and their agencies focus on a wide range of businesses in a broad scope of markets. Visit the following websites and familiarize yourself further with the nature and scope of the advertising world:

   Advertisers

   - Global–International Advertising Association (IAA): www.iaaglobal.org
   - National–Association of National Advertisers (ANA): www.ana.net

   Advertising Agencies

   - National (United States)–American Association of Advertising Agencies (AAAA): www.aaaa.org

   Advertising Practitioners

   - International–Institute of Practitioners in Advertising (IPA): www.ipa.co.uk
   - National–American Advertising Federation (AAF): www.aaf.org
   - Regional–Advertising Federation of Minnesota: www.adfed.org
   - Local–AdClub of Greater Boston: www.adclub.org

   Advertising Publications

   - National–*Advertising Age:* www.adage.com
   - Regional/local–*Adweek:* www.adweek.com

Answer the following questions for each site:

a.   What advertising group (advertiser, ad agency, practitioner, trade press) sponsors the site? Who is the intended audience?

b.   What are the size and scope of the organization?

c.   What is the organization's purpose? The site's purpose?

d.   What benefit does the organization provide individual members? The advertising community at large?

e.   How is this organization important to the advertising industry? Why?

2.   **Developing a Brand Image**
     After visiting at least three of the websites listed in Exercise 1, develop a mission statement for two hypothetical new advertising

agencies. The first agency is small, has an irreverent edge, and is primarily dedicated to working on social justice issues. The second agency would like to represent luxury goods companies looking to add young professionals to its clientele.

3.   How well do these brand sites engage consumers? What are the principles of engagement that emerge from your review?

a.   Scentos: https://scentos.com/

b.   Mountain Dew: www.mountaindew.com/

c.   Mercedes-Benz USA: www.mbusa.com/en/home

d.   Sandals Resorts: www.sandals.com/bahamas/

End Notes

1.   U.S. Census, "Business & Industry," www.census.gov/econ.
2.   "Rubio's Coastal Grill," *Wikipedia*, https://en.wikipedia.org/wiki/Rubio%27s_Coastal_Grill.
3.   Jim Rowe, "Integrated Marketing Tips? Study Retail Trade," *Advertising Age*, April 4, 1994, p. 32.
4.   Henry A. Laskey, J. A. F. Nicholls, and Sydney Roslow, "The Enigma of Cooperative Advertising," *Journal of Business and Industrial Marketing* 8, no. 2 (1993), pp. 70–79.
5.   Kathy Crosett, "Best of 2012: CPG Trade Promotion, Co-op Ads Shifting to Digital in 2012," *Audience Scan*, December 19, 2012, www.audiencescan.com/best-of-2012-cpg-trade-promotion-co-op-ads-shifting-to-digital-in-2012/.
6.   David Barkholz, "Ford Co-op Program Pushes More Digital Ads," *Automotive News*, June 19, 2015, www.autonews.com/article/20140113/RETAIL/301139986/ford-co-op-program-pushes-more-digital-ads.
7.   "Helping Dealers Sell More Tires," *Printing Impressions* 48, no. 4 (2005), p. 96.
8.   "100 Leading National Advertisers, 2014," *Ad Age DataCenter*, June 23, 2014, http://adage.com/article/datacenter-advertising-spending/100-leading-national-advertisers/293054/.
9.   "100 Leading National Advertisers, 2014," *Ad Age DataCenter*, June 23, 2014, http://adage.com/article/datacenter-advertising-spending/100-leading-national-advertisers/293054/.
10. "Brands," *General Mills*, www.generalmills.com/en/Brands/Overview.
11. William O. Bearden, Thomas N. Ingram, and Raymond W. LaForge, *Marketing Principles & Perspectives* (Burr Ridge, IL: Irwin, 1995), p. 96.
12. "Investor Relations," *P&G*, www.pginvestor.com/.
13. "100 Leading National Advertisers, 2014," *Ad Age DataCenter*, June 23, 2014, http://adage.com/article/datacenter-advertising-spending/100-leading-national-advertisers/293054/.
14. Alan Mitchell, "P&G Drops Old Job Tags in Rejig," *Marketing* (UK), October 14, 1993, p. 4.
15. Aelita G. B. Martinsons and Maris G. Martinsons, "In Search of Structural Excellence," *Leadership & Organization Development Journal* 15, no. 2 (1994), pp. 24–28.
16. Ellen Byron, "P&G's Internal Memo on Management Shakeup," *The Wall Street Journal*, October 22, 2014, http://blogs.wsj.com/corporate-intelligence/2014/10/22/pgs-internal-memo-on-management-shakeup/.
17. E. Jerome McCarthy and William D. Perreault Jr., *Basic Marketing*, 11th ed. (Burr Ridge, IL: Irwin, 1993), p. 593.
18. "Global Marketer's Index," *Ad Age DataCenter*, December 7, 2014, http://adage.com/article/datacenter-advertising-spending/global-marketers-index/106350/.
19. Eric N. Berkowitz, Roger A. Kerin, Steven W. Hartley, and William Rudelius, *Marketing*, 3rd ed. (Burr Ridge, IL: Irwin, 1992), p. 609.
20. Kathleen How, "Meet Estée Lauder's Newest Supermodel Face," The Cut, May 15, 2018, www.thecut.com/2018/05/grace-elizabeth-is-este-lauders-newest-spokesmodel.html.
21. James E. Ellis, "Why Overseas? 'Cause That's Where the Sales Are," *BusinessWeek*, January 10, 1994, p. 63; "How CAA Bottled Coca-Cola," *Fortune*, November 15, 1993, p. 156; Deborah Hauss, "Global Communications Come of Age," *Public Relations Journal*, August 1993, pp. 22–23; Sally Solo, "How to Listen to Consumers," *Fortune*, January 11, 1993, pp. 77–78; Jennifer Lawrence, "Delta Gears Up for Global Fight," *Advertising Age*, August 19, 1991, pp. 3, 44; Charles Hennessy, "Global-degook," *BusinessLondon*, March 1990, p. 131; Raymond Serafin, "W. B. Doner Hits a Gusher," *Advertising Age*, June 6, 1988, p. 43.
22. Jim Patterson, "Viewpoint: Global Communication Requires a Global Understanding," *Adweek*, October 31, 1994, p. 46; "Efficacy of Global Ad Prospects Is Questioned in Firm's Survey," *The Wall Street Journal*, September 13, 1984, p. 29.
23. Jim Patterson, "Viewpoint: Global Communication Requires a Global Understanding," *Adweek*, October 31, 1994, p. 46.
24. Aelita G. B. Martinsons and Maris G. Martinsons, "In Search of Structural Excellence," *Leadership & Organization Development Journal* 15, no. 2 (1994), pp. 24–28.
25. Frederick R. Gamble, *What Advertising Agencies Are—What They Do and How They Do It*, 7th ed. (New York: American Association of Advertising Agencies, 1970), p. 4.
26. "Brands on Trial," *Adweek*, May 24, 1993, pp. 24–31.
27. Melanie Wells, "The Interactive Edge—Part II: Desperately Seeking the Super Highway," *Advertising Age*, August 22, 1994, pp. 14–19.
28. Jennifer Gilbert, "Gotham Gathers Interactive under Hinkaty," *Advertising Age*, July 31, 2000, p. 42, http://webgate.sdsu.edu.
29. Andrew McMains, "Debunking the Consolidation Myth," *Adweek*, February 20, 2006, www.adweek.com/aw/national/article_display.jsp?vnu_content_id=1002035233.
30. *Advertising Age* Data Center, "World's 10 Largest Media Agencies," 2014.
31. Beth Snyder, "True North Unites Modem, Poppe into Digital Force," *Advertising Age*, May 1998 (Articles & Opinions, http://adage.com); Kate Maddox, "Agency Pitch Heats Up Camp Interactive Show," *Advertising Age*, August 1998 (Articles & Opinions, http://adage.com); "Think New Ideas Takes Answer-Think Moniker," *Advertising Age*, April 3, 2000 (Interactive Daily, http://adage.com).

32. "Fact Sheet: Inside the AAAA," *American Association of Advertising Agencies,* August 15, 2000, *www.aaaa.org/inside/about_us.html*.

33. Kevin Goldman, "IBM—Account Fight Lifts Planner Profile," *The Wall Street Journal,* October 26, 1993, p. B8.

34. Nancy D. Holt, "Workspaces/A Look at Where People Work," *The Wall Street Journal,* January 22, 2003, p. B6.

35. Sally Goll Beatty, "Leo Burnett Group to Decentralize U.S. Operations," *The Wall Street Journal,* September 17, 1997, p. B10; Sally Goll Beatty, "Leo Burnett to Offer Small-Agency Style," *The Wall Street Journal,* September 18, 1997, p. B4; Dottie Enrico, "Ad Agency Ready for a New Day," *USA Today,* September 19, 1997, p. 5B.

36. Alison Fahey, "Agencies Look to Shape Up, Slim Down," *Adweek,* August 16, 1993, p. 4.

37. William F. Arens and Jack J. Whidden, "La Publicité aux Etats-Unis: Les Symptómes et les Stratégies d'une Industrie Surpleuplée," *L'Industrie de la Publicité au Québec* (Montreal: Le Publicité-Club de Montréal, 1992), pp. 383–84.

38. Jon Lafayette and Cleveland Horton, "Shops to Clients: Pay Up—4A's Members Call for an End to Free Services," *Advertising Age,* March 19, 1990, pp. 1, 66.

39. Andrew Jaffe, "Has Leo Burnett Come to the End of the 'Free Overservice' Era?" *Adweek,* December 6, 1993, p. 46; Melanie Wells and Laurel Wentz, "Coke Trims Commissions," *Advertising Age,* January 31, 1994, p. 2.

40. Nikki Kria, "4A's Unveils Enlightened Workplace Certification® Program," *American Association of Advertising Agencies,* February 12, 2018, *www.aaaa.org/4as-unveils-enlightened-workplace-certification-program/*.

41. Shareen Pathak, "'The Schoolyard Has Been Replaced by the Office': The Bullying Problem at Agencies," *Digiday,* February 19, 2018, *https://digiday.com/marketing/schoolyard-replaced-office-bullying-problem-agencies/*.

42. Shareen Pathak, "'The Schoolyard Has Been Replaced by the Office': The Bullying Problem at Agencies," *Digiday,* February 19, 2018, *https://digiday.com/marketing/schoolyard-replaced-office-bullying-problem-agencies/*.

43. Nikki Kria, "4A's Announces Open Enrollment and In-Market Training Tour for Its Enlightened Workplace Certification Program," *Cision,* May 21, 2018, *www.prweb.com/releases/2018/05/prweb15503025.htm*.

44. John Micklethwait, "Cut the Ribbon," *The Economist,* June 9, 1990, pp. S16–S17; Tom Eisenhart, "Guaranteed Results' Plan May Suit Business Marketers," *Business Marketing,* July 1990, p. 32; Jim Kirk, "Miller Sets Free Rates," *Adweek,* January 24, 1994, p. 4.

45. James R. Willis Jr., "Winning New Business: An Analysis of Advertising Agency Activities," *Journal of Advertising Research,* September/October 1992, pp. 10–16.

46. Andrew Jaffe, "The Fine Art of Keeping Clients Happy While Chasing New Business," *Adweek,* May 9, 1994, p. 38.

47. Melanie Wells, "Courtship by Consultant," *Advertising Age,* January 31, 1994, pp. 10–11; "Accounts on the Move," *Advertising Age,* June 2, 1997, *http://adage.com*; "H&R Block Review Down to 3," *Advertising Age,* May 17, 2000 (Daily Deadline, *http://adage.com*); "Monster, L.L. Bean Open Account Review," *Advertising Age,* July 12, 2000 (Daily Deadline, *http://adage.com*); "Deutsch Tunes in $70 Mil DirecTV Account," *Advertising Age,* August 18, 2000 (Daily Deadline, *http://adage.com*).

48. Thorolf Helgesen, "Advertising Awards and Advertising Agency Performance," *Journal of Advertising Research,* July/August 1994, pp. 43–53.

49. Daniel B. Wackman, Charles T. Salmon, and Caryn C. Salmon, "Developing an Advertising Agency–Client Relationship," *Journal of Advertising Research,* December 1986/January 1987, pp. 21–28.

50. Kevin Goldman, "FCB Bumps Ayer as AT&T's Top Agency," *The Wall Street Journal,* November 22, 1994, p. B8.

51. Kevin Goldman, "Ties That Bind Agency, Client Unravel," *The Wall Street Journal,* November 16, 1994, p. B6.

52. Yumiko Ono, "Apple Picks TBWA," *The Wall Street Journal,* August 11, 1997, p. B3.

53. Burt Helm and David Kiley, "Wal-Mart Leaves Draft Out in the Cold," *Bloomberg Businessweek,* December 7, 2006.

54. Steven Raye, "Agencies, Clients: It's Mutual Contribution for Mutual Gain," *Brandweek,* September 12, 1994, p. 20; Ed Moser, "Inside Information," *Adweek,* January 24, 1994, p. 22; Mat Toor, "Fear and Favour in Adland," *Marketing* (UK), November 15, 1990, pp. 30–32.

55. Paul C. N. Mitchell, Harold Cataquet, and Stephen Hague, "Establishing the Causes of Disaffection in Agency–Client Relations," *Journal of Advertising Research,* March/April 1992, pp. 41–48.

56. Isabelle T. D. Szmigin, "Managing Quality in Business-to-Business Services," *European Journal of Marketing* 27, no. 1 (1993), pp. 5–21.

57. Ron Jackson, "If You Hire a Vendor, You Get a Vendor Mindset," *Marketing News,* April 25, 1991, pp. 13–14.

58. Steven A. Meyerowitz, "Ad Agency Conflicts: The Law and Common Sense," *Business Marketing,* June 1987, p. 16.

59. Andrew Jaffe, "For Agencies, Conflict Taboo Seems Strong as Ever," *Adweek,* January 24, 1994, p. 46.

60. Betsy Sharkey, "New Suit," *Adweek,* June 20, 1994, p. 20.

61. Newspaper Association of America, "Total Paid Circulation," *www.naa.org/TrendsandNumbers/Total-Paid-Circulation.aspx*.

62. "Average Paid and Verified Weekday Circulation of the New York Times from 2000 to 2018," *Statista, www.statista.com/statistics/273503/average-paid-weekday-circulation-of-the-new-york-times/*.

63. Number of magazines in the United States from 2002 to 2017. Statista, *www.statista.com/statistics/238589/number-of-magazines-in-the-united-states/*.

64. U.S. Census Bureau, "Information and Communications," *Statistical Abstract of the United States, www.census.gov*.

65. Sean Savage, "For Firms on Network, Net Gains Can Be Great," *ComputerLink,* Knight Ridder News Service, November 29, 1994, pp. 3–4.

66. Lindsay Stein, "What to Expect at the 4A's Annual Conference, Including John Leguizamo," *AdAge,* March 28, 2018, *https://adage.com/article/agency-news/4a-s-leader-marla-kaplowitz/312895/*.

67. Bennett Bennett, "Marla Kaplowitz on 4A's Relationship with ANA," *The Drum,* December 12, 2017, *www.thedrum.com/news/2017/12/12/marla-kaplowitz-4a-s-relationship-with-ana-it-takes-time-make-sure-the-trust-and*.

68. "4A's Chief Seeks 'Client of the Future,' Launches Inclusion Certification Program," *Beet TV, www.beet.tv/2018/04/marla-kaplowitz.htm*.

69. Katie RIchards, "Why the 4A's Chose MEC North America CEO Marla Kaplowitz as Its Next Leader," *Adweek,* February 27, 2017, *www.adweek.com/agencies/why-the-4as-chose-mec-north-america-ceo-marla-kaplowitz-as-its-next-leader/*.

70. Megan Graham, "4A's Accelerate: Industry Talks #WHATIF, Harassment and 'Frenemies,'" *https://adage.com/article/agency-news/4a-s-conference-industry-talks-whatif-harassment-frenemies/313078/*.

71. Think Marketing, The country on a can; Coca Cola Egypt latest campaign, April 18, 2017, *https://thinkmarketingmagazine.com/the-country-on-a-can-coca-cola-egypt-latest-campaign/*.

CHAPTER

5

Marketing and Consumer Behavior: The Foundations of IMC

LEARNING OBJECTIVES

To underline the importance of the marketing process in business and to define the role of advertising and other marketing communications tools in presenting the company and its products to the market. The successful advertising practitioner must understand the relationship between marketing activities and the way consumers behave. Ideally, it is this relationship that shapes the creation of effective advertising.

After studying this chapter, you will be able to:

LO5-1   Define marketing and explain the relationship between consumer needs and product utility.

LO5-2   Identify the key participants in the marketing process.

LO5-3   Explain why consumer behavior is the key to IMC strategy.

LO5-4   Outline the psychological processes in consumer behavior.

LO5-5   Describe the fundamental motives behind consumer purchases.

LO5-6   Elaborate on the interpersonal influences on consumer behavior.

LO5-7   Explain how nonpersonal influences affect consumer behavior.

On January 24th,
Apple Computer will introduce
Macintosh.
And you'll see why 1984
won't be like "1984."

Imagine you've created the most amazing product in the world. Wouldn't you want to introduce it with one of the greatest ads of all time? Steve Jobs thought so, and fought to make it happen. But it almost didn't. ∎ Apple's origins date to the late 1970s when Jobs and his engineering buddy Steve (Woz) Wozniak bonded over a shared obsession with building a machine that allowed someone to hack AT&T and make free (illegal) long-distance phone calls.[1] ∎ Amazingly, they created a simple device that worked as promised. After a potential "customer" demanded the machine and pointed a gun at Jobs' stomach, he decided to find other things to build. ∎ So they turned to the new technology of personal computers. The Apple I was little more than a motherboard sold directly to hobby shops. Realizing the value of a more polished and consumer-friendly product, Jobs and Wozniak created a true computer, the Apple II. The machine was an immediate hit, beloved by technology enthusiasts, and it helped the company attract significant venture capital. ∎ But trouble was brewing. Jobs had a unique talent for rubbing people the wrong way. Intense, abrasive, moody, self-absorbed, and thoroughly unconventional, he was thought by many to be too immature to lead a growing firm. ∎ Jobs was relegated to a development team. Worse, it was a "B-team" assigned to a secondary product. Apple's hopes rested with a successor to the Apple II named "Lisa." Jobs was given the task of developing a "backup," which came to be called the Macintosh. ∎ True to form, Jobs became obsessed with making the Mac a dream computer. Intensely competitive, he wanted a device that would not only outsell the IBM PC, the industry's leader, but that would also crush the Lisa. Jobs believed computers could be instruments of personal liberation and empowerment. So he infused the Mac with an assortment of cutting-edge technologies, including a revolutionary graphical user interface (GUI). The interface was beautiful, incorporating a variety of fonts, colors, and graphics. The machine could even talk. ∎ By the end of 1983, the Mac was ready. Apple enlisted a well-known California ad agency, Chiat/Day, to help introduce the machine. Jobs told agency executives that the popular IBM PC represented a bland, almost sinister technology, one that turned individuals into drones. But the beautifully designed Macintosh, he explained, was an instrument of freedom, creativity, and self-expression.[2] ∎ Chiat/Day pitched an idea that positioned the Mac against the PC using the metaphor of George Orwell's novel *1984*. If the PC helped to "enslave the masses," the Mac would liberate the individual. Jobs loved it.

■ Film director Ridley Scott (*Blade Runner, Alien, Gladiator*) was hired to direct the ad. The script depicted a future in which gray drones stare blankly at a giant screen depicting Big Brother (IBM). Suddenly, a young woman with a sledge hammer runs toward the screen, chased by guards. She twirls, tosses her hammer into the screen, and changes the future forever. The ad ends with the tag line "On January 24th, Apple Computer will introduce Macintosh. And you'll see why 1984 won't be like '1984.'" ■ Jobs, Woz, and everyone at Chiat/Day loved it. But the Apple board was not so sure. Expensive to produce, the ad was supposed to run during the most costly ad buy of the year, the 1984 Super Bowl. A single showing would cost well over a million dollars, big money for a young technology company struggling to generate profits. Getting cold feet at the last minute, Apple's board decided to cancel the buy and Chiat/Day was instructed to sell back the airtime. ■ Jobs was furious, as was Chiat/Day. The agency claimed it could not find a buyer for the ad time, although legend has it that this wasn't true. ■ And so "1984" debuted during the Super Bowl. Audiences and critics alike were awestruck. It became an instant classic, even though it ran on network television just once. In fact, the "1984" ad helped to establish the Super Bowl as the place where the very best ads premiere each year.[3] Cannes named the spot the best of the year, and *Ad Age* eventually ranked it 12th in its list of the 100 greatest ads of the century. Best of all, the Macintosh was introduced to broad acclaim and became a big seller for Apple. ■ Unfortunately, even this sweet success could not prevent conflicts between Jobs and Apple execs from boiling over. In 1985, things became so bad that he was asked to leave the company. He would return years later to lead Apple to new heights and oversee the development of amazing products, such as the iPhone and iPad. And Apple would continue to be associated with a variety of great ad campaigns. ■ But no Apple campaign would achieve greater respect than "1984." Beautifully produced, the ad was much more than great entertainment. It communicated in a powerful, almost irresistible way Jobs' belief that Apple was the future of computing.[4] By vividly comparing IBM to Big Brother, and Apple to a beautiful young rebel, the spot may well have been the greatest example of positioning in advertising history.[5]

Marketing: Creating Satisfying Exchanges by Creating Utility

LO 5-1

All marketers are challenged about how to best present their products, services, and ideas effectively. To do this, they must comprehend the important relationship between the product and its market. This is the task of marketing.

A company prospers only if it can attract and keep customers who are willing to pay for its offerings. Marketers must be able to identify and locate prospective customers—where they live, work, and play—and then understand their needs, wants, and desires; create products and services that satisfy such desires better than the firm's competitors; and finally communicate information about the company's offerings in a powerful, clear, and credible way.

This chapter will help you better understand IMC's role in the marketing function and introduce the human factors that ultimately shape responses to advertising.

The Relationship of Marketing to IMC

In Chapter 1 we noted that **marketing** is used by management to plan and execute the *conception, pricing, promotion,* and *distribution* of its products. The ultimate purpose of marketing is to create exchanges that satisfy the perceived needs, wants, and objectives of individuals and organizations.

Integrated marketing communications (IMC) is just one of many tools used in the promotional aspect of marketing. But how the IMC is done, and where it is placed, depends largely on the other aspects of the marketing mix and for whom the messages are intended.

Customer Needs and Product Utility

Companies use marketing research to discover the needs and wants that exist in the marketplace. The goal is to use this information for *product shaping* and development—designing products, through manufacturing, repackaging, or IMC, to satisfy more fully the customers' needs and wants.

This definition of marketing shows that one of the important elements is the special relationship between a customer's *needs* and a product's *need-satisfying potential.* This is known as the product's utility. **Utility** is the product's ability to satisfy both functional needs and symbolic (or psychological) wants.[6] One of the roles of IMC is to communicate this utility. Thus, some messages suggest how well a product works; others tout glamor, sex appeal, or status.

To consider one example, the Ram 1500 truck competes in a challenging market. While its overall sales are good, it trails rivals Ford (F150) and Chevrolet (Silverado). In 2019 Ram introduced cabin upgrades that appeal to a new kind of utility, the "luxury truck." While the motives people think consumers would have for purchasing a pickup truck might involve the need to perform outdoor work or a desire for off-road driving, the new Ram Limited has standard features that include a lush cabin, Harmon Kardon speakers, and a 12-inch touchscreen console that gives Tesla a run for its money. These new features represent changes in the utilities sought by truck buyers and show how closely effective marketers must understand utility in the marketplace.[7]

Exchanges, Perception, and Satisfaction

Recall that the purpose of marketing is "to create exchanges that satisfy the perceived needs, wants, and objectives of individuals and organizations." Three important ideas are expressed in this definition: *exchanges, perception,* and *satisfaction.* Let's take a brief look at each.

Exchanges: The Purpose of Marketing and IMC

Any transaction in which one person or organization trades something of value with another is an **exchange.** Exchange is the traditional, theoretical core of marketing. We all engage in exchanges. It's a natural part of our human self-interest. Buyers do it to acquire more things and improve their lives or the lives of others. Sellers do it to grow their businesses and make a profit.

Marketing facilitates these exchanges, thus increasing everyone's potential for satisfaction. How? In a variety of ways: by developing products people want, by pricing them attractively, by distributing them to convenient locations, and by informing consumers about them through advertising and other promotional tools. By providing information, IMC makes people aware of the availability of products and of the selection alternatives among different brands. It helps communicate product features and benefits, price options, and locations where the product can be purchased. In the case of *direct marketing,* IMC may even close the sale.

Perception Is Everything

The essence of a successful marketing transaction is that each party is satisfied with the exchange. Companies must therefore sell their goods at a profit. Customers must believe they got their money's worth. But sometimes the people who are about to engage in a business exchange feel apprehensive. They may worry that the exchange is not equal, even when it is truly fair. This is where *perception* comes in. The perception of inequity is more likely if the customer has little knowledge of the product. In this case, the more knowledgeable party (the seller) must reassure the buyer—perhaps through IMC—that a satisfactory exchange is possible. If the seller can provide the information and inspiration the buyer seeks, both parties may recognize the potential for a *perceived equal-value exchange.* Without this perception, though, an exchange is unlikely. For example, if people don't believe the benefits of an iPhone XS Max are worth $1,400, they won't buy one, no matter how much Apple spends on IMC.

Apple advertising fits with Apple products. They are both "cool" and, at a deeper level, the ads and the products share other features: simplicity, elegance, and style. As shown in the two Apple ads on this page, both share common design elements, yet both are also strikingly different. What are some of the differences in the two ads and, despite those differences, why do you think both are effective examples of advertising?

(both): The Advertising Archives

So marketers must first acquire an understanding of their customers. What do they need? What do they want? How do they see us now? Once marketers develop a deep understanding of their customers, they can be more effective in trying to change their customers' perception of the product (awareness, attitude, interest) and their customers' belief in the product's ability (value) to satisfy their perceived wants or needs (utility).

IMC can do this in many ways. By using just the right mood lighting or music, for example, a commercial can simultaneously capture customers' attention and stimulate their emotions toward the goal of need or want fulfillment. If customers are aware of the product and its value, and if they decide to satisfy the particular want or need the product addresses, they are more likely to act.[8] Because perception is so important to advertisers, we discuss it in greater detail later in this chapter.

Satisfaction: The Goal of the Customer

Even after an exchange occurs, *satisfaction* remains an issue. Satisfaction must occur every time customers use the product, or people won't think they got an equal-value exchange. Satisfaction leads to more exchanges: Satisfied customers repurchase, and satisfied customers tell their friends. Positive word of mouth creates even more sales and contributes to a good reputation. And while word of mouth has always been important, it is crucial in the new age of social media such as Facebook. Thus, while satisfaction is the goal of the customer, it must also be the fundamental goal of any sophisticated marketer.

IMC *reinforces* satisfaction by reminding customers why they bought the product, helping them defend the purchase against skeptical friends, and enabling them to persuade others to buy it. It should be easy to see why messages founded on false or empty promises won't prove effective. If a product performs poorly, the negative effect will be even more far-reaching. And good campaigns for a poor product can actually hasten the brand's demise. The better the campaign, the more people will try the product—once. And the more who try an unsatisfactory product, the more who will reject it—and tell their friends.

The greenest family of notebooks

Apple's ads succeed because they speak to Apple consumers and address the utilities these consumers want.

Xinhua/eyevine/Redux Pictures

The Key Participants in the Marketing Process

LO **5-2**

Customers

People's needs and wants change regularly, and marketers constantly promote a variety of products for customer attention and interest. This makes the marketing process very dynamic. At times, it seems like everybody is searching for an exchange. At other times, it seems nobody is. Marketing exchanges depend on three types of participants: *customers, markets* (groups of customers), and *marketers.*

Customers are the people or organizations that consume goods and services. They fall into three general categories: *current customers, prospective customers,* and *centers of influence.*

Current customers have already bought something from a business or brand; in fact, they may buy regularly. One way to measure a business's success is by calculating the number of its current customers and their repeat purchases. **Prospective customers** are people about to make an exchange or considering it. **Centers of influence** are those people or groups whose ideas and actions others respect. A center of influence is often the link to many prospective customers.

Markets

The second participant in the marketing process is the **market,** which is a group of current customers, prospective customers, and noncustomers who share a common interest, need, or desire; who have the money or resources to spend to satisfy needs or solve problems; and who have the authority to buy.[9] As we discuss more fully in Chapter 6, a market never includes everybody. Companies design messages for four broad classifications of markets:

1. **Consumer markets** are made up of people who buy for their own use. Both Ram and BMW, for example, aim at the consumer market. But they cater to different groups within that market. They promote some vehicles to single women, others to upscale young families, and still others to retired people. The consumer market is huge, accounting for a significant amount of spending in the U.S. economy.[10] Chapter 6 discusses ways to categorize consumer segments.

2. **Business markets** are made up of organizations that buy services, natural resources, and component products that they resell, use to conduct their business, or use to manufacture another product. While you are likely more familiar with

How does this ad, showing empty-nest parents holding a bag of Celebrations Candy, appeal to the important Boomer market? Do you think the ad also appeals to younger consumers?

Source: Mars, Incorporated

consumer promotions, almost half of all marketing is business-to-business. In the United States, business buyers purchase trillions of dollars' worth of manufactured goods every year, billions more of raw materials, and billions more for the services of law firms, accountants, airlines, and advertising agencies.[11] The two most important business markets are *reseller markets* and *industrial markets.*

Reseller markets buy products to resell them. Ram, for example, distributes trucks to consumers through a network of independently owned dealers. Similarly, Minute Maid relies on retail grocers to carry its brand of juices, or they will never be sold to consumers. Apple sells its technologies in its own stores, but also sells through retailers such as Best Buy.

Industrial markets include millions of firms that buy products used to produce other goods and services.[12] Manufacturers of plant equipment and machinery promote to industrial markets, as do office suppliers, computer companies, and telephone companies. Chapter 6 categorizes industrial markets by factors of industry segment, geographic location, and size.

3. **Government markets** buy products for municipal, state, federal, and other government activities. Some firms are immensely successful selling only to government markets. They promote post office vehicles, police and military weapons, and tax collector office equipment to government buyers.

For the high-involvement consumer, information is everything. This ad for Charles Schwab offers useful facts to potential investors. The information helps consumers decide if an account with Charles Schwab fits their investment needs.

Source: Charles Schwab & Co.

Apple's products appeal to many different markets. While consumers view iPads as entertainment devices, the product is also attractive to millions of businesspeople.

Mahod84/Shutterstock

4. **Transnational (or global) markets** include any of the other three markets located in foreign countries. Every country has consumers, resellers, industries, and governments. So what's the difference between the transnational market and the domestic U.S. or Canadian market for the same product? Environment. The environment in France differs from that in Japan. The environment in Brazil differs from that in Saudi Arabia. Sometimes, as in the case of Switzerland, environments even vary widely within a single country. Targeting markets across national boundaries presents challenges and opportunities for contemporary marketers, so we deal with the subject wherever applicable throughout this book.

Marketers

The third participant in the marketing process, **marketers,** includes every person or organization that has products, services, or ideas to sell. Manufacturers market consumer and business products. Farmers market wheat; doctors market medical services; banks market financial products; and political organizations market philosophies and candidates. To be successful, marketers must know their markets intimately—*before* they create messages.

Consumer Behavior: The Key to IMC Strategy

LO **5-3**

Think about your friends or the people you work with. How well do you know them? Could you describe their lifestyles and the kinds of products they prefer? Do they typically eat out or cook for themselves? Do they ski? Play tennis? If so, what brands do they buy? Do you know how often they use social media? What TV programs they watch? What websites they frequent? If you were Apple's advertising manager and wanted to advertise a new iPhone to these people, what type of appeal would you use? What media would you use to reach them?

The Importance of Knowing the Consumer

Marketers spend a lot of money to keep individuals and groups of individuals (markets) interested in their products. To succeed, they need to understand what makes potential customers behave the way they do. The goal is to get enough market data to develop profiles of buyers—to find the common ground (and symbols) for communication. This involves the study of **consumer behavior:** the mental and emotional processes and the physical activities of people who purchase and use goods and services to satisfy needs and wants.[13] The behavior of **organizational buyers** (the people who purchase products and services for use in business and government) is also important. We examine this in Chapter 6.

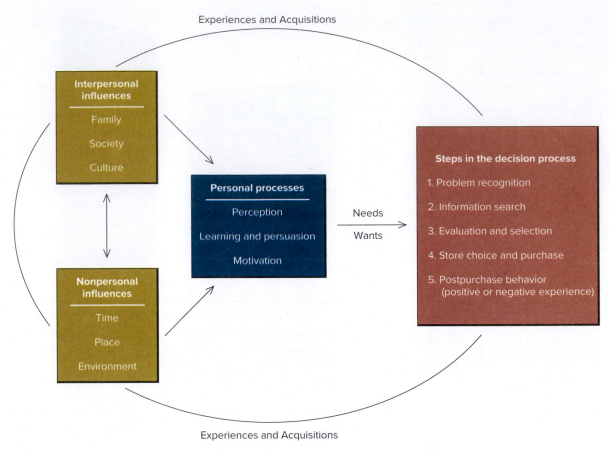

Experiences and Acquisitions

Interpersonal influences

Family

Society

Culture

Nonpersonal influences

Time

Place

Environment

Personal processes

Perception

Learning and persuasion

Motivation

Needs

Wants

Steps in the decision process

1. Problem recognition

2. Information search

3. Evaluation and selection

4. Store choice and purchase

5. Postpurchase behavior (positive or negative experience)

Experiences and Acquisitions

Exhibit 5-1
The basic consumer decision process comprises a set of fundamental steps that the consumer experiences during and after the purchase process. Advertising can affect the consumer's attitude at any point in this process.

The Consumer Decision Process: An Overview

Social scientists develop many theories of consumer behavior to explain the process of making a purchase decision. Let's look at this information from the viewpoint of the advertiser.

The moment someone recognizes a need that might be satisfied by a purchase, he or she begins the **consumer decision process.** Exhibit 5-1 presents the basic steps of this process. It involves a sequence of activities: *problem recognition* (which may occur as a result of seeing an ad), *information search, evaluation and selection, store choice and purchase,* and, finally, *postpurchase behavior.* For simple, habitual, everyday purchases, the decision-making process is short. But in those situations where the consumer is highly involved in the purchase, it's not at all unusual for the consumer to substantially extend the decision process.

Whether the process is limited or extended, many factors play a role in the way consumers behave. These include a series of personal subprocesses that are shaped by various influences.

The three **personal processes** govern the way we discern raw sensory information (*stimuli*) and translate it into feelings, thoughts, beliefs, and actions. The personal processes are *perception, learning and persuasion,* and *motivation.*

Second, our mental processes and behavior are affected by two sets of influences. **Interpersonal influences** include *family, society,* and *culture.* **Nonpersonal influences**—factors often outside the consumer's control—include *time, place,* and *environment.*

After engaging these processes and responding to these influences, we face the pivotal decision: to buy or not to buy. Taking that final step requires **evaluation of alternatives,** in which we choose brands, sizes, styles, and colors. If we do decide to buy, our **postpurchase evaluation** will affect whether or not we buy again.

Psychological Processes in Consumer Behavior

LO 5-4

Assume you are the brand manager preparing to launch Apple's newest campaign. What's your first objective?

The first task in promoting any new product is to create awareness (*perception*) that the product exists. The second is to provide enough compelling information (*learning and persuasion*) about the product for prospective customers to find interest and make an informed decision. Finally, you want your advertising to stimulate customers' desire (*motivation*) to satisfy their needs and wants by trying the product. Apple generates great excitement with its product rollouts. Rumors, perhaps some even planted by the company, typically precede the announcements. Technology reporters trek to Apple's headquarters on the exciting day news about a new line of phones or computers is shared. After the announcements, Apple's website is given an immediate overhaul to feature the new products. And advertising spending is ramped up to be sure everyone is aware of the new features consumers can expect.

By focusing on the three personal processes of consumer behavior—perception, learning and persuasion, and motivation—advertisers can better evaluate how their messages are perceived.

The Consumer Perception Process

As we noted before, perception is everything. It guides all our activities from the people we associate with to the products we buy. How a consumer perceives each of the different brands in a category determines which ones he or she uses.[14] The perception challenge, therefore, is the first and greatest hurdle advertisers must cross. Some marketers spend millions of dollars on national advertising, sales promotion, point-of-purchase displays, and other marketing communications only to discover that many consumers don't remember the product or the promotion. And really, why should they? The average adult may be exposed to thousands of ads each day but notices only a handful and remembers even fewer.[15] How does this happen? The answer lies in the principle of perception.

The term **perception** refers to the information we receive through our five senses. There are several key elements to the consumer perception process, as shown in Exhibit 5-2.

A **stimulus** is something (light, sound, scent) that impacts our senses. It may originate within our bodies, as when we notice that we feel hungry at lunchtime. Or it may originate from outside our bodies, as when we see an ad for an iPhone and decide it looks beautiful.

IMC messages are external stimuli that can appear in a variety of forms: a window display at a local department store, the brightly colored labels on cans of Campbell's tomato soup, or even the red price tag on a pair of skis at REI. These objects are all physical in nature; they stimulate our senses (with varying degrees of intensity) in ways that can be measured.

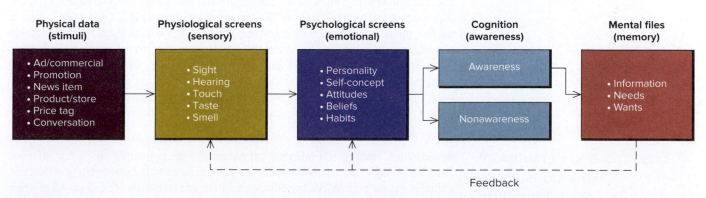

Exhibit 5-2
This model of the consumer perception process portrays how consumers perceive, accept, and remember an ad or other stimulus to buy.

Screens are the barriers that IMC must penetrate. How does the appearance of Katy Perry in this Super Bowl ad for Pepsi help attract attention and break through perceptual and psychological barriers?

Source: PepsiCo Inc.

Physiological Screens

Before a stimulus can be perceived, it must first penetrate a set of **physiological screens,** subconscious filters that shield us from unwanted messages.

The physiological screens comprise the five senses: sight, hearing, touch, taste, and smell. They detect the incoming data and measure the dimension and intensity of the physical stimuli. A sight-impaired person can't read an ad in *Sports Illustrated.* And if the type in a movie ad is too small for the average reader, it won't be read. Similarly, if the music in a TV commercial for a furniture store is not complementary to the message, the viewer may tune out, change channels, or even turn off the TV. A message is effectively screened out when the viewer can't detect it; perception does not occur, and the furniture goes unsold.[16]

Cognition

The third key element in perception is **cognition:** comprehending the stimulus. Once we detect the stimulus and allow it through our perceptual screens, we can comprehend and accept it.

But each of us has his or her own reality. For example, some people admire Apple products for their simplicity and beauty. Others buy Apple products because they are best sellers and find it comforting to use the same technology as most others. Still others are Apple fanatics, closely monitoring the technology press for any word on new product developments. And some people, perhaps wanting to be seen as different from the masses, would never consider an Apple product, no matter how good. That person's reality is considerably different.

Just as we have screens at the level of perception, so too do screens exist at the level of cognition. Each consumer uses **psychological screens** to evaluate, filter, and personalize information according to subjective emotional standards. These screens evaluate data based on *innate factors,* such as the consumer's personality and instinctive human needs, and *learned factors,* such as self-concept, interests, attitudes, beliefs, past experiences, and lifestyle. They help consumers summarize unwieldy or complex data. For example, perceptual screens help us accept or reject symbolic ideas, such as the sexy commercial for Levi's Dockers in which a man and a number of women dance provocatively in a nightclub. Prospective partners pull at the man by grabbing his belt loops. When he finally leaves with one, the voice-over says, "You'll get worn out before they do." The campaign is targeted toward upscale, fashion-forward men in the 25-to-34 age group who critically influence others.

Psychologists believe[17] that people use two systems for thinking, one that is relatively fast, uncontrolled, and immediate ("I'm hungry and that burger looks amazing!") and one that is slower and more deliberate ("But remember you are on a diet. Get a salad"). We use the fast, intuitive system to make many decisions and only call on the slower, effortful system when we stop ourselves and recall that the decision requires deliberation and caution. Advertising, through provocative imagery and powerful copy, is remarkably effective at engaging the fast system. For many low-priced, low-involvement purchases (buying a soft drink), the fast system works fine, but for important purchases (e.g., a computer), consumers may find themselves experiencing an internal dialog ("That laptop is gorgeous; I have to have it. But should I really spend that much money?").

Learning and Persuasion: How Consumers Process Information

By definition, **learning** is a relatively permanent change in thought process or behavior. Learning produces our habits and skills. It also contributes to the development of interests, attitudes, beliefs, preferences, prejudices, emotions, and standards of conduct—all of which affect, among other things, our eventual purchase decisions.

Mental Files

Cognition is not just about how we respond to things we perceive, it is also about how we store information for later use. Many promotional messages rely on consumers making a purchase long after they are exposed to a brand message. According to psychologists, information in memory is not stored randomly, but rather in **mental files.**

Memory is a limited resource, and one susceptible to some well-known biases. As an example, pause for a moment and consider whether there are more words that begin with the letter *k* (i.e., *kangaroo*) versus words that have *k* in the third position (i.e., *Arkansas*). What is your guess? Many people are surprised to discover there are nearly three times more words (*ask, askance, ark*) with *k* in the third position. But when we search through memory, our mental files make it easier to retrieve words by their first letter. We then confuse this ease of retrieval with the frequency of occurrence. This "availability" heuristic is just one example of how the structure of our cognitive system influences what we recall and how we decide.[18] For another, see Ad Lab 5–A.

Because screens are such a major challenge to advertisers, it's important to understand what's in the consumer's mental files and, if possible, modify them in favor of the advertiser's product. That brings us to the second process in consumer behavior: *learning and persuasion.*

Theories of Learning

Conditioning theories suggest that learning occurs when consumers associate stimuli or behaviors with things they desire. **Classical conditioning** is a kind of learning first reported by the Russian psychologist Ivan Pavlov. Pavlov knew that dogs salivate when they are presented with food. He wanted to test whether another stimulus, one that had no significant meaning to his dogs, could also elicit salivation if it became associated with the food. Pavlov called food an *unconditioned stimulus* and salivation an *unconditioned* (naturally occurring) *response* for the dogs. In his experiment, he began consistently ringing a bell just before giving his dogs food. He found that after a number of occasions the dogs began salivating just from the sound of the bell. The bell was now a *conditioned stimulus*. The dogs associated the bell with something desirable.[19]

The American psychologist B. F. Skinner developed another theory of learned association, which he labeled **operant conditioning.** Operant conditioning involves the reinforcement of behavior with a reward or punishment. Skinner's "subjects" were frequently pigeons who received food when they performed a desired activity, such as pecking a bar. Both *positive reinforcement* (a reward such as food) and *negative reinforcement* (removing a noxious stimulus such as a loud noise) increase the likelihood of a reinforced behavior.

Of course, consumers are not pigeons or dogs, and some people find it hard to believe that they learn this way. In fact, much knowledge is not from direct experience at all but from seeing what happens to others. You don't need to smoke to know it is dangerous or practice poor dental hygiene to know it leads to cavities. This was an insight that guided Albert Bandura, an American psychologist, to expand on conditioning theories and propose that people learn in a variety of ways, not just from personal experience. For example, people can watch what happens to other people (my friend Sam studied hard this semester, and as a result made the dean's list) and deduce the implications for themselves. Bandura's **social cognitive theory** provides a richer, cognitive perspective on how people learn. It suggests that consumers pay attention to the rewards and costs experienced by others in response to their actions. When people we know (called models by Bandura) experience good outcomes, we are motivated to imitate the behaviors that led to them. When they experience bad outcomes, we are motivated to avoid the behaviors that led to them. This is true whether the models are our friends and neighbors, or people appearing on our TV screens or YouTube videos.[20]

"Free" is a word that most people respond to positively. In operant conditioning, people associate rewards with specific behaviors. Pizza Hut uses operant conditioning effectively in the above ad.

The Advertising Archives

AD Lab 5–A

The Context of Choice: How a Product's Perceived Value Varies by the Products It Is Compared With

How much is something worth? Economists would say, "whatever someone is willing to pay for it." But the value of a thing can change based on its context. A fountain cola might cost you a dollar at a convenience store. The same drink will cost four or five dollars in a movie theater. How is that possible? And why would people pay so much more in the theater?

If a convenience store charges you four dollars for a drink, you just drive to the next place soft drinks are sold, where you know it will be cheaper. In the theater, your choice is different: pay four dollars or watch the movie without a drink. So context matters.

Interestingly, context can matter even in ads, as is demonstrated by marketing professor Dan Ariely in his fascinating book *Predictably Irrational: The Hidden Forces That Shape Our Decisions.* Ariely describes an experiment in which he asked students to choose the magazine subscription they would prefer.

> **Economist.com subscription**—US$59.00
>
> One-year subscription to Economist.com. Includes online access to all articles from *The Economist* since 1997.
>
> **Print subscription**—US$125.00
>
> One-year subscription to the print edition of *The Economist.*
>
> **Print & web subscription**—US$125.00
>
> One-year subscription to the print edition of *The Economist* and online access to all articles from *The Economist* since 1997.

Assuming you wanted to read *The Economist,* which of these options would be your first choice? Think about it for a moment before reading further.

When Ariely presented the choice to his students, the preferred option was the combined print and web subscription for $125. In fact 84 percent of the students chose this option. An additional 16 percent choose the cheaper web-only subscription for $59. No one chose the print-only subscription of $125.

In fact, the print-only option seems almost silly. Given that the combined print and web option costs exactly the same amount as print only, who in their right mind would choose the latter? Why offer consumers an option in an ad that no one would choose?

But if you think the unchosen print subscription option is presenting useless information, you would be mistaken. In fact, Ariely calls it a decoy. What is the purpose of the decoy? To make the print and web combination offer look particularly enticing. And Ariely proved it.

He created a different version of the ad that mimicked the one you just read, except that option 2, the print-only option, was not included.

> **Economist.com subscription**—US$59.00
>
> One-year subscription to Economist.com. Includes online access to all articles from *The Economist* since 1997.
>
> **Print & web subscription**—US$125.00
>
> One-year subscription to the print edition of *The Economist* and online access to all articles from *The Economist* since 1997.

Students who saw the second ad reversed their preferences, with more than two-thirds preferring the web-only subscription and just 32 percent preferring the print and web combination. The preferred option from the first ad became the distant loser in the second. And this happened because "useless" information from the first ad was deleted from the second. How can this be?

Ariely traces the effect to relativity. In the ad that features the decoy, the combination offer looks like a great deal. For the same amount of money as the print subscription, you can get the web version too. In the second ad, minus the decoy, that combination web plus print offer looks rather pricey.

The smart IMC professional understands that rational people are influenced by a variety of irrational pieces of information. And as Ariely demonstrates, information in IMC messages can influence perceptions of product value even when that information is "useless."

Laboratory Application

Type up the first version of *The Economist* ads that Ariely used above and give it to your friends. Ask them to choose their preferred options. For those friends who select option 3, point out that they were likely influenced by the "print-only" option. Do you think they will agree? Can you explain the decoy effect to them in a way that will help them understand the importance of context?

Visit a retail store that sells small appliances such as coffee makers or microwaves. See if you can spot "decoys" on the shelves, that is, models that no one would buy but that might steer shoppers towards pricier models.

Conditioning theories are more applicable to the simple, basic purchases consumers make every day—soap, cereal, toothpaste, paper towels, and so forth. And it is here that reinforcement advertising plays its most important role—along with superior product performance and good service. If learning is reinforced enough and repeat behavior is produced, a purchasing habit may result.

Learning and persuasion are closely linked. **Persuasion** occurs when people change a belief, attitude, or behavioral intention in response to a message (including advertising or personal selling).[21] Naturally, advertisers are very interested in persuasion and how it takes place.

Exhibit 5-3
The Elaboration Likelihood Model.

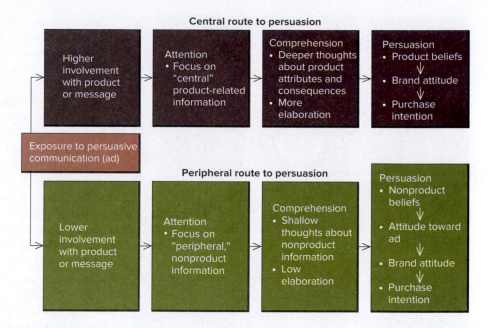

A Theory of Persuasion: The Elaboration Likelihood Model

In the 1970s, a pair of young psychologists, Richard Petty and John Cacioppo, discovered that persuasion can occur via two very different routes. One involves deliberation and thinking, while the other involves emotions and associations. Their discovery has direct implications for how marketers should try to persuade consumers to try or use a product. This is because these two different routes, the *central* (or deliberate) and the *peripheral* (or emotional), are best used in specific situations. Specifically, when consumers are highly involved with a product (an expensive purchase, for example), marketers would be wise to take advantage of factors known to be effective in central-route persuasion. On the other hand, when consumers have low involvement with a purchase (such as buying a soft drink or a pack of gum), smart marketers will leverage techniques known to be effective as facilitating persuasion via the peripheral route.[22]

The two routes are part of the **Elaboration Likelihood Model** in Exhibit 5-3. In the **central route to persuasion,** the high involvement that consumers have with the product or the message motivates them to pay attention to product-related information, such as product attributes and benefits or demonstrations of positive functional or psychological consequences. Because of their high involvement, consumers tend to learn cognitively and comprehend the ad-delivered information at deeper, more elaborate levels. This can lead to product beliefs, positive brand attitudes, and purchase intention.[23]

Suppose you are in the market for a significant purchase, say, a new phone. Because the purchase is relatively expensive, your level of involvement is higher. Perhaps you ask for advice from some friends or family members. You go online to check out expert reviews. And you probably read ads thoroughly to understand the variety of product features and benefits. That's central processing. And in that situation, a well-written, informative ad that addresses the important questions a consumer has about the product can be very persuasive.

The **peripheral route to persuasion** is very different. People who are not in the market for a product typically have low involvement with the product message. They have little or no reason to pay attention to it or to comprehend the factual information in an ad. As a result, consumers form few if any strong brand beliefs, attitudes, or purchase intentions. However, these consumers might attend to some peripheral aspects—say, the pictures or the colors in an ad or the actors in a commercial—for their entertainment value. And whatever they feel or think about these peripheral, nonproduct aspects might integrate into a positive attitude toward the ad. At some later date, if a purchase occasion does arise and the consumer needs to make some brand evaluation, these ad-related associations could be activated to form a brand attitude or purchase intention.

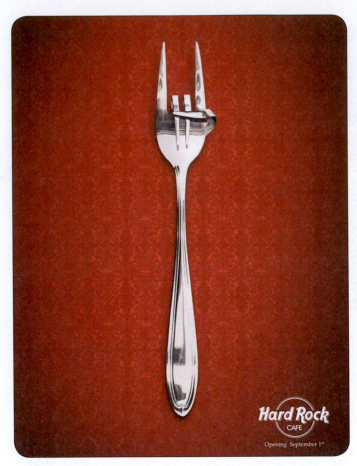

The bold image and clever use of a hand sign familiar to rockers suggest this ad by the Hard Rock Cafe is capitalizing on the peripheral route to persuasion.

Source: Hard Rock Cafe International, Inc.

Whether you like Coke or Pepsi better, both companies do a great job of using powerful peripheral cues to induce persuasion.

Most consumer ads are designed to facilitate peripheral processing for the simple reason that few of the messages we see have relevance to our immediate goals or needs. Our involvement is very low. That's why we also have very little recall of promotions we saw yesterday. In cases where there is little product differentiation, marketers may actually *want* us to engage in peripheral processing. Their campaigns focus more on image or entertainment than product features. This is typical for everyday low-involvement purchases such as soap, cereal, toothpaste, and chewing gum.

But when a product has a distinct advantage, the company's goal should be to encourage central route processing by increasing consumers' involvement with the message. One way is to use comparative advertising.[24]

A common tactic useful for both learning and persuasion is repetition. Just as a student prepares for an exam by repeating key information to memorize it, marketers should repeat key information to prospective customers so they remember the product's name and its benefits. Repeat messages penetrate consumer screens by rekindling memories of information from prior messages. Repeated messages are harder to forget, even when they receive little attention. Finally, research suggests that repeated exposure to something increases liking and persuasion. Repetition is a powerful, if expensive, tactic, so long as the message is strong.[25]

Learning Produces Attitudes and Interest

An **attitude** is our acquired evaluation of some idea or object. It is the positive or negative feelings or action tendencies that we learn and often cling to. For most companies, creating and maintaining positive consumer attitudes are critical to success.

In Japan, for instance, dishwashers are not a common household appliance. Not only is there very little space for them, Japanese homemakers feel guilty about using the labor-saving device. As a result, dishwasher manufacturers have designed smaller, space-saving machines and then promoted them using good hygiene themes rather than convenience appeals.[26]

For mature brands in categories with familiar, frequently purchased products, *brand interest* is even more critical for motivating action. **Brand interest** is an individual's openness or curiosity about a brand.[27] Enjoyable, entertaining campaigns can enhance interest in the brand and reduce the variety-seeking tendencies of consumers who become bored with using the same old product.[28]

Learning Leads to Habits and Brand Loyalty

Attitude is the mental side and *habit* the behavioral side of the same coin. **Habit**—the acquired behavior pattern that becomes nearly or completely automatic—is the natural extension of learning. We really are creatures of habit.

Most consumer behavior is habitual for three reasons: It's safe, simple, and essential. First, regardless of how we learned to make our purchase decision (through either central or peripheral route processing), if we discover a quality product, brand, or service, we feel *safe* repurchasing it through habit.

Second, habit is *simple*. To consider alternatives we must evaluate, compare, and then decide. This is difficult, time-consuming, and risky. If our utilities are met by a brand, the simplest thing to do is to keep buying it. Advertising for popular brands should reinforce

Apple seeks to offer users an "end-to-end" experience. In iTunes, this means everything the consumer wants to do with music can be done with Apple technologies. Apple is capitalizing on people's habits: If you know how to use one of the company's technologies, you are comfortable with them all.

Susan Van Etten/PhotoEdit

such thinking, while advertising for new brands or brands with distinctive benefits should challenge consumers to break their habits.

Finally, because habit is both safe and easy, we rely on it for daily living. Imagine rethinking every purchase decision. It would be virtually impossible, not to mention impractical. So it's really *essential* to use habit in our lives.

The major objective of all brand marketers is to produce *brand loyalty,* a direct result of the habit of repurchasing and the reinforcement of continuous advertising. **Brand loyalty** is the consumer's conscious or unconscious decision, expressed through intention or behavior, to repurchase a brand continually.[29] It occurs because the consumer *perceives* that the brand offers the right product features, image, quality, or relationship at the right price. Recall earlier we suggested that a decision about what brand of smartphone to buy is a highly involving one. But if a consumer's utility is satisfied, the next smartphone purchase may not be involving at all. The consumer may simply decide that a particular brand has everything that she or he could want.

In the quest for brand loyalty, companies have three aims related to habits:

1. *Breaking habits.* Get consumers to unlearn an existing purchase habit and try something new. Marketers frequently offer incentives to lure customers away from old brands or stores. Or they may use comparative advertising to demonstrate their product's superiority. Breaking habits is hard, and advertising designed to make consumers reevaluate a previous decision must be especially powerful.

2. *Acquiring habits.* Teach consumers to repurchase their brand or repatronize their establishment. Many car companies incentivize a repeat purchase when a consumer is ready to buy again. This helps convince consumers that their utilities can always be met by staying with a known brand.

3. *Reinforcing habits.* Remind current customers of the value of their original purchase and encourage them to continue purchasing. JetBlue, like many major airlines, offers frequent flyer miles to loyal customers. Mature brands capitalize on loyalty programs to ensure customers don't stray.

Developing brand loyalty is difficult due to consumers' sophistication and to the legions of habit-breaking, *demarketing* activities of competitive advertisers.[30] Practitioners of IMC are constantly weighing the costs and benefits of breaking consumer habits (among those who use competing brands) versus encouraging habits (among loyal brand users). One rule of thumb is that sales promotion activities break habits by encouraging consumers to switch brands because of the promotion. Conversely, advertising generally provides consumers with benefit information intended to convince them that they should pay full price for the products or services they already use.

Apple is able to maintain high levels of consumer loyalty and and thus rarely competes on price. Many Apple customers buy its products out of habit. Apple believes that IMC activities devoted to brand building, rather than sales promotion, are the key to reinforcing loyalty and maintaining market share.[31] Just as important, it is essential for maintaining profitability. While sales promotions increase sales in the short run, they do so at the expense of profits. We revisit this topic in our discussion of sales promotion in Chapter 10.

Learning Defines Needs and Wants

Learning is both immediate and long term. The moment we file information, some learning takes place. When we see a succulent food ad, we may suddenly feel hungry; we *need* food. This leads to the next personal process, motivation.

Superstars like LeBron James ensure an ad is noticed and remembered. Kia expects that the value of his popularity and attractiveness will help not only in attracting new customers, but also in building loyalty among existing users of the brand.

Source: Kia Motors Corporation

Exhibit 5-4

The hierarchy of needs suggests that people meet their needs according to priorities. Physiological and safety needs carry the greatest priority. In advertising, the message must match the need of the market or the ad will fail. Advertisers use marketing research to understand the need levels of their markets and use this information in determining the marketing mix.

Need	Product	Promotional appeal
Self-actualization	Golf lessons	"Realize your full potential"
Esteem	Luxury car	"Be in control of the road"
Social	Pendant	"Show her you care"
Safety	Tires	"Bounces off hazards"
Physiological	Breakfast cereal	"The natural energy source"

The Consumer Motivation Process

LO 5-5

Motivation refers to the underlying forces (or motives) that contribute to our actions. These motives stem from the conscious or unconscious goal of satisfying needs and wants. **Needs** are the basic, often instinctive, human forces that motivate us to do something. **Wants** are "needs" that we learn during our lifetime.[32]

Motivation cannot be observed directly. When we see people eat, we assume they are hungry, but we may be wrong. People eat for a variety of reasons besides hunger: They want to be sociable, it's time to eat, or maybe they're nervous or bored.

People are usually motivated to satisfy some combination of needs, which may be conscious or unconscious, functional or psychological. *Motivation research* offers some insights into the underlying reasons for unexpected consumer behavior. The reasons *(motives)* some people buy a hybrid car may be environmental concern, sensitivity to gas prices, or a desire to be seen as progressive and sensitive to carbon emissions. Any or all of these factors might make a car buyer switch to a hybrid, even though he or she may give up many desirable features to do so.

To better understand what motivates people, Abraham Maslow developed the classic model shown in Exhibit 5-4 called the **hierarchy of needs.** Maslow maintained that the lower physiological and safety needs dominate human behavior and must be satisfied

Advertisers realize that English speakers are not the only market in the United States. Other linguistic and ethnic cultures exist and offer enormous markets for the culturally savvy. Here, the U.S. Army (www.goarmy.com) suggests to the Spanish-speaking audience that the soldier pictured followed his heart, and now "others follow it."

Source: U.S. Army

My IMC Campaign 5-A

Understanding What Consumers Look for in a Product

Your client's hope is that you can offer helpful advice on creating promotional messages that will get people to do something. In most cases, that something will be buying the client's product or using the service. If your client is a nonprofit, it might involve donating time and/or money.

This seems like common sense, but in fact persuading people to do something they are not already doing can be quite difficult. To help you organize your approach, it may be useful to review what marketing and psychology scholars have learned about consumers and how they are persuaded.

Your challenge at this point in the campaign is to understand the consumer and to get a sense of how the product or service your client offers relates to the consumer's life. Doing this well will require at least two things: a complete understanding of the product and its possible benefits, and a thorough understanding of the consumer.

Maslow's hierarchy of needs suggests that individuals have a range of needs they seek to satisfy in life.

Here is Maslow's hierarchy and some examples that involve food. Consider whether your client's product or service might have benefits that relate to one or more needs:

Need	Examples Involving Food
Self-actualization	Culinary arts degree
Esteem	Cooking lessons
Social	What everyone is eating
Safety	Healthful, organic foods
Physiological	Something that satisfies your hunger

Informational motives involve eliminating a problem, whereas transformational motives involve getting a reward. Consider the possible informational and transformational motives that exist in your consumers that might be addressed by your product.

Informational Motives	
Motive	**Solution**
Problem removal	"Eliminates your headache fast"
Problem avoidance	"Stay out in the sun—you're protected"
Incomplete satisfaction	"The diet drink that doesn't taste like a diet drink"
Mixed approach–avoidance	"Pain-free dental care"
Normal depletion	"Last gas station for 20 miles"

Transformational Motives	
Sensory gratification	"These headphones sound like you are at the show"
Intellectual stimulation	"Hours of fun with challenging puzzles"
Social approval	"Your spouse will love the way you look"

The Foote, Cone & Belding grid below was developed to classify how consumers learn about different types of products. Although it was originally designed with the idea that different products would fit in different quadrants, some believe that the quadrants can also be used to classify competing brands within a product category (e.g., luxury brands versus discount brands). Where would you place your client's brand? What does that suggest for how you might persuade consumers?

The following guides can help you determine where your client's brand belongs in the FCB grid:

Involvement

1. Is the decision to buy or use the product an important or an unimportant one?
2. Does the consumer stand to lose a great deal or very little if he or she chooses the wrong brand?
3. Does the decision require a great deal of consideration or very little?

Think versus Feel

Think

1. The decision is based on objective criteria.
2. The decision is based primarily on factual information.

Feel

1. The decision is based on a feeling.
2. The decision is closely related to the consumer's personality.
3. The decision is based on the senses (taste, touch, etc.).

FCB Grid

	Think	Feel
High Involvement	I. Informative Learn—Feel—Do (products: major purchases such as insurance, appliances, computers) Strategy: Follow steps of the creative pyramid, beginning with awareness.	II. Affective Feel—Learn—Do (products: expensive car, jewelry, high-end apparel) Strategy: Focus on self-esteem and ego benefits of product purchases.
Low Involvement	III. Habitual Do—Learn—Feel (products: car fuel, detergents, razors) Strategy: Focus on offering samples and creating habits in consumer purchasing.	IV. Satisfaction Do—Feel—Learn (products: experiential products such as beer, chewing gum, greeting cards, pizza) Strategy: Focus on social factors and peer use of the product.

before the higher, socially acquired needs (or wants) become meaningful. The highest need, self-actualization, is the culmination of fulfilling all the lower needs and reaching to discover the true self.

The promise of satisfying a certain level of need is the basic promotional appeal for many ads. In affluent societies such as the United States, Canada, western Europe, and Japan, most individuals take for granted the satisfaction of their physiological needs. So advertising campaigns often portray the fulfillment of social, esteem, and self-actualization needs, and many offer the reward of satisfaction through personal achievement.

In focus groups for Nabisco SnackWells, for example, it became apparent that middle-aged women today have a high sense of self-worth. Wellness, to them, is no longer about looking good in a bathing suit; rather, it's about celebrating what they do well. The advertiser wondered if it could use women's positive attitude about themselves to change their attitude toward the concept of snacking. Nabisco's agency, Foote, Cone & Belding, capitalized on the idea in a new campaign aimed at boosting women's self-esteem. The message: "Snacking is not about 'filling' yourself, but 'fulfilling' yourself."[33]

We all have needs and wants, but we are frequently unaware of them. Before the advent of the laptop computer, people were completely unaware of any need for it. But the moment a consumer consciously recognizes a product-related want or need, a dynamic process begins. The consumer first evaluates the need and either accepts it as worthy of action or rejects it. Acceptance converts satisfaction of the need into a goal, which creates the dedication (the motivation) to reach a particular result. In contrast, rejection removes the necessity for action and thereby eliminates the goal and the motivation to buy.

Modern researchers have translated Maslow's theory about needs and motives into more strategic concepts for use by marketers and advertisers. Rossiter and Percy, for example, identify eight fundamental purchase and usage motives (see Exhibit 5-5). They refer to the first five as *negatively originated (informational) motives* and the last three as *positively originated (transformational) motives.*[34]

Negatively Originated (Informational) Motives

The most common energizers of consumer behavior are the **negatively originated motives,** such as problem removal or problem avoidance. Whenever we run out of something, for instance, we experience a negative mental state. To relieve those feelings, we actively seek a new or replacement product. Thus, we are temporarily motivated until the time we make the purchase. Then, if the purchase is satisfactory, the drive or motivation is reduced.

These are also called **informational motives** because the consumer actively seeks information to reduce the mental state. In fact, Rossiter and Percy point out, these could also be called "relief" motives because consumers work to find relief from the negative state.

Positively Originated (Transformational) Motives

From time to time, we all want to indulge ourselves by buying some brand or product that promises some benefit or reward. With the **positively originated motives,** a positive bonus is promised rather than the removal or reduction of some negative situation. The goal is to use positive reinforcement to increase the consumer's motivation and to energize the consumer's investigation or search for the new product.

The three positively originated motives—sensory gratification, intellectual stimulation, and social approval—are also called **transformational motives** because the consumer expects to be transformed in a sensory, intellectual, or social sense. They could also be called "reward" motives because the transformation is a rewarding state.[35]

For some consumers, the purchase of a particular product (say, a new suit) might represent a negatively originated motive (they don't really want to spend the money on it, but they have to have it for work). But for other consumers, it might be positively originated (they love to shop for new clothes). This suggests two distinct target markets that marketers must understand and that may call for completely different strategies.

Exhibit 5-5
Rossiter and Percy's eight fundamental purchase and usage motives.

Negatively originated (informational) motives

1. Problem removal
2. Problem avoidance
3. Incomplete satisfaction
4. Mixed approach–avoidance
5. Normal depletion

Positively originated (transformational) motives

6. Sensory gratification
7. Intellectual stimulation or mastery
8. Social approval

Before creating messages, companies must carefully consider the goals that lead to consumer motivations. Chili's restaurants would make a costly mistake if its ads portrayed the reward of a romantic interlude if the real motive of most Chili's customers is simply to satisfy their need to reduce hunger with a filling, low-priced meal.

The issues of high-involvement and low-involvement products and informational and transformational motives are so important that we will revisit them in Chapter 8 when we discuss the planning of IMC strategies.

Interpersonal Influences on Consumer Behavior

Understanding the personal processes of perception, learning, persuasion, and motivation is not enough for marketers. Important **interpersonal influences** can affect—sometimes dominate—consumer behavior. These influences can be categorized as the *family,* the *society,* and the *cultural environment* of the consumer.

Family Influence

From an early age, family communication affects our socialization as consumers—our attitudes toward many products and our purchasing habits. This influence is usually strong and long lasting. A child who learns that the "right" headache relief is Bayer aspirin and the "right" name for appliances is Samsung has a strong foundation for adult purchasing behavior.

From 1960 to 2016 the percentage of children living in families with two parents declined from 88 percent to 69 percent. This suggests that family influence has changed in the United States over the last 30 years.[36] As this happens, the influence of the social and cultural environments intensifies.

Societal Influence

Our communities exert a strong influence on all of us. When we affiliate with a particular societal division or identify with some reference group or value the ideas of certain opinion leaders, it affects our views on life, our perceptual screens, and eventually the products we buy.

Societal Divisions: The Group We Belong To

Sociologists traditionally divided societies into **social classes:** upper, upper-middle, lower-middle, and so on. They believed that people in the same social class tended toward similar attitudes, status symbols, and spending patterns.

But today this doesn't apply to most developed countries. U.S. society, especially, is extremely fluid and mobile—physically, socially, and economically. Americans believe strongly in getting ahead, being better than their peers, and winning greater admiration and self-esteem.

Because of this mobility, increases in immigration, and the high divorce rate, social class boundaries have become quite muddled. Single parents, stockbrokers, immigrant shopkeepers, retired blue-collar workers, and bankers all see themselves as part of the great middle class. So "middle class" doesn't mean anything anymore. From the advertiser's point of view, social class seldom represents a functional or operational set of values.

To deal with these often bewildering changes, marketers seek new ways to classify societal divisions and new strategies for advertising to them. We discuss some of these in Chapter 6. Exhibit 5-6 outlines some of the classifications marketers use to describe society today: for example, Upper Crust; Brite Lites, Li'l City; Young Influentials; and Urban Achievers. People in the same group tend to have similar patterns of behavior and product usage.

Reference Groups: The People We Relate To

Most of us care how we appear to people whose opinions matter. We may even pattern our behavior after members of some groups we value. This is the significance of **reference groups**—people we try to emulate or whose approval concerns us. Reference

Upper Crust	Blue-Chip Blues
The nation's most exclusive address, Upper Crust is the wealthiest lifestyle in America—a haven for empty-nesting couples over 55 years old. No segment has a higher concentration of residents earning over $200,000 a year or possessing a postgraduate degree. And none has a more opulent standard of living.	Blue-Chip Blues is known as a comfortable lifestyle for young, sprawling families with well-paying blue-collar jobs. Ethnically diverse—with a significant presence of Hispanics and African Americans—the segment's aging neighborhoods feature compact, modestly priced homes surrounded by commercial centers that cater to child-filled households.
Brite Lites, Li'l City	**Old Glories**
Not all of America's chic sophisticates live in major metros. Brite Lights, Li'l City is a group of well-off, middle-aged couples settled in the nation's satellite cities. Residents of these typical DINK (double income, no kids) households have college educations, well-paying business and professional careers, and swank homes filled with the latest technology.	Old Glories are the nation's downscale suburban retirees, Americans aging in place in older apartment complexes. These racially mixed households often contain widows and widowers living on fixed incomes, and they tend to lead home-centered lifestyles. They're among the nation's most ardent television fans, watching game shows, soaps, talk shows, and newsmagazines at high rates.
Young Influentials	**City Startups**
Once known as the home of the nation's yuppies, Young Influentials reflects the fading glow of acquisitive yuppiedom. Today, the segment is a common address for young, middle-class singles and couples who are more preoccupied with balancing work and leisure pursuits. Having recently left college dorms, they now live in apartment complexes surrounded by ball fields, health clubs, and casual dining restaurants.	In City Startups, young, multiethnic singles have settled in neighborhoods filled with cheap apartments and a commercial base of cafés, bars, laundromats, and clubs that cater to twentysomethings. One of the youngest segments in America—with 10 times as many college students as the national average—these neighborhoods feature low incomes and high concentrations of Hispanics and African Americans.
Urban Achievers	**Low-Rise Living**
Concentrated in the nation's port cities, Urban Achievers is often the first stop for up-and-coming immigrants from Asia, South America, and Europe. These young singles and couples are typically college-educated and ethnically diverse; about a third are foreign-born, and even more speak a language other than English.	The most economically challenged urban segment, Low-Rise Living is known as a transient world for young, ethnically diverse singles and single parents. Home values are low—about half the national average—and even then, less than a quarter of residents can afford to own real estate. Typically, the commercial base of Mom-and-Pop stores is struggling and in need of a renaissance.

Exhibit 5-6

Contemporary social classes. The social groups outlined in this exhibit are just a few of the 66 lifestyle segments defined by Claritas. This division of Equifax wants to know what financial services various consumers, from the wealthiest (Upper Crust) to the poorest (Low-Rise Living), are likely to need.

groups can be personal (family, friends, coworkers) or impersonal (political parties, religious denominations, professional associations). A special reference group, peers, exerts tremendous influence on what we believe and how we behave. They determine which brands are cool and which are not.[37] To win acceptance by our peers (fellow students, coworkers, colleagues), we may purchase a certain style or brand of clothing, choose a particular place to live, and acquire behavioral habits that will earn their approval.

Often an individual is influenced in opposite directions by two reference groups and must choose between them. For example, a college student might feel pressure from some friends to join a Greek house and from others to live independently off campus. In ads targeted to students, a local apartment complex might tap the appeal of reference groups by showing students splashing in the complex's pool.

Opinion Leaders: The People We Trust

An **opinion leader** is some person or organization whose beliefs or attitudes are respected by people who share an interest in some specific activity. All fields (sports, religion, fashion, politics) have opinion leaders. An opinion leader may be a knowledgeable friend or some expert we find credible. We reason, "If Keira Knightley thinks Chanel is the best perfume, then it must be so." Thus, the purchasing habits and testimonials of opinion leaders are important to advertisers.

When choosing an opinion leader as a spokesperson for a company or product, advertisers must understand the company's target market thoroughly. Even if executives in the company do not relate to the spokesperson, they must follow market tastes and

Ethics, Diversity & Inclusion

Helping an Industry Look Like America

Advertising agencies have long struggled to represent the diversity of the U.S. population within their ranks. There is no question that the backgrounds of those working in ad agencies have, for many years, differed from those of the broader population. As late as the middle of the 20th century, for example, most jobs and all senior management positions were held by white males. In this respect, agencies were no better (but also perhaps no worse) than most other businesses.

The agency world can even point to some dramatic successes in promoting people from diverse backgrounds. For example, in 1967 Mary Wells Lawrence, a savvy creative head at Doyle, Dane, Bernbach, made history as the first female agency CEO at Wells Rich Greene. With clients like IBM, Procter & Gamble, and Sheraton Hotels, WRG was a major advertising shop. Lawrence eventually became the highest-paid agency head in the business and the first female leader of an NYSE-listed company.

But many, both within and outside the agency business, believe that diversity is still a problem in the world of advertising. Some even contend that agencies have a special obligation to take a leadership role on the issue. After all, they say, how can agencies develop effective and responsible messages for diverse audiences if their own employees lack diversity? According to Rick Milentha, CEO of TenUnited, "It is a travesty that our industry, which is supposed to market to all of America, does not reflect all of America. . . . I think it's incumbent on us to find a way for this not to be the case in the future. The truth is, it's just plain good business. If we're going to do our job for our clients, we can't be predominantly white and male."[38]

Diversity became much more than an abstract issue in the fall of 2006 when the New York City Commission on Human Rights issued a barely veiled threat to the industry: institute specific practices that can help with minority recruitment or face public humiliation.

To understand what happened between the commission and America's biggest ad agencies, a bit of history is in order. The commission is charged with eliminating discrimination in employment practices. In 1967 it surveyed 40 agencies with branches in New York and discovered that only 634 blacks and about 300 Hispanics could be found among the nearly 18,000 agency employees. That math worked out to a workforce of about 5 percent minorities in a metropolitan labor force that was about 25 percent minority. The commission urged agencies to do a better job in hiring and retaining blacks and Hispanics.

In 1977 the commission once again examined the agency workforce. In seven large agencies, the percentage of black and Hispanic employees was nearly 12 percent. Two other large agencies, both of which had agreed to specific affirmative action plans, had workforces that were almost 14 percent minority. It was progress, but the commission continued to believe agencies could do more. By 2006, the commission had apparently had enough. It announced that it would hold hearings on industry practices in hiring and retaining minorities. Perhaps not coincidentally, the hearings would take place during an annual New York event called Advertising Week. Advertising Week is, according to its own promotional materials, the "largest assembly of advertising and media leaders in North America" (you can find out more at www.advertisingweek.com). The event is a celebration of the ad industry.

But the commission threatened to make Advertising Week anything but a celebration when it issued subpoenas to 16 senior agency executives, including the CEOs of the four big conglomerates: Omnicom, WPP, Interpublic, and Publicis. The subpoenas required that the executives testify regarding their hiring practices and their failures to diversify.

Fearing a humiliating grilling during the most widely publicized event of the year, three of the four conglomerates immediately agreed to the commission's demands, including pledging money to historically black colleges and setting hiring goals. The goals ranged from 5 to 30 percent for minority hires and promotions. But one conglomerate, Omnicom, held out. Omnicom was not ignoring diversity; indeed, it pledged more than $2 million for its own initiatives, including creating an advertising curriculum at Medgar Evers College, a historically black institution. The group argued that it merely wished to address diversity in its own way, rather than follow dictates from the commission. But after several weeks of bad press, Omnicom buckled and signed.

How much of a difference were these concessions likely to make? Not much, according to *Advertising Age*, which commented, "Why do we—along with 93% of those responding [to an industry poll]—get the feeling that we'll be reading something similar in another 30 years?" The magazine argued, "Both sides need to get real. The commission needs to cease grandstanding attempts to embarrass the industry into action . . . and acknowledge the fact that in a supply-demand market, qualified and interested minority applicants can get a lot more out of their degrees in other sectors." Turning to the industry, it noted it could "be a little less defensive and a great deal more proactive. Poaching qualified minority applicants already in the system doesn't boost numbers. And time spent whining that there aren't enough black kids [in ad programs] could be better spent looking for undergraduates in other programs. Training and mentoring would help. As would breaking up the good ol' boy vibe prevalent in many agencies."[39]

But perhaps *Advertising Age* is missing the bigger picture. Nancy Hill, former CEO of the AAAA, made diversity a priority, and her successor, Marla Kaplowitz (see People behind the Ads: Marla Kaplowitz, in Chapter 4), has done the same. Even the appointments of these two women as president, the first women in the 90-plus-year history of the organization, suggests a change in perspective. And the AAAA is a sponsor of the Minority Advertising Internship Program (MAIP), which places students of underrepresented backgrounds in top agency internships where they receive mentoring and develop valuable contacts (find out more about the MAIP and how you might become a participant at https://maip.aaaa.org/). These efforts, and many others by ad agencies across the United States, may finally make it more likely that the ad industry begins to look like America.

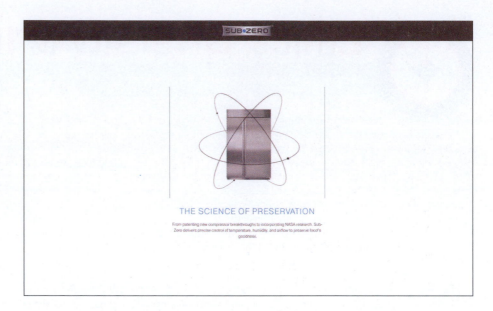

interests. A spokesperson out of sync with the market undermines his or her credibility—and the company's. On the other hand, an internal person such as Steve Jobs, before he passed away in 2011, turned out to be a highly credible spokesperson without the risks associated with outside celebrities and athletes.[40]

Opinion leaders don't even have to be real people. Even fictional ones will do. That's why it is not surprising that Apple laptops turn up on many highly rated shows and feature films. The fact that key characters in these entertainment media use the brand represents a belief that viewers will notice and be influenced by the choices of their favorite characters.[41]

Cultural and Subcultural Influence

Culture has a tenacious influence on consumers. **Culture** refers to the whole set of meanings, beliefs, attitudes, and ways of doing things that are shared by some homogeneous social group and are typically handed down from generation to generation.[42] Americans love hot dogs, peanut butter, corn on the cob, and apple pie. Canada, Russia, Germany—every country has its own favorite specialties. And companies find it much easier to work with these tastes than try to change them.

Global marketers are especially concerned with the purchase environment. According to Professor Carolyn Lin, of all business functions, marketing activities are the most susceptible to cultural error.[43]

For example, while both demographic and psychographic traits figure importantly in U.S. consumer marketing, age and sex are better indicators of behavior and lifestyles in Japan, where income is largely proportional to seniority and sex roles tend to be standardized.[44] In international markets, companies must consider many environmental factors: cultural trends, social norms, changing fads, market dynamics, product needs, and media channels.[45]

In countries where people earn little income, demand for expensive products is low. So the creative strategy of an automobile advertiser might be to target the small group of wealthy, upper-class consumers. In a country with a large middle class, the same advertiser might be better off mass-marketing the car and positioning it as a middle-class product.

The United States and Canada embrace many subcultures, some of them quite large. They may be based on race, national origin, religion, language, or geographic proximity. The marketer must understand these subcultures because differences among them may affect responses to both products and messages.

The United States, in particular, is a great patchwork of minority subcultures. A **subculture** is a segment within a culture that shares a set of meanings, values, or activities that differ in certain respects from those of the overall culture.[46] According to the U.S. Census, 39 million African Americans, 48 million Hispanics, and 14 million Asians live in the United States. These three minority groups alone account for more than a third of the American population.[47] Canada has two major subcultures, anglophones and franco-phones, based on language (English and French), plus a mosaic of many other cultures based on ethnic and national origin.

Racial, religious, and ethnic backgrounds affect consumers' preferences for styles of dress, food, beverages, transportation, personal care products, and household furnishings, to name a few. As we saw in Chapter 4, many agencies now specialize in minority markets. Recognizing the rapid growth of the Hispanic population, for example, Procter & Gamble spends more than $153 million per year to understand and promote to this market. Other major Hispanic marketers include Ford Motor Co., AT&T, and Sears.[48] Global marketers also face cultural challenges. In North America, advertising encourages us to keep our mouths clean, our breath fresh, and our teeth scrubbed. But people in some southern European countries consider it vain and improper to overindulge in toiletries. Consumers in the Netherlands and the United Kingdom use three times as much toothpaste as those in Spain and Greece. To communicate effectively with Spanish consumers, who view toothpaste as a cosmetic product, marketers use chic creative executions rather than dry, therapeutic pitches.[49]

Clearly, many interpersonal factors influence consumers. They have an important effect on our purchase decisions. Awareness of these interpersonal influences helps marketers, both domestic and international, create the strategies on which much IMC is based.

Nonpersonal Influences on Consumer Behavior

Numerous nonpersonal influences affect a consumer's final purchase decision. The most important **nonpersonal influences** are *time, place,* and *environment.*

Time

LO 5-7

The old saw "timing is everything" certainly applies to marketing. A special weekend sale may provide just the added incentive to penetrate customers' perceptual screens and bring them into a store. But running an ad for that sale on Sunday evening would be a waste of advertising dollars.

Likewise, the consumer's particular need may be a function of time. Forecasts of an unusually wet winter from the El Niño phenomenon motivated special ads from a variety of national companies as well as many small retailers of linens, boots, snow shovels, and rock salt. Consumers don't need snow tires and rock salt in the summer (although some off-season promotions do work). But if we unexpectedly get a flat on the highway, tire campaigns suddenly become timely. As we will see in our chapters on media, companies must plan all their marketing activities with the consumer's clock in mind.

Place

Once consumers decide to purchase a certain product, they will still hesitate if they don't know where to buy it or if it isn't available in a convenient or preferred location. Similarly, if consumers believe a particular brand is a specialty good but it suddenly appears everywhere, their perception of the product's "specialness" may diminish. Thus, marketers carefully weigh consumer demand when planning distribution strategy, and they devote much of their promotional activities to communicating the convenience of location. Distribution is an important element of the marketing mix and will be discussed further in Chapter 6.

Environment

Many **environments**—ecological, social, political, technical, economic, household, and point-of-sale location, to mention a few—can affect the purchase decision. For example, during a recession, companies can't expect to accomplish much with consumers who don't have enough money to buy. And no matter how good the message or how low the price, memberships in the National Rifle Association aren't likely to be a hot item with members of the Audubon Society. On the other hand, an enticing display next to the cash register can improve sales of low-cost impulse items. Marketers must consider the influence of the purchase environment on the consumer's decision processes.

Likewise, the state of technological development affects economic and social conditions—and the prospects for advertisers of certain products and services. For example, countries that don't manufacture computers might be poor markets for components such as hard drives and microprocessors. On the other hand, campaigns for low-priced, imported computers might do very well.

Finally, some governments exert far greater control over their citizens and businesses than does the U.S. government. For example, for many years, virtually no American-made products could be sold in former Eastern bloc countries or China. It simply wasn't allowed. Political control often extends to which products companies may advertise and sell, which media they use, and what their ads say.

The Purchase Decision and Postpurchase Evaluation

Now that you've learned about the elements in the consumer purchase decision process, let's see how they might work in a typical situation. Ad Lab 5-B demonstrates an advertiser's approach, but it is also important to look through the eyes of a consumer. A hypothetical consumer named Chris is thinking about buying a tablet.

> Chris is enrolled at a state university and financed in part by a small scholarship. He also has a part-time job but must act conservatively when it comes to spending money because tuition, books, and other expenses are costly.
>
> One day, thumbing through a consumer electronics magazine, Chris sees an exciting ad for a new top-of-the line tablet. A beautiful photograph shows the product's modern yet understated design. The copy highlights the tablet's special features. They exude high-tech class—it's just the right style. The ad's signature: "Exclusively at TechMart."
>
> In a split second Chris leaps from perception to motivation. Got to have it! He is highly involved and he wants this personal reward for all his hard work.
>
> The next day Chris visits TechMart. While looking for the advertised tablet, he encounters a variety of alternative styles and models by well-known manufacturers.

The ad has already done its work; the purchase decision process is well under way. At the point of making a purchase decision, though, consumers typically search, consider, and compare alternative brands.

Consumers evaluate selection alternatives (called the **evoked set**). To do this, they establish **evaluative criteria,** the standards they use to judge the features and benefits of alternative products. Not all brands make it to the evoked set. In fact, based on their mental files, most consumers usually consider only four or five brands—which presents a real challenge to advertisers. If none of the alternatives meet the evaluative criteria, the consumer may reject the purchase entirely or postpone the decision.

> Chris finally finds the advertised product. But it looks larger on the shelf than it did in the ad. Two other good tablets are also displayed; both are attractive, both expensive. While looking over the beautiful screen, Chris considers other unique qualities of style and design. "This one may be a little too bulky." "This one syncs easily with my phone." "This one is less expensive."
>
> Using central route processing, Chris compares the tablets, considering their style, technology, possible advantages, and price. The advertised unit really is the best buy and would be the most satisfying. The purchase decision is complete when Chris uses his debit card to make the purchase.
>
> On the way home, the **postpurchase evaluation** begins. Chris suddenly envisions some friends' possible negative reactions to the purchase. Maybe it wasn't wise to spend so much money on a high-end device. Chris starts to worry—and to plan.
>
> "It's really a great piece of technology. It's excellent quality and worth the money. I'll get a lot of use out of it."

A key feature of the postpurchase evaluation is *cognitive dissonance.* The **theory of cognitive dissonance** (also called **postpurchase dissonance**) holds that people strive to justify their behavior by reducing the dissonance, or inconsistency, between their cognitions (their perceptions or beliefs) and reality.[50] In fact, research shows that, to combat

AD Lab 5–B

Applying Consumer Behavior Principles to Ad Making

When Polaroid needed to capture the attention of photo enthusiasts, it turned to the creatives at Leonard/Monahan to design a series of ads that would exhibit the advantages of the instant film over other photo products.

Source: Polaroid

The first challenge for the creative design team was to break through the consumers' resistance, the subtle barrier that begins with the perceptual screens. Second, the team had to present the picture as being worth a thousand words while avoiding clichés.

The advertisement's headline—"The victim refuses to speak. The pictures refuse to keep quiet."—commands your attention and expresses the big idea with urgency. The ad's black-and-white visual of a battery victim suggests the subject's grave nature while allowing the color Polaroid pictures to jump out, emoting a raw portrayal of reality. The ad becomes credible by demonstrating the benefits of Polaroid pictures and how they can be successfully used (to investigate, prosecute, and win). The tagline, "Instant evidence," sums up the product's features and helps the prospective consumer recall the product's benefits. These factors show clearly the product's benefits to those who may be critical of their purchase decision.

Laboratory Application

Choose an ad from a popular magazine and explain how the visuals, the words, and the overall design of the ad accomplish the following tasks. Provide specific details to support your answers.

1. Penetrate consumer perceptual screens.
2. Stimulate consumer learning.
3. Use the consumer's existing beliefs.
4. Tap consumer wants and needs to achieve motivation.

---

dissonance, consumers are more likely to read ads for brands they've already purchased than for new products or competing brands.[51]

> As soon as he leaves the store, Chris begins thinking that the other tablets were pretty attractive too, and some were cheaper or had more features. This begins creating an uneasy feeling in Chris that he might not have made a wise decision. He also knows that the money he used to buy the tablet could have been used for many more practical purchases. Chris is anxious to get confirmation that he made the right choice so that he'll begin feeling better. He decides to go online and find some cool apps he can download. He also visits Facebook to share a photo of the new device. Chris is relieved to see many friends weigh in with "likes" and positive comments. Later, when he sees an ad for the tablet on TV, Chris is proud that he decided to buy one.

During the postpurchase period, the consumer may enjoy the satisfaction of the purchase and thereby receive reinforcement for the decision. Or the purchase may turn out to be unsatisfactory for some reason. In either case, feedback from the postpurchase evaluation updates the consumer's mental files, affecting perceptions of the brand and similar purchase decisions in the future.

This story is common for a high-involvement purchase decision. Of course, if Chris's decision had merely involved the purchase of a pack of gum, the process would have been significantly simpler.

Chris may typify a particular group of consumers, and that is important to marketers. Marketers are interested in defining target markets and developing effective marketing strategies for groups of consumers who share similar characteristics, needs, motives, and buying habits. These are the subjects of market segmentation and the marketing mix, the focus of Chapter 6.

People BEHIND the Ads

Jon Steel: Advertising Legend

Courtesy of Jon Steel

Jon Steel has been named "West Coast Executive of the Year," "Agency Innovator," one of the "100 smartest people in the Bay Area," and a member of the Advertising Federation Hall of Achievement for executives under 40. Lee Clow, the famous CEO of TBWA Chiat/Day, called him "one of the great practitioners in advertising today."

What has Steel done to earn such accolades? The answer, at least in part, is that he helped change the way advertising is done in the United States. During a wildly successful run at Goodby Silverstein & Partners, Steel became both the greatest advocate for and greatest practitioner of account planning.

Steel traces the origins of the planner role to the kind of advertising created by industry legend William Bernbach (see People behind the Ads in Chapter 2). You might remember that Bernbach was a strong critic of the formulaic ads of the 1950s. More than anything, Bernbach believed that advertising should respect rather than pander to the consumer.

And just what is account planning? Some view it as a hybrid of research and strategy that places the consumer front and center. At Steel's first agency, England's Boase Massimi Pollitt (BMP), account planning developed when founder Stanley Pollitt insisted that account managers and researchers work together in teams, much as copywriters and art directors do in creative departments. Pollitt thought the consumer was often forgotten after researchers handed control of a campaign over to account people and

creatives. The account planner would maintain a consumer focus throughout the campaign and serve, in Steel's words, as the "conscience" of the agency.

Would you make a good account planner? Steel believes that great planners share some obvious characteristics such as intellect, curiosity, facility with both left- and right-brain thinking, and well-honed written and oral communication skills. Less obvious but equally important are modesty and humility, an interest in listening rather than speaking, and talent for building relationships with a broad range of people. And least obvious of all, Steel believes that account planners have to be, well, just a little weird. "Almost all of the good planners I have known are a little out of the ordinary. This manifests itself in two main ways: In a somewhat off-center perspective on situations and a rather eclectic mix of background and interests." To prove the point he lists the backgrounds of some of the best: professional chess player, musician, aeronautical engineer, classics scholar, and a killer whale trainer at Sea World.

Jon Steel was born and grew up in England, earning a degree from Nottingham University in geography. He was interviewed for an account management position at BMP, but his interviewer spotted skills that fit better with a planning job. It was Steel's good fortune that BMP had pioneered account planning as early as 1968 and was well known for using the approach.

By the late 1980s, U.S. agencies recognized that the best ads in the world were being done in England, not the United States. A big factor in London's excellence was the widespread use of account planning. But there really wasn't anyone practicing it in the United States.

Goodby Silverstein & Partners, a respected San Francisco agency, went right to the source and recruited Steel to develop account planning at the agency in 1989. Steel came to America prepared to shake things up. For example, believing that focus groups are often designed more for the comfort of brand managers sitting behind one-way mirrors than for the consumer, Steel insisted that planners venture out into consumers' "native habitats." So to help pitch a campaign for Sega, Steel and his colleagues invaded the bedrooms of kids to watch them playing video games. His book recounts a funny story of a six-year-old bounding out of a closet in a super-hero costume and biting the arm of one of the Goodby planners. Goodby got the account.

Clearly account planning was a different way to do developmental research, and as the Sega work demonstrated, it could even be a bit dangerous! But was it a better way to develop great ads? By almost any measure the answer is yes. During Steel's tenure at Goodby, the agency's billings surged tenfold. The creative work was stunning as well, as the agency produced award-winning ads for clients like Sega, Norwegian Cruise Lines,

Porsche, the Partnership for a Drug-Free America, and the California Fluid Milk Processors Advisory Board (the famous "Got Milk" campaign).

Steel eventually left Goodby and now works for one of the largest advertising companies in the world, the WPP group, where he directs the marketing fellowship program. He has also produced two wonderful books on the advertising business, *Truth, Lies & Advertising,* published in 1998, and more recently *Perfect Pitch.*

Jon Steel graciously answered some questions for students of *Contemporary Advertising:*

CA: How did you help to bring planning to America?

JS: At the time I joined GS&P, planning was still in its infancy in the United States. Jay Chiat had introduced it a few years before, famously declaring it "the best new business tool ever invented." And with great planners like Jane Newman, M. T. Rainey, and Rob White, Chiat/Day did indeed win a lot of new business. For a while, planning was Chiat/Day's Unique Selling Proposition, but planning alone was not responsible for the agency's success. Chiat/Day won new business and produced great work because of the combination of some very good planners with an excellent creative department.

When I moved from BMP in London to start a planning department in San Francisco, many people assumed that I would be "introducing BMP-style planning to Goodby." That was never my intention because the most effective planning evolves from an agency culture; it's never the other way around. Goodby Silverstein was founded on the desire to be the best advertising agency in the world ("as judged by our peers and by our effectiveness in the marketplace"). That meant that creative excellence and relevance walked hand-in-hand from the start, and thus it was a fertile environment for planners who shared those beliefs.

I'd like to think that in the time I was responsible for planning at Goodby, I developed a model of planning that was more agile than that traditionally practiced at BMP and other British agencies. If we had six months to develop strategic recommendations, then we could take six months, but if we only had six days, then we were still capable of delivering something interesting. Our aim was always to create the best possible solution, not to show how clever we were. The planners were there both as an aid to creativity and as a reality check. But most important, the style of planning we practiced was designed solely for that agency. It's not easily transplanted elsewhere, and it was very hard for experienced planners to come in from the outside and ply their trade effectively. (Many of my most successful planners were homegrown, hired straight out of school, and trained inside the agency environment.)

CA: Two of your own advertising heroes are Howard Gossage and William Bernbach. What did you admire most about each man? How have they influenced your own career?

JS: Bill Bernbach changed the face of advertising by putting art directors and copywriters together for the first time. It probably seems ridiculous now, but there was a time when the copy department and the art department were separate, and copy was sent along the corridor or to a different floor for someone else to make it look nice. The idea of the creative team ultimately changed the way all agencies work, and the campaigns that came out of Doyle, Dane, Bernbach inspired generation after generation of creative talent to come into the business.

Even if he never employed anyone in his agency with the word *planner* on their business card, Bill Bernbach valued human insights and substance as much as the artistry and poetry that his "new advertising" embodied. "At the heart of an effective creative philosophy," he once said, "is the belief that nothing is so powerful as an insight into human nature, what compulsions drive a man, what instincts dominate his action, even though his language so often camouflages what really motivates him." For the last 20 years, I have found myself searching for such insights, attempting to fuse research and creativity so that my clients don't talk at people but rather *with* them; so that members of our audience don't just hear a message and understand it, but instead *feel* it.

Gossage is a legend in San Francisco, but not as well known and, therefore, less influential than Bernbach in the wider world of advertising. But Jeff Goodby, Andy Berlin, and Rich Silverstein were big fans of Gossage's work and for that reason he probably had the greater direct influence on my career.

"Is advertising worth saving?" he wrote. "From an economic point of view I don't think that most of it is. From an aesthetic point of view I'm damn sure it's not; it is thoughtless, boring, and there is simply too much of it." In his view advertising was an uninvited guest in people's homes, and being uninvited he felt it should not only behave impeccably, but also give something in return for the attention paid to it. Gossage believed in interactive advertising about 40 years before technology made it possible for lesser mortals; he put a coupon on every print ad, not as a simple transactional device but rather as a way of establishing a two-way dialogue with his readers.

CA: What else would you like to share with students of the industry?

JS: My advice? Always remember: it's only advertising. No one's going to die, so don't take it so seriously. And the less seriously you take it, the better the work will be.

Courtesy of Jonathan Steel.

Chapter Summary

Marketing is the process companies use to make a profit by satisfying their customers' needs. Marketing focuses on the special relationship between a customer's needs and a product's utility. The essence of marketing is the perceived equal-value exchange. Need satisfaction is the customer's goal and should be the marketer's goal as well.

Advertising is concerned with the promotion aspect of the marketing process. It is one of several tools marketers use to inform, persuade, and remind groups of customers (markets) about the need-satisfying value of their products and services. Advertising's effectiveness depends on the communication skill of the advertising person. It also depends on the extent to which firms correctly implement other marketing activities, such as market research, pricing, and distribution.

There are three categories of participants in the marketing process: customers, markets, and marketers. To reach customers and markets, advertisers must effectively blend data from the behavioral sciences with the communicating arts. Advertisers study the behavioral characteristics of large groups of people to create advertising aimed at those groups.

Successful advertising people understand the complexity of consumer behavior, which is governed by three personal processes: perception, learning and persuasion, and motivation. These processes determine how consumers see the world around them, how they learn information and habits, and how they actualize their personal needs and motives. Two sets of influences also affect consumer behavior: interpersonal influences (the consumer's family, society, and culture) and nonpersonal influences (time, place, and environment). These factors combine to determine how the consumer behaves, and their influence differs considerably from one country to another. Advertisers evaluate the effect of these factors on groups of consumers to determine how best to create their messages.

Once prospects are motivated to satisfy their needs and wants, the purchase process begins. Based on certain standards, they evaluate various alternative products (the evoked set). If none of the alternatives meet their evaluative criteria, they may reject or postpone the purchase. If they do buy, they may experience cognitive dissonance. The result of the postpurchase evaluation will greatly affect the customer's attitude toward future purchases.

Important Terms

attitude, *162*

brand interest, *162*

brand loyalty, *163*

business markets, *153*

centers of influence, *153*

central route to persuasion, *161*

classical conditioning, *159*

cognition, *158*

consumer behavior, *155*

consumer decision process, *156*

consumer markets, *153*

culture, *170*

current customers, *153*

Elaboration Likelihood Model, *161*

environments, *171*

evaluation of alternatives, *156*

evaluative criteria, *172*

evoked set, *172*

exchange, *151*

government markets, *154*

habit, *162*

hierarchy of needs, *164*

industrial markets, *154*

informational motives, *166*

interpersonal influences, *156, 167*

learning, *158*

market, *153*

marketers, *155*

marketing, *150*

mental files, *159*

motivation, *164*

needs, *164*

negatively originated motives, *166*

nonpersonal influences, *156, 171*

operant conditioning, *159*

opinion leader, *168*

organizational buyers, *155*

perception, *157*

peripheral route to persuasion, *161*

personal processes, *156*

persuasion, *160*

physiological screens, *158*

positively originated motives, *166*

postpurchase dissonance, *172*

postpurchase evaluation, *156, 172*

prospective customers, *153*

psychological screens, *158*

reference groups, *167*

reseller markets, *154*

social classes, *167*

social cognitive theory, *159*

stimulus, *157*

subculture, *170*

theory of cognitive dissonance, *172*

transformational motives, *166*

transnational (global) markets, *155*

utility, *151*

wants, *164*

Review Questions

1. What is marketing, and what is the role IMC plays in the marketing process?

2. How does product utility relate to IMC?

3. Why is the perceived equal-value exchange an important campaign issue?

4. What is the difference between a *customer* and a *market?* What are the different types of markets?

5. What does the term *consumer behavior* refer to, and why is it important to marketers?

6. Which consumer behavior process presents the greatest challenge to marketers?

7. What is the difference between the central route and the peripheral route to persuasion?

8. What is the significance of negatively originated motives and positively originated motives for IMC planners?

9. What are some of the environmental influences on consumer behavior in international markets?

10. How does the theory of cognitive dissonance relate to IMC?

The Advertising Experience

1. **Cognitive Dissonance**
   Describe an incident of cognitive dissonance that you (or someone you interview) felt after a significant purchase. Discuss the feelings generated by this purchase and what happened to those feelings. For example, perhaps the purchaser felt better over time as the quality and value of the product became evident. Finally, discuss what the company could have done to make the buyer feel better during the period of cognitive dissonance.

2. **Consumer Behavior**
   Understanding consumer behavior is essential to the contemporary advertiser. Browse the websites listed below, keeping in mind what you learned about culture/subculture, social class, reference groups, family/household, and opinion leaders. Identify and describe the major social influences that enable each organization to be successful in reaching its consumers.

   - Beech-Nut: www.beechnut.com
   - Ben & Jerry's: www.benjerry.com
   - CNN: www.cnn.com
   - Motorola: www.motorola.com
   - Music Television (MTV): www.mtv.com
   - Oprah: www.oprah.com
   - PetSmart: www.petsmart.com

   - Facebook: www.facebook.com
   - See's Candies: www.sees.com
   - Google: www.google.com
   - Xbox: www.xbox.com

3. **Motivation and Interpersonal Influences**
   Review the websites in Exercise 2 in terms of Maslow's hierarchy of needs. Find three instances of appeals to each of the five basic needs. Next, discuss what kind of people might seek to satisfy each of these needs with the particular products. Finally, consider opinion leaders whose testimonies could be added to each site. How could these leaders strengthen the appeal of the site for the consumers who have unsatisfied needs?

4. Write narratives for two hypothetical customers (similar to the one about Chris and his purchase decision in the section "The Purchase Decision and Postpurchase Evaluation"): one deciding between an Apple Watch and a Fitbit and one choosing between Chick-fil-A and McDonald's. Use Exhibit 5-1 for guidance.

5. Analyze Apple's advertising strategies using theories of learning and the Elaboration Likelihood Model (see Exhibit 5-3). Which routes to persuasion does the company use? What is your evidence? How does Apple help consumers to learn about its products?

End Notes

1. Walter Isaacson, *Steve Jobs* (New York: Simon & Schuster, 2011).

2. Ted Friedman, "Apple's 1984: The Introduction of the Macintosh in the Cultural History of Personal Computers," revised version of a paper presented at the Society for the History of Technology Convention, Pasadena, CA, 1997, *www.duke.edu/~tlove/mac.htm*.

3. Caroline McCarthy, "Remembering the '1984' Super Bowl Mac Ad," *CNET,* January 23, 2009, *http://news.cnet.com/8301-13577_3-10148380-36.html*.

4. Tom Hormby, "The Story behind Apple's 1984 Ad," *Low End Mac,* January 24, 2014, *http://lowendmac.com/orchard/06/1984-apple-superbowl-ad.html*.

5. "1984 Apple's Macintosh Commercial," *www.youtube.com/watch?v=OYecfV3ubP8*.

6. William Perreault Jr., Joseph Cannon, and E. Jerome McCarthy, *Essentials of Marketing,* 16th ed. (New York: McGraw Hill, 2019), pp. 5–6; Eric N. Berkowitz, Roger A. Kerin, Steven W. Hartley, and William Rudelius, *Marketing,* 3rd ed. (Burr Ridge, IL: Irwin, 1992), p. 27.

7. Dee-Ann Durbin, "Americans Are Becoming Obsessed with $80,000 Luxury Pickups," *Business Insider,* October 12, 2017, *www.businessinsider.com/american-truck-buyers-want-luxury-features-2017-10*.

8. James J. Kellaris, Anthony D. Cox, and Dena Cox, "The Effect of Background Music on Ad Processing: A Contingency Explanation," *Journal of Marketing,* October 1993, pp. 114–25.

9. William O. Bearden, Thomas N. Ingram, and Raymond W. LaForge, *Marketing Principles and Perspectives,* 2nd ed. (Burr Ridge, IL: Irwin/McGraw-Hill, 1997), p. 49.

10. *Consumer Expenditures in 2016,* U.S. Bureau of Labor Statistics, *www.bls.gov/opub/reports/consumer-expenditures/2016/pdf/home.pdf.>*

11. Bureau of Economic Analysis, "Gross Domestic Product by Industry, 1st Quarter 2018," press release, July 20, 2018, *www.bea.gov/news/2018/gross-domestic-product-industry-1st-quarter-2018.*

12. Bureau of Economic Analysis, "Gross Domestic Product by Industry, 1st Quarter 2018," press release, July 20, 2018, *www.bea.gov/news/2018/gross-domestic-product-industry-1st-quarter-2018.*

13. William O. Bearden, Thomas N. Ingram, and Raymond W. LaForge, *Marketing Principles and Perspectives,* 2nd ed. (Burr Ridge, IL: Irwin/McGraw-Hill, 1997), p. 99.

14. S. Kent Stephan and Barry L. Tannenholz, "The Real Reason for Brand Switching," *Advertising Age,* June 13, 1994, p. 31.

15. "Ad Nauseum," *Advertising Age,* July 10, 2000.

16. James J. Kellaris, Anthony D. Cox, and Dena Cox, "The Effect of Background Music on Ad Processing: A Contingency Explanation," *Journal of Marketing,* October 1993, p. 123.

17. Alice Z. Cuneo, "Dockers Takes a Sexier Approach in New Ad Push," *Advertising Age,* January 19, 1999, p. 8.

18. Daniel Kahneman, *Thinking Fast and Slow* (New York: Farrar, Straus and Giroux, 2011).

19. Elnora W. Stuart, T. A. Shimp, and R. W. Engle, "Classical Conditioning of Consumer Attitudes: Four Experiments in an Advertising Context," *Journal of Consumer Research* 14 (1987), pp. 334–49.

20. Albert Bandura, "Social Cognitive Theory," *in Handbook of Social Psychological Theories,* ed. P. A. M. van Lange, A. W. Kruglanski, and E. T. Higgins (London: Sage, 2011), pp. 349–73.

21. J. Paul Peter and Jerry C. Olson, *Consumer Behavior and Marketing Strategy,* 4th ed. (Burr Ridge, IL: Irwin, 1996), p. 554.

22. R. E. Petty, J. T. Cacioppo, and D. Schumann, "Central and Peripheral Routes to Advertising Effectiveness: The Moderating Role of Involvement," *Journal of Consumer Research* 10 (1983), pp. 135–46.

23. This section and the model are adapted from J. Paul Peter and Jerry C. Olson, *Consumer Behavior and Marketing Strategy,* 4th ed. (Burr Ridge, IL: Irwin, 1996), pp. 554–55.

24. J. Paul Peter and Jerry C. Olson, *Consumer Behavior and Marketing Strategy,* 4th ed. (Burr Ridge, IL: Irwin, 1996), pp. 556–57.

25. John T. Cacioppo and Richard E. Petty, "Effects of Message Repetition on Argument Processing, Recall, and Persuasion," *Basic and Applied Social Psychology* 10 (1989), pp. 3–12.

26. Yumiko Ono, "Overcoming the Stigma of Dishwashers in Japan," *The Wall Street Journal,* May 19, 2000, p. B2.

27. Karen A. Machleit, Chris T. Allen, and Thomas J. Madden, "The Mature Brand and Brand Interest: An Alternative Consequence of Ad-Evoked Affect," *Journal of Marketing,* October 1993, pp. 72–82.

28. Karen A. Machleit, Chris T. Allen, and Thomas J. Madden, "The Mature Brand and Brand Interest: An Alternative Consequence of Ad-Evoked Affect," *Journal of Marketing,* October 1993, pp. 72–82.

29. J. Paul Peter and Jerry C. Olson, *Consumer Behavior and Marketing Strategy,* 4th ed. (Burr Ridge, IL: Irwin, 1996), p. 513.

30. Ken Dychtwald and Greg Gable, "Portrait of a Changing Consumer," *Business Horizons,* January/February 1990, pp. 62–74; Larry Light, "Trust Marketing: The Brand Relationship Marketing Mandate for the 90s," address to the American Association of Advertising Agencies annual meeting, Laguna Niguel, CA, April 23, 1993.

31. Colin McDonald, "Point of View: The Key Is to Understand Consumer Response," *Journal of Advertising Research,* September/October 1993, pp. 63–69.

32. William Perreault Jr., Joseph Cannon, and E. Jerome McCarthy, *Essentials of Marketing,* 16th ed. (New York: McGraw Hill, 2019), pp. 5–6.

33. Vanessa O'Connell, "Nabisco Portrays Cookies as Boost to Women's Self-Esteem," *The Wall Street Journal,* July 10, 1998, p. B7.

34. John R. Rossiter and Larry Percy, *Advertising Communications and Promotion Management,* 2nd ed. (New York: McGraw-Hill, 1997), pp. 120–22.

35. John R. Rossiter and Larry Percy, *Advertising Communications and Promotion Management,* 2nd ed. (New York: McGraw-Hill, 1997), p. 121.

36. U.S. Census Bureau, "The Majority of Children Live with Two Parents, Census Bureau Reports," press release, November 17, 2016, *www.census.gov/newsroom/press-releases/2016/cb16-192.html.*

37. "The Worth of the Cool: Asking Teenagers to Identify the Coolest Brands," *Adweek,* May 9, 1994, p. 18.

38. Marla Martzer Rose, "Advertising Industry Working Fast to Boost Minority Hiring, Increase Internships," *Target Market News Inc.,* February 11, 2007.

39. "The Ad Industry Diversity Hiring Controversy: Will We Be Reading This Same Story Again in 2036?" editorial, *Advertising Age,* September 17, 2006, *https://adage.com/article/news/editorial-ad-industry-diversity-hiring-controversy/111896.*

40. Greg Farrell, "Star Search," *Adweek,* December 6, 1993, p. 26.

41. Ashley Bergner, "Have Product Placements in Films Become a Necessary Evil?," *Morning Sun,* April 23, 2012, *www.morningsun.net/news/entertainment/x1780488795/Have-product-placements-in-films-become-a-necessary-evil.*

42. William Perreault Jr., Joseph Cannon, and E. Jerome McCarthy, *Essentials of Marketing,* 16th ed. (New York: McGraw Hill, 2019), pp. 5–6; J. Paul Peter and Jerry C. Olson, *Consumer Behavior and Marketing Strategy,* 4th ed. (Burr Ridge, IL: Irwin, 1996), p. 368.

43. Carolyn A. Lin, "Cultural Differences in Message Strategies: A Comparison between American and Japanese TV Commercials," *Journal of Advertising Research,* July/August 1993, pp. 40–48.

44. Carolyn A. Lin, "Cultural Differences in Message Strategies: A Comparison between American and Japanese TV Commercials," *Journal of Advertising Research,* July/August 1993, pp. 40–48.

45. Carolyn A. Lin, "Cultural Differences in Message Strategies: A Comparison between American and Japanese TV Commercials," *Journal of Advertising Research,* July/August 1993, pp. 40–48.

46. J. Paul Peter and Jerry C. Olson, *Consumer Behavior and Marketing Strategy,* 4th ed. (Burr Ridge, IL: Irwin, 1996), p. 413.

47. U.S. Census Bureau, *Statistical Abstract of the United States: 2010, www.census.gov.*

48. "Hispanic Fact Pact 2005," *Advertising Age, http://adage.com/article?article_id=46168.*

49. Rebecca Purto, "Global Psychographics," *American Demographics,* December 1990, p. 8.

50. The classic studies on cognitive dissonance were initiated by Leon Festinger, *A Theory of Cognitive Dissonance* (Evanston, IL: Row, Peterson, 1957), p. 83; for more recent views, see Hugh Murray, "Advertising's Effect on Sales—Proven or Just Assumed?" *International Journal of Advertising* (UK) 5, no. 1 (1986), pp. 15–36; Delbert Hawkins, Roger Best, and Kenneth Coney, *Consumer Behavior,* 7th ed. (Burr Ridge, IL: McGraw-Hill/Irwin, 1998), pp. 609–10; Ronald E. Milliman and Phillip J. Decker, "The Use of Post-Purchase Communication to Reduce Dissonance and Improve Direct Marketing Effectiveness," *Journal of Business Communication,* Spring 1990, pp. 159–70.

51. Larry Light, "Advertising's Role in Building Brand Equity," speech to annual meeting of the American Association of Advertising Agencies, April 21, 1993.

CHAPTER

6

Market Segmentation and the Marketing Mix: Determinants of Campaign Strategy

LEARNING OBJECTIVES

To describe how marketers use behavioral characteristics to cluster prospective customers into market segments. Because no product or service pleases everybody, marketers need to select specific target markets that offer the greatest sales potential. Thus, they can fine-tune their mix of product-related elements (the four Ps), including IMC, to match the needs or wants of the target market.

After studying this chapter, you will be able to:

LO 6-1   Define market segmentation and describe its purposes.

LO 6-2   Explain the target marketing process.

LO 6-3   Show how IMC is used with the product element in marketing.

LO 6-4   Illustrate how IMC is used with the price element in marketing.

LO 6-5   Review how IMC is used with the place element in marketing.

LO 6-6   Discuss how IMC is used with the communication element in marketing.

SMELL LIKE A MAN, MAN.
Old Spice

Source: Procter and Gamble

IMC success is not just about what you say, but to whom you say it. Case in point, perhaps the best IMC campaign of 2011, the Old Spice "Man your man could smell like" promotion. A key secret to the campaign's success? Addressing the ads for a male body wash . . . to women. Targeting women for a male brand was certainly not a conventional approach, but then, just about everything about this campaign was unusual. To fully appreciate the ads, let's see why Old Spice needed to produce a game-changing campaign in the first place. ■ Old Spice was first sold in the 1930s as a men's after-shave lotion. Later, as male consumers showed interest in other grooming products, including deodorants and liquid soaps, Old Spice, acquired by Procter & Gamble, introduced brand extensions to meet those demands. ■ In 1983 P&G's global archrival, Unilever, introduced Axe. As a younger product, Axe had credibility in positioning itself as a sexy alternative. While Old Spice ads over the years tended to be safe and conventional, Axe used provocative spots suggesting the brand makes men irresistible to beautiful women.[1] ■ However implausible the "irresistibility" appeal

may seem, it's worked. By the 2000s, Axe established a healthy lead in share of the market. ■ In 2010, Proctor & Gamble had to consider whether to invest in a mature brand or move on. It decided to assign the challenge of reinvigorating Old Spice to one of the world's greatest agencies, Wieden+Kennedy. W+K built its reputation by making Nike a world leader in footwear. Its new challenge would be making Old Spice fresh, relevant, even hip.[2] ■ Before starting, the agency and client made a big decision. It would create ads that appealed to men (who use body wash) but spoke directly to women (who often buy it for them). The campaign slogan would be "the man your man could smell like." ■ In the first commercial, former NFL player Isaiah Mustafa, standing in front of a running shower, dressed only in a bath towel, addressed the intended audience right from the start. "Hello, ladies," he confidently intoned, "Look at your man, now back to me, now back at your man, now back to me. Sadly, he isn't me. But if he stopped using lady-scented body wash and switched to Old Spice, he could smell like he's me."[3] ■ The fast-paced and somewhat absurd style and pacing, along with Mustafa's charm and humor, made the ad an immediate hit. Old Spice was back. ■ But now what? Advertising is filled with "one-hit wonder" campaigns that quickly fizzle. So Wieden+Kennedy changed the game. After the Old Spice campaign drew national attention, the agency began using Mustafa in social media, developing dozens of different, personalized executions for key influencers like Ellen DeGeneres. Naturally, Ellen was flattered and invited Mustafa on her show. More buzz for Old Spice. And a Cannes Grand Prix for the campaign.[4] ■ W+K still wasn't done. It decided to create a viral story line for Mustafa's "Old Spice guy." Jason Bagley, creative director at Wieden, settled on a story line in which an older celebrity would try to usurp Mustafa as spokesperson. The agency picked Fabio, an Italian model known for serving as a cover model for countless romance novels. The theme of over 100 viral videos shot featuring the two was "Mano a Mano en el Bañó." ■ The results? Another win for Old Spice. During a single week, the videos were watched more than 20 million times. The number one and four spots for most-viewed channels on YouTube were held by Old Spice and New Old Spice Guy Fabio. And the brand attracted nearly 70,000 new fans on Facebook.[5] And best of all, Old Spice regained its share of market lead from Axe as sales increased dramatically. The Old Spice ads have received about as many accolades as a campaign can attract. And W+K has solidified its reputation as an amazing creative shop. And it all started with a decision to tout the benefits of male body wash to women.[6]

Market Segmentation

LO 6-1

Marketing people constantly search for clusters of consumers who might be better satisfied. The process of **market segmentation** involves two steps: *identifying groups of people* (or organizations) with certain shared needs and *aggregating* (combining) these groups into larger market segments according to their interest in the brand's utility. This process should result in market segments large enough to target and reachable through a mix of marketing activities.

Markets often consist of many segments. A company may offer different products and use distinct marketing strategies for every segment, or concentrate its marketing activities on only one or a few segments. Either task is far from simple. Toyota, a company best known for selling cars to middle-class Americans, developed its Scion line to appeal to younger drivers. It also markets Lexus to wealthier, older consumers. Catering to all these needs on a global level requires a sophisticated marketing and communications system. In this chapter, we look first at how marketers identify and categorize *consumer markets* and second at the techniques they use to segment *business markets*. Then we discuss various IMC strategies companies use to match their products with markets and create profitable exchanges.

Segmenting the Consumer Market

The concept of *shared characteristics* is critical to market segmentation. Marketing and advertising people know that consumer needs and wants can be identified from consumer "footprints in the sand"—the telltale signs of where people live and work, what they buy, and how they spend their leisure time. By following these footprints, marketers can locate and define groups of consumers with similar needs and wants, create messages for them, and know how and where to deliver their messages. The goal is to find that particular niche, or space in the market, where the marketer's product or service will fit. Consider the Old Spice story you read at the beginning of the chapter. For a moment, think about what you can determine about the brand's target market. Research revealed that men will use the product if women buy it for them. The campaign encourages women to help their partners stop using "lady-scented body wash." The category of "men" is narrowed to men with the following characteristics: they are in relationships and already use liquid soap. This is a smaller, but more valuable segment than just "men." Why more valuable? Because these are consumers who are most likely to respond to the advertiser's message.

Marketers group these shared characteristics into categories (*behavioristic, geographic, demographic,* and *psychographic*) to identify and segment consumer markets (see Exhibit 6-1). Most marketers have two goals: first, to identify people who are likely to be interested in a brand's benefits, and second, to develop a mix of effective messages that can help these consumers understand the benefits.

Old Spice helped keep the buzz going and fans flocking to its social media by introducing Fabio to the campaign.

Source: Procter and Gamble

Variables	Typical Breakdowns	Variables	Typical Breakdowns
Geographic		**Demographic**	
Region	Pacific; Mountain; West North Central; West South Central; East North Central; East South Central; South Atlantic; Middle Atlantic; New England	Age	Under 6, 6–11, 12–19, 20–34, 35–49, 50–64, 65+
County size	A, B, C, D	Sex	Male, female
Climate	Northern; southern	Family size	1–2, 3–4, 5+
City or SMSA size	Under 5,000; 5,000–19,999; 20,000–49,999; 50,000–99,999; 100,000–249,000; 250,000–499,999; 500,000–999,999; 1,000,000–3,999,999; 4,000,000 or over	Family life cycle	Young, single; young, married, no children; young, married, youngest child under 6; young, married, youngest child 6 or over; young, unmarried, with children; older, married, with children; older, unmarried, with children; older, married, no children under 18; older, single; other
Density	Urban, suburban, rural	Income	Under $10,000; $10,000–19,999; $20,000–29,999; $30,000–39,999; $40,000–59,999; $60,000–99,999; $100,000–149,999; $150,000 and over
Behavioristic			
Purchase occasion	Regular occasion, special occasion	Occupation	Professional and technical; managers, officials, and proprietors; clerical, sales; craftspeople; supervisors; operatives; farmers; retired; students; homemakers; unemployed
Benefits sought	Economy, convenience, prestige		
User status	Nonuser, ex-user, potential user, first-time user, regular user		
Usage rate	Light user, medium user, heavy user	Education	Grade school or less; some high school; high school graduates; some college; college graduates
Loyalty status	None, medium, strong, absolute		
Readiness stage	Unaware, aware, informed, interested, desirous, intending to buy	Religion	Catholic, Protestant, Jewish, Muslim, other
Marketing factor sensitivity	Quality, price, service, advertising, sales promotion	Race	White, Black, Asian, other
		Nationality	American, British, French, German, Scandinavian, Italian, Latin American, Middle Eastern, Japanese, other
Psychographic			
Societal divisions	Upper crust, movers and shakers, successful singles, social security, middle of the road, metro ethnic mix		
Lifestyle	Strivers, achievers, actualizers		
Personality	Compulsive, gregarious, authoritarian, ambitious		

Exhibit 6-1
Methods for segmenting consumer markets.

Behavioristic Segmentation

A straightforward way to segment markets is to group consumers by buying behavior. This is called **behavioristic segmentation.** Behavioral segments are determined by many variables, but the most important are *user status, usage rate, purchase occasion,* and *benefits sought.* These categories tell us who our customers are now, when and why they buy, and how much they consume.

Old Spice is a mature brand. But with the use of clever, witty, and even somewhat absurd advertising, the brand rebounded strongly. Wieden+Kennedy's great work suggests that with the right message, brands can find their own Fountain of Youth, as exemplified in the ad above depicting a robot in a hot tub on a date with two attractive models.

Source: Procter & Gamble

User-Status Variables   Many markets can be segmented by the **user status** of prospective customers. Researchers Stephan and Tannenholz have identified six categories of consumers based on user status.

Sole users choose one brand exclusively. These consumers are the most brand loyal and require the least amount of promotion. *Semi-sole users* typically use Brand A but have an alternative in mind if Brand A is not available, or are willing to use the alternative when it is discounted. *Discount users* are the semi-sole users of competing Brand B. They don't buy Brand A at full price but will consider buying it at a discount. *Aware nontriers* use competitive products in the category but haven't taken a liking to Brand A. A different advertising message could help, but these people rarely offer much potential. *Trial/rejectors* responded to Brand A's IMC messages but didn't like the product. More promoting won't help; only a reformulation of Brand A will bring them back. *Repertoire users* perceive two or more brands to have superior attributes and will buy at full price. They are the primary

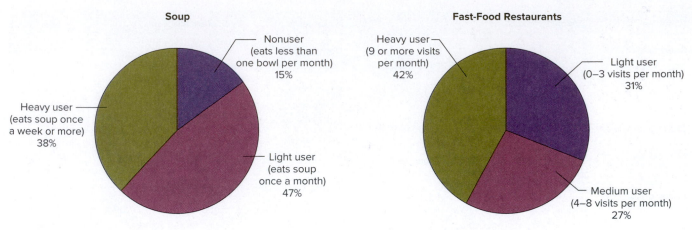

Soup

Nonuser
(eats less than
one bowl per month)
15%

Heavy user
(eats soup once
a week or more)
38%

Light user
(eats soup
once a month)
47%

Fast-Food Restaurants

Heavy user
(9 or more visits
per month)
42%

Light user
(0–3 visits per month)
31%

Medium user
(4–8 visits per month)
27%

Exhibit 6-2
Usage rates vary for different products.

Source: Mediamark Research and Intelligence. *Journal of Advertising Research* (www.warc.com/jar).

brand switchers and respond to persuasive information based on their fluctuating wants and desires. Therefore, they should be the primary target for brand messages.[7]

Usage-Rate Variables   Heavy users are more valuable than light users, for the obvious reason that they buy more of the product. In **volume segmentation,** marketers measure people's **usage rates** to define consumers as light, medium, or heavy users of products (see Exhibit 6-2). One rule of thumb suggests that 20 percent of all users consume 80 percent of the product. Marketers want to identify that 20 percent and target them with ads.

Hardee's, a fast-food chain owned by CKE Restaurants Inc., even has a pet name for its prized 17- to 34-year-old male market segment: the HFFU (pronounced who-foo). According to Andrew Pudzer, CKE's CEO, "That's the 'heavy fast-food user,' someone who eats there four or five times a week. . . . It is the sweet spot of the industry and what appeals to him is drippy, messy burgers. He is not interested in little 99-cent burgers or low-carb anything. He's not a big calorie counter."[8]

By finding similarities among heavy users of their products, marketers can define product differences and focus campaigns more effectively. For example, independent businesspeople who travel at their own expense, the group that Fallon Worldwide describes as "road warriors," are heavy users of budget hotel chains, with some spending over a hundred nights a year on the road. In creating a campaign that targeted this group for Holiday Inn Express, Fallon also discovered that road warriors make their travel plans at the beginning of the week and like to watch ESPN, CNN, and the Weather Channel. Such knowledge helped Fallon media people schedule messages when and where the target audience would be attentive.

Marketers of one product sometimes find their customers are also heavy users of other products and can define target markets in terms of the usage rates of the other products. Research indicates that heavy users of organic foods spend more on fruits and vegetables and less on prepared foods than do non–organic food users. Additionally, organic shoppers tend to be less religious, better educated, and younger than those who do not shop for organics.[9] Similarly, Claritas[10] suggests that the cluster it refers to as "Second City Elite" is much more likely than the typical American to enjoy cultural activities (books, attending theater and dance productions) and is more likely to read magazines and to drive Lexus cars.

Purchase-Occasion Variables   Buyers can also be distinguished by when they buy or use a product or service—the **purchase occasion.** Air travelers, for example, may fly for business or vacation, so one airline might promote business travel while another promotes tourism. The purchase occasion might be affected

Repertoire users are concerned with quality. In this ad, by associating Rolex with an accomplished performer, the ad conveys added luxury and suggests that individuals with taste prefer the brand.

Source: Rolex

The Crest website does a great job of highlighting the benefits of using Crest toothpaste.

Source: Procter & Gamble

by frequency of need (regular or occasional), a fad (candy, computer games), or seasons (water skis, raincoats). The Japan Weather Association tracked buying patterns on 20,000 items and correlated them to the outside temperature. Not surprisingly, when the temperature goes up, people buy more sunshades, air conditioners, watermelons, and swimwear. When there's a chill in the air, sales of suits, sweaters, and heaters take off.[11] A marketer who discovers common purchase occasions for a group has a potential target segment and can better determine when to run specials and how to promote certain product categories.

Benefits-Sought Variables   Marketers frequently segment according to the *benefits* being sought. Consumers seek various **benefits** in the products they buy—high quality, low price, status, sex appeal, good taste, health consciousness. A teenaged consumer getting lunch at McDonald's may be searching for an inexpensive, filling meal, while a parent with two young children might be looking for a place to enjoy a hot cup of coffee while the kids eat Happy Meals. In addition to tangible benefits, customers are often motivated by *symbolism*—what the brand name means to them, to associates, or to some social reference group. **Benefit segmentation** is the prime objective of many consumer attitude studies and the basis for many successful ad campaigns.

Some product categories are characterized by substantial *brand switching* from one purchase occasion to the next. Researchers have determined that switching occurs in response to different "need states" that consumers may experience from one occasion to another. Thus, a soft drink company competes not just for *drinkers* (users) but for *drinks* (occasions) based on the benefits the consumer is seeking at that moment. For example, a consumer who might not ordinarily buy ginger ale may do so during the holidays when he or she is having family visit. By measuring the importance of occasion-based motives, marketers can determine if a campaign needs to reposition the product.[12]

Using behavioristic segmentation, we can accomplish the first step of identifying likely prospects for our marketing efforts. The next step in developing rich profiles of these customers involves the use of geographic, demographic, and psychographic characteristics.

Geographic Segmentation

Markets can also be defined using **geographic segmentation.** People in one region of the country (or the world) have needs, wants, and purchasing habits that differ from those in other regions. People in Sunbelt states, for example, buy more sunscreen. Canadians buy special equipment for dealing with snow and ice—products many Floridians have never seen in stores.

When marketers analyze geographic data, they study sales by region, county size, city size, zip code, and types of stores. Many products sell well in urban areas but poorly in suburban or rural ones, and vice versa. As we'll see in Chapter 9, geographic information is critical in developing advertising media schedules because, with limited budgets, marketers want to advertise in areas where their sales potential is best.

**Louisville, KY:
S. Hancock St. & E. Market St.**

5 and 10 Mile Radii Showing Dominant PRIZM Cluster by ZIP Code

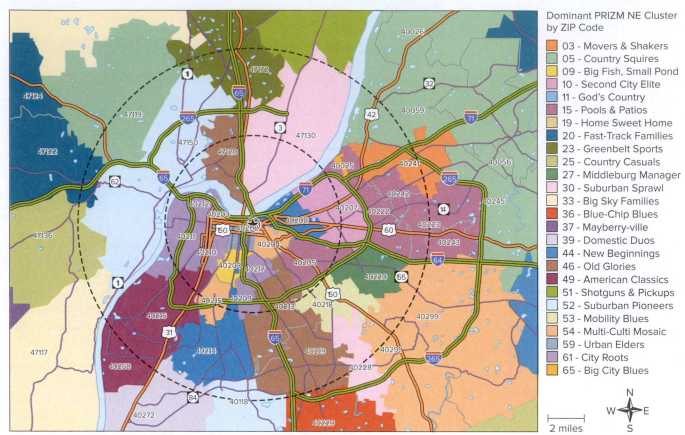

Dominant PRIZM NE Cluster
by ZIP Code

- 03 - Movers & Shakers
- 05 - Country Squires
- 09 - Big Fish, Small Pond
- 10 - Second City Elite
- 11 - God's Country
- 15 - Pools & Patios
- 19 - Home Sweet Home
- 20 - Fast-Track Families
- 23 - Greenbelt Sports
- 25 - Country Casuals
- 27 - Middleburg Manager
- 30 - Suburban Sprawl
- 33 - Big Sky Families
- 36 - Blue-Chip Blues
- 37 - Mayberry-ville
- 39 - Domestic Duos
- 44 - New Beginnings
- 46 - Old Glories
- 49 - American Classics
- 51 - Shotguns & Pickups
- 52 - Suburban Pioneers
- 53 - Mobility Blues
- 54 - Multi-Culti Mosaic
- 59 - Urban Elders
- 61 - City Roots
- 65 - Big City Blues

2 miles

Exhibit 6-3

Claritas offers several tools for companies to research consumers in their area. Claritas's products PRIZM® and P$YCLE® sort customers by lifestyles, ethnic affinity, shopping, and financial behaviors. This exhibit shows how Claritas's PRIZM system classifies prospective customers in the Louisville area by census tract and labels each area by the residents' shared characteristics.

Source: Claritas's PRIZM NE System from Claritas.

Even in local markets, geographic segmentation is important. For example, a local progressive politician might send a mailer only to precincts where voters typically support liberal causes, and a retail store rarely draws customers from outside a fairly limited *trading area.*

One of the most respected geographic segmentation systems is PRIZM, a product of Claritas.[13] Marketers have used the PRIZM system for more than 30 years, and it is updated every 10 years with census results, most recently in 2010. PRIZM analyzes urbanization measures, as well as household and neighborhood characteristics, in order to assign every U.S. zip code to one of 66 geographic segments with vivid descriptions that include "Young Digerati," "Money and Brains," "Bohemian Mix," and "American Dreams" (see Exhibit 6-3) Young Digerati live in urban areas, are wealthy, have kids, and often have advanced degrees. They are more likely than most to own an Audi, grab a coffee at Starbucks, and use Uber. American Dreams are also urban-dwellers, but they make less money and have less education than Young Digerati. Claritas suggests that they are overrepresented as owners of Volvos and as shoppers at Nordstrom Rack.

Demographic Segmentation

Demographic segmentation is a way to define population groups by their statistical characteristics: sex, age, ethnicity, education, occupation, income, and other quantifiable factors. Demographics are often combined with geographic segmentation to select target markets for advertising. This is called **geodemographic segmentation.** For example, research shows that

Exhibit 6-4

Projected U.S. Hispanic population and largest advertisers in Hispanic media (ranked by U.S. measured-media spending.

Year	Hispanic	Total U.S.	Hisp. %Total
2000	35,621,721	282,124,631	12.6
2005	41,800,971	295,507,134	14.1
2010	47,755,585	308,935,581	15.5
2015	53,647,237	322,365,787	16.6
2020	59,755,555	335,804,546	17.8
2025	66,190,911	349,439,199	18.9
2030	73,055,166	363,584,435	20.1
2035	80,242,372	377,886,238	21.2
2040	47,584,907	391,945,658	22.3
2045	95,025,560	405,862,392	23.4
2050	102,559,846	419,853,587	24.4

Rank	Advertiser	2017 spending (millions)
1	Procter & Gamble Co.	$335
2	Genomma Lab International	260
3	T-Mobile	116
4	Dish Network	116
5	AT&T	108
6	Molson Coors Brewing	106
7	L'Oréal	104
8	Softbank Group Corp.	100
9	Johnson & Johnson	95
10	Anheuser-Busch InBev	94

Source: AdAge Hispanic Fact Pack, 2018. Crain Communications, Inc.

people who identify themselves as "strongly Hispanic" tend to be very loyal to certain brands. And, as Exhibit 6-4 reveals, the numbers of Americans with Hispanic ancestry are expected to grow at a rate much faster than that of the overall population well into this century. This has meant a surge in advertising dollars allocated to Hispanic media. Many blue-chip advertisers, such as AT&T, McDonald's, and General Motors, now aim a significant portion of their advertising specifically at this market, which reached $1.3 trillion in 2018.[14] To do so efficiently, they measure the size of the "strongly Hispanic" community in each marketing area they plan to target, as well as its income, age distribution, and attitudes. JCPenney, for example, discovered that its Sandra Salcedo line of clothing for Hispanic women sold well in Texas and Northern California stores but not in heavily Mexican American Los Angeles, where urban influences hold greater sway. This is an excellent reminder that focusing on one consumer influence to the exclusion of others is usually overly simplistic.[15]

Best Buy discovered a large untapped market after data-mining technology revealed that women customers were being underserved in the company's stores. In an effort to boost sales to this demographic group, Best Buy opened 68 concept stores staffed with salespeople trained to provide information tailored to the needs of female shoppers. "We are enabling her transformation into a big-time electronics buyer by talking her language," noted Best Buy vice president Nancy Brooks.[16]

As people mature and their incomes change, so do their interests in various product categories (see Exhibit 6-5). The biggest generational cohort as of 2015[17] is Millennials, whose numbers now just slightly exceed those of Baby Boomers. Millennials are consumers who in 2015 were between 18 and 34, and they numbered about 75 million.[18] Naturally, many businesses want to better understand how to successfully market to these affluent young consumers. Car seller AutoTrader interviewed a large sample of Millennials and found commonalities

Exhibit 6-5
Heavy usage patterns of various age groups.

Age	Name of Age Group	Merchandise Purchased
0–5	Young children	Baby food, toys, nursery furniture, children's wear
6–19	Schoolchildren and teenagers	Clothing, sporting goods, CDs and DVDs, school supplies, fast food, soft drinks, candy, cosmetics, movies
20–34	Young adults	Cars, furniture, housing, food and beer, clothing, diamonds, home entertainment equipment, recreational equipment, purchases for younger age segments
35–49	Younger middle-aged	Larger homes, better cars, second cars, new furniture, computers, recreational equipment, jewelry, clothing, food and wine
50–64	Older middle-aged	Recreational items, purchases for young marrieds and infants, travel
65 and over	Senior adults	Medical services, travel, pharmaceuticals, purchases for younger age groups

and differences between the cohort and those that came before it. For example, Millennials, like other groups, are status-conscious and like luxury car brands. In response, car makers such as BMW are creating lower-priced, entry-level models such as the BMW X2. But unlike other generations, Millennials spend much more time shopping online, especially on their phones. Auto dealerships should expect that their Millennial customers will arrive in showrooms well-educated about their options. And when the haggling begins, these young consumers will grab their phones and check prices over a new car purchase.[19]

Demographic segmentation is vital in the fast-food industry, or QSR (quick-serve restaurant) industry, as it now prefers to be called. McDonald's, the industry's creator and perpetual frontrunner, runs the table. Once stigmatized as unsanitary meat fit only for poor people, chains like White Castle and McDonald's helped change the hamburger's image, fashioning it into the national cuisine by the 1950s.[20] Now, children are McDonald's primary target consumers. Decades of ads for Happy Meals and toys have made an impression. Among fictional characters, Ronald McDonald's cultural penetration is surpassed only by Santa Claus: 96 percent of schoolchildren in the United States can identify the yellow-jumpsuited clown.[21] Against this giant's brand value and advertising expenditures, competitors have returned to the hamburger's traditional consumer, the young male. In the segment where McDonald's is slightly weaker, Hardee's intends to be strong. Thickburger TV spots proclaim that consumers should "eat like you mean it."

"Eat like you mean it" is a great tagline because it identifies the audience (individuals looking for a juicy, large hamburger) and the benefit (you can find those burgers at Hardee's).

Source: Carl's Jr. Restaurants LLC

In international markets, the demographics of many populations are changing rapidly. From India to Brazil to Poland, comfortable lives and discretionary spending are becoming available to more people. This emerging middle class has an insatiable appetite for consumer goods—everything from smartphones and iPads to cars and refrigerators.[22] Currently, nearly 1.6 million Indian families spend an average of $9,000 annually on high-end goods.[23] China's emergence as one of the world's fastest-growing advertising markets is a direct result of the country's increasingly wealthy consumers. According to CTR Market Research, China now ranks just behind the United States and Japan in the global advertising market.[24]

Ad spending in any country is a function of two factors: the amount spent on each consumer and the total population. So, while the total Chinese market is huge (the nation has 1.4 billion people, or nearly 19 percent of the world's population), the amount spent per person is small, just $48.66 in 2018. Conversely, the highest amount of spending per person in any nation is still the United States, where marketers spend an estimated $670.65 on every man, woman, and child.[25]

Geographic and demographic data provide information about markets but little about the psychology of individuals. In many instances, people in the same demographic or geographic segment have widely differing product preferences and TV viewing habits. Rarely can demographic criteria alone predict purchase behavior.[26] That's why marketers use *psychographics.*

Psychographic Segmentation

With **psychographics,** marketers group people by their values, attitudes, personality, and lifestyle. Psychographics enables marketers to view people as individuals with feelings and inclinations. Then they can classify people according to what they believe, the way they live, and the products, services, and media they use.[27]

Perhaps the best-known psychographic classification system is VALS ("Values, Attitudes And Lifestyles"), a product of SRI Consulting Business Intelligence (SRIC-BI). VALS assigns consumers to one of eight groups based on two dimensions: **primary motivation** and **resources.** According to SRIC-BI, individuals are primarily motivated by one of three things: ideals (or basic principles), achievement (tangible markers of success or accomplishment), or self-expression (a desire for experiences or to take risks). In addition, people possess varying levels of resources, which include money, education, or self-confidence. Those with the fewest resources are placed near the bottom of the VALS typology, while those with the most are at the top.[28]

The purpose of VALS is to help marketers identify whom to target, uncover what the target group buys and does, locate where concentrations of the target group live, identify how best to communicate with them, and gain insight into why the target group behaves the way it does. The system has been applied to a variety of areas: new product development and design, target marketing, product positioning, advertising message development, and media planning, to name a few.[29]

In one case, for example, a foreign car manufacturer used VALS to reposition its sports utility vehicle after its award-winning but ineffective television campaign failed to result in higher sales. Using VALS, the company targeted a new "rebellious" consumer group with a new campaign using a "breaking the rules" theme. Nothing changed but the advertising, but sales increased 60 percent in six months.[30]

Later, SRIC-BI developed additional VALS products: Japan-VALS, to determine the consumer effect of changing values and social behavior in Japan, and GeoVALS, to determine where target customers live and show why they behave the way they do. This helps advertisers select the best site locations, target direct-mail campaigns effectively, and maximize advertising dollars.[31]

In Europe and Asia, numerous lifestyle studies have produced a variety of other classification systems intended to help marketers understand the product use of different target groups across national boundaries. The research company RISC investigated how people react to social changes in 12 European countries. The basis of the research was the belief that when individuals share similar values, perceptions, and sensitivities, their purchasing behavior will also show consistent similarities. Roper Starch Worldwide has developed its ValueScope service to help marketers find "shared patterns of market space behavior" around the world in order to conduct global campaigns. The Roper model uses three drivers of consumer behavior—nationality, lifestage, and values—to define six consumer segments: creatives, fun seekers, intimates, strivers, devouts, and altruists.[32] An interesting aspect of Roper's research was the discovery of the top 10 values shared by people around the world (see Exhibit 6-6).

Another psychographic segmentation scheme is MindBase, which divides consumers into eight psychological categories, including "I am driven" (motto: nothing ventured, nothing gained) and "I measure twice" (motto: an ounce of prevention). Kantar, a global research firm, uses the system to demonstrate how people with similar demographic backgrounds can have very different in motives and feelings. The company's data also suggest that the groups differ in their receptivity to marketing messages and rely on different media.[33]

Simmons, an Experion brand, offers a psychographic tool called BehaviorGraphics. This classification scheme is based on attitudes and lifestyle measures, including information about the products that consumers like and the media they consume. The tool aggregates consumers into 31 different segments, with names such as Trendsetters (teens heavily attracted to media and to current styles, who make greater use of the Internet than any of the other 30 groups), Kid Focused (middle-class families whose activities and media use revolve around their children), and Sarcastics (predominantly young men who enjoy television programs on Comedy Central and are heavily into sports).[34]

Exhibit 6-6
The world's top 10 values shared by people around the world.

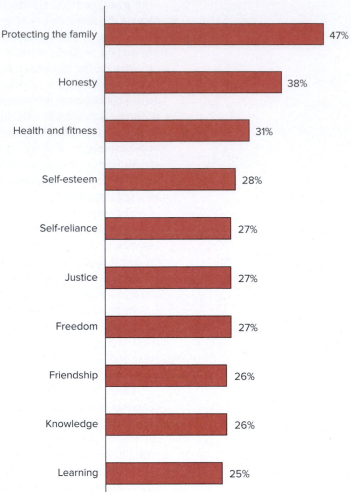

Protecting the family	47%
Honesty	38%
Health and fitness	31%
Self-esteem	28%
Self-reliance	27%
Justice	27%
Freedom	27%
Friendship	26%
Knowledge	26%
Learning	25%

In an influential book, *The Tipping Point,* cultural observer Malcolm Gladwell suggests another reason why advertisers may wish to psychologically segment consumers: to identify that small groups of people can have a great impact on the rest of us. Gladwell argues that certain types of people create what he calls *social epidemics,* typified by the almost overnight increase in the popularity of a product, fashion, or idea. He offers the example of Hush Puppy shoes, which sold in low numbers for many years before suddenly surging in popularity again among young, cool consumers. This happened, Gladwell believes, because a small group of influentials began using the brand, leading to imitation by others. Gladwell proposes that epidemics most often follow the actions of three types of people: *Connectors, Mavens,* and *Salesmen.* Connectors have very wide social circles. While ordinary people may have a few dozen acquaintances, Connectors often know and keep tabs on hundreds. With such a large social network, Connectors can link different social groups that would not ordinarily influence one another. This increases the chances that an idea prevalent in one group will transfer to others. Mavens spend the time and energy accumulating knowledge that most people can't be bothered to find out. A Maven will know where to get the best steak in town, where to find the best deal on a new TV, and what brand of phone provides the best options. Just as important, Mavens love sharing this information. Connectors and Mavens are important sources of information about new products, trends, and ideas, but persuading people to embrace these things falls to Salesmen. Salesmen are people others find to be credible, trustworthy, and authoritative. Unlike the "hard sell" stereotype that the term may invoke, Gladwell's archetype is low-key, attractive, and, most of all, influential.

Ethics, Diversity & Inclusion

The Youngest Target Market

Imagine you are a brand manager looking to uncover opportunities with a new target market. What is the youngest age group you would consider from the perspective of effectiveness? How about from the perspective of ethics?

Would you consider marketing to infants or children under 3? Seem too young? Not to Disney, or a growing number of other marketers. The following story was reported in *Adweek:*

> Jenny Gill was in [the] hospital earlier this year for the birth of her son, Jack, when a photographer stopped by to take snapshots of the mother and newborn. The practice is common in hospitals, but what the photographer did next surprised Gill. "In the middle of taking the pictures, she pulls out this cutely wrapped onesie and says, 'Oh, here's a free Disney onesie. We'll just need your e-mail address,'" Gill recalls. "It weirded me out. I just gave birth, please lay off with the Disney already!"

Disney wasn't marketing to Jenny, but to her baby. The idea is to make logos and brand characters visible to young children, even infants, to establish the brand as early as possible.

But why? What benefits come from imprinting brands on consumers who can't read, talk, or use a credit card? *Adweek* suggests several:

- Young children can recognize brands at an early age, and do form early brand preferences.

- Families are more attentive to product preferences of young children.

- Brand loyalty with very young kids can last a (very long) lifetime.

And Disney's efforts don't stop with onesies. The company has developed an extensive line of "baby apps" for phones and tablets. And if you think pretoddlers are too young to use apps, think again. One child advocacy organization estimates that 14 percent of kids under 2 spend at least a couple of hours a day with digital media. It seems Mom and Dad are increasingly likely to reach for a mobile phone instead of a pacifier when the little one gets cranky.

Companies are sensitive to criticisms about marketing to kids, even ones much older than infants, if, for no other reason, in order to prevent the FCC from strengthening its already stringent guidelines for television ads in children's programming. Some familiar complaints about kid-centered ads include kids are too young to evaluate product claims or understand an ad's purpose and ads encourage kids to influence family consumption decisions, often in unhealthy ways. Defenders of the practice say families should teach children about what ads are and about buying decisions. Dr. Susan Linn doesn't agree, "It's unfair and naïve to expect that parents, on their own, are going to be able to do a great job of coping with this . . . they need help from the government."

When dealing with the youngest consumers, those under 3, even many defenses of the practice of kid-focused marketing seem weak or irrelevant. For example, some point out that older children, say those aged 7 to 14, would have little media content directed to them without ad-sponsored shows. But should a 2-year-old ever find him- or herself in the target audience of a product?

Questions

1. Is it ever ethically justified to market to a child under 3? Why or why not?

2. Do you agree with Susan Linn that parents are not able to determine how best to respond to marketing efforts for their children?

3. From an ethical perspective, who are the stakeholders in this situation, and what values or conception of what is right is important to consider? Are the concerns about very young children more important than those of others?

Sources: Brian Braiker, "The Next Great American Consumer: Infants to 3-Year-Olds: They're a New Demographic Marketers Are Hell-Bent on Reaching," *Adweek,* September 26, 2011, retrieved December 31, 2011, from www.adweek.com/news/advertising-branding/next-great-american-consumer-135207; Christine Lagorio, "The Hard Sell: Marketing to Kids," *CBS Interactive,* May 14, 2007, retrieved December 31, 2011, from www.cbsnews.com/8301-18563_162-2802643.html.

AD Lab 6–A

Market Segmentation: A Dog of a Job

Market segmentation doesn't have to be boring. A Michael Reinemer article in *Advertising Age* described a market he could have fun with—dogs (or, at least, dog owners).

Reinemer shared what prompted his thinking. He saw a video for dogs in an upscale pet store. And an ad for dogs who can't brush after every meal. And an article about dog health insurance, puppy psychotherapy, and Prozac for canines. He suddenly realized that many dogs in the United States probably enjoy better nutrition and health care than millions of people in the world. His reaction: "How do I cash in on this thing?"

Reinemer thought of launching a new consulting firm called "Dog Trend$" to sniff out every conceivable emerging dog-related trend or fad and sponsor a Dog Marketing Conference.

Then he created a few trends of his own for man's best friend[37]:

Dog fitness centers. While the baby boomers pursue fitness, why not let the dog work out, too (SpaDog and DogAerobics)?

Dog video games. Interactive games that improve the dog's eye–paw coordination (Mortal Dogfight, Hydrant Finder, Car Chase).

Fashion magazines for dogs. When it's a cold winter day and you put that warm sweater on to keep you warm, why not put a fashionable sweater on your dog (*Dogmopolitan, smELLE, Dogue,* and *DQ*)?

Dog retirement communities (Sunset Leisure Kennels).

Cable networks (DoggieVision).

Upscale department stores (BloomingDog's).

Maybe Reinemer's ideas are more than fun. Could they really be the next phase in marketing?

Laboratory Applications

1. Come up with a market segment that you think would be fun to work with. What five products could you market?

2. Come up with your own trends for dogs (or cats if you prefer). Suggest five new business ideas that can capitalize on people's love for their animal companions.

Gladwell's analysis suggests that relatively small groups of people are very influential in affecting the consumption of much larger segments of society. The influence of his analysis is already incorporated in several segmentation tools, including BehaviorGraphics.[35]

Limitations of Consumer Segmentation Methods

Advocates of psychographic systems claim they help address the factors that motivate consumers. However, because the markets for many products comprise such a broad cross section of consumers, psychographics may in fact offer little real value—especially since it oversimplifies consumer personalities. Some typologies, such as VALS, are also criticized for being complicated and lacking proper theoretical underpinnings.[36]

Still, it's important for marketers to monitor and understand their customers. It helps them select target markets, create ads that match the attributes and images of their products with the types of consumers who use them, develop effective media plans, and budget their advertising dollars wisely. (For an amusing twist on satisfying market needs, see Ad Lab 6–A.)

Segmenting Business and Government Markets: Understanding Organizational Buying Behavior

Business (or *industrial*) **markets** include manufacturers, government agencies, wholesalers, retailers, banks, and institutions that buy goods and services to help them operate. These products may include raw materials, electronic components, mechanical parts, office equipment, vehicles, or services used in conducting business. Many business marketers sell to **resellers,** such as retail businesses. Some brands are produced, merchandised, and resold under their own names, like Levi's jeans. Other resellers offer both brand-name products and unbranded products. For example, much of Hardee's food is supplied by Siméus Foods International, a processing, production, and distribution conglomerate. Siméus's two plants produce and freeze menu items, such as hamburger and chicken patties, to the specifications of customers like Hardee's and Denny's. The end product is resold by Hardee's with no mention of Siméus. Hardee's reselling contract with Coca-Cola, however, is a

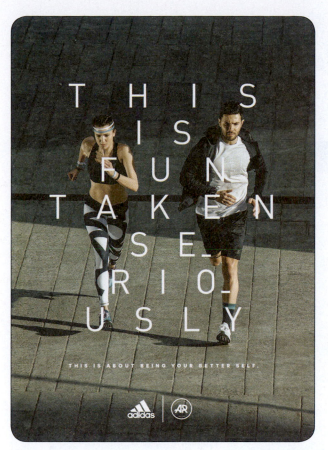

THIS IS FUN TAKEN SERIOUSLY

THIS IS ABOUT BEING YOUR BETTER SELF.

adidas | AR

Ads for adidas (www.adidas.com) capture the attitude and lifestyle of its target market: athletic young people around the world who define themselves by their athletic achievements. Fun taken seriously positions adidas in the lives of active young people.

Source: Adidas America Inc.

much more visible "brand partnership"; Coke products are often featured in Hardee's advertising.

Identifying target markets of prospective business customers is just as challenging as identifying consumer markets. Many of the criteria used to identify consumer markets can also be used for business markets—for example, geography and behavior (purchase occasion, benefits sought, user status, and usage rate).

Business Purchasing Procedure

When businesspeople evaluate new products, they use a process far more complex than the consumer purchase process described in Chapter 5. Business marketers must design their promotional programs with this in mind.

Large firms have purchasing departments that act as professional buyers. They evaluate the need for products, analyze proposed purchases, weigh competitive bids, seek approvals from managers, make requisitions, place orders, and supervise all product purchasing. This structured purchase decision process implies a rational approach. According to recent research, however, professional buyers often show a willingness to pay a substantial premium for their favorite brand. This suggests that advertising may play a larger role in business-to-business marketing than previously thought.[38]

Making a sale in business markets may take weeks, months, or even years, especially to government agencies. Purchase decisions often depend on factors besides price or quality, among them product demonstrations, delivery time, terms of sale, and dependability of supply. Marketers often emphasize these issues in promotional appeals.

Before choosing a target market, business marketers should consider how the purchase decision process works in various segments. New companies, for instance, may want to target smaller firms where the purchase decision can be made quickly. Or they may use commission-only reps to call on the larger prospects that require more time.

Industrial Classification System

Industrial customers need different products, depending on their business. For example, apparel manufacturers such as Levi's are customers for buttons and zippers. Marketing managers need to focus their sales and advertising efforts on firms that are in the right business for their products.[39] The U.S. Census Bureau classifies all U.S. businesses—and collects and publishes industry statistics on them—using the **North American Industry Classification System (NAICS) codes.** The NAICS (pronounced "nakes") system includes many new industries that are relevant to today's changing economy. The system was developed in cooperation with Canada and Mexico to ensure consistency throughout North America.

NAICS organizes all the industries into 20 broad sectors such as mining, manufacturing, wholesale trade, and information. These are then subdivided into four hierarchical levels of classification, including subsectors, industry groups, industries, and finally distinct U.S. industries. (See Exhibit 6-7 for a breakdown of NAICS codes in the information

Exhibit 6-7
NAICS hierarchy and codes. A business marketer selling goods or services to firms in the paging industry can use the NAICS codes to locate prospective companies in directories or in subscription databases.

Level	Code	Sector
Sector	51	Information
Subsector	513	Broadcasting and telecommunications
Industry group	5133	Telecommunications
Industry	51332	Wireless telecommunications carriers (except satellite)
U.S. industry	513321	Paging

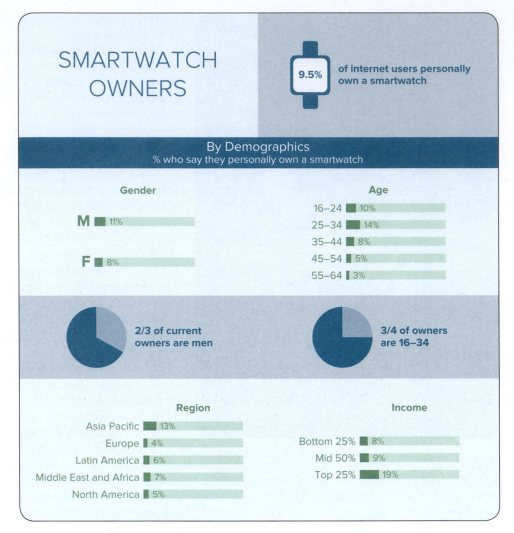

SMARTWATCH OWNERS

9.5% of internet users personally own a smartwatch

By Demographics
% who say they personally own a smartwatch

Gender

M 11%

F 8%

Age

16–24 10%
25–34 14%
35–44 8%
45–54 5%
55–64 3%

2/3 of current owners are men

3/4 of owners are 16–34

Region

Asia Pacific 13%
Europe 4%
Latin America 6%
Middle East and Africa 7%
North America 5%

Income

Bottom 25% 8%
Mid 50% 9%
Top 25% 19%

Technology users are also segmented. Consider the importance of age, gender, global region and annual income in the appeal of a smart watch.

and wireless telecommunications industry.) The U.S. Census Bureau uses NAICS to offer marketers useful information, such as the number of firms, sales volumes, and number of employees by geographic area. Thus, the NAICS codes help companies segment markets and do research, and marketers can even obtain lists of companies in particular NAICS divisions for direct mailings.[40]

Market Concentration

Many countries' markets for industrial goods are concentrated in one region or several metropolitan areas. In the United States, for example, the industrial market is heavily concentrated in the Midwest, the South, and California. Market concentration reduces the number of geographic targets for an advertiser.

Moreover, business marketers deal with fewer buyers than consumer marketers. Less than 7 percent of U.S. manufacturing firms account for almost 80 percent of all manufacturing dollars.[41] Customer size is important for market segmentation. A firm may concentrate its marketing and advertising efforts on a few large customers, many smaller ones, or both.

Levi Strauss markets through three channels: independent department stores, specialty stores (such as Urban Outfitters), and chain stores (such as JCPenney). Its top

100 accounts provide 80 percent of the company's annual sales and are made through 13,000 retail outlets. Its remaining accounts represent another 13,000 stores. Major accounts are served by sales reps from Levi's various divisions, smaller accounts by telemarketers and pandivisional sales reps. Bartle Bogle Hegarty creates and coordinates advertising for most Levi Strauss divisions in the United States.

Business marketers can also segment by end users. For example, a firm may develop software for one industry, such as banking, or for general use in a variety of industries. That decision, of course, affects advertising media decisions.

Aggregating Market Segments

After marketers identify broad product-based markets with shared characteristics (behavioristic, geographic, demographic, or psychographic), they can proceed to the second segmentation step. This involves (1) selecting groups that have a mutual interest in the product's utility and (2) reorganizing and aggregating (combining) them into larger market segments based on their potential for sales and profit. Let's take a look at how this process might work for Levi Strauss.

First, management needs to know the market potential for jeans and casual pants in various market areas; that is, it needs to discover the **primary demand trend** of the total U.S. market for pants. To do this it uses a variety of *marketing research* techniques (discussed in Chapter 7).

Then management must identify the needs, wants, and shared characteristics of the various groups within the casual apparel marketplace who live near the company's retail outlets. It may use the services of a large marketing information company such as Nielsen, which collects data on people's purchasing behavior and creates profiles of geographic markets across the country.

The company finds a huge market of prospective customers throughout the United States: students, blue-collar workers, young singles, professional people, homemakers, and so on. It then measures and analyzes household groups in each major retail area by demographic, lifestyle, and purchasing characteristics; sorts them into 66 geodemographic segments; and refers to them with terms such as those in Exhibit 6-3: Upper Crust, Movers & Shakers, Bedrock America, Pools & Patios, and the like. All these people have apparel needs, and many may be interested in the style, cachet, and durability of the Levi's brand.

Selecting Groups Interested in Product Utility

Levi Strauss next selects groups that would like and be able to afford the utilities or benefits of Levi's apparel—suitability for work or play, comfort, style, reasonable cost, durability, and so on. Groups interested in all these features make up the total possible market for Levi's clothes.

Part of the challenge of market segmentation is estimating the profits the company might realize if it (1) aims at the whole market or (2) caters only to specific market segments. Apparel is a highly competitive market, but 10 percent of 1,000 is always larger than 90 percent of 100. So for a company such as Levi Strauss, the target market must be a large mass market or it won't be profitable.[42]

Combining Groups to Build Target Market Segments

The company needs to find groups that are relatively homogeneous (similar) and offer good potential for profit. Market data turn up a large number of demographic and lifestyle groups, including ethnically diverse families, young singles, and seniors with lower education and income who often live in rented homes or apartments: New Empty Nest (1.1 percent), Park Bench Seniors (1.1 percent), and Low Rise Living (1.3 percent). Because of their minimal retail or credit activity, these groups are not prime targets for premium-branded department store products.

Other segments offer greater potential—young to middle-aged households with medium to high incomes and average to high retail activity: Movers & Shakers (1.63 percent), Bohemian Mix (1.8 percent), and Home Sweet Home (1.8 percent). By combining these (and similar) groups with the young professionals in the Young Influentials (1.5 percent)

Levi's has introduced several product lines in an effort to satisfy needs and wants of different consumer segments. One of its successful lines is the Dockers brand of casual clothes. This beautiful ad cleverly expresses the image of the user and draws attention to the brand; the campaign is still running in 2019.

Source: Levi Strauss & Co.

and New Beginnings (1.5 percent) segments, Levi Strauss can target young to middle-aged people on their way up. Nationally, that amounts to 20 million U.S. households. That's not everybody, but it's a large and potentially very profitable mass-market segment. These people might like the style and comfort of Levi's 550s as well as the tradition of a brand they know and trust, and the company could develop a campaign to appeal to their particular needs, wants, and self-images.

LO 6-2

The Target Marketing Process

Target Market Selection

Levi's returned to sales growth and profitability with the expansion to new markets. This ad, which appeared in China, demonstrates that the power of the Levi's brand extends far from the country in which jeans were first invented.

Source: Levi Strauss & Co.

Once the market segmentation process is complete, a company can proceed to the **target marketing process.** This will determine the content, look, and feel of its advertising.

The first step in target marketing is to assess which of the newly created segments offer the greatest profit potential and which can be most successfully penetrated. The company designates one or more segments as a **target market**—that group of segments the company wishes to appeal to, design products for, and tailor its marketing activities toward.[43] It may designate another set of segments as a secondary target market and aim some of its resources at it.

Let's look at the most likely target market for loose-fitting jeans: customers between 30 and 50 years of age with moderate to high income and education who like the style, comfort, and fashion of Levi's apparel. This group represents a large percentage of the apparel market and, if won, will generate substantial profits. Levi's offers what these prospects need and want: the style and fashion of the jeans they grew up with, updated to be more comfortable for the adult body.

But the middle-class, comfort-oriented segment is not enough for Levi's to be profitable, so it also caters to at least two other important markets. Beginning in the early 2000s, in response to the enormous numbers of consumers shopping at giant, low-cost retailers like Walmart and Target, Levi's developed a new line, Levi's Signature, priced lower than its regular collection. These jeans appealed to budget-conscious families with children such as Family Thrifts and Big Sky Families. In addition, Levi's has found it profitable to cater

AD Lab 6–B

Understanding the Product Element: Amazon

When you think of Amazon, what comes to mind? The company dates to the early days of the internet boom. Jeff Bezos, Amazon founder and current CEO, left a lucrative job on Wall Street in the early 1990s to participate in the early growth phase of the internet. Why walk away from a high-paying job to start a risky new venture? Bezos coined the term "regret minimization framework" to describe his feeling that the time was right to take a gamble and not live with regrets that he missed the chance.

Since its founding in 1995, Amazon has been many "products." In its earliest incarnation it was an online bookstore. That conception actually led to a lawsuit. Barnes & Noble took Amazon to court over the website's description of itself as "the world's largest bookstore." To Barnes & Noble, the site was a book broker, not a store. After the companies settled, Amazon continued to make the same claim.

Amazon soon expanded beyond books and began selling a wide variety of goods, both from its massive warehouses and by using partner firms that sell to Amazon customers via the website.

While most people continue to think of Amazon as an online retailer, its products go far beyond that. These products include technologies such as the Amazon Echo, cloud storage for many of the nation's web servers, neighborhood groceries (after its acquisition of Whole Foods), and TV and movie production (original series for Amazon Prime). The company is even a partner of the U.S. Postal Service, which includes Sunday mail delivery.

With so many ways to consider what Amazon is as a product, it seems obvious the company can no longer accurately call itself the world's largest bookstore. So how does Amazon capture its ambitions, its audacity, and its relentless focus on evolving its product focus to serve the needs of billions of people globally? The company's new slogan is: Earth's Most Customer-centric Company.

Laboratory Application

Amazon has become one of the world's most successful companies by changing the way people think about the company's product. Name another company that has done this successfully. How did it do so? Try to think of a company that has not been successful at evolving its product. What factors hindered its success?

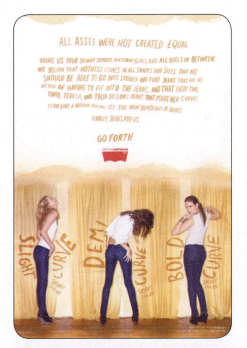

Levi's understands that brands represent a bundle of values. How is the product concept depicted in the above ad an aggregation of all of the utilitarian and symbolic values embodied by a brand?

Source: Levi Strauss & Co.

to young, 20-something, image-conscious consumers who like premium designer jeans, which can cost upward of $200 or more. Even so, the company struggled throughout much of the early 2000s, with sales declining from $7.1 billion in 1997 to just $4 billion by 2005.[44] Under the leadership of CEO Chip Bergh, the company came roaring back. Among the reasons: marketing and distributing to new markets hungry for jeans in Russia, China, and India. For more about segmentation, look at Ad Lab 6–B and consider how Amazon selected its new target market.

The Marketing Mix: A Strategy for Matching Products to Markets

Once a company defines its target market, it knows exactly where to focus its attention and resources. It can shape the product concept and even design special features for its target market (such as certain colors or special sizes). It can establish proper pricing. It can determine the need for locating stores or dealers and prepare the most convincing advertising messages.

As we discussed in Chapter 5, a product offers a number of utilities, perceived by the consumer as a *bundle of values.* With this in mind, marketers and advertisers generally try to shape their basic product into a total **product concept:** the consumer's perception of a product as a bundle of utilitarian and symbolic values that satisfy functional, social, psychological, and other wants and needs.

Companies have many strategic options they can employ to enhance the product/service concept and effect marketing exchanges (make sales). Marketers categorize these options under four headings: (1) *product,* (2) *price,* (3) *distribution,* and (4) *communication.*[45] The way the marketer mixes and blends these different elements creates the company's marketing strategy—often called the **marketing mix.** For convenience, marketing educator E. Jerome McCarthy developed a mnemonic device to help recall these four functions: *product, price, place,* and *promotion*—or the **four Ps (4Ps).**[46]

My IMC Campaign 6-A

Segmenting the Audience

What is the target market for your product? The answer to this question is rarely simple; thus, your choices again will require the application of strategic thinking. To make the decision, you will need to gather as much information from your client and from secondary sources as you can, focusing on the product's market, users, and the competition. The information you gathered about the consumer in the My IMC Campaign from Chapter 5 will be important as well. And in some instances it may make sense to conduct primary research with current customers or with individuals who use competing products.

You may have the opportunity to offer counsel to your client about whether it is pursuing the right target market. Check to be sure before offering such advice; some clients may not wish to receive it. If the client is so interested, consider whether there are underserved segments that offer sales or profit potential. For example, if your client is a local pizzeria located near campus, it may be focusing on attracting students. This is to be expected since students normally represent a sizable market in any college town. In addition, your client is doubtless using the timeworn strategy of attracting hungry, cash-strapped undergrads with messages that emphasize low prices, large servings, and coupons. But while students may represent a large market for pizza, there are probably dozens of other food businesses competing for this segment. If so, it might be smarter to refocus on a smaller but underserved segment, especially one that offers great profit potential. If your town lacks an upscale pizzeria that serves specialty pies, the client might be better served by improving its offerings and dining facility, raising prices, and promoting to nonstudents who would be willing to pay more for quality pizzas.

Of course, to evaluate opportunities in a market you will need to segment. Many advertisers find that it makes sense to segment on the basis of standard demographic characteristics such as age, gender, ethnicity, location, social class, or income level. Dividing your market according to product loyalty or product usage levels is also worth strongly considering. Understanding your market with respect to psychographics and lifestyles can be incredibly valuable, especially later when you begin to develop your creative brief. Such data can be more difficult to obtain, however.

Defining the Target Market

	Your Client's Customers	The Competition's Customers	Nonusers
Demographics			
Age			
Gender			
Ethnicity/race			
Location/region			
Social class			
Income			
Education			
Behaviors			
Product usage (light, medium, heavy)			
Brand loyalty (loyal, switchers)			
Psychographics			
Principle-oriented			
Status-oriented			
Action-oriented			
Benefits Sought			
Low price			
Quality			

The 4Ps are a simple way to remember the basic elements of the marketing mix. But within each element, a company can employ numerous marketing activities to fine-tune its product concept and improve sales. Advertising, for example, is one instrument of the communication (promotion) element. The remainder of this chapter focuses on the relationship between advertising and the other elements of the marketing mix.

IMC and the Product Element

Product Life Cycles

LO 6-3

In developing a marketing mix, marketers generally start with the **product element.** Major activities typically include the way the product is designed and classified, positioned, branded, and packaged. Each of these affects the way the product is advertised.

Marketers theorize that just as humans pass through stages in life from infancy to death, products (and especially product categories) also pass through a **product life cycle** (see Exhibit 6-8).[47] A product's position in the life cycle influences the target market selected and the kind of advertising used. The product life cycle has four major stages: *introduction, growth, maturity,* and *decline.*

When a company introduces a new product category, nobody knows about it. By using market segmentation, though, the company may try to identify those prospects who are known to be **early adopters**–willing to try new things–and begin promoting the new category directly to them. The idea is to stimulate **primary demand**–consumer demand for the whole product category, not just the company's own brand.

During the **introductory (pioneering) phase** of any new product category, the company incurs considerable costs for educating customers, building widespread dealer distribution, and encouraging demand. It must spend significant advertising sums at this stage to establish a position as a market leader and to gain a large share of market before the growth stage begins.

When mobile telephones were introduced in the late 1980s, advertisers had to first create enough consumer demand to pull the product through the channels of distribution (called a **pull strategy**). IMC educated consumers about the new product and its category, explaining what such phones are, how they work, and the rewards of owning one. **Sales promotion** efforts aimed at the retail trade (called a **push strategy**) encouraged distributors and dealers to stock, display, and advertise the new products (see Chapter 10).

When sales volume begins to rise rapidly, the product enters the **growth stage.** This period is characterized by rapid *market expansion* as more and more customers, stimulated

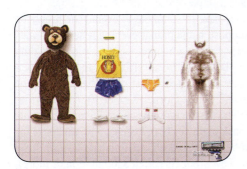

The grooming habits of the American male have evolved over the years, creating an opportunity for established brands to develop new product uses. This funny ad from Gilette uses subtle imagery and a straightforward tag line: take it all off.

Source: Procter and Gamble

Exhibit 6-8
A product's life cycle curve may vary, depending on the product category. Marketing objectives and strategies change as the product proceeds from one stage to the next.

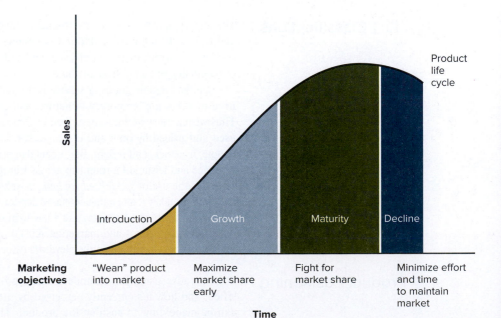

| Marketing objectives | "Wean" product into market | Maximize market share early | Fight for market share | Minimize effort and time to maintain market |

by mass advertising and word of mouth, make their first, second, and third purchases. Competitors jump into the market, but the company that established the early leadership position reaps the biggest rewards. As a percentage of total sales, advertising expenditures should decrease, and individual firms will realize their first substantial profits.

During the early 1990s, the demand for phones exploded, and category sales quadrupled every year. Many competitors suddenly appeared. With increased production and competition, prices started to fall, which brought even more people into the market. By 2005, 70 percent of all U.S. families owned mobile phones.[48]

In the **maturity stage,** the marketplace becomes saturated with competing products and the number of new customers dwindles, so industry sales reach a plateau. Competition intensifies and profits diminish. Companies increase their promotional efforts but emphasize **selective demand** to impress customers with the subtle advantages of their particular brand. At this stage, companies increase sales only at the expense of competitors (conquest sales). The strategies of market segmentation, product positioning, and price promotion become more important during this shakeout period as weak companies fall by the wayside and those remaining fight for small increases in market share. By the mid-1990s, for example, phones that once sold for $1,500 were suddenly advertised regularly for $100 to $200. Ads emphasized features and low prices, and the product became a staple of discount merchandisers.[49]

Late in the maturity stage, companies may have to scramble to extend the product's life cycle. Without innovation or marketing support, name brands eventually see their sales erode. As of 2011, for example, BlackBerry devices, once market leaders, were struggling in their competition with Apple and Google phones. If the advertised brand has no perceived advantage, people will buy whatever is cheapest or most convenient. Professor Brian Wansink, who directs the Food and Brand Lab at Cornell University, suggests that the reason many old brands die is less for life cycle reasons and more for marketing neglect. He points out that aging brands often pack plenty of brand equity. The challenge for marketers is to determine which brands can be revitalized and then decide how to do it. But with today's high price tag on introducing new products (often $100 million or more), revitalization should be the strategy of choice whenever possible. Marketers may try to find new users for the brand, develop new uses for the product, change the size of packages, design new labels, improve quality, or use promotion to increase frequency of use.[50]

If they're not revitalized, products will finally enter the **decline stage** because of obsolescence, new technology, or changing consumer tastes. At this point, companies may cease all promotion and phase out the products quickly, as in the case of record turntables and LP albums, or let them fade slowly with minimal advertising, like most sheer hosiery brands.

Product Classifications

The way a company classifies its product is important in defining both the product concept and the marketing mix. As Exhibit 6-9 shows, there are many ways to classify tangible goods: by markets, by the purchasing habits of buyers, by the consumption rate or degree of tangibility, or by physical attributes.

Unlike tangible goods, a **service** is a bundle of *intangible* benefits that satisfy some need or want, are temporary in nature, and usually derive from completion of a task.[51] Thus we have *task utility,* as described in Chapter 5. Rail service, for example, is transitory, used and priced by time and distance. It offers the functional benefits of transporting people, livestock, and freight. But it can also offer psychological benefits. Just think of the romance and leisure of a train trip across Europe aboard the Orient Express. The railroad relies on the use of *specialized equipment*—vehicles able to pull huge loads over a unique track. This makes it an **equipment-based service.**

In contrast, an ad agency, like a law firm or a bank, is a **people-based service;** it relies on the creative talents and marketing skills of individuals. As one agency CEO said, "My inventory goes up and down the elevators twice a day."[52]

Product Positioning

Once an advertising person understands a product's stage in the life cycle, how it's classified, and how it's currently perceived by the marketplace, the first strategic decision can be made: how to **position** the product. The basic goal of positioning strategy is to

By Market	By Rate of Consumption and Tangibility	By Purchasing Habits	By Physical Description
Consumer goods Products and services we use in our daily lives (food, clothing, furniture, cars). **Industrial goods** Products used by companies for the purpose of producing other products (raw materials, agricultural commodities, machinery, tools, equipment).	**Durable goods** Tangible products that are long-lasting and infrequently replaced (cars, trucks, refrigerators, furniture). **Nondurable goods** Tangible products that may be consumed in one or a few uses and usually need to be replaced at regular intervals (food, soap, gasoline, oil). **Services** Activities, benefits, or satisfaction offered for sale (travel, haircuts, legal and medical services, massages).	**Convenience goods** Purchases made frequently with a minimum of effort (soda, food, newspapers). **Shopping goods** Infrequently purchased items for which greater time is spent comparing price, quality, style, warranty (furniture, cars, clothing, tires). **Specialty goods** Products with such unique characteristics that consumers will make special efforts to purchase them even if they're more expensive (fancy electronic equipment, special women's fashions, computer components). **Unsought goods** Products that potential customers don't yet want (insurance) or don't know they can buy (new products), so they don't search them out.	**Packaged goods** Cereals, hair tonics, and so forth. **Hard goods** Furniture, appliances. **Soft goods** Clothing, bedding. **Services** Intangible products.

Exhibit 6-9
Product classifications.

own a word that ranks the product in the prospect's mind. Levi's owns "jeans." FedEx owns "overnight." And Volvo owns "safety." By developing a unique position for the brand in the consumer's mind, the marketer helps the consumer remember the brand and what it stands for.

Products may be positioned in many different ways. Generally, they are ranked by the way they are differentiated, the benefits they offer, the particular market segment to which

Microsoft had a big hit with its Surface Pro. It used explicit comparisons with the Macbook Air to highlight the Surface Pro's unique features, which include a detachable keyboard and interactive screen. This is product differentiation at its finest.

Source: Microsoft Corporation

Product	Competitor	Differentiator	Life
Microsoft Zune	Apple iPod	Sharing music	2006–2012
U.S. Football League	NFL	Summer schedule	1982–1986
Crystal Pepsi	Coke	No coloring	1992–1994
Apple III	IBM PC	No cooling fans	1980–1984
Burger King "Big King"	McDonald's Big Mac	King Sauce, grilled patty	2016–2017
3D television	2D television	Three dimensions	2011–2018

they appeal, or the way they are classified. Xerox has repositioned itself as "The Document Company," moving from the narrow, glutted, copier market to the broader, growing, document-handling market. With one stroke, Xerox redefined the business it is in, differentiated itself from the competition, and created a new number one position for itself.[53]

Product Differentiation

Product differentiation involves explaining how a brand offers something unique and desirable to a market segment. In any campaign, nothing is more important than being able to tell prospects truthfully that your product is new and different. Marketers know that for many products development cycles are short due to competitive pressures, innovation and technology, and constraints on distribution. As a result, brand managers often find themselves launching new products that are "only 85 percent there."[54] So it's not surprising that most "new" products fail to impress consumers. (For some underperforming products by major U.S. marketers, see Exhibit 6-10.) Simply adding new colors might differentiate a product enough to attract a new set of customers, but not all product differences need be that obvious. Differences between products may be *perceptible, imperceptible (hidden),* or *induced.*[55]

Perceptible differences are readily apparent to the consumer. Snapple, for example, received its initial impetus because of its unique taste, and to promote this difference to consumers nationwide, the company employed a variety of nontraditional marketing techniques, including sole sponsorship of a Boston radio station for 40 days.[56] **Hidden differences** are not so readily apparent. Trident gum may look and taste the same as other brands, but it is differentiated by the use of artificial sweeteners. While hidden differences can enhance a product's desirability, IMC is usually needed to let consumers know about them.

For many product classes, such as aspirin, salt, gasoline, packaged foods, liquor, and financial services, advertising can create **induced differences.** Banks, brokerage houses, and insurance companies, for example, which offer virtually identical financial products and services, use promotion to differentiate themselves. They also know the value of consistent advertising campaigns, favorable publicity, special-event sponsorship, and good word of mouth.[57]

Product Branding

As discussed in Chapter 1, the fundamental differentiating device for products is the **brand**—that combination of name, words, symbols, or design that identifies the product and its source and distinguishes it from competing products. Without brands, consumers couldn't tell one product from another.

Branding decisions are difficult. A manufacturer may establish an **individual brand** for each product it produces. Unilever, for example, markets its toothpastes under the individual brand names Aim, Pepsodent, and Close-Up. Such companies designate a distinct target market for each product and develop a separate personality and image for each brand. However, this strategy is very costly.

On the other hand, a company might use a **family brand** and market different products under the same umbrella name. When Heinz promotes its ketchup, it hopes to help its relishes too.

Because it is so expensive for manufacturers to market **national brands** (also called *manufacturer's brands*), some companies use a *private-labeling strategy.* They manufacture the product and sell it to resellers (distributors or dealers), who put their own brand on the product. **Private labels,** typically sold at lower prices in large retail chain stores,

Chanel is one of the top cosmetic brands in the world. To reinforce its image of luxury and glamour, Chanel ads feature top models.

Source: Chanel

Exhibit 6-11
World's most valuable brands.

Rank	Brand	2018 Brand Value (in billions)
1	Apple	$182.8
2	Google	132.1
3	Microsoft	104.8
4	Facebook	94.8
5	Amazon	70.9
6	Coca-Cola	57.3
7	Samsung	47.6
8	Disney	47.5
9	Toyota	44.7
10	AT&T	41.9

Source: "The Worlds's Most Valuable Brands," *Forbes*, 2018, retrieved at www.forbes.com/powerful-brands/list/#tab:rank.

Product packaging is important around the globe. Packaging and advertising converge as Amazon leverages the value of its global shipping materials to provide advertisers a new platform. These boxes help promote the release of the movie Minions.

Source: Amazon.com, Inc.

include such familiar names as Kenmore, Craftsman, Cragmont, Kroger, and Party Pride. They now account for almost 20 percent of grocery purchases.[58] The responsibility for creating brand image and familiarity rests with the distributor or retailer, who is also the principal benefactor if the brand is successful. Recent trends have moved toward premium private labels, such as President's Choice, which has enjoyed immense success. These products feature better packaging, superior quality, and a higher price, comparable to national brands.

Branding decisions are critical because the brands a company owns may be its most important capital asset. Imagine the value of owning a brand name such as Coca-Cola, Nike, Porsche, or Levi's (see Exhibit 6-11).[59] Some companies pay a substantial fee for the right to use another company's brand name. Thus, we have **licensed brands** such as Sunkist vitamins, Coca-Cola clothing, Porsche sunglasses, and Mickey Mouse watches.

The Role of Branding

For consumers, brands offer instant recognition. They also promise consistent, reliable standards of quality, taste, size, or even psychological satisfaction, which adds value to the product for both the consumer and the manufacturer. In a survey conducted by TWICE/Campaigners, 44 percent of consumers ranked brand name as the most important factor when making a major electronics purchase. Price ranked second.[60]

Brands are built on differences in images, meanings, and associations. Marketers attempt to differentiate their products clearly and deliver value competitively. The product has to taste better, or get clothes cleaner, or be packaged in a more environmentally friendly container.[61] Advertising for an established brand, particularly a well-differentiated one, is much more effective if it exploits the brand's positioning.[62] Ideally, when consumers see a brand on the shelf, they instantly comprehend the brand's promise and have confidence in its quality. Of course, they must be familiar with and believe in the brand's promise (a function of IMC effectiveness). As we pointed out in Chapter 5, marketers seek *brand loyalty*—because it serves both the consumer and the marketer. For the consumer, it reduces uncertainty and shopping time. For the marketer, it builds **brand equity,** the totality of what consumers, distributors, dealers—even competitors—feel and think about the brand over an extended period of time. In short, it's the value of the brand's capital.

High brand equity offers a host of blessings to the product marketer: customer loyalty, price inelasticity, long-term profits. The value of retaining customers and building loyalty is substantial. For example, finding new customers costs four to ten times as much as retaining current ones. Repeat buyers spend more with a company than new ones. And repeat buyers continue to spend more with a company over time.[63] But building brand equity requires time, effort, and money. Brand value and preference drive market share, but these benefits are usually won by the advertisers who spend the most. And increasing brand loyalty may require a spending increase of 200 to 300 percent to affect loyalty dramatically.[64] Charlotte Beers, the former head of J. Walter Thompson, points out the importance of "brand stewardship." She believes companies must maintain consistency in their message by integrating all their marketing communications—from packaging and advertising to sales promotion and publicity—to maintain and reinforce the brand's personality in a real-life context and avoid doing something foolish such as changing the distinctive color of a Ryder rental truck.[65]

Product Packaging

The product's package is a component of the product element and is also an *exhibitive medium* that plays a vital role in retail shelf competition. In fact, packaging may be a brand's one differential advantage—and it's the marketer's last chance to communicate at the point of sale. Package designers (who sometimes work in ad agencies) must make the package exciting, appealing, and functional. The four considerations in package design are *identification;*

Gatorade helps remind consumers of a brand they love while introducing a new benefit with G Organic. The colorful labels help attract people interested in a sports beverage made from natural ingredients.

Sheila Fitzgerald/Shutterstock

containment, protection, and convenience; consumer appeal; and *economy.* These functions may even become **copy points**—copywriting themes—in the product's advertising.

Identification

Why do some companies use the same package and label design for years? Because the unique combination of trade name, trademark, or trade character, reinforced by the package design, quickly identifies the brand and differentiates it from competitors. For example, the traditional contoured Coke bottle was so unusual and popular that in the 1990s Coca-Cola reintroduced it to U.S. markets. The company never stopped using it in many international markets because it differentiated Coke so well from other colas.

Packages should offer high visibility and legibility to penetrate shoppers' *physiological screens.* Product features must be easy to read, and color combinations must provide high contrast to differentiate the product. To penetrate consumers' *psychological screens,* the package design must reflect the tone, image, and personality of the product concept. In many product categories (wine, cosmetics), the package quality largely determines the consumer's perception of the product's quality.

Containment, Protection, and Convenience

The purpose of any package is to hold and protect the product and make it easy to use. Marketers also try to ensure it will keep the product fresh and protect its contents from damage, water vapor (for frozen goods), grease, infestation, and odors. And packages must adhere to legal protection requirements.

Retailers want packages that are easy to stack and display; they also want a full range of sizes to fit their customers' needs. Consumers want packages that are easy to carry, open, and store, so these are important design considerations.

Consumer Appeal

Consumer appeal in packaging is the result of many factors: size, color, material, and shape. Certain colors have special meanings to consumers. Even a subtle change in color can result in as much as a 20 percent change in sales.[66]

In this age of environmental awareness, *green marketing* is an important issue for companies and consumers alike. New technology has made ecologically safe packaging available and affordable for many product categories. Many companies now advertise their packages as environmentally responsible.

A package's shape also offers an opportunity for consumer appeal based on whimsy, humor, or romance. Heart-shaped packages of Valentine's Day candy instantly tell what the product is. Some tins and bottles even become collectibles (Chivas Regal). These packages are really premiums that give buyers extra value.

Economy

Investments in identification, protection, convenience, and consumer appeal add to basic production costs, but this increase may be more than offset by increased customer appeal. These benefits may make a considerable difference to the consumer and affect both the product concept and IMC messages.

LO 6-4

IMC and the Price Element

Many companies, especially small ones, request input from their advertising people about pricing strategies. That's because the **price element** of the marketing mix influences consumer perceptions of the brand dramatically.

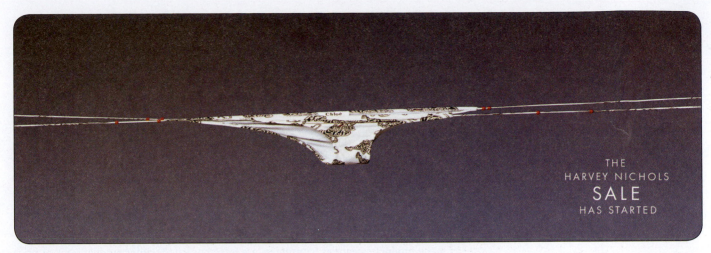

THE
HARVEY NICHOLS
SALE
HAS STARTED

This print ad for Harvey Nichols in London was awarded a Silver Lion at Cannes. The stretched bathing suit is an apt metaphor for consumers who are interested in stretching their money. Of course, the ad could be read another way: This image might depict what happens when frantic shoppers fight for the same item.

Harvey Nichols

Key Factors Influencing Price

Companies set their prices based on market demand for the product, costs of production and distribution, competition, and corporate objectives. As a practical matter, though, a company may have relatively few options for determining its price strategy, depending on the desired product concept.

Market Demand

If the supply of a product is stable but the desire (demand) for it increases, the price tends to rise. If demand drops below available supply, the price tends to fall. This may affect IMC messages in a major way (see Exhibit 6-12).

In the last recession, auto manufacturers faced a glut of unsold new cars and declining demand. Several companies offered substantial factory rebates—price cuts—to motivate prospective buyers. Dealers immediately sold more cars. Hyundai, in another example of innovation, offered to take back a new car purchase if the buyer became unemployed. The result was a jump in sales. No amount of image or awareness advertising would have had the same effect. But, of course, advertising was essential to communicate that the time to buy was now.

Some marketing researchers theorize that for new durable goods, advertising works with word-of-mouth and social media communication to generate awareness of and belief

Exhibit 6-12

This graph plots demand versus price and supply versus price. The demand curve shows the amounts purchased at various prices. The supply curve shows the amounts offered for sale at various prices. The point where the two curves cross is called the market clearing price, where demand and supply balance. It is the price that theoretically sells out the product.

in the product's benefits. Once consumers perceive that the product's value warrants the purchase price, sales occur. As product experience and information spread, the risks associated with new products diminish, which increases consumers' willingness to purchase at a higher price.[67]

Production and Distribution Costs

The price of goods depends to some extent on the costs of production and distribution. As these costs increase, they must be passed on to the consumer, or the company will be unable to meet its overhead and will be forced out of business. One common IMC strategy is to tout the materials used in manufacturing a product. This can also help justify the prices manufacturers must charge to cover their production costs.

Competition

In many product categories, consumers are less concerned with a product's actual price than with its perceived price relative to competitors. For the marketer, maintaining the value perception during periods of intense price competition and fluctuation is challenging but important.[68]

Corporate Objectives and Strategies

A company's objectives also influence price. When introducing new products, companies often set a high price initially to recover development and start-up costs. In other cases, if the objective were to position the brand as an inexpensive convenience item aimed at a broad target market, ads would stress the product's economy.

Price also depends on the company's marketing strategy, and image advertising may be used to justify a higher price. Many premium-priced brands, such as L'Oréal, are touted for the very fact that they do cost more. The important thing is that the price be consistent with the brand image; you can't charge a Rolex price for a Timex watch.

As products enter the maturity stages of their life cycles, corporate objectives tend to aim at increasing, or at least maintaining, market share. To accomplish this, competitive advertising and promotion heat up, and prices tend to drop.

Variable Influences

Economic conditions, consumer income and tastes, government regulations, marketing costs, and other factors also influence prices and thus advertising. Marketing management must consider all these to determine an appropriate pricing strategy and then create advertising that justifies the product's price.

IMC and the Distribution (Place) Element

Before the first message can be created, the **distribution element,** or *place,* must be decided. It is important for marketers to understand that the method of distribution, like the price, must be consistent with the brand's image. To understand Starbucks' distribution strategy, see Ad Lab 6–C, "Starbucks and the Place Element." Companies use two basic methods of distribution: *direct* or *indirect.*

Direct Distribution

LO 6-5

When companies sell directly to end users or consumers, they use **direct distribution.** Avon, for example, employs sales reps who work for the manufacturer rather than for a retailer and sell directly to consumers. Technology giants such as Dell and Microsoft sell a large percentage of their products directly to customers who order on the web. In these cases, the promotional burden is carried entirely by the manufacturer.

Network marketing (also called *multilevel marketing*) takes advantages of personal and family ties by having individuals act as independent distributors for a manufacturer or private-label marketer. These people sign up friends and relatives to consume the company's

AD Lab 6–C

Starbucks and the Place Element

The "place" (or distribution) element of marketing strategy is always integral to successful business. You may have the most wonderful product in the world—but potential customers won't buy it if they can't find it.

Starbucks (www.starbucks.com) is a phenomenon that changed the way people view coffee. This can be explained, in large part, by the creative use of the place element. You'll notice that Starbucks cafés are found in high-traffic, easily noticeable locations in each market area. In some markets, a Starbucks seems to appear on virtually every street corner. Although the average consumer may find this excessive, Starbucks actually picks and plans each retail location with great care.

For a company like Starbucks, street space is like shelf space. In this sense, buying out existing coffeehouses is the same as Coca-Cola buying shelf space in a supermarket. Starbucks management believes that chain expansion is as much a part of the company's success as is its coffee bar and customer service concepts. Since its opening, stores have sprouted up in virtually every major city across the globe, and Starbucks has no intention of stopping. As of 2017 there are more than 27,000 Starbucks worldwide, including 15,000 in the U.S.

Aside from its store locations, Starbucks' unique coffee blends are now found in selected airlines, restaurants, hotels, and supermarkets. Additional venues include a mail-order business with catalog distribution, a coast-to-coast alliance with Barnes & Noble bookstores, a partnership with Star Markets in Boston and Publix in the U.S. southeast, and distribution to the Washington State Ferry system, Holland America Line–Westours cruises, Safeco Field in Seattle, and Chicago's Wrigley Field.

Obviously, Starbucks intends to fully saturate every coffee market. When consumers go shopping for groceries, they aren't likely to make a separate trip to Starbucks for coffee. So Starbucks now competes directly with other specialty coffees sold in supermarkets. In 1998 Kraft Foods agreed to distribute and market Starbucks coffee beans in more than 25,000 grocery stores in the United States. This collaboration is a major stepping stone for Starbucks to surpass Folgers as the leading supermarket coffee brand in the United States.

Laboratory Application

Take the product you used in Ad Lab 6–B and compare the distribution principles used by Starbucks with your product. In addition, think about the factors that should be considered when placing your product or service in other venues. How does it compare with Starbucks?

---

products and recruit others to join. Through a gradual, word-of-mouth process, they form a "buying club" of independent distributors who buy the products wholesale directly from the company, use them, and tout them to more and more friends and acquaintances.

If successful, the rewards for the network marketing company (and many of the distributors) can be staggering. Amway International, the granddaddy of network marketing, now boasts U.S. sales in excess of $8 billion, and many of its longtime distributors became multimillionaires in the process.[69] Other companies have broken the billion-dollar sales mark, too, among them Nikken (Japan), Herbalife, and Shaklee. These companies brag about the fact that they do *no media advertising*. Because they usually sell consumer products (which typically carry a heavy advertising and sales promotion burden), they save money. Most marketing communications are simply word of mouth, including digital word of mouth on platforms such as Facebook, Pinterest, and Instagram. So Avon lets its network marketers create their own digital groups for friends to follow.

Indirect Distribution

Manufacturers usually don't sell directly to consumers. Most companies market their products through a *distribution channel* that includes a network of *resellers*. A **reseller** (or *middleman*) is a business firm that operates between the producer and the consumer or industrial purchaser. It deals in trade rather than production.[70] Resellers include both wholesalers and retailers, as well as manufacturers' representatives, brokers, jobbers, and distributors. A **distribution channel** includes all the firms and individuals that take title, or assist in taking title, to the product as it moves from the producer to the consumer.

Indirect distribution channels make the flow of products available to customers conveniently and economically. Appliance companies, for example, contract with exclusive regional distributors that buy the products from the factory and resell them to local dealers, who then resell them to consumers. Many industrial companies market their products through reps or distributors to *original equipment manufacturers (OEMs)*. These OEMs may use the product as a component in their own product, which is then sold to their customers.

The advertising a company uses depends on the product's method of distribution. Much of the advertising we see is not prepared or paid for by the manufacturer, but by the distributor or retailer. Members of a distribution channel give enormous promotional support to the manufacturers they represent.

A part of marketing strategy is determining the amount of coverage necessary for a product. Procter & Gamble, for example, distributes Crest toothpaste to virtually every supermarket and discount, drug, and variety store. Other products might need only one dealer for every 50,000 people. Consumer goods manufacturers traditionally use one of three distribution strategies: *intensive, selective,* or *exclusive*.

Intensive Distribution

Soft drinks, candy, Timex watches, and other convenience goods are available at every possible location because of **intensive distribution.** In fact, consumers can buy them with a minimum of effort. The profit on each unit is usually very low, but the volume of sales is

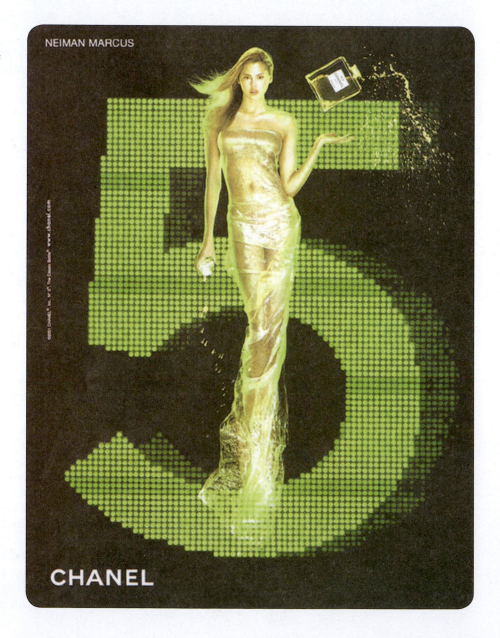

Cooperative (co-op) advertising involves a manufacturer and a retailer sharing the costs of an ad that benefits both. A great example is this beautiful ad featuring Chanel and Neiman Marcus.

Source: Chanel USA Corporate Office Headquarters HQ

high. The sales burden is usually carried by the manufacturer's national advertising. Ads in trade magazines *push* the product into the retail "pipeline," and in mass media they stimulate consumers to *pull* the products through the pipeline. As a manufacturer modifies its strategy to more push or more pull, special promotions may be directed at the trade or at consumers to increase sales (see Chapter 10).

Selective Distribution

By limiting the number of outlets through **selective distribution,** manufacturers can cut their distribution and promotion costs. Many hardware tools are sold selectively through discount chains, home improvement centers, and hardware stores. Some pet foods are available at vet offices or pet stores, but not at grocery stores. Manufacturers may use national advertising, but the sales burden is normally carried by the retailer. The manufacturer may share part of the retailer's advertising costs through a **cooperative (co-op) advertising** program, as we discussed in Chapter 4. For example, a Levi's retailer may receive substantial allowances from the manufacturer for advertising Levi's clothing in its local area. In return, the retailer agrees to advertise and display the clothing prominently.

Exclusive Distribution

Under an **exclusive distribution** agreement, selected wholesalers or retailers are granted exclusive rights to distribute a particular product. For example, coffee retailer Starbucks was the exclusive seller of a CD of previously unreleased Bob Dylan songs.[71] The Rolling Stones released a concert video DVD that could be purchased only at Best Buy. This is also common in high fashion, major appliances, and furniture lines. What is lost in market coverage is often gained in the ability to maintain a prestige image and premium prices. Exclusive distribution agreements also force manufacturers and retailers to cooperate closely in advertising and promotion programs.

Vertical Marketing Systems: The Growth of Franchising

To be efficient, members of a distribution channel need to cooperate closely. This need gave rise to the **vertical marketing system (VMS),** a centrally managed distribution system that serves a group of stores or other businesses.

There are many types of vertical marketing systems. For the last quarter century, the greatest growth has been in **franchising**—such as Chick-fil-A or Mailboxes, Etc.—in which retail dealers (or *franchisees*) pay a fee to operate under the guidelines and direction of the parent company or manufacturer (the *franchisor*).

Franchising and other vertical marketing systems offer both manufacturers and retailers numerous advantages, not the least of which are centralized coordination of marketing efforts and substantial savings and continuity in advertising. Perhaps most important is consumer recognition: The moment a new McDonald's opens, the franchisee has instant customers. Moreover, a single newspaper ad can promote all of a chain's retailers in a particular trading area.

Many marketers find that franchising is the best way to introduce their services into global markets. Subway

The vertical marketing system gave rise to a number of successful business plans, like franchising, in which franchisees pay a fee and operate under the guidelines of a parent company. For instance, independent owners and operators serve customers in thousands of Chick-fil-A restaurants. The company supports those efforts with national advertising campaigns, which in turn guide ads in local markets paid for by franchisees.

Source: Chick-fil-A

sandwich shops, for example, is one of the fastest-growing franchise operations in the world with a total of more than 25,000 stores in 84 different countries.[72]

In the last decade, the European Union, a market of nearly 462 million people, has opened its doors to innovative marketers. As a result, franchising has grown rapidly, especially in the United Kingdom, France, Germany, Spain, Belgium, and the Netherlands. Some 10,000 franchised brands are now operating in 20 European countries.[73] Although franchising is less regulated in Europe, advertising is more regulated. This again points out the need for local experts to manage the advertising function in foreign markets.

IMC and the Communication (Promotion) Element

LO 6-6

Once it determines product, price, and distribution, a company is ready to plan its marketing communications, of which advertising is just one component. (See Ad Lab 6–D.)

The **communication element** includes all marketing-related communications between the seller and the buyer. A variety of marketing communications tools comprise the **communications mix.** These tools can be grouped into *personal* and *nonpersonal communication* activities.

Personal communication includes all person-to-person contact with customers. **Nonpersonal communication** activities—which use some medium as an intermediary for communicating—include *advertising, direct marketing,* certain *public relations* activities, *collateral materials,* and *sales promotion.* Today, successful marketing managers blend all these elements into an *integrated marketing communications program.*

Personal Selling

Advertising is nonpersonal selling. However, like personal selling, it can be used to close the sale, especially in mail order. This humorous direct-mail piece from Land Rover touts an "edible survival guide."

Source: Land Rover

Some consumer products are sold by clerks in retail stores, others by salespeople who call on customers directly. Personal selling is very important in business-to-business marketing. It establishes a face-to-face situation in which the marketer can learn firsthand about customer wants and needs, and customers find it harder to say no. We discuss personal selling further in Chapter 10.

Advertising

Advertising is sometimes called *mass* or *nonpersonal selling.* Its usual purpose is to inform, persuade, and remind customers about particular products and services. In some cases, like mail order, advertising even closes the sale.

Certain products lend themselves to advertising so much that it plays the dominant communications role. The following factors are particularly important for advertising success:

- A high primary demand trend.
- The chance for significant product differentiation.
- Hidden qualities that are important to consumers.
- The opportunity to use emotional appeals.
- The availability of substantial sums to support advertising.

Where these conditions exist, as in the cosmetics, auto, or wireless phone industries, companies spend large amounts on advertising, and the ratio of advertising to sales dollars is often quite high. For completely undifferentiated products, such as sugar, salt, and other raw materials or commodities, price is usually the primary influence, and advertising is minimally important. Sunkist is an interesting exception. This farmers' cooperative successfully brands an undifferentiated commodity (citrus fruit) and markets it internationally.

Direct Marketing

Direct marketing is like taking the store to the customer. A mail-order house that communicates directly with consumers through ads and catalogs is one type of company engaged in direct marketing. It builds its own database of customers and uses a variety of media to communicate with them.

AD Lab 6–D

China Airlines and the Promotion Element

A lot of research suggests that consuming experiences, such as travel, bring greater satisfaction than buying things. Not surprisingly, companies that offer travel services (airlines, hotels, etc.) frequently feature glamorous images of destinations in their ads.

China Airlines decided to take a different approach. The tagline sounds like every other travel spot you've ever seen: "You never know what travel will bring into your life, Let's go find out." But the experiences? One traveler is depicted as looking nothing like her license photo after getting cosmetic surgery in South Korea. In a playful twist on the phrase, "A whole new life," a woman is shown learning of an unexpected pregnancy following her Australian adventure. Another traveler has trouble remembering exactly where on his trip he got that new tattoo on his back.

While these incidents are played for humor, it still seems risky to highlight the undesirable aspects of travel. But Leo Burnett

Taiwan seems to be on to something. The agency has been thrilled with the attention the campaign is attracting. It was viewed 6 million times in one month alone and attracted lots of media attention.

The success of the China Airlines ad is more proof that promotions require freshness and originality. When everyone else zigs, a smart brand zags.

Laboratory Application

When constructing the marketing mix for your chosen product or service (refer to Ad Labs 6–B and 6–C), consider these last two elements: price and promotion. What should your product's price be and why? How do most brands in your product's category advertise? How can you break the mold with with your promotions, the way China Airlines did?

The field of direct marketing is growing rapidly because companies like the benefits of control, cost efficiency, and accountability. For example, many companies such as Levi Strauss use **telemarketing** (a direct marketing technique) to increase productivity through person-to-person phone contact. By using the phone to follow up direct-mail advertising, a company can increase the response rate substantially. Moreover, through telemarketing, it can develop a valuable database of customers and prospects to use in future mailings and promotions.[74] We discuss this topic more thoroughly in Chapter 10.

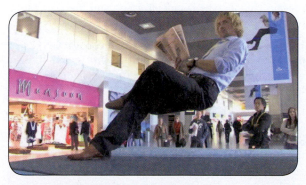

What better way to suggest that KLM Economy Comfort is like sitting on air, than to stage a publicity event at an airport suggesting a man is doing just that?

Source: KLM Royal Dutch Airlines

Public Relations

Many firms supplement (or replace) their advertising with various public relations activities such as **publicity** (news releases, feature stories) and **special events** (open houses, factory tours, VIP parties, grand openings) to inform various audiences about the company and its products and to build corporate trustworthiness and image. As Al and Laura Ries point out, through decades of overuse and overpromising, advertising today has lost some of its effectiveness and credibility.[75] On the other hand, public relations activities, as we discuss in Chapter 11, are extremely credible brand-building tools that should always be integrated into a company's communication mix.

Collateral Materials

As mentioned in Chapter 4, **collateral materials** are the many accessory items companies produce to integrate and supplement their advertising or PR activities. These include booklets, catalogs, brochures, films, sales kits, promotional products, and annual reports. Collateral materials should always be designed to reinforce the company's image or the brand's position in the minds of customers.

Sales Promotion

As we discuss in Chapter 10, sales promotion is a special category of communication tools and activities. Designed to supplement the basic elements of the marketing mix for

People BEHIND the Ads

Tere and Joe Zubi, Zubi Advertising

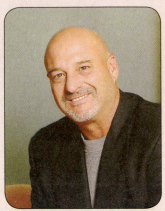 

(both): Courtesy of Zubi Advertising

The surging growth of Latino population numbers and economic power is one reason advertisers are shifting large portions of their promotional budgets to Hispanic media.

Coral Gables, near Miami, is home to one of the largest independent Hispanic agencies in America, Zubi Advertising. Zubi is short for Zubizarreta, and the agency was founded by Tere Zubi, after she and her husband fled Cuba for a better life in the United States. Of course, as with many immigrants, Tere did not find success easily or immediately. In fact, as she relayed to PBS in an interview, her own career was launched by necessity after her husband's small business failed in the early 1970s. Tere applied for jobs as a secretary to help make ends meet.

The second job (interview) I went to was an advertising agency. And I didn't know anything about advertising. I didn't even know how to use an electric typewriter because I had learned on a manual. And the person that interviewed me—everything he asked me—he would say, "Do you know anything about advertising?" And my answer would be, "I don't know, but I'll learn," and so forth. So that was a Friday. And Monday morning, I get the call that I got the job.

And then I asked later on—Mr. Gilmore, who was my boss, Al Gilmore, I said, "Why did you hire me?" He said, "Because I have never met a more honest answer in interviewing any person, because you did not try to fool me. You know, you were straightforward and said, 'I don't know, but I will learn.'"

And learn Tere did. Encouraged by friends, she went on to open her own small South Florida agency with little money or equipment and in office space loaned by friends. Within two decades, Zubi Advertising was handling $80 million in billings for clients like Ford and American Airlines.

A commitment to learning is still a part of Zubi Advertising today. Although Mama Zubi, as Tere was known to coworkers and clients alike, passed away in 2007, the business is still run by the Zubizarreta family, including son Joe and daughter Michelle.

As COO, Joe oversees Zubi's business development, strategic planning, and client relations. He joined Zubi after eight years with Beber, Silverstein and Partners, where within five years he became the youngest account supervisor.

As chief administrative officer, Michelle handles the agency's financial, budgetary, and operational matters, including personnel and management relations, as well as employee recruitment, retention, and benefits.

Current blue-chip accounts include Dunkin' Donuts, Ford Motor Company, Chase, Walgreens, and many others.

Joe Zubi shared some thoughts with us on the unique issues that confront a multicultural advertising agency.

CA: *What is the role of a multicultural agency?*
JZ: The role is twofold: First, we provide our clients with the cultural insights that can drive effective communication platforms. Second, we partner with general market advertising agencies to help them be more effective with campaigns that target all residents of the United States.

CA: *How do you keep track of all the changes that are taking place in the demographic makeup of the United States?*
JZ: It's a challenge. We regularly consult all of the important secondary sources of information, including the U.S. Census, Simmons Market Research Bureau reports, and research from pollsters such as Yankelovich and Nielsen. We also examine customized proprietary studies that are category specific. The adaptation to change is based on the category, its competitive set, and the brand's position in its life cycle.

CA: *What are you looking for in the people that you will be hiring at Zubi Advertising over the next several years?*
JZ: We want people who can grow beyond their potential—people who are confident, passionate, and eager to learn. We are looking for people who are willing to take chances.

CA: *Is there anything else that you would like to share with students of advertising?*
JZ: Yes. Don't hesitate to take on anything that is thrown your way. Take on any challenge, learn from your mistakes, and celebrate your successes. Life is too short to take this too seriously; have fun! It's just advertising. If you want a serious career, be a doctor.

Courtesy of Tere and Joe Zubi, Zubi Advertising.

short periods of time, sales promotion is aimed at stimulating customers or members of the distribution channel to some immediate, overt behavior.[76] This broad category includes trade deals, free samples, displays, trading stamps, sweepstakes, cents-off coupons, and premiums, among others. *Reader's Digest,* for example, is famous for its annual sweepstakes designed to increase circulation. One recent survey found that 90 percent of U.S. shoppers use coupons, saving $3.1 billion annually.[77]

Some promotions are linked mainly to the communications function of the marketing mix (displays, events, trade shows), while others are linked more to the product element (free samples, premiums) or the price element (coupons, volume discounts, end-of-month sales). And some complement the distribution element (trade deals, sales contests). Sales promotion (often referred to simply as *promotion*) is used primarily as a tactical adaptation to some external situation such as competitive pressure, changing seasons, declining sales, or new product introductions.[78] Because advertising people are frequently called on to solve a variety of marketing problems, it is critical that they understand and know how to integrate the whole mix of communications techniques.

The Marketing Mix in Perspective

With the target market designated and the elements of the marketing mix determined, the company has a complete product concept and a strategic basis for marketing to that target. Now it can formalize its strategies and tactics in a written marketing and advertising plan. As part of the planning process, companies use marketing and advertising research. We discuss this in Chapter 7 before dealing with the formal planning process in Chapter 8.

Chapter Summary

Market segmentation is the process of identifying groups of people with certain shared characteristics within a broad product market and aggregating these groups into larger market segments according to their mutual interest in the product's utility. From these segments, companies then select a target market. Marketers use a number of methods to identify behavioral groups and segment markets. The most common are behavioristic, geographic, demographic, and psychographic.

Business markets are often segmented in the same way as consumer markets. They may also be grouped by business purchasing procedures, NAICS code, or market concentration.

In the target marketing process, companies designate specific segments to target and develop their mix of marketing activities. The product concept is the consumer's perception of the product as a bundle of utilitarian and symbolic need-satisfying values.

Every company can add, subtract, or modify four major elements in its marketing program to achieve a desired marketing mix. These elements are product, price, distribution (place), and communications (promotion)—the 4Ps.

The *product* element includes the way the product is designed and classified, positioned, branded, and packaged. Just as humans pass through a life cycle, so do products—and product categories. The stage of a product's life cycle may determine how it is promoted.

To satisfy the variety of consumer tastes and achieve competitive advantages, marketers build differences into their products. Even the product's package is part of the product concept. The concept may also be developed through unique positioning against competing products.

Price refers to what and how a customer pays for a product. Companies use many common pricing strategies. Some products compete on the basis of price, but many do not.

Distribution refers to how the product is placed at the disposal of the customer: where the product is distributed, how it is bought, and how it is sold. Companies may use direct or indirect methods of distribution. Consumer goods manufacturers use several types of distribution strategies.

Communications refers to all marketing-related communications between the seller and the buyer. Tools of the communications element include personal selling, advertising, direct marketing, public relations activities, collateral materials, and sales promotion. Marketers try to integrate all their marketing communications programs for greater effectiveness and consistency.

Important Terms

behavioristic segmentation, *183*

benefits, *185*

benefit segmentation, *185*

brand, *202*

brand equity, *203*

business markets, *192*

collateral materials, *211*

communication element, *210*

communications mix, *210*

cooperative (co-op) advertising, *209*

copy points, *204*

decline stage, *200*

demographic segmentation, *186*

direct distribution, *206*

direct marketing, *210*

distribution channel, *207*

distribution element, *206*

early adopters, *199*

equipment-based service, *200*

exclusive distribution, *209*

family brand, *202*

Review Questions

1. How does the concept of shared characteristics relate to the market segmentation process?

2. How could you use VALS to develop the marketing strategy for a product of your choice?

3. How does the segmentation of business markets differ from that of consumer markets?

4. What is the most important factor to consider when determining the elements of the marketing mix?

5. What is the difference between a product and a product concept?

6. What are some examples of product positioning not discussed in this chapter?

7. What effect does the product life cycle have on the advertising a company uses?

8. What factors influence the price of a product?

9. How do the basic methods of distribution affect advertising?

10. What product characteristics encourage heavy advertising? Little advertising? Why?

The Advertising Experience

1. **Product Life Cycles**

   Many well-established American brands may seem to be in the decline stage of the product life cycle, perhaps because changing tastes or new technologies have rendered the products obsolete. Choose one of these and describe a plan for revitalizing the product, especially in terms of the 4Ps.

2. **World of Marketing**

   Part I: Marketing. You have already learned the importance of marketing to the study and application of advertising. Visit the sites below to get a wider view of the scope of the marketing world and the importance of a good marketing strategy. Answer the questions below for each site:

   - American Marketing Association (AMA): www.ama.org
   - Business Marketing Association (BMA): www.marketing.org
   - B to B: www.btobonline.com

   - AdWeek Brand Marketing: www.adweek.com/brand-marketing/
   - Sales & Marketing Management: www.salesandmarketing.com

   a. What group sponsors the site? Who is the intended audience?

   b. What is the site's purpose? Does it succeed? Why?

   c. What are the size and scope of the organization? What is the organization's purpose?

   d. Who makes up the organization's membership? Its constituency?

   Part II: Marketing Mix. Visit Mountain Dew's site (www.mountaindew.com/) and then answer the following questions about one of its products:

   a. Identify the product, price, place, and promotion. (If there are multiple products, choose one.)

    b.   Identify the product's stage in the product life cycle.

    c.   What is the product's positioning?

    d.   What are the key elements of the product's differentiation?

3. **Market Segmentation and Target Marketing**
   Segmenting markets and generating sound demographic, geographic, psychographic, and behavioristic profiles are critical to formulating advertising strategy. An abundance of market segmentation data are available on the internet from both the government and the private sector. Peruse the following sample of online resources for target market information:

   - Claritas: www.claritas.com
   - Forrester Research: www.forrester.com
   - Target Marketing: www.targetonline.com
   - U.S. Census Bureau American FactFinder: http://factfinder.census.gov

   Now choose a company with a website and use one of these online resources to answer the following questions. Be sure to cite any online resources you used in addition to the above.

    a.   What type of segmentation approach did the company take (single-market, multiple-market, aggregate market)?

    b.   Develop a demographic profile, including age, income, education, and gender, for the target market.

    c.   Describe the general geographic skew for the company's market.

    d.   What consumption patterns are evident in the company's consumers?

4. The Old Spice campaign revitalized a brand whose image may have grown stale in the minds of consumers. Identify another brand whose image, in your opinion, needs revamping. Explain why the image is dated. Propose a new brand identity and suggest a way that an advertisement might help the brand acquire that identity. Be sure to describe how your new identity relates to characteristics of the target audience for the product.

5. Another important way that the Old Spice campaign succeeded was it identified an unusual target audience. The ads were directed at consumers who buy the product (women) rather than those who use it (men). Identify another brand whose buyers are different from its users. Which group does the brand target in its advertising and why?

End Notes

1. Axe Ads, http://axeads.blogspot.com/.
2. Jeff Hirsch, "Reinvigorating the 'Solid Citizen' Brand," July 11, 2011, www.therightbrainstudio.com/reinvigorating-the-%E2%80%9Csolid-citizen%E2%80%9D-brand/.
3. "Old Spice: The Man Your Man Could Smell Like," www.youtube.com/watch?v=owGykVbfgUE.
4. Todd Wasserman, "How Old Spice Revived a Campaign That No One Wanted to Touch," Mashable.com, http://mashable.com/2011/11/01/old-spice-campaign/.
5. Todd Wasserman, "How Old Spice Revived a Campaign That No One Wanted to Touch," Mashable.com, http://mashable.com/2011/11/01/old-spice-campaign/.
6. Noreen O'Leary and Todd Wasserman, "Old Spice Campaign Smells Like a Sales Success, Too," *Adweek*, July 25, 2010, www.adweek.com/news/advertising-branding/old-spice-campaign-smells-sales-success-too-107588?page=2.
7. S. Kent Stephan and Barry L. Tannenholz, "The Real Reason for Brand Switching," *Advertising Age*, June 13, 1994, p. 31; S. Kent Stephan and Barry L. Tannenholz, "Six Categories That Hold Elusive Consumers," *Advertising Age*, June 20, 1994, p. 32.
8. Quoted in Al Stewart, "Edgy Ads, Burgers Drive CKE," *Orange County Business Journal* 27, no. 30 (July 26, 2004), p. 5.
9. L. Zepeda and J. Li, "Characteristics of Organic Food Shoppers," *Journal of Agricultural and Applied Economics* 39, no. 1 (2007), pp. 17–28, doi:10.1017/S1074070800022720; "Descriptive Materials for the VALS2 Segmentation System," *Values and Lifestyles Program* (Menlo Park, CA: SRI International, 1989).
10. "Second City Elite," Nielsen: My Best Segments, 2014 PRIZM Segmentation Systems, www.claritas.com/MyBestSegments/Default.jsp?ID=37&id1=1027&id2=10.
11. "Weather or Not to Sell," *Personal Selling Power*, September 1994, p. 79.
12. Joel S. Dubow, "Occasion-Based vs. User-Based Benefit Segmentation: A Case Study," *Journal of Advertising Research*, March/April 1992, pp. 11–18.
13. "PRIZM Premier," *Claritas*, https://claritas360.claritas.com/mybestsegments/#.
14. "Hispanic Consumer Expenditure in the United States from 2018 to 2024 (in Billion U.S. Dollars)," Statista, www.statista.com/statistics/899107/hispanic-consumer-expenditure-us/.
15. Leon E. Wynter, "Business and Race: JCPenney Launches Diahann Carroll Line," *The Wall Street Journal*, July 2, 1997, p. B1.
16. Pallavi Gogoi, "Retailing, the High-Tech Way," *BusinessWeek Online*, July 6, 2005, www.businessweek.com/technology/content/jul2005/tc2005076_5703.htm?campaign_id=search.
17. Richard Fry, "This Year, Millennials Will Overtake Baby Boomers," Pew Research Center, January 16, 2015, www.pewresearch.org/fact-tank/2015/01/16/this-year-millennials-willovertake-baby-boomers/.
18. Richard Fry, "This Year, Millennials Will Overtake Baby Boomers," Pew Research Center, January 16, 2015, www.pewresearch.org/fact-tank/2015/01/16/this-year-millennials-willovertake-baby-boomers/.
19. Mark Huffman, "Millennials Buy Cars Differently Than Their Parents," *Consumer Affairs*, September 15, 2014, www.consumeraffairs.com/news/millennials-buy-cars-differently-than-their-parents-091514.html.
20. Eric Schlosser, "Meat & Potatoes," *Rolling Stone* 800, November 26, 1998 (retrieved via EBSCO).
21. Eric Schlosser, "The True Cost of America's Diet," *Rolling Stone* 794, September 3, 1998 (retrieved via EBSCO).
22. Peter D. Kiernan, "The World's Middle Class Is Growing—and America Is Getting Left Behind," *Business Insider*, June 18, 2015, www.businessinsider.com/world-is-more-middleclass-2015-6.
23. Shoba Narayan, "India's Lust for Luxe," *Time.com*, April 3, 2006, www.time.com/time/nation/article/0,8599,1179415,00.html.
24. "Global Ad Spending Growth to Double This Year," eMarketer, July 9, 2014, www.emarketer.com/Article/Global-Ad-Spending-Growth-Double-This-Year/1010997.
25. Emarketer, "Total Media Ad Spending per Person Worldwide, by Country, 2012–2018," as reported in "Global Ad Spending

Growth to Double This Year," HispanicAd.com, July 10, 2014, http://hispanicad.com/agency/business/global-ad-spending-growth-double-year.

26. Henry Assael and David F. Poltrack, "Can Demographic Profiles of Heavy Users Serve as a Surrogate for Purchase Behavior in Selecting TV Programs?," *Journal of Advertising Reserach,* January/February 1994, p. 11.

27. Sulekha Goyat, "The Basis of Market Segmentation: A Critical Review of the Literature," *European Journal of Business and Management* 3, no. 9 (2011), pp. 45–55.

28. SRI Consulting Business Intelligence, "Welcome to VALS," www.sric-bi.com/vals.

29. SRI Consulting Business Intelligence, "Welcome to VALS," www.sric-bi.com/vals.

30. SRI Consulting Business Intelligence, "Welcome to VALS," www.sric-bi.com/vals.

31. Strategic Business Insights, "VALS Links Global Strategies to Local Efforts through GeoVALS," www.sric-bi.com/vals/geovals.shtml; SRI Consulting Business Intelligence, "Japan-VALS," www.strategicbusinessinsights.com/vals/international/japan.shtml.

32. "Re-Mapping the World of Consumers," special advertising section by Roper Starch Worldwide, *American Demographics,* October 2000.

33. "MindBase," Kantar Consulting, https://consulting.kantar.com/our-solutions/monitor/monitor-analytics/mindbase/.

34. www.experian.com/simmons-research/behavioral-targeting.html/about.html.

35. Malcolm Gladwell, *The Tipping Point: How Little Things Can Make a Big Difference* (New York: Little, Brown, 2002).

36. Lewis C. Winters, "International Psychographics," *Marketing Research: A Magazine of Management & Application,* September 1992, pp. 48–49.

37. Michael Reinemer, "It's a Dog's Life, and Its Time to Cash In," Advertising Age, October 03, 1994, https://adage.com/article/news/a-dog-s-life-time-cash-trend/89886.

38. James Hutton, "A Theoretical Framework for the Study of Brand Equity and a Test of Brand Sensitivity in an Organizational Buying Context," dissertation, University of Texas, Austin, 1993.

39. William D. Perreault Jr. and E. Jerome Mccarthy, *Basic Marketing,* 12th ed. (Burr Ridge, IL: Irwin, 1996), p. 261.

40. U.S. Bureau of the Census, Economic Classification Policy Committee, *New Data for a New Economy* (Washington, DC: U.S. Department of Commerce, 1998).

41. U.S. Bureau of the Census, *Statistical Abstract of the United States: 1999,* 119th ed. (Washington, DC: U.S. Department of Commerce, 1999), pp. 741–42, 744.

42. Michael Schrage, "Think Big," *Adweek,* October 11, 1993, p. 25.

43. William D. Perreault Jr. and E. Jerome McCarthy, *Basic Marketing,* 12th ed. (Burr Ridge, IL: Irwin), pp. 48–49, 91–112.

44. Walter Loeb, "How the Retail Industry Can Learn from Levi Strauss' Transformation," *Forbes,* September 28, 2017, www.forbes.com/sites/walterloeb/2017/09/28/how-the-retail-industry-can-learn-from-levi-strauss-transformation/#423e34c245bf.

45. Walter van Waterschoot and Christophe Van den Bulte, "The 4P Classification of the Marketing Mix Revisited," *Journal of Marketing,* October 1992, pp. 83–93.

46. The now widely popularized conceptual model of the 4Ps was developed by E. J. McCarthy, *Basic Marketing* (Homewood, IL: Irwin, 1960); the usage of the marketing mix derived from Neil H. Borden, "The Concept of the Marketing Mix," *Journal of Advertising Research,* June 1964, p. 27.

47. William D. Perreault Jr. and E. Jerome McCarthy, *Basic Marketing,* 12th ed. (Burr Ridge, IL: Irwin, 1996), pp. 310–21.

48. Gene Koprowski, "Cell Phone Services Vendors Banking on Mobile Gaming Apps," *TechNewsWorld,* April 8, 2006, www.technewsworld.com/story/49707.html.

49. Decision Analyst Inc., "Use of Cellular Phones Trends Upward, Survey Shows," press release, July 24, 1998; Matthew Klein, "More Callers Unleashed," *Forecast,* September 1998, www.demographics.com.

50. Brian Wansink, "Making Old Brands New," *American Demographics,* December 1997, www.demographics.com.

51. Adapted from William O. Bearden, Thomas N. Ingram, and Raymond W. LaForge, *Marketing: Principles & Perspectives* (Burr Ridge, IL: Irwin, 1995), pp. 211–13; and from Philip Kotler and Gary Armstrong, *Principles of Marketing* (Englewood Cliffs, NJ: Prentice Hall, 1994), pp. 640–43.

52. Hank Seiden, *Advertising Pure and Simple, The New Edition* (New York: AMACOM, 1990), p. 11.

53. Pat Sabena, "Tough Market for New Products Requires Partnership," *Marketing Review,* June 1996, pp. 12–13.

54. Adrienne Ward Fawcett, "In Glut of New Products, 'Different' Becomes Key," *Advertising Age,* December 13, 1993, p. 28.

55. Hank Seiden, *Advertising Pure and Simple, The New Edition* (New York: AMACOM, 1990), pp. 23–30; Robert Pritikin, *Pritikin's Testament* (Englewood Cliffs, NJ: Prentice Hall, 1991), pp. 25–33.

56. "Snapple Promotional Campaign Pays for 40 Ad-Free Days on WFNX-FM," *Boston Business Journal,* May 26, 2006, http://boston.bizjournals.com/boston/stories/2006/05/22/daily64.html.

57. Haim Oren, "Branding Financial Services Helps Consumers Find Order in Chaos," *Marketing News,* March 29, 1993, p. 6.

58. Frank Bilorsky, "Grocers Labels Offer a New Kind of Branding," *Rochester Democrat and Chronicle,* July 11, 2004, www.rochesterdandc.com.

59. "The Best Global Brands; *BusinessWeek* and Interbrand Tell You What They're Worth," *BusinessWeek* Special Report, August 5, 2007, www.businessweek.com.

60. Alan Wolf, "TWICE/Campaigners Poll Shows Shoppers Choose Brand over Price," *Twice: This Week in Consumer Electronics,* December 5, 2005, p. 18.

61. C. Manly Molpus, "Brands Follow New Shopping Patterns," *Advertising Age,* February 14, 1994, p. 22.

62. S. Kent Stephan and Barry L. Tannenholz, "The Real Reason for Brand Switching," *Advertising Age,* June 13, 1994, p. 31.

63. Mathew Draper, "What Is the True Value of Customer Retention?," *Liferay,* September 27, 2017, www.liferay.com/blog/en-us/customer-experience/what-is-the-true-value-of-customer-retention-.

64. Larry Light, "Brand Loyalty Marketing Key to Enduring Growth," *Advertising Age,* October 3, 1994, p. 20.

65. Andrew Jaffe, "A Compass Point Out of Dead Calm: 'Brand Stewardship,'" *Adweek,* February 7, 1994, p. 38.

66. Linda Trent, "Color Can Affect Success of Products," *Marketing News,* July 5, 1993, p. 4.

67. Kristin Zhavago, "How Customers Choose a Product or Service: Debunking Common Marketing Myths," *Business 2 Community,* November 15, 2012, www.business2community.com/customer-experience/how-customers-choose-a-product-or-service-debunking-common-marketing-myths-part-2-of-4-0333002.

68. Nielsen Global Retail-Growth Strategies Survey, "Valuable Variables: Consumers Want More Than Low Prices from Retailers," news release, June 20, 2016, www.nielsen.com/us/en/insights/news/2016/valuable-variables-consumers-want-more-than-low-prices-from-retailers.html.

69. Amway, "Amway Announces Sales of $8.6 Billion USD for 2017," news release, February 12, 2018, www.amwayglobal.com/amway-announces-sales-8-6-billion-2017-emphasis-product-innovation-technology-leads-companys-future-focus/.

70. William D. Perreault Jr. and E. Jerome McCarthy, *Basic Marketing,* 12th ed. (Burr Ridge, IL: Irwin, 1996), p. 16.
71. Mya Frazier, "Retailers Scramble for Exclusive Music Rights," *Advertising Age,* September 19, 2005, *http://adage.com/article .php?article_id=46812*.
72. Subway, *www.subway.com/subwayroot/index.aspx*.
73. Sean McGarry, "Is Europe a Fit for Your Franchise?" *Franchising World* 42, no. 6 (June 2010), p. 58.
74. Jim Emerson, "Levi Strauss in the Early Stages of Shift to Database Marketing," *DM News,* December 7, 1992, pp. 1–2; Lisa Benenson, "Bull's-Eye Marketing," *Success,* January/February 1993, pp. 43–48.
75. Al Ries and Laura Ries, *The Fall of Advertising and the Rise of PR* (New York: HarperBusiness, 2002), pp. 8–12.
76. Walter van Waterschoot and Christophe Van den Bulte, "The 4P Classification of the Marketing Mix Revisited," *Journal of Marketing,* October 1992, p. 89.
77. Doreen Christensen, "Coupons by the Numbers: Savings Up, Redemption Down in 2017," *Sun Sentinel,* October 6, 2018, *www.sun-sentinel.com/features/deals-shopping/fl-bz-doreen-christensen-2017-coupon-redemption-down-story.html*.
78. Walter van Waterschoot and Christophe Van den Bulte, "The 4P Classification of the Marketing Mix Revisited," *Journal of Marketing,* October 1992, pp. 89–90.

7

Research: Gathering Information for IMC Planning

To examine how advertisers gather intelligence about the marketplace and how they apply their findings to marketing and advertising decision making.

After studying this chapter, you will be able to:

LO7-1   Elaborate on the purposes of IMC research.

LO7-2   Explain the basic steps in the research process.

LO7-3   Distinguish qualitative and quantitative research.

LO7-4   Describe the differences between pretesting and posttesting of campaign messages.

LO7-5   List the important considerations in effective IMC research.

Anheuser Busch

"The Budweiser puppy has done what the Seattle Seahawks could not—it won back-to-back Super Bowls," glowed *USA Today* writer Bruce Horovitz.[1] The commercial, "Lost Dog," focuses on a lost puppy aided by Budweiser's iconic Clydesdales. You can watch it here: www.youtube.com/watch?v=otCxSnu_HXA. ■ The ad is a heart warmer, to be sure. But it seems reasonable to ask whether the spot can be justified based on strategic considerations. First, a 30-second spot in the Super Bowl sold for $4 million in 2015, and this does not include the costs of production. Does Budweiser earn a return on its investment that justifies spending that much on a single showing? ■ Some might question the focus of the ad as well. The commercial causes many viewers to feel a variety of emotions, ending with the warm glow of the puppy's reunion with its owner. Emotional response to advertising is generally good. But the emotions created by this ad center on a cute puppy, some brave Clydesdales, and a pet owner's joy at the reunion. Because the true "star" of the campaign is supposed to be a brand of beer, did the ad miss the mark? ■ No advertiser would spend the kind of money ponied up (no pun intended) by Budweiser without answers to such questions. And based on careful, deliberate, and quantitative research, Anheuser Busch was reasonably certain its investment was justified. ■ To begin with, consumers loved the ad. Evidence for this comes from a variety of sources, including the popular *USA Today* AdMeter. The company obtains ratings from approximately 7,000 consumer panelists, each of whom evaluated every one of the 61 ads that appeared in the game. "Lost Dog" finished first, beating every other slickly produced spot shown during the game. ■ But advertisers consider liking a means to an end, not an end in itself. A more relevant goal is using advertising to persuade consumers to like the brand. Can a cute puppy create positive feelings about a global brand of beer? The answer seems to be yes, based on research by a company named Bully Pulpit Interactive.[2] The company measured a sampled group of consumers' brand attitudes toward Super Bowl advertisers both before the game and immediately following. Budweiser saw a greater lift in brand favorability than any other game advertiser save one. Budweiser also topped all other brands save one in getting consumers interested in buying and was the most recalled ad of the game. ■ Still, a cynic might argue, liking, recall, brand favorability—these are surrogates for the real metric of interest, sales. What about sales? ■ To answer that question, it is important to recall that a purchase is the final step in a sequence of consumer responses. As you learned in Chapter 5, ads need to pass through perceptual and cognitive filters in order to affect consumers. The favorable reaction of viewers to the spot suggests the ad was successful. And as you will see in Chapter 8, a decision to take action, in this case a decision to purchase the brand, flows from a series of earlier steps that include brand awareness, message comprehension, conviction,

and desire. Triggering these psychological responses is an important advertising goal, and research confirmed "Lost Dog" achieved these goals. ■ But back to sales. What evidence do we have that the ad's psychological effectiveness produced the desired increase in sales? Research was able to address this question as well. Wesley Hartmann, a marketing professor at Stanford University, analyzed data collected from 55 markets around the United States as well as sales figures provided by Nielsen. The analysis showed that Budweiser's ad spending on the big game produced sales increases of $96 million, or a return on investment (ROI) of 172 percent.[3] All-in-all, a pretty satisfactory return. ■ When agencies spend their clients' money, the stakes are high. Jon Wanamaker, an advertising professional from many years ago, famously said, "I know 50 percent of my advertising is wasted. I just don't know which 50 percent." With modern research techniques, ignorance about advertising results is no longer inevitable. Or acceptable.

The Need for Research in Marketing and IMC

LO 7-1

Every year companies spend millions of dollars creating ads and promotions that they hope their customers and prospects will notice and relate to. Then they spend millions more placing their communications in media, hoping their customers will see and hear them and eventually respond.

Advertising is expensive. In the United States, the cost of a single 30-second commercial on AMC's popular series *Walking Dead* is nearly $334,000.[4] Likewise, a single, full-page color ad in a national business magazine averages $100 to reach every thousand prospects.[5] That's too much money to risk unless companies have good information about who their customers are, what they want and like, and where they spend their media time. And that's why marketers need research. Research provides the information that drives marketing decision making. Without that information, firms are forced to use intuition or guesswork. In a fast-changing, highly competitive, global economy, that invites failure.

What Is Marketing Research?

To help managers make marketing decisions, companies develop systematic procedures for gathering, recording, and analyzing new information. This is called **marketing research** (it should not be confused with *market research,* which is information gathered about a *particular* market or market segment).[6] Marketing research does a number of things: It helps identify consumer needs and market segments; it provides the information for developing new products and marketing strategies; and it enables managers to assess the effectiveness of promotional activities. Marketing research is also useful in financial planning, economic forecasting, and quality control.

Research has become big business. Worldwide, the top 10 research companies had revenues of more than $5.5 billion for marketing, advertising, and public opinion research. Led by The Nielsen Company, with offices in more than 100 countries, the top 25 have corporate parents in the United Kingdom, Sweden, Brazil, France, Germany, Japan, the Netherlands, and the United States. But more than half of their revenues come from

Exhibit 7-1

Top 10 research companies ranked by U.S. research revenues in 2018 ($ in billions).

U.S. Rank 2018	Company	Headquarters	Worldwide Revenue (billions)	Website
1	Nielsen Holdings	New York	$6.57	nielsen.com
2	IQVIA	Durham, NC	3.46	iqvia.com
3	Kantar	London	3.99	kantar.com
4	IRI	Chicago, IL	1.14	iriworldwide.com
5	Ipsos	Paris, France	1.97	ipsos-NA.com
6	Westat	Rockville, MD	0.55	westat.com
7	comScore	Reston, VA	0.40	comscore.com
8	GfK	Nuremberg, Germany	1.65	gfk.com
9	NPD Group	Port Washington, NY	0.38	npd.com
10	ICF International	Fairfax, VA	0.23	icfi.com

Source: Diane Bowers, "The 2018 AMA Gold Top 50 Report," *American Marketing Association* (November 13, 2018), retrieved at: www.ama.org/publications/MarketingNews/Pages/2018-ama-gold-top50-report.aspx.

operations outside their home countries.[7] Exhibit 7-1 lists the top 10 research companies ranked by U.S. revenues.

Research is used to gather a lot of different types of information. It may be easiest to think of all these in terms of the *three Rs* of marketing: *recruiting* new customers, *retaining* current customers, and *regaining* lost customers.[8]

For example, to *recruit* new customers, researchers study different market segments and create *product attribute models* to match buyers with the right products and services. Marketers have many questions: What new products do consumers want? Which ideas should we work on? What product features are most important to our customers? What changes in the product's appearance and performance will increase sales? What price will maintain the brand's image, create profits, and still be attractive and affordable? Answers may lead to decisions that directly affect the product's nature, content, packaging, pricing—and IMC.[9]

On the other hand, to *retain* existing customers, a marketer may use *customer satisfaction studies*. Likewise, *databases* of customer transactions may identify reasons for customer satisfaction or dissatisfaction.[10] Today, companies realize that the best sales go to those who develop good relationships with individual customers.[11] As a result, customer satisfaction is now the fastest-growing field in marketing research.

Information gained for the first two Rs helps the third, *regaining* lost customers. For example, if an office equipment manufacturer discovers through research that an increase in service calls typically precedes cancellation of a service contract, it can watch for that pattern and take preventive action. Moreover, it can review service records of former customers and (if the pattern holds true) devise some marketing action or appeal to win them back.[12]

In short, good marketing research enables companies to devise a sophisticated, integrated mix of product, price, distribution, and communication elements. It gives them the information they need to decide which strategies will enhance the brand's image and lead to greater profits. Finally, it enables them to judge the effectiveness of past marketing programs and campaigns.

What Is IMC Research?

Before developing any campaign, a company needs to know how people perceive its products, how they view the competition, what brand or company image would be most credible, and what messages offer the greatest appeal. To get this information, companies use *IMC research*. While marketing research provides the information necessary to make marketing decisions, **IMC research** uncovers the information needed for making IMC decisions. By definition, it is the systematic gathering and analysis of information to help develop or evaluate message strategies, individual promotions, and whole campaigns.

A 30-second spot in Super Bowl XLIX cost $4.5 million. At those prices, advertisers are smart to do everything they can to make sure their ads resonate with consumers. Budweiser's "Lost Dog" spot topped the charts of many ad measures, including those employed by research company "Ace Metrix."

Courtesy of Ace Metrix

In this chapter, we consider the importance of information gathering to the development of IMC plans and strategies; we look at how companies use research to test the effectiveness of ads before and after they run; and we explore a number of specific research techniques.

Applying Research to IMC Decision Making

IMC research serves various purposes, most of which can be grouped into four categories: *strategy research, creative concept research, pretesting,* and *posttesting.*

1. *IMC strategy research.* Used to help define the product concept or to assist in the selection of target markets, messages, or media.

2. *Creative concept research.* Measures the target audience's acceptance of different creative ideas at the concept stage.

3. *Message pretesting.* Used to diagnose possible communication problems before a campaign begins.

4. *Message posttesting.* Enables marketers to evaluate a campaign after it runs.

As Exhibit 7-2 shows, marketers use the different categories of research at different stages of campaign development. The techniques they use at each stage also vary considerably. We'll examine each of these categories briefly before moving on to discuss the research process.

Message Strategy Research

Companies develop a message strategy by blending elements of the *creative mix.* These include the *product concept,* the *target audience,* the *communication media,* and the *creative message.* To seek information about any or all of these various elements, companies use **IMC strategy research.**

Product Concept

As we saw at the beginning of this chapter, marketers need to know how consumers perceive their brands. They also want to know what qualities lead to initial purchases and, eventually, to brand loyalty.

	Advertising Strategy Research	Creative Concept Research	Pretesting	Posttesting
Timing	Before creative work begins	Before agency production begins	Before finished artwork and photography	After campaign has run
Research Problem	Product concept definition Target audience selection Media selection Message element selection	Concept testing Name testing Slogan testing	Print testing TV storyboard pretesting Radio commercial pretesting	Advertising effectiveness Consumer attitude change Sales increases
Techniques	Consumer attitude and usage studies Media studies	Free-association tests Qualitative interviews Statement comparison tests	Consumer juries Matched samples Portfolio tests Storyboard tests Mechanical devices Psychological rating scales	Aided recall Unaided recall Attitude tests Inquiry tests Sales tests

Exhibit 7-2
Categories of research in advertising development.

Using this information, they try to establish a unique *product concept* for their brand—that bundle of values we discussed in Chapter 6 that encompasses both utilitarian and symbolic benefits to the consumer.

The opening vignette of this chapter offers an illustration of how research informs the development of a product concept. Budweiser knew that its warm, emotional messages, created with a heavy emphasis on symbolism and storytelling, would be effective in creating favorable attitudes toward the brand. It is one reason why Bud has purchased an exclusive Super Bowl ad buy in the beer category.[13]

It's this kind of information that can lead to an effective positioning strategy for the brand. IMC can shape and magnify a brand's position and image over time. But to use message strategies effectively, strategy research should inform a blueprint for creatives to follow.[14]

IMC works differently for different product categories and, often, even for different brands within a category. This means that each brand must develop a template for the creative based on an understanding of its particular consumers' wants, needs, and motivations. Only if this is done correctly over time (say, one to two years) can brand equity be built.[15]

To determine how brands are built and how they derive their strength, the Young & Rubicam agency developed a model called the BrandAsset Valuator. It measures brands in terms of differentiation, relevance, esteem, and familiarity, in that order. According to Y&R's theory, a brand must first develop differentiation—it must offer something unique and different—to survive. Second, it must be perceived by the target market as relevant to their needs and wants. Finally, it needs to build stature through esteem and knowledge. Once all these steps are accomplished, a brand achieves leadership status. Y&R performed a study in 19 countries and found that Disney scored high on all these dimensions.[16]

Following Y&R's lead, other agencies have developed their own brand equity studies. In 1998, WPP Group introduced a research tool titled "BRANDZ." Then, in 2000, DDB Worldwide introduced "Brand Capital," and Leo Burnett unveiled its research tool, which it dubbed "Brand Stock." All of these systems are designed to help agencies understand how consumers connect with brands before clients spend millions on creating and placing messages.[17]

Target Audience Selection

The second element of the creative mix is the target audience. We pointed out in Chapters 5 and 6 that no market includes everybody. Therefore, an important purpose of research is to develop a rich profile of the brand's target markets. The marketer will want to know which customers are the primary users of the product category and will study them carefully to understand their demographics, geographics, psychographics, lifestyles, and purchase behaviors.

With any new product, there is never enough money to attack all geographic or demographic markets effectively at the same time. So the marketer will often decide to employ the *dominance concept*—researching which markets (geographic or otherwise) are most important to product sales and targeting those where it can focus its resources to achieve promotional dominance.

Fallon Worldwide, a Minneapolis agency, worked closely with Holiday Inn Express to identify the target audience for the client's famous "Stay Smart" campaign. The agency believed it was important to find a target audience that would be heavy users of hotels but were being ignored by other hotel chains. A group the agency labeled "Road Warriors," consisting of independent-minded male businessmen, typically working for small companies or for themselves, fit the bill perfectly. As heavy users of hotels, they represented a highly profitable market segment. And because Road Warriors believed that no hotel brand was particularly interested in them, Fallon could design a campaign that targeted their needs and concerns.

Media Selection

To develop media strategies, select media vehicles, and evaluate their results, agencies use a subset of IMC research called **media research.** Agencies subscribe to syndicated research services (such as ACNielsen, Arbitron, Simmons, or @plan) that monitor and publish information on the reach and effectiveness of media vehicles—radio, TV, newspapers,

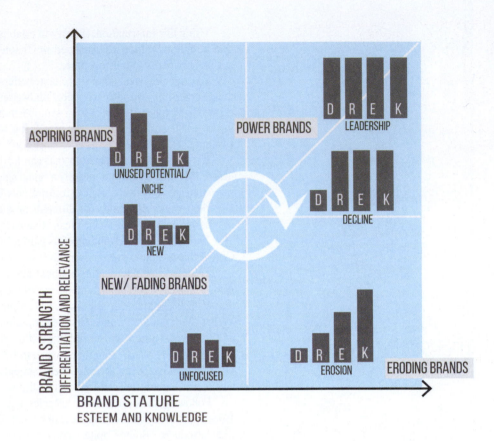

websites, and so on—in every major geographic market in the United States and Canada. (We'll discuss these further in Chapter 9.)

For Holiday Inn Express, Fallon researched the media habits of drive-ups and discovered that they tended to watch cable fare focused on news and sports, including programs on ESPN, CNN, and the Weather Channel. Research also suggested that the target audience formulated travel plans early in the week, so Fallon ran ads only on Sunday and Monday nights. While the overall ad budget was comparatively small, the concentration of ads on two evenings using a small number of networks gave the campaign a larger presence on those occasions when drive-ups would actually be watching TV and thinking about travel. In addition, because the campaign was so fresh and unusual, it got an additional boost from unpaid references to the "No, but I did stay at a Holiday Inn Express last night" slogan on ESPN, *Late Night with David Letterman,* NPR, and *The Washington Post.*

Message Element Selection

The final component of IMC strategy is the message element. Companies hope to find promising messages by studying consumers' likes and dislikes in relation to brands and products. Kraft Foods, for example, was looking for ways to dissuade parents from switching to less-expensive brands of processed cheese. While its Kraft Singles brand dominated the processed cheese slices category, it was concerned that the brand wasn't keeping up with overall growth in the market.

Working with several research companies and its agency, J. Walter Thompson, the company conducted a series of qualitative consumer attitude studies to figure out how women, particularly mothers, felt about Kraft Singles with the hope of discovering possible message themes. The mothers said they felt good giving their kids Kraft Singles because of the brand's nutritional value. But there was a catch—they also said they'd switch to a competitive product if it were cheaper. Fortunately, a phone survey provided some clues for solving the problem. Among these polled, 78 percent considered the brand an extra source of calcium for their kids. And 84 percent of women with kids under 12 said they'd be motivated to buy the brand because of that added benefit.[18]

From this information, the agency used concept testing to determine which message element options might prove most successful. This was now category 2 research aimed at developing creative concepts.

Developing Creative Concepts

Once it develops an IMC strategy, the company (or its agency) will begin developing creative concepts. Here again, research is helpful in determining which concepts to use.

From all their studies, Kraft researchers came up with two concepts that might keep mothers from defecting to competitive brands. First, show how much kids like Kraft Singles, and second, emphasize the fact that the brand provides the calcium kids need. J. Walter Thompson prepared two tentative TV spots and then conducted focus groups of mothers to get their reactions. With a discussion leader moderating the conversation, each group viewed the commercials. The groups' reactions were measured, taped, and observed by JWT and Kraft staff behind a one-way mirror. Immediately, problems surfaced. The idea that kids love the taste of Kraft Singles just didn't come across strongly enough. And the statement that Kraft provides calcium wasn't persuasive. Parents said, "Of course it has calcium; it's cheese." The agency had to find a newsier way to communicate the information.

Tweaking the commercials, JWT came up with a new spot showing youngsters gobbling gooey grilled-cheese sandwiches while a voice-over announcer stated that two out of five kids don't get enough calcium. More focus groups ensued. Now the parents agreed that the shots of kids devouring sandwiches communicated the great taste theme, but some thought the two-out-of-five statement played too much on their guilt.

To soften the message, the agency switched to a female announcer and then brought in the Dairy Fairy, a character from an earlier campaign, to lighten the whole tone of the spot. This seemed to work better, so the agency proceeded to copy testing.

Pretesting and Posttesting

IMC is one of the largest costs in a company's marketing budget. Companies want to know what they are getting for their money—and whether their messages are working. And they'd like some assurance before their ads run.

Kraft was no exception. Millward Brown Research performed a number of copy tests to see how the agency's latest spot would perform. The tests showed that the spot performed significantly better than the norm on key measures such as branding and persuasion. Following the copy tests, the company aired "The Calcium They Need" commercial in five test markets to see how it would affect sales. Kraft quickly achieved a 10 percent increase in sales in those markets. Based on such a strong showing, Kraft rolled the campaign out nationally, and sales took off. Base volume soared 14.5 percent, and sales grew 11.8 percent.[19]

The campaign was so successful that the Advertising Research Foundation named Kraft and J. Walter Thompson finalists for its prestigious David Ogilvy Research Award, given to the most effective campaign guided by research.

The Purpose of Testing

Testing is used to ensure IMC dollars are spent wisely. Testing can prevent costly errors, especially in judging which strategy or medium is most effective. And it can give the marketer some measure of a campaign's value.

To increase the likelihood of preparing the most effective messages, companies use **pretesting.** Pretesting is somewhat controversial among creatives because it is believed it can lead to bland, safe copy. But large clients frequently insist on it, and the practice is now becoming common even in digital campaigns.[20] When companies don't pretest, they may encounter a surprising reaction from the marketplace. Schering Canada received a torrent of complaint letters from customers who said they didn't like its commercial introducing the antihistamine Claritin to the over-the-counter market in Canada. Most negative responses, though, are more insidious: Consumers simply turn the page or change the channel, and sales mysteriously suffer. This is why it's also important to evaluate the effectiveness of a campaign *after* it runs. **Posttesting** (also called *tracking*) provides the marketer with useful guidelines for future advertising.

Testing Helps Marketers Make Important Decisions

Companies use pretesting to help make decisions about a number of variables. It may be helpful to think of these as the five Ms: *merchandise, markets, motives, messages,* and *media.* Many of these can be posttested too. We'll discuss each of the five Ms briefly.

Merchandise   For purposes of alliteration, we refer to the product concept here as **merchandise.** Companies may pretest many things: the package design, how a message positions the brand, or how well it communicates the product's features.

Markets   Companies may pretest a strategy or particular commercials with different **markets.** The information they gain may cause them to alter their strategy and target the campaign to new segments. In posttesting, advertisers want to know if the campaign succeeded in reaching its target markets. Changes in awareness and increases in market share are two indicators of success.

Motives   Consumers' **motives** are outside a company's control, but the messages they create to appeal to those motives are not. Pretesting helps marketers identify and appeal to the most compelling needs and motives, and to evaluate whether consumers consider brand claims about meeting such needs as compelling and credible. Posttesting can indicate how effective they were.

Messages   Pretesting helps identify outstanding, as well as underperforming, messages. It helps determine what (from the customer's point of view) a **message** says and how well it

Exhibit 7-3
Media categories.

Media Classes	Print	Electronic	Digital Interactive	Direct Mail	Out-of-Home
Media subclasses	Newspaper Magazines	Radio Television	Internet Social media Smartphone	Catalog Brochure	Outdoor transit
Media vehicles	*The N.Y.* *Times* *Elle*	KNX-AM *Wheel of* *Fortune*	App, website, e-mail Facebook	Lands' End	Billboards Bus stations Subway stations
Media units	Half page Full page	30-second spot Infomercial	Banner Digital video App game appearance	16 pages Letter size	Poster panel Inside card

says it. If the message is an ad, an agency might test the headline, the text, the illustration, the typography—or the message concept. Most important, pretesting guides the improvement of commercials.

However, pretesting is not foolproof. The only way to know for sure if a message is effective is through posttesting. Here the marketer determines to what extent the message was seen, remembered, and believed. Virtually all testing assesses both cognitive change (e.g., increased awareness of a brand or the memorability of a slogan or benefit) and evaluative change (e.g., brand interest or more positive brand attitudes).

Media   The cost of media advertising is soaring, and marketers hold their agencies accountable for demonstrating the effectiveness of media buys. Information gained from pretesting can influence several types of media decisions: classes of media, media subclasses, specific media vehicles, media units of space and time, media budgets, and scheduling criteria.

The broad media categories of print, electronic, digital interactive, direct mail, and out-of-home are referred to as **media classes.** Conversely, **media subclasses** refer to newspapers or magazines, radio or TV, and so on. The specific **media vehicle** is the particular publication or program. **Media units** are the size or length of an ad: half-page or full-page ads, 15- or 30-second spots, 60-second commercials, and so forth (see Exhibit 7-3).

After a campaign runs, posttesting can determine how effectively the media mix reached the target audience and communicated the desired message. We discuss audience measurement further in Chapters 13 through 17.

A constant question facing all advertisers is how large the company's promotional budget should be. How much should be allocated to various markets and media? To specific products? Companies can use a number of pretesting techniques to determine optimum spending levels before introducing national campaigns. (Chapter 8 provides further information on budgeting.)

Media scheduling is another nagging question for many advertisers. Through pretesting, marketers can test consumer response during different seasons of the year or days of the week. They can test whether frequent advertising is more effective than occasional or one-time insertions, or whether year-round advertising is more effective than advertising concentrated during a gift-buying season. (Chapter 9 discusses the most common types of media schedules.)

Testing in Digital Media   A big appeal of digital media is the ease with which even small advertisers can test potential messages. Advertising with search engine Google can be prohibitively expensive unless a marketer knows which keywords are being used by potential customers. Google's *Keyword Planner* allows advertisers to view how many people are searching the web for a word or phrase at a given time.[21] Similarly, Google tools can be used to test the effectiveness of mobile ads in Google's mobile ios.[22]

Facebook also encourages advertisers to test campaigns before committing large resources to running ads and provides valuable help on how to do so.[23] Effective online marketing is not just about attracting an audience, however; it is also about converting those who've been attracted into customers. Google Analytics is a well-known tool for tracking visits to a website, but Twitter offers sophisticated tools for determining whether social media activity on the platform has resulted in a sale.[24]

Exhibit 7-4
The marketing research process begins with evaluation of the company's situation and definition of the problem.

Overall Results   Finally, marketers want to measure overall results to evaluate how well they accomplished their objectives. Posttesting is most helpful here to determine whether and how to continue, what to change, and how much to spend in the future. We'll discuss the methods used for pretesting and posttesting in the next section on conducting primary research.

Steps in the Research Process

LO 7-2

Now that we understand the various types of decision-related information that marketers seek, let's explore how they gather this information by looking at the overall research process and some of the specific techniques they use.

There are five basic steps in the research process (see Exhibit 7-4):

1. Situation analysis and problem definition.
2. Informal (exploratory) research.
3. Construction of research objectives.
4. Primary research.
5. Interpretation and reporting of findings.

Step 1: Analyzing the Situation and Defining the Problem

The first step in the marketing research process is to *analyze the situation* and *define the problem*. Many large firms have in-house research departments. Often the marketing department also maintains a **marketing information system (MIS)**—a sophisticated set of procedures designed to generate a continuous, orderly flow of information for use in making marketing decisions. These systems ensure that managers get the information they need when they need it.[25]

Most smaller firms don't have dedicated research departments, and their methods for obtaining marketing information are frequently inadequate. These firms often find the problem definition step difficult and time-consuming. Yet good research on the wrong problem is a waste of effort.

Step 2: Conducting Informal (Exploratory) Research

The second step in the process is to use **informal** (sometimes *exploratory* or *formative*) **research** to learn more about the market, the competition, and the business environment, and to better define the problem. Researchers may discuss the problem with wholesalers, distributors, or retailers outside the firm; with informed sources inside the firm; with customers; or even with competitors. They look for whoever has the most information to offer. In creating the Super Bowl campaign for Budweiser, agency account planners spoke with individuals from the target market, but also with company executives, franchise owners, and consumers of competing beverages.

Research into Budweiser's award-winning Super Bowl ad also rested on a foundation of storytelling.[26] The 60-second commercial followed a familiar arc of storytelling: (1) an ordinary person (or puppy) (2) encounters a challenge that he or she is able to overcome, followed by (3) a return to normalcy, albeit with growth or change. Budweiser's focus on storytelling also follows research showing the effects of powerful stories on the brain.[27]

There are two types of research data: *primary* and *secondary*. Information collected by the company or agency about a specific problem is called **primary data;** acquiring it is typically expensive and time-consuming. So during the exploratory stage, researchers frequently use **secondary data**—information previously collected or published, usually for some other purpose. This information is readily available, either internally or externally, and can be gathered more quickly and inexpensively than primary data. To give specific examples, when Fallon planners interviewed drive-ups, they were collecting primary data. When they searched the web for information on hotel chains, they were collecting secondary data.

Assembling Internal Secondary Data

Company records are often a valuable source of secondary information. Useful internal data include product shipment figures, billings, warranty card records, advertising expenditures, sales expenses, customer correspondence, and records of meetings with sales staff.

A well-developed marketing information system can help researchers analyze sales data, review past tracking studies, and examine previous marketing research data. This information might point the way toward an interesting headline or positioning statement such as Jiffy Lube's "The Well-Oiled Machine."

Gathering External Secondary Data

Much information is available, sometimes for little or no cost, from the government, market research companies, trade associations, various trade publications, or computerized databases. Most large companies subscribe to any of a number of syndicated research reports about their particular industry. For example, as the advertising manager for a large nutritional company introducing a new line of vitamins, you might need to know the current demand for vitamins and food supplements, the number of competitors in the marketplace, the amount of advertising each is doing, and the challenges and opportunities the industry faces.

In the United States, frequently used sources of secondary data include

- Library reference materials (*Business Periodicals Index* for business magazines, *Reader's Guide to Periodical Literature* for consumer magazines, *Public Information Service Bulletin, The New York Times Index,* and the *World Almanac and Book of Facts*).
- Government publications (*Statistical Abstract of the United States*).
- Trade association publications (annual fact books containing government data gathered by various industry groups listed in the *Directory of National Trade Associations*).
- Research organizations and their publications or syndicated information (literature from university bureaus of business research, Nielsen retail store audits, MRCA consumer purchase diaries, Simmons' Study of Media and Markets, Jupiter Research, IRI's InfoScan market tracking service, and Standard Rate & Data Service).
- Consumer/business publications (*Bloomberg Businessweek, Forbes, Fortune, American Demographics, Advertising Age, Prevention,* and thousands more).
- Computer database services (Dialog Information Service, ProQuest, Electric Library, Lexis-Nexis, and Dow Jones News Retrieval Service).
- Internet search engines (Google, Bing, Digg, and others).
- Google research tools, including Think Insights,[28] Google Trends,[29] and the Google Keyword Tool.[30]

Step 3: Establishing Research Objectives

Once the exploratory research phase is completed, the company may discover it needs additional information that it can get only from doing primary research. For example, it may want to identify exactly who its customers are and clarify their perceptions of the company and the competition. To do so, the company must first establish *specific research objectives.*

A concise written statement of the research problem and objectives should be formulated at the beginning of any research project. A company must be clear about what decisions it has to make that the research results will guide. Once it knows the application, it can set

An extraordinary amount of secondary data can be found on the web. Services such as EDGAR Online (www.edgar-online.com) create databases of news articles published in a wide range of trade and business journals.

Source: EDGAR® Online

down clear, specific research objectives.[31] For example, a department store, noticing that it is losing market share, might write its problem statement and research objectives as follows:

Market Share

Our company's sales, while still increasing, seem to have lost momentum and are not producing the profit our shareholders expect. In the last year, our market share slipped 10 percent in the men's footwear department and 7 percent in the women's fine apparel department. Our studies indicate we are losing sales to other department stores in the same malls and that customers are confused about our position in the market. We need to make decisions about how we position ourselves for the future marketplace.

Research Objectives

We must answer the following questions: (1) Who are our customers? (2) Who are the customers of other department stores? (3) What do these customers like and dislike about us and about our competitors? (4) How are we currently perceived? (5) What do we have to do to clarify and improve that perception?

This statement of the problem is specific and measurable, the decision point is clear, and the questions are related and relevant. The research results should provide the information management needs to decide on a new positioning strategy for the company. The positioning strategy facilitates the development of marketing and advertising plans that will set the company's course for years to come.

Step 4: Conducting Primary Research

When a company wants to collect its own data about a specific problem or issue, it uses **primary research.** There are two types of primary research: qualitative and quantitative.

To get a general impression of the market, the consumer, or the product, marketers typically start with **qualitative research.** This enables researchers to gain insight into both the population whose opinion will be sampled and the subject matter itself. Then, to get hard numbers about specific marketing situations, they may perform a survey or use some other form of **quantitative research.** Sophisticated agencies use a balance of both qualitative and quantitative methods, understanding the limits of each and how they work together.[32] (See Exhibit 7-5.)

Step 5: Interpreting and Reporting the Findings

The final step in the research process involves interpreting and reporting the data. Research is very costly (see Exhibit 7-6), and its main purpose is to help solve problems. The final report must be comprehensible to the company's managers and relevant to their needs.

Tables and graphs are helpful, but they must be explained in words management can understand. Technical jargon (such as "multivariate analysis of variance model") should be avoided, and descriptions of the methodology, statistical analysis, and raw data should be

Exhibit 7-5
Differences between qualitative and quantitative research.

	Qualitative	Quantitative
Main techniques for gathering data	Focus groups and in-depth interviews.	Survey and experiments (copy or message testing).
Kinds of questions asked	Why? Through what thought process? In what way? In connection with what other behavior or thoughts?	How many? How much?
Role of interviewer	Critical: Interviewer must think on feet and frame questions and probes in response to whatever respondents say. A highly trained professional is advisable.	Important, but interviewers need only be able to read scripts. They should not improvise. Minimally trained, responsible employees are suitable.
Questions asked	Questions vary in order and phrasing from group to group and interview to interview. New questions are added, old ones dropped.	Should be exactly the same for each interview. Order and phrasing of questions carefully controlled.
Number of interviews	Fewer interviews tending to last a longer time.	Many interviews in order to give a projectable scientific sample.
Kinds of findings	Develop hypotheses, gain insights, explore language options, refine concepts, flesh out numerical data, provide diagnostics on advertising copy.	Test hypotheses, prioritize factors, provide data for mathematical modeling and projections.

My IMC Campaign 7-A

Research

Research is a complicated aspect of preparing a campaign, and without at least one course in advertising research, you may find it tough going. However, without research, you will find it difficult to make some of the tough creative and strategic decisions that lie ahead. Even without an extensive research background, you can do some secondary and qualitative research that can result in better choices for your campaign.

Secondary Research

Secondary research involves obtaining information from existing sources, including your client. Be sure to obtain all that you can, with the understanding that information shared by your client is valuable and that most clients will insist on strict confidentiality. Breaking a confidentiality agreement is a very serious transgression and should not happen under any circumstances, whether deliberately or through neglect.

Qualitative Research

You can also plan some qualitative research studies. Two of the most common are focus groups and observational research. In a focus group, you bring together a collection of carefully chosen participants (users of your brand, users of competing brands, etc.) and lead a group discussion that has the potential to offer strategic insights.

Qualitative Research: Focus Groups

For a tutorial on using focus groups, see www.cse.lehigh.edu/~glennb/mm/FocusGroups.htm. Tips for using focus groups can be found at www.groupsplus.com/pages/mn091498.htm.

Observational Research

Observational research techniques involve monitoring the consumer in his or her native environment (the mall, a restaurant, a skateboard park, etc.). The goal is to see how the consumer behaves in a natural setting. Careful attention is ordinarily paid to language, dress, interactions, symbols, and style.

See the observational research tutorial at http://writing.colostate.edu/guides/research/observe/index.cfm. Tips for observational research can be found at www.quirks.com/articles/a1997/19971208.aspx?searchID=625728.

Quantitative Research

Your project may also involve administering a survey. Google Forms, introduced in My IMC Campaign 2, from Chapter 2, may be useful for creating an online survey that is easy and inexpensive to administer. The hard part is writing a good survey instrument and then choosing data analysis techniques that will provide you and your client with useful information. Some web tutorials are listed below:

Surveys

Writing good questions: www.accesswave.ca/~infopoll/tips.htm
Response options: https://explorable.com/survey-response-scales
Create an online survey using Google forms: www.google.com/forms/about/

Data Analysis Using Excel

www.ncsu.edu/labwrite/res/gt/gt-menu.html

Exhibit 7-6

The cost of professional research.

Type of Research	Features	Cost	Cost per Respondent	Factors That Can Affect Quality and Costs
Telephone and mail surveys	500 20-minute interviews, with report	$30,000 to $55,000	$60 to $110	Response rates Interview time Incidence of qualified respondents Level of analysis required in the report
Online surveys	500 surveys, with report	$15,000 to $35,000	$30 to $70	Extent population can be reached via web Response rates Level of analysis required in the report
Focus group	2 groups with 10 respondents each, with report	$8,000 to $12,000	$400 to $600	Cost of focus group facilities Moderator costs Respondent costs

Sources: Dave Glantz, "Let's Talk Price: How Much Does Research Cost?—(Archived)," Market Connections, Inc., www.marketconnectionsinc.com/lets-talk-price-how-much-does-research-cost/, accessed October 14, 2018; Vernon Research Group, "How Much Does Research Cost?," www.vernonresearch.com/wp-content/uploads/2018/01/HowMuchDoesMarketResearchCost_ebook.pdf, accessed October 14, 2018.

confined to an appendix. The report should state the problem and research objective, summarize the findings, and draw attention to important conclusions. The researcher should make recommendations for management action, and the report should be discussed in a presentation to allow for questions and to highlight important points.

Understanding Qualitative and Quantitative Research Approaches

LO 7-3

In this section we'll discuss the basic methods companies use for conducting qualitative and quantitative research, and then we'll look at how they apply these techniques to testing campaigns.

Methods of Qualitative Research

To get people to share their motives, beliefs, and perceptions, researchers use **qualitative research** that encourages consumers to openly discuss their thoughts and feelings in response to questions from an interviewer. Some marketers refer to this as *motivation research.* Unfortunately, no matter how skillfully posed, some questions are uncomfortable for consumers to answer. When asked why they bought a particular status car, for instance, consumers might reply that it handles well or is economical or dependable, but they rarely admit that it makes them feel important. Digging down to uncover unarticulated or even unacknowledged motivation takes special skill. The methods used in qualitative research are usually either *projective* or *intensive techniques.*

Projective Techniques   Advertisers use **projective techniques** to unearth people's underlying or subconscious feelings, attitudes, interests, opinions, needs, and motives. By asking indirect questions (such as "What kind of people do you think shop here?"), the researcher tries to involve consumers in a situation where they can express feelings about the problem or product. A technique used by one researcher includes asking individuals to find pictures that, for that individual, exemplify a brand, company, or person. These pictures are used as the starting point for a discussion of why the pictures were chosen and what they mean.

Projective techniques were adapted for marketing research after their use by psychologists in clinical diagnosis. But such techniques require the skill of highly experienced researchers.

Intensive Techniques   **Intensive techniques,** such as in-depth interviews, also require great care to administer properly. In the **in-depth interview,** carefully planned but loosely structured questions help the interviewer probe respondents' deeper feelings. The big pharmaceutical company Schering-Plough, for example, uses in-depth interviews with physicians to find out what attributes doctors consider most important in the drugs they prescribe and to identify which brands the doctors associate with different attributes.[33]

While in-depth interviews help reveal individual motivations, they are also expensive and time-consuming, and skilled interviewers are in short supply.

One of the most common intensive research techniques is the **focus group,** in which the company invites six or more people typical of the target market to a group session to discuss the product, the service, or the marketing situation. The session may last an hour or more. A trained moderator guides the often freewheeling discussion, and the group interaction reveals the participants' true feelings or behavior toward the product. Focus group meetings are usually recorded and often viewed from behind a one-way mirror.

Focus groups aren't a representative sample of the population, but the participants' responses are useful for several purposes. They can provide input about the viability of prospective spokespeople, determine the effectiveness of visuals and strategies, and identify elements in ads that are unclear or claims that don't seem plausible. Focus groups are best used in conjunction with surveys. In fact, focus group responses often help marketers design questions for a formal survey.[34] Following a survey, focus groups can put flesh on the skeleton of raw data.[35]

Focus groups are particularly useful to gain a deeper understanding of particular market segments. A *show-and-tell* focus group conducted by Grieco Research Group in Colorado provides a glimpse of the core values of baby boomers. Participants were asked to bring to the session three or four items that they felt represented their ideal environment. Items ranged from photographs to magazine pictures to mementos and souvenirs. One mother of two brought tickets to a retro rock concert; a conservative corporate executive brought in a pack of cigarettes to show he was still rebellious; a middle-aged father brought a lucky fishing lure his own father had given his kids.

The process uncovered five key themes regarding what matters most to urban boomers. Family love and support and a good home life are viewed as important achievements. Long-term friendships are also very important and provide continuity to boomers. City-dwelling boomers are driven to "get away from it all" and escape to the big outdoors. Spiritual fitness is as important as physical fitness, so they love to develop their intellectual potential. They also feel that they're never too old to improve themselves. Clearly, all these values can translate into interesting platforms for ads and commercials.[36]

Basic Methods of Quantitative Research

Companies use **quantitative research** to gain reliable, hard statistics about specific market conditions or situations. Three basic research methods can be used to collect quantitative data: *observation, experiment,* and *survey.*

Observation   In the **observation method,** researchers monitor consumer activities, typically in their native environments, such as a store, a park, or the workplace. They may count the traffic that passes by a billboard, count a TV audience through instruments hooked to TV sets, or study consumer reactions to products displayed in the supermarket. Most observation method research is performed by large, independent marketing research companies, such as ACNielsen and Information Resources Inc. Healthtex, for example, subscribes to the services of NPD (National Panel Diary), which tracks the clothing purchases of 16,000 homes as a nationwide sample. From this, Healthtex can find out its market share and better understand statistical trends in the marketplace.

An important tool for assessing user experiences with new websites and other digital content is called user experience testing, or more commonly **UX** for short. The testing is an important step in the development of an effective site given the need to ensure a straightforward, friction-free experience on the part of visitors.[37]

The Universal Product Code on packaging is scanned at checkout counters. It improves checkout time and inventory control, and it provides a wealth of accessible data for use in measuring advertising response.

pikepicture/Shutterstock

Technology has greatly improved the observation method. One example is the **Universal Product Code (UPC)** label. By reading the codes with optical scanners, researchers can tell which products are selling and how well. The UPC label not only increases speed and accuracy at the checkout counter; it also enables timely inventory control and gives stores and manufacturers accurate point-of-purchase data sensitive to the impact of price, in-store promotion, couponing, and advertising.

ACNielsen's ScanTrack provides data on packaged-goods sales, market shares, and retail prices from more than 4,800 stores representing 800 retailers in 52 markets. A companion service, Homescan, uses in-home bar-code scanners to collect data on consumer purchases and shopping patterns. As a result, marketers have reliable data on the effectiveness of IMC. With that information, they can develop models to evaluate alternative marketing plans, media vehicles, and promotional campaigns.[38] In one case, for instance, data might indicate that a 40-cent coupon for toothpaste would create $150,000 in profits, but a 50-cent coupon on the same item would create a $300,000 loss.

Companies used to assume that changes in market share and brand position happen slowly. But observation shows that the packaged-goods market is complex and volatile. At the local level, weekly sales figures may fluctuate considerably, making it difficult to measure advertising's short-term effectiveness.

Other technologies have also been effective in observation research. Envirosell, a New York–based research company, uses security-type cameras to capture consumer in-store shopping habits. To determine the effectiveness of packaging and displays, the company analyzes how much time people spend with an item and how they read the label.[39]

Experiment   To measure cause-and-effect relationships, researchers use the **experimental method.** An experiment is a scientific investigation in which a researcher randomly assigns different consumers to two or more messages or stimuli. For example, a marketer might develop two print ads that feature different spokespeople, then randomly expose different consumers to each to determine who is more effective. This type of research is used often for new product and new campaign introductions. As we saw in the Kraft story, marketers go to a **test market,** and introduce the product in that area alone or test a new ad campaign or promotion before a *national rollout.* For example, a new campaign might run in one geographic area but not another. Sales in the two areas are then compared to determine the campaign's effectiveness. However, researchers must use strict controls so the variable that causes the effect can be accurately determined.

Survey   A common method of gathering primary research data is the **survey,** in which the researcher gains information on attitudes, opinions, or motivations by questioning current or prospective customers (political polls are a common type of survey). Surveys can be conducted by personal interview, by telephone, by mail, or on the Internet. Each has distinct advantages and disadvantages (see Exhibit 7-7). An important consideration in evaluating the validity of a survey is whether it has been administered to a randomly selected sample. If not, survey results cannot be treated as representative of the population of interest. We'll discuss some important issues regarding survey research in the last section of this chapter.

Juhi Singh helps companies with shopper experience research. Find out more about Juhi at http://cargocollective.com/juhisingh.

(both): Courtesy of Juhi Singh

Exhibit 7-7
Comparison of data collection methods.

	Personal	Telephone	Internet
Data collection costs	High	Medium	Low
Data collection time required	Medium	Low	Medium
Sample size for a given budget	Small	Medium	Large
Data quantity per respondent	High	Medium	Low
Reaches widely dispersed sample	No	Maybe	Yes
Reaches special locations	Yes	Maybe	Yes
Interaction with respondents	Yes	Yes	No
Degree of interviewer bias	High	Medium	None
Severity of nonresponse bias	Low	Low	Medium
Presentation of visual stimuli	Yes	No	Yes
Field worker training required	Yes	Yes	No

Message Testing before and after a Campaign

Although there is no infallible way to predict a campaign's success or failure, pretesting and posttesting can give a marketer useful insights if properly applied. Pretesting refers to message testing that takes place before a campaign launches. Posttesting, on the other hand, describes testing activities that occur after a campaign has begun.

Pretesting Methods

LO 7-4

Companies pretest ads for likability and comprehension by using a variety of qualitative and quantitative techniques.

For example, when pretesting print ads, researchers often ask direct questions: What does the advertising say to you? Does the advertising tell you anything new or different about the company? If so, what? Does the advertising reflect activities you would like to participate in? Is the advertising believable? What effect does it have on your perception of the merchandise offered? Do you like the ads?

Through **direct questioning,** researchers can elicit a full range of responses from people and thereby infer how well advertising messages convey key copy points. Direct questioning is especially effective for testing alternative messages in the early stages of development, when respondents' reactions and input can best be acted on. There are numerous techniques for pretesting print messages, including *focus groups, order-of-merit tests, paired comparisons, portfolio tests, mock magazines, perceptual meaning studies,* and *direct-mail tests.* (See My IMC Campaign 7–B, "Methods for Pretesting.")

Several methods are used specifically to pretest radio and TV commercials. In **central location tests,** respondents are shown test commercials, usually in shopping centers, and questions are asked before and after exposure. In **clutter tests,** test commercials are shown with noncompeting control commercials to determine their effectiveness, measure comprehension and attitude shifts, and detect weaknesses.

A company's own employees are an important constituency. Some companies, in fact, pretest new commercials by prescreening them on their in-house cable TV systems and soliciting feedback.

The Challenge of Pretesting

Choosing the right way to pretest a message can be difficult because each has its own advantages and disadvantages.

Pretesting helps distinguish strong messages from weak ones. But because the test occurs in an artificial setting, respondents may assume the role of expert or critic and give answers that don't reflect their real buying behavior. They may invent opinions to satisfy the interviewer, or be reluctant to admit they are influenced, or vote for the messages they think they *should* like.

Researchers encounter problems when asking people to rank messages. Respondents often rate the ones that make the best first impression as the highest in all categories (the **halo effect**). Also, questions about the respondent's buying behavior may be invalid; behavior *intent* may not become behavior *fact.* And some creative people mistrust testing because they believe it stifles creativity.

Despite these challenges, the issue often comes down to dollars. Small marketers rarely pretest, but their risk isn't as great, either. When companies risk millions of dollars

My IMC Campaign 7-B

Methods for Pretesting

Companies rarely trust intuition alone when evaluating their creative work. There is simply too much on the line. Pretesting is what occurs when agencies or marketers test prototypes of their messages before they are run in the mass media. Below is a comprehensive list of ways that real agencies test their work. You don't have the resources to do many of them. But you can use some of these methods to test your creative ideas with a small sample drawn from your target audience. Doing so will give you added ammunition for persuading your client that you've developed a strong strategy for his or her brand.

Print Advertising

- **Direct questioning.** Asks specific questions about ads. Often used to test alternative ads in early stages of development.
- **Focus group.** A moderated but freewheeling discussion and interview conducted with six or more people.
- **Order-of-merit test.** Respondents see two or more ads and arrange them in rank order.
- **Paired comparison method.** Respondents compare each ad in a group.
- **Portfolio test.** One group sees a portfolio of test ads interspersed among other ads and editorial matter. Another group sees the portfolio without the test ads.
- **Mock magazine.** Test ads are "stripped into" a magazine, which is left with respondents for a specified time. (Also used as a posttesting technique.)
- **Perceptual meaning study.** Respondents see in timed exposures.
- **Direct-mail test.** Two or more alternative ads are mailed to different prospects on a mailing list to test which ad generates the largest volume of orders.

Broadcast Advertising

- **Central location projection test.** Respondents see test commercial films in a central location such as a shopping center.
- **Trailer test.** Respondents see TV commercials in trailers at shopping centers and receive coupons for the advertised products; a matched sample of consumers just gets the coupons. Researchers measure the difference in coupon redemption.
- **Theater test.** Electronic equipment enables respondents to indicate what they like and dislike as they view TV commercials in a theater setting.
- **Live telecast test.** Test commercials are shown on closed-circuit or cable TV. Respondents are interviewed by phone, or sales audits are conducted at stores in the viewing areas.
- **Sales experiment.** Alternative commercials run in two or more market areas.

Physiological Testing

- **Pupilometric device.** Dilation of the subject's pupils is measured, presumably to indicate the subject's level of interest.
- **Eye movement camera.** The route the subject's eyes traveled is superimposed over an ad to show the areas that attracted and held attention.
- **Galvanometer.** Measures subject's sweat gland activity with a mild electrical current; presumably, the more tension an ad creates, the more effective it is likely to be.
- **Voice pitch analysis.** A consumer's response is taped, and a computer is used to measure changes in voice pitch caused by emotional responses.
- **Brain pattern analysis.** A scanner monitors the reaction of the subject's brain.

---

on a new campaign, they must pretest to be sure the message is interesting, believable, likable, and memorable—all while creating or reinforcing the brand image.

Posttesting Methods

Posttesting can be more costly and time-consuming than pretesting, but it can test a campaign under actual market conditions. As we saw with Kraft, some marketers benefit from pretesting *and* posttesting by running ads in select test markets before launching a campaign nationwide.

As in pretesting, marketers use both quantitative and qualitative methods in posttesting. Most posttesting techniques fall into five broad categories: *aided recall, unaided recall, attitude tests, inquiry tests,* and *sales tests.* (See My IMC Campaign 7-C, "Methods for Posttesting.")

Posttesting involves assessing the impact of a campaign after it has run. It is an important way that companies judge whether their messages have helped them to achieve their objectives (see Chapter 8). You will most likely not do posttesting for your client. However, it is good practice for you to propose HOW the client might posttest your campaigns. This

My **IMC** Campaign 7-C

Methods for Posttesting

- **Aided recall (recognition–readership).** To jog their memories, respondents are shown certain messages and then asked whether their previous exposure was through reading, viewing, or listening.

- **Unaided recall.** Respondents are asked, without prompting, whether they saw or heard promotional messages.

- **Attitude tests.** Direct questions, semantic differential tests, or unstructured questions measure changes in respondents' attitudes after a campaign.

- **Inquiry tests.** Additional product information, product samples, or premiums are given to readers or viewers; messages generating the most responses are presumed to be the most effective.

- **Sales tests.** Measures of past sales compare campaign efforts with sales. Controlled experiments test different media in different markets. Consumer purchase tests measure retail sales from a given campaign. Store inventory audits measure retailers' stocks before and after a campaign.

is material that you can incorporate in your campaigns book. Be sure to reference your objectives when you propose a posttesting technique.

Some use **attitude tests** to measure a campaign's effectiveness in creating a favorable image for a company, its brand, or its products. Presumably, favorable changes in attitude predispose consumers to buy the company's product.

IAG Research has developed a syndicated data service called IAG Ad that the company administers for such clients as American Express, General Motors, and Procter & Gamble. Using more than 80,000 surveys, IAG Ad collects key data about the ads that viewers watched the night before and generates a detailed performance analysis that includes brand recall, message understanding, likability, and purchase intent. This tool helps companies understand the actual effectiveness of their campaigns.[40]

Similarly, Nissan interviews 1,000 consumers every month to track brand awareness, familiarity with vehicle models, recall of commercials, and shifts in attitude or image perception. If a commercial fails, it can be pulled quickly.[41]

Children's clothing manufacturer Healthtex conducted some print-ad posttesting and discovered that, while new mothers appreciated the information in the long copy format, more experienced mothers didn't. For them, the headline and one line of copy were sufficient to get the point across. They already understood the rest. As a result, the company used the shorter format and redesigned the ads aimed at experienced parents.

Consumers love extra perks and ads perform better when they inform consumers about unexpected benefits. Getting cash back on purchases is a key to the success of this ad for Santander Bank. The ad was created by Arnold Worldwide.

Source: Santander Bank, N. A.

Ethics, Diversity & Inclusion

Diversity Among Market Researchers

How well do marketing researchers represent America? According to one professional, Rill Hodari (Hodari is the founding president of the Association of Minority Market Research Professionals), not terribly well. Hodari compares percentages of minorities in the adult population to the incidence of those groups working in marketing research and finds that blacks (13 percent of the population, 5 percent incidence in marketing research) and Hispanics (16 percent versus 2 percent) are underrepresented while Asians (6 percent versus 10 percent) and white, non-Hispanics (63 percent versus 71 percent) are overrepresented.

Why do such differences exist? Hodari offers a couple of explanations. First, there may be low awareness of marketing research careers among some ethnic groups. Further, educational barriers may play a role.

The AMA considered marketplace diversity important enough to devote a special issue of the *Journal of Public Policy and Marketing* to the topic. It broadened diversity to go beyond ethnicity and include nationality, gender, sexual orientation, physical differences, religion, and other sociocultural differences.

Research is ultimately about understanding. Clearly, the people who are easiest for us to understand are people like ourselves. It is a greater challenge to understand those from different backgrounds, cultures, or experiences. Ultimately, then, better understanding of a diverse marketplace may require more diverse marketing researchers.

Questions

1. Why might consumer understanding improve if marketing researchers come from more diverse backgrounds?

2. Is it possible for marketing researchers to understand people from backgrounds different from their own? What experiences might make this more likely?

Sources: Rill Hodari, "Analyzing the Current Representation of Minorities in Market Research," *Quirks Media,* August 20, 2015, www.quirks.com/articles/analyzing-the-current-representation-of-minorities-in-market-research; "Diversity in the Marketplace," *Journal of Public Policy and Marketing,* November 2014, www.researchgate.net/publication/281865085_From_Exclusion_to_Inclusion_An_Introduction_to_the_Special_Issue_on_Marketplace_Diversity_and_Inclusion.

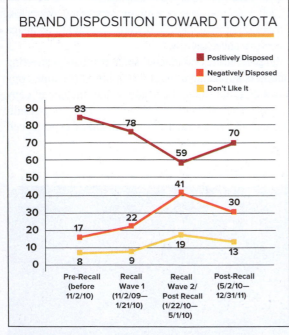

BRAND DISPOSITION TOWARD TOYOTA

GfK MRI Starch tracked consumer sentiments toward Toyota through two product recalls and attempts by the company to address consumer concerns. This is an example of posttesting following both undesired environmental events and efforts by the company to deal with the issue.

Source: GfK MRI Starch

The Challenge of Posttesting

Each posttesting method has limitations. **Recall tests** reveal the effectiveness of message components, such as size, color, or themes. But they measure what respondents noticed, *not* whether they actually buy the product.

For measuring sales effectiveness, attitude tests are often better than recall tests. An attitude change relates more closely to product purchase, and a measured change in attitude gives management the confidence to make informed decisions about advertising plans. Unfortunately, many people find it difficult to determine and express their attitudes. For mature brands, brand interest may be a better sales indicator, and companies now measure that phenomenon.[42]

By using **inquiry tests**—in which consumers respond to an offer for information or free samples—researchers can test a message's attention-getting value, readability, and understandability. These tests also permit fairly good control of the variables that motivate reader action, particularly if a *split-run* test is used (split runs are covered in Chapter 12). The inquiry test is also effective for testing small-space ads.

Unfortunately, inquiries may not reflect a sincere interest in the product, and responses may take months to receive. When advertising is the dominant element or the only variable in the company's marketing plan, **sales tests** are a useful measure of advertising effectiveness. However, many other variables usually affect sales (competitors' activities, the season of the year, and even the weather). Sales response may not be immediate, and sales tests, particularly field studies, are often costly and time-consuming.

For consumer packaged goods, though, the cost of sales tests has been greatly reduced thanks to grocery store scanners. Finally, sales tests are typically more suited for gauging the effectiveness of campaigns than of individual messages or promotions.

Important Issues in IMC Research

When marketers conduct primary research, there is always one legitimate concern—the accuracy of the findings. This is especially true when conducting formal quantitative research and when doing research in international markets.

Considerations in Conducting Primary Quantitative Research

LO 7-5

Quantitative research requires formal design and rigorous standards for collecting and tabulating data to ensure their accuracy and usability. When conducting primary research, marketers must consider certain issues carefully, especially whether the research is *valid* and *reliable*. For more on the pros and cons of research statistics, see the Ethics, Diversity and Inclusion feature on bias in marketing services.

Validity and Reliability

Assume you want to determine whether a new toy will sell in a particular market. The market consists of 10 million individuals. You show a prototype of the toy to five people and four say they like it (an 80 percent favorable attitude). Is that test valid? Hardly. For a test to have **validity,** *results must be free of bias and reflect the true status of the market.*[43] Five people aren't enough for a minimum sample, and liking a toy is not necessarily a predictor of whether these people would buy it.

Moreover, if you repeated the test with five more people, you might get an entirely different response. So your test also lacks **reliability.** For a test to be reliable, it must be *repeatable*—it must produce approximately the same result each time it is administered (see Exhibit 7-8).

Validity and reliability depend on several key elements: the sampling methods, the survey questionnaire design, and the data tabulation and analysis methods.

Validity

High   Low

Reliability

High

Low

Exhibit 7-8

The reliability–validity diagram. Using the analogy of a dartboard, the bull's-eye is the actual average of a value among a population (say, the average age in the community). The top row shows high reliability (repeatability) because the darts are closely clustered. When reliability drops, the darts land more randomly and spread across a wider area, as in both examples in the bottom row. The left column demonstrates high validity because in both examples the darts center around the bull's-eye. The right column represents low validity because bias in the testing process drew all the darts to one side. In the upper right quadrant, members of a fraternity are in the same age group (high reliability or repeatability), but their ages do not reflect the average of the community (low validity). The lower left quadrant suggests that the testing of our average age sample is highly valid, but it is not reliable because it includes people with a wide range of ages. The upper left quadrant reflects the truest picture of the data.

Sampling Methods

When a company wants to know what consumers think, it can't ask everybody. But its research must reflect the **universe** (the entire target population) of prospective customers. Researchers select from that population a **sample** that they expect will represent the population's characteristics. To accomplish this, they must decide whom to survey, how many to survey, and how to choose the respondents. Defining **sample units**—the individuals, families, or companies being surveyed—is very important.

A sample must be large enough to achieve precision and stability. The larger the sample, the more reliable the results. Statisticians note that the margin of error, an estimate of how likely sample statistics will diverge from numbers in the universe, is three times greater if a sample of 10 is chosen rather than a sample of 100. It is ten times greater for a sample of 10 compared to a sample of 1,000. Five hundred survey participants or more are generally recommended for accurate samples. There are two types of samples: random probability samples and nonprobability samples.

The greatest accuracy is gained from **random probability samples** because everyone in the universe has an equal chance of being selected.[44] For example, a researcher who wants to know a community's opinion on an issue starts with a complete list of all people in the community and selects members at random. But this method has difficulties. Every unit (person) must be known, listed, and numbered so each has an equal chance of being selected—an often prohibitively expensive and sometimes impossible task, especially with customers of nationally distributed products.

Instead, researchers use **nonprobability samples** extensively because they're easier than probability samples, as well as less expensive and time-consuming. Nonprobability samples don't give every unit in the universe an equal chance of being included, so there's no guarantee the sample is representative. As a result,

Exhibit 7-9

A personal questionnaire like this helps determine shoppers' feelings toward a chain of stores, its merchandise, and its advertising. Questions 1–3 are dichotomous (only two choices). Question 4 is multiple choice, asking consumers to make a single selection, while Question 6 is a multiple-choice question allowing consumers to choose as many responses as needed. Question 5 uses rating scales. Finally, Question 7 is an open-ended question.

1. Do you intend to shop at _(Store name)_ between now and Sunday?
   Yes   1   No   2   (If no, skip to question 5)

2. Do you intend to buy something in particular or just to browse?
   Buy   1   Browse   2

3. Have you seen any of the items you intend to buy advertised by _(Store name)_ ?
   Yes   1   (continue)   No   2   (skip to question 5)

4. Where did you see these items advertised? Was it in a _(Store name)_ advertising insert included with your newspaper, a _(Store name)_ flyer you received in the mail, the pages of the newspaper itself, on TV, or somewhere else?

   ☐ Insert in newspaper   ☐ On TV
   ☐ Flyer in mail   ☐ Somewhere else (specify)_____
   ☐ Pages of newspaper   ☐ Don't recall

5. Please rate the _(Store name)_ advertising insert on the attributes listed below. Place an X in the box at the position that best reflects your opinion of how the insert rates on each attribute. Placing an X in the middle box usually means you are neutral. The closer you place the X to the left or right phrase or word, the more you believe it describes the _(Store name)_ insert.

Looks cheap								Looks expensive
Unskillful								Cleverly done
Unappealing								Appealing
Does not show clothing in an attractive manner								Shows clothing in an attractive manner

   1   2   3   4   5   6   7

6. Please indicate all of the different types of people listed below you feel this _(Store name)_ advertising insert is appealing to.

   ☐ Young people   ☐ Quality-conscious people
   ☐ Bargain hunters   ☐ Low-income people
   ☐ Conservative dressers   ☐ Budget watchers
   ☐ Fashion-conscious people   ☐ Older people
   ☐ Rich people   ☐ Middle-income people
   ☐ Professionals   ☐ Blue-collar people
   ☐ High-income people   ☐ Women
   ☐ Men   ☐ Office workers
   ☐ Someone like me   ☐ Smart dressers
   ☐ Career-oriented women   ☐ Other (specify)_____

7. What aspects of (Store name) advertising are most appealing to you? What aspects are least appealing?

   _____
   _____
   _____
   _____

researchers can't be confident in the accuracy of the responses.[45] Most marketing research needs only general measures of the data. For example, the nonprobability method of interviewing shoppers in malls may be sufficient to determine the shopping preferences, image perceptions, and attitudes of customers.

How Questionnaires Are Designed

Constructing a good questionnaire requires considerable expertise. Much bias in research is blamed on poorly designed questionnaires. Typical problems include asking the wrong types of questions, asking too many questions, using the wrong form for a question (which makes it too difficult to answer or tabulate), and using the wrong choice of words. Exhibit 7-9 shows some typical questions that might be used in a survey for a retail store.

My IMC Campaign 7-D

Developing an Effective Questionnaire

In many years of teaching an advertising research class, I have always told students that the hardest thing they will do is write a good survey. When they hear this, students are often skeptical; after all, many of them are good writers. But writing a survey is surprisingly tough if you've never done it before. The key is to write questions and statements that get to the heart of your objectives. Every survey item must be relevant, clear, and useful. Don't waste your respondents' time (or your own) with items that hold little potential for helping you better serve your client. Here are some tips for writing items that can help you make better decisions:

- **List specific research objectives.** Don't spend money collecting irrelevant data.
- **Write short questionnaires.** Don't tax the respondent's patience; you may get careless or flip answers.
- **State questions clearly** so there is no chance for misunderstanding. Avoid generalities and ambiguities.
- **Write a rough draft first;** then polish it.

- **Use a short opening statement.** Include the interviewer's name, the name of the organization, and the purpose of the questionnaire.
- **Put the respondent at ease** by opening with one or two inoffensive, easily answered questions.
- **Structure questions so they flow logically.** Ask general questions before more detailed ones.
- **Avoid questions that suggest an answer or could be considered leading.** They bias the results.
- **Include a few questions that cross-check earlier answers.** This helps ensure validity.
- **Put the demographic questions (age, income, education) and any other personal questions at the end of the questionnaire.**
- **Pretest the questionnaire** with 20 to 30 people to be sure they interpret the questions correctly and that it covers all the information sought.

Consider the simple question, "What kind of soap do you use?" The respondent may be confused. Does the question reference hand soap, shampoo, laundry detergent, or dishwashing soap? Does *kind* mean brand, size, or type? Finally, what constitutes use? What a person buys (perhaps for someone else) or uses personally—and for what purpose? In fact, one person probably uses several different kinds of soap, depending on the occasion. It's impossible to answer this question accurately. Worse, if the consumer does answer it, the researcher doesn't know what the answer means and will likely draw an incorrect conclusion. For these reasons, questionnaires must be pretested. (See My IMC Campaign 7-D, "Developing an Effective Questionnaire.")

Effective survey questions have three important attributes: focus, brevity, and clarity. They focus on the topic of the survey. They are as brief as possible. And they are expressed simply and clearly.[46] These qualities have a common purpose: to ensure respondents read and understand the questions in the same way.

The four most common types of questions are *open-ended, dichotomous, multiple-choice,* and *scale.* But there are many ways to ask questions within these four types. Exhibit 7-10 shows examples of each of these. Neutral responses can be removed from the scale question so the respondent must answer either positively or negatively.

Exhibit 7-10
Different ways to phrase research questions.

Type	Questions
Open-ended	How would you describe (**Store name**) advertising?
Dichotomous	Do you think (**Store name**) advertising is too attractive? _____ Yes _____ No
Multiple choice	What description best fits your opinion of (**Store name**) advertising? _____ Modern _____ Unconvincing _____ Well done _____ Old-fashioned _____ Believable
Scale	Please indicate on the scale how you rate the quality of (**Store name**) advertising. ____ ____ ____ ____ ____ 1 2 3 4 5 Poor Excellent

Questions should elicit a response that is both accurate and useful. By testing questionnaires on a small subsample, researchers can detect any confusion, bias, or ambiguities.

Data Tabulation and Analysis

Collected data must be validated, edited, coded, and tabulated. Answers must be checked to eliminate errors or inconsistencies. For example, one person might answer two years, while another says 24 months; such responses must be changed to the same units for correct tabulation. Some questionnaires may be rejected because respondents' answers indicate they misunderstood the questions. Finally, the data must be analyzed on a computer.

Many researchers want *cross-tabulations* (e.g., product use by age group or education). Software programs such as SPSS and SAS make it possible for small businesses as well as large corporations to tabulate data on a personal computer and apply advanced statistical techniques. Many cross-tabulations are possible, but researchers must use skill and imagination to select only those that answer the right questions.

Collecting Primary Data in International Markets

International marketers face a number of challenges when they collect primary data. For one thing, research overseas is often more expensive than domestic research. Many marketers are surprised to learn that research in five countries costs five times as much as research in one country; there are no economies of scale.[47]

But marketers must determine whether their messages will work in foreign markets. (Maxwell House, for example, had to change its "great American coffee" campaign when it discovered that Germans have little respect for U.S. coffee.)

Control and direction of the research is another problem. Some companies want to direct research from their headquarters but charge it to the subsidiary's budget. This creates an instant turf battle. It also means that people less familiar with the country—and therefore less sensitive to local cultural issues—might be in charge of the project, which could skew the data. Marketers need more than just facts about a country's culture. They need to understand and appreciate the nuances of its cultural traits and habits, a difficult task for people who don't live there or speak the language. Knowledgeable international companies such as Colgate-Palmolive work in partnership with their local offices and use local bilingual marketing people when conducting primary research abroad.[48]

For years, Mattel tried unsuccessfully to market the Barbie doll in Japan. It finally sold the manufacturing license to a Japanese company, Takara, which did its own research. Takara found that most Japanese girls and their parents thought Barbie's breasts were too

This example from Procter & Gamble's Bonux detergent campaign in Lebanon illustrates some of the difficulties inherent in international IMC. Lebanese housewives take great pride in clean washing, so much so that they even brag about laundry secrets and hang their laundry on balconies to be seen by neighbors. Bonux created the "housewives' moment of fame" campaign and bought space on the roofs of buses so the ads could be seen from balconies. Radio spots featured interviews with housewives riding the buses. The campaign raised awareness 85 percent, increased market share by 20 percent, and won a Media Lion at the Cannes Advertising Festival.
(both) Source: Procter & Gamble

People BEHIND the Ads

Hulton Archive/Archive Photos/Getty Images

Understand the opinions, beliefs, and intentions of a sample of 2,000 or so people, chosen properly, and you can understand the country. Even in this day and age, that remains a pretty astonishing fact—so astonishing, perhaps, that you may have difficulty believing it, but it is true.

Opinion polls don't contact everyone when they examine social issues, only a sample of two or three thousand people. Nielsen doesn't have a meter in every home when it reports TV show ratings, just a small subset of representative households. And Simmons Market Research Bureau doesn't phone every American to find out about product usage or media consumption, just a carefully chosen group of several thousand.

In fact, almost everything we know about public opinion comes from small groups chosen using probability sampling. These are samples chosen in a way that ensures that every member of the population has an equal chance of being selected. Today we know that, properly used, such samples have tremendous predictive power. And no one has done more to advance our understanding of the power of properly conducted surveys than George Gallup.

Gallup was born in the small town of Jefferson, Iowa, in 1901. He attended college at the University of Iowa and stayed long enough to earn a doctorate in psychology. Gallup then taught journalism courses at Drake, Northwestern, and Columbia.

While teaching college, Gallup developed a lifelong passion for understanding public opinion. His interests ranged from understanding attitudes about important issues of the day to understanding what people attend to when they read newspapers and magazines. He was particularly interested in finding out what types of advertisements caught people's eye, realizing the value of such information to the burgeoning ad industry.

In 1932 Young & Rubicam, one of New York's top agencies, lured Gallup to New York to become head of its research and marketing departments. While at Y&R, Gallup extended his investigations from understanding print effectiveness to methods for tracking radio ad performance. Of course, years later when television became the dominant broadcast medium, Gallup was one of the first to measure the effects of TV commercials.

Gallup eventually left the agency and began running his own polling firm. He first broke into broad national awareness by accurately forecasting the results of the 1936 presidential election. America's most famous opinion poll at the time, the *Literary Digest* Poll, picked Alfred Landon to win against Franklin D. Roosevelt. However, Gallup correctly predicted Roosevelt would win (which he did by an almost 2–1 margin!). Celebrating the accuracy of his methods, Gallup promised that opinion polling would be transformed "from a glorified kind of fortune telling into a practical way of learning what the nation thinks."

And Gallup seemed to be living up to his boasting, appearing on *Time* magazine's cover as the "Babe Ruth of the polling profession." Unfortunately, Gallup would soon face his greatest professional embarrassment.

In 1948 Gallup, like a lot of pollsters, proclaimed that President Harry Truman would go down in defeat to challenger Thomas Dewey. In fact, Gallup claimed, it would not even be close. As it turned out, the election was close, and Truman, not Dewey, won.

It is never easy or enjoyable to be wrong. But his mistake led Gallup to focus even more attention on improving sampling techniques. Key insights came when he realized the value of probability sampling over quota sampling, and found ways to reduce systematic bias introduced by survey interviewers. The year 1948 would be the last year Gallup incorrectly predicted a presidential election winner.

Eventually, both the public and the industry would embrace Gallup's methods. Today, no major advertiser or agency would launch a campaign without extensive use of social science methods to carefully test and calibrate the campaign. No advertiser would buy time on a TV show without careful study of who is watching and what they are like. And no manufacturer would consider distribution to a new market without access to mountains of data on the consumers who live there. These methodologies, and many others described in this chapter, have been influenced by Gallup's insights. George Gallup may have hailed from a small Iowa town, but he discovered methods that allowed him, and others, to understand the world.

big and her legs too long. It modified the doll accordingly, changed the blue eyes to brown, and sold 2 million dolls in two years.

In Malaysia, Nestlé performed extensive research to build up its knowledge and adapt its products to local tastes and customs. As a result, some of its Malaysian products are now gelatin-free out of respect for Muslim sensitivities.[49]

Conducting original research abroad can be fraught with problems. First, the researcher must use the local language, and translating questionnaires can be tricky.

Second, many cultures view strangers suspiciously and don't wish to talk about their personal lives. U.S. companies found that mail surveys and phone interviews don't work in Japan; they have to use expensive, time-consuming personal interviews.[50]

Despite these problems—or perhaps because of them—it's important for global marketers to perform research. Competent researchers are available in all developed countries, and major international research firms have local offices in most developing countries. The largest of these companies, which serve the largest multinational clients, organize their services globally based on the type of specialized research they conduct regularly. Research International Group, for instance, has global research directors for advertising research and for customer satisfaction research and global account directors for clients' projects worldwide.[51]

Marketers are often surprised by some of the differences they encounter when trying to conduct international research. Lead times to begin projects are typically longer, with the Far East being particularly troublesome. Groups can take twice as long to set up overseas. The structures differ too. Focus groups, for instance, rarely use more than 4 to 6 people rather than the 8 to 10 typical of the United States. Screening requirements for participants abroad are typically less rigid, and foreign moderators tend to be much less structured than their U.S. counterparts. Finally, the facilities don't usually have all the amenities of U.S. offices, but the costs are frequently twice as high in Europe and three times as high in Asia.[52]

Two goals for international research are flexibility and standardization, and both are necessary for the best results. Flexibility means using the best approach in each market. If you're studying the use of laundry products, it's just as irrelevant to ask Mexicans about soy sauce stains as it is to ask Thais how they get salsa out of their clothes.[53]

On the other hand, standardization is important so that information from different countries can be compared.[54] Otherwise the study will be meaningless. Balance is required to get the best of flexibility and standardization.

Thanks to a combination of computer-based interviewing, the internet, e-mail, telephones, faxes, and courier services, the time required to conduct worldwide business-to-business research has been drastically reduced. Today, nearly three-quarters of market research firms use the internet to conduct some form of market research.[55] With the global adoption of the internet, experts anticipate further cuts in costs and time for getting valuable customer input for marketing and advertising decision making.

Chapter Summary

Marketing research is the systematic procedure used to gather, record, and analyze new information to help managers make decisions about marketing goods and services. Marketing research helps management identify consumer needs, develop new products and communication strategies, and assess the effectiveness of marketing programs and promotional activities. The many types of information gathered can help marketers recruit, retain, and regain customers.

IMC research, a subset of marketing research, is used to gather and analyze information for developing or evaluating advertising. It helps advertisers develop strategies and test concepts. The results of research help define the product concept, select the target market, and develop the primary message elements.

Businesses use testing to make sure their dollars are spent wisely. Pretesting helps detect and eliminate weaknesses before a campaign runs. Posttesting helps evaluate the effectiveness of an ad or campaign after it runs. Testing is used to evaluate several variables including merchandise, markets, motives, messages, media, and overall results.

The research process involves several steps: analyzing the situation and defining the problem, conducting informal (exploratory) research by analyzing internal data and collecting external secondary data, setting research objectives, conducting primary research using qualitative or quantitative methods, and, finally, interpreting and reporting the findings.

Marketers use qualitative research to get a general impression of the market. The methods used may be projective or intensive. Quantitative techniques include observation, experiment, and survey.

Techniques used in pretesting include central location tests, clutter tests, and direct questioning. Pretesting has numerous problems, including artificiality, consumer inaccuracy, and the halo effect of consumer responses. The most commonly used posttesting techniques are aided recall, unaided recall, attitude tests, inquiry tests, and sales tests.

The validity and reliability of quantitative surveys depend on the sampling methods used and the design of the survey questionnaire. The two sampling procedures are random probability and nonprobability. Survey questions require focus, brevity, and simplicity.

In international markets, research is often more expensive and less reliable than in the United States. But marketers must use research to understand cultural traits and habits in overseas markets.

Important Terms

attitude test, *237*

central location test, *235*

clutter test, *235*

direct questioning, *235*

experimental method, *234*

focus group, *232*

halo effect, *235*

IMC research, *221*

IMC strategy research, *222*

in-depth interview, *232*

informal research, *228*

inquiry test, *238*

intensive techniques, *232*

marketing information system
(MIS), *228*

marketing research, *220*

markets, *226*

media classes, *227*

media research, *223*

media subclasses, *227*

media units, *227*

media vehicles, *227*

merchandise, *226*

message, *226*

motives, *226*

nonprobability samples, *239*

observation method, *233*

posttesting, *226*

pretesting, *225*

primary data, *228*

primary research, *230*

projective techniques, *232*

qualitative research, *230, 232*

quantitative research, *230, 233*

random probability samples, *239*

recall test, *238*

reliability, *239*

sales test, *238*

sample, *239*

sample unit, *239*

secondary data, *228*

survey, *234*

test market, *234*

Universal Product Code (UPC), *234*

universe, *239*

validity, *239*

Review Questions

1. How does research help advertisers meet the challenge of the three Rs of marketing?

2. Give an example that demonstrates the difference between marketing research and market research.

3. Which kind of research data is more expensive to collect, primary or secondary? Why?

4. How might you use observational research to understand a consumer behavior?

5. How could the halo effect bias a pretest for a soft drink ad?

6. When might research offer reliability but not validity?

7. How would you design a controlled experiment to test the advertising for a new restaurant?

8. When could research help in the development of an advertising strategy for an international advertiser? Give an example.

The Advertising Experience

1. **Marketing Research Organizations and Publications**
   Many advertisers choose to perform their own research. When collecting research data by themselves, they can use a number of advertising- and marketing-specific research sources available on the web. Visit the research organizations' and publications' websites listed below and answer the questions that follow:

   - Advertising Research Foundation (ARF): www.thearf.org
   - American Marketing Association: www.ama.org
   - Journal of Advertising Research: www.journalofadvertisingresearch.com/
   - Marketing Research Association (MRA): www.insightsassociation.org/issues-policies/glossary/marketing-research-association-mra

   a. What research group sponsors the site? Who is/are the intended audience(s)?

   b. What is the site's purpose? Does it succeed? Why?

   c. What range of services is offered?

   d. What is the organization's purpose?

2. **Market Research Companies**
   Marketers and advertisers depend heavily on timely and accurate research in preparation for advertising planning. Many market research companies are available to serve nearly every marketing and advertising research need. Visit the following syndicated and independent research companies' websites and answer the questions that follow:

   - Nielsen: www.acnielsen.com
   - Burke: www.burke.com
   - Dun & Bradstreet: www.dnb.com
   - The Gallup Organization: www.gallup.com
   - GfK NOP: www.gfkamerica.com
   - International Data Corporation (IDC): www.idc.com
   - Ipsos Connect: www.ipsos.com/en-us
   - J. D. Power and Associates: www.jdpower.com
   - Kantar: www.kantar.com
   - Qualtrics Online Sample: www.qualtrics.com/online-sample/

a. What types of research does the company specialize in?

b. What industries/companies would be best suited to utilize the company's resources?

c. What specific services, products, or publications does the company offer?

d. Are the information services offered by the company primary or secondary data?

e. How useful is the company for conducting advertising and marketing research? Why?

3. **Market Research for Politics**
Silver-maned Armand LeMouche, state senator for your district for 30 years, passed away recently, and his appointed replacement, Millard Frumpe, lacks a solid political base. Sally Daily, a self-made millionaire and the owner of a string of bakeries, would like to challenge Millard, but she wants to do some research first. She firmly believes that advertising research helped her get where she is. What research would Sally need in order to find out if her campaign is feasible or not, and, if it is, how she could win.

4. What were the research challenges that Budweiser faced in creating a great Super Bowl ad? What research techniques did the agency use, and what kinds did it choose not to use? Why do you think that it made the decisions it did, and do you agree with them?

5. Do an "emotion" experiment with the Budweiser spot by identifying the emotions that you feel for each scene in the ad. Make an "emotion map" that can be tagged to each key scene. Compare the emotion map you generate with that of a classmate.

End Notes

1. Bruce Horovitz, "Budweiser 'Lost Dog' Finds Way to Top of Super Bowl Ad Meter," *USA Today,* February 2, 2015, www.usatoday.com/story/money/business/2015/02/01/usa-today-ad-meter-2015-super-bowl-money/22378605/.

2. "Here Are the Super Bowl Advertisers That Got the Biggest Brand Lifts," *Adweek,* February 5, 2015, www.adweek.com/news/advertising-branding/here-are-super-bowladvertisers-got-biggest-brand-lifts-162805.

3. Clifton B. Parker, "Super Bowl Ads Not Profitable for Competing Brands, Stanford Scholar Says," *Stanford News,* January 26, 2015, http://news.stanford.edu/news/2015/january/super-bowl-ads-012615.html.

4. Wayne Friedman, "'The Walking Dead' Posts Top 30-Second Ad Pricing for Season's End," *Media Post,* July 24, 2018, www.mediapost.com/publications/article/322657/the-walking-dead-posts-top-30-second-ad-pricing.html.

5. Media kits: www.businessweek.com and www.forbes.com, October 2000; Chad Rubel, "Some Cute Super Spots Now Just a Memory," *Marketing News,* March 13, 1995, p. 15.

6. William Perreault Jr., Joseph Cannon, and E. Jerome McCarthy, *Basic Marketing: A Marketing Strategy Planning Approach* (New York: McGraw-Hill Education, 2013).

7. "Top 50 Research Organizations," *American Marketing Association,* www.data.marketingpower.com.

8. Edward F. McQuarrie, *The Market Research Toolbox* (Thousand Oaks, CA: Sage, 2016).

9. Livia Marian, Polymeros Chrysochou, Athanasios Krystallis, and John Thorgersen, "The Role of Price as a Product Attribute in the Organic Food Context: An Exploration Based on Actual Purchase Data," *Food Quality and Preference,* October 2014, pp. 52–60.

10. Livia Marian, Polymeros Chrysochou, Athanasios Krystallis, and John Thorgersen, "The Role of Price as a Product Attribute in the Organic Food Context: An Exploration Based on Actual Purchase Data," *Food Quality and Preference,* October 2014, pp. 52–60.

11. Dennis B. Arnett and C. Michael Wittman, "Improving Marketing Success: The Role of Tacit Knowledge Exchange Between Sales and Marketing," *Journal of Business Research,* March 2014, pp. 324–31.

12. V. Kumar, Yashoda Bhagwat, and Zi (Alan) Zhang, "Regaining 'Lost' Customers: The Predictive Power of First-Time Behavior, the Reason for Defection, and the Nature of the Win-Back Offer," *Journal of Marketing* 79, no. 4 (2015).

13. Clifton B. Parker, "Super Bowl Ads Not Profitable for Competing Brands, Stanford Scholar Says," *Stanford News,* January 26, 2015, http://news.stanford.edu/news/2015/january/super-bowl-ads-012615.html.

14. Tom Alstiel and Jean Grow, *Creative Strategy, Copy, Design* (Menlo Park, CA: Sage, 2013).

15. Tom Alstiel and Jean Grow, *Creative Strategy, Copy, Design* (Menlo Park, CA: Sage, 2013).

16. "BrandAsset Valuator," *Landor,* retrieved at www.bavgroup.com/about-bav.

17. Kathryn Kranhold, "Agencies Boost Research to Spot Consumer Views," *The Asian Wall Street Journal,* March 10, 2000, p. 6.

18. Story adapted from "Cheese, Please!," *American Demographics,* March 2000, pp. S6–S8 (Copyright Primedia Intertec, March 2000).

19. Story adapted from "Cheese, Please!," *American Demographics,* March 2000, pp. S6–S8 (Copyright Primedia Intertec, March 2000).

20. Jack Neff, "Copy Testing Coming to Digital Marketing," *Advertising Age,* February 27, 2011, http://adage.com/article/digital/copy-testing-coming-digital-marketing/149100/.

21. Perry Marshall, Mike Rhodes, and Bryan Todd, *Entrepreneur Ultimate Guide to Google AdWords,* 4th ed. (Irvine, CA: Entrepreneur Press, 2014).

22. "Test Ads," *Google,* https://developers.google.com/admob/android/test-ads.

23. "How Can I A/B Split Test My Facebook Ads?" *Facebook Help Center,* www.facebook.com/help/community/question/?id=10152988283170078.

24. "Conversion Tracking for Websites," Twitter Help Center, https://support.twitter.com/articles/20170807-conversion-tracking-for-websites.

25. William Perreault Jr., Joseph Cannon, and E. Jerome McCarthy, *Basic Marketing: A Marketing Strategy Planning Approach* (New York: McGraw-Hill Education, 2013), p. 153.

26. Harrison Monarth, "The Irresistible Power of Storytelling as a Strategic Business Tool," *Harvard Business Review,* March 11, 2014, https://hbr.org/2014/03/the-irresistible-power-of-storytelling-as-a-strategic-business-tool; Joyce Steinberg, "How Stories Impact the Brain," *LinkedIn,* July 26, 2017, www.linkedin.com/pulse/how-stories-impact-brain-joy-steinberg/.

27. Harrison Monarth, "The Irresistible Power of Storytelling as a Strategic Business Tool," *Harvard Business Review,* March 11, 2014, *https://hbr.org/2014/03/the-irresistible-power-of-storytelling-as-a-strategic-business-tool*; Joyce Steinberg, "How Stories Impact the Brain," *LinkedIn,* July 26, 2017, *www.linkedin.com/pulse/how-stories-impact-brain-joy-steinberg/.*

28. *www.google.com/think/.*

29. *https://trends.google.com/trends/?geo=US.*

30. *https://adwords.google.com.*

31. Economic and Social Research Council, "Setting Objectives," *https://esrc.ukri.org/research/impact-toolkit/developing-a-communications-and-impact-strategy/step-by-step-guide/setting-objectives/.*

32. Michael L. Garee and Thomas R. Schori, "Focus Groups Illuminate Quantitative Research," *Marketing News,* September 23, 1996, p. 41.

33. Robert West, Schering Canada, personal interview, May 17, 1993.

34. William Weylock, "Focus: Hocus Pocus?" *Marketing Tools,* July/August 1994, pp. 12–16; Thomas L. Greenbaum, "Focus Groups Can Play a Part in Evaluating Ad Copy," *Marketing News,* September 13, 1993, pp. 24–25.

35. Pat Sloan and Julie Liesse, "New Agency Weapon to Win Clients: Research," *Advertising Age,* August 30, 1993, p. 37.

36. Rex Hartson and Partha S. Pyla, *The UX Book: Process and Guidelines for Ensuring a Quality User Experience* (Amsterdam: Elsevier, 2012).

37. Rex Hartson and Partha S. Pyla, *The UX Book: Process and Guidelines for Ensuring a Quality User Experience* (Amsterdam: Elsevier, 2012).

38. Jack Honomichl, "The Honomichl 50," *Marketing News,* June 10, 2002, p. H2; Don E. Schultz, Stanley I. Tannenbaum, and Robert F. Lauterborn, *Integrated Marketing Communications: Putting It Together and Making It Work* (Lincolnwood, IL: NTC Business Books, 1993), pp. 149–50; ACNielsen, *http://us.acnielsen.com/products.*

39. Leah Rickard, "Helping Put Data in Focus," *Advertising Age,* July 11, 1994, p. 18.

40. IAG Research, *www.iagr.net.*

41. Richard Gibson, "Marketers' Mantra: Reap More with Less," *The Wall Street Journal,* March 22, 1991, p. B1.

42. Karen A. Machleit, Chris T. Allen, and Thomas J. Madden, "The Mature Brand and Brand Interest: An Alternative Consequence of Ad-Evoked Affect," *Journal of Marketing,* October 1993, pp. 72–82.

43. Pamela L. Alreck and Robert B. Settle, *The Survey Research Handbook,* 2nd ed. (Burr Ridge, IL: Irwin, 1995), pp. 56–59.

44. Pamela L. Alreck and Robert B. Settle, *The Survey Research Handbook,* 2nd ed. (Burr Ridge, IL: Irwin, 1995), p. 40.

45. William Perreault Jr., Joseph Cannon, and E. Jerome McCarthy, *Basic Marketing: A Marketing Strategy Planning Approach* (New York: McGraw-Hill Education, 2013), p. 173.

46. Pamela L. Alreck and Robert B. Settle, *The Survey Research Handbook,* 2nd ed. (Burr Ridge, IL: Irwin, 1995), pp. 88–90.

47. George S. Fabian, panelist, "Globalization: Challenges for Marketing and Research," *Marketing Review,* February 1993, p. 23.

48. Maureen R. Marston, panelist, "Globalization: Challenges for Marketing and Research," *Marketing Review,* February 1993, pp. 20–21.

49. Suzanne Bidlake, "Nestlé Builds Database in Asia with Direct Mail," *Advertising Age International,* January 1998, p. 34.

50. Michael Brizz, "How to Learn What Japanese Buyers Really Want," *Business Marketing,* January 1987, p. 72.

51. Simon Chadwick, panelist, "Globalization: Challenges for Marketing and Research," *Marketing Review,* February 1993, p. 18.

52. Thomas L. Greenbaum, "Understanding Focus Group Research Abroad," *Marketing News,* June 3, 1996, pp. H14, H36.

53. Maureen R. Marston, panelist, "Globalization: Challenges for Marketing and Research," *Marketing Review,* February 1993, p. 24.

54. Maureen R. Marston, panelist, "Globalization: Challenges for Marketing and Research," *Marketing Review,* February 1993, p. 24.

55. Deborah Szynal, "Big Bytes," *Marketing News,* March 18, 2002, p. 3.

CHAPTER 8

Marketing and IMC Planning

LEARNING OBJECTIVES

To describe the process of marketing and IMC planning. Marketers need to understand the various ways plans are created. They must also know how to analyze situations; set realistic, attainable objectives; develop strategies to achieve them; and establish budgets for marketing communications.

After studying this chapter, you will be able to:

LO8-1   Explain strategic planning using a marketing plan.

LO8-2   Detail the tactical or "bottom-up" approach favored by smaller businesses.

LO8-3   Differentiate the IMC planning approach from the tactical.

LO8-4   Describe the important components of an IMC plan.

LO8-5   Explain how IMC budgets are determined.

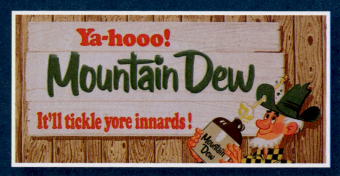

The changes in Mountain Dew advertising from inception to the present represent the evolution of the brand from a beverage popular in rural America to one that is more urban, youth-oriented, and high energy.

Source: PepsiCo

Kevin Hart launched Mountain Dew's latest campaign, "Give your head a MTN DEW KICKSTART" in late 2018. The series of ads includes a look inside the popular comedian's head as he drinks a Dew. The ad cements the evolution of the brand as a popular choice among urban, cool, young consumers. To know how far the brand has come, it helps to start at the beginning. ■ More than 60 years ago, Ally and Barney Hartman of Knoxville, Tennessee, produced a lemon-lime soft drink for family and friends. When neighbors began clamoring for some, they started bottling and distributing it to the locals. Their first label featured a gun-toting hillbilly and in honor of the mountain moonshine famous in Tennessee, they named their drink "Mountain Dew." The brothers believed they had a good thing going, but the public disagreed. Mountain Dew was a sales failure. ■ As we showed with Coca-Cola in Chapter 2, sometimes a brand just needs someone who understands marketing. For Mountain Dew, that man was Bill Jones. Jones, a salesman, convinced Ally Hartman to become an investor during a dinner meeting. In addition to his money, Ally offered the Mountain Dew brand under the condition that Jones spring for dinner. ■ Over the course of time, the brand grew. The moonshine-drinking Willy the Hillbilly and the apt slogan, "Ya-hoo Mountain Dew," helped build it into a regional player. The Pepsi-Cola Company took notice and purchased Mountain Dew in 1964. For some years, Pepsi continued using the old advertising approach. But as sales flattened, Pepsi decided a new direction was called for. ■ In 1973, it completely repositioned and relaunched Mountain Dew as a high-energy, youth-oriented, flavored soft drink. New ads created by BBDO New York featured active young people enjoying outdoor activities to the theme "Hello Sunshine, Hello Mountain Dew." By 1978, the action-oriented approach sent Dew sales over the 100-million-case mark. In the 1980s Pepsi added high-octane sports and adventure to the advertising.[1] ■ Since that time, Mountain Dew has set a standard of how to remain true to its own definition of exuberance across a variety of marketing platforms. "We have a great unity of message and purpose that has been consistent over time about what we are and what we aren't," says Scott Moffitt, director of marketing for Mountain Dew.[2] "The brand is all about exhilaration and energy, and you see that in all that we do, from advertising and community to grass-roots programs and our sports-minded focus. We have a very crystal clear, vivid positioning." ■ The positioning concept has allowed Mountain Dew great latitude: The brand's marketing extends from skateboarding parks and alternative events to mainstream extravaganzas such as the Super Bowl. Marketing across such a broad spectrum is known within PepsiCo as "mass intimacy."[3] ■ One Pepsi-Cola executive puts it this way: "It's our way of saying we haven't sold out. We have to make sure with programs like advertising on the Super Bowl that we are still letting customers see the brand in a way that is designed for them."[4] So whether Dew is talking advertising, events, endorsements, or simply premiums, a "Dew-x-perience" is paramount when talking to the brand's two key consumer groups: teenagers and 20- to 39-year-olds. ■ Mountain Dew's unique selling proposition remains the same—it is the "ultimate, indulgent, thirst-quenching soft drink." This positioning took it to the top of the "heavy citrus" soda category in the early 1990s. In 1999 it briefly passed Diet Coke to become the number three soft drink in the United States after Classic Coke and Pepsi. In the $62 billion carbonated soft drink industry, that is a huge success. ■ In the 2000s, the carbonated soft drink market stalled as people spent more on flavored drinks and bottled water. To stem the trend, PepsiCo introduced Code Red, a cherry-flavored Mountain Dew line extension. With a stealth launch, and using only limited radio ads targeting trend-setting teenagers, Code Red was a smashing success. ■ An early adopter of IMC, Mountain Dew eschewed ads in the early 2000s and instead financed a documentary on the history of snowboarding. The movie, called *First Descent*, included subtle rather than overt references to the brand, primarily through Mountain Dew's sponsorship of two of the featured athletes. The decision to finance a film, which carried a cost close to that of a traditional 30-second TV spot, originated in the marketers' recognition that its target audience watches less TV than other groups.[5] ■ By understanding its consumers, defining its brand clearly and creatively, and ensuring that its messages are compelling, exciting, and on-strategy, Mountain Dew has proven that its growth is no flash in the pan. Can the Dew success story continue? Despite the declining popularity of carbonated soft drinks, Mountain Dew keeps growing and gaining market share within its category. The reason? One of the world's strongest brand images, bolstered by some of the world's best IMC.[6] ■

Strategic Planning: The Marketing Plan

In spite of the brilliant creativity employed by BBDO in its ads for Mountain Dew, the Dew story actually demonstrates that business success often depends more on careful marketing and IMC planning than on creativity. Yet, every year, companies waste millions of dollars on ineffective messages due to a lack of planning. To prevent this, most companies engage in what is often referred to as "top-down" marketing planning. This process begins with a review of a company's mission, an audit of the current situation (referred to as a situation analysis), and strategies and tactics that logically flow from this audit (see Exhibit 8-1).

A **marketing plan** is a written guide for the present and future marketing activities of an organization. Marketing plans generally do a number of important things, including (1) clarifying the organization's mission; (2) assessing the brand's current marketing situation and identify factors, both within the company and in the environment, that may help or hinder achieving marketing objectives; (3) presenting clear, measurable, time-delineated marketing objectives; (4) describing strategies that can be used to achieve marketing objectives with specific target markets; (5) describing tactics or action programs for implementing the marketing strategy; (6) explaining how marketing efforts will be evaluated; and (7) proposing a budget for these activities (see the Marketing Plan Outline in Appendix A).

The marketing plan has a profound effect on an organization's IMC. It dictates the role of promotional messages in the marketing mix. It enables better implementation, control, and continuity of campaigns, and it guides the allocation of promotional dollars. Successful organizations do not separate IMC plans from marketing. They view each as a vital building block for success.

The Mission Statement

A good marketing plan generally begins with the organization's mission statement. The **mission statement** is a short description of the organization's purpose and philosophy. It is intended to be both aspirational and inspirational. Starting the plan with a mission

Exhibit 8-1
Traditional top-down marketing plan.

statement helps remind planners and marketing partners about what the organization is and what it stands for. PepsiCo.'s mission is to be

> The world's premier consumer products company, focused on convenient foods and beverages. We seek to produce healthy financial rewards to investors as we provide opportunities for growth and enrichment to our employees, our business partners and the communities in which we operate. And in everything we do, we strive to act with honesty, openness, fairness and integrity.[7]

This mission statement nicely summarizes who Pepsi is, what it does, and how it does it. The following table presents mission statements of some other prominent brands.

Company	Corporate Mission Statements
Google	To organize the world's information and make it universally accessible and useful.
Life is Good	To spread the power of optimism.
Facebook	To give people the power to build community and bring the world closer together.
IKEA	To create a better everyday life for the many people.
Trader Joe's	To give our customers the best food and beverage values that they can find anywhere and to provide them with the information required to make informed buying decisions.
JetBlue	To inspire humanity—both in the air and on the ground

The Situation Analysis

The second part of the marketing plan is the **situation analysis,** a detailed description of the brand's current marketing situation. You can see a sample outline for one in My IMC Campaign 8-A. The situation analysis presents all facts relevant for planning a marketing strategy. Most situation analyses include a description of the brand's history, market share, growth, profitability, promotional expenditures, key competitors, and so on. Good marketing plans also provide the context for the facts they contain. For example, Diet Mountain Dew's sales growth of 8 percent during the most recent year is put into a context when the marketing plan notes that overall sales of carbonated beverages declined. In that context, 8 percent growth is outstanding.

Planners draw attention to the most important aspects of a brand's situation through a **SWOT analysis.** The SWOT analysis draws on the facts contained in the situation analysis to determine the strengths, weaknesses, opportunities, and threats for the brand. *Strengths* and *weaknesses* are internal elements that represent the company's capabilities, while *opportunities* and *threats* represent external, environmental factors. One obvious strength for Mountain Dew is its well-defined, attractive brand image as a high-energy, full-flavored, carbonated beverage. A possible weakness could be the brand's age or could be a distribution challenge faced by parent brand PepsiCo. An opportunity for Mountain Dew might be the increased interest in energy drinks. Because Mountain Dew is a highly caffeinated beverage, it might profit from such a trend. Threats to Mountain Dew might include rising prices for the commodities used in production (sugar, flavorings) that would force Mountain Dew to raise prices to remain profitable. Other threats might be changes in the beverage choices of its target markets (some of the fastest-growing soft drinks today are vitamin-infused beverages such as Pepsi's Tava).

The Marketing Objectives

Marketing objectives, the third part of the marketing plan, are clear, quantifiable, realistic marketing goals that are to be accomplished within a defined time period. Marketing objectives generally fall into one of two broad categories: *sales-target objectives* and *communication objectives.*

Sales-target objectives include goals related to increasing or maintaining sales volume and market share. Such objectives, of course, must be realistic in light of the issues

My IMC Campaign 8-A

Developing the Situation Analysis

In previous chapters you've honed your understanding of the consumer, segmented the audience, and conducted research. It is time to pull all of this information together and create an assessment of your client's current situation. Marketers call such an assessment a situation analysis. Use the list below to organize your analysis.

The Industry

- **Companies in industry:** Dollar sales, strengths.
- **Growth patterns within industry:** Primary demand curve, per capita consumption, growth potential.
- **History of industry:** Technological advances, trends.
- **Characteristics of industry:** Distribution patterns, industry control, promotional activity, geographic characteristics, profit patterns.

The Company

- **The company story:** History, size, growth, profitability, scope of business, competence, reputation, strengths, weaknesses.

The Product or Service

- **The product story:** Development, quality, design, description, packaging, price structure, uses, reputation, strengths, weaknesses.
- **Product sales features:** Exclusive and nonexclusive differentiating qualities, competitive position.
- **Product research:** Technological breakthroughs, improvements planned.

Sale History

- **Sales and sales costs:** By product, model, sales districts.
- **Profit history.**

Share of Market

- **Sales history industrywide:** Share of market in dollars and units.
- **Market potential:** Industry trends, company trends, demand trends.

The Market

- **Who and where is the market:** How was market segmented; how can it be segmented; what are consumer needs, attitudes, and characteristics? How, why, when, where do consumers buy?
- **Past IMC appeals:** Successful or unsuccessful.
- **Who are our customers:** Past and future? What characteristics do they have in common? What do they like about our product? What don't they like?

Distribution

- **History and evaluation:** How and where product is distributed, current trend.
- **Company's relationship:** With the distribution channel and its attitudes toward product/company.
- **Past policies:** Trade advertising, deals, co-op programs.
- **Status:** Trade literature, dealer promotions, point-of-purchase displays.

Pricing Policies

- **Price history:** Trends, relationship to needs of buyers, competitive price situation.
- **Past price objectives:** Management attitudes, buyer attitudes, channel attitudes.

Competition

- **Who is the competition:** Primary, secondary, share of market, products, services, goals, attitudes. What is competition's growth history and size?
- **Strengths and competition:** Sales features, product quality, size. Weaknesses of competition.
- **Marketing activities of competition:** Advertising, promotion, distribution, sales force. Estimated budget.

Promotion

- **Successes and failures:** Past promotion policy, sales force, advertising, publicity.
- **Promotion expenditures:** History, budget emphasis, relation to competition, trend.
- **IMC programs:** Review of strategies, themes, campaigns.
- **Sales force:** Size, scope, ability, cost/sale.

described in the situation analysis. In good economic times and in a new product category, a company might set very ambitious sales-target objectives. Because Mountain Dew is an established brand in a mature product category, it might propose a sales-target objective of 5 percent growth in overall sales over a period of one year. This overall sales objective might be a result of even more specific objectives by distribution point. For example, Mountain Dew might propose modest sales-target objectives at one distribution point (grocery stores) and higher objectives at another (restaurants).

Communication objectives are outcomes that can reasonably be associated with promotional activities, such as increases in brand recognition or awareness, increased comprehension of a brand's attributes or benefits, more positive attitudes about a brand or a more favorable image of the brand or its typical user, and stronger intentions to try or buy a brand. Mountain Dew's IMC is meant to help consumers view the brand as a flavorful, high-energy drink for youthful-thinking people looking for an alternative to colas.

Experts suggest that good marketing plans should place greater emphasis on communication objectives and less on sales-target objectives. This may seem counterintuitive. After all, isn't the purpose of IMC to drive sales? In one way, the answer is yes. Companies spend money on campaigns to generate an even greater return in sales. But viewing IMC effectiveness only in terms of sales overlooks some key issues. For example, a campaign's impact on sales usually works through intermediate steps (see Exhibit 8-5 later in this chapter). In many instances consumers must navigate a sequence of awareness, comprehension, conviction, and desire before they take action and buy a product. These intermediate steps are best achieved by specifying communications objectives.

In addition, the relationship between sales and IMC is a complex one. An effective campaign can make a consumer want to try a product, but a repeat sale is typically influenced by the consumer's product experiences. So even great campaigns can fail if consumers are dissatisfied with the product when they try it. Finally, many factors unrelated to IMC (a recession, new competitors, government regulation, and the like) can have a large impact on sales no matter how good or poor the advertising.

A Traditional Model for Setting Objectives: DAGMAR

Determining the objectives for a marketing program can be difficult, especially for planners without years of experience. The task was simplified considerably when Russell Colley introduced a system for *d*efining *a*dvertising *g*oals for *m*easured *a*dvertising *r*esults (DAGMAR). The **DAGMAR** approach emphasizes communication objectives because Colley believed that the proper way to evaluate a campaign is to determine how well it communicates information, within a given budget, to the target audience.

Planners who follow DAGMAR formulate objectives related to one of four outcomes: *awareness* (knowing the brand exists), *comprehension* (knowing about the brand's benefits or attributes), *conviction* (a favorable attitude toward the brand), and *action* (purchasing and using the brand). Like other hierarchical models, DAGMAR assumes that consumers travel through these stages in order. Thus, a marketer knows that if there is little awareness of the brand in the target market, focusing on later objectives in the sequence may not be a good strategy.

DAGMAR is also clear about the qualities of a good objective. Good objectives specify an audience and define outcomes that are concrete and measurable. They are also clear about the current situation, the desired situation, and the time frame for moving from the former to the latter.

Let's consider a fictional example to see how a company might formulate objectives. Our fictional brand is a tax software program called EasyFile. The key difference between EasyFile and other tax software programs (or doing taxes without a software program) is that it dramatically simplifies tax preparation. The marketing planners at EasyFile know that simplifying tax preparation is a benefit that appeals to people who do their own taxes. The planners also believe that if they convince their target audience that EasyFile is much easier than other programs, sales will increase substantially. The sales-target objective for EasyFile could be stated this way: "EasyFile will increase unit sales to the target market of people who file their own taxes from 165,000 in 2020 to 355,000 in 2021." This optimistic assumption is based on the situation analysis, which shows that the product category of tax preparation software is growing rapidly and that people are frustrated with the difficulty of existing programs.

Note that the sales-target objective described above offers little insight as to the strategy that could help EasyFile accomplish its sales increase. This is why communication objectives are so important in a marketing plan. Communication objectives help define what IMC should do in order to help a brand achieve its sales goals. The communication objective for EasyFile might be stated this way: "Research shows the most sought-after benefit in tax software is ease-of-use. While 90 percent of the target market is aware of EasyFile, only 10 percent believes that EasyFile is the easiest way to prepare income taxes. In 2020 we will increase that percentage to 35 percent of the target market."

The Marketing Strategy

The **marketing strategy** describes how the company plans to meet its marketing objectives (see Ad Lab 8–A, "The Strategies of Marketing Warfare"). Marketing strategy typically involves three steps: (1) defining the particular target markets, (2) determining the strategic position, and (3) developing an appropriate marketing mix for each target market. A company's marketing strategy has a dramatic impact on its advertising. It determines the role and amount of advertising in the marketing mix, its creative thrust, and the media to be employed.

Advertisers find it useful to frame their marketing strategies in terms of need-satisfying objectives. Mountain Dew is positioned as the beverage choice of young, hip, rebellious urbanites. This ad featuring comedian Kevin Hart for Kickstart is intended to resonate with that group. For more on positioning, see Ad Lab 8–A.

Source: PepsiCo

Selecting the Target Market   The first step in strategy development is to define and select the target market, using the processes of market segmentation and research discussed in Chapters 6 and 7.

Tesla's Model X, first introduced in 2015, is an all-electric SUV that targets "ultra-luxury" consumers for the simple reason it can sell for close to $150,000 with available options. When Jaguar recently launched its I-Pace, another all-electric SUV, it decided to "slide" under Tesla's demographic and target luxury buyers. Why? The I-Pace sells for just under $70,000, where it competes with luxury gas-powered SUVs by Mercedes and BMW. By bringing desired benefits (lower fuel costs and environmental friendliness) to a new segment, Jaguar stands to have a hit on its hands.[8]

Similarly, Mountain Dew defines its target market as active, young people in their teens as well as young adults 20 to 39 years old. In addition, the brand aims a significant portion of its marketing activities at urban youth, especially African Americans and Latinos.[9] To Mountain Dew, the prototypical consumer is an 18-year-old, street-smart, male teen.[10]

Positioning the Product   The famous ad executive David Ogilvy said one of the first decisions in marketing is also the most important: how to position the product. Positioning, which we introduced in Chapter 1, refers to the place a brand occupies in the minds of consumers relative to other brands it competes with. Every product has some position—whether intended or not—even if the position is "nowhere." Positions are based on consumer beliefs, which may or may not reflect reality. Strong brands have a clear, often unique position in the target market. Ogilvy's agency differentiated Dove soap in 1957 by positioning it as a "complexion bar" for women with dry skin. Now, over a half-century later, the company still emphasizes natural beauty as a theme, and Dove is consistently the number one brand, with twice the share of market of its nearest competitor.[11]

AD Lab 8–A

The Strategies of Marketing Warfare

Jack Trout and Al Ries's *Marketing Warfare* is based on the classic book of military strategy, *On War*, written by Prussian general Carl von Clausewitz and published in 1832. The book outlines the principles behind all successful wars, and two simple ideas dominate: *force* and the *superiority of defense*.

The Strategic Square

How do the principles of warfare apply to marketing? It comes down to the "strategic square":

Out of every 100 companies:
One should play defense.
Two should play offense.
Three should flank.
And 94 should be guerrillas.

Defensive Warfare

Datril opened its war on Tylenol with a price attack. Johnson & Johnson immediately cut Tylenol's price, even before Datril started its price advertising. Result: It repelled the Datril attacks and inflicted heavy losses on the Bristol-Myers entry.

Here are the rules for defensive marketing warfare:

1. Participate only if you are a market leader.
2. Introduce new products and services before the competition does.
3. Block strong competitive moves by copying them rapidly.

Offensive Warfare

Colgate had a strong number one position in toothpaste. But rival Procter & Gamble knew a thing or two about von Clausewitz.

P&G launched Crest toothpaste with not only a massive $20 million advertising budget but also the American Dental Association "seal of approval." Crest went over the top to become the best-selling toothpaste in the country.

But overtaking the leader is not that common. Most companies are happy if they can establish a profitable number two position.

The rules for waging offensive marketing warfare are these:

1. Consider the strength of the leader's position.

2. Launch the attack on as narrow a front as possible, preferably with single products.

3. Launch the attack at the leader's weakest position.

Flanking Warfare

The third type of marketing warfare is where the action is for many companies. In practice, it means launching products where there is no competition. Unilever introduced Mentadent, the first baking soda/peroxide toothpaste, which became very successful.

Here are the principles of flanking marketing warfare:

1. Make flanking moves into uncontested areas.
2. Use surprise. Too much research often wastes precious time.
3. Keep up the pursuit; too many companies quit after they're ahead.

Guerrilla Warfare

Most of America's companies should be waging guerrilla warfare. The key to success in guerrilla wars is flexibility. A guerrilla should abandon any product or market if the tide of battle changes.

Here are the principles of guerrilla marketing warfare:

1. Find a market segment small enough to defend.
2. No matter how successful you become, never act like the leader.
3. Be prepared to "bug out" at a moment's notice.

Bottom Up

Trout and Ries's later book, *Bottom-Up Marketing* (discussed later in this chapter), continues the military analogy.

"Deep penetration on a narrow front is the key to winning a marketing war," they say. By this they mean that smaller companies should keep their products narrowly focused on single concepts. Too many companies spread their forces over a wide front. In fact, most large corporations today must fend off focused attacks by smaller companies.

Laboratory Applications

1. Think of a successful product and explain its success in terms of marketing warfare.
2. Select a product and explain how marketing warfare strategy might be used to gain greater success.

Many positions are available in a market. The big mistake many companies make is not staking out any position. They can't be everything, but they don't want to be nothing.[12] A company might pick a position similar to a competitor's and fight for the same customers. Or it might find a position not held by a competitor—a hole in the market—and fill it quickly, perhaps through product differentiation or market segmentation.

Positioning is important for both the advertiser and the consumer because it helps differentiate products from the competition. Shieldtox Naturgard uses natural ingredients to formulate its insect repellent. That creates a position against larger-selling brands that use chemicals.

Source: Reckitt Benckiser

Professor Ernest Martin proposes seven distinct approaches to developing a positioning strategy:

1. *Product attribute*—setting the brand apart by stressing a particular product feature important to consumers. *Example:* Crest 3D White Whitening Therapy Enamel Care toothpaste.
2. *Price/quality*—positioning on the basis of price or quality. *Examples:* No-AD Suncare (price); BMW, "The ultimate driving machine" (quality).
3. *Use/application*—positioning on the basis of how a product is used. *Example:* Arm & Hammer's website lists solutions for infants, bathrooms, carpets, households, kitchens, outside, and personal hygiene; see http://armandhammerbakingsoda.ca/solutions.
4. *Product class*—positioning the brand against other products that, while not the same, offer the same class of benefits. *Example:* Starbucks' Nitro Cold Brew versus hot coffee.
5. *Product user*—positioning using the particular group that consumes the product. *Examples:* Bates Waterproof boots, which advertises that it is used by the U.S. Marine Corps.
6. *Product competitor*—positioning against competitors (using the strength of the competitor's position to help define the subject brand). *Examples:* Apple Macs versus PCs; Ram trucks versus Ford F-150s.
7. *Cultural symbol*—positioning apart from competitors through the creation or use of some recognized symbol or icon. *Examples:* AirBnB, Lyft, Snap.[13]

We add an eighth approach: by category—positioning by defining or redefining the business category. A simple way for a company to get the number one position is to invent a new product category. This has been labeled the "Blue Ocean Strategy," defined by authors Kim and Mauborgne as "the simultaneous pursuit of differentiation and low cost to open up a new market space and create new demand. It is about creating and capturing uncontested market space, thereby making the competition irrelevant."[14] A classic example cited by the authors is Cirque du Soleil, which created a form of entertainment quite unlike any other.

Successful positioning can bring enormous benefits. Although Apple was founded as a computer company, its greatest successes came with innovations that defined new categories: tablets, an online music store, and smartphones. These were possible because of the original brand's strong position.[15]

With all its high energy and exhilaration, "youth" is not only the positioning of Mountain Dew; it's the heartbeat of the brand.[16] PepsiCo defines the Dew positioning this way:

> To 18-year-old males who embrace excitement, adventure, and fun, Mountain Dew is the great-tasting soft drink that exhilarates like no other because it is energizing, thirst-quenching, and has a unique citrus flavor.[17]

Determining the Marketing Mix   The next step in developing the marketing strategy is to determine a cost-effective marketing mix for *each* target market the company pursues. As we discussed in Chapter 6, the mix blends the various marketing elements the company controls: *product, price, distribution,* and *communications.*

Mountain Dew was blessed with a broad marketing toolbox to draw upon. First, it offered consumers an energizing, thirst-quenching soft drink *product* with a unique citrus flavor and an image of youthful exuberance, exhilaration, and adventure. Then, to build *distribution,* it used a variety of promotions to the trade that would enable grocers and other resellers to increase both volume and profits. While its *price* was competitive with other soft drinks, Mountain Dew promoted itself aggressively with free samples, premiums, and prizes at various street and sporting events—which effectively lowered the price to consumers.

Finally, Mountain Dew initiated an integrated *communications* program that included extensive advertising on TV, radio, outdoor and print media, and the internet; sports and event sponsorships; appearances at grass-roots geographical events; plus a host of public relations activities—all designed to develop and promote the distinct Mountain Dew personality.

Companies have a wide variety of marketing strategy options. They might increase distribution, initiate new uses for a product, change a product line, develop entirely new markets, or start discount pricing. Each option emphasizes one or more marketing mix elements. The choice depends on the product's target market, its position in the market, and its stage in the product life cycle.

Marketing Tactics

A company's objectives indicate where it wants to go; the strategy indicates the intended route; and the **tactics** determine the specific short-term actions to be taken, internally and externally, by whom, and when. Advertising campaigns live in the world of marketing tactics.

What are some tactics that major marketers have employed to achieve their strategies? GoPro wanted to demonstrate the power of the device for capturing intense moments of life. To do so, they encouraged users to post videos on popular video sites such as YouTube (see www.youtube.com/watch?time_continue=19&v=CjB_oVeq8Lo). Demian Farnworth, writing for Copyblogger.com, demonstrates some great examples of the tactic of native advertising, ads designed to subtly promote a brand by looking like publisher content. Examples include IBM-sponsored content on big data in the *Atlantic* and Iclick eyeware-sponsored content on Gawker for the article "How to Transform into a Total Nerd-Babe." Finally, the Ice-Bucket challenge, which encouraged people to video themselves being doused with ice water while pledging to support a charity, has to be considered one of history's greatest marketing tactics (see the opening vignette in Chapter 16).

Tactical Planning: Small Company "Bottom-Up" Marketing

LO 8-2

In a small company, everybody is both player and coach, and the day-to-day details seem to come first, leaving little or no time for formal planning. However, there is a solution to this dilemma: **bottom-up marketing** (see Exhibit 8-2).

Jack Trout and Al Ries think one of the best ways for a company to develop a competitive advantage is to focus on an ingenious tactic first and then develop that tactic into a strategy. By reversing the normal process, marketers sometimes make important discoveries.[18] Researchers at Vicks developed an effective liquid cold remedy but found it put people to sleep. Rather than throw out the research, Vicks positioned the formula as a nighttime cold remedy. NyQuil went on to become the number one cold remedy and the most successful new product in Vicks's history.

Ethics, Diversity & Inclusion

Subliminal Persuasion

Absolut Vodka pokes fun at popular accounts of subliminal ad campaigns with this print ad. The name of the brand is readily seen on the ice cubes.

Source: Absolut Spirits Co.

Imagine you could inject an ad message directly into people's minds, bypassing ordinary perception. Consumers would be unable to challenge or ignore your communication because they would never notice it in the first place.

Incredibly, in 1957 James Vicary claimed he had such a technique. The market researcher said that during a movie he had flashed the phrases "Drink Coca-Cola" and "Hungry? Eat popcorn" subliminally (shown the words so quickly people could not detect them). Vicary claimed that sales of popcorn and Coke shot up by 18 percent and 58 percent, respectively.

The public took notice. As psychologist Anthony Pratkanis observed, "people were outraged and frightened by a technique so devilish that it could bypass their conscious intellect and beam subliminal commands directly to their subconscious." Great Britain and Australia banned **subliminal advertising** and the FCC threatened to revoke the license of any TV station that showed subliminal ads.

Concerns abated when Vicary could not reproduce his effects under supervised tests. He later admitted he made the whole thing up. But fascination with subliminal advertising reappeared in the early 70s when Wilson Bryan Key published books that claimed to find the word *sex* in hundreds of ads, from ice cubes in a gin ad to the surface of a Ritz cracker! And while almost nobody else could see these "embeds," Key sold plenty of books.

Case closed? Well, not quite. It helps to separate subliminal advertising (demonstrating that a real advertiser has affected product sales with a hidden message embedded in a commercial) from subliminal influence (demonstrating that people can be affected by an undetectable message). Surprisingly, current evidence is conclusive: *People can be influenced subliminally.*

Demonstrating subliminal influence requires a couple of things. First, you have to present the message (a picture, word, or phrase) so quickly that people can't tell it was there. Psychologists say that something shown for 120 milliseconds (0.12 of a second) or less is undetectable. Second, it has to be demonstrated that the message influences people in some way. For example, a group shown a subliminal message must think, feel, or act differently from a control group that doesn't see the subliminal message.

Dozens of published research studies have provided such demonstrations. Consider one example: A group of researchers wondered what would happen if people who are snake phobic are subliminally presented with a picture of a snake. Phobics typically begin sweating and become anxious when they see a snake photograph, whereas most people are fine. So what happens if snake photos are presented subliminally? The researchers found that even though subjects could not "see" the snake pictures, they responded as if they could: Phobics were anxious; nonphobics were not. So much for the idea that we are immune to messages we can't detect.

Exhibit 8-2
Bottom-up marketing plan.

The *tactic* is a specific action for helping to accomplish a strategy. By planning from the bottom up, entrepreneurs can find unique tactics to exploit. Small company tactics often focus on local communities. This makes a great deal of sense because this is where a small company can have an edge over a large national or multinational corporation. *Forbes* suggests the following small company tactics: (1) partner with other local companies; (2) use transit ads; (3) build relationships with local tech groups; (4) make use of vivid, powerful stories; (5) sponsor or attend events; (6) organize industry events; (7) get involved in charities or causes; and (8) turn users into advocates.[19]

The artful combination of tactic and strategy creates a position in the consumer's mind. When Tom Monaghan thought of the tactic of delivering pizza within 30 minutes to customers' homes, he focused his whole strategy on that singular idea. He ended up making a fortune and marketing history with Domino's Pizza.

But snakes and phobias are far removed from the concerns of most advertisers. Advertisers want to influence buying behaviors, not fears. This brings us to research done by three business professors, Yael Zemack-Rugar, James Bettman, and Gavan Fitzsimons. In an ingenious experiment, they subliminally presented words related to either sadness or guilt to study participants. Both sadness words (i.e., *sad, miserable*) and guilt words (*guilty, blameworthy*) describe bad feelings. But people act differently when they feel sad as opposed to when they feel guilty. Sad people look for rewards to cheer themselves up, but guilty people deny themselves rewards. So the researchers predicted that in response to subliminal presentation of guilt words, guilt-prone people (as opposed to non–guilt-prone people) would be less likely to buy themselves an indulgence. Conversely, in response to sad words, guilt-prone people as compared with others would be just as likely to buy an indulgence. In fact, their experiments demonstrated these patterns of results. By subliminally influencing specific emotions, the researchers influenced purchase behaviors.

An even more direct demonstration that subliminal advertising can work comes from a study done by psychologists Johan Karremans, Wolfgang Stroebe, and Jaspar Claus. They argued that subliminal advertising influences brand preference only when someone is motivated to buy in the first place. In their experiment, people tracked strings of letters on a computer screen. Unbeknownst to the participants, subliminal messages were being flashed every so often. Half of the participants were exposed to the subliminal message "Lipton Ice," and half were exposed to a control word. Later, in a supposedly unrelated second study, participants were asked both how thirsty they were and whether they preferred Lipton or a competing brand. The results: When subjects were not thirsty, the two groups showed the same preference for Lipton. But thirsty participants showed a different pattern: Those exposed to the Lipton subliminal message showed a strong preference for Lipton; those in the control group did not. The authors' explanation: Motivation plus subliminal prime equals increased preference for the primed brand.

Taken together, these studies and many others show conclusively that we can be affected by messages presented outside of awareness. Score one for Vicary. But it is a long way from saying this *can* be done to showing that it *is* done. In fact, as stated earlier, no one has ever shown that an ad campaign has used subliminal stimuli. And no research backs up Key's claims about "embeds" in print ads.

But can we be sure that no advertiser ever used subliminal advertising? Proving that something has never happened is pretty difficult (can you really "prove" that Aunt Lois wasn't abducted by aliens returning home from school back in 1975?). But the risks an advertiser would court by using a subliminal message far outweigh the likely rewards. What would consumers think of a company that was caught using subliminal ads? What would the legal repercussions be? Moreover, why would a company choose subliminal advertising when the nonsubliminal type can work so well?

People seem both repelled and attracted by the thought that they can be influenced below the threshold of awareness. It seems to imply a hidden power and dovetails nicely with a universal interest in the idea that not everything is what it seems. Interest in the phenomenon of subliminal advertising won't be going away soon, especially now that we know it CAN work.

Questions

1. What are the ethical concerns that subliminal advertising would create? Who are the stakeholders (people or groups that would be affected by this practice)?

2. How does subliminal advertising relate to the free-market principle of complete information we discussed earlier?

Sources: Anthony R. Pratkanis, "The Cargo-Cult Science of Subliminal Persuasion," *Skeptical Inquirer*, 1992, retrieved March 4, 2007, from http://csicop.org/si/9204/subliminal-persuasion.html; P. J. Lang, D. N. Levin, G. A. Miller, and M. J. Kozak, "Fear Behavior, Fear Imagery, and the Psychophysiology of Emotion: The Problem of Affective Response Integration," *Journal of Abnormal Psychology* 92 (1983), pp. 276–306; A. Ohman, A. Flykt, and D. Lundqvist, "Unconscious Emotion: Evolutionary Perspectives, Psychophysiological Data, and Neuropsychological Mechanisms," in *Cognitive Neuroscience of Emotion*, ed. R. D. Lane, L. Nade, and G. Ahern (New York: Oxford University Press, 2000), pp. 296–327; Y. Zemack-Rugar, J. R. Bettman, and G. J. Fitzsimons, "The Effects of Nonconsciously Priming Emotion Concepts on Behavior," *Journal of Personality and Social Psychology* 93 (2007), pp. 927–39; J. C. Karremans, W. Stroebe, and J. Claus, "Beyond Vicary's Fantasies: The Impact of Subliminal Priming and Brand Choice," *Journal of Experimental Social Psychology* 42 (2006), pp. 792–98.

Managers of small companies have an advantage here. Surrounded by the details of the business, they are more likely to discover a good tactic that can be developed into a powerful strategy. However, that's not to say that a large company cannot profit from bottom-up marketing. Many have, like 3M with its Post-it notes.

LO 8-3

The IMC Approach to Marketing and Campaign Planning

Integrated marketing communications suggests a new approach to planning marketing and communications activities. It differs from the traditional processes by mixing marketing and communications planning together rather than separating them. Using the outside-in process, the IMC approach starts with the customer. Marketers learn about what media customers use, the relevance of their message to the customers, and when customers and

Exhibit 8-3
IMC macro model.

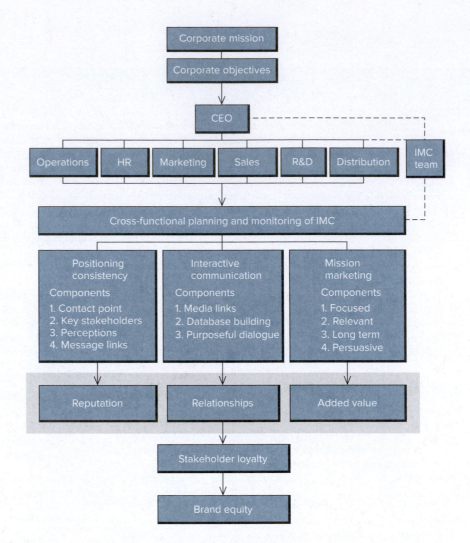

prospects are most *receptive* to the message. As depicted in Exhibit 8-3 (starting at the bottom), IMC activities begin with the customer and work back to the brand.[20] In turn, all corporate marketing functions are dedicated to building and maintaining brand equity through a united focus on stakeholder loyalty.

Thanks to technology, marketers have a wealth of information at their fingertips. With supermarket scanner data, for instance, packaged-goods marketers can (1) identify specific users of products and services, (2) measure their actual purchase behavior and relate it to specific brand and product categories, (3) measure the impact of various advertising and marketing communications activities and determine their value in influencing the actual purchase, and (4) capture and evaluate this information over time.[21]

But this is really just the start. Mobile payment devices and plans (Apple pay, PayPal) offer marketers even richer data on consumption behavior. Big data behemoth Amazon can easily link buying behaviors in its Whole Foods stores (it acquired the chain in 2017) to all of the other information it maintains about its consumers (including users of Prime video).[22]

This ever-expanding database of customer behavior can be the basis for planning future marketing and communications activities, especially if the database contains information on customer demographics, psychographics, purchase data, and brand or product category attitudes (see Exhibit 8-4).

Starting the planning process with a database focuses the company on the consumer, or prospect, not the company's sales or profit goals. These marketing objectives are moved farther down in the planning process.[23]

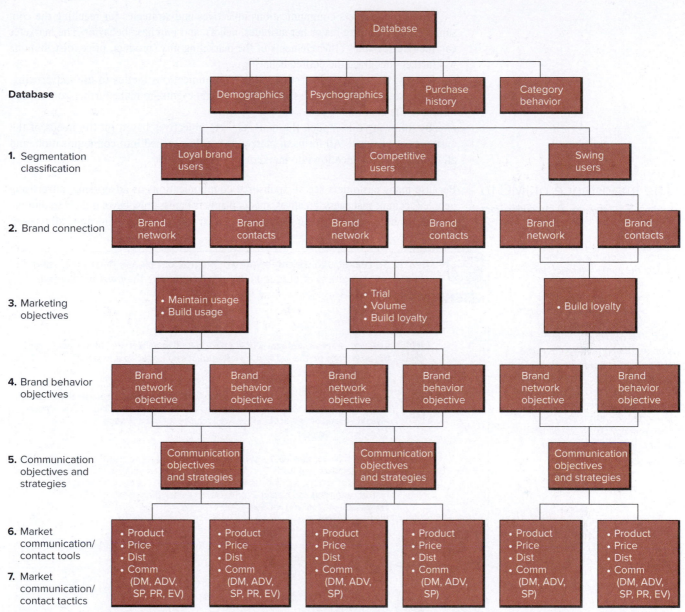

Database

1. Segmentation classification

2. Brand connection

3. Marketing objectives

4. Brand behavior objectives

5. Communication objectives and strategies

6. Market communication/contact tools

7. Market communication/contact tactics

DM = Direct marketing   ADV = Advertising   SP = Sales promotion   PR = Public relations   EV = Event marketing
Dist = Distribution   Comm = Marketing communications

Exhibit 8-4
Wang–Schultz IMC planning model.

So how does planning proceed under an integrated approach? Wang and Schultz developed a seven-step IMC planning model. The first step segments the customers and prospects in the database—either by brand loyalty, as illustrated, or by some other measurable purchase behavior (usage, for instance).

The second step analyzes information on customers to understand their attitudes, their history, and how they discover and interact with the brand or product. The goal is to find the best time, place, and situation to build and maintain relationships.

Next, the planner sets marketing objectives based on this analysis. In the illustrated example, these objectives relate to building and maintaining usage or nurturing brand loyalty.

The marketer then identifies what brand contacts and what changes in attitude are required to support the consumer's continuance or change of purchase behavior.

The fifth step sets communications objectives and strategies for reaching the consumer and influencing his or her attitudes, beliefs, and purchase behavior. The marketer can then decide what other elements of the marketing mix (product, price, distribution) will further encourage the desired behavior.

Finally, the planner determines what communications tactics to use—advertising, direct marketing, publicity, sales promotion, special events—to make further contact and influence the consumer's behavior.[24]

By following this model, the marketer sets objectives based on the needs of the customer or prospect. All forms of marketing are thus turned into communication, and all forms of communication into marketing.[25]

The Importance of IMC to the Study of Advertising

Because many customers see all sponsored communications as advertising, advertising people (account managers, creatives, media planners) must grow beyond their traditional specialty to become enlightened generalists, familiar with and able to integrate all types of

Companies have control over their advertising, but they must be careful about any unplanned messages they may inadvertently engender as the open exchange of opinions and beliefs promoted by social media can't be managed. The adjacent screenshot shows an exchange between a Nestlé employee and some consumers on Facebook over Nestlé's request to not use an altered version of the company's logo as a profile picture. Do you think the exchange is an example of bad social networking? Could Nestlé have handled this in a different manner?

Source: Facebook.com/Nestle

marketing communications. Conversely, marketers traditionally viewed advertising as IMC. In other words, marketers failed to look beyond traditional advertising approaches when creating campaigns, and failed to acknowledge that effective communications can (and should) come from a variety of media, platforms, and sources. The IMC approach helps broaden the company's perspective, so that message tactics come from a consideration of broader marketing strategies, rather than the other way around.

In a survey of 122 *Fortune* 500 marketing, advertising, and communications executives, most respondents indicated a general understanding of integrated marketing and agreed that synergy is the key benefit of IMC.[26] However, the study also showed that confusion remains concerning IMC use. Many practitioners today still lack the broad knowledge required to develop, supervise, and execute full IMC programs.[27]

The IMC Plan

The **IMC plan** is a natural outgrowth of the marketing plan and is prepared in much the same way. Appendix B at the end of the book outlines both a traditional advertising plan and an IMC plan.

Reviewing the Marketing Plan

The brand manager first reviews the marketing plan to understand where the company is going, how it intends to get there, and the role of IMC in the marketing mix. The first section of the plan should summarize briefly the situation analysis and SWOT analysis, review the target market segments, itemize the long- and short-term marketing objectives, and restate decisions regarding market positioning and the marketing mix.

Setting Objectives

LO 8-4

The brand manager then determines what tasks IMC must accomplish. What strengths and opportunities can be leveraged? What weaknesses and threats need to be addressed? Unfortunately, some corporate executives (and advertising managers) state vague goals, like "increasing sales and maximizing profits by creating a favorable impression of the product in the marketplace." When this happens, no one understands what the messages are intended to do, how much they will cost, or how to measure the results. Objectives should be specific, realistic, and measurable.

Understanding What Campaigns Can Do

Most IMC programs encourage prospects to take some action. However, it is usually unrealistic to assign IMC the whole responsibility for achieving sales. Sales goals are marketing objectives, not advertising objectives. Before a company can persuade customers to buy, it must inform, persuade, or remind its intended audience about the company, product, service, or issue. A simple adage to remember when setting objectives is "Marketing sells; IMC tells." In other words, IMC objectives should always be related to communication effects.

Earlier we suggested that communications objectives are important for the overall marketing plan too. Does the IMC plan merely restate these? In most cases, the communications objectives stated in the IMC plan will be those that message campaigns are best suited to accomplish. Objectives best achieved by other communication tools may be dealt with in separate plans.

The IMC Pyramid: A Guide to Setting Communications Objectives

Suppose you're advertising a new brand in a new product category, but you're not sure what kind of results to expect. The pyramid in Exhibit 8-5 shows some of the tasks IMC can perform. Obviously, before your product is introduced, prospective customers are completely unaware of it. Your first communication objective, therefore, is to create *awareness*—to acquaint people with the company, product, service, and brand.

Exhibit 8-5
The IMC pyramid depicts the progression of communications effects on mass audiences—especially for new products. The initial message promotes awareness of the product to a large audience (the base of the pyramid). But only a percentage of this large group will comprehend the product's benefits. Of that group, even fewer will go on to feel conviction about, then desire for, the product. In the end, compared with the number of people aware of the product, the number of people who take action is usually quite small.

In the social media age, savvy marketers understand that audiences can receive negative brand information from a variety of sources. The above screenshot is a review for a restaurant from the popular website www .tripadvisor.com. The restaurant received both negative and positive reviews. Do you as a consumer place more value on the negative reviews over the positive reviews? Would these reviews influence your decision to eat at this establishment? How important are the comments and overall number of reviews to your decision?

Source: TripAdvisor LLC

The next task might be to develop *comprehension*—communicating enough information about the product so that some percentage of the aware group recognizes the product's purpose, image, or position, and perhaps some of its features.

Next, you need to communicate enough information to develop *conviction*—persuading a certain number of people to actually believe in the product's value. Once convinced, some people may be moved to *desire* the product. Finally, some percentage of those who desire the product will take *action*. They may request additional information, send in a coupon, visit a store, or actually buy the product.

The pyramid works in three dimensions: time, dollars, and people. Campaign results may take time, especially if the product is expensive or not purchased regularly. Over time, as a company continues communicating with prospects and customers, the number of people who become aware of the product increases. As more people comprehend the product, believe in it, and desire it, more take the final action of buying it.

Let's apply these principles to a hypothetical case. Suppose you are in charge of the new "Lightning Bug," a hybrid car built by Volkswagen. Your initial objectives for this fictional car might read as follows:

1. Within two years, communicate the existence of the Lightning Bug to half of the more than 500,000 people who annually buy foreign economy cars.
2. Inform two-thirds of this "aware" group that the Lightning Bug is a superior economy car with many design, safety, and environmentally friendly features; that it is a brand new nameplate backed with unmatched service, quality, and value; and that it is sold only through dedicated Volkswagen dealers.
3. Convince two-thirds of the "informed" group that the Lightning Bug is a high-quality car, reliable, economical, and fun to drive.
4. Stimulate desire within two-thirds of the "convinced" group for a test drive.
5. Motivate two-thirds of the "desire" group to visit a retailer for a test drive.

These IMC objectives are specific as to time and degree and are quantified. Theoretically, at the end of the first year, research could determine how many people are aware of the Lightning Bug, how many people understand the car's primary features, and so on, thus measuring the program's effectiveness. See how IMC objectives can help a marketer succeed in My IMC Campaign 8–B.

Volkswagen's campaign may accomplish the objectives of creating awareness, comprehension, conviction, desire, and action. But once the customer is in the store, it's the retailer's responsibility to close the sale with effective selling and service.

With the advent of integrated marketing communications, we can look at the pyramid in another way. By using a variety of marketing communication tools and a wide menu of traditional and nontraditional media, we can accomplish the communication objectives suggested by the pyramid in a more efficient manner. For instance, for creating awareness of the new Lightning Bug as well as a brand image for the car and the company, public relations activities supported by mass media advertising might be the communication tools of choice. Comprehension, interest, and credibility can be augmented by media advertising, press publicity, direct-mail brochures, and special events such as a sports car show. Desire can be enhanced by a combination of the buzz created by good reviews in car enthusiast magazines, plus media advertising, beautiful brochure photography, and the excitement generated by a sales promotion (such as a sweepstakes). Finally, action can be stimulated by direct-mail solicitation, sales promotion, and the attentive service of a retail salesperson in an attractive new car showroom. Following the sale, direct mail could continue to reinforce the purchase decision. Calls from the retailer can be used to thank the customer, solicit feedback on that customer's experience, and offer assistance. This acknowledges that the sale was just the beginning of a valuable relationship. In fact, to maintain and deepen the relationship between marketer and customer, new buyers might be asked to like the Lightning Bug's Facebook page, be encouraged to follow the brand on Twitter, and receive a Groupon discount for buying "Bug" accessories at the

My IMC Campaign 8-B

Developing IMC Objectives

For the next big sets of decisions you will make, both media and creative, it will be essential that you specify what advertising and other promotions should *do*. Use the checklist below to focus your thinking on your objectives.

Does the message aim at immediate sales? If so, objectives might be

_____ Perform the complete selling function.

_____ Close sales to prospects already partly sold.

_____ Announce a special reason for buying now (price, premium, and so forth).

_____ Remind people to buy.

_____ Tie in with special buying event.

_____ Stimulate impulse sales.

Does the message aim at near-term sales? If so, objectives might be

_____ Create awareness.

_____ Enhance brand image.

_____ Implant information or attitude.

_____ Combat or offset competitive claims.

_____ Correct false impressions, misinformation.

_____ Build familiarity and easy recognition.

Does the message aim at building a "long-range consumer franchise"? If so, objectives might be

_____ Build confidence in company and brand.

_____ Build customer demand.

_____ Select preferred distributors and dealers.

_____ Secure universal distribution.

_____ Establish a "reputation platform" for launching new brands or product lines.

_____ Establish brand recognition and acceptance.

Does the message aim at helping to increase sales? If so, objectives would be

_____ Hold present customers.

_____ Convert other users to advertiser's brand.

_____ Cause people to specify advertiser's brand.

_____ Convert nonusers to users.

_____ Make steady customers out of occasional ones.

_____ Suggest new uses.

_____ Persuade customers to buy larger sizes or multiple units.

_____ Remind users to buy.

_____ Encourage greater frequency or quantity of use.

Does the message aim at some specific step that leads to a sale? If so, objectives might be

_____ Persuade prospect to write for descriptive literature, return a coupon, enter a contest.

_____ Persuade prospect to visit a showroom, ask for a demonstration.

_____ Induce sampling (trial offer).

How important are supplementary benefits of message? Objectives would be

_____ Help salespeople open new accounts.

_____ Help salespeople get larger orders from wholesalers and retailers.

_____ Help salespeople get preferred display space.

_____ Give salespeople an entrée.

_____ Build morale of sales force.

_____ Impress the trade.

Should the message impart information needed to consummate sales and build customer satisfaction? If so, objectives may be to use

_____ "Where to buy it" messages.

_____ "How to use it" messages.

_____ New models, features, package.

_____ New prices.

_____ Special terms, trade-in offers, and so forth.

_____ New policies (such as guarantees).

Should the message build confidence and goodwill for the corporation? Targets may include

_____ Customers and potential customers.

_____ The trade (distributors, dealers, retail people).

_____ Employees and potential employees.

_____ The financial community.

_____ The public at large.

What kind of images does the company wish to build?

_____ Product quality, dependability.

_____ Service.

_____ Family resemblance of diversified products.

_____ Corporate citizenship.

_____ Growth, progressiveness, technical leadership.

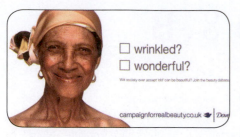

□ wrinkled?
□ wonderful?

Will society ever accept 'old' can be beautiful? Join the beauty debate.

campaignforrealbeauty.co.uk ☜ Dove

Not every message follows the learn–feel–do approach. This ad for Dove invites readers to feel–learn–do through challenging conventional standards of beauty.

Source: Unilever

Exhibit 8-6
Messages go to the customer through advertising and other communication channels. Messages come back via direct response, surveys, and a purchase behavior database. The marketer's message can evolve based on this feedback.

IMC Strategy and the Creative Mix

company's store. Whereas the traditional advertising approach often terminated with a sale, the IMC approach treats the sale as part of the broader relationship between the customer and the brand.

Different Ways Consumers Learn about Brands

The IMC pyramid represents the *learn–feel–do* model of effects. That is, it assumes that people rationally consider a prospective purchase, and once they feel good about it, they act. The theory is that IMC affects attitude, and attitude leads to behavior. That may be true for certain expensive, high-involvement products that require a lot of consideration (buying a home or car, or choosing a college). But other purchases may follow a different pattern. For example, impulse purchases at the checkout counter may involve a *do–feel–learn* model, in which behavior leads to attitude (picking up a pack of gum or a magazine after every visit to the supermarket). Other purchases may follow some other pattern. Thus, there are many marketing considerations when objectives are being set, and they must be thought out carefully.

The pyramid also reflects the traditional mass marketing monologue. The marketer talks and the customer listens.[28] That was appropriate before the advent of computers and databases, and it may still be appropriate in those categories where the marketer has little choice or does not expect a repeat purchase (as when a family has a garage sale or a shop at a vacation destination sells t-shirts).

But today, as the IMC model shows, many marketers have databases detailing where their customers live, what they buy, and what they like and dislike. When marketers can have a dialogue and establish a relationship, the model is no longer a pyramid but a circle (see Exhibit 8-6). Consumers and business customers can send messages back to the marketer in the form of coupons, phone calls, e-mail, social media posts, surveys, and database information on purchases. With interactive media, responses are in real time. This feedback can help the marketer's product, service, and messages evolve.[29] And reinforcement IMC, designed to build brand loyalty, will remind people of their successful experience with the product and suggest reuse.

By starting with the customer and then integrating all aspects of their marketing communications—package and store design, personal selling, advertising, public relations activities, special events, and sales promotions—companies hope to accelerate the communications process, make it more efficient, and achieve lasting loyalty from *good* prospects, not just prospects.[30]

The IMC *objective* declares what the marketer wants to achieve with respect to consumer awareness, attitude, and preference; the advertising (or creative) *strategy* describes how to get there.

IMC strategy blends the elements of the **creative mix:** *target audience, product concept, communications media,* and *advertising message.*

The Target Audience: Everyone Who Should Know

The **target audience,** the specific people the IMC will reach, is typically larger than the target market. Marketers need to know who the end user is, who makes the purchase, and who influences the purchasing decision. Children, for example, often exert a strong influence on where the family eats. So while McDonald's target market is adults, its target audience also includes children, and it spends much of its promotional budget on campaigns directed at kids.

Similarly, while companies may target heavy users of a product, many light users and nonusers are exposed to the campaign as well. That's good because research shows that brand popularity (which IMC is uniquely good at creating) cuts across all levels of purchasing frequency.[31] The dominant brands are purchased most by both heavy and light users (see Exhibit 8-7). It's the accumulation of all these sales that makes a product dominant.

Exhibit 8-7

Brand popularity. Dominant brands are the most popular at each level of purchasing frequency.

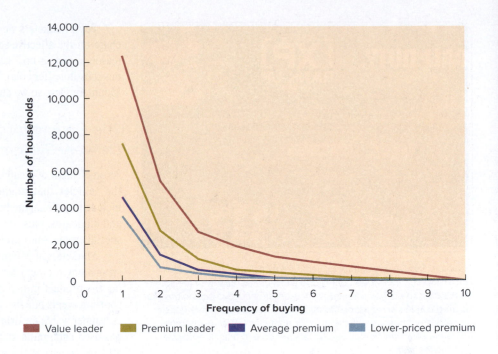

Value leader   Premium leader   Average premium   Lower-priced premium

The Product Concept: A "Bundle of Values"

The "bundle of values" the marketer presents to the consumer is the **product concept.** General Motors markets essentially the same truck to two different audiences but presents two different product concepts. The Silverado is marketed to the vast middle class with campaigns that stress its rugged, macho durability. Promotions for the Sierra, on the other hand, are aimed at white-collar professionals and emphasize the vehicle's snob appeal.[32]

When writing the IMC plan, the brand manager must develop a simple statement to describe the product concept—that is, how IMC will present the product. To create this statement, the company first considers how consumers perceive the product and then weighs this against the company's marketing strategy.

Recall from Chapter 5 our discussion of the Elaboration Likelihood Model and the role of involvement with the product message. Some years ago, Richard Vaughn at Foote, Cone & Belding noted that different kinds of products typically evoke different levels of consumer involvement (either high or low) and different types of involvement, either *cognitive* (think) or *affective* (feel). This means different products call for different kinds of advertising. He created a two-dimensional model known as the FCB grid, which categorized consumer products into four quadrants based on "high involvement" or "low involvement" and "think" or "feel." By positioning brands in the grid based on the degree and type of involvement consumers brought to the purchase decision, the agency could determine which type of advertising would be most appropriate. Rossiter and Percy extended this research with the grid you saw in Exhibit 5-3, which also suggested different creative executions.

More recently, academics Kim and Lord recognized that people can be both cognitively and affectively involved at the same time. So they developed the Kim-Lord grid, shown in Exhibit 8-8. It too depicts the degree and the kind of involvement a consumer brings to the purchase decision for different products. Some purchases, like cars, require a high degree of personal involvement on both the cognitive and affective levels.[33] For others, like detergent, involvement is low on both axes. Sometimes a marketer uses an advertising strategy aimed at shifting the product to higher involvement on either axis. A product's location on the grid also indicates how the product is purchased (learn-feel-do or feel-learn-do) and how campaign copy should be written (more emotional or more rational).[34]

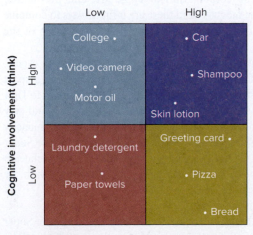

Exhibit 8-8

The Kim–Lord grid.

Mountain Dew excels at maintaining a relationship with its users. Understanding that video games and chips are popular with the soft drink's consumers helps Mountain Dew create effective campaigns. As illustrated in this screenshot, Mountain Dew and Doritos have done numerous promotions with the popular game Call of Duty, whereby Mountain Dew and Doritos purchasers are able to unlock exclusive perks in the game.

Source: Pepsi Cola Company

Pepsi marketers view Mountain Dew as a high-involvement purchase on the affective scale. "We continually need to give people a reason to pick us up," says one executive, "because we're not an obvious substitute [for cola]. People make a conscious choice to consume Mountain Dew, so we push to keep the positioning pure."[35]

The Communications Media: The Message Delivery System

As an element of creative strategy, the **communications media** are all the vehicles that might transmit the marketer's message. They include traditional media such as radio, TV, newspapers, magazines, and billboards, plus the Internet, direct marketing, public relations, special events, sales promotion, and personal selling.

Marketers at Mountain Dew use a variety of media to create a special environment for the product. This means not only promoting the product in mainstream media and sampling the product at sporting events but also creating the particular environment that the consumer wants for drinking the Dew. For example, Mountain Dew has used cars, radio stations, computer game demos, and extreme athletes as part of the experience. One summer, marketers decked out a subway car with "Do the Dew" memorabilia and hauled it around the country to major youth-oriented events where they passed out branded premiums such as snowboards, gear, and T-shirts—all relevant to the target market.

While balancing Dew on both ends of the grass-roots and mass-appeal spectrum, Pepsi marketers realize that not all teens are into alternative sports. The one-time hillbilly drink aggressively targets African American and Latino youth. Endorsement deals with hip-hop artists allow the Dew to appeal to the fast-growing ethnic market—which also coincides with the regional urban markets it targets.[36] "Mountain Dew is a brand whose core is inextricably linked to a pervasive human need for fun and exhilaration," says one executive. "That basic need has not changed over time, so we have to stick with that and be as current and leading edge as possible."[37]

The IMC Message: What the Campaigns Communicate

What the company plans to say and how it plans to say it, both verbally and nonverbally, make up the **IMC message.** As we discuss in Chapter 12, the combination of copy, art, and production elements forms the message, and there are infinite ways to combine these elements (see the Portfolio Review, "Strategic Use of the Creative Mix").

Dew personifies its product concept not only through events, but via a team of 10 extreme athletes, each representing a sport more daring than the next. That same attitude is passed on to Dew campaigns. With longtime agency BBDO helping the brand stay true to its youthful feel, its campaigns have an edginess and audacity that stand in stark contrast to the big cola brands. In one Super Bowl commercial, a Dew Dude on a bicycle chases down a cheetah and wrestles it to the ground. Reaching into the cat's mouth, he retrieves a stolen can of Dew.

"Bad cheetah," he says.

The ad was the second-highest rated commercial of the Super Bowl broadcast. In another highly rated spot, the Dew Dudes did a spoof version of the Queen classic "Bohemian Rhapsody." A third

Mountain Dew has a special relationship with consumers. Engaging them on Instagram is about more than exchanging messages. It is about sharing the brand with its most passionate users. Mountain Dew partnered with its fans in developing marketing messages and even a new flavor.

Source: Instagram/PepsiCo

Setting a brand apart from its competitors requires a marriage of creative thinking and imaginative creative ideas. This ad for the 2019 Ram 1500 departs from typical pickup truck executions featuring off-road driving and towing and instead features a deluxe interior more reminiscent of a luxury car. By emphasizing a less traditional approach, is Ram taking a risk? Does unique positioning like this warrant a greater investment? Which of the budgeting strategies we've discussed seems most useful for developing this Ram campaign?

Source: Fiat Chrysler Automobiles

popular commercial, called "Showstoppers," featured choreographed mountain bikes in a spectacular extravaganza reminiscent of a 1930s MGM musical, with the Dew Dudes playing the role of directors. According to *USA Today,* teenagers loved the spot. "Retro is in with teens," said Dawn Hudson, senior vice president of marketing for Pepsi. "We try to see things through the eyes of a teenager, and that's full of energy and exhilaration. Besides, the brand can't keep relying on skateboarding high jinks. Mountain Dew should always have a fresh perspective on things. It can't be cookie cutter."[38]

Ted Sann, the chief creative director at BBDO, says, "The idea is to evolve the campaign—take it to the next plateau."[39]

The sales numbers suggest it's working. Moreover, the campaign has long legs—"Do the Dew" is the longest-running continuous campaign in the soft drink category. Even so, Mountain Dew knows fresh creativity is the engine of its brand success, and it continues to evolve both its brand and its messages.

The Secret to Successful Planning

Whether the marketer is a large corporation or a small company, the key to successful planning is information. But the genius of business is in interpreting what the information means. This leads to direction, which makes planning easier and more rewarding.

IMC Budgeting Approaches

In early 2008, the United States and Canada experienced the first throes of what would prove to be the longest recession in modern history. Consumer confidence declined, real estate sales dropped, construction of new homes slowed, and unemployment began to rise. To make matters worse, turmoil in the Middle East led to higher fuel prices.

When sales drop, many executives cut back their marketing communication budgets, some to zero. Later, when the recession is over, these executives will wonder why sales are still down and how their companies lost so much market share.

Money is the motor that drives every marketing and IMC plan. If you suddenly shut off the motor, the car may coast for a while, but before long it will stop running. The marketing department has the tough job of convincing top management that communication spending makes good business sense, even during adverse economic conditions.

IMC: An Investment in Future Sales

Accountants and the Internal Revenue Service consider many promotional expenditures to be a current business expense. Consequently, executives treat IMC as a budget item to be trimmed like other expense items when sales drop. This is understandable but frequently shortsighted.

The cost of a new plant or distribution warehouse is an investment in the company's future ability to produce and distribute products. Similarly, IMC—as one element of the marketing mix—is an investment in a product or brand. While IMC is often used to stimulate immediate sales, its greatest power is in its cumulative, long-range, reinforcement effect.[40]

Campaigns build consumer preference and promote goodwill. This, in turn, enhances the reputation and value of the company name and brand. And it encourages customers to make repeat purchases.

So while IMC is a current expense for accounting purposes, it is also a long-term capital investment. For management to see IMC as an investment, however, it must understand how message campaigns relate to sales and profits.

The Relationship of IMC to Sales and Profits

Economists have long studied the relationship between the amount a company spends on advertising, traditionally one of the most important IMC elements, and subsequent increases or decreases in sales or profitability. Such analyses are imperfect, as they occur in the real world rather than inside a laboratory, and most conclusions have followed from

(continued on page 273)

Portfolio Review

:: Strategic Use of the Creative Mix

During the marketing and advertising planning process, companies need to carefully consider who their target markets are and then who should be the targets of their advertising. They also need to consider the other elements of advertising strategy. This brings up a lot of questions: What product concept are we trying to communicate; what various media will be used to communicate the message; and what should the nature of our advertising message be? Once these things are decided, the creative team can begin its work.

• The ads in this portfolio demonstrate some good creative thinking, but more important, some outstanding strategic thinking. See if you can determine which element or elements of the creative mix are emphasized in each ad.

IKEA's brand is simple and unpretentious. This ad draws on the same qualities and adds just a bit of humor to promote Valentine's Day shopping at the store.

Source: Inter IKEA Systems B.V.

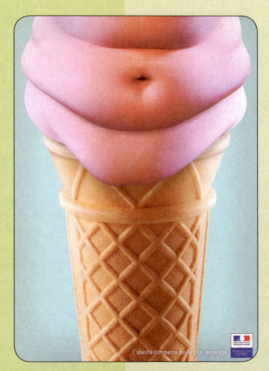

Good health follows from good habits, a point this ad from the French Ministry of Health notes in promoting healthy childhood nutrition. The copy translates as "obesity starts at a young age."

Source: Ministère des Affaires sociales et de la Santé

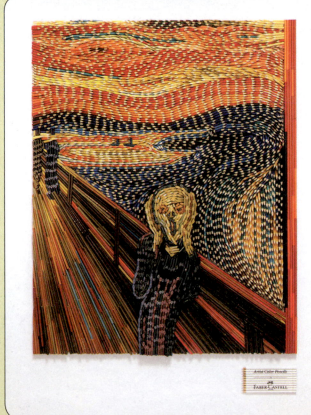

Achieving maximum impact in magazines requires bold, powerful images. Ads that occupy two adjacent pages really stand out. An unavoidable problem of this execution is the fold, which can diminish the beauty of an ad. Unless you are adidas, which uses the fold to heighten the creative appeal of these ads.

Source: Adidas America Inc.

A great use of advertising is to demonstrate the possibilities of even a simple product. Faber-Castell, maker of premium pencils, accomplishes that with this stunning reimagining of Edvard Munch's famous "The Scream."

Source: Faber-Castell USA, Inc.

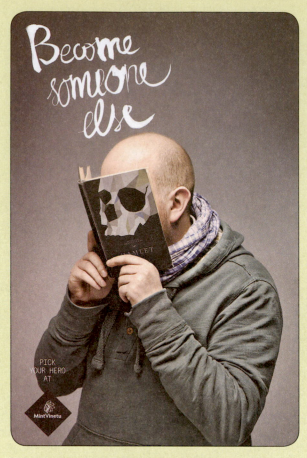

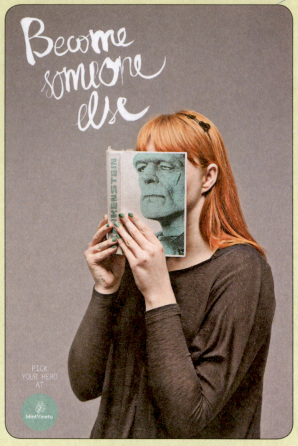

How can an advertiser show that books help you to "Become someone else" without using words? The answer is beautifully demonstrated in these ads for Mint Vinetu, a bookstore in Vilnius, Lithuania.

Source: Mint Vinetu

One way to make yourself an icon is to associate with other icons. Since these ads first appeared, Apple has clearly achieved iconic status. But when the Think Different campaign ran in the late 1990s, it had yet to introduce many technologies we know today, including the iPod, iPhone, and iPad.

Source: Apple, Inc.

(continued from page 269)

Why are popular console games the perfect pairing for Dew? And, properly executed, how might this pairing convince consumers to buy more Dew, thereby increasing sales, and value the brand over its competitors, thereby increasing profits?

Source: PepsiCo

the study of advertising rather than IMC more broadly considered. However, substantial research does support the following principles:

- In consumer goods marketing, increases in market share are closely related to increases in the marketing budget. And market share is a prime indicator of profitability.[41]

- Sales normally increase with additional advertising. At some point, however, the rate of return plateaus and then declines. (See Ad Lab 8–B, "The Economic Effect of Advertising on Sales.")

- Sales response to advertising may build over time, but the durability of advertising is brief, so a consistent investment is important.

- Advertising expenditures below certain minimum levels have no effect on sales.

- Some sales will occur even if there is no advertising.

- Culture and competition impose saturation limits above which no amount of advertising can increase sales.

To management, these facts might say, spend more until it stops working. In reality, the issue isn't that simple. IMC isn't the only marketing activity that affects sales. A change in market share may occur because of quality perceptions, word of mouth, the introduction of new products, competitive trade promotion, the opening of more attractive outlets, better personal selling, seasonal changes in the business cycle, or shifts in consumer preferences.

In 2019, Payless Shoes, Gymboree, and Kona Grill all filed for bankruptcy. These filings followed declines of other famous brands, such as Toys R Us, Brookstone, Sears, and Rockport. Simply increasing expenditures on IMC would not have prevented their declines. While each proved successful for a while, capitalism's ruthless edict requires that companies meet consumer needs and wants, or perish.

One thing remains clear. Because the response to promotional messages is spread out over time, IMC should be viewed as a long-term investment in future profits. Like all expenditures, campaigns should be evaluated for wastefulness. But historically, companies that make IMC the scapegoat during tough times end up losing substantial market share before the economy starts growing again.[42]

The corollary is also true. Sustained spending during difficult times protects, and in some cases even increases, market share and builds brands. During a previous global recession, the leading European marketers recognized this fact, and fewer than 40 percent of the top spenders in Italy, Austria, Germany, France, and Spain cut their budgets.[43]

The Variable Environments of Business

Before attempting to determine IMC allocations, the brand manager must consider the company's economic, political, social, and legal situations. These factors affect total industry sales and corporate profits on sales. The manager must consider the institutional and competitive environments. What is the level of sales within the industry? How much are competitors spending, and what are they doing that might either help or hinder the company's marketing efforts?

Finally, the manager must consider the internal environment. Do the company's current policies and procedures allow it to fulfill the promises its campaign intends to make?

Developing an IMC Budget

Most business executives will spend more on IMC as long as they are assured it will mean more profit. However, the point of equilibrium is hard to predict when budgets are being developed.

Companies use a number of methods to determine how much to spend on IMC, including the *percentage of sales, percentage of profit, unit of sale, competitive parity, share of market,* and *objective/task methods* (see My Ad Campaign 8–C, "Ways to Set IMC Budgets").

AD Lab 8–B

The Economic Effect of Advertising on Sales

As a rule, the level of sales of a product is proportional to the level of advertising expenditure—that is, within reasonable limits, the more you spend, the more you sell (assuming the advertising program is not too repugnant). Yet, even the most enthusiastic ad agency will admit, reluctantly, that it is possible to spend too much.

Ideally, managers would like to know how much more they will be able to sell per additional dollar of advertising and when additional advertising dollars cease being effective. They need to have not a fixed number representing potential demand, but a graph or a statistical equation describing the relationship between sales and advertising.

In our illustration, most of the curve goes uphill as we move to the right (it has a *positive* slope). This means that additional advertising will continue to bring in business until (at a budget of *x* million dollars) people become so saturated by the message that it begins to repel them and turn them away from the product.

Even if the saturation level cannot be reached within the range of outlays the firm can afford, the curve is likely to level off, becoming flatter and flatter as the amount spent on advertising gets larger and larger and saturation is approached. The point at which the curve begins to flatten is the point at which returns from advertising begin to diminish. When the total advertising budget is

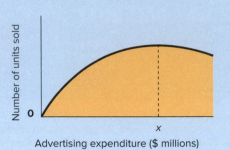

small, even a $1 addition to the campaign may bring in as much as $10 in new sales. But when the market approaches saturation, each additional dollar may contribute only 30 cents in new sales, if anything at all.

Laboratory Application

1. When would an advertising expenditure curve have a negative slope?

2. Economists suggest that the quantity sold depends on the number of dollars the company spends on advertising. Is that a safe assumption? Discuss.

No technique is adequate for all situations. The methods discussed here are used primarily for national advertising budgets. However, local retailers can use them too.

Percentage of Sales Method

The **percentage of sales method** is one of the most popular techniques for setting promotional budgets. It may be based on a percentage of last year's sales, anticipated sales for next year, or a combination of the two. Businesspeople like this method because it is simple, it doesn't cost them anything, it is related to revenue, and it is considered safe. The problem is knowing what percentage to use. As Exhibit 8-9 shows, marketing spending can vary considerably across industries. In the categories listed below, promotional expenditures range from just 2.4 percent of sales to nearly 19 percent. Looking over the exhibit, what factors do you think lead to a higher or lower amount for spending as a percentage of sales?

Usually the percentage is based on an industry average or on company experience. Unfortunately, it is too often determined arbitrarily. An industry average assumes that every company in the industry has similar objectives and faces the same marketing problems. Company experience assumes that the market is highly static, which is rarely the case.

However, when applied against anticipated future sales, this method often works well. It assumes that a certain number of dollars will be needed to sell a certain number of units. If the company knows what the percentage is, the correlation between IMC spending and sales should remain constant, assuming the market is stable and competitors' spending remains unchanged. And because this method is common in the industry, it diminishes the likelihood of competitive warfare.

A big shortcoming of the percentage of sales method is that it violates a basic marketing principle. Marketing activities are supposed to *stimulate* demand and, thus, sales, not occur as a *result* of sales. If IMC automatically increases when sales increase and declines when sales decline, it ignores all other factors that might encourage an opposite move.

My IMC Campaign 8-C
Ways to Set IMC Budgets

How much should you recommend that your client spend on promotions? Here is a list of ways companies set their marketing budgets.

- **Percentage of sales.** Budget is determined by allocating a percentage of last year's sales, anticipated sales for next year, or a combination of the two. The percentage is usually based on an industry average, company experience, or an arbitrary figure.

- **Percentage of profit.** Percentage is applied to profit, either past years' or anticipated.

- **Unit of sale.** Also called the *case-rate method*. A specific dollar amount is set for each box, case, barrel, or carton produced. Used primarily in assessing members of horizontal co-ops or trade associations.

- **Competitive parity.** Also called the *self-defense method*. Allocates dollars according to the amounts spent by major competitors.

- **Share of market/share of voice.** Allocates dollars by maintaining a percentage share of total industry spending comparable to or somewhat ahead of desired share of market. Often used for new product introductions.

- **Objective/task.** Also referred to as the *budget buildup method*, this method has three steps: defining objectives, determining strategy, and estimating the cost to execute that strategy.

- **Empirical research.** Companies determine the most efficient level by running experimental tests in different markets with different budgets.

- **Quantitative mathematical models.** Computer-based programs developed by major advertisers and agencies rely on input of sophisticated data, history, and assumptions.

- **All available funds.** Go-for-broke technique generally used by small firms with limited capital, trying to introduce new products or services.

The percentage of sales method also ignores the strategic nature of marketing. Rather than encouraging planners to think carefully about the proper budget for accomplishing objectives, it forces them to develop objectives that fit the budget. This means planners often miss opportunities for building brand equity or long-term relationships with consumers.

Share of Market/Share of Voice Method

In markets with similar products, a strong relationship usually exists between a company's share of the market and its share of industry IMC.

The **share of market/share of voice method** is an attempt to link promotional dollars with sales objectives.[44] It holds that a company's best chance of maintaining its share of a market is to keep a share of IMC (voice) somewhat ahead of its market share. For example, a

Exhibit 8-9
Marketing expenditures as a percent of company revenues by industry. The numbers vary considerably, such that a consumer services company with revenues of $1 million will, on average, spend almost $190,000, while a manufacturing company earning the same amount would spend just $24,000.

Rank	Industry	Marketing Spending as a Percentage of Sales
1	Consumer Services	18.9%
2	Education	12.0
3	Tech/Software/Biotech	9.7
4	Banking/Finance/Insurance	9.2
5	Consumer Package Goods	9.1
6	Communications/Media	9.0
6	Healthcare	9.0
8	Transportation	8.5
9	Energy	8.3
10	Service/Consulting	7.5
11	Retail/Wholesale	4.4
12	Mining/Construction	3.0
13	Manufacturing	2.4

Source: Deloitte, "The CMO Survey: The Latest Results and Insights: What's on the Mind of Marketing Leaders?" 2018, https://cmo.deloitte.com/xc/en/pages/articles/cmo-survey.html; The CMO Survey, Highlights and Insights Report, August 2018.

People **BEHIND** the Ads

Samantha Avivi, Brand Strategist at Jim Stengel Company

Courtesy of Samantha Avivi

As the daughter of advertising giant Stan Harris, Samantha Avivi had IMC in her blood from the start. After earning an advertising degree from the University of Florida, Sam spent two years learning her craft at her dad's agency before joining Young & Rubicam, where she handled accounts with Advil and Fisher Price. Next came stints with DMB&B and BBDO before her biggest client, Procter & Gamble, convinced Sam to jump ship and become an assistant brand manager for Luvs. Next came a stint as Global Marketing Director at Kimberly-Clark, before joining marketing consultancy Jim Stengel Company, where she works as a brand strategist. We had a chance to catch up with Samantha when she was honored as an alumna of distinction at UF.

CA: Tell us about your professional journey

SA: I have a passion for building businesses through consumer-led, purpose-driven brands. This was fueled from over 20 years of client, agency, and retail experience with some of the world's largest companies, including Procter & Gamble, Kimberly Clark, Wal-Mart, BBDO and Y&R. I've led iconic brands such as M&M's, Pampers, Head and Shoulders, Fisher Price, and ADT. As a consultant I've advised brands in categories that include automotive, business & professional services, consumer packaged goods, energy & utilities, entertainment and sports, food and beverage, heath care, media, nonprofits, and pharmaceuticals. I love developing talent and inspiring others to the possibility of revolutionary brand building.

CA: What do you look for in students who would like to be you someday?

SA: I look for students who are smart, demonstrate leadership ability, and have the right attitude. A good GPA is important, but I know someone is a smart thinker when they prove they can gather and synthesize data to drive sound conclusions. Proven leadership ability is also important. Even at the beginning of someone's career he/she will need to lead projects and people. Finally, the right attitude sets someone apart from their peers. I look for someone with passion and commitment to their work.

CA: How do large companies think about their consumers, brands, and communications objectives?

SA: A good example is Kimberly-Clark. The company places the consumer at the center of everything it does. They prioritize all work to meet the needs of our consumers around the world. This is clearly evident in the vision, "Leading the World in Essentials for a Better Life."

Each of the company's brands, including Kleenex, Huggies, and Kotex, represent a promise to the consumer. Communications are also critical at Kimberly-Clark. This function of marketing is to help connect, engage, influence, and inspire consumers.

The ad above shows a digital ad for the online master's program in the University of Florida's College of Journalism and Communication. Industry spending is relatively high among educational institutions, as shown in Exhibit 8.9.

Source: University of Florida

company with a 30 percent share of the market should spend 35 percent of the industry's promotional dollars.

The share of market/share of voice method is commonly used for new product introductions.[45] According to this formula, when a new brand is introduced, the budget for the first two years should be about one and a half times the brand's targeted share of the market in two years. This means that if the company's two-year sales goal is 10 percent of the market, it should spend about 15 percent of promotional spending during the first two years. The company's share of all promotional spending is what is meant by "share of voice."

To see how this method works, consider three leading American car producers: GM, Ford, and DaimlerChrysler. The domestic market, based on sales of the big three, is about $290 billion. DaimlerChrysler, with almost $80 billion in sales, had roughly 27.6 percent of U.S. auto company sales. What was advertising share of voice? It turns out that DaimlerChrysler spent nearly $1.9 billion on advertising, which was only about 24 percent of U.S. automaker expenditures. To grow its market share, a larger share of voice may have been required.

The right communications is at the heart of all our marketing activities.

CA: What have been the biggest changes you've seen over the past 10 years in brand promotions?

SA: The lines between brand promotions and "equity building" advertising have been blurred. It's all about building the business now and, as such, brands need to build their equity while driving immediate revenue.

CA: What value do you see in newer forms of media (social media, search, etc.) as compared to traditional forms?

SA: Social media has so much benefit. For one, it is a way to develop a two-way relationship with our consumers. Consumers now have the upper hand to tell manufacturers and their closest friends (the entire world on the internet) what they think of our products. Companies that create great products and have strong brands will disproportionately win in those types of situations. Another benefit of social media is it provides a way to do low-cost research. Consumers want to give us their opinion. We need to find a way to productively use their input.

CA: How important are benchmarks for brands, and what are some of the most important ones? Do you have different benchmarks for evaluating the performance of social as compared with traditional media?

SA: Benchmarks are critical to evaluate in-market potential. It helps in many aspects of my job, including evaluation of product performance; commercial effectiveness; ROI; consumer attitudes, habits, and practices; and most quantitative research. We haven't been able to use historical benchmarks on social media because it's so new. I have backed into the benchmarks for this medium by tying it back to our overall goals for an initiative.

CA: What does IMC mean to you and how does that affect KC's relationships with its agencies?

SA: Integrated Marketing Communications means that all agencies work with a common big creative idea that can drive business results. It does not mean that creative work is identical.

CA: You've been on both sides of the agency–client divide. What stands out about the differences and/or similarities of those experiences?

SA: Both sides are looking to build the business. Everyone feels ownership, love, and responsibility for the brand. Both have a deep understanding of the consumer. The difference is in the approach. The agency uses creative solutions, while the client focuses more on analytics and data. The agency goes deep on one component, the communication. The client has a wider scope of responsibility that covers the entire brand experience.

CA: What excites you about your career over the next five years?

SA: It's funny. The same thing excites me now as what excited me when I started my career. Over the next five years I'm excited to better understand and meet the needs of consumers. In the past, I've overheard people talking about work I've executed and how it's made a difference in their life. There's nothing more rewarding than to know that you were part of that effort. I hope to have more experiences like that in the next five years.

CA: Anything else you'd like to comment on or that would be helpful to advertising and IMC students?

SA: My advice is to identify your passion and not give up. Careers have ups and downs. It takes twists and turns. What's most important is to learn from all experiences. Take chances that support your passion and work hard to make the most of each experience.

Courtesy of Samantha Avivi.

An IMC focus helps to remind us that advertising is just one component of IMC, and for some marketers, not the most important one. The top national packaged-goods marketers spend 25 to 30 percent of their marketing budgets on consumer and trade promotion rather than consumer advertising.[46] That's how they get more shelf space in the store. And in certain packaged-goods categories, in-store trade promotions may generate 25 percent of a brand's short-term volume, while advertising may be responsible for only 5 percent.[47]

Strategic Budgeting: Objective/Task Method

The **objective/task method,** also known as the *budget buildup method,* is used by many large national marketers in the United States. It treats IMC as a marketing tool for generating sales.

The task method has three steps: defining objectives, determining strategy, and estimating cost. After setting specific, quantitative communication objectives, the company develops programs to attain them. If the objective is to increase awareness of Mountain Dew Code Red by 40 percent, PepsiCo determines which campaign approach will work best, how often messages must run, and which media to use. The estimated cost of the program becomes the basis for the budget. Of course, the company's financial position is always a consideration. If the cost is too high, objectives may have to be scaled back.

If results are better or worse than anticipated after the campaign runs, the next budget may need revision.

The task method forces companies to think in terms of accomplishing goals. Its effectiveness is most apparent when campaign results can be readily measured. The task method is adaptable to changing market conditions and can be easily revised.

However, it is often difficult to determine in advance the amount of money needed to reach a specific goal. Techniques for measuring campaign effectiveness still have many weaknesses.

Additional Methods

Advertisers also use several other methods to allocate funds. In the **empirical research method,** a company runs a series of tests in different markets with different budgets to determine the best level of advertising expenditure.

Computers can generate quantitative mathematical models for budgeting and allocating promotional dollars. Many sophisticated techniques facilitate marketing planning, budget allocation, new product introductions, and media and promotion analysis. However, most are not easily understood by line executives, and all rely on data that may be unavailable or estimated. These methods require very sophisticated users and, for the most part, are still too expensive for the average small business.

The Bottom Line   Unfortunately, all these methods rely on one of two fallacies. The first is that IMC is a *result* of sales. Marketers know this is not true, yet they continue to use the percentage of sales method.

The second fallacy is that IMC *creates* sales. In certain circumstances (where direct-response messages are used), advertising closes the sale. But a campaign's real role is to reinforce current customers, locate new prospects, position the product competitively, build brand equity, and stimulate demand. It may even stimulate inquiries and product trial and, on the local level, build retail traffic.

But the principal job of IMC is to influence consumers by informing, persuading, and reminding. IMC *affects* sales, but it is just one of many influences on consumers. Brand managers must keep this in mind when preparing their plans and budgets.

Chapter Summary

The marketing plan may be the most important document a company possesses. It assembles all the pertinent and current facts about a company, the markets it serves, its products, and its competition. It sets specific goals and objectives and describes the precise strategies to use to achieve them. It musters the company's forces for the marketing battlefield and, in so doing, dictates the role of IMC in the marketing mix and provides focus for IMC creativity.

There are three types of marketing planning models: top-down, bottom-up, and integrated marketing communications planning.

The top-down marketing plan contains four principal sections: situation analysis, marketing objectives, marketing strategy, and tactics (action programs). A company's marketing objectives should be logical deductions from an analysis of its current situation, its prediction of future trends, and its understanding of corporate objectives. They should relate to the needs of specific target markets and specify sales objectives. Sales-target objectives should be specific, quantitative, and realistic.

The first step in developing a marketing strategy is to select the target market. The second step is to determine the product's positioning. The third step is to construct a cost-effective marketing mix for each target market the company pursues. The marketing mix is determined by how the company blends the elements it controls: product, price, distribution, and communications. IMC is a communications tool.

One way for small companies to construct the marketing and IMC plan is to work from the bottom up, taking an ingenious tactic and building a strategy around it.

Integrated marketing communications can help build long-term relationships with customers. IMC planning is driven by technology. Thanks to computers and databases, marketers can learn more about their customers' wants and needs, likes and dislikes.

IMC is a natural outgrowth of the marketing plan, and the IMC plan is prepared in much the same way as the top-down marketing plan. It includes a SWOT (strengths, weaknesses, opportunities, and threats) analysis, advertising objectives, and strategy.

IMC objectives may be expressed in terms of moving prospective customers up through the IMC pyramid (awareness, comprehension, conviction, desire, action). Or they may be expressed in terms of generating inquiries, coupon response, or attitude change.

The IMC (or creative) strategy is determined by the marketer's use of the creative mix. The creative mix is composed of the target audience, product concept, communications media, and the message. The target audience includes the specific groups of people IMC will address. The product concept refers to the bundle of product-related values the company presents to the customer. The communications media are the vehicles used to transmit the marketer's message. The message is what the company plans to say and how it plans to say it.

Several methods are used to allocate advertising funds. The most popular are the percentage of sales approach and the objective/task method. The share of market/share of voice method is often used in markets with similar products.

Important Terms

bottom-up marketing, *257*

communication objectives, *253*

communications media, *268*

creative mix, *266*

DAGMAR, *253*

empirical research method, *278*

IMC message, *268*

IMC plan, *263*

IMC strategy, *266*

marketing objectives, *251*

marketing plan, *250*

marketing strategy, *254*

mission statement, *250*

objective/task method, *277*

percentage of sales method, *274*

product concept, *267*

sales-target objectives, *251*

share of market/share of voice method, *275*

situation analysis, *251*

subliminal advertising, *258*

SWOT analysis, *251*

tactics, *257*

target audience, *266*

Review Questions

1. What is a marketing plan, and why is it a company's most important document?

2. What examples illustrate the difference between need-satisfying objectives and sales-target objectives?

3. What are the three types of marketing plans? How do they differ?

4. What basic elements should be included in a top-down marketing plan?

5. How can small companies use bottom-up marketing to become big companies?

6. What are the elements of an advertising plan and an IMC strategy?

7. What types of involvement do consumers bring to the purchase decision?

8. What is the best method of allocating advertising funds for a real estate development? Why?

9. What types of companies tend to use the percentage of sales method? Why?

10. How could a packaged-foods manufacturer use the share of market/share of voice method to determine its advertising budget?

The Advertising Experience

1. **The Importance of Planning**

   Why is planning so important for the success of brand messages? How did planning help Mountain Dew to evolve not only its ads and other promotional activities, but its core identity?

2. **Strategic IMC Planning**

   You have explored various means of planning advertising strategy—top-down, bottom-up, and IMC. Browse through the websites of the following marketers, and then answer the questions regarding the various means of planning IMC strategy:

   - American Automobile Association (AAA): www.aaa.com
   - Bristol-Myers Squibb: www.bms.com
   - ProFlowers: www.proflowers.com
   - Hudson Moving & Storage: www.moving-storage.com
   - Metro Goldwyn Mayer/UA: www.mgm.com
   - General Electric: www.ge.com

   - Hewlett-Packard: www.hp.com
   - Intel: www.intel.com
   - Kellogg's: www.kelloggs.com
   - Walt Disney: www.disney.com

   a. What are the size and scope of the company and its business? What is the company's purpose?

   b. Identify the target audience, product concept, communications media, and advertising message for each.

   c. What is the company's position within the industry? What is the type of communication used? Target market?

   d. Where does the company's product(s) fall within the Kim–Lord grid?

3. **Websites and IMC**

   IMC can involve many different elements, and a website can be an integral part of a company's marketing efforts. Discuss how the following three companies might make a site part of an overall IMC effort:

a.   The Green Threads clothing retailer described in Chapter 1.

b.   A medium-sized candy maker with some brands that are nearly 100 years old.

c.   A small company that publishes books, CDs, and DVDs for a motivational speaker who has just had her first big break with an appearance on *The Dr. Phil Show*.

4.   Mountain Dew has "owned" an association with extreme sports and youth since the early 1990s, and this strategy continues to be successful for the brand. What cultural or societal trends must the brand monitor in order to know how to communicate with its audience? Does its image also limit growth possibilities? If so, in what ways? How might it circumvent these limits?

5.   The University of Florida's Online graduate program in communications wants to determine its marketing budget for the coming year. UF has 20 percent of the market in online graduate education with overall revenues of $1 million for the current year. It expects revenues next year will be $1.5 million and wants to achieve 25 percent of the market by revenue. It's primary challenger is Acme University, which spends $2 million each year on marketing and has 25 percent of the market. Total spending on education marketing for all programs is $8 million. How much should UF spend on marketing using the following approaches? (Be sure to reference Exhibit 8.9 in this chapter.)

■   The percentage of current sales using industry averages.

■   Percentage of future sales using industry averages.

■   Share of voice (against Acme).

End Notes

1.   Updated promo sheet and letter from BBDO-NY, 1995.

2.   Theresa Howard, "Brand Builders: Being True to Dew," *Brandweek,* April 24, 2000, p. 28.

3.   Theresa Howard, "Brand Builders: Being True to Dew," *Brandweek,* April 24, 2000, p. 30.

4.   Theresa Howard, "Brand Builders: Being True to Dew," *Brandweek,* April 24, 2000, p. 30.

5.   Christopher Lawton, "PepsiCo's Mountain Dew Backs Film," *The Wall Street Journal,* September 12, 2005, p. B4.

6.   Jillian Berman, "Here's Why Mountain Dew Will Survive the Death of Soda," *Huffington Post,* January 26, 2015, *www .huffingtonpost.com/2015/01/26/mountain-dew-regions_n_ 6524382.html*.

7.   PepsiCo Inc., "Our Mission & Vision," 2011.

8.   Mathew DeBord, "Tesla's Newest Rival Has Highlighted a Big Problem That No One Is Talking About," *Business Insider,* March 29, 2018, *www.businessinsider.com/tesla-faces-a-problem-with-market-segmentation-2018-3*.

9.   Kate MacArthur and Hillary Chura, "Urban Youth," *Advertising Age,* September 4, 2000, pp. 16–17.

10.   Duane Stanford, "Mountain Dew Wants Some Street Cred," *Bloomberg Business,* April 26, 2012, *www.bloomberg.com/bw/ articles/2012-04-26/mountain-dew-wants-some-street-cred*.

11.   "U.S. Population: Most Used Brands of Bar Soap from 2011 to 2018," *Statista, www.statista.com/statistics/285772/brands-of-bar-soap-in-the-us-trend/*.

12.   Automation Marketing Strategies, "The Art of Market Position-ing," *Strategic Advantage Newsletter,* January 2000.

13.   Ernest Martin, "Target Marketing: Summary and Unit Learning Outcomes," Course Syllabus CADV 213.

14.   "What Is Blue Ocean Strategy?" *Blue Ocean, www. blueoceanstrategy.com/what-is-blue-ocean-strategy/*; W. Chan Kim and Renée Mauborgne, *Blue Ocean Strategy: How to Create Uncontested Market Space and Make the Competition Irrelevant,* Expanded ed. (Boston: Harvard Business Review Press, 2015).

15.   Carmine Gallo, "The 7 Innovation Secrets of Steve Jobs," *Forbes,* May 2, 2014, *www.forbes.com/sites/carminegallo/ 2014/05/02/the-7-innovation-secrets-of-steve-jobs/*.

16.   Greg Farrell, "Dew Poses Real Pepsi Challenge to Coke," *USA Today,* 2000, p. B2.

17.   PepsiCo Inc., "Positioning Strategy," 2019.

18.   Adapted from Al Ries and Jack Trout, *Bottom-Up Marketing* (New York: McGraw-Hill, 1989), p. 8.

19.   Forbes Chicago Business Council, "12 Marketing Strategies That Work for Small Businesses in Chicago," *Forbes,* May 23, 2018, *www.forbes.com/sites/forbeschicagocouncil/2018/05/23/ 12-marketing-strategies-that-work-for-small-businesses-in-chicago/ #35576bf1dcfb*.

20.   Don E. Schultz, "Integration Helps You Plan Communications from Outside-In," *Marketing News,* March 15, 1993, p. 12.

21.   Regis McKenna, "Marketing Is Everything," *Harvard Business Review,* January/February 1991, p. 65.

22.   Greg Petro, "Amazon's Acquisition of While Foods Is about Two Things: Data and Product," *Forbes,* August 2, 2017, *www.forbes.com/sites/gregpetro/2017/08/02/amazons-acquisition-of-whole-foods-is-about-two-things-data-and-product/#5138f0d9a808*.

23.   Don E. Schultz, Stanley I. Tannenbaum, and Robert F. Lauterborn, *Integrated Marketing Communications: Putting It Together & Making It Work* (Lincolnwood, IL: NTC Business Books, 1993), pp. 55–56.

24.   Paul Wang and Don E. Schultz, "Measuring the Return on Investment for Advertising and Other Forms of Marketing Communication, Using an Integrated Marketing Communications Planning Approach," paper presented at the annual conference of the Association for Education in Journalism and Mass Communication, Kansas City, August 13, 1993.

25.   Don E. Schultz, Stanley I. Tannenbaum, and Robert F. Lauterborn, *Integrated Marketing Communications: Putting It Together & Making It Work* (Lincolnwood, IL: NTC Business Books, 1993), p. 58.

26.   Wayne Henderson, "The IMC Scale: A Tool for Evaluating IMC Usage," *Integrated Marketing Communications Research Journal* 3, no. 1 (Spring 1997), pp. 11–17.

27.   Wayne Henderson, "The IMC Scale: A Tool for Evaluating IMC Usage," *Integrated Marketing Communications Research Journal* 3, no. 1 (Spring 1997), pp. 11–17 ; Cyndee Miller, "Everyone Loves 'IMC,' but . . . ," *Marketing News,* August 16, 1993, pp. 1, 6.

28.   Don E. Schultz and Paul Wang, "Real World Results," *Marketing Tools,* premier issue, May 1994, pp. 40–47.

29.   Don E. Schultz and Paul Wang, "Real World Results," *Marketing Tools,* premier issue, May 1994, pp. 40–47.

30.   Don E. Schultz, "Integrated Marketing Communications: A Competitive Weapon in Today's Marketplace," *Marketing Review,* July 1993, pp. 10–11, 29.

31. Ned Anschuetz, "Point of View: Building Brand Popularity: The Myth of Segmenting to Brand Success," *Journal of Advertising Research,* January/February 1997, pp. 63–66.

32. Sally Beatty, "Two GM Divisions Try to Create Different Images for Their Trucks," *The Wall Street Journal,* October 14, 1998, p. B8.

33. Chung K. Kim and Kenneth R. Lord, "A New FCB Grid and Its Strategic Implications for Advertising," *in Proceedings of the Annual Conference of the Administrative Sciences Association of Canada* (Marketing), ed. Tony Schellinck (Niagara Falls, Ontario: Administrative Sciences Association of Canada, 1991), pp. 51–60.

34. Johan C. Yssel and Mark W. Walchle, "Using the FCB Grid to Write Advertising Strategy," paper presented at the annual conference of the Association for Education in Journalism and Mass Communication, 1992.

35. Theresa Howard, "Brand Builders: Being True to Dew," *Brandweek,* April 24, 2000, p. 30.

36. Theresa Howard, "Brand Builders: Being True to Dew," *Brandweek,* April 24, 2000, p. 31; Kate MacArthur, "Mountain Dew: Dawn Hudson," *Advertising Age,* June 26, 2000, p. 27.

37. Theresa Howard, "Brand Builders: Being True to Dew," *Brandweek,* April 24, 2000, p. 31.

38. Greg Farrell, "Dew Poses Real Pepsi Challenge to Coke," *USA Today,* 2000, p. B2; Greg Farrell, "Star Search," *Adweek Eastern Edition,* 1993.

39. Greg Farrell, "Dew Poses Real Pepsi Challenge to Coke," *USA Today,* 2000, p. B2.

40. Gregg Ambach and Mike Hess, "Measuring Long-Term Effects in Marketing," *Marketing Research: A Magazine of Management and Applications* (American Marketing Association), Summer 2000, pp. 23–30.

41. Robert D. Buzzell and Frederick D. Wiersema, "Successful Share-Building Strategies," *Harvard Business Review,* January/February 1981, p. 135; Siva K. Balasubramanian and V. Kumar, "Analyzing Variations in Advertising and Promotional Expenditures: Key Correlates in Consumer, Industrial, and Service Markets," *Journal of Marketing,* April 1990, pp. 57–68.

42. Bernard Ryan Jr., *Advertising in a Recession: The Best Defense Is a Good Offense* (New York: American Association of Advertising Agencies, 1991), pp. 13–29; Priscilla C. Brown, "Surviving with a Splash," *Business Marketing,* January 1991, p. 14; Edmund O. Lawler, "A Window of Opportunity," *Business Marketing,* January 1991, p. 16; Rebecca Colwell Quarles, "Marketing Research Turns Recession into Business Opportunity," *Marketing News,* January 7, 1991, pp. 27, 29.

43. Fabiana Giacomotti, "European Marketers Keep Up Ad Budgets," *Adweek,* January 24, 1994, pp. 16–17.

44. Leo Bogart, *Strategy in Advertising,* 2nd ed. (Chicago: Crain Books, 1984), pp. 45–47.

45. John Philip Jones, "Ad Spending: Maintaining Market Share," *Harvard Business Review,* January/February 1990, pp. 38–42; James C. Schroer, "Ad Spending: Growing Market Share," *Harvard Business Review,* January/February 1990, pp. 44–49.

46. Peter Breen, "Seeds of Change," *Promo Sourcebook Supplement,* Copyright 2000, INTERTEC, p. 18, *www.global.lexisnexis.com/us*.

47. Gregg Ambach and Mike Hess, "Measuring Long-Term Effects in Marketing," *Marketing Research: A Magazine of Management and Applications* (American Marketing Association), Summer 2000, pp. 23–30.

9

Planning Media Strategy: Disseminating the Message

In collaboration with Jordan Alpert, University of Florida

LEARNING OBJECTIVES

To show how communications media help advertisers achieve marketing and advertising objectives. To get their messages to the right people in the right place at the right time, media planners follow the same procedures as marketing and advertising planners: setting objectives, formulating strategies, and devising tactics. To make sound decisions, media planners must possess marketing savvy, analytical skill, and creativity.

After studying this chapter, you will be able to:

LO9-1 Define media planning and indicate why it is important in advertising and IMC.

LO9-2 Explain the role of media in the marketing framework.

LO9-3 Describe how planners define media objectives.

LO9-4 Discuss how reach, frequency, and continuity are optimized in media planning.

LO9-5 Outline how media planners create a media strategy.

LO9-6 List the tactics that can be used to implement a media strategy.

LO9-7 Explain how computer technologies change media planning.

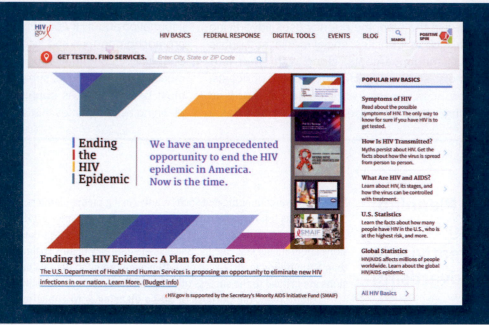

Source: U.S. Department of Health & Human Services

Media plans help companies identify vehicles that effectively deliver ads to desirable audiences. But they are equally important to nonprofits and government agencies that serve the public interest. One such agency is HIV.gov. As with any organization that relies on media to accomplish its communication goals, HIV.gov needs to identify who it should target and then how to get those audiences the right message at the right time. ■ The federal government's efforts to combat the devastation caused by HIV is a responsibility of many agencies, but the communications element is a primary responsibility of HIV.gov. HIV.gov formulates its media efforts around three critical objectives: (1) expand the visibility of timely and relevant federal HIV policies, programs, and resources to the public; (2) increase the use of new media tools by government, minority, and other community partners to extend the reach of HIV programs to at-risk communities; and (3) increase knowledge about HIV and access to HIV services for people at risk of HIV. ■ As with any organization trying to disseminate its message to the right audience at the right time, HIV.gov faces numerous communication challenges. Among these are determining what behaviors will make the greatest impact on stopping the spread of the disease. ■ HIV.gov determined that an underserved population is the

group of people who live with HIV.[1] When HIV-infected persons receive test results, they typically adopt healthy behaviors. However, with the passage of time, people sometimes revert to risky behaviors that put their own health and that of others at risk. As a result, HIV.gov determined that a prevention campaign should target individuals living with HIV and encourage them to make healthy choices. ■ Persons living with HIV/AIDS constitute one important target audience for HIV.gov, but they are not the only one. Other important audiences include infectious disease specialists, primary care providers who treat people with HIV, personnel at health centers and clinics that treat people with HIV, and medical students. Health care providers are particularly important because research suggests that they can influence people living with HIV to adopt behaviors that limit the spread of the disease.[2] ■ HIV awareness is high, but the disease has receded somewhat as a national and global priority following the development of newer and more effective treatments. Even so, the challenge of living with HIV is significant, as demonstrated in a video recorded by Janne (see www.youtube.com/watch?v=KBylQxZMEjE), a Finnish man with HIV who challenged strangers with the following sign: "I am HIV-positive—Touch me."[3] ■ To meet the challenge, HIV.gov requires a communication strategy. You can see its plan on page 285. As outlined in the plan, the agency uses advertising media such as websites, social media, and public service announcements, along with other IMC channels, such as conference calls, podcasts, conferences, press releases, and in-person meetings. Each of these channels in turn has a specific communications goal, such as providing information about HIV basics and federal resources, promoting partners, and listening, monitoring, and engaging.[4] Communication about the disease is crucial to preventing its spread; therefore, HIV.gov must be every bit as sophisticated about media planning as companies that sell consumer brands.

Media Planning: Integrating Science with Creativity in Advertising

LO 9-1

In today's overcommunicated society, advertising media planners need to be as analytically competent as top financial officers and as creative as senior art directors and copywriters. The emergence of digital media has placed greater focus on data analytics to drive decisions about media placements. Because most money in advertising is spent on media, more than $206 billion in 2017 with over 40 percent going to digital channels,[5] solid media decisions are critical to the success of the overall marketing communications plan.

Traditionally, the purpose of **media planning** is to conceive, analyze, and creatively select channels of communication that will direct advertising messages to the right people in the right place at the right time. However, as the media landscape continues to evolve, consumers have more control than ever about when, where, and how they view content. In fact, as we will see in this and several other chapters, consumers are often content creators.

Media planners approach campaigns knowing that the following issues must be carefully considered and articulated:

- Where should we advertise? (In what countries, states, or parts of town?)
- Which media vehicles should we use and why?
- When during the year should we amplify our advertising? When is it in our interests to cut back on advertising?
- How often should we run the advertising?
- What opportunities are there to integrate advertising with other communication opportunities?

Some of these decisions require data and detailed analysis, aided by sophisticated software programs. But understanding and interpreting what all the numbers really mean, and then designing and implementing a truly masterful media plan, demand human intelligence and creativity.[6]

The Challenge

Historically, the people who plan and buy media have enjoyed relative anonymity compared to the "stars" in the creative and account service departments.

Today the media planner's assignment is just as critical as the creative director's: One media planner can be responsible for millions of client dollars. The planner's work is focused on an agency's strategic ability to understand the target market and the most optimal time and place to communicate with it. Some agencies have gone so far as to integrate the strategic planning and media planning groups into one department, effectively giving media planners a seat at the creative strategy table.

The media department gained this new prominence in the late 1990s. Clients started taking an à la carte approach to agency services, and agencies began competing for media planning and buying assignments separately from the creative business.[7] By the early 2000s, media wins had become big news: Universal McCann won the $150 million Nestlé account, Gillette awarded its $600 million media account to Mindshare, and Kraft consolidated its $800 million media business at Starcom MediaVest Group.[8] More recently, Carat was awarded the $3 billion GM account and MediaVest won the $100 million Cox Communications account.[9]

/// COMMUNICATION TOOLS WE USE

Our primary focus is on tools and channels with the highest return on our investment and greatest insights into the needs of the HIV community. Our criteria for selecting these tools and channels are the following:

- has a large number critical mass of individuals from our target audience;
- responds to an expressed information need; and/or
- provides a significant opportunity to engage with our audiences.

We use some tools and channels on a secondary basis in order to communicate about selected, specific events, resources or campaigns.

COMMUNICATION CHANNEL	HOW WE USE IT					
	Provide information about HIV basics and federal resources	Highlight news and events	Share HIV/AIDS Awareness Day information	Provide training and technical assistance	Listen, monitor, and engage	Promote our partners
PRIMARY FOCUS/PRESENCE						
RESPONSIVE WEBSITE *www.hiv.gov*	✓	✓	✓	✓		✓
BLOG *http://positivespin.hiv.gov*	✓	✓	✓	✓	✓	✓
TWITTER *www.twitter.com/hivgov*	✓	✓	✓	✓	✓	✓
FACEBOOK *www.facebook.com/hivgov*	✓	✓	✓		✓	✓
YOUTUBE *www.youtube.com/hivgov*		✓	✓		✓	✓
PINTEREST *www.pinterest.com/AIDSgov*	✓	✓	✓		✓	✓
PODCASTS *www.hiv.gov/topics/podcasts*	✓	✓	✓			✓
HIV/AIDS PREVENTION & SERVICE PROVIDER LOCATOR *www.locator.hiv.gov*	✓					✓
CONFERENCES, TRAININGS, IN-PERSON MEETINGS	✓	✓	✓	✓	✓	✓
MEETINGS WITH FEDERAL & COMMUNITY PARTNERS	✓	✓	✓	✓	✓	✓
SECONDARY FOCUS/PRESENCE						
PRESS RELEASES/STATEMENTS	✓	✓	✓			✓
WEBINARS & CONFERENCE CALLS	✓	✓	✓	✓	✓	✓
INSTAGRAM *www.instagram.com/hivgov*	✓	✓	✓		✓	✓
PUBLIC SERVICE ANNOUNCEMENTS	✓	✓	✓			✓
FOURSQUARE *www.foursquare.com/AIDSgov*			✓		✓	✓
SLIDESHARE *www.slideshare.net/AIDSgov*	✓	✓	✓	✓	✓	✓
FLICKR *www.flickr.com/photos/AIDSgov*		✓	✓		✓	✓
STORIFY *www.storify.com/AIDSgov*		✓	✓		✓	✓
EMAIL NEWSLETTER	✓	✓	✓			✓

HIV.gov provides a clear plan for which channels it will use and what it hopes to achieve with each.

Source: U.S. Department of Health & Human Services

AD Lab 9–A

Buying Traditional Local Media

What is it like selecting media for a local ad campaign? You can find out by working through this lab exercise.

The Choices

For this lab, imagine you are working to select media on behalf of a small boot store in Amarillo, Texas, called Sole Solutions. Amarillo has a population about 200,000 people. You decide to focus on four local vehicles, the town's newspaper, radio station KRRR, TV station WGBC, and TV station WCAB. The client has budgeted $15,000 for your campaign.

Starting Point

As you think about this challenge, even before you dive into data considerations, what are the pros and cons of using the newspaper, radio, and television for your client? Would you eliminate any of these options before knowing something about their audiences and costs? Why or why not?

Total Audience for Each Vehicle

As noted before, Amarillo has about 200,000 total residents. You start your analysis by verifying the total audience for each of the options. You discover that the newspaper has 50,000 daily readers. Radio station KRRR has about 10,000 listeners during peak times. Finally, TV station WGBC has 30,000 viewers and TV station WCAB has 50,000 viewers on a typical day. Say you ran a campaign that involved placing a single ad in each vehicle (four ads total). From the information above, how many gross impressions would the campaign generate? How many gross impressions would you generate if your campaign instead involved running four ads only on TV station WGBC?

Target Audience for Each Vehicle

Not everyone who lives in Amarillo is in the Sole Solutions target market, which consists of men and women ages 21 to 45. In fact, the total number of Amarillo residents who fit that profile is 100,000

Table 9.1

Audiences for Amarillo, TX, Media Options

Audience	Amarillo Total	Newspaper	Radio KCGC	TV WGBC	TV WCAB
Total audience	200,000	50,000	10,000	30,000	50,000
Target audience	100,000	9,000	3,000	14,000	16,000

people. You do research to find out how many in each vehicle's audience fit are in your target market and discover the following: newspaper, 9,000; radio KCGC, 3,000; TV WGBC, 14,000; and TV WCAB, 16,000. See Table 9.1 for a summary of the audience data we've presented so far.

The total audiences of the newspaper and TV WCAB are the largest at 50,000 each. The vehicle with the largest number from the target audience is WCAB, with 16,000.

Costs

Running ads costs money, of course, so while audience size and composition are important, so is knowing how much an audience will cost if advertising in a particular vehicle. Newspapers charge on the basis of the print ad, with larger ads and the use of color costing more than smaller ads or black and white. The newspaper tells you that a full-page, four-color ad on a weekday will cost $1,000.

Broadcast stations, both TV and radio, price ads on the basis of the length of the ad (15-second, 30-second, etc.) and the size of the audience. The radio station charges $15 each time it runs a 30-second commercial. WGBC charges $700 and WCAB charges $1,000 for each 30-second spot. These figures are summarized in Table 9.2.

Frequency Considerations

You now have enough information to start thinking about how far your budget will go choosing among the different options. One

As the complexity of the field increases, media decisions become more critical and clients more demanding. Advertisers want agencies to be more than efficient: They want accountability and information, particularly about media options, and they want creative buys, such as those executed by AIDS.gov.

What makes media planning today so much more complicated and challenging than it was just a few years ago?

Increasing Media Options Increase Audience Fragmentation

With the spread of digital technologies and the natural maturation of the marketplace, many more vehicles are available, and each offers a dizzying array of possibilities for connecting

Table 9.2
Ad Costs for the Campaign

	Newspaper	Radio	TV WGBC	TV WCAB
Ad cost	$1,000	$15	$700	$1,000
Ad format	Full-page, full-color print	30-second commercial	30-second commercial	30-second commercial

way to start is to calculate how many ads you could buy, within budget, in each option if you only spent on that option. For example, if you only ran newspaper ads in the campaign, your budget of $15,000 would allow you to run a full-page color ad 15 times. You can figure this quickly by dividing your total budget ($15,000) by the cost generated each time you place an ad ($1,000). Knowing that, how many radio ads could you afford if you only used the radio station? How many TV ads could you run on WGBC? How many on WCAB?

Now consider the following: Your client tells you that you must run a minimum of two ads every day of the coming year, both weekdays and weekends. Does this information help to guide your selection? How?

Reach

Frequency is not the only consideration, or even always the most important consideration, in a campaign. Imagine that you learn that the target audience across your four options is rarely duplicated.

Table 9.3
Comparing the costs of the target audience across vehicles

Station	Ad Cost	Target Impressions	CPM?	Rating	CPRP
WGBC	$ 700	14,000	?	14	?
WCAB	1,000	16,000	?	16	?

In other words, the people who use any one of the options rarely use the others. If you wanted to emphasize reach in your campaign, how does that information guide your thinking?

Audience Cost

Now assume you've narrowed your focus to just the two TV stations. Both seem attractive, but your client wants to know the better value between the two. In other words, he wants to know which station delivers a target audience member for the lower amount of money.

Media experts make such comparisons using cost per thousand (CPM) and cost per rating point (CPRP) estimates. CPM is more common when evaluating print, and CPRP when considering broadcast options like radio and TV. But both calculations can be used if desired. Table 9.3 provides information you can use to generate a CPM and CPRP number for each of the two stations.

Calculate the target audience CPM and CPRP for the two stations. Which is more efficient (cheaper)? Use these formulas:

- CPM = (Ad cost/Impressions) × 1,000
- CPRP = Ad cost/Program rating

Interpreting your numbers: Smaller numbers are good here because it means the costs of a thousand impressions or a rating point are cheaper.

Laboratory Applications

1. After working through the exercise, which vehicle, or which combination of vehicles, would you recommend? Why?
2. Given the client you are working with, what day part should your client focus on with its ads? What day of the week? When do consumers make a decision about buying a boot? How could you find out?
3. What information that was not provided might you want to know to be sure you made the right decision?

with audiences. As we mentioned earlier, it wasn't long ago that major advertisers could ensure a big audience by simply advertising on TV. Not anymore. Even though consumers are spending more time with media than ever before—an average of over 11 hours daily[10]—it's much more difficult to reach a big audience today. Although media usage has grown as a result of the reliance on digital media, especially for young consumers, many consumers are overwhelmed by an overabundance of choices,[11] causing them to be less satisfied with their brand experiences, and leading to brand abandonment.[12]

TV is now fragmented into network, syndicated, spot, local, and OnDemand, as well as cable. Specialized magazines now aim at every possible population and business segment. Even national magazines publish editions for particular regions or demographic groups. For example, in early 2009 *Parent* magazine became three separate magazines to better appeal to its diverse and divergent audiences: *Baby Talk, Parent: The Preschool Years,* and *Parent: The*

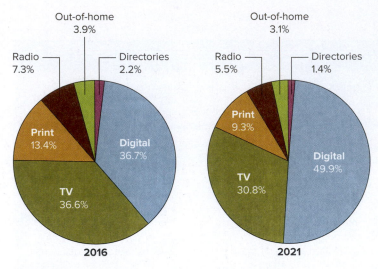

Exhibit 9-1

Percent of ad dollars allocated across media categories in the United States.

Source: "US Programmatic Ad Spending Forecast 2017," eMarketer.com

School Years. Finally, the incredible growth of the internet has brought with it a host of new media options. But it has also added to the complexity of media work as planners face the challenge of staying current with the constantly expanding technology and mastering a whole new lexicon of associated terminology (to experience the challenge of selecting media try Ad Lab 9–A). Exhibit 9-1 shows how spending across major categories of media has changed in the United States. The exhibit illustrates a trend that will continue into the future: the growth of spending on digital media at the expense of traditional media.

Nontraditional media—from DVD and movie advertising to interactive kiosks and even shopping carts—also expand the menu of choices. In addition, many companies spend a considerable portion of their marketing budgets on specialized communications like direct marketing, sales promotion, public relations activities, and personal selling, topics we'll discuss in the last two chapters. In fact, these "below-the-line" (noncommissionable) activities are the fastest-growing segments at some of the large agency holding companies, like WPP and Interpublic.[13]

For companies practicing integrated marketing communications, the "media menu" needs to include everything that carries a message to and/or from customers and other stakeholders. The proliferation of apps, mobile platforms, e-mail, websites, and social media choices makes it easy and cost-effective to generate customer feedback. The result is that advertisers can be very creative in designing systems for both sending and receiving messages. That means that companies and agencies need to think in terms of *message handling,* being as responsible for *receiving* messages as for sending them. Mark Goldstein, the president of integrated marketing at Fallon in Minneapolis, said, "Media is no longer planned and bought; instead it's created, aggregated, and partnered." As with other technology disruptions, those that challenge the practice of placing content efficiently and collaboratively have led some to question whether the traditional media planning agency is obsolete.[14]

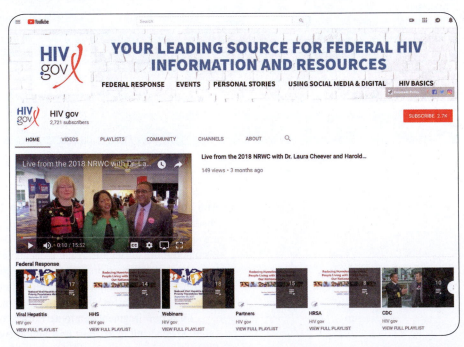

HIV.gov makes full use of a variety of platforms to ensure it reaches audiences effectively and often. Social media site YouTube is one such platform.

Source: YouTube/U.S. Department of Health & Human Services

Increasing Costs

At the same time that there are more media choices, the number of messages that need to be communicated has also proliferated—so much so, in fact, that they have outstripped the ability of consumers to process them. People can cope with only so many messages, so the media have to restrict the number of ads they sell. As a result, the cost of reaching target audiences is increasing.

In the last decade, the cost of exposing 1,000 people to each of the major media (called *cost per thousand*) rose faster than inflation. Television shows that can deliver a big audience are sold at a premium. A 30-second spot on *Sunday Night Football* costs over $700,000, while the rate for a 30-second spot during the Super Bowl is over $5 million. Rising costs make media planning more challenging than ever, especially for advertisers with small budgets. Clients want proof that planners are squeezing the most they can out of every media dollar.[15]

Increasing Complexity in Media Buying and Selling

As the process of buying media has become more complex, so has the process of selling media. This complexity is largely the result of the ever-changing media landscape. The world of media has converged as traditional media companies expand and acquire digital media companies. For instance, CBS Corporation owns hundreds of radio stations, cable networks including Showtime, book publisher Simon & Schuster, as well as their main broadcasting networks. In recent years, CBS has acquired digital properties, like the websites CNET and Metacritic. The media landscape is constantly consolidating, as the telecommunications company Verizon acquired Yahoo, and AT&T acquired both Time Warner and DirecTV. AT&T has 159 million wireless and 40 million pay-TV subscribers. Owning Time Warner will allow the telecommunications company to transform into a media company, delivering content from its publishers: TNT, TBS, CNN, and HBO. And AT&T can place ads across multiple platforms, including TV, mobile phones and other digital devices. The company can even bundle personal selling and sales promotion opportunities for its marketing clients because it has retail stores all across the United States. The lesson: the larger the media conglomerate, the greater the ability to earn advertising dollars by bundling content and IMC opportunities.

In the constant battle for additional sales, many media companies developed "value-added" programs to provide extra benefits. Besides selling space or time at rate-card prices or below, these companies now offer reprints, merchandising services, special sections, event sponsorships, and mailing lists. To get a bigger share of the advertiser's budget, larger media companies are bundling the various stations, publications, or properties they own and offering them in integrated combos as further incentives. The Discovery Networks, for example, which include the Travel Channel, TLC, Animal Planet, and Discovery, offer their advertisers "multiplatform content sponsorships." What this unwieldy name means is that each advertiser gets a major internet/TV sponsorship with four or five commercials in a special-event Discovery show and webcast. Specially created TV spots promote the program and the webcast, as well as Discovery's website and even the advertiser's website.

Television networks work with major sports associations and professional teams to develop integrated marketing "partnerships" for sports and event sponsors. General Motors and NBC, for example, raised the bar on Olympic sponsorships in 1997 with a 12-year,

Value-added packages are exemplified nicely in Wayfair's sponsorship of the reality show Brother vs. Brother, *appearing on HGTV. The company sells home products that include "looks" from the hit show.*

Source: Wayfair LLC

TV advertisers sometimes find it is better to weave their brands right into the shows rather than run traditional commercials. Popular television shows like America's Got Talent *and* Modern Family *offer advertisers unique opportunities to draw attention to their brands.*
NBC/Photofest

$600 million deal to make GM the official domestic car and truck of the U.S. Olympic Team. The NBC portion of the deal gave GM domestic category exclusivity and media placement for the network's coverage of the 2000, 2002, 2004, 2006, and 2008 Olympics. GM spent an estimated additional $300 million to leverage its Olympics involvement. As Phil Guarasco, GM's VP/general manager of marketing and advertising, said, "This isn't about dollars; it's about value. What we have here is a strong, cost-effective marketing initiative for the company."[16]

Value-added packages often employ communications vehicles outside traditional media planning, such as public relations activities, sales promotion, and direct marketing. *Brother vs. Brother,* a popular home renovation reality television show on the cable network HGTV, partnered with the home furnishing e-commerce website Wayfair. Episodes feature the siblings, who are licensed contractors, competing against one another to renovate and redesign rooms in houses. The brothers order items from Wayfair, showcasing its quick delivery and a wide selection of home decor. On its website, Wayfair features a special *Brother vs. Brother* section where consumers can view each room of the renovated house by episode and add items to their shopping cart. In another example, *The Next Iron Chef International* on the Food Network allowed product integration for the premier sponsor, Kikkoman, into the competition and also recorded one of the episodes on-site at Kikkoman headquarters in Japan. These types of integrations allow advertisers to gain associative value that basic advertising cannot accomplish. But placing a value on these deals is difficult because the nonmedia elements are hard to quantify.

The trend toward integrated marketing communications and relationship marketing is creating a new breed of media planner: younger, computer literate, and schooled in marketing disciplines beyond traditional media. The good media specialist today is actually a real advertising generalist. And with many of the biggest client changes happening in *media-only* agency reviews, it's apparent that the media professionals have finally come into their own.

Increasing Competition

The final element making media planning more challenging today is the competitive environment, which in just a few years completely changed the structure of the advertising business. In the early 1990s, as clients sought greater efficiency with their media dollars, independent media-buying services came to the fore, attracting some of the best and brightest talent in the business to compete with agencies for what was once their private domain. Initially, the independents bought advertising space and time at lower bulk rates and then sold it at a higher rate to advertisers or ad agencies that didn't have a fully staffed media department. As the media specialists grew, though, clients came to realize the virtues of scale, and financial clout emerged as a potent weapon in negotiating media buys.[17] By 1994, independents handled more than one-fourth of all national advertising media accounts.[18]

Modern audiences are exposed to a fragmented media landscape. In response, some advertisers have placed less emphasis on traditional advertising formats and instead used clever (and expensive) product placements. The example above shows Audi prominently featured in the smash hit movie Black Panther.
Source: Black Panther/Marvel Studios and Walt Disney Studios Motion Pictures

To respond to the competitive pressure, ad agencies started unbundling their own media departments, setting them up as separate subsidiaries. These companies could compete with the independents as well as with other agencies for media-only accounts. Over time, all these firms became quite expert at the media function. With the rapid increase in billings, they were able to pour a substantial amount of money into the development of new research tools, which was critical given the continued fragmentation of the mass media into smaller and smaller niches.

However, the rise of digital media has allowed companies, both big and small, to have greater control over their media spending. It is no longer necessary to partner with a media agency to purchase media placements because technology companies like Google and Facebook provide easy-to-use tools for selecting audiences and delivering advertisements. For instance, Google AdWords has the capability to display ads on over two million websites and in over 650,000 apps.[19] Therefore, anyone with a Google account can become a media planner! The interface makes it easy to identify a target audience and set a budget. Similarly, Facebook enables anyone with an account to place ads on Facebook.com that can reach 2 billion people every month and 500 million Instagram users every day.[20] Just like Google, data such as demographics, behaviors, and contact information can be easily accessed and reporting tools display results in an easy-to-use dashboard. Marketers can test different ads and determine which creative elements and placements deliver the best results.

The Role of Media in the Marketing Framework

LO 9-2

As we've discussed in previous chapters, the key to successful advertising is proper planning. Thus, before media planning begins—indeed, before advertising is even considered—companies must first establish their overall marketing and advertising plans for their products.

Marketing Objectives and Strategy

In Chapter 8 you read how the top-down marketing plan defines the market need and the company's sales objectives and details strategies for attaining those objectives. Exhibit 9-2 on page 294 shows how objectives and strategies result from the marketing situation (or SWOT) analysis, which defines the company's *strengths* and *weaknesses* and uncovers any marketplace *opportunities* and *threats.* Marketing objectives may focus on solving a problem ("regaining sales volume lost to major competitive introductions over the past year") or seizing an opportunity ("increasing share in the female buyer segment of the athletic-shoe market").

Marketing strategies lay out the steps for meeting these objectives by blending the four elements of the marketing mix. A company whose marketing objective is to increase sales of a particular brand in a certain part of the country has many options. For example, it can adapt the product to suit regional tastes *(product);* it can lower the price to compete with local brands *(price);* it can devise deals to gain additional shelf space in retail outlets *(place);* and it can reposition the product through intensive trade and consumer advertising *(promotion).* Thus, advertising is just one of the many strategic tools a company may use to achieve its marketing objectives.

Although the 4Ps of marketing (product, place, price, promotion) is a valuable concept, University of North Carolina at Chapel Hill professor Bob Lauterborn suggests modernizing the 4Ps to the 4Cs[21]:

- Consumer: Instead of focusing on a product, marketers should consider the consumer's wants and needs. Marketers should ask themselves questions like "What problem is the consumer experiencing?" and "What is frustrating the consumer?" to provide a helpful solution.
- Cost: Lauterborn says that "price is almost irrelevant." He suggests marketers consider the cost of time to drive to the store, the price of shipping, and other factors that result in a cost to the consumer in order to satisfy the want or need.
- Convenience: Consumers can purchase almost anything online with ease, but marketers should consider the most cost-effective and convenient method of how consumers can attain the product. Convenience has become a major factor in the way consumers shop for things like groceries and clothes.
- Communication: Social media has placed even more importance on communication. In addition to advertisements, consumers are learning about brands through friends they follow on social media, influencers, and consumers writing online reviews.

Ethics, Diversity & Inclusion

Diversity and Inclusion in Media Planning

While the aim of media planning is to deliver messages to groups of people with commonalities, it is not uncommon that some groups are inadvertently overlooked and excluded in the process. For instance, such groups as same-sex couples and Hispanics are not often represented in advertising, although the number of Americans who identify as lesbian, gay, bisexual, or transgender increases every year, and Hispanics constitute almost 20 percent of the nation's total population.

Diversity in Advertisements

As the demographic makeup of the United States continues to change, some brands have prioritized greater inclusivity. In 2014, Coca-Cola ran a Super Bowl ad with children singing "America the Beautiful" in different languages. It is also believed to be the first Super Bowl ad to show same-sex parents. Again in 2018, Coca-Cola's Super Bowl ad featured people from a variety of races, nationalities, and geographic regions. Jennifer Healan, group director of integrated marketing content at Coca-Cola, believes the ad is a "message of inclusion." Other brands that have successfully featured diversity include Chevrolet, which featured families consisting of gay and interracial couples. Cheerios's 2014 campaign depicted a multiracial family, and the lingerie retailer Aerie has prominently featured real women proudly proudly living with disability or illness. Their 2018 campaign included a model with Down syndrome and other women modeling underwear with a colitis bag and an insulin pump.

Diversity in Media Placements

Brands are also customizing the content of their advertisements based on media placements to highlight cultural aspects of diverse groups. For example, Toyota has created different versions of commercials designed to resonate specifically with African American, Hispanic, and Asian American audiences. Each spot represents the different groups in a positive and authentic way. The Asian American spot dispels stereotypes by depicting the not-often-seen behavior of a father and daughter connecting with one another while joyfully listening to music as they drive. Each commercial was aired on television shows with high numbers of viewers representing each ethnicity. Toyota developed the campaign because it believes that people want to see messaging that resonates with how they see themselves. The brand collaborated with several ad agencies that specialize in ethnic targeting and creative.

Diverse Media Habits

The placement of ads can impact exposure of brands and products to individuals based on their media habits. According to the Interactive Advertising Bureau (IAB), more than one-third of viewers watching ad-supported, original digital video are cord-cutters or cord-nevers. Advertisers are unable to reach them through traditional pay-TV because they have canceled their subscriptions or never subscribed in the first place. About 60 percent of these individuals are 34 years old or younger, and 43 percent of the viewership of original digital video is nonwhite. It is important for media planners to recognize how engagement with media is changing so that appropriate target audiences can be identified and segmented.

Consequences of Targeting

Technology has made it possible to tailor advertisements so that individuals can be exposed to ads based on their gender, race, household income, and other demographics. However, there are negative consequences of utilizing such technology, as it can be purposefully used to exclude groups from receiving advertisements. For example, companies advertising rental

Advertising Objectives and Strategy

The objectives and strategies of an advertising plan unfold from the marketing plan. But advertising objectives focus on communication goals, such as

- Convincing 25 percent of the target market during the next year of the brand's need-satisfying abilities.
- Positioning the brand as a cost-effective alternative to the market leader in the minds of 30 percent of men ages 18 to 34 during the next two years.
- Increasing brand preference by 8 percent in the South during the next year.
- Improving the target stakeholder group's attitude toward the company's environmental efforts by at least 15 percent by campaign end.

To achieve these objectives, companies devise advertising strategies that employ the elements of the **creative mix:** the product concept, target audience, IMC message, and communications media.

listings and employment opportunities on Facebook discriminated against certain groups, including African Americans, mothers of high school kids, people with disabilities, individuals of Jewish descent, and Spanish speakers. This occurred by using targeting technology to display the ads to whites only. This is not the first time Facebook has encountered difficulties with its targeting capabilities. Its lack of policing enabled users to use derogatory keywords to reach users who posted offensive material, and derogatory phrases like "kill muslim radicals" were auto-suggested by the targeting tool. The company has vowed to make changes, but these incidents expose the problematic nature of freely available user data. As user targeting and data-driven media planning become commonplace, media companies have to be mindful about how their targeting tools may be used negatively and need to implement safeguards to avoid the spread of discriminatory content.

Inclusion in the Media Workplace

Leadership positions within most agencies are largely constituted of white males. Although women make up nearly 50 percent of those working in the advertising industry, only 11 percent are creative directors, according to the 3 Percent Movement. To connect with different types of consumers, advertising and media agencies should reflect all varieties of consumers. Brands are aware of this problem and are urging agencies to embrace diversity. Recently, Verizon, General Mills, and HP Inc. asked for "action plans" from major agencies about how they will address the diversity gap to hire more women and minorities. Diversity in advertising is a competitive differentiator that imparts insights about markets and customers, and companies with more diverse workforces perform better financially, according to a McKinsey study.

Questions

1. In your experience, how has working with diverse groups, either in school or in the workplace, contributed to positive outcomes?

2. What are some of the ethical challenges that come with the ability to target consumers based on their gender, race, and other demographics?

3. Provide an example of a brand that has showcased diversity in its advertising. How has this change altered your opinion of the brand?

Sources: U.S. Census Bureau, *Facts for Features: Hispanic Heritage Month*, August 31, 2017, www.census.gov/newsroom/facts-for-features/2017/hispanic-heritage.html; Brian Steinberg, "Coke Adds Diversity to Super Bowl by Playing Ad for Many Audiences," *Variety*, February 1, 2018, https://variety.com/2018/tv/news/super-bowl-commercials-coca-cola-1202683895/; Sapna Maheshwari. "Different Ads, Different Ethnicities, Same Car," *The New York Times*, October 12, 2017, www.nytimes.com/interactive/2017/10/12/business/media/toyota-camry-ads-different-ethnicities.html; Benjamin Mullin, "Who's Watching Digital Video? A Diverse, Expanding Audience, IAB Says," August 26, 2018, *The Wall Street Journal*, www.wsj.com/articles/whos-watching-digital-video-a-diverse-expanding-audience-iab-says-1524760278; Jessica Guynn, "Facebook Halts Ads That Exclude Racial and Ethnic Groups," *USA Today*, November 29, 2017, www.usatoday.com/story/tech/2017/11/29/facebook-stop-allowing-advertisers-exclude-racial-and-ethnic-groups-targeting/905133001/; The 3% Movement, *What Women Want*, March 2016, www.3percentmovement.com/sites/default/files/resources/WhatWomenWant%20-%20Final.pdf; Sapna Maheshwari, "Brands to Ad Agencies: Diversify or Else," *The New York Times*, September 30, 2016, www.nytimes.com/2016/10/01/business/media/brands-to-ad-agencies-diversify-or-else.html; Vivian Hunt, Dennis Layton, and Sara Prince, "Why Diversity Matters," *McKinsey & Company*, January 2015, www.mckinsey.com/business-functions/organization/our-insights/why-diversity-matters.

The media department's job is to make sure the advertising message (developed by the creative department) gets to the correct target audience (established by the marketing managers and account executives) in an effective manner (as measured by the research department).

The Media-Planning Framework

In the age of integrated marketing communications, many agencies have moved the task of media planning earlier in the advertising management process because people typically make contact with the brand through some medium. Before determining what creative approach to employ, it's important to know when, where, and under what conditions contact can best be made with the customer or other stakeholder and to plan for that. This sets the strategic direction for the creative department.

That's also why we present the topic of media planning now, in Part Two, "Planning the Campaign," because media planning is part of the strategic work done prior to developing creative concepts. Later, in Part Three, "Executing and Evaluating the Campaign," we'll discuss the tactical details of each medium, how it's used, and how it's bought—activities that typically occur after the creative process.

The situation analysis
Purpose: To understand the marketing problem. The company and its competitors are analyzed on
1. Internal strengths and weaknesses.
2. External opportunities and threats.

The marketing plan
Purpose: To plan activities that will solve one or more of the marketing problems.
Includes the determination of
1. Marketing objectives.
2. Product and spending strategy.
3. Distribution strategy.
4. Which marketing mix to use.
5. Identification of "best" market segments.

The advertising plan
Purpose: To determine what to communicate through ads.
Includes the determination of
1. How product can meet consumer needs.
2. How product will be positioned in ads.
3. Copy themes.
4. Specific objectives of each ad.
5. Number and sizes of ads.

Setting media objectives
Purpose: To translate marketing and advertising objectives and strategies into goals that media can accomplish.

Determining media strategy
Purpose: To translate media goals into general guidelines that will control the planner's selection and use of media. The best strategy alternatives should be selected.

Selecting broad media classes
Purpose: To determine which broad class of media best fulfills the criteria. Involves comparison and selection of broad media classes: newspapers, magazines, radio, television, and others. Audience size is a major factor used in comparing the various media classes.

Selecting media within classes
Purpose: To compare and select the best media within broad classes, again using predetermined criteria. Involves making decisions about the following:
1. If magazines were recommended, then which magazines?
2. If television was recommended, then
   a. Broadcast or cable TV?
   b. Network or spot TV?
   c. If network, which program(s)?
   d. If spot, which markets?
3. If radio or newspapers were recommended, then
   a. Which markets shall be used?
   b. What criteria shall buyers use in making purchases in local media?

Media use decisions—broadcast
1. What kind of sponsorship (sole, shared participating, or other)?
2. What levels of reach and frequency will be required?
3. Scheduling: On which days and months are commercials to appear?
4. Placement of spots: In programs or between programs?

Media use decisions—print
1. Numbers of ads to appear and on which days and months.
2. Placement of ads: Any preferred position within media?
3. Special treatment: Gatefolds, bleeds, color, etc.
4. Desired reach or frequency levels.

Media use decisions—other media
1. Billboards:
   a. Location of markets and plan of distribution.
   b. Kinds of outdoor boards to be used.
2. Direct mail or other media: Decisions peculiar to those media.
3. Interactive media:
   a. Which kind of interactive media?
   b. How will responses be handled?

Evaluation Criteria
How will success be measured?
1. Campaign: Depending on the media used, which analytics are best to gauge whether the campaign met or exceeded expectations?
2. Attitudinal: How do consumers think and feel about the brand? Usage studies and surveys can be employed to understand consumer sentiment.
3. Behavioral: How are consumers responding? Monitoring website visits, social media interaction, and key performance indicators, such as sales, may indicate whether consumers are taking the desired actions of the brand.
4. Optimizations: Data should be closely monitored, allowing for modifications to show how the budget is allocated in each medium. If a particular medium is a high-performer, funds can be removed from low performers to improve the overall performance of the campaign.

Exhibit 9-2
This diagram outlines the scope of media-planning activities.

Development of a media plan involves the same process as marketing and advertising planning. First, review the marketing and advertising objectives and strategies and set relevant, measurable objectives that are both realistic and achievable by the media. Next, try to devise an ingenious strategy for achieving these objectives. Finally, develop the specific tactical details of media scheduling and selection.

Defining Media Objectives

LO 9-3

Media objectives translate the advertising strategy into goals that media can accomplish. Exhibit 9-3 shows general media objectives for a hypothetical new food product. They explain who the target audience is and why, where messages will be delivered and when, and how much advertising weight needs to be delivered over what period of time.

Media objectives have two major components: *audience objectives* and *message-distribution objectives.*

Audience Objectives

Audience objectives define the specific types of people the advertiser wants to reach. Media planners typically use geodemographic classifications to define their target audiences. In Exhibit 9-3, for example, the target audience is food purchasers for large families who live in urban areas across the country.

The target audience may consist of people in a specific income, educational, occupational, or social group—any of the segments we discussed in Chapter 6. And the target audience is not necessarily the same as the product's target market. Often it is considerably larger. For example, in the case of a new product introduction, the target audience will often include members of the distribution channel, key opinion leaders, the financial community, and even the media itself—in addition to potential customers.

Many advertisers have to defend their media decisions with the retailers who stock and resell their products. Why? If these people construed a change in media strategy as a loss of advertising support, they might reduce the shelf space for the advertiser's products. Therefore, most consumer campaigns are supported by a concurrent campaign directed to the trade.

The consumer target audience may be determined from the marketer's research. However, planners rely largely on secondary research sources, such as Arbitron and Nielsen Media Research, which provide basic demographic characteristics of media audiences. Others, such as Simmons Market Research Bureau (SMRB) and Mediamark Research, Inc. (MRI), describe media audiences based on purchase tendencies (see Exhibit 9-4). These syndicated reports give demographic profiles of heavy and light users of various products and help planners define the target audience. The reports also specify which TV programs or magazines heavy and light users watch and read, which helps planners select media with large audiences of heavy users. Planners can then select **media vehicles**—particular magazines or shows—according to how well they "deliver" or expose the message to the media audience that most closely resembles the desired target consumer.

Advertisers using the IMC planning model start by segmenting their target audiences according to brand-purchasing behavior (e.g., loyal users, brand switchers, new prospects) and then ranking them by profit to the brand.[22] Communications objectives are then stated in terms of reinforcing or modifying customer purchasing behavior or creating a perceptual change about the brand over time.[23]

Unfortunately, due to cost restraints, much media research does not provide the specificity that marketers would really like. Most radio, TV, newspaper, and outdoor audience reports, for example, are limited to age and gender. So media planners often have to rely on their judgment and experience to select the right media vehicles.[24]

Message-Distribution Objectives

Distribution objectives define where, when, and how often advertising should appear. To answer these questions, a media planner must understand a number of terms, including *message weight, reach, frequency,* and *continuity.*

ACME Advertising
Client: Econo Foods
Product/Brand: Chirpee's Cheap Chips
Project: Media plan, first year introduction

Media Objectives

1. To target large families with emphasis on the family's food purchaser.
2. To concentrate the greatest weight of advertising in urban areas where prepared foods traditionally have greater sales and where new ideas normally gain quicker acceptance.
3. To provide extra weight during the announcement period and then continuity throughout the year with a fairly consistent level of advertising impressions.
4. To deliver advertising impressions to every region in relation to regional food store sales.
5. To use media that will reinforce the copy strategy's emphasis on convenience, ease of preparation, taste, and economy.
6. To attain the highest advertising frequency possible once the need for broad coverage and the demands of the copy platform have been met.

Exhibit 9-3
How media objectives are expressed.

Exhibit 9-4
A media planner's toolbox.

Secondary sources of information help media planners do their jobs.

- **GfK MRI (mri.gfk.com)** reports data on product, brand, and media usage by both demographic and lifestyle characteristics.
- **Broadcast Advertisers Reports (BAR), Leading National Advertisers (LNA), and Media Records** report advertisers' expenditures by brand, media type, market, and time period.
- **Kantar Media/SRDS (www.srds.com)** provides information on media rates, format, production requirements, and audience.
- **Alliance for Audited Media (www.auditedmedia.com)** verifies circulation figures of publishers.
- **Kantar/TNS Global (www.tnsglobal.com)** delivers strategic advertising intelligence to advertising agencies, advertisers, broadcasters, and publishers. The tracking technologies collect occurrence and expenditure data, as well as the creative executions of over 2.2 million brands across 21 media.
- **Nielsen (www.nielsen.com/us/en.html)** is a privately held global information and media company and one of the world's leading suppliers of marketing information (ACNielsen), media information and TV ratings (Nielsen Media Research), online intelligence (Nielsen Online), mobile measurement (Nielsen Mobile), purchase behavior and consumption (Nielsen Homescan), media consumption across platforms and devices (Nielsen Total Audience), trade shows, and business publications (*Billboard, The Hollywood Reporter, Adweek, R&R*).
- **eMarketer (www.emarketer.com/)** is the go-to source for information on digital and mobile advertising.
- **Comscore (www.comscore.com)** delivers innovative and comprehensive analytics across multiple platforms. Products include Ad Metrix to track display advertising, Mobile Metrix for audience behavior on smartphones and tablets, and Comscore Box Office Essentials, reporting on how many people go to the movies and how much they spend.
- **Google AdWords Reach Planner (www.adwords.google.com/home/tools/reach-planner/)** allows advertisers to forecast the reach and frequency achievable on YouTube and across Google's video partners.

Audience Size and Message Weight

Marketers are naturally interested in having their messages exposed to as many customers and prospects as they can afford. So they are also logically most interested in those media opportunities that offer the largest audiences.[25] The basic way to express audience size is simply to count the number of people in a medium's audience. This is what media research firms like Nielsen and Arbitron do for the broadcast media, typically using a statistical sample to project the total audience size. For print media, firms like the Audit Bureau of Circulations actually count and verify the number of subscribers (the **circulation**) and then multiply by the estimated number of **readers per copy (RPC)** to determine the total audience.

Media planners often define media objectives by the schedule's **message weight,** the total size of the audience for a set of ads or an entire campaign, because it gives some indication of the scope of the campaign in a given market. There are two ways to express message weight: *gross impressions* and *gross rating points.*

If planners know the audience size, they can easily calculate the number of advertising impressions in a media schedule. An **advertising impression** is a possible exposure of the advertising message to one audience member. It is sometimes referred to as an **opportunity to see (OTS).** By multiplying a medium's total audience size by the number of times an advertising message is used during the period, planners arrive at the **gross impressions,** or potential exposures, possible in that medium. Then, by summing the gross impressions for each medium used, they know the total gross impressions for the schedule (see Exhibit 9-5).

Exhibit 9-5
Gross impressions analysis for Brand X in the second quarter, 2020.

Media Vehicle	Target Audience*	Messages Used	Gross Impressions
TV *Channel 6 News*	140,000	15	2,100,000
Daily newspaper	250,000	7	1,750,000
Spot radio	10,000	55	550,000
Total gross impressions			4,400,000

*Average.

Exhibit 9-6
Gross rating points analysis for Brand X in the second quarter, 2020.

Media Vehicle	Adult Rating*	Messages Used	Gross Rating Points
TV *Channel 6 News*	14	15	210
Daily newspaper	25	7	175
Spot radio	1	55	55
Total gross rating points			440

*Assumes market size of 1 million people.

With large media schedules, though, gross impressions can run into the millions and become very awkward to handle, so that's where the concept of *ratings* came from. The **rating** is simply the percentage of homes (or individuals) exposed to an advertising medium. Percentages are not only simpler numbers to deal with, they are also more useful in making comparisons. Thus, one rating point is equal to 1 percent of a given population group. When we hear that a particular TV show garnered a 20 rating, it means 20 percent of the households with TV sets (expressed as **television households or TVHH**) were tuned in to that show. The higher a program's rating, the more people are watching.[26] This definition applies to many media forms, but it is most commonly used for radio and TV.

By adding the ratings of several media vehicles (as we did for gross impressions), we can determine the message weight of a given advertising schedule, only now it's expressed as **gross rating points (GRPs)** (see Exhibit 9-6). When we say a schedule delivered 180 GRPs, that means the gross impressions generated by our schedule equaled 180 percent of the target market population. For broadcast media, GRPs are often calculated for a week or a month. In print media, they're calculated for the number of ads in a campaign. For outdoor advertising, they're calculated on the basis of daily exposure.

Media planners may use GRPs to determine the optimal level of spending for a campaign. The more GRPs they buy, the more it costs. However, because of discounting, the unit cost per GRP decreases as more GRPs are bought. Beyond a certain point, the effectiveness of additional GRPs diminishes.

Through the use of computer models and certain assumptions based on experience, sophisticated planners can detect the relative impact of ad-related variables on sales and determine the *return on investment (ROI)* from each. This can potentially save clients substantial sums of money.[27]

In the calculation of message weight, advertisers disregard any overlap or duplication. As a result, certain individuals within the audience may see the message several times while others don't see it at all. While message weight gives an indication of size, it does not reveal much about who is in the audience or how often they are reached. This fact necessitated the development of other media objectives, namely *reach, frequency,* and *continuity*.

Reach

The term **reach** refers to the total number of unique (or different) people or households exposed, at least once, to a medium during a given period of time, usually four weeks.[28] For example, if 40 percent of 100,000 people in a target market tune in to radio station WKKO at least once during a four-week period, the reach is 40,000 people. Reach may be expressed as a percentage of the total market (40 percent) or as a raw number (40,000). Reach should not be confused with the number of people who will actually be exposed to and consume the advertising, though. It is just the number of people who are exposed to the medium and therefore have an *opportunity to see* the ad or commercial.

An advertiser may accumulate reach in two ways: by using the same media vehicle continuously or by combining two or more media vehicles.[29] Naturally, as more media are used, some

While traditional media buys are still made by a buyer contacting a seller and negotiating a price for placing an ad, digital media space is often purchased by computer programs efficiently matching sellers (content providers such as news websites) with buyers (firms looking to place ads that match specific audience characteristics). A key player in this type of programmatic advertising is DoubleClick, which is owned by Google.

Source: Google

		25	30	35	40	45	50	55	60	65	70	75	80	85	90	95
							Reach of First Medium									
Reach of Second Medium	25	46	47	51	55	59	62	66	70	74	77	81	85	89	92	95
	30	—	51	54	58	61	65	68	72	75	79	82	86	90	93	95
	35	—	—	58	61	64	67	71	74	77	80	84	87	90	93	95
	40	—	—	—	64	67	70	73	76	79	82	85	88	91	94	95
	45	—	—	—	—	70	72	75	78	81	83	86	89	92	94	95
	50	—	—	—	—	—	75	77	80	82	85	87	90	92	95	95
	55	—	—	—	—	—	—	80	82	84	86	89	91	93	95	95
	60	—	—	—	—	—	—	—	84	86	88	90	92	94	95	95
	65	—	—	—	—	—	—	—	—	88	89	91	93	95	95	95
	70	—	—	—	—	—	—	—	—	—	91	92	94	95	95	95
	75	—	—	—	—	—	—	—	—	—	—	94	95	95	95	95
	80	—	—	—	—	—	—	—	—	—	—	—	95	95	95	95
	85	—	—	—	—	—	—	—	—	—	—	—	—	95	95	95
	90	—	—	—	—	—	—	—	—	—	—	—	—	—	95	95
	95	—	—	—	—	—	—	—	—	—	—	—	—	—	—	95

Exhibit 9-7

Random combination table. Find the reach of the first medium on the horizontal axis. Find the reach of the second medium on the vertical axis. The point of intersection shows the combined reach of the two media. If three or more media forms are combined, use the same procedure, finding the combined reach of the first two media on the horizontal axis and reading down to the intersection with the reach of the third medium.

duplication occurs. Exhibit 9-7 is a statistical table that shows how unduplicated reach builds as additional media are added.

Frequency

To express the number of times the same person or household is exposed to a message—a radio spot, for example—in a specified time span, media people use the term *frequency*. **Frequency** measures the *intensity* of a media schedule, based on repeated exposures to the medium or the program. Frequency is important because repetition is the key to memory.

Frequency is calculated as the *average* number of times individuals or homes are exposed to the medium. For instance, suppose in our hypothetical 100,000-person market that 20,000 people tune in to WKKO and have three OTSs during a four-week period, and another 20,000 have five OTSs. To calculate the average frequency, divide the total number of exposures by the total reach:

$$\text{Average frequency} = \text{Total exposures} \div \text{Audience reach}$$

$$= [(20,000 \times 3) + (20,000 \times 5)] \div 40,000$$

$$= 160,000 \div 40,000$$

$$= 4.0$$

For the 40,000 listeners reached, the average frequency, or number of exposures, was four.

Once we understand reach and frequency, we have another simple way to determine the message weight. To calculate gross rating points, just multiply a show's reach (expressed as a rating percentage) by the average frequency. In our radio example, 40 percent of the radio households (a 40 rating) had the opportunity to hear the commercial an average of four times during the four-week period:

$$\text{Reach} \times \text{Frequency} = \text{GRPs}$$

$$40 \times 4 = 160 \text{ GRPs}$$

Thus, the message weight of this radio campaign would be equal to 160 percent of the total market—or 160,000 gross impressions.

Continuity

Media planners refer to the duration of an advertising message or campaign over a given period of time as **continuity.** Few companies spread their marketing efforts evenly throughout the year. They typically *heavy up* before prime selling seasons and slow down during the off-season. Likewise, to save money, a media planner for a new product might decide that after a heavy introduction period of, say, four weeks, a radio campaign needs to maintain *continuity* for an additional 16 weeks but on fewer stations. We'll discuss some common scheduling patterns in the section on media tactics.

While frequency is important to create memory, continuity is important to *sustain* it. Moreover, as people come into and out of the market for goods and services every day, continuity provides a means of having the message there when it's most needed. Ads that hit targets during purchase cycles are more effective and require less frequency.[30]

Optimizing Reach, Frequency, and Continuity: The Art of Media Planning

LO 9-4

Good media planning is both an art and a science. The media planner must get the most effective exposure on a limited budget. As Exhibit 9–8 shows, the objectives of reach, frequency, and continuity have inverse relationships to each other. To achieve greater reach, some frequency and/or continuity has to be sacrificed, and so on. Research shows that all three are critical. But because all budgets are limited, which is most critical? This is currently the subject of hot debate in advertising circles.

Effective Reach

One of the problems with reach is that, by themselves, the numbers don't take into account the *quality* of the exposure. Some people exposed to the medium still won't be aware of the message. So, on the surface, reach doesn't seem to be the best measure of media success. Media people use the term **effective reach** to describe the quality of exposure. It measures the number or percentage of the audience who receive enough exposures to truly receive the message. Some researchers maintain that three OTSs over a four-week period are usually enough to reach an audience.[31]

Effective Frequency

Similar to the concept of effective reach is **effective frequency,** defined as the average number of times a person must see or hear a message before it becomes effective. In theory, effective frequency falls somewhere between a minimum level that achieves message awareness and a maximum level that becomes overexposure, which leads to "wearout" (starts to irritate consumers).

Following the publication of Michael Naples's classic book *Effective Frequency* in 1979, most of the industry fell in love with his claim that, in most cases, effective frequency could be achieved by an average frequency of three over a four-week period. Here was a nice, simple conclusion that all the low-level media planners could use. Naples's conclusion seemed to be intuitively correct, and it was supported by some researchers who viewed advertising effects as a learning situation. While this might be true for some new products, most of the time advertising is for established products and therefore is not about "learning" but rather about "reminding." Syracuse University professor John Philip Jones writes that "a massive, multitiered edifice" of belief was built on the evidence in Naples's book—evidence that he believes led the industry down the wrong path.[32]

While the concepts of effective reach and frequency are now hotly debated, virtually all agencies still use them. Cannon and Riordan point out that conventional media planning is based on *media vehicle exposure* (the number of people in a medium's audience), but effectiveness should relate to *advertising message exposure*. For example, only 20 percent of viewers may pay attention when a commercial runs. It may take 10 opportunities-to-see to reach an average frequency of one!

Cannon and Riordan would replace effective frequency with *optimal frequency*. Most studies of the **advertising response curve** indicate that incremental response to advertising

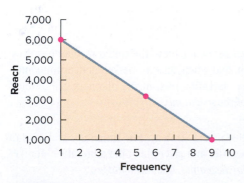

Exhibit 9-8

Reach, frequency, and continuity have an inverse relationship to one another. For instance, in the example, an advertiser can reach 6,000 people once, 3,000 people 5.5 times, or 1,000 people 9 times for the same budget. However, to gain continuity over time, the advertiser would have to sacrifice some reach and some frequency.

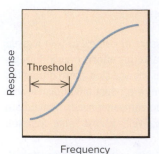
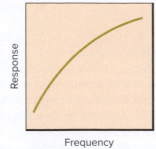

a. **S-shaped response curve**   b. **Convex response curve**

Exhibit 9-9
Two advertising response curves. The S-shaped curve would be applicable for products that require a frequency of more than one to reach a threshold of greatest response. After that threshold is reached, the response diminishes for each subsequent exposure. The convex curve applies to products for which the first exposure produces the best return and all subsequent exposures produce a slightly lower response.

actually diminishes, rather than builds, with repeated exposures (see Exhibit 9-9). The optimal frequency concept moves the focus of media planning from exposure effectiveness to *effective exposures per dollar.*

With a response curve that is characterized by continually diminishing returns, the first ad will be the most profitable. But subsequent exposures–advertising frequency–are still important. How important depends on the slope of the response curve and the cost of advertising. Obviously, the less money it costs per exposure to advertise, the more the firm can afford to advertise. The profit-maximizing firm will continue to spend until the revenue resulting from an additional advertisement placed is offset by its cost.[33]

The implications of Cannon and Riordan's theory are immense. Historically, media planning has emphasized frequency as the most important media objective. This assumes an S-shaped advertising response curve in which the first two or three exposures don't count. But Cannon and Riordan's analysis indicates that response curves are convex. The first exposure is the most effective, followed by diminishing returns. If that's the case, then the basic emphasis in advertising should switch from maximizing frequency to maximizing target market reach, adding less profitable second exposures only as the budget permits.[34]

This approach is now supported by numerous researchers who believe effective frequency planning is seriously flawed and who make a strong case for the primacy of reach and continuity as the most important media objectives.[35] In fact, for fast-moving consumer products, researcher Erwin Ephron suggests the concept of **recency planning,** based on "the sensible idea that most advertising works by influencing the brand choice of consumers who are ready to buy." Therefore, the important thing for advertising is to be there when the consumer is ready to buy, and that suggests continuity.[36] His theories have gained the attention of many of the nation's largest advertisers, among them Procter & Gamble, Kraft Foods, and Coca-Cola.[37]

One problem with all these theories is that they assume all exposures are equal. If that's the case, then where does advertising creativity come in? And what about the programs where the advertising appears? Doesn't that have some effect on the quality of exposure?

For most media planners, the only solution to this debate is to establish first which type of response curve is most likely to apply to the particular situation and then to develop the campaign's media objectives accordingly.

Once the media objectives have been determined–that is, the optimum levels of message weight, reach, frequency, and continuity–the media planner can develop the strategy for achieving them.

Developing a Media Strategy: The Media Mix

The media strategy describes how the advertiser will achieve the stated media objectives: which media will be used, where, how often, and when. Just as marketers determine marketing strategy by blending elements of the marketing mix, media planners can develop media strategies by blending the elements of the *media mix.*

Elements of the Media Mix

Many factors go into developing an effective media strategy. For simplicity and ease of memory, we have sorted them into five categories and given them the alliterative moniker of the **five Ms (5Ms):** *markets, money, media, mechanics,* and *methodology.*

Markets refers to the various targets of a media plan: trade and consumer audiences; global, national, or regional audiences; ethnic and socioeconomic groups; or other stakeholders. In an integrated marketing communications plan, the IMC planner wants to find the reasons and motivations for the prospect's purchase and usage patterns and then create a media plan based on those findings.[38]

Guided by the client's budget and using intuition, marketing savvy, and analytical skill, the media planner determines the second element, **money**–how much to budget and where

Online Media Consumption Behaviors: 2012 vs. 2016
Number of hours and minutes per day typically devoted to the following

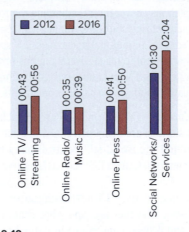

Offline Media Consumptions Behaviors: 2012 vs. 2016
Number of hours and minutes per day typically devoted to the following

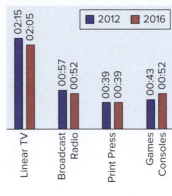

Exhibit 9-10
Average Time Devoted to Online and Offline Media: 2012–2016.
Source: Insight Report, "Digital vs. Traditional Media Consumption," *Global Web Index,* January 2017.

to allocate it. How much for digital media, how much in TV, how much to nontraditional or supplemental media, how much to each geographic area? We discuss this issue in depth in the chapters on using and buying media (Chapters 13 through 17).

From the IMC perspective, **media** include *all* communications vehicles available to a marketer. This includes radio, TV, newspapers, magazines, out-of-home, digital, and direct mail, plus sales promotion, direct marketing, public relations activities and publicity, special events, sponsorships, brochures, and even shopping bags. In today's dynamic media landscape, change is the norm, not the exception. This is particularly true in the increased time people are spending with online media (see Exhibit 9-10). Media planners must stay abreast of the emergence of new platforms and integrate these into their plans.

Good media planners champion the integration of all marketing communications to help achieve their companies' marketing and advertising objectives. They look at the media element both analytically and creatively.

The media planner also has to deal with the complex **mechanics** of advertising media and messages. Radio and TV commercials come in a variety of time units, and print ads are created in a variety of sizes and styles. IMC planners may also deal with the mechanics of nontraditional media, everything from shopping bags to multimedia kiosks to the internet. The myriad media options now available offer exciting, creative ways to enhance consumer acceptance of the advertiser's message and offer the consumer a relevant purchase incentive.

The **methodology** element refers to the overall strategy of selecting and scheduling media vehicles to achieve the desired message weight, reach, frequency, and continuity objectives. It offers the opportunity for creativity in planning, negotiating, and buying.

Factors That Influence Media Strategy Decisions

Media decisions are greatly influenced by factors over which the media planner has little or no control. These include the scope of the media plan, sales potential of different markets, competitive strategies and budget considerations, availability of different media vehicles, nature of the medium, mood of the message, message size and length, and buyer purchase patterns.

Scope of the Media Plan

The location and makeup of the target audience strongly influence the breadth of the media plan, thereby affecting decisions regarding the *market,* the *money,* and the *media* elements.

Domestic Markets   A media planner normally limits advertising to areas where the product is available. If a store serves only one town, or if a city has been chosen to test-market a new product, then the advertiser will use a *local* plan.

A *regional* plan may cover several adjoining metropolitan areas, an entire state or province, or several neighboring states. Regional plans typically employ a combination of local media, regional editions of national magazines, TV spots and radio, and the internet.

Advertisers who want to reach several regions or an entire country use a *national* plan. This may call for network TV and radio, full-circulation national magazines and newspapers, nationally syndicated Sunday newspaper supplements, and the internet.

International Markets   Foreign media can be a challenge for U.S. advertisers. While many broadcast stations are being privatized in countries as diverse as Israel and Russia, governments around the world still control many broadcast media, and some still do not permit commercials. Others limit advertising to a certain number of minutes per hour or per day.

In countries that do allow TV advertising, advertisers face other problems: how many people own TV sets, who they are, and what channels they receive. While this is not an issue in Europe and is becoming less so in Latin America, it is still a problem in many of the less-developed nations of Africa and Asia. There, TV ownership may be limited to upper-income consumers, or the availability of commercial channels may be severely limited. In those markets, advertisers must use a different media mix. Likewise, internet access may be severely limited—or too expensive for consumers to afford. So that option may not even be available for some markets.

In many countries of Europe, about 48 percent of total advertising expenditures are still spent in print media versus about 35 percent on television.[39] However, like the United States, Europe and Asia are experiencing a virtual explosion of new media and technology. Advertisers and agencies alike are realizing the importance of developing integrated marketing communications plans to build their brands and establish long-term relationships with their customers.

Most marketers develop an international media plan by formulating individual national plans first. But it's not as simple as it sounds. Depending on the country, precise media information may not be available, circulation figures may not be audited, audience demographics may be sketchy, and even ad rates may be unreliable. Finally, the methodology used in media research may be considerably different from one market to another, making comparisons virtually impossible. At the same time, in some European countries, media research and planning may be more sophisticated than in the United States, which creates another problem for U.S. advertisers who are unfamiliar with European terms, concepts, and methodologies.[40]

Because of the media variations from country to country, most international and global advertisers entrust national media plans to in-country foreign media specialists or the local foreign branches of global media agencies such as MindShare, OMD Worldwide, Mediaedge:cia, or Carat, rather than risk faulty centralized media planning.[41]

Sales Potential of Different Markets

The *market* and *money* elements of the media mix also depend on the sales potential of each area. National advertisers use this factor to determine where to allocate their advertising dollars. Planners can determine an area's sales potential in several ways.

The Brand Development Index   The **brand development index (BDI)** indicates the sales potential of a particular brand in a specific market area. It compares the percentage of the brand's total U.S. sales in an area to the percentage of the total U.S. population in that area.

Global brands like Coca-Cola must simultaneously adapt to local cultures and retain the essence of a strong brand. This ad shows how well Coke handles the challenge.

Source: The Coca-Cola Company

The larger the brand's sales relative to the area's percentage of U.S. population, the higher the BDI and the greater the brand's sales potential. BDI is calculated as

$$BDI = \frac{\text{Percent of the brand's total U.S. sales in the area}}{\text{Percent of total U.S. population in the area}} \times 100$$

Suppose sales of a brand in Los Angeles are 1.58 percent of the brand's total U.S. sales, and the population of Los Angeles is 2 percent of the U.S. total. The BDI for Los Angeles is

$$BDI = \frac{1.58}{2} \times 100 = 79$$

An index number of 100 means the brand's performance balances with the size of the area's population. A BDI index number below 100 indicates poor potential for the brand.

The Category Development Index   To determine the potential of the whole product category, media planners use the **category development index (CDI),** which works on the same concept as the BDI and is calculated in much the same way:

$$CDI = \frac{\text{Percent of the category's total U.S. sales in the are}}{\text{Percent of total U.S. population in the area}} \times 100$$

If category sales in Los Angeles are 4.92 percent of total U.S. category sales, the CDI in Los Angeles is

$$CDI = \frac{4.92}{2} \times 100 = 246$$

The combination of BDI and CDI can help the planner determine a media strategy for the market (see Exhibit 9-11). In our example, low BDI (under 100) and high CDI (over 100) in Los Angeles indicate that the product category has high potential, but the brand is not selling well. This may represent a problem or an opportunity. If the brand has been on the market for some time, the low BDI raises a red flag; some problem is standing in the way of brand sales. But if the brand is new, the low BDI may not be alarming. In fact, the high CDI may indicate the brand can grow substantially, given more time and greater media and marketing support. At this point, the media planner should assess the company's share of voice (discussed in Chapter 8) and budget accordingly.

Competitive Strategies and Budget Considerations

Advertisers always consider what competitors are doing, particularly those that have larger advertising budgets. This affects the *media, mechanics,* and *methodology* elements of the media mix. Several services, like TNS Media Intelligence, detail competitive advertising expenditures in the different media. By knowing the size of competitors' budgets, what

Exhibit 9-11
Media buyers compare the brand development index with the category development index for their products to better understand which markets will respond best to advertising. Advertising can be expected to work well when BDI and CDI are both high, but probably not when both are low.

	Low BDI	High BDI
High CDI	Low market share *but* Good market potential	High market share *and* Good market potential
Low CDI	Low market share *and* Poor market potential	High market share *but* Monitor for sales decline

media they're using, the regionality or seasonality of their sales, and any new-product tests and introductions, advertisers can better plan a counterstrategy.

Again, the media planner should analyze the company's share of voice in the marketplace. If an advertiser's budget is much smaller than the competition's, the brand could get lost in the shuffle. Advertisers should bypass media that competitors dominate and choose other media that offer a strong position.

When Anne Myers, media director of Palmer Jarvis DDB, Toronto, had to develop a media plan for Panasonic Canada's Power Activator batteries, she didn't have the budget of Energizer or Duracell to work with. So she didn't want to place her ads where theirs were. Myers and her team creatively fashioned a guerrilla media plan that targeted a cynical, hard-to-reach audience, 15- to 22-year-olds, right where they lived—in the clubs, on the street, and on the internet. The campaign included posters in the dance clubs; sponsorship of popular DJs and VJs; free PA T-shirts, hats, posters, and stickers; an eight-week run of television spots on popular music shows tied to a month-long cross-promotion with a new CD release; and a special contest run on a microsite that linked back to Panasonic Canada's main site. The response was excellent: Sales were up 136 percent over the previous year, and the contest promotion generated more than 16,300 entries on the site with a click-through rate of 35 percent.[42]

It sometimes makes sense to use media similar to the competition's if the target audiences are the same or if the competitors are not using their media effectively.

Media Availability and Economics: The Global Marketer's Headache

North American advertisers are blessed—or cursed—with an incredible array of media choices, locally and nationally. Such is not always the case in other areas of the world, which is one reason their per capita advertising expenditures are so much lower than in the United States.

Every country has communications media, but they are not always available for commercial use (especially radio and television) and coverage may be limited. Lower literacy rates and education levels in some countries restrict the coverage of print media. Where income levels are low, TV ownership is also low. These factors tend to segment markets by media coverage.

A global media strategy requires understanding options available around the world. China restricts or denies access to social media sites popular in the United States and Europe but has functional "equivalents" that advertisers can use to reach consumers in this enormous market, as shown in this beautiful exhibit from China Business Review.

Courtesy of Ogilvy

To reach lower-income markets, radio is the medium of choice, as both Coke and Pepsi have demonstrated successfully for years. Auto manufacturers make good use of TV and magazine advertising to reach the upper class. And movie advertising can reach whole urban populations where TV ownership is low because motion picture attendance in such countries is very high.

Some companies are attempting to become true global marketers of their brands with centralized control of media and standardized creative. As a group, global media are growing, which is good news for global marketers.[43] However, there are still few true global media. So these major advertisers must continue to use local foreign media in the countries where they do business and localize their campaigns for language and cultural differences.

Finally, there's the problem of **spillover media,** local media that many consumers in a neighboring country inadvertently receive. For example, media from Luxembourg regularly spill over into France, Belgium, and the Netherlands. Media often spill over into countries lacking indigenous-language publications, particularly specialty publications. English and German business media enjoy a large circulation in Scandinavian countries, for example, where there are relatively few specialized trade publications written in Swedish, Danish, or Norwegian.

Spillover media pose a threat for the multinational advertiser because they expose readers to multiple ad campaigns. If the advertiser runs both international and local campaigns for the same products, discrepancies in product positioning, pricing, or advertising messages could confuse potential buyers. Advertisers' local subsidiaries or distributors need to coordinate local and international ad campaigns to avoid such confusion. On the positive side, spillover media offer potential cost savings through regional campaigns.

Nature of the Medium and Mood of the Message

An important influence on the *media* element of the mix is how well a medium works with the style or mood of the particular message.

Advertising messages differ in many ways. Some are simple messages: "Just do it" (Nike). Others make emotional or sensual appeals to people's needs and wants: "The great taste of fruit squared" (Jolly Rancher candies). Many advertisers use a reason-why approach to explain their product's advantages: "Twice the room. Twice the comfort. Twice the value. Embassy Suites. Twice the hotel."

Complex messages, such as ads announcing a new product or concept, require more space or time for explanation. Each circumstance affects the media selection as well as the *methodology* of the media mix.

A new or highly complex message may require greater frequency and exposure to be understood and remembered. A dogmatic message like Nike's may require a surge at the beginning, then low frequency and greater reach.

Once consumers understand reason-why messages, pulsing advertising exposures at irregular intervals is often sufficient. Emotionally oriented messages are usually more effective when spaced at regular intervals to create enduring feelings about the product. We discuss these scheduling methods further in the next section on media tactics.

And sometimes, as educator, philosopher, and scholar Marshall McLuhan famously claimed, "the medium is the message." The very medium that an advertiser chooses can have as much or more of an impact on an audience as the communication. For instance, a local jeweler who chooses to advertise on TV may present the perception of being a successful business, which will appeal to some consumer groups, regardless of the message being conveyed in the 30-second spot.

Message Size, Length, and Position Considerations

The particular characteristics of different media, over which the media planner has no control, affect the *mechanics* element of the media mix. For example, in print, a full-page ad attracts more attention than a quarter-page ad and a full-color ad more than a black-and-white one. Color and larger units of space or time cost dearly in terms of reach and

Exhibit 9-12

Top performing ad sizes by click-through rate on mobile and tablet devices (analytics derived from more than 300 billion data points)

Source: From *Medialets H1-2014 Mobile & Tablet Advertising Benchmarks Report,* August 27, 2014.

frequency. In digital media, where engagement is important, the best ad dimensions vary across handsets (phones) and tablets, as shown in Exhibit 9-12.

Should a small advertiser run a full-page ad once a month or a quarter-page ad once a week? Is it better to use a few 60-second commercials or many 15- and 30-second ones? The planner has to consider the nature of the advertising message; some simply require more time and space to explain. Competitive activity often dictates more message units. The product itself may demand the prestige of a full page or full color. However, it's often better to run small ads consistently rather than one large ad occasionally. Unfortunately, space and time units may be determined by someone other than the media planner—creative or account service, for example—in which case the planner's options are limited.

The position of an ad is another consideration. Preferred positions for magazine ads are front and back covers; for TV, sponsorship of prime-time shows. Special positions and sponsorships cost more, so the media planner must decide whether the increased reach and frequency are worth the higher costs. The position of search engine results on Google or Bing can dictate whether an organic or paid search result is ever seen. If a search result doesn't appear on the first page, it is unlikely that users will view the second page of results. Similarly, search results appearing above the fold, the first half of the screen before a user scrolls down, generate the most clicks. According to a study by the Internet Marketing Ninjas, the number one ranked search result is clicked over 21 percent of the time, whereas the number six result receives less than 3 percent.[44]

The digital environment provides the opportunity for a variety of ad sizes. Websites typically allow advertisers to display image-based ads that animate. Common sizes are banner ads (468 × 60 pixels) or squares (250 × 250) that appear throughout the website,

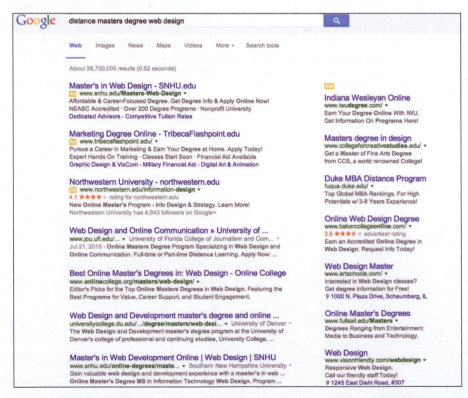

Online advertising plays by different rules than does conventional. Advertisers pay for behavior (clicks) rather than for exposure.

Source: Google

My IMC Campaign 9–A

Developing Media Objectives and Strategies

Over the past 20 years, the media landscape has changed dramatically, becoming much more fragmented and full of choice. This has elevated the complexity of the media planning role. In this part of your assignment, you are nonetheless considering all types of media to help distribute your message. You will most likely be given a media budget and asked to formulate a plan of attack. To better support your choices, it is imperative that you develop sound objectives and strategies.

In some cases, your professor may have given you a set of marketing objectives, or your research on clients may have indicated their main goals for advertising. It is important to note here that marketing objectives do not equal media objectives. They do, however, help us shape our media objectives, which in turn help us develop sound media strategy.

Developing Media Objectives

The first place to start in developing media objectives is with the marketing objectives themselves. You should view media objectives as the goals that become the building blocks of the media plan and that ultimately help clients meet their marketing goals.

Here are some examples of marketing objectives, translated into media objectives:

Marketing Objectives

- Increase awareness among target audience by 23 percent.
- Steal 2 percent share of sales from competitors.
- Build customer database of 5,000 individuals.

Media Objectives

- Generate mass awareness among target audience.
- Differentiate brand from competitors.
- Generate leads/requests for more information.

While the media objectives seem very similar to marketing objectives, they are actually quite different. Media objectives should focus on only what the media can achieve. Remember that the media plan is one of many components that go into building a successful promotional or communications plan, and it has a distinct role, which is what you are trying to highlight in the objectives.

Developing Media Strategies

Media strategies are born out of the media objectives and describe a specific plan of action for achieving stated objectives. The strategy seeks to accomplish two things: setting the foundation for media ideas that help you meet the objective or goal and providing a position of advantage over your client's competitors.

The media strategy itself is built on key plan parameters on which the entire communications team has had input:

- Target audience
- Seasonality
- Geography
- Overall communication goals
- Budget
- Creative
- Competitive analysis

So how do media objectives translate into strategies? Let's look at the three we detailed earlier:

Media Objectives

- Generate mass awareness among target audience.
- Differentiate brand from competitors.
- Generate leads/requests for more information.

Media Strategies

- Use mass media (broadcast) to build reach against M18–34.
- Secure high-profile sponsorship with category exclusivity.
- Use interactive media to elicit registration.

In the subsequent media chapters (Chapters 12–14), we'll discuss the different ways to better evaluate the opportunities within each of the media.

while leaderboards (728 × 90) are typically placed on the very top of websites. When running video ads, media planners can choose from in-stream video, ads within a video player that appear before (pre-roll), during (mid-roll) or after (post-roll) a piece of video content; out-stream video, ads that automatically play on mute as soon as a page loads; and in-banner ads, standard banner ads (i.e., 300 × 250 pixels) with videos embedded inside that can expand when rolled over.[45] Websites are constantly testing to determine the length of video that will adequately hold the user's attention. Websites such as Facebook and YouTube have introduced 6-second video ads, which can produce higher engagement without interrupting the user's experience, compared to 15- and 30-second ads.

As we can see, the nature of the creative work has the potential to greatly affect the media strategy. This means that media planners have to be flexible because the initial media plan may well have been determined prior to beginning the creative work.

Buyer Purchase Patterns

Finally, the customer's product-purchasing behavior affects every element of the media mix. The media planner must consider how, when, and where the product is typically purchased and repurchased. Products with short purchase cycles (convenience foods and paper towels) require more constant levels of advertising than products purchased infrequently (refrigerators and furniture).

Stating the Media Strategy

A written rationale for the media strategy is an integral part of any media plan. Without one, it's difficult for client and agency management to analyze the logic and consistency of the recommended media schedule.

Generally, the strategy statement begins with a brief definition of target audiences (the *market* element) and the priorities for weighting them. It explains the nature of the message and indicates which media types will be used and why (the *media* element). It outlines specific reach, frequency, and continuity goals and how they are to be achieved (the *methodology* element). It provides a budget for each medium (the *money* element) including the cost of production and any collateral materials. Finally, it states the intended size of message units, any position or timing considerations (the *mechanics* element), and the effect of budget restrictions.

 LO 9-6

Once the strategy is delineated, the plan details the tactics to be employed, the subject of the next section.

Media Tactics: Selecting and Scheduling Media Vehicles

Once the general media strategy is determined, the media planner can select and schedule particular media vehicles. The planner usually considers each medium's value on a set of specific criteria (see Ad Lab 9-B).

Criteria for Selecting Individual Media Vehicles

In evaluating specific media vehicles, the planner considers several factors: overall campaign objectives and strategy; size and characteristics of each medium's audience; attention, exposure, and motivational value of each medium; and cost efficiency.

Overall Campaign Objectives and Strategy

The media planner's first job is to review the nature of the product or service, the intended objectives and strategies, and the primary and secondary target markets and audiences. The characteristics of the product often suggest a suitable choice. A product with a distinct personality or image, such as a fine perfume, might be advertised in media that reinforce this image. The media planner considers how consumers regard various magazines and TV programs—feminine or masculine, highbrow or lowbrow, serious or frivolous—and determines whether they're appropriate for the brand.

The content and editorial policy of the media vehicle and its compatibility with the product are important considerations. *Tennis* magazine is a poor vehicle for alcohol ads even though its demographic profile and image might match the desired target audience.

Consumers choose a particular media vehicle because they gain some "reward": self-improvement, financial advice, career guidance, or simply news and entertainment. Advertising is most effective when it positions a product as part of the solution that consumers seek. Otherwise, they may see it as an intrusion.[46]

If the marketing objective is to gain greater product distribution, the planner should select media that influence potential dealers. If the goal is to stimulate sales of a nationally distributed product in isolated markets, ads should be placed in local and regional media that penetrate those markets. Pricing strategy influences media choices too. A premium-priced product should use prestigious or classy media to support its market image.

AD Lab 9–B

Media Selection: A Quick List of Advantages

Medium	Advantages
Newspapers	Many ad sizes available. Quick placement, local targeting. Audience interest.
Magazines	High-quality graphics/reproduction. Prestige factor. Color. Selective targeting.
TV	Combines sight, sound, movement. A single message. Demonstration. Social dominance.
Radio	Intimacy. Loyal following. Ability to change message quickly. Repetition and frequency.
Internet	Immediate response. Interactive. Highly selective targeting. Global.
Direct mail	Measurable. Graphics, color. 3-D. Highly personal. Adaptable message length.
Outdoor/Transit	Local targeting. Graphics, color. Simple message. Larger than life. Repetition.
Mobile	Immediate response. Interactive. Personal. Fastest-growing medium.

Laboratory Applications

1. If you wanted a set of complementary media to cover all the creative advantages, which mix would you select?
2. What creative advantages can you add to the list?

Advertising in digital media changes the planning process substantially when it is accomplished through **programmatic advertising.** Programmatic advertising buys are done largely via computer programs that match content sites (such as CNN.com or MTV.com) to advertisers via an advertising exchange (see Exhibit 9-13).

Characteristics of Media Audiences

An **audience** is the total number of people or households exposed to a medium. The planner needs to know how closely the medium's audience matches the profile of the target market and how interested prospective customers are in the publication or program. A product intended for a Latino audience, for example, would likely appear in specific media directed toward Hispanics. Simmons Market Research Bureau provides research data on age, income, occupational status, and other characteristics of magazine readers. Simmons also publishes demographic and psychographic data on product usage of consumers. Likewise, Nielsen provides audience statistics for television programs and Arbitron for radio stations.

The *content* of the medium usually determines the type of people in the audience. Some radio stations emphasize in-depth news or sports; others feature jazz, rock, or classical music. Each type of programming attracts a different audience.

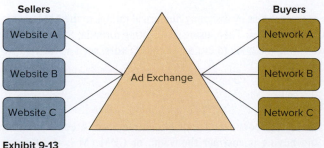

Sellers   **Buyers**

Exhibit 9-13
Ad exchange

Exposure, Attention, and Motivation Value of Media Vehicles

The media planner has to select media that will not only achieve the desired exposure to the target audience, but also attract *attention* and *motivate* people to act.

Exposure   To understand the concept of **exposure value,** think of how many people an ad "sees" rather than the other way around. How many of a magazine's 3 million readers will an ad actually see? How many of a TV program's 10 million viewers will a commercial actually see?

As we discussed earlier, just because someone reads a particular magazine or watches a certain program doesn't mean he or she sees the ads. Some people read only one article, set the magazine aside, and never pick it up again. Many people change channels during commercial breaks or leave to get a snack. Comparing the exposure value of different media vehicles, therefore, is very difficult. Without statistics, media planners have to use their best judgment based on experience.

Five main factors affect the probability of ad exposure:

1. The senses used to perceive messages from the medium (e.g., scratch-and-sniff ads really improve the exposure value of magazines).
2. How much and what kind of attention the medium requires (higher involvement suggests greater ad exposure).
3. Whether the medium is an information source or a diversion (e.g., radio news programs offer greater ad exposure than elevator music).
4. Whether the medium or program aims at a general or a specialized audience (exposure value will be higher with specialized audiences).
5. The placement of the ad in the vehicle (placement within broadcast programs gives greater exposure than placement between programs; ads placed next to editorial material get greater exposure than ads placed next to other print ads).

Attention   Degree of attention is another consideration. As we discussed in Chapter 5, consumers with no interest in motorcycles or cosmetics won't typically remember ads for those products. For a variety of reasons, they fail to penetrate the viewer's perceptual screens. But someone in the market for a new car tends to notice every car ad.

Exposure value relates only to the medium; **attention value** concerns the advertising message and copy, as well as the medium. Special-interest media, such as boating magazines, offer good attention value to a marine product because the reader is in the boating mindset. But what kind of attention value does the daily newspaper offer such a product? Do sailors think about boats while reading the newspaper? Much research still needs to be done, but six factors are known to increase attention value:[47]

1. Audience involvement with editorial content or program material.
2. Specialization of audience interest or identification.
3. Number of competitive advertisers (the fewer, the better).
4. Audience familiarity with the advertiser's campaign.
5. Quality of advertising reproduction.
6. Timeliness of advertising exposure.

Motivation   These same factors affect a medium's **motivation value,** but in different ways. Familiarity with the advertiser's campaign may affect attention significantly but motivation very little. The attention factors of quality reproduction and timeliness can motivate someone, however.

Media planners analyze these values by assigning numerical ratings to their judgments of a medium's strengths and weaknesses. Then, using a weighting formula, they add them up. Planners use similar weighting methods to evaluate other factors, such as the relative importance of age versus income.

Cost Efficiency of Media Vehicles

Finally, media planners analyze the cost efficiency of each medium. A common term used in media planning and buying is **cost per thousand, or CPM** (M is the Roman numeral for 1,000). If a daily newspaper has 300,000 subscribers and charges $5,000 for a full-page ad, the cost per thousand is the cost divided by the number of thousands of people in the audience. Because there are 300 thousand subscribers, you divide $5,000 by 300:

$$CPM = \frac{\$5,000}{300,000 \div 1,000} = \frac{\$5,000}{300} = \$16.67 \text{ per thousand}$$

However, media planners are more interested in **cost efficiency**—the cost of exposing the message to the target audience rather than to the total circulation. Let's say the target audience is males ages 18 to 49, and 40 percent of a weekly newspaper's subscriber base of 250,000 fits this category. If the paper charges $3,000 for a full-page ad, the CPM is computed as follows:

$$\text{Total audience} = 0.40 \times 250,000 = 100,000$$

$$CPM = \frac{\$3,000}{100,000 \div 1,000} = \$30 \text{ per thousand}$$

The daily paper, on the other hand, might turn out to be more cost efficient if 60 percent of its readers (180,000) belong to the target audience:

$$CPM = \frac{\$5,000}{180,000 \div 1,000} = \$27.78 \text{ per thousand}$$

Comparing different media by CPMs is important but does not take into account each medium's other advantages and disadvantages. The media planner must evaluate all the criteria to determine

1. How much of each medium's audience matches the target audience, also described as *composition*.
2. How each medium satisfies the campaign's objectives and strategy.
3. How well each medium offers attention, exposure, and motivation.

To evaluate some of these issues in broadcast, the media planner may want to calculate the **cost per point (CPP)** of different programs. This is done the same way as cost per thousand, except you divide the cost by the rating points instead of the gross impressions.

Economics of Foreign Media

The main purpose of media advertising is to communicate with customers more efficiently than through personal selling. In some developing countries, though, it's actually cheaper to send people out with baskets of samples. For mass marketers in the United States, this kind of personal contact is virtually impossible.

In many foreign markets, outdoor advertising enjoys far greater coverage than in the United States because it costs less to have people paint the signs and there is also less government restriction.

Cost inhibits the growth of broadcast media in some foreign markets, but most countries now sell advertising time to help foot the bills. China and Vietnam, for example, have recently become booming markets for advertising.[48] As more countries allow commercial broadcasts and international satellite channels gain a greater foothold, TV advertising will continue to grow.

The Synergy of Mixed Media

A combination of media is called a **mixed-media approach.** There are numerous reasons for using mixed media:

- To reach people who are unavailable through only one medium.
- To provide repeat exposure in a less-expensive secondary medium after attaining optimum reach in the first.
- To use the intrinsic value of an additional medium to extend the creative effectiveness of the ad campaign (such as music on radio along with long copy in print media).

- ■ To deliver coupons in print media when the primary vehicle is broadcast.
- ■ To produce **synergy,** where the total effect is greater than the sum of its parts.

Newspapers, for example, can be used to introduce a new product and give immediacy to the message. Magazine ads can then follow up for greater detail, image enhancement, longevity, and memory improvement.

A mixed-media campaign was effective for General Electric's lighting products. The promotion used a combination of network TV spots, print advertising, Sunday supplement inserts, in-store displays in more than 150,000 stores, and a highly creative publicity program. By using an integrated, mixed-media approach, the campaign produced "unprecedented" consumer awareness and dealer support. It achieved synergy.[49]

Methods for Scheduling Media

After selecting the appropriate media vehicles, the media planner decides how many space or time units to buy of each vehicle and schedules them for release over a period of time when consumers are most apt to buy the product.

Continuous, Flighting, and Pulsing Schedules

To build continuity in a campaign, planners use three principal scheduling tactics: *continuous, flighting,* and *pulsing* (see Exhibit 9-14).

In a **continuous schedule,** advertising runs steadily and varies little over the campaign period. It's the best way to build continuity. Advertisers use this scheduling pattern for products consumers purchase regularly. For example, a commercial is scheduled on radio stations WTKO and WRBI for an initial four-week period. Then, to maintain continuity in the campaign, additional spots run continuously every week throughout the year on station WRBI.

Flighting alternates periods of advertising with periods of no advertising. This intermittent schedule makes sense for products and services that experience large fluctuations in demand throughout the year (tax services, lawn-care products, cold remedies). The advertiser might introduce the product with a four-week flight and then schedule three additional four-week flights to run during seasonal periods later in the year.

The third alternative, **pulsing,** mixes continuous and flighting strategies. As the consumer's purchasing cycle gets longer, pulsing becomes more appropriate. The advertiser maintains a low level of advertising all year but uses periodic pulses to heavy up during peak selling periods. This strategy is appropriate for products like soft drinks, which are consumed all year but more heavily in the summer.

Additional Scheduling Patterns

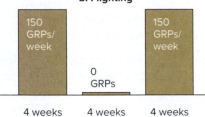

Exhibit 9-14
Three ways to schedule the same number of total gross rating points: continuous, flighting, and pulsing.

For high-ticket items that require careful consideration, **bursting**—running the same commercial every half hour on the same network during prime time—can be effective. A variation is **roadblocking,** buying air time on all three networks simultaneously. Chrysler used this technique to give viewers the impression that the advertiser was everywhere, even if the ad showed for only a few nights. Digital Equipment used a scheduling tactic called **blinking** to stretch its slim ad budget. To reach business executives, it flooded the airwaves on Sundays (on both cable and network TV channels) to make it virtually impossible to miss the ads.[50]

Once the scheduling criteria are determined, the media planner creates a flowchart of the plan. The flowchart is a graphic presentation of the total campaign to let the creative department, media department, account services, and the client see the pattern of media events that will occur throughout the campaign, usually over one year (see Exhibit 9-15).

LO 9-7

Artificial Intelligence in Media Selection and Scheduling

As suggested earlier in the chapter, programmatic advertising relies on computers to match messages and audiences in real time based on complex algorithms of what advertisers are willing to pay and content providers are willing to sell. While programmatic advertising is largely found in digital media buys, some believe it will become a bigger part of the

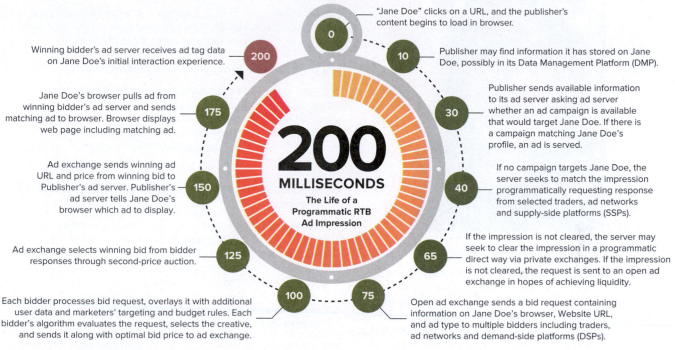

200MS: The Life of a Programmatic RTB Ad Impression

0 — "Jane Doe" clicks on a URL, and the publisher's content begins to load in browser.

200 — Winning bidder's ad server receives ad tag data on Jane Doe's initial interaction experience.

10 — Publisher may find information it has stored on Jane Doe, possibly in its Data Management Platform (DMP).

175 — Jane Doe's browser pulls ad from winning bidder's ad server and sends matching ad to browser. Browser displays web page including matching ad.

30 — Publisher sends available information to its ad server asking ad server whether an ad campaign is available that would target Jane Doe. If there is a campaign matching Jane Doe's profile, an ad is served.

150 — Ad exchange sends winning ad URL and price from winning bid to Publisher's ad server. Publisher's ad server tells Jane Doe's browser which ad to display.

40 — If no campaign targets Jane Doe, the server seeks to match the impression programmatically requesting response from selected traders, ad networks and supply-side platforms (SSPs).

125 — Ad exchange selects winning bid from bidder responses through second-price auction.

65 — If the impression is not cleared, the server may seek to clear the impression in a programmatic direct way via private exchanges. If the impression is not cleared, the request is sent to an open ad exchange in hopes of achieving liquidity.

100 — Each bidder processes bid request, overlays it with additional user data and marketers' targeting and budget rules. Each bidder's algorithm evaluates the request, selects the creative, and sends it along with optimal bid price to ad exchange.

75 — Open ad exchange sends a bid request containing information on Jane Doe's browser, Website URL, and ad type to multiple bidders including traders, ad networks and demand-side platforms (DSPs).

200 MILLISECONDS — The Life of a Programmatic RTB Ad Impression

Exhibit 9-15

Media Crossing, a leading independent digital media trading company, created this graphic that sequences the 200-millisecond birth of a programmatic ad. You can watch a video of the process here: www.youtube.com/watch?v=rTg9I4d8MU4.

Courtesy of Media Crossing.

way traditional media are bought and sold as well. Exhibit 9-15 shows how quickly a variety of complicated processes take place during programmatic advertising. While programmatic advertising is largely found in digital media buys, it is becoming a bigger part of the way other media are bought and sold. In fact, programmatic spending in TV will increase over 82 percent from 2018 to 2019, to $3.8 billion.[51] Mobile and digital display programmatic spending are also on the rise, with mobile reaching over $36 billion and digital display over $45 billion in 2019.[52]

Even when not relying on programmatic advertising, most planners use software to determine optimized buys of traditional media. Telmar was the first company to provide media planning systems on a syndicated basis. Today, it is the world's leading supplier of media planning software and support services. More than 3,500 users in 85 countries, including the majority of the world's top agencies, use Telmar systems for media and marketing decision making.[53]

Telmar's software suite is designed to help media planners, buyers, research analysts, and sellers work more efficiently and make better judgments in the evaluation or sales process. The software allows advertising executives to estimate the effectiveness of multifaceted marketing plans that use various combinations of media including print, broadcast, in-store, special promotions, special events, PR, and other "new media." Its flexibility permits the user to analyze the potential effectiveness of any and every marketing tool used to reach the consumer.

Similarly, Bionic provides a wide range of information systems for the advertising industry. The company produces easy-to-use, sophisticated media planning and analysis

People BEHIND the Ads

Tria Chingcuangco, Director, Strategy & Planning, at PowerPhyl Media

Courtesty of Tria Chingcuangco

As Director of Strategy & Planning at PowerPhyl Media Solutions, Tria leads planning teams for a wide range of clients. After nearly a decade, as a director at Tangible Media, she oversaw national and local media campaigns encompassing digital media (display, social, search engine marketing, video, and mobile), traditional media (TV, radio, outdoor, print, and experiential) as well as leading new business initiatives. Clientele included fragrance, health care, and tourism accounts. She previously worked at Allscope Media and Universal McCann.

Tria earned a bachelor of arts degree in art history with a minor in philosophy from the University at Buffalo.

We asked Tria to comment on the dramatic changes taking place in media and on the skills and qualities that make for a top media planner:

CA: What are the biggest changes right now in the world of media planning?

TC: Consumer media behaviors are extremely segmented. People consume content in various ways, using multiple devices, whenever they want. It's an even bigger challenge to find the most qualified audiences across a plethora of media partners.

CA: What do you do to stay current and abreast of these changes?

TC: We educate ourselves and then we test. The only way we stay relevant is by testing new opportunities. When beta opportunities are available, or when brand study opportunities are presented, we jump at the opportunity.

CA: What qualities do you consider important in a media planner?

TC: It is important to be able to exhibit critical thinking and exceptional analytical skills. As media planners, we are consistently challenged to prove the success of our media campaigns.

CA: What was your own path to your present career?

TC: I was lucky to start this career right out of college. A recruiter introduced me to this field, and I never looked back. I worked for some big agencies, with big clients, but I've also worked for more boutique shops. You have to find what works best for you. I find that in smaller shops, you'll have greater autonomy and more room to learn and grow.

CA: What kind of strategic resources do you use to help clients plan media?

TC: The first place we look is within our internal and historical data. That seems to yield better results when we know the reasons behind successes and failures. As an agency, we are a Google Premier Partner, which means we have access to Google's proprietary research tools and other insights not available to the public.

CA: How has programmatic advertising changed the way you plan media?

TC: In theory, programmatic advertising should make planning easier, and in a lot of ways it does. But it can also introduce other challenges such as brand safety and campaign delivery. Is it really reaching the audience you want to target? It becomes important that you implement verification tools as a safety measure. A lot of clients are willing to pay for that kind of assurance.

CA: How does media planning integrate with the account planning and creative teams?

TC: At PowerPhyl, we are responsible for the roles of both account planning and media planning. We have direct access to the client, which streamlines the process. Most of our clients have their own creative agencies, so we'll directly work with them on projects.

CA: What advice do you have for students beginning a career in media and advertising?

TC: Go on interviews even while you are still in school. Observe the agency culture, ask a lot of questions, and just soak it all in. If possible, find an opportunity that you are passionate about. Always do your research and never come to an interview without a copy of your résumé.

Courtesy of Tria Chingcuangco

software that planners use to analyze both industry and proprietary research. The software enables media planners to track planned spending and other crucial information by brand, campaign, market, and region.[54]

AdSense by Google is an invaluable tool for media planning, especially for small websites as it allows them to generate revenue from visitors. And it offers ad buyers access to tens of thousands of niche markets.

Source: Google

Programmatic advertising is forcing media planners to rethink the way they go about planning media. The ability to communicate with consumers throughout the decision-making journey is an opportunity to provide insightful and meaningful information to assist in the customer's moment of need. Engaging creative advertising can be tailored and customized to consumers depending on the channel they are on, the device they are using, and the individual's exposure to the brand. Reporting can be viewed in real time, enabling optimizations to ensure that ads are only shown to people who are likely to buy the product or service. Return on investment can be maximized because target setting can be altered instantly. Due to real-time bidding, there is no risk of overpayment because advertisers can set the price they are willing to pay.

Despite the benefits of programmatic advertising, there are some disadvantages. Employing the technology can be expensive. For example, it would take five full-time employees to spend a $100 million national broadcast budget, while the same number would be needed for a $5 million programmatic buy. Ad-serving and technology targeting fees can amount to more than 50 cents out of every dollar.[55]

The automation of programmatic advertising can also lead to poorly and inappropriately placed ads. For example, Citibank placed an ad in *People* with a smiling couple enjoying a skiing vacation next to an article about a man who tragically died on a snow mountain in Argentina.[56] Programmatic advertising also opens up the potential for fraud. In 2015, the U.S. ad industry lost a total of over $8 billion from ad fraud.[57] This occurs through nonviewable ads, in which ads are placed but never reach a user. Several organizations have implemented services to defend against fraudulent practices. DoubleVerify evaluates the quality of each impression delivered, and the Interactive Advertising Bureau (IAB) has initiated the ads.txt project. Ads.txt stands for Authorized Digital Sellers and is a secure method that publishers and distributors can use to publicly declare the companies they authorize to sell their digital inventory.[58] These tools are creating greater transparency in the inventory supply chain, making it more difficult for counterfeit and fraudulent activity to occur.

Even with all the technological timesavers and shortcuts that programmatic advertising affords, it's still up to the media planner to know the product, the market, and the media, and to then make the call. Computers can't decide which medium or environment is best for the message. They can't evaluate the content of a magazine or the image of a TV program. They can't judge whether the numbers they're fed are valid or reliable, and they can't interpret the meaning of the numbers. What they can do is help the process along.

Chapter Summary

Traditionally, professionals have defined media planning as the analysis and selection of channels that direct advertising messages to the right people in the right place at the right time. As with all IMC functions, changes in technology have dramatically changed the practice of media planning.

Media plans follow from earlier decisions that have been made about marketing strategies and advertising objectives and strategies. Advertising strategies include the elements of the creative mix: the product concept, the target audience, the message, and communications media. The media department ensures the advertising message goes to the right target audience in an effective manner.

The media function involves two basic processes: planning media strategy and selecting media vehicles. Media plans begin by defining audience objectives—the specific types of people the advertising message will be directed to—and then establishing goals for communicating with those audiences.

Planners who follow an IMC model start by segmenting their audiences according to brand purchasing behavior and then ranking these segments by profit to the brand. Once the target audience is determined, the planner sets the message-distribution objectives. These specify where, when, and how often the advertising should appear. They may be expressed in terms of message weight, reach, frequency, and continuity. In this process, the planner considers the amount of advertising needed to achieve effectiveness.

To create the media strategy, a planner blends the five Ms: markets, money, media, mechanics, and methodology. There may be many uncontrollable variables: the scope of the media plan, which is determined by the location and makeup of the target audience; the sales potential of different markets for both the brand and the product category; competitive strategies and budget considerations; media availability and economics; the nature of the medium and the mood of the message; the size, length, and position of the message in the selected media; and buyer purchase patterns. IMC planners try to discover the reasons and motivations for people's purchase and usage patterns and then create media plans based on those findings.

After the media strategy is developed, the planner implements specific media tactics that include the choice of vehicles. Vehicles are selected to maximize exposure, attention, and the motivation value of their audiences. Other factors that influence the selection process include vehicle cost efficiency and the advisability of a mixed-media approach.

Once media vehicles are selected, the media planner decides on scheduling—how many of each medium's space or time units to buy over what period of time. A media campaign can run continuously or in erratic pulses. These decisions are affected by consumer purchase patterns, the product's seasonality, and the balance of reach, frequency, and continuity that meets the planner's media objectives and budget. Once the campaign launches, data are monitored and optimizations are made to improve performance based on the predetermined evaluation criteria.

Media planning is changing as a result of artificial intelligence, sophisticated computer programs and networks, and the growth of digital media. Programmatic advertising, in which advertisers place bids for desired audiences, is growing at a fast rate and is likely to become a dominant method for placing ads in the not-too-distant future.

Important Terms

advertising impression, *296*

advertising response curve, *299*

attention value, *310*

audience, *309*

audience objectives, *295*

blinking, *312*

brand development index (BDI), *302*

bursting, *312*

category development index (CDI), *303*

circulation, *296*

continuity, *299*

continuous schedule, *312*

cost efficiency, *311*

cost per point (CPP), *311*

cost per thousand (CPM), *310*

creative mix, *292*

distribution objectives, *295*

effective frequency, *299*

effective reach, *299*

exposure value, *309*

five Ms (5Ms), *300*

flighting, *312*

frequency, *298*

gross impressions, *296*

gross rating points (GRPs), *297*

markets, *300*

mechanics, *301*

media, *301*

media planning, *284*

media vehicles, *295*

message weight, *296*

methodology, *301*

mixed-media approach, *311*

money, *300*

motivation value, *310*

opportunity to see (OTS), *296*

programmatic advertising, *309*

pulsing, *312*

rating, *297*

reach, *297*

readers per copy (RPC), *296*

recency planning, *300*

roadblocking, *312*

spillover media, *305*

synergy, *312*

television households (TVHH), *297*

Review Questions

1. What major factors contribute to the increased complexity of media planning?

2. What must media planners consider before they begin?

3. What secondary research sources are available to planners?

4. How does the IMC approach differ from the top-down media planning approach?

5. What are the "right" reach and frequency for a given message?

6. How are GRPs and CPMs calculated?

7. What are the 5Ms of the media mix, and how are they determined?

8. What major factors influence the choice of individual media vehicles?

9. Why might an advertiser use a mixed-media approach?

10. What are the principal methods used to schedule media?

The Advertising Experience

1. **Diversity in Media Planning**

   As a planner working on behalf of a large toy company, it is your job to buy media space for the launch of the Kitchi Kiss doll, which all advertising research shows will be a tremendous profit maker for the company. The product is expected to have greatest appeal to girls aged 5–11. How can you ensure that the diversity considerations outlined in this chapter's Ethics, Diversity and Inclusion box can be incorporated in your media plan?

2. **Media-Buying Service**

   There are three sides to the media business: planning, buying, and selling. Media planning and media buying are often in-house functions at an advertising agency, while sellers are those who represent the various media to clients, agencies, and media-buying services.

   Visit the websites for the media companies listed below, consider the impact and importance of each to advertisers and their agencies, and answer the questions that follow.

   - The Davis Group: www.thedavisgrouptx.com
   - Initiative Media: www.initiative.com
   - Wavemaker: www.wavemakerglobal.com
   - Media Solutions: www.mediasol.com
   - Worldata: www.worldata.com
   - Zenith: www.zenithmedia.com

   a. Who is the intended audience(s) of the site?

   b. What is the site's purpose? Does it succeed? Why or why not?

   c. What is the company's purpose?

   d. Does the company specialize in any particular segment (consumer, business-to-business, agriculture, automotive)?

3. **Media Organizations**

   The world of media is vast and constantly changing. Many media giants own properties in several media categories and are major forces in the world of advertising. Visit the websites for the following media companies and answer the questions below.

   - Valassis: www.valassis.com
   - Cox Enterprises: www.coxenterprises.com
   - Gannett: www.gannett.com
   - Hearst Corporation: www.hearst.com
   - McGraw-Hill: www.mheducation.com
   - Warner Media: www.warnermediagroup.com
   - Tribune Company: www.tribune.com
   - Viacom: www.viacom.com

   a. Who is the intended audience of the site?

   b. What are the size and scope of the organization?

   c. What is the organization's purpose? The site's purpose?

   d. How important is this organization to the advertising industry? Why?

4. Reread the HIV.gov chapter opening vignette. Next, answer the following questions:

   a. What media options are not being used that perhaps should be?

   b. What target audiences that are not being targeted should be?

   Be sure to justify your answers to both questions.

5. Imagine you were a media planner and a client suggested using Snapchap to help provide information about preventing the spread of HIV to teens. How would you evaluate that request? What are the pros and cons of using Snapchat as an advertising medium for this target audience? Do some research to justify your recommendations.

End Notes

1. "Campaigns," HIV.gov, www.hiv.gov/federal-resources/campaigns/.
2. "Prevention IS Care," Centers for Disease Control and Prevention, March 26, 2009, www.cdc.gov/actagainstaids/campaigns/pic/index.html.
3. Ana Swanson, "Video: What Happens When a Man with HIV Asks Strangers to Touch Him?," *The Washington Post,* June 27, 2015, www.washingtonpost.com/blogs/wonkblog/wp/2015/06/27/video-what-happens-when-a-manwith-hiv-asks-strangers-to-touch-him/.
4. AIDS.gov, "Communication Strategy: Internal Working Plan," January 2013, https://docplayer.net/4673208-Communication-strategy.html.
5. Corey McNair, *US Ad Spending: The eMarketer Forecast for 2017,* September 19, 2017.
6. "The Year's 23 Best Media Plans Sparked Conversation with Next-Level Innovation and Creativity," *Adweek,* September 16, 2018, www.adweek.com/brand-marketing/2018s-23-most-effective-media-plans-used-next-level-innovation-and-creativity-to-reach-consumers/.
7. Yumiko Ono, "Cordiant Puts Hamilton in Key U.S. Post," *Advertising Age,* July 18, 1997, p. B2.
8. Stephanie Thompson, "Universal McCann Gets $150 Million Nestlé Account," *Advertising Age,* April 12, 2002, http://adage.com; Richard Linnett and Jack Neff, "Mindshare Wins $600 Million Gillette Media Account," *Advertising Age,* September 26, 2002, http://adage.com.
9. Alexandra Bruell, "GM Parks $3 Billion Media Account at Carat," *Advertising Age,* January 24, 2012, http://adage.com; Alexandra Bruell, "MediaVest Emerges Winner in Cox Communications Review," *Advertising Age,* December 7, 2011, http://adage.com.
10. Lisa E. Phillips, "Trends in Consumers' Time Spent with Media," *eMarketer,* December 28, 2010, www.emarketer.com.
11. Jasper Jackson, "Know Your Audience: How the Digital Native Generation Consume Media," *The Media Briefing,* August 30, 2013, www.themediabriefing.com/analysis/know-your-audience-how-the-digital-native-generation-consume-media.

12. *2018 Accenture Interactive Personalization Pulse Report,* www.accenture.com/us-en/service-propelling-growth-through-personalization.

13. "Business: Hi Ho, Hi Ho, Down the Data Mine We Go," *The Economist,* August 23, 1997, pp. 47–48.

14. Larry Allen, "The Traditional Media Buying Agency Is Dead," *Business Insider,* January 17, 2012, www.businessinsider.com/the-traditional-media-buying-agency-is-dead-2012-1.

15. Callum Borchers, "In Ad Wars, Clients Want Proof of Success," *Boston Globe,* May 8, 2015, www.bostonglobe.com/business/2015/05/07/firms-face-new-pressure-deliver/y9gLXbmWHwBkMEgoonIcPM/story.html.

16. Rick Klein and Jeff Jensen, "GM's Huge Pact Raises Olympics Bar," *Advertising Age,* August 4, 1997, p. 6.

17. Christina Merrill, "Media Rising," *Adweek,* November 9, 1998.

18. Joe Mandese, "Boost for Media Buyers," *Advertising Age,* March 7, 1994, p. 47.

19. "Display Campaigns," Google, https://ads.google.com/intl/en_us/home/campaigns/display-ads/

20. "Facebook Ads," Facebook, www.facebook.com/business/products/ads.

21. Bob Lauterborn, "New Marketing Litany; Four P's Passe; C-Words Take over," *Advertising Age,* October 1, 1990, http://rlauterborn.com/pubs/pdfs/4_Cs.pdf.

22. Jullie Liesse, "Inside Burnett's Vaunted Buying Machine: Giant Agency Opens Classroom to Integrated Marketing, AA Reporter," *Advertising Age,* July 25, 1994, p. S6, https://adage.com/article/news/rethinking-media-burnett-style-chart-inside-burnett-s-vaunted-buying-machine-giant-agency-opens-classroom-integrated-marketing-aa-reporter/90860.

23. Don E. Schultz, Stanley I. Tannenbaum, and Robert F. Lauterborn, *Integrated Marketing Communications: Putting It Together & Making It Work* (Lincolnwood, IL: NTC Business Books, 1993), pp. 81–82, 108.

24. Adapted from Donald W. Jugenheimer, Arnold M. Barban, and Peter B. Turk, *Advertising Media: Strategy and Tactics* (Dubuque, IA: Brown & Benchmark, 1992), p. 131.

24. Donald W. Jugenheimer, Arnold M. Barban, and Peter B. Turk, *Advertising Media: Strategy and Tactics* (Dubuque, IA: Brown & Benchmark, 1992), pp. 131–33.

26. Jim Surmanek, *Introduction to Advertising Media: Research, Planning, and Buying* (Chicago: NTC Business Books, 1993), p. 54.

27. Shula Bigman, "First, Let's Find Out How Media Works: Making Media Accountable Means Creating New Tools," *Advertising Age,* October 5, 1998, p. 40.

28. Adapted from Jim Surmanek, *Introduction to Advertising Media: Research, Planning, and Buying* (Chicago: NTC Business Books, 1993), p. 106.

29. Donald W. Jugenheimer, Arnold M. Barban, and Peter B. Turk, *Advertising Media: Strategy and Tactics* (Dubuque, IA: Brown & Benchmark, 1992), p. 135.

30. Joe Mandese, "Revisiting Ad Reach, Frequency," *Advertising Age,* November 27, 1995, p. 46.

31. George B. Murray and John G. Jenkins, "The Concept of 'Effective Reach' in Advertising," *Journal of Advertising Research* 32, no. 3 (1992), pp. 34–44.

32. John Philip Jones, *When Ads Work: New Proof That Advertising Triggers Sales* (New York: Simon & Schuster/Lexington Books, 1995); Colin McDonald, "From 'Frequency' to 'Continuity'—Is It a New Dawn?," *Journal of Advertising Research,* July/August 1997, p. 21.

33. Hugh M. Cannon and Edward A. Riordan, "Effective Reach and Frequency: Do They Really Make Sense?," *Journal of Advertising Research,* March/April 1994, pp. 19–28.

34. Hugh M. Cannon and Edward A. Riordan, "Effective Reach and Frequency: Do They Really Make Sense?," *Journal of Advertising Research,* March/April 1994, pp. 27–28; John Philip Jones, "What Does Effective Frequency Mean in 1997?" *Journal of Advertising Research,* July/August 1997, pp. 14–20.

35. Kenneth A. Longman, "If Not Effective Frequency, Then What?" *Journal of Advertising Research,* July/August 1997, pp. 44–50; Hugh M. Cannon, John D. Leckenby, and Avery Abernethy, "Overcoming the Media Planning Paradox: From (In)Effective to Optimal Reach and Frequency," *Proceedings of the 1996 Conference of the American Academy of Advertising,* pp. 34–39.

36. Erwin Ephron, "Recency Planning," *Journal of Advertising Research,* July/August 1997, pp. 61–64.

37. Laurie Freeman, "Added Theories Drive Need for Client Solutions," *Advertising Age,* August 4, 1997, p. S18.

38. Don E. Schultz, Stanley I. Tannenbaum, and Robert F. Lauterborn, *Integrated Marketing Communications: Putting It Together & Making It Work* (Lincolnwood, IL: NTC Business Books, 1993), pp. 116–22, 132–33; Julie Liesse, "Buying by the Numbers? Hardly," *Advertising Age,* July 25, 1994, p. S16.

39. "The European Advertising & Media Forecast," *European Advertising & Media Forecast,* April 2006.

40. Joe Mandese, "Cultures Clash as 'Optimizers' Sort Out U.S. Media," *Advertising Age,* August 4, 1997, p. S2.

41. Rein Rijkens, *European Advertising Strategies* (London: Cassell, 1992), pp. 86–87.

42. Special Report: Best Media Plan Competition, "Guerrilla Tactics Get Panasonic Noticed," *Strategy* (Canada), March 27, 2000, p. BMP10.

43. Todd Pruzan, "Global Media: Distribution Slows, but Rates Climb," *Advertising Age International,* January 16, 1995, p. I19.

44. Dan O'Leary, "Announcing: 2017 Google Search Click Through Rate Study," *Internet Marketing Ninjas,* July 24, 2017, www.internetmarketingninjas.com/blog/google/announcing-2017-click-rate-study/.

45. Sara Jabbari, "What Are the Different Video Ad Formats Available?" *Pulpix,* June 8, 2017, www.pulpix.com/insights/blog/what-are-different-video-ad-formats/.

46. Neil Kelliher, "Magazine Media Planning for 'Effectiveness': Getting the People Back into the Process," *Journal of Consumer Marketing,* Summer 1990, pp. 47–55.

47. Kenneth Longman, *Advertising* (New York: Harcourt Brace Jovanovich, 1971), pp. 211–12.

48. Kevin Goldman, "With Vietnam Embargo Lifted, Agencies Gear Up for Business," *The Wall Street Journal,* February 7, 1994, p. B8.

49. "The Power of Partnership," NBC Marketing Supplement, *Advertising Age,* November 16, 1992, p. 13.

50. Kevin Goldman, "Digital Warms Couch Potatoes with Only-on-Sunday TV Ads," *The Wall Street Journal,* November 22, 1994, p. B8.

51. "US Programmatic TV Ad Spending, 2015–2019 (billions, % change and % of TV ad spending)," *eMarketer,* June 3, 2019, www.emarketer.com/Chart/US-Programmatic-TV-Ad-Spending-2015-2019-billions-change-of-TV-ad-spending/209351.

52. "eMarketer Releases New Programmatic Advertising Estimates," *eMarketer,* April 18, 2017, *www.emarketer.com/ Article/eMarketer-Releases-New-Programmatic-Advertising-Estimates/1015682*.

53. Telmar, July 2006, *www.telmar.com*.

54. Bionic, *www.bionic-ads.com/planner/.*

55. Alexandra Bruell, "Inside the Hidden Costs of Programmatic," *Advertising Age,* September 14, 2015, *http://adage.com/ article/print-edition/inside-hidden-costs-programmatic/ 300340/*.

56. Vivienne Tay, "LOOK Citibank Digital Ad Placement Gone Wrong," *Marketing,* October 19, 2016, *www.marketing-interactive.com/look-citibank-digital-ad-placement-gone-wrong/*.

57. "Digital Ad Industry Will Gain $8.2 Billion by Eliminating Fraud and Flaws in Internet Supply Chain, IAB & EY Study Shows," *IAB,* December 1, 2015, *www.iab.com/news/digital-ad-industry-will-gain-8-2-billion-by-eliminating-fraud-and-flaws-in-internet-supply-chain-iab-ey-study-shows/*.

58. Ads.txt—Authorized Digital Sellers, *https://iabtechlab.com/ ads-txt/*.

10

Creative Strategy and the Creative Process

LEARNING OBJECTIVES

To show how IMC strategies are translated into creative briefs and message strategies that guide the creative process. The chapter examines the characteristics of great campaigns, styles of thinking, the nature of creativity and its importance in advertising, and the role of the agency creative team. We discuss how research serves as the foundation for creative development and planning, and we review common problems and pitfalls faced by members of the creative team.

After studying this chapter, you will be able to:

LO10-1   Explain the attributes of great creative.

LO10-2   Describe how creative strategy is developed and used.

LO10-3   Show how creativity enhances advertising.

LO10-4   Demonstrate the role that agency talent plays in the creative process.

Source: Target Brands, Inc.

Walmart fundamentally changed the retail world, a result of its relentless focus on offering a broad selection of goods at low prices. This approach has made it the largest public company by annual revenue in the world. ■ For stores that compete with Walmart (and in this day and age, that is most stores), finding the right strategy for success is an ongoing challenge. ■ Some focus on a single product category, like clothes, electronics, pet supplies, or toys, and present a broader selection within that category. Sometimes that strategy pays off (American Eagle); sometimes it doesn't (Circuit City, Sharper Image, Toys R Us). ■ An even riskier strategy is going head-to-head, as Kmart, Sears, Montgomery Ward, and others have learned the hard way. But standing tall among the scattered ruins of Walmart's direct competitors is one company that has found a way to prosper. And that is Target. ■ Target's origins date to 1962 when the Dayton Company opened the first store in a Minneapolis suburb. The company grew through a strategy of both store openings and competitor acquisitions.[1] ■ With nearly 1,700 stores throughout the United States, Target ranked 39 in the 2019 *Fortune 500* and is eighth in overall revenue among U.S. retailers. Not bad for an organization whose greatest expansion occurred during the same years that Walmart conquered the world. ■ How has Target succeeded where other retail giants have not? In part by being one of the greatest practitioners of positioning, a concept we introduced in Chapter 8. Everyone knows that Walmart is synonymous with the concept of a "big box store." To the individual who is looking to save money but finds Walmart's offerings just a bit ordinary or who wants a more attractive shopping environment, Target proudly proclaims, "Expect more, pay less." ■ The slogan says it all. You'll save money at Target (compared to many retailers) and you'll have more fun shopping (compared to Walmart). The promise of a better shopping experience (the "expect more" part of the equation) has been the key. ■ Start with the merchandise. Lots of the things you find at Target you can find at Walmart as well, but Target displays them with more style and space. And some things you can't get at Walmart, or anywhere else— in-house lines like Xhilaration[2] and Universal Thread, and specially produced products from Opalhouse and Heyday.[3] ■ Then, there is the red. Lots of red. As Michael Francis, senior VP of marketing at the retailer, notes, "Trust us, red does go with everything." The strategy at Target is to "own red," that is, have the consumer associate the color with the brand. ■ One means for communicating that Target owns red is through its retail stores. But the color plays a prominent role in Target advertising as well and helps tie the many executions together in a seamless campaign. ■ Target spends nearly four times as much on its advertising as a percentage of sales than does Walmart.[4] Its ads are fun and quirky, in direct contrast to Walmart's more conservative, "hard-sell," approach. Target uses lifestyle themes to suggest ways that its products help shoppers to express themselves. The campaigns have been remarkably effective, and have helped fuel Target's growth. "Value" means different things to different people. Target's creative and captivating ads have helped the company position itself as a more enjoyable place to shop than its biggest competitor. The strategy has helped Target thrive even in the midst of Walmart's successes. ■

This chapter focuses on advertising creation, as advertising is the component of IMC over which creative people have the greatest control. Many of the more general creative processes are equally important for other IMC elements as well. In the next chapter we'll explain several of the unique considerations in developing copy and art for other elements of IMC.

The creative spark begins with a team typically composed of an art director and a copywriter. The **copywriter** is responsible for the *verbal* message, the copy (words) communicated by the ad's imaginary persona. The **art director** is responsible for the *nonverbal* aspect of the message, the design, which determines the visual look and intuitive feel. Together, they work under the supervision of a **creative director** (typically, a former copywriter or art director), who is ultimately responsible for the creative product—the form the final message takes. In large agencies, there are many creative teams working under a creative director. In a very small agency the creative director may be a team of one. As a group, these people are referred to as **creatives.**

This chapter focuses on the creative process: how it starts, develops, and relates to marketing and advertising strategy. We then examine production: the events between the creative ideas and the ultimate execution.

What Makes for Great Creative?

Pause for a moment and think of some ads you've seen that you would describe as great— the ones you'll always remember. As you think of these different ads, what are their common characteristics? In your opinion, what makes an ad great?

Some of the classic ads in history offer a few clues about greatness: Think of Volkswagen's famous "Think small" ad; DeBeers' "A diamond is forever" line; Clairol's "Does she or doesn't she?"; Burger King's "Have it your way"; Nike's "Just do it"; and Coca-Cola's "The real thing." What makes these campaigns great?

This is a very important question because research indicates that "ad liking" helps predict "ad success." No wonder, then, that agencies want to create ads that people like. But is liking all that is required for an ad to be great?

Bright colorful images, geometric shapes, and strong contrasts in both copy and graphics are qualities for great creative ads. Not only do they successfully draw the reader's attention, they help brand Target as an "upscale" discount store.

Source: Target Brands, Inc.

Whether it's a billboard, a print ad, an Instagram story, or a website, great ads do have certain commonalities. We can group most of these characteristics into two dimensions: *audience impact* and *strategic relevance.*

The Impact Dimension

The first thing an ad must do is capture an audience member's attention and then hold it. For this reason, a great ad makes an impact on its intended audience. It *resonates.*

Why? Because of the boom factor.

When a cannon goes "boom," it gets your attention—right now. So it is with an ad. It's the surprise element—the "aha." It not only gets your attention, it catches your imagination. In this sense it's like great art. It invites you to stop and think about the message.

Other ads have an impact for different reasons. Look at the Target ad, juxtaposing colors, the expressions of the models, and copy (i.e., "all about warm" versus "all about sparkle.") The ad is unusual, even for Target, so we stop to examine it more closely. And as

One way Target communicates that it offers an extraordinary shopping experience is through the use of extraordinary ads that successfully capture the attention of its consumers. Consider all of the ways this ad showcases the boom factor, from effective use of color to the positions and expressions of the models.

Source: Target Brands, Inc.

we do so, the colors and the familiar logo convey so much about Target. Ads like this help the retailer convincingly claim you should "expect more." The ad resonates.

Unfortunately, most ads, whether they're informational or transformational, have little impact. Why? Because they lack a "big idea" or they fail in the *execution.* The copy may be uninspiring, the visual may be less than attractive, or the production techniques may be of low quality. From the consumer's point of view, these ads are just a waste of time. From the client's, they are a waste of money.

The Relevance Dimension

The second dimension of great advertising is strategic relevance. An ad may get you to think, but what does it get you to think about? A classic example is the old Taco Bell "Yo Quiero Taco Bell" campaign featuring a speaking chihuahua. It captured everyone's imagination, but it reinforced the wrong feeling—people took delight in the cute dog, not the menu items.

Behind every creative team's choice of tone, words, and ideas lies an advertising strategy. When the ad is completed, it must be relevant to the strategy, or it will fail—even if it resonates with the audience. In other words, it may be great *entertainment,* but not great *advertising.* Great advertising always has a strategic mission to fulfill.

Recall from Chapter 5 our discussion of consumer motives. *Negatively originated motives,* such as problem avoidance or problem removal, provide the foundation for many great ads. Ads can achieve relevance by being highly **informational,** that is, by offering relief from some problem (e.g., one gym's advertising headline reads, "Need to lose 30 pounds?"). Other motives are *positively originated* as consumers seek sensory gratification, intellectual stimulation, or social approval. Here, ads achieve greatness by being **transformational,** using positive reinforcement to offer a reward (Microsoft's headlines for Office read, "I want to make it great," followed by reasons, such as "for a VIP presentation at work" or "so I can get an A at school").

Perhaps the best example of the importance of relevance is the success of search engine advertising. As we will demonstrate in Chapter 14, Google ads may not be the prettiest or most creative, but they are usually relevant because Google displays ads based on the words users input during their search. Google's massive revenues are proof that when an IMC message is relevant, people respond.

Developing and Implementing the Creative Strategy

Let's look at the advertising strategy that Target and its agencies developed. Then we'll see how they translated that into a message strategy and a big idea and, finally, into effective ads.

Recall from Chapter 8 that creative strategy consists of four elements: the *target audience,* the *product concept,* the *communications media,* and the *message.*

What is Target's **target audience?** Target focuses on value-conscious shoppers, usually adults ages 25 to 49 with families, who seek products that are nicer than those typically found at deep-discount stores. These shoppers are not poor, but they do look to save money (Target reports that the median household income of its shoppers, or "guests," as the company calls them, is $60,000). This group is Target's *primary market*—that's who the company sells to. So Target definitely wants them to see and like its advertising. Because Target offers both value and a sense of style, 18- to 25-year-olds are another important market. While this group as a whole may not spend as much as the primary market, they act as *centers of influence* (or *key influentials*). This group is a *secondary target market*. And, of course, with the passage of time, 18- to 25-year-olds will eventually enter the primary target market.

What is Target's **product concept?** Target has been described by some as "cheap chic." In other words, it is a mass merchandiser that appeals to those with a sense of style. The product concept is exemplified by the stores themselves, and Target continues to reimagine the shopping experience. How? By opening small-store formats that serve neighborhoods, by continuing to include exclusive brands found only at Target, and by integrating personal shopping with online.[5]

With respect to **communications media,** Target spends nearly three out of four ad dollars on television commercials and newspaper ads. TV is perfect for nationally focused brand-building campaigns, and newspapers are ideal for informing local shoppers about sales and promotions in towns with a Target. Some money is also spent on outdoor and radio as a means for reaching consumers while they drive. And like many companies, Target is increasing its spending on digital media, including e-mail, Instagram, and Facebook.

What is Target's **IMC message?** In its simplest terms, message strategy is determined by *what* a company wants to say and *how* it wants to say it. Target's ads stress the dual benefit proposition, "Expect more, pay less." While Walmart ads are product focused, Target's campaigns emphasize the consumer and her lifestyle. This reinforces the "expect more" benefit. To do this effectively, the messages have to exude an aura of quality. So the agency creative team chose a message strategy that is simple yet thoughtful, entertaining, credible, and, most of all, distinctive.

The agency and client team must understand and agree to these four elements of the IMC strategy—target, product, media, and message—before creative work begins. In most agencies, the account management group is responsible for developing the campaign strategy. In some large agencies, account planners spend a great deal of time researching the market. Then they prepare the campaign strategy with input from, and the approval of, account management. When the strategy-development task is completed, the account executives prepare a *creative brief* to communicate the strategy to the creative department.

Writing the Creative Brief (Copy Platform)

After message objectives and strategy are determined, the account managers write a brief statement of the intended strategy. The **creative brief** is a creative team's guide for writing and producing the campaign. In some agencies it may be referred to as a *copy platform,* a *work plan,* or a *copy* (or *creative*) *strategy document.* Regardless of the name, it is a simple written statement of the most important issues to consider in the development of the campaign: the who, why, what, where, and when.

- *Who?* Who is the prospect in terms of behavioristic, geographic, demographic, and/or psychographic qualities? What is the typical prospect's personality? The goal is to specify the important qualities of the individuals the ads will be created for.
- *Why?* Does the consumer have specific wants or needs the ad should appeal to? Marketers use two broad categories of appeals. **Rational appeals** are directed at the consumer's practical, functional need for the product or service; **emotional appeals** target the consumer's psychological, social, or symbolic needs. For a sampling of specific appeals within these categories, see Exhibit 10-1.

Exhibit 10-1
Selected IMC appeals.

Approach Needs	Selected IMC Appeals		
	Rational	Emotional	
Self-actualization	Opportunity for more leisure Efficiency in operation or use	Ambition Avoidance of laborious task Curiosity Entertainment	Pleasure of reaction Simplicity Sport/play/physical activity
Esteem	Dependability in quality Dependability in use Enhancement of earnings Variety of selection	Pride of personal appearance Pride of possession	Style/beauty Taste
Social	Cleanliness Economy in purchase	Cooperation Devotion to others Guilt Home comfort Humor	Romance Sexual attraction Social achievement Social approval Sympathy for others
Safety	Durability Protection of others Safety	Fear Health	Security
Physiological	Rest or sleep	Appetite	Personal comfort

- *What?* What features of the product will satisfy the consumer's needs? What is the "proof" the company offers to support its claims? How is the product positioned? What personality or image (of the product or the company) can be or has been created?

- *Where* and *when* will these messages be communicated? Through what media? At what times of year? In what parts of the country?

- Finally, *what style, approach,* or *tone* will the campaign use? And, generally, what will the copy say?

Procter & Gamble and Leo Burnett use a simple creative brief with three parts:

1. *An objective statement.* A specific, concise description of what the campaign is supposed to accomplish or what problem it is supposed to solve. The objective statement also includes the name of the brand and a brief, specific description of the target consumer. For example,

   The campaign will convince value-conscious consumers that Target stores offer them a way to save money on their everyday purchases. In addition, Target offers a vast selection of products that make life better.

2. *A support statement.* A brief description of the evidence that backs up the product promise. For example,

   Support is found in two types of ads that Target regularly runs. Newspaper ads, including weekly inserts, demonstrate to consumers the low prices of the products sold at Target. Television ads emphasize the quality and value of the everyday products found at Target. Both TV and newspaper ads should do more than focus on the product alone; rather, they should help demonstrate that the products sold at Target make life easier and better. Social media efforts will also reinforce value and a better life by focusing on ways Target products brighten up the household even for families on tight budgets.

3. *A tone or brand character statement.* A brief statement of either the advertising's tone or the long-term character of the brand. Tone statements are short-term emotional descriptions of the advertising strategy. Brand character statements are long-term descriptions of the enduring values of the brand—things that give the product brand equity. A tone statement might be phrased

   The tone of Target ads should convey a spirit of optimism and energy. The ads should suggest that Target understands the consumer and the challenges she faces in her life. They should suggest that shopping at Target is fun and that Target is the value shopping venue that best fits with the shopper's personality and lifestyle.

Target ads are quirky and creative. But the nonverbal elements of the red and white colors and repetition of the Target logo make them instantly recognizable.

Source: Target Brands, Inc.

On the other hand, a brand character statement might be phrased

Target offers consumers the selection and value typical of a mass merchandiser in stores that have elegance and flair. Target is the place where shoppers can save money and have a fun shopping experience.

The delivery of the creative brief to the creative department concludes the process of developing an IMC strategy. It also marks the beginning of the next step: the *campaign creative process,* in which the creative team develops a *message strategy* and begins the search for the *big idea.* After writing the first message, the copywriter should again check the brief to see if the message measures up on the resonance and impact dimensions. If it doesn't, the team must start again.

Elements of Message Strategy

Armed with the brief, the creative team is ready to develop creative ideas. The first step is to create a message strategy.

The **message strategy** (or **rationale**) is a simple description and explanation of a campaign's overall creative approach—what the campaign says, how it says it, and why. The message strategy has three components:

- ■ **Verbal.** Guidelines for what the messages should say, considerations that affect the choice of words, and the relationship of the copy approach to the medium (or media) that will carry the message.

- ■ **Nonverbal.** Overall nature of the campaign's graphics, any visuals that must be used, and the relationship of the graphics to the media in which the message will appear.

- ■ **Technical.** Preferred execution approach and mechanical outcome, including budget and scheduling limitations (often governed by the media involved); also any **mandatories**—specific requirements such as addresses, logos, and slogans.

Because all these elements of the message strategy intertwine, they typically evolve simultaneously. Language affects imagery, and vice versa. However, the verbal elements are the starting point for many campaigns.

The message strategy helps the creative team sell the campaign concept to the account managers and helps the managers explain and defend the creative work to the client. Of course, the message strategy must conform to the strategy outlined in the creative brief or it will probably be rejected.

In the development of message strategy, certain basic questions need to be answered: How is the market segmented? How will the product be positioned? Who are the best prospects for the product? What is the key consumer benefit? What is the product's (or company's) current image? What is the product's unique advantage?[6] At this point, research data are important. Research helps the creative team answer these questions.

How Creativity Enhances IMC

The powerful use of imagery, copy, and even humor in the Target campaign demonstrates how creativity enhances IMC. But what exactly is creativity or the creative process? What is the role of creativity? And where does creativity come from?

What Is Creativity?

For a seemingly simple concept, a definition of creativity can be surprisingly elusive. Social media expert Lee Odden writes, "creativity is seeing and communicating ideas in ways that are unique, compelling, and unexpected."[7] Marketing expert David Meerman Scott suggests it involves seeing "patterns that others don't and effectively communicating them." Providing creative definitions of creativity, writer Seth Godin suggests it involves imagining and thinking, "This might not work," while author Daniel Pink argues it is giving "the world something it didn't know it was missing."[8] To create means to originate, to conceive a thing or idea that did not exist before. Typically, though, **creativity** is thought of as combining two or more previously unconnected objects or ideas into something new.

Many people think creativity springs directly from human intuition. But the creative process can also follow from a disciplined approach. We'll discuss such an approach in this chapter.

The Role of Creativity in IMC Campaigns

Companies often select an agency specifically for its creative style and its reputation for coming up with bold, original concepts. While creativity is important to a campaign's basic mission of informing, persuading, and reminding, it is vital to achieving the boom factor.

Creativity Helps Messages Inform

A campaign's ability to inform is greatly enhanced by creativity. Good creative work makes a campaign more vivid, and many researchers believe vividness attracts attention, maintains interest, and stimulates thinking.[9] A common technique is to use word plays and verbal or visual metaphors, such as "Think different," "Go further," or "You're in good hands." The metaphor describes one concept in terms of another, more familiar one, helping the audience member learn about the product.[10]

Ads like this out-of-home execution communicate a great deal with very little copy. How does Target meld a creative design and simultaneously imply great selection with this billboard? Aesthetic cues such as lighting, the pose of the model, setting, and clothing style can instantly communicate meaning to viewers nonverbally.

Source: Target Brands, Inc.

Other creative techniques can also improve a message's ability to inform. Writers and artists must arrange visual and verbal message components according to a genre of social meaning so that readers or viewers can easily interpret the message using commonly accepted symbols. For example, aesthetic cues such as lighting, the pose of the model, setting, and clothing style can instantly signal viewers nonverbally whether a fashion ad reflects a romantic adventure or a sporting event.[11]

Creativity Helps Messages Persuade

The ancients created legends and myths about gods and heroes—symbols for humankind's instinctive, primordial longings and fears—to affect human behavior and thought. To motivate people to some action or attitude, copywriters have created new myths and heroes, like the Marlboro man and the Energizer Bunny. A creative story or persona can establish a unique identity for the product in the collective mindset, a key factor in helping a product beat the competition.[12]

Creativity also helps position a product on the top rung of consumers' mental ladders. The Target ads featured in this chapter, for example, metaphorically suggest that ordinary products can be combined creatively to make life better. The higher form of expression creates a grander impression. And when such an impression spreads through the market, the product's perceived value also rises.

To be persuasive, the verbal message must be reinforced by the creative use of nonverbal message elements. Artists govern the use of these elements (color, layout, and illustration, for example) to increase vividness. Research suggests that, in print and digital media, *info graphics* (colorful explanatory charts, tables, and the like) can raise the perception of quality.[13] Artwork can also stimulate emotions. Color, for example, can often motivate consumers, depending on their cultural background and personal experiences (see Ad Lab 10–A, "The Psychological Impact of Color"). So it should be no surprise that Michael Francis, brand czar at Target, wants the retailer to "own red." Translation? When you see red in a campaign, you should anticipate that it is a Target message, even before the brand is identified.[14]

The Psychological Impact of Color

National origin or culture can play a role in color preferences. For example, warm colors—red, yellow, and orange—tend to stimulate, excite, and create an active response. People from warmer climes, apparently, are most responsive to these colors. Certain color combinations stimulate ethnic connotations. Metallic golds with reds, for example, are associated with China. Turquoise and beige are associated with the Indian tribes of the American Southwest.

Colors can impart lifestyle preferences. Vivid primary colors (red, blue, yellow) juxtaposed with white stripes exude decisiveness and are often used in sporting events as team colors. Thus, they are associated with a sporting lifestyle.

The colors we experience during the four seasons often serve as guides for combining colors and for guessing the temperaments of individuals who dress themselves or decorate their house in specific seasonal colors. Spring colors such as yellows, greens, and light blues, for example, suggest a fresh, exuberant character. Winter colors such as dark blues, deep violets, and black are associated with cool, chilly attitudes.

Because we usually feel refreshed after sleeping, we associate the colors of the morning—emerald green, raspberry, and pale yellow—with energy. And because the mellow colors of sunset predominate when we're usually home relaxing after work, we may associate sunset colors—peach, turquoise, and red-orange—with relaxation and reflective moods.

Some colors are ambiguous. Violet and leaf-green fall on the line between warm and cool. They can be either, depending on the shade.

Here are some more observations:

Red

Symbol of blood and fire. Second to blue as people's favorite color but more versatile, the hottest color with highest "action quotient." Appropriate for soups, frozen foods, and meats.

Brown

A masculine color, associated with earth, woods, mellowness, age, warmth, comfort. Used to sell anything, even cosmetics.

Yellow

High impact to catch consumer's eye, particularly when used with black. Good for corn, lemon, or suntan products.

Green

Symbol of health and freshness; popular for environmentally friendly products.

Blue

Coldest color with most appeal; effective for frozen foods (ice impression); if used with a lighter tint it becomes "sweet" (Lowenbrau beer, Wondra flour).

Black

Conveys sophistication and high-end merchandise, and is used to stimulate purchase of expensive products. Good as background and foil for other colors.

Orange

Most "edible" color, especially in brown-tinged shades; evokes autumn and good things to eat.

Laboratory Application

Explain the moods or feelings that are stimulated by two-color ads or packages illustrated in this text.

Creativity Helps IMC Remind

Imagine using the same invitation, without any innovation, to ask people to try your product again and again, year after year. Your invitation would become stale very quickly. Only creativity can transform boring reminders into interesting, entertaining messages. Nike is proof. Many of Nike's campaigns, including the recent one with former NFL player Colin Kaepernick, never mention the company name. Instead, they tell stories. And the only on-screen cue identifying the sponsor is the single, elongated "swoosh" logo. A Nike spokesperson said this approach wasn't risky "given the context that the Nike logo is so well known."[15] We are entertained daily by creative campaigns—for soft drinks, snacks, and cereals—whose primary mission is simply to remind us to indulge again.

Creativity Puts the "Boom" in Campaigns

Successful comedy also has a boom factor—the punchline. It's that precise moment when the joke culminates in a clever play on words or turn of meaning, when the audience suddenly gets it and shows its approval.

Good news. There are still some snakes left.

Good news there are snakes in Ireland? Audi thinks so. The car manufacturer targets Irish consumers with an ad that resonates. Great design, a headline that stops the reader in his or her tracks, and all completely unexpected. That's the boom factor in action.

Source: Audi of America

Good punchlines are the result of taking an everyday situation, looking at it creatively, adding a bit of exaggeration, and then delivering it as a surprise. Great campaigns often do the same thing. The long-running Progressive campaign featuring Flo uses all of these elements to help brand Progressive insurance.

The boom doesn't always have to be funny. It may come from the sudden understanding of an unexpected double-meaning, as in the case of Target ads. Or from a funny or charming response from a Dell social media rep. Or the breathtaking beauty of a magnificent nature photograph for Timberland shoes. In a business-to-business situation, it may come from the sudden recognition that a new high-tech product can improve workplace productivity. In short, the boom factor may come from many sources. But it always requires the application of creativity.

Understanding Creative Thinking

Some people may exhibit more of it than others, but creativity lives within all of us. Human creativity, developed over millions of years, enabled our ancestors to survive. As individuals, we use our natural creativity every time we try to solve a problem or create something beautiful or meaningful.

Styles of Thinking

The German sociologist Max Weber proposed that people think in two ways: an objective, rational, fact-based manner and a qualitative, intuitive, value-based manner. Sometimes we use both simultaneously. For example, while buying a car, we consider price, mileage, and warranties, but also styling, beauty, and how we think others will judge us making the purchase. The first set of criteria draws on our rational, fact-based style of thinking, while the second calls on taste, intuition, and emotions.

Roger von Oech defined this dichotomy as hard and soft thinking. *Hard thinking* refers to concepts like logic, reason, precision, consistency, work, reality, analysis, and specificity. *Soft thinking* refers to less-tangible concepts: metaphor, dream, humor, ambiguity, play, fantasy, hunch. On the hard side, things are right or wrong, black or white. On the soft side, there may be many right answers and many shades of gray.[16]

Fact-Based versus Value-Based Thinking

Most theories of thinking fit into two general categories: value-based or fact-based. Let's examine these styles of thinking more closely.

People whose preferred style of thinking is **fact-based** tend to fragment concepts into components and to analyze situations to discover the one best solution. Although fact-based people can be creative, they tend to be linear thinkers and prefer to have facts and figures—hard data—they can analyze and control. They are not comfortable with ambiguous situations. They like logic, structure, and efficiency.

In contrast, **value-based** thinkers make decisions based on intuition, values, and ethical judgments. They are better able to embrace change, conflict, and paradox. This style fundamentally relies on blending concepts together. Value-based thinkers, for example, attempt to integrate the divergent ideas of a group into an arrangement that lets everyone win. They are good at using their imagination to produce a flow of new ideas and synthesizing existing concepts to create something new.

How Styles of Thinking Affect Creativity

If the creative team prefers a value-based thinking style, it tends to produce ads such as those in the Target and Nike campaigns—emotional and metaphorical. That's fine if the client also prefers that style of thinking.

On the other hand, clients who prefer a fact-based style often seek agencies that produce practical, hard-edged work characterized by simple, straightforward layouts; rational appeals; and lots of data. A fact-based client may even find a value-based campaign to be unsettling.

One Saatchi & Saatchi ad campaign for Hewlett-Packard's laser printers, for example, created a stir internally. The ads simulated interviews. The actors portrayed harried customers talking about how they didn't have time to think about their printers. "Some people

Every kid deserves
a brush with inspiration.

Target is on track to give
$1 BILLION FOR EDUCATION
by the end of 2015

Target.com/Education

within Hewlett-Packard are somewhat uncomfortable with the direction of the campaign," reported Arlene King, a marketing communications manager for HP, "because we are a high-tech company and the ads don't focus on any aspect of the technology."[17]

The creative team must understand the campaign's target audience. In some market segments (high-tech, for example), customers may tend toward one style of thinking over another—and that could dictate which approach to use.

As we shall see in the next section, the best art directors and copywriters use both styles to accomplish their task. In the creative process, they need to use their imagination (value-based thinking) to develop a variety of concepts. But to select the best alternative and get the job done, they have to use the fact-based style.

The Creative Process

LO 10-4

The **creative process** is the step-by-step procedure used to discover original ideas and reorganize existing concepts in new ways. By following it, people can improve their ability to unearth possibilities, cross-associate concepts, and select winning ideas.

The new generation of creatives will face a world of ever-growing complexity. They must handle the many challenges of integrated marketing communications (IMC) as they help their clients build relationships with highly fragmented target markets. They will need to understand the wide range of new technologies affecting advertising. And they will have to learn how to advertise to emerging international markets. To do this, they need a model that handles many situations simply.

Over the years, many notions of the creative process have been proposed. Although most are similar, each format has unique merits. Roger von Oech published a four-step creative model that many *Fortune* 100 companies employ. It offers flexibility for fact-based and value-based thinkers alike. Von Oech describes four distinct, imaginary roles (Explorer, Artist, Judge, and Warrior) that every art director and copywriter has to adopt at some point in the creative process:[18]

1. The *Explorer* searches for new information, paying attention to unusual patterns.
2. The *Artist* experiments and plays with a variety of approaches, looking for an original idea.
3. The *Judge* evaluates the results of experimentation and decides which approach is most practical.
4. The *Warrior* overcomes excuses, idea killers, setbacks, and obstacles to bring a creative concept to realization.

The Explorer Role: Gathering Information

Copywriters and art directors thrive on the challenge of creating advertising messages—the encoding process. But first they need the raw materials for ideas: facts, experiences, history, knowledge, feelings.

Taking on the role of the **Explorer,** the creatives examine the information they have. They review the creative brief and the marketing and advertising plan; they study the market, the product, and the competition. They may seek additional input from the agency's account managers and from people on the client side (sales, marketing, product, or research managers).

When the creative team developed ads for Target, they first assumed the Explorer role. They spoke with people about the nature of the company, its products, its marketing history, its competitors, and the competitors' styles of advertising.

Develop an Insight Outlook

It's important that when creatives play the Explorer role, they get off the beaten path to look in new and uncommon places for information—to discover new ideas and to identify unusual patterns. One reviewer of Target campaigns asked whether its campaigns or store designs would have been possible without the influence of Andy Warhol. In all likelihood, the answer is no. Creative inspiration in this case came from the world of art.

Target spends more money than most retailers on national efforts to brand the stores. But that doesn't mean it ignores advertising in newspapers to emphasize sales, bargains, and specials relevant to its shoppers.

Source: Target Brands, Inc.

Von Oech suggests adopting an "insight outlook" (a positive belief that good information is available and that you have the skills to find and use it). This means opening up to the outside world to receive new knowledge. Ideas are everywhere: in museums, art galleries, hardware stores, and history books. The more diverse the sources, the greater your chance of uncovering an original concept.

Sam Cannon leads creative teams at the digital agency Razorfish. In his view, creativity comes from constraints, usually found in the creative brief. Limits, rather than unfettered thoughts, provide deep insights. He also cautions against habit, arguing, "If you tend toward comedy, stop yourself with the next assignment and try to do something a little more serious." He continues, "Take a different turn and see where it leads you."[19]

Know the Objective

Philosopher John Dewey said, "A problem well-stated is a problem half-solved." This is why the creative brief is so important. It helps define what the creatives are looking for. The creatives typically start working on the message strategy during the Explorer stage because it helps them define what they're looking for.

To get their creative juices flowing, most copywriters and art directors maintain an extensive library of award books and trade magazines. Many also keep a *tickler* (or *swipe*) *file* of ads they like that might give them direction.

Head creative Conor Bady offers specific advice for kickstarting creative thinking: "Get away from the computer; get out of the office as a team; socialize together; hash out problems over a beer; be open to being lucky; do thinks outside of digital; go see a film or a play and learn how those people solve problems."[20]

Brainstorm

As Explorers, the creative team looks first for lots of ideas. One technique is **brainstorming,** a process in which two or more people get together to generate new ideas. A brainstorming session is often a source of sudden inspirations. To succeed, it must follow a couple of rules: All ideas are above criticism (no idea is "wrong") and all ideas are written down for later review. The goal is to record any inspiration that comes to mind, a process that psychologists call *free association,* allowing each new idea an opportunity to stimulate another.

Von Oech suggests other techniques for Explorers: Leave your own turf (look in outside fields and industries for ideas); shift your focus (pay attention to a variety of information); look at the big picture (stand back and see what it all means); don't overlook the obvious (the best ideas are right in front of your nose); don't be afraid to stray (you might find something you weren't looking for); and stake your claim to new territory (write down any new ideas or they will be lost).

The Explorers' job is to find new information. To be effective Explorers, they must exercise flexibility, courage, and openness.[21]

The Artist Role: Developing and Implementing the Big Idea

The Artist's role is both the toughest and the longest. But it's also the most rewarding. The **Artist** must actually accomplish two major tasks: searching for the big idea and then implementing it.

Task 1: Develop the Big Idea

The first task for Artists is the long, tedious process of reviewing all the pertinent information gathered during the Explorer role, analyzing the problem, and searching for a key verbal or visual concept.

Creating a mental picture of the message, also called **visualization** or **conceptualization,** is important. It's where the search for the **big idea**—that flash of insight—takes place. The big idea is a bold, creative initiative that builds on the strategy; joins the product benefit with consumer desire in a fresh, involving way; brings the subject to life; and makes the audience stop, look, and listen.[22]

What's the difference between a strategy and a big idea? A strategy describes the direction the message should take. A big idea gives it life. For example, the creative brief discussed earlier for Target contains a strategic brand character statement:

> Target offers consumers the selection and value typical of a mass merchandiser in stores that have the elegance and flair of a department store.

Target could have used that strategy statement as a headline. But it would have been dreadfully dull. It lacks what a big idea headline delivers: a set of multiple meanings that create interest, memorability, and, in some cases, drama. Note the short, punchy headline that Target chose to convey the same strategic concept:

> Expect more. Pay less.

John O'Toole said, "While strategy requires deduction, a big idea requires inspiration."[23] The big idea is almost invariably expressed through a combination of art and copy. Target's approach is to use short but witty copy, beautiful photography, and the immediately recognizable red "target" logo to visually communicate the essence of the brand.

Transforming a Concept: Do Something to It   Von Oech points out that when we take on the Artist role, we have to do something to the information we collected as Explorers to give it value. That means asking lots of questions: What if I added this? Or took that away? Or looked at it backward? Or compared it with something else? The Artist changes patterns and experiments with various approaches.

For example, one Target ad for cosmetics uses a traditional, high-fashion layout. The twist is found in the multiple headlines in which the suffix "less" is highlighted. This simple yet powerful change transforms the ad from a somewhat snobbish appeal to a value proposition. It suggests the Target consumer can buy a great product for a low price.

At this point in the creative process, a good Artist may employ a variety of strategies for transforming things. Von Oech suggests several techniques for manipulating ideas:[24]

1. *Adapt.* Change contexts. Think what else the product might be besides the obvious. A Campbell's Soup ad showed a steaming bowl of tomato soup with a headline: "HEALTH INSURANCE."

2. *Imagine.* Ask what if. Let your imagination fly. What if people could do their chores in their sleep? What if there was one place where people could leave all disagreements behind? Clyde's Bar in Georgetown actually used that idea. The ad showed a beautifully illustrated elephant and donkey dressed in business suits and seated at a table toasting one another. The headline: "Clyde's. The People's Choice."

3. *Reverse.* Look at it backward. Sometimes the opposite of what is expected has great impact and memorability. A cosmetics company ran an ad for its moisturizing cream under the line: "Introduce your husband to a younger woman." A vintage Volkswagen ad used "Ugly is only skin deep."

4. *Connect.* Join two unrelated ideas together. Ask yourself: What ideas can I connect to my concept? A Target ad showed the rear view of a high-fashion-type model clad only with a backpack and a lampshade–the latter wrapped around her middle like a miniskirt. Next to the Target logo the ad said simply, "fashion and housewares."

5. *Compare.* Take one idea and use it to describe another. Ever notice how bankers talk like plumbers? "Flood the market, laundered money, liquid assets, cash flow, take a bath, float a loan." The English language is awash in metaphors. Jack in the Box advertised its onion rings by picturing them on a billboard and inviting motorists to "Drive thru for a ring job." An elegant magazine ad for the Parker Premier fountain pen used this sterling metaphor: "It's wrought from pure silver and writes like pure silk."

6. *Eliminate.* Subtract something. Or break the rules. In IMC there's little virtue in doing things the way they've always been done. Seven-Up became famous by advertising what it wasn't ("the Uncola") and thereby positioned itself as a refreshing alternative. To

My IMC Campaign 10-A

The Creative Brief

Every agency has a slightly different twist on a creative brief. In this chapter, we outline the components of most briefs this way:

- Who (the prospect).
- Why (specific wants or needs the ad should appeal to).
- What (what are the product features that can satisfy consumer needs?).
- Where and when (will the messages be transmitted?).
- Style, approach, tone.

We also describe the creative brief that Leo Burnett uses for P&G. It is even simpler:

- An objective statement (what are you trying to do?).
- A support statement (the evidence that backs up the promised benefit).
- A tone or brand character statement (emotional descriptions of the advertising strategy).

Are you interested in creativity? Visit one of the best agency resources on the web, Ogilvy.com, for lots of information about effective creative, including the agency's take on creative briefs, summarized here:

1. What are the communications objectives?
2. What should consumers do differently? Why?
3. How will messages affect consumer beliefs and actions?
4. How are our competitors advertising? How can we make our ads different?
5. Who is the target audience and what is their shared need that the brand can fulfill?
6. Demographics of the audience, but even more importantly, shared attitudes.
7. The brand:

    - How does the brand address the shared need?
    - How should the brand experience (as defined by both planned and unplanned messages) be defined?
    - What is the proposition (or benefit)?
    - What evidence gives people a reason to believe the proposition?
    - What is the personality of the brand?
    - How can the mood or tone of the ads be matched to the personality of the brand?

The Ogilvy site is filled with a lot more useful information, including suggestions for maximizing the likelihood that the brief will spark a big idea. Check it out.

introduce its new models one year, Volkswagen used a series of humorous teaser ads that didn't show any cars. In one, a shaggy dog sat patiently in front of a fan. He was presumably replicating what dogs do in cars, sticking their heads out the window to catch the breeze. The only difference was he was doing it indoors.

Metaphor is a powerful creative tool. Consider the metaphor of the artwork in this ad and the way the artist transformed the balloons in this image to make it more effective.

Source: Smith & Milton, London

Embarrassing Bodies
Channel 4. Tuesdays. 9pm

Many of Roger von Oech's suggestions for transforming a concept are embodied in Target's ads. How many can you spot in this execution?

Source: Target Brands, Inc.

7. *Parody.* Fool around. Have some fun. Tell some jokes—especially when you're under pressure. There is a close relationship between the *ha-ha* experience of humor and the *aha!* experience of creative discovery. Humor stretches our thinking and, used in good taste, makes for some great advertising. A classical radio station ran a newspaper ad: "Handel with care." William Shatner parodies the public's image of himself in Priceline.com ads. In one, he was even "fired" and replaced by fellow Star Trek castmember Leonard Nimoy.

Blocks to Creativity   Everybody experiences times when the creative juices just won't flow. There are many causes: information overload, mental or physical fatigue, stress, fear, insecurity. Often, though, the problem is simply the style of thinking being used.

In the Explorer stage, when creatives study reams of marketing data, the facts and figures on sales and market share may put them in a fact-based frame of mind. But to create effectively, they need to shift gears to a value-based style of thinking.

As von Oech says, "Creative thinking requires an attitude that allows you to search for ideas and manipulate your knowledge and experience." Unfortunately, it is sometimes difficult for creatives to make that mental switch instantly. Von Oech recommends some techniques to stimulate integrative thinking. For example: Look for the second right answer (there is usually more than one answer to any problem, and the second may be more creative); seek cross-fertilization (TV people could learn a lot from teachers, and vice versa); slay a sacred cow (sacred cows make great steaks); imagine how others would do it (stretch the imagination by role playing); laugh at it (make up jokes about what you're doing); and reverse your viewpoint (open up your thinking and discover things you typically overlook).[25]

George Gier, cofounder of the Leap Partnership, says, "The only thing agencies have left to sell to clients that they can't get anywhere else is creative ideas."[26] Perhaps this is why Derek Walker, owner of a small agency in South Carolina, writes that in advertising, "the client is not always right."[27]

Creative blocking may occur when people in the agency start "thinking like the client," especially if the client is a fact-based thinker. This can also be hazardous to the agency's creative reputation and is one reason agencies sometimes resign accounts over "creative differences." An agency can eliminate a lot of frustration and wasted time and money by evaluating the client's corporate culture, its collective style of thinking, and its creative comfort level in advance.

Creative fatigue sometimes happens when an agency has served an account for a long time and all the fresh ideas have been worked and reworked. It can also happen when a

Because Target focuses on lifestyle, its ads must reflect the aspirations and concerns of its consumers. This ad demonstrates a commitment to the Salvation Army. What role does the artist play in the development of this type of advertisement?

Source: Target Brands, Inc.

Creative thinking knows no boundaries, as shown in this ad for Pantene. Research by the company showed that air pollution, which is significant in Bangkok, damages hair even more than it damages skin. To illustrate this, a billboard was constructed that dropped giant strands when air pollution levels were high. The strands symbolized falling hair. The campaign simultaneously drew attention to the dangers of unhealthy air and the healing qualities of Pantene shampoo.

Source: Procter & Gamble

client has rejected a series of concepts; the inspiration is lost and the creatives start trying to force ideas. They suddenly find it hard to shift their style of thinking or to crank up the creative process again. If this becomes chronic, the only solutions may be to appoint an entirely new creative team or resign the account.

Incubating a Concept: Do Nothing to It   When the brain is overloaded with information about a problem, creatives sometimes find it's best to just walk away from it for a while, do something else, and let the unconscious mind mull it over. This approach yields several benefits. First, it puts the problem back into perspective. It also rests the brain, lets the problem incubate in the subconscious, and enables better ideas to percolate to the top. When they return to the task, creatives frequently discover a whole new set of assumptions.

Task 2: Implement the Big Idea

Once creatives latch onto the big idea, they have to implement it. This is where the real art of advertising comes in—writing the exact words, designing the precise layout. To have a sense of how advertising creatives do that, it helps to understand what *art* is in advertising, how artistic elements and tools are selected and used, and the difference between good art and bad art.

Art shapes the message into a complete communication that appeals to the senses as well as the mind. So while **art direction** refers to the act or process of managing the visual presentation of the message, the term **art** actually refers to the whole presentation—visual, verbal, and aural. For example, the artful selection of words not only communicates information but also stimulates positive feelings for the product. An artfully designed typeface not only makes reading easier, it also evokes a mood. By creatively arranging format elements—surrounding the text with lines, boxes, and colors, and relating them to one another in proportion—the art director can further enhance the appeal. Art also shapes the style of photography and illustration. An intimate style uses soft focus and close views, a documentary style portrays the scene without pictorial enhancements, and a dramatic style features unusual angles or blurred action images.

In short, if *copy* is the verbal language of a message, *art* is the body language. TV uses both sight and sound to involve viewers. Radio commercials use sound to create *word pictures* in the minds of listeners. The particular blend of writing, visuals, and sounds makes up an ad's expressive character. So while the quality may vary, every ad uses art.

In advertising, balance, proportion, and movement are guides for uniting words, images, type, sounds, and colors into a single communication so they relate to and enhance each other. We'll discuss more of these concepts in Chapter 11.

The Creative Pyramid: A Guide to Formulating Copy and Art

The **creative pyramid** is a model that can help the creative team convert the advertising strategy and the big idea into the actual physical ad or commercial. It uses a simple five-step structure (see Exhibit 10-2).

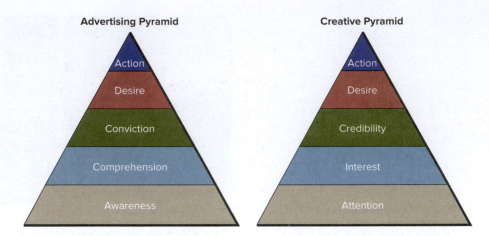

The purpose of much copy and design is either to persuade prospective customers to take some action to satisfy a need or want, or to remind them to take the action again. In a new-product situation, people may first need to be made aware of the problem or, if the problem is obvious, that a solution exists. For a frequently purchased product, the marketer simply has to remind people of the solution close to the purchase occasion. In either case, the company must first get the prospect's *attention.* The second step is to stimulate *interest*—in either the message or the product itself. Next, it's important, especially for new products, to build *credibility* for the product claims. Then the campaign can focus on generating *desire* and finally on stimulating *action.* These five elements should be addressed in just about every marketing appeal. We'll deal with each step briefly.

Attention   A product message is a *stimulus.* It must break through consumers' physiological screens to create the kind of attention that leads to perception. *Attention,* therefore, is the first objective of any campaign and the fundamental building block in the creative pyramid. The Artist may spend as much time and energy figuring out how to express the big idea in an interesting, attention-getting way as searching for the big idea itself.

Print ads often use the headline as the major attention-getting device. The copywriter's goal is to write a headline that expresses the big idea with verve. Usually designed to appear in the largest and boldest type in the ad, the headline is often the strongest focal point conceptually as well as visually. Many other devices also help gain attention. In print media, they may include dynamic visuals, unusual layout, vibrant color, or dominant ad size. In electronic media, they may include special sound effects, music, animation, or unusual visual techniques.

Some factors are beyond the creatives' control. The budget may determine the size of a sponsorship or length of the viral video. And that may influence how well or quickly it breaks through consumers' screens. Similarly, a TV spot's position in a cluster of commercials between shows or an ad's position in a publication may determine who sees it.

The attention-getting device should be dramatic, powerful, and intense. It must also be appropriate, relating to the product, the tone of the campaign, and the needs or interests of the intended audience. This is especially true in business-to-business campaigns where rational appeals and fact-based thinking dominate. The natural attention-drawing value of sexual themes is often exploited by marketers. See our "Ethics, Diversity & Inclusion" box on page 340 to find out more about the pros and cons of using sex as an attention-getting device.

Headlines that make a promise lacking in credibility won't make a sale; in fact, they may alienate a potential customer. Messages that use racy headlines or nude figures unrelated to the product often lose sales because prospects can't purchase the item that first attracted their attention.

Interest   The second step in the creative pyramid, *interest,* carries the prospective customer—now paying attention—to the heart of the message. The message must keep the prospect excited or involved as the information becomes more detailed. To do this, the copywriter may answer a question asked in the attention step or add facts that relate to the headline.

How many steps in the creative pyramid does this Target ad achieve?

Courtesy of Outdoor Advertising Association of America

To maintain audience interest, the tone and language should be compatible with the target market's attitude. As we discussed earlier, the successful message has impact.

The writer and designer must lead prospects from one step to the next. Research shows that people read what interests them and ignore what doesn't, so the writer must maintain prospects' interest at all times.[28] One way to do so is to credibly demonstrate that the sponsor understands the prospect and knows about his or her problems, needs, and how the product or service will answer them. Copywriters use the word *you* a lot.

There are many effective ways to stimulate interest: a dramatic situation, a story, cartoons, charts. In radio, copywriters use sound effects or catchy dialogue. Television frequently uses quick cuts to maintain interest. We discuss some of these techniques in the chapter on advertising production.

Credibility   The third step in the creative pyramid is to establish *credibility* for claims about the product or service. Customers are skeptical. They want proof. Comparison ads can build credibility, but they must be relevant to customers' needs—and fair.

Well-known presenters may lend credibility to a campaign. For example, actress Keira Knightley effectively represents Chanel with her glamorous and elegant style, just as snowboarder Shaun White represents Mountain Dew with a personality that is athletic and free-spirited.

Marketers often show independent test results to substantiate product claims. To work, such "proofs" must be valid, not just statistical manipulation. Many consumers have extensive product knowledge, even in specialized areas.

Desire   In the *desire* step, the writer encourages prospects to picture themselves enjoying the benefits of the product or service. Essentially, they are invited to visualize.

In print, copywriters initiate visualization by using phrases like "picture yourself" or "imagine." In film or video, Jenny Craig shows before and after images of customers who've lost weight, while e-Harmony shows happily married couples who met through the service. The not-so-subtle message: "This could be you!"

The desire step hints at the possibilities and lets the consumer's mind take over. If prospects feel they're being led by the nose, they may feel insulted, resent the ad, and lose interest. In some cases, writers maintain this delicate balance by having a secondary character agree with the main character and prattle off a few more product benefits. The secondary character allows the main character, the one audiences relate to best, to retain integrity.

Action   The final step up the creative pyramid is *action*. The purpose is to motivate people to do something—send in a coupon, visit a website, visit the store—or at least to agree with the advertiser.

Ethics, Diversity & Inclusion

Is It Ethical to Use Sex in Advertising?

In 2018 the #metoo hashtag was a powerful reminder to everyone of the atrocious treatment endured by many women in the workplace from sexual harassment and mistreatment. The powerful stories of women called into question the casual use of sexuality in advertising.

It's one of the more blatant uses of sex in advertising in recent memory: A billboard features a young woman, holding a grease gun cartridge in each hand and leaning over to exhibit an ample amount of cleavage. The headline reads, "This is Debbie. She wants you to have this pair in your car." The ad is for auto parts, but the implication seems to be that if you buy *this manufacturer's* auto parts, you'll get Debbie or someone like Debbie in the bargain. Nothing in the ad says so explicitly, but the innuendo is all that's required to capture the viewer's attention.

Advertisers frequently use the power of suggestion to imply sex, encouraging viewers to come to their own conclusions. However, advertisers who run such risqué ads must contend with the critics and with the often-tricky legal distinction between obscenity and indecency. Obscenity is illegal and carries criminal charges, whereas indecency does not. To be considered obscene, an ad must meet three conditions: It appeals to prurient interests, it is patently offensive, and it lacks any redeeming social value.

In general, most ads with sexual appeals don't meet the criteria for obscenity, but they may still be considered indecent because indecency is in the eyes of the beholder. If enough people believe sexually oriented material is indecent, then "community standards" reflect this belief. In such cases, citizen pressure groups, along with media organizations and local courts, enforce community standards by disallowing advertising that offends those standards.

Consider Abercrombie & Fitch. The clothing retailer once sparked controversy at a mall in Omaha when its window posters featured a topless model covering her breasts with her hands. A Christian group, Family First, quickly objected, claiming that Abercrombie's posters created a "sexualized walkway." Commenting on the objections, a spokesperson for A&F said the displays might have been "sexy" but were not the "sexually charged monstrosities" that Family First asserted. Nevertheless, the community standards had been revealed. Family First began pressuring shoppers and other retailers in the mall to object to the photographs, and within nine days the window displays were changed.

Were the posters obscene or indecent? Advertisers like A&F, who continue to strive for the "sexy" appeal, are beginning to find it increasingly difficulty to draw the line between simple sex appeal and unethical exploitation.

There is no easy solution to this dilemma, especially because research shows that sexual appeals can be effective when sexuality relates to the product. However, when it doesn't, it can distract audiences from the main message and severely demean the advertiser in the consumer's eyes. This brings up an important and rather common paradox about sexually oriented advertising. How is a naked model in a window poster an advertisement for clothing? Many argue that it is not, making such ads not only a distraction, but also a source of negative *externalities*—the social costs to consumers outside the target market, such as children who might be indirectly affected.

Advertisers must examine, on a case-by-case basis, at what point sexual appeals become counterproductive. In one case, an executive on the Valvoline advertising account justified using "girlie calendars" for mechanics by noting that "the calendar may offend some groups—but they aren't our customers."

This block of the pyramid reaches the smallest audience but those with the most to gain from the product's utility. So the last step is often the easiest. If the copy is clear about what readers need to do and asks or even nudges them to act, chances are they will (see Ad Lab 10-B, "Applying the Creative Pyramid").

The call to action may be explicit—"Call for more information"—or implicit—"Fly the friendly skies." Designers cue customers to take action by placing dotted lines around coupons to suggest cutting and by highlighting the company's telephone number with large type or a bright color.

Marketers use technology to make it easy for people to act, sometimes through either a toll-free phone number or an attractive website. In relationship marketing, the campaign enables people to select themselves as being interested in a relationship. Then the marketer can use more efficient one-on-one media to develop the relationship.

The Judge Role: Decision Time

The next role in the creative process is the **Judge.** This is when the creatives evaluate the value of their big ideas and decide whether to implement, modify, or discard them.[29]

The Judge's role is delicate. On the one hand, the creatives must be self-critical enough to ensure that when it's time to play the Warrior, they will have an idea worth fighting for. On the other hand, they need to avoid stifling the imagination of their internal Artist. It's easier to be critical than to explore, conceptualize, or defend. But the Judge's purpose is to produce good ideas, not to revel in criticism. Von Oech suggests

Miller Lite's "Catfight" campaign raised many eyebrows. The campaign appeared to signal the company's return to "beer and babes" ads, depicting women as sexual objects. In the commercial, two women in a restaurant begin the classic "tastes great/less-filling" debate over Miller Lite. The debate quickly turns into a full-fledged catfight, with the two women stripped down to their underwear, splashing around in an adjacent fountain. Moments later, we see the two brawlers going at it in a soggy cement pit. The ad cuts to a bar. It turns out the fight was only the fantasy of two guys in a bar who were dreaming of the perfect beer commercial, much to the shock and disgust of their girlfriends, who were with them at the time. The cable TV version then takes things a little further as it cuts back to the women with one saying to the other, "Do you want to make out?"

So what does any of this have to do with selling beer? Hillary Chura, who covers the beer industry for *Advertising Age,* explains that ads such as the "Catfight" commercial are "aspirational." After watching these two beautiful women wrestle around for 30 seconds, Miller wants guys to say, "Hey, if I drink Miller Genuine Draft, I'll get those hot women." And Miller wants women to think, "If I drink this beer, I'll look like those women."

But what is the social cost of these unrealistic "aspirations"? In a society rife with confidence-related disorders, should advertisers exploit consumer insecurities in an effort to sell more of their product? At what point do advertisers need to accept some ethical responsibility for the interests of the society to which they owe their existence? And to the interests of women who face workplace harassment?

Some will argue that sex sells. Perhaps. But the casual use of sex in advertising raises ethical issues, and the cultural shift created by #metoo is making many advertisers rethink their approach. Reliance on sexual appeals in advertising may no longer be lazy. It may be just plain wrong.

Questions

1. How would you explain the "redeeming value" of sexual appeals in advertising?

2. If sexual appeals are considered OK by the audiences that are directly targeted, what responsibility does the advertiser have for any effect on indirect targets, such as women who face sexual harassment in the workplace? What is your stance on the use of sexuality in advertising?

Sources: Erin Cooksley, "Sex Sells, Ethics Absent from Advertising Industry," *The Daily Skiff,* February 11, 2004, retrieved from www.skiff.tcu.edu/2004/spring/issues/02/11/sex.html; Florence Kennel, "Burgundy Ads Banned for Sexual Innuendo," *Decanter,* January 23, 2004, retrieved from www.decanter.com; "Does Sex Really Sell?," *Adweek,* October 17, 2005; Robynn Tysver, "Family Group Protests 'Sexualized' Ads at Stores in Lincoln Mall," *Omaha World-Herald,* February 12, 2003, retrieved from www.nexis.com; Deborah Alexander, "Family Group Ends Protest after Shop Changes Displays," *Omaha World-Herald,* February 21, 2003, retrieved from www.nexis.com; Rance Crain, "Relevance Is Operative Word in 'Catfight' or Chip-Dip Ads," *Advertising Age,* January 27, 2003; Basem Boshra, "Uh, Can You Say Appallingly Sexist?" *Montreal Gazette,* February 1, 2003, retrieved from www.nexis.com; Julie Dunn, "The Light Stuff. Coors Loves the Young Male Demographic—and Twins!" *Denver Westword,* January 23, 2003, retrieved from www.nexis.com; Tom Daykin, "Miller Gets Down and Dirty with Lite Ad; Reaction Mixed, but Commercial Is Being Noticed," *Milwaukee Journal Sentinel,* January 26, 2003, retrieved from www.nexis.com.

focusing first on the positive, interesting aspects of a new idea. The negatives will come soon enough.

When playing the Judge, the creatives ask certain questions: Is this idea an aha! or an uh-oh? (What was my initial reaction?) What's wrong with this idea? (And what's right with it?) What if it fails? (Is it worth the risk?) What is my cultural bias? (Does the audience have the same bias?) What's clouding my thinking? (Am I wearing blinders?)

In an effort to create world-class campaigns, Michael Conrad, formerly the worldwide chief creative officer for Leo Burnett and currently the dean of the new Cannes Lions Academy, developed the rating scale shown in Exhibit 10-3. Leo Burnett's Global Product Committee now uses this scale to evaluate every message before presenting it to a client. Ones that score 4 or below don't get presented. The objective is to develop campaigns that score 8 and above, and those receive full agency support. The top rating, world-class, means "best in the world, bar-none."

Risk is an important consideration. When the campaign is a hit, everybody's happy, sales go up, people get raises, and occasionally there's even positive publicity. But when a campaign flops, sales may flatten or even decline, competitors gain a couple of points in market share, distributors and dealers complain, and the phone rings incessantly with calls from disgruntled client executives. Perhaps worst of all is the ridicule in the trade. Advertising pundits say nasty things about the campaign in TV interviews; reviewers write articles in *Advertising Age* and *Adweek;* and even the big daily papers get in their licks. This is not good for either the agency's stock or the client's. And it's how agencies get replaced. So the Judge's role is vital.

AD Lab 10–B

Applying the Creative Pyramid

Notice how the five objectives of advertising copy apply to the ad shown here for the Salvation Army.

Attention The photograph of a man in what appears to be a superhero outfit draws the reader's attention quickly. What's happened to Superman?

Interest The reader quickly realizes that something is amiss. This is no superhero, but a destitute man living in squalid conditions. In a flash, the reader has moved from one set of assumptions about the ad to ones that are completely different. Because his situation looks so bleak, the reader might start losing interest, thinking he or she can do little to help. That's when the headline maintains interest by suggesting that helping is easy.

Credibility Is helping easy? Sure it Is. Take the old clothes you'd just throw away, and bring them to a nearby Salvation Army location. What could be easier?

Desire The man's plight is contrasted with the ease of giving away unwanted clothing. The ad is respectful in tone, asking the reader to "Please donate your unwanted clothes to the homeless this winter." By phrasing the request this way, the ad makes clear that the reader's actions will have a direct impact on the population in need.

Action If the previous steps have been accomplished, then the key to success is to get people to act now, while the plight of the homeless is fresh in their minds. The ad makes it easy to help by asking the reader to "Call the Salvation Army" and giving the phone number to call.

Source: The Salvation Army

Laboratory Applications

1. Find an ad that exhibits the five elements of the creative pyramid. *(A print ad will be the easiest to find and talk about, but radio and TV commercials also feature the five elements. Beware: The desire step may be hard to find.)*

2. Why do so many good ads lack one or more of the five elements listed here? How do they overcome the omission?

10	World-class
9	New standard in advertising
8	New standard in product category
7	Excellence in craft
6	Fresh idea(s)
5	Innovative strategy
4	Cliché
3	Not competitive
2	Destructive
1	Appalling

Exhibit 10-3
Leo Burnett Global Product Committee's rating scale.

Robert Smith, an Indiana University scholar, drew on psychological research in creativity to create a set of questions any creative judge can ask about his or her ideas:

1. Is the ad "out of the ordinary"?
2. Does it depart from stereotypical thinking?
3. Is it unique?
4. Does the ad contain ideas that move from one subject to another?
5. Does it contain different ideas?
6. Does it shift from one idea to another?
7. Does the ad contain numerous details?
8. Does it extend basic ideas and make them more intricate?
9. Does it contain more details than expected?
10. Does the ad connect objects that are usually unrelated?
11. Does it contain unusual connections?
12. Does it bring unusual items together?
13. Is the ad visually or verbally distinctive?
14. Does it make ideas come to life graphically or verbally?
15. Is it artistic in its production?[30]

If the Artist-as-Judge does a good job, the next role in the creative process, the Warrior, is far easier to perform.

AD Lab 10–C

The Creative Gymnasium

The Explorer

The explorer looks for fresh, new ways to see things. To become an explorer, be conscious of how you see the world, and try to discover the new and unusual patterns that exist right below the surface.

Juriah Mosin/Shutterstock

The Judge and the Warrior

As a creative person, what verdict would your Judge give to ads that feature creative gymnastics? How would your Warrior present ads like this to a client for approval?

The Artist

The Artist uses humor and absurd what-if questions to mentally loosen up. Try these warm-up techniques:

1. Think up a new set of conversion factors:

    10^{12} microphones = 1 megaphone

10^{12} pins = 1 terrapin

$3\frac{1}{3}$ tridents = 1 decadent

4 seminaries = 1 binary

10^{21} piccolos = 1 gigolo

1 milli-Helen = the amount of beauty required to launch 1 ship

2. Another mental muscle stretcher is to change the context of an idea. You can turn the Roman numeral for 9 into a 6 by adding only a single line:

    IX

    Some people put a horizontal line through the center, turn it upside down, and then cover the bottom. This gives you a Roman numeral VI. A more artistic solution might be to put "S" in front of the IX to create "SIX." What we've done here is take the IX out of the context of Roman numerals and put it into the context of "Arabic numerals spelled out in English."

    Another right answer might be to add the line "6" after the IX. Then you get IX6, or one times six.

Laboratory Applications

1. Attempt to solve the exercises above. Explain your choices.
2. Create a metaphor for each of these paired concepts:
    a.   Boxing + Water.
    b.   Magnet + Library.
    c.   Rainbow + Clock.

The Warrior Role: Overcoming Setbacks and Obstacles

In the final step of the creative process, the **Warrior** wins territory for big new ideas in a world resistant to change. The Warrior carries the concept into action. This means getting the big idea approved, produced, and placed in the media. Von Oech says Warriors must be bold, sharpen their sword (skills), strengthen their shield (examine criticism in advance), follow through (overcome obstacles), use their energy wisely, be persistent, savor their victories, and learn from defeat.

To get the big idea approved, the Warrior has to battle people within the agency and often the client, too. So part of the Warrior's role is turning the agency account team into co-warriors for the presentation to the client. At this point, it's imperative that the creatives finish their message strategy document to give their rationale for the copy, art, and production elements in the concept they're trying to sell. And the message strategy had better mesh with the creative brief, or the valiant Warrior will likely face a wide moat with no drawbridge (see Ad Lab 10-C, "The Creative Gymnasium").

Part of the Warrior's task may be to help the account managers present the campaign to the client. So how can the artist, or the account manager representing him or her, increase the odds of getting creative idea approval?[31]

(continued on page 348)

:: The Creative Director's Greatest Ads as Named by *Ad Age*

The creative director always wants to produce the most effective advertising possible in order to give the client the greatest bang for the buck. That means first conceiving a brilliant idea that will both resonate with the particular target audience and relate to the client's marketing and advertising strategy. Then the idea must be executed in a masterful way.

• *Ad Age,* the bible of the advertising agency world, selected the ads below as the best (so far) of the 21st century. Visit here to see how they picked: https://adage.com/lp/top15/#intro.

• How do these ads achieve greatness?

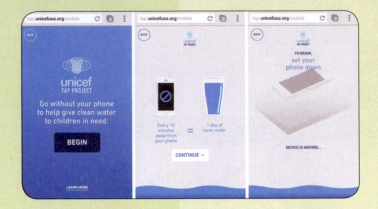

At number 15 is Unicef's Tap Project. When Esquire challenged David Droga, the Australian chairman and founder of Droga5, to launch a brand for positive change, he responded with this campaign. Making it simple, easy, and convenient to use your phone to make a difference proved key to its success. Unicef believes the project has brought more than half a million people healthy drinking water.

Source: UNICEF

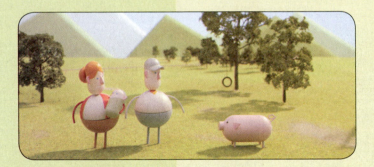

Number 14 is Chipotle's "Back to the Start," its first national ad campaign featuring a short, animated film promoting family farming. Running first in small theaters and online, the campaign eventually ran during the 2012 Grammy Awards. Interestingly, the restaurant does not use an ad agency but does all of its work in-house.

Source: Chipotle Mexican Grill

The boom factor was unusually evident in *Ad Age*'s pick for number 13. Budweiser's ads had a simple premise: focus on a group of friends checking in and finding out "Whassup" with each other. The unique spots were intended to reach younger members of Budweiser's target market. The campaign was popular enough to spawn a host of unauthorized imitators.

Source: Anheuser-Busch

Do people fear death more if the cause of their death is dumb? That was the assumption of this campaign, which showcased amazing creativity in the "Dumb Ways to Die" ad focused on preventing risky behaviors around trains. Read more about this campaign in the beginning of the next chapter.

Source: Metro Trains Melbourne

Dos Equis tapped its inner David Ogilvy (creator of the Man in the Hathaway suit and Commander Schweppes) when it introduced America to the "most interesting man in the world." *Ad Age*'s pick for the eleventh best campaign of the 21st century amused and encouraged us to "Stay Thirsty."

Source: Cervezas Mexicanas

The tenth best campaign of this century originated in the mind of Chapter 11's "People behind the Ads" subject, Alex Bogusky. Changing the frame from health to the reputation of the tobacco industry helped make the Truth campaign especially memorable.

Source: Truth Initiative

On the left, campaign number nine celebrates a hero for many more people than those who idolize athletes or celebrities: moms. As obvious as that seems, it fell to P&G to come up with the idea and execute it brilliantly. On the right, in the eighth position, Apple's "I'm a Mac" commercials showed that comparative advertising could be gentle, but still have a bite.

(left) Source: Procter & Gamble; (right) Source: Apple, Inc.

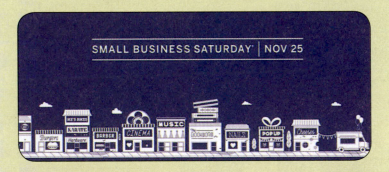

The seventh-ranked ad, from American Express, celebrates Small Business Saturday, ensuring small businesses notice the support they receive from the credit company. Number six, from Burger King, is another Alex Bogusky–inspired creation. How do you remind consumers that at Burger King they can "Have it your way"? Bring back the Subservient Chicken, who does whatever he's asked.

(top) Source: American Express Company; (bottom) Source: Burger King Corporation

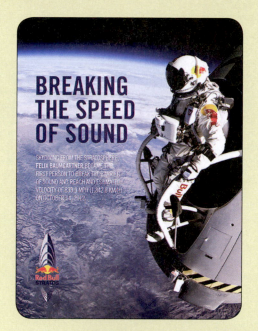

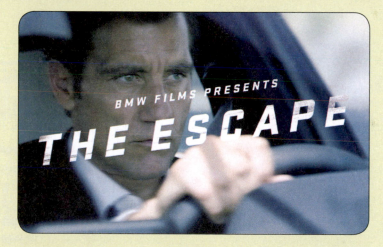

When Felix Baumgartner jumped into space to begin a free-fall that hit a top speed of over 1300 km/h for Red Bull, he guaranteed a big audience would be watching. Check that, with an audience of 7.5 million, making this campaign the fifth best of this century. At number four, Old Spice's "Man your man could smell like" used the boom factor to explode sales of the brand. Finally, at number three, BMW's James Bond–inspired online movie shorts featuring Clive Owen helped ensure BMW continues its reputation as "The ultimate driving machine." Numbers two and one? Visit *Ad Age* to see the two best campaigns of this century at https://adage.com/lp/top15/#getamac.

(top left) Source: Red Bull; (top right) Source: Procter & Gamble; (bottom) Source: BMW of North America

People BEHIND the Ads

Tim Piper, Writer/Director for PiRo, Former Associate Creative Director, Ogilvy & Mather, Toronto

Courtesy of Tim Piper

After all is said and done, creativity is the fuel that makes the ad agency business run.

So it must please Ogilvy & Mather, Toronto, that it can count among its employees an individual named one of the top 100 creative people in the world by *Time* magazine in 2008, a person named the top art director in the world by *Strategy* magazine, AND someone named the second-best copywriter in the world by *The Big Won,* a database that tracks industry recognition.

And what's really remarkable is that all of this recognition is for the same guy.

Tim Piper, former associate creative director for Ogilvy & Mather, Toronto, is currently at work at PiRo, an agency that he co-founded. The native-born Australian helped O&M, Toronto, draw rave reviews for creative for several years. And 2007 was an exceptionally good year. Piper served as copywriter and art director for *Evolution,* winner of the 2007 Cannes Grand Prix, the industry's most prestigious award.

Evolution is the commercial for Dove that helped drive home the "Real Beauty" campaign big idea. A pretty but ordinary-looking young woman sits in a studio. Using time-lapse photography,

makeup crews transform the woman into a model-quality beauty. But because that is still not beautiful enough, her image is then digitally altered to lengthen her neck and sharpen her face lines. The new photo, which hardly resembles the original woman at all anymore, is shown in a final shot as a billboard on the street near a place where young girls walk by. The message is clear: Sometimes even the models can't live up to the beauty industry's standards. So why should girls try to?

The campaign resonated with women in a powerful way and started thousands of discussions about beauty and the expectations foisted on girls. It remains an example of how advertising has the potential to surprise and move us.

Of course, with success, the big question becomes what next? Piper did not disappoint, as he helped create *Evolution's* successor, *Onslaught. Onslaught* begins with a close-up on the freckled face of a young girl, looking innocently at the camera. We are then treated to a blitz of images of women modeling, dieting, exercising, using beauty products. These early images suggest the power of the beauty industry to compel women to focus on their looks as a standard for happiness. But then the images get worse, and we are treated to brief but emotionally powerful flashes of women enduring plastic surgery, going through drastic weight fluctuations, and, finally, demonstrating eating disorder behaviors. The commercial ends with an admonition to "talk to your daughter before the beauty industry does."

That's how you follow up the best ad in the world. With a better one.

Like everyone else, Piper admits he runs into creative blocks. He told *Strategy* that his solution is to "watch a movie, read a book, send an abusive e-mail that could get me fired, that sort of thing."

Piper's career began as a graphic designer, working freelance, in the small town of Adelaide, Australia. When *Strategy* asked him what his first job taught him, he said wryly, "I didn't want to be a freelance graphic designer." He admits that the Grand Prix was his most coveted award but said that the best feeling he'd ever had about his work was "when my family back in Australia told me they saw it on the news there."

Based on the quality of his work so far, we just have one piece of advice for Tim Piper: Get used to that feeling.

(continued from page 343)

1. *Reach out early.* Test your idea with key decision makers. This often helps the Warrior anticipate questions that will come up later during a formal presentation. Testing has other benefits, including obtaining buy-in, showing you want input, and making your idea better.

2. *Be prepared.* Presentations involve questions and answers. Not knowing how to answer a question can damage the Warrior's credibility. Harvard Business School's Michael Norton says, "When you watch someone stumble through an answer, you make an inference that they don't know what they're talking about."[32] Expect people will attack your idea. Rather than avoiding criticisms, develop thoughtful, detailed, and honest responses to tactics like personal attacks, sowing confusion, or raising fears or anxieties about your idea.

3. *Who are you talking to?* Just as great ads have a target audience in mind, so should great pitches. Michael Norton says, "You absolutely want to tailor the specifics of

your presentation to your audience." How will your idea solve their problems? Make them look good? Address their concerns? Offer them rewards or benefits?

4. *Simple trumps complicated.* With respect to your idea, you know more than your audience, and sharing everything you know is rarely achievable or desirable. Many poorly prepared presentations go long, leaving the big idea underdeveloped. So focus on the essentials. Share data judiciously. Don't be distracted from the essential points you are trying to get across.

5. *Responding with confidence.* Warriors face questions that are posed in a variety of ways: Some may seem friendly, others hostile, still others off-point. Whichever way questions are posed, the Warrior's job is to "come off as a statesman," according to John Kotter, Chief Innovation Officer at Kotter International. "Treat [your questioner] like a reasonable person with a reasonable question." What if the question is so off-point that there is no way to answer it without distracting from your key message? Michael Norton suggests you "dodge," by which he means offering a response that touches on the question but quickly segues back to the idea you are trying to advance.[33]

For clients, recognizing a big idea and evaluating it are almost as difficult as coming up with one. (For some examples of big ideas, see the Portfolio Review, "The Creative Director's Greatest Ads.") When the agency presents the concepts, the client is suddenly in the role of the Judge, without having gone through the other roles first. David Ogilvy recommended that clients ask themselves five questions: Did it make me gasp when I first saw it? Do I wish I had thought of it myself? Is it unique? Does it fit the strategy to perfection? Could it be used for 30 years?[34]

As Ogilvy pointed out, campaigns that run five years or more are the superstars: Dove soap (33 percent cleansing cream), BMW ("the ultimate driving machine"), the U.S. Army("Be all you can be"). Some of these campaigns are still running today, and some have run for as long as 30 years. Those are big ideas!

When the client approves the campaign, the creative's role as a Warrior is only half over. Now the campaign has to be executed. That means the Warriors shepherd it through the intricate details of design and production to see that it is completed on time, under budget, and with the highest quality possible. At the same time, the creatives revert to their Artist roles to design, write, and produce the ads.

The next step in the process, therefore, is to implement the big idea, to produce the ads for print and electronic media—the subject of our next two chapters.

Chapter Summary

In the marketing communications process, the creative team is responsible for conceiving and designing advertising messages. It is the author of the communications. The creative team is commonly made up of an art director and a copywriter who report to a creative director.

Their job is to create great advertising for their clients. Great campaigns are characterized by two dimensions: audience impact and strategic relevance. To truly resonate, messages need the boom factor—that element of surprise that attracts the audience's attention, gets them involved, and stirs their imagination. Some campaigns are informational and resonate with the audience by offering relief from a problem. Others are transformational and achieve resonance by offering a reward.

The second dimension of great campaigns, strategic relevance, is behind the visuals and the text of every message. Relevance is an important reason for the success of digital advertising. In fact, strategy is the key to great creative work.

Typically written by the account management team, the creative strategy includes four elements: the target audience, the product concept,

the communications media, and the message. Once the general parameters of the plan are developed, account managers prepare a creative brief that outlines the key strategic decisions. The creative brief should contain at least three elements: an objective statement, a support statement, and either a tone statement or a brand character statement. The brief gives strategic guidance to the art director and copywriter, but it is their responsibility to develop a message strategy that lays out the specifics of how the message will be executed. The three elements of message strategy are copy, art, and production.

Copy is the verbal and art is the nonverbal (visual) presentation of the message strategy. Production refers to the mechanical details of how the promotional messages will be produced.

To create means to originate, and creativity involves combining two or more previously unconnected elements, objects, or ideas to make something new. Creativity helps to inform, persuade, and remind customers and prospects by making the campaign more vivid. All people have creativity; they just differ in degree.

Scholars believe certain styles of thinking are more conducive to creativity than others. The two basic thinking styles are fact-based and value-based. People who prefer the fact-based style tend to be linear thinkers, analytical, and rational. Value-based thinkers tend to be less structured, more intuitive, and more willing to use their imagination. They are good at synthesizing diverse viewpoints to arrive at a new one. And, with their ability to think metaphorically, they tend to be more creative.

In one model of the creative process, the creative person must play four roles along the way to acceptance of a new idea: the Explorer, Artist, Judge, and Warrior. The Explorer searches for new information, paying attention to unusual patterns. The Artist experiments with a variety of approaches looking for the big idea. The Artist also determines how to implement it. For this, the creative pyramid may help. The pyramid models the formation of an ad after the way people learn new information, using five steps: attention, interest, credibility, desire, and action.

The Judge evaluates the results of experimentation and decides which approach is most practical. The Warrior overcomes excuses, idea killers, setbacks, and obstacles to bring a creative concept to realization. Each role has unique characteristics, and there are many techniques for improving performance in each role. During the creative process, it's better to use a value-based style of thinking. During the Judge and Warrior phases, a fact-based style is more effective.

One of the worst blocks to creativity is getting stuck in the wrong mindset, the wrong style of thinking, for the task at hand. However, there are numerous techniques for escaping these mental blocks.

Important Terms

art, *337*

art direction, *337*

art director, *322*

Artist, *333*

big idea, *333*

brainstorming, *333*

communications media, *325*

conceptualization, *333*

copywriter, *322*

creative brief, *325*

creative director, *322*

creative process, *332*

creative pyramid, *337*

creatives, *322*

creativity, *328*

emotional appeal, *325*

Explorer, *332*

fact-based thinking, *330*

IMC message, *325*

informational, *324*

Judge, *340*

mandatories, *327*

message strategy (rationale), *327*

nonverbal, *327*

product concept, *325*

rational appeal, *325*

target audience, *325*

technical, *327*

transformational, *324*

value-based thinking, *330*

verbal, *327*

visualization, *333*

Warrior, *343*

Review Questions

1. Select an ad from an earlier chapter in the book. What do you believe is the sponsor's advertising and message strategy? What is the ad's boom factor?

2. Choose an ordinary product and create a strategic brief for it, focusing on the target audience of students at your school.

3. What are the elements of message strategy, and how do they differ from those of advertising (or creative) strategy?

4. In what ways have you exercised your personal creativity in the last week?

5. What qualities characterize the two main styles of thinking? Think of an occasion when you usually employ one of these.

Now think of a time you typically use the other. Why do the styles fit these occasions?

6. What are the four roles of the creative process? Have you played those roles in preparing a term paper? How?

7. What is the difference between a strategy statement and a big idea?

8. Select five creative ads from a magazine. What techniques of the Artist can you recognize in those ads?

9. In those same ads, can you identify each step of the creative pyramid?

10. Consider a real situation in which you wish to be persuasive. How can you use tactics of the Warrior to advance your idea?

The Advertising Experience

1. **Impact of Color**
   Different colors create subtle differences in the impression an image makes. Find a black-and-white print advertisement. Recreate it in color three times, each time using different color combinations. Ask different audiences (such as your classmates, your friends, or your family) for their impressions of each color scheme. Write an analysis of the results for each, explaining how the colors enhance or diminish the ad's message.

2. **Effective Creative Strategy and Execution**
   Apply the creative process and the various means of deriving and judging "good" advertising to the following websites, noting the quality of the creative and the strategic intent behind the work. Be sure to answer the questions below.

   - adidas: www.adidas.com
   - Energizer: www.energizer.com
   - Xbox: www.xbox.com
   - Harley-Davidson: www.harley-davidson.com
   - AT&T: www.att.com
   - SeaWorld: www.seaworld.com
   - Taco Bell: www.tacobell.com

a. Who is the intended audience of the site?

b. What is it that makes the site's creativity good or bad? Why?

c. Identify the "who, why, what, when, where, style, approach, and tone" of the communication.

d. Write an objective statement, support statement, and brand character statement for each.

3. **Account Planning**

Account planners help ensure that the research process has reaped the proper information for the creatives. The importance of account planning—namely the gathering of research and the formulation of strategy for the creative team—cannot be understated. The Account Planning Group (APG) is an organization that brings together 700 account planners and communications strategists. Browse through

the documents held on the APG website (www.apg.org.uk) and answer the questions that follow.

a. Who is the intended audience of the site?

b. What is account planning? Why is it important?

c. What is the primary document that the account planning function generates? What are the main elements in the document?

d. Choose an essay or article on any of the APG sites and discuss at length, explaining the relevance of the topic to account planning and the advertising business.

4. **How Strategy Dictates Execution**

Target's value-based advertising tends to take a humorous and unexpected approach to communicating its message to the reader. But Target also uses "hard-sell" ads in newspaper inserts. Why?

End Notes

1. "Target Through the Years," Target Corporate, *https://corporate.target.com/about/history/Target-through-the-years*.
2. "xhiliaration," Target.com, *www.target.com/bp/xhiliaration*.
3. Corinne Ruff, "8 Target Private Label Brands That Launched This Year," *RetailDive*, November 20, 2018, *www.retaildive.com/news/8-target-private-label-brands-that-launched-this-year/541814/*.
4. Steve McKee, "What Should You Spend on Advertising?" *Bloomberg Business*, February 1, 2009, *www.businessweek.com/smallbiz/content/feb2009/sb20090210_165498.htm*.
5. A Bullseye View, "Investing to Grow: Target Commits More Than $7 Billion to Adapt to Rapidly Evolving Guest Preferences," February 28, 2017, *https://corporate.target.com/article/2017/02/financial-community-meeting*.
6. Pat Fallon and Fred Senn, *Juicing the Orange: How to Turn Creativity into a Powerful Business Advantage* (Cambridge, MA: Harvard Business School Press, 2006).
7. Damian Farnworth, "What Is Creativity? 21 Authentic Definitions You'll Love," *Copyblogger*, April 11, 2016, *www.copyblogger.com/define-creativity/*.
8. Damian Farnworth, "What Is Creativity? 21 Authentic Definitions You'll Love," *Copyblogger*, April 11, 2016, *www.copyblogger.com/define-creativity/*.
9. J. Scott Armstrong, *Persuasive Advertising: Evidence-Based Principles* (New York: Palgrave Macmillan, 2006).
10. Maja Petricevic, "Bring Out the Power of Metaphors!" *creitive*, September 23, 2015, *www.creitive.com/blog/bring-out-the-power-of-metaphors*.
11. Charles Forceville, "The Strategic Use of the Visual Mode in Advertising Metaphors," in *Critical Multimodal Studies of Popular Discourse*, ed. Emilia Djonov and Sumin Zhao (Abingdon, UK: Routledge, 2013).
12. Matt Britton, *Youthnation: Building Remarkable Brands in a Youth-Driven Culture* (Hoboken, NJ: John Wiley & Sons, 2015).
13. Andrea Ovans, "What Makes the Best Infographics So Convincing," *Harvard Business Review*, April 22, 2014, *https://hbr.org/2014/04/what-makes-the-best-infographics-soconvincing*.
14. Aleksi Tzatzev, "10 Colors That Might Get You Sued," *Business Insider*, September 29, 2012, *www.businessinsider.com/colors-that-are-trademarked-2012-9*.
15. Cam Wolf, "Colin Kaepernick Is the Star of Nike's New Ad Campaign—and the Protests Against It Are Hilarious," *GQ*, September 4, 2018, *www.gq.com/story/nike-colin-kaepernick-sock-protest*.
16. Roger von Oech, *A Whack on the Side of the Head* (New York: Warner Books, 1990).
17. Kevin Goldman, "Nike, H-P Gamble on New Sales Pitches," *The Wall Street Journal*, April 8, 1994.
18. Roger von Oech, *A Kick in the Seat of the Pants* (New York: HarperPerennial, 1986).
19. Tim Nudd, "Genius or Process? How Top Creative Directors Come Up with Great Ideas," *Adweek*, September 25, 2013, *www.adweek.com/brand-marketing/genius-or-process-how-top-creative-directors-come-great-ideas-152697/*.
20. Tim Nudd, "Genius or Process? How Top Creative Directors Come Up with Great Ideas," *Adweek*, September 25, 2013, *www.adweek.com/brand-marketing/genius-or-process-how-top-creative-directors-come-great-ideas-152697/*.
21. Adapted with permission from Roger von Oech, *A Kick in the Seat of the Pants* (New York: HarperPerennial, 1986).
22. Eleftheria Parpis, "What's the 'Big Idea'?" *Adweek*, September 13, 2010, *www.adweek.com/news/advertising-branding/whats-big-idea-103274*.
23. John O'Toole, *The Trouble with Advertising*, 2nd ed. (New York: Random House, 1985), p. 132; Fred Danzig, "The Big Idea," *Advertising Age*, November 9, 1988, pp. 16, 138–40.
24. Roger von Oech, *A Whack on the Side of the Head* (New York: Warner Books, 1990).
25. Roger von Oech, *A Whack on the Side of the Head* (New York: Warner Books, 1990).
26. Kevin Goldman, "Leap Partnership Touts All-Creative Shop," *The Wall Street Journal*, December 23, 1993.
27. Derek Walker, "If the Client Was Always Right, It Wouldn't Need an Ad Agency," *Advertising Age*, July 29, 2011, *http://adage.com/article/small-agency-diary/client-adagency/228932/*.
28. Joseph Sugarman, *The Adweek Copywriting Handbook* (New York: John Wiley & Sons, 2012).
29. Adapted with permission from Roger von Oech, *A Kick in the Seat of the Pants* (New York: HarperPerennial, 1986).
30. Werner Reinartz and Peter Saffert, "How to Assess an Ad's Creativity," *Harvard Business Review*, May 21, 2013, *https://hbr.org/2013/05/how-to-assess-an-ads-creativity*.
31. Amy Gallo, "How to Get Your Idea Approved," *Harvard Business Review*, November 15, 2010, *https://hbr.org/2010/11/how-to-get-their-approval.html*.
32. Amy Gallo, "How to Get Your Idea Approved," *Harvard Business Review*, November 15, 2010, *https://hbr.org/2010/11/how-to-get-their-approval.html*.
33. Amy Gallo, "How to Get Your Idea Approved," *Harvard Business Review*, November 15, 2010, *https://hbr.org/2010/11/how-to-get-their-approval.html*.
34. David Ogilvy, *Ogilvy on Advertising* (New York: Random House, 1985).

CHAPTER

11

Creative Execution: Art and Copy

LEARNING OBJECTIVES

To present the role of art and copy—the nonverbal and verbal elements of message strategy—in print, radio, television, and on the web. Artists and copywriters include a variety of specialists who follow specific procedures for conceptualizing, designing, writing, and producing IMC messages. To be successful, creatives must be conversant with the copywriting and commercial art terms and formats used in the business. They must also develop an aesthetic sensitivity so they can recognize, create, evaluate, or recommend quality work.

After studying this chapter, you will be able to:

LO11-1   Describe the tools and principles important for effective design in print layouts.

LO11-2   Explain how to create great copy in print.

LO11-3   Identify the important aspects of writing for radio and TV.

LO11-4   Review ways to develop great spots in radio and TV.

LO11-5   Suggest ways to write effectively for digital media.

LO11-6   List the challenges involved in creating messages for international markets.

Source: Metro Trains Melbourne

Can creativity save lives? Maybe, if the creativity is exceptional and the strategy is perfect. A small campaign focused on convincing people not to take foolish risks around trains illustrates this perfectly. ■ Nothing has been more frustrating in the history of PSAs than the failure of campaigns to get people to quit smoking, not use drugs, not drink too much, not have unprotected sex, etc. ■ Why do so many campaigns fail? Reasons vary, but there are some common mistakes planners make. For one, many falsely assume people don't know they are taking risks. Smokers, for example, know perfectly well that smoking is dangerous. They do it anyway. Second, planners forget that people resent being preached at or told what to do. ■ These realities were understood by McCann's Melbourne, Australia, office when the Metro Trains network asked it to develop a campaign that would reduce fatal accidents around trains. Specific behaviors included running across the tracks, walking along tracks, standing too close to a platform's edge, and racing around a lowered crossing gate. ■ Why would people do these things? One reason could be ignorance, but it's also possible that certain individuals see risky behaviors around trains as brave or as showing a devil-may-care attitude. For example, one news article reported on a gang of teens standing on subway tracks until the last possible moment as an initiation.[1] ■ Given all of that, what message would you recommend to reduce accidents around trains? Messages that scare or frighten most people could actually incentivize daredevils. And messages that preach turn most people off. ■ McCann went in a different direction. Its message would reframe "brave" as dumb. To make that point, it developed a campaign named by *Advertising Age* one of the best campaigns of the 21st century, "Dumb Ways to Die." ■ The hook is simple: Show cartoon characters taking risks (and perishing) from actions that most would consider incredibly stupid. The natural horror of death is softened by child-like music, cartoonish geometric figures, and an overall sense of silliness that helps to keep viewers watching. You can watch the video here: www.youtube.com/watch?v=IJNR2EpS0jw.

Dumb Ways to Die
(from public service announcement campaign by Metro Trains)
Set fire to your hair
Poke a stick at a grizzly bear
Eat medicine that's out of date
Use your private parts as piranha bait

[Refrain:]

Dumb ways to die
So many dumb ways to die

Dumb ways to di-ie-ie
So many dumb ways to die
Get your toast out with a fork
Do your own electrical work
Teach yourself how to fly
Eat a two-week-old un-refrigerated pie

[Refrain]

Invite a psycho-killer inside
Scratch a drug dealer's brand new ride
Take your helmet off in outer space
Use a clothes dryer as a hiding place

[Refrain]

Keep a rattlesnake as a pet
Sell both your kidneys on the Internet
Eat a tube of superglue
I wonder, what's this red button do?

[Refrain]

Dress up like a moose during hunting season
Disturb a nest of wasps for no good reason
Stand on the edge of a train station platform
Drive around the boom gates at a level crossing
Run across the tracks between the platforms

They may not rhyme but they're quite possibly
The dumbest ways to die

The dumbest ways to die
The dumbest ways to di-ie-ie-ie
So many dumb
So many dumb ways to die

Be safe around trains . . . a message from Metro[2]

■ The three-minute video attracted 30 million views in its first two weeks and as of 2017 had been watched 140 million times.[3] ■ It was also a big winner at Cannes, perhaps advertising's top festival. In fact, by winning five awards, "Dumb Ways to Die" (DWTD) became the most successful campaign in Cannes history.[4] ■ Whether the hoped-for reduction in preventable accidents and deaths has resulted is a matter of some dispute. The client, Metro Trains, claimed a 21 percent decrease,[5] but that has been challenged by some, including judges at Australia's Effie Awards.[6] The Effies, unlike awards at Cannes, require evidence of advertising effectiveness. The debate over the final impact of the campaign on train deaths may not be resolved anytime soon. But there is no debate about the reach, influence, or success of the spots to raise awareness about dangerous behaviors around trains. ■ McCann's success calls to mind the words of Bill Bernbach, perhaps the greatest creative mind in the history of advertising, who once said, "You can say the right thing about a product and nobody will listen. You've got to say it in such a way that people will feel it in their gut. Because if they don't feel it, nothing will happen."

As "Dumb Ways to Die" shows, how you say something is just as important as what's said. That's why creativity is so important in advertising. In the DWTD video, the nonverbal aspects of the message carry at least half the burden of communicating. This is true more generally as well. Nonverbal message components help position the product and create personality for the brand. They create the mood and determine the way a campaign *feels* to the audience. That mood flavors the verbal message, embodied in the *copy*.

In this chapter, we discuss how creative concepts are executed from the standpoints of both art and copy. We examine the visual and the verbal details, first of print and then of electronic and digital media. Campaigns must inform (see My IMC Campaign 11–A), but they should do so in a clear, attractive, and engaging way. Design is about making that happen. More so than others, this chapter focuses on planned messages, like advertising, because marketers and agencies have the greatest control over their look and content. Design is a less important consideration in sites that compel certain layouts (such as Facebook or other social media), and it is least important in many kinds of public relations activities, especially publicity.

You will also learn about production. Production involves the steps between a great idea and a finished commercial message. A great idea can still fail if it is poorly executed. Even though many think of creativity in terms of idea generation, it is also an enormously important part of production.

Designing Print Layouts

LO **11-1**

Design refers to how the art director and graphic designer choose and structure the artistic elements of an ad. A designer establishes a *style*—the manner in which a thought or image is expressed—by choosing artistic elements and uniquely blending them.

Several designers, working under the art director, may produce initial layouts of the ad concept. Working with copywriters, these artists draw on their expertise in graphic design (including photography, typography, and illustration) to create the most effective ad, brochure, or website.

The Use of Layouts

A **layout** is an overall orderly arrangement of the format elements of an ad: visual(s), headline, subheads, body copy, slogan, seal, logo, and signature. Layouts serve several purposes. First, they help the agency and the client consider, in advance, how the ad will look and feel. It gives a client something tangible to correct, change, question, and approve.

Second, a layout helps the creative team develop the message's psychological elements: the nonverbal and symbolic components. Sophisticated marketers expect messages to create a personality for the product and to build the brand's (and the company's) equity with the consumer. To do this, the "look" of the message should elicit a mood that reflects and enhances both the marketer and the product. In the "Dumb Ways to Die" commercial, the choice of geometric figures, bright colors, and child-like music were very deliberate. The comical elements help soften the appeal and make it easier for the audience to consider the message.

Third, once the best design is chosen, the layout serves as a blueprint. It shows the size and placement of each element in the ad. Once the production manager knows the dimensions of the ad, the number of photos, the amount of typesetting, and the use of art elements such as color and illustrations, he or she can determine the cost of producing the ad (see Ad Lab 11-A, "The Role of the Artist").

Design and Production: The Creative and Approval Process

The design process is both a creative and an approval process. In the creative phase, the designer uses thumbnails, roughs, dummies, and comprehensives—in other words, *nonfinal art*—to establish the message's look and feel. Historically, during the *prepress* phase, the time between the creation of the layout and printing,[7] the artist would prepare a

This ad for upscale workout brand Equinox uses the nonverbal element and symbolic components successfully to help attract attention and position the brand. The campaign included multiple executions tied together by the "Commit to Something" theme. None of them show exercise machines or a workout facility, a deliberate choice by the ad's creators.

Source: Equinox Fitness Company

My IMC Campaign 11-A

Product Facts for Creatives

Art directors and copywriters must have a thorough understanding of the brand to create advertising that resonates. Make sure your creatives have the information that will help them write copy that sizzles and create layouts that stop consumers dead in their tracks.

- **Proprietary information**

  Product's trade name

  Trademark

  Product symbol

  Other copyrighted or patented information

- **History**

  When was the product created or invented?

  Who introduced it?

  Has it had other names?

  Have there been product changes?

  Is there any "romance" to it?

- **Research**

  Are research results available?

  What research about the product does the supplier have?

  Which research will be most useful for each medium?

- **Life cycle**

  What is the product's life or use span?

  What stage is it in now and what style of copy should be used for that stage?

  What stages are competitors in?

- **Market position**

  What is the product's share of the total market?

  Does its market share suggest a positioning strategy?

  What position does the company wish to occupy?

- **Competitive information**

  Who are the product's competitors?

  Does the product have any advantages over them?

  Does it have any disadvantages?

  Are they all about the same?

  Do rival products present problems that this one solves?

- **Product image**

  How do people view the product?

  What do they like about it?

  What do they dislike about it?

  Is it a luxury?

  Is it a necessity?

  Is it a habit?

  Is it self-indulgent?

  Do people have to have it but wish they didn't?

- **Customer use**

  How is the product used?

  Are there other possible uses?

  How frequently is it bought?

  What type of person uses the product?

  Why is the product bought?

  Personal use

mechanical: the final artwork with the actual type in place along with all the visuals the printer or the media will need to reproduce the ad. Today, virtually all commercial prepress work is done via desktop publishing using products such as Adobe Creative Suite.

The approval process takes place at each step along the way. At any point in the design and production process, the ad—or the ad concept—may be altered or even canceled.

Thumbnail Sketches

The thumbnail sketch, or **thumbnail,** is a small, rough, rapidly produced drawing that the artist uses to visualize layout approaches without wasting time on details. Thumbnails are very basic. Blocks of straight or squiggly lines indicate text placement, and boxes show placement of visuals. The best sketches are then developed further.

Rough Layout

In a rough, the artist draws to the actual size of the ad or website. Headlines and subheads suggest the final type style, illustrations and photos are sketched in, and body copy is simulated with lines. The agency may present roughs to clients, particularly cost-conscious ones, for approval.

Gift

Work

What type of person uses the product most (heavy user)?

How much does the heavy user buy?

Where do the best customers live?

■ **Performance**

What does the product do?

What might it be expected to do that it does not?

How does it work?

How is it made or produced?

What's in it?

Raw materials

Special ingredients

Preservatives

Chemicals

Nutrients

■ **What are its physical characteristics?**

Smell

Appearance

Color

Texture

Taste

Others

■ **Effectiveness**

Is there proof the product has been tested and works well?

Do any government or other regulations need to be mentioned or observed?

How does it work compared to its competitors?

■ **Manufacturing**

How is the product made?

How long does it take?

How many steps are in the process?

How many people are involved in making it?

Are any special machines used?

Where is it made?

■ **Distribution**

How widely is the product distributed?

Are there exclusive sellers?

Is there a ready supply or a limited amount?

Is it available for a short season?

What channels of distribution must be reached?

■ **Packaging**

Unit size or sizes offered.

Package shape

Package design

Styling

Color

Special protection for product

A carrier for product

Package label

Comprehensive

The **comprehensive layout,** or **comp,** is a highly refined facsimile of the finished ad. A comp is generally quite elaborate, with colored photos, the final type styles and sizes, subvisuals, and a glossy spray coat. Copy for the comp is typeset on a computer and positioned with the visuals, and then printed as a full-color proof. At this stage, all visuals should be final.

Dummy

A **dummy** presents the handheld look and feel of brochures, multipage materials, or point-of-purchase displays. The artist may assemble the dummy by hand, using color markers and computer proofs, mounting them on sturdy paper, and then cutting and folding them to size. A dummy for a brochure, for example, is put together, page by page, to look exactly like the finished product.

The Use of Computers in Publishing

Desktop computers are now powerful enough to create print and digital messages of the highest professional quality. Preparing print or digital materials for commercial purposes using a computer and publishing software is called **desktop publishing**.

AD Lab 11–A

The Role of the Artist

All the people employed in commercial art are called artists, but they may perform entirely different tasks. Some can't even draw well; instead, they're trained for different artistic specialties.

Art Directors

Art directors are responsible for the visual presentation of the ad. Along with a copywriter, they develop the initial concept. They may do initial sketches or layouts, but after that they may not touch the ad again. Their primary responsibility is supervising the ad's progress to completion.

The best art directors excel at presenting ideas in both words and pictures. They are usually experienced graphic designers with a good understanding of consumers. They may have a large or small staff, depending on the organization. Or they may be freelancers (independent contractors) and do more of the work themselves.

Web Designers

Website designers help plan and compose the layouts and content for websites. Web designers are able to compose pages using HTML, CSS, JavaScript, PHP, and other languages that can be read by web browsers. Web programmers have more extensive coding skills and help build applications that let websites perform certain tasks, such as link to databases or process purchases.

Compared to other creatives, web designers have two unique challenges. First, their messages have to work across a variety of different viewing platforms. While a print ad will appear in only one execution, websites are viewed in a variety of browsers, each of which may handle code differently. In addition, people view web pages on mobile devices such as phones and tablets so content must automatically adjust to the screen a viewer is using. The second challenge for web designers is that sites are not a single page, but a collection of different, linked pages. Conceptualizing the structure of this collection is an important design consideration.

Graphic Designers

Graphic designers are precision specialists preoccupied with shape and form. In advertising they arrange the various graphic elements (type, illustrations, photos, white space) in the most attractive and effective way possible. While they may work on ads, they usually design and produce collateral materials, such as posters, brochures, and annual reports.

In an agency, the art director often acts as the designer. Sometimes, however, a separate designer is used to offer a unique touch to a particular ad.

Illustrators

Illustrators paint or draw the visuals in an ad. They frequently specialize in creating visuals for products such as automotive, fashion, or furniture. Very few agencies or advertisers retain full-time illustrators; most advertising illustrators freelance. Typically, agencies hire different illustrators for different jobs, depending on an ad's particular needs, look, and feel.

Photographers

Like the illustrator, the advertising photographer creates a nonverbal expression that reinforces the verbal message. Photographers use the tools of photography—cameras, lenses, and lights—to create images. They select interesting angles, arrange subjects in new ways, carefully control the lighting, and use many other techniques to enhance the subject's image quality. A studio photographer uses high-powered lights to photograph products in front of a background or as part of an arranged setting. A location photographer generally shoots in real-life settings such as those in the Timberland ads. Many photographers specialize—in cars, celebrities, fashion, food, equipment, or architecture. Agencies and advertisers rarely employ staff photographers. They generally hire freelancers by the hour or use stock photography, photos on file or that can be purchased from a vendor.

Laboratory Applications

1. Select an ad in the Chapter 10 Portfolio Review. Explain which advertising artists were probably involved in its creation and what the responsibility of each artist was.

2. Which ad in the Chapter 10 Portfolio Review do you think needed the fewest artists? How many?

Most print and web ads are created today using desktop publishing because it offers extraordinary benefits over traditional methods. First, it speeds the development and design of publications. Whereas designers once had to carefully count type and use detailed measurements to fit visuals and text, these functions are handled automatically by a computer. In addition, design elements in digital media can be saved and reused through **style sheets,** or on websites through the use of **cascading style sheets.** Second, it significantly lowers the cost of publishing, in part because a single person can do much of the work that used to be required by a team. Third, it allows for rapid and inexpensive changes to the layout of an ad. Finally, the same computer and software suites can be used to create messages that will be seen in a digital format (such as a web page) or print format.

Exhibit 11-1

The copy approval process begins within the agency and ends with approval by key executives of the client company. Each review usually requires some rewrite and a presentation to the next level of approvers. When the agency and the advertiser are large companies, the process can require long lead times.

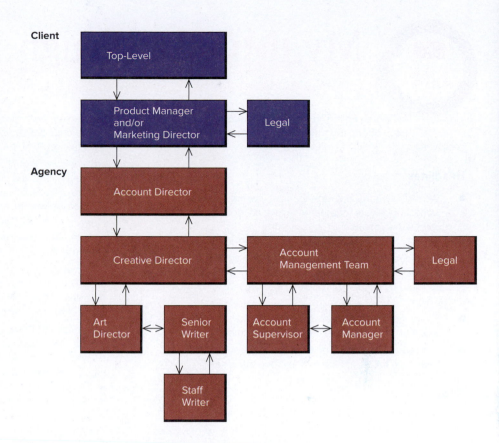

Approval

The work of the copywriter and art director always requires approval. The larger the agency and the larger the client, the more formidable this process becomes (see Exhibit 11-1). A new ad concept is first approved by the agency's creative director. Then the account management team reviews it. Next, the client's product managers and marketing staff review it, often changing a word or two or sometimes rejecting the whole approach. Both the agency's and client's legal departments scrutinize the copy and art for potential problems. Finally, the company's top executives review the final concept and text.

The biggest challenge in approval is keeping approvers from corrupting the style of the ad. The creative team works hard to achieve a cohesive style. Maintaining artistic purity is extremely difficult and requires patience, flexibility, maturity, and the ability to articulate an important point of view and explain why artistic choices were made. Bringing decision makers great copy right from the start is a good way to build credibility and smooth the approval process. For tips on writing great copy and headlines, see some suggestions from one of the best, George Felton, in My IMC Campaign 11-B.

Creating Effective Layouts: Tools and Formats

Small Windows- and Mac-based systems are ideal for computer design, and sophisticated graphics software is now available for page layouts (InDesign), painting and drawing (Adobe Illustrator), image manipulation (Adobe Photoshop), and web design (Adobe Dreamweaver and Animate).[9] Today's graphic artist, illustrator, and retoucher, in addition to having a thorough knowledge of aesthetics, must be skilled in the use of design software.

Promotional appeals are designed to attract consumers, but they have a lot of competition. Indeed, studies show that the average American sees 3,000 ads each day. At the same time, a majority of consumers, about 53 percent, believe that "most marketing is a bunch of B.S."[10] Studies also show virtually no relationship between how much the marketer spends and how well the ad is recalled. But the quality of the message's appearance is important. Good design not only commands attention but holds it. Alex Palmer, writing for

My IMC Campaign 11–B

Creating Great Headlines and Copy

George Felton, in his book *Advertising Concept and Copy*, offers the following suggestions for aspiring copywriters:

Headlines

- "Achieve synergy, not redundancy." The headlines and artwork should work together to create an idea, but not be completely redundant.

- "Let the consumer do some of the work." It is ok to create headlines that prompt thought or even puzzlement. Avoid ads that insult the audience's intelligence (a philosophy articulated by Bill Bernbach. (See "People behind the Ads" in Chapter 2.)

- "Combine overstatement and understatement." If the visual is BIG, make the headline small. And vice versa.

- "Emphasize one idea per ad." If you have several ideas, show how they combine to make one big idea.

Copy

Demian Farnworth at Copyblogger offers the following ways to write "damn good copy":

1. *Plain copy:* Make it simple, short, and to the point. This works well in search advertising. Example: "College scholarships that you likely qualify for."

2. *Storytelling copy:* Use the elements of a story (opening, conflict, dialog, and solution). Example: Arielle wanted to feel better about how she looked and felt, and with her wedding just months away, she was ready for change (opening). For years she had been yo-yo dieting (conflict). Then a friend told her how she could lose weight with Weight Watchers (dialog). All it took was the easy Weight Watchers plan for tracking food, activity, and water intake (solution).

3. *Conversational copy:* Write as though you are speaking with your prospect. Example: "Today I want to share the three lessons that really helped me connect to my kids."

4. *Imagine copy:* Invite the prospect to dream or imagine that a problem is removed or a transformation is possible. "Imagine looking at that swimsuit you love and finding out about an easy, inexpensive way you can wear it next summer with confidence."

5. *Long copy:* Farnworth notes, "The more you tell, the more you sell." This is especially useful when the benefit is not simple or easily communicated.

6. *Killer poet copy:* Combining style with selling. The best example may be this copy from ad legend David Ogilvy: "At 60 miles an hour the loudest noise in this new Rolls-Royce comes from the electric clock."

7. *Direct-from-CEO copy:* Let the boss sell by communicating directly with prospects or users. Example: Pete Coors appeared in a commercial for Coor's Light. With snow-covered mountains behind him, Coors looked directly at the camera and said, "Some brewers look out their windows and see smokestacks. Some don't."

8. *Frank copy:* Admit the elements of the product that aren't easy, simple, convenient, or perfect. This honesty earns credibility and also helps the consumer see him- or herself as unique. Examples: The admired campaign by luxury gym brand Equinox with the tagline "Commit to something" or Patagonia's "Don't buy this jacket."

9. *Superlative copy:* Outrageous claim? That's what you're going for. Examples: Patagonia's "The President Stole Your Land," Mountain Dew's "Dew or die," and Monster Energy's "Unleash the Beast."

10. *Rejection copy:* Who doesn't want to be part of an exclusive club? Farnworth cites American Express's Black Card and the Beautiful People dating site as examples of "not everyone is good enough."[8]

UX Mastery, notes, "Design is meant to show the intent that exists behind an action or an object in a clear way. Great design strips away all possible interpretations of intent, leaving only one."[11]

Creatives use many different types of layouts (see Portfolio Review, "The Art Director's Guide to Layout Styles," later in this chapter). Traditionally, the ads that score the highest recall employ a standard, **poster-style format** (also called a **picture-window layout** and **Ayer No. 1** in the trade) with a single, dominant visual that occupies 60 to 70 percent of the ad's total area.[12] The visuals are intended to stop the reader and arouse interest, so their content must be interesting.

As we discuss in the next section, headlines should stop the reader and contribute to the memorability of the ad's key points.[13] As a design element, the total headline area is typically no more than 10 to 15 percent of the ad, so the type need not be particularly large. Headlines may appear above or below the visual, depending on the situation. As Altstiel and Grow note, the effectiveness of a headline ultimately relates to how well it works within its context.[14]

Research also shows that readership drops considerably if ads have more than 50 words. So to attract a large number of readers, copy blocks should be kept to less than 20 percent of the ad. However, with certain high-involvement products, the more you tell, the more you sell. If selling is the objective, then informative body copy becomes important. And long copy works when it's appropriate—when the advertiser is more interested in *quality* of readership than *quantity*.[15]

Finally, most people want to know who placed the ad. Company signatures or logos need not be large or occupy more than 5 to 10 percent of the area. For best results, they should be placed in the lower right-hand corner or across the bottom of the ad.

Advertising author Roy Paul Nelson points out that the principles of design are to the layout artist what the rules of grammar are to the writer. The basic rules include the following:

- A design must be in *balance.*
- The space within the ad should be distributed in pleasing *proportions.*
- A directional pattern should be evident so the reader knows in what *sequence* to read.
- Some force should hold the ad together and give it *unity.*
- One element, or one part of the ad, should have enough *emphasis* to dominate all others.[16]

For more on the basic principles of advertising design (balance, proportion, sequence, unity, and emphasis), see My IMC Campaign 11–C, "Design Principles."

The Use of Typography in Print

The look of an ad is also a function of the typefaces chosen for the printed words. Art directors select type styles to enhance the desired personality of the product and complement the tone of the ad. Typefaces affect an ad's appearance, design, and readability. Good type selection can't compensate for a weak headline, poor body copy, or an inappropriate illustration, but it can create interest and attract readers.

Typography is the art of selecting and setting type. Advertising artists know the five major type groups, the artistic variations within type families, and the structure of type. The most important considerations in selecting type are *readability, appropriateness, harmony or appearance,* and *emphasis.* Ad Lab 11–B, "The Characteristics of Type," describes these and other type-related topics.

The Use of Visuals in Print

The artists who paint, sketch, and draw in advertising are called **illustrators.** The artists who produce pictures with a camera are **photographers.** Together they are responsible for the **visuals,** or pictures, we see in IMC.

Purpose of the Visual

When confronted with a print ad, most prospects spot the picture first, then read the headline, and then peruse the body copy, in that order. Because the visual carries so much responsibility for an ad's success, it should be designed with several goals in mind. Some of the most obvious follow:

- Capture the reader's attention.
- Clarify claims made by the copy.
- Identify the subject.
- Show the product actually being used.
- Qualify readers by stopping those who are legitimate prospects.
- Help convince the reader of the truth of copy claims.
- Arouse the reader's interest in the headline.
- Emphasize the product's unique features.
- Create a favorable impression of the product or advertiser.
- Provide continuity for the campaign by using a unified visual technique.

My IMC Campaign 11–C

Design Principles

Make sure your layout follows these rules of thumb for creating attractive, informative ads.

Balance

The optical center is the reference point that determines the layout's balance. The optical center is about one-eighth of a page above the physical center of the page. Balance is achieved through the arrangement of elements on the page—the left side of the optical center versus the right, above the optical center versus below.

_____ **Formal balance.** Perfect symmetry is the key to formal balance: matched elements on either side of a line dissecting the ad have equal optical weight. This technique strikes a dignified, stable, conservative image.

_____ **Informal balance.** A visually balanced ad has elements of different size, shape, color intensity, or darkness at different distances from the optical center. Like a teeter-totter, an object of greater optical weight near the center can be balanced by an object of less weight farther from the center. Many ads use informal balance to make the ad more interesting, imaginative, and exciting.

Movement

Movement is the principle of design that causes the audience to read the material in the desired sequence. It can be achieved through a variety of techniques.

_____ People or animals can be positioned so that their eyes direct the reader's eyes to the next important element.

_____ Devices such as pointing fingers, boxes, lines, or arrows (or moving the actors or the camera or changing scenes) direct attention from element to element.

_____ Design can take advantage of readers' natural tendency to start at the top left corner of the page and proceed in a Z motion to the lower right.

_____ Comic-strip sequence and pictures with captions force the reader to start at the beginning and follow the sequence in order to grasp the message.

_____ Use of white space and color emphasizes a body of type or an illustration. Eyes will go from a dark element to a light one, or from color to noncolor.

_____ Size itself attracts attention because readers are drawn to the biggest and most dominant element on the page, then to smaller elements.

Proportion

_____ Elements should be accorded space based on their importance to the entire ad. Attention-getting elements are usually given more space. Avoid the monotony of giving equal amounts of space to each element.

White Space (Isolation)

_____ White space is the part of the ad not occupied by other elements (note that white space may be some color other than white). White space helps focus attention on an isolated element—it makes the copy appear to be in a spotlight. White space is an important contributor to the ad's overall image.

Contrast

_____ An effective way of drawing attention to a particular element is to use contrast in color, size, or style; for example, a reverse ad (white letters against a dark background) or a black-and-white ad with a red border.

Clarity and Simplicity

_____ Any elements that can be eliminated without damaging the overall effect should be cut. Too many type styles; type that is too small; too many reverses, illustrations, or boxed items; and unnecessary copy make for an overly complex layout and an ad that is hard to read.

Unity

_____ Unity means that an ad's many different elements must relate to one another in such a way that the ad gives a singular, harmonious impression. Balance, movement, proportion, contrast, and color may all contribute to unity of design. Many other techniques can be used: type styles from the same family, borders around ads to hold elements together, overlapping one picture or element on another, judicious use of white space, graphic tools such as boxes, arrows, or tints.

Continuity

_____ Continuity is the relationship of one ad to the rest of the campaign. This is achieved by using the same design format, style, and tone; the same spokesperson; or the same graphic element, logo, cartoon character, or catchy slogan.

Determining the Chief Focus for Visuals

The visuals capture a mood and create a feeling, a context for the consumer's perception of the product.

Selecting the focus for visuals is a major step in the creative process. It often determines how well the big idea is executed. Print promotions use many standard subjects for ad visuals, including

1. *The package containing the product.* Especially important for packaged goods, it helps the consumer identify the product on the grocery shelf.
2. *The product alone.* This usually does not work well for nonpackaged goods.
3. *The product in use.* Cosmetic ads usually show the product in use with a close-up photo of a beautiful woman or a virile man.
4. *How to use the product.* Recipe ads featuring a new way to use food products have historically pulled very high readership scores.
5. *Product features.* Automobile ads frequently show the technologies used in the car that distinguish it from competitors.
6. *Comparison of products.* The marketer shows its product next to a competitor's and compares important features.
7. *User benefit.* It's often difficult to illustrate intangible user benefits. However, marketers know that the best way to get customers' attention is to show how the product will benefit them, so it's worth the extra creative effort.
8. *Humor.* If used well, a humorous visual can make an entertaining and lasting impression. But it can also destroy credibility if used inappropriately.

Strong visuals come from an artist's vision and from understanding principles of design. The photo at the top left illustrates formal balance, while the upper right photo demonstrates informal balance. Both use principles of design to draw the reader's attention and create a sense of beauty. Finally, the photo at the bottom left demonstrates movement.

(top left): Daniel Ingold/Cultura/Image Source; (top right): THEPALMER/iStock/Getty Images; (bottom left): filmfoto/iStock/Getty Images

AD Lab 11–B

The Characteristics of Type

Readability

The most important consideration in selecting a typeface is readability. General factors that contribute to readability include the type's style, boldness, and size; the length of the line; and the spacing between words, lines, and paragraphs. An ad is meant to be read, and reduced readability kills interest. Difficult-to-read typefaces should be used infrequently and only to create special effects.

Large, bold, simply designed typefaces are the easiest to read. However, the amount of space in the ad and the amount of copy that must be written limit the use of these type forms. For ads, columns of copy should be less than 3 inches wide.

Spacing between lines also influences an ad's readability. Space between lines of type allows for descenders (the part of the letter that extends downward, as in the letters *j, g, p*) and ascenders (the part of the letter that extends upward, as in the letters *b, d, k*). When this is the only space between lines, type is said to be "set solid." Sometimes an art director adds extra space between lines (called **leading,** pronounced "ledding") to give a more "airy" feeling to the copy.

Kerning (spreading or narrowing the spaces between letters) also improves an ad's appearance and readability. The narrower the kerning, the more type can fit into the available space. Narrow kerning is effective in headlines because people read large type faster when the letters are close together. But narrow kerning is hard to read in smaller type sizes.

Appropriateness

A typeface must be appropriate to the product being advertised. Each typeface and size convey a mood and feeling quite apart from the meanings of the words themselves. One typeface whispers "luxury"; another screams "bargain!" A typeface that looks old-fashioned is probably inappropriate for a smartphone.

Harmony/Appearance

Advertising novices often mix too many typefaces, creating disharmony and clutter. Type should harmonize with the other elements of an ad, including the illustration and layout. Skilled artists choose typefaces in the same family or faces that are similar in appearance.

Emphasis

Contrast creates emphasis. Artists often use more than one type style or mix italic and roman, small and large type, lowercase and uppercase. But they must be careful not to emphasize all elements or they won't emphasize any.

Classes of Type

Two classes of type are used in advertising.

Display type is larger and heavier than text type; it is useful in headlines, subheads, logos, and addresses, and for emphasis.

Text type is smaller and finer, used in body copy.

Type Groups

Serif *(roman)* type is the most popular type group due to its readability and warm personality. It is distinguished by small lines or tails called serifs that finish the ends of the main strokes and by variations in the thickness of the strokes. It comes in a wide variety of designs and sizes.

Sans serif *(gothic)* type is the second most popular type group; it is also referred to as block or contemporary. Characterized by lack of serifs (hence the name *sans serif*) and relatively uniform thickness of the strokes, it is not as readable as roman but is widely used because the simple, clean lines give a slick, modern appearance (see **a**).

Roman type	Square serif type
Typography	Typography
Typography	
Typography	Script type
Typography	*Typography*
	Typography
Sans serif type	
Typography	Ornamental type
Typography	Typography
TYPOGRAPHY	**Typography**

a.

To contrast sans serif and serif faces, compare the letters in this lab with those in the main text.

9. *Testimonial.* Before-and-after endorsements are very effective for weight-loss products, skin-care lotions, and bodybuilding courses.

10. *Negative appeal.* Sometimes visuals point out what happens if you don't use the product. If done well, that can spark interest.

Selecting the Visual

The kind of picture used is often determined during the conceptualization process. But frequently the visual is not determined until the art director or designer actually lays out the ad.

Square serif type combines sans serif and serif typefaces. It has serifs, but letter strokes have uniform thickness.

Cursive or *script type* resembles handwriting; letters often connect and may convey a feeling of femininity, formality, classicism, or beauty. It is difficult to read and is used primarily in headlines, formal announcements, and cosmetic and fashion ads.

Ornamental type uses novel designs with a high level of embellishment and decorativeness. It adds a "special effects" quality but is often difficult to read.

Type Families

A **type family** is made up of related typefaces. The serif typeface used in this text is called Garamond Book. Within a family, the basic design remains the same but varies in the proportion, weight, and slant of the characters. The type may be light, medium, bold, extra bold, condensed, extended, or italic. Variations enable the typographer to provide contrast and emphasis without changing the family (see **b**).

Garamond Book	Garamond Condensed Book
Garamond Book Italic	*Garamond Condensed Book Italic*
Garamond Bold	**Garamond Condensed Bold**
Garamond Bold Italic	***Garamond Condensed Bold Italic***
Garamond Light	Garamond Condensed Light
Garamond Light Italic	*Garamond Condensed Light Italic*
Garamond Ultra	**Garamond Condensed Ultra**
Garamond Ultra Italic	***Garamond Condensed Ultra Italic***

b.

A **font** is a complete assortment of capitals, small capitals, lowercase letters, numerals, and punctuation marks for a particular typeface and size.

Measuring Type

Type characters have height, width, weight, and, for some ornamental typefaces, depth. They also come in shapes called a case. And with the advent of computers, type comes in a variety of resolutions.

Size is the height of a character (or letter) measured in **points** (72 points to the inch) from the bottom of the descenders to the top of the ascenders (see **c**).

Text type	Display type
6 pt. Type size	16 pt. Type size
8 pt. Type size	18 pt. Type size
9 pt. Type size	20 pt. Type size
10 pt. Type size	24 pt. Type size
12 pt. Type size	30 pt. Type size
14 pt. Type size	36 pt. Type size

c.

The set width of a letter, known as an *em space,* is usually based on the maximum width and proportions of the capital letter M for that particular typeface. The set width of the letter N is called an *en space.*

Resolution refers to the fineness of the type. The goals of fine typesetting are readability, clarity, and smoothness of appearance. The preferred level of quality for magazines and brochures begins at 1,000 dpi (dots per inch); advertisers often use resolutions of 2,400 to 3,750 dpi.

Laboratory Applications

Use the various figures and terms in this Ad Lab to answer the following:

1. Find examples of each of the five type groups listed above in ads that appear in magazines or online. How well do these typefaces complement the designs of the ads?

2. Identify an ad that, in your opinion, uses an inappropriate typeface. How would you improve it?

If the art director determines that a visual is required, how many should there be: one, two, or more? Should the visual be black-and-white or color? These may be budgetary decisions. The art director must then decide the subject of the picture. Should it be one of the standard subjects listed earlier? Or something else altogether? And how relevant is that subject to the advertiser's creative strategy?

Finally, the art director has to know what technical and/or budgetary issues must be considered. With so many options, selecting visuals is obviously no simple task. In Chapter 13, we'll see how all these decisions come together in the process of producing the final ad.

:: The Art Director's Guide to Layout Styles

Art directors use many different types of layouts. Creating an ad for the fictitious Imperial Cruise Lines, Tom Michael, the president and creative director of Market Design (Encinitas, CA), first prepared several thumbnail sketches using a variety of different layout styles and headlines to see which ideas would work best.

Note how the copy in each ad is indicated by lines of recurring gibberish. The computer programs art directors use frequently offer an option to represent layout text with such incoherent ramblings, referred to in the business as "greek."

• Study the different layouts and discuss the advantages and disadvantages of each. Which approach would you recommend for Imperial Cruise Lines? Why? What additional layout or copy ideas can you come up with?

Picture-window layout—"Warm up to the beauty of Alaska." Also called a *poster-style layout*, note how the single, large visual occupies about two-thirds of the ad. The headline and copy may appear above or below the "window."

Source: Tom Michael/Market Design

Mondrian grid layout—"Alaska: The last frontier for family fun." Named after Dutch painter Piet Mondrian, the Mondrian layout uses a series of vertical and horizontal lines, rectangles, and squares within a predetermined grid to give geometric proportion to the ad.

Source: Tom Michael/Market Design

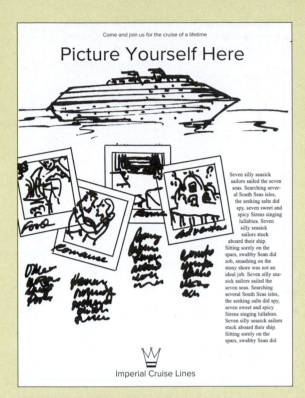

Circus layout—"Picture Yourself Here." Filled with multiple illustrations, oversize type, reverse blocks, tilts, or other gimmicks to bring the ad alive and make it interesting.

Source: Tom Michael/Market Design

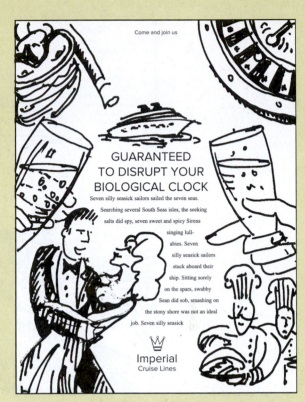

Frame layout—"Guaranteed to disrupt your biological clock." The copy is surrounded by the visual. Or, in some cases, the visual may be surrounded by the copy.

Source: Tom Michael/Market Design

Copy-heavy layout—"Get rocked to sleep on our water bed." When you have a lot to say and visuals won't say it, use text. But be sure the headlines and subheads make it interesting. In this case, the heavy copy actually frames the headline and visual to add visual interest. However, the headline might just as well have run above or below the copy.

Source: Tom Michael/Market Design

Come and join us for a romantic cruise of a lifetime

Seven silly seasick sailors sailed the seven seas. Searching several South Seas isles, the seeking salts did spy, seven sweet and spicy Sirens singing lullabies. Seven silly seasick sailors stuck aboard their ship. Sitting sorely on the spars, swabby Sean did sob, smashing on the stony shore was not an ideal job. Seven silly seasick sailors sailed the seven seas. Searching several South Seas isles, the seeking salts did spy, seven sweet and spicy Sirens singing lullabies.

GET ROCKED TO SLEEP ON OUR WATER BED

Seven silly seasick sailors stuck aboard their ship. Sitting sorely on the spars, swabby Sean did sob, smashing on the stony shore was not an ideal job. Seven silly seasick sailors sailed the seven seas. Searching several South Seas isles, the seeking salts did spy, seven sweet and spicy Sirens singing lullabies. Seven silly seasick sailors stuck aboard their ship. Sitting sorely on the spars, swabby Sean did sob, smashing on the stony shore was not an ideal job. Seven silly seasick sailors sailed the

seven seas. Searching several South Seas isles, the seeking salts did spy, seven sweet and spicy Sirens singing lullabies. Seven silly seasick sailors stuck aboard their ship. Sitting sorely on the spars, swabby Sean did sob, smashing on the stony shore was not an ideal job. Seven silly seasick sailors sailed the seven seas. Searching several South Seas isles, the seeking salts did spy, seven sweet and spicy Sirens singing lullabies. Seven silly seasick sailors stuck aboard their ship. Sitting sorely on the spars, swabby Sean did sob, smashing on the stony shore was not an ideal job. Seven silly seasick sailors sailed the seven seas. Searching several South Seas isles, the seeking salts did spy, seven sweet and spicy Sirens singing lullabies. Seven silly seasick sailors stuck aboard their ship. Sitting sorely on the spars, swabby Sean did sob, smashing on the stony shore was not an ideal job. Seven silly seasick sailors sailed the seven

Imperial Cruise Lines

Montage layout—"Open all night. Loitering encouraged." Similar to the circus layout, the montage brings multiple illustrations together and arranges them by superimposing or overlapping to make a single composition.

Source: Tom Michael/Market Design

Combo layout—"Warm up to Alaska." Creativity often involves combining two or more unrelated elements to make a new element. The same is true in design. To make an ad more interesting or contemporary, the art director may combine two or more layout types to make a combo layout. This ad, for instance, starts out with a grid layout, but in the center of the grid note how the copy surrounds the headline and logo as in a frame layout.

Source: Tom Michael/Market Design

These images demonstrate the design principle of unity. The trained eyes of a professional designer create images that are pleasing . . . and impossible to ignore.

Source: Apple, Inc.

Writing Great Print Copy

LO 11-2

Now that you understand the objectives and format elements of good design, let's examine some basic copywriting formats to see how art and copy are linked.

In print, the key layout elements are the *visual(s), headlines, subheads, body copy, slogans, seals, logos,* and *signatures.* As Exhibit 11-2 shows, copywriters can correlate the visual, headline, and subhead to the *attention* step of the creative pyramid. The *interest* step typically corresponds to the subhead and the first paragraph of body copy. Body copy handles *credibility* and *desire,* and the *action* step takes place with the logo, slogan, and signature block. We'll discuss these elements first and then look at the formats for radio and television commercials.

If your interests lie in copywriting, pay careful attention to the messages you are exposed to every day. Try not to read them only as a consumer, but also as a student of creative work. Think carefully about the choices the writer has made in the words and structure of the message. And remember that while good copy may come from imitating others (see the Ethics, Diversity & Inclusion box), great copy comes from true originality.

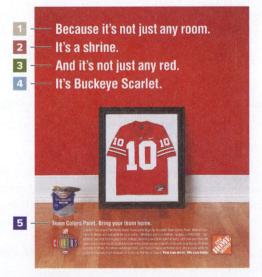

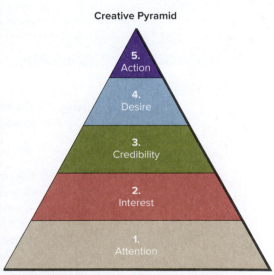

Exhibit 11-2
An ad's success depends on the viewer's ability to go through steps of the creative pyramid. Not every ad is as successful in using the format elements (headlines, subheads, body copy, slogan, image) in transporting the prospect through each step as is this one from the Home Depot.

(left) Source: Homer TLC, Inc.

Ethics, Diversity & Inclusion

Empathy: Understanding That Ads Can Hurt or Empower

As this chapter emphasizes, words and ideas matter—not only in terms of selling and persuading, but in empowering or harming. Today's ethical creative should be sensitive to the responsibility he or she has to impact more than just the target audience.

Consider just a few examples.

One of the most important social media movements of the last few years has been the #MeToo movement. Initiated in part by charges of assault and rape against Hollywood producer Harvey Weinstein, the movement has been traced to social activist Tarana Burke. Burke used social media to call attention to "empowerment through empathy" by using the hashtag. The movement quickly grew and fostered understanding of the challenges faced by many women in their lives.

In light of the seriousness of sexual harassment and abuse, it seems unimaginable that Bloomingdales would run an ad with the headline "Spike your best friend's eggnog when they are not looking." The ad featured a man looking at a beautiful woman whose attention is directed elsewhere. Ditto for Bud Light's decision to label its can with the phrase "The perfect beer for removing 'no' from your vocabulary for the night. #UpForWhatever." These ads were meant to be funny. They aren't.

Insensitive and even hurtful ads need not deal with a topic as serious as sexual harassment. An ad for a retail diamond dealer showed a beautiful gem alongside copy that read "Make her speechless. For a change." PETA sponsored a billboard advocating vegetarianism that showed the back of an overweight woman and the headline "Save the whales." Again, the intent was not to harm, but it is hard to avoid the possibility that such messages reinforce stereotyping and shaming.

Advertising causes harm in other ways. Some people believe that in a post-modern society, everything is fair game for humor. An alternative view is that there are things that should never be made light of or used to sell a product. Consider the following: In 1978 a demented cult leader named Jim Jones convinced over 900 of his followers, including men, women, and children, to commit suicide by drinking Kool-Aid laced with poison. If you think that an event of such evil would be off limits for an ad, think again. Hacienda Mexican Restaurants placed a billboard ad with the headline "We're like a cult with better Kool-Aid." Next to the image of a frozen cherry drink the ad featured the tag line "To die for."

The encouraging news is that some marketers are discovering the value of respect, dignity, and virtue. Case in point: Procter & Gamble's ad that reframes the casual insult "like a girl" (as in "you throw like a girl") through a campaign highlighting the harm of such phrases (see more here: www.adweek.com/creativity/girl-no-longer-insult-inspiring-ad-pgs-always-158601/).

Another marketing leader, Coca-Cola, partnered with the Ad Council to create ads centered on an inclusive vision of the idea of who is an American. The campaign, "Love has no labels," celebrates tolerance and inclusion for all Americans (see more here: www.youtube.com/watch?time_continue=2&v=0MdK8hBkR3s)

Advertising Age summed up the power of great marketing to make society better by arguing that the goal of such ads is "driving empathy, not sympathy." The article goes on to note, "At the end of the day, good feelings and supportive words are nice, but to really make a difference, decision-makers should bring the rational decision of supporting diversity back to the human level. . . ."[17]

Questions

1. Some would argue that many people are too sensitive and take themselves too seriously when they object to ads such as the examples shown above. How would you respond to this criticism?

2. What things can you do to gain a better understanding of people who are different from yourself? Why is such understanding important if you hope to work in advertising or IMC?

Headlines

The **headline** contains the largest type on the page—the words that will be read first and are situated to draw the most attention.

Role of Headlines

Effective headlines attract attention, engage the audience, explain the visual, lead the audience into the body of the ad, introduce the brand, and present the selling message.

Another goal of a headline is to engage the reader—fast—and give a reason to read the rest of the ad. If the headline lacks immediacy, prospects turn their attention to another subject and pass the ad's message by.[18]

An ad for Esser's wine store is a good example of a headline leading the reader into the body copy.

Headline: "Esser's Knows."
Body copy: "Manfred Esser's nose knows a good wine . . ."

The headline is the most important thing an ad communicates to the prospect. It explains the visual and dictates the marketer's position in that person's mind, whether or not the prospect chooses to read on.

The creativity embodied by this headline for IFAW comes from more than its meaning. It is also present in the artistic typography. The headline also does a great job of driving home the product's benefit, which is protecting wildlife.

Source: International Fund for Animal Welfare

Ideally, headlines present the complete selling idea. Research shows that three to five times as many people read the headline as read body copy. So if the message doesn't sell in the headline, the advertiser is wasting money.[19] Nike uses beautiful ads featuring only an athlete, the logo, and the memorable headline: "Just do it." Working off the visual, the headline creates the mood and tells the reader, through implication, to take action—buy Nike products. Headlines help trigger a recognition response, which reinforces brand recognition and brand preference.

Many experts believe that headlines with 10 words or more gain greater readership. But one researcher's effort to confirm this failed to find an impact of headline length, at least for ad recall. He concluded, "For the time being, we must assume that for magazine advertising, what you have to say in a headline is more important than how many words you use to say it."[20] David Ogilvy said the best headline he ever wrote contained 18 words—and became a classic: "At 60 miles an hour, the loudest noise in the new Rolls-Royce comes from the electric clock."[21]

Headlines should offer a benefit that is compelling and easy to grasp. For example: "Please do not drive faster than your GPS satellite can fly" (Lamborghini), or "Not all mind expanding substances are illegal" (*The Economist*). A simple print ad honored at Cannes was little more than a headline that read, "Cancer cures smoking." Alstiel and Grow cite a classic example of brevity and punch from a 1934 newspaper ad: "It pays to buy at Brooks Brothers."[22]

Finally, headlines should present *product news.* Consumers look for new products or new uses or improvements from established ones. If they haven't been overused in a category, "power" words that suggest newness can increase readership and improve the boom factor of an ad. They should be employed whenever *honestly* applicable.[23] Examples include *free, now, amazing, suddenly, announcing, introducing, it's here, improved, at last, revolutionary, just arrived, new,* and *important development.*

Types of Headlines

Copywriters use many variations of headlines depending on the strategy. Typically, they use the headline that presents the big idea most successfully. Headlines may be classified by the type of information they carry: *benefit, news/information, provocative, question,* and *command.*

Benefit headlines promise the audience that experiencing the utility of the product or service will be rewarding. Benefit headlines shouldn't be too cute or clever, just simple statements of the product's most important benefit. Two good examples are

America runs on Dunkin   and   Speak a foreign language in 30 days or your money back.

Note that both of these headlines focus on the benefit of using the product, not the features of the product itself.[24]

The **news/information headline** announces news or promises information. SeaWorld began its TV announcement of a new baby whale with the headline "It's a girl." The information must be believable, though. A claim that a razor "shaves 200% smoother" probably isn't.[25]

Copywriters use **provocative headlines** to arouse the reader's curiosity—to stimulate questions and thoughts. "Bet you can't eat just one" (Lay's Potato Chips) is an example. Another example is William Bernbach's famous headline for Volkswagen, "Lemon." To learn more, the reader must read the body copy. The danger, of course, is that the reader won't read on. To avoid this, a compelling visual can clarify the message or provide story appeal.

A **question headline** raises uncertainty, encouraging readers to search for the answer in the body of the ad. An ad for a tire retailer asked: "What makes our tire customers smarter & richer than others?" A good question headline piques the reader's curiosity and imagination. But if a headline asks a question the reader can answer quickly (or even worse, negatively), the rest of the ad may not get read. If a headline asks: "Do you want to buy insurance?" and the reader answers, "No," the ad will accomplish very little.

A **command headline** orders the reader to do something, so it might seem negative. But readers pay attention to such headlines. Sprite ads instruct prospects to "Obey your thirst." American Express used the popular command "Don't leave home without it" for many years.

Many headline types are easily combined. But the type of headline used is less important than the way it's used. Copywriters must always write with style—for the audience's pleasure, not their own.

Headlines in Digital Ads

When headlines are used in search-related ads, such as the sponsored ads that appear next to Google's search results, several additional considerations come into play, largely driven by the primary purpose of the headline: the click. WordStream, an online advertising company, offers a number of suggestions for effective PPC headlines (pay-per-click). These are a sampling: (1) include keywords specific to the advertiser's offering, (2) solve the prospect's problem, and (3) limit characters to 25. The limit relates to restrictions in characters shown in sponsored search headlines.[26]

Some topics are so frightening that a direct representation could overwhelm the reader. In this ad, Reporters Without Borders uses metaphor to communicate the dangers its members face in bringing news to the world, and the headline helps clarify the significant issue that the pencil metaphor is illustrating.

Source: Reporters Without Borders

Hootsuite analyzed thousands of Facebook display ads looking for the right combination of elements found in the ones that are most effective. It concluded that the ideal Facebook ad headline is short (in some cases just five words), features a testimonial, offers a benefit that is verifiable, presents a numbered list ("4 traits to look for when hiring"), and solves a problem ("How to . . .").[27]

Subheads

The **subhead** is an additional smaller headline that can appear above the headline or below it. Subheads are less common in contemporary advertising but still appear in ads with relatively large amounts of text. They can help break up copy and attract attention to the benefits that a reader is searching for. Subheads are longer and more like sentences than headlines. They serve as stepping stones from the headline to the body copy, telegraphing what's to come.

Subheads are usually set smaller than the headline but larger than the body copy or text. Subheads generally appear in **boldface** (heavier) or **italic** (slanted) type or a different color. Like a headline, the subhead transmits key sales points fast. But it usually carries less important information than the headline. Subheads are important for two reasons: Most people read only the headline and subheads, and subheads usually support the interest step best.

Body Copy

The advertiser tells the complete sales story in the **body copy,** or **text.** The body copy comprises the interest, credibility, desire, and often even the action steps. It is a logical continuation of the headline and subheads, set in smaller type. Body copy covers the features, benefits, and utility of the product or service. Most importantly, body copy is proof of the provocative claims made by the headline or visual.

My IMC Campaign 11-D

Writing Effective Copy

- **Get to the main point—fast.**
- **Emphasize one major idea simply and clearly.**
- **Be single-minded.** Don't try to do too much. If you chase more than one rabbit at a time, you'll catch none.
- **Position the product clearly.**
- **Keep the brand name up front and reinforce it.**
- **Write with the consumer's ultimate benefit in mind.**
- **Write short sentences.** Use easy, familiar words and themes people understand.
- **Don't waste words.** Say what you have to say—nothing more, nothing less. Don't pad, but don't skimp.
- **Avoid bragging and boasting.** Write from the reader's point of view, not your own. Avoid "we," "us," and "our."
- **Avoid clichés.** They're crutches; learn to get along without them. Bright, surprising words and phrases perk up readers and keep them reading.
- **Write with flair.** Drum up excitement. Make sure your own enthusiasm comes through in the copy.

- **Use vivid language.** Use lots of verbs and adverbs.
- **Stick to the present tense, active voice.** It's crisper. Avoid the past tense and passive voice. Exceptions should be deliberate, for special effect.
- **Use personal pronouns.** Remember, you're talking to just one person, so talk as you would to a friend. Use "you" and "your" whenever appropriate.
- **Use contractions.** They're fast, personal, natural. People talk in contractions (listen to yourself).
- **Don't overpunctuate.** It kills copy flow. Excessive commas are the chief culprits. Don't give readers any excuse to jump ship.
- **Read the copy aloud.** Hear how it sounds; catch errors. The written word is considerably different from the spoken word so listen to it.
- **Rewrite and write tight.** Edit mercilessly. Tell the whole story and no more. When you're finished, stop.

The body copy is typically read by only a fraction of readers, so it must speak to the reader's self-interest, explaining how the product or service satisfies the customer's need. The best ads focus on one big idea or one clear benefit. Copywriters often read their copy aloud to hear how it sounds, even if it's intended for print media. The ear is a powerful copywriting tool.[28]

Some of the best copywriting techniques of leading experts are highlighted in My IMC Campaign 11-D, "Writing Effective Copy."

Body Copy Styles

Experienced copywriters look for the technique and style with the greatest sales appeal for the idea being presented. Common copy styles include *straight sell, institutional, narrative, dialogue/monologue, picture caption,* and *device.*

In **straight-sell copy,** writers immediately explain or develop the headline and visual in a straightforward, factual presentation. The straight-sell approach appeals to the prospect's reason. Because it ticks off selling points and reasons why in order of importance, straight-sell copy is particularly good for high-involvement products or products that are difficult to use. It's very effective for direct response advertising, search advertising, and industrial or high-tech products.

Advertisers use **institutional copy** to promote a philosophy or extol the merits of an organization rather than product features. Institutional copy is intended to lend warmth and credibility to the organization's image. Banks, insurance companies, public corporations, and large manufacturing firms use institutional copy in both print and electronic media. However, David Ogilvy warned against the "self-serving, flatulent pomposity" that characterizes the copy in many corporate ads.[29]

Copywriters use **narrative copy** to tell a story. Ideal for the creative writer, narrative copy sets up a situation and then resolves it at the last minute by having the product or service come to the rescue. Narrative copy offers good opportunities for emotional

too many wrinkles to be in an anti-aging ad

but this isn't an anti-aging ad. this is pro-age.
a new line of skin care from dove. beauty has no age limit.

Breaking through the clutter requires fresh approaches. How many ways, in both the visual and the copy, does this Dove ad challenge your expectations?

Source: Unilever

appeals. An insurance company, for example, might tell the poignant story of the man who died unexpectedly but, fortunately, had just renewed his policy.[30]

By using **dialogue/monologue copy,** the copywriter can add the believability that narrative copy sometimes lacks. The characters portrayed in a print ad do the selling in their own words. A caution: Poorly written dialogue copy can come off as dull or, even worse, false and manipulative.

Sometimes it's easier to tell a story with illustrations and captions. A photo with **picture-caption copy** is especially useful for products that have different uses or come in a variety of styles or designs.

With any copy style, the copywriter may use some device copy to enhance attention, interest, and memorability. **Device copy** uses figures of speech (such as puns, alliteration, assonance, and rhymes) as well as humor and exaggeration. Copywriter Paul Suggett offers an example: "Dead batteries, now free of charge." Some believe that verbal devices help people remember the brand and affect attitude favorably. But Suggett argues that device copy should be avoided.

Humor can be effective when the advertiser needs high memorability in a short time, wants to dispel preconceived negative images, or needs to create a distinct personality for an undifferentiated product. However, humor should always be used carefully and never be in questionable taste.

Formatting Body Copy

The keys to good body copy are simplicity, order, credibility, and clarity. Or, as John O'Toole says, prose should be "written clearly, informatively, interestingly, powerfully, persuasively, dramatically, memorably, and with effortless grace. That's all."[31]

Four basic format elements are used to construct long copy ads: *the lead-in paragraph, interior paragraphs, trial close,* and *close.*

The **lead-in paragraph** bridges the headline and the sales ideas presented in the text. Like a subhead, the lead-in paragraph is part of the *interest* step. It must engage and convert a prospect's reading interest into product interest.

The **interior paragraphs** develop *credibility* by providing proof for claims and promises and they should build *desire* by using imaginative language. Advertisers

NO ONE TRUSTS ME. THE LADIES JUST USE ME FOR MY BODY. AND I THINK I HAVE FLEAS.

carlos@myspace.com

MEERKAT MANOR
FRIDAYS 8:30PM E/P

A great headline and a well-chosen illustration are the key elements in this print ad.

Source: Discovery Communications, Inc.

should support their product promises with research data, testimonials, and warranties. Such proofs help convince customers of the value of the product, improve goodwill toward the advertiser, and stimulate sales.

Interspersed in the interior paragraphs should be suggestions to *act*. Good copy asks for the order more than once; mail-order ads ask several times. Consumers often make the buying decision without reading all the body copy. The **trial close** gives them the opportunity to make the buying decision early.

The **close** is the real *action* step. A good close asks consumers to do something and tells them how. The close can be indirect or direct (a subtle suggestion or a direct command). A *direct close* seeks immediate response in the form of a purchase, a store or website visit, or a request for further information.

The close should simplify the audience's response, making it easy for them to order the merchandise, send for information, or visit a showroom or a website. A business reply card or a toll-free phone number may be included.

Of course, not all ads sell products or services. Advertisers may want to change attitudes, explain their viewpoints, or ask for someone's vote. By giving a website address, the advertiser can offer additional information to those wanting it.

Slogans

Many **slogans** (also called **themelines** or **taglines**) begin as successful headlines, like AT&T's "Reach out and touch someone." Through continuous use, they become standard statements, not just in advertising but for salespeople and company employees.

Slogans have two basic purposes: to provide continuity to a series of ads in a campaign and to reduce an advertising message strategy to a brief, repeatable, and memorable positioning statement. Wheaties cereal, for example, positions itself as the "Breakfast of Champions." And ads for DeBeers still use the famous "Diamonds are forever" slogan. But Miller Lite's corny "It's it and that's that" was "major league pathetic," according to one *Wall Street Journal* article. Lacking the creativity, freshness, and power to become a full-fledged slogan, it was short-lived.[32]

Seals, Logos, and Signatures

A **seal** is awarded only when a product meets standards established by a particular organization, such as the Organic Crop Improvement Association, the Good Housekeeping Institute, Underwriters Laboratories, or Parents Institute. Because these organizations are recognized authorities, their seals provide an independent, valued endorsement for the advertiser's product.

Logotypes (*logos*) and **signature cuts** (*sig cuts*) are special designs of the advertiser's company or product name. They appear in all company ads and, like trademarks, give the product individuality and provide quick recognition at the point of purchase.

Cash Back
3+x at US Supermarkets
2x at US Gas Stations
2x at select US Department Stores
1x on other purchases
No Annual Fee

Blue Cash Everyday Card from American Express

Backed by...
Purchase Protection
Extended Warranty
Return Protection
Mobile Fraud Alerts
Zero Liability on Fraudulent Charges
Purchase Assistance hotline
24/7 Phone & Online Oral Customer Service
Welcome to the service and security of Membership.

Blue Cash Everyday Card from American Express

American Express uses these two ads to show two kinds of problems brands can solve: the expected one (cash back) and the unexpected one (a purchase guarantee).

Source: American Express Company

Writing Great Radio and TV Copy

For audio and video media, the fundamental elements—the five steps of the creative pyramid—remain the primary guides, but the copywriting formats differ. Radio and television writers prepare *scripts* and *storyboards*.

Writing Radio Copy

A **script** resembles a two-column list. On the left side, speakers' names are arranged vertically, along with descriptions of any sound effects and music. The right column contains the dialogue, called the **audio.**

LO 11-3

Radio provides entertainment or news to listeners who are usually doing something else—driving, washing dishes, reading the paper, or even studying. To be heard, an advertising message must be catchy, interesting, and unforgettable. Radio listeners usually decide within seconds if they're going to pay attention. To attract and hold the attention of listeners, particularly those not attracted to a product category, radio copy must be intrusive.

A radio script format resembles a two-column list, with speakers' names and sound effects on the left and the dialogue in a wider column on the right. This national public service announcement (PSA) was created by McCann and is one of many in a campaign designed to inspire Americans to take small steps toward a healthier lifestyle.

Healthier America
Lost Campaign
Radio: 60
"Neighbor"
Expiration date: 2/23/05

SFX: Phone ringing

Bill: Hello . . . ?

George: Hi, Bill? This is George Dewey from up the street.

Bill: Hey, George. How ya doin?

George: Good, good. Say, I noticed you've been walking to work these days instead of driving . . . and I, uh, don't quite know how to say this, but . . . but . . .

Bill: But what?

George: *(stammering)* But . . . But . . . Your butt, your buttocks, your butt—I think I found your butt on my front lawn. Have you recently lost it?

Bill: As a matter of fact, I have, George. *(pleased)* It's about time someone noticed.

George: *(playful)* Well, it was kinda hard to miss if you know what I mean . . . . . . Anyways, would you like it back?

Bill: Would I like it back? No, not really.

George: So, it's okay if I throw it out?

Bill: Sure, that's fine. Take it easy, George.

SFX: Phone ringing

Announcer: Small step #8—Walk instead of driving whenever you can. It's just one of the many small steps you can take to help you become a healthier, well, you. Get started at www .smallstep.gov and take a small step to get healthy.

Legal: A public service announcement brought to you by the U.S. Department of Health and Human Services and the Ad Council.

Intrusive, yes; offensive, no. An insensitive choice of words, overzealous effort to attract listeners with irritating everyday sounds (car horn, alarm clock, screeching tires), or characters that sound too exotic, odd, or irritating can cause listener resentment and ultimately lose sales. Other guidelines are given in My IMC Campaign 11-E, "Creating Effective Radio Commercials."

One of the most challenging aspects is making the script fit the time slot. The delivery changes for different types of commercials, so writers read the script out loud for timing. With digital compression, recorded radio ads can now include 10 to 30 percent more copy than text read live. Still, the following are good rules of thumb:

10 seconds: 20–25 words	30 seconds: 60–70 words
20 seconds: 40–45 words	60 seconds: 130–150 words[33]

Radio writing has to be clearer than other kinds of copy. For example, the listener can't refer back, as in print, to find an antecedent for a pronoun. Likewise, the English language is so full of homonyms (words that sound like other words) that one can easily confuse the meaning of a sentence ("who's who is whose").

My IMC Campaign 11-E

Creating Effective Radio Commercials

Writing for radio takes a sharp ear, empathy for the listener, and the ability to create pictures inside the consumer's head. These tips will help you create great radio spots.

- **Make the big idea crystal clear.** Concentrate on one main selling point. Radio is a good medium for building brand awareness, but not for making long lists of copy points or complex arguments.

- **Mention the advertiser's name early and often.** If the product or company name is tricky, consider spelling it out.

- **Take time to set the scene and establish the premise.** A 30-second commercial that nobody remembers is a waste of money. Fight for 60-second spots.

- **Use familiar sound effects.** Ice tinkling in a glass, birds chirping, or a door shutting can create a visual image. Music also works if its meaning is clear.

- **Paint pictures with your words.** Use descriptive language to make the ad more memorable.

- **Make every word count.** Use active voice and more verbs than adjectives. Be conversational. Use pronounceable words and short sentences.

- **Be outrageous.** The best comic commercials begin with an absurd premise from which subsequent developments follow logically. But remember, if you can't write humor really well, go for drama.

- **Ask for the order.** Request listeners to take action.

- **Remember that radio is a local medium.** Adjust your commercials to the language of your listeners and the time of day they'll run.

- **Presentation counts a lot.** Even the best scripts look boring on paper. Acting, timing, vocal quirks, and sound effects bring them to life.

Writing Television Copy

A TV script is created in a two-column format with the left side titled "Video" and the right side "Audio." The video column describes what the viewer will see: camera angles, action, scenery, and special effects, for instance. The audio describes what is heard: dialog, sound effects, music, etc.

Video commercials must be believable and relevant. And even outlandish or humorous commercials must exude quality in their creation and production to reflect well on the product's quality. While the art director's work is very important, the copywriter sets the tone of the commercial, establishes the language that determines which visuals to use, and pinpoints when the visuals should appear. Research and the experience of professionals suggest the techniques given in My IMC Campaign 11-F, "Creating Effective TV Commercials," work best.

An effective campaign for Lubriderm skin lotion illustrates these principles nicely. People want smooth, soft skin and consider a patch of rough, flaky skin a disappointment. If you were the copywriter for Lubriderm, how would you approach this somewhat touchy, negative subject?

The creatives at J. Walter Thompson crafted an artistic solution by choosing an alligator as the big idea. The reptile's scaly sheath was a metaphor for rough, flaky skin. When a large gator walked by a beautiful, sophisticated woman with smooth, feminine skin, people's survival instincts were ignited and they paid attention, But the woman appeared completely unruffled by the passing gator. The swing of the animal's back and tail echoed the graceful curves of the two simple pieces of furniture on the set, and its slow stride kept the beat of a light jazz tune.

This commercial opened with an attention-getting big idea that was visually surprising, compelling, dramatic, and interesting. It was also a quasi-demonstration: we saw the alligator's scaly, prickly skin and the woman's confidence and willingness to touch the alligator as it passed by, which symbolized the confidence Lubriderm can bring.

This ad follows the creative pyramid. The alligator captures attention visually while the announcer's first words serve as an attention-getting headline: "A quick reminder." The ad commands us to listen and sets up the interest step that offers this claim: "Lubriderm restores lost moisture to heal your dry skin and protect it." Now for the credibility step: "Remember, the one created for dermatologists is the one that heals and protects." Then a

My IMC Campaign 11-F

Creating Effective TV Commercials

- **Begin at the finish.** Concentrate on the final impression the commercial will make.
- **Create an attention-getting opening.** An opening that is visually surprising or full of action, drama, humor, or human interest sets the context and allows a smooth transition to the rest of the commercial.
- **Use a situation that grows naturally out of the sales story.** Avoid distracting gimmicks. Make it easy for viewers to identify with the characters.
- **Characters are the living symbol of the product.** They should be appealing, believable, nondistracting, and, most of all, relevant.
- **Keep it simple.** The sequence of ideas should be easy to follow. Keep the number of elements in the commercial to a bare minimum.

- **Write concise audio copy.** The video should carry most of the weight. Fewer than two words per second is effective for demonstrations. For a 60-second commercial, 101 to 110 words is most effective; more than 170 words is too talky.
- **Make demonstrations dramatic but believable.** They should always be true to life and avoid the appearance of camera tricks.
- **Let the words interpret the picture and prepare viewers for the next scene.** Use conversational language; avoid "ad talk," hype, and puffery.
- **Run scenes five or six seconds on average.** Rarely should a scene run less than three seconds. Offer a variety of movement-filled scenes without "jumping."
- **Keep the look of the video fresh and new.**

quick trial close (action): "Lubriderm." And then the desire step recaps the primary product benefit and adds a touch of humor: "See you later, alligator."

Generating Effective Ideas for Radio and TV Commercials

Former *Advertising Age* columnist Bob Garfield, asked to name the year's best ad, described one created by Delvico Bates, Barcelona, for Esencial hand cream. The spot opens with a woman riding her bicycle to the persistent squeak of its unlubricated chain. She dismounts, opens a jar of Esencial, and rubs some of the cream onto the chain. Then she rides away—but the squeak is still there. Why? Because, as the voice-over points out, "Esencial moisturizes, but it has no grease."

No big production. No digital effects. No jingle. No celebrity. No big comedy payoff. Just a pure creative idea: a problem-resolution spot where the brand pointedly cannot solve the problem. It's a vivid demonstration of brand nonattributes. Inspired. Cunning. Brilliant. And a demonstration of what creatives mean by "the big idea."[34]

Developing the Artistic Concept for Commercials

Creating the concept for a commercial is similar to creating the concept for print ads. Start with the big idea. Then the art director and copywriter must decide what commercial format to use. Should a celebrity present the message? Or should the ad dramatize the product's benefits (or deficiencies) with a semifictional story? The next step is to write a script containing the necessary copy or dialogue plus a basic description of any music, sound effects, and/or camera views.

In both radio and TV, the art director assists the copywriter in script development. But in television, artistic development is much more extensive. Using the TV script, the art director creates a series of **storyboard roughs** to present the artistic approach, the action sequences, and the style of the commercial. When the storyboard is approved, it serves as a guide for production.

Good casting is critical. The most important consideration is relevance to the product; agencies don't use a comic to sell financial products—or cremation services. Should the ad feature someone famous? Some experts don't believe in using celebrities. David Ogilvy, for example, thought viewers remember the celebrity more than the product.[35] Conversely, celebrities can accomplish several necessary tasks in an ad: attracting and holding attention, and establishing credibility. Many radio and podcast ads are read by the program host, to whom listeners often show great loyalty.

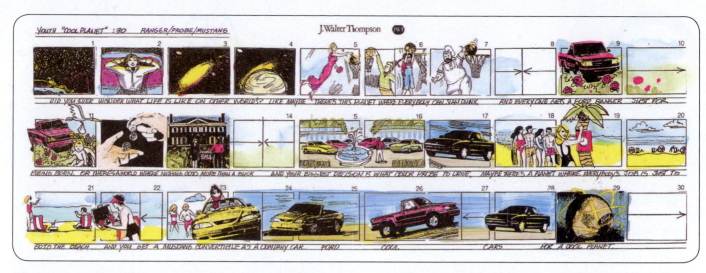

After the initial concepts for a television ad are finalized, creatives develop a storyboard rough composed of small sketches that depict the various scenes of the ad. The storyboard rough, including camera angles and script, is used to provide a visual guideline for shooting the various scenes during the final production phase.

Source: J. Walter Thompson/Ford Motor Company

As the concept evolves, the creative team defines the characters' personalities in a detailed **casting brief.** These descriptions serve as guides in casting sessions when actors audition for the roles. Sometimes agencies discover new, unknown stars who evolve into solid, memorable characters and who go beyond the simple role by actually creating a personality or image for the product. Flo, the famous spokesperson for Progressive Insurance, has represented the brand for almost two decades. She is, for most people, better known than the actress who portrays her, Stephanie Courtney.

Formats for Radio and TV Commercials

Similar to print advertising, the format for a broadcast ad serves as a template for arranging message elements into a pattern. Once the art director and copywriter establish the big idea, they must determine the commercial's format.

Many radio and TV commercial styles have been successful. Some of these are listed in Ad Lab 11-C, "Creative Ways to Sell on Radio." Hank Seiden, the former chair of Ketchum Advertising, developed the Execution Spectrum: 24 basic formats that range from frivolous to serious (see Exhibit 11-3). Here we consider eight common commercial formats that can be used in either radio or television: *straight announcement, presenter, testimonial, demonstration, musical, slice of life, lifestyle,* and *animation.*

Straight Announcement

The oldest and simplest type of radio or TV commercial is the **straight announcement.** One person, usually a radio or TV announcer, delivers the sales message. Music may play in the background. Straight announcements are popular because they are adaptable to almost any product or situation. In radio, a straight announcement can also be designed as an **integrated commercial**—that is, it can be woven into a show or tailored to the style of a given program.

For TV, an announcer may deliver the sales message **on camera** or off screen, as a **voice-over,** while a demonstration, slide, or film shows on screen. If the script is well written and the announcer convincing, straight announcements can be very effective. Because they don't require elaborate production facilities, they save money, too.

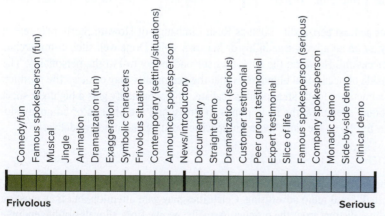

Exhibit 11-3
The Execution Spectrum, developed by Hank Seiden, shows 24 execution formats ranging in style from frivolous to serious, for both print and electronic advertising.

Source: Hank Seiden. "Advertising Pure and Simple," American Management Association, March 1, 1977.

AD Lab 11–C

Creative Ways to Sell on Radio

Product demo The commercial tells how a product is used or the purposes it serves.

Voice power A unique voice gives the ad power.

Electronic sound Synthetic sound-making machines create a memorable product-sound association.

Customer interview A spokesperson and customer discuss the product advantages spontaneously.

Humorous fake interview The customer interview is done in a lighter vein.

Hyperbole (exaggeration) statement Overstatement arouses interest in legitimate product claims that might otherwise pass unnoticed; often a spoof.

Fourth dimension Time and events are compressed into a brief spot involving the listener in future projections.

Hot property Commercial adapts a current sensation: a hit show, performer, or song.

Comedian power Established comedians do commercials in their own unique style, implying celebrity endorsement.

Historical fantasy Situation with revived historical characters is used to convey product message.

Sound picture Recognizable sounds involve the listener by stimulating imagination.

Demographics Music or references appeal to a particular segment of the population, such as an age or interest group.

Imagery transfer Musical logo or other sound reinforces the memory of a TV campaign.

Celebrity interview Famous person endorses the product in an informal manner.

Product song Music and words combine to create a musical logo, selling the product in the style of popular music.

Editing genius Many different situations, voices, types of music, and sounds are combined in a series of quick cuts.

Improvisation Performers work out the dialogue extemporaneously for an assigned situation; may be postedited.

Laboratory Applications

1. Select three familiar radio commercials and discuss which creative techniques they use.

2. Select a familiar radio commercial and discuss how a different creative technique would increase its effectiveness.

Straight announcements are commonly used on late-night TV programs, by local advertisers, and by nonprofit or political organizations.

Presenter

The **presenter commercial** uses one person or character to present the product and carry the sales message. Some presenters are celebrities, such as David Harbour for Tide. Others may be corporate officers of the sponsor, such as John Schnatter, who spoke for Papa John's (Schnatter was forced out of his own company as of 2018), or they may be actors playing a role (the Allstate "Mayhem" character is portrayed by actor Dean Winters).

A **radio or podcast personality,** such as Rush Limbaugh or Howard Stern, may read a script, or may *ad lib* an ad message in his or her own style. Done well such commercials can be very successful. However, the advertiser surrenders control to the personality. The main risk, outside of occasional blunders, is that the personality may criticize the product. Even so, this sometimes lends an appealing realism. The personality gets a highlight sheet listing the product's features, the main points to stress, and the phrases or company slogans to repeat. But he or she can choose the specific wording and mode of delivery.

Testimonial

The true **testimonial**—where a satisfied user tells how effective the product is—can be highly credible in both TV and radio advertising. Celebrities may gain attention, but they must be believable and not distract from the product. Actually, people from all walks of life endorse products, from known personalities to unknowns and nonprofessionals. Which type of person to use depends on the product and the strategy. Satisfied customers are the best sources for testimonials because their sincerity is usually persuasive. Ogilvy suggested shooting candid testimonials when the subjects don't know they're being filmed.[36] One of top creative

"More Cat Chow" :30
(Open on Sue sitting on her living room floor giving one of her cats a pedicure)
Super: Sue Collister's "Cat Chat"

Sue: Yes, I like the dusty rose on you too . . . Oh . . . Hello, welcome back to "Cat Chat." Today we're having a spa day, so let's all be extra quiet. (Reveal the room filled with cats. Cats are resting on their backs, cucumber slices over their eyes. This continues for about 10 seconds. It is silent and peaceful. Cut to Jack, sitting in his office. He means business.)

Jack: You thought I was bluffing? Try my new smokehouse bacon cheddar burger with grilled onions, barbecue sauce, and melting cheese or it's gonna be a "Cat Chat" summer.
Super: Limited time only

(Cut back to all the cats sleeping)
Sue: Shhh. Evanka is in her happy place. Who's next for a mani-pedi?

(Bag drops)
Bag 1: Stop Cat Chat.
Bag 2: New Smokehouse Bacon Cheddar Burger.
Super: Jack in the Box logo.

Advertisers often use presenter commercials to carry out their sales message. In this humorous example, Jack in the Box's spokesperson, Jack, threatens to air the awful show "Cat Chat" if people don't buy the featured sandwich.

Source: Jack in the Box, Inc.

Alex Bogusky's greatest concepts, the Whopper Freakout, involved secretly filming the reactions of real customers to (the fictional) news the Whopper was being discontinued.

Demonstration

Television is well suited for visual demonstration. And a **demonstration** convinces an audience better and faster than a spoken message. So don't say it, show it. Naturally, it's easier to demonstrate the product on TV than on radio, but some advertisers have used the imaginative nature of radio to create humorous, tongue-in-cheek demonstrations.

Products may be demonstrated in use, in competition, or before and after. These techniques help viewers visualize how the product will perform for them.

Musical

The **musical commercials,** or **jingles,** we hear on radio and TV are among the best—and worst—ad messages produced. Done well, they can bring enormous success, well beyond the average nonmusical commercial. Done poorly, they can waste the advertising budget and annoy audiences beyond belief.

Ads that appeal to a lifestyle present the type of user associated with the product, rather than the product itself. This ad for IBM uses Harley-Davidson employees to illustrate how IBM can help every business—large and small.
Source: IBM

Musical commercials have several variations. The entire message may be sung; jingles may be written with a **donut** in the middle (a hole for spoken copy); or orchestras may play symphonic or popular arrangements. Many producers use consistent musical themes for background color or to close the commercial. An example is McDonald's brief musical snippet ("ba da ba ba ba, I'm loving it") at the end of each of its ads. This is called a **musical logo.** After many repetitions of the advertiser's theme, the listener begins to associate the musical logo with the product. To achieve this, the jingle should have a **hook**—that part of the song that sticks in your memory.[37]

Advertisers have three sources of music. They can buy the right to use a tune from the copyright owner, which is usually expensive. They can use a melody in the public domain, which is free. Or they can hire a composer to write an original song. Some original tunes, including Coke's famous "I'd like to teach the world to sing," or the "Dumb Ways to Die" song featured in the chapter opener, have become hits.

Slice of Life (Problem–Solution)

Commercials that dramatize real-life situations are called **slice of life.** This approach usually starts with just plain folks, played by professional actors, discussing some problem or issue. Often the situation deals with a problem of a personal nature: bad breath, loose dentures, dandruff, body odor, or yellow laundry. A relative or a co-worker drops the hint, the product is tried, and the next scene shows the result—a happier, cleaner, more fragrant person off with a new date. The drama always concludes with a successful trial. Such commercials can get attention and create interest, even though they are often irritating to viewers and hated by copywriters. An excellent and creative example was Amazon's "Alexa Loses Her Voice" commercial, one of the most effective of the 2018 Super Bowl (see http:// admeter.usatoday.com/commercials/alexa-loses-her-voice/).

The key to effective slice-of-life commercials is simplicity. The ad should concentrate on one product benefit and make it memorable. Often a **mnemonic device** can dramatize the product benefit and trigger instant recall. Users of Imperial margarine, for example, suddenly discover crowns on their heads.

Believability in slice-of-life commercials is difficult to achieve. People don't really talk about "the sophisticated taste of Taster's Choice," so the actors must be highly credible to put the fantasy across. That's why most *local* advertisers don't use the slice-of-life technique. Creating that believability takes very professional talent and money. In all cases, the story should be relevant to the product and simply told.

Lifestyle

To present the user rather than the product, advertisers may use the **lifestyle technique.** For example, Diesel pitches its denim to urbanites by showing characters working and playing while wearing its latest line. Likewise, beer and soft drink advertisers frequently target their messages to active, outdoorsy young people, focusing on who drinks the brand rather than on specific product advantages.

Animation

Cartoons, puppet characters, and demonstrations with computer-generated graphics are very effective **animation** techniques for communicating difficult messages and reaching specialized markets, such as children. The way aspirin or other medications affect the human system is difficult to explain. Animated pictures of headaches and stomachs can simplify the subject and make a demonstration clear and understandable.

Computer animation requires a great deal of faith on the part of advertisers. Because most of this very expensive work is done on the computer, there's nothing to see until the animation is well developed and a good bit of money has been spent.

Basic Mechanics of Storyboard Development

After the creative team selects the big idea and the format for a TV commercial, the art director and the writer develop the script. Television is so visually powerful and expressive that the art director's role is particularly important. Art directors must be able to work with a variety of professionals—producers, directors, lighting technicians, and set designers—to develop and produce a commercial successfully.

Storyboard Design

Once the basic script is completed, the art director must turn the video portion of the script into real images. This is done with a **storyboard,** a sheet preprinted with a series of 8 to 20 blank windows (frames) in the shape of TV screens. Below each frame is room to place the text of the commercial, including the sound effects and camera views as abbreviated in Exhibit 11-4. The storyboard works much like a cartoon strip.

Through a process similar to laying out a print ad (thumbnail, rough, comp), the artist carefully designs how each scene should appear, arranging actors, scenery, props, lighting, and camera angles to maximize impact, beauty, and mood. The storyboard helps the creatives visualize the commercial's tone and sequence of action, discover any conceptual weaknesses, and make presentations for management approval. It also serves as a guide for filming.

Even when designed to the level of a comp, though, the storyboard is only an approximation of the final commercial. Actual production often results in many changes in lighting, camera angle, focal point, and emphasis. The camera sees many things that the artist couldn't visualize, and vice versa.

Exhibit 11-4
Common abbreviations used in TV scripts.

CU: Close-up. Very close shot of person or object.
ECU: Extreme close-up. A more extreme version of the above. Sometimes designated BCU (big close-up) or TCU (tight close-up).
MCU: Medium close-up. Emphasizes the subject but includes other objects nearby.
MS: Medium shot. Wide-angle shot of subject but not whole set.
FS: Full shot. Entire set or object.
LS: Long shot. Full view of scene to give effect of distance.
DOLLY: Move camera toward or away from subject. Dolly in (DI), dolly out (DO), or dolly back (DB).
PAN: Scan from one side to the other.
ZOOM: Move in or out from the subject without blurring.
SUPER: Superimpose one image on another (as showing lettering over a scene).
DISS: Dissolve (also DSS). Fade out one scene while fading in another.
CUT: Instantly change one picture to another.
WIPE: Gradually erase picture from screen. (Many varied effects are possible.)
VO: Voice-over. An off-screen voice, usually the announcer's.
SFX: Sound effects.
DAU: Down and under. Sound effects fade as voice comes on.
UAO: Up and over. Voice fades as sound effects come on.

Animatic: The Video Comp

To supplement the storyboard or pretest a concept, a commercial may be taped in rough form using the writers and artists as actors. Or an **animatic** may be shot—a video of the sketches in the storyboard accompanied by the audio portion of the commercial synchronized on tape. Computers have cut the costs involved in producing a standard animatic. Avid Technologies, for example, developed an editing system that lets the agency process and edit moving pictures on the screen, lay sound behind them, and transfer the entire package to the client. Apple produces a similar high-performance digital nonlinear editing system called Final Cut Studio. This kind of technology has enabled agencies to serve clients' needs better for less money.

Writing Effectively for Digital Media

LO 11-5

Most college students don't remember a time without the internet. Globally, the internet is used by over half the population, a staggering 4 billion people as of 2018.[38] In the United States, majorities of all age groups, save adults over 65, use the medium. But within these millions of users are an especially important group that deserves special attention from web copywriters.

According to research by Burson Cohn & Wolfe, a large New York public relations firm, there are 11 million especially influential online users in the United States, and their opinions affect the buying decisions of 155 million consumers both online and off. Burson Cohn & Wolfe refers to these opinion leaders as *e-fluentials.*

"An e-fluential is the rock that starts the ripple," said Chet Burchett, president and chief executive officer. "Each one communicates with an average of 14 people." E-fluentials can be reputation builders or busters.[39]

Interestingly, Burson's research found that, across a wide variety of sectors—technology, retail, finance, pharmaceutical, and automotive—90 percent of e-fluentials use company websites to verify advertising information, but only 20 percent report that they find the corporate websites credible.

So writing effectively for the internet, especially for the e-influential audience, is critical. Company websites that provide e-fluentials with straightforward, easy-to-use information are crucial to building and enhancing brand value. And in an age of social media, content must be more than clear and compelling; it must be shareable.

Reid Goldsborough, a widely syndicated technology columnist and former copywriter, maintains that although image is everything in traditional advertising, on the internet content is king. He points to research showing that, unlike readers of newspapers and magazines, people using the internet typically focus on the text first, looking at photos and graphics later. Said another way, the words are most important. The words connote substance, and substance triumphs over style.

Second, internet users don't read deeply, rather they scan content, so the information presented must be at once concise and comprehensive. Numbered lists and bulleted items can be used more than in print media. Rather than scanning down the page like newspaper readers, digital consumers just read the first text screen of any site and then move on. But if they like what they see, then they will want more, and they will stay on the site to search for more information. Having fewer space limitations than any other medium, the internet is ideal for in-depth elaboration. But dumping screen after screen of text on a site is, according to Goldsborough, reader abuse.

Finally, websites should always offer interactivity—a way for the reader to respond, either through e-mail or internet response forms. The internet is about interactivity. Companies that forget that feature are wasting their money.

Of course, digital media involve more than websites. They include social media like Facebook, Instagram, and Twitter, platforms that allow companies like Dell, Apple, Starbucks, and others to remain in regular, instant contact with loyal customers. Part of Twitter's initial appeal was its 140-character limit, which ensured that messages were focused and to the point. However, in 2017 the company announced it would double the length of tweets to 280 characters, making the blog a bit less "micro."

Other suggestions for ways companies can communicate effectively with customers come from Joel Comm, author of *Twitter Power.* His suggestions for companies that want to practice "the art of the tweet" include (1) don't spam, (2) follow Twitter style rules (e.g., texting abbreviations are a no-no on Twitter), (3) give credit for retweets, (4) stick to the character limit, and (5) follow people who follow you. We have more to say about social media in Chapter 15.[40]

Web copy plays a roll in attracting search engines, so Jason Falls recommends that copywriters get to "know SEO" (search engine optimization). Creatives should also emphasize short, exciting messages that will get the audience to "click, share, and respond." Falls suggests that copywriters keep in mind that while "messages are two-way now," it is also more than a dialogue because "you can also watch them talking to each other. That's powerful."[41]

Falls notes that "your message needs to be more human. . . . 'We're here to hang out with you. If you want to talk about your car repairs, we know a thing or two about that.'" In fact, it's best if the message doesn't appear to be "copywritten" at all. Put the brand "in a natural environment" that allows someone to "show off the product and show how cool, smart or helpful the company is." The less staged, the better.[42]

Creating Ads for International Markets

In international markets, the most important consideration for copywriters and creative directors is language. In western Europe, people speak at least 15 different languages and more than twice as many dialects. A similar problem exists in Asia, Africa, and, to a lesser extent, South America.

International advertisers have debated the transferability of campaigns for years. One side believes it's too expensive to create a unique campaign for each national group. They simply translate one overall campaign into each language. Another method is to think globally but act locally, creating ads in various languages and reflecting the needs of different groups, but maintaining a consistent theme worldwide. Other advertisers believe the only way to ensure success is to create a special campaign for each market. Citigroup uses a variation of this approach. With branches in more than 100 countries, the financial service giant adapts its ads and products to the needs of each market. For example, the large Indian population working abroad can open checking accounts in rupees instead of the local currency; family members back home can access the accounts via Citibank ATMs in 34 cities in India, avoiding the steep fees usually associated with transferring money. Some advertisers find such solutions expensive and unnecessary. They run their ads in English worldwide, promoting their products generically rather than specifically.

Marketers must address their unique situations. Moreover, they have to weigh the economics of various promotional strategies.

People BEHIND the Ads

Courtesy of Alex Bogusky, photo by Jason Leiva

Certain people in advertising become recognized as the best talents of their times. Claude Hopkins was the preeminent creative of the time before broadcast media. In the 1950s, David Ogilvy defined creative genius. In the 1960s Bill Bernbach was widely acknowledged as the greatest mind in the business. Who in the 2000s will be remembered by future generations as the greatest creative working in U.S. advertising?

Trade journal *Adweek's* choice is Alex Bogusky, once and current creative director and cochair at Crispin Porter Bogusky. You've seen his work: the Burger King spots where customers "freak out" that their favorite burger, the Whopper, has been "discontinued." The "subservient chicken" website that was so popular it recently reappeared. The hysterical "Square Butts" spots that promote Sponge Bob Kids Meals. The powerful "Truth" ads that shine a harsh light on the tobacco industry. The early MINI Cooper promotions and, more recently, the great campaigns for Volkswagen. Unique, even quirky? Undeniably. But they also demonstrate a special flair for slashing through the clutter and for building brands. And that has helped make CPB one of America's best-known and most respected ad agencies.

To the shock of many, Bogusky walked away from it all in 2010 to pursue other interests. Then, in 2018, he returned to the creative helm of Crispin, ready for new challenges. Bogusky explained his return this way: "CPB is in my blood, and MDC Partners continues to be the network where real innovation can thrive," he wrote, adding, "the timing is right."

Contemporary Advertising spoke with Bogusky just before he left the agency. Here is what he shared:

Things You May Know about Alex Bogusky

He started at what was then called Crispin and Porter Advertising in 1989 as an art director. He was employee number 16. He became creative director of the agency five years later, was named a partner in 1997, and became cochair in January 2008. Under his direction, the agency has grown to over 700 employees and has become the world's most awarded advertising agency over the last few years. Alex has been profiled in *Communication Arts, Adweek, Ad Age, Fast Company,* and *BusinessWeek.* His work has been featured in *The New York Times, The Wall Street Journal, USA Today, Newsweek,* and *Time,* as well as on national television and radio. And in 2002, Alex was inducted into the American Advertising Federation's Hall of Achievement.

Things You May Not Know About Alex Bogusky

Alex Bogusky loses his wallet way more often than most people. He would be perfectly content eating Tex-Mex food every day for the rest of his life. Most Mondays, he will come to work with at least one bloody, puss-oozing injury. He rarely drinks anymore, but when he does, he goes straight for the tequila. He has the attention span of a mating fruit fly. In grade school, his teacher recommended he be put in a special class. He owns 11 bicycles, four dirt bikes, and one crotch rocket. He has a photographic memory, but only for ads. He has an irrational dislike of St. Louis. Yet many of his favorite people are from St. Louis. At one time, he was a good enough motocross racer to turn pro. His mom and dad are both designers and more talented than he is. And he cuts his own hair. With a Flowbee.

Alex spoke with *Contemporary Advertising* about his influences, the things he finds rewarding, his philosophy of managing a creative department, and his advice for students finding their career paths. Not long after speaking with us, Bogusky left his position with CP+B and started his own consulting firm.

CA: You've often acknowledged the role your parents played in your creative development. How did they do that?

AB: Both my parents are more creative people than I am. My mom taught art at an elementary school and our house always had books on art and design. When my parents threw parties, they'd play a game where people had to come up with the best logo for a product in three minutes.

CA: So did they encourage you to go in a creative direction?

AB: Not directly. They were so good I actually found it a bit discouraging. But my mom taught me some practical creative skills, like doing paste-ups and mechanicals. It helped me to get my first agency job.

CA: Did you respond to feeling less creative than your parents as a challenge?

AB: Not really. I just came to terms with it and accepted it. Ultimately, I think it gave me a very healthy work ethic. I realized that there is no shortcut for putting in the time. Being smart can take the place of talent and because of that some people don't put the rigor they should into their work.

CA: So humility is an important asset for a creative person?

AB: Humility is an asset for any person, but certainly for a creative. It helps you realize that your ideas are not good just because you've thought of them. In an ad agency, ideas get built up and torn down all the time. You can't see that happen to your ideas if you have a big ego. I like to think that I have millions of ideas, so I don't worry too much about any one of them. If others think an idea is a bad one, I'm always confident I can come up with another.

CA: Over the years you've talked a lot about the collaborative nature of the creative department at CP+B. The phrase you've used is that your creatives are willing to "jump on hand grenades" for each other. What do you mean by that?

AB: At CP+B we trust the process. You can spend too much time wondering and worrying about what you will come up with. At the agency we believe that you have a role, others have a role, and we try to help each other out when we need to. It gives you some comfort, and it helps you enjoy the work.

CA: How important is that sense of enjoyment?

AB: If you've done it for a while, you realize that the job never changes, it never gets easier. The creative process can be torture, so you have to love it. Each time you achieve something or win some award, you realize that you go back to work on Monday and the job is exactly the same. The work is the benefit.

CA: As a creative director, your job is a lot less about creating the ad and a lot more about overseeing and working with creative people. How do you do that?

AB: The job is different from being a copywriter or art director; it is more about helping people to find their own process, about mentoring.

CA: What is your philosophy about mentoring and getting great work from people?

AB: Realizing that everyone wants to contribute. Sometimes there is just not that much for a creative director to do. We have great people at CP+B and they know how to do their job. I think some creative directors have a hard time standing back from the work, but I don't. Of course, sometimes there are days where you are just praying for someone to come in with a good idea. But even when I have to give a lot of feedback, I'll write my comments in the margins of a draft. I don't ever get on someone's computer and start writing. After I scratch up a piece of paper, I give it back to them and let them do it themselves. It's important that a creative person is allowed to have that sense of contribution.

CA: What else is important?

AB: One of the hardest parts of my job is keeping the bar high. What level of work do we need to keep our aim high? It can be easy to lower the bar and wherever you put it, that's where people aim. Having the energy to keep the bar high is critical. I think it can be easy for a creative director to say, "I'm really good, but the people around me are not." I believe that is death; you have to expect as much from the people around you as you expect from yourself.

CA: What advice do you have for students looking for a career at an agency like CP+B?

AB: Well, I've gotten lots of advice over the years, and I've learned to be cautious about giving it. When I talk to interns, I like to say that I've never made a tough decision. When I've made decisions, even about tough matters, I've always sensed what feels right to me. In making decisions about my own career, I've always tried to move closer to a place that feels like the sweet spot, that lets me do what I enjoy. So many people get into advertising with a preconceived idea about what the business is like. Maybe they've seen it on TV or read about it. They often don't allow themselves to slide and move. But there are so many places to go in this business, literally millions of niches. To me, so much success depends on simply finding the right niche. I always felt that I didn't have to find it right away, so I've done a lot of jobs in advertising, but inevitably I try to gravitate toward the jobs that give me satisfaction and pleasure. I like to call it the feeling of "running downhill." I've had jobs where I felt like I was pushing uphill, and there is no point in staying in a job like that. I think you should go with the momentum, with your energies. Don't fight those things; go with what makes you happy. I think a lot of students are too worried about money. My favorite example is Michael Jordan. He found his exact right thing. MJ is a very talented guy, a good baseball player, a good marketer. But he found his thing in basketball.

CA: Does that carry over to what you look for in the people you hire?

AB: Yes. I interviewed one person, actually a very talented person who is one of our top creative people now. I asked him what he would like to do if he didn't get the job. He began describing a career as a musician, playing small clubs, maybe making a few small recordings. He had really thought this through and I could see his passion for it. Midway through the story, he knew he had blown the interview.

CA: But the story has a happy ending?

AB: A few years later, he was interviewing with us again. He knew how to answer that question the second time! What we are really looking for is somebody who wants to do advertising more than anything else. That's how we feel and that's who we want to work with.

Courtesy of Alex Bogusky.

Translating Copy

Regardless of strategy, translation remains a basic issue. Classic examples of mistranslations and faulty word choices abound in international advertising. A faulty Spanish translation for Perdue chickens reads, "It takes a sexually excited man to make a chick affectionate," instead of, "It takes a tough man to make a tender chicken."[43]

A poorly chosen or badly translated product name can undercut advertising credibility in foreign markets. A classic case was when Coke's product name was widely translated into Chinese characters that sounded like "Coca-Cola" but meant "bite the wax tadpole."[44]

People in the United States, Canada, England, Australia, and South Africa all speak English, but with wide variations in vocabulary, word usage, and syntax. Similarly, the French spoken in France, Canada, Vietnam, and Belgium may differ as much as the English spoken by a British aristocrat and a Tennessee mountaineer. Language variations exist even within countries. The Japanese use five lingual "gears," ranging from haughty to servile, depending on the speaker's and the listener's respective stations in life. Japanese translators must know when to change gears.

Global marketers often use a single promotional piece, such as a web page, and translate it into the languages of the various countries where it will run. Lexus uses different approaches in America, its most important market; Japan, its country of origin; and Germany, where it competes with German luxury brands like Mercedes and BMW.

Source: Toyota Motor Corporation

Companies should follow some basic rules in using translators:

■ *The translator must be an effective copywriter.* In the United States and Canada, most people speak English, yet relatively few are good writers and even fewer are good copywriters. Too often marketers simply let a translation service rewrite their ads in a foreign language. That's not good enough.

■ *The translator must understand the product.* The translator must also know the product's features and its market. It is always better to use a translator who is a product or market specialist rather than a generalist.

■ *Translators should translate into their native tongue.* Ideally, they should live in the country where the ad will appear. This way the company can be sure the translator has a current understanding of the country's social attitudes, culture, and idioms.

■ *Give the translator easily translatable English copy.* The double meanings and idiomatic expressions that make English such a rich language for an advertiser rarely translate well. They only make the translator's job more difficult.

There is no greater insult to a national market than to misuse its language. The translation must be accurate and punctuated properly, and it must also be good copy.

English is rapidly becoming the universal language for corporate campaigns directed to international businesspeople, and some firms print their instructional literature and brochures in English as well. But this approach can incite nationalistic feelings against the company. Worse yet, it automatically limits a product's use to people who understand technical English.

Art Direction for International Markets

Philosophers often refer to the arts as a kind of international language whose nonverbal elements translate freely regardless of culture—a nice idea but, in advertising, a very costly one. People ascribe different meanings to color depending on their culture. When designing ads for use in other countries, the art director must be familiar with each country's artistic preferences and peculiarities.

Some consider color to indicate emotion: Someone "has the blues" or is "green with envy" (refer back to Ad Lab 10-A, "The Psychological Impact of Color"). National flags—the Canadian maple leaf; the red, white, and blue of the United States; the tricolor of France—are nonverbal signals that stir patriotic emotions, thoughts, and actions. However, these same symbols could hurt sales. For example, a promotion using the colors in the U.S. and French flags could easily fail in Southeast Asia, where some people still have painful memories of wars fought against the two countries.

An **icon,** a visual image representing some idea or thing, can have a meaning that cuts across national boundaries and reflects the tastes and attitudes of a group of cultures. An ad with a snake (an icon for the devil and eroticism in many Western cultures) could easily lose sales in North American markets. But in the Far East, where the snake represents renewal (by shedding its skin), the same visual might work as a dynamic expression of a product's staying power.

On a more personal level, a culture's icons can express social roles. When an agency calls a casting company or talent agent in search of a model, the agency, in essence, seeks an icon. It hopes the model will effectively symbolize the product's benefits or help the target market relate better to the ad. A model considered attractive in one culture is not necessarily seen that way in another, however.

Catchy phrases popular in a local culture are often used for advertising. But even if the idea translates verbally into another language, which is rarely the case, the art director may still have difficulty using the same imagery. Advertisers working in global markets must pretest art and design concepts with natives of each country.

Legal Restraints on International Marketers

Finally, all advertising creativity, including what the ads say, show, or do, is at the mercy of foreign governments and cultures. As we discussed in Chapter 3, many countries strongly regulate advertising claims and the use of particular media.

Chapter Summary

The nonverbal aspect of a message carries half the burden of communicating the big idea. In fact, the nonverbal message is inseparable from the verbal. Either can enhance the other or destroy it.

Design refers to how the art director and graphic artist conceptually choose and structure the artistic elements that make up a message's appearance or set its tone. For print, the first work from the art department is a simple, undeveloped design of the layout. The layout has several purposes: It shows where the parts are to be placed; it is an inexpensive way to explore creative ideas; it helps the creative team check the message's psychological or symbolic function; and it serves as a blueprint for the production process.

As copy goes through the editing process, copywriters must be prepared for an inevitable (and sometimes lengthy) succession of edits and reedits from agency and client managers and legal departments. Copywriters must be more than creative; they must be patient, flexible, mature, and able to exercise great self-control.

Typography affects an ad's appearance, design, and legibility. There are four important concepts when selecting type: readability, appropriateness, harmony or appearance, and emphasis.

Several steps are used to develop a design: thumbnail sketch, rough layout, and comprehensive layout. The mechanical is the final art ready for reproduction. Brochures and other multipage materials use a three-dimensional rough called a dummy.

The computer has dramatically affected graphic design. Software suites allow artists to paint and draw, make up pages, and manipulate images in ways that would not be possible manually. Every graphic designer must now be computer literate.

In print, the visual has a great deal of responsibility for a message's success. The picture may be used to capture the reader's attention, identify the subject, create a favorable impression, or serve a host of other functions.

The two basic devices for illustrating a message are photos and drawings. Photography can contribute realism; a feeling of immediacy; a feeling of live action; the special enhancement of mood, beauty, and sensitivity; and speed, flexibility, and economy. Drawn illustrations do many of these

things, too, and may be used if the artist feels they can achieve greater impact than photos. The chief focus for visuals may be the product in a variety of settings, a user benefit, a humorous situation, a testimonial, or even some negative appeal.

The key format elements for writing print are headlines, subheads, body copy, slogans, seals, logos, and signatures. Many headline types and copy styles are used in print. There are five basic types of headlines: benefit, provocative, news/information, question, and command. Copy styles also fall into several categories: straight sell, institutional, narrative, dialogue/monologue, picture caption, and device.

The creative pyramid and the format elements come together in creating effective print messages. The headline carries the attention step, the subhead and lead-in paragraph hold the interest step, and the interior paragraphs, trial close, and close of body copy contain the credibility and desire steps. The action step takes place with the last line of copy or with the logo, slogan, and signature block.

In electronic media, copy is normally spoken dialogue that is prepared using a script; it is referred to as the audio portion of the commercial. The copy may be delivered as a voice-over by an unseen announcer or on camera by an announcer, spokesperson, or actor.

Radio commercials must be intrusive to catch and hold the attention of people who are usually doing something else. Radio copy must be more conversational than print copy and should paint word pictures for listeners to see in their mind's eye.

Television copywriters use scripts and storyboards to communicate the verbal and nonverbal ideas of a commercial. When writing TV ads, the creative team must strive for credibility, relevance, and consistency in tone. While TV commercials should be entertaining, the entertainment should not interfere with the selling message.

In radio and TV, art plays an important role. Art includes concept development, character definition, set and scene design, costuming, lighting, scripting, camera angles—everything having to do with the visual value of the commercial.

Common formats for radio and TV commercials include straight announcement, presenter, testimonial, demonstration, musical, slice of life, lifestyle, and animation. The art director works with a writer to develop the artistic qualities of the big idea, the format, and the storyboard. The storyboard, the basic rough design of a TV commercial, contains sketches of the scenes along with the script. To supplement the storyboard and pretest a commercial, an animatic may be used.

Writing for digital media requires understanding how consumers find and respond to information online. Content is king in digital, and most audiences scan rather than read. Social media is about audiences sharing content and addressing one another, so copywriters should use styles of writing that encourage such behaviors.

When creating campaigns for international markets, advertisers must consider the variations in language and the legal restrictions imposed by foreign governments or cultures. Art direction for international markets requires an in-depth knowledge of the foreign culture. Even if the verbal message translates well, the icons and images may not.

Important Terms

animatic, *384*

animation, *383*

audio, *375*

Ayer No. 1, *360*

benefit headline, *371*

body copy, *372*

boldface, *372*

cascading style sheets, *358*

casting brief, *379*

close, *375*

command headline, *372*

comprehensive layout (comp), *357*

demonstration, *381*

design, *355*

desktop publishing, *357*

device copy, *374*

dialogue/monologue copy, *374*

display type, *364*

donut, *383*

dummy, *357*

font, *365*

headline, *370*

hook, *382*

icon, *390*

illustrator, *361*

institutional copy, *373*

integrated commercial, *379*

interior paragraph, *374*

italic, *372*

jingle, *381*

kerning, *364*

layout, *355*

leading, *364*

lead-in paragraph, *374*

lifestyle technique, *383*

logotype, *375*

mnemonic device, *383*

musical commercial, *381*

musical logo, *382*

narrative copy, *373*

news/information headline, *371*

on camera, *379*

photographer, *361*

picture-caption copy, *374*

picture-window layout, *360*

points, *365*

poster-style format, *360*

presenter commercial, *380*

provocative headline, *371*

question headline, *371*

radio or podcast personality, *380*

sans serif, *364*

script, *375*

seal, *375*

serif, *364*

signature cut, *375*

slice of life, *382*

slogan, *375*

storyboard, *383*

storyboard rough, *378*

straight announcement, *379*

straight-sell copy, *373*

style sheet, *358*

subhead, *372*

tagline, *375*

testimonial, *380*

text, *372*

text type, *364*

themeline, *375*

thumbnail, *356*

trial close, *375*

type family, *365*

typography, *361*

visuals, *361*

voice-over, *379*

Review Questions

1. What is a layout? What is its purpose?
2. What are the elements of design? How do they work to attract and direct attention?
3. What is the purpose of white space?
4. From any chapter in the book, select an ad that contains a visual. What is the visual's purpose? How would you improve the visual if you were the art director?
5. What kind of headline does the ad from Question 4 have? How well has the creative team followed the steps up the creative pyramid? Explain.
6. Choose an ad you don't like. Rewrite the headline using three different styles.
7. What is a storyboard, and what is its role? Choose a commercial you enjoy and create a storyboard for it.
8. Give examples of television spots that typify the eight major types of TV commercials.
9. Find an international ad or commercial you like. What is its message strategy? Can you discern the copy style? Do you think the copy and headline reflect the strategy? What do you like about the ad? Why?
10. What guidelines can you cite for preparing an ad in a foreign language?

The Advertising Experience

1. Big Stan's Tri-State Mattress Outlet usually advertises by sponsoring monster truck shows or demolition derbies. However, Big Stan wants to expand his business and has decided to try radio advertising. Using the script format found in the section "Writing Radio Copy," create the kind of radio ad that would please Big Stan and his potential customers.

2. **Creative Boutiques**
   One of the growing trends in advertising is the increased use of creative boutiques. Many of these smaller shops have won clients previously handled by larger, full-service advertising agencies. Peruse the small sampling of creative boutiques below and answer the questions that follow.
   - Brolik: http://brolik.com/
   - Crispin Porter Bogusky: www.cpbgroup.com
   - The Idea Boutique: www.theideab
   - Love & War: www.loveandwar.com

   a. What is the focus of the company's work (consumer, business-to-business, ethnic, general market)?

   b. What are the scope and size of the company's business?

   c. What services does the company offer?

   d. What is your overall impression of the company and its work? Why?

3. **Creative Resources**
   As you saw when reading this chapter, a lot goes into writing good copy or scripts and developing effective visuals. Because of the internet, many new resources are available to the creative team that is developing a concept.

   Copywriters often rely on different sources to aid them in developing their copy. Visit the following websites and explain how each relates to copywriters and their task of developing effective copy.
   - Copy Chef: www.copychef.com
   - The Slot: www.theslot.com
   - Writers Guild of America: www.wga.org

   Like copywriters, art directors require many resources while developing their art. Familiarize yourself further with art direction by browsing the following websites. Be sure to discuss the importance of each site to art directors.
   - American Institute of Graphic Arts: www.aiga.org
   - The One Club: www.oneclub.org
   - Creativity Cafe: www.creativity.net
   - Graphic Design & Publishing Center: www.graphic-design.com
   - PhotoDisc: www.photodisc.com
   - Photographers Index: www.photographersindex.com
   - GoCreate: www.gocreate.com

4. How does the "Dumb Ways to Die" campaign use metaphor to change behaviors around trains? How, and why, does the campaign suggest that there is something even worse than death for those who might be tempted to take risks around trains?

End Notes

1. Hannah Rand, "Horrifying Video Shows Gang of Youths Risking Death by Playing Game of Chicken on New York Subway Tracks," *Daily Mail,* April 18, 2012, www.dailymail.co.uk/news/article-2131549/Horrifying-video-shows-gang-youths-riskingdeath-playing-game-chicken-New-York-subway-tracks.html.

2. ©Metro Trains Melbourne, Dumb Ways to Die.™ All rights reserved.

3. Tim Nuddl, "5 Years Later, 'Dumb Ways to Die' Remains Advertising's Most Delightfully Horrible Creation," *Adweek,* April 11, 2017, www.adweek.com/creativity/5-years-later-dumb-ways-to-die-remains-advertisings-most-delightfully-horrible-creation/.

4. Mark Sweney, "Cannes Lions: Dumb Ways to Die Scoops Top Award," *The Guardian,* June 22, 2013, www.theguardian.com/media/2013/jun/22/cannes-lions-advertisingawards.

5. "Top Ad Campaigns of the 21st Century: Metro Trains: Dumb Ways to Die," *Advertising Age,* http://adage.com/lp/top15/#tapproject.

6. Miranda Ward, "Has Dumb Ways to Die Been Effective?" *mUmBRELLA,* January 30, 2015.

7. "The History of Prepress," Prepressure.com, www.prepressure.com/prepress/history.

8. Demian Farnworth, "10 Ways to Write Damn Good Copy," *Copyblogger,* January 28, 2013, www.copyblogger.com/good-copywriting/.

9. "Adobe Agency Partner Program," *Adobe,* www.adobe.com/solutions/advertising.html.

10. "The State of Online Advertising," *Adobe,* www.adobe.com/aboutadobe/pressroom/pdfs/Adobe_State_of_Online_Advertising.pdf.

11. Alex Palmer, "The Difference between Good and Great Designers," *UX Mastery,* August 9, 2016, https://uxmastery.com/difference-good-great-designers/.

12. Robyn Blakeman, *Advertising Campaign Design: Just the Essentials* (Armonk, NY: M. E. Sharpe, 2015).

13. Nathan Collins, "Poorly Chosen Headlines Can Hurt Your Memory," *Pacific Standard,* November 6, 2014, www.psmag.com/politics-and-law/headlines-hurt-memory-94053.

14. Tom Altstiel and Jean Grow, *Advertising Creative: Strategy, Copy, Design* (Thousand Oaks, CA: Sage, 2013).

15. Tom Altstiel and Jean Grow, *Advertising Creative: Strategy, Copy, Design* (Thousand Oaks, CA: Sage, 2013).

16. Roy Paul Nelson, *The Design of Advertising* (Dubuque, IA: Brown & Benchmark, 1994).

17. Shelley Zalis, "Diversity and Inclusion, Rewriting the Rules for Marketing," *Advertising Age,* November 14, 2017, https://adage.com/article/deloitte-digital/diversity-inclusion-rewriting-rules-marketing/311262/.

18. Tom Altstiel and Jean Grow, *Advertising Creative: Strategy, Copy, Design* (Thousand Oaks, CA: Sage, 2013); Neil Raphel and Murray Raphel, "Rules to Advertise By," *Progressive Grocer,* December 1993, pp. 13–14; Murray Raphel, "How to Get Ahead in Direct Mail," *Direct Marketing*, January 1990, pp. 30–32, 52.

19. Nathan Safran, "5 Data Insights into the Headlines Readers Click," *Moz Blog,* July 17, 2013, https://moz.com/blog/5-data-insights-into-the-headlines-readers-click.

20. David A. Wesson, "Headline Length as a Factor in Magazine Ad Readership," *Journalism Quarterly, Summer* 1989, p. 468.

21. David Ogilvy, *Ogilvy on Advertising* (New York: Random House, 1985).

22. Tom Altstiel and Jean Grow, *Advertising Creative: Strategy, Copy, Design* (Thousand Oaks, CA: Sage, 2013).

23. Philip Ward Burton, *Advertising Copywriting,* 6th ed. (Lincolnwood, IL: NTC Business Books, 1991), p. 54; Arthur J. Kover and William J. James, "When Do Advertising 'Power Words' Work? An Examination of Congruence and Satiation," *Journal of Advertising Research,* July/August 1993, pp. 32–38.

24. MCNG Marketing, "Market the Benefits, Not the Features of Your Product," *From the Blog,* May 16, 2013, http://www.mcngmarketing.com/market-the-benefits-not-the-features-of-your-product/#.VZgsdflVhBc.

25. Tom Altstiel and Jean Grow, *Advertising Creative: Strategy, Copy, Design* (Thousand Oaks, CA: Sage, 2013).

26. Dan Shewan, "21 Tips for Writing Great Ad Headlines," *WordStream,* February 2, 2015, www.wordstream.com/blog/ws/2015/02/02/ppc-ad-headlines.

27. Brad Smith, "7 Facebook Headline Hacks to Drive Clicks through the Roof," *AdEspresso by Hootsuite,* June 28, 2017, https://adespresso.com/blog/headline-hacks-high-click-rate/.

28. Margo Berman, *The Copywriter's Toolkit* (Malden, MA: Wiley-Blackwell, 2012).

29. David Ogilvy, *Ogilvy on Advertising* (New York: Random House, 1985).

30. Philip Ward Burton, *Advertising Copywriting,* 6th ed. (Lincolnwood, IL: NTC Business Books, 1991); Marjorie Zieff-Finn, "It's No Laughing Matter," *Direct Marketing,* September 1992.

31. John O'Toole, *The Trouble with Advertising,* 2nd ed. (New York: Random House, 1985).

32. Joanne Lipman, "It's It and That's a Shame: Why Are Some Slogans Losers?" *The Wall Street Journal,* July 16, 1993.

33. Herschell Gordon Lewis, "Radio Copywriting—Not as Easy as You May Think," *Direct Marketing,* July 1992.

34. Adapted with permission from Bob Garfield, "The Best Ad Missed the Boat to Cannes," *Advertising Age,* June 23, 1997.

35. David Ogilvy, *Ogilvy on Advertising* (New York: Random House, 1985).

36. David Ogilvy, *Ogilvy on Advertising* (New York: Random House, 1985).

37. Fast Company Staff, "The 10 Most Addictive Sounds in the World," *Fast Company,* February 22, 2010, www.fastcompany.com/1555211/10-most-addictive-sounds-world.

38. Simon Kemp, "Digital in 2018: World's Internet Users Pass the 4 Billion Mark," *We Are Social,* January 30, 2018, https://wearesocial.com/blog/2018/01/global-digital-report-2018.

39. "Corporate Advertising Study," *Burson-Marsteller,* October 13, 2003, www.efluentials.com/documents/pr_101303.pdf.

40. Joel Comm and Dave Taylor, *Twitter Power 3.0* (Hoboken, NJ: John Wiley & Sons, 2015).

41. Jason Falls, "Why You Shouldn't Trust Social Media to an SEO Consultant," *Social Media Explorer,* March 9, 2009, www.socialmediaexplorer.com/search-enginemarketing/why-you-shouldnt-trust-social-media-to-an-seo-consultant/.

42. Jason Falls, "Copywriting for Social Media," *Social Media Explorer,* June 9, 2010, www.socialmediaexplorer.com/digital-marketing/copywriting-for-social-media/.

43. John Freiralds, "Navigating the Minefields of Multilingual Marketing," *Pharmaceutical Executive,* September 1994.

44. Phil Mooney, "Bite the wax tadpole?" Coca Cola History, March 6, 2008, www.coca-colacompany.com/stories/bite-the-wax-ta.

LEARNING OBJECTIVES

To examine how print advertising enhances the advertiser's media mix. Newspapers and magazines, with their unique qualities, can complement broadcast, direct mail, and other media. By using print wisely, advertisers can significantly increase the reach and impact of their campaigns and still stay within their budget.

After studying this chapter, you will be able to:

LO12-1   Explain the advantages and disadvantages of magazine advertising.

LO12-2   Discuss the various ways to analyze a magazine's circulation.

LO12-3   Analyze how rates are determined for print media.

LO12-4   List the advantages and disadvantages of newspaper advertising.

LO12-5   Show how newspapers are categorized.

LO12-6   Define the major types of newspaper advertising.

LO12-7   Detail how newspaper space is purchased.

LO12-8   Describe how print ads are produced.

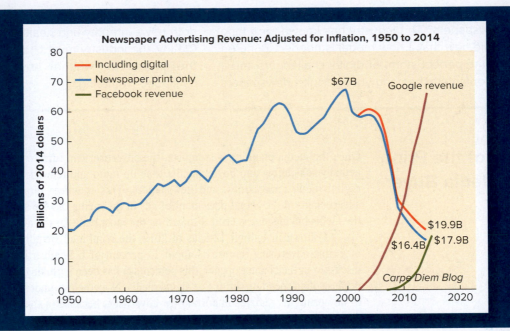

Newspaper Advertising Revenue: Adjusted for Inflation, 1950 to 2014

Including digital
Newspaper print only
Facebook revenue

$67B

Google revenue

$19.9B
$16.4B $17.9B

Carpe Diem Blog

Billions of 2014 dollars

Source: Newspaper Association of America

Whither newspapers? ■ The word "whither," with an "h," refers to place and in the first sentence means "what will happen to print media?" Drop the "h," as in "wither," and the term refers to shriveling. Sadly, both words are appropriate in discussing the oldest advertising medium. ■ The digital revolution has challenged all media, but especially newspapers. To see why, it is helpful to consider several trends that started years ago and are continuing today. ■ First are the trendlines in the graph above showing the decline in newspaper and surge in Google and Facebook ad revenues. The data, shared in the Baekdal/Plus blog (see www.baekdal.com/thoughts/what-killed-the-newspapers-google-or-facebook-or/) show a disruption of the most significant kind as new media replace old. Additional data come from the Pew Research Center's "Newspapers Fact Sheet." You can read the original report here: www.journalism.org/fact-sheet/newspapers/. ■ The report shows that circulation of newspapers in 2017, both paper and digital, was only 31 million for weekdays, a decline of 11 percent for just one year. Even digital circulation has fallen.[1] ■ Newspapers are more likely to be read by the better educated, so it should be a positive development that U.S. citizens, on average, have more education today than they did in times past. For example, in 1947 just 5 percent of Americans held a four-year degree, but by 2012 that number had reached 30 percent, a historic high. However, college-educated adults are less likely to read a newspaper than at any other time in history.[2] ■ While the declines in newspaper readership are consistent and significant, they pale in comparison to the decline in advertising revenue. In 2006 revenues from print and online ads peaked at about $49 billion.[3] By 2017 that number had shrunk to $16 billion. ■ Where has the money gone? If you guessed the internet, you would be right. Advertisers have shifted major portions of their spending to online and social media. In fact, in 2018 online spending reached over $110 billion and in 2019 digital represents 55 percent of all money spent on advertising.[4] ■ Newspapers have long hoped that digital ad revenue would be the savior of the industry. However, newspapers still only receive a small fraction of advertising and circulation revenues from their online products. Pew reports that for every $1 newspapers gain in digital advertising income, they are losing $7 from print ads.[5] ■ The pain has been felt by most papers, including top brands. Advertising revenue at *The Wall Street Journal* declined 11 percent from 2014 to 2015, leading to staff layoffs.[6] *The New York Times* saw ad revenues slip just under 6 percent in 2018, although it saw increases in subscriber revenues.[7] Digital revenues at Gannett, parent company of *USA Today,* grew in 2018 but failed to offset declines in print revenues.[8] ■ So whither newspapers? The industry has known for a long while now that a new model is needed. Buffeted by the perfect storm of digital challengers and a lack of interest among young adults, newspapers have struggled to find an approach that promises both news integrity and healthy revenue growth. Clearly, the industry must find an answer soon if the answer to "whither newspapers?" is not continued "withering."

The Role of the Print Media Buyer

Once the media planning is complete, the advertiser can turn to the tactical details of actually scheduling and buying media time on radio and television and media space in digital media, magazines, and newspapers. This is where most money is spent in advertising—on the actual placement of ads in the media. So the skilled performance of the media-buying task is critical to getting the most bang for the advertiser's buck.

As shown in Exhibit 12-1, as of 2019, the combined spending on newspaper and magazine advertising represents about 13 percent of U.S. advertising expenditures. As discussed in the chapter opener, this percentage has been shrinking throughout the 2000s because of ad spending shifting to digital media. Nonetheless, understanding how and why to buy print ads remains important for advertisers because of the unique opportunities afforded by these media.

The person tasked with negotiating and contracting with media is called a **media buyer.** Media buyers often used to specialize, so there were print media buyers, spot TV media buyers, network media buyers, and so on. But media have evolved and provide increased value to advertisers by offering cross-platform opportunities. An advertiser interested in ESPN's audience can choose the firm's magazine, website, retail outlets, social media feeds, Spanish-language channel, and so on.[9] Contemporary media buyers must therefore understand the synergies that come from mixing media to achieve their objectives.

The size and scope of the agency and client also affect how media planning is practiced. In small agencies, for example, media buyers rarely specialize. One person may perform both planning and buying tasks. Some agencies, employing hundreds, do only media-related functions and work for large multinational companies. These big media agencies routinely buy so much time and space that they qualify for big discounts, which they pass along to clients. Carat is a media agency that plans buys for all of General Motor's brands, including Chevrolet, Cadillac, and Buick.

Success as a *print media buyer* requires a broad understanding of all available print media and the terminology used in the field. Buyers need to know, for example, how magazines and newspapers are categorized, the advertising possibilities each form offers, and the pros and cons of using various types of vehicles. They should also have an understanding of the impact of new technologies on print media.

Second, buyers need to know how to buy magazine and newspaper space. They must understand how to analyze circulation, read rate cards, get reliable information, and calculate and negotiate the most efficient media buys.

Finally, media buyers call on creativity for developing ingenious, sophisticated ways to integrate the advertiser's print media efforts into the whole creative mix.

These are not small tasks. But for the student of advertising beginning his or her career in a media department, the opportunities are great. Choosing media is every bit as strategic, and important, as other important facets of IMC. The purpose of this chapter is to bring clarity to these subjects.

Using Magazines in the Creative Mix

Advertisers use magazines in their creative mix for many reasons. First and foremost, magazines allow an advertiser to reach a particular target audience with a high-quality presentation. In 2018, Pfizer, Johnson & Johnson, L'Oréal, and Procter & Gamble were four of the biggest spenders on magazines in their creative mix.

Newspaper and Magazine Ad Spending as a Percentage of All U.S. Ad Spending 2018

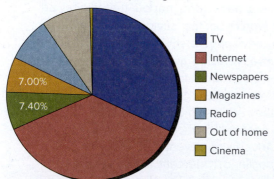

- TV
- Internet
- Newspapers
- Magazines
- Radio
- Out of home
- Cinema

7.00%

7.40%

Exhibit 12-1
U.S. Spending on Newspapers and Magazines
Source: Advertising Age Fact Pack, "200 Leading National Advertisers 2018 Fact Pack."

My IMC Campaign 12-A

The Pros and Cons of Magazine Advertising

The Pros

- **Flexibility** in readership and advertising. Magazines cover the full range of prospects; they have a wide choice of regional and national coverage and a variety of lengths, approaches, and editorial tones.

- **Color** gives readers visual pleasure, and color reproduction is best in slick magazines. Color enhances image and identifies the package. In short, it sells.

- **Authority and believability** enhance the commercial message. TV, radio, and newspapers offer lots of information but lack the depth needed for readers to gain knowledge or meaning; magazines often offer all three.

- **Permanence,** or long shelf life, gives the reader time to appraise ads in detail, allowing a more complete education/sales message and the opportunity to communicate the total corporate personality.

- **Prestige** for products advertised in upscale or specialty magazines such as *Architectural Digest, Connoisseur,* and *Town and Country.*

- **Audience selectivity** is more efficient in magazines than any other medium except direct mail. The predictable, specialized editorial environment selects the audience and enables advertisers to pinpoint their sales campaigns. Examples: golfers *(Golf Digest),* businesspeople *(Bloomberg Businessweek),* 20-something males *(Details),* or teenage girls *(Seventeen).*

- **Cost efficiency** because wasted circulation is minimized. Print networks give advertisers reduced prices for advertising in two or more network publications.

- **Selling power** of magazines is proven, and results are usually measurable.

- **Reader loyalty** that sometimes borders on fanaticism.

- **Extensive pass-along readership.** Circulation, which is the number of issues printed, is usually much lower than readership because subscribers share their magazines with others.

- **Merchandising assistance.** Advertisers can generate reprints and merchandising materials that help them get more mileage out of their ad campaigns.

The Cons

- **Lack of immediacy** that advertisers can get with digital or broadcast media.

- **Shallow geographic coverage.** They don't offer the national reach of broadcast media.

- **Inability to deliver mass audiences at a low price.** Magazines are costly for reaching broad masses of people.

- **Inability to deliver high frequency.** Magazines are the poorest performer among major media for building frequency. The reason: weekly or monthly publication schedules.

- **Long lead time** for ad insertion, sometimes two to three months. The world, and the advertiser's competitive situation, can change a lot in that period of time.

- **Heavy advertising competition.** The largest-circulation magazines have 52 percent advertising to 48 percent editorial content.

- **High cost per thousand.** Average black-and-white cost per thousand (CPM) in national consumer magazines is high; some trade publications with highly selective audiences have a CPM over $50 for a black-and-white page.

- **Declining circulations,** especially in single-copy sales, is an industry-wide trend that limits an advertiser's reach.

The Pros and Cons of Magazine Advertising

LO 12-1

Why do media planners choose magazines for their creative mix? Magazines offer a host of features: flexible design options, prestige, authority, believability, and long shelf life. They may sit on a coffee table or shelf for months and be reread many times. People can read a magazine ad at their leisure; they can pore over the details of a photograph; and they can carefully study the information presented in the copy. This makes magazines an ideal medium for high-involvement think and feel products. The presence of major pharmaceutical companies like Pfizer and Johnson & Johnson among top spenders on magazine advertising suggests another benefit: the ability to present large amounts of information as text, images, or both.

Magazines also have a number of drawbacks (see My IMC Campaign 12-A, "The Pros and Cons of Magazine Advertising"). They are expensive (on a cost-per-thousand basis), especially for color ads. And because they typically come out only monthly, or weekly at best, it's difficult to build frequency quickly. To compensate, many advertisers use magazines in conjunction with other media—such as newspapers, TV, and digital media (see Ad Lab 12-A, "Magazines and the Creative Mix").

AD Lab 12–A

Magazines and the Creative Mix

Read My IMC Campaign 12–A, "The Pros and Cons of Magazine Advertising," and see if you can apply that information to the following situation:

You manage an elegant French restaurant in Los Angeles that is known for its intimate setting, excellent service, and lovely outdoor garden patio. You decide to build the business by promoting the special ambience your restaurant offers. To enhance the sense of romance, you plan to give away a long-stemmed rose and a glass of champagne with each entrée. Your clientele consists primarily of wealthy, educated business leaders and celebrities. However, a growing segment of your customers includes tourists and middle-class couples out for a special evening.

Laboratory Applications

1. Is a magazine the best way to advertise this special? Can a magazine be used along with other media? Which type of magazine would be best?

2. How can magazine advertising help you build the restaurant's image? What qualities of magazine advertising make it attractive for this opportunity?

3. Look at Exhibit 12-2 and identify a layout for your magazine ad that would be ideal for this advertiser. Describe your ad and explain your choice of layout.

Special Possibilities with Magazines

Media buyers are aware of the many creative possibilities magazines offer advertisers through various features. These include bleed pages; cover positions; inserts and gatefolds; and special sizes, such as junior pages and island halves.

When the dark or colored background of the ad extends to the edge of the page, it is said to **bleed** off the page. Most magazines offer bleed pages, but they charge 10 to 15 percent more for them. The advantages of bleeds include greater flexibility in expressing the advertising idea, a slightly larger printing area, and more dramatic impact.

If a company plans to advertise in a particular magazine consistently, it may seek a highly desirable **cover position.** Few publishers sell ads on the front cover, commonly called the *first cover.* They do sell the inside front, inside back, and outside back covers (the *second, third,* and *fourth covers,* respectively), usually through multiple-insertion contracts at a substantial premium.

A less expensive way to use magazine space is to place the ad in an unusual place on the page or dramatically across spreads. A **junior unit** is a large ad (60% of the page) placed in the middle of a page and surrounded with editorial matter. Similar to junior units are **island halves,** surrounded by even more editorial matter. The island sometimes costs more than a regular half-page, but because it dominates the page, many advertisers consider it worth the extra charge. Exhibit 12-2 shows how space combinations can be used to create impact.

Sometimes, rather than buying a standard page, an advertiser uses an **insert.** The advertiser prints the ad on high-quality paper stock to add weight and drama to the message, and then ships the finished ads to the publisher for insertion into the magazine at a special price. Another option is multiple-page inserts. Calvin Klein once promoted its jeans in a 116-page insert in *Vanity Fair.* The insert reportedly cost more than $1 million, but the news reports about it in major daily newspapers gave the campaign extra publicity value. Advertising inserts may be devoted exclusively to one company's product, or they may be sponsored by the magazine and have a combination of ads and special editorial content consistent with the magazine's focus.

A **gatefold** is an insert whose paper is so wide that the extreme left and right sides have to be folded into the center to match the size of the other pages. When the reader opens the magazine, the folded page swings out like a gate to present the ad. Not all magazines provide gatefolds, and they are always sold at a substantial premium.

Some advertisers create their own **custom magazines.** These look like regular magazines and are often produced by the same companies that publish traditional magazines. However, they are essentially magazine-length ads, which readers are expected to purchase

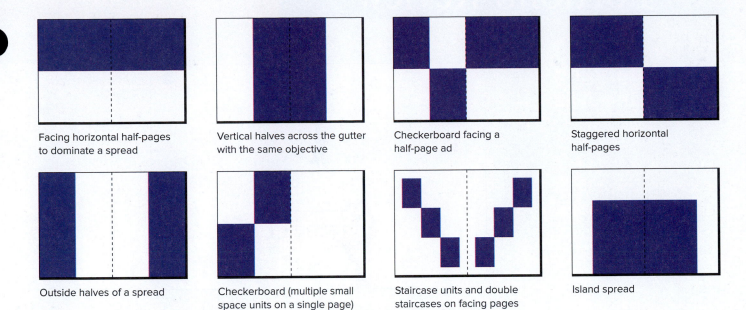

Facing horizontal half-pages to dominate a spread

Vertical halves across the gutter with the same objective

Checkerboard facing a half-page ad

Staggered horizontal half-pages

Outside halves of a spread

Checkerboard (multiple small space units on a single page)

Staircase units and double staircases on facing pages

Island spread

Exhibit 12-2
An ad's position on the page influences its effectiveness. The size and shape of the ad often determine where it will fall on the page. These eight two-page spreads show most of the positions an ad can take.

at newsstands. Custom magazines have been published for Sony, General Motors, General Electric, Jenny Craig, and Ray-Ban sunglasses. Kraft Foods decided to expand its free, custom-published magazine *Food & Family,* which offers recipes and cooking tips, to 1 million U.S. households. This came after Kraft's successful test in Canada of another custom magazine, *What's Cooking.* The popularity of that publication even inspired a TV spin-off of the same name.[10] Ad Lab 12-B discusses another innovation in magazine advertising similar to the custom magazine: native advertising.

Among the most important developments in recent years is native advertising. **Native advertising** is defined by the Native Advertising Institute as "paid advertising where the ad matches the form, feel and function of the content of the media on which it appears."[11] In essence, native ads are sponsored content that does not look like advertising. Examples can include articles or advertorials in newspapers and magazines, but also video content on the web or TV and promoted content in social media. It's effectiveness is linked to the similarity of the sponsored content to editorial matter. For more on native advertising in magazines, see Ad Lab 12-B.

How Magazines Are Categorized

In the jargon of the trade, magazines are called books, and media buyers commonly categorize them by content, geography, and size.

Content

The broadest classifications of content are *consumer magazines, farm publications,* and *business magazines.* Each may be broken down into hundreds of categories.

- **Consumer magazines,** purchased for entertainment, information, or both, are edited for consumers who buy products for their own personal consumption: *Time, Maxim, Glamour, Good Housekeeping.* The Portfolio Review, "Outstanding Magazine Ads," shows the range of creativity in consumer magazine advertising.
- **Farm publications** are directed to farmers and their families or to companies that manufacture or sell agricultural equipment, supplies, and services: *Farm Journal, Progressive Farmer, Prairie Farmer, Successful Farming.*

(continued on page 403)

:: Outstanding Magazine Ads

Magazines provide creatives with an unlimited palette of colorful opportunities for their imagination. Offering permanence, color, unmatched reproduction quality, and excellent credibility, magazines are a powerful weapon in the advertiser's arsenal. In this portfolio, we've selected some outstanding examples of magazine advertising.

• See if you can look past the beauty of these ads and determine the underlying strategy that guided the artists' thinking. Who is the target audience? Is that different from the target market? What are they trying to say about the advertiser? How is the advertiser positioned? Once you've determined the strategy, which magazines would you place these ads in?

Can a Pedigree treat control a dog's behavior as effectively as a game controller can run a console? This clever ad suggests so.

Source: Mars, Incorporated

Taste and smell might be the only senses not affected by print ads. Well, usually not affected. This attention-grabbing magazine ad from Fanta encourages users to "tear off a piece of this page, pop in your mouth, and enjoy a Fanta by tasting this ad!"[13]

Source: The Coca-Cola Company

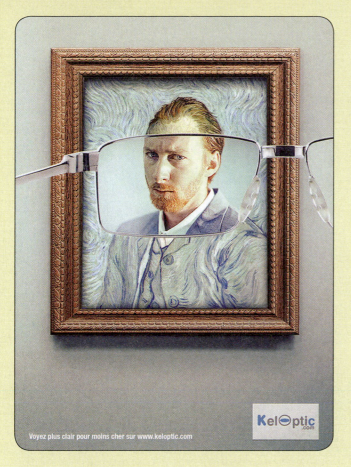

Changing the familiar in an inspired way by calling attention to the brand benefit is advertising at its best. This optical ad for KelOptic is a showcase example.

Source: KelOptic

Why do the ants avoid the candy? Because it is sugar-free, of course. This is just one example in a long line of inspired Chupa Chups advertising.

Source: Perfetti Van Melle

Creative consultant Roger Von Oech emphasizes the power of metaphor to communicate in a powerful yet simple way. This Nivea magazine ad, comparing the product to a beautiful evening moon, uses a metaphorical approach to draw attention and persuade.

Source: Beiersdorf

Another of Von Oech's suggestions is to use ambiguity when thinking creatively. This ad, focused on improving marriages, is somewhat ambiguous. By inviting deeper scrutiny, it packs a punch when it delivers its message.

Source: StrongerMarriage.org

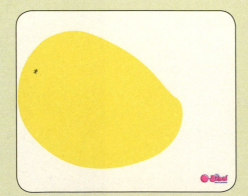 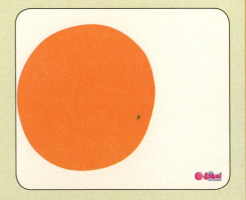

Perfetti Van Melle is a worldwide manufacturer and distributor of candy products. These bright ads convey the sweet bold flavors of the candy through great color and design.

Source: Perfetti Van Melle

AD Lab 12–B

Native Advertising

The line between advertising and content in many magazines is blurring with the growth of native advertising, a form of sponsored content that appears to be editorial matter. Magazines work closely with advertisers to develop this kind of advertising.

According to FIPP and the Native Advertising Institute, in 2020 revenue from native advertising will account for an astounding 40 percent of magazine ad revenue, up from 21 percent in just 2016. For an industry experiencing regular year-over-year declines in revenues, native advertising is an important opportunity.

However, the practice is not without its critics. For a humorous (but bawdy) critique of native advertising, watch HBO's John Oliver criticize the use of native ads here: https://adage.com/article/the-media-guy/watch-john-oliver-s-hilarious-attack-native-advertising/294448/.

The gist of Oliver's critique, and that of many others, is that native advertising succeeds for an unethical reason: It deceives people into thinking that what they are reading is content that has been vetted by editors of the publication. In fact, it is content designed to sell or persuade.

Why disguise the ads? Credit the success of technology, consumer sophistication, and even advertising's critics. Because consumers have so many ways to avoid ads, advertisers are ready to embrace new, more slippery methods of gaining exposure. The disguised nature of the ads helps bypass the cynicism many consumers feel toward sponsored content.

The flipside, of course, is that native advertising changes the nature of the relationship between publishers and their readers. Readers have long believed that strong editorial review helps ensure the value and validity of magazine content. The choice to allow native ads means publishers are turning over some of that content to others. While some readers may be skeptical of sponsored content,

research suggests that at least half of all consumers don't really know what native advertising is, or why they should be suspicious of it.

The key to successful native advertising is content. A good example is Hennessy's ad in *Vanity Fair* about Sir Martin Campbell, the first person to drive faster than 300 miles per hour. The piece, titled "Hennessy Fuels Our Chase for the Wild Rabbit . . . but What Does It All Mean?" was described by blog Wordstream as "genuinely interesting." The review also noted, "The content's inevitable product placement is handled well, and it doesn't feel gratuitous or tenuously positioned alongside the subject matter. Finally, the piece is as stylish as a regular *Vanity Fair* feature, which results in an engaging experience for the reader."[12]

Wordstream also highlighted some examples of the poor use of native advertising, including an *Atlantic Magazine* piece about a prominent leader in the Church of Scientology and a *New York Times* advertorial entitled "Will Millennials Ever Completely Shun the Office?" The review noted, "the 'Millennial work ethic' angle is so tired it's practically comatose. Even the question posed by the article is ridiculous—no, Millennials will not 'shun' offices, because most of them are saddled with back-breaking student loan debt and can't find work."

Like it, hate it, or feel indifferent, native advertising is here to stay. The most effective will focus on content attractive to readers and styles that tell compelling stories and make only subtle references to sponsored brands.

Laboratory Application

Identify some story themes that could be used to create native magazine ads for the following products:

- Detergent
- Organic foods
- Electric cars

(continued from page 399)

- **Business magazines,** by far the largest category of titles, target business readers. They include *trade publications* for retailers, wholesalers, and other distributors *(Progressive Grocer, Packaging World); business* and *industrial magazines* for businesspeople involved in manufacturing and services *(Electronic Design, American Banker);* and *professional journals* for lawyers, physicians, architects, and other professionals *(Archives of Ophthalmology).*

Geography

A magazine may also be classified as *local, regional,* or *national.* Today, most major U.S. cities have a **local city magazine:** *San Diego Magazine, New York, Los Angeles, Chicago, Palm Springs Life.* Their readership is usually upscale business and professional people interested in local arts, fashion, and business.

Regional publications are targeted to a specific area of the country, such as the West or the South: *Sunset, Southern Living.* National magazines sometimes provide special market runs for specific geographic regions. *Time, Newsweek, Woman's Day,* and *Sports Illustrated* allow advertisers to buy a single major market. Exhibit 12-3 shows the nine major geographic breakdowns of regional editions of *U.S. News.* This is important for local or regional advertisers who want the benefit of advertising in larger, more well-known publications while staying geographically relevant to the audience that may be reading the magazine.

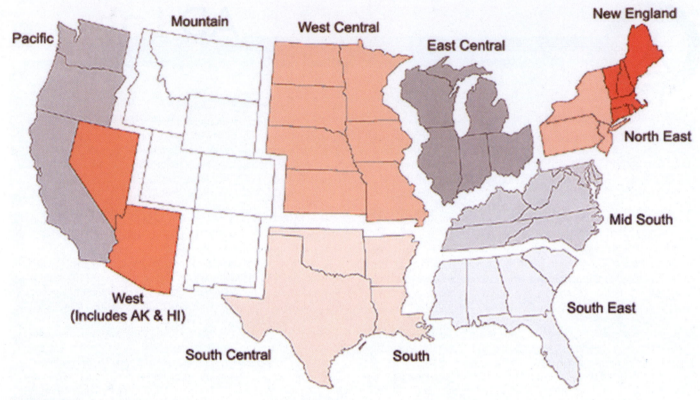

Exhibit 12-3
Advertisers benefit from selecting regional print editions similar to the nine geographic regions shown on the map. With regional binding and mailing, advertisers can buy ad space for only the amount of distribution they need.
Source: U.S. News & World Report, L.P., 2007.

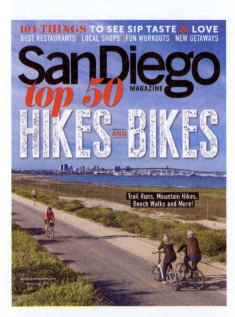

Magazines that cater to specific geographic areas are regional publications. Most metropolitan areas publish magazines specific to their city. San Diego Magazine gives its readers information on everything they need to know about San Diego from the best places to dine, shop, and even hike and bike.
Source: SDM, LLC

National magazines range from those with enormous circulations, such as *TV Guide,* to small, lesser-known national magazines, such as *Nature* and *Volleyball.* The largest circulation magazine in the United States today is *AARP The Magazine,* distributed to the 22.4 million members of the AARP.[14]

Size

It doesn't take a genius to figure out that magazines come in different shapes and sizes, but it might take one to figure out how to get one ad to run in different-size magazines and still look the same. Magazine sizes run the gamut, which can make production standardization a nightmare. The most common magazine sizes follow:

Size Classification	Magazine	Approximate Size of Full-Page Ad
Large	*Spin, Rolling Stone*	4 col. × 170 lines (9½ × 11⅓ inches)
Flat	*People, Entertainment Weekly*	3 col. × 140 lines (7 × 10 inches)
Standard	*National Geographic*	2 col. × 119 lines (6 × 8½ inches)
Digest	*Reader's Digest, Jet*	2 col. × 91 lines (4½ × 6½ inches)

Buying Magazine Space

When analyzing a magazine, media buyers consider readership, cost, mechanical requirements, and ad closing dates (deadlines). Information about these statistics is included in a magazine's **rate card.**

Understanding Magazine Circulation

LO 12-2

The first step in analyzing a publication's potential effectiveness is to assess its audience. The buyer studies circulation statistics, primary and secondary readership, subscription and vendor sales, and any special merchandising services the magazine offers.

Guaranteed versus Delivered Circulation

A magazine's rates are partially based on its circulation. The **rate base** is the circulation figure on which the publisher bases its rates; the **guaranteed circulation** is the number of copies the publisher expects to circulate. This assures advertisers they will reach a certain number of people. If the publisher does not reach its *delivered figure,* it must provide a refund. For that reason, guaranteed circulation figures are often stated safely below the average actual circulation. However, this is not always true. Circulation actually gets overstated more often than people think. As many as 30 percent of consumer magazines audited by the **Alliance for Audited Media (AAM),** formerly the Audit Bureau of Circulation (ABC), each year don't meet the circulation levels they guarantee to advertisers.[15]

So media buyers expect publications to verify their circulation figures. Publishers pay thousands of dollars each year for a **circulation audit**—a thorough analysis of the circulation procedures, outlets of distribution, readers, and other factors—by companies such as AAM. Directories such as those published by Standard Rate & Data Service (SRDS) feature the logo of the auditing company in each listing for an audited magazine.

Primary and Secondary Readership

Data from the AAM or other verified reports tell the media buyer the magazine's total circulation. This **primary circulation** represents the number of people who buy the publication, either by subscription or at the newsstand. **Secondary (or pass-along) readership,** which is an estimate determined by market research of how many people read a single issue of a publication, is very important to magazines. Some have more than six readers per copy. Multiplying the average pass-along readership by, say, a million subscribers can give a magazine a substantial audience beyond its primary readers.

Vertical and Horizontal Publications

Business publications are classified in two ways based on readership: *vertical* and *horizontal.* A **vertical publication** covers a specific industry in all its aspects. For example, Cahners Publishing produces *Restaurants & Institutions* strictly for restaurateurs and food-service operators. The magazine's editorial content includes everything from news of the restaurant industry to institutional-size recipes.

Horizontal publications, in contrast, deal with a particular job function across a variety of industries. Readers of *Purchasing* work in purchasing management in many different industries. Horizontal trade publications are very effective advertising vehicles because they usually offer excellent reach and they tend to be well read.[16]

Subscription and Vendor Sales

Media buyers also want to know a magazine's ratio of subscriptions to newsstand sales. Today, subscriptions account for the majority of magazine sales. Newsstands (which include bookstore chains) are still a major outlet for single-copy sales, but no outlet can handle more than a fraction of the many magazines available.

From the advertiser's point of view, newsstand sales are impressive because they indicate that the purchaser really wants the

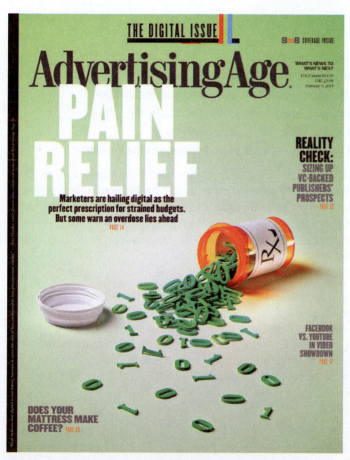

Advertising Age is a good example of a vertical publication. The magazine is geared toward a variety of issues specific to the advertising industry. Unlike horizontal publications, which focus on a single job function across various industries, Ad Age is read by a wide range of people throughout the industry.

Source: Crain Communications

magazine and is not merely subscribing out of habit. According to the Magazine Publishers Association, single-copy sales account for 34 percent of total revenues for a representative sampling of leading magazines.

Paid and Controlled Circulation

Business publications may be distributed on either a *paid-circulation* or *controlled-circulation* basis. A paid basis means the recipient pays to receive the magazine. *Bloomberg Businessweek* is a **paid-circulation** business magazine.

In **controlled circulation,** the publisher delivers the magazine free to individuals believed important to advertisers. Executives at *Fortune* 1000 corporations receive a *strategy + business* magazine. To qualify for the free subscription, people must specify that they want to receive the magazine and must give their professional title and information about the size of their company. Dues-paying members of organizations often get free subscriptions. For example, members of the National Association for Female Executives receive free copies of *Executive Female.*

Publishers of paid-circulation magazines say subscribers who pay are more likely to read a publication than those who receive it free. But controlled-circulation magazines can reach valuable prospects for the goods and services they advertise.

Merchandising Services: Added Value

Magazines, and newspapers too, often provide liberal *added-value services* to their regular advertisers, such as:

- Special free promotions to stores.
- Marketing services to help readers find local outlets.
- Response cards that allow readers to request brochures and catalogs.
- Help handling sales force, broker, wholesaler, and retailer meetings.
- Advance editions for the trade.
- Research into brand preferences, consumer attitudes, and market conditions.

If a publication's basic factors—editorial, circulation, and readership—are strong, these additional services can increase the effectiveness of its ads.[17] Magazines offer great potential for relationship marketing because they already have a relationship with their subscribers. New added-value options might include using magazines' custom publishing, editorial, and production knowledge, along with their databases, to help clients develop videos, books, and websites that create added value for the brand.[18]

Reading Rate Cards

Magazine rate cards follow a standard format. This helps advertisers determine costs, discounts, mechanical requirements, closing dates, special editions, and additional costs for features like color, inserts, bleed pages, split runs, or preferred positions.

Three dates affect magazine purchases. The **cover date** is the date printed on the cover. The **on-sale date** is the date the magazine is actually issued. And the **closing date** is the date all ad material must be in the publisher's hands for a specific issue. Lead time may be as much as three months.

Rates

As we discussed in Chapter 9, one way to compare magazines is to look at how much it costs to reach a thousand people based on the magazine's rates for a one-time, full-page ad. You compute the **cost per thousand (CPM)** by dividing the full-page rate by the number of *thousands* of subscribers:

$$\frac{\text{Page rate}}{(\text{Circulation} \div 1,000)} = \text{CPM}$$

If the magazine's black-and-white page rate is $10,000, and the publication has a circulation of 500,000, then:

$$\frac{\$10,000}{500,000 \div 1,000} = \frac{\$10,000}{500} = \$20 \text{ CPM}$$

Consider this comparison. Recently the page rate for a full-color, one-page ad in *Car & Driver* was $196,632 on total paid circulation of 1,200,000. *Road & Track* offered the same ad for $105,309 on total paid circulation of 600,000. Which was the better buy on a CPM basis (keeping in mind that lower is better)?[19]

Discounts

Magazines and newspapers often give discounts. **Frequency discounts** are based on the number of ad insertions, usually within a year; **volume discounts** are based on the total amount of space bought during a specific period. Most magazines also offer *cash discounts* (usually 2 percent) to advertisers who pay right away, and some offer discounts on the purchase of four or more consecutive pages in a single issue. In fact, many magazine publishers now negotiate their rates. According to publisher Harold Shain, "Every piece of business is negotiated."[20]

Premium Rates

Magazines charge extra for special features. Color normally costs 25 to 60 percent more than black and white. Some publications, such as *Money,* even offer metallic inks and special colors. Bleed pages can add as much as 20 percent to regular rates, although the typical increase is about 15 percent.

Second and third cover rates (the inside covers) typically cost less than the fourth (back) cover. According to SRDS, however, in 2008, *ESPN the Magazine* charged $208,000 for a normal color page, $457,600 for the second cover, and $270,400 for the fourth cover.[21]

Magazines charge different rates for ads in geographic or demographic issues. **Geographic editions** target geographic markets; **demographic editions** reach readers who share a demographic trait, such as age, income level, or professional status. *Time* offers one-page, four-color ads (one-time insertion) in its Boston edition for $21,495 (135,000 circulation) and in its New York edition for $34,708. For full-page, four-color ads, advertisers in the top management edition pay $90,000 (circulation 805,489). To run the same ad in *Time Gold,* which is targeted to baby boomers and has a circulation of more than 1 million, advertisers pay $69,000.

Software for Buying Print Media

One of the most important tasks in advertising is the placement of ads in various media. So the role of the media buyer is critical to the overall success of the campaign.

Placing an ad in a magazine or newspaper is not as easy as it may seem, especially when there are hundreds of newspapers and magazines around the country with different deadlines, different mechanical requirements, and different rates. To say the least, the job can be very tedious and time-consuming.

Fortunately, thanks to technology, print media buyers now have a variety of software programs available to assist them.

STRATA Marketing Inc., for example, has developed media-buying software for each form of media. Its print software programs offer media buyers various ways to keep track of orders, clients, and rate information, while providing a large variety of formats for insertion order reports. This program also allows media buyers to copy insertion orders to numerous publications, all with a single keystroke.

These programs, and others similar in function, save media buyers a lot of time, thereby increasing productivity and efficiency. More time can be spent analyzing information, evaluating various print vehicles, and exercising creativity. By using software like this, media buyers gain flexibility and control over the placement of ads in print media.

People BEHIND the Ads

Nancy Berger Cardone, VP/Publisher and CRO at _Marie Claire_

Courtesy of Nancy Berger Cardone

When _Advertising Age_ wrote that "_Marie Claire_ keeps on outdoing itself," it gave much of the credit to VP, Publisher, and Chief Revenue Officer Nancy Berger Cardone and her team. In fact, it named her Publisher of the Year and placed her on the Magazine A-List. When CA spoke with Nancy, we knew she would have energy, passion for her job, and excitement about the future. But Nancy's real secret is a talent for great ideas every bit as developed and sophisticated as that of a top agency creative director. Evidence? _Marie Claire_ has little trouble attracting conventional "women's" brands. But Nancy drove ad growth by showing the value of _Marie Claire_ to brands that often don't target the magazine's readers, such as Ruth's Chris Steak Houses. We asked Nancy to tell us a bit about her job and to offer advice to those who will follow in her footsteps.

CA: Describe the culture of your group at Marie Claire.

NBC: _MC_ is a media brand in the print, digital, social, broadcast, and event space. We have a total audience of 16 million educated, stylish, and influential women across all channels. The magazine is the largest piece of our revenue, but other platforms are growing quickly. _Marie Claire_ is a global brand, published in 33 additional countries around the world. We are an organization of passionate media executives who are committed to innovation, relevance, and story telling.

CA: Describe a "typical" day that highlights your career responsibilities.

NBC: We publish the magazine on a monthly basis, and close each issue two months ahead of the month published on the cover. Our digital and social closing dates are more timed to the actual delivery of the communications, so in effect, we are constantly closing business. My day consists of a lot of meetings, internal and external. I typically have a business breakfast and lunch appointment every day. I travel about 25 percent of the time around the country (bigger advertising markets like Chicago, Dallas, San Francisco, Los Angeles), as well as internationally (mostly London, Paris, and Milan). I consume a lot of media, to stay on top of what is happening in the industries that affect my business.

CA: What are the most important changes taking place in media selling today? How will things be different in the future?

NBC: When I started in this business, my job was to sell advertising pages and that was it. And my competition was other magazines. Today, we are selling content on all delivery channels and competing for marketing dollars within every media category. A typical sale today encompasses multiple engagement points to bring an advertiser closer to our audience. We host events, create advertising, do custom research, connect and create marketing partnerships, create ideas, create ownership opportunities for clients. And the sale is on-going all year long. The future will continue to evolve and change as new products and measurement tools are being developed.

CA: How important is approaching selling from an IMC perspective? From a global perspective? Would you say it is increasing in importance? How can students become more globally aware?

NBC: _Marie Claire_ is a global brand and a majority of our advertisers are also global brands. In the past, each country has operated independently, but we have all realized the benefits of communicating with a common position and DNA around the world. As clients begin to do this more as well, we have been able to spearhead some exciting global initiatives. We have had great successes over the past few years, and look forward to continuing this momentum on the global stage.

CA: What do you look for in new talent?

NBC: I look for ambition. I look for creativity and pro-activeness. I look for a strong work ethic. I want to see a passion for the work. I want someone who always wants to learn and improve. I respect someone who wants my job one day.

CA: What is the most enjoyable part of your job?

NBC: I love mentoring people. I love creating things/ideas that have never been done before. I love finding a white-space opportunity and filling it. I love interacting with other informed and passionate people.

CA: What should a university student be doing to prepare to follow in your footsteps someday?

NBC: A university student should always bring a strong sense of curiosity, ambition, and knowledge that they have honed throughout their years at university into the workforce.

CA: What do you do in your spare time?

NBC: I do a lot of charity work. My youngest son, Jakob, was diagnosed with Type 1 diabetes 5 years ago, and I am committed to raising funds and awareness. I am addicted to Soul Cycle. I love to cook, spend time with my family, travel, and learn new things.

CA: What is your favorite place in the world?

NBC: My favorite place in the world is home.

My second favorite place in the world is Italy . . . for the people, for the food, and for the shoes!

Used with permission of Nancy Berger Cardone.

Using Newspapers in the Creative Mix

When a small, alternative newspaper in New York asked one of the hottest creative shops in the city for help in promoting subscriptions, it had no idea what the little agency with the funny name, Mad Dogs & Englishmen, would do for it.

The *Village Voice* newspaper had always knocked the Establishment with its opinionated coverage of social issues, politics, media, and culture. So perhaps it shouldn't have come as a surprise when the Mad Dogs took the newspaper's own prose style and turned it around in a series of impertinent, self-mocking ads.

"Hell, I wouldn't have my home contaminated with a subscription to your elitist rag if you were giving away five-speed blenders," rants one ad in the series. "You people think New York is the friggin' center of the world." But then a second paragraph offers a dramatic alternative: "YES, I want to buy a year's subscription to the *Village Voice,*" along with a coupon.

The paper's readers aren't spared either. One ad skewers New Age tree-huggers: "Murderers! Trees are being systematically swallowed up by the jaws of industry and still you insist I take part in this horror by subscribing?"

Mad Dogs principal Nick Cohen said he thought the *Voice* would like the campaign because the newspaper is honest. "It really stands behind the freedom of the writers, even when they criticize the management itself," he said.

Selecting the medium was easy. Because most people who would be interested in a subscription are *Village Voice* readers, the campaign ran in the paper itself. It proved to be a wise choice. In the first year of the campaign, the *Voice* saw a 30 percent increase in its subscriber base, surpassing all expectations.[22]

Who Uses Newspapers?

Newspapers are now the third-largest medium (after television and magazines) in terms of advertising volume, receiving 13.7 percent of the dollars spent by advertisers in the United States.[23]

Newspapers can be an important medium in the creative mix, when used strategically.
Source: Home Box Office, Inc.

Rank	Advertiser	Newspaper Ad Spending in 2017 ($ in Billions)
1	News Corp.	$83
2	Andersen Corp.	83
3	Macy's	76
4	Rooms To Go	55
5	LVMH Moet Hennessy Louis Vuitton	55
6	Realogy Holdings Corp.	51
7	Comcast Corp.	50
8	Target Corp.	49
9	Berkshire Hathaway	48
10	Kohl's Corp.	43

Exhibit 12-4

Top Newspaper Advertisers

Source: Advertising Age Fact Pack, "200 Leading National Advertisers 2018 Fact Pack," Crain Communications.

Consider these important facts:

- The total circulation of newspapers (digital and print combined) is 31 million each weekday and 34 million on Sundays.[24]

- Advertising revenue for the U.S. newspaper industry is about $16.5 billion as of 2018, down from a high of nearly $50 billion in 2006.[25]

- About 23% of Americans questioned said they read a print newspaper the previous day (the survey was administered in 2012), a drop of 18 points over a 10-year period.[26]

- The median age of a person reading a daily newspaper as of 2017 is 58. Newspaper website visitors are younger, with a median age of 41.[27]

- Newspaper readers, according to Nielsen, are more likely to be college graduates and have six-figure incomes than are nonreaders. This is especially true of digital editions.[28]

Although the newspaper is an important community-serving medium for both news and advertising, national advertisers are shifting to radio and television. As a result, radio and TV carry most of the national advertising in the United States, while 84 percent of newspaper advertising revenue comes from local advertising. As Exhibit 12-4 shows, a diverse group of brands is represented among top national advertisers in newspapers.

The Pros and Cons of Newspaper Advertising

LO **12-4**

The *Village Voice* promotion shows how small businesses with even smaller budgets can benefit from creative newspaper advertising. Print ads in general and newspapers in particular provide a unique, flexible medium for advertisers to express their creativity—especially with businesses that rely on local customers.

Newspapers offer advertisers many advantages. One of the most important is *timeliness;* an ad can appear very quickly, sometimes in just one day. Newspapers also offer geographic targeting, a broad range of markets, reasonable cost, and more. But newspapers suffer from lack of selectivity, poor production quality, and clutter. And readers criticize them for lack of depth and follow-up on important issues.[29]

Use My IMC Campaign 12–B, "The Pros and Cons of Newspaper Advertising," to answer the questions in Ad Lab 12–C, "Newspapers and the Creative Mix."

How Newspapers Are Categorized

LO **12-5**

Newspapers can be classified by *frequency of delivery, physical size,* or *type of audience.*

Frequency of Delivery

A **daily newspaper** is published as either a morning or evening edition at least five times a week, Monday through Friday. Of the 1,400 or so dailies in the United States, most are morning papers.[30] Morning editions tend to have broader geographic circulation and a larger male readership; evening editions are read more by women.

With their emphasis on local news and advertising, **weekly newspapers** characteristically serve small urban or suburban residential areas and farm communities. Although not as well known as dailies, there are many more weekly papers in the U.S., almost 7,000. A weekly newspaper's cost per thousand is usually higher than a daily paper's, but a weekly has a longer life and often has more readers per copy.

Physical Size

There are two basic newspaper formats, standard size and tabloid. The **standard-size newspaper** is about 22 inches deep and 13 inches wide and is divided into six columns. The **tabloid newspaper** is generally about 14 inches deep and 11 inches wide. National tabloid newspapers such as the *National Enquirer* and the *Star* use sensational stories to fight for single-copy sales. Other tabloids, such as the *New York Post,* emphasize straight news and features.

My IMC Campaign 12-B

The Pros and Cons of Newspaper Advertising

The Pros

- **Mass medium** penetrating every segment of society. Most consumers read the newspaper.
- **Local medium** with broad reach. Covers a specific geographic area that comprises both a market and a community of people sharing common concerns and interest.
- **Comprehensive in scope,** covering an extraordinary variety of topics and interests.
- **Geographic selectivity** is possible with zoned editions for specific neighborhoods or communities.
- **Timeliness.** Papers primarily cover today's news and are read in one day.
- **Credibility.** Studies show that newspaper ads rank highest in believability. TV commercials are a distant second.
- **Selective attention** from the relatively small number of active prospects who, on any given day, are interested in what the advertiser is trying to tell them or sell them.
- **Creative flexibility.** An ad's physical size and shape can be varied to give the degree of dominance or repetition that suits the advertiser's purpose. The advertiser can use black and white, color, Sunday magazines, or custom inserts.

- **An active medium** rather than a passive one. Readers turn the pages, clip and save, write in the margins, and sort through the contents.
- **A permanent record,** in contrast to the ephemeral nature of radio and TV.
- **Reasonable cost.**

The Cons

- **Declining circulation,** especially among young and diverse audiences. Many consumers get their news elsewhere.
- **Lack of selectivity** of specific socioeconomic groups. Most newspapers reach broad, diverse groups of readers, which may not match the advertiser's objectives.
- **Short life span.** Unless readers clip and save the ad or coupon, it may be lost forever.
- **Low production quality.** Coarse newsprint generally produces a less impressive image than the slick, smooth paper stock of magazines. Weekly papers are sometimes still printed in black and white.
- **Clutter.** Each ad competes with editorial content and with all the other ads on the same page or spread.
- **Lack of control** over where the ad will appear unless the advertiser pays extra for a preferred position.

Newspapers used to offer about 400 different ad sizes. But in 1984, the industry introduced the **standard advertising unit (SAU)** system, which standardized the newspaper column width, page sizes, and ad sizes. An SAU **column inch** is $2\frac{1}{16}$ inches wide by 1 inch deep. There are now 56 standard ad sizes for standard papers and 32 for tabloids. Virtually all dailies converted to the SAU system (some at great expense) and so did most weeklies.

Type of Audience

Some dailies and weeklies serve special-interest audiences, a fact not lost on advertisers. They generally contain advertising oriented to their special audiences, and they may have unique advertising regulations.

Some serve specific ethnic markets. Today, more than 200 dailies and weeklies are oriented to the African American community. Others serve foreign-language groups. In the United States, newspapers are printed in 43 languages other than English.

Specialized newspapers also serve business and financial audiences. *The Wall Street Journal,* the leading national business and financial daily, enjoys a circulation of 1.8 million. Other papers cater to fraternal, labor union, or professional organizations, religious groups, or hobbyists.

Other Types of Newspapers

The United States has 919 Sunday newspapers, mostly Sunday editions of daily papers, with a combined circulation of about 34 million.[31] Sunday newspapers generally combine standard news coverage with special functions like these:

- Increased volume of classified ads.
- Greater advertising and news volume.

AD Lab 12-C

Newspapers and the Creative Mix

Study My IMC Campaign 12–B, "The Pros and Cons of Newspaper Advertising," and see if you can apply that information to the following situation:

You're the product manager for a major brand of bar soap and you wish to go nationwide with an ad featuring a coupon.

Laboratory Applications

1. Which newspaper would be best?
   a. A weekly.   b. A daily.

2. If you use a daily, in what section of the paper do you want your ad to appear?

3. If you decided on the Sunday supplement, which of the following would you choose and why?
   a. *Parade* magazine.   b. Color coupon insert.

Newspapers create special sections. In turn, these are attractive to advertisers interested in their unique readership. The Sunday Times *is Britain's largest-selling Sunday newspaper. The* Sunday Times *also publishes several supplement magazines, including* The Sunday Times Rich List, The Sunday Times Magazine, *and* The Sunday Times Travel Magazine.

Source: The Sunday Times

- In-depth coverage of business, sports, real estate, literature and the arts, entertainment, and travel.
- Review and analysis of the past week's events.
- Expanded editorial and opinion sections.

Most Sunday newspapers also feature a **Sunday supplement** magazine. Some publish their own supplement, such as *Los Angeles Magazine* of the *Los Angeles Times.* Other papers subscribe to syndicated supplements; *Parade* magazine has a readership of more than 54 million based on a circulation of 22 million.[32]

Printed by rotogravure on heavier, coated paper stock, Sunday supplements are more conducive to color printing than newsprint, making them attractive to national advertisers who want better reproduction quality.

Another type of newspaper, the **independent shopping guide** or free community newspaper, offers advertisers local saturation. Sometimes called *pennysavers,* these shoppers offer free distribution and extensive advertising pages targeted at essentially the same audience as weekly newspapers—urban and suburban community readers. Readership is often high, and the publishers use hand delivery or direct mail to achieve maximum saturation.

North Americans also read national newspapers, including the *Globe and Mail* in Canada, *USA Today,* and the *Christian Science Monitor.* With a circulation of 2.3 million, *The Wall Street Journal* is the largest national newspaper, followed by *The New York Times* (2.2 million) and *USA Today* (1.0 million).[33]

Types of Newspaper Advertising

The major classifications of newspaper advertising are *display, classified, public notices,* and *preprinted inserts.*

Display Advertising

LO 12-6

Display advertising includes copy, illustrations or photos, headlines, coupons, and other visual components—such as the ads for the *Village Voice* discussed earlier. Display ads vary in size and appear in all sections of the newspaper except the first page of major sections, the editorial page, the obituary page, and the classified advertising section.

One common variation of the display ad, the **reading notice,** looks like editorial matter and sometimes costs more than normal display advertising. To prevent readers from mistaking it for editorial matter, the word *advertisement* appears at the top.

As we discussed in Chapters 4 and 6, retailers often run newspaper campaigns through **cooperative (or co-op) advertising** sponsored by the manufacturers whose products they sell. The manufacturer pays fully or partially to create and run the ad, which features the manufacturer's product and logo along with the local retailer's name and address.

Classified Advertising

Classified ads provide a community marketplace for goods, services, and opportunities of every type, from real estate and new-car sales to employment and business opportunities. A newspaper's profitability often depends on a large and healthy classified section.

Classified ads usually appear under subheads that describe the class of goods or the need the ads seek to satisfy. Most employment, housing, and car advertising is classified. To promote the use of classified ads in the *Village Voice,* Mad Dogs & Englishmen created a series of display ads that used humorous "Situation Wanted" ads as the main visuals.

Classified rates are typically based on how many lines the ad occupies and how many times the ad runs. Some newspapers accept **classified display ads,** which run in the classified section of the newspaper but feature larger type and/or photos, art borders, abundant white space, and sometimes even color.

Public Notices

For a nominal fee, newspapers carry legal **public notices** of changes in business and personal relationships, public governmental reports, notices by private citizens and organizations, and financial reports. These ads follow a preset format.

Preprinted Inserts

Like magazines, newspapers carry **preprinted inserts.** The advertiser prints the inserts and delivers them to the newspaper plant for insertion into a specific edition. Insert sizes range from a typical newspaper page to a double postcard; formats include catalogs, brochures, mail-back devices, and perforated coupons.

Some large metropolitan dailies allow advertisers to limit their inserts to specific circulation zones. A retail advertiser that wants to reach only those shoppers in its immediate trading area can place an insert in the local-zone editions. Retail stores, car dealers, and large national advertisers are among those who find it less costly to distribute their circulars this way compared to mailing them or delivering them door to door.

Ads that provoke an emotional reaction are often developed for video. But as this ad for McDonald's shows, print can be creatively exploited to do the same thing. This ad, with the headline "Leave your Morning Mood Behind," playfully illustrates the power of print advertising. Do you think this style of print advertising would be effective in newspapers? What type of newspaper would you run this advertisement in?

Source: McDonald's

Buying Newspaper Space

To get the most from the advertising budget, the media buyer must know the characteristics of a newspaper's readership: the median age, sex, occupation, income, educational level, and buying habits of the typical reader.

Understanding Readership and Circulation

LO 12-7

Readership information is available from most newspapers and is often verified by the Alliance for Audited Media in the U.S. Most large papers also provide extensive data on print and digital subscribers.

In single-newspaper cities, reader demographics typically reflect a cross section of the general population. In cities with two or more newspapers, however, these characteristics may vary widely. The *Los Angeles Times* is directed to a broad cross section of the community while *La Opinion* targets L.A.'s large Hispanic population.

Advertisers must understand the full extent of the newspaper's circulation. The paper's total circulation includes subscribers and single-copy newsstand buyers, as well as secondary readers.

Rate Cards

Like the magazine rate card, the newspaper **rate card** lists advertising rates, mechanical and copy requirements, deadlines, and other information. Because rates vary greatly, advertisers should calculate which papers deliver the most readers and the best demographics for their money.

Local versus National Rates

Many newspapers charge local and national advertisers different rates. The **national rate** can be as much as 75 percent higher.[34] Newspapers attribute higher rates to the added costs of serving national advertisers. For instance, an ad agency usually places national advertising and receives a 15 percent commission from the paper.

But many national advertisers reject the high rates and take their business elsewhere. Only a small percentage of national ad money now goes to newspapers.[35] In response to declining national advertising revenue, newspapers are experimenting with simplified billing systems and discount rates for their national clients.

Newspapers are also revising their business models in response to the collapse of advertising revenue. Led by *The New York Times,* many papers are charging more for subscriptions to remain in business.[36]

Flat Rates and Discount Rates

Many national papers charge **flat rates,** which means they allow no discounts; a few newspapers offer a single flat rate to both national and local advertisers.

Newspapers that offer volume discounts have an **open rate** (their highest rate for a one-time insertion) and **contract rates,** whereby local advertisers can obtain discounts of up to 70 percent by signing a contract for frequent or bulk space purchases. **Bulk discounts** offer advertisers decreasing rates (calculated by multiplying the number of inches by the cost per inch) as they use more inches. Advertisers earn **frequency discounts** by running a given ad repeatedly in a specific time period. Similarly, advertisers can sometimes get **earned rates,** a discount applied retroactively as the volume of advertising increases through the year. Many newspapers also participate in Newsplan, a program that gives national and regional advertisers discounts for purchasing six or more pages per year.

Short Rate

An advertiser who contracts to buy a specific amount of space during a one-year period at a discount and then fails to fulfill the promise is charged a **short rate,** which is the difference between the contracted rate and the earned rate for the actual inches run. Conversely, an advertiser who buys more inches than contracted may be entitled to a rebate or credit because of the discounted earned rate for the additional advertising space.

Combination Rates

Combination rates are often available for placing a given ad in (1) morning and evening editions of the same newspaper; (2) two or more newspapers owned by the same publisher; and (3) in some cases, two or more newspapers affiliated in a syndicate or newspaper group.

Run of Paper versus Preferred Position

Run-of-paper (ROP) advertising rates entitle a newspaper to place a given ad on any newspaper page or in any position it desires. Although the advertiser has no control over where the ad appears in the paper, most newspapers try to place an ad in the position the advertiser requests.

The advertising rates for Pacific NW, a magazine publication of the Seattle Times, shows the ad units that are available along with their costs.

Source: The Seattle Times Company

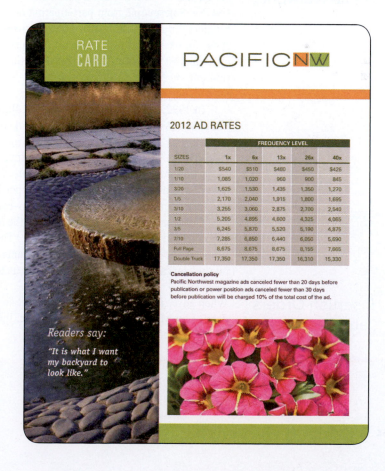

An advertiser can ensure a choice position for an ad by paying a higher **preferred-position rate.** A tire manufacturer, for example, may pay the preferred rate to ensure a position in the sports section.

There are also preferred positions on a given page. The preferred position near the top of a page or at the top of a column next to reading matter is called **full position.** It's usually surrounded by reading matter and may cost the advertiser 25 to 50 percent more than ROP rates. Slightly less desirable is placement *next to reading matter (NR),* which generally costs 10 to 20 percent more than ROP rates.

Color Advertising

Color advertising is available in many newspapers on an ROP basis. Because of their high-speed presses and porous paper stock, newspapers are not noted for high-quality color printing. So advertisers frequently preprint ads using processes known as HiFi color and Spectracolor. The cost of a color ad is usually based on the black-and-white rate plus an extra charge for each additional color.

Split Runs

Many newspapers (and magazines) offer **split runs** so that advertisers can test the *pulling power* of different ads. The advertiser runs two ads of identical size, but different content, for the same product on the same day in the same or different press runs. The idea is to eliminate as many variables as possible. By measuring responses to the two ads, the advertiser is able to compare and contrast the effectiveness of each. For this service, newspapers typically charge extra and set a minimum space requirement.

Co-ops and Networks

As an aid to national advertisers, the NAB created the Newspaper Co-op Network (NCN). Salespeople from participating newspapers helped national advertisers line up retailers for dealer-listing ads. The advertiser would produce the ad and include a blank space for each paper to insert local retailers' names. The system also helped manufacturers manage local advertising tie-ins to national campaigns and themes. Before the development of NCN, national advertisers had to place ads and recruit local dealers individually.

In 1992, the Newspaper Advertising Bureau merged with the American Newspaper Publishers Association and five other marketing associations to form the Newspaper Association of America. More recently the group has reorganized under a new name, the **News Media Alliance (NMA),** which continues to simplify national newspaper ad buys. In 1994, the group launched a *one-order, one-bill system* for national advertising, allowing advertisers to make multimarket newspaper buys by placing one order and paying one bill, instead of having to contact—and pay—each paper individually.

Chrysler was the first marketer to use the new network, placing ads for its national mini-van sale in 75 newspapers in March 1994.[38] The Newspaper National Network offers advertisers competitive CPM pricing and guaranteed positioning, in addition to its one-order, one-bill appeal.[39] It also allows smaller papers to participate in national advertising.[40]

Insertion Orders and Tearsheets

When advertisers place an ad, they submit an **insertion order** to the newspaper stating the date(s) on which the ad is to run, its size, the desired position, the rate, and the type of artwork accompanying the order.

Ethics, Diversity & Inclusion

What's at Stake with Sweepstakes?

Have you ever received an envelope in the mail with the phrase "You Are a Winner!"—or something similar—plastered in large, bold type behind the front window? Perhaps, for a split second you believed that you had won the $100,000 prize. Then you discovered the disclosure, in tiny, almost-unreadable print, telling you otherwise. There have been some who didn't notice the disclosure and traveled to the sweepstakes' headquarters believing that they had won the jackpot. Others, believing that purchasing advertised products would increase their chances of winning, spent thousands of dollars on magazine subscriptions. Were these people deceived?

Although any company can use sweepstakes, it was magazine publishers that were the most frequent user—and beneficiary of consumer confusion.

According to the Direct Marketing Association, sweepstakes are, by definition, "an advertising or promotional device by which items of value (prizes) are awarded to participating consumers by chance, with no purchase or 'entry fee' required in order to win."[37] However, by entering a sweepstakes you are volunteering your name, address, and possible tastes in the advertised product to be put on lists for other direct marketers to acquire. In turn, you are offered a chance to win what can seem like easy money. For years it was difficult for recipients to tell whether or not they had a winning entry. With statements claiming "You are a winner," simulated checks, and material resembling communications from the government, the line separating promotion and deception became very thin.

All of this changed in 2000. Following investigations of sweepstakes firms in more than 40 states, state regulators took three of the biggest sweeps marketers—Publisher's Clearing House (PCH), Time Inc., and U.S. Sales Corp.—to court, alleging that their promotions were deceptive. In California alone, state officials claimed that 5,000 consumers spent more than $2,500 each a year in unnecessary magazine subscriptions through PCH because they believed that it improved their odds of winning. The companies defended their marketing practices, claiming they believed their mailings were clear. One PCH spokesperson stated that 98 percent of the consumers who purchased magazines through their promotions spent less than $300 a year. But in the end each company decided to settle and agreed to reform its practices. Combined, the companies refunded more than $50 million in fines and restitution to state regulators and consumers.

The reforms these companies agreed to were in accord with the Deceptive Mail Prevention and Enforcement Act that became effective in April 2000. The act changed how direct-mail sweepstakes are presented and packaged. Among the most significant changes were abandoning any "winner" proclamations unless the recipient had truly won a prize and displaying a "fact box" that "clearly and conspicuously" explained all the terms and rules of the sweepstakes, including the odds of winning. Each mailing was also required to include the statements "No purchase is necessary to enter" and "A purchase does not improve your chances of winning" in boldfaced capital letters in the mailing, in the rules, and on the order/entry form itself.

The legislation largely ended the practice. Only Publisher's Clearing House now uses sweepstakes to promote magazines. This may be because the law had teeth. In 2010 Publisher's Clearing House paid a $3.5 million fine for violating the agreement.

How much harm, if any, are sweepstakes really causing? Some sweepstakes, such as McDonald's Monopoly game, strike many as fun and harmless. And isn't part of promotion getting consumers to believe that they want what is being advertised? Without question, the ethical issues involved are complicated, but at least now you won't have to read the fine print to get the whole story.

Now that state governments have ended most sweepstakes, what has taken their place? A case can be made that it has been state lotteries. Indeed, the decline of sweepstakes correlates almost perfectly with the growth of lotteries. From 2009 to 2016, lottery sales jumped from $58 billion to almost $81 billion.

Questions

1. Are sweepstakes companies really at fault for misleading their consumers? Why or why not?

2. Do you believe it is ethical for sweepstakes to "disguise" their promotions for the purpose of advertising?

3. Are lotteries more ethical than sweepstakes? Why or why not?

An insertion order serves as a contract between the advertiser (or its agency) and the publication. If an advertiser fails to pay the agency, the agency still must pay the publication. To avoid this liability, many agencies now place a disclaimer on their insertion orders stating that they are acting solely as an *agent for a disclosed principal* (legal terminology meaning the agency is just a representative for the advertiser and is therefore not liable for the payment). Some publications refuse to accept insertion orders with disclaimers unless payment accompanies the order. In 1991, the American Association of Advertising Agencies recommended to its agency members that they no longer accept sole liability for their clients' bills.[41] However, many agencies do still accept liability, perhaps out of some insecurity about possibly losing their agency commission—or their client.

When a newspaper creates ad copy and art, it gives the advertiser a **proof copy** to check. In contrast, most national advertising arrives at the newspaper *camera ready,* either in the form of a photo print or an electronic file via e-mail. To verify that the ad ran, the newspaper tears out the page on which the ad appeared and sends it to the agency or advertiser. Today, most **tearsheets** for national advertisers are handled through a private central office, the Advertising Checking Bureau.

When a tearsheet arrives, the advertiser examines it to make sure the ad ran according to instructions: in the right section and page position, and with the correct reproduction. If the ad did not run per instructions, the agency or advertiser is usually due an adjustment, a discount, or even a free rerun.

Producing Ads for Print

In advertising, production refers to the steps between a draft of an ad to the finished version that is shown to consumers. The **print production process** varies according to whether manual or computerized processes are used. For a simple model of this process, see Exhibit 12-5.

The Preproduction Phase: Planning the Project

The first step, **preproduction,** begins when the creative department submits the approved creative concepts—rough or comprehensive layout and copy—to the production department. The production department's first task is to consider the general nature of the job and answer several questions pertinent to managing it efficiently. For example,

- What equipment will be needed?
- How will we get it? (Will we have to lease another machine?)
- What materials are necessary? (If this is a packaging job, what material will we be printing on: tin, paper, cardboard?)
- What human resources are needed? (Do we need to hire any freelancers?)
- Will there be any special expenses associated with the job? (Do we need to do location photography, for example?)
- How many production artists will be needed? (Is the deadline so near that we'll have to call up the reserves?)

Once these general questions are answered, the production manager can look more closely at the specific needs of the project.

Working backward from publication **closing dates** (deadlines), the traffic and production managers decide when each step of the work must be completed. Deadlines can vary from months to hours. The manager tries to build extra time into each step because every word and aesthetic choice may need some last-minute change.

LO 12-8

Classic manual print production process

Rough or comprehensive layout

Type specification and typesetting

Pasteup and mechanical

Printer

Prepress
- Color separations
- Negatives
- Stripping
- Platemaking

Presswork
- Printing
- Cutting
- Binding

Computerized print production process

- Design
- Type
- Mechanicals
- Color separations
- Negatives
- Stripping

Platemaking

Printer

Presswork
- Printing
- Cutting
- Binding

Exhibit 12-5
The print production process.

Planning the Job

The overall purpose of the preproduction phase is to plan the job thoroughly, which usually entails making a number of strategic choices before launching into full production. For example, because the art director's conceptual rough layouts are often made with marker colors that do not match printing inks, the production managers consult with art directors to formally select a color palette in advance, using a color guide such as the PANTONE system.

For brochures, there is also the question of which printing process and which type of printing press to use for the job. This will affect the budget and dictate how art is prepared in the production and prepress phases.

Similarly, the art director and production manager usually consult on the paper to be used. Three categories of paper are used for advertising purposes: *writing, text,* and *cover stock.* Letters and fliers, for example, commonly use **writing paper.** Bond writing paper is the most durable and most frequently used. For brochures, there are many types of **text papers,** such as news stock, antique finish, machine finish, English finish, and coated. These range from the inexpensive to the smooth, expensive, coated stocks used in upscale magazines. **Cover papers,** available in many finishes and textures, are used on soft book covers, direct-mail pieces, and brochure covers, so they're thicker, tougher, and more durable.

To create the art for an ad, brochure, or package, the production artist normally begins by marking out a grid on which to lay the type and art. Art directors use computers to do this with commands for setting up columns and guides. The grid provides an underlying consistency to the spacing and design of the piece.

The production artist then specifies the style and size of the typefaces for the text and inputs this information, along with the copy, into the computer.

The art elements must be properly positioned in the artwork (whether mechanical or computer generated) because the printer needs to have layers of art that can be reproduced individually. The total image is then constructed as each layer is printed over the previous one. Because the printer must photograph each layer to make separate plates, this kind of artwork is called **camera-ready art.**

This procedure is easily performed in the computer. The various elements of art are assigned to a layer the operator names and can be run out as separate film negatives or paper positive images as needed.

The Production Phase: Creating the Artwork

The **production phase** involves completing ancillary functions such as illustrations or photography, setting up the artwork and typesetting, and then melding all these components into a final form for the printer.

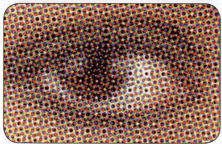

A halftone screen breaks up continuous-tone artwork into tiny dots. The combination of printed dots produces an optical illusion of shading, as in a photograph: The color dots show the separation for the color photo above. The other set of dots show the range that would appear in a black-and-white photo.

Lori Kramer/McGraw-Hill Education

In a multicolor piece of art, the printer needs layers that can be reproduced individually. This is done by computer or assembled by hand with plastic overlays. The total image is then reconstructed as each layer is printed over the other.

(left): Zigy Kaluzny-Charles Thatcher/Getty Images; (right): Didier Maillac/REA/Redux Pictures

Creating the Visual

Almost every ad has some kind of a visual besides typography, and many ads have several pictures. The visual may be an illustration or a photograph. But where do these pictures come from?

When reviewing the layout with the art director, the decision will be made whether to use illustration or photography and how to get just the pictures the creatives envision. In many cases, to save money, the art director or producer will choose to use stock photography for a reasonable licensing fee. The fee will typically be based on the intended usage and the length of time the usage will continue.

Most expensive is commissioning an illustrator to draw an original picture or hiring a photographer to go on location to shoot a specific visual. Producers must plan for hiring the right photographer. Some are well versed in photojournalistic techniques. Others are especially good at shooting interiors. And some specialize in food or fashion photography.

Printing in Color

Designs that don't need full color are printed in blended inks rather than process colors. For example, it would take two process colors (magenta and yellow) to make red or three process colors (magenta, yellow, and cyan) to make burgundy. To print a brochure in black and burgundy, it's cheaper to use only two ink colors rather than black plus three process colors.

A PANTONE color, one of a spectrum of colors that makes up the **PANTONE Matching System (PMS),** is a single ink premixed according to a formula and given a specific color number. The PANTONE swatch book features more than 100 colors in solid and screened blocks printed on different paper finishes.[42]

Four-Color Separations

Four separate halftone negatives are needed to make a set of four-color plates: one each for cyan, yellow, magenta, and black. Each of the resulting negatives appears in black and white, and the set is called the **color separation.** In printing, the process color inks are translucent, so two or three colors can overlap to create another color. For example, green is reproduced by overlapping yellow and cyan dots.

My IMC Campaign 12-C

Planning and Evaluating Print Media

At this point in your project you should have decided whether or not to use print (magazine and newspaper) as a communication vehicle. The next step is deciding which of the thousands of options makes the most sense for your client's brand.

The beauty of media planning and buying is that you have a blank slate from which to build your plan. As you start to build your plan, however, you need to consider what you are working toward. By answering a set of simple questions, you can build the foundation of your recommendation. You should approach planning print media in the same way you would approach planning the brand strategy:

- Whom do you want to reach?
- Why use print?
- What are the brand objectives?
- Where do you want to place your advertising to best achieve your objectives?
- How should you execute your plan?

When you have answered these questions, it is time to analyze and evaluate your opportunities and develop your plan.

Selecting publications requires both critical thinking and hard and fast numbers. For instance monthly magazines can take up to 12 weeks to gain full readership (called "to cume" their audience). This can obviously be an issue if your communication objectives are centered on building reach quickly. On the other hand, weekly magazines cume their audience in approximately one to two weeks, making them great to generate reach around key events. Finally, the number of insertions by title also depends on your strategy. If you are telling a sequenced story through three ads, then you need to plan for three insertions in each publication (pub). This will obviously be expensive and likely will reduce the number of pubs on the plan, ultimately limiting your reach.

The great thing about print advertising is that it offers a large number of opportunities for brands to engage consumers in niche environments, thereby limiting brand wastage. However, not all brands want or need such niche vehicles, and lucky for those brands there are more mass-oriented publications too:

Targeted	Mass Books
Golf	*People*
Field and Stream	*TV Guide*
Baby Talk	*Parade*
Ski	*National Enquirer*
Martha Stewart Living	*Reader's Digest*

Some of you will be focusing on large national advertisers and can utilize nearly all types of print options. But what opportunities exist for the local advertiser? First, newspapers are typically a staple of any large local advertiser. Second, most of the print publications that we have discussed thus far will allow you to layer in location-based targeting to help fine-tune your plan. Take this into account as you build your plan. It doesn't make sense to advertise in a national pub if your client is only located in the southeastern United States.

See My IMC Campaigns 12–A and 12–B for checklists of the pros and cons of magazine and newspaper advertising.

As you can see, common sense plays a major role in planning print campaigns, especially for large advertisers. But for other brands, advertising in print is a bit more difficult because the names of the targeted publications don't just roll off the tongue like *Sports Illustrated* or *People*. To plan for those campaigns, most advertisers use syndicated research such as GfK's MRI product. This is a piece of planning software that indexes, through surveys, people's readership of tens of thousands of different publications. So when Microsoft wants to reach IT decision makers in the enterprise (in companies with over 100 employees), MRI tells the media planner that she can find a high composition (concentration of overall readership) of that target in publications like *eWeek, InformationWeek,* and *Baseline* magazine.

While we detail a number of tools in this chapter, for the large majority of projects, access to these tools will be limited. Therefore, think about the medium in terms of the mindset of the readers when you place an ad in front of them. The closer you can get that mindset to match the category, industry, or association of your brand's product, the better off you are.

Today, sophisticated electronic scanning systems—such as the workstations from Silicon Graphics, Hell ScriptMaster, Scitex, and Crosfield—can produce four-color separations and screens in one process, along with enlargements or reductions.

The Duplication and Distribution Phase: Printing, Binding, and Shipping

The last phase of the traditional print production process involves the actual printing, proofing, and finishing steps of drying, cutting, binding, and shipping.

The Press Run

Once the paper, plates, and ink are readied, the press is started and stopped a few times to adjust the image's alignment on the paper. In multicolored printing, proper alignment of all the colors is critical. When the initial proofs show good alignment, the presses are sped up to maximum output.

Finishing

Once all the pieces are printed, the ink must dry (unless heat-set or cold-set inks were used). Then the excess paper (or other material) is cut away using huge cutting machines. Depending on the nature of the job, the pieces may be delivered to special subcontractors who emboss or die-cut or perform other special techniques to enhance the final printed piece. The final stop may be the bindery for two- and three-hole drilling, wire stapling, and folding.

Chapter Summary

The printed page—in magazines and newspapers—provides a unique, flexible medium for advertising creativity.

In selecting magazines for advertising, the media buyer must consider a publication's circulation, its readership, its cost, and its mechanical requirements. A magazine's rates may be determined by several factors: its primary and secondary readership, the number of subscription and vendor sales, and the number of copies guaranteed versus those actually delivered.

Magazine rate cards follow a standard format so advertisers can readily compare advertising costs. They list black-and-white and color rates, discounts, issue and closing dates, and mechanical requirements.

Magazines offer distinct advantages. They are the most selective of all mass media and are flexible in both readership and advertising. They offer unsurpassed color, excellent reproduction quality, authority and believability, long shelf life, and prestige at an efficient cost. However, they often require long lead times, have problems offering reach and frequency, and are subject to heavy advertising competition. The cost of advertising in some magazines is also very high.

The newspaper is a mass medium that almost everybody reads. It offers great flexibility, which assists creativity, and its printed message lasts longer than ads in electronic media. However, newspapers also have disadvantages: lack of audience selectivity, short life span, poor production quality, heavy advertising competition, potentially poor ad placement, and overlapping circulation. Still, the newspaper is the major community-serving medium today for both news and advertising.

The newspaper's rate card lists prices, deadlines, mechanical requirements, and other pertinent information. Rates vary for local and national advertisers. Also listed are the newspaper's short-rate policy, combination rates, frequency discounts, run-of-paper rates, and other data.

Specialists are involved in the production of print ads. Among the important jobs are production manager and art director. The increased use of computer technology has transformed the printing process and made print production much easier and more user-friendly.

Newspapers and magazines are making alliances with cable, regional telephone, and online computer companies to enter the interactive information market. They are still experimenting with ways to sell advertising on their electronic publications. Some experts believe that the convergence of text, video, and graphics will cause a creative revolution in advertising, with targeted, information-rich messages able to lead consumers step by step to a transaction without ever leaving home.

The print production process consists of four phases: preproduction, production, prepress, and printing and distribution. In the preproduction phase, the manager plans the overall job carefully and then starts to deal with the specific needs of the job.

Important Terms

Alliance for Audited Media (AAM), *405*

bleed, *398*

bulk discount, *414*

business magazines, *403*

camera-ready art, *419*

circulation audit, *405*

classified ad, *413*

classified display ad, *413*

closing date, *406, 418*

color separation, *420*

column inch, *411*

combination rate, *414*

consumer magazines, *399*

contract rate, *414*

controlled circulation, *406*

cooperative (co-op) advertising, *413*

cost per thousand (CPM), *406*

cover date, *406*

cover paper, *419*

cover position, *398*

custom magazines, *398*

daily newspaper, *410*

demographic editions, *407*

display advertising, *412*

earned rate, *414*

farm publications, *399*

flat rate, *414*

frequency discount, *407, 414*

full position, *416*

gatefold, *398*

geographic editions, *407*

guaranteed circulation, *405*

horizontal publication, *405*

Review Questions

1. If you worked in the advertising department of a premium-priced furniture manufacturer, would you recommend magazine advertising? Why or why not?

2. If you were the advertising manager for a magazine aimed at senior citizens, what advantages would you cite to potential advertisers?

3. What is the advantage of magazine advertising to businesses that sell to other businesses?

4. What is the importance of the Alliance for Audited Media?

5. Why do retailers advertise so heavily in local newspapers?

6. How can advertisers improve the selectivity of their newspaper ads?

7. What factors should advertisers consider in deciding among several local papers (including dailies and weeklies)?

8. Should national advertisers be charged a higher rate than local advertisers? Support your position.

9. Should agencies be liable for their clients' advertising bills? Why or why not?

10. How could a local newspaper use an online database service or the internet to help itself or its advertisers?

The Advertising Experience

1. **Using Print Advertising**

   As a maker of soy-based products, you are very excited about your new chocolate soy-milk drink. As long as they don't know it contains soy, children actually prefer its taste to that of milk. The product, now named Swoosh and represented by a toothy cartoon surfer, is all set for a print campaign. Choose a geographic area similar to the ones shown in Exhibit 12-3, examine the leading regional magazines and newspapers, and decide how to allocate funds for advertising. Explain why you chose newspapers, magazines, or both.

2. **Print Media Organizations**

   Visit the following print industry websites and familiarize yourself further with the size and scope of the print media world. Be sure to answer the questions for each site.

   - American Society of Newspaper Editors (ASNE): www.asne.org
   - International News Media Association (INMA): www.inma.org
   - National Newspaper Association (NNA): www.nnaweb.org
   - National Newspaper Publishers Association (NNPA): www.nnpa.org

   - News Media Alliance (NMA): www.newsmediaalliance.org

   a. What is the purpose of the organization that sponsors this site?

   b. Who is(are) the intended audience(s) of this site?

   c. Who makes up the organization's membership? Its constituency?

   d. How important do you feel this organization is to the advertising industry? Why?

3. **Print Media Tools**

   Were it not for the products and services offered by the following companies, planning and buying print vehicles could be an overwhelming task for media professionals. From audit reports to media kits, agencies and media houses are aided every day by companies that specialize in easing the lives of media planners and buyers. Visit the following syndicated and independent media companies' websites and answer the questions that follow:

   - Advertising Checking Bureau: www.acbcoop.com
   - Advertising Media Internet Community (AMIC): www.amic.com

- Alliance for Audited Media: https://auditedmedia.com/
- BPA Worldwide (BPA): www.bpaww.com
- MediaCentral: www.mediacentral.net
- MediaFinder: www.mediafinder.com
- Vividata: http://vividata.ca
- Nielsen Scarborough: www.nielsen.com/us/en/solutions/capabilities/scarborough-local/

- Kantar SRDS Media Planning Platform: http://next.srds.com
- *a.* Who is the intended audience of the site?
- *b.* What are the size and scope of the company?
- *c.* What type(s) of print media information does the company specialize in?
- *d.* How useful do you believe the company or organization is for obtaining print media information? Why?

End Notes

1. "Newspapers Fact Sheet," Pew Research Center, June 13, 2018, www.journalism.org/fact-sheet/newspapers/.
2. Daniel de Vise, "Number of U.S. Adults with College Degrees Hits Historic High," *The Washington Post,* February 23, 2012, www.washingtonpost.com/national/highereducation/number-of-us-adults-with-college-degrees-hits-historichigh/2012/02/23/gIQAi80bWR_story.html.
3. Rick Edmonds, "Newspapers: By the Numbers," State of the News Media 2013, May 7, 2013, www.stateofthemedia.org/2013 /newspapers-stabilizing-but-still-threatened/newspapers-by-the-numbers/.
4. US Ad Spending 2018," *eMarketer*, October 16, 2018, www .emarketer.com/content/us-ad-spending-2018
5. Tom Rosenstiel, Mark Jurkowitz, and Hon Ji, "The Search for a New Business Model," Pew Research Center, March 5, 2012, www.journalism.org/2012/03/05/searchnew-business-model.
6. "Wall Street Journal Hit with Layoffs That Could Top 100," *CNN Money,* June 18, 2015, retrieved at http://money.cnn .com/2015/06/18/media/wall-street-journal-layoffs/.
7. Jaclyn Peiser, "New York Times Co. Reports Revenue Growth as Digital Subscriptions Rise," *The New York Times,* May 3, 2018, www.nytimes.com/2018/05/03/business/media/new-york-times-earnings.html.
8. Mike Snider, "Gannett Swings to a Q2 Profit, Beats Expectations as Digital Revenue Continues to Rise," *USA Today*, August 9, 2018, www.usatoday.com/story/money/media/2018/08/09/gannett-posts-q-2-profit-surpassing-expectations-digital-revenue-rises/937161002/.
9. "ESPN Digital," ESPN Consumer Marketing and Sales, https://espncms.com/digital/.
10. Audit Bureau of Circulation, December 31, 2008, http://abcas3 .accessabc.com/ecirc/magtitlesearch.asp.
11. Anders Vinderslev, "What Is the Definition of Native Advertising?" *Native Advertising Institute,* https://nativeadvertisinginstitute.com/blog/the-definition-of-native-advertising/.
12. Dan Shewan, "Native Advertising Examples: 5 of the Best (and Worst)," *WordStream,* December 18, 2017, www.wordstream .com/blog/ws/2014/07/07/native-advertising-examples.
13. World's first tastable print ad. The Coca-Cola Company.
14. Audit Bureau of Circulation, June 30, 2011, http://adage.com/datacenter/datapopup?article id=229488.
15. Patrick M. Reilly and Ernest Beck, "Publishers Often Pad Circulation Figures," *The Wall Street Journal,* September 30, 1997, p. B12.
16. Shu-Fen Li, John C. Schweitzer, and Benjamin J. Bates, "Effectiveness of Trade Magazine Advertising," paper presented to the annual conference of the Association for Education in Journalism and Mass Communication, Montreal, Quebec, August 1992.

17. Gene Willhoft, "Is 'Added Value' Valuable?" *Advertising Age,* March 1, 1993, p. 18.
18. Stephen M. Blacker, "Magazines' Role in Promotion," *Advertising Age,* June 30, 1994, p. 32.
19. *Car and Driver,* www.caranddrivermediakit.com/hotdata/publishers/cardrivermk/cardrivermk/materials/Car_and_Driver_General_Rates.pdf; *Road and Track,* www.roadandtrackmediakit.com/r5/showkiosk.asp?listing_id=4182649.
20. Lisa I. Fried, "New Rules Liven Up the Rate-Card Game," *Advertising Age,* October 24, 1994, p. S8.
21. SRDS Media Solutions, "Sample SRDS Listing," www.srds.com/frontMatter/ips/consumer/sample.html.
22. Joyce Rutter Kaye, *Print Casebooks 10/The Best in Advertising,* 1994–95 ed. (Rockville, MD: RC Publications, 1994), pp. 63–65; Tony Case, "Getting Personal," *Editor & Publisher,* February 1, 1992, pp. 16, 31; Ann Cooper, "Creatives: Magazines—Believers in the Power of Print," *Adweek* (Eastern ed.), April 12, 1993, pp. 34–39.
23. "ZenithOptimedia: U.S. Ad Spending Forecasts through 2012," http://adage.com/datacenter/datapopup.php?article_id=228231.
24. "Newspapers Fact Sheet," Pew Research Center, June 13, 2018, www.journalism.org/fact-sheet/newspapers/.
25. "Newspapers Fact Sheet," Pew Research Center, June 13, 2018, www.journalism.org/fact-sheet/newspapers/.
26. Russell Heimlich, "Number of Americans Who Read Print Newspapers Continues Decline," Pew Research Center, October 11, 2012, www.pewresearch.org/fact-tank/2012/10/11/number-of-americans-who-read-print-newspapers-continues-decline/.
27. Jim Conaghan, "Young, Old and In-Between: Newspaper Platform Readers Ages Are Well-Distributed," News Media Alliance, May 17, 2017, www.newsmediaalliance.org/age-newspaper-readers-platforms/.
28. "Newspapers Deliver across the Ages," *Nielsen Insights,* December 15, 2016, www.nielsen.com/us/en/insights/news/2016/newspapers-deliver-across-the-ages.html.
29. Ronald Redfern, "What Readers Want from Newspapers," *Advertising Age,* January 23, 1995, p. 25.
30. National Newspaper Association, "Community Newspaper Facts & Figures," July 3, 2018, www.nnaweb.org/about-nna?articleCategory=community-facts-figures#2.
31. "Newspapers Fact Sheet," Pew Research Center, June 13, 2018, www.journalism.org/fact-sheet/newspapers/.
32. Sara Guaglione, "Correction: 'Parade' Magazine Circulation, Readership Is Weekly," *Publishers Daily,* February 27, 2017; "Newspapers Fact Sheet," Pew Research Center, June 13, 2018, www.journalism.org/fact-sheet/newspapers/.
33. Douglas A. McIntyre, "America's 100 Largest Newspapers," Yahoo! Finance, January 24, 2017, https://finance.yahoo.com/news/america-100-largest-newspapers-180528599.html; "USA Today," *Wikipedia,* https://en.wikipedia.org/wiki/USA_Today.

34. *Newspaper Rate Differentials* (New York: American Association of Advertising Agencies, 1990); Christy Fisher, "NAA Readies National Ad-Buy Plan," *Advertising Age,* March 1, 1993, p. 12.

35. *The Source: Newspapers by the Numbers,* Newspaper Association of America, *www.naa.org/thesource*.

36. Derek Thompson, "The Print Apocalypse and How to Survive It," *The Atlantic,* November 3, 2016, *www.theatlantic.com/business/archive/2016/11/the-print-apocalypse-and-how-to-survive-it/506429/*.

37. *Sweepstakes Assistance: A Caregiver's Guide* (Data & Marketing Association, 2018).

38. Christy Fisher, "Chrysler's One-Stop Ad Buys Boost Ailing Newspapers," *Advertising Age,* March 7, 1994, p. 49.

39. Dorothy Giobbe, "One Order/One Bill System Gets a Dress Rehearsal," *Editor & Publisher,* March 12, 1994, pp. 26, 46.

40. Christy Fisher, "Chrysler's One-Stop Ad Buys Boost Ailing Newspapers," *Advertising Age,* March 7, 1994, p. 49; Dorothy Giobbe, "One Order/One Bill System Gets a Dress Rehearsal,"*Editor & Publisher,* March 12, 1994, pp. 26, 46.

41. Joe Mandese and Scott Donaton, "Wells Rich Tests 4A's Liability Clause," *Advertising Age,* April 22, 1991, pp. 1, 40; Willie Vogt, "Defining Payment Liability," *AgriMarketing,* May 1992, pp. 42–43.

42. PANTONE® is a registered trademark of PANTONE Inc.

CHAPTER

13

Using Electronic Media: Television and Radio

LEARNING OBJECTIVES

To present the important factors advertisers need to evaluate when considering the use of radio and television in the creative mix. Each medium has its own characteristics, advantages, and drawbacks. Advertisers must be able to compare their merits and understand the most cost-effective ways to buy advertising time.

After studying this chapter, you will be able to:

LO13-1 Describe the advantages and drawbacks of broadcast and cable TV as advertising media.

LO13-2 Explain the challenge to traditional TV arising from streaming video.

LO13-3 Give an overview of TV audience trends.

LO13-4 Describe the kinds of TV advertising buys that are available.

LO13-5 Review the important measures of TV viewership.

LO13-6 Discuss the main factors to consider when buying television time.

LO13-7 Analyze the pros and cons of using radio in the creative mix.

LO13-8 Indicate how radio ads are bought.

LO13-9 Summarize how audio and video spots are produced.

Source: Mars, Incorporated

M&M's started with a bang, literally, as Forrest Mars invented them after seeing soldiers gulp Smarties, a coated English chocolate candy, during the Spanish Civil War. Returning to the U.S., Mars created his own version and named them M&M's after his father, Forrest E. Mars, and Bruce Murrie, the son of Hershey's president William Murrie. ■ The candy went on to become a popular diversion during another war, World War II. Although sold exclusively to soldiers, demand was so high the company opened a bigger factory to keep the confections in the mess kits of soldiers in Europe. ■ Right after the war, M&M's introduced what would become its iconic tagline. Mars had noticed that soldiers loved that the candy did not melt when transported, even in heat—hence, a slogan that perfectly captured the brand's USP, "melts in your mouth, not in your hand." ■ By the 1990s, some of M&M's marketing magic was beginning to wear thin and sales began slowing. Mars chose to work with a new ad agency to try to turn things around and selected one of the best, BBDO. ■ BBDO's creative director was Susan Credle, who immediately grasped the flagging sales were linked to weak branding. "They'd become just candy. An aisle store candy brand versus an icon brand."[1] ■ The solution was the introduction of six funny brand "advocates." Yellow is "plump, yellow, and all smiles" whose best friend is Red "because he seems to know a lot." Red has a hidden talent of turning "simple chores into complicated tasks" and thinks his best features are "genius IQ and physical prowess." To put this in context, his shortcoming is he "Thinks he knows more than he does." Orange has a dream "to be on the endangered species list" and is turned off by "people who want to eat him." Blue is turned off by "squares, man . . . squares" and lists his turn-ons as "moonlit nights, jazz" and "the ladies." Ms. Brown lists her best attribute as "her big beautiful brain" and her hidden talent as "always being right." Finally, Green insists that she "melts for no one" and owns up to the shortcoming that she "can sometimes be intimidating."[2] ■ These iconic figures have provided M&M's with nearly two decades of great TV and cinema advertising, including a beloved spot in Super Bowl LI where Red, wishing to become human, turns into Danny DeVito. More importantly, they have helped M&M's become America's best-selling candy. In 2017, M&M's had sales of nearly $700 million, more than sales of second place Hershey's and third place Reese's combined.[3] ■ The most successful ad campaign ever? The case can be made that it is, and all owing to a powerful, yet simple idea of making the candy the star. ■ Susan Credle, who no longer works for BBDO, deserves much of the credit. And Credle's ideas have kept coming (among her other creations is the popular Mayhem character for Allstate). In 2018 she took on new challenges as global chief creative officer at FCB New York. Her advice for other CMOs is,

"Dream bigger, build legacies, be ambitious. Not just about the bottom line. We're going to do things you never thought you're going to do. The Times Square M&Ms store is there because of Paul Michaels' [former Mars president] big dreams."[4]

Broadcast and Cable Television and Streaming Video

LO 13-1

In 1950 U.S. advertisers spent $171 million, or just 3 percent of total U.S. advertising volume, on the new medium of television. It didn't take long, though, for the nation's advertisers to discover the power of this new medium to reach mass audiences quickly and frequently. TV offered advertisers unique creative opportunities to imbue their brands with personality and image like never before. In 2018, advertisers spent nearly $68 billion on cable and broadcast TV. This number, impressive as it is, was not enough for TV to remain the largest category of spending, a title that now falls to internet advertising.[5] Exhibit 13-1 lists the top network television advertisers in the United States and their annual expenditures.

Until recently, television was available to advertisers in two principal forms: broadcast and cable TV. **Broadcast TV** reaches its audience by transmitting electromagnetic waves through the air across some geographic territory. **Cable TV** reaches its audience through wires, which may be strung from telephone poles or laid underground. Today, a third option, growing much faster than broadcast or cable, called streaming video, offers advertisers new ways to connect to audiences. **Streaming video** involves accessing either free or paid content via an internet connection. Examples include YouTube, Hulu, and Netflix.

Broadcast TV

Until the advent of the internet, broadcast television grew faster than any other advertising medium in history. From its beginnings in the 1950s, TV rapidly emerged as the only in-home medium that offered sight, sound, and motion. As TV's legions of viewers grew, national-brand advertisers quickly discovered its power to efficiently expand distribution across the country and sell products like never before. Not only that, the medium was ideal for branding, even better than magazines, which had previously been the image-building medium of choice. It didn't take long for marketers to switch their budgets from radio, newspapers, and magazines.

Radio and Television Ad Spending as a Percentage of All U.S. Ad Spending 2018

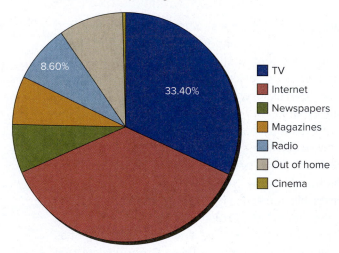

- TV
- Internet
- Newspapers
- Magazines
- Radio
- Out of home
- Cinema

Radio and television ad spending.

Source: Zenith forecast for 2018 total U.S. ad spending (via *Advertising Age*'s 200 Leading National Advertisers report).

Exhibit 13-1

Top 10 network TV advertisers in the United States (2017).

Source: "Biggest U.S. Spenders by Medium, Broadcast Network TV," *Ad Age* 200 Leading National Advertisers 2018 Fact Pack, Crain Communications.

Rank	Advertiser	($ in Millions) 2017
1	Procter & Gamble	$1,029
2	Ford Motor Co.	692
3	Pfizer	686
4	AT&T	634
5	General Motors Co.	610
6	Berkshire Hathaway	607
7	T-Mobile	545
8	Verizon	538
9	Apple	521
10	Samsung	444

The United States now has 1,761 commercial TV stations. About 656 of these are **VHF** (very high frequency, channels 2 through 13); the rest are **UHF** (ultrahigh frequency, channels 14 and above).[6] Stations in the United States operate as independents unless they are affiliated with a network (ABC, NBC, CBS, Fox, CW). Both network affiliates and independent stations may subscribe to nationally syndicated programs as well as originate their own programming. However, increasing competition from cable and other viewing options is taking viewers from national network programs. To compensate, some networks invest in cable TV systems or create their own. NBC, for example, started CNBC and MSNBC, and ABC has a majority stake in ESPN. Disney (which owns ABC), 21st Century Fox (which owns Fox Broadcasting), Comcast (which owns NBC), and Warner Media (HBO, Turner, TBS, and CNN) have joined forces to create their own streaming platform, Hulu.

Cable TV

The origins of cable date to the 1940s. Initially, cable was developed to provide TV to areas with poor reception such as rural and mountainous regions. But in the 1970s, the advent of satellite TV signals, the proliferation of channels, and the introduction of uncut first-run movies via pay-cable channels such as Home Box Office and Showtime made cable TV more attractive to all viewers

A variety of advertiser-supported cable networks soon appeared with specialized programming in arts, history, sports, news, and comedy, along with diversified pay services and many more local shows. As the number of cable customers grew, viewers began abandoning programs on the big broadcast networks.

For three decades, cable's growth was extraordinary. In 1975, only 13 percent of TV households in the United States had cable. By 2010, cable reached almost 90 percent of all homes.[7] Since that time, however, cable has been in retreat, as consumers find less expensive and more responsive ways to consume content. In fact, by 2018 only 78 percent of homes subscribed to cable.[8] Although cable subscribers may receive more than 100 channels, most households watch only 15 to 20.[9] The My IMC Campaign 13–A guides you through the planning process for all of these choices for TV.

Most channels are privately owned and commercially operated. These include local network affiliates and independents, cable networks, superstations, local cable system channels, and community access channels. The cable fees represent about one-third of cable TV revenues; advertising makes up the remainder. Networks such as CNN, USA, the Discovery Channel, Arts & Entertainment, Lifetime, Comedy Central, and Spike TV now compete for advertisers' dollars, each selling its own niche audience.[11] For an additional price, subscribers can receive premium services such as HBO, Showtime, and Cinemax and see special events such as first-run films, championship boxing matches, and sports.

There are now more than 900 cable networks in the United States. Exhibit 13-2 lists the most popular ones. There are also a handful of *superstations,* local over-the-air TV stations whose signals are delivered via satellite to cable systems across the country and that carry some national advertising.

Exhibit 13-2
Most viewed cable networks in 2018.

Fox News	2.4 million
MSNBC	1.6 million
HGTV	1.4 million
USA	1.3 million
History	1.1 million
Discovery	1.1 million
Hallmark	1.0 million
Investigation Discovery	1.0 million
TBS	1.0 million
CNN	0.9 million

Source: A. J. Katz, "The Top Basic Cable Networks for July 2018 Are . . . ," *TV Newser* (Adweek, LLC), August 1, 2018, *www.adweek.com/tvnewser/the-top-basic-cable-networks-for-july-2018-are/372335.*

Streaming Video

LO 13-2

The origins of streaming video are older than you might think. George Owen Squier was born during the three weeks before the end of the U.S. Civil War in 1865. A decorated soldier and graduate of West Point, Squier received a doctorate from Johns Hopkins University and went on to develop several patents and inventions. One involved a method for transmitting music over electrical wires, a method he labeled "Wired Radio." Shortly before his death in 1934, Squier changed the name to Muzak.

Muzak, which today is still responsible for the music heard in many offices and retail outlets, was the earliest alternative to using the broadcast spectrum for delivering mass audio content. But between its invention and the late 1990s there were few developments in alternatives to broadcast other than cable.

This changed when personal computers started becoming popular in the late 1980s. The first home computers were little more than digital typewriters until early attempts to

My IMC Campaign 13-A

Planning and Buying TV and Radio

Media planners use syndicated and proprietary research tools to plan and buy TV and radio ads. These tools help identify the larger concentrations (composition) of a target audience in specific programming and the cost associated with those audiences. The currency for both media is a rating point, which represents 1 percent of the target audience. Both TV and radio, therefore, are bought based on demographics. So when certain prime-time shows have a rating of 14 for A25–49, it means that a particular program reaches 14 percent of all adults between the ages of 25 and 49. A buyer's cost per point (CPP) is her way of determining a vehicle's (program's) efficiency in delivering her target audience. Ratings points are additive, so two spots on shows with 14 targeted rating points means that the advertiser has purchased 28 gross rating points, or GRPs.

You won't have access to the types of tools that help you plan and optimize broadcast TV or radio media plans, so your focus should be on the merits of each of these media in achieving your marketing and advertising objectives and how they match your overall media strategies. (Refer back to My IMC Campaign 9–A for a refresher on building media strategies.)

Streaming Video

Streaming video may be an option for your campaign because buying ads or placing videos on YouTube, now owned by Google, is very feasible, even if you are working for a small client. YouTube provides lessons in creating, placing, monetizing, and evaluating video spots in free tutorials you can see at www.youtube.com/yt/advertise/how-it-works/. Brand messages on YouTube can either be in the content that people want to watch or appear just before, after, or embedded within the content.

And YouTube is not the only game in town. Other streaming services that include ads are Hulu, Spotify, Pandora, Google Play Music, and DirectTV Now.

Television

About 115 million homes in America have at least one TV set. However, TV-land is becoming a fragmented marketplace. While the average viewer watches only 15 channels on a regular basis, those channels may not be the same 15 channels as the ones his neighbor watches, making the media planner's job that much more difficult in building mass audiences.

Besides large audiences, the other core benefit of TV is that it builds awareness relatively quickly. If you are launching a new product or trying to gain a high level of awareness in a relatively short period of time, TV is your medium. While TV will take up a large portion of your budget, its dynamic nature and its ability to include sight, sound, and motion in the advertisement make it great for telling stories.

Last, TV is still the best medium to generate excitement around a brand, whether that is with internal constituents (employees) or external audiences. As stated in Chapter 9, the medium is the message, and no medium, to date, gives people the same perception of legitimacy as a well-produced TV advertisement.

Radio

Why do advertisers use radio? One reason is that radio is much more efficient than TV; CPPs are sometimes one-tenth those of TV. Radio also is much less expensive to produce; in fact, typically all you need is copy and talent, making the lead time to go live with radio as short as one to two weeks. It also happens to be more promotional in nature—stations typically have a loyal audience following, and advertisers can usually be a part of any local station events and get the station personalities to endorse the brand. Testimonials, and especially personality testimonials, can be very valuable to advertisers that are looking to build legitimacy in themselves or their product.

So while you think about what your TV and radio ads will do for your brand(s), it is important to reflect on what part of the objectives and strategies each will fulfill and how they might work in concert with each other. Think of starting a new advertising campaign with TV messages and the support of radio. The TV will generate awareness and legitimacy immediately, and the radio will allow you to get out of the higher-cost media quickly while allowing for long-term continuity of messaging at a more efficient rate.

Podcasts

Advertisers can purchase time in a podcast either by purchasing directly from the podcaster or via increasingly common podcast networks. Singlegrain, a digital marketing consultancy, writes that there are over 500,000 active podcast shows.[10] It suggests the two biggest benefits to advertisers are that podcasts engage their listeners and that listeners rate podcast hosts as high in credibility. To this we would add that podcasts attract audiences based on lifestyles, interests, values, and goals. In other words, podcast audiences offer unique segmentation opportunities.

link them through phone lines and modems. This technology was enough for e-mail, but neither computers nor phone lines were powerful enough to link people to streaming video or audio content.

By the early 2000s several developments changed the game for streaming technology. These included greater bandwidth in home internet connections, more powerful computers, and increasingly sophisticated software algorithms for compressing video and audio content.

In 2005, YouTube, founded by three young PayPal employees, posted its first video on April 23 (watch YouTube's first posted video, Me at the Zoo, at https://en.wikipedia.org/wiki/Me_at_the_zoo). That same year, Netflix, already anticipating the end of DVD rentals, began working on a streaming system called Netflix Box. Two years later, that technology was already obsolete and the company introduced internet video on demand.

From these recent and humble beginnings, streaming video has become remarkably popular. As of 2017, 59 percent of all adults reported that cable or satellite subscription was the primary way they watch TV, while only 9 percent reported using a digital antenna. The remainder, 28 percent, indicated they use an online streaming service as the primary way they watch. Even more impressively, among viewers between 18 and 29, the advertising "sweet spot," 61 percent said streaming was their primary way of TV watching.[12]

Streaming video is a disruptive force for the traditional players in TV. Why? First, much streaming video is ad-free (Netflix, HBO, some Hulu subscriptions) because subscribers pay for it. Second, streaming has replaced cable and broadcast as must-watch TV, with the result that millions are canceling their cable subscriptions. Third, one of the most appealing aspects of streaming video is video-on-demand, where consumers can watch what they want, when they want, where they want. The old model of "appointment viewing" is disappearing, even on broadcast TV, forcing Nielsen to create a new measure of audiences: Live+3 (live viewers plus those who time-shift their viewing for up to 3 days).

The old model supported a number of groups that will struggle if the streaming video approach of Netflix should triumph. These include the broadcast networks, which try to appeal to large numbers of people with broadcast standards and restrictions companies like Netflix can safely ignore. It also includes local TV affiliates, which have no role in streaming video and therefore have no way to make money from it. And it includes cable companies, who have no good rationale for requiring $100+ subscriptions that require dozens of channels people don't want. There is also a clear set of winners in streaming video. On Netflix, it is the producers and actors who benefit from the company's billion-dollar content binge. And on YouTube it is young stars and entrepreneurs who attract large audiences through cleverness and talent, bypassing Hollywood's system entirely.

TV Audience Trends

LO 13-3

As a way to reach a mass audience, no other medium has the unique creative abilities of television: the combination of sight, sound, and motion; the opportunity to demonstrate the product; the potential to use special effects; the chance to develop the empathy of the viewer; and the believability of seeing it happen right before your eyes (see My IMC Campaign 13-B, "The Pros and Cons of Broadcast TV Advertising"). Over half of viewers believe TV is the most authoritative advertising source, compared to only 15.4 percent for newspapers, 10.8 percent for magazines, 8.6 percent for radio, and 4.4 percent for the internet. Television is also rated as the most influential, persuasive, and exciting medium.[13]

The heaviest viewers of broadcast TV are middle-income, high school–educated individuals and their families, so most programming is directed at this group. People with considerably higher incomes and more education typically have a more diverse range of interests and entertainment options.

TV has many competitors for audience leisure time, but viewing hours remain high. *Advertising Age* estimates that the average American watches nearly two hours of TV each day.[14]

Around the world, older women watch TV the most (36 hours per week in both the United States and Canada). This makes the medium very popular with advertisers whose primary target is middle-aged and older women. Conversely, the attractive audience between 18 and 29 watches the least amount of TV.

Cable in North American homes has significantly altered TV viewing patterns and the use of other media. Households with cable spend less time watching broadcast TV. They also spend less time listening to the radio, reading, or going to the movies. Cable seems to reach an audience that is difficult to get to in any other way.[15] As a result of this *audience fragmentation,* advertising on broadcast networks has become less cost-effective.

My IMC Campaign 13-B

The Pros and Cons of Broadcast TV Advertising

The Pros

Contemporary broadcast television offers advertisers many advantages over competing media.

- **Mass coverage.** A full 98 percent of all U.S. homes have a TV (most have more than one), and viewing time for the average household increased from about five hours a day in 1960 to more than eight hours in 2004.

- **Relatively low cost.** Despite the often huge initial outlays for commercial production and advertising time, TV's equally huge audiences bring the cost per exposure down to $2 to $10 per thousand viewers.

- **Some selectivity.** Television audiences vary a great deal depending on the time of day, day of the week, and nature of the programming. Advertising messages can be presented when potential customers are watching, and advertisers can reach select geographic audiences by buying local and regional markets.

- **Impact.** Television offers a kind of immediacy that other forms of advertising cannot achieve, displaying and demonstrating the product with sound, motion, and full color right before the customer's eyes.

- **Creativity.** The various facets of the TV commercial—sight, sound, motion, and color—permit infinite original and imaginative appeals.

- **Prestige.** Because the public considers TV the most authoritative and influential medium, it offers advertisers a prestigious image. Hallmark, Xerox, Coca-Cola, and IBM increase their prestige by regularly sponsoring cultural programs on network TV.

- **Social dominance.** In North America, most people under age 35 grew up with TV as a window to their social environment. They continue to be stirred by TV screenings of the Olympics, space travel, assassinations, wars, and political scandals around the world.

The Cons

Sometimes broadcast TV just doesn't "fit" the creative mix because of cost, lack of audience selectivity, inherent brevity, or the clutter of competitive messages.

- **High production cost.** One of broadcast TV's greatest handicaps is the high cost of producing quality commercials. Depending on the creative approach, the cost of filming a national commercial today may run from $200,000 to more than $1 million.

- **High airtime cost.** The average cost of a prime-time network commercial ranges from $200,000 to $400,000. A single 30-second commercial for a top-rated show in prime time may cost more than $500,000, and in special attractions like the Super Bowl more than $2 million. The cost of wide coverage, even at low rates, prices small and medium-size advertisers out of the market.

- **Limited selectivity.** Broadcast TV is not cost-effective for advertisers seeking a very specific, small audience. And it is losing some of its selectivity because of changing audience trends. More women are working outside the home or watching cable TV, hurting advertisers on network soap operas.

- **Brevity.** Studies show that most TV viewers can't remember the product or company in the most recent TV ad they watched—even if it was within the last five minutes. Recall improves with the length of the commercial; people remember 60-second spots better than 30-second spots.

- **Clutter.** TV advertising is usually surrounded by station breaks, credits, and public service announcements, as well as six or seven other spots. All these messages compete for attention, so viewers become annoyed and confused and often misidentify the product.

- **Zipping and zapping.** DVR users who skip through commercials when replaying recorded programs are zipping; remote-control users who change channels at the beginning of a commercial break are zapping.

National advertisers have been using cable since the late 1970s, and cable advertising revenues have grown steadily, reaching more than $21 billion in 2010.[16] One reason is that cable's upscale audience buys proportionately more goods and services than noncable subscribers (see Exhibit 13-3). Procter & Gamble traditionally spends the most on network cable. However, local retailers also find local cable a good place to advertise.

Nielsen studies indicate that the average U.S. household receives well over 100 TV channels. A larger number of channels, however, doesn't translate into more TV viewing. The Nielsen data indicate that the more channels a household has, the lower the percentage of channels watched. Households with the most channels (more than 150) regularly watch only 16.[17]

While there is no doubt that the media play an ever-expanding role in our daily lives, there is a finite limit to the number of advertising exposures people can absorb. When that limit is reached, any new media will simply be fighting for market share. This is the reason for the increasing fragmentation of the audience and the precipitous decline in the huge

Exhibit 13-3

Cable households provide advertisers with attractive demographics (Index of 100 = U.S. average).

Cable versus Noncable Household Characteristics			
Upscale Profiles	**Cable HH vs. U.S. Average (Index)**	**Noncable HH vs. U.S. Average (Index)**	**% Advantage Cable HH**
Occupation: Professional	108	88	+23%
Education: Graduated college+	110	85	+29%
Occupation: Management/financial	105	93	+ 13%
Household Income: $75,000+	112	80	+40%
Value of Home: $500,000+	109	87	+25%
Downscale Profiles	**Cable HH vs. U.S. Average (Index)**	**Noncable HH vs. U.S. Average (Index)**	**% Advantage Cable HH**
Education: Did not graduate HS	86	122	−30%
Employment: Not working	99	101	−2%
Occupation: Construction/maintenance	87	120	−17%
Household Income: <$20,000	87	121	−28%
Value of Home: <$60,000	83	127	−35%

Source: Cable Viewer Summary, Cable TV Advertising Bureau, 2018.

share of audience once held by the broadcast networks. This is also why media buyers and planners are growing in importance as advertisers search for the elusive audience and fight for their share of that audience in an overcrowded media environment.

The Use of Television in IMC

Television is very versatile. For many years it was strictly a mass medium, used to great advantage by the manufacturers of mass consumption goods: toiletries and cosmetics, food, appliances, and cars (see Exhibit 13-4). But today, thanks to the narrowcasting ability of cable TV, television can also be a highly selective niche medium. It's not unusual, for instance, to see ads for special feed for thoroughbreds and show horses on ESPN's *Grand Prix of Jumping.* And thanks to local cable, TV is now affordable for even small local advertisers. This makes it a very viable option for use in an IMC program.

While single programs don't deliver the mass audience they once did, television is still the most cost-effective way to deliver certain kinds of messages to large, well-defined audiences. When it comes to awareness and image advertising, for instance, television has no rival. The same is true for brand reinforcement messages.[18]

Because marketing integrators are looking to establish, nourish, and reinforce relationships with many groups of stakeholders, television serves another role quite efficiently. It can speak to many different kinds of stakeholders—not just customers—at the same time. Moreover, through its unique ability to deliver a creative big idea, television can impart *brand meaning* (the symbolism or personality of the brand) to either attract people to the brand or reinforce their current relationship with it.

Television is also a good leverage tool. That is, an advertiser might take advantage of the relatively low CPM of television to reach out to many prospects. Prospects can identify themselves by responding to the commercial, and then the advertiser can follow up with less expensive, one-to-one or addressable media.[19]

What's important to remember in all this is that the high visibility of TV forces the sponsor to create ads that people find interesting and that consistently reinforce the brand's strategic position (remember our definition of great advertising). The brands that succeed are the ones that are the most popular. And "ad liking" has a lot to do with brand popularity.

Exhibit 13-4

Top 10 cable network advertisers (2017).

Rank	Advertiser	Cable TV Spending (in Millions)
1	Procter & Gamble	$724
2	Berkshire Hathaway	513
3	PepsiCo	437
4	Yum Brands	416
5	AT&T	358
6	General Motors Co.	295
7	General Mills	293
8	Comcast Corp.	278
9	Hershey Co.	270
10	Unilever	267

Source: "Biggest U.S. Spenders by Medium, Cable TV Network," *Ad Age* 200 Leading National Advertisers 2018 Fact Pack, Crain Communications.

My IMC Campaign 13-C

The Pros and Cons of Cable TV Advertising

The Pros

- **Selectivity.** Cable offers specialized programming aimed at particular types of viewers. Narrowcasting allows advertisers to choose programming with the viewer demographics that best match their target customers.

- **Audience demographics.** Cable subscribers are younger, better educated, and more affluent; have higher-level jobs; live in larger households; and are more likely to try new products and buy more high-ticket items, such as cars, appliances, and high-tech equipment.

- **Low cost.** Many small companies get TV's immediacy and impact without the enormous expenditures of broadcast TV. Cable advertising can sometimes cost as little as radio. Many national advertisers find sponsorship attractive because an entire cable series can cost less to produce than a single broadcast TV commercial.

- **Flexibility.** Broadcast TV commercials need to be short because of the high costs of production and airtime, but cable ads can run up to two minutes and, in the case of infomercials, much longer. They can also be tailored to fit the programming environment.

- **Testability.** Cable is a good place to experiment, testing both new products and various advertising approaches: ad frequency, copy impact, and different media mixes.

The Cons

Like every medium, cable TV has its drawbacks.

- **Limited reach.** About 23 percent of households don't have cable. This was cable's main weakness in the past, but it is less so today.

- **Fragmentation.** With more than 50 channels at their disposal, cable viewers do not watch any one channel in enormous numbers. To reach the majority of the cable audience in a particular market, ads must run on many stations.

- **Quality.** Cable, particularly local cable, sometimes has poorer production quality and less desirable programming than broadcast TV.

- **Zipping and zapping.** Cable TV has some of the same drawbacks as broadcast TV, such as zipping and zapping.

Types of TV Advertising

LO 13-4

Advertisers use different strategies to buy time on broadcast and cable television. The major broadcast networks offer a variety of programs that appeal to different audiences. So the advertiser buys ads based on the viewing audience of each program. A national advertiser that wants to reach a broad cross section of women ages 25 to 45, for example, might find *Grey's Anatomy* an efficient buy at a cost of $203,078 for a 30-second commercial.[20] When identifying a market segment to target, advertisers should consider the ethics of their appeal. For example, children represent a target market for some brands, but targeting kids carries significant responsibilities. See the Ethics, Diversity & Inclusion box later in this chapter for the guidelines on advertising to children.

When buying cable TV, an advertiser can buy ads over the full schedule of a channel because cable networks typically aim their overall programming to relatively specific *audiences.* The Lifetime and Family channels heavily weight programs toward women; MTV targets viewers 16 to 25. Cable companies sell their network channels in bundles at a discount and offer discounts for *run-of-schedule* positioning—multiple ad purchases they can place throughout a channel's daily schedule (see My IMC Campaign 13-C, "The Pros and Cons of Cable TV Advertising").

Advertisers can buy time on TV in several ways. They include sponsoring an entire network program, participating in a network program, purchasing spot announcements from a network affiliate, purchasing spots from syndicators, and purchasing spots from cable companies.

Network Advertising

Historically, major U.S. advertisers purchased airtime from one of the national broadcast **networks:** ABC, CBS, NBC, or Fox. In 1995, relaxed FCC rules enabled two of the biggest producers of prime-time shows, Warner Bros. and Paramount, to launch their own broad-

Television plays an important role in its ability to impart brand personality. Television communicates with many stakeholders simultaneously and can deliver a "big idea" in a uniquely creative manner. This commercial for M&M's keeps the idea that the candies are personalities and alive by having Red wish he was human and then turn into Danny DeVito.

Source: Mars, Incorporated

cast networks—WB and UPN—giving them captive distribution outlets for programs they produce and buy.[21] With 31 affiliated stations, UPN immediately covered 80 percent of the country, even though it initially programmed only a couple of nights a week. In 2006, UPN and WB merged to become CW.[22]

Cable has eroded the audience of the broadcast networks. At one time the big three (ABC, CBS, and NBC) had more than 90 percent of the prime-time audience. Today their total share is about 38.3 percent, with ad-supported cable networks comprising 60 percent.[23]

Networks offer large advertisers convenience and efficiency because they broadcast messages simultaneously across many affiliate stations throughout the country. Broadcast networks tend to reach masses of American consumers representing a cross section of the population, while cable networks tend to reach more selective niches.

An advertiser who underwrites the cost of a program is engaging in **sponsorship.** In a sole sponsorship, the advertiser is responsible for both the program content and the total cost of production. Sponsorship is so costly that single sponsorships are usually limited to specials. Companies that sponsor programs (e.g., AT&T, Xerox, and Hallmark) gain two important advantages. First, the public more readily identifies with the product(s) due to the prestige of sponsoring first-rate entertainment. Second, the sponsor controls the placement and content of its commercials. The commercials can be fit to the program and run any length the sponsor desires so long as they remain within network or station regulations. Further, because networks are centralized, the advertiser gets only one bill.

Sponsorship offers many opportunities. When the popular drama series *24* started its second season, the first episode was presented commercial-free, thanks to a full sponsorship by Ford Motor Company. The episode also featured numerous Ford vehicles in the show. To save money and reduce risks, many advertisers cosponsor programs, sponsoring on alternate weeks or dividing the program into segments. NFL games, for instance, are always sold as multiple sponsorships.

Most network TV advertising is sold on a **participation basis,** with several advertisers buying 30- or 60-second segments within a program. This enables them to spread their budgets and avoid long-term commitments to any one program. It also lets smaller advertisers buy a limited amount of time and still get the nationwide coverage they need.

Network advertising also has several disadvantages: lack of flexibility, long lead times, inconvenient restrictions, and forced adherence to network standards and practices, not to mention high prices. Cable, which now offers shows with audiences that match or exceed those on the networks, suffers from fewer restrictions but equally high prices. As shown in Exhibit 13-5, advertisers need a big budget to appear on the most popular programs. For this reason, many advertisers decide to buy *spot announcements.*

Exhibit 13-5

Advertising cost per 30-second spot on the 10 most popular prime-time shows 2017.

Rank	Show and Network	Price (000)	Viewership (millions)
1	*Big Bang Theory* (CBS)	$286	18.5
2	*Sunday Night Football* (NBC)	670	18.4
3	*The Good Doctor* (ABC)	126	17.8
4	*NCIS* (CBS)	140	17.7
5	*This is Us* (NBC)	394	16.5
6	*The Voice Monday* (NBC)	259	16.0
7	*Fox NFL Sunday Post Game* (Fox)	289	15.8
8	*The Walking Dead* (AMC)	236	15.1
9	*The Voice Tuesday* (NBC)	230	14.7
10	*Bull* (CBS)	129	14.4

Source: "Top Broadcast and Cable TV Prime-Time Shows in 2017," *Ad Age* Marketing Fact Pack 2018, Crain Communications Inc.

Movie product placements also benefit the advertiser when the films are later shown on TV. Apple and Pepsi have found this to be a useful strategy for promoting products.

AF archive/Alamy Stock Photo

Spot Announcements

National **spot announcements** run in clusters between programs. They are less expensive than participations and more flexible than network advertising because they can be concentrated in specific regions of the country. An advertiser with a small budget or limited distribution may use spots to introduce a new product into one area at a time. Or an advertiser can vary its message for different markets to suit promotional needs.[24]

Spots may run 10, 15, 30, or 60 seconds and be sold nationally or locally. Spot advertising is more difficult to buy than network advertising because it involves contacting each station directly. This is a headache with cable channels because one city may be served by 10 or more cable companies. For the broadcast stations, the *national rep system,* in which individuals act as sales and service representatives for a number of stations, alleviates this problem through the use of *electronic data interchange (EDI).*[25] This technology enables agency buyers to electronically process orders, makegoods (free advertising time to compensate for problems), and revisions, and to maintain an electronic audit trail through the life of a schedule. Likewise, reps can transmit orders directly to their stations via satellite while keeping in day-to-day contact with agency buyers.[26]

Meanwhile, a number of large cable rep firms are also working to make the purchase of spot cable more convenient for national advertisers through satellite technology and digital systems that interconnect various cable companies in a region.[27]

Spot advertising is available only at network station breaks and when network advertisers purchase less than a full lineup, so spot ads may get lost in the clutter—which is why they tend to have fewer viewers and a smaller piece of the ad spending pie.

Syndication

As audiences fragment, syndicated programs become an increasingly popular adjunct or alternative to network advertising. Over the years, the syndication industry has grown from almost nothing into a $4.1 billion advertising medium.[28]

Syndication is the sale of programs on a station-by-station, market-by-market basis. In other words, the producer (e.g., Warner Bros. or Disney) deals directly with the stations, often through a distribution company, rather than going through the networks. This efficient "direct-from-the-factory" approach gives local TV stations more programming control and greater profits. It also gives advertisers access to **inventory** (commercial time) for their spots that they might not get on network programs—often at better prices.[29] Syndication has become an important source of programming in the United States (see Exhibit 13-6).

Television syndication comes in three forms: off-network, first-run, and barter. In **off-network syndication,** former popular network programs (reruns) are sold to individual stations for rebroadcast. Examples include *Seinfeld* and *Friends.* **First-run syndication** involves original shows, like *Ellen, Inside Edition,* and *Extra,* that are produced specifically for the syndication market. One of the fastest-growing trends in television is **barter syndication** (also called *advertiser-supported syndication*). These are first-run programs offered free or for a reduced rate, but with some of the ad space (usually 50%) presold to national advertisers. *Wheel of Fortune* and *Jeopardy,* distributed by King World Productions, are two of the most popular examples.[30]

Syndication is a powerful tool for building reach. Advertisers like it because they can affiliate with popular programs and maximize their use of broadcast TV, gaining back much of the audience they used to reach through the networks (see Exhibit 13-7).

Ethics, Diversity & Inclusion

Should Kids Ever Be a Target Audience?

From its inception, parents, regulators, and advocates have looked warily at television as a platform for advertising to kids. Until the internet, TV was the one medium offered advertisers a straight path to young hearts and minds.

It could be argued that ads directed at youngsters are wasted because parents control the purse strings. Nothing could be farther from the truth. A report published in 2012 by ad agency Digitas estimated that young children and tweens had purchasing power in the neighborhood of $1.2 trillion. That figure includes the money kids control for themselves as well as their ability to influence parents' purchases. The report suggests that 6 in 10 tweens have "substantially influenced" adult decisions about a car purchase! According to one expert, the minivan was created because children demanded more room. Then, when kids decided the vehicle was "uncool," their opinions helped to develop the SUV.

Madison Avenue seems keenly aware of the power of these small "influencers," and as a result kids see lots of commercials. One study estimated kids between 6 and 11 see up to 20,000 every year—easy to do when that group spends close to 30 hours a week watching TV.

Of course, it can be argued that parents play a primary role in regulating what children watch and consume. Still, against a tide of commercial messages, parents can't seem to get the upper hand. In response, the World Health Organization, focusing on one especially pernicious problem, childhood obesity, has recommended that advertisers reduce "food and beverage marketing directed at little children that is high in sugar, fat and sodium in order to help reduce the burden of obesity worldwide."[31] In the U.S., the FTC notes that since 1980, "childhood obesity rates have tripled among adolescents and doubled among younger children." While acknowledging that the causes of this health problem are complex, the agency concludes that "regardless of the causes, responsible marketing can play a positive role in improving children's diets and physical activity level."[32]

Some have made the affirmative case for ads directed at kids. Among the most common arguments is that child-oriented programming on nonpublic stations might not exist if ad revenues dried up—a point that is both true and insufficient. Between an advertising ban and an all-out attempt to persuade youngsters to buy or pester their parents is a middle ground, one that acknowledges a role for advertisers to play in protecting kids.

Questions

1. Should advertising directed to kids be banned entirely? Why or why not?

2. If ads to kids are not banned outright, what might responsible advertising look like?

Exhibit 13-6
TV network and syndication distribution.
a. The networks are essentially middlemen.
b. Syndication is often a more efficient way of financing and distributing programs.

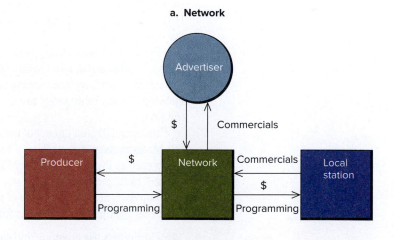

Exhibit 13-7
Syndication viewing shares for total and daytime dayparts. Although syndication holds a respectable 13 percent share relative to total overall viewing, it commands a full one-third of viewing share of all national broadcast. During prime-time dayparts, when competing with network sitcoms and dramas, syndication's share of audience drops way off. But during early prime time it is responsible for over 75 percent share of national broadcast viewing, and during late fringe it commands close to 50 percent share. Syndication ranks high in early prime time and late fringe segments because the only broadcast competition comes from early evening news programs and late-night talk shows.

Source: Billboard/Howard Appelbaum Publisher.

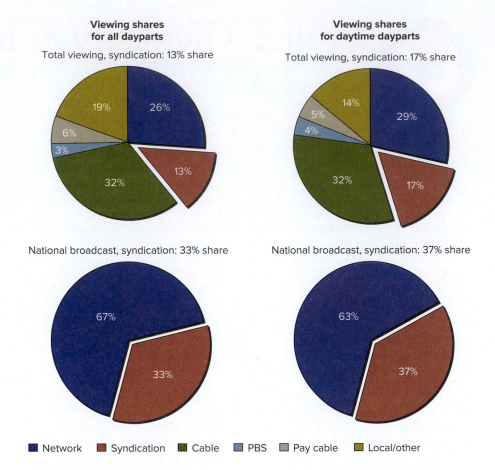

Direct-Response Television

In the fall of 1992, independent presidential candidate Ross Perot sat in front of a TV camera for 30 minutes with homemade flip charts and a down-home pitch for the White House and drew 20 million viewers. A month later, he pulled a respectable 19 percent of the vote.

Perot made advertising history by catapulting the **program-length advertisement (PLA),** or **infomercial,** into the limelight. He also proved what companies that produce and sell infomercials have been saying for years: Long-form advertising can communicate a message in a way other forms can't.[33] As a result, *Advertising Age* named Perot its adman of the year.

Infomercials aren't new, but their respectability is. Before Perot, most PLA users were off–Madison Avenue marketers of hand mixers, juicers, and car waxes. Today, major marketers such as Pfizer, Microsoft's MSNTV2, and Voom have ventured into the infomercial arena.[34] In Colorado, long-form ads were used as a negotiating tool in a labor dispute.[35] And now even networks air some of these ads, which were once relegated to independents and cable channels.[36] The reasons for this sudden growth are simple:

1. Consumers pay attention and can respond immediately.
2. Brand managers may be able to gain a competitive advantage by going where the competition is not.
3. PLAs can fulfill some message objectives, like product demonstration and brand differentiation, far better than 30-second commercials.
4. Results are measurable.
5. The ad campaign can pay for itself while supporting the retail trade.
6. PLAs combine the power of advertising, direct response, and sales promotion.[37]

Infomercials are examples of long-form messages. They engage audiences with entertaining content and take time to discuss the benefits of products people are not likely to be familiar with. Increasingly, this content can be put on the web as well. Squatty Potty, using the metaphor of a unicorn, delivers an entertaining message on a delicate subject. You can see the ad here: www.youtube.com/ watch?v=KlEovr29KBU.

Source: Squatty Potty, LLC

In addition to infomercials, direct-response TV (DRTV) includes shorter ads (often 60 seconds to two minutes) that ask consumers to order a product, as well as cable networks (Home Shopping Network) that feature round-the-clock sales. It's easy to see why national marketers have jumped on the bandwagon. The market for DRTV has grown to over a $7.8 billion market.[38]

Local TV Advertising

Local businesses and retailers, often in cooperation with nationally known manufacturers, now spend over $16 billion annually on local broadcast and cable TV.[39] Most local stations sell spot announcements, but some local advertisers develop and sponsor local programs or buy the rights to a syndicated series.

Efficient advertisers study the audiences of various programs and analyze their impact and cost-effectiveness against other media vehicles. To do this, they must understand the techniques and terminology used in television audience measurement.

The companies that measure the program audiences of TV and radio stations for advertisers and broadcasters are called **rating services.** These firms attempt to pick a representative sample of the market and furnish data on the number and characteristics of the viewers or listeners. Several research organizations gather the data at their own expense and publish it. Companies subscribe to a service and use it as a basis for planning, buying, or selling media advertising.

In the United States, Nielsen Media Research is the major rating service for television. Its flagship service, the Nielsen Television Index (NTI), uses a national sample of 5,100 households equipped with *people meters* to develop audience estimates for all national TV programming sources: 7 broadcast networks, 47 cable networks, 3 Spanish-language networks, and more than 200 syndicators. At the local level, Nielsen uses people meters in the 55 largest markets and diary surveys in 210 TV markets to measure viewing for more than 1,500 local TV stations, 140 cable operators, 48 syndicators, and 2,000 local advertising agencies.[40] It publishes the information at least twice a year in a publication commonly called *The Book* (see Ad Lab 13–A).

Digital video recorders (DVRs) have helped change the face of TV ratings measurement. Because of the perception that audiences were taking measures to skip commercials and only watching the programs, even before DVRs were invented, advertisers and agencies have been lobbying Nielsen to measure commercial minutes rather than program minutes. Commercial minutes have long been thought to be the holy grail of TV audience measurement. But with DVRs, programming companies have been pushing to include measures of shows that are not watched live, which program ratings do not take into account. In 2007 the commercial rating was rolled out, with the new designation of C3 for the commercial rating plus the addition of any commercial viewing up to three days after airing. This new measurement replaces a 65-year-old standard of measurement. Rollout began in 2008 of these new measurements.[42]

AD Lab 13–A

Where Do Those Infamous TV Ratings Come From?

Variety reported that the 2018 Oscars, the movie industry's famous awards show, was the least-watched Academy Awards broadcast in history. The show drew just over 26 million viewers, down from the prior year's show, which was watched by 33 million.

The drop in viewers has a number of implications, both for Hollywood and for the advertisers who pay to participate in the show. But you may find yourself asking a different question: How do they know 26 million people watched?

Sam Lothridge/CBS/Getty Images

American viewing habits are reported primarily by one company, Nielsen. Nielsen was founded in the 1930s to track the audiences for radio shows and shifted its techniques to TV in 1950 at the start of the television era. It remains the de facto standard to the present day.

But how does it do it? How does it know, for example, if you were watching Jimmy Kimmel's Oscars program?

The answer, bluntly, is it doesn''t know if *you* watched. Rather, it determines viewership using a powerful technique, known as random sampling, to identify a group of households that look like America.

Nielsen households agree to allow the company to monitor their viewing habits with technologies that track what each household member is watching. A box placed on a TV requires viewers to enter codes that indicate who is watching. The data are transmitted to Nielsen every night.

Seems simple enough. But Nielsen's challenge has grown significantly in recent years. For example, how should sports audiences be measured when many people watch in sports bars or other people's homes? (Nielsen research shows significant numbers of people only or usually watch sports out-of-home.)[41]

An interesting development in audience measurement is the single-source data made available by supermarket scanners. Once information on a family's viewing habits has been gathered, its packaged-goods purchases are measured. The implications are monumental for marketing and media planners. The leaders in single-source measurement today are Information Resources Inc. (IRI), with its BehaviorScan service, and Nielsen, with its Home Scan service.

Laboratory Applications

1. What are the advantages and disadvantages of the various measurement methods?
2. Which method do you consider the best? Why?

For demographic studies of TV audiences, advertisers also use the Simmons Market Research Bureau and Mediamark Research, Inc. These companies perform extensive surveys of the U.S. marketplace and publish their findings on consumer lifestyles, product usage, and media habits. Advertisers use the results for strategic planning purposes.

Product Placement

Another way to reach movie and television audiences is to pay a fee to have the product written into the movie or program. Such **product placement** is common. Notice the number of identifiable products in the next movie or TV program you see.

By getting brand appearances, and sometimes roles, in TV shows and movies, companies benefit from the association with top actors. Nokia has had great success with this technique: Its phones were so prominent in the film *The Matrix* that 31 percent of moviegoers thought that characters in *The Matrix Reloaded* sequel were still using Nokia phones, when in fact they had switched to Samsung.[43]

Constantly fretting about viewers' newfound ability to avoid commercials by using TiVo, advertisers are also embedding their products more frequently in television programs. Ford and Coca-Cola both had high-profile presences on *American Idol*—judges drank from red cups with the Coca-Cola logo and contestants performed in Ford vehicles—just one example of the emerging "brand casting" trend, worth an estimated $1.5 billion in the United States in 2005. Product placement growth is expected to significantly outpace that of traditional advertising. According to *PQ Media,* U.S. paid product placement reached almost $9 billion in 2017.[44]

However, controversy surrounds some product placement categories. In response to severe new laws prohibiting most forms of tobacco advertising, the Canadian Tobacco Manufacturers' Council withdrew all product placements in films, TV programs, and computer games.

Defining Television Markets

Television rating services define geographic television markets to minimize the confusion of overlapping TV signals. The Nielsen station index uses the term **designated market areas (DMAs)** for geographic areas (cities, counties) in which the *local* TV stations attract the most viewing. For example, the DMA for Columbus, Georgia (see Exhibit 13-8), is the 17 counties in which the local area TV stations are the most watched.

Audience Measures

Rating services and media planners use many terms to define a station's audience, penetration, and efficiency. **TV households (TVHH)** refers to the number of households that own television sets. The number of TVHH in a particular market gives an advertiser a sense of the market's size. Likewise, the number of TVHH tuned in to a particular program helps the advertiser estimate the program's popularity and how many people a commercial is likely to reach.

The percentage of homes in a given area that have one or more TV sets turned on at any particular time is expressed as **households using TV (HUT).** If there are 1,000 TV sets in the survey area and 500 are turned on, HUT is 50 percent.

The **program rating** refers to the percentage of TV households in an area that are tuned in to a specific program. The rating is computed as follows:

$$\text{Rating} = \frac{\text{TVHH tuned to specific program}}{\text{Total TVHH in area}}$$

Exhibit 13-8

This map of the area surrounding Columbus, Georgia, shows media planners which counties are included in the designated market area (DMA) and will be reached by advertising placed on the local television stations. Columbus, Georgia, is the 125th largest DMA in the United States and contains over 200,000 TV households.

Networks want high ratings because they measure a show's popularity. More popular shows can command higher advertising rates. Local stations often change their programming (e.g., buy different syndicated shows) to attract more viewers and thereby their ratings (and their revenues).

The percentage of homes with sets in use (HUT) tuned to a specific program is called the audience **share.** A program with only 500 viewers can have a 50 *share* if only 1,000 sets are turned on. *Ratings,* in contrast, measure the audience as a percentage of all TVHH in the area, whether the TV sets are on or off.

The total number of homes reached by some portion of a program is called **total audience.** This figure is normally broken down to determine **audience composition** (the distribution of the audience into demographic categories).

Gross Rating Points

In television, **gross rating points (GRPs)** are the total rating points a particular media schedule achieves over a specific period. As we discussed in Chapter 9, a weekly schedule of five commercials on programs with an average household rating of 20 would yield 100 GRPs. Recall that GRPs are computed as follows:

$$\text{Reach (average rating)} \times \text{Frequency} = \text{Gross rating points}$$

GRPs allow advertisers to draw conclusions about the different markets available for a client's ads by providing a comparable measure of advertising weight. However, GRPs do not reflect a market's size. For example, while campaigns in Knoxville and Charlotte might have the same GRPs, Charlotte is a much larger city (859,000) than Knoxville (187,000) so a ratings point has over four times as many people in it.

	TV Homes (000s)	Average Cost per Spot	Average Rating	No. of Spots	GRPs
Knoxville	638	$ 1,100	15	5	75
Charlotte	2,640	5,782	15	5	75

To better determine the relative value of television advertising markets, other measures are used, such as *cost per rating point (CPP)* and *cost per thousand (CPM),* which were described in Chapter 9.

Buying Television Time

The process of buying TV time can be lengthy and, depending on the number of stations in the buy, quite involved. Advertisers or media buyers must

- Determine which programs are available at what cost.
- Analyze the various programs for efficiency.
- Negotiate price with station reps.
- Determine what reach and frequency they are achieving.
- Sign broadcast contracts.
- Review affidavits of performance to be sure the commercials ran as agreed.

These procedures are so complex that most large advertisers use ad agencies or media-buying services. Buying services have gained in popularity because they charge less and can save advertisers money by negotiating for desirable time slots at reduced rates. Local advertisers typically rely on station reps to determine the best buys for the money.

Requesting Avails

To find out which programs are available, media buyers contact stations' sales reps–local station salespeople, national media rep organizations that sell for one station in each market, or network reps. The media buyer gives the rep information about the advertiser's media objectives and target audiences and asks the rep to supply a list of **avails** (available time slots) along with prices and estimated ratings. Many media buyers ask for the information based on the last few Nielsen books to see whether a show's ratings are consistent, rising, or falling.

Selecting Programs for Buys

The media buyer selects the most efficient programs in relation to the target audience using the **CPP** and the **CPM** for each program:

$$CPP = \frac{Cost}{Rating} \qquad CPM = \frac{Cost}{Thousands\ of\ people}$$

For example, assume *CSI* has a rating of 25, reaches 200,000 people in the primary target audience, and costs $2,000 for a 30-second spot with a fixed guarantee on station WALB-TV in Albany, Georgia. Then,

$$CPP = \frac{\$2,000}{25} = \$80 \qquad CPM = \frac{\$2,000}{(200,000 \div 1,000)} = \$10$$

By calculating CPP, the media buyer can compare the cost of a rating point from one program or network to another. That's good information for beginning negotiations. But rating points relate to the whole market. The real important figure is the cost of reaching 1,000 prospects in the *target* market. That's why the CPM must be calculated against the size of the target audience, not the whole market. The lower the cost per 1,000 target audience (CPM-TA), the more efficient the show is at reaching real prospects.

To get the best buys within the available budget, then, the media buyer substitutes stronger programs for less efficient ones (see Ad Lab 13–B, "Getting 'You're Out' on TV").

Negotiating Prices and Contracts

TV stations and cable companies publish rate cards to sell their airtime. However, because TV audiences are estimated at best, television reps will always negotiate prices.

The media buyer contacts the rep and explains what efficiency the advertiser needs in terms of delivery and CPM to make the buy. The buyer has numerous ways to negotiate lower rates: work out a package deal, accept *run-of-schedule positioning* (the station chooses when to run the commercials), or take advantage of preemption rates. A **preemption rate** is lower because the advertiser agrees to be "bumped" (preempted) if another advertiser pays the higher, nonpreemption rate.

The media buyer must read the advertising contract carefully before signing it. The contract indicates the dates, times, and programs on which the advertiser's commercials will run, the length of each spot, the rate per spot, and the total amount. The reverse side of the contract defines payment terms and responsibilities of the advertiser, agency, and station. After the spots run, the station returns a signed and notarized **affidavit of performance** to the advertiser or agency, specifying when the spots aired and what makegoods are available. **Makegoods** refer to free advertising time an advertiser receives to compensate for spots the station missed or ran incorrectly or because the program's ratings were substantially lower than guaranteed.[45]

Electronic Media Buying Software

With the internet, today's broadcast media buyers don't ever have to leave the office but can, right from their desktops, pore over SRDS and Simmons research data to create and even buy media schedules with electronic avails.

With software like Arbitron's SmartPlus media-buying suite, media planners and buyers can analyze, plan, and report from one application. Most spot broadcasts are revised many times, and SmartPlus allows for revisions and transfers seamlessly in the planning process. Nowadays software can integrate with almost everything through a simple XML/API feed. SmartPlus integrates with Outlook, increasing the efficiency of communications between buyers and sellers.

Nielsen's PAL software is a national media planning system. It takes into account market-by-market differences in media delivery for network TV, syndicated TV, cable TV,

AD Lab 13–B

Getting "You're Out" on TV

"You're Out" baseball mitts are planning a campaign on TV. The mitts are for kids so they are your target market. As the marketing director, you choose to examine the gross rating points (GRPs) for placing your advertising. You have an idea of the days and times you want the ads to be placed. Chart 1 indicates the best programs for Memphis, Tennessee, and relevant planning data your assistant has gathered according to your preferences. Due to time constraints, the chart is incomplete, but enough data are available for you to finish the chart.

Laboratory Applications

1. Using the formulas in the text as a guide, complete Chart 1.
2. Assuming your budget is $68,000, use Chart 1 to decide which two programs would be most effective for reaching just kids. Explain your selection.

Chart 1: Best Programs for Memphis, TN

Program	Rating	Cost	Spots	GRP
KC Undercover (*early* evening daily, rerun, 30/70 adults to kids)	15	$34,000	32	_____
Saturday morning cartoons (kids ages 2–12)	_____	34,000	30	300.0
Major League Baseball game (weekends, mostly adults)	7.8	34,000	29	_____
After-school special (kids ages 7–13, afternoon, daily)	_____	34,000	27	205.0

and magazines. PAL can be used in different ways. First, it evaluates market-by-market performance of a national media schedule in terms of GRPs and/or budgets. Also, PAL can define your marketing objectives by using BDI or sales data, along with selected spot weight.

Alternatively, Nielsen's Clear Decisions and Reach and Frequency help media planners generate schedule results with minimal effort, identify insights from a suite of reports, and even create presentation-ready charts and graphs from one screen. The planner can perform R&F analyses using Clear Decisions to get to the answers faster.

Considerations in Buying TV Time

Advertisers must decide *when* to air commercials and on *which programs.* Unlike radio listeners, TV viewers are loyal to programs, not stations. Programs continue to run or are canceled depending on their *ratings* (percentage of the population watching). Ratings also depend on the time of day a program runs.

Television time is divided into dayparts as follows:

Daytime:	9 a.m.–4 p.m. (EST)
Early fringe:	4–5:30 p.m. (EST)
Early news:	5 or 5:30–7:30 p.m. (EST)
Prime access:	7:30–8 p.m. (EST)
Prime:	8–11 p.m. (EST)
Late news:	11–11:30 p.m. (EST)
Late fringe:	11:30 p.m.–1 a.m. (EST)

Viewing is highest during **prime time** (8 to 11 p.m. Eastern Standard Time; 7 to 10 p.m. Central Standard Time). Late fringe ranks fairly high in most markets among adults, and daytime and early fringe tend to be viewed most heavily by women. To reach the greatest percentage of the advertiser's target audience with optimal frequency, the media planner determines a **daypart mix** based on TV usage levels reported by the rating services.

Radio

Radio is a personal, one-on-one medium; people listen alone. And radio is mobile. It can entertain people who are driving, walking, at home, or away from home. This makes it a particularly strong way to reach people who commute by car.

Radio is also adaptable to moods. In the morning, people may want to hear the news, upbeat music, or interesting chatter; in the afternoon, they may want to unwind with classical or easy-listening music.

Contemporary radio exists in three primary forms. The oldest, terrestrial or **broadcast radio,** transmits over the electromagnetic broadcast spectrum (with frequencies between 300 and 3,000 kHz for AM and 30–300 MHz for FM) and can be received by anyone with an inexpensive tuner. **Satellite radio** is broadcast from space satellites that remain in orbit over North America (Sirius XM) or other parts of the world, including Africa, Eurasia, and Japan. Finally, radio content can be accessed via the internet through **streaming radio.**

This chapter also will review a competitor to radio, one that is posing an increasing challenge to the radio business model: podcasts. **Podcasts** are internet-only shows that listeners stream on demand. Originally developed as part of Apple's ecosystem, podcasts are now played on many devices and are important vehicles for many advertisers.

Who Uses Radio?

In an average week, 93 percent of the U.S. population listens to broadcast radio; in an average day, about 72 percent. As shown in Exhibit 13-9, broadcast radio remains the most popular way of accessing radio content, although alternatives are becoming more popular. The average American listens to the radio for close to two hours each day. In fact, during the prime shopping hours of 6 a.m. to 6 p.m., the average U.S. adult spends more time with radio than with broadcast and cable TV combined.[46] Radio is also cost-effective. In the last decade, the CPM for radio advertising has risen less than for any other major medium and substantially less than the consumer price index.[47]

LO 13-7

More national advertisers are discovering radio's reach and frequency potential. Certainly it has worked well for brands like Motel 6, which for over 30 years has featured folksy Tom Bodett assuring listeners that the chain will "leave the lights on." The campaign remains fresh even as the spots are instantly identifiable from Bodett's voice, the country music sound, the wry humor, and leisurely pacing. As proof the ads are still going strong, the campaign won "Best of Show" at the Radio Mercury Awards in 2016. Listen to a spot mocking smartphone autocorrection that ran during the Super Bowl at http://wyrk.com/listen-to-the-funniest-motel-6-radio-commercial/.

The Use of Radio in IMC

While television tends to be a passive medium that people simply watch, radio actively involves people. They listen intently to their favorite personalities; they call in to make requests, participate in a contest, or contribute to a discussion; they use their ears and imaginations to fill in what they cannot see. Most people listen faithfully to two or three different radio stations with different types of programming. This means that smart advertisers can use the medium to establish an immediate, intimate relationship with consumers and other stakeholders. That makes radio an ideal medium for integrated marketing communications.

With radio, national companies can tie in to a local market and target the specific demographic group they want to reach. Most important, radio enables advertisers to maintain strategic consistency and stretch their media dollars through **imagery transfer.** Research shows that when advertisers run a schedule on TV and then convert the audio portion to radio commercials, fully 75 percent of consumers replay the video in their minds when they hear the radio spot. That extends the life and builds the impact of a TV campaign at greatly reduced cost.[48] In an IMC campaign, where message consistency is a primary objective, this is a very important feature of radio.

Local retailers like the medium for the same reasons. Also, they can tailor it to their needs. It offers defined audiences; its recall characteristics are similar to TV's; and retailers can create an identity by doing their own ads. Finally, because radio is so mobile, retailers can reach prospects just before they purchase. Hence, recent years have seen major spending increases by local grocery stores, car dealers, banks, and home-improvement, furniture, and apparel stores.[49]

Exhibit 13-9

Daily reach of radio for people 18 and older

Source	Daily Reach
AM/FM radio	72%
Owned music	26
YouTube music videos	20
Ad-free SiriusXM	11
Ad-supported Pandora	11
TV music channels	9
Podcasts	8
Other streaming audio	7
Ad-supported SiriusXM	4
Ad-supported Spotify	4
Amazon Music	3
Ad-free Pandora	2
Apple Music	2

Source: Edison Research, "Share of Ear," Q2–Q4 2017, Q1 2018, Persons 18+.

Radio Programming and Audiences

Radio stations plan their programming carefully to reach specific markets and to capture as many listeners as possible. The larger the audience, the more a station can charge for commercial time. Therefore, extensive planning and research go into radio programming and program changes.

Stations can use tried-and-true formats, subscribe to network or syndicated programming, or devise unique approaches. Programming choices are greatly influenced by whether a station is on the AM or FM band. FM has much better sound fidelity, fewer commercial interruptions, and more varied programming.

Depending on a company's advertising needs, radio has many uses within the IMC model. This ad for Lindsay Olives (www.lindsayolives.com) personifies the quality and selectivity that define the brand in a humorous and memorable way.

Source: Zeimer's Advertising Shoppe, "Born Homely"

MUSIC UP AND UNDER THROUGHOUT.

MALE VOICEOVER: I was a homely looking olive when I was born. Not ugly . . . but homeliness is next to nothingness if you're trying to be a handsome Lindsay Olive.

So I tried to change . . . to become one of the beautiful olives. I wore contact lenses . . . I had my pimento styled by Mr. Joe . . . Nothing helped.

So, I turned to olive surgery. I mean, I was desperate to become a quality Lindsay Olive! Now, some surgeons wouldn't touch an olive that looked like me; they said it was too risky. But you can always find someone who'll take out a wrinkle here, or inject an imitation of that great Lindsay flavor there.

The Lindsay people gave me a second look, and I almost got in! . . . But one inspector saw a scar and I was through. I guess the Lindsay people were right after all: Beauty is only skin deep, but ugliness goes all the way to the pit . . .

FEMALE VOICEOVER ANNOUNCER: An olive is just an olive, unless it's a Lindsay.

MALE VOICEOVER ANNOUNCER: Well, maybe another olive company will give me a break.

MUSIC UP AND OUT.

To counteract FM's inroads, many AM stations switched to programs that don't rely on sound quality, such as news, talk, and sports. Some stations are experimenting with all comedy, midday game shows with audience participation, or formats geared to specific regions, such as KHJ's "car radio" in Los Angeles. AM stations are also trying to win back music listeners by improving their sound quality and offering stereo broadcasting.

When buying radio time, advertisers usually buy the station's *format,* not its programs. Most stations adopt one of the dozen or so standard **programming formats:** contemporary hit radio (CHR-TOP 40), adult contemporary, country, rock, easy listening, news/talk, adult standards, classical, religious, and so on, as shown in Exhibit 13-10. Each format tends to appeal to specific demographic groups. The most popular format is country music, which is programmed by 18.9 percent of the stations in the United States (both AM and FM) and appeals to a broad cross section of Americans from 25 to 54 years old.

Contemporary hit radio (CHR), always found on FM stations, appeals to teenagers and women under 30. It provides a constant flow of top 40 hits, usually with minimal intrusion by disk jockeys. Another popular format, adult contemporary (or "easy oldies"), is often advertised as "light rock, less talk." This format aims at the desirable target group of working women between 25 and 54. The news/talk, easy-listening, and nostalgia formats tend to have high listenership among men and women over 35.[50]

There are now more than 20 national radio networks, including the multiple "mini-networks" of ABC, CBS, Westwood One, and Unistar, and numerous syndicators offer programs from live rock concerts to public-affairs discussions. To stand out, 80 percent of licensed radio stations are opting for syndicated and network offerings.[51] As more stations carry these programs and more listeners tune in, national advertisers find them increasingly attractive.

Although spending on radio advertising accounts for only about 4 percent of all ad spending, consumers spend about 44 percent of their total time with media listening to the radio.[52] Clearly, although it is much cheaper to produce than television advertising, radio ad spending has room to grow. In 2017, however, revenue for radio measured $7.6 billion, down slightly from the previous year.[53] The largest national radio advertisers are major retailers and telecommunications companies (see Exhibit 13-11).

Exhibit 13-10

Top radio formats among U.S. listeners.

Top 10 Radio Formats 2016—All Persons

	All persons share	
Rank	**Format**	**Share**
1	News Talk Information	9.6%
2	Pop Contemporary Hit Radio (CHR)	8.1%
3	Adult Contemporary (AC)	7.5%
4	Country*	7.4%
5	Hot Adult Contemporary (AC)	6.4%
6	Classic Hits	5.3%
7	Classic Rock	5.1%
8	Urban Adult Contemporary (AC)	4.8%
9	All Sports	4.7%
t10	Mexican Regional	3.7%
t10	Urban Contemporary	3.7%

Top 10 Radio Formats 2016—Persons 18–34

	Persons 18–34 Share	
Rank	**Format**	**Share**
1	Pop Contemporary Hit Radio (CHR)	12.2%
2	Country*	8.6%
3	Hot Adult Contemporary (AC)	7.3%
4	Urban Contemporary	6.6%
5	Adult Contemporary (AC)	6.5%
6	Rhythmic Contemporary Hit Radio (CHR)	5.1%
t7	Mexican Regional	5.0%
t7	Alternative	5.0%
9	Classic Rock	4.5%
10	News Talk Information	4.1%

*Country *is a combination of Country and New Country formats*

Source: "What Were 2016's Most Popular Radio Formats?" *Marketing Charts*, January 4, 2017, www.marketingcharts.com/demographics-and-audiences/youth-and-gen-x-73353.

Exhibit 13-11

Top 10 national spot radio advertisers 2017.

Rank	Advertiser	National Spot Radio Spending ($ in Millions)
1	T-Mobile	$188
2	Comcast	185
3	Home Depot	112
4	AT&T	104
5	Berkshire Hathaway	97
6	Sprint	94
7	Mattress Firm	89
8	Fiat Chrysler	81
9	Macy's	56
10	McDonald's	56

Buying Radio Time

Advertisers need a basic knowledge of the medium to buy radio time effectively: the types of radio advertising available for commercial use, a basic understanding of radio terminology, and the steps involved in preparing a radio schedule.

Types of Radio Advertising

LO 13-8

An advertiser may purchase network, spot, or local radio time. Advertisers like the reach and frequency, selectivity, and cost efficiency of radio (see My IMC Campaign 13-D, "The Pros and Cons of Radio Advertising").

Networks

Advertisers may use one of the national radio networks to carry their messages to the entire national market simultaneously via stations that subscribe to the network's programs. In addition, more than 100 regional radio networks in the United States operate with information oriented toward specific geographic markets.

My IMC Campaign 13-D

The Pros and Cons of Radio Advertising

The Pros

The principal advantages of radio are high reach and frequency, selectivity, and cost efficiency.

- **Reach and frequency.** Radio offers an excellent combination of reach and frequency. The average adult listens more than three hours a day, radio builds a large audience quickly, and a normal advertising schedule easily allows repeated impact on the listener.

- **Selectivity.** Specialized radio formats, with prescribed audiences and coverage areas, enable advertisers to select the market they want to reach: a specific sex, age group, ethnic or religious background, income group, employment category, educational level, or special interest.

- **Cost efficiency.** Radio offers its reach, frequency, and selectivity at one of the lowest costs per thousand, and radio production is inexpensive. National spots can be produced for about one-tenth the cost of a TV commercial. And local stations often produce local spots for free.

- **Other advantages.** Radio also offers timeliness, immediacy, local relevance, and creative flexibility.

The Cons

In spite of these advantages, radio has limitations: It's an aural medium only, its audience is highly segmented, the advertiser's commercials are short-lived and often only half-heard, and each ad must compete with the clutter of other advertising.

- **Limitations of sound.** Radio is heard but not seen, a drawback if the product must be seen to be understood. Some agencies think radio restricts their creative options.

- **Segmented audiences.** If a large number of radio stations compete for the same audience, advertisers that want to blanket the market have to buy at multiple stations, which may not be cost-effective.

- **Short-lived and half-heard commercials.** Radio commercials are fleeting. They can't be kept like a newspaper or a magazine ad. Radio must compete with other activities for attention, and it doesn't always succeed.

- **Clutter.** Stations with the greatest appeal for advertisers have more commercials. Advertisers must produce a commercial that stands out from the rest.

Networks provide national and regional advertisers with simple administration and low effective net cost per station. Disadvantages include lack of flexibility in choosing affiliated stations, the limited number of stations on a network's roster, and the long lead times required to book time.

Spot Radio

Spot radio affords national advertisers great flexibility in their choice of markets, stations, airtime, and copy. They can put commercials on the air quickly—some stations require as little as 20 minutes' lead time, and advertisers can build local acceptance by using local personalities. Radio rep firms, like Katz Radio, represent a list of stations and sell spot time to national advertisers and agencies.

Local Radio

Local time denotes radio spots purchased by a local advertiser or agency. It involves the same procedure as national spots.

Radio advertising can be either live or taped. Most radio stations use recorded shows with live news in between. Likewise, nearly all radio commercials are prerecorded to reduce costs and maintain broadcast quality.

Radio Terminology

For the most part, the terminology used for radio is the same as for other media, but some terms are particular to radio. The most common of these are the concepts of *dayparts, average quarter-hour audiences,* and *cumes* (cumulative audiences).

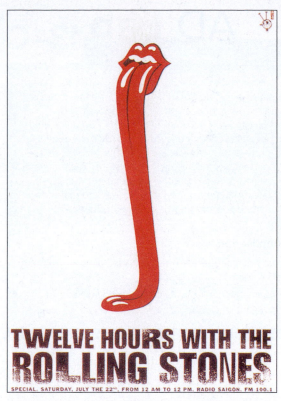

Radio stations that choose to accept programming from external sources, like the Westwood One Radio Network (www.westwoodone.com), can increase their market share during instances of special programming. Westwood One is well known for bringing high-quality recordings of top-name concerts, such as The Rolling Stones, to radio stations that might not otherwise be able to acquire such programming.

Source: Westwood One, Inc.

Dayparts

The radio day is divided into five dayparts:

6 a.m.–10 a.m.	Morning drive
10 a.m.–3 p.m.	Daytime
3 p.m.–7 p.m.	Afternoon (or evening) drive
7 p.m.–midnight	Nighttime
Midnight–6 a.m.	All night

Rating services measure audiences for only the first four dayparts because all-night listening is very limited and not highly competitive. Ad Lab 13-C describes the major radio audience rating services. Heaviest radio use occurs during **drive times** (6–10 a.m. and 3–7 p.m.) during the week (Monday through Friday), when many listeners are commuting to or from work or school.

Radio stations base their rates on the time of day the advertiser wants commercials aired, but the rates are negotiable according to supply and demand at any given time. For the lowest rate, an advertiser orders spots on a **run-of-station (ROS)** basis, similar to ROP in newspaper advertising. However, this leaves total control of spot placement up to the station. So most stations offer a **total audience plan (TAP)** package rate, which guarantees a certain percentage of spots in the better dayparts if the advertiser buys a total package of time.

Average Quarter-Hour Audience

Average quarter-hour audience (AQH persons) identifies the average number of people listening to a specific station for at least five minutes during a 15-minute period of any given daypart. For example, station KKDA in Dallas–Fort Worth, Texas, has an average quarter-hour listenership of 33,800, meaning that any day, during any 15-minute period between 3 and 7 p.m., about 33,800 people ages 12 and older are tuned in.

The **average quarter-hour rating** expresses the AQH persons as a percentage of the population. Because KKDA is located in an area of 3,072,727 people, its average quarter-hour persons could be expressed as an average quarter-hour *rating* of 1.1:

$$\frac{\text{AQH persons}}{\text{Population}} \times 100 = \text{AQH rating}$$

$$\frac{33,800}{3,072,727} \times 100 = 1.1\%$$

The same idea can be expressed in terms of **average quarter-hour share:** the station's audience (AQH persons) expressed as a percentage of the total radio listening audience in the area. For example, if the total average quarter-hour persons for all stations is 676,000, then radio station KKDA's average quarter-hour *share* is 5:

$$\frac{\text{AQH persons of a station}}{\text{AQH persons of all stations}} \times 100 = \text{AQH share}$$

$$\frac{33,800}{676,000} \times 100 = 5\%$$

The **gross rating points** of a radio schedule are the sum of all ratings points delivered by that schedule, or the *gross impressions* (see Chapter 9) expressed as a percentage of the population being measured:

$$\text{AQH rating} \times \text{Number of spots} = \text{GRPs}$$

$$1.1 \times 24 = 26.4$$

AD Lab 13–C

The Challenge of Measuring Audio Audiences

Media buyers used to get data from three major audience rating services, Arbitron, Birch, and RADAR, to determine which programs delivered the greatest number of target listeners. However the decline in radio's overall audience has left just one large company, Nielsen. Nielsen is also the major player in television audience measurement.

A problem for small stations is that Nielsen will only measure audiences in communities that match its criteria, which include metro size, average listening levels, and commuting habits. A small challenger, Eastlan, has attempted to fill the gap in small markets.

But many stations have given up on audience measurement altogether. This means that advertisers have little to go on other than station assurances.

Audience measurement is also compromised by tech disruptions. For example, a local station may be picked up on a broadcast antenna or an internet stream. And terrestrial stations compete with other audio options including streaming radio, streaming music, cable music, satellite radio, podcasts, and audiobooks.

Podcasts typically have accurate information about the number of listeners because consumers subscribe. However, obtaining demographics on listeners can be tricky. Apple has very user-friendly privacy protections in its iTunes ecosystem, which means advertisers cannot learn much about who is listening. Conversely, newer podcast networks are actively seeking ways to make podcast sponsorship more responsive to advertiser requirements.

Laboratory Application

1. What are the advantages and disadvantages of radio versus podcast advertising?

2. When might an advertiser buy time on a radio station that does not measure its audience?

or

$$\frac{\text{Gross impressions}}{\text{Population}} \times 100 = \text{GPRs}$$

$$\frac{33{,}800 \times 24}{3{,}072{,}727} \times 100 = 26.4$$

Cume Estimates

The **cume persons** is the total number of *different* people who listen to a radio station for at least five minutes in a quarter-hour within a reported daypart (also called *unduplicated audience*).

In the example, our schedule on station KKDA generated 811,200 gross impressions, but that does not mean that 811,200 different people heard our commercials. Many people heard the commercials three, four, or five times. By measuring the cumulative number of different people who listened to KKDA, rating services provide the *reach potential* of our radio schedule, which in this case is 167,800.

The **cume rating** is the cume persons expressed as a percentage of the population being measured. For example,

$$\frac{167{,}800 \times 100}{3{,}072{,}727} = 5.5\%$$

Satellite Radio

A challenge to "terrestrial" radio has been mounted by networks that transmit signals nationwide via satellite. In 2008, **satellite radio** began its steady growth beginning with competition between first-out-of-the-block XM and Sirius. Subsequently the two companies merged and as of 2019 just under 30 million people subscribe to the service.[54]

In order to receive satellite radio, an audience member must pay a monthly subscription fee and invest in a receiver capable of receiving one of the two networks' signals. Sirius attempted to convince people that radio is worth paying for by offering two important

People BEHIND the Ads

Felix Arvid Ulf Kjellberg (PewDiePie), YouTube Influencer

Vincent Sandoval/WireImage/Getty Images

It is highly likely that your parents don't know who PewDiePie is. And maybe you don't know either, unless you spend a lot of time on YouTube, love video games, or just keep up with cultural trends.

On the other hand, it's hard to call something obscure if millions of people are followers. About 75 million to be more precise. That number makes Felix Arvid Ulf Kjellberg, a 29-year-old Swede, the post popular star on YouTube.

For comparison, consider that the highest-rated program on network television, *Bull,* was watched by an average of about 14 million people each week. About the same number listen to PBS's *Morning Edition*, the highest-rated radio program. America's most popular magazine (aside from AARP and Costco publications, which are sent to members) is *Better Homes and Gardens,* which circulates just under 8 million copies a month. And the newspaper highest in circulation, *USA Today*, distributes about 4 million copies a day.

What does PewDiePie do that attracts a larger audience than the most popular titles in U.S. television, radio, newspapers, and magazines combined? According to *Wired* magazine, his popularity is traceable to humorous expressions he offers during video game commentary and trolling (making random or offensive remarks about something in an effort to provoke a response).

In recent years, the young star has begun to arouse considerable controversy. *The Wall Street Journal* reported in February 2017 that a video at PewDiePie's channel featured two men laughing as they held a sign with an anti-Semitic message. When the *Journal* contacted one of the YouTuber's sponsors, Walt Disney Co., the family-friendly company canceled its contract. Still, PewDiePie continued to create content that many found racist and anti-Semitic.

And PewDiePie is not alone in courting controversy. Another streaming celeb named Logan Paul generated significant criticism after visiting a Japanese forest known as a place where people commit suicide. In his video he showed the body of someone who had hung himself from a tree. Paul later apologized.

These events call attention to the disruptions created by new media, contrasting standards of "mass" media versus "new" media, and the future of both advertising and content. PewDiePie's reaction to being called out by *The Wall Street Journal* and losing his Disney contract was to apologize. Sort of. He told the *Journal,* "I acknowledge that I took things too far and that's something I definitely will keep in mind going forward. But the reaction and the outrage have been nothing but insanity."

The reason sites such as YouTube are attractive in the first place is they are a sandbox for anyone. Theoretically, there are no rules. PewDiePie, a college dropout who spent time as a hot dog stand vendor, created a unique online personality that proved attractive, first to hard-core gamers, then to a much larger audience. In turn, he made millions from ads that ran on his site and from YouTube's financial model of paying for content that attracts subscribers.

But YouTube was forced to act after advertisers demanded their ads not be associated with racist or controversial channels. YouTube canceled PewDiePie's show on its subscription service and removed nine different clips of what they deemed offensive material. YouTube also changed its system for how creators could financially benefit from advertising and viewership. But PewDiePie remains on the channel and continues to influence tens of millions. He regularly endorses the sites of others and products that he likes. How the transition from old to new will end up remains, as of now, unresolved.

benefits not available to terrestrial radio listeners: a large number of program choices including sports, news, entertainment, and a variety of commercial-free music formats) and exclusive programming, such as Howard Stern, Jenny McCarthy, and Dr. Laura.

How significant is satellite radio as an alternative to terrestrial radio? With millions of subscribers, the short answer is very. Sirius has been successful in leveraging exclusive talent, programming, and commercial-free music to attract subscribers.[55] It is also partnering with Google to extend its AdWords program to bidding on radio ads on non-commercial-free channels.[56] Conversely, the disruptive technology of satellite may face challenges from even newer, possibly more nimble competitors iavailable on mobile networks, such as Pandora, Apple Music, and Spotify.[57]

Because advertisers typically buy radio spots according to station format rather than by specific program, the AQH is typically a strong indicator of the most opportune time to run ads. Commercial ads, like this humorous spot from Hooked on Phonics (www.hookedonphonics.com), are frequently aired during dayparts with high listenership, such as drive times. This works especially well for Hooked on Phonics, whose listener base—parents of younger children—are very likely to be in the car with their children at this time.

Source: Zeimer's Advertising Shoppe.

(DAD READING TO DAUGHTER)

DAD: OK, honey. One story, then it's bedtime . . .

LITTLE GIRL: OK, Daddy!

DAD: Once upon a time, there was the Letter A. But A couldn't find any other letters to play with . . .

LITTLE GIRL: Ohhh . . . that's so sad!

DAD: Wait, it gets better . . .

So A called a meeting. There, he met Letter B, who thought they should merge . . .

LITTLE GIRL (LAUGHING): Daddy, you're silly!

DAD: I know. Then, they did a leveraged buyout for letters C through L . . .

LITTLE GIRL: Really? . . .

DAD: And offered stock options for M through Z . . .

LITTLE GIRL: What's that? . . .

DAD: And they all lived happily ever after! . . .

LITTLE GIRL: Yayyyy!

SEGUE TO ANNOUNCER VOICEOVER OVER DISTINCTIVE NEEDLEDROP MUSIC. If you're a parent, you don't have to invent stories to get your kids to love reading. Just go to the best place in cyberspace for help . . . the Hooked on Phonics Website. Visit us today at A-B-C-D-E-F-G dot-com. Take the FREE personalized reading assessment to find out how to help your child become a more confident reader.

So for all this—and much, much more—log onto Hooked on Phonics at the most memorable web address anywhere: A-B-C-D-E-F-G dot-com. (Musical logo played under VO.)

NEEDLEDROP MUSIC OUT.

The Seven Steps in Preparing a Radio Schedule

The procedure advertisers use to prepare radio schedules is similar to that used for TV schedules.

1. Identify stations with the greatest concentration (cume) of the advertiser's target audience by demographics (say, men and women ages 35 to 49).
2. Identify stations whose format typically offers the highest concentration of potential buyers.
3. Determine which time periods (dayparts) on those stations offer the most (average quarter-hour) potential buyers.
4. Using the stations' rate cards for guidance, construct a schedule with a strong mix of the best time periods. At this point, it is often wise to give the advertiser's media objectives to the station reps, suggest a possible budget for their station, and ask what they can provide for that budget. This gives the media buyer a starting point for analyzing costs and negotiating the buy.
5. Assess the proposed buy in terms of reach and frequency.
6. Determine the cost for each 1,000 target people each station delivers. The key word is *target;* the media buyer isn't interested in the station's total audience.
7. Negotiate and place the buy.

Producing Audio and Video Spots
Producing Radio and Podcast Spots

LO 13-9

Radio commercials, called **spots,** are relatively quick, simple, and easy to produce. In fact, many stations provide production services free to local advertisers.

Some commercials are delivered live by the announcer, in which case the station gets a script. The material must be accurately timed. A live commercial script should run about 130 to 150 words per minute so the announcer can speak at a normal, conversational pace. The best way to do this is to use a popular DJ and let him or her improvise. It's entertaining and links the DJ's credibility to the product.[58]

The disadvantages of live commercials are inconsistent announcers and limited sound effects. Uniform delivery requires a recorded commercial. The process of producing a recorded commercial includes *preproduction, production,* and *postproduction* (or finishing) phases (see Exhibit 13-12).

Exhibit 13-12

Radio commercials have three production phases. The preproduction and finishing phases are usually the most complex. Preproduction and postproduction editing and mixing typically require far more time than the actual recording session.

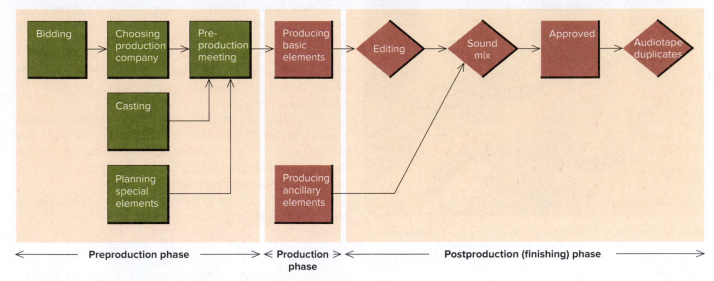

Preproduction

In the **preproduction phase,** the advertiser and agency make plans that ensure production will run smoothly, on time, and within budget. The agency assigns a radio producer from its staff or hires a freelancer. Based on the script, the producer selects a studio and a director, determines what talent will be needed, estimates costs, and prepares a budget for the advertiser's approval.

To get the finest sound reproduction, most ad agencies use independent recording studios. The best audio studios have experienced sound directors and technicians, close ties to well-known talent, and the latest recording equipment.

In evaluating talent, the advertiser and agency consider several factors: the person's tone of voice, vocal acting skills and creativity, intelligence, style of thinking, and reputation. If the script calls for music, the producer decides whether to use prerecorded music or hire a composer and/or arranger.

Any needed sound effects can be created or, most often, collected from prerecorded sources. Each decision affects the budget, but also has a dramatic impact on the effectiveness of the spots.

Once the talent is hired and music prepared, the **director** supervises rehearsals until everything is ready for recording.

Production: Cutting the Spot

All the elements to be used in the commercial—voices, music, sound effects—are recorded at a **session.** Depending on the nature of the spot, a session can last from a half-hour to more than a day. Because studios charge by the hour, rehearsals are important in the preproduction phase.

The Sound Studio   The session is recorded in a studio, which has sound-dampening surfaces, microphones, a window to a control room, and wall plugs for connecting equipment and instruments to the control room.

Standard items in the sound studio are microphones, headphone sets, and speakers. Announcers and singers wear headphones to hear instructions from the director in the control room or to monitor prerecorded instrumental tracks as they sing.

A sophisticated audio console manipulates sound electronically, making sounds sharper or fuzzier, with more echo, or more treble or bass. Its multitrack mixing and sound enhancement capabilities are most useful during postproduction.

Exactostock/Digital Vision/SuperStock

Studio engineers carefully select, disperse, and aim the appropriate microphones to capture the full spectrum of sounds.

The Control Room   The agency producer, director, and sound engineer (and often the client and account executive) sit in the **control room,** where they can monitor all the sounds generated in the sound studio. The control room is separated from the studio by a thick glass window and soundproofed walls, so the people monitoring the session can hear the sounds on quality speakers and discuss the various takes.

The director and sound engineer work at a **console** (also called a **board**), the central "switchboard" for controlling the sounds and channeling them to the appropriate recording devices. As they monitor the sounds coming from the studio, they keep the pitch and loudness within acceptable levels for broadcast.

The board also serves as a sound mixer, blending both live and prerecorded sounds for immediate or delayed broadcast.

Postproduction: Finishing the Spot

After the commercial is recorded a number of times, a selection is made from the best takes. The sound engineer usually records music, sound effects, and vocals separately and then mixes and sweetens them during the **postproduction** (or *finishing*) **phase.** High-end digital audio equipment can cost a lot of money, but free or low-cost digital audio programs are available for anyone who wants to make professional-sounding audio. Avid Pro Tools costs about $600 for a license, but a powerful program called Audacity is available in a free version.

Producing Video Spots

The Role of the Commercial Producer

Video production is, as you might expect, considerably more complex than radio production. People who work in production require months or years of training. But all advertising students can benefit from an understanding of basic video production concepts to understand how commercials are made, why production is so expensive, and what methods they can use to cut costs without sacrificing quality or effectiveness.

As with radio, the process of producing a TV commercial always involves three stages, as shown in Exhibit 13-13:

1. Preproduction: all the work prior to the actual day of filming.
2. Production: the actual day (or days) the commercial is filmed.
3. Postproduction (or finishing): all the work done after shooting to edit and finish the commercial.

Each step has a dramatic effect on cost and quality.

The Preproduction Phase

Good planning before production can save advertisers a lot of money. That's the purpose of the **preproduction phase.** The first thing the producer must do, therefore, is study the script and storyboard and analyze the production techniques that will be called for in the commercial. Three major categories of production techniques are used: *live action, animation,* and *special effects.*

If a commercial calls for live action, the producer must consider whether the action will be staged indoors in a studio, outside on a studio lot, or on location away from the studio. Will it be taped or filmed? All these factors have a bearing on what equipment and personnel are required, where costumes are obtained, what permissions may be required, what talent can be used, and, of course, what the commercial costs.

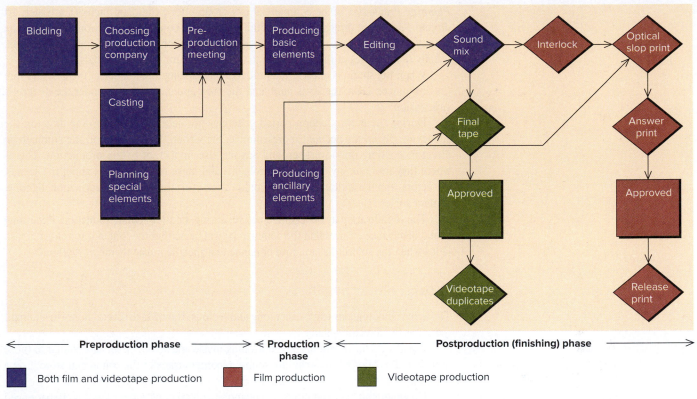

Preproduction phase	Production phase	Postproduction (finishing) phase

■ Both film and videotape production   ■ Film production   ■ Videotape production

Exhibit 13-13

The production processes for video are very similar to that for audio until the sound-mixing stage. Computerized editing speeds up the finishing phase for digital video.

In the preproduction stage, art directors, copywriters, and producers carefully hash out the details required for filming a 30-second commercial. During this stage, the production team will develop and sketch a storyboard that depicts, in rough form, how the ad will appear. Any major changes should be made at this time because alterations in script or direction after filming begins can drive production costs up exponentially.

Source: Saatchi & Saatchi, Los Angeles

Planning Production   The commercial is a group effort; the team includes a writer, art director, producer, director, and sometimes a musical composer and choreographer. The agency producer, who is responsible for completing the job on schedule and within budget, usually sends copies of the storyboard to three studios for competitive bids.

When the studio is chosen, the producer and casting director select the cast and hire the announcer. Next, the set is built, and the crew and cast rehearse under the director's supervision.

During the preproduction period, meetings are necessary between the director, the agency producer, the account representative, the writer, the art director, the commercial director, possibly the advertiser, and anyone else important to the production. This is where they iron out any last-minute problems and make final decisions about the scenes, the actors, and the announcer. They should review everything—music, sets, action, lighting, camera angles.

The soundtrack may be recorded before, during, or after actual production. Recording sound in advance ensures that the commercial will be neither too long nor too short; it also helps when the subject has to move or dance to a specific music theme or rhythm.

Production: The Shoot

The actual shooting day can be very long and tedious. It may take several hours just to light the set to the director's liking.

Procedures for recording and controlling music and sound effects are similar to those used in radio. Microphones capture sound; recorders transfer the sound and store it on a medium.

Cinematographers and directors collaborate on creating proper lighting. Experienced **cinematographers** (motion picture photographers) can guess the range and intensity of light by briefly studying its source. However, they use light meters to determine how to set the camera's lens **aperture,** the opening that controls the amount of light that reaches the film or digital media. To record the correct color and brightness, all light sources must be in balance.

Lighting helps establish a visual mood. Intense light from a single source gives a harsh appearance and may be used to create anxiety in the viewer. By using filters, warmer lights, diffusion screens, and reflectors, the cinematographer can create a reddish, more consistent, softer illumination—and a more romantic mood.

Professional film cameras used for making TV commercials shoot 16-millimeter (mm; the diagonal measure of one frame), 35-mm, and 75-mm film and digital.

Heavy-duty studio video cameras mounted on a stand with wheels can carry a number of accessories. One of the most important is the lens-mounted **teleprompter,** which allows the camera to see a spokesperson through the back of a two-way mirror while he or she reads moving text reflected off the front.

Staging for a commercial may be done in the isolation of a studio, outside on a studio lot, or on location. The studio offers the most control.

Most film and video studios have heavy soundproofing to eliminate outside noises such as sirens and low-flying aircraft. The studios are lightproof, which allows for complete lighting control. Special equipment is easier to use in the controlled environment of a studio. But studio lighting can make a scene appear artificial.

For scenes requiring large amounts of space, scenery, and the full effect of outdoor lighting, the studio lot offers the best control. The **lot** is outside acreage shielded from stray, off-site sounds.

Although it adds realism, **location** shooting is often a technical and logistical nightmare. Every location has natural and manufactured features that create obstacles. Natural lighting creates bright highlights that contrast with harsh shadows. Large reflective screens and high-intensity lights are required to brighten up shadows for a more even-toned exposure. Energy sources for lighting and equipment may be insufficient, requiring long cables and mobile generators.

Digital equipment provides advertisers the option to create an illusion of almost any background. Green elements on the set are replaced with digital elements in postproduction.

Courtesy of Ultimatte Corporation

Whether at the studio or on location, most scenes require several takes for the **talent** (actors) to get them right. Lighting may need readjusting as unexpected shadows pop up. Each scene is shot from two or three different angles: one to establish the characters, one to show only the speaker, and one to show the listener's reaction.

A long time may be needed between scenes to move the camera, reset the lights, reposition the talent, and pick up the action, sound, and look to match the other scenes. Each action must match what comes before and after. Commercials with disconcerting jumps destroy credibility. The adoption of digital technology allows for green studios. In these studios, elements that are colored green are replaced in postproduction using computer technologies. The backgrounds that can then be substituted are almost limitless.

In any commercial production, it's typical to have many more people behind the camera than in front of it. In addition to the director and assistant director, other important players behind the scenes may include a sound editor, lighting technicians, electricians, and grips.

Hero Images/Getty Images

In the postproduction phase, the director and editor use computerized video and sound editing equipment for the assembly of the final product. At this stage, the director and editor will select and edit scenes into their respective order, removing all the unneeded footage. Next, they add off-camera special effects, like supers, and incorporate any necessary music or voice-overs.

Yanyong/iStock/Getty Images

Postproduction

In the **postproduction phase,** the film editor, sound mixer, and director actually put the commercial together.

With digital technology, editors can add effects such as wipes and dissolves electronically. Although a director will spend many hours editing a commercial shot on video, it will still be considerably less than what is needed for film editing and lab work.

Chapter Summary

As a means of reaching the masses, no other medium today has the unique creative ability of television. Broadcast TV grew faster than any previous advertising medium because of the unique advantages it offered advertisers: mass coverage at efficient cost, impact, prestige, and social dominance.

Television is a powerful creative tool, but the medium still has many drawbacks, including high cost, limited selectivity, brevity, clutter, and susceptibility to zipping and zapping.

Broadcast TV dominance is being challenged by new electronic media, particularly cable and streaming video. Cable offers the visual and aural appeal of TV at much lower cost and with greater flexibility. Cable audiences are highly fragmented, which helps advertisers target specific markets but is a drawback for those wanting to reach a mass audience. Younger audiences are abandoning both broadcast and cable TV for on-demand streaming video from companies like YouTube and Netflix.

TV advertising can be done at the national, regional, or local level and can take the form of program sponsorships, segment sponsorships, and spots of varying lengths, including program-length infomercials.

To determine which shows to buy, media buyers select the most efficient ones for their target audience. They compare the packages of each station, substitute stronger programs for less efficient ones, and negotiate prices to get the best buy. Media buyers must have a firm grasp of certain important terms: *designated market areas (DMAs), TV households (TVHH), households using TV (HUT), program rating, share of audience, gross rating points,* and *cost per thousand.*

Like television, radio is a highly creative medium. Its greatest attribute is its ability to offer excellent reach and frequency to selective audiences at a very efficient price. Its drawbacks are the limitations of sound, segmented audiences, and its short-lived and half-heard commercials. Broadcast radio, like broadcast TV, is facing challenges from newer technologies, including satellite radio, streaming radio, and podcasts.

Radio stations are normally classified by the programming they offer and the audiences they serve. Radio stations may be AM or FM. They may use network or syndicated programs and follow any of a dozen or more popular formats. Advertisers purchase radio time in one of three forms: local, spot, or network. Buying radio time requires a basic understanding of radio terminology. The most common terms are *dayparts, average quarter-hour,* and *cumulative audiences.*

Radio spots are among the quickest, simplest, and least expensive ads to produce. A producer manages the production process through the preproduction, production, and postproduction stages. The producer contracts with a recording studio, selects talent, and collects music and sound effects for the recording session. At the session, the talent works in a studio, while the director and sound engineer work in the control room at a console, monitoring and modulating the sound as it's recorded.

In the postproduction phase, the director and sound engineer select the best takes, splice them together, mix in sound effects and music, and then edit the sound until the master tape is completed. Dubs are made from this and sent to radio stations for airing.

Television production involves the same three stages. In preproduction, the producer determines which production technique is most suitable for the script. The studio is chosen, the cast selected, and rehearsals held. As much work as possible is done during preproduction to reduce the shooting time required.

The production phase is when the commercial is actually shot, in a studio, on a lot, or on location. Specialized technicians are responsible for the sound, lights, and cameras, all of which can diminish the commercial if not handled correctly. Scenes are shot and reshot until the director and producer feel they have a good take. For cost reasons, scenes are frequently not shot in order.

In the postproduction stage, the commercial is actually put together. External sound, music, and special effects are added to the video until the spot is completed.

Important Terms

affidavit of performance, *443*

aperture, *456*

audience composition, *442*

avails, *442*

average quarter-hour audience (AQH persons), *449*

average quarter-hour rating, *449*

average quarter-hour share, *449*

barter syndication, *436*

board, *454*

broadcast radio, *445*

broadcast TV, *428*

cable TV, *428*

cinematographer, *456*

console, *454*

control room, *454*

cume persons, *450*

cume rating, *450*

daypart mix, *445*

designated market areas (DMAs), *441*

director, *453*

drive time, *449*

first-run syndication, *436*

gross rating points (GRPs), *442, 449*

households using TV (HUT), *441*

imagery transfer, *445*

infomercial, *438*

inventory, *436*

local time, *448*

location, *456*

lot, *456*

makegoods, *443*

networks, *434*

off-network syndication, *436*

participation basis, *435*

podcast, *445*

postproduction phase, *454, 458*

preemption rate, *443*

preproduction phase, *453, 454*

prime time, *444*

product placement, *440*

program-length advertisement (PLA), *438*

programming format, *446*

program rating, *441*

rating services, *439*

run of station (ROS), *449*

satellite radio, *445, 450*

session, *453*

share, *442*

sponsorship, *435*

spot announcement, *436*

spot radio, *448*

spots, *452*

streaming radio, *445*

streaming video, *428*

talent, *457*

teleprompter, *456*

total audience, *442*

total audience plan (TAP), *449*

TV households (TVHH), *441*

UHF, *429*

VHF, *429*

Review Questions

1. What are the advantages of broadcast TV advertising for a product like milk?

2. What steps can advertisers take to overcome zipping and zapping?

3. Why has advertising on network TV become less desirable in recent years?

4. In what ways is cable TV's selectivity a strength? A drawback?

5. What are the various ways to buy broadcast television time?

6. How can TV be best used in an integrated marketing communications program?

7. How can radio be best used in an IMC program?

8. What is the format of the radio station you listen to most? How would you describe the demographics of its target audience?

9. What is the difference between average quarter-hour and cume audiences? Which is better?

10. What is the significance of dayparts in radio and TV advertising? What are the best dayparts for each?

The Advertising Experience

1. Radio Advertising

Valentine's Day is approaching, and as the owner of Dream Flower Florists, you want to increase your share of local business by advertising on the radio. After researching local stations, choose one whose format suits your target audience. Decide what kind of buys you will make and when they will be aired.

2. TV Organizations

The size of the television industry and the advertising dollars that are spent within it are extraordinary. Many TV-related organizations were formed to help serve the industry. Discover a little more about the nature and scope of the television industry as you peruse the following websites. Be sure to answer the questions that follow.

- Broadcast Education Association (BEA): www.beaweb.org
- Cable/Telecommunications Association for Marketing (CTAM): www.ctam.com
- NCTA: www.ncta.com/
- National Association of Broadcasters (NAB): www.nab.org

a. Who is the intended audience(s) of the site?

b. What is the site's purpose? Does it succeed? Why?

c. What is the organization's purpose?

d. What benefit does the organization provide individual members/subscribers? The overall advertising and television and cable communities?

3. Broadcast Media Tools

Broadcast advertising reports and audience studies are critical to the development and implementation of effective media strategy. As with print media, advertisers have a set of "staple" companies and reports they regularly use to help plan and implement their broadcast media buys. Visit the following syndicated and independent broadcast media companies' websites and answer the questions that follow:

- Nielsen Media Research: www.nielsenmedia.com
- Numeris: http://en.numeris.ca/
- Radio Advertising Bureau (RAB): www.rab.com/
- Television Bureau of Advertising: www.tvb.org
- TV RunDown: www.tvrundown.com

a. What type(s) of broadcast media information does the company specialize in and what specific services, products, or publications does the company offer?

b. What industries/companies would be best suited to utilize the company's media resources?

c. Does the company represent syndicated or independent research?

d. How useful do you feel the company is for gathering broadcast media information? Why?

4. If Hyundai asked its agency to come up with a corresponding radio complement to its Assurance TV campaign, what would its agency want to keep in mind when converting this concept to an audio-only format?

5. Given the audience for Hyundai's Assurance campaign—middle-class America—in what daypart do you think its TV commercial would be most effectively broadcast?

End Notes

1. Lara O'Reilly, "How 6 Colorful Characters Propelled M&M's to Become America's Favorite Candy," *Business Insider,* March 26, 2016, *www.businessinsider.com/the-story-of-the-mms-characters-2016-3.*

2. "Characters," M&M's, *www.mms.com/en-us/experience-mms/characters.*

3. "Sales of the Leading Chocolate Candy Brands of the United States in 2017," *Statista, www.statista.com/statistics/190393/top-chocolate-candy-brands-in-the-united-states/.*

4. Jenny Rooney, "New to FCB, Creative Chief Susan Credle Reflects on Her Move, CMO Skills and Agency Relevance," *Forbes Media LLC,* February 29, 2016.

5. Zenith, "Advertising Expenditure Forecasts," June 2018 (numbers rounded). More info at *www.zenithmedia.com.* Reported in *Advertising Age*'s Marketing Fact Pack, 2018.

6. "Broadcast Station Totals," FCC.gov, September 30, 2018, *www.fcc.gov/document/broadcast-station-totals-september-30-2018.*

7. "Broadcast Station Totals," FCC.gov, September 30, 2018, *www.fcc.gov/document/broadcast-station-totals-september-30-2018.*

8. "Pay TV Penetration Rate in the United States from 2010 to 2018," *Statista, www.statista.com/statistics/467842/pay-tv-penetration-rate-usa/.*

9. "Broadcast Station Totals," FCC.gov, September 30, 2018, *www.fcc.gov/document/broadcast-station-totals-september-30-2018.*

10. Eric Siu, "Podcast Advertising: What You Need to Know," *Singlegrain, www.singlegrain.com/blog-posts/content-marketing/podcast-advertising-what-you-need-to-know/.*

11. "TV Basics: Channels—Receivable versus Tuned," Television Bureau of Advertising Inc., *www.tvb.org.*

12. "About 6 in 10 Young Adults in U.S. Primarily Use Online Streaming to Watch TV," Pew Research, September 13, 2017, *www.pewresearch.org/fact-tank/2017/09/13/about-6-in-10-young-adults-in-u-s-primarily-use-online-streaming-to-watch-tv/.*

13. "2008 Media Comparisons Study," Television Bureau of Advertising Inc., *www.tvb.org.*

14. "Marketing Fact Pack, 2018" *Advertising Age,* Crain Publications.

15. "Cable Viewership Summary," Cable Advertising Bureau, *www.onetvworld.org.*

16. AdAge DataCenter, "Measured-Media Spending by Medium," *https://adage.com/section/datacenter-advertising-spending/305.*

17. Nielsen, "Average U.S. Home Now Receives a Record 118.6 TV Channels, According to Nielsen," news release, June 2008, *http://en-us.nielsen.com/main/news/newsreleases/2008/june/averageushome.*

18. Thomas R. Duncan and Sandra E. Moriarty, *Driving Brand Value: Using Integrated Marketing to Manage Stakeholder Relationships* (New York: McGraw-Hill, 1997), pp. 101–102.

19. Thomas R. Duncan and Sandra E. Moriarty, *Driving Brand Value: Using Integrated Marketing to Manage Stakeholder Relationships* (New York: McGraw-Hill, 1997), pp. 101–102.

20. "What a Spot Costs 2011," *Advertising Age* Annual 2011, *http://adage.com.*

21. Eric Schmuckler, "Betting on a Sure Thing," *MediaWeek,* January 23, 1995, pp. 18–20; Steve Coe, "UPN Beats . . . Everybody," *Broadcasting & Cable,* January 23, 1995, pp. 4, 10; T. L. Stanley, "Network Branding," *Brandweek,* January 9, 1995, pp. 30–32; Ronald Grover, "Are Paramount and Warner Looney Tunes?" *BusinessWeek,* January 9, 1995, p. 46; David Tobenkin, "New Players Get Ready to Roll," *Broadcasting & Cable,* January 2, 1995, pp. 30–33.

22. Kristen Baldwin and Henry Goldblatt, "The Story behind the WB-UPN Merger," EW, January 26, 2006, *https://ew.com/ article/2006/01/21/story-behind-wb-upn-merger/.*

23. "Why Ad-Supported Cable?" Cabletelevision Advertising Bureau, April 19, 2012, *www.thecab.tv/main/bm~doc/why-cable 2012-p.pdf.*

24. Kathy Haley, "Spot TV Is Power Tool," *The Power of Spot TV,* supplement to *Advertising Age,* September 29, 1993, p. T3.

25. "National Sales Reps Are Key to the Spot TV Mix," *The Power of Spot* TV, supplement to *Advertising Age,* September 23, 1992, pp. T10, T12.

26. Kathy Haley, "Spot TV Is Power Tool," *The Power of Spot TV,* supplement to *Advertising Age,* September 29, 1993, p. T3; Kathy Haley, "Reps Zero In on Advertiser Goals," *The Power of Spot TV,* supplement to *Advertising Age,* September 29, 1993, p. T6.

27. Michael Burgi, "Cable TV: Welcome to the 500 Club," *Adweek,* September 13, 1993, p. 45; Christopher Stern, "Advertisers Hear Promise of Smooth Spot Cable Buys," *Broadcasting & Cable,* April 26, 1993, pp. 56, 58.

28. "100 Leading National Advertisers," *Advertising Age,* June 26, 2006.

29. "What Is Syndication?" *1994 Guide to Advertiser-Supported Syndication,* supplement to *Advertising Age* (New York: Advertiser Syndicated Television Association, 1994), p. A6; David Tobenkin, "Action Escalates for Syndicators," *Broadcasting & Cable,* August 29, 1994, pp. 29–35.

30. "Syndication Showcase," *Broadcasting & Cable,* January 24, 1994, pp. 82–86.

31. World Health Organization: Europe, *Marketing of Foods High in Fat, Salt and Sugar to Children: Update 2012–2013* (Copenhagen, Denmark: World Health Organization, 2013).

32. Federal Trade Commission, "Food Marketing to Children and Adolescents," 2018.

33. Kathy Haley, "The Infomercial Begins a New Era as a Marketing Tool for Top Brands," *Advertising Age,* January 25, 1993, p. M3.

34. James B. Arndorfer, "Guthy-Renker Gives the Infomercial Street Cred," *Advertising Age,* May 2, 2005.

35. Jim Cooper, "Long-Form Ad Used in Contract Dispute," *Broadcasting & Cable,* May 24, 1993, p. 71.

36. Kevin Goldman, "CBS to Push Videotaping of Infomercials," *The Wall Street Journal,* November 15, 1993, p. B7.

37. Kevin Goldman, "CBS to Push Videotaping of Infomercials," *The Wall Street Journal,* November 15, 1993, p. B7; Tom Burke, "Program-Length Commercials Can Bring These Six Benefits to a Major Brand Campaign," *Advertising Age,* January 25, 1993, p. M5.

38. "AdSphere Reports Impressive Growth for Brand-Direct & Direct Response Industry," DRMetrix, January 20, 2018, *www .drmetrix.com/2017study.html .*

39. "100 Leading National Advertisers," *Advertising Age,* June 26, 2007.

40. Jack Honomichl, "Top 25 Global Firms Earn $6.1 Billion in Revenue," *Marketing News,* August 18, 1997, p. H2; Nielsen Media Research, *www.nielsenmedia.com;* "Media Measured," *www .nielsenmedia.com/monitor-plus.*

41. John Lafeyette, "Nielsen Finds Out of Home Sports Viewing in Many Places," *B+C,* September 27, 2018, *www.broadcastingcable. com/news/nielsen-find-out-of-home-sports-viewing-in-many-places*

42. Nielsen, "C3 TV Ratings Show Impact of DVR Ad Viewing," Nielsen Media and Entertainment, October 14, 2009, retrieved at *www.nielsen.com/us/en/insights/news/2009/c3-tv-ratings-show- impact-of-dvr-ad-viewing.html.*

43. Emma Hall, "Young Consumers Receptive to Movie Product Placement," *Advertising Age,* March 29, 2004, *https://adage .com/article/news/young-consumers-receptive-movie-product- placement/98097.*

44. "U.S. Product Placement Market Grew 13.7% in 2017, Pacing for Faster Growth in 2018, Powered by Double-Digit Growth in Television, Digital Video and Music Integrations," *PRWeb,* June 13, 2018, *www.pqmedia.com/wp-content/uploads/2018/06/ US-Product-Placement-18.pdf.*

45. Kevin Goldman, "CBS Pays Price for Losing Bet on Ratings," *The Wall Street Journal,* November 30, 1993, p. B4; Kevin Goldman, "CBS Again Must Offer Make-Good Ads," *The Wall Street Journal,* October 27, 1994, p. B6; Kevin Goldman, "'Scarlett' Make-Goods," *The Wall Street Journal,* November 21, 1994, p. B8.

46. "As the Audio Landscape Evolves, Broadcast Radio Remains the King," *N Insights,* February 14, 2018, *www.nielsen.com/us/ en/insights/news/2018/as-the-audio-landscape-evolves-broadcast- radio-remains-the-comparable-king.html.*

47. Judann Pollack, "Radio's Health Is Better than You Think, but What's the Long-Term Prognosis?" *Ad Age,* April 17, 2018, *https://adage.com/article/media/mixed-signals-radio-s-health/313110*

48. "Media Comparisons," *1997 Radio Marketing Guide and Fact Book for Advertisers; Imagery Transfer Study* (New York: Network Radio Association, 1993); Media Facts: *The Complete Guide to Maximizing Your Advertising* (New York: Radio Advertising Bureau, 1994), pp. 8–9.

49. "Maximize Your Marketing Message with Radio," *1997 Radio Marketing Guide and Fact Book for Advertisers; Radio Marketing Guide and Factbook for Advertisers: 1993–1994,* pp. 29–33.

50. "There's a Radio Format for Everybody," *1997 Radio Marketing Guide and Fact Book for Advertisers.*

51. *Network Radio: Targeting the National Consumer,* supplement to *Advertising Age,* September 6, 1993, pp. R2, R4; *Marketer's Guide to Media,* Fall/Winter 1992–93, pp. 69–70.

52. *2006 Marketing Guide and Fact Book,* Radio Advertising Bureau, *www.rab.com.*

53. "200 Leading National Advertisers 2018 Fact Pack," *Advertising Age.*

54. "SiriusXM Beats 2018 Subscriber Guidance and Issues 2019 Guidance," SiriusXM press release, January 8, 2019, *http://investor .siriusxm.com/investor-overview/press-releases/press-release- details/2019/SiriusXM-Beats-2018-Subscriber-Guidance-and- Issues-2019-Guidance/default.aspx*

55. Abbey Klaassen, "XM and Sirius Satellite Radio Report Continuing Losses," *Advertising Age,* August 1, 2006.

56. Abbey Klaassen, "Google Inks First Satellite Radio Ad Sales Deal," *Advertising Age,* August 2, 2006.

57. Gary Bourgeault, "Challenges Sirius XM Holdings Must Overcome to Ensure Future Growth," *Seeking Alpha,* January 18, 2018, *https://seekingalpha.com/article/4182429-challenges-sirius-xm- holdings-must-overcome-ensure-future-growth.*

58. Bonnie L. Drewniany and A. Jerome Jeweler, *Creative Strategy in Advertising,* 10th ed. (Boston: Wadsworth, 2011).

CHAPTER

14

Using Digital Interactive Media

LEARNING OBJECTIVES

To explore the important factors advertisers weigh when considering digital interactive media. This medium has its own distinct characteristics, unique advantages, and drawbacks. Advertisers must be able to understand the merits of this medium and identify the most cost-effective ways to use them in the media mix.

After studying this chapter, you will be able to:

LO14-1   Discuss the various opportunities and challenges presented by digital interactive media.

LO14-2   Describe the evolution of interactive media.

LO14-3   Explain how the internet audience is measured.

LO14-4   Describe how programmatic advertising works.

LO14-5   Define the various kinds of digital advertising.

LO14-6   Debate the pros and cons of the internet as an advertising medium.

If by magic you could choose to be the CEO of either of two of the biggest companies in the world, Walmart or Google, which would you choose? Google parent Alphabet recorded revenues of $136 billion in 2018. Walmart brought in $500 billion. Not bad either way. ■ But how about a third choice, which is leveraging the strengths of both Walmart and Google? That company is Amazon, and 2018 was a big year for the online giant. One of the five digital leaders represented in the acronym FAANG (Facebook, Amazon, Apple, Netflix, and Google), the company reported record profits, conducted a highly followed search for a second corporate headquarters, and continued to introduce new technologies, including numerous devices powered by its Alexa technology. ■ The company's goal is as simple as it is enormous: to be a part of almost every interaction of people and their devices. An overstatement? Perhaps. But consider that when someone arrives at your door, the button he or she presses may be connected to a smart doorbell made by Nest. You check your phone to see who is at the door and see on your Nest security camera that it is an invited guest. Once inside, your guest experiences climate controls monitored by a Nest thermostat (Nest is owned by Amazon). As you both head to your living room, the music you hear is played by an Echo device connected to Amazon Prime Music. Feeling hungry, you select leftovers from your LG refrigerator (with voice-activated features of Alexa), pop them in a GE microwave, and tell Alexa to heat the food. After you stream some Amazon Prime Video content on your Amazon Firestick-connected device, you head out for a ride in your friend's new BMW. Like all 2018 BMWs, the car comes standard with Alexa and does not require a smartphone to play music or understand commands. ■ Impressive, you may say, but what has this got to do with advertising. Actually, everything.

■ For many people, Amazon is first and foremost a retailer, one sometimes blamed for the demise of such memorable competitors as B. Dalton Booksellers, Camelot Music, Office Warehouse, Toys 'R' Us, F.A.O. Schwarz, Wickes Furniture, Radio Shack, and Sports Authority, not to mention countless local small businesses. Whether or not Amazon is in fact to blame for a string of retail bankruptcies, it is true that the company sells a lot of stuff. It reported sales of $233 billion in 2018 and is on pace to surpass Walmart by 2020.[1] ■ To become the world's largest retailer, Amazon wants to be everywhere, which means Alexa will be everywhere. ■ Walmart has dominated retail from the end of the 20th century until very recently. Sam Walton grew his company to the point where its power vis à vis suppliers became enormous.

Companies know that without access to Walmart shelves they can't be successful, so they offer Walmart sweeter deals than ones offered to anyone else. That means Walmart can operate with higher margins and fatter profits than competitors can achieve. ■ Amazon now dominates sales on the internet and is the preferred venue of young consumers. A survey conducted by the Max Borges agency of 1,100 people ages 18 to 34 who shopped on Amazon found 77 percent would choose Amazon over alcohol for a year, and 44 percent would choose Amazon over sex.[2] ■ Besides its advantage with young shoppers, Amazon has one other advantage that Walmart doesn't. Search. When people shop at Amazon, they often search for products at the company's website. Sponsored listings appearing on search are the foundation of Google's empire. Amazon is now promoting "sponsored listings" for retailers who pay for the privilege. These are becoming so popular that Amazon's advertising division is its fastest-growing profit center. ■ Any company would be thrilled to leverage the unique advantage of either Walmart or Google. But only one company is leveraging the advantages of both.

Digital Interactive Media

This chapter focuses on digital interactive media, including websites, mobile media, blogs, and other content accessible from a phone or computer. We do not discuss social media, an important form of digital media, here. Rather we present it in Chapter 15 because its importance in contemporary advertising merits extensive coverage. The year 2018 marks the first time in many decades that spending on television advertising is not the largest category of total U.S. ad spending. The reason is the ascendance to the top spot and continued growth of ad spending on digital media: the internet and mobile. Nor will this trend stop any time soon. It is safe to say that the future of advertising is digital.

In truth, technology has always disrupted advertising practice. Consider that at the birth of television many advertisers counted on people sitting through ads simply because it was irritating to get up and change channels. The remote control was the first step toward convenient interactivity, and it had a major impact on commercial viewership. Instead of watching commercials, people could now use the station breaks to channel surf, effectively slamming the door once again in the salesperson's face.

Right on the heels of the remote came the widespread popularity of cable TV. In little more than a decade, the network TV audience plunged from 90 to 50 percent.

Then came the VCR, and succeeding devices such as TiVo. People could now record shows and watch them later at their convenience, zipping through the commercials. Or they could just rent a movie and skip the commercials altogether. TiVo brought ad-avoidance into the digital age, allowing viewers to customize their entertainment schedules.

And as we saw in Chapter 13, technology keeps on going and going and going. It's already given us the 8K TV, tablets, smartphones, the internet, YouTube, surround sound—and the software to make it all simple enough for virtually anybody to use. With growing consumer acceptance of all this wizardry, prices have plummeted, making much of it affordable for almost everyone.

Internet and Mobile Ad Spending as a Percentage of All U.S. Ad Spending 2018

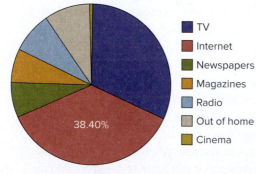

- TV
- Internet
- Newspapers
- Magazines
- Radio
- Out of home
- Cinema

38.40%

Internet and mobile ad spending as a percentage of total U.S. ad spending.

These are not just advertising media. In many cases, they represent completely new ways of living and doing business. The fastest-growing advertising medium in history has also opened the door to electronic commerce.

From the convenience of your phone, you can cash a check, buy a car or a beautiful piece of art, trade stocks, book airline reservations, purchase concert tickets, buy a complete new wardrobe from your favorite department store, or even order your week's groceries and have them delivered to your door.

The internet has also changed the way people communicate, eliminating the need for an overseas airmail stamp if you want to communicate with your brother in Berlin. You can do library research in the comfort of your den, or you can start your own home-based business and market your products worldwide.

Digital media are truly revolutionary in their effect on our daily lives, and it's a revolution for marketers, too. As the nation's biggest traditional advertisers realized that digital offers wonderful opportunities for achieving real, bottom-line results, they shifted their ad

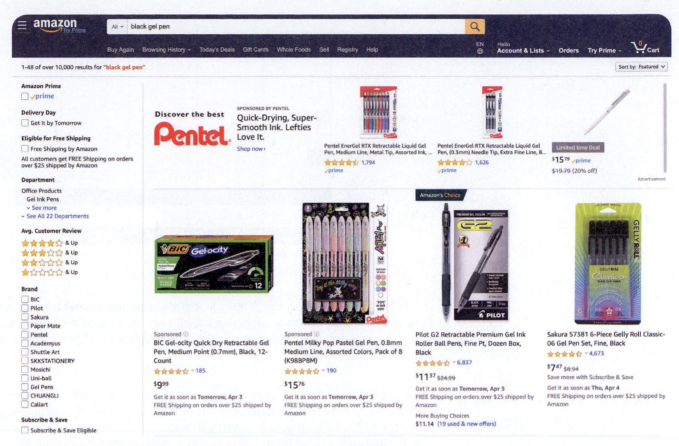

Amazon sponsored listings represent the opportunity for brands to gain exposure at the most critical time: just when a consumer is making a buying decision. For that reason, Amazon is increasingly profiting from advertising revenue.

Source: Amazon.com, Inc.

spending dramatically. Digital advertising spending reached $59 billion in 2012, rose to $94 billion in 2018, and is projected to reach nearly $130 billion in 2021.[3] This growth has occurred even as spending on other media is flat or declining.

In addition to this phenomenal growth, by offering true interactivity, digital media enable businesses and other organizations to develop and nurture relationships with their customers and other stakeholders, in a way never before available, on a global scale and at a very efficient cost.

Digital interactive media are more than computers and the internet. Brands are more interested in mobile devices today, and more people access digital content on their devices than on computers.

manaemedia/Shutterstock

Exhibit 14-1
U.S. digital ad spending by format (billions), 2019.
Source: eMarketer inc.

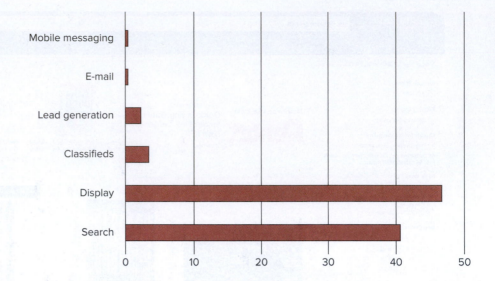

In just 15 years as a commercial medium, digital has become a mass forum for advertising as well as other communications (see Exhibit 14-1). In recognition of this explosive growth, it's important to understand how advertisers buy internet advertising and use it in their marketing plans.

Digital Interactive as a Medium

Digital interactive media have come a long way from their simple roots. While some assume it is new, the technological infrastructure of the internet, the oldest form of digital interactive media, has been around for nearly 60 years.

The **internet** is a global network of devices that communicate through **protocols,** common rules for linking and sharing information. It began in the early 1960s in the Defense Department's Advanced Research Projects Agency (ARPA) plan to create a network that could survive a nuclear war. ARPAnet had little commercial value; its primary users were governmental organizations and research universities, and the internet of today is a far different medium. However, ARPAnet was important because its structure, a **distributed network,** was revolutionary. Traditionally, media content is delivered through **centralized networks,** in which a hub, such as a TV station, a publisher, or a cable company, distributes content to many receivers (see Exhibit 14-2). In a centralized system, if the hub is knocked out, receivers go dark. But a distributed network is characterized by many different hubs and links, which allows continuous communication even if some connections stop working.

Exhibit 14-2
In a centralized network, a hub distributes content to many receivers. A distributed network has many different hubs and links.

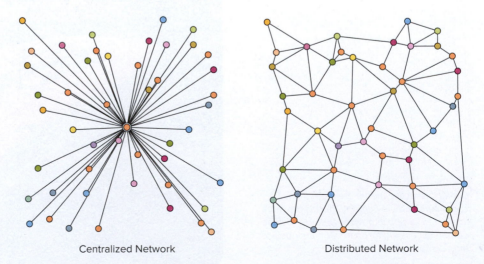

Centralized Network   Distributed Network

There are at least three other important distinctions between digital and traditional media. The first is the cost of time and/or space. In traditional media, time (on TV or radio) and space (in print) are precious, limited, and costly resources. Network TV commercials average 30 seconds, which is a very small window, and that window is expensive, averaging in the hundreds of thousands of dollars. In contrast, space on digital media is vast and relatively inexpensive. Websites or servers can store as much information as a company wishes to share. For consumers who require lots of facts before they make a decision to buy, this is a real plus.

The second distinction between traditional and digital media centers on how people consume content. In traditional media, audiences adapt to a schedule created by the provider. For instance, NBC schedules a show on a day and at a time each week and, if you enjoy it, that day and time is when you watch. But digital media deliver content any time, so consumers watch when they want. As "appointment" viewership numbers decrease and digital media use increases, more content creators will use a strategy that allows for on-demand viewing. Hulu.com provides content from over 50 providers, such as FOX, NBC, MGM, Sony Pictures Television, and others; allows users to watch full-length episodes of their favorite TV shows, old and new; and gives users the ability to cut out and create "clips" of their favorite scenes for reposting on social media. People can, and do, binge watch an entire season of content in a single sitting. While obviously appealing to the consumer, Hulu also gives advertisers the opportunity to connect their brands with premium content online, to interact with highly engaged consumers, and to extend their reach via Hulu's broad distribution network.

A third distinction is the relationship between those who create content and those who consume it. Traditional media create content for audiences to consume. In our

A quality website helps companies define their brands and entice customers to make immediate purposes. It is the conjoining of action and awareness messaging. Campos uses its award-winning site to do just that.

Source: Campos Coffee

previous NBC example, NBC is the creator and you are the consumer. But digital media are *interactive,* blurring the line between content providers and consumers. The digital audience consumes, interacts with, and creates content. As an example, imagine a teenager who uploads a video to YouTube. The teen is both a content creator (of her video or blog) and a consumer (when she watches other videos). In addition, the internet makes it easy and cheap for the teen to promote her video. She can e-mail friends and ask them to watch it or she can create links to the video on Instagram. If her friends like it, they may recommend the video to others on their own social platforms. If the content is interesting, thousands may watch the teen's video, even though it was produced very inexpensively. If she chooses, and draws a sizeable audience to her video, the teen can even monetize it by allowing YouTube to run ads alongside.

A Brief History of the Internet

How did the internet become so pervasive? As mentioned earlier, it was created with military and scientific purposes in mind. However, in the early 1980s, the National Science Foundation expanded ARPAnet by supporting a fast data network. At the same time, new companies such as AOL, Prodigy, and CompuServe helped attract people online by providing news, information, and e-mail services to subscribers. These services anticipated the web by encouraging people to use their computers to find information and communicate with others. But these content providers did not link to one another and shared information via relatively slow phone lines.

During the 1990s, the numbers of people using the internet doubled annually. Fueling the medium's growth was the increasing popularity and affordability of personal computers. The 1990s also introduced people to a part of the internet known then as the **World Wide Web (WWW).** The web, as its name implies, was a distributed network of content providers and users, communicating through a protocol known as **HTML,** or HyperText Markup Language. HTML allowed for the relatively easy creation of displays, called **web pages,** that link to all kinds of content, including other web pages or sites (and, later, photographs, movies, databases, sound files, etc.). Viewing web pages was made easy by the development of **web browsers,** software that interpreted HTML (and later other code that permitted greater interactivity, such as Javascript, PhP, and Flash).

In the 2000s, the internet became a global medium. People around the world began using it to post photos, research products, stay in touch with friends, and find out what is new. The introduction of high-speed *broadband* access made it easy to watch videos, listen to audio programming, and download large files.

This new medium has proven highly popular. The number of websites has grown from 50 in 1993 to more than 1.94 billion in 2019 (many with almost no visitors). And the number of internet users globally now exceeds 4 billion.

Exhibit 14-3

Top 10 most-visited websites.

Rank	Site	Country	Daily Time on Site
1	Google.com	USA	7:38
2	Youtube.com	USA	8:40
3	Facebook.com	USA	9:43
4	Baidu.com	China	7:19
5	Wikipedia.org	USA	4:11
6	Qq.com	China	4:02
7	Amazon.com	USA	8:05
8	Taobao.com	China	8:02
9	Yahoo.com	USA	4:03
10	Tmall.com	China	7:27

Source: "The Top 500 Sites on the Web," Alexa, an Amazon.com company.

The Digital Audience

In the past several years, we have seen a steady migration of people who used to spend time in front of the TV moving over to the computer. A 2006 study by Nielsen//NetRatings suggested that some internet users reduce TV watching by 25 percent. According to Mainak Mazumdar, Nielsen vice president of product marketing and measurement science, "It's not that people are abandoning TV for the Internet. Sometimes they do both. We only have 24 hours a day. . . . (That's) a finite amount of time to consume media."[4] Of course, some TV networks also maintain popular websites, and this strategy pays dividends in the digital age. For example, although overall TV use is down among internet users, this same group watches more programming on cable networks such as Bravo and Comedy Central than do non-internet users. This is doubtless due, at least in part, to the strong, feature-rich website that each channel maintains (see www.comedycentral.com and www.bravotv.com). Exhibit 14-3 indicates which websites were most popular in 2018. Google, the top site, serves more

Exhibit 14-4
Number of people online (in millions).

Region	Population 2018 est. (000,000)	Internet Users 2018 (000,000)	Internet Users 2011 (000,000)	Penetration 2018 (%)	Penetration 2011 (%)
Africa	1,287	464	139	36.1%	13.5%
Asia	4,207	2,062	1,016	49.0	26.2
Europe	827	705	500	85.2	61.3
Latin America/Caribbean	652	438	237	67.2	39.5
Middle East	254	164	77	64.5	35.6
North America	363	345	273	95.0	78.6
Oceania/Australia	41	28	24	68.9	67.5
World total	7,634	4,208	2,267	55.1	32.7

Source: "Internet World Stats Usage and Population Statistics," Miniwatts Marketing Group, 2018.

than a trillion (yes, trillion) search requests each year, over half of which originate from mobile devices.

Who Uses the Internet

The percentage of the U.S. population able to access the internet on a regular basis continues to climb. In 1997, only 50 million people were connected. This number had doubled by 2000 and has since doubled again. In 2011, more than 273 million people in the United States accessed the internet each month.[5] Worldwide, the active internet audience is estimated at 2.3 billion, with many more occasional users (see Exhibit 14-4). According to Internet World Stats (www.internetworldstats.com), internet penetration is currently growing fastest in Africa. Iceland (98%) and Norway (97%) top the list of the most wired nations.

Media budgets tend to be very pragmatic. As audiences migrate, so do the media dollars. As a result, media spending on internet advertising has grown substantially. One of the great draws of the internet from the marketer's point of view is its demographics.

Historically, the majority of people who surfed the internet were well-educated, upscale, white males who used the internet for business or scientific purposes. Yet, recent surveys of internet demographics suggest the reach of the medium is much more diverse and in most ways closely resembles the U.S. population (see Exhibit 14-5). Because the medium is near saturation, the few groups where adoption lags are found are age (older Americans), income (poorer Americans), education (less well educated), and community (rural Americans).

The Pew Internet & American Project Life Study suggests that one of the biggest changes in the past five years is the number of people who access the internet using a phone rather than a computer. Among young adults, nearly 26 percent do not have **broadband** at home but instead use their phone to connect. The number for all Americans is 20 percent.

In 2018 about two-thirds of adult Americans had home broadband, although this percentage is in decline. Why? Because mobile phone speeds are getting faster and the phone is a popular "screen" for accessing content. The trend is only likely to accelerate with the coming introduction of **5G** ("fifth generation") phone service, which began rolling out in 2019. The promise of 5G is much faster download speeds without cable connections. If the reality is as great as the promise, it will likely be highly disruptive to cable.

5G will prove disruptive in other ways too. Fast data access means people will consume large amounts of information when they are out of their homes, including when they are driving. Cars will become even smarter than they are now, and quite soon may possess the ability to drive, park, and return home without human assistance. Devices such as virtual reality aids will prove much more practical when people have fast, untethered connections. The central device in many people's lives is already their smartphone, not their computer. This trend will accelerate with the diffusion of 5G technology.

Exhibit 14-5
Percentage of demographic groups that use the internet, according to a 2018 Pew Internet & American Life Project survey.

% Who Use the Internet	
All Adults	
Men	89
Women	88
Race/Ethnicity	
White, non-Hispanic	89
Black, non-Hispanic	87
Hispanic (English- and Spanish-speaking)	88
Age	
18–29	98
30–49	97
50–64	87
65+	66
Household Income	
Less than $30,000/yr	81
$30,000–$49,999	93
$50,000–$74,999	97
$75,000+	98
Educational Attainment	
No high school diploma	65
High school grad	84
Some college	93
College+	97
Community	
Rural	78
Suburban	90
Urban	92

Source: "Internet/Broadband Fact Sheet," Pew Research Center, 2018.

Measuring the Digital Audience

Audience activity in digital media presents many challenges to those who would measure it. People gain access using different devices (phones, tablets, computers) and across a variety of content (websites, streaming content, e-mail, social media, and multiple content sources simultaneously). Audience members may simultaneously use traditional and digital media (as when watching TV on cable and accessing a show's site online). The audience is, in other words, fragmented.[6]

For all of the challenges, companies are drawn to digital media because audience behavior generates data, and lots of it. It is not an exaggeration to say that companies can now learn more about customers and prospective customers than at any other time in history. This reality, however, has both positive and negative aspects.

While companies are excited to learn more about what people do with their brands, the wealth of data raises significant privacy issues. Just because a company can measure almost anything someone is doing online, should it? How much permission should a company obtain from someone before it spies on what that person is doing? While this issue has been present from the very origins of digital media, it has become the focus of much greater scrutiny now. The turning point may have been the 2016 presidential election. During the campaign, Russian operatives sponsored activities on Facebook that were intended to influence the outcome. Additionally, a British political consulting firm called Cambridge Analytica accessed the personal data of nearly 87 million Facebook users by exploiting an app. Most of these users had not given the company permission to access their data.

It soon became clear that Cambridge Analytica was just the tip of the iceberg. Congress demanded testimony from executives at Facebook, Google, and other large internet companies about the data they collect and how they use it. The story is not pretty. It was revealed that Facebook shared user data with companies to a far greater extent than the company had ever admitted and that in doing so it had relaxed its own privacy rules. For example, Facebook permitted Microsoft's search engine, Bing, to obtain users' friends without requesting permission and allowed Netflix to read private Facebook messages.[7] Google, meanwhile, stood accused by European consumer organizations of deceiving internet users about tracking user locations.[8]

Privacy is an important issue when considering what reputable companies do with audience data, but the ramifications go far beyond that. In recent years, it has become clear that data security at many companies is lax or ineffective against intrusions from criminal actors and organizations as well as foreign governments. As shown in Exhibit 14-6, internet users are at serious risk of having their personal data, including social security and credit card numbers, seriously compromised.

Regulators are finally catching up. In 2018 Alabama, Arizona, Colorado, Iowa, Louisiana, Nebraska, Oregon, South Dakota, Vermont, and Virginia all passed new or revised data breach laws. The laws vary in their particulars, but among their provisions are notification requirements, disclosures about privacy practices, supervision of third parties that manage data, and civil penalties for violations. The bottom line is with access comes responsibility. Companies must do more to protect consumers, even though doing so will put limits on their access to and use of data.

Media Planning Tools

LO 14-3

As with other media, there are companies that specialize in delivering audited measurement to help media planners choose the right vehicles for their target audience. Two of the larger companies that help in the media planning process on the internet are Nielsen and Comscore. Both companies offer advertisers and agencies tools that help define target market size, behavior, and composition relative to each major website on the internet. They also provide views into how other advertisers are using the internet, thereby giving competitive insights into industry and category best practices.

Nielsen, the dominant company in broadcast and cable TV ratings, seeks to play the same role in digital through several initiatives. Nielsen's *Digital Ad Ratings* offer what the company calls "a comprehensive, next-day view of an ad's computer and mobile audience in a way that is comparable to Nielsen TV ratings."[9] The technology, first introduced

Exhibit 14-6
Prominent data breaches and the number of individuals affected in 2018.

TicketFly 27,000,000	**LocalBlox** 48,000,000	**SKY Brasil** 32,000,000	**Facebook** 50,000,000

NMBS 1,460,000 — **Click2 Gov** 300,000 — **Dell** 100,000 — **Health care.gov** 75,000

British Airways 380,000

Saks and Lord & Taylor 5,000,000

T-Mobile 2,000,000

WordPress 76,500,000

Amazon 5,000,000

Sing Health 1,500,000

Panerabread 37,000,000

Newegg 45,000,000

Vision Direct 100,000

Orbitz 880,000

Cathay Pacific Airways 9,400,000

Chinese résumé leak 202,000,000

Grindr 3,000,000

Aadhaar 1,100,000,000

Twitter 330,000,000

GovPay Now.com 14,000,000

MyFitnessPal 150,000,000

Firebase 100,000,000

High Tail Hall 411,000 — **MBM Company** 1,300,000

Aadhaar 1,000,000,000

Health South East 3,000,000

Quora 100,000,000

Ticketmaster 40,000

Facebook 29,000,000

MyHeritage 92,283,889

Marriott Hotels 383,000,000

View Fines 934,000

Texas voter records 14,800,000

CMS 93,689

Dixons Carphone 10,000,000

Urban Massage 309,000

Nametests 120,000,000

Google+ 52,500,000

Amazon 100,000

Careem 14,000,000

Source: David McCandless, Tom Evans, Paul Barton, and Stephanie Tomasevic, "World's Biggest Data Breaches & Hacks," *Information Is Beautiful,* December 5, 2018, https://informationisbeautiful.net/visualizations/worlds-biggest-data-breaches-hacks/.

in the United States, is now available in a number of international markets, including China, Ireland, New Zealand, Poland, South Africa, Taiwan, and Turkey.

Nielsen randomly recruits individuals to download and utilize a *desktop meter* so all internet activity on that computer is then tabulated, measured, and recorded. This is very similar to the methods Nielsen utilizes to measure TV audiences. Using the sample, Nielsen then projects these numbers to the rest of the internet audience. For instance, if a panel identifies that 50 percent of all men aged 18–34 go to ESPN.com daily, whereas on average most sites garner only 25 percent of the male panel audience, Nielsen will project an index of 200 for ESPN.com relative to the entire internet for men between the ages of 18 and 34. Media planners utilize these numbers to identify the highest concentration, or **composition,** of the target they are trying to reach. However, because of lack of standardization, many companies report many different numbers, and it is a media planner's job to make heads or tails of the data. (See Ad Lab 14–A for a deeper explanation.)

In 2018 the company introduced a more comprehensive measurement tool, *Nielsen Total Audience.* The tool is designed to measure traditional viewing metrics (reach, frequency, GRPs) across digital and traditional video platforms in all 210 local markets. Previously this capability had only been possible on a national scale. In addition, as of 2018 Nielsen has virtually eliminated diaries as a measure of audience activity in favor of Local People Meters. A sample snapshot of adult viewing patterns can be seen in Exhibit 14-7.

AD Lab 14–A

Internet Ratings: A Call for Standards

With the increased popularity of the internet as an advertising medium comes increased reliance on measurement. However, because of a lack of standards, many measurement methods are available and it can be challenging to make heads or tails of the various solutions.

Each measurement company has its own way of "counting" and measuring, but for the most part there are two main buckets of measurement. There are planning tools from Comscore and Nielsen and tracking tools such as Doubleclick, Omniture, and WebTrends. All of these companies help quantify internet usage, but the main difference between the sets is that one is based on projected activity from samples of consumers and the others are census-based, where census means complete records of activity at a site or ad campaign level.

The panel-based, or sample, approach has to date been widely accepted in the planning community for the main reason that it offers demographic and targeting-based information that is still considered unreliable from the census companies. However, both Comscore and Nielsen have come under tremendous pressure to come up with a better solution as they have been highly scrutinized for undercounting by up to two to three times what most publishers count from their own server logs.

However, everything isn't all peaches and cream on the census side either. In fact, anyone can perform a basic search for internet measurement information and find a number of blogs, articles, and press releases about the monumental discrepancies between all of the various census-based reporting tools, and there are many.

The discrepancies stem from a multitude of reasons: different data collection methods, unique data models, untagged pages, blocking software, cookie issues, and many more reasons. In fact, Google Analytics, Google's free-to-use website tracking tool, has pages on its help site about why Google AdWords' clicks don't match Google Analytics' page visits. So is there hope? Yes, and it comes in two forms: Media Rating Council (MRC) and start-ups.

The MRC's number one objective is **To secure for the media industry and related users audience measurement services that are valid, reliable, and effective.** Hallelujah . . . right? It is definitely a step in the right direction; however, because the MRC is an organization that can tell you only what you "should do," not what you "must do," it is up to the advertisers and publishers to come to resolution if the industry really wants to see a change happen.

Or you rely on the start-ups to make a better black box. Companies like Alexa, Quantcast, and even Google AdPlanner are coming up with different, possibly more acceptable, ways to measure internet usage. But as with all start-ups, they have yet to truly prove themselves. Their task is to engage with advertisers and publishers and reliably deliver numbers that both sides feel comfortable with.

Laboratory Applications

1. What are some of the problems of internet audience measurement?

2. Do you think these problems can be fixed? How?

Average Time Spent Per Adult 18+ Per Day
Based on Total U.S. Population

Legend:
- Live TV
- Time Shifted TV
- Radio
- DVD/Blu-ray Device
- Game Console
- Internet Connected Device
- Internet on a Computer
- App/Web on a Smartphone
- App/Web on a Tablet

Exhibit 14-7
Nielsen Total Audience snapshot, Q1, 2018.

Source: "The Nielsen Total Audience Report: Q1 2018," *Advertising Research Foundation*, August 16, 2018, https://thearf.org/category/news-you-can-use/the-nielsen-total-audience-report-q1-2018/.

Nielsen's biggest competitor in both traditional and online audience measurement is *Comscore*. The company, founded in 1999, uses consumer panels composed of people who permit monitoring software to be installed on their computers. The company estimates that 2 million people participate in its panels and, in exchange, receive gifts and the chance to win cash prizes. A significant problem with these panels is that they are self-selected (people choose to participate) rather than randomly chosen. Comscore uses weights to adjust their results in an attempt to match the panels to the broader population.

Both Nielsen and Comscore face challenges in creating a standard for measuring digital audiences. Interestingly, some of the challenges come from the companies that stand to benefit most from such a standard. For example, NBCUniversal, which owns a large stake in Hulu, convinced Nielsen to limit the rollout of Nielsen Total Content Ratings (TCR), a metric that would offer more accurate audience metrics across all platforms. Why the concern? Simply put, there is a tension between those who sell ads and those who buy them. Companies that sell ads (networks, cable companies, streaming services) like measures that imply their audiences are large because they can charge advertisers higher rates for more eyeballs. While accuracy is a value, any change in measuring an audience that suggests it is smaller than originally thought may cost companies that sell ads millions of dollars.

Variety, a media trade publication, summarized the current state of audience measurement this way:

> Nielsen's effort to implement TCR shows how much discord the industry must resolve: To make the measurement work, media companies need to install software code across a wide variety of distribution points—mobile apps, video-on-demand interfaces, and more. But the process varies from TV network to TV network, and depends upon each network's individual priorities. Perhaps one media company places more emphasis on measuring desktop video-streaming, while another is eager to aggregate viewership from a particular mobile app. Because each network is pursuing a different agenda, the fear is that industry-wide rankings might wind up being incongruous, rather than measuring the same thing in every instance.[10]

No matter who is measuring, they face the challenge of tracking new groups with the names **cord-cutters** (people who end their cable subscriptions), **cord-shavers** (people who cut back on the cable services they use, including premium tiers, digital recording devices, or internet service), and **cord-nevers** (people who have never subscribed to cable).[11] These groups still access digital content (through their phones or through broadband) and are still important to advertisers even though they've abandoned or limited cable.

Another group of interest to advertisers is people who access what is called OTT inventory. **OTT, or "over-the-top," inventory** is video content accessed via the internet rather than through cable or broadcast. Think Netflix, Hulu, and Amazon Prime, as well as others. OTT is contrasted with what is now called **linear TV,** or TV the way everyone used to watch (cable, broadcast). For the moment, the threat of traditional cable erosion is mitigated by the fact that many people access OTT on cable internet services; this may change with the introduction of 5G mobile technology, as mentioned earlier.

ESPN uses both subscriptions for premium content and advertising to make its popular website profitable.

Source: ESPN Enterprises, Inc.

Behavioral Targeting

Behavioral targeting is the ability to track people's behavior on the internet in order to display unique, targeted content. Although software developers claim that the users are tracked anonymously with encrypted identification numbers, privacy advocates believe the marketing method is too invasive into consumers' lives (see Ethics, Diversity & Inclusion: Who's Watching You? in the next section).

How does tracking work? Online activities are followed quite regularly by a variety of companies. Visitors to sites often don't realize that they've acquired small code files, saved on their devices or in their browsers, that are known as **cookies**. Cookies track whether the user has ever visited a specific site that is part of an **ad network**, a large collection of advertisers and content providers, or **internet publisher**. This allows the site to serve visitors unique information depending on their digital behaviors. Cookies also indicate the users' frequency of visits, the time of last visit, and the domain from which they arrived. Additionally, cookies give marketers valuable metrics, such as the number of times users call for an ad, time of day, type of browsers they use, whether or not they click, and so on.

A behavioral tracking experience might work this way. A user goes to Amazon to look at dresswear. Finding nothing, she leaves to do email and access social media. Later in the day, she goes to the CNN website to read the day's news. As depicted on the next page an ad at the site offers dresses for sale.

How did the dress ad show up on CNN? Both the advertiser and publisher are part of an ad network. After looking at dresses on Amazon's site, a cookie was written to the surfer's computer. Later that day, she visited a publisher that served up an ad for the clothing company. The cookie recorded that the woman had earlier looked at dresses but did not make a purchase. Valuable information indeed.

Amazon tracking ad.
Source: Cable News Network

Measure what matters to make cross-platform audiences and advertising more valuable.

LEARN MORE

Comscore is the trusted currency for planning, transacting, and evaluating media across platforms.

One reason media budgets are shifting to the internet is that the medium offers a variety of ways to track interactions of consumers with ads. One company that helps provide such metrics is comScore (www.comscore.com).
Source: Comscore, Inc.

Ad networks employ the services of **third-party ad servers.** Third-party ad servers deliver ads from one central source, or server, across multiple web domains, allowing advertisers the ability to manage the rotation and distribution of their advertisements. The best-known companies are DoubleClick, owned by Google, and Atlas DMT, owned by Microsoft. These companies allow advertisers to monitor the performance of their buys on a daily basis all the way down to conversion to sales or any other action advertisers desire. By placing a line of code on the last page of the sales process (in this case, the confirmation page), DoubleClick and/or Atlas can match the user back to the last advertisement he or she saw or clicked on, via the cookies and credit that advertisement with the sale. This allows the agency to understand direct metrics from advertising to sales in near real time.

More sophisticated technology provides marketers with additional details about the consumer. The computer first assigns each user an anonymous and encrypted identification number for tracking purposes. A user profile is then created with data on the content of the pages read, what keywords may have been used in a search, the time and day that a web page was viewed, the frequency with which an ad is seen, the sequence of ads that are seen, the computer operating system of the user, the browser type, and the IP address. From these data, marketers' computers can again guess the user's ISP, telephone area code, and NAIC code. Marketers may then match these data with demographic information gathered offline to create a clearer picture of consumer behavior than has ever been available.

Seeking Standardization

As much as Madison Avenue may want web metrics to resemble traditional media measurements, this is not possible at present. But progress has been made. For most advertisers, the basic questions remain the same: Do people see our ads? Are they effective? Until fairly recently, when a task force of the Internet Advertising Bureau (IAB) provided some practical definitions, internet audience measurement information lacked the standardization needed to be able to compare its advertising effectiveness to other media.

The most simple measurement, yet an area of great controversy, is the **advertising impression.** The IAB defines an ad impression as "an opportunity to deliver an advertising element to a Website visitor."[12] When a user loads a web page with ads on it, the browser will pull the advertisement from an ad server and bring it up as a banner, button, or interstitial. The number of ad requests received can then be translated into the familiar cost form. The problem with this definition, from the point of view of advertisers and agencies, is that the advertiser is not guaranteed that a user will ever see an ad. People often click away to some other site before the requested ad ever comes up. Under the IAB definition, an advertiser would be charged for an ad that might never have been seen. The AAAA prefers to define an ad request as an ad that is actually delivered to users' screens. This controversy over definitions has a huge impact on the business because it also creates reporting differences between what web publishers count and what the agencies count and are willing to pay for. These considerations prevent marketers from obtaining the foolproof numbers they want. But as technology improves the speed and methods of online advertising, we can anticipate increased accuracy in measurement. For more on internet ratings, see Ad Lab 14-A.

A second measurement, unique to the internet, is the **click-through rate,** or *click rate.* A click occurs when a visitor moves the mouse's pointer to a web link and clicks on the mouse button to get to another page. The click rate is the number of clicks on an ad divided by the number of ad impressions. In essence, marketers are measuring the frequency with which users try to obtain additional information about a product by clicking on an advertisement. Clicks are an important metric behind the success of internet giants such as Google and Amazon because clicks deliver a potential buyer to an advertiser's website or product.

Buying Time and Space on the Internet

Media planners cannot think of the internet in mass media terms. Interactive media are *personal audience venues.* That means one on one. So cost per thousand, rating points, and share of audience don't really mean the same things in the interactive world. With interactive media, sales volume often takes a back seat to relationship building, one customer at a time. And the care companies exercise in buying and developing their interactive programs and integrating them with their other media programs will determine overall success.

Digital media spending is the fastest-growing segment both in the U.S. and worldwide. Online display advertising spending amounted to $8.1 billion in 2017 and measured search marketing ad spending totaled $18.3 billion.[13] Exhibit 14-8 lists the top 10 digital display advertisers ranked by spending. The best marketers are testing extensively. That means being willing to lose money for a while, which is, of course, not exciting to most advertisers or agencies.

Exhibit 14-8
Top internet display marketers.

Rank	Company	Estimated Spending (Millions) 2017
1	Expedia	$251
2	Newchic	122
3	Cox Enterprises	113
4	Walmart	110
5	Harry's	96
6	Qurate Retail Group	92
7	AT&T	91
8	Dyson	79
9	Comcast Corp.	77
10	Capital One	77

Source: *Ad Age* 200 Leading National Advertisers 2018 Fact Pack, Crain Communications.

Pricing Methods

Advertising space on the internet can be purchased in several different ways, as discussed later in the chapter. The most common means is the display ad, typically billed on a cost-per-thousand basis determined by the number of ads displayed. On most web pages, the base display rate pays for exposure on a rotation that randomly selects which ads to show.

The real marketing power of digital, however, is the ability to specifically target an audience in a way that is virtually impossible in traditional media. In addition to general display ads, media buyers may opt to purchase more selective space. For example, ads may be purchased in a portal's information categories and subcategories, such as finance, news, travel, or games. Prices vary according to category and increase as the buyer targets a more selective audience. Costs are tiered according to thousands, hundreds of thousands, or even millions of page requests per month.

Today advertisers increasingly rely on **programmatic advertising** as a way to purchase digital space. In programmatic advertising, many of the human tasks of buying and selling ads are replaced by computer algorithms. In a typical programmatic ad buy, an advertiser places a bid on the audience she or he wishes to reach. The bid is informed by many strategic considerations, including the value of the audience, the ROI ad spends, and other factors. Bids from all advertisers are analyzed by computers in real time, and prime space goes to the highest bidders. This is also known as **real-time bidding.**

Programmatic advertisers are really buying audiences rather than publishers. This sounds good, but in a number of instances advertisers have discovered their ads being served on controversial or political sites that are inconsistent with their brands. In response, advertisers have demanded greater accountability from programmatic companies.

Bidding is also essential to the **keyword** purchase, available on major search engines. Advertisers may buy specific keywords that bring up their ads when a user's search request contains these words. Keywords may be purchased individually or in packages that factor in the information categories and subcategories of a search engine site.

Some publishers charge their clients according to **click-throughs**—that is, when a user actually clicks on a display ad to visit the advertiser's landing page. Although the CPM for simple impressions is considerably lower, this method is still popular with publishers. When an advertiser buys on a per-click basis, the publisher may expose many users to an advertiser's message without being able to charge for the service.

For advertisers involved in e-commerce, some publishers offer an **affiliate marketing program** whereby they charge a percentage of the transaction cost. For example, a site devoted to music reviews may have a banner link to an online music retailer. When consumers buy music from the retailer, the site publisher receives a percentage of the sale for showing the banner.

Types of Internet Advertising

LO 14-5

Digital media constantly evolve. Therefore, advertisers have new and interesting ways to reach target audiences that extend beyond the more standard ad placements (see Exhibit 14-9). In approaching this topic, we will work our way back up the generic online "sales funnel." The internet is truly unique as a medium in its ability to lead directly to sales, but beware of pigeonholing the internet as a direct marketing medium. It has often been said that the accountability factor is not only the internet's saving grace, it is also the bane of its existence. (See the Portfolio Review on "Digital Advertising" for different online creative executions discussed in this section.)

Websites, Microsites, and Landing Pages

A **website** is a collection of web pages, images, videos, or data assets that is hosted on one or more web servers, usually accessible via the internet. Wikipedia.org lists 22 different types of websites. We will be primarily referencing two: corporate and commerce sites. A corporate site offers background information about an organization, product, or service. A commerce site is used to sell a product or service. Of course, there is a fine line between these definitions; for companies like Amazon.com, the corporate site is the commerce site and the advertising site. Good marketers use web assets for multiple purposes. They understand that the website is an extension of the brand and that the website experience is synonymous with a brand experience. Many marketers use microsites and landing pages to deliver the desired experience.

A **microsite** is used as a supplement to a website. A great example, and one that fits well with the Ethics, Diversity & Inclusion box, is The Data That Lies Beneath (http://interactive.columnfivemedia.com/lucidworks/dark-data/), where you can discover how your data are used for both good and not-so-good purposes.

For advertisers, microsites are typically singular in focus and deliver on the current advertising message. For instance, when Electronic Arts (EA) launched the *Return of the King* video game after the very popular movie trilogy *The Lord of the Rings,* it had Freestyle Interactive build a robust microsite that gave users cheats, codes, game screens, and exclusive videos and also gave users a chance to win a replica sword from the movie. The kicker was that to unlock the content, users actually had to go on an internet-based scavenger hunt to find four pieces, or shards, of the sword. Each piece unlocked more content until the sword was "reforged" and the user could open the cheats and enter to win the replica sword. The microsite was able to identify how many pieces each user had found from cookies placed on the user's browser.

Any web page can be a **landing page**—the term used to describe direct links to deeper areas of the website beyond the homepage to which advertising drives consumers. Typically, advertisers use landing pages to give consumers a more relevant experience as it relates to the message from the advertising. For instance, if someone searches for "men's dress pants" on Google, Dockers wants to send them directly to the *men's apparel* section, and more specifically all the way to the pants page, rather than making the user click two or three more times just to find the relevant products. Advertisers use landing pages to streamline the selling or information-gathering process, as studies have found that people's attention spans are limited online. If they cannot find what they are looking for right away, they may be lost forever. Consumers are fickle, and anything to help them on their online journey is typically a smart approach.

Search Engine Marketing

Most people looking to find information on the web use a **search engine.** Search engines are web tools or sites that allow people to type a word or phrase into a text box and then quickly receive a listing of information on a **search-results page.**

In the late 1990s, several companies competed to be the leading brand for searches. The clear winner is Google, which has an astounding 92 percent share of search worldwide as of November 2018.[14] Moreover, the story of how Google used a superior search capability to become one of the biggest and most profitable companies in the world offers important lessons for digital advertising.

Exhibit 14-9
U.S. digital advertising spending 2018–2019.

($ billions)		
Category	2018	2019 Expected Growth
Search	$47.7	12.2%
Mobile	70.3	20.7
Desktop	36.3	−5.3
Video	13.0	19.4

Source: Greg Sterling, "Report: Digital Now Makes up 51% of US Ad Spending," *Marketing Land* (Third Door Media Inc.), September 20, 2018.

Ethics, Diversity & Inclusion

Who's Watching You?

Because this is a college-level text, it is likely that most readers fall within the adult 18–24 demographic. This isn't hard to extrapolate, nor is it all that intrusive to the reader that someone somewhere has this information. But what if the knowledge was much deeper? For example, what if an unknown organization knew where you are from, what your marital status is, what college you are attending, if you are female or male, and what type of cologne or perfume you like? That might be a bit scary. If the information could go even deeper, well, most people would consider that unsettling.

It is just these types of feelings that drive consumer privacy issues online. Throughout this chapter we've highlighted the various ways in which consumers are targeted and messaged when they access information online. Much of this is possible due to a few lines of code, called *cookies*, that track, categorize, and filter your every click.

Companies like BlueKai, an online behavioral data company, supply marketers with access to online consumers who've behaved in a way that matches their intended target audience. For instance, if Audi wanted consideration from a potential new car buyer, it could pay BlueKai to identify and target all relevant people who've recently visited an auto site, spent a lot of time on that site, and frequently returned over a specific time period. Companies like BlueKai can even suggest what type of car the person is interested in. If Audi wanted to deliver a message to people considering rival BMW's cars, it could potentially buy information about BMW "Auto Intenders," as classified by BlueKai.

BlueKai partners with sites like Expedia.com to help them

(a) capture these data
(b) mine the data for insights
(c) organize and categorize the information
(d) sell it to advertisers

In exchange, BlueKai shares the information and the revenue it creates with its partners. This allows its partners to have multiple revenue streams and do a better job of classifying their monthly internet traffic that they too sell to advertisers.

When polled, 62 percent of consumers say they do not want their online activities tracked. However, behaviorally targeted advertising represents some of the highest-performing online ads. So how does a marketer deal with this, as consumers are clearly more responsive to targeted ads but don't trust how the data used to target them is gathered and used?

To further complicate the issue, when an advertiser also has a popular web property, like Amazon.com, then the question of who owns the data arises. While some argue that the data of any individual is owned by that individual, until recently there have been no clear directions for consumers, nor any industry-wide practices that allow customers to limit the data companies can access.

Any consumer can turn off cookies in his or her browser. However, by doing so the consumer no longer gets a personalized online experience.

The Federal Trade Commission (FTC) has investigated the issue, much like it did in the early 2000s when it ultimately passed the CAN-SPAM Act, making it illegal to spam—send e-mail without permission. In late 2011, the FTC issued a privacy report that called for a "do not track" system to be put in place, but it took the EU to actually legislate privacy policies with teeth. In 2018 the EU issued the General Data Protection Regulation (GDPR), which specifies that any marketer who does business in Europe must meet specific data protection and privacy rules. And because every major online company does business in Europe, it means Americans receive these same benefits.

Among the many requirements of the GDPR are that sites must disclose that they collect data, describe how long they will retain the data, and indicate whether the data are to be shared with third parties. Most importantly, sites must obtain consent to the company's data policies from visitors.

Does the regulation have teeth? Immediately on its implementation, websites around the world began complying with its requirements. And in November 2018, Google was charged with GDPR violations by seven European countries. So it appears that what U.S. regulators could not accomplish, Europe has done for them.

Questions

1. Why would companies want to track everyone's online behavior?

2. Think of the last five websites you were on. What did you look at? How do you think advertisers could use that information to better target you?

3. Has the online media industry taken tracking too far? Do you think it is okay, or not okay, to watch people's behavior online?

When Google's creators, Sergey Brin and Larry Page, first met as graduate students at Stanford, profits were not their main interest. Brin and Page were interested in helping users find information and believed they had a better algorithm for doing so.

Their search engine, using a process they eventually named *Pagerank,* analyzed the links and relationships of internet sites to create rankings. As did other search engines at the time, when a keyword is entered in a search, Google looked for websites that feature the word. But Google separated itself from the competition by analyzing site links to determine what sites are considered useful.

Consider two sites that each use the term *marketing* five times. If a web user typed *marketing* as a search term, Google's search engine would locate both. But which site should be listed relatively high in the search results and which should be listed much lower? This is where Pagerank comes in. Sites with links from many other sites, especially highly ranked sites, get higher Pageranks and show up prominently in search results. The net result is a fast search engine that returns remarkably relevant search results.

Because the company created a better search engine, Google users surged. But throughout the 1990s Brin and Page did not know how to monetize search. Like many companies at the time, Google sustained itself on venture capital investments. That ended with the dot-com bust of the early 2000s, when Google investors forced Brin and Page to develop a revenue model. Their response was two advertising programs, AdWords and AdSense (these are now integrated into a program called "Google Ads"). It is difficult to overstate how successful these programs have been because, in a few short years, Google has used them to create an annual revenue stream that topped $100 billion in 2018.

AdWords

When you search on Google, you'll notice that the first listings are often labeled "Sponsored Links." **Sponsored links** are paid listings. For advertisers there is really no better place to put a message. The power of a sponsored link is that it offers a solution at the very moment someone is indicating he or she has a problem. This is relevance, and it has helped Google crush many other types of advertising. Consider an example. You are a brand manager at Dockers and are targeting men seeking business attire. All things being equal, would you choose to purchase a magazine ad or an AdWords placement for the word *dress pants?*

Google's search results page is thus composed of two distinct areas: **organic search results**, which are unaffected by sponsorship and sponsored links, and sponsored links. Google's sponsored links have three important characteristics. First, advertisers do not pay just for being seen, a common practice with banner ads. Instead, advertisers pay Google only when a search engine user clicks on the link and visits the sponsor's site. This performance-based pay-per-click model has proven very attractive to advertisers. Second, the amount that an advertiser owes for each click-through is not actually set by Google. Instead, it is determined in an auction, where companies can bid for keywords used in searches, such as the term *marketing.* Higher bids generally lead to better listings, such as those located on the first search results page and located near the top of the page. These are locations where the search engine user is most likely to see them. Holding true to its relevancy algorithm for organic searches, Google adds one additional twist to its AdWords: The ranking of sponsored listings is not completely determined by how much a company bids on a keyword but on its ad's performance as well. Text ads that attract lots of clicks rise in the rankings, while links that are ignored fall. Third, Google benefits from the targeted nature of search. When people are hunting for a term like *marketing,* they often find that the sponsored links are as useful as the search results. Google estimates that almost 15 percent of searches result in click-throughs to sponsors, an astonishingly high *conversion rate* in comparison with other media, interactive or traditional. Google's model clearly emphasizes performance.

AdSense

Google's other major ad program, AdSense, helps websites and blogs monetize audiences by running ads. Websites that use AdSense set aside a portion of pages for Google text ads. The ads themselves are selected by Google software and inserted automatically, without any input from the website. Google software attempts to insert ads that are relevant to the site's content.

The revenue model for the AdSense program is very similar to AdWords in that advertisers pay Google only when web users click the link and visit the sponsor sites. In this case, the owner of the site in which the ad appeared also gets revenue. For popular websites, this can generate significant income, and it is thus a powerful incentive for site owners to participate in the Google program.

(continued on page 485)

:: Digital Advertising

As the fastest-growing medium in history, digital advertising offers incredible opportunities for a wide range of people in both business and advertising, despite a number of unknown factors of the medium. For advertisers, there is a whole new world of potential customers out there, waiting to be engaged. But for advertising's historically television-oriented creatives, just learning the new rules of creative is challenging, especially with the medium's ever-changing technologies. Of course, this is exactly the same challenge that took place when TV was first introduced some 70 years ago.

•   In this portfolio, study digital ads and evaluate how they capitalize on interactivity. Try to determine how each fits into the company's overall strategy and how the site either complements or perhaps replaces a more traditional media approach. Could the company benefit from incorporating additional features into its content? What features would you suggest?

Based in Sydney, Australia, The Horse curates exceptional Australian gift items. Its beautiful website won an award designation as an exceptional e-commerce site.
Source: The Horse

Ultranoir is a Paris digital boutique that creates stunning websites for its clients. You can see its work at www.ultranoir.com/en/#!/home/.
Source: Ultranoir

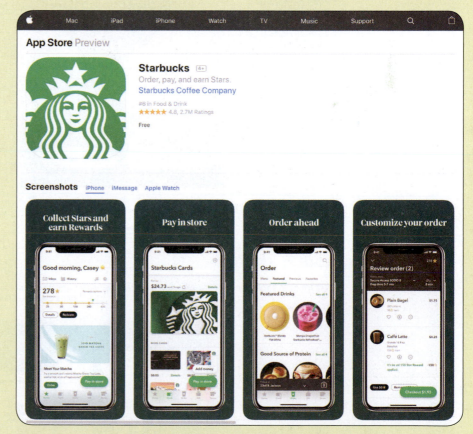

Mobile phone users can't live without their apps, and smart brands develop ones that are functional and beautiful. Great examples are these award winners from iTranslate Converse and Starbucks (above) and Warby Parker and Weight Watchers (on next page).

(top) Source: Apple, Inc.; (bottom) Source: Starbucks/Apple, Inc.

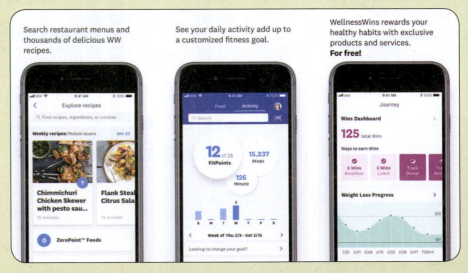

(top) Source: Warby Parker; (bottom) Source: WW International, Inc./Apple Inc.

The highly interactive nature of Airbnb's site ensures that customers come back often.

Source: Airbnb, Inc.

Southwest's award-winning heart campaign has its own microsite.

Source: Southwest Airlines Co.

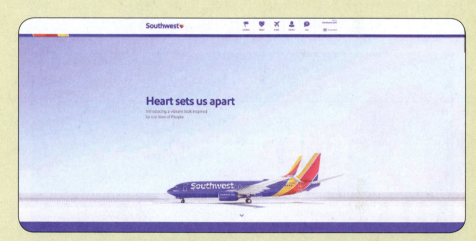

Apple's challenge is clear: As a brand known for design, it must have a website that reinforces the company's reputation for taste, beauty, and elegance.

Source: Apple, Inc.

If you want to buy new furniture, why not see what it will look like in your home before you pick it up? IKEA has an app for that.

Source: Ikea/Apple, Inc.

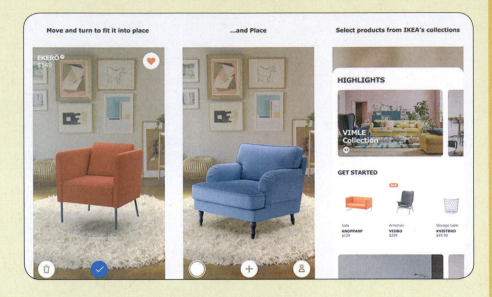

Interactivity is the name of the game, and Virgin Mobile used an interactive app called "Game of Phones" to attract over 40,000 players in an effort to win $200,000 worth of prizes.

Source: Virgin Mobile USA, L.P.

(continued from page 479)

Large websites, such as those listed in Exhibit 14-3, generally don't use programs such as Google Ads, preferring to sell ad space themselves. But the program has helped thousands of small to midsized sites and blogs develop steady revenue streams. Tiny, targeted, and text-based ads have revolutionized the web and leveled the playing field for small businesses competing against larger ones.

Of course, to benefit from search-based ad programs, companies must have websites that convert visitors into customers. Businesses ranging from your local florist to global manufacturers are using the internet to present multimedia content that includes interesting or entertaining information, product data, video, and even games. Many of them, like Ameritrade and Amazon .com, conduct all their commerce right on the web. Users move from page to page and site to site depending on what they are looking for. In other words, the user is in control. The consumer chooses what screens to experience, which banners to click, and which to ignore.

That means marketers have to provide information that is useful and relevant. They have to keep updating it to get repeat visits—and a little entertainment with a few freebies tossed in doesn't hurt. Even Ragú (www.ragu.com) spaghetti sauce has a colorful site that offers Italian phrases, recipes, and occasionally a sweepstakes. Learning how to use this new medium challenges the creativity of the whole advertising community. And with the amount of daily updating that is required to keep websites current, the opportunity for career growth and specialization is great.

Internet Display Ads

The basic form of web display advertising is the ad banner. A **banner** is a little billboard that spreads across the top or bottom of the web page. When users click their mouse pointer on the banner, it sends them to the advertiser's site or a buffer page. The standard size for an ad banner is 468 pixels (picture elements) wide by 60 pixels high. That means that on a standard 8½- by 11-inch page, the banner would measure just over 4½ inches wide by ½-inch high.

Banners have existed since the first days of the internet, and web advertisers quickly learned that without a clear strategy, they were not very effective. Through the use of behavioral tracking, described earlier, banner ads are now "smarter." Banner ads served to someone on the basis of their online behaviors are known as **retargeting ads.**[15]

The group most responsible for standards in internet and other digital ad formats is the **Interactive Advertising Bureau (IAB),** an association of digital publishers. Its first attempt at standardization was the Universal Ad Package, introduced in 2003. Since then the organization has continued to determine requirements that help both advertisers and publishers standardize digital ad buying.

Full motion, animation, and user interaction are now commonplace through the broad adoption of **rich-media advertising.** Originally these ads were developed in Adobe Flash, but in recent years the formats rely on other codes, such as HTML 5. This type of ad includes graphical animations and ads with audio and video elements that overlay the page or even float over the page. Many of the rich-media ads complement the standard banners endorsed by the IAB, as each of these can display 15-second animations.[16]

Rich mail incorporates graphics, video, and audio in an e-mail message. When you open up a rich e-mail, your e-mail client automatically calls up your internet connection and launches an HTML page in your e-mail window. E-mail clients that are offline will invite you to click on the link when you have your internet connection open again. If your e-mail client does not support graphics, you will receive the e-mail in text only. We can anticipate seeing more audio and animation integrated into these ads as improving technology accommodates them.

Preroll is now a fast-growing advertising segment. With more bandwidth comes the consumption of more video entertainment online, and companies such as Broadband Enterprises and YuMe Networks are trying to capitalize on this by aggregating much of this content and placing 5-second to 30-second video advertisements as a **third-party ad server.** How is this different from TV? As we discussed previously, the internet's ability to hypertarget is one of the many ways it sets itself apart. So, imagine if you could get the great qualities of TV advertising—sight, sound, and motion—to a highly targeted audience, at prices lower than those of TV.

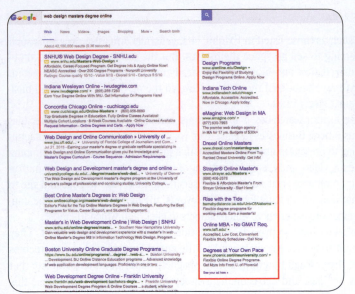

Google's advertising revenue comes primarily from its Google Ads program. The company earns revenue when web users click sponsored links during search. AdSense does the same when users visit websites, like "How to Clean Anything," that are part of Google's program.

Source: (left) Google; (right) howtocleananything.com

Sponsorships and Added-Value Packages

A form of advertising on the internet that is growing in popularity is the **sponsorship** of web pages. Corporations sponsor entire sections of a publisher's web page or sponsor single events for a limited period of time, usually calculated in months. In exchange for sponsorship support, companies are given extensive recognition on the site. Sometimes an added-value package is created by integrating the sponsor's brand with the publisher's content, as a sort of advertorial, or with banners and buttons on the page.

Google's AdSense helps thousands of sites earn revenue in exchange for providing space for targeted advertising. PaperCut offers educators free graphics tools and earns money when visitors click the ads.

Source: Teachnology, Inc.

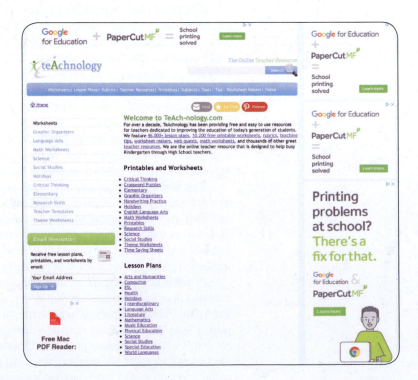

This screenshot from Dell's ecommerce site is notable for two reasons. First, Dell does not make televisions so the TVs listed here are being offered through the computer manufacturer's site. Second, the banner ad on the right from Vizio is an example of sponsorship on the page. Vizio is advertising on an ecommerce site for another brand.

Source: Dell, Inc.

IBM has exclusively sponsored the Super Bowl web page, at an estimated cost of $1 million for each event. Other forms of sponsorships have included web serials, sites devoted to women's issues, contests, and giveaways.

Classified Ads

Another growing area for internet advertisers, and an excellent opportunity for local advertisers, is the plethora of **classified ad websites,** like Craigslist. Many of these offer *free* classified advertising opportunities because they are typically supported by ad banners of other advertisers. In style, the classifieds are very similar to what we are all familiar with from newspapers. You can search for homes, cars, jobs, computer equipment, business opportunities, and so on. Moreover, the search can be narrowed to your city or expanded nationwide. Many of these sites are sponsored by the search engines themselves or by local newspapers around the country.

E-Mail Advertising

According to *Forbes*'s "Ad Effectiveness Study," 74 percent of marketers send **e-mail advertising** to customers who have asked for it. Marketers have always known that direct-mail advertising (discussed in Chapter 17) is the most effective medium for generating inquiries and leads and for closing a sale. It's also been the most expensive medium on a cost-per-exposure basis. Now, thanks to the internet, the power of direct mail is increased even more, and the cost is reduced dramatically.

It's important to differentiate responsible e-mail advertising from **spam,** which is just electronic junk mail. Spam generally refers to unsolicited, mass e-mail advertising for a product or service that is sent by an unknown entity to a purchased mailing list or newsgroup. Spammers face the wrath of frustrated customers, tired of having their inboxes filled with unwanted e-mails. Since January 2004, spammers also face litigation under the CAN-SPAM Act (Controlling the Assault of Non-Solicited Pornography and Marketing). Legitimate e-mail advertisers are required to (1) clearly mark the e-mail as advertising, (2) provide a valid reply-to e-mail address, and (3) allow recipients to opt out of future mailings. The first lawsuits under the act were filed in April 2004 against two companies that had sent nearly a million e-mails advertising bogus diet patches and growth hormones.[17] With this in mind, wary marketers are focusing their e-mail efforts on **customer retention and relationship management (CRM)** rather than on prospecting.

One of the hottest trends on the internet today actually started as an application of e-mail but has been enhanced by social media. Thanks to *viral marketing,* Amazon.com, eBay, and Blue Mountain Arts all made it big on the web, reaching unexpected heights in short time spans, most with surprisingly low marketing budgets.[18] **Viral marketing** is the internet version of word-of-mouth advertising. The term was coined in 1997 by Steven Jurvetson and his partners at the venture capital firm Draper Fisher Jurvetson. They were describing free e-mail provider Hotmail's incredible growth to 12 million users in just 18 months through the use of a little message at the bottom of every e-mail.[19] The message invited recipients to sign up for their own free Hotmail account.

Since that time, many other marketers have come up with ways to induce their satisfied customers to recommend their product or service to friends and family members. One of the keys to viral marketing success is to present an offer with real perceived value—one that people will want to share with one another. Audible, an Amazon digital audiobooks site, and Dropbox, a cloud storage site, make effective use of referral programs whereby members receive benefits each time someone they refer to the site becomes a member.

Microsoft shows how to do banner ads right with this collection. First, use color and layout in a way that attracts attention. Second, avoid clutter. Third, make the offer simple and compelling.

Source: Microsoft

My IMC Campaign 14-A

Using Interactive Media

Every medium offers unique creative options that media planners can incorporate into each campaign to help break through the clutter. However, no other medium has the same degree of flexibility as the internet does. While the IAB has done a good job of setting banner ad standards, the development of new technologies continually pushes the boundaries of what advertisers can do online. In concert with technological advancements, now-standard technologies are also decreasing in cost.

For every new campaign, advertisers need to think about how each element of their online presence communicates the company's message. From the website, to the banner advertisements, to social media, a brand appears on multiple online sites, and coordinating its image across all of them is time-consuming. It can also be very creative and rewarding. Here is a list of avenues you should explore, but not limit yourself to, as you think about building your online campaigns:

- Website, microsites, and landing pages
- Search engine marketing
- Display ads
- Rich media
- E-mail

As you embark on the online portion of your campaign, think of the online platform as a blank canvas for you to meet your objectives. Start by determining the website's purpose and move out into the online world. Think about what users will do after seeing your print or TV ads and how you will capture the interest and demand generated by that promotion. The internet, while extremely important in your communication strategies, may not be the first place your audience notices your ads. However, remember that most online sessions start with a web search, whether that occurs on sites like Google or Gmail, or on the intended website itself. So it is imperative that you have a good search strategy in place for all online activity.

To understand what sites your audience regularly uses, look to free services like Quantcast and/or Google AdPlanner as a means of identifying sites where you will want to advertise. When you plug in some information about your target at these sites, you will get a list of sites your intended audience frequently uses. This is a helpful guide in determining the appropriate venues to capture your target's mindshare. While the internet is in a constant state of evolution, savvy marketers commonly use some technologies associated with it, such as rich media. *Rich media* is the term for web ads that have a high degree of interactivity or motion or that pull info directly from the advertiser's website into the banner ad. Today rich media is so widely accepted that almost any site where you are thinking about advertising will be able to handle its creative demands. That wasn't always so, but companies with a long-standing history of producing great rich media executions, such as PointRoll, Eyeblaster, DART Motif, and Atlas Rich Media, have paved the way for turnkey solutions.

Last, think about ways to connect with loyalists of your brand in ways outside of push communications. How do you create a conversation with them and empower that audience to help you in your marketing efforts? We are speaking, of course, of social media. Does your brand warrant a Facebook page or a Twitter feed? If so, how will you use these arenas creatively and how will you incite participation and pass-along?

Online media can be fun, but they can also be daunting because the virtual sky is the limit. Remember to make sound judgments and to put yourself in the consumers' shoes. Are you asking too much of them with your online strategies, or will your approach resonate?

Because members enjoy the sites so much, it's natural that they would want to share with their friends and families. Another example is Blendtec's "Will It blend" series, which was started on Youtube.com (it can now be found at www.willitblend.com) and has brought a new consumer market to a blender company that formerly served industry. See the My IMC Campaign 14-A box "Using Interactive Media" to better understand interactive media and how to effectively choose the different types of online media.

Problems with Digital as an Advertising Medium

LO 14-6

Digital media have their drawbacks. They are not mass media in the traditional sense, and may never offer mass media efficiency. Some marketers may decide they're too complex, too cumbersome, too cluttered, or not worth the time and effort.

Digital media have also presented big headaches to traditional advertising agencies, who are staffed with people trained in creating and evaluating traditional media. The background of someone working in digital media today is as likely to be from computer science or engineering as it is from marketing or communication.

Some have even wondered if advertising agencies have an important role to play in the digital age. Companies such as Facebook and Google provide marketers (and you!) with an extensive toolset for creating, researching, monitoring, and measuring ad effectiveness. They also provide, free of charge, the learning materials to master these tools. Advertisers may start, and some are, wondering what additional value they receive from paying an agency. On the other hand, agencies argue that mastering digital requires expertise, judgment, and an understanding of audiences that people from other backgrounds may lack.

Finally, digital media are still so new that it is unclear whether anyone has the right rules for success. Privacy failures and security breaches have demonstrated that in a rush to enjoy the benefits of digital marketing, many companies have failed to consider the costs. Security (e.g., for credit card purchases online) has become a major concern (and failure) for many prominent marketers. The final drawback is also one of the internet's greatest appeals: It is the most democratic of media—anybody can get on it and do or say just about anything. That's both good and bad.[20]

Other Interactive Media

In addition to the internet, advertisers now also use other new media vehicles, such as interactive TV and mobile advertising. While they are not major media forms, they do warrant some brief discussion.

Craigslist provides internet users a free marketplace to buy and sell products. The rapid growth and dramatic success of such sites have come at the expense of newspaper classified sections.

Source: Craigslist Inc.

Interactive Media

The TV of the future will be the size of a wall. Wander to any part of the room and your perspective will remain perfect. That's because the TV knows who you are and follows where you go. In response, it adapts its perspective to give you ideal viewing. Additionally, it will interact with you on the basis of voice commands or direct touch, rather than remote controls. A complete fantasy? A prototype, the Panasonic Life Wall, was first shown back in 2008.[21]

Interactive TVs are not a technology of the future, but of the present. Most people take for granted technologies such as digital video recorders (DVRs, sometimes also called *personal video recorders*) and interactive remote controls. Apple TV, now in its third generation, added voice-control and apps to the mix.

Amazon demonstrated that Apple is not the only tech company to create an entire new category of devices with its **Amazon Echo** device. The original Echo was a small cylinder that responded to voice commands to play music, report the news, provide a weather report, or look up an interesting fact. It was an immediate hit and has spawned dozens of devices, some from Amazon and some from its competitors. For example, Amazon introduced the Dot, which sacrifices sound quality for affordability (it only costs $30), as well as the Spot and Show, both with displays. Amazon also licensed its technology to Sonos and Bose, manufacturers of high-quality speakers and headsets.

Google, Apple, and Facebook quickly followed with their own devices, labeled Google Home, Apple HomePod, and Facebook Portal. The battle is on for the voice assistant of the American household.

The benefit of the device for Amazon is quite clear. Among its many uses, the Echo is a shopping tool. When an Echo owner says, "Alexa, order batteries," the user's account is billed and batteries are on their way. But wait, whose batteries? Amazon will happily recommend what it calls "Amazon's Choice." What is an Amazon's Choice brand? The company claims the product is popular, is highly rated, is available in Amazon Prime, and has a lower-than-average return rate. It typically bears a "competitive" price as well. Does Amazon earn higher-than-average margins on these products? The company won't say, but returned items are a serious cost of business for the company, so that factor alone means Amazon benefits when you accept its recommendation.

There is no question anymore that interactivity has influenced TV content and ad pricing. For example, some of the highest advertising rates are for sports and live shows. Why? People do not timeshift these types of programs to the extent they do other content.

People BEHIND the Ads

Brian Green, Senior Director, Property and Advertiser Solutions, Yahoo!

Courtesy of Brian Green

For just under 20 years now, Yahoo! has been a staple in the lives of numerous online surfers—so much so that it still has one of the largest daily reach vehicles on the internet. On any given day, well over 100 million unique users traffic Yahoo!'s pages, according to Yahoo!'s Advertising Solutions page. Name a TV program with that type of reach that doesn't involve helmeted players throwing a pigskin.

On nearly all Yahoo! pages you'll find an advertisement, and with all of those users turning multiple pages, the resulting amount of ad inventory is staggering—so staggering in fact that Yahoo! has a group dedicated to monetizing all that traffic. The group is called the Marketing Solutions Group, and it's their responsibility to package, price, and present the opportunity to advertisers, working in conjunction with the client-facing sales team.

One of the men leading this group of skilled negotiators—and by that we mean internal negotiation, as they have to work with multiple groups to do their jobs, such as product, sales, and yield management—is Brian Green, Senior Director, Property and Advertiser Solutions. Brian has been in the digital advertising industry since early 2000. His résumé includes big brand agencies like Foote, Cone and Belding (now a part of Draftfcb), and publishers such as Fox Interactive Group and IGN. He's worked as a media planner, a digital sales representative, and a performance marketing specialist—truly a well-rounded set of skills that make him just right for this group within Yahoo!.

Contemporary Advertising sat down with Brian Green to learn more about his role and how he faces the challenges of the fast-moving digital advertising industry.

CA: How does Yahoo! set its prices for advertising?

BG: In most cases we act like most large internet companies—we use a variety of tools that help price our products—from third-party research tools like Comscore and Nielsen, to proprietary programs and databases that give us a robust history on our prices and their respective fill rates. We use these tools to give us a healthy picture on our competition, supply and demand, and industry trends that may affect our rates.

In other cases, we are given objectives from our clients, and our work is less analytical and more creative in how we package our various offerings together to truly achieve that objective. This is where knowledge, experience, and a little marketing know-how are actually more effective than the most efficient of CPMs (cost per thousand).

CA: What types of advertisers seem most interested in buying on Yahoo!?

BG: Most advertisers are actually not classified by their industry categorization, for example, auto, but rather by the tactics they are trying to achieve. Because of Yahoo!'s broad reach, we are big enough to reach all advertisers' objectives and therefore have a healthy cross section of advertisers that include those trying to achieve branded metrics, direct marketing measures, and those that seek a hybrid approach—building brand through direct marketing methods.

This ability to work with advertisers of any ilk is what makes Yahoo! still, after all these years, a very relevant vehicle for brands. And because Yahoo! continues to innovate and push the envelope, we have been able to maintain a healthy audience at a time when audiences migrate to the next big thing, seemingly daily.

CA: Your homepage is one of the most expensive one-day advertising placements on the web; why can you continue to sell it at such a high out-of-pocket cost?

BG: Yahoo!'s stable and massive one-day reach makes it unique to the internet. Most web properties accrue their reach over a 30-day period. Very few properties can actually give an advertiser tens of millions of eyeballs with one advertising placement. Because of that, the out-of-pocket is definitely high, but what we have found is that our rate is actually extremely competitive.

CA: How do you feel you help advertisers meet their objectives better than your competition?

BG: Because of Yahoo!'s size, it's difficult to point to just one thing as the reason we are so unique. Saying that, we have invested a lot of time and money in ensuring that we have a unique mix of ad products such as search, targeted content, and ad exchanges, along with a unique programming and content strategy that gives ample opportunity for advertisers of all objectives.

CA: Lastly, with so many people using phones and tablets to access Yahoo!, how does Yahoo! handle cross-channel engagement?

BG: Like any other brand, it's important for Yahoo! to think of its users and their customers in an integrated way; therefore, we provide an integrated sales process that is solution-oriented to meet the needs of the advertisers. We also have been very bullish on our distribution strategies, ensuring that our users can access all of the Yahoo! content in a variety of ways within a robust set of internet-enabled devices such as mobile phones, tablets, and even on internet-connected TVs.

Courtesy of Brian Green.

The Amazon Echo is a fully realized interactive device that ensures Amazon orders are just a simple command away.

James W Copeland/Shutterstock

Mobile Advertising

When mobile advertising was first introduced, phone companies controlled a lot of the inventory as they limited the amount of traffic that went outside their **deck.** The deck refers to the content and experience that the carrier made available to its users when they loaded a web browser on their phones. This was due in large part to the carriers' desire to boost revenues from their own data services and not bog down their networks with massive data downloads from off-deck web surfing. However, iPhone has revolutionized the mobile phone business and the way consumers interact with their phones.

The iPhone has increased data plan usage, or non–voice-related consumption over the carriers' networks. iPhone users are 12 times more likely to use their phones for video and mobile TV.[22] Because of this increase, people routinely use phones to download applications and games, watch videos, and send multimedia messages. All of this presents opportunities to advertisers. Apps, available on most phones, connect periodically to the network to check for updates, identify a person's location, or connect one user with another. The appeal to advertisers is that unlike any other medium, the phone is the only real portable and personally identifiable medium.

Mobile ad spending is the fastest-growing area of digital advertising and surged past desktop digital advertising in 2018.[23] The most common form of mobile advertising, banner advertising (also called WAP, Wireless Access Protocol, Banner), is very similar to online banner advertising. Banner advertising is standardized by the Mobile Marketing Association (MMA), which, much like the Interactive Advertising Bureau (IAB) for online banner advertising, has issued guidelines and standards for mobile web advertising (they can be found here: http://mmaglobal.com/policies/global-mobile-advertising-guidelines). Banner ads can also be placed into applications that have been downloaded to a user's phone, and can be swapped as those applications reconnect with the network.

The other form of advertising, and the one that represents the largest inventory, is sponsored SMS (Short Message System). Companies like 4INFO, in the United States, offer news, horoscopes, and sports scores, among other things, for free to users via SMS, and advertisers sponsor these messages. The carriers have set up very strict guidelines in the use of SMS and act as a gatekeeper for all messages that go over their networks in an effort to reduce SMS spam. A person can reply back to the SMS message to opt in to the marketing message that has been displayed, or can go directly from that SMS, via a link, to a mobile web page.

QR codes, mobile coupons, and video present other opportunities, as the prevalence of smartphones allows people to easily use these technologies.

Chapter Summary

Digital interactive media, which include online database services, the internet, interactive media, and mobile advertising, are a revolution in the making. From an advertising standpoint, these media offer an opportunity to develop customer relationships rather than volume. Technology is racing ahead at a rapid pace.

The commercialization of the internet really began with the commercial online services that offered a large subscriber base to potential advertisers. However, the internet itself dwarfed the online services in potential because it reached so many people around the globe. Once web browser software became available, it made the internet user-friendly to noncomputer specialists.

Similarly, search engines made sites on the web available to PC users with just the click of a mouse. When people began migrating to the web, so did advertisers.

Web users tend to be upscale, college-educated men and women. This is an ideal target, especially for business-to-business advertisers. This group is rapidly broadening, which will make the web even more attractive to many mainline advertisers.

The most common types of online advertising are search, display, and classifieds. Like all media, the internet has many advantages and disadvantages.

Most internet advertising is sold by CPM. Some, though, is sold by click-through or results. Today the biggest advancements are in social media, which present a relationship opportunity to brands never before realized. Mobile advertising is a burgeoning medium that presents advertisers the opportunity to reach on-the-go consumers.

Interactive media are gaining a bigger foothold in homes with the popularity of Amazon's Echo devices. The Echo is a part of Amazon's strategy to ensure people can easily order products from the company anywhere, anytime.

Important Terms

Review Questions

1. How did the internet evolve to its present status as an advertising medium?

2. Which companies on the internet receive the greatest amount of advertising revenue? Why?

3. What are the different ways of advertising online?

4. What are cookies, and what are they used for?

5. What are the different ways web publishers charge for advertising?

6. How would you describe the advantages the internet offers advertisers over traditional media?

7. How does audience measurement on the web differ from that for traditional media?

8. What is the importance of interactive media to small advertisers?

9. What do best practices suggest that advertisers first do before engaging in social media?

The Advertising Experience

1. **Internet Advertising**

    Advertising display ads on the internet are akin to outdoor billboards and fill the web with advertising messages, corporate signage, and hyperlinks. Companies like DoubleClick (www.doubleclick.com) are flourishing as they introduce new and better ways of managing web advertising—helping advertisers feel more confident about the ad programs they place.

    Visit the following advertising-related sites on the internet and discover more about this fast-changing segment of the advertising industry. Then answer the questions that follow.

    - DoubleClick: www.doubleclick.com
    - Clickz: www.clickz.com
    - iMedia Connection: www.imediaconnection.com
    - Banner Report: www.bannerreport.com
    - mediapost: www.mediapost.com

    a. What group sponsors the site, and what is the organization's purpose?

    b. What are the size and scope of the organization?

    c. Who is the intended audience(s) of the website?

    d. What services does the organization offer web advertisers?

2. **Designing a Banner Ad**

    X-Scream magazine, which is dedicated to extreme sports of all kinds, would like to dedicate some of its advertising budget to banner ads. Taking into account the target market this magazine would have, find three websites its consumers might visit, and design a banner ad that would motivate them to learn more about (and subscribe to) the magazine.

3. Visit Dove's special website, www.dove.com/us/en/stories/campaigns.html, and watch some of their ads. The brand promotes the idea of "real beauty," suggesting that beauty comes in many

forms, shapes, sizes, and colors. What do you think of the ads? What do you think are the advantages of placing them on the web?

4. In 2006 Dove asked visitors to its website to open a free account and create a Dove ad. The company provided tools that allowed visitors to construct the ad easily at the site. The best ad was then featured in the 2007 Academy Awards program. What communications objectives do you think were behind this effort? What metrics do you think Dove used to gauge the success of this web initiative?

5. At present a relatively small number of items are ordered on Amazon's Echo compared to its website. Will that change in the future? Make a case for why or why not.

6. Assume that you are an interactive media designer working on the Kitchen View project, and you have been assigned the task of developing a banner ad to promote the website. What information would be essential to present? How might this be accomplished given the inherent limitations of display ads?

End Notes

1. Thomas Franck, "Amazon's US Sales to Match Walmart's within Three Years, JP Morgan Predicts," *CNBC,* May 15, 2018, *www.cnbc.com/2018/05/15/amazons-us-sales-to-match-walmarts-within-three-years-jp-morgan-predicts.html.*

2. Kate Taylor, "Almost Half of Millenials Say They'd Rather Give up Sex Than Quit Amazon for a Year, According to a New Survey," *Business Insider,* December 6, 2018, *www.businessinsider.com/millennials-pick-amazon-over-sex-survey-2018-12.*

3. "Digital Advertising Spending in the United States from 2015 to 2021 (in billion U.S. dollars)," *Statista, www.statista.com/statistics/242552/digital-advertising-spending-in-the-us/.*

4. Frank Barnako, "Bravo, Comedy Central Get Boost from Net Homes," *MarketWatch,* October 11, 2006, *www.marketwatch.com/story/bravo-comedy-central-get-boost-from-net-homes.*

5. "Share of Adults in the United States Who Use the Internet in 2018, by Age Group," *Statista, www.statista.com/statistics/266587/percentage-of-internet-users-by-age-groups-in-the-us/.*

6. Bennett Bennett, "The Future of Audience Measurement Is Getting Clearer, but Nielsen May Not Carry the Torch," *The Drum,* May 3, 2018, *www.thedrum.com/news/2018/05/03/the-future-audience-measurement-getting-clearer-nielsen-may-not-carry-the-torch.*

7. Gabriel J. X. Dance, Michael LaForgia, and Nicholas Confessore, "As Facebook Raised a Privacy Wall, It Carved an Opening for Tech Giants," *The New York Times,* December 18, 2018, *www.nytimes.com/2018/12/18/technology/facebook-privacy.html.*

8. Jon Porter, "Google Accused of GDPR Privacy Violations by Seven Countries," *The Verge,* November 27, 2018, *www.theverge.com/2018/11/27/18114111/google-location-tracking-gdpr-challenge-european-deceptive.*

9. "Nielsen Digital Ad Ratings," Nielsen LLC, 2019, *www.nielsen.com/us/en/solutions/capabilities/digital-ad-ratings.html.*

10. Brian Steinberg, "TV Industry Struggles to Agree on Ratings Innovation," *Variety,* April 11, 2017.

11. Adam Levy, "Cord Cutting, Cord Shaving, and Cable Gaming: How Consumers Save Money on Their Cable Bills," *Motley Fool,* July 5, 2015, *www.fool.com/investing/general/2015/07/05/cord-cutting-cord-shaving-and-cable-gaming-how-con.aspx.*

12. Media Measurement Task Force, Internet Advertising Bureau, "Metrics and Methodology," September 15, 1997.

13. *Ad Age* 200 Leading National Advertisers 2018 Fact Pack (Crain Communications, 2018).

14. Statcounter GlobalStats, *http://gs.statcounter.com/search-engine-market-share.*

15. "Online Ads: A Guide to Online Ad Types and Formats," *Wordstream, www.wordstream.com/online-ads#PPC%20Ads.*

16. Claudia Kuehl, "Spam's Good Twin. If E-mail Is Done Just Right, People Will Want to Receive It. Really," *The DMA Interactive,* Library White Papers, May 2000, *www.the-dma.org/library/whitepapers/spamsgoodtwin.shtml.*

17. Federal Trade Commission, "FTC Announces First Can-Spam Act Cases," press release, April 29, 2004, *www.ftc.gov/news-events/press-releases/2004/04/ftc-announces-first-can-spam-act-cases.*

18. Amanda Beeler, "Word-of-Mouth Pitches Mutate into New Forms on the Internet," *Advertising Age,* April 2000, *http://adage.com.*

19. Steve Jurvetson and Tim Draper, "Viral Marketing: Viral Marketing Phenomenon Explained, *DFJ.com,* January 1, 1997, retrieved at *http://dfj.com/news/article_26.shtml.*

20. Tom Risen, "Is the Internet Bad for Society and Relationships?" *U.S. News,* February 27, 2014, *www.usnews.com/news/blogs/data-mine/2014/02/27/is-the-internet-bad-for-society-and-relationships.*

21. Dinesh C. Sharma, "Study: DVR Adoption on the Rise," *CNET News.com,* March 30, 2004, *http://news.com.com/Study+DVR+adoption+on+the+rise/2100-1041_3-5182035.html?tag=nl.*

22. Steve Miller and Mike Beirne, "The iPhone Effect," *Brandweek,* April 28, 2008, *www.adweek.com/aw/content_display/news/agency/e3ibef1ad200773laba65le6216ba3b6267.*

23. IAB, "Digital Ad Spending Reaches an All-Time High of $88 Billion in 2018, with Mobile Upswing Unabated, Accounting for 57 Percent of Revenue," news release, May 10, 2018, *www.iab.com/news/digital-ad-spend-reaches-all-time-high-88-billion-2017-mobile-upswing-unabated-accounting-57-revenue/.*

Social Media

LEARNING OBJECTIVES

To explore how social media are changing the way that advertisers think about engaging with their audiences. Advertisers must understand how to effectively employ social strategies that enhance the relationships they have with their current and potential customers.

After studying this chapter, you will be able to:

LO15-1   Discuss how social media differ from traditional media.

LO15-2   Explain the various ways that social media can be used.

LO15-3   Discuss how social media have changed consumer's behavior.

LO15-4   Explain how to manage social media on behalf of a brand.

LO15-5   Define the different applications of social media.

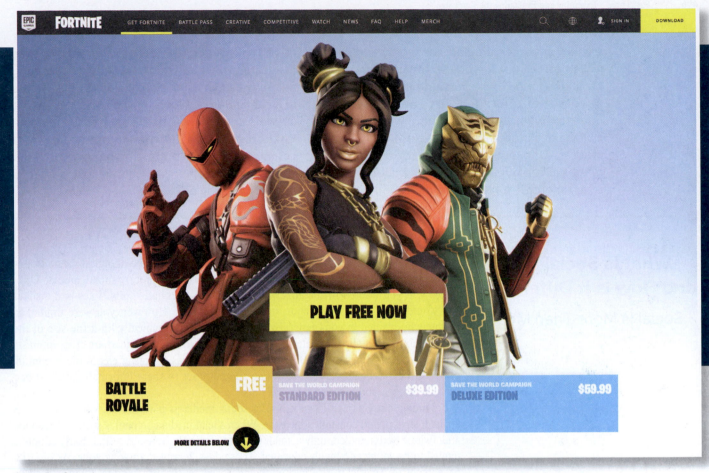

Tim Sweeney had a problem. His new, interactive, highly social game, *Fortnite,* was selling more slowly than expected. He had launched the game in July 2017 and sold it for $40 a pop. Unsatisfied with the revenues, he used an unexpected strategy: He gave the game away for free. "That strategy," noted *Ad Age,* "has made him a billionaire."[1] ■ If you haven't played, it may be difficult to understand the excitement the game arouses in its players. But the number of non-players shrinks by the day—as of March 2019, 250 million had played around the globe. It's appeal is likely due to its fast, enjoyable interface; its highly social nature (players join up with friends and communicate in the game); and the ability of players to choose their personae, weapons, armor, and gear. ■ If the game is free, how has Epic Games, Sweeney's company, made over $2 billion in 2018? If you are a smartphone user, you probably already know. Many "free" apps require "in-app purchases" to really get the most out of the program. It is the same with *Fortnite.* Addicted players can customize many aspects of their experience but must pay to do so. ■ The game does not carry many overt ads, so you may be wondering why it leads off this chapter. Or perhaps you are unsure why a game is a useful way to introduce social media, which for many are better exemplified by Facebook, Instagram, Twitter, and Snap. ■ Let's start with the ads: The game does offer branding opportunities, which are a source of revenue. For example, *Fortnite* produced a cross-promotion with Marvel for the film *Avengers: Infinity War.*[2] Advertising opportunities are also available for a secondary market: video game streamers. These are people recognized among hardcore gamers for their skills who attract fans by posting video recordings of their matches online. One such player, code-named "Ninja," streams his games on social service Twitch and claims revenues of $500,000 a month. The money comes from advertisers who are featured on his stream.[3] ■ What about the claim that *Fortnite* is not social media? In fact, the game fits the description of social media in almost every way. Like other social media, it permits virtually unlimited interactions among participants. Like other social media, the game is the platform, but user content and actions are the draw. And like social media, the interactions and excitement of the medium are highly addictive. ■ Games are not a place for every brand. The audience tends to skew young and male. They have little tolerance for messages that interrupt what they want to do, which is play. But make no mistake—games are not a small market. One estimate suggests that mobile games are played by nearly 3 billion people every month.[4] ■ As for the mind behind all of this? Tim Sweeney is nearly 50 years old, likes fast cars, and spends his money on creating nature preserves. For all of his riches, he prefers to lunch at Burger King. And while he may not be as well known (yet) as Jeff Bezos and Mark Zuckerberg, he shares one important commonality with both: the genius, and the courage, to try something different, risky, and big. And watch it pay off.

What Is Social Media and How Is It Different?

Social Is More Than Media

LO 15-1

Chapter 14 describes a variety of digital media. However one type of digital media is now important enough to deserve the spotlight in its own chapter, social media. Until recently, if you wanted to socialize with individuals who had similar likes and dislikes you would join a group or a club, such as a book club. However, you were limited to people who resided in your general vicinity, which would typically limit the size of the club. Social media allow people to "meet" virtually to discuss and share their interests with each other. Merriam-Webster defines **social media** as "forms of electronic communication through which users create online communities to share information, ideas, personal messages, and other content."[5]

Throughout Chapter 15 we consider social media as platforms in which content is created, shared, and consumed by users. When social media companies such as Facebook and Twitter were founded, only a small number of people were interested. Early adopters tended to be young and highly educated. Those days, however, are long gone. As of 2018, 68 percent of Americans use Facebook and 35 percent use Instagram. Snap is used by 27 percent and Twitter by 24 percent.

The numbers are even higher for young people, especially those 18 to 24 years old (the advertising "sweetspot"). Nearly 8 out of 10 people in this age group use Snap, and most of those users visit it several times each day.[6]

Harnessing social media content is big business. When someone posts a review on TripAdvisor, comments on another's blog, or bookmarks a page using Digg, that information is open for anyone to see. A host of tools collect all of this information using keywords. Companies like Nielsen's BuzzMetrics or J.D.Power's Umbria Communications help marketers aggregate the information being posted about their brands or products to understand what people think and feel about them. In turn, large advertisers like Electronic Arts, Coca-Cola, Virgin America, and Procter & Gamble all have a social media component for each brand they market. But practicing IMC in social media is challenging because people interact with each product or brand differently, and the brand promise must really shine through.

The visual beauty of Pinterest is reminiscent of the importance of design in traditional print media.

Source: Pinterest

Our Social Media Personas

We noted in Chapter 14 how the web gave rise to the consumer as content creator. Social media platforms are the catalyst for this behavior change. Their value proposition is primarily centered on ease of use. Social media make it easier to maintain more friendships, to find people with similar interests, and to share information with

Exhibit 15-1

Seven user types identified by Forrester Research.

Source: Forrester, "Global Social Media Adoption in 2011" (white paper, January 23, 2012), retrieved from *www.mindjumpers.com/blog/2012/01/global-social-media-adoption-2011/*.

 I am a Creator: I publish blogs or web pages, or I post videos, music, or writings that I created

 I am a Conversationalist: I often update my status on social networking

 I am a Critic: I post reviews or contribute to online forums

 I am a Collector: I use RSS feeds or add "tags" to photos

 I am a Joiner: I visit social networking sites or maintain my profile on at least one site

 I am a Spectator: I read or listen to content others have posted

 I am Inactive: I do none of the above

friends. Used in conjunction with search engines, social media also make it easier to find content.

Forrester Research described the many different ways in which consumers engage with social media. Exhibit 15-1 illustrates the seven user types. From creators to inactives, each of us falls into a bucket that broadly defines how we use social media. Unlike traditional media, where consumption is inherently passive, social media consumption can be both passive and active.

Social media resist easy classification because they are as much technology as they are media and can take on many different forms, including magazines, forums, weblogs, social blogs, microblogs, wikis, podcasts, photographs or pictures, games, videos, ratings, and social bookmarking. As one author suggests,

> there are six different types of social media: collaborative projects (e.g., Wikipedia), blogs and microblogs (e.g., Twitter), content communities (e.g., YouTube), social networking sites (e.g., Facebook), virtual game worlds (e.g., World of Warcraft), and virtual social worlds (e.g., Second Life). Technologies include: blogs, picture-sharing, vlogs, wall-postings, e-mail, instant messaging, music-sharing, crowdsourcing and voice over IP, to name a few. Many of these social media services can be integrated via social network aggregation platforms. Social media sites are sites like Facebook, Twitter, Bebo and MySpace.[7]

From YouTube to TripAdvisor to Facebook, the appeal of social media is accessing content created by ordinary people. And for some, an additional appeal is the opportunity for self-expression and content sharing.

The Rise of Social Media and Influencer Marketing

Many brands today have little choice but to participate in popular social media channels. This is because their customers and prospects live in these channels and expect to find their favorite brands there.

Using social media strategically starts with understanding what people use it for. Many believe that a desire to feel connected to others is what drives social media use. Fostering connections and building relationships with customers can be the catalyst for creating **influencers,** who will share their brand experiences with friends and family. Of course, brands hope that influencers will share positive experiences, but that is not always the case. People also share bad or unexpected experiences.

The potency of influencers has led to a rise in what is sometimes called **influencer marketing.** Influencer marketing is the strategic collaboration between brands and people who are highly credible with important audiences in brand promotion. Influencers can be celebrities, but in many cases they are individuals less widely known than sports stars or actors.

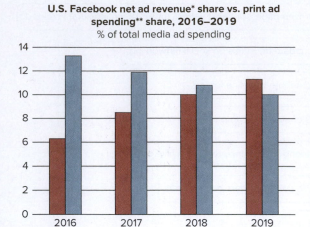

U.S. Facebook net ad revenue* share vs. print ad spending** share, 2016–2019

% of total media ad spending

■ Facebook net ad revenues*   ■ Print ad spending**

Note: *includes advertising that appears on desktop and laptop computers as well as mobile phones, tablets, and other internet-connected devices, and includes all the various formats of advertising on those platforms; net ad revenues after companies pay traffic acquisition costs (TAC) to partner sites; **excludes digital

Exhibit 15-2
Facebook versus print as a percentage of total media ad spending.

Source: eMarketer editors, "Social Media Will Hit Major Milestones in 2018," *eMarketer,* January 9, 2018, www.emarketer.com/content/social-media-will-hit-major-milestones-in-both-ad-revenues-and-usage-in-2018.

Helping to connect audiences to a brand seems relatively straightforward, but it can be anything but. As you will learn in this chapter, social media are open environments, and some companies find that to be a scary proposition. Engagement requires that brands relinquish control over the message, which cuts against lessons many marketers were taught. Conservative or risk-averse brands inevitably find that engaging in social media can be difficult and cumbersome, even as newer, more nimble brands like Orange Theory and Zappos.com (now owned by Amazon.com) are reaping the benefits.

Adoption of Social Media

The promise of social media has not been missed by advertisers. In 2013 it was estimated that social ad revenue was about $6.1 billion in the United States. Considering only Facebook, Twitter, LinkedIn, and Snapchat, ad revenue had risen to nearly $23 billion in 2018. In fact, beginning in 2018, advertising revenues for Facebook alone exceeded those for all print media combined (see Exhibit 15-2). And a big reason for that growth is the power of social media in the technology that most people use to access digital content: the smartphone.

Another attraction of social media for advertisers is the ability to target. As can be seen in Exhibit 15-3, while social media was primarily of interest to younger audiences in the mid-2000s, today a majority of people from all age groups, except those 65 and over, use social media.

While Facebook is the king of the mountain (Exhibit 15-4 shows that Facebook owns a whopping 36% of visit market share), it is by no means the only social site people use, and it was not the first social site either. In fact, if you were asked to identify the first social media site that reached 50 million users, what would you guess? Alumni-focused social site Classmates.com reached 50 million users in the late 1990s. And it wasn't until 2002–2004 that social media really took off when companies like Friendster, LinkedIn, MySpace, and a small college-oriented social network named Facebook experienced their monumental growth. Another trend visible in Exhibit 15-4 is the new players in the social media space. Instagram, Tumblr, and Reddit were no-shows back in 2012, while they are top ten and growing in 2018. Facebook is currently on top but its share of visits is shrinking.

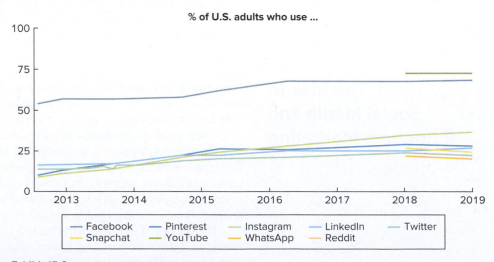

% of U.S. adults who use ...

— Facebook   — Pinterest   — Instagram   — LinkedIn   — Twitter
— Snapchat   — YouTube   — WhatsApp   — Reddit

Exhibit 15-3
Demographics of Popular Social Media Platforms.

Source: "Social Media Fact Sheet," Pew Research Center, June 12, 2019, www.pewinternet.org/fact-sheet/social-media/.

Exhibit 15-4

Visit market share 2018.

Source: FE International company.

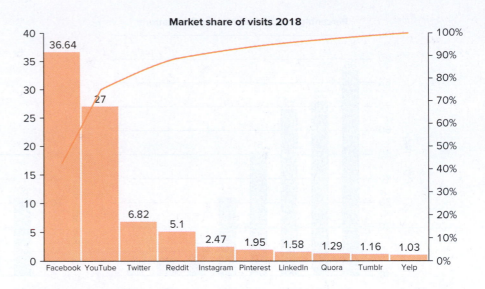

Market share of visits 2018

Facebook 36.64
YouTube 27
Twitter 6.82
Reddit 5.1
Instagram 2.47
Pinterest 1.95
LinkedIn 1.58
Quora 1.29
Tumblr 1.16
Yelp 1.03

Social Trends

After it first launched, some felt that Facebook and even social media generally were flashes in the pan. A poll in 2012 found that a majority of Americans thought that Facebook's appeal was just a fad.[8] Given the rapid turnover in the list of top-ten social sites and the company's bad publicity surrounding privacy in 2018, it is difficult to predict whether Zuckerberg's company will remain popular. But regardless of what may become of Facebook, the reality is that social media technologies are integral to our lives. The simple act of sharing, connecting, and keeping up with friends, family, and acquaintances thus far has made social networking one of the most popular ways people use digital media. Perhaps social media reign over traditional media, too, if you add up the sheer mass of global users that Facebook has attracted. At the end of 2018, Facebook claimed 2.27 billion monthly users, most of whom are outside North America. And the company reports that Facebook's suite of programs, including WhatsApp, Messenger, Instagram, and Facebook itself, are accessed by more than 2 billion people a day.[9]

Trending is a term used by tweeters to describe what people are talking, or tweeting, about on Twitter. And as we mentioned earlier, because social media platforms are open, in some cases what's being tweeted isn't actually happening on Twitter but in a third-party tool, application, or website. Facebook Connect and Twitter's open **application protocol interface (API)** mean that any site, tool, or application can feed and extract information from the social network sites in accordance with how the user has granted permissions. For instance, if a person wants to find friends in her local area and see what they are doing, she might load up Foursquare on her iPhone and see where her friends have "checked-in." She might check in too, and that information is then fed to Twitter or Facebook or both as a tweet or status update. But how did Foursquare know who her friends were? Easy—when our subject signed up for the service, she used Facebook Connect. This allows her not to have to input any information on yet another site. It also allows Foursquare to see all the people she is connected with on Facebook, cross-referencing those friends with active Foursquare users and instantly attaching them to her account.

Twitter offers advertisers several programs to engage users, from modest efforts like Promoted Posts to expensive, cross-platform campaigns such as Promoted Trends. In the middle, and useful for gaining followers, is the Promoted Account campaign, illustrated here.

Source: McDonald's

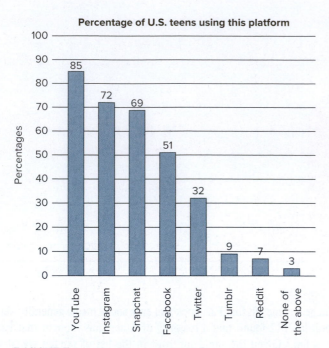

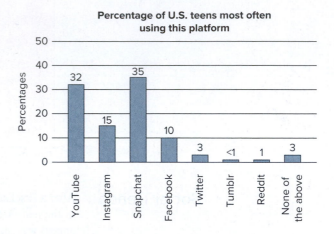

Exhibit 15-5

Teen use of social media platforms.

Source: "YouTube, Instagram and Snapchat Are the Most Popular Online Platforms among Teens," Pew Research Center, May 29, 2018, www.pewinternet.org/2018/05/31/teens-social-media-technology-2018/pi_2018-05-31_teenstech_0-01/.

Who Uses Social Media

Earlier, in Exhibit 15-3, we showed a broader demographic breakdown of social media sites. In Exhibit 15-5, we present usage rates for a group of great interest to advertisers: teens. As can be seen in the exhibit, YouTube, Instagram, and Snap have far more appeal with this group than with older age groups. This is important as brands begin to wonder if they should be actively participating in the medium. Naturally, brands that cater to the older demographic are not so quick to adopt social practices. As the penetration continues to grow for the 65 and older segment, however, those same brands will quickly move to participate in social media.

Types of Social Media

Social media include any web- or mobile-based technology that is used for interactive communication between groups, communities, companies, and individuals. This broad definition helps explain why there are so many different types of technologies that fall under the social media umbrella. Worldwide there are over 2.8 billion social media profiles, which represents about half of all internet users.[10] Here are some of the most common types of social media.

Forums

Forums are typically sections of sites that connect individuals around a specific topic. For instance, a Mustang forum will have users conversing about the iconic automobile. Some technology companies like Disqus and Livefyre actually connect people horizontally on different forums, meaning a user can manage one Disqus login for several forums on many sites about different topics. In 2011, monthly forum contribution declined significantly from the previous year, from 38 to 32 percent of total internet users.[11]

Weblogs (Blogs)

A **blog** is a reverse chronological journaling site. Typically, blogs are personal in nature; however, they have become so pervasive that some websites use a blog format as their

Ethics, Diversity & Inclusion

Kids and Victimhood in Social Media

The popularity of social media can mask some serious issues that are caused by overuse or misuse. Problems that were unheard of 10 years ago are now experienced by significant numbers of people, especially teens and preteens. What responsibilities do social sites share for these problems? And what about the advertisers and sponsors who support them?

Cyberbullying, according to the U.S. government's website, Stopbullying.gov, "is bullying that takes place over digital devices like cell phones, computers, and tablets. Cyberbullying can occur through SMS, Text, and apps, or online in social media, forums, or gaming where people can view, participate in, or share content. Cyberbullying includes sending, posting, or sharing negative, harmful, false, or mean content about someone else. It can include sharing personal or private information about someone else causing embarrassment or humiliation. Some cyberbullying crosses the line into unlawful or criminal behavior."[13] Between 9 and 15 percent of U.S. students say they've been cyberbullied. Among LGBTQ students the number is 55 percent.[14] The U.S. government considers cyberbullying to be of special concern because it can be persistent (happen at all hours of the day), permanent (shared widely and publicly, impacting many personal and professional areas of life), and hard to notice (teachers and parents may not see bullying posts).

The issue of cyberbullying sparked discussion at the national level when college student Tyler Clementi killed himself after his roommate and another student recorded and shared on social media a video of Clementi kissing a male friend in his dorm.

Because young children are often the victims of cyberbullying, it is essential that parents, teachers, and family members work to prevent it. Warning signs include increases or decreases in texting, strong emotions in response to texts and posts, a child hiding his or her device when others come near it, deactivated social accounts, avoidance, withdrawal, depression, and isolation.[15]

Kids can face threats from other uses of social media as well. A variety of sites have evolved to help people locate others interested in casual sexual relationships, including AdultFriendFinder,

Tinder, Pure, Clover, Her, Match, and iHookup. Such sites may be appropriate for consenting adults who understand the risk but are clearly not for children below the age of consent.

Unfortunately, pedophiles need not use these sites to victimize kids. Many parents would be surprised to know that photos of children doing perfectly ordinary things are often found on the computers of criminals who downloaded them from Facebook and other traditional social media.

Pedophilia may seem to be a rare and unusual facet of modern life, but statistics suggest otherwise. The FBI reports child pornography is one of the fastest-growing crimes and that child porn arrests have surged 2,500 percent over the past 30 years. More than half of state prison sex offenders are serving time for crimes against kids. And the National Center for Missing and Exploited Children estimates that 100,000 American kids are victimized by sexual exploitation.[16]

How do the monsters who pursue children locate and gain the trust of their intended victims? Frequently through social media accounts where children post about their pastimes, hobbies, friends, likes, dislikes, etc. This information also sometimes identifies the child's school, home address, e-mail, and social accounts.

This suggests that the characteristics of social media that make them attractive to many can also lead to terrible misuse. Who, ultimately, bears responsibility for ensuring that kids can enjoy connecting with others in a safe, protected environment?

Questions

1. Is it ethical for parents to let children have unsupervised social media accounts? At what age?

2. Imagine a parent allows her/his child to have a social media account but secretly monitors it without letting the child know. Is the parent's behavior ethical?

3. What responsibility, if any, do social media brands have for ensuring the safety of their users? Do advertisers who practice IMC on social sites have a role to play as well?

---

main page. WordPress and Blogger (owned by Google) are two of the more common blog content management systems (CMSs). These CMSs are web-publishing tools that allow for nontechnical users to **post** content easily. Twenty-seven percent of global internet users actively engage in blog-writing on a monthly basis.[12]

Blogs can also be multimedia in nature whereby the post is a photo or a video, like Flickr and YouTube. While some of the nomenclature describing the activities on these sites differs, in essence they feature the same easy-to-use web publishing format. However, in Flickr and YouTube, the user creates channels rather than pages and uploads content rather than posting content. Uploading video has increased from 21 to 27 percent among global internet users.[17]

Microblogs

A **microblog,** according to *PC Magazine,* is a blog that contains brief entries about the daily activities of an individual or company. The most popular microblog on the web today is Twitter. Much like blogs, microblog postings are organized in reverse chronological order, but users are allowed a limited number of characters of text in their posts (or tweets). This allows for the transfer of small bits of information or content among many people at the same time, giving it a broadcast characteristic.

After making a big splash and experiencing rapid growth following its launch, Twitter struggled for several years with both user growth and profitability. The company was criticized for its culture, in which employees were accused of harassment. From an advertising perspective, the discovery that a majority of tweets in the system were not from people but automated systems, known as "bots," suggested Twitter's popularity had been significantly overstated. The company, to its credit, made strides to address its problems and as of 2018 returned to user growth and financial stability with two profitable quarters.[18]

Wikis

A **wiki** is a user-collaborated content site, typically text in nature. Wikis allow the community to create, edit, or delete content. They are typically used to share knowledge across diverse groups of individuals. Wikipedia is the most well-known but, because it does not accept advertising, is largely ignored by marketers.

Social Bookmarking

A once-popular form of sharing content on the web, **social bookmarking** has recently declined in popularity. However, out of this form of social media came a very important categorization tool—tagging. Tagging is the act of self-classification with key words that make content easier to search for and therefore find. Tags are now used in every form of social media as a way to organize the information. Popular social bookmarking sites are reddit.com, Mix, and Tumblr.com.

Social Networking

Social networking is the term used to describe websites where people congregate based on some shared interest. In the case of Facebook, that interest is information on people; on Twitter, the shared interest is news and trends; and so on. Exhibit 15-6 shows the top social network sites based on unique visitors. Many more of the sites are used primarily by Chinese citizens, representing the growing influence of China in global communication.

The Data Explosion

In Chapter 14 we wrote of the tracking mechanisms that allow marketers to measure usage and patterns of behavior. Couple that information with the data flowing into and out of these social platforms and you have more data being produced in two days than that from the beginning of recorded history through 2003.[19] This information gives marketers a greater understanding of how their audience interacts with, shares, likes, dislikes, and feels about their brand. This unprecedented feedback mechanism is the advertiser's holy grail; however, most advertisers haven't had the wherewithal to truly take advantage of this opportunity. There might be a number of explanations as to why, but most likely the reasons stem from a lack of resources and not enough understanding about how some indirect measures, like brand likability, ultimately affect the companies' bottom line.

This is starting to change; as advertisers ask these tough questions, handfuls of entrepreneurs seek to answer them. Companies like Turn, a media technology company, are building **software as a service (SaaS)** for marketers to truly harness the

Exhibit 15-6

Most popular social network sites worldwide as of October 2018, ranked by number of active users.

Site	Estimated Unique Monthly Visitors
Facebook	2,230,000,000
YouTube	1,900,000,000
WhatsApp	1,500,000,000
Facebook Messenger	1,300,000,000
WeChat	1,058,000,000
Instagram	1,000,000,000
QQ	803,000,000
QZone	548,000,000
Douyin/Tik Tok	500,000,000
Sina Weibo	431,000,000
Twitter	335,000,000
reddit	330,000,000

Source: "Most Popular Social Networks Worldwide as of January 2019, Ranked by Number of Active Users (in millions)," Statista, Inc., 2019, www.statista.com/statistics/272014/global-social-networks-ranked-by-number-of-users/.

power of these data. Their technology, and others like it, is so powerful that it will take data from the marketers' existing databases (CRM, Transactions/Sales, Newsletters, etc.) along with data from third-party data providers (BlueKai and Targus Info) and website traffic to give a view of the makeup of the brand's customers. Then the marketers are able to use those data to target them and people like them on the internet, all in real time while optimizing the campaign based on the actions people take on the ads and the effect on the sales or transactional data. This technology allows marketers to make split-second decisions on whom to send a message to, on what site, and with what execution to increase the probability of a desired action, such as a sale. Sounds a lot like what we discussed in Chapter 9 about the role of a media planner. No wonder advertising agencies are scrambling to figure out how to thrive in this world of new social media and technology.

Managing Social Media

One of the biggest differences between social media and traditional media is that social media consist of 20 percent planning and 80 percent execution and management, whereas traditional media are the exact opposite: 80 percent planning and 20 percent execution and management. This means that social media are more labor- and resource-intensive. Another way of saying this is to note that social media use tends to be tactical, rapid, and responsive rather than strategic and deliberate. A great example is shown below in the "battle" between Kit-Kat and Oreo in response to a chocolate lover's tweet that she loved both brands. Kit-Kat challenged Oreo to a "duel" for the consumer's affection in a game of Tic Tac Toe. Oreo's response, according to Mashable, "could have gone many ways, with fans encouraging the two brands to duke it out on the Tic Tac Toe board, but Oreo chose the safest, funniest and most unexpected route: a compliment to Kit-Kat."[20]

Owned Media and Fragmentation

LO 15-3

In the early days of social media, brands paid very little for a presence. Rather, most brands spent time and effort in *owned properties*. The distinction here is that an owned property, like a website, is not a place where you have to pay a media company to gain a presence to distribute your message. Like the brand website, social media worked the same way: The various pages or groups that a brand deploys were free in that no money changed hands from Disney to Facebook, for example, despite Disney having multiple pages for its parks,

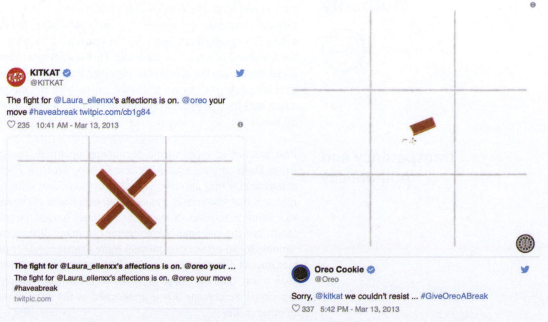

(left) Source: Nestlé/Twitter; (right) Source: Mondeléz International/Twitter

M&M's, liked by over 10 million followers, builds engagement with fans through Facebook, Instagram, YouTube, Pinterest, and other social sites.

Source: Mars, Incorporated/Facebook

movies, TV channels, cruises, and more. In recent years social sites have found ways to charge brands and organizations for their pages, but the challenging part remains the need to continually create and update these presences with engaging content that doesn't bore or overwhelm the audience. The biggest reason "unfollowing" happens on Twitter is overtweeting.

Going back to our Disney example, with so many brands and so many avenues to deploy their owned presence, managing the fragmentation is resource-intensive and requires several policies and procedures to ensure accurate portrayal of the brand in these arenas. But like everything else in our new technology era, where there's a headache, aspirin is being made. Buddy Media (owned by Salesforce) and Hootsuite are two young companies that help brands and agencies take control of all their social presences from one dashboard. They provide analytics and measurement tools that help define success from every promotion, tweet, poll, or other content mechanism that is deployed. Trend analysis will help brands explain the effects of every action they take on social media sites.

Listening tools, discussed later in the chapter, also are beneficial in understanding what's going on in the *blogosphere* (the aggregation of all blogs online). For example, how is a company's brand being talked about, and is it negative or positive? Text analytics—the measurement and analysis of text-based **user-generated content (UGC)**—is a burgeoning field in the social space, giving rise to unprecedented insights from the mere words and syntax we use when expressing our opinion about a product, brand, or service on the internet.

These tools help make the fragmentation of social media a bit easier to manage; however, the tools are only as good as the people using them. Therefore, it is still a very labor-intensive way of connecting with an audience.

Building Social Authority

Social media bring a new element into advertising and marketing—the human element. This means that the consumers know they can connect with actual people from a company in real time. The effect is that a relationship is started between consumers and brand that can elevate the perception of the company as an authority in the area where they are selling their products or services. The subsequent increase in brand favorability increases the likelihood of a sales increase too. This is what most companies strive for when adding social media into the media mix. However, building authority is not as easy to accomplish as it is to describe. As we discussed earlier with the mommy bloggers and Motrin, it is sometimes hard to predict the outcomes of the human interactions, just like in the physical world.

Transparency and Authenticity

Best practice in social media encourages openness, transparency, and authenticity. As Brian Stolis, principal at Altimeter Group, wrote in *Forbes*, "I actually see businesses changing how they approach social media to deliver value to the customer."[21] What Stolis means is that historically, value was an expression of the relative cost of a product or service being advertised. Nowadays value goes beyond just the pricing or product and extends into the customer's life, perhaps in many different ways, such as Nike creating a running social network to connect more joggers together under the Nike brand. This service doesn't directly sell shoes, but it connects the brand with the heart of the customer in such a way that the brand is linked to his or her passion. This is a very powerful and emotional attachment that is unmatched by the more in-your-face promotional messages of other media.

In social media, the only thing needed to build a following is creativity, passion, and a sense of what audiences find interesting. Red Bull was one of the first brands to take advantage of Instagram's advertising platform. Its campaign involved posting both its own images and those of its many followers.

Source: Red Bull

Driving traffic to a brand's website is not the sole purview of Google. Facebook's "Click to website" posts can accomplish the same objective.

Source: Facebook

However, many companies aren't built to be as open and connected as social media platforms demand. These companies need to figure out whether, if they cannot embrace openness, it's worth their participation in the media. And then what? Do they walk away from social media as a viable marketing tactic? Or do they fundamentally change their business philosophy to encourage conversations in social media?

Two-Way Brand Communication

Market research is nothing new to brands. Understanding the perspective of the target audience has helped brands create better products, services, and communications. However, the instantaneous feedback mechanism that social media provide is new and is so immediate that most companies, until recently, haven't been able to handle the demands of social media. Consider that just 10 years ago, getting information about how a brand's audience felt about its product required weeks to recruit, administer, compile, and report the findings. Now it can happen within seconds by just typing a few key words into a **social listening** tool and poof, you have information not only about the brand, but also about the competition, the category, and the industry. Best of all, you can assess sentiment based on the syntax of the text.

It has also been known that **word of mouth (WOM)**—for example, a friend's recommendation—is the most effective form of communication in persuading a future sale. In social media, WOM is replicated on sites that post user reviews. Here audiences can find detailed and helpful perspectives on businesses of all kinds. This kind of social intelligence rewards businesses that provide value. It also punishes businesses that fail to serve customers well.

Just how important are reviews in social media for local businesses? Bright Local, which surveys consumers annually, reports that 86 percent of consumers read reviews for local businesses and 27 percent use the internet to find a local business every day. A local business looking to cultivate trust should know that consumers require an average of 10 reviews before they find business ratings to be credible. Over half of all consumers will only frequent a business if it has four stars or higher. And among young consumers, aged 18–34, 9 out of 10 trust online reviews as much as a friend's recommendation.[22]

Social media platforms are tools that amplify WOM and make it measurable. A brand can now know how often an asset (link, photo, video, promotion) has been shared and how many people it has reached. This makes social media very powerful in their ability to move the proverbial needle on WOM recommendations. Most brands want to figure out how to encourage that behavior, and social media provide that platform. Through branded pages, Facebook, Pinterest, Twitter, and others can engage in the conversation and hopefully move the conversation in the right direction.

But brands need to be very clear on what it means to be truly authentic and truly transparent. Clearly, it would make bad business sense for a company to be 100 percent transparent or authentic because chances are its competition is listening. Besides that, we are dealing with humans, and humans have a tendency to say one thing and mean another. Consider the word *convenience* as an explanation for banking services. For different people that word means different things; it might mean that the bank makes it easy by offering mobile services, or that the bank is located nearby for easy walk-in service, or that the bank has customized the experience especially for the individual customer. All of those elements are convenient, so it isn't enough to just suggest that authenticity and transparency are the tent poles of the business's social strategy. The brand needs to define how authentic and transparent it is going to be, and typically what this two-way communication really offers is an opportunity for the brand to be helpful in its own way (authentic) and not just push promotional offers, but rather give the customer greater opportunity to explore behind the scenes with the product or service (transparency).

Customer Service in Social Media

As we suggested in the last section, being helpful is a very powerful mechanism for a company to engender trust and loyalty within a customer base. This was evidenced by Zappos.com, Comcast, and many other brands that utilize social media as an extension to their customer service efforts.

Log in to Twitter and search @comcastcares, and you'll find a stream of questions, comments, and statements from customers to @comcastcares with near-immediate responses. There are even updates from the Comcast Twitter feed when they are stepping away from the computer for a few minutes so no one gets angry if Comcast doesn't reply right away. What started out as a project quickly became an initiative for reducing support costs at the company.

Other companies like Casper provide forums for their customers to self-support. They will even bring in top volunteer commenters to be "beta customers" on new products and services, asking for their valued feedback. This keeps the customers happy, and the beta customer now feels obligated to help others and to maintain goodwill within the forum of frustrated and irate customers. By playing to the ego of some of these top influential customers, DirecTV customer service reps, who are usually not as knowledgeable on technical issues, deal with a lot fewer customer issues, saving millions of dollars a year.

Consider the implications of this story. A man arrives late to the Four Seasons hotel in Palo Alto and gets bumped to a room that doesn't meet his standards. Not happy about this, he tweets his displeasure. The Four Seasons sees the tweet immediately and rectifies the situation. As it turns out, the guest visits Palo Alto nearly 60 times a year. He then tweets his pleasure, and the Four Seasons has just created a loyal customer.[23] Prior to the advent of social media, the guest would have channeled his frustration in ways that the hotel could never have known about, and could possibly have lost him as a guest forever. As the best-selling author and creator of @comcastcares, Frank Eliason, says, social media mark the end of business as usual.

How Social Media Have Transformed Business

There are countless ways to describe how social media are changing the business environment. The flurry of engagement created by social media is not useful for branding alone. It has real consequences for revenues from e-commerce. Here are some demonstrations of how social media platforms continue to push the boundaries of what is standard practice:

- Financial and credit brands invest heavily in Facebook ads to target Millennials.
- Local businesses, able to capitalize on current events and local concerns, frequently have an advantage over big brands in social media.
- Comcast has at least 11 full-time employees dedicated to customer service via social media sites.
- Dell attributes well over $6.5 million in revenue directly from Twitter.
- JetBlue website visitors who also visited Twitter were 35 percent more likely to complete a booking than visitors who did not visit Twitter.[24]
- 36 percent of social media users post brand-related content.
- 85 percent of small to medium-sized firms use Twitter to provide customer service.
- 25 percent of U.S. marketers run video ads on Instagram.[25]
- 75 percent of companies now use Twitter as a marketing channel.
- 41 percent of the class of 2011 used social media sites in their job search.
- Over 5 million businesses rely on Facebook advertising, up from 3 million as recently as 2016.[26]
- The average user spends almost 50 minutes a day on Facebook's channels (Facebook, Instagram, Messenger).[27]
- Twitter advertising options include promoted tweets that cost up to $2 an engagement and promoted trends that run to $200,000 a day.[28]

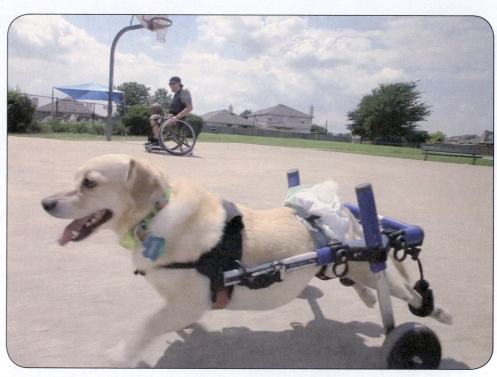

Kleenex attracted 27 million views and nearly as many comments with its viral "unlikely best friends." Chance needed a break when he lost the use of his hind legs after being struck by a car. Michael, who lives with a disability himself, found him at a shelter and created a way to give the dog mobility. While the sharing statistics are important, it was the heartfelt stories that people posted that made this viral so powerful.

Source: Kimberly-Clark Worldwide, Inc.

Application of Social Media

Social media are not one-size-fits-all marketing tools. So much is predicated on the type of company, the audience, and objectives for using the medium. We'll cover some of the more common uses of social media in the following sections.

Common Uses of Social Media

Although not all brands are active in social media—and not all brands have to be—there are some common ways in which advertisers are starting to harness the power of social media.

Blogs

One of the easiest and best ways to get started in social media is to be a practitioner. Blogs are simple, reverse-chronological-order web pages that are typically opinionated in nature. Many brands deploy blogs as a way for customers to hear the voice of the brand and get to know the brand on a deeper, more personal level. Zappos.com has an extensive site that lists blogs by category of shopping items: outdoor, running, or housewares, to name a few. We'll revisit Zappos.com later in the chapter.

Brand Monitoring and Social Listening

We've talked briefly in this chapter about listening tools such as Nielsen's BuzzMetrics. These tools allow brands to aggregate all of the commentary, positive, negative, or otherwise, into a user-friendly dashboard with robust analytics and trend analysis of how conversations are growing and sentiment is changing over time. These tools are great for learning how peo-

My IMC Campaign 15-A

Using Social Media

Unlike any other media choice, social media platforms aren't necessarily about placing ads in the areas that have the highest concentration of a company's target audience. In fact, that traditional process simply doesn't apply.

Social media are about engagement. However, *engagement* is a tricky word because it is typically defined differently for each brand. But defining what engagement means for your brand is what will help you determine how you will approach social media appropriately. Take a moment to think about how your target audience uses social media and where there might be entry points for you to engage the users. This is the first step in figuring out how to use social media for IMC.

As you have read throughout this chapter, the use of social media is now a very important part of integrated marketing communications. Basically, social media's function is to make brands remember that their target audiences are actually just people, and that they need to treat them like that.

The great thing about social media is that they allow you to be very creative. But don't go overboard on one creative idea because social media are as much about sustained and consistent presence as they are about having a one-off creative execution. Also remember that social media are inherently open, which means that seemingly disparate technologies can actually work together to create something new, rather than having to invent a new "thing."

Approach the use of social media for your campaign as a way to connect with your loyalists, and perhaps provide them with the tools to share your brand. Remember that word of mouth is the king of communications, and who better than your loyalists to sing your praises? There are many different ways in which people interact with social media, and you need to understand how the loyalists for your particular brand use them to achieve their goals. If you can identify that, and come up with some creative ideas that deliver on those goals, then you will have a winning strategy.

Here are some sites that can help you use popular social media sites to market, including Instagram (https://rosssimmonds.com/how-market-instagram/), Facebook (www.facebook.com/business/marketing/facebook) and Twitter (www.practicalecommerce.com/25-ways-to-use-twitter-for-marketing).

ple are actively talking about your brand. There are many different ways you can use these data. A very common way is to track new product launches and gauge the receptiveness from the customer base.

Remarketing

It used to be standard for brands to give their web audience the ability to sign up for newsletters right from their website. They would then take those names and remarket to them on an ongoing basis until they opted out of the communications. In some cases, the brands became so sophisticated they could tell you the exact number of sales from each newsletter drop based on the day, time, and offer. Nowadays these customer databases have moved to the social web, where likes and followers dominate the way in which most brands remarket to their customers. There are efficiencies to this replacing e-mail as the main form of remarketing, mostly around scale—it is much easier to follow or friend a brand than to fill in a lead form. Also, the message is distributed in multimedia formats where a customer *wants* to interact with the brand or company, and not necessarily in his or her inbox. A brand can create a channel on YouTube.com or Vimeo.com, have a Twitter page and Facebook page, and even have a LinkedIn group or Slideshare.net or Flickr channel—all of which allow the brand to distribute communications to its *own* **network.**

Marketing Research Online Communities (MROCs)

Communispace and Passenger are the largest suppliers of online communities for marketing research purposes. Imagine that you were a brand and you had what you thought was the next big idea. Well, if you had a marketing research online community (MROC), you could ask your loyal customer advocates what they thought of the idea or the communications or all of it. Communispace and Passenger recruit and manage these small communities on behalf of the brands, giving them valuable feedback prior to spending large sums of media dollars only to find that the new product would ultimately flop. Starbucks is a good example of an online community that works. The community allows users to submit to Starbucks their ideas and suggestions, which are then voted on. Starbucks promotes the ideas that make it into actual products or services in its blog *Ideas in Action.*

Customer Service

What can a brand do with 140 characters (or 280 as of late 2017) of text? For Comcast and Zappos.com, they can build brand loyalty that is unmatched in their category. What started out as one "guy" behind the @Comcastcares Twitter account has become a team of support personnel answering questions about everything from what channel is my regional Fox Sports network, to how do I program my remote, to even managing complaints about billing issues. For Zappos.com, those 280 characters can encourage every employee to be active on all things social media, including and especially Twitter. This allows the company to distribute its already legendary customer service to nearly every tweeter in the United States. Anytime someone talks about Zappos.com, an answer or a retweet (RT) will surely follow, and it is quite possible that the person answering you is Tony Hsieh, the CEO of Zappos.com.

Social Ads

Advertising in social media requires a strategy and set of objectives in the same way that advertising in other media does. A firm should have a clear sense of who they want to reach and what they hope to accomplish. Is the purpose of the advertising to grow contacts for a list, grow a group of followers, increase knowledge of the product or brand, drive people to a website, or make a sale? Who is the market, and how can social media tools ensure the campaign targets only prospects?

Facebook

As several of the exhibits in this chapter make clear, Facebook remains the 900-pound gorilla in social media. The site has global reach (not including China, which limits social media access to nonapproved sites) and can be accessed by almost a third of the entire internet audience. Almost 700 million people use the site every day.

Companies that wish to advertise on Facebook can take advantage of several opportunities:

A **boosted post** gives a company the opportunity to make a post more prominent in the News Feeds of individuals who are fans of the company. This increases the chance more fans will see the post, like or share it, or engage in some other way. Boosted posts are useful with people who are already fans and can increase a brand's followers if fans share the post with others. For extra money, Facebook will promote the post with friends of a brand's fans.

Ads called **click to website** operate much as Google search ads do: They bring the user to the firm's site outside of Facebook. For a company looking to make a sale or elicit some other behavior from Facebook users, this is a good option.

Page likes ads are intended to grow the fans of a company or brand. The ads feature the like button right in the ad, which makes it easy for a user to become a fan. There is some controversy about exactly how meaningful it is for a brand to cultivate "likes," but most marketing experts agree that likes are not an end in themselves but the beginning of an opportunity for a brand to build a relationship.

Variations of this type of ad may try to encourage deeper relationships, such as a purchase. Additionally, the ads may feature product videos, maps, or other engaging content. While some ads appear in the News Feed, others may appear to the right of the feed or in the user sidebar.

Mobile app installs are another category of ads on Facebook that, as the name suggests, ask users to install apps on their smartphones or other devices. Examples of apps include "Band Profile," which allows musicians to share music with fans; "Causes," an app that helps nonprofits raise money; and "Where I've Been," an app sponsored by social media company TripAdvisor that allows users to share their journeys with others.

The performance of these different advertising opportunities varies somewhat according to data collected over a variety of campaigns. Data for mobile app installs and page posts suggest click-through rates (CTRs) of approximately 2 percent.

Finally, Facebook allows advertisers to restrict exposures of their campaigns to the right demographic mix, including selecting audiences on the basis of education, geographics, or gender, but also likes and interests.

Twitter

Twitter offers a similar menu of choices for advertising, beginning with the **promoted tweet.** Promoted tweets help to raise the prominence of a tweet to the top of followers' feeds, the Twitter equivalent of Facebook's news wall. Twitter does extend the reach of promoted tweets to users who are not brand followers but whose interests and behaviors are similar. This makes it easier for a brand to grow followers.

Another option for Twitter advertisers is the **promoted account.** These appear in a user's "Who to Follow" tab and are an even better choice for increasing followers as the primary audience are not current followers of the brand. Twitter suggests that promoted accounts are most useful for driving purchases, leads, downloads, and signups; for increasing brand awareness and WOM sharing; and for driving web traffic.

A third Twitter opportunity is **promoted trends.** These are an expensive option; Twitter charges companies $200,000 a day to purchase a promoted trend. In exchange, companies get their hashtag near the list of trending topics on Twitter, which can be seen by all users. This has proven attractive not only to big brands like Coke and Disney but to presidential campaigns.

The performance of ad campaigns on Twitter is a bit more difficult to assess as the company shares less information with advertisers than does Facebook. However, industry estimates suggest that CTRs on Twitter campaigns are consistent with those in Facebook.

Other Social Media

Advertising is now a part of almost every popular social media platform, including Instagram, Snapchat, and Pinterest. These companies have built loyal, active audiences that are immensely attractive to advertisers. They are also proving effective in mobile, which advertisers like because people are accessing the web more and more from phones and tablets.

Social media organizations have not been shy about asking brands to pay large sums of money for their audiences either. The $200,000 that Twitter demands for a promoted trend is steep enough to match rates that television networks will require for a prime-time commercial. And Snapchat's asking price of $750,000 for advertising on the platform exceeds the costs of almost every TV prime-time commercial save those that run during the Super Bowl.

Crowdsourcing

To come up with a new logo or a website redesign, companies can spend tens of thousands to hundreds of thousands of dollars. Or they could go to 99designs.com or Crowdspring, create a brief, and allow people to showcase how they might produce your logo. People from all over the world congregate on these sites looking for new projects. Next, they create mockups of designs for you to peruse and decide which ones you like best. Then you can work with the designers to tweak the logo or advertisement to get it to your liking. The final price tag? Just under $800. This can save companies lots of money that they can use in other ways. It is quite possible that the person who had the winning design sits in another country where $800 goes a long way. This is the power of crowdsourcing.

People BEHIND the Ads

The Asahi Shimbun/Getty Images

No one ever made it big by thinking small. Proof positive: Mark Zuckerberg, CEO of Facebook. "A lot of companies get grouped as social networking," Zuckerberg told *Fortune* magazine. "Lots are dating sites, or media sites or sites for community. But our mission is helping people understand the world around them."

So how does someone go from nearly broke college kid to web tycoon in just a few short years? The best answer may be a unique combination of smarts, ambition, determination, guts, and a bit of hacker mentality.

Zuckerberg was born in Dobbs Ferry, a suburb of New York. Like many of his generation, he grew up with computers and became a self-taught programmer. A bit of code Zuckerberg and a friend wrote for creating customized music playlists caught the attention of Microsoft, which offered the teens jobs. But Zuckerberg had been admitted to Harvard, so he turned the company down and headed for Cambridge.

Once on campus, Zuckerberg got his first taste of both fame and controversy. The Ivy League school lacked an online photo directory, and administrators claimed it would be impossible to create one. That statement proved to be a challenge that Zuckerberg could not resist. Breaking into Harvard's computers, he posted photos on a website he named Facemash. To build traffic, he invited Harvard students to visit Facemash and pick who was "hotter" among pairs of undergrad photos. A short time later, the school closed him down.

But Zuckerberg wasn't finished, and his first incarnation of Facebook was birthed in February 2004. Zuckerberg himself describes Facebook as a "social utility that helps people communicate more efficiently with their friends, families and coworkers." It proved to be an immediate success, and within a couple of weeks a majority of Harvard students had joined. A short time later, Facebook was expanded to other schools and proved equally successful.

Zuckerberg now had to decide whether to stay in school or build a company. He chose the latter, leaving Harvard for Palo Alto, California, close to the headquarters of nearly all the major web and software firms. By 2006 Facebook had attracted nearly $40 million in venture capital and had almost 7 million users, predominantly college students.

But with success came new challenges. Although Facebook's trajectory was remarkable, its size was still tiny in comparison to MySpace, then America's most popular social networking site. In 2006 MySpace membership hovered around 100 million. Zuckerberg's plans to expand his site outside of college campuses had not been successful, and Facebook's growth rate was flattening. The question that was likely in his mind was, Is this the top?

In addition, Facebook's success was getting attention, and big companies were making offers. Viacom offered $750 million, but Zuckerberg turned it down. A short while later Yahoo! came calling. Few people know what it's like to be 24 years old and get a $1 billion offer for your company. One of them is Mark Zuckerberg. He told Yahoo! he would accept the offer, but at the last minute Yahoo! changed the bid—it announced it would pay "only" $800 million for Facebook. Zuckerberg decided to walk away.

How has the company achieved such phenomenal success? Admirers say that Zuckerberg turned the site into more than a social network. *Wired* magazine calls it a "full-fledged platform that organizes the entire Internet." In fact, a big part of what separates Facebook from other social network sites is its willingness to open its platform to third-party developers. These developers help generate the applications that make the site so addictive.

When *Time* magazine asked Zuckerberg in 2007 about his grand plans, including plans for advertising, he responded, "It's tough to say, exactly, what things will look like in three to five years. . . . [There are] a lot of different applications that are going to be developed to allow people to share information in different ways. I would expect the user base will grow [and there will be] more ways for advertisers to reach people and communicate in a very natural way, just like users communicate with each other. All these things will just get more and more evolved."

Zuckerberg's leadership paid off when on May 18, 2012, the company set records at its initial public offering (IPO) for volume traded, and Facebook generated over $14 billion in cash. Subsequently the stock fell significantly before recovering and beginning a path of steady growth.

The recent past has presented trials for Facebook, as the company has faced scrutiny over its privacy practices. It has also been a target of political criticism for both allowing forums for speech some find offensive and for censoring speech that some do not. In early 2019, there were even some calls for Zuckerberg's resignation.

But Mark Zuckerberg has made clear he is not going anywhere. While Facebook's success story has been uneven, the company has continually found ways to innovate, grow, and remain important to its audiences.

The future? Facebook is investing heavily in virtual reality. If the past is any guide, it will continue to evolve along with the benefits sought by its users. And its advertisers.

Entertainment

Social media platforms aren't always about being serious; some brands utilize social media to breathe life into their company culture, like Zappos.com, or bring entertainment in unique ways to their fan base. Take these two companies as examples: Burger King and Blendtec. Burger King created a Facebook application that asked people to sacrifice 10 friends by defriending them. For sacrificing those 10 friends, they earned a free Whopper. After 20,000 users defriended over 200,000 "friends," Facebook shut down the application for privacy concerns. Sometimes bad news is actually good for a brand image. We mentioned Blendtec, an industrial blender manufacturer, in Chapter 14. It created a YouTube.com channel called "Will It Blend." In a campy and methodical way, the CEO of Blendtec took to video to literally show everyone that his blenders could blend just about anything. From skis to iPhones to batteries and glow sticks, this channel became a phenomenon, and Blendtec quickly stopped all other marketing efforts to focus on creating these episodic videos on what the blenders could handle.

Games and Gamification

We opened this chapter with the example of *Fortnite*. While the combat game is the latest example of connecting people around the world who share a gaming passion, this is really nothing new. People have been playing chess, Scrabble, and Hangman with others for a while now. In fact, it is the rare digital game that does not encourage online competition. You probably don't have to imagine very hard because the explosion of companies like Zynga, the maker of *Words with Friends* and other social games, has made what once was impossible, downright easy. Millions play every day from their PC, console, or phone.

Helping gamers and others in social media stay longer on sites is fostered by **gamification,** the use of rewards, badges, points, or other "game-like" benefits to encourage engagement. Earning points and advancing to levels has also been a massively addictive rewards system. Massively multiplayer online role-playing games (MMORPG) such as *Fortnite* were quite possibly some of the first social communities that existed online. And their leveling and badging system has been adopted for other more utilitarian applications like Foursquare, creating a whole new way of engaging consumers in gamification. And it works. People crave the immediate rewards and feedback mechanism. These short-term bits of happiness keep consumers engaged far longer than if the gamification didn't exist. So apply this gamification with branded online communities and you have a recipe for a long-term engagement with consumers around your brand, quite possibly without having to sell that person anything.[29]

Reviews and Opinions

We discussed earlier the impact that social media have on word of mouth. Through reviews, everyday people can let the world know what they think of certain products or services. Imagine that you are about to be one of the first to buy the latest shiny new toy, and you look it up online only to find that the three people who bought it before you have commented about how disappointed they were in the product and that they are going to return it. That type of information is invaluable to the consumer and a product killer to brands. CNet.com was one of the first websites to build around the user-generated content of reviews and opinions. And Yelp.com brings that same infrastructure to local service providers. Wondering if that local plumbing service is any good? Look it up on Yelp.com and read 25 reviews from people like you.

Chapter Summary

Social media are unlike any other media to date. They can't be measured simply by time and place. In fact, there are no standardized advertising placements that can be sponsored. This makes social media platforms unique and challenging. The sharing aspect of social media has helped scale the media and makes them the fastest media of all time to reach 50 million users. They have also quickly changed social media users' behavior in the number of people they stay in touch with and how they communicate with them. A status update is the new phone call. Social media have changed how companies communicate with their customers as well. They have ushered in a more transparent and open

relationship between brand and consumer. Social media platforms are a component of almost every website on both the wired and mobile internet. From reviews, to forums, to social networks, the connections that form within social media have helped usher in a new era of IMC. There are many different ways in which brands can use social media. From research, to remarketing, to crowdsourcing and entertainment, social media provide brands different ways of connecting with their audience to better understand them, provide products that meet their needs, and create a feedback loop that is unprecedented in the history of advertising and IMC.

Important Terms

application protocol interface (API), *499*

blog, *500*

boosted post, *509*

click to website, *509*

forum, *500*

gamification, *512*

influencer marketing, *497*

influencers, *497*

microblog, *502*

mobile app installs, *509*

network, *508*

page likes, *509*

post, *501*

promoted account, *510*

promoted trends, *510*

promoted tweet, *510*

social bookmarking, *502*

social listening, *505*

social media, *496*

social networking, *502*

software as a service (SaaS), *502*

trending, *499*

user-generated content (UGC), *501*

wiki, *502*

word of mouth (WOM), *505*

Review Questions

1. What are ways that social media are different than traditional media?
2. What are the ways in which social media have changed consumer behavior?
3. What are the different ways consumers engage within social media?
4. What are examples of social media ads and what are they used for?
5. Why is transparency so important for companies?
6. What are the different types of social media?
7. How would you describe the advantage of deploying a social media campaign?

The Advertising Experience

1. **Using Social Media**

   As the communications director of a new start-up, you are very excited to tell the world that your company is the next best thing to sliced bread. To be successful, your company needs to reach a lot of people very quickly. What are some of the tactics that you would use to spread the word through social media?

2. **Social Media Organizations**

   Visit the following social media industry websites and familiarize yourself with the size of the social media world. Be sure to answer the questions for each site.

   - Review Trackers: www.reviewtrackers.com/ social-media-marketing/
   - Influencer Marketing Hub: https://influencermarketinghub.com
   - International Network for Social Network Analysis: www.insna.org
   - Hootsuite: https://signup.hootsuite.com

   a. What is the purpose of the organization that sponsors this site?

   b. Who is (are) the intended audience(s) of this site?

   c. Who makes up the organization's membership? Its constituency?

   d. How important do you feel this organization is to the advertising industry? Why?

3. Social media not only allow fans and users to participate in campaigns, they often encourage it. Create a video for your favorite brand and post it. Track to see if your video is acknowledged by the company, how often it is shared, etc.

4. Identify a passion (exercise, photography, novels, sports) and consider who might be an influencer in that sphere. What brands might form an influencer marketing relationship with this person?

End Notes

1. Devon Pendleton and Christopher Palmeri, "Fortnite Phenomenon Turns a Game Developer into a Billionaire," *Ad Age,* July 24, 2018, *https://adage.com/article/media/fortnite-phenomenon-turns-game-developer-into-a-billionaire/314357/.*

2. Alissa Fleck, "Fornite's Explosion in Popularity Is Opening New Doors for Marketers," *Adweek,* June 5, 2018, *www.adweek.com/brand-marketing/fortnites-explosion-in-popularity-is-opening-new-doors-for-marketers/.*

3. Alissa Fleck, "Fornite's Explosion in Popularity Is Opening New Doors for Marketers," *Adweek,* June 5, 2018, *www.adweek.com/brand-marketing/fortnites-explosion-in-popularity-is-opening-new-doors-for-marketers/.*

4. Maximus Live, "Fortnite's Branded Crossovers Show Just How Much Fun Native Advertising Can Be," *Medium.com,* June 8, 2018, *https://medium.com/@maximuslive.mediabuying/https-medium-com-maximuslive-mediabuying-fortnites-branded-crossovers-fun-native-advertising-6a6071cf28a9.*

5. *Merriam-Webster,* s.v. "social media," *www.merriam-webster.com/dictionary/social%20media.*

6. Aaron Smith and Monica Anderson, "Social Media Use in 2018," Pew Research Center, March 1, 2018, *www.pewinternet.org/2018/03/01/social-media-use-in-2018/.*

7. "Classification of Social Media," Wikipedia.org, May 2012, *http://en.wikipedia.org/wiki/social_media.*

8. "Half of Americans Call Facebook a 'Fad,'" Associated Press/CNBC, May 15, 2012, *www.psfk.com/2012/05/americans-call-facebook-fad-headlines.html.*

9. Jason Abbruzzese, "Facebook Hits 2.27 Billion Monthly Active Users as Earnings Stabilize," *NBC News,* October 30, 2018, *www.nbcnews.com/tech/tech-news/facebook-hits-2-27-billion-monthly-active-users-earnings-stabilize-n926391.*

10. Cara Pring, "100 Social Media Statistics for 2012," *The Social Skinny,* January 11, 2012, *http://thesocialskinny.com/100-social-media-statistics-for-2012/.*

11. Cara Pring, "100 Social Media Statistics for 2012," *The Social Skinny,* January 11, 2012, *http://thesocialskinny.com/100-social-media-statistics-for-2012/.*

12. Cara Pring, "100 Social Media Statistics for 2012," *The Social Skinny,* January 11, 2012, *http://thesocialskinny.com/100-social-media-statistics-for-2012/.*

13. "What Is Cyberbullying," stopbullying.gov, *www.stopbullying.gov/cyberbullying/what-is-it/index.html;* "What Is Cyberbullying?" U.S. Department of Health and Human Services, 2018.

14. "Facts About Bullying," Stopbullying.gov, *www.stopbullying.gov/media/facts/index.html#stats.*

15. "Prevent Cyberbullying," Stopbullying.gov, *www.stopbullying.gov/cyberbullying/prevention/index.html.*

16. Dwight Falk, "Pedophilia Is More Common Than You Think," *The Trumpet,* April 26, 2018, *www.thetrumpet.com/17188-pedophilia-is-more-common-than-you-think.*

17. Cara Pring, "100 Social Media Statistics for 2012," *The Social Skinny,* January 11, 2012, *http://thesocialskinny.com/100-social-media-statistics-for-2012/.*

18. Jacob Kastrenakes, "Twitter's Numbers Are Actually Growing Again," *The Verge,* April 25, 2018, *www.theverge.com/2018/4/25/17274828/twitter-earning-q1-2018-profit-user-growth.*

19. M. G. Siegler, "Eric Schmidt: Every 2 Days We Create as Much Information as We Did up to 2003," *Techcrunch.com,* August 4, 2010, *http://techcrunch.com/2010/08/04/schmidt-data/.*

20. Taylor Casti, "The 5 Most Notorious Brand Feuds on Twitter," *Mashable,* October 12, 2013, *https://mashable.com/2013/10/12/twitter-brand-feuds/#7YQjSc3Zkmq4.*

21. Jennifer Leggio, "The Battle for Social Media Authenticity," *Forbes,* October, 13, 2011, *www.forbes.com/sites/jenniferleggio/2011/10/13/the-battle-for-social-media-authenticity/2/.*

22. Bright Local, "Local Consumer Review Survey 2018," December 7, 2018, *www.brightlocal.com/learn/local-consumer-review-survey/#local-business-review-habits.*

23. Rohit Bhargava, "9 Ways Top Brands Use Social Media for Better Customer Service," *Mashable.com*, October 28, 2011, *http://mashable.com/2011/10/28/social-customer-service-brands/.*

24. Kipp Bodnar, "The Ultimate List: 300+ Social Media Statistics," *Hubspot,* May 13, 2010, *https://blog.hubspot.com/blog/tabid/6307/bid/5965/the-ultimate-list-300-social-media-statistics.aspx.*

25. "28 Twitter Statistics All Marketers Need to Know in 2018," *Hootsuite,* January 17, 2018, *https://blog.hootsuite.com/twitter-statistics/.*

26. "28 Twitter Statistics All Marketers Need to Know in 2018," *Hootsuite,* January 17, 2018, *https://blog.hootsuite.com/twitter-statistics/.*

27. Keran Smith, "25 Facebook Advertising Statistics That Will Blow Your Mind," *Lyfe,* December 2, 2017, *www.lyfemarketing.com/blog/facebook-advertising-statistics/.*

28. Brandon Bailey, Peter Delevett, and Steve Johnson, "Facebook IPO Huge, but No 'Pop,'" *Mercury News,* May 18, 2012, *www.mercurynews.com/business/ci_20656753/facebook-ipo-huge-but=no-pop.*

29. David DiSalvo, *What Makes Your Brain Happy and Why You Should Do the Opposite* (Amherst, NY: Prometheus Books, 2011), pp. 225–26.

Using Out-of-Home, Exhibitive, and Supplementary Media

To present the factors advertisers consider when evaluating various out-of-home, exhibitive, and supplementary media. Many advertisers use these media to either complement or replace print and electronic media, so it's important to understand how advertisers buy these media and the advantages and disadvantages of each.

After studying this chapter, you will be able to:

LO16-1   Discuss the pros and cons of out-of-home advertising.

LO16-2   Describe the types of standard out-of-home advertising structures.

LO16-3   Explain how to measure exposure to out-of-home media.

LO16-4   Detail the various options available in transit advertising.

LO16-5   Identify the influences on the cost of transit and other out-of-home media.

LO16-6   Discuss the importance of exhibitive media in a company's marketing mix.

LO16-7   Explain the issues advertisers face when considering a change in packaging.

LO16-8   Identify several types of supplementary media.

The most common form of out-of-home advertising is the billboard. And pity the poor billboard. With all of the excitement advertisers have about the digital and social media platforms you read about in the last two chapters, who gets worked up about billboards? ■ One reason for the lackluster appeal of billboards is their tactical nature. Think of a billboard you've seen recently and you're likely to recall one letting you know there is a Shell station at the next interstate exit. In other words, billboards and IMC just don't seem to go together. ■ Such a view would be shortsighted. It is true there are many dull, uninspiring examples of billboards. However, in the hands of creatives, boards can make powerful IMC statements. ■ One great example is a 2018 campaign by Corona in support of World Ocean's Day. The campaign combines a traditional board featuring a photo of movie star Chris Hemsworth surfing, over what appears to be a foaming blue wave. ■ But on closer inspection, the "wave" is a carefully constructed pile of plastics, all harvested from ocean waters. A nearby sign for the London billboard reads, "This wave of waste contains the average amount of marine plastic pollution found on every two miles of beach in the UK."[1] ■ The billboard catches the eye, but how does this execution square with IMC? To start, Corona, the world's best-selling Mexican beer, has spent years advertising a connection between the brand and lazy, tropical, beautiful beach scenes. So the connection of oceans and beach is well established. ■ In addition, Corona is partnering with Parley, an advocacy group for clean oceans, to bring meaningful change to the beverage industry. Here again, Corona, the first beer brand marketed in clear glass bottles, each label painted, and each bottle brewed in Mexico, has an edge. The Corona-Parley collaboration will focus specifically on protecting islands in Mexico, the Maldives, Australia, Chile, Italy, and the Dominican Republic. ■ Adding even more IMC elements that are rare in an out-of-home campaign, Corona is marketing Hawaiian-style shirts created from plastic. The shirts emphasize a typical tropical scene until you see, on close inspection, that the imagery is again plastic ocean pollution. Finally, consumers who walk by the display are encouraged to take a role by dropping off plastic waste at nearby bins. The donated plastics will be used in further modifications of the board. ■ Corona's efforts demonstrate that billboards need not be boring or just tactical. In an effort to make a difference, Corona's creativity demonstrates to other advertisers that out-of-home advertising can do more. And do good. ■

Exhibit 16-1
Breakdown of out-of-home media.
Source: Adapted from Out of Home Advertising Association of America, Inc.

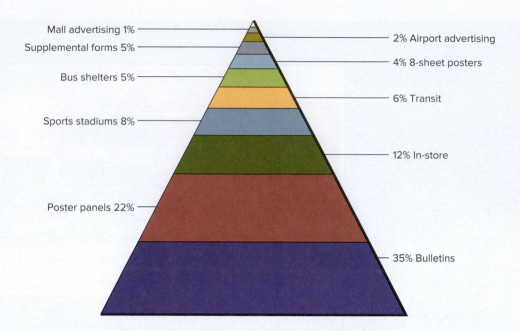

Mall advertising 1%
Supplemental forms 5%
Bus shelters 5%
Sports stadiums 8%
Poster panels 22%

2% Airport advertising
4% 8-sheet posters
6% Transit
12% In-store
35% Bulletins

Out-of-Home (OOH) Media

LO **16-1**

Ads that reach prospects exclusively outside of their homes—like billboards (sometimes called bulletins), bus and taxicab advertising, subway posters, terminal advertising, even skywriting—are part of the broad category of **out-of-home (OOH) advertising** (see Exhibit 16-1). Today, there are more than 100 different types of out-of-home media, generating $7.7 billion in revenues in 2017.[2] While not considered OOH (because they are not measured or bought), the most common are *on-premise signs,* which promote goods and services, or identify a place of business, on the property where the sign is located.[3] The golden arches at McDonald's franchises are a good example. On-premise signs are important for helping people find a place of business, but they don't provide market coverage, and they aren't an organized, purchasable medium.

In the past three chapters, we've looked at the traditional mass media forms as well as some of the interesting new media vehicles that have burst upon the advertising scene. Now, to round out our discussion of advertising media, we'll present in this last media chapter some of the other vehicles that advertisers use today.

We start with the last major category: organized out-of-home media. These include standardized outdoor advertising and transit advertising. We also briefly discuss some other out-of-home vehicles that are gaining in popularity: mobile billboards, electronic signs and displays, and even the ads that now frequent unusual places such as phone booths and parking meters.

Next we'll discuss a category we call *exhibitive media,* which includes product packaging and trade shows and exhibits. Finally, we'll examine media that advertisers typically consider supplementary to their other advertising activities—things like promotional products (specialty advertising) and **directories**—as well as some emerging media that are beginning to gain advertiser interest.

Out-of-Home Ad Spending as a Percentage of All U.S. Ad Spending 2018

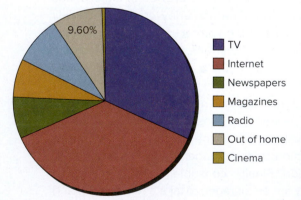

9.60%

- ■ TV
- ■ Internet
- ■ Newspapers
- ■ Magazines
- ■ Radio
- ■ Out of home
- ■ Cinema

OOH Advertising

As a national and global medium, outdoor advertising has achieved great success. It was the first advertising medium ever used, dating back more than 5,000 years to when hieroglyphics on obelisks directed travelers. In the Middle Ages, bill posting was an accepted form of advertising in Europe. And in the nineteenth century, it evolved into a serious art form, thanks to the poster paintings of both Manet and Toulouse-Lautrec.[4]

Today, around the globe, marketers use OOH for the same reasons: to communicate a succinct message or image in the local language to a mass audience quickly and frequently at the lowest cost per thousand of any major medium.

Engagement can be important in outdoor advertising, especially in urban settings. This clever Mountain Dew ad not only gets people to interact with a billboard that is 40 feet off the ground, but it encourages people to take pictures, ensuring a longevity beyond the time the ad will run.

(all): Source: Pepsi Cola Company

Growth in OOH has been steady compared to other traditional media. Expenditures rose from $7 billion in 2014 to $7.7 billion in 2017, and the numbers for 2018 show a continued rise.[5] And this growth is expected to continue as advertisers seek alternatives to the declining audiences and ad clutter of traditional media. Now that TV viewers can choose from hundreds of channels, it has become increasingly difficult for national advertisers to tell their story to mass audiences. But there's still one medium that can carry their message 24 hours a day, seven days a week, without interruption. It's never turned off, zipped, zapped, put aside, or left unopened. That's OOH. For that reason, some experts refer to billboards as the *last* mass medium.[6]

Another reason for the growth of OOH is it has integrated digital technologies in a fashion that exceeds other traditional media. Conventional billboards, terminal signs, and stadium ads are going digital. As we show later, this increases the creative possibilities for

Exhibit 16-2

Number of displays within OOH categories.

Source: "Number of Out of Home Displays (2019)," Out of Home Advertising Association of America, retrieved at: https://oaaa.org/AboutOOH/Factsamp;Figures.aspx.

Number of Out of Home Displays (2019)

Billboards	Street Furniture	Transit	Place-based OOH
Bulletins 164,370	**Bus Shelters** 63,239	**Airports** 29,476	**Arenas and Stadiums** 961
Digital Billboards 8,800	**Urban St. Furniture** 39,128	**Digital Airport** 2,350	**Cinema** 35,800
Posters 147,029	Bus benches Newsracks	**Buses** 1.05 million	**Digital Place-based** 1.25 million
Junior Posters 19,818	Newsstands Phone kiosks	**Rail/Subway** 365,113	**Interior Place-based** Convenience stores
Wall Murals 2,289	Urban panels	**Digital Rail/Subway** 5,454	Health clubs Restaurants/bars
	Digital St. Furniture 5,742	**Digital transit** 7,847	**Exterior Place-based** Airborne
		Mobile Billboards 514	Marine Resorts and leisure
		Taxis 44,008	**Shopping Malls** 21,700
		Digital Taxis 33,800	**Digital Shopping Mall** 5,830
		Truckside 3,501	

the medium. And, as can be seen in Exhibit 16-2, advertisers have many choices for reaching people outside of their homes. Finally, out-of-home advertising may be used for a variety of purposes. For example, nothing beats outdoor as a directional medium for motorists. But in an IMC program, OOH also greatly enhances awareness of or reinforces the advertiser's core message with high frequency at a very reasonable cost.

Standardization in OOH

Standardized outdoor advertising uses scientifically located structures to deliver an advertiser's message to markets around the world.

In the United States, more than 400,000 outdoor ad structures are owned and maintained by some 3,000 outdoor advertising companies, known as *plants.*[7] Plant operators find suitable locations (usually concentrated in commercial and business areas), lease or buy the property, acquire the necessary legal permits, erect the structures in conformance with local building codes, contract with advertisers for poster rentals, and post the panels or paint the bulletins. Plant operators also maintain the outdoor structures and keep surrounding areas clean and attractive.

The plant operator may have its own art staff to supply creative services for local advertisers; ad agencies usually do the creative work for national advertisers. The biggest outdoor advertisers are traditionally in the entertainment and amusement category. The next largest category is local retail. Typically, the smaller the market, the larger the percentage of local advertisers.

Types of OOH Advertising

LO 16-2

Outdoor advertising options are plentiful. According to the Out of Home Advertising Association of American (OAAA), there are six major kinds of out-of-home media: billboards, street furniture (bus shelters, store displays, urban furniture, kiosks), transit (buses, subway and rail, airports, truckside, taxi display, and wrapped vehicles), broadcast using place-based TVs (stores, schools, bars), radio (drive time, in-office, in-store), and alternative (elevators, stadiums, airborne, shopping malls). We begin our discussion with a focus on the category that is probably most familiar to you, billboards. Standardized structures come in three basic forms: *bulletins, poster panels,* and *junior posters.* For extra impact, some companies may use the nonstandard *spectacular.*

This ad for LEGO blends in with the street where it's been placed. Using existing surroundings to accent an ad is a creative and memorable strategy.

Source: The Lego Group

Bulletins

Where traffic is heavy and visibility is good, advertisers find that large **bulletin structures** work best, especially for long-term use. Bulletins measure 14 by 48 feet, plus any extensions, and may carry either painted or printed messages. They are created in sections in the plant's shop and then brought to the site, where they are assembled and hung on the billboard structure.

Painted displays are normally illuminated at night and repainted several times each year (color is very important for readability; see Ad Lab 16-A). Some bulletins are three-dimensional or embellished by extensions (or cutouts) that stretch beyond the frames of the structure. Variations include cutout letters, backlighting, moving messages, and electronic time and temperature units called jump clocks.

Painted bulletins are very costly, but some advertisers overcome this expense by rotating them to different choice locations in the market every 60 or 90 days. Over time, this gives the impression of wider coverage than the advertiser is actually paying for. The dominating effect of bulletins frequently makes them well worth the extra cost—especially in small markets.

Poster Panels

The **poster panel** (or *standard bulletin*) is less costly per unit and is the basic outdoor advertising structure. A poster consists of a steel structure created with a standardized size and border. Its message is first printed at a lithography or screen plant on large sheets of vinyl, then mounted by hand on the panel. In some instances, painters may be hired to create a message directly on plywood. In many instances, the frame of the panel can be lifted off the steel pole that supports it and moved to different locations to increase a campaign's reach.[8]

Some local advertisers get high-quality outdoor advertising at reduced cost by using **stock posters.** These ready-made posters are available in any quantity and often feature the work of first-class artists and lithographers. Local florists, dairies, banks, or bakeries simply place their name in the appropriate spot.

Junior Posters

 LO 16-3

Manufacturers of grocery products, as well as many local advertisers, use smaller poster sizes. Called **junior posters** (or *junior panels*), these offer a 5- by 11-foot printing area on a panel surface 6 feet high by 12 feet wide. They are typically concentrated in urban areas, where they can reach pedestrian as well as vehicular traffic. In an integrated marketing communications campaign, they are also an excellent medium for coverage close to the point of purchase.

Spectaculars are expensive, elaborate animated signs found primarily in the hearts of large cities. They incorporate movement, color, and flashy graphics to grab attention in high-traffic areas.

TongRo Images/Alamy Stock Photo

Spectaculars

Times Square in New York is well known for its **spectaculars**—giant electronic signs that incorporate movement, color, and flashy graphics to grab attention in high-traffic areas. Spectaculars are very expensive to produce and are found primarily in the world's largest cities, such as Tokyo, London, Atlanta, Los Angeles, and, of course, Las Vegas (see the Portfolio Review, "Out-of-Home Advertising").

Buying OOH Advertising

Advertisers use OOH advertising for a variety of purposes. For example, Spotify used digital billboards to share data about listening trends around the 2016 holidays. Delta and its agency, Wieden + Kennedy, partnered with dating app Tinder to show photos of

AD Lab 16–A

How to Use Color and Type in Out-of-Home Advertising

These 14 color combinations represent the best use of color contrast for advertising readability. The chart evaluates primary and secondary color combinations taking into account hue and value. Example 1 is the most legible color combination while example 14 is the least legible.

Hue is the identity of color, such as red, yellow, or blue.

Value is the measure of lightness or darkness and can be separated into shades and tints.

Shades are the relative darkness of colors. Tints are the relative lightness of colors.

A standard color wheel illustrates the importance of contrast in hue and value. Like sound waves, light rays have varying wave lengths or frequencies. Some pigments absorb light while others reflect it. Reflected frequencies are perceived as color.

Opposite colors on a wheel are complementary. An example is red and green. They represent a good contrast in hue, but their values are similar. It is difficult for the cones and rods of the human eye to process the wavelength variations associated with complementary colors. Consequently, a quivering or optical distortion is sometimes detected when two complementary colors are used in tandem.

Adjacent colors, such as blue and green, make especially poor combinations because their contrast is similar in both hue and value. As a result, adjacent colors create contrast that is hard to discern.

Alternating colors, such as blue and yellow, produce the best combinations because they have good contrast in both hue and value. Black contrasts well with any color of light value and white is a good contrast with colors of dark value. For example, yellow and black are dissimilar in the contrast of both hue and value. White and blue are also a good color combination.

Typestyles

Fonts selected for OOH designs must be easy to read from variable distances. Use large and legible typefaces. Choose fonts that

Source: Victors & Spoils

romantic getaways on posters around New York. Smirnoff, a vodka brand, tweaked the Trump administration with billboards that proclaimed "Made in America (but we'd be happy to talk about our ties to Russia under oath."[9]

The basic unit of sale for billboards, or posters, is *100 gross rating points daily,* or a **100 showing.** One rating point equals 1 percent of a particular market's population. Buying 100 gross rating points does *not* mean the message will appear on 100 posters; it means the message will appear on as many panels as needed to provide a daily exposure theoretically equal to the market's total population. Actually, a showing of 100 gross rating points achieves a *daily* reach of about 88.1 percent of the adults in a market over a 30-day period.[10]

For less saturation, units of sale can be expressed as fractions of the basic unit, such as 75, 50, or 25 gross rating points. If a showing provides 750,000 total impression opportunities daily in a market with a population of 1 million, it delivers 75 GRPs daily. Over a period of 30 days, the showing would earn 2,250 GRPs (30 × 75).

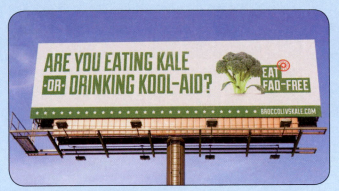

Bolthouse Farms ■ Without mentioning a single health benefit, Bolthouse used bold messaging to establish a persona for broccoli that was difficult to ignore.
Source: Victors & Spoils

are easily read at long distances. Fonts with thin strokes or ornate script will be difficult to read.

Adequate spacing between letters, words, and lines will enhance visibility. The relative size of letter characters is also an important consideration. When designing for roadside displays, a one-foot letter height is unreadable, while a two-foot letter height is marginal. A letter height greater than three feet is clearly readable. Words comprised of both upper- and lowercase characters are generally easier to read than words constructed solely of capital letters.

Laboratory Applications

1. Which billboard ads in this chapter use color most effectively? Explain.

2. What billboard ads have you seen that don't use color effectively? How can they be improved?

Text Legibility Guide

Distance in Feet	Print Resolution	Resolution for LED	Examples	Minimal Readable Text Height in Inches
5'-50'	High	3mm-8mm	Malls, Airports, Retail, Lobbies, Offices, etc.	1"-2"
50'-100'	High	6mm-12mm	Window, Street Display, Drive Through	2"-4"
100'-200'	Normal	12mm-25mm	Posters, Surface Streets	4"-8"
200'-300'	Normal	25mm-34mm	Posters, Surface Streets and Highway Bulletins	8"-10"
300'-350'	Normal	34mm-66mm	Highway Bulletins, Highway Posters	10"-15"
350'-500'	Normal	34mm-66mm	Highways, Spectaculars	15"-20"
500'-600'	Low - Normal	66mm-76mm	Highways, Spectaculars, Stadiums	20"-24"
600' +	Low	76mm-90mm	Skyscrapers, Spectaculars, Set back from road	24"-40"

Source: Reprinted with permission of Out of Home Advertising Association of America.

A showing, as indicated above, has historically been measured by a rudimentary equation that takes the number of people who pass by an out-of-home display as its measure of reach. This measurement is called Daily Estimated Circulation, or DEC. However, in 2009, the Outdoor Advertising Association of America (OAAA), now the Out of Home Advertising Association of America, and the Traffic Audit Bureau developed a new method of measuring out-of-home's true reach and frequency. Their new rating system is called **Eyes on Impressions (EOI).** EOI actually takes into account many factors besides the number of people who pass a display. These factors include the size of the display, its angle to the road, format, street type, distance from the road, and roadside position. This new rating system then integrates these factors into a formula for determining the number of people who *actually* see the ad in a week. The key difference between DECs and EOIs is the former estimates traffic on a daily basis versus the latter's focus on *exposures*

(continued on page 528)

:: Out-of-Home Advertising

As the oldest medium on earth, outdoor advertising benefits from its inherent nature as a "sign" as well as the modern features of graphic design and technology. In fact, thanks to technology, advertisers can do things in outdoor today they couldn't have dreamed of just a few years ago. Plus, no other medium is this big—commanding attention from motorists and pedestrians 24 hours a day, seven days a week, at a fraction of the cost of other media. However, outdoor is limited in what it can say. For normal outdoor structures on the highway, seven words is the rule of thumb. That places an additional burden on the nonverbal (artistic) aspects of the ad, and this definitely challenges the creative muscle of every advertising ad agency.

• Study the ads in this portfolio to see how big, strategic ideas get translated into outstanding outdoor or transit advertising. Then consider why the advertiser chose this particular medium. Was outdoor or transit the right choice for this advertiser? Why? Or why not? Could the same concept be used in other media? How?

Kiwi, a shoe polish brand, won accolades at Cannes for ads showing "completed" masterworks of art highlighting the subject's shoes.
Source: S. C. Johnson & Son, Inc.

In this ad the art is everything, creating the contrast of luxury and poverty that the sponsor wishes to highlight. The sparse copy makes the message credible by indicating that the photo has not been altered.
Source: Delta Air Lines, Inc.

Consider the importance of color, space, and repetition in the effectiveness of these OOH brand messages.

Bhubeth Bhajanavorakul/Shutterstock

Ads can now easily be applied to the exterior of cars, trucks, buses, and subways. What are some of the advantages, and possible drawbacks, of messages appearing on moving vehicles?

BobNoah/Shutterstock

Technology now allows OOH advertising to target consumers based on location. Location-based advertising delivers ads to audiences who enter or occupy a defined geographic area. In social media, serving a promoted Tweet or Instagram ad to consumers in a specified location is sometimes called geofencing.

TotallyMJ/Shutterstock

The ubiquity of mobile phones has also made QR codes and Near Field Communication (NFC) more prevalent and common in OOH advertising. Consumers have the ability to quickly access sales information and even purchase products while walking down the street.

Imagine China/Newscom

Absolut Vodka went above and beyond with this bulletin, which displays a typical Manhattan apartment.

Jorge Vasconcelos/Moment/Getty Images

Creativity is at the heart of every great media placement. Here, the World Wildlife Foundation uses the depletion of paper towels to convey their conservation message.

Source: World Wildlife Foundation

Innovative users of OOH can create ads that are impossible to ignore. Here the advertiser takes advantage of consumer expectations that subway ads exist in two dimensions by surprising them with three.

Francois Guillot/AFP/Getty Images

This ad for KitchenAid uses an unusual execution to say something important about the brand. How does the beauty of the ad speak to the quality and beauty of the product?

Source: KitchenAid

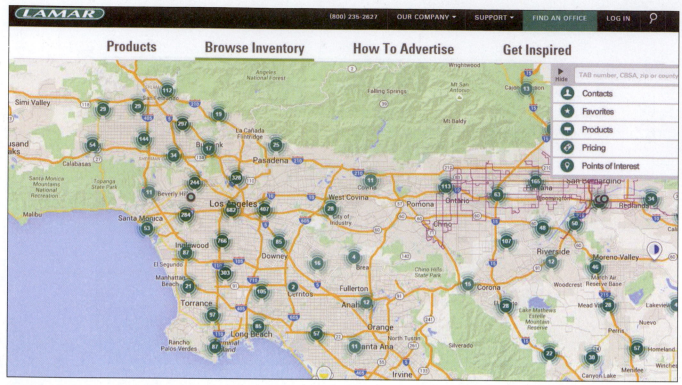

Exhibit 16-3
Billboard and other OOH Locations in Los Angeles.
Source: Reprinted with permission of Lamar Advertising.

(continued from page 523)

to the ad on a weekly basis. The net effect is twofold: (1) Out-of-home is now the only ad medium that tracks viewers of ads, rather than just the potential to see ads, and (2) the frequency of out-of-home has been drastically reduced over a monthly period where the reach difference is negligible.[11]

Location, Location, Location

As in real estate, location is everything in outdoor advertising. Advertisers that want more saturation can increase the number of posters or purchase better locations to achieve 200 or 300 GRPs per day. The map in Exhibit 16-3 shows billboard locations in Los Angeles, California. Rates vary considerably from market to market due to variations in property rentals, labor costs, and market size. As a rule of thumb, a standard billboard offers the lowest cost per thousand of any major mass medium.[12]

Technology in Outdoor Advertising

In the past it was always a problem for a media buyer in New York to adequately supervise the posting of outdoor boards in Peoria, Illinois. A buyer can't just jump on a plane and travel to all the cities where the client's boards are posted to verify the value of the locations. Fortunately, though, new technology has helped solve this dilemma and has thus made outdoor an even more attractive medium to national advertisers. OOH companies use **global positioning systems (GPSs)** to give the exact location of particular boards using satellite technology. Media buyers, equipped with sophisticated software, can then integrate this information with demographic market characteristics and traffic counts to determine the best locations for their boards.[13]

Some outdoor companies even provide digitized video of their locations so the buyer can see the actual board and the environment in which it is located. Bar coding technology allows materials to be tracked, posted, and authenticated, all by computer. Computerized painting on flexible vinyl guarantees a high-quality, high-resolution, faithful reproduction of

Geo-targeting involves serving ads to consumers based on their geographic locations. Related to this are two other location-based tactics, geofencing, and beaconing. In geofencing ads are served to people using smartphones when they enter a specific area. Beaconing is a strategy for placing Bluetooth devices around retail areas to signal a phone, open a relevant app, and provide the user with information.

Transit Advertising

the advertiser's message regardless of the market. Additional advances include the use of LED technology on billboards. Because LED screens can change instantly, advertisers can connect better with consumers by displaying up-to-the minute messages that can be fine-tuned or updated depending on the time of day.[14]

Exciting new technologies may change the future of how we "see" outdoor and other out-of-home ads. TeamOne launched a revolutionary campaign for Lexus that included a full-size hologram of the new IS sedan. Using interactive kiosks located in Times Square and other prime U.S. locations, the display featured a hologram of the Lexus in motion and touch pads that allowed visitors to change the car's color and other features.[15] This opens up many thrilling possibilities for advertisers: Imagine a bulletin-size structure on the highway promoting the latest Batman film, with a larger-than-life superhero coming at you in 3-D.

The newest entry into OOH advertising is **location-based advertising**. Location-based advertising, at the broadest level, is targeting audiences within well-defined geographical boundaries with messages that are highly relevant in those areas. **Geofencing** takes this notion one step further by taking advantage of technologies such as smartphones that can be identified and communicated with via Bluetooth or other localized transmitting devices. Social media companies use geofencing to serve ads when consumers are close to advertisers. The idea is simple: Because people are on their phones throughout the day, why not capture their attention with an offer or service that is close by? So, for example, a person walking near a Starbucks might find a coupon for a latte in his or her news feed. Facebook, not to be outdone, is already distributing technologies to companies that will make it easy to do.

Regulation of Outdoor Advertising

The Highway Beautification Act of 1965 controls outdoor advertising on U.S. interstate highways and other federally subsidized highways. It was enacted partly in response to consumer complaints that outdoor advertising was spoiling the environment. Over 700,000 billboards were removed by 1991, the year Congress banned the construction of new billboards on all scenic portions of interstate highways.[16] Since that time, the image of outdoor advertising has improved dramatically, and most people polled say they like billboards, believe they promote business, and find them useful travel information for drivers.[17]

Each state also regulates, administers, and enforces outdoor advertising permit programs through its department of transportation. Some states (Maine, Vermont, Hawaii, and Alaska) prohibit billboards altogether. Ironically, though, some of these states use outdoor advertising themselves in other states to promote tourism (see Ethics, Diversity & Inclusion).

When Campbell Soup started advertising in 1910, the company spent its first $5,000 placing ads on one-third of the buses in New York City for one year. The ads were so successful that after only six months, Campbell enlarged the contract to include all surface vehicles in the city. People started trying more Campbell's and soon sales were up 100 percent. For the next 12 years, transit advertising was the only medium Campbell employed. Today, Campbell is still a major user of transit advertising.

Transit advertising is a category of out-of-home media that includes bus and taxicab advertising as well as posters at transit shelters, terminals, and subways. Although transit is not considered a major medium by most advertising practitioners, standardization, better research, more statistical data, and measured circulation have made transit advertising more attractive to national advertisers. Other advantages of transit include its attention-grabbing power, its unique audience, and advertiser options for the size and location of the ad.[20]

Transit advertising is a cost-effective way for marketers to reach a large audience of people. Buses and taxis provide high ad exposure by traversing the busiest streets of a city many times a day. A 1-800-Flowers.com campaign promoting the company's specialty bouquets featured ads on buses, on subway stations, and in other urban locations. The company's sales were seven times higher in markets where the outdoor campaign ran.[21]

Transit advertising is equally popular with local advertisers. Retailers can expand their reach inexpensively and often receive co-op support from national marketers, which thrive on the local exposure.[22]

Ethics, Diversity & Inclusion

Does Spillover Need Mopping Up?

When laws and self-regulatory efforts banished products like tobacco and hard liquor from the airwaves, many brands moved their budgets to OOH. The rub, however, is that OOH advertising may be the most difficult medium for restricting audience exposure. In fact, it is virtually impossible to shield minors from being exposed to such advertising due to the *spillover* nature of OOH. The ethical issues involved with spillover media are complex, including the kind of advertising appeals used to target audiences.

Today it is not uncommon to find sexually explicit ads, especially in dense urban areas. The Out of Home Advertising Association of America's (OAAA) Code of Principles says that they "support the right to reject advertising that is misleading, offensive, or otherwise incompatible with community standards."[18] But it is unknown how often this clause is invoked. Indeed, when the Los Angeles City Council passed an ordinance prohibiting alcohol ads on virtually all publicly visible sites, even store windows, the OAAA, and other local Los Angeles trade associations filed a federal civil rights action, claiming that the ordinance violates the the First Amendment.

As technology advances, so do the venues for advertising. Taxicabs and buses have carried ads for years; however, now appearing on Boston cabs are electronic billboards that have the ability to change their message minute by minute—depending on a few desired variables. Using a satellite feed and wireless internet links, messages change depending on time of day and location. Different neighborhoods see different ads and, if appropriate, even different languages. The taxi's location is monitored by an internet link to a satellite tracking system. This new technology is inexpensive for advertisers and may become a common feature in taxicabs across America. However, it raises legal and ethical questions. Should mobile billboards be subjected to the same restrictions as stationary billboards? Neighborhoods and schools may theoretically be protected from unwanted advertising, but can concerned parents protect their children from viewing advertising that travels on taxis? While the increasing prevalence of Uber and Lyft may change the game for now, does anyone doubt that these private cars may one day also generate revenue from ads?

Spillover also reaches children in other media vehicles besides out-of-home. Films, for example, consistently show people smoking. And if the smoker is a celebrity, an impressionable child might interpret that as an endorsement. In a study conducted by Dartmouth Medical School, researchers found that actor endorsements of tobacco brands jumped tenfold in the 1990s. The study also found that 87 percent of popular movies contain tobacco use and about one-third display identifiable brand-name logos. Minors make up a large percentage of moviegoers, and through movies they may be getting more exposure to smoking endorsements than in real life. Young people who look up to sport stars and movie celebrities may be vulnerable to intentional and unintentional endorsements. Benedict Carey of the *Los Angeles Times* calls today's movies "almost as smoke-laden as the stock car racing circuit."[19]

Many people think that ads are not to blame for social problems like teen sexual activity and tobacco and alcohol use. Others believe that advertisers have a greater responsibility to separate youth from the adult world of unhealthy and explicit activity. Regardless of who is right, advertisers, agencies, and media companies must be sensitive to public opinion and seek creative solutions to protect impressionable children. Otherwise, the industry will risk severe restriction and regulation for having failed to responsibly and conscientiously assert firm ethical standards itself.

Questions

1. Do you believe the goal of protecting children justifies banning advertising for legal products? Which products specifically?

2. Should ads in spillover media be censored for sexually explicit content or other objectionable content? If so, who should the censors be and what specifically should they prohibit?

3. What alternatives might be available to fight teenage smoking, drinking, and risky sexual practices besides banning advertising for legal adult products?

Types of Transit Advertising

Transit advertising targets the millions of people who use commercial transportation (buses, subways, elevated trains, commuter trains, trolleys, and airlines), plus pedestrians and car passengers, with a variety of formats: transit shelters; station, platform, and terminal posters; inside cards and outside posters on buses; and taxi exteriors.

Transit Shelters   In cities with mass-transit systems, advertisers can buy space on bus shelters and on the backs of bus-stop seats. **Transit shelter advertising** is a relatively new out-of-home form enjoying great success. It reaches virtually everyone who is outdoors: auto passengers, pedestrians, bus riders, motorcyclists, bicyclists, and more. It is extremely inexpensive and available in many communities that restrict billboard advertising in business or residential areas. In fact, shelter advertising is sometimes the only form of outdoor advertising permitted.

Outdoor advertising doesn't consist of billboards only. Creative transit ads can leverage the characteristics of vehicles to highlight a product feature or benefit. This Dr. Best's transit ad uses the door to call attention to the flexible brush.

Source: GlaxoSmithKline

It's also an excellent complement to outdoor posters and bulletins, enabling total market coverage in a comprehensive outdoor program.

Terminal Posters   In many bus, subway, and commuter train stations, space is sold for one-, two-, and three-sheet **terminal posters.** Major train and airline terminals offer such special advertising forms as floor displays, island showcases, illuminated cards, dioramas (3-D scenes), and clocks with special lighting and moving messages.

In Paris, Nike made a splash at the French Open tennis tournament even though a competitor had locked up advertising rights within the stadium. Nike covered the city by buying space on some 2,500 buses during the tournament. As the coup de grace, it bought up every bit of signage space at the Porte d'Auteuil metro (subway) station close to the stadium and turned it into a Nike gallery of terminal posters featuring famous tennis players from around the world.[23]

Inside and Outside Cards and Posters   The **inside card** is placed above the seats and luggage area in a wall rack. Cost-conscious advertisers print both sides of the card so it can be reversed to change the message, saving on paper and shipping charges. Inside **car-end posters** (in bulkhead positions) are usually larger than inside cards, but sizes vary. The end and side positions carry premium rates.

Outside posters are printed on high-grade cardboard and often varnished for weather resistance. The most widely used outside posters are on the side, rear, and front of a bus.

Advertisers may also buy space on **taxicab exteriors,** generally for periods of 30 days, to display internally illuminated, two-sided posters positioned on the roofs. Some advertising also appears on the doors or rear of taxicabs. In some major areas, sponsors can buy cards mounted on the trunks. In Southern California, advertisers can rent cards mounted on the tops of cabs that travel throughout Los Angeles, Orange, and San Diego counties, serving major airports and traveling the busiest freeways in the country. Costing from $110 to $130 per month per cab, this is a very cost-effective way to reach the mobile public.

Buying Transit Advertising

The unit of purchase is a **showing,** also known as a *run* or *service.* A **full showing** (or *No. 100 showing*) means that one card will appear in each vehicle in the system. Space may also be purchased as a *half* (No. 50) or *quarter* (No. 25) *showing.*

Rates are usually quoted for 30-day showings, with discounts for 3-, 6-, 9-, and 12-month contracts. Advertisers supply the cards at their own expense, but the transit company can help with design and production.

Cost depends on the length and saturation of the showing and the size of the space. Rates vary extensively, depending primarily on the size of the transit system. Advertisers get rates for specific markets from local transit companies.

Special Inside Buys   In some cities, advertisers gain complete domination by buying the **basic bus**—all the inside space on a group of buses. For an extra charge, pads of business reply cards or coupons (called **take-ones**) can be affixed to interior ads for passengers to request more detailed information, send in application blanks, or receive some other benefit.

Special Outside Buys   Some transit companies offer **bus-o-rama signs,** jumbo full-color transparencies backlighted by fluorescent tubes and running the length of the bus. A bus has two bus-o-rama positions, one on each side. A single advertiser may also buy a **total bus**—all the exterior space, including the front, rear, sides, and top.

Compelling visuals help ads attract attention. In this ad, placed on the side of a taxi, the driver actually becomes part of the message.

Tom Gilks/Alamy Stock Photo

My IMC Campaign 16–A

Using Out-of-Home, Exhibitive, and Supplementary Media

Go to Google.com and do an image search for the keyword phrase "creative outdoor advertising" and you will most likely see some of the most outrageous and ingenious advertisements in the world. Because most other media are set to standards that deal with time and space delivered in a linear programming mechanism (think TV, radio, and print), rather than just space, creativity is restricted to what can be construed in that limited window. Out-of-home (OOH), on the other hand, is typically constrained only by space, and even then most creative OOH placements end up breaking out of their dimensional boxes.

Planning for OOH can be challenging and fun. Marshall McLuhan coined the phrase "the medium is the message," suggesting that the medium embeds itself in the message, affecting how the message is interpreted. In no other medium is this truer than OOH; in fact, the best ads have little to no copy and rely on the medium to do the heavy lifting of communicating.

The major limitations to OOH center on the fact that because you are dealing with physical real estate, exposure is limited to the geographical location of the ad. If people do not pass by your billboard or ride public transportation, they won't see your message. So most advertisers weigh the reach restrictions and focus their OOH efforts in a handful of important markets. For instance, there is no reason a surfboard company should be advertising in Kansas City, Missouri, but it would be appropriate to choose San Diego, Los Angeles, Miami, and the like. Sometimes the decision to use OOH actually comes down to a strategic decision in which an advertiser would rather focus on quality impressions rather than volume or quantity of impressions.

As you come up with your IMC campaigns, think of how you might be able to represent the message in a clever way in OOH. But also remember that to build your plan, you will have to consider these factors:

- What types of OOH make the most sense for my brand? If the medium is the message, what does it say to my consumer if I am advertising on billboards versus bus shelters versus inside bars?
- In which cities will I be advertising?
- How does this fit with the other media that I am choosing?
- Am I getting enough reach, or is OOH going to be my main reach driver?

Another thing to consider is how the digital revolution is affecting OOH advertising. Today, through companies like Captivate Network, National Outdoor Media, Rich Media Group, and Clear Channel Outdoor, an advertiser can run a national OOH campaign on video displays that exist in coffee shops, gas stations, doctors' offices, office buildings, restaurant juke boxes, elevators, and even airports, all from the comfort of their digital device. By delivering a digitized version of a video advertisement, advertisers can deliver the ads to their thousands of displays reaching people in a variety of different ways. This is a great way for advertisers to extend their TV campaigns and possibly gain a bit more reach at a much lower cost.

If you are planning to have a TV spot for your campaign, don't forget to leverage all the different ways that you can syndicate that spot. The 30-second spot has been set free from the lonely confines of the TV set.

Last, don't limit yourself to traditional ways of thinking. Media can be derived from a number of things. In one case study from Initiative Media, tune-in messages for a new fall show on CBS were stamped onto eggs so that people received an ad impression when they opened the cartons at the store. You have probably heard of the phrase "location, location, location," and in no other medium is that more of a mantra.

For years, New York subways have been running **brand trains,** which include all the subway cars in a particular corridor. However, with the July 2004 opening of its monorail system, the city of Las Vegas has taken the concept further. The glitz of the city's strip extends to its public transportation: Each of the nine monorail trains and seven stations has a corporate sponsor, and many feature elaborate **immersive advertising** themes. City officials banked on the monorail system, which is entirely funded by passenger fares and sponsorship instead of tax dollars, to generate at least $6.5 million annually in advertising revenue. Things started promisingly when a deal was struck with Nextel (now part of Sprint), for an estimated $50 million. But while the company signed on for a 12-year sponsorship of the system's "crown jewel," the main station at the Las Vegas Convention Center, it cancelled the sponsorship after only five years. The system subsequently filed for bankruptcy protection.[24] See My IMC Campaign 16–A to better understand how to choose from all the various forms of transit and other outdoor advertising.

The final messaging point prior to purchase occurs when the consumer encounters the product. Smart companies invest in packaging that embellishes the brand's image. Infuzions uses a colorful display of the fresh fruits that comprise its key ingredients. Meiji uses an artful layout that conveys what the Japanese call shibui, or subtle, harmonious beauty.

Source: (left): Infuzions, Ltd and Parker Williams; (right): Meiji

Exhibitive Media

Some media are designed specifically to help bring customers eyeball-to-eyeball with the product—often at the point of sale or close to it. These **exhibitive media** include *product packaging* and *trade-show booths and exhibits.* When successful, the synergy of combining exhibitive media with other media can improve product or brand awareness by as much as 500 percent.[25]

Product Packaging

In 2018, one estimate suggests global companies spent close to $975 billion on packaging.[26] Because upward of 70 percent of all buying decisions are made at the point of purchase, packages play a major role in both advertising and selling. And in the world of integrated marketing communications, the package is not only the last "ad" a consumer sees before purchasing the product; it is the only "ad" the consumer sees when using the product. So it is more than just another *planned message.* Packaging influences the *product message* as well because (as we discussed in Chapter 6) it is often an intrinsic aspect of the basic product concept. Perhaps this is why, according to a 2018 survey, most brand owners planned to spend more on packaging. Additional findings from the survey suggest that many brand managers are adopting more sustainable packaging and 80 percent agree that packaging is critical to their brand's success.[27]

Packaging encompasses the physical appearance of the container and includes design, color, shape, labeling, and materials. Packaging serves marketers in four major ways: protection, preservation, information, and promotion.[28] Although the protection and preservation aspects reduce the costly effects of damage, pilferage, and spoilage, the importance of packaging as an informational and promotional tool cannot be underestimated. An attractive package can create an immediate relationship with the customer, influence in-store shopping decisions, help set the product apart from competitors, and inform customers of the product's features and benefits.

Designers consider three factors: the package's stand-out appeal, how it communicates verbally and nonverbally, and the prestige or image desired.

Consumers have their own desires with respect to packaging (see Exhibit 16-4), so packaging design can be as important as advertising in building a product's brand image. Packaging establishes or reinforces the brand's personality at the point of sale. So if status is the goal, the package designer must consider what consumers regard as prestigious. This is especially important for so-called nonrational products—cosmetics and perfumes, sports accessories, confection gifts, and certain luxury products—in which fantasy, impulsiveness, or mystique may overrule rational choice.

To sell products off the shelf, packages may use shape, color, size, interesting visuals, or even texture to deliver a marketing message, give product information, and indicate

Consumers	Manufacturers	Marketing Intermediaries (Retailers/Wholesalers)	Consumer Advocacy Groups	Government Agencies
Ease (to handle and store)	Sturdiness	Sturdiness (of case and packages)	Package safe to	Free of deception
Convenience	Suppleness	Convenience (of removal)	– Handle	Free of harmful effects to ecology
List of ingredients	Attractiveness	Tamperproof	– Use	Biodegradable
Instructions	Safety (to users and for the product)	Identifiable	Environmentally safe (biodegradability, etc.)	Free of health hazards
Life of product	Cost of	Safety (to users and for the product)	Package free of health hazards	All-around safety
Disposal method	– Materials	Ease of	Self-informative	– Safe to handle
Toll-free phone number for emergencies	– Fabrication	– Storage	– List of ingredients	– Safe to use
Performance guarantees	– Labor	– Shelving stocking	– Instructions	Labeled properly
Safety guarantees	– Inventory	– Package stacking	– Disposal method	– List of ingredients
Environmental safety (biodegradability)	– Shipping	– Inventory (by computer)	– Toll-free phone number for emergencies	– Nutritional facts with guidelines
Reusable	– Storage	Room for price	– Warranties	Expiration date for certain products
Recyclable	Need to change	Stickers	– Expiration date	Recyclable
	Lighter weight (with safety)		Recyclable	Adherence to federal and local regulations
	Tamperproof		Adherence to federal and local regulations	
	Package size (promotion space versus materials cost and environmental safety)			
	Availability of materials			

Exhibit 16-4
Expectations and concerns in packaging development.

Source: W. Wossen Kassage and Dharmendra Verma, "Balancing Traditional Packaging Functions with the New 'Green Packaging Concerns,'" *SAM Advanced Management Journal* 57, no. 4 (Autumn 1992), pp. 15–23, 29.

application. After they are purchased, packages continue promoting the product in the home, reinforcing the brand's image, so they should open and close with minimal effort and be easy to handle.

Buying packaging includes two major phases: *concept* and *production.* The *conceptual process* involves input from five major groups: consumers, manufacturers, marketing intermediaries, consumer advocacy groups, and government agencies.[29] The conflicting concerns of these groups strongly influence the nature and the cost of packaging (see Exhibit 16-4).

Environmental Issues in Packaging

As manufacturers continue to produce environmentally safe packaging, the marketer's cost of materials rises. And what some consumers expect from *green packaging* is not necessarily what manufacturers traditionally offer or what marketing intermediaries prefer to use.[30]

With the public's growing concern for the environment, especially in international markets, recyclable tin-coated steel and aluminum packages are enjoying a resurgence in popularity. Because European countries are so densely populated, their regulations requiring environmentally friendly packaging are far more stringent than in North America. Marketers need to take this into consideration because such regulations add to the cost of doing business overseas.

Government Impact on Packaging

Government agencies also affect package design. The Food and Drug Administration (FDA), for example, and the Nutrition Labeling and Education Act of 1990 (which went into effect in 1994) imposed stricter labeling requirements for nutrition and health products. And sometimes a state's packaging requirements differ from the federal government's, adding even more complexity for manufacturers.

Package Manufacturing

Packages may come in many forms: wrappers, cartons, boxes, crates, cans, bottles, jars, tubes, barrels, drums, and pallets. And they may be constructed of many materials, from paper and steel ("tin" cans) to wood, glass, and burlap. Newer packaging materials include

Bags aren't simply for carrying purchased goods. Savvy marketers have realized that shoppers frequently carry their bags all day and that well-designed bags can be an efficient and productive use of a marketing budget.

SMXRF/Star Max/GC Image/Getty Images

plastic-coated papers, ceramics, metal foils, and even straw. The plastic film pouch for food products has become a substitute for tin cans and is more flexible, light, and compact. For pharmaceutical products, consumers prefer plastic containers.[31]

The second phase of packaging, the *production process,* may require the use of many packaging specialists: experts in package engineering (box designers, packaging materials consultants, and specialists in equipment configuration), graphic artists (designers, production/computer artists, illustrators, and photographers), label producers (printers and label manufacturers), die-cutters for custom packages, and package warehousing companies (wholesalers of prefabricated packages and package manufacturers).

Ad agencies are not usually involved in packaging decisions. This is typically the realm of specialists. However, it's not uncommon for an agency to be consulted on the design of labels and packages, and some may even prepare the copy that goes on them. In an IMC program, the agency can be very helpful in coordinating this work with the overall theme of the ad campaign.

Generally, the package's design should be kept simple for three reasons: Typical packaging materials (such as corrugated cardboard) cannot support high-resolution printing, intricate folding and die-cutting can be very expensive, and packaging that requires exact folding and fitting often creates excessive assembly costs and leads to structural challenges that most cost-effective packaging materials cannot support.[32]

Knowing When a Package Should Change

There are many reasons to change a package: product alteration or improvement, substitution in packaging materials, competitive pressure, environmental concerns, changes in legislation, the need to preserve product safety or freshness, the need to prevent damage, and the need to increase brand recognition.[33]

Packages are changed as parts of continual brand updating efforts too. Brands change products, logos, colors, and slogans in an effort to stay fresh and relevant. As a result, advertisers spend millions researching and promoting new images. And packages have to reflect a contemporary brand image consistent with constantly changing consumer perceptions and desires. However, marketers should always exercise caution. Designers often change packaging very gradually to avoid confusing consumers.

Coca-Cola, often thought of as a fairly traditional brand, has made many changes to its famous bottle. The image on the left, from the early 1900s, shows the famous Coke logo but not the red and white coloring that are so iconic. The image on the right is Coke's PET bottle, made from 30 percent plant material and introduced in 2009.

Source: The Coca-Cola Company

Want to stand out from the rest of the booths at a trade show? This unique interactive experience, sponsored by Volkswagen, helps people experience the company's brands with zero risk of an accident.

Kobby Dagan/VW PICS/UIG/Getty Images

Trade-Show Booths and Exhibits

Every major industry sponsors annual **trade shows**—exhibitions where manufacturers, dealers, and buyers get together for demonstrations and discussion. More than 14,000 industrial, scientific, and medical shows are held in the United States and Canada each year, and many companies exhibit at more than one show. Trade shows are also very important for global marketers because they may be the only place where an advertiser can meet the company's major international prospects at one time. Moreover, some of the world's largest trade shows (e.g., the Paris Air Show) are held overseas.

The construction of trade-show **booths** and **exhibits** has become a major factor in sales promotion plans. To stop traffic, a booth must be simple and attractive and have good lighting and a large visual. It should also provide a comfortable atmosphere to promote conversation between salespeople and prospects. Many regular trade-show exhibitors use state-of-the-art technology, such as holograms, fiber optics, and interactive computer systems to communicate product features quickly and dramatically.

When establishing an exhibit booth program, managers should consider planning, budgeting, promotion, people, and productivity.[34]

Planning

Planning pivots on four major areas: the budget, the image of the company or brand, the frequency of the shows, and the flexibility of booth configuration.[35] In planning the actual exhibits or trade-show booths, advertisers need to consider numerous factors: size and location of space; desired image or impression of the exhibit; complexities of shipping, installation, and dismantling; number of products to be displayed; need for storage and distribution of literature; use of preshow advertising and promotion; and the cost of all these factors.

Budgeting

Trade shows are expensive, and costs have increased substantially in the last decade. A large company may spend $1 million or more on a booth for one trade show. With staffers' travel, living, and salary expenses added to booth costs and preshow promotion, the cost per visitor reached rises to more than $195.[36] Despite the expense, trade shows can still be a cost-effective way to reach sales prospects, especially if the trade show visitors are key decision makers for large purchases.

Budgeting for trade shows and a booth may require an extensive review of more than 60 factors.

Promotion

To build traffic for a trade-show booth or exhibit, marketers send out personal invitations, conduct direct-mail campaigns, place ads in trade publications, issue news releases, and perform telemarketing. The pie chart in Exhibit 16-5 portrays how customers typically learn about the trade shows they attend.[37]

At the show itself, activities at the booth and promotional materials (handouts, brochures, giveaway specialty items, raffles) can stimulate customer interest and improve product exposure. 3M's Telcomm Products Division mailed 6,000 potential show attendees a Pony Express theme folder that invited them to pick up a trail map at the booth. The map guided the visitors (Pony Express riders) through a series of stations shared by seven product groups within the huge booth. Once the visitors' maps had been stamped at each station, they were given a "pay envelope" containing replicas of 1850 coins and vouchers redeemable for merchandise awards.[38]

Exhibit 16-5

How do customers learn about trade shows?

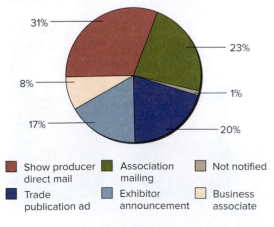

- 31%
- 23%
- 8%
- 1%
- 17%
- 20%

Legend:
- Show producer direct mail
- Association mailing
- Not notified
- Trade publication ad
- Exhibitor announcement
- Business associate

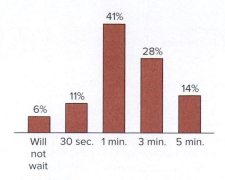

Exhibit 16-6

How long a visitor will wait for a sales rep at a trade-show booth.

Source: INCOMM Research.

People

The company representatives staffing the booth personify the kind of service the customer can expect to receive. They should be articulate, people-oriented, enthusiastic, knowledgeable about the product, and empathetic listeners.[39]

The primary goal of a trade-show booth is to meet with qualified prospects face-to-face. However, research shows that 58 percent of the people visiting a booth will not wait more than one minute to meet a representative (see Exhibit 16-6). Ideally, 80 percent of the salesperson's time should be spent listening and 20 percent talking.[40]

Productivity

A company's trade-show effort may be wasted if prospects' names are not collected and organized properly. Each lead should be evaluated as to the prospect's readiness to receive another contact (A = now; B = 2 weeks; C = 6 months; D = never).[41] The resulting lead list is the link to future sales and augments the company's prospect database.

Supplementary Media

Many promotional media are difficult to classify because they are tailored to individual needs. Such supplementary media include specialty advertising, directories and Yellow Pages, and a variety of emerging alternative media vehicles.

Specialty Advertising

LO **16-8**

The Promotional Products Association International (PPAI) defines an **advertising specialty** as a promotional product, usually imprinted with an advertiser's name, message, or logo, that is distributed free as part of a marketing communications program.[42] Today, nearly every business uses advertising specialties of some sort. As many as 15,000 different specialty items, ranging from coffee mugs to ballpoint pens, key chains, and T-shirts, represent an annual volume of more than $17.0 billion.[43]

An advertising specialty is different from a premium. **Premiums** are also promotional products; they are typically more valuable and usually bear no advertising message. However, to get a premium, recipients must buy a product, send in a coupon, witness a demonstration, or perform some other action advantageous to the advertiser. An advertising specialty, on the other hand, is always given *free* as a goodwill item. Some specialty items may be kept for years and serve as continuous, friendly reminders of the advertiser's business. Companies often spend substantial sums for goodwill items to promote their businesses, and studies indicate that this investment pays off: An extensive survey conducted by L. J. Market Research found that promotional items produced higher product recall than print ads. More than 75 percent of respondents could recall the name of the advertiser on a promotional item from the past year, but only 53 percent could name an advertiser in a print publication from the last week.[44]

Business-to-Business Specialties

In the business-to-business arena, companies use more structured specialty promotions to improve their goodwill standing over competitors. Over half of those surveyed in the L. J. Market Research study claimed their impression of the promotional-product advertiser was "somewhat" or "significantly" more favorable after they had received the item.[45]

The dollar amount spent on each promotional item may be less important than the sponsorship itself. In one test, a group of Realtors received a $1.49 ballpoint pen imprinted with a mortgage company's name, a second group received a $10 sports bag (also imprinted), and a third group got nothing. In a follow-up questionnaire, Realtors who received nothing were least inclined to recommend the product, but both the sports bag and ballpoint pen groups responded equally

Advertisers use specialty products as gifts to consumers. When consumers keep the specialty, the brand is exposed on a regular basis and the gift generates positive feelings.

Anthony Pidgeon/Getty Images

People BEHIND the Ads

Cliff Marks, CineMedia

Courtesy of Cliff Marks

For quite a while now, if you've arrived at a movie theater a bit early, instead of staring at a blank screen or a curtain, you've been able to watch branded entertainment while waiting for the show to start.

The man behind the "pre-movie" showings is Clifford ("Cliff") Marks, president of sales and marketing at National CineMedia (NCM).

The idea that consumers waiting to see a film might actually enjoy polished, entertaining advertising content seems so sensible that you might wonder why it hasn't been tried before, especially when you consider the power of the movie theater: big screens, high-definition content, Dolby sound systems, and zero distractions. But the truth is, the logistics of making the thousands of screens in U.S. theaters available to advertisers are more difficult than they might seem at first blush.

Marks and NCM found a way to make it happen. Using agreements with large theater chains such as the Regal Entertainment Group, Marks and his company introduced *The 2wenty,* a digitally transmitted entertainment and advertising pre-feature program. *The 2wenty* featured both traditional (30-second) and longer-format ads that placed a premium on entertainment value. Audiences were happy to have something to watch while waiting for the film to begin, and advertisers were thrilled to be getting an audience that could not be reached as efficiently in any other medium—making it a win-win situation.

The successor to the *2wenty* is *FirstLook. FirstLook* takes pre-movie advertising to an even higher level, providing advertisers with bundled offerings of on-screen and lobby marketing products that provide multiple ways to interact with theater goers. Using digital transmission, NCM can target advertising and content to specific auditoriums and lobby areas within a network of more than 1,600 network affiliate movie theaters, including over 20,150 digital screens nationally. In 2015, NCM estimates that its programming reached approximately 700 million movie patrons.

Before creating these innovative cinema programs, Marks served as president of sales and marketing with Regal Entertainment Group's media subsidiary, Regal CineMedia Corporation. Before joining NCM Marks was a 14-year veteran of ESPN/ABC Sports, where as senior vice president, he oversaw its $2 billion sales organization. Working with top national advertisers such as Anheuser Busch, Circuit City, MCI, Toyota, AT&T, Pizza Hut, Taco Bell, and KFC, Marks was instrumental in developing vertically integrated advertising packages for clients across multiple platforms including ABC Sports programming, ESPN, ESPN2, ESPN Classic, ESPNews, ESPN.com, *ESPN Magazine,* ESPN radio, and ESPNZone restaurants.

Cliff Marks shared some of his thoughts about cinema advertising with *Contemporary Advertising.*

CA: *How was the idea for nationwide cinema advertising born?*

CM: It was born in Europe many years ago, primarily as a result of the lack of advertising in European TV. While North America has always had a very mature commercial television industry and Americans have grown up with commercials being a staple of their television experience, the same is not true in Europe, where government-owned broadcast stations were created to be noncommercial "public service" programmers. The cinema became the place where marketers could communicate with consumers using the big screen to market to captive audiences who are entertainment focused and receptive to messaging portrayed in an entertaining and respectful way.

CA: *When you speak with advertisers, how do you distinguish the opportunities they can get from cinema advertising from other channels, especially other out-of-home?*

CM: We explain that cinema has the best elements of out-of-home and broadcast television, a unique combination of sight, sound, and motion. Unlike most out-of-home, advertisers can reach a national audience—it has scale. Plus, there is NO MIGA

positively. Evidently, gift recipients felt obliged to reciprocate, but the value of the gift was not crucial. So the $1.49 pen was the better return on investment.[46]

Inappropriate specialty items can backfire no matter what the cost. A recipient may perceive an overly expensive gift as a form of bribery, yet a cheap trinket could make a quality-conscious business look cheap. Finally, marketers should realize that the value and nature of gifts may raise ethical issues.

Emerging Opportunities for OOH

As traditional advertising media become more expensive and audiences become more fragmented, many advertisers seek new ways to reach their customers. Several types of

(Make It Go Away) device for consumers to avoid the commercials. Cinema has much in common with television; for example, it is a scalable national medium with touch points in every major market in America and can be bought nationally, regionally, or locally. Cinema has also invested in digital satellite delivery technology allowing marketers to target specific messages in any way they desire. A brand may target by market, by region, by film rating (PG/PG 13/R), or by film genre—comedy, suspense, horror, romance or chick flicks, guy films, kid films, etc. . . . The investment in digitizing America's movie theaters has changed the advertising landscape forever as marketers are now empowered to hyper-target their audiences with no additional cost to the marketer. This makes cinema in many ways more valuable than broadcast.

Cinema is primarily sold to national marketers as a complement to national broadcast. We tell advertisers that cinema is itself just another network. Of course, cinema's affiliates are not TV stations, but movie theaters. But that's really where the network model difference ends. We also stress the unique aspects of cinema, which include a 40-foot screen, complete attention captivity, digital targeting ability, lobby and other sampling and consumer-centric assets, and a reasonable barrier to entry making new competitors unlikely.

CA: How do you do market research on cinema advertising? What does it tell you about your audience?

CM: Our research is generally comparable to other media, allowing for some direct apples-to-apples comparisons. Of course, cinema has the luxury of knowing exactly how many people attend a film as they share the revenue with their studio partners and must account for every single ticket sold. There is a lot of syndicated research on the movies and the kinds of people that attend different genres. The research shows that cinema casts a pretty wide net—we reach everybody from 4-year-olds to 84-year-olds, depending on the kind and rating genre. Cinema's sweet spot is 12–34-year-olds, as this audience is more likely to see a film several times, and most likely to go over six times per year. They are the "heavy users."

CA: What is the future of cinema advertising? How will it evolve?

CM: Cinema advertising has grown by strong double digits every year since 2002 and the future is very bright. Cinema will evolve to compete with both network TV and spot TV for both national and local funds. We've invested heavily in digital technologies, which allow advertisers to carve up the network and target specific kinds of audiences or specific markets. These technologies make cinema a highly targetable medium with mass scale.

Advertisers will view cinema the same way they view TV networks. If you look at an NCM *FirstLook* program prior to the movies, it fits this definition because it plays on over 17,000 screens throughout the United States.

One other interesting development in the evolution of cinema advertising is alternative content, which is played over the digital screens when movies are not the predominant product. We have seen various events like music concerts, opera, sports, and other specialty events make their big screen debut with varying degrees of success. This model will be perfected and the cinema will become a common venue to view alternative content over an HD satellite network.

CA: Which advertisers seem most interested in cinema? My impression is that many of the advertisers are TV networks. What do they like about cinema?

CM: Most brands that take advantage of cinema make highly entertaining, brand-image advertising. Cinema is less strong with very retail-centric ads, ads that have an immediate call to action. One thing all advertisers know is that there are no refrigerators, computers, phones, changing the baby, using the men's room, and, of course, no remote controls or TiVo machines and other common distractions that affect advertising on television.

CA: Any other thoughts about the future of this exciting new advertising medium?

CM: The world is changing a lot and I would suspect that many more companies are going to reevaluate their media options in the coming years. I do not think that networks will go away. They are still a reasonably good deal for marketers as they still sell their time at a reasonable price (especially cable nets). But cinema stands to be one of the big winners (certainly not the only big winner!) as other digital networks that offer scale, sight, sound, motion, and measurability will help marketers reach their designated target audiences.

Courtesy of Cliff Marks.

alternative opportunities are now viable options, including cinema advertising, new locations, augmented reality advertising, target and retarget digital advertising, programmatic advertising, mobile billboards and display panels.

Cinema Advertising

Advertising in movie theaters (**cinema advertising**) is a growing but controversial practice. Although some movie-going audiences resent watching ads, cinema advertising is becoming more and more attractive to marketers. "Unlike traditional media, we don't have to

Product placement *is an increasingly popular way to advertise consumer products. For product placement to work, the brand must be prominent, identifiable, and credible in the context. If you see a prominent car brand in a film or TV series it is highly likely it's been sponsored.*

Walt Disney Studios Motion Pictures/Photofest

Congress removed a long-standing ban on advertisements appearing on stamps, opening the doors to yet another subtle form of media to influence and persuade consumers.

Source: Stamps.com

Digital technologies are revolutionizing many media forms, including jukebox screens. The vast number of such machines guarantees advertiser interest.

Source: TouchTunes

fight for our audience's attention; they don't flip channels," says Bob Martin, president and chair of the Cinema Advertising Council.[47] Cinema advertising grew to a $456 million industry in 2006, up 15 percent from 2005. Nonetheless, some movie theater chains prohibit filmed advertising for fear of offending their audience.

New Locations

OOH ads are invading previously unutilized spaces to present messages in created and unexpected ways. Consumers now regularly encounter advertising on ATM screens, at gas station pumps, in the offices of physicians and dentists, at the supermarket, or in retail and even restaurant spaces. An interesting example is shown in the photo of space reserved on postage stamps. Advertisements can also be found on trucks, and even passenger cars in some cities. For the owners of places where people congregate, advertising means revenue. And for advertisers, it means an opportunity for exposure in an unexpected place.

Augmented Reality Advertising

The use of newer technologies that are available to many consumers has fostered an emerging category of augmented reality. The popular smartphone is now an augmented-reality device in a number of campaigns. Coca-Cola, for example, integrated augmented reality in its Arctic Home Campaign, co-sponsored with the World Wide Fund for Nature. Visitors to London's Science Museum were able to interact with virtual polar bears in an Arctic landscape.

Unsurprisingly, both Google and Facebook are at the fore of augmented reality technology. Google introduced *Google Glass* in 2013. The product faced backlash over privacy concerns and was withdrawn, but was reintroduced in 2017. The device is essentially a pair of glasses that allow for interactive experiences with virtual entities in a native environment. Imagine walking down a street and seeing digitally projected information about the buildings, statues, restaurants, and shops. The promise is an execution as natural and seamless as the "first-down" lines that are digitally projected on your TV screen when you watch an NFL football game.

Target and Retarget Advertising

Combine digital OOH with geofencing technology and suddenly OOH offers advertisers the chance to build frequency by serving outdoor travelers ads in sequence. For example, a consumer who takes a subway ride and sees digital signage for Starbucks in the station can emerge outside and see a large billboard pointing the way to a Starbucks nearby. In other words, someone who sees an ad at one location can be tracked and served related advertising messages throughout the day. Conversely, if the person goes into the Starbucks for a coffee, the digital messages can change to a different brand.

Programmatic Advertising in OOH

We discussed programmatic advertising in Chapter 14, but the technology is not limited to the internet. The introduction of digital OOH means the same use of computers and bidding to purchase audiences on the internet can be used to purchase them OOH. Bidders can customize their buys to leverage different audiences, dayparts, weather conditions, or any of the many circumstances that might be relevant.

Mobile Billboards

The **mobile billboard,** a cross between traditional billboards and transit advertising, was conceived as advertising on the sides of tractor-trailer trucks. Today in some large cities, specially designed flatbed trucks carry long billboards up and down busy thoroughfares. Local routes for mobile ads are also available on delivery trucks in major cities around the U.S.

Display Panels

Display panels display text and graphic messages much like the big screens in sports stadiums. The signs transmit commercial messages to retail stores, where shoppers see them. The stores pay nothing for the signs and receive 25 percent of the advertising revenue. In Montreal, Telecite used its new visual communication network (VCN) technology to install electronic display panels on subway cars. Advertisers got a powerful, inexpensive, and flexible medium with a large, captive audience; the transit authority got a modern, self-financed emergency and public information system; and passengers got something to watch while they rode.[48] Telecite is negotiating with numerous U.S. and European cities to install the systems in their subway and metro cars.

Chapter Summary

Media that reach prospects outside their homes are called out-of-home media. They include outdoor advertising, transit advertising, and exotica like electronic signs and parking meters. Of the major advertising media, outdoor advertising is the least expensive per message delivered. It also offers other attractive features: instant broad coverage (reach), very high frequency, great flexibility, and high impact. Drawbacks include the limits of brief messages, long lead times, high initial preparation costs, and the difficulty of physically inspecting each billboard.

The standardized outdoor advertising industry consists of about 3,000 local and regional plant operators. National advertising makes up the bulk of outdoor business. The three most common forms of outdoor advertising structures are the poster panel, the junior poster, and the bulletin. A form of outdoor available in some cities is the spectacular, an expensive electronic display. The basic unit of sale for outdoor advertising is the 100 showing, or 100 GRPs, which means the message will appear on enough panels to provide a daily exposure equal to the market's total population.

Transit advertising includes transit shelters; station, platform, and terminal posters; inside cards and outside posters on buses; and taxi exteriors. This medium offers high reach, frequency, exposure, and attention values at very low cost. It gives long exposure to the advertiser's message and offers repetitive value and geographic flexibility. In addition, advertisers have a wide choice in the size of space used. But transit advertising does not cover some segments of society. Also, it reaches a nonselective audience, it lacks prestige, and copy is still somewhat limited.

Exhibitive media include product packaging and trade-show booths and exhibits. These media are designed to help bring consumers or business customers eyeball-to-eyeball with the product, often at the point of sale or close to it. Brands are investing more than ever in product packaging in response to the need to keep brands fresh and affect consumer experiences. Every major industry sponsors annual trade shows—exhibitions where manufacturers, dealers, and buyers get together for demonstrations and discussion. Trade shows are also very important for global marketers because they may be the only place where an advertiser can meet the company's major international prospects at one time.

Supplementary media include specialty advertising and emerging media like movie theaters and product placements. Product placement occurs in films, videos, computer games, and the internet. The advantage of film is that it creates brand association with top movies and actors.

Important Terms

advertising specialty, *537*

basic bus, *531*

booth, *536*

brand trains, *532*

bulletin structure, *521*

bus-o-rama sign, *531*

car-end poster, *531*

cinema advertising, *539*

directories, *518*

display panels, *541*

exhibit, *536*

exhibitive media, *533*

Eyes on Impressions (EOI), *523*

full showing, *531*

geofencing, *529*

global positioning system (GPS), *528*

immersive advertising, *532*

inside card, *531*

junior poster, *521*

location-based advertising, *529*

mobile billboard, *540*

100 showing, *522*

out-of-home (OOH) advertising, *518*

outside poster, *531*

packaging, *533*

premium, *537*

product placement, *540*

showing, *531*

spectaculars, *521*

standardized outdoor advertising, *520*

stock poster, *521*

take-ones, *531*

taxicab exterior, *531*

terminal poster, *531*

poster panel, *521*

total bus, *531*

trade show, *536*

transit advertising, *529*

transit shelter advertising, *530*

Review Questions

1. Why is OOH advertising sometimes referred to as the last mass medium?

2. Which advertising objectives are OOH media most suitable for?

3. Is OOH an effective advertising medium for a local political candidate? Why?

4. How do gross rating points for outdoor media differ from GRPs for electronic media?

5. What are the principal categories of transit advertising?

6. What is a brand train and what advantages does it offer over less expensive forms of transit advertising?

7. Which are the exhibitive media and why are they called that?

8. What is the principal benefit of trade shows and exhibitions?

9. How does specialty advertising differ from premiums? How could a local computer store use these media, and which would be better for the store to use?

The Advertising Experience

1. **Using Billboard Advertising**
Upshaw Books, the largest independent bookstore in the area, wants to advertise on billboards along the main commuter route. Create a series of three standard billboards that would grab commuters' attention and motivate them to visit the store.

2. **Outdoor Advertising**
As you have learned in this chapter, out-of-home advertising and communication have been a mainstay in consumers' lives for quite some time. The outdoor advertising industry certainly makes up the largest portion of such advertising.

   Although often overlooked in advertising and media decision making, outdoor advertising can have a powerful effect as a supplemental medium to broader print or broadcast campaigns. To find out more about this side of the advertising business, visit five of the websites for the outdoor advertising organizations listed below and answer the questions that follow.

   - Burkhart Advertising: www.burkhartadv.com
   - Outfront Media: www.outfrontmedia.com
   - Clear Channel Outdoor: www.clearchanneloutdoor.com
   - Kinetic: www.kineticww.com
   - Lamar Outdoor Advertising: www.lamar.com
   - Out of Home Advertising Association of America Inc. (OAAA): www.oaaa.org
   - *SignCraft* magazine: www.signcraft.com
   - SignIndustry.com: www.signindustry.com
   - Wilkins Media Company: www.wilkins-media.com

   a. What organization sponsors the site? Who is (are) the intended audience(s)?
   b. What is the purpose of the site? Does it succeed? Why?
   c. What services (if any) does the organization provide advertisers?
   d. How important do you believe this organization is to outdoor advertising today and in the future? Why?

3. **Specialty Advertising**
Promotional specialty items are, perhaps, one of the oldest forms of media. Though consumers do not always think of these items as "advertising," they most certainly are—being clearly composed, nonpersonal communications by an identified sponsor. Many organizations and firms are involved in specialty advertising and the industry is still growing today. Peruse some of the websites below and learn more about the products, processes, and promotional power of specialty ad items. Then answer the questions that follow.

   - BCG Creations: www.bcgcreations.com
   - Wearables: www.wearables.com
   - Cowan Imaging Group: www.cowan.ca
   - Image Pointe: www.imagepointe.com
   - PromoMart: www.promomart.com
   - PROMO'S: www.coolgifts.com
   - Promotional Products Association International (PPAI): www.ppai.org
   - PromosOnline: www.promosonline.com
   - S-N-T Graphics: www.sntgraphics.com

   a. What is the focus of the organization sponsoring this site?
   b. Who is the intended audience of the site?
   c. What services (if any) does the organization offer?
   d. What is your overall impression of the organization and its work? Explain?

4. Some companies are known for their beautiful packaging. Apple comes to mind. Identify three other brands that enhance the value of their brands by using exceptionally designed packages.

5. If, at the time of the launch of the Corona campaign featured at the start of the chapter, it had decided that a transit medium would have better suited the advertiser's objectives, how would the campaign have been adjusted to meet the needs of this new format?

End Notes

1. James Herring, "Corona Unveil Ocean Plastic Billboard linstallation for #worldoceansday," *PR Examples,* June 8, 2018, www.prexamples.com/2018/06/corona-unveil-ocean-plastic-billboard-installation-for-worldoceansday/.

2. Out of Home Advertising Association of America, "Out of Home Advertising Up 1.2% to $7.7 Billion in 2017," news release, March 22, 2018, https://oaaa.org/StayConnected/NewsArticles/IndustryRevenue/tabid/322/id/5232/Default.aspx.

3. "Introduce Yourself to Outdoor Advertising," Out of Home Advertising Association of America Inc., *www.oaaa.org*.
4. *Billboard Basics* (New York: Outdoor Advertising Association of America, 1994), p. 5.
5. "Historical Revenue," Out of Home Advertising Association of America Inc., *https://oaaa.org/AboutOOH/Factsamp;Figures/HistoricalRevenue.aspx*.
6. Mary Jo Haskey, "The Last Mass Medium," *MediaWeek,* December 6, 1993, p. 17.
7. Mary Jo Haskey, "The Last Mass Medium," *MediaWeek,* December 6, 1993, pp. 11, 21; Kevin Goldman, "Billboards Gain Respect as Spending Increases," *The Wall Street Journal,* June 27, 1994, p. B5.
8. "IBillboard," How Products Are Made, *www.madehow.com/Volume-5/Billboard.html*.
9. Tim Nudd, "13 Brilliant Outdoor Ads That Stopped People in Their Tracks in 2017," *Adweek,* December 14, 2017, *www.adweek.com/creativity/13-brilliant-outdoor-ads-that-stopped-people-in-their-tracks-in-2017/*.
10. Institute of Outdoor Advertising, press release, 1991.
11. Traffic Audit Bureau, "Eyes on—Out-of-Home Media Measurement: The Basics 2009," *www.eyesonrating.com*.
12. "Facts and Figures," OAAA about Outdoor, *www.oaaa.org/outdoor/facts/cpmcomparison.asp*.
13. "Technology Standards," Out of Home Advertising Association of America, *www.oaaa.org/presscenter/technology.asp*.
14. "Technology Standards," Out of Home Advertising Association of America, *www.oaaa.org/presscenter/technology.asp*.
15. Karl Greenberg, "Lexus Accelerates into All Venues in Push for Revamped IS Sedan," *Brandweek,* August 31, 2005, *www.brandweek.com/bw/news/autos/article_display.jsp?vnu_content_id=1001052022*.
16. Cyndee Miller, "Outdoor Advertising Weathers Repeated Attempts to Kill It," *Marketing News,* March 16, 1992, pp. 1, 9; *Billboard Basics* (New York: Outdoor Advertising Association of America, 1994), pp. 15–16.
17. "Surveys Show Americans Like Their Billboards," Outdoor Advertising Association of America, 1997, *www.oaaa.org*.
18. "OAAA Code of Industry Principles," Out of Home Advertising Association of America, *https://oaaa.org/AboutOAAA/WhoWeAre/OAAACodeofIndustryPrinciples.aspx*.
19. Benedict Carey, "Cigarettes Are Doing Big Box Office," *Los Angeles Times,* January 8, 2001.
20. Kathy J. Kobliski, "The Advantages of Transit Advertising," *Entreprenuer*, March 18, 2005, *www.entrepreneur.com/article/76826*
21. Melissa Korn, "Bricks Rivaling Clicks in Ad Spending," *Financial Times,* July 21, 2006, *http://search.ft.com/searchArticle?queryText=1-800-flowers&y=4&javascriptEnabled=true&id=060721008312&x=8*; "Outdoor Grows Online Sales: 1-800-Flowers.com Sales 7 Times Greater in Outdoor Markets," CBS Outdoor, *www.cbsoutdoor.com/news.php*.
22. Riccardo A. Davis, "Retailers Open Doors Wide for Co-op," *Advertising Age,* August 1, 1994, p. 30.
23. "Advertising That Imitates Art," *Adweek,* June 20, 1994, p. 18.
24. Kyle B. Hansen, "Las Vegas Monorail Files for Bankruptcy Protection," *Las Vegas Sun,* January 13, 2010, *https://lasvegassun.com/news/2010/jan/13/las-vegas-monorail-files-bankruptcy-protection/*.
25. *The Point of Purchase Advertising Industry Fact Book* (Englewood, NJ: Point of Purchase Advertising Institute, 1992), p. 51.
26. "Global Packaging Market to Reach $975 Billion by 2018," Smithers Pira, *www.smitherspira.com/news/2013/december/global-packaging-industry-market-growth-to-2018*.
27. Patti Zarling, "Half of Brand Managers Plan to Spend More on Packaging, Survey Finds," *Grocery Dive,* May 16, 2018, *www.grocerydive.com/news/grocery-half-of-brand-managers-plan-to-spend-more-on-packaging-survey-finds/534014/*.
28. W. Wossen Kassaye and Dharmendra Verma, "Balancing Traditional Packaging Functions with the New 'Green' Packaging Concerns," *SAM Advanced Management Journal* 57, no. 4 (Autumn 1992), pp. 15–23.
29. W. Wossen Kassaye and Dharmendra Verma, "Balancing Traditional Packaging Functions with the New 'Green' Packaging Concerns," *SAM Advanced Management Journal* 57, no. 4 (Autumn 1992), pp. 15–23.
30. W. Wossen Kassaye and Dharmendra Verma, "Balancing Traditional Packaging Functions with the New 'Green' Packaging Concerns," *SAM Advanced Management Journal* 57, no. 4 (Autumn 1992), pp. 15–23.
31. Chris Baum, "10th Annual Packaging Consumer Survey 1994: Consumers Want It All—and Now," *Packaging,* August 1994, pp. 40–43.
32. Wayne Robinson, *How'd They Design and Print That?* (Cincinnati, OH: North Light Books, 1991), pp. 74–75.
33. W. Wossen Kassaye and Dharmendra Verma, "Balancing Traditional Packaging Functions with the New 'Green' Packaging Concerns," *SAM Advanced Management Journal* 57, no. 4 (Autumn 1992), pp. 15–23.
34. Susan A. Friedmann, *Exhibiting at Trade Shows* (Menlo Park, CA: Crisp, 1992), p. V.
35. Susan A. Friedmann, *Exhibiting at Trade Shows* (Menlo Park, CA: Crisp, 1992), p. 16.
36. Carla Waldemar, "Show Selection—The Five-Step Shuffle," *Exhibitor Online, www.exhibitoronline.com/topics/article.asp?ID=1220&catID=32*.
37. Susan A. Friedmann, *Exhibiting at Trade Shows* (Menlo Park, CA: Crisp, 1992), p. 24.
38. Susan A. Friedmann, *Exhibiting at Trade Shows* (Menlo Park, CA: Crisp, 1992), pp. 34–39.
39. Susan A. Friedmann, *Exhibiting at Trade Shows* (Menlo Park, CA: Crisp, 1992), p. 44.
40. Susan A. Friedmann, *Exhibiting at Trade Shows* (Menlo Park, CA: Crisp, 1992), pp. 70–71.
41. Susan A. Friedmann, *Exhibiting at Trade Shows* (Menlo Park, CA: Crisp, 1992), p. 90.
42. "Promotional Products Fact Sheet," Promotional Products Association International, Irving, TX, 1995.
43. "Promotional Products Industry in the US," IBIS World, November 18, 2018, *www.ibisworld.com/industry-trends/market-research-reports/professional-scientific-technical-services/professional-scientific-technical-services/promotional-products.html*.
44. Leslie Joseph and Rick Ebel, "Promotional Strategies: Research That Can Put Money in Your Pocket," *www.epromos.com/educationCenter/research.jsp*.
45. Leslie Joseph and Rick Ebel, "Promotional Strategies: Research That Can Put Money in Your Pocket," *www.epromos.com/educationCenter/research.jsp*.
46. Avraham Shama and Jack K. Thompson, "Promotion Gifts: Help or Hindrance?" *Mortgage Banking,* February 1989, pp. 49–51.
47. Shahna Mahmud, "Cinema Ad Revenue up 15 Percent," *Adweek,* October 15, 2007.
48. James Ferrier, "Spotlight on Technology—Telecite," *Advertising Age,* November 22, 1993, p. SS10.

Relationship Building: Direct Marketing, Personal Selling, and Sales Promotion

LEARNING OBJECTIVES

To emphasize the importance of relationships in today's high-tech, overcommunicated world and to demonstrate how marketing communications can be integrated with advertising to manage an organization's relations with its stakeholders. Relationship marketing and IMC are two of the most important trends in marketing today. Direct marketing, personal selling, and sales promotion play different but often overlapping roles in IMC programs. Each offers many opportunities but also has limitations.

After studying this chapter, you will be able to:

LO17-1   Define direct marketing and explain its role in IMC.

LO17-2   Distinguish personal selling from other forms of IMC.

LO17-3   List the activities that constitute sales promotion, including push and pull tactics, and explain their roles in IMC.

Sponsorship is big business in global marketing, especially in the sports world. Famous athletes including Roger Federer, LeBron James, Rory McIlroy, and Kei Nishikori are rewarded with income in the tens of millions of dollars every year for endorsing brands including Nike, Under Armour, adidas, and others. ■ But sports are not the only avenue for sponsorship and, as detailed in Chapter 3, the benefits of big-money sponsorships with celebrities and athletes don't always justify the risk. ■ What if sponsors could leverage an opportunity at venues that attract more visitors than the NHL, more than the NBA, and more than even the NFL? Well, they can, and they can do so in an environment that is about as wholesome and happy as it gets: the four theme parks and two water parks of the Walt Disney World complex. ■ It may seem strange to associate Disney, a powerful global brand, with sponsorship opportunities. In fact, there are many. Consider, for example, Test Track, one of Disney's newest rides, sponsored by and infused with Chevrolet. As guests queue up to take the ride, they can look over concept cars and watch videos of how they were designed.[1] ■ EPCOT (the acronym stands for Experimental Prototype City of Tomorrow) is divided into two halves, one with technology-themed pavilions and the other with nation-related ones. In all cases, the costs of construction and maintenance of these pavilions is to a significant degree borne by sponsors. While details are difficult to come by, one recent article suggested that the newest nation pavilion, thought to be Brazil, will cost almost $450 million, and that sponsorship would cover half of the costs.[2] The national pavilions are falsely thought to be sponsored by the relevant government—while some governments (such as Norway) have contributed funds, both national and technology pavilions primarily rely on corporate sponsors. For example, when EPCOT first opened, the American Adventure was sponsored by American Express and Coca-Cola, while the UK exhibit was funded by Bass Export, Pringle of Scotland, and Royal Doulton.[3] ■ Although sponsorships may be most obvious in EPCOT, they are found throughout the parks. Wondering what the "official phone case" of Disney World might be? The answer is OtterBox. How about the official "timepiece" of both Disney World and Disneyland? Citizen. Does Toy Story Land have a sponsor? It does: Babybel cheese. Participants in the Kidcot experience get to gather cards around the World Showcase that feature Disney characters and information about the pavilion-related nations. The sponsor is Ziploc, which becomes clear when guests are encouraged to store their cards in a special Ziploc bag.[4] ■ Is the whole idea of a sponsorship pretty out of date in a social media world? Hardly. As we suggested in Chapter 13, advertisers are concerned about the measurement of audiences on video screens. By comparison, the measure of a park visitor is pretty straightforward.

Additionally, a theme park visit is an immersive, joyful, and family-centered activity. While social media are pervasive, sponsored tweets have a hard time matching a ride down Space Mountain (sponsored by RCA and FedEx over its history).[5] ■

Throughout the text, we've suggested that the key to building brand equity in the 21st century is the development of interdependent, mutually satisfying relationships with customers and other stakeholders. Further, to benefit from these relationships, companies should consciously (and *conscientiously*) integrate their marketing communications activities with all their other functions so that the messages the marketplace receives about the company are consistent. However, this is a lot easier said than done because everything a company does (and doesn't do) sends a message. Seamless, consistent communication—from every corner of the company—is how a firm earns a good reputation. And that is the principal objective of IMC.

It is important for communications specialists to understand how to integrate the various tools of marketing communications. As they plan a campaign, practitioners need a basic understanding of what other communications tools are available to them and how they can best be used in the overall marketing communications mix. In this chapter, we will discuss the interactive, one-to-one communication tools of direct marketing and personal selling. We'll also look at sales promotion, which might be called the "value-added" tool. In the next chapter, we'll address the "credibility" tools companies use to enhance their reputations. These include various public relations activities, sponsorships, and corporate advertising.

Understanding Direct Marketing

LO 17-1

There is a lot of confusion surrounding the term *direct marketing,* even among the experts.

The ANA (a combination of what was formerly the Direct Marketing Association and the Association of National Advertisers) defines **direct marketing** as "an interactive process of addressable communication that uses one or more advertising media to effect, at any location, a measurable sale, lead, retail purchase or charitable donation, with this activity analyzed on a database for the development of ongoing mutually beneficial relationships between marketers and customers, prospects or donors."[6]

Direct Marketing magazine goes even further: "Direct marketing is a measurable system of marketing that uses one or more advertising media to effect a measurable response and/or transaction at any location, with this activity stored in a database."[7] From this definition, a virtually synonymous term has emerged: **database marketing.** Database marketers build and maintain databases of current and prospective customers (and other stakeholders) and communicate with them using a variety of media (from personal contact to direct mail to mass media). Database marketing is a widely adopted marketing method because it has proven to be a cost-efficient way to increase sales. A good **database** enables marketers to target, segment, and grade customers. It helps them to know who their customers and prospects are, what and when they buy, and how to contact them. That, of course, leads to the possibility of a relationship.

The various definitions of direct marketing share much in common. First and foremost, direct marketing is a *system of marketing* and it is *interactive,* meaning buyers and sellers exchange information with each other directly. A second shared part of the definition is the concept of *one or more advertising media.* Part of the confusion with the name is its similarity to *direct mail.* But direct mail is just one of the many media that direct marketers use.

Consider one effective direct marketer, insurance giant GEICO. While many insurance companies rely on local agencies and personal selling to generate business, GEICO has mastered how to use a mass medium—television—to develop leads among customers who might be interested in saving on insurance. GEICO uses other media as well, including radio and direct mail, to reach its target audience. In fact, GEICO spends more than twice as much on consumer advertising as the next highest-spending brand. Experienced direct marketers have known for years that cross-media campaigns are more productive than relying on a single channel.[8]

The third key point of the direct marketing definition is that responses are *measurable*. In fact, the kind of advertising direct marketers use is called **direct-response (or action) advertising.** This is because direct marketing efforts are always aimed at stimulating an action or measurable response on the part of the customer or prospect. While it can be argued that all advertising is ultimately directed at getting consumers to take action, the response intended by a direct-response ad is meant to happen relatively quickly. It may be in the form of a request for information, a store visit, or an actual purchase. Because these responses can be tallied and analyzed, direct marketing is accountable. And that, more than any other reason, is responsible for the tremendous growth of direct marketing in recent years. Managers like it because they can see what they got for their money.

Direct marketing is intended to stimulate a response in the form of a request for information, an actual purchase, or a visit. GEICO revolutionized the sale of insurance with clever, clear, and compelling ads that show the benefit and make the request for a customer response.

Source: GEICO

GEICO

The other guy.

| Helping people since 1936 | 24/7 licensed agents | 97% customer satisfaction | 2nd-largest auto insurer |

The choice is yours, and it's simple.

Why enjoy just a slice of an apple when you can have the whole thing?

The same goes for car insurance. Why go with a company that offers just a low price when GEICO could save you hundreds and give you so much more? You could enjoy satisfying professional service, 24/7, from a company that's made it their business to help people since 1936. This winning combination has helped GEICO to become the 2nd-largest private passenger auto insurer in the nation.

Make the smart choice. Get your free quote from GEICO today.

GEICO.

geico.com | 1-800-947-AUTO | Local Office

By including its gecko spokesperson, GEICO is able to launch an integrated campaign through a variety of media, including direct response TV, print ads, and web banners, which helps ensure its messages will work together.
Source: GEICO

Finally, the definition notes that the response can be at *any location*. In other words, direct marketing is *not* restricted to mail order or catalog sales. Customers may respond by telephone, via mail-in coupons, via social media, at a retail store or other place of business, or online. GEICO processes the vast majority of its quote requests by phone and via the web.

The Role of Direct Marketing in IMC

Today, sophisticated companies use the skills developed by direct marketers to establish, nourish, and maintain relationships, not just with customers, but with all stakeholders.

GEICO, for instance, uses TV advertising as one of its **linkage media**—media that help prospects and customers link up with a company—to inform prospects how to inquire about its products. Next, it uses these responses to build its database of names, addresses, and e-mail addresses. Then it uses the database to communicate with prospects, create a dialogue, and establish a relationship. It may send a mail piece with ordering information or direct people to its website to enable prospects to connect with GEICO directly.

The Evolution of Direct Marketing

Direct marketing is the oldest marketing method, and today it is growing incredibly fast, propelled by the major social and technological changes. About 57 percent of American women work outside the home.[9] So while families have more income, they have less time to spend shopping, thus making the convenience of phones and digital media important factors in direct marketing. Likewise, the expanding use of credit cards has revolutionized the way consumers buy goods and services. Electronic, cashless transactions make products (especially large, costly items) easier and faster to purchase. And now, with advances in credit card security technology, more and more people are shopping right from their computers.

In 2018, sales driven by direct marketing grew by 4.3 percent, a pace that is faster than overall U.S. sales. In fact, nearly 9 percent of the U.S. GDP originates in direct marketing.[10]

Working with direct-response specialists, marketers are fueling this growth by pouring money into direct marketing campaigns. Exhibit 17-1 shows the largest direct-response agencies in the United States. The greatest overall spending increases in 2015 were expected to be in search (11%), display and mobile advertising (21%), and e-mail (9.7%).[11]

Globally, certain challenges in foreign markets have limited the growth of direct marketing efforts. Foreign markets have a wide variety of laws and regulations, and some

Exhibit 17-1
Largest direct marketing networks in the United States.
Source: "Marketing Fact Pack 2016," *Ad Age* Datacenter.

Rank 2017	Agency [Company]	U.S. Revenue (Million) 2017
1	Epsilon	$1,611
2	Deloitte Digital	1,452
3	Acxiom Corp.	820
4	Wunderman	716
5	Merkle	619
6	Rapp	531
7	Digitas	502
8	PwC Digital Services	414
9	Ogilvy	299
10	Harte Hanks	295

Direct-response ads allow Geico to save marketing dollars. The effective ads help save money compared to the cost of an elaborate personal sales force.

Source: GEICO

focus to a much greater extent (compared with the U.S.) on privacy. Likewise, payment and postal systems vary considerably, as do conventions for addressing mail. And finally, cultural nuances and language can get in the way.[12]

The Impact of Databases on Direct Marketing

Computer technology enables marketers to compile and analyze important customer information in unprecedented ways. Pitney Bowes, for instance, is the dominant company in the postal meter business. However, its growth rate and profitability were flattening. So the company used its database to identify its best customers, their value to the organization, and their needs and buying behavior. From this information, Pitney Bowes created a **customer lifetime value (LTV)** model based on historical and potential share of business. Computing and ranking the *lifetime value* of all of its 1.2 million customers showed that more than two-thirds of the customer base value existed in less than 10 percent of the customers. The company also found it had a major retention problem within its low-volume, low-cost accounts. Cancellation rates were running as high as 40 percent per year in some segments. This analysis enabled Pitney Bowes to develop a distinct direct marketing strategy for both its best and its worst customers. It began a sophisticated *loyalty program* for its best customers and a *retention program* for its problem accounts. By the end of the first year, the program had reduced attrition by 20 percent, and the reduction in cost of sales alone paid back the entire direct marketing investment.[13] In another situation, a company might determine from its LTV analysis that its best course of action is simply to drop the most unprofitable customers.

The database is the key to direct marketing success, especially in an IMC program. It enables marketers to target, segment, and grade customers. It is the corporate memory of all important customer information: name and address, telephone number, e-mail address, NAIC code (if a business firm), source of inquiry, cost of inquiry, history of purchases, and so on. It should record every transaction across all points of contact with both channel members and customers. The company that understands its customers' needs and wants better than any of its competitors, and retains more of its best customers, will create a sustainable competitive advantage. Strategically, therefore, companies have to determine if they focus on share of market or on retention and loyalty (share of customer).[14] More often than not, this is a short-term versus long-term trade-off.

The database also lets the company measure the efficiency of its direct-response advertising efforts to see, for instance, which radio or TV commercials, or which mailing lists, perform the best. Working with a marketing database requires two processes: data management and data access. **Data management** is the process of gathering, consolidating, updating, and enhancing the information about customers and prospects that resides in the database.

Most important, the database gives marketers **data access,** enabling them to manipulate, analyze, and rank all the information to make better marketing decisions. Thanks to new software, this can now usually be accomplished on PCs connected to client–server computers. Rob Jackson, coauthor of *Strategic Database Marketing,* suggests that database marketing should start with *customer profiling.* Profiling allows marketers to get a snapshot of what their customers look like at any given time by identifying common characteristics and ranking their relative importance in different segments.[15]

In the same vein, direct marketing experts Stone and Jacobs use an **RFM formula** (recency, frequency, monetary) to identify the best customers—the ones most likely to buy again (see Exhibit 17-2). The best customers have bought recently, buy frequently, and spend the most money. Customers may be further ranked by the type of merchandise or services they buy, information that becomes very useful in the effort to cross-sell other merchandise.[16]

Some companies may simply purchase a mailing list as its initial database. Three types of data are typically available for purchase: demographics, lifestyle (leisure interests), and behavioristics (purchase habits).[17] Perhaps the greatest reason for direct marketing's current growth is that marketers and agencies realize they can't do the job with just one medium

Exhibit 17-2

RFM (recency, frequency, monetary) analysis of accounts.

Account Number	Month of Purchase	Recency Points	No. of Purchases	Frequency Points	Dollar Purchases	Monetary Points	Total Points	Carryover Points	Cumulative Points
701	7	12	1	4	37.45	3.75	19.75	16	35.75
701	10	24	2	8	17.86	1.79	33.79	16	49.79
702	6	6	2	8	25.43	2.54	16.54	4	20.54
703	4	6	1	4	33.22	3.32	13.32	7	20.32
703	8	12	2	8	42.34	4.23	24.23	7	44.56
703	11	24	1	4	18.95	1.90	29.90	7	74.45
704	9	12	1	4	109.45	9.00	25.00	23	48.00
705	5	6	2	8	37.65	3.77	17.77	0	17.77
705	7	12	3	12	49.63	4.96	28.96	0	46.73
706							0.00	43	43.00

Notes:
- Points assigned by recency of purchase: current quarter—24 points; last 6 months—12 points; last 9 months—6 points; and last 12 months—3 points.
- Frequency points: number of purchases × 4.
- Monetary points: 10 percent of dollar purchase, with a ceiling of 9 points.
- Carryover points: Points carried over from previous calendar year.
- Cumulative total points: Total account points plus carryover from previous calendar year.

The RFM formula is a mathematical model that provides marketers with a method for determining the most valuable customers in a company's database, according to recency, frequency, and monetary variables. Recency points are assigned according to the date of the customer's last purchase (24 points if the purchase was made within the current quarter, 12 points if within the last 6 months, 6 points if within the last 9 months, and 3 points if the purchase was made within the last 12 months). Frequency points are equal to the number of purchases made multiplied by a factor of 4. Monetary points are equal to 10 percent of the dollar purchase, with a maximum of 9 points to prevent artificial distortion by an unusually large purchase. The R, F, and M variables are summed to provide total points. The cumulative total is a measure of relative customer importance to the company—the larger the value, the more likely a customer is to make additional purchases of significant value. The higher-value customers, such as account numbers 701 and 703, who make multiple purchases, are likely prospects for targeted mailings and special offers.

anymore. As the mass audience fragmented and companies began to integrate their marketing communications, customer databases became key to retaining and growing customers.

Direct marketing is the best way to develop a good database. The database enables the marketer to build a relationship by learning about customers in depth: what and where they buy, what they're interested in, and what they need. With a database, companies can choose the prospects they can serve most effectively and *profitably*—the purpose of all marketing. "You don't want a relationship with every customer," says Philip Kotler. "In fact, there are some bad customers out there."[18] Retailer Best Buy uses direct mail to send sales promotions materials, but only to its best customers.[19]

People like to see themselves as unique, not part of some 100-million-member mass market. Through direct marketing, especially addressable electronic media, companies can send discrete messages to individual customers and prospects. With different types of sales promotion (discussed in the last part of this chapter), a company can encourage individuals, not masses, to respond and can develop a relationship with each person. By responding, the prospect *self-selects,* giving the marketer permission to begin a relationship.[20] The direct marketing database, then, becomes the company's primary tool to initiate, build, cultivate, and measure the effectiveness of its loyalty efforts.[21]

By providing a tangible response, direct marketing offers accountability. Marketers can count the responses and determine the cost per response. They can also judge the effectiveness of the medium they're using and test different creative executions.

Direct marketing offers convenience to time-sensitive consumers, and it offers precision and flexibility to cost-sensitive marketers. For example, to reach small BTB markets, there is no more cost-effective method than the database-driven direct-response media. That said, the economics of direct marketing are becoming more competitive. It used to be easy for big companies to spend a few million dollars for prime-time network TV spots when everybody was home watching and the average cost was only a penny to 10 cents per person. But those days are over. Not everyone is watching anymore, and if they are, they're watching 150 different channels or streaming Netflix. They have a remote control to mute

Ethics, Diversity & Inclusion

Unethical Marketing to Seniors

The sweet spot for many marketing campaigns is the person aged 18–34. They are independent earners with an expected long lifetime of spending on brands.

That doesn't mean that every ad campaign targets young adults, however. Elderly Americans, aged 55+, are also prime marketing targets. In many cases, this is because they need unique services and products. In some cases, it may be because they are often vulnerable.

The National Adult Protective Services Association notes that one in nine seniors is abused, neglected, or exploited in a given year. Even at that high rate, many believe elder abuse is underreported.

Unethical marketers target the elderly because of challenges some older Americans face from cognitive impairment and their need for assistance with ordinary activities of daily life. These scams can include lotteries and sweepstakes, "home repair" sales people, fake charities, predatory lending (reverse mortgages, other risky loans), pyramid schemes, identity theft, medical scams, and other unethical or illegal marketing ploys.

Ethical marketing begins with ethical norms. The AMA states that its member marketers should be guided by these principles: (1) do no harm; (2) foster trust in the marketing system; and (3) embrace ethical values, such as truthfulness, products that offer value, and honoring promises. These principles are an excellent start. However, the elderly represent a vulnerable population. As such, special precautions should be taken.

One blog suggests the following about marketing to seniors: (1) use relatable language (seniors just want to know what problem your product will solve); (2) don't assume seniors are helpless; (3) understand that seniors look for benefits, not products; (4) make things easy for them (no fine print, make it clear); (5) use multi-channel marketing (including catalogs); (6) give them something familiar; (7) personalize their experience; and (8) make sure your message is received.[22] Actually, that seems like pretty good advice for marketing to all audiences.

---

ads and a DVR to skip them. Further, network TV advertising is far more expensive than it used to be. Thus, targeted direct-response media (magazines, niche TV, direct mail, e-mail, kiosks) are more cost-effective than ever before.

Finally, unlike the public mass media, direct-response media can be more private. A company can conduct a sales letter campaign without the competition ever knowing about it. In politics, the ability to target "stealth" messages to different voting blocs is a tactic heavily used by both major parties (see the Ethics, Diversity & Inclusion box).

Drawbacks to Direct Marketing

At the same time, direct marketing still faces some challenges. In the past, direct marketers were sales oriented, not relationship oriented. This gave direct marketing a bad reputation. Many people enjoy the experience of visiting retail stores and shopping. They like to see and feel the goods personally, and they are hesitant to buy sight unseen. This is why the objective of many direct marketing campaigns is now to help drive traffic to retail locations.

Direct marketing efforts often have to stand on their own without the content support of the media that advertising enjoys. They don't always get the prestigious affiliation offered by some media. This makes it more difficult (and costly) to build image for the product, something mass media advertising is particularly good at.

Direct marketing also suffers from clutter. People are deluged with mail from commercial sponsors and drum-beating politicians. Cable channels are filled with infomercials for food processors. And telemarketing pitches for insurance plans intrude on consumers at home and at work.

Many consumers are also concerned with privacy. They don't like having their names sold by list vendors. And as a result, Congress frequently applies pressure to companies, including large ones like Google, to account for their privacy policies on a regular basis.[23] Wise marketers heed these

Database marketing was much more difficult before the development of computers because of the intense data management requirements. Today, with low-cost PCs, even the smallest companies can engage in complex database building and marketing strategies.

Source: Microsoft

warnings and develop methods for responsible direct marketing. Using IMC theory, they integrate all their marketing communications and focus on building the *relationship value* of their brands.

Types of Direct Marketing Activities

All direct marketers face two basic strategy decisions: the extent to which they will use *direct sales* and the extent to which they will use *direct-response advertising.* They can use either or both.

Direct Sales

In a **direct-sales strategy,** marketers' representatives sell to customers directly, either at home or at work, rather than through a retail establishment or some other intermediary. Direct sales feature *personal* (face-to-face) *selling* or *telemarketing.*

Personal Direct Selling   Professors Robert Peterson and Thomas Wotruba define **direct selling** as face-to-face selling away from a fixed retail location. In this sense, direct selling usually refers to a method of marketing consumer goods—everything from encyclopedias and insurance to cosmetics and nutritional products.[24] Companies such as Avon, Amway, Herbalife, Mary Kay Cosmetics, World Book, and Tupperware have achieved very high levels of success in direct sales. In personal direct selling, the representative introduces the product to the customer, convinces the customer of the product's value, and, if successful, completes the sale. Personal selling takes two main forms: person-to-person and group sales. In some *network marketing* organizations, such as Amway, Nikken, and Shaklee, the direct salespeople are both distributors (sellers) and end users. They often do very little actual retailing of the products. Their effort is usually to recruit new distributors who will buy the products at wholesale and consume them personally.

The Peterson–Wotruba definition of direct selling could also apply to business-to-business marketing because it typically occurs "away from a fixed retail location." However, the common term for this is simply *personal selling.* And because it is so important to B2B marketers, we will deal with that subject more completely in the next section of this chapter.

Telemarketing   As a method of direct sales, telemarketing has been used for decades. **Telemarketing** includes selling and prospecting by telephone, answering phone inquiries, and providing sales-related services to callers. The resulting information updates the company's customer database. Telemarketing is the major source of income for some companies and organizations, such as nonprofit and charitable causes, political candidates, and home-study courses. With the surge in digital spending, however, telemarketing has been in decline in recent years. This is in part a shift in consumers from landlines to mobile phones (and who likes a marketing call on their mobile?).[25]

It would be wrong to write off telemarketing entirely. First, telemarketing costs a lot less money than personal selling. In the insurance business, for example, the expense ratio for car and home insurance is currently running at 27 percent for all insurers. The most efficient insurers, like GEICO, employ high-tech database marketing techniques from phone centers and operate at around a 20 percent expense ratio.[26] That difference goes straight to the bottom line.

Second, some people do like to shop by phone. It's convenient, hassle-free, and inexpensive. In the United States, the toll-free telephone business is booming. In any given week, 30,000 to 50,000 toll-free numbers are added across North America. Heavy demand caused the pool of 800 numbers to run dry in 1996. Soon thereafter, concern grew that even the 888 numbers faced depletion, leading to limits on their allocation, and 877 and 866 numbers were introduced, with other numbers to be added for toll-free use as needed.[27]

As an IMC medium, telemarketing is the next best thing to a face-to-face, personal sales call. In the business-to-business arena, for example, good telemarketers can develop strong, lasting relationships with customers they have never met but with whom they speak

Although the use of telemarketing has declined in recent years, it is still used by companies in certain industries. Telemarketing also integrates easily into database management campaigns for gathering new data and for utilizing the collected data.

Bojan Milinkov/Shutterstock

every week. Stand Out Designs in San Diego employs highly skilled telemarketers who call on zoos, museums, and boutique retailers all across the country to get them to order and stock the company's unique line of silk-screened T-shirts. The telemarketers don't just take orders; they counsel the dealers with display and promotion suggestions, offer advertising tips, and arrange for special imprints on the shirts when appropriate.

When combined with other direct-response media, telemarketing becomes even more effective. For example, experience shows that when telemarketing is combined with direct mail, there is usually at least a 10 percent increase in responses—often more.

Direct-Response Advertising

Advertising that asks the reader, viewer, or listener to provide feedback to the source is called **direct-response advertising.** Any medium can be used for direct response, but the most common in addition to direct mail are catalogs, traditional print, radio, TV, and digital media. Direct-response is one of the fastest-growing areas of the advertising industry. Today almost every major marketer expects its agencies to incorporate direct-response in their final plans book (for an example of a plans book, see My IMC Campaign 17–A).

Direct Mail: The Addressable Medium   Next to personal selling and telemarketing, direct mail is the most effective method for closing a sale or generating inquiries. All forms of advertising sent directly to prospects through a government, private, or electronic mail delivery service are called **direct-mail (action) advertising.** It's very useful to direct marketers seeking an immediate response. Direct-mail spending has declined in recent years, another victim of digital advertising growth. But some believe it is poised to make a big comeback. Why? Digital ad blockers. As more browsers and apps allow digital audiences to block ads, direct mail starts to look pretty good again.[28]

Both large and small companies use direct mail. New firms often use direct mail as their first advertising medium. The reason is clear: Of all media, direct-mail advertising offers the straightest line to the desired customer. Decades of mailboxes stuffed with catalogs, credit card offers, and music club packets have made today's advertising-weary consumers harder to reach, though.

Types of Direct Mail   Direct mail comes in a variety of formats, from handwritten postcards to dimensional mailings like ShipShapes. The message can be one sentence or dozens of pages. And within each format—from tiny coupon to thick catalog or box—the creative options are infinite. In addition to the dimensional direct-mail category are the following:

Sales letters, the most common direct-mail format, are often mailed with brochures, price lists, or reply cards and envelopes. **Postcards** are used to announce sales, offer discounts, or generate customer traffic. National postal services regulate formats and dimensions. Some advertisers use a double postcard, enabling them to send both an advertising message and a perforated reply card. A recipient who wants the product or service tears off the reply card and mails it back to the advertiser. To encourage response,

Creativity in direct mail is paramount for making a campaign stand out. Optimum uses correlation to hammer home its message. It correlates conventional phone service with using carrier pigeons to send mail—an archaic way to send messages.

Source: Optimum Lightpath and its agency, Hawkeye

My IMC Campaign 17–A

Developing a Plans Book

A plans book, quite simply, is the representation of all the hard work you have put in to develop the ideas for your project. For some of you, this is an actual deliverable for the project; for the rest of you, it is good practice and good process management to develop a plans book to ensure that all of your thinking exists in one place.

Don't let the word *book* fool you—what we are talking about here is a binder or a set of binders that house information relevant to your client's problem. Whether it is competitive news and information, industry news, research on target audiences, and/or SWOT analysis, this binder should comprise all of that organized information. The plans book is the foundation you will use to build the final presentation (we talk about the final presentation in Chapter 18), a concise explanation of how you will utilize the information in the plans book to put your campaign ideas into action.

Here is the information that should be represented in your plans book:

- Objectives
- Challenges
- SWOT analysis
- Target audience analysis
- Communications strategy
- Creative and media brief(s)
- Creative concepts
- Media strategy and plan
- Evaluation or success metrics

Objectives

This is a statement or a set of statements that describe what you hope to achieve from advertising for your client's product. Some common goals are lifting awareness within a new audience, stealing share from competitors, or changing perceptions of consumers. It is better to stay focused and not try to do too much.

Challenges

Think about what you are trying to achieve and what barriers exist that make your work that much harder. If you are trying to lift sales for your client's products, one challenge may be that there is little to no awareness.

SWOT or Situation Analysis

Understanding the strengths, weaknesses, opportunities, and threats for your client's product(s) helps you focus on the appropriate strategy to market the brand. Along with target analysis, the SWOT analysis should lead right into your strategy for marketing the product/brand.

Target Audience Analysis

Hopefully you have done a combination of primary research (interviews) and secondary research (syndicated or already done by a third party) to help understand what motivates your consumers to take action. Once you understand this, advertising becomes much easier; this section should highlight the research done and the insights from that work.

Communications Strategy

Your communications strategy is an overarching guide to how you will approach reaching your target with your client's message. All of your tactics should easily fall out of your strategy statements.

Creative and Media Brief(s)

This can be a single document or a set of documents, but either way it should present the parameters for all of your creative and media work. Look back to Chapter 10 for how to develop a brief.

Creative Concepts

The creative concept is a visual representation of your idea or set of ideas, complete with messaging and layouts.

Media Strategy and Plan

Like the communication strategy, the media strategy should act as a framework for all of your tactical media ideas. The media plan itself is just a representation of the tactical ideas with timing included. (See Exhibit 9-13 in Chapter 9 for an example of a media plan.)

Evaluation or Success Metrics

Of course all of your ideas will work because you have done all of your homework, but what if one of them didn't . . . how would you know? This is where you detail how you plan to track and measure your campaign's effectiveness. This could be as simple as sales growth or more complex, like a pre/post attitudinal study.

---

some advertisers use **business reply mail** so the recipient can respond without paying postage. The advertiser needs a special first-class postal permit and must print the number on the face of the return card or envelope. On receiving a response, the advertiser pays postage plus a handling fee of a few cents. "Postage-free" incentives usually increase response rates.

Folders and **brochures** are usually printed in multiple colors with photos or other illustrations on good paper stock that reproduces printed images well. **Broadsides** are larger than folders and are sometimes used as window displays or wall posters in stores. They fold to a compact size to fit in a mailbag.

Self-mailers are any form of direct mail that can travel without an envelope. Usually folded and secured by a staple or seal, they have special blank spaces for the prospect's name and address to be written, stenciled, or labeled.

Statement stuffers are ads enclosed in monthly customer statements from department stores, banks, oil companies, and the like. To order, customers write in their credit card number and sign the reply card.

House organs are publications produced by associations or business organizations—for example, stockholder reports, newsletters, consumer magazines, and dealer publications.

Using Direct Mail in the Media Mix   Direct mail is an efficient, effective, and economical medium for sales and business promotion. That's why a wide variety of companies, charity and service organizations, and individuals use it. Direct mail can increase the effectiveness of ads in other media. Publishers Clearinghouse uses TV spots to alert viewers to the impending arrival of its direct-mail sweepstakes promotions.

Direct mail has two main drawbacks: cost and the "junk mail" image, both of which are almost inescapable. No other medium (except personal selling and consumer targeting on the internet) has such a high cost per thousand. For this reason, many small marketers participate in cooperative mailings with companies such as ADVO, which serves most major U.S. cities. ADVO mails an envelope containing a coupon for each participating company to targeted zip codes.

Some large companies don't send unsolicited mail. To locate prospects, they use other direct-response media. Then they use direct mail to respond to inquiries. They save money by mailing only to qualified prospects, and by sending higher-quality materials, they build their image and improve their chances of establishing a worthwhile relationship.

Buying Direct Mail   Direct mail has three basic costs: list acquisition, creative production, and distribution.

The heart of any direct-mail program is the mailing list. Each list actually defines a market segment. Direct-mail advertisers use three types of lists: *house, mail-response,* and *compiled.*

The company's relational database of current, recent, and long-past customers as well as future prospects comprises the **house list** for direct-mail programs. Because customers are its most important asset, every company should focus sufficient resources on developing a rich database of customer and prospect information and profiles. There are several ways a company can build its own house list, from offering credit plans to sending useful information to exchanging names with other businesses with similar customer profiles.

Consumer product companies like General Electric gather customer data by enclosing an owner registration form with their products. On the mail-in form, purchasers give their name, address, phone number, birth date, occupation, income range, credit card preferences, home ownership status, and number of children. They also indicate their hobbies and interests (such as golf, foreign travel, photography, or bowling). Companies use this information for their own mailings and sell it to other direct-mail advertisers.

The marketer's second most important prospects are people who respond to direct-mail pieces from other companies—especially those with complementary products or services. **Mail-response lists** are the house lists of other direct-mail advertisers, and they can be rented with a wide variety of demographic breakdowns.

The most readily available lists are those that some entity compiles for a different reason and then rents or sells—for example, lists of car owners, new-home purchasers, business owners, and so on. **Compiled lists,** which are lists purchased from list vendors, typically offer the lowest response rate, so experts suggest using numerous sources, merging them on the computer with mail-response and house lists, and then purging them of duplicate names.[29]

Direct-mail lists can be bought or rented. Purchased lists can be used without limit; rented lists may be used for a single mailing only. List owners plant decoy names in the list to be sure renters don't use it more than once.

Exhibit 17-3

Typical listing of direct-mail rates and data, published by DirectMail.com.

Source: DirectMail.com™

Some list owners pay a **list broker** a commission (usually 20%) to handle the rental details. The company, in turn, benefits from the broker's knowledge of list quality without having to pay more than the rental cost.

Lists can be brokered or exchanged with list houses or other noncompetitive companies. And they can be tailored to reflect customer location (zip code); demographics such as age, income, and credit card ownership; or psychographic characteristics such as personality and lifestyle. The DirectMail.com list contains detailed records that include hundreds of classifications (see Exhibit 17-3).

The quality of mailing lists varies enormously. The wrong list can have out-of-date addresses and names of people who live too far away, don't use the product advertised, and can't afford it anyway. Mailing list prices vary according to quality. The more stringent the advertiser's selection criteria, the more expensive the list. An extra $10 per thousand is often well worth the savings in mailers and postage that would otherwise be wasted.

The average mailing list changes more than 40 percent a year as people relocate, change jobs, get married, or die. So mailing lists must be continually updated (*cleaned*) to be sure they're current and correct. Marketers can also test the validity and accuracy of a given list. They rent or buy every *n*th name and send a mailer to that person. If the results are favorable, they purchase additional names, usually in lots of 1,000.

To create a direct-mail package, the marketer may use in-house staff, an ad agency, or a freelance designer and writer. Some agencies specialize in direct mail.[30]

The direct-mail piece normally goes through the same production process as any other print piece. The size and shape of the mailing package, as well as the type, illustrations, and colors, all affect printing costs. Special features such as simulated blue-ink signatures, cardboard pop-ups, and die-cutting (the cutting of paper stock into an unusual shape) add to the cost. But the larger the printing volume, or *run,* the lower the printing cost per unit (see Ad Lab 17–A, "Developing Effective Direct-Mail Packages").

AD Lab 17–A

Developing Effective Direct-Mail Packages

Good direct-mail campaigns help build relationships between advertisers and customers. As with an ad, the effectiveness of a direct-mail campaign relies strongly on both its message and its overall appearance.

Shaping the Message

When the AICPA (American Institute of Certified Public Accountants) wanted to present the cooler side of accounting to high school and college students, it contacted Wunderman. The AICPA had created a recruiting website called "Start Here. Go Places." that featured a trivia game. Wunderman's task was to get the students to the website where they would play the game and learn more about the accounting profession as a result. Lucky players of the game could win prizes like cash, iPods, and gift cards. Wunderman created the highly graphic, attention-getting postcard shown here, which was sent to targeted high school and college students.

To develop the message element in direct mail, experts suggest several techniques: stress the benefits; repeat your offer more than once; offer an incentive; offer a guarantee; don't be afraid of long copy; don't write copy that is over the reader's head; and give the customer more than one option for responding.

Integrating the Message with the Direct-Mail Pieces

Creating direct mail involves fitting the message with the key physical components of the direct-mail package. As discussed in Chapter 10, the five steps of the creative pyramid (attention, interest, credibility, desire, and action) may be guidelines for forming the message. Next, this information must be incorporated into all the components of the direct-mail package.

The AICPA postcard attracts *attention* with its colorful and humorous graphics. The mismatched fonts and image of the Contador beckon the recipient to look further. The specifics within the postcard build *credibility* by providing data that the offer is real and important. The prizes offered further attract the target's *desire* to visit the site. What student could turn down a chance at winning cash or an iPod? The desired *action* (playing the game) is made easy by providing the web address of the game on both the front and the back of the postcard.

Some Secrets of Direct Mail

Research has revealed countless direct-mail techniques that improve response rates: indent type and set it flush left with a ragged right edge; avoid printing in reverse type; list dollars saved in your offer rather than percentages; use the word *you* in the text; provide a reason for sale pricing (almost any will do); and do not paste labels over old addresses—print new materials.

Laboratory Applications

1. Locate a direct-mail package that has the four components common to most mailings and list how the elements of the creative pyramid are integrated throughout the components.

2. Review the copywriting in your direct-mail package and identify how many of the techniques mentioned in this Ad Lab are used or could be improved.

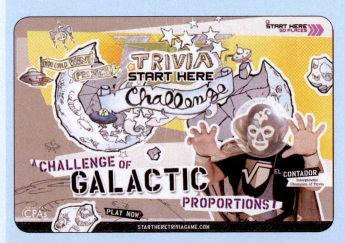

This colorful, attention-grabbing mail piece is meant to attract high school and college students who might be interested in accounting.

Source: AICPA and Wunderman

Remaining production and handling tasks can be done by a local **letter shop** (or *mailing house*), or the company can do them internally.[31] On a cost-per-thousand basis, letter shops stuff and seal envelopes, affix labels, calculate postage, and sort, tie, and stack the mailers. Some shops also offer creative services. If the marketer is using third-class bulk

Winning political office now frequently requires large amounts of cash. So while some ads try to convince voters to support a candidate with their votes, direct-response ads are used to raise money.

Source: Habitat for Humanity International

Because millions of consumers are comfortable shopping on the web, direct-response messages only need to provide a compelling benefit and a memorable web address. Priceline.com is successful at both of these objectives.

Source: The Priceline Group

mail, the letter shop separates mailers by zip code and ties them into bundles to qualify for low bulk rates. Then the letter shop delivers the mailers to the post office.

Distribution costs are based chiefly on the weight of the mailer and the delivery method. U.S. advertisers can use the U.S. Postal Service, air freight, or private delivery services like UPS and FedEx. The most common, the U.S. Postal Service, offers several types of delivery.[32] Direct-mail advertising is most effective when it arrives on Tuesdays, Wednesdays, or Thursdays.[33]

Catalogs   The largest direct marketers are the catalog companies. **Catalogs** are reference books that list, describe, and picture the products sold by a manufacturer, wholesaler, or retailer. With more high-income families shopping at home, specialized catalogs are becoming very popular. Some catalog retailers prosper with specialized approaches like lifestyle clothing (L.L.Bean, Anthropologie, Lands' End), electronic gadgets (Sharper Image), and gourmet foods (Dean & Deluca).

Catalogs remain big business. As of 2017, it estimates suggest catalogs return roughly $3 for every $1 spent.[34] The top 10 catalog companies did over $92.2 billion in business in 2005. The industry experienced a significant decline after the recession of 2007 but, unlike some other traditional media, had staged a comeback as of 2015.[35]

Direct-Response Print Advertising   Newspaper ads and inserts featuring coupons or listing toll-free phone numbers can be very effective at stimulating customer responses. Today, the same is true with magazines. Moreover, in magazines, advertisers can devote most of the space to image-building, thus maximizing the medium's power. We discussed the use of print media in Chapter 12.

Direct-Response Broadcast Advertising   Direct marketers' use of TV and radio has increased dramatically in recent years. Total Gym, whose products are normally sold through health care and physical fitness professionals, worked with American Telecast to develop a 30-minute infomercial featuring TV star Chuck Norris and supermodel Christie Brinkley. The campaign exceeded their wildest expectations, producing more than $100 million in the first year and continuing to generate similar returns for the next four years.[36] As Exhibit 17-4 shows, more people are watching infomercials and buying the advertised products. In fact, one survey found that 60 percent of infomercial purchasers preferred this type of shopping to buying items in a store.[37]

For many years, radio commentator Paul Harvey was very successful pitching a wide variety of products to his loyal audience. Likewise, talk jocks Howard Stern and Rush Limbaugh made Snapple an overnight success by drinking the product and touting its good taste on the air. Still, until fairly recently, radio has rarely been the medium of choice for direct-response advertising. But that has made the medium all the more intriguing to some marketers.[38]

Exhibit 17-4
Who watches (and buys from) infomercials.

	Total Viewers	Total Nonviewers	Total Buyers
Primary gender	Female, 53.2%	Male, 55.4%	Female, 51.7%
Mean age	41.2	45.2	45.9
Primary ethnicity	Caucasian	Caucasian, 76.4%	Caucasian
Primary employment	Full time	Not employed	Full time
Marital status	Married, 49.3%	Married, 52.8%	Married, 60.3%
Children present	Yes, 40.1%	Yes, 38.5%	Yes, 43.1%
Residence	Suburban	Small town, 31.5%	Suburban
Mean household income	$56,000	$49,000	$55,000

Direct response can occur in a variety of media. The Home Shopping Network is a great example of how to use television to sell directly to consumers.

Source: HSN, Inc.

Radio industry executives now expect to see a dramatic increase in the number of direct-response ads on radio. Radio, TV, and infomercials are discussed in depth in Chapter 13.

Direct-Response Digital Advertising   Direct-response advertising represents the vast majority of online advertising efforts. Using e-mail to distribute marketing messages remains popular because of its low cost and effectiveness. Online direct response includes display, or banner, ads and search ads. Social media sites are increasingly featuring ads that allow an immediate response. Mobile is another popular direct-response medium. Mobile includes SMS (short message service or text ads), MMS (multimedia message service, or text plus images, audio, or video), mobile applications (better known as apps), QR (or quick-response) bar codes, and mobile banner ads.

Understanding Personal Selling

LO 17-2

"If it is to be, it is up to me."

Ten little words, two letters each. That was Sid Friedman's philosophy for success. Typical sales rep, right?

Well, not exactly. Sid Friedman sold insurance. He'd been doing it for some time. He was the president and chair of the Philadelphia-based insurance, financial planning, and consulting firm Corporate Financial Services. Friedman managed his 200-plus employees, ran three other companies, and directed the Philadelphia chapter of the children's Make-a-Wish Foundation. *Forbes* magazine's article "People at the Top, What Do They Earn?" included Sid, along with the likes of Arnold Schwarzenegger, Tom Clancy, and Ralph Lauren.

Sid made the *Forbes* article because his selling techniques, augmented by the use of direct marketing, resulted in personal commissions of $2.6 million—in one year. Sid liked telephone marketing. It worked for him. Every week he called 100 people, got 15 appointments, sold three, and earned lots of money.

"Sometimes," he said, "you earn even more money, but only when you do three things: See the people, see the people, and see the people."[39]

That's what personal selling is all about: seeing the people. And that's also why personal selling is the best marketing communication tool for relationship building—because the sales rep and the customer are face-to-face. It's the ultimate one-to-one medium. It's also the most expensive medium. For most companies, personal selling expenditures far exceed expenditures for advertising. And in many companies, the primary role of advertising is to lend support to the sales force either directly by producing leads or indirectly by creating a positive atmosphere for the sales call. That is certainly true for all of the GEICO ads that direct audiences to the company's toll-free number.

Personal selling can be defined in a number of ways, depending on the orientation of the company using it. In an integrated marketing communications program, though, the sales effort of the reps must be consistent with the mission, vision, and strategies of the firm and with all the firm's other communications.

Therefore, for our purposes we define **personal selling** as the *interpersonal communication process* by which a seller ascertains and then satisfies the needs of a buyer, to the mutual, long-term benefit of both parties.[40]

Thus, the task of personal selling is a lot more than just making a sale. In an IMC program, the objective of personal selling is to build a relationship, a partnership, that will provide long-term benefits to both buyer and seller (a win–win situation). The salesperson discovers the buyer's needs by helping the customer identify problems, offers information about potential solutions, assists the buyer in making decisions, and provides after-sale service to ensure long-term satisfaction. Influence and persuasion are only one part of selling. The major part is problem solving.

Apple's creation of retail stores that allow the company to engage in personal selling was a bold move by the late Steve Jobs. The result has been nothing short of spectacular, as Apple generates higher sales per square foot of floor space than any other retailer.

Xaume Olleros/Bloomberg/Getty Images

Types of Personal Selling

Everyone sells, at one time or another. Children sell lemonade, magazine subscriptions, and Girl Scout cookies. Students sell prom tickets, yearbook ads, and term papers. Doctors sell diets to unwilling patients. Lawyers sell briefs to skeptical juries. And cops sell traffic safety to nervous motorists.

As a business process and a profession, though, personal selling is something else. It's just one of a company's mix of communications tools, and its relative importance depends on the type of business or industry, the nature of the product or service, and the strategy of the business.

The fact is that everything has to be sold, by someone to somebody. A retail clerk may sell you a cell phone. Behind that clerk is a virtual army of other salespeople who sold processed materials to the manufacturer, capital equipment for use in the manufacturing process, business services such as human resources and accounting, plant and office furniture, vehicles, advertising services, media space and time, and insurance. Then the manufacturer's salespeople sold the phone (and a few others) to a wholesaler who, of course, had to buy transportation services and warehousing from other salespeople. And then the wholesaler's sales reps sold the phone to the retail outlet where you bought it.

As this scenario shows, people in sales work for a wide variety of organizations and call on an equally wide variety of customers. They may call on other businesses to sell products or services used in the manufacture of other products. They may call on resellers or sell to consumers, either in a retail store or, as we discussed earlier, in a direct selling situation away from a retail location.

Because marketing messages are designed to support and reinforce a company's sales efforts, marketers (whether in the company or at an agency) have to understand the selling environment in which their companies or clients deal. Many companies have their marketing people make calls with the sales force for this very reason. They can experience firsthand what questions prospects ask, how customers view the company (and its competitors), how people use the company's product, and what information (in either an ad or a piece of sales material) might help the salesperson communicate better with the prospect.

Advantages of Personal Selling

The greatest strength of personal selling is its personal nature. Nothing is as persuasive as personal communication. A skilled salesperson can observe a prospect's body language and read between the lines to detect what's troubling the customer. The rep can ask questions and provide answers. And the rep has the flexibility to adjust the presentation, tailoring it specifically to the needs and interests of the particular prospect. Not only that, the salesperson can demonstrate the product live. And the rep can negotiate, finding those terms that best suit the buyer's needs.

Time is on the rep's side, too. The sale doesn't have to be made today. The relationship has to be established, though, and a human being is better at doing that than any nonpersonal medium.

One of the major jobs of personal selling is to gain distribution for new products—a task no other communication tool can do as well. In fact, in many trade and industrial situations, personal contact may be vital to closing the sale. This is also true for certain high-ticket or technical consumer products such as camcorders, health care, and estate planning. In these cases, personal selling is well worth its high cost—because it gets the job done.

Because of the potential of personal selling, an entire industry is devoted to educating and informing salespeople about the skills needed for success. Selling Power magazine is an excellent tool for the salesforce.

Source: Personal Selling Power, Inc.

Drawbacks of Personal Selling

Personal selling is labor intensive, making it the most costly way to communicate with prospects. This is its single biggest weakness. A business-to-business sales call costs well in excess of $300. Not only that, it's very time-consuming. Because it is a one-on-one medium, there are few economies of scale. In fact, two or three salespeople will sometimes go to an important customer's office to make a presentation. In personal selling, we don't talk about cost per thousand.

This is why one important role of IMC is to *reduce the cost of sales* by communicating as much relevant information as possible about the company and its products to prospects and customers before the salesperson even calls. That information may be functional (specifically about the product) or symbolic (building image and credibility for the company).

Another drawback is the poor reputation of personal selling with many people. Decades of "suede shoe" salesmen employing high-pressure tactics, usually in retail venues, have sullied the profession—thus, the common jibe: "Would you buy a used car from that man?" In health care services, for example, selling activities have limited philosophical acceptance. Salespeople are frequently given fancier titles such as marketing associate, marketing representative, admissions coordinator, clinical liaison, professional services representative, or program manager in an attempt to avoid the tarnished image associated with personal selling.[41] Of course, the advertising profession doesn't fare much better when it comes to image and reputation—or fancy titles.

There's an old saying about one bad apple ruining a barrel. Imagine spending millions of dollars on a nationwide advertising campaign to communicate your expertise and good customer service, and then sending an unprofessional sales force out that is ignorant of product features and benefits and lacks empathy for customer needs. Unfortunately, it happens all the time. The salesperson has the power to either make or break a delicate relationship. As a result, sophisticated firms go to great lengths to screen sales applicants to find the right personality attributes and then invest heavily in training. Of course, this goes both ways. A tasteless advertising campaign can hurt a company's national reputation more than one bad salesperson. As always, it's the responsibility of marketing management to ensure consistency between what the advertising presents, what the sales force promises, and what the company actually delivers.

The Role of Personal Selling in IMC

Salespeople are the company's communicators. They are the human medium. In fact, to the customer who doesn't know anybody else at the company, the salesperson doesn't just represent the firm; he or she *is* the firm. The customer's impression of the salesperson, therefore, will frequently govern his or her perception of the company. Again, this makes the sales rep a very important person.

In an integrated marketing communications program, personal selling can play a very important role. Salespeople provide four distinct communications functions: information gathering, information providing, order fulfillment, and relationship building. We'll discuss each of these briefly.

Gathering Information

Sales reps often serve as the eyes and ears of the company. Because they are out in the field talking to customers or attending trade shows, they have access to information and they can see trends. For example, salespeople provide information on who's new in the business, how customers are reacting to new products or styles, what the competition is doing, and where new sales might be made. Generally, information gathering by the sales force relates to three areas: prospecting; determining customer wants, needs, and abilities; and monitoring the competition.

Providing Information

Salespeople also impart information. In fact, the stereotype (both negative and positive) of a good salesperson is someone who is a good talker, articulate, and persuasive. In truth, a superior salesperson is a good listener first and a good talker second. Salespeople impart information both upstream and downstream within their organization. They deliver information to customers about the company and its products, recommend solutions to problems, and use information to communicate value and to build relationships and trust.

Personal selling incorporates all three legs of the IMC triangle, the "say → do → confirm," because what the rep says and does will either confirm or contradict the

Amazon's success can be directly traced to the sophisticated fulfillment centers it uses to ship products quickly to customers. This photo of the center near Phoenix shows both the complexity and organization that make the company so effective.

Joshua Lott/Bloomberg/Getty Images

Nordstrom strives to provide exceptional service to its customers. An engaging and helpful website is part of that effort. So is the company's lenient returns policy and justifiably famous focus on consumer satisfaction.

Source: Nordstrom

company's other messages. The rep's skill, therefore, will definitely color the relationship between the company and the customer. It's critically important that the salesperson's performance be consistent with the firm's positioning and reinforce its other marketing communications.

Fulfilling Orders

There comes a time in every relationship when someone has to make a commitment. Asking for that commitment can be difficult if the preceding steps have not been handled well. The tasks of personal selling are to motivate the customer to action, close the sale, and then make sure the goods and services are delivered correctly.

An important part of personal selling is following up after the sale, making sure the goods or services are delivered in a timely fashion, and seeing to it that the customer is completely satisfied. This is a combination of the "do" and "confirm" steps, and it's critical to continued relationship building.

This is also where cross-functional management and open communication come back into play. If there is any kind of manufacturing glitch or delay in shipping, the salesperson needs to notify the customer immediately. But to do that, the salesperson must be

Snapple's clever promotion of its Mango Madness flavor demonstrates an ingenious integration of sales promotion and product positioning. By placing a sticker ad on actual mangoes in the fresh-fruit section, Snapple reinforced its slogan of "100% natural" and grabbed the attention of customers not necessarily looking to buy the beverage. The marketing strategy was supported by placing bottles of Mango Madness in close proximity to the fruit.

Source: Snapple Beverage Corp.

informed. Similarly, goods need to be protected and shipped with care. Salespeople hate to receive calls from new customers saying their first shipment arrived with damaged goods. Every employee, including those in the warehouse, needs to understand the impact of *unplanned* product messages.

Likewise, if the company is advertising a certain model of a product and the salesperson closes the sale on the product, that model had better be in stock. Again, good internal communication is a key to good external relationships.

Building Relationships

A company's sales staff should be the ultimate relationship marketers. When all things are equal, people naturally want to buy from the salesperson they like and trust. Salespeople build relationships by paying attention to three simple things: keeping commitments, servicing their accounts, and solving problems.

Here again, marketers can help. When a company communicates, it is making a commitment to its customers and prospects. It is very difficult for a salesperson to keep those commitments if the IMC has overpromised.

Likewise, it's difficult for customer service reps to adequately service their accounts if every time people call they get a busy signal. This happened to the giant telephone utility U.S. West when it downsized and reengineered the company. It continued running ads touting its great service, but nobody could get through to them. Not smart. Marketers have to know what's going on in the company, and sometimes they need to recommend that advertising be stopped.

Finally, advertising as well as salespeople should be concerned with solving problems. If the sales staff uncovers a problem that customers frequently encounter, and the company's product can help solve that problem, then that should become the focus of some planned communications—advertising, publicity, or company-sponsored events.

Understanding Sales Promotion

LO **17-3**

Imagine walking into the fresh-fruit section of your local grocery store; picking up a big, juicy mango; and discovering a sticker on it stating: "Now available in Snapple. Mango Madness." You turn around and suddenly notice that there, right next to the fresh-fruit bin, stands a big Snapple display of, you guessed it, Mango Madness.

It actually happened. New York agency Kirshenbaum, Bond & Partners launched Snapple's new Mango Madness drink nationally with stickers on the back of 30 million pieces of fruit. Talk about out-of-the-box thinking and creative media planning! Moreover, it was an outstanding example of how sales promotion can be perfectly integrated with a company's positioning, in this case Snapple's overall "100% natural" message strategy.

The term *sales promotion* is often misunderstood or confused with advertising or publicity. This may be because sales promotion activities often occur simultaneously and use both advertising and publicity as part of the process. In truth, though, it is a very specific marketing communications activity.

Sales promotion is a direct inducement that offers extra incentives anywhere along the marketing route to enhance or accelerate the product's movement from producer to consumer. Within this definition, there are three important elements to consider. Sales promotion:

■   May be used anywhere in the marketing channel: from manufacturer to wholesaler, wholesaler to dealer, dealer to customer, or manufacturer to customer.

■   Normally involves a direct inducement (such as money, prizes, extra products, gifts, or specialized information) that provides an incentive to buy now or buy more, visit a store, request literature, display a product, or take some other action.

■   Is designed to change the timing of a purchase or to shift inventory to others in the channel.

Let's see how this definition applies to Snapple. In an interesting combination of both consumer advertising and *trade promotion* (sales promotion aimed at members of the distribution channel), Snapple used the fresh mangoes as an unusual new advertising medium to introduce its Mango Madness to consumers and to stimulate initial demand for the drink. The magnitude of that media effort (30 million pieces of fruit) served as a huge incentive to retailers to grant Snapple extra floor space (very expensive real estate, by the way) to display Mango Madness right next to the fresh-fruit stand. The result: Snapple, and the retailers, sold a lot more Mango Madness a lot faster, and for a lot less money, than they would have if they had run ads in consumer magazines or on TV. Moreover, by creatively integrating different forms of marketing communications, Snapple simultaneously bolstered its positioning strategy and enhanced its relationship with the retail trade—its primary customer.

Sales promotion is expensive. But it's also effective. Unfortunately, it has serious drawbacks, which lead to furious battles in marketing circles between proponents of sales promotion and proponents of advertising. Each approach has an important role to play, but advertisers must consider the positives and negatives and get the balance right.

The Role of Sales Promotion in IMC

Effective sales promotion accomplishes a number of things. First of all, it adds tangible, immediate added value to the brand. Snapple's creative media buy suddenly made Mango Madness more valuable to the retail trade. This induced retailers to stock up on the new product and display it prominently. Similarly, when McDonald's runs its Monopoly game, it's adding instant value to the products it sells. This is why we refer to sales promotion as the *value-added tool.*

Second, by adding immediate value, sales promotion *maximizes* sales volume. A short-term price cut or rebate, for instance, may be very effective at boosting sales. While advertising helps develop and reinforce a quality, differentiated brand reputation, and build long-term *market value,* sales promotion helps build *market volume.* To become a market leader, therefore, a brand needs both advertising and sales promotion.

Finally, when all brands appear to be equal, sales promotion can be more effective than advertising in motivating customers to try a new brand or to select one brand over another. It can also motivate some customers who might be unmoved by advertising efforts. And certain sales promotions generate a more immediate, measurable payoff than traditional advertising campaigns. This is why we might also refer to sales promotion as the "sales accelerator."

To succeed, sales promotions should be creative and hard to imitate. Kirshenbaum, Bond & Partners certainly demonstrated that with its Snapple labels.

Advertisers need to understand the negative effects of sales promotion, too. For instance, excessive sales promotion at the expense of advertising hurts profits. Some marketers believe a proper expenditure balance for consumer packaged-good products is approximately 60 percent for trade and consumer promotion and 40 percent for advertising.

A high level of trade sales promotion relative to advertising and consumer sales promotion has a positive effect on short-term market share but may have a negative effect on brand attitudes and long-term market share. Without an effective advertising effort to emphasize brand image and quality, customers become deal-prone rather than brand loyal. And overemphasis on price (whether in advertising or sales promotion) eventually destroys brand equity.[42]

Another drawback of sales promotion is its high cost. One analysis showed that only 16 percent of sales promotions were profitable. In other words, the manufacturer spent more than $1 to generate an extra $1 of profits.[43]

Finally, overly aggressive sales promotion or advertising can draw competitors into a price war, which leads to reduced sales and profits for everyone.

Thus, if too much of the marketing mix is allocated to advertising, the brand may gain a high-quality, differentiated image but not enough volume to be a market leader. On the other hand, as Larry Light, McDonald's chief global marketing officer says, "Too much [sales] promotion, and the brand will have high volume but low profitability. Market leadership can be bought through bribes, but enduring profitable market leadership must be earned through building both brand value as well as volume."[44]

Exhibit 17-5
Two marketing communications approaches.

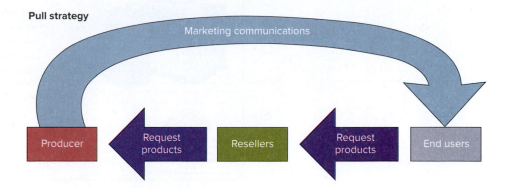

Sales Promotion Strategies and Tactics

To move their products through the distribution channel from the point of manufacture to the point of consumption, marketers employ two types of strategies: push and pull. **Push strategies** are primarily designed to secure the cooperation of retailers, gain shelf space, and protect the product against competitors. **Trade promotions**—sales promotions aimed at members of the distribution channel—are one of the principal tactics marketers use to *push* products through the distribution pipeline and gain shelf space. We'll discuss some of these tactics in the next section. Marketers may also use **trade advertising** (advertising in publications read by members of the trade) as a push tactic.

Pull strategies, on the other hand, are designed to attract customers and increase demand for the product (see Exhibit 17-5). Consumer advertising and **consumer sales promotions** are examples of pull strategies because they are designed to induce consumers to seek out or ask for the product, in effect pulling the product through the pipeline. Today, some national advertisers spend more dollars on trade sales promotions than on either consumer sales promotions or media advertising. But that is often the price they have to pay to gain distribution, without which they cannot make any sales.

Giving Brands a Push with Trade Promotions

In supermarkets today, shelf space and floor space are hard to come by. To maintain their own images, department stores set standards for manufacturers' displays. This means that retailers often can't use the special racks, sales aids, and promotional literature manufacturers supply.

These are minor problems; major ones have to do with control of the marketplace. **Trade concentration**—more products going through fewer retailers—gives greater control to the retailers and less to the manufacturers. Increased competition for shelf space gives retailers even more power, enabling them to exact hefty deals and allowances. As a result, manufacturers of national brands often don't have enough money left to integrate consumer advertising or sales promotion.[45]

Despite these problems, many manufacturers still implement effective push strategies. And the smart ones safeguard enough money for consumer advertising. Trade tactics include slotting allowances, trade deals, display allowances, buyback allowances, advertising allowances, cooperative advertising and advertising materials, dealer premiums and contests, push money, and company conventions and dealer meetings.

Allowances and Trade Deals   In response to the glut of new products, some retailers charge manufacturers **slotting allowances**—fees ranging from $15,000 to $40,000 for the privilege of obtaining shelf or floor space for a new product. The practice is controversial because

THE SECOND LINE THAT'S NO SECOND STRINGER.

It's your business, your time and your reputation. Choose a second line that will help you protect it. Payne offers a range of low-cost high quality heating and cooling options. Durable and dependable, we can help you increase your margins without increasing your maintenance costs. With easy-to-sell and easy-to-install products like our ENERGY STAR® labeled 12 SEER cooling and 90% heating systems, Payne can help you make the most of every opportunity.

A MEMBER OF THE UNITED TECHNOLOGIES CORPORATION FAMILY. STOCK SYMBOL: UTX.

www.payne.com

With the energy crisis here to stay, your customers are going to be looking for this symbol. Low-cost, high-efficiency Payne models can help you stay ahead of the game.
Energy Star and the Energy Star logo are registered U.S. marks.

PAYNE
HEATING & COOLING
RIGHT FOR YOU.

some manufacturers think they're being forced to subsidize the retailer's cost of doing business. On the other side of the coin, small-scale sellers, such as family farms trying to market their produce, complain that the allowances shut out all but the largest suppliers. Although a 1994 ruling by the Federal Trade Commission and the Bureau of Alcohol, Tobacco and Firearms determined that they were acceptable as long as the same promotional allowances were offered to all retailers on "proportionally equal terms," the allowances remain controversial, and the FTC has recommended further research.[46]

In an effort to avoid slotting allowances, some marketers have made major shifts in strategy. Following a four-year investigation, the FTC signaled its willingness to fight egregious slotting allowance abuses by taking legal action against spice giant McCormick. Through agreements with "favored purchasers," the company had managed to command 90 percent of shelf space set aside for spices and offered a range of prices for its customers. The FTC ordered McCormick to refrain from selling its products to a purchaser at a net price that was higher than that charged to the purchaser's competitors. The order's narrow scope dismayed some critics, but overall the action was hailed as "a thoughtful beginning to the evolution of a sound and measured antitrust response to slotting fee abuses."[47]

Manufacturers make **trade deals** with retailers by offering short-term discounts or other dollar inducements. To comply with the Robinson-Patman Act, trade deals must be offered proportionally to all dealers. Dealers usually pass the savings on to customers through sale prices, or "specials."

Excessive trade deals threaten brand loyalty because they encourage customers to buy whatever brand is on sale. Furthermore, marketers who use trade discounts extensively find themselves in a vicious circle: If they cut back on the promotions, they may lose shelf space and then market share.

Some retailers capitalize on trade discounts by engaging in forward buying and diverting. With **forward buying,** a retailer stocks up on a product when it is on discount and buys smaller amounts when it sells at list price. **Diverting** means using the promotional discount to purchase large quantities of an item in one region, then shipping portions of the buy to areas where the discount isn't offered. These tactics enable both the manufacturer and the dealer to shift inventory when they need to.

Retailers often charge manufacturers **display allowances**—fees assessed in exchange for featuring an item prominently on end caps or displays. In-store displays include counter stands, floor stands, shelf signs, and special racks that give the retailer ready-made, professionally designed vehicles for selling more of the featured products.

When introducing a new product, manufacturers sometimes offer retailers a **buyback allowance** for the old product that hasn't sold. To persuade retailers to take on their

product line, some manufacturers even offer a buyback allowance for a competitor's leftover stock.

Manufacturers often offer **advertising allowances** as either a percentage of gross purchases or a flat fee. Advertising allowances are more common for consumer than industrial products. They are offered primarily by large companies, but some smaller firms give them to high-volume customers.

Co-op Advertising and Advertising Materials   With **cooperative (co-op) advertising,** national manufacturers reimburse dealers for advertising the manufacturer's products or logo. The manufacturer usually pays 50 to 100 percent of the dealer's advertising costs based on a percentage of the dealer's sales. Special co-op deals are used to introduce new products, promote profitable lines, or combat aggressive competitors.

Unlike advertising allowances, co-op programs typically require the dealer to submit invoices and proof of the advertising (tearsheets from the newspaper or affidavits of performance from radio or TV stations). Many manufacturers also give their dealers prepared advertising materials: ads, glossy photos, sample radio commercials, and so on. To control the image of their products, some advertisers insist that dealers use these materials to qualify for the co-op advertising money.

Other Push Strategies   To encourage retail dealers and salespeople to reach specific sales goals or stock a certain product, manufacturers may offer special prizes and gifts. Ethics can be a thorny issue when companies award prizes and gifts to dealers and salespeople.

Retail salespeople are often encouraged to push the sale of particular products. One inducement is called **push money (PM),** or **spiffs.** For example, a shoe salesperson may suggest shoe polish or some other high-profit extra; for each item sold, the salesperson receives a 25- to 50-cent spiff.

Most major manufacturers hold **company conventions and dealer meetings** to introduce new products, announce sales promotion programs, or show new advertising campaigns. They may also conduct sales and service training sessions. Meetings can be a dynamic sales promotion tool for the manufacturer.

Push strategies are virtually invisible to consumers. Yet successful inducements mean the product gets more shelf space, a special display, or extra interest and enthusiasm from salespeople. And extra interest can spell the difference between failure and success.

Using Consumer Promotions to Pull Brands Through

One reason for today's increased focus on consumer sales promotions is the change in TV viewing habits. With cable TV, DVRs, and DVDs, fewer people watch any one program. Advertising audiences are more fragmented, and major manufacturers must turn to new methods to reach these moving targets.

Common consumer sales promotions include point-of-purchase materials, coupons, electronic coupons and convenience cards, cents-off promotions, refunds, rebates, premiums, sampling, combination offers, contests, and sweepstakes. A successful IMC campaign may integrate several of these techniques along with media advertising, product publicity, and direct marketing. Ad Lab 17–B offers the opportunity to apply what you've learned about push and pull strategies to the marketing of textbooks.

Point-of-Purchase (P-O-P) Materials   Walk into any store and notice the number of display materials and advertising-like devices that are designed to build traffic, exhibit and advertise the product, and promote impulse buying. Collectively, these are all referred to as **point-of-purchase (P-O-P) materials.**

P-O-P works best when used with other forms of IMC. For example, by advertising its gum and candy, one marketer increased sales by about 150 percent. But when P-O-P was added to the same program, the purchase rate jumped 550 percent.[48]

In one poll, 56 percent of mass-merchandise shoppers and 62 percent of grocery shoppers said they noticed point-of-purchase materials. More than half reported noticing signs and displays, 18 percent remembered coupon dispensers, and 14 percent could recall samplings and demonstrations.[49]

Pull campaigns rely on the power of consumers to pull brands through the distribution chain. A product called Full Core makes it easy for consumers to demand its product by supplying them with this ad.

Source: Full Core, LLC

Most coupons, such as this one for L'Oréal's EverPure Moisture Shampoo, reach consumers through newspaper freestanding inserts (FSIs), which have a higher redemption rate than regular newspaper or magazine coupons.

Source: L'Oréal Paris

Today's consumers make their decisions in the store 66 percent of the time and make unplanned (impulse) purchases 53 percent of the time, so P-O-P can often be the major factor in stimulating purchases.[50]

P-O-P materials may also include window displays, counter displays, floor and wall racks to hold the merchandise, streamers, and posters. Often, the product's shipping cartons are designed to double as display units. A complete information center may even provide literature, samples, product photos, or an interactive computer in a kiosk.

The trend toward self-service retailing has increased the importance of P-O-P materials. With fewer and less-knowledgeable salespeople available to help them, customers are forced to make purchasing decisions on their own. Eye-catching, informative displays can give them the nudge they need. Even in well-staffed stores, display materials can offer extra selling information and make the product stand out from the competition.

The proliferation of P-O-P displays has led retailers to be more discriminating in what they actually use. Most are beginning to insist on well-designed, attractive materials that will blend harmoniously with their store atmosphere.

The emphasis on P-O-P has led to a variety of new approaches, including ads on shopping carts, "talking" antacid boxes, beverage jingles activated when in-store refrigerator doors are opened, and interactive computers for selecting everything from shoe styles to floor coverings. Digital technology has led to Hallmark Cards' Touch-Screen Greetings interactive kiosks, which print a customer's personal message onto any card. To send it, look for one of the new Automated Postal Centers rolled out by the U.S. Postal Service. The kiosks allow customers to weigh materials to be mailed, buy postage, and even look up zip codes.

Coupons   A **coupon** is a certificate with a stated value presented to the retail store for a price reduction on a specified item. More than 278 billion coupons were distributed by consumer packaged goods companies in the United States in 2005, but only about 3 billion were ever redeemed.[51]

Coupons may be distributed in newspapers or magazines, door to door, on packages, in stores, and by direct mail. Most reach consumers through colorful preprinted newspaper ads called **freestanding inserts (FSIs).** FSIs have a higher redemption rate than regular newspaper and magazine coupons; coupons in or on packages have the highest redemption levels of all.[52]

Manufacturers lose hundreds of millions of dollars annually on fraudulent coupon submissions. Some coupons are counterfeited; others are submitted for products that were never purchased. To fight this problem, some companies have developed computerized systems to detect fraudulent submissions and charge them back to the retailers who made them.

Digital Coupons and Convenience Cards   High-tech **digital coupons** work like paper coupons in that they entitle the shopper to a discount, but their method of distribution is entirely different.

Membership implies commitment, which is why large discount retailers like Costco offer benefits to people who join their programs.

dennizn/Shutterstock

Interactive touch-screen videos at the point of purchase generate instant-print discounts, rebates, and offers to try new brands. Digital coupons are common in the nation's supermarkets.

Digital couponing gives the retailer access to information about consumers that would not be available with paper coupons. Many supermarket chains now issue customers convenience cards entitling them to instant discounts at the checkout counter. When customers use the card, a record of their purchases is sent to a database and sorted into various lifestyle groups. The card saves customers the hassle of clipping paper coupons, and it allows retailers to better understand its customers' purchasing behaviors.

Similar systems are used in Europe. Multipoints is an interactive system that lets customers collect points for visiting stores or watching commercials on TV. The points can be redeemed for prizes and discounts on various products at participating stores. Quick Burger, France's second-largest restaurant chain, noticed a significant increase in traffic after joining Multipoints, even when the system was less than a year old.[53]

Cents-Off Promotions, Refunds, and Rebates   **Cents-off promotions** are short-term reductions in the price of a product in the form of cents-off packages, one-cent sales, free offers, and boxtop refunds. Some packages bear a special cents-off sticker, which the clerk removes and credits at the checkout counter.

Some companies offer *refunds* in the form of cash or coupons that can be applied to future purchases of the product. To obtain the refund, the consumer must supply proof of purchase, such as three boxtops.

Rebates are larger cash refunds on items from cars to household appliances. Large rebates (like those given on cars) are handled by the seller. For small rebates (like those given for coffeemakers), the consumer sends in a certificate.

Research indicates that many people purchase a product because of an advertised rebate but never collect the rebate because of the inconvenience.[54] More than $500 million worth of rebates goes unclaimed every year.

Premiums   A **premium** is an item offered free or at a bargain price to encourage the consumer to buy an advertised product. Premiums affect purchase behavior the same way as rebates but tend to be more effective at getting consumers to buy a product they don't really need (see Exhibit 17-6). Premiums are intended to improve the product's image, gain goodwill, broaden the customer base, and produce quick sales.

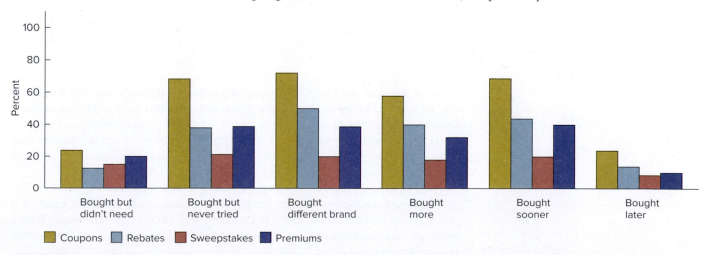

Exhibit 17-6

Next to coupons, premiums are one of the most effective sales promotion techniques for changing consumer behavior.

Source: Adapted from the American Marketing Association.

People BEHIND the Ads

Dayana Falcon, Sales Marketing Manager, Disney Advertising

Courtesy of Dayana Falcon

CA: Dayana, tell us what you do for the Walt Disney Co.

Dayana Falcon: I am a Sales Marketing Manager for the Disney Advertising Sales team, a division within the Direct to Consumer and International segment. My responsibilities consist of bringing our go-to-market strategy to life for Disney Advertising Sales. This ranges from thought leadership to strategic positioning of Disney in the advertising industry, client relations at industry tentpole events, creation of best-in-class collateral to support our sales team, and exploration of revenue strategies. Our Sales Communication team is responsible for developing persuasive content and experiences to bring our ad propositions to life. Whether it's a one-on-one meeting or large-group setting, we are the source for compelling category, client, and portfolio narratives.

CA: What is a typical day in your life like?

DF: No day is the same. One day I could be creating the go-to-market strategy for our sales organization for the Consumer Electronics Show (CES) and another for our stage at the Interactive Advertising Bureau (IAB) Newfronts. Ensuring the highest quality for our client check-in, premiums, visuals of sizzle-loop videos on screens, presentations to share our thought leadership ideas on the main stage, and provision of white-glove customer service are examples of what a day in my life at Disney looks like.

CA: What do you love most about your job?

DF: I love bringing the creativity of our franchises (Disney, Pixar, Star Wars, Marvel, ABC, ESPN, etc.) to life through innovative and unexpected experiences. From Mickey Mouse on a hologram to showcasing a demo of our partnership with Samsung's AR Emoji to infusing thought leadership into that narrative of "so what?" and "what's next?"—bringing Disney franchises to life through innovation for our clients is everything to me!

CA: What are the advertisers that you deal with looking for when working with Disney?

DF: Our clients are looking for solutions that work across the breadth of our portfolio and are associated with the favorability of Disney's franchises. This spans capabilities from digital to linear, emerging platforms, experiential, etc. Instead of them having to negotiate with multiple partners for one campaign, they can come to Disney Advertising Sales to get emotional, live, and award-winning moments across the breadth of our portfolio from *Good Morning America* to binge-watching Freeform to short-form content on the Disney Princess's Facebook page.

CA: What unique benefits does advertising with Disney offer?

DF: We take storytelling to new heights and deliver on everyday, emotional, and winning moments. . . . It's what sets us apart. The power of Disney's stories are memorable. And advertising is

A premium should have strong appeal and value and should be useful or unusual. It may be included in the product's package *(in-pack premium),* on the package *(on-pack premium),* mailed free or for a nominal sum on receipt of proof of purchase (boxtop or label), or given with the product at the time of purchase. Cosmetics companies often hold department store promotions in which scarves, purses, and cosmetic samplers are given free or for a low price with a purchase.

The purchased cosmetics sampler is an example of a *self-liquidating premium:* The consumer pays enough that the seller breaks even but doesn't make a profit. A variation is the *continuity premium,* given weekly to customers who frequent the same store. With a minimum dollar purchase of other items, the customer receives a dish or book each week to complete a set.

Sampling   **Sampling** is the most costly of all sales promotions. It is also one of the most effective for new products because it offers consumers a free trial in hopes of converting

remembered better and performs better when surrounded with compelling stories so there is a tremendous opportunity for our clients.

CA: What (if you can share!) are you doing to partner with Amazon on Echo devices or Google on Google Home devices?

DF: Technology and innovation have always been at the forefront of TWDC since its inception, and Disney continues to be a leader in technology-powered entertainment. We excel at innovative storytelling on emerging tech platforms, such as voice technology. By embedding content experiences using personal assistants, Disney can leverage immersive storytelling and deepen engagement. We are focused on bringing storytelling to life in new and exciting ways.

CA: What are some examples?

DF: On Amazon's Echo you can say: "Alexa, open Disney Stories"—or request a specific franchise by saying, "Alexa, ask Disney Stories for a Cinderella story"—to create a screen-less bedtime story experience for your family. Or on Google Home you can say: "Hey Google, play Mickey Mouse Adventure," and choose an adventure experience where kids can have a one-to-one conversation with Mickey Mouse.

CA: What is the best advice you received from a professional mentor?

DF: "Step out of your comfort zone and BE PASSIONATE." If you are comfortable, you stay stagnant and don't grow. Always put yourself in environments where you are constantly learning and in industries where, at your core, you are drawn to the subject matter. You will grow so much faster when you are in an industry role that allows you influence and fulfills your passions.

CA: How do you keep up with the industry changes?

Thanks to Association of National Advertisers' *Smart Brief Newsletter,* e-marketer reports, and a combination of LinkedIn and Twitter feeds, I am able to stay abreast of new technologies, client activities, and the latest and greatest in marketing trends. I also closely watch conferences such as CES, Mobile World Congress in Barcelona, and the ANA's Brand Master's Conferences.

CA: What can a student of this text do to jumpstart her or his career?

DF: Find what you are passionate about (i.e., travel, dance, sports, meeting new people, etc.). Then find brands that you love because of their social impact, customer service, or the longevity of business models.

Figure out if you want to begin your career client side, agency side, or publisher side. **Clients** are the big brands: Nike, Lyft, Mercedes Benz, Macy's Tesla, Taco Bell, etc. **Agencies** include WPP, Omnicom, Publicis, etc. (remember that agencies span functions from media to creative, data, e-commerce, experiential, multicultural, and public relations, to name a few). **Publishers** include Facebook, Instagram, Apple, Disney, Amazon, Spotify, Buzzfeed, etc. Now:

1. Build a list of your Top 10 dream companies and create a Twitter RSS feed that includes them so you can follow their daily communications. Track which ones you gravitate towards.

2. Build connections with alumni from your school or by applying for an internship in the companies on your dream list

3. Don't forget to nurture those connections by checking in with your connections, sharing an article, tagging them in a post, etc.

Now, go find your dream company!

CA: Your life is so busy! Do you have other professional passions?

DF: Who doesn't?! I am also the Chief Marketing Officer of Millennial Women Inc. Our mission and vision is to create a multimedia platform for women from our generation to rely on as a source of inspiration and to provide them with the resources to become the best version of themselves. My focus as CMO is building the brand, business development, and branded partnerships and creating the Millennial Womanhood community worldwide.

Courtesy of Dayana Falcon.

In-store sampling displays allow consumers to test products in an environment where they may be readily purchased.

Noel Hendrickson/Photodisc/Getty Images

them to habitual use. Sampling should be supported by advertising and must involve a product available in small sizes and purchased frequently. Successful sampling depends heavily on the product's merits. It offers the greatest credibility and can turn a nonuser into a loyal customer instantly—if the product lives up to its promise.

Samples may be distributed by mail, door to door, via coupon advertising, or by a person in the store. They may be given free or for a small charge. Sometimes samples are distributed with related items, but this limits their distribution to those who buy the other product. In **polybagging,** samples are delivered in plastic bags with the daily newspaper or a monthly magazine. This enables distribution to targeted readers and lets publications give their subscribers added value at no cost.[55]

In-store sampling is very popular. Most in-store sampling programs are tied to a coupon campaign. Depending on the nature of the product, samples can be used as either a push strategy or a pull strategy.

Combination Offers   Food and drug marketers use **combination offers,** such as a razor and a package of blades or a toothbrush with a tube of toothpaste, at a reduced price for the two. For best results, the items should be related. Sometimes a combination offer introduces a new product by tying its purchase to an established product at a special price.

Contests and Sweepstakes   A **contest** offers prizes based on entrants' skill. A **sweepstakes** offers prizes based on a chance drawing of entrants' names. A **game** has the chance element of a sweepstakes but is conducted over a longer time (like local bingo-type games designed to build store traffic). A game's big marketing advantage is that customers must make repeat visits to the dealer to continue playing.

Both contests and sweepstakes encourage consumption of the product by creating consumer involvement. These devices pull millions of entries. Usually contest entrants must send in some proof of purchase, such as a boxtop or label. For more expensive products, consumers may only have to visit the dealer to pick up an entry blank.

To encourage entries, sponsors try to keep their contests as simple as possible. The prize structure must be clearly stated and all the rules listed. National contests and sweepstakes are handled and judged by independent professional contest firms.

Sweepstakes and games are now more popular than contests because they are much easier to enter and take less time. Sweepstakes require careful planning by the advertiser. Companies cannot require a purchase as a condition for entry or the sweepstakes becomes a lottery and therefore illegal. Marketers must obey all postal laws. If they run the sweepstakes in Canada, they may have to pay a percentage of the prizes to the Quebec government.

Contests and sweepstakes must be promoted and advertised to be successful, and this can be expensive. And sales promotions need dealer support. To ensure dealer cooperation, many contests and sweepstakes require the entrant to name the product's local dealer. They may also award prizes to the dealer who made the sale.

Chapter Summary

The key to building brand equity in the 21st century is to develop interdependent, mutually satisfying relationships with customers and other stakeholders. To manage these relationships, companies consciously integrate their marketing communications activities with their other company functions so that all the messages the marketplace receives about the company are consistent.

As part of this process, it is important to understand how to integrate the various tools of marketing communications. Advertising practitioners need to have a basic understanding of what other tools are available to them and how they can best be used in the overall communications mix.

In direct marketing, the marketer builds and maintains a database of customers and prospects and uses anything from personal contact to mass media to communicate with them directly in the effort to generate a response, a transaction, or a visit to a retail location.

The database is the key to direct marketing success, especially in an IMC program. Databases let marketers target, segment, and grade customers. This allows them to identify their best customers, their value to the organization, and their needs and buying behavior. They can then calculate the customer's lifetime value. The database is the corporate memory of all important customer information. It should record every transaction across all points of contact with both channel members and customers. The database also enables the company to measure the efficiency of its direct-response advertising efforts.

Direct marketing is a rapidly growing industry, but it still suffers from problems of cost, clutter, and image.

Direct marketers use a variety of activities, from direct sales (personal selling and telemarketing) to direct-response advertising. Telemarketing, followed by direct mail, is the medium of choice for most direct marketers, but more are beginning to use other media, especially TV infomercials. Interactive TV may be the direct-marketing medium of the future.

Direct mail has historically been the most expensive major medium on a cost-per-exposure basis, it has also been effective in terms of tangible results. Marketers like direct mail for its accountability. There are many types of direct-mail advertising, from catalogs and brochures to statement stuffers. While it has declined in recent years, digital ad blockers may be sparking a comeback for direct mail.

One of the great features of direct mail is that it can increase the effectiveness of ads in other media. However, direct mail has many drawbacks too—primarily its cost and the junk-mail image.

The two most important things that affect direct-mail success are the mailing list and the creativity used. The direct-mail piece normally goes through the same production process as any other print piece. The size and shape of the mailing package, as well as the type, illustrations, and colors, all affect printing costs.

Personal selling is actually the ultimate interactive medium. It is the interpersonal communication process by which a seller ascertains and then satisfies the needs of a buyer, to the mutual, long-term benefit of both parties.

There are many types of personal selling: retail, business-to-business, and direct selling. Because advertising is a support service for a company's sales efforts, advertising people have to understand the selling environment their companies deal in.

The greatest strength of personal selling is its personal nature. Nothing is as persuasive as personal communication. The one-to-one situation facilitates instant feedback. And the rep has the flexibility to adjust the presentation, tailoring it specifically to the needs and interests of the particular prospect.

Like all communications tools, personal selling also has some drawbacks. It is very expensive. Additionally, the salesperson has the power to make or break a delicate relationship. So one of the risks is that one bad apple can ruin a previously unblemished association.

Salespeople provide four communications functions: information gathering, information providing, order fulfillment, and relationship building.

Sales promotion complements advertising and personal selling by stimulating sales. It includes direct inducements (such as money, prizes, or gifts) aimed at salespeople, distributors, retailers, consumers, and industrial buyers.

Marketers must balance sales promotion with advertising. Advertising creates market value for a brand; promotion creates market volume. Advertising has a positive effect on profits; promotion can have a negative effect. Sales promotion techniques are used in the trade to push products through the distribution channels and with consumers to pull them through.

Manufacturers use many sales promotion techniques with dealers: slotting allowances, trade deals, display allowances, buyback allowances, advertising allowances, co-op advertising and advertising materials, dealer premiums and contests, push money, and company conventions and dealer meetings. Sales promotions aimed at the ultimate purchaser include point-of-purchase materials, coupons, digital coupons and convenience cards, cents-off promotions, refunds, rebates, premiums, sampling, combination offers, contests, and sweepstakes.

Important Terms

advertising allowance, *567*

broadsides, *554*

brochures, *554*

business reply mail, *554*

buyback allowance, *566*

catalog, *558*

cents-off promotion, *569*

combination offer, *572*

company conventions and dealer meetings, *567*

compiled lists, *555*

consumer sales promotion, *565*

contest, *572*

cooperative (co-op) advertising, *567*

coupon, *568*

customer lifetime value (LTV), *549*

data access, *549*

database, *546*

database marketing, *546*

data management, *549*

digital coupon, *568*

direct-mail (action) advertising, *553*

direct marketing, *546*

direct-response (action) advertising, *547*

direct-sales strategy, *552*

direct selling, *552*

display allowance, *566*

diverting, *566*

folders, *554*

forward buying, *566*

freestanding insert (FSI), *568*

game, *572*

house lists, *555*

house organs, *555*

in-store sampling, *571*

letter shop, *557*

linkage media, *548*

list broker, *556*

mail-response lists, *555*

personal selling, *559*

point-of-purchase (P-O-P) materials, *567*

polybagging, *571*

postcards, *553*

premium, *569*

pull strategies, *565*

push money (PM), *567*

push strategies, *565*

rebate, *569*

RFM formula, *549*

sales letters, *553*

sales promotion, *563*

sampling, *570*

self-mailers, *555*

slotting allowance, *565*

spiffs, *567*

statement stuffers, *555*

sweepstakes, *572*

telemarketing, *572*

trade advertising, *565*

trade concentration, *565*

trade deal, *566*

trade promotion, *565*

Review Questions

1. Who are a company's best prospects for additional sales and profits? Why?

2. How should a large insurance company view integrated marketing communications?

3. What are the basic strategic and tactical decisions direct marketers face?

4. How can an advertiser use a newspaper for direct-response advertising?

5. What distinct communications functions do salespeople provide?

6. What are the three things salespeople must do to build relationships?

7. What are the main purposes of sales promotion?

8. Why is trade promotion controversial?

9. What are the most common pull strategies? Which would you use to launch a new soft drink?

10. Why is there a trend away from push strategies and toward pull strategies?

11. How could you use direct mail in an integrated marketing communications program? Give an example.

12. What factors have the greatest influence on the success of a direct-mail campaign?

The Advertising Experience

1. **Push and Pull Techniques**

   Advertisers commonly use both push and pull techniques. Explore the situation of a company of your choice, identifying its pull techniques and also tracking down its push techniques. (Push techniques might be more difficult to find.) Trade publications are a good place to look. Create a report detailing the overall strategy of the company and discuss why you think one area might be emphasized over another.

2. **Direct Marketing and Direct Response**

   Direct marketing is not only vast, it's ever changing in all its facets—direct sales, direct mail, direct response. Likewise, direct marketing agencies tend to differ from traditional advertising agencies in strategy, organization, and clientele. Take a look at some of the websites below and answer the questions that follow for each site.

   Direct Marketing Organizations

   - Canadian Marketing Association (CMA): www.the-cma.org
   - Association of National Advertisers (ANA): www.ana.net
   - Direct Marketing News: www.dmnews.com
   - Give to Get Marketing: www.givetogetmarketing.com
   - Los Angeles Digital Marketing Association: www.ladma.org
   - Direct Marketing Association of Northern California: www.dmanc.org/
   - Federation of European Direct Marketing: www.fedma.org

   a. What group sponsors the site? Who is (are) the intended audience(s)?

   b. What are the size, scope, and purpose of the organization?

   c. What benefits does the organization provide to individual members or subscribers? To the overall advertising and direct marketing communities?

   d. How important do you believe this organization is to the direct marketing industry? Why?

   Direct Marketing Firms

   Select five of the following direct marketing firms, visit their websites, and answer the questions that follow.

   - Acxiom Digital: www.acxiom.com
   - GEICO: www.geico.com
   - Harte-Hanks: www.hartehanks.com
   - Wunderman: www.wunderman.com

   a. Who is the intended audience of the site?

   b. How does the agency position itself (i.e., creative-driven, strategy- (account) driven, media-driven, etc.)?

   c. What is your overall impression of the agency and its work? Why?

3. **Direct Mail**

   Despite its junk-mail image, direct mail requires a great deal of creativity. Jones Educational Services, which provides GMAT, GRE, and MCAT preparation, has agreed that a direct-mail campaign may be the best way to increase its market share. Create a campaign for your college or university designed to attract top high school recruits. Browse the direct-mail related websites below for ideas.

   - Association of National Advertisers (ANA): www.ana.net
   - U.S. Postal Service: www.usps.com

4. **Sales Promotion**

   Sales promotion vehicles are often key elements in integrated marketing communication campaigns. Browse the websites of the following support organizations for the sales promotion field and answer the questions for each site.

   Sales Promotion Organizations

   - Promotional Products Association International (PPAI): www.ppai.org/
   - *Creative* Magazine: www.creativemag.com

   a. What group sponsors the site? Who is (are) the intended audience(s)?

   b. What is the organization's purpose?

   c. Who makes up the organization's membership? Its constituency?

   d. What benefit does the organization provide individual members/subscribers? The overall advertising and sales promotion communities?

   Sales Promotion Agencies

   Promotional companies, like their direct marketing counterparts, differ somewhat from traditional advertising firms. Visit the websites for the following sales promotion companies, and answer the questions below for each.

   - AdSolution: www.adsolution.com
   - BIC Graphic: www.bicgraphic.com
   - InterPromo, Inc.: www.interpromo.com
   - Valpak Coupons: www.valpak.com

   a. What is the focus of the company's work (i.e., consumer or trade)?

   b. What are the scope and size of the company's business?

   c. What promotional services does the company offer?

   d. What is your overall impression of the company and its work? Why?

5. Other insurance companies rely more heavily on a sales force to gain customers than does GEICO. Given what you know about direct-response advertising and personal selling, what are the pros and cons of each approach?

6. How does GEICO use advertising to both get an immediate response from prospects *and* build brand equity? Who else do you think does this well?

End Notes

1. Christian Sylt, "How Disney Cast Its Spell on Sponsorship," *Forbes,* July 12, 2018, www.forbes.com/sites/csylt/2018/07/12/how-disney-cast-its-spell-on-sponsorship/#5d1db176303d.

2. Ken Storey, "Disney Is Rumored to Be Spending $450 Million on a New Epcot Pavilion," *Orlando Weekly,* August 6, 2018, www.orlandoweekly.com/Blogs/archives/2018/08/06/disney-is-rumored-to-be-spending-450-million-on-a-new-epcot-pavilion.

3. Werner Weiss, "Two Myths About World Showcase at Epcot," *Myths & Legends About Disney at Yesterland.com,* August 31, 2018, www.yesterland.com/worldshowcase.html.

4. Amanda Kondoljy, "Disney Is Quietly Adding More Brands to Walt Disney World," *Theme Park Tourist,* July 16, 2018, www.themeparktourist.com/news/20180716/34071/disney-sponsorships.

5. Christian Sylt, "How Disney Cast Its Spell on Sponsorship," *Forbes,* July 12, 2018, www.forbes.com/sites/csylt/2018/07/12/how-disney-cast-its-spell-on-sponsorship/#5d1db176303d.

6. "What Is the Direct Marketing Association?" Association of National Advertisers.

7. "What Is the Direct Marketing Association?" Association of National Advertisers.

8. Bob Stone and Rob Jacobs, *Successful Direct Marketing Methods,* 8th ed. (New York: McGraw-Hill, 2007).

9. "12 Stats About Working Women," *U.S. Department of Labor Blog,* March 1, 2017, https://blog.dol.gov/2017/03/01/12-stats-about-working-women.

10. "Marketing Fact Pack 2018," *Advertising Age.* http://adage.com/d/resources/resources/whitepaper/marketing-fact-pack-2019

11. Ginger Conlon, "Marketing Spending in 2015," *DIrect Marketing News,* January 27, 2015, www.dmnews.com/marketing-strategy/marketing-spending-in-2015-infographic/article/400487/.

12. Ulatus, "Understanding Cultural Nuance in Your Translation," Feb. 5, 2016, www.ulatus.com/translation-blog/understanding-cultural-nuance-in-your-translation/

13. www.pitneybowes.com/us/rewards.html

14. Chris Luo, "Customer Acquisition vs. Retention: Which One Should You Choose?" *Fivestars,* 2016, https://blog.fivestars.com/customer-acquisition-vs-retention-which-one-should-you-choose/.

15. Rob Jackson, "Database Doctor," *Direct,* January 9, 1996.

16. Bob Stone and Rob Jacobs, *Successful Direct Marketing Methods,* 8th ed. (New York: McGraw-Hill, 2007).

17. Rob Jackson, "Database Doctor," *Direct,* January 9, 1996.

18. Thomas E. Caruso, "Kotler: Future Marketers Will Focus on Customer Data Base to Compete Globally," *Marketing News,* June 8, 1992, pp. 21–22.

19. Tom Van Riper, "The Why of Best Buy," *Forbes,* April 2, 2008, www.forbes.com/2008/04/02/retail-best-buy-biz-commerce-cx_tvr_0402retail.html#781c52183a9a.

20. Steven MacDonald, "GDPR for Marketing: The Definitive Guide for 2019," *SuperOffice,* January 4, 2019, www.superoffice.com/blog/gdpr-marketing/.

21. Nicholas G. Poulos, "Customer Loyalty and the Marketing Database," *Direct Marketing,* July 1996, pp. 32–35.

22. Larry Alton, "7 Tips for Marketing Effectively to Seniors," *SEMrush Blog,* May 12, 2017, www.semrush.com/blog/7-tips-for-marketing-effectively-to-seniors/.

23. Makena Kelly, "Google Faces Mounting Pressure from Congress over Google+ Privacy Flaw," *The Verge,* October 11, 2018, www.theverge.com/2018/10/11/17964134/google-plus-congress-privacy-data-vulnerability.

24. Robert A. Peterson and Thomas R. Wotruba, "What Is Direct Selling?—Definition, Perspectives, and Research Agenda," *Journal of Personal Selling and Sales Management* 16, no. 4 (Fall 1996), pp. 1–16.

25. Andy DIckens, "Telemarketing Is Dead. Here's Why," *VSL,* April 5, 2017, www.virtual-sales.com/telemarketing-dead-heres/.

26. Kailey Fralik, " Geico Home Insurance Review," *The Simple Dollar,* August 12, 2019, www.thesimpledollar.com/insurance/reviews/geico-home-insurance-review/

27. "Brief History of Toll-Free Numbers," www.tollfreenumbers.com.

28. Dave Sutton, "5 (Surprising?) Marketing Trends That Will Continue to Blow up in 2019," *Business to Community,* October 12, 2018, www.business2community.com/marketing/5-surprising-marketing-trends-that-will-continue-to-blow-up-in-2019-02129656.

29. Robert H. Hallowell III, "The Selling Points of Direct Mail," *Trusts & Estates,* December 1994, pp. 39–41.

30. Ami Miyazaki, *New Absolute Appeal: Direct Mail Design* (Tokyo: PIE International, 2010).

31. Ken Boone, Terry Woods, and John Leonard, *Direct Mail Pal: A Direct Mail Production Handbook* (Sewickley, PA: GATF Press, 2002).

32. U.S. Postal Service, www.usps.com.

33. Gwen Moran, "Postal Power—Direct Mail Tips for Small Business," 2002, www.bnet.com.

34. Courtney Reagan, " Millennials Are More Interested in Catalogs than Your Grandmother Is," *CNBC,* December 21, 2017, www.cnbc.com/2017/12/21/millennials-are-more-interested-in-catalogs-than-your-grandmother-is.html

35. Denise Lee Yohn, "Why the print catalog is back in style," *Harvard Business Review,* February 25, 2015, https://hbr.org/2015/02/why-the-print-catalog-is-back-in-style

36. Personal Interview with Tom Campanaro, President, Total Gym Inc., December 2000.

37. Electronic Retailing Association, "Consumer Spending Shows Electronic Retailing Shopper as Loyal, Satisfied, and Likely to Return for More Purchases," press release, June 9, 2004, www.retailing.org.

38. Nancy Colton Webster, "Radio Tuning in to Direct Response," *Advertising Age,* October 10, 1994, pp. S14, S15.

39. Murray Raphel, "Meet One of America's Top Salespeople," *Direct Marketing,* March 1994, p. 31.

40. Adapted from Barton A. Weitz, Stephen B. Castleberry, and John F. Tanner Jr., *Selling: Building Partnerships* (Burr Ridge, IL: Irwin, 1992), p. 5.

41. Edwin Klewer, Robert Shaffer, and Bonnie Binnig, "Sales Is an Investment, Attrition an Expense," *Journal of Health Care Marketing,* September 1995, p. 12.

42. Jayne Thompson, "Advantages and Disadvantages of Sales Promotions," *BizFluent,* October 25, 2018, https://bizfluent.com/list-6673344-advantages-disadvantages-sales-promotions.html.

43. Magid M. Abraham and Leonard M. Lodish, "Getting the Most Out of Advertising and Promotion," *Harvard Business Review,* May/June 1990, p. 51.

44. Larry Light, "Trustmarketing: The Brand Relationship Marketing Mandate for the 90's," address to American Association of Advertising Agencies, Laguna Niguel, CA, April 23, 1993.

45. Larry Light, "At the Center of It All Is the Brand," *Advertising Age,* March 29, 1993, p. 22.

46. Federal Trade Commission, *Report of the Federal Trade Commission Workshop on Slotting Allowances and Other Marketing Practices in the Grocery Industry,* February 2001, p. 69.

47. Robert A. Skitol, "FTC Spices Up Debate over Slotting Fees and the Robinson-Patman Act with Its McCormick Action," March 13, 2000, American Antitrust Institute FTC: Watch #540, www.antitrustinstitute.org.

48. *The Point of Purchase Advertising Industry Fact Book* (Washington, DC: POPAI, 1997), p. 51.

49. Kelly Shermach, "Study: Most Shoppers Notice P-O-P Material," *Marketing News,* January 1995, p. 27.

50. *The Point of Purchase Advertising Industry Fact Book* (Washington, DC: POPAI, 1997), p. 39; Kelly Shermach, "Great Strides Made in P-O-P Technology," *Marketing News,* January 2, 1995, pp. 8–9.

51. Angela Lawson, "The End of the Line," June 18, 2004, www.kioskmarketplace.com/article.php?id=13673.

52. Carol Angrisani, "Coupon Competition," *SN: Supermarket News,* March 3, 2006, pp. 23–25.

53. Bruce Crumley, "Multipoints Adds Up for Quick Burger," *Advertising Age,* November 29, 1993, p. 14.

54. Stephanie Moore, "Rebate Madness—How to Avoid the Rebate Trap," www.consumeraffairs.com.

55. Lorraine Calvacca, "Polybagging Products to Pick Up Customers," *Folio: The Magazine for Magazine Management,* January 1993, p. 26.

Relationship Building: Public Relations, Sponsorship, and Corporate Advertising

---

LEARNING OBJECTIVES

To explain the role of public relations, sponsorships, and corporate advertising in relationship marketing and integrated marketing communications. By integrating public relations, event sponsorships, and institutional advertising with general advertising activities, a company can improve the effectiveness of its marketing efforts.

After studying this chapter, you will be able to:

LO 18-1   Define public relations and distinguish it from advertising.

LO 18-2   List the functions performed by public relations professionals.

LO 18-3   Identify the tools public relations practioners use.

LO 18-4   Explain the growing interest in sponsorships and describe when sponsorships should be included in an IMC plan.

LO 18-5   Define corporate advertising and list the activities that are included under this concept.

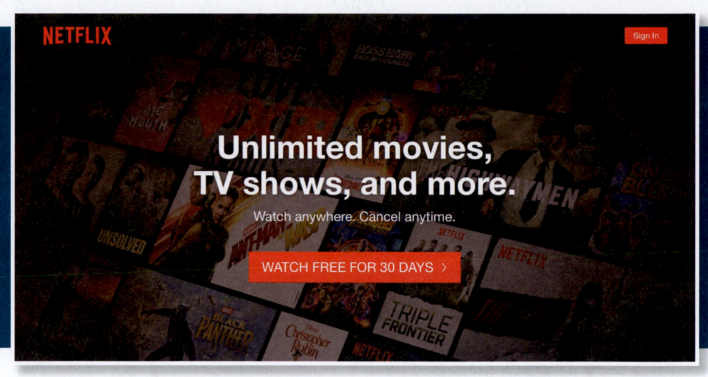

Source: Netflix, Inc.

This vignette might be subtitled: how to squander ten years of goodwill and then compound the damage with poor public relations. But get it back in the end. ■ It begins with one of today's successful companies, Netflix. Most people know of Netflix as a company that streams movies and TV shows. But in its original incarnation, the firm disrupted an earlier model of content distribution: DVD rentals. Legend has it that founder and CEO Reed Hastings launched his company after balking at fees he owed for a late DVD rental. His great idea was to deliver DVD rentals without three annoyances: late fees, return dates, and the need to drive to the store. ■ Launched in 1998, Netflix allowed consumers to get movies in the mail, keep them as long as they wanted, and drop them in the mailbox for returns. All for one low monthly fee. ■ The company grew from 1 million subscribers in 2002 to nearly 14 million just eight years later. And while not profitable until 2003, when Netflix's model took hold, the writing was on the wall for brick-and-mortar companies like Blockbuster and Hollywood Video. ■ Netflix leveraged a number of technologies in its rise to the top, including the internet. Customers could go to the company's website and order their next selection. But by

2010, the internet also ensured that Netflix would face a new, nimbler, faster-growing, and more convenient challenger: itself. Netflix began competing with itself when it allowed a small portion of its catalog to be streamed. The streaming service was offered for no additional charge to individuals on the traditional plan. ■ While most customers, at first, still ordered their DVDs by mail, streaming was clearly the future. But with two delivery models the company was competing with itself. Supporting both models was expensive. Profit margins began tanking as the service grew. ■ So Hastings made a decision: Customers who wanted to get DVDs by mail and enjoy unlimited streaming would see their monthly rate jump from $9.99 to $15.98. When the company introduced the price increase, it called it "a terrific value." That's not how Netflix customers saw it. In fact, many, shocked at the price jump, were outraged. Austin Carr, writing for Fastcompany.com, wrote, "Subscribers saw right through this corporate boilerplate, leaving nearly 13,000 comments on Netflix's blog, creating a social media nightmare for the company on Twitter and Facebook, and overwhelming Netflix's call center with complaints."[1] ■ But there was more to come. Hastings decided to split mail delivery and streaming into two different companies. Netflix would focus on streaming delivery, and a new independent subsidiary, Qwikster, would deliver DVDs by mail. The companies would be completely separate and require separate subscriptions. The response? More outrage. ■ Hastings understood that he had done a poor job explaining his decisions. He blogged,

> When Netflix is evolving rapidly . . . I need to be extra-communicative. This is the key thing I got wrong . . . In hindsight, I slid into arrogance based upon past success. We have done very well for a long time by steadily improving our service, without doing much CEO communication. Inside Netflix I say, "Actions speak louder than words," and we should just keep improving our service. But now I see that given the huge changes we have been recently making, I should have personally given a full justification to our members of why we are separating DVD and streaming, and charging for both.[2]

Hastings also dove into the comments section of his blog to deal with consumers directly. Fastcompany.com recounts the following exchange between Hastings and a customer:

> Customer: "Seriously, you thought a good idea to make up for miscommunications was to separate the websites and make it more complicated for us to manage our queues? Really?"
>
> Hastings: "We think the separate websites (a link away from each other) will enable us to improve both faster than if they were single websites." (Only 54 Likes, at last count.)[3]

Consumers were unhappy, and Netflix estimated that it lost nearly a million subscribers in the third quarter of 2011. But while it was easy for consumers to dislike the company's decisions, in truth Hastings had little choice. Offering both services for under $10 was unsustainable. Netflix needed to alter its pricing model, or face the financial losses dictated by the marketplace. Could it have done so in a better way, one that would have allowed its customers to better understand the need for the company's actions? ■ Perhaps. But Netflix has survived this bump in the road. By the fourth quarter of 2011, it was adding subscribers again, finishing the year with over 20 million subscribers. And by 2019, the company had an amazing 146 million subscribers.[4] Hastings may have stumbled early in his explanations to the loyal customers of Netflix, but by showing a willingness to engage, listen to complaints, and respond proactively, he was able to quickly right the ship. And calm waters and smooth sailing have characterized the company's growth ever since.

Public Relations: IMC and More

LO 18-1

The primary role of public relations is to manage a company's reputation and help build public consent for its enterprises. Today's business environment has become so competitive that public consent can no longer be assumed; it must be earned.[5]

The term *public relations* is widely misused. Part of the confusion is because the term covers a broad range of activities. Depending on the context and one's point of view, it can be a concept, a profession, a management function, or a practice. For our purposes, we define **public relations (PR)** as the strategic management of the relationships and messages that individuals and organizations have with other groups for the purpose of creating mutual goodwill.

Every company, organization, or government body has relationships with people who are affected by what it does or says. They may be employees, customers, stockholders, competitors, suppliers, legislators, or the community in which the organization resides. Marketing professionals refer to these people as *stakeholders* because they have some vested interest in the company's actions. In PR terminology, these groups are considered the organization's **publics,** and the goal of PR is to develop and maintain

Reed Hastings, pictured above, has always understood the need to consider public relations activities with loyal customers. The changes Hastings made to Netflix, and his poor way of communicating about them, cost the company goodwill and subscribers. But Hastings remained engaged with customers and improved his product, ultimately returning Netflix to growth and profitability.

Juan Naharro Gimenez/Getty Images

goodwill with most, if not all, of a company's publics. Failure to do so may mean loss of customers and revenues, time lost dealing with complaints or lawsuits, unwanted regulation or legislation that negatively impacts the firm, and loss of esteem (which weakens the organization's brand equity as well as its ability to secure financing, make sales, and grow).

A company's publics change constantly. When its founders sold the business to a large multinational company, Ben & Jerry's faced criticism from previously silent, content publics. It still generally projects a sunny, laid-back image even though it is now part of global marketing giant Unilever, but this did not quell the critics. The Center for Science in the Public Interest (CSPI) accused Ben & Jerry's of misleading the public by claiming that some of its products were "all-natural" when they in fact contained hydrogenated oils and artificial flavors. CSPI called on the FDA to take action against the company.[6] Ben & Jerry's hedged response was that the term "all-natural" had various definitions in the food industry, but that it would work with natural food organizations on the issue.[7] Subsequently, the company voluntarily recalled pints of its Karamel Sutra ice cream that contained peanuts not mentioned on the label. After receiving one illness complaint about this common food allergen, the recall went forward, with CEO Yves Couette stating, "Our primary concern is always for the health and safety of our consumers."[8] These issues have not gone away, even many years after Unilever's acquisition. In the summer of 2018, the company was sued by the Organic Consumers Association, which challenged Ben & Jerry's claim that its ice cream is manufactured from milk from "happy cows" residing in "caring Dairies." The suit also charged that the ice cream is not 100 percent organic.[9]

Because of the powerful effect of public opinion, companies must consider the breadth of impact of their actions. This is especially true in times of crisis. But it also holds true for major policy decisions: changes in management or pricing, labor negotiations, introduction of new products, or changes in distribution methods. Each decision affects stakeholders in different ways. Effective public relations can channel groups' opinions toward mutual understanding and positive outcomes.

In short, the goals of public relations are to improve public opinion, build goodwill, and establish and maintain a satisfactory reputation for the organization. PR efforts may rally public support, obtain public understanding or neutrality, or simply respond to inquiries. Well-executed public relations is an ongoing process that molds good long-term relationships and plays an important role in relationship marketing and IMC.[10]

The Difference between Advertising and Public Relations

Advertising and public relations are similar—but they're not the same. Advertising reaches its audience through paid media. It appears just as the advertiser designed it, with the advertiser's bias built in. Knowing this, the public views ads with some skepticism. So in an IMC program, advertising claims are often viewed as lacking credibility.

Many public relations messages, like publicity, are not openly sponsored (see the ethical issues this raises in the Ethics, Diversity & Inclusion box). People receive these communications in the form of reviews, news articles, corporate blogs, or feature stories. Such messages are reviewed and edited—filtered—by the media. Because the public thinks they come from a news organization rather than a company, it trusts public relations messages more readily. For building credibility, therefore, public relations is usually the better approach. Netflix, for example, benefited heavily from favorable press reviews during its heady growth years.

However, while advertising is carefully placed to gain particular reach and frequency objectives, PR is less precise. Public relations objectives are not as easy to quantify. In fact, the results gained from public relations activities depend greatly on the experience and skill of the people executing them and the relationship they have with the press. But PR can go only so far. Editors won't run the same story over and over. An ad's memorability, however, comes from repetition. While PR activities may offer greater

Ellen DeGeneres has enormous influence with millions of consumers who enjoy her shows. So when Ellen suggests she has a strong brand preference, the impact on sales is substantial.

Neil Rasmus/BFA/Sipa/Newscom

Ethics, Diversity & Inclusion

Public Relations—Meet Social Media and the Web

What happens when unregulated meets anonymous? Welcome to public relations in the internet age.

PR practitioner Todd Defren raises several real-world digital public relations ethical issues in his blog "PRsquared." In one, Defren asked, "What would you do if a client contact—who had a pretty solid Twitter following—asked you to tweet from his account as if you were him? Crazy? Wrong? Unethical?"[11]

Defren raises the same issue about a corporate blog. He refers to the practice of a PR agency writing unattributed posts for a client as "ghostblogging." "You can rail against it as a black mark against authenticity," notes Defren, "but it is happening and it is a trend that will only grow. Not enough people see this as a bright line separating 'good' from 'bad' . . ."

And speaking of blogs, how ethical is it to pay people to give a brand or company favorable coverage? The site payperpost.com encourages visitors to "Make money blogging! PayPerPost lets you pick your advertisers, name your own price and negotiate your own deals. You can get paid to blog on virtually any subject. Sign up below!"[12] How credible would you find such posts if you knew they were sponsored?

Even big brands are getting in on the game. Coach collaborates with bloggers, even asking them to appear in its ad campaigns. WWD.com quotes David Duplantis, executive VP of global and digital media, as saying, "We see bloggers as editors, influencers and entrepreneurs who reach a very specific and unique audience. We find great value in working with those who are relevant to our brand, and are willing to pay fairly for projects."[13] Duplantis believes that while Coach benefits from bloggers, the bloggers in turn benefit from working with a brand as important as Coach. But how do consumers benefit if they are unaware of a brand–blogger relationship?

The analyst firm Forrester thinks it's smart for companies to pay bloggers to engage in "sponsored conversations." Marshall Kirkpatrick at ReadWriteWeb.com, disagrees, noting, "We respectfully disagree with Forrester's recommendations on this topic. In fact, we think that paying bloggers to write about your company is a dangerous and unsavory path for new media and advertisers to go down."[14]

Maybe all of this has convinced you that if you are looking for advice, you might want to skip blogs. Better to use a search engine, like Google, that can deliver search results that reflect the wisdom of millions of consumers. But what if a company tried to take advantage of Google's search engine? JCPenney decided it would try. Thousands of fake pages were created featuring key words valuable to the store. The initiative was designed to take advantage of Google's PageRank system and send shoppers to JCPenney's website. Not illegal, certainly. But ethical? Google eventually intervened and made it less likely JCPenney's results would show up in "organic" search.

But if Google polices JCPenney, who polices Google? The company admitted that it paid bloggers to promote its Chrome browser. Dailytech.com reported that Google indicated it had "investigated" and that it would be "taking manual action to demote www.google.com/chrome and lower the site's PageRank for a period of at least 60 days."[15] Maybe all of this seems so frustrating to you that you've resolved to stick to Twitter, where at least you can judge a source's credibility by observing the number of followers that the individual or group has. After all, millions of followers can't be wrong. Unfortunately, the number of "followers" of a Twitter source may be very misleading because sources can actually buy followers. *The New York Times* and *USA Today* have reported that up to 70 percent of Barack Obama's followers, and 71 percent of Lady Gaga's, are "fake" or "inactive."

The web is an evolving medium, and companies are searching for ways to profit from it. The history of advertising suggests that consumers will reject companies that try to take advantage of them unfairly, unethically, or dishonestly. That is something every brand manager might want to keep in mind.

Questions

1. Do any of the activities described above strike you as unethical? Why?

2. Do you agree that consumers will not long stand for deceptive or underhanded practices? What actions, both corporate and governmental, will evolve if consumers lose faith in social media and the web as sources of marketing information?

credibility, advertising offers precision and control. This is why some companies relay their public relations messages through *corporate advertising,* which we discuss later in this chapter.

Advertising and PR in the Eyes of Practitioners

Another major difference between public relations and advertising is the orientation of professional practitioners. Advertising professionals see *marketing* as the umbrella process companies use to determine what products and services the market needs and how to distribute and sell them. To advertising professionals, advertising and public relations are marketing tools used to promote sales.

Public relations professionals take a different view. With their background typically in journalism rather than marketing, they believe *public relations* should be the umbrella

Exhibit 18-1
Top global public relations agencies 2018.

Firm (Country)	Fee Income (000,000)	% Fee Change from 2017
1. Edelman (USA)	$894	2.1%
2. Weber Shandwick (USA)	805	−2.4
3. FleishmanHillard (USA)	570	0
4. Ketchum (USA)	550	−2.1
5. Burson-Marsteller (USA)	463	−3.5
6. MSL (France)	460	0
7. Hill+Knowlton Strategies (USA)	400	1.3
8. Ogilvy (USA)	354	−1.9
9. BlueFocus (China)	322	19.8
10. Cohn & Wolfe (USA)	246	9.8

Note: Burson-Marsteller and Cohn & Wolfe have since merged to become Burson Cohn & Wolfe.

Source: "Global Top 250 PR Agency Rankings 2018," *The Holmes Report,* www.holmesreport.com/ranking-and-data/global-pr-agency-rankings/2018-pr-agency-rankings/top-250.

Every company makes mistakes. Smart ones address them head on and renew their commitment to great products and service. When David Neeleman, founder and CEO of JetBlue, offered an apology to customers for a week of operational snafus, he did not mince words: "JetBlue was founded on the promise of bringing humanity back to air travel, and making the experience of flying happier. . . . We know we failed to deliver on this promise last week. . . . You deserved better—a lot better . . . and we let you down."

Leonard Zhukovsky/Shutterstock

process. They think companies should use PR to maintain relationships with all publics, including consumers. As *Inside PR* magazine says, "Public relations is a management discipline that encompasses a wide range of activities, from *marketing and advertising* to investor relations and government affairs."[16] To PR professionals, public relations should be integrated "corporate" or strategic communications, which is broader than integrated "marketing" communications. Public relations people, for example, are also concerned with employee relations and investor relations. Marketing and advertising people rarely are.

Apple is one of the world's most popular brands, but it too discovered the value of good public relations. Like many companies, Apple uses Chinese factories to produce iPads and other technologies at relatively low costs. This in turn helps Apple market iPads for a price that makes it difficult for competitors to beat in the marketplace. Offering a strong value proposition is, of course, an important marketing goal. But when rumors of terrible factory conditions at its Chinese plant began circulating, Apple faced a problem that went beyond marketing. Acting on the basis of its public relations counsel, Apple invited ABC news to tour its Chinese partner's factory. ABC found that the rumors were false and that employees were well treated. Crisis averted.

To date, though, few companies are structured with a public relations orientation; most are still marketing oriented, perhaps due to marketing's bottom-line orientation. But in a world of downsizing, reengineering, and total quality management (TQM), marketing people would be well advised to adopt the multiple-stakeholder approach and relationship consciousness that PR people bring to the table.

Moreover, in times of crisis, the candid, open-information orientation of PR is invariably the better perspective to adopt. Fortunately, with the growing interest in relationship marketing, two-way interactivity, and IMC, companies are finally beginning to embrace a public relations philosophy. Exhibit 18-1 shows some indicators of the PR industry's health and growth.

When PR activities are used for marketing purposes, the term **marketing public relations (MPR)** is often used. In support of marketing, public relations activities can raise awareness, inform and educate, improve understanding, build trust, make friends, give people reasons or permission to buy, and create a climate of consumer acceptance.[17] Marketing strategists Al and Laura Ries believe the best way to build a brand is through publicity—a PR activity. They cite numerous examples of leading companies that achieved their cachet with relatively little advertising but extensive publicity: Starbucks, The Body Shop, and Walmart, to name a few.[18]

In an integrated marketing communications program, advertising and MPR need to be closely coordinated. Many ad agencies now have PR departments for this very purpose. And many companies now have communications departments that manage both advertising and PR.

LO 18-2

Information

TO PRESERVE OUR OCEANS: ADIDAS TO PRODUCE MORE SHOES USING RECYCLED PLASTIC WASTE IN 2019

January 21, 2019—

In 2018 adidas produced more than five million pairs of shoes containing recycled plastic waste. The company now plans to more than double that figure this year. As outcome of a cooperation between the sporting goods manufacturer and the environmental organization and global collaboration network Parley for the Oceans, plastic waste is intercepted on beaches, such as the Maldives, before it can reach the oceans. That upcycled plastic waste is made into a yarn becoming a key component of the upper material of adidas footwear. In addition to footwear, the company also produces apparel from the recycled material, such as the Champions League jersey for FC Bayern Munich and Alexander Zverev's outfit for the Australian Open.

> With adidas products made from recycled plastic, we offer our consumers real added value beyond the look, functionality and quality of the product, because every shoe is a small contribution to the preservation of our oceans. After one million pairs of shoes produced in 2017, five million in 2018, we plan to produce eleven million pairs of shoes containing recycled ocean plastic in 2019.

ERIC LIEDTKE, ADIDAS EXECUTIVE BOARD MEMBER RESPONSIBLE FOR GLOBAL BRANDS

"Sustainability at adidas goes far beyond recycled plastic," added Executive Board member Gil Steyaert, responsible for Global Operations. "We also continue to improve our environmental performance during the manufacturing of our products. This includes the use of sustainable materials, the reduction of CO_2 emissions and waste prevention. In 2018 alone, we saved more than 40 tons of plastic waste in our offices, retail stores, warehouses and distribution centers worldwide and replaced it with more sustainable solutions."

Recently, adidas signed the Climate Protection Charter for the Fashion Industry at the UN Climate Change Conference in Katowice, Poland, and agreed to reduce greenhouse gas emissions by 30 percent by 2030. In addition, adidas is committed to using only recycled polyester in every product and on every application where a solution exists by 2024. As a founding member of the Better Cotton Initiative, adidas meanwhile sources only sustainably produced cotton. Since 2016, adidas stores no longer use plastic bags.

Where the use of plastics—for example in transport packaging—is still unavoidable, adidas is relying on counterbalancing measures and promoting sustainable alternatives. The company is currently supporting the global innovation platform Fashion for Good with a donation of €1.5 million which equates to the company's environmental impact of plastic packaging. The foundation is driving the development of innovative, durable and reusable materials for the fashion industry. adidas has been a partner of the foundation since the beginning of 2018.

This adidas press release is a good example of a company notifying both current shareholders and prospective shareholders of a business practice relevant to sustainability and corporate social responsibility.

Source: Adidas, "Adidas to Produce More Shoes Using Recycled Plastic Waste in 2019," press release, January 21, 2019.

The Public Relations Job

Public relations involves a variety of activities, from crisis communications to fund-raising. And PR practitioners use many tools besides press conferences and news releases.

PR Planning and Research

The first function of a PR practitioner is to plan and execute the public relations program. Part of this task may be integrated with the company's marketing efforts (for instance, product publicity), but the PR person typically takes a broader view. He or she must prepare a public relations program for the whole organization.

Effective planning requires that public relations professionals constantly monitor, measure, and analyze changes in attitudes and behaviors among a variety of publics. When some Belgian consumers became ill after drinking Coca-Cola, the investment firm of Goldman, Sachs & Co. monitored Coke's standing with the general consuming public so that it could make better investment recommendations to its clientele. Analysts realized that rebuilding consumer confidence would probably require substantial marketing investment. And invest Coke did. Coke sponsored a "Coca-Cola Beach Party" featuring Beach Boys songs and dancing over tons of imported sand. Summer tours and thousands of premiums were also supported. Within three months of lifting a ban on the sale of Coke products, Coke's primary consumers had purchase intentions that matched those of the pre-crisis period.[19] Some 19 percent of consumers polled in Belgium, France, and Germany expressed at least some reservations about drinking Coke products in the future—even after Coke had begun airing a new campaign. However, 77 percent of Belgians, 70 percent of French, and 61 percent of the Germans said they had complete faith in the company's products.[20]

A common form of public relations research is **opinion sampling** using techniques discussed in Chapter 7: shopping center or phone interviews, focus groups, analysis of incoming mail, and field reports. Some companies set up toll-free phone lines and invite consumer feedback.

The practitioner analyzes the organization's relationships with its publics; evaluates people's attitudes and opinions toward the organization; assesses how company policies and actions relate to different publics; determines PR objectives and strategies; develops and implements a mix of PR activities, integrating them whenever possible with the firm's other communications; and solicits feedback to evaluate effectiveness.

Social media provide PR experts a window into the minds of consumers, especially "influentials," the individuals whose opinions matter a great deal to others (we referred to these individuals as "centers of influence" in earlier chapters). Influentials are easy to spot online—they have large numbers monitoring their tweets, blog postings, or comments (although see the Ethics, Diversity & Inclusion box for a different take on "followers"). It is no surprise then that the arrival of social media has transformed public relations so dramatically that some now refer to it as "public relations 2.0."[21]

Reputation Management

One of the principal tasks of public relations is managing the standing of the firm with various publics. **Reputation management** is the name of this long-term strategic process. PR practitioners employ a number of strategies and tactics to help them manage their clients' reputation, including publicity and press agentry, crisis communications management, and community involvement.

Publicity and Press Agentry

Many public relations professionals focus primarily on generating news and placing it in the media for their companies or clients. **Publicity** is the generation of news about a person, product, or service that appears in print or electronic media. Companies employ this activity either for marketing purposes or to enhance the firm's reputation.

Some people think of publicity as "free" because the media don't charge firms to run it (they also don't guarantee they'll use it). This is a misnomer, though. Someone still gets paid to write the release and coordinate with the press. However, as a marketing communications vehicle, publicity often offers a considerably greater return on money invested than other communications activities. A large ad campaign might require an investment of 5 to 20 percent of sales; a major publicity program, only 1 to 2 percent.

To attract media attention, publicity must be *newsworthy*. Typical publicity opportunities include new-product introductions, awards, company sales and earnings, major new contracts, mergers, retirements, parades, and speeches by company executives. Sometimes publicity accrues unintentionally, such as when Netflix instituted its price increases. And because publicity can originate from any source, it may be difficult—or impossible—to control. In IMC terms, unintentional publicity is an *unplanned message*.

The planning and staging of events to generate publicity is called **press agentry.** Press agentry helps bring attention to new products or services or to portray their organizations favorably. For print media, the publicity person deals with editors and feature writers. For broadcast media, he or she deals with program directors, assignment editors, or news editors. Successful PR practitioners maintain close, cordial relations with their editorial contacts. An MPR professional practicing IMC sees the press as an important *public,* and writers and editors as important *stakeholders.* PR people pay attention to the phenomenon of stakeholder overlap: A company's customer might also work for the press. An employee might also be a stockholder and a customer. Awareness of these potentially multifaceted relationships helps create consistent communications, the hallmark of IMC. To learn about an intriguing example of press agentry, listen to the father of American Public Relations (and Freud's nephew) Edward Bernays describe his early campaign to get Americans to eat eggs and bacon for breakfast. You can see it at www.youtube.com/watch?v=KLudEZpMjKU.

Crisis Communications Management

One of the most important public relations tasks for any corporation is **crisis management.** Brand value can be quickly destroyed if "damage control" is not swift and thorough. For example, Martha Stewart's formerly profitable marketing persona quickly became a liability in 2002 when her involvement in an insider-trading scheme surfaced (she was later tried and sentenced to a prison term). Even though her company, Martha Stewart Living Omnimedia, immediately began efforts to distance itself from its founder's legal troubles by removing her name from some products and publications, its stock value and revenues both dropped by more than 30 percent.[22]

The classic case of exemplary crisis communication management was Johnson & Johnson's handling of a product-tampering episode in 1982. Several people died when a criminal laced bottles of J&J's Extra-Strength Tylenol with cyanide on retail shelves. The

VERY FEW CRIME REPORTS START WITH "THE SUSPECT, A FORMER CUB SCOUT, WAS LAST SEEN..."

CUB SCOUT ENROLLMENT IS HERE. WWW.JOINCUBS.COM

Nonprofits and service organizations also rely on publicity to educate others about the good that they do. This clever message for the Cub Scouts creates goodwill, even among people who are not parents of Scouts, by speaking to a broader social benefit provided by the organization.

Source: Northern Star Council, BSA

moment they received the news, management strategists at J&J and McNeil Products (the J&J subsidiary that markets Tylenol) formulated three stages of action:

1. Identify the problem and take immediate corrective action. J&J strategists got information from the police, FBI, FDA, and press; identified the geographic area affected; corrected rumors; and immediately withdrew the product from the marketplace.

2. Actively cooperate with authorities in the investigation. Johnson & Johnson was proactive. It helped the FBI and other law enforcement agencies generate leads and investigate security at the plants, and it offered a $100,000 reward.

3. Quickly rebuild the Tylenol name and capsule line, including Regular Strength capsules, which were recalled too. Although J&J believed the poisoning had taken place at the retail end of the chain, it first made sure that the tampering hadn't occurred at McNeil. The company's two capsule production lines were shut down, and dog teams were brought in to search for cyanide.

The insatiable appetite of the news media plus a flood of inquiries from anxious consumers put J&J's PR people under enormous pressure. All communications between the media and the company were channeled through the corporate communications department. All customer, trade, and government communications were coordinated within the company. This way, J&J maintained open, clear, consistent, legal, and credible communications and avoided rumors, political backbiting, and corporate defensiveness.

In the first 48 hours after the news broke, phone calls to Johnson & Johnson and McNeil were incessant. In the basement at McNeil, a bank of phones usually used for sales was staffed by employees who were briefed on what to say, what not to say, and where to refer tough questions.

At the same time, management and employees had to be informed, authorities contacted, and many others notified. J&J and McNeil public relations managers and staff had to plan, coordinate, and supervise this enormous task.

As infrequent as disasters are, there is no more important activity for PR professionals and public information officers than crisis communications management—especially those in highly sensitive fields such as airlines, government agencies, the military, law enforcement, chemical and oil companies, health, and public utilities.

Since the Tylenol incident, many companies in normally nonsensitive industries have prepared crisis management plans. The manner in which a company handles communications during emergencies or catastrophes will determine to a great extent how the public responds to the news. When corporations have no plans for coping with crisis, the resulting press coverage can be disastrous. Experts on crisis management encourage all companies to follow J&J's example by being open and candid. Withholding information or evading questions inevitably backfires, as many politicians have learned.

Attitudes toward a former crisis can soften over time. Netflix, after losing subscribers over its botched growth plans, eventually resumed growth. And Martha Stewart, Michael Vick, Tiger Woods, and many others have had "second chances" after bad publicity.

Community Involvement

The goal of **community involvement** is to develop a dialogue between the company and the community.[23] This is best done by having company officers, management, and employees contribute to the community's social and economic development. Every community offers opportunities for corporate involvement: civic and youth groups, charitable fund-raising drives, cultural or recreational activities, and so on. As we discussed in Chapter 8, a company should ideally adopt one program relevant to its expertise and focus its *mission marketing* activities. The PR department may help set up such programs and publicize them to the community (see Ad Lab 18–A).

AD Lab 18–A

"Green" Advertising

Since its introduction in the mid-1980s, environmental advertising has become a significant aspect of marketing. Advertisers saw the consumer desire for environmentally safe products and tried to meet the demand as quickly as possible. Many advertisers embraced genuine concern for the environment. But it didn't take long for consumers to catch on to the fact that some companies were making false claims, using such vague terms as *environmentally friendly* and *green*.

In a short time, consumers grew wary of the environmental appeal, and advertisers reacted by reducing its emphasis. To avoid future trouble, many companies waited for state and federal governments to define terms and provide legal guidelines. Over the past decade, the Federal Trade Commission (FTC) has established rules and guidelines, while several states adopted a set of laws setting definitions for terms like *ozone friendly, biodegradable,* and *recycled*. In 1995, California's Truth in Environmental Advertising law was enacted. It was shortly repealed and introduced again in 1997 without success.

Presently, there are no federal laws governing what a seller can say about a product. The FTC, in cooperation with the Environmental Protection Agency (EPA), has developed new guidelines for advertisers to ensure that their environmental marketing claims do not mislead consumers. These Guidelines for the Use of Environmental Advertising Claims carry no force of law, and compliance is voluntary.

Several companies and organizations act as intermediaries between advertisers and consumers regarding environmental claims. Scientific Certification Systems (SCS) (www.planetinc.com/certification.htm), for instance, verifies claims of recycled content in products. It uses an environmental report card, which measures a product's total environmental impact.

Green Seal (www.greenseal.org), an independent, nonprofit organization, promotes the manufacture and sale of environmentally responsible consumer products. It awards a Green Seal of Approval to products that cause less harm to the environment than other similar products. Founded in 1994, Green Seal "focuses on the measure of environmental damage that scientists have found to be most important in certain product categories," says Norman Dean, president.

Today's new marketing sensitivity toward the environment and social consciousness focuses on consumer purchasing behavior. Seventy-nine percent of Americans consider themselves environmentalists, 83 percent say they have changed their shopping habits to help protect the environment, and 67 percent say they would be willing to pay 5 to 10 percent more for environmentally friendly products. The data, however, are contradicted by more recent studies that reveal that people in America do not actually buy the products they claim to prefer. Even though studies show a high concern for the environment, the public lacks a behavior consistent with such concerns. Researchers believe that this attitude–behavior gap exists when the competitive advantage of green products is overcome by factors of price, quality, and convenience.

But in an increasingly competitive marketplace, firms must ultimately benefit from their green actions. A new environmental management tool called SPINE was developed to help industries achieve environmental recognition. SPINE makes it possible for customers to verify marketers' environmental claims by following a product's manufacturing process through every step.

Even with organizations such as Scientific Certification Systems and Green Seal, and reference tools such as SPINE, it is still a major challenge to get businesses and consumers to understand the value of green advertising, especially when no stringent regulations are in effect. Today, the consumer can only speculate how "environmentally friendly" a company actually is. Thinking about the future, either through regulation or voluntary action, companies will have to provide consumers with more information about the environmental friendliness of their products so customers may decide for themselves how well a product suits their needs.

Laboratory Applications

1. Imagine you are marketing a new product that sells for $1.25 and is environmentally safe. Would you spend thousands of dollars for a green seal on your impulse product if consumers are ambivalent toward such environmentally safe goods, as observed in the first wave? Explain.

2. Imagine that you just made manufacturing changes to your product so that it is now easily recyclable. Would you advertise these changes, knowing the restrictions on the term *recycle*?

Other Public Relations Activities

In addition to planning and reputation management, public relations professionals are often involved in activities such as public affairs and lobbying, speechwriting, fund-raising and membership drives, creation of publications, and special-events management.

Public Affairs and Lobbying

Organizations often need to deal with elected officials, regulatory and legislative bodies, and various community groups—the realm of **public affairs.** Public affairs usually requires a specialist. Many experts think PR and public affairs should become more integrated to combine the skills and policy expertise of the specialist with the PR person's media and community relations savvy.

The internet has created new methods of public relations activities. Corporate blogs, such as this example from Netflix, are an important way for companies to stay in touch with the press, customers, and other publics.

Source: Netflix, Inc.

Lobbying refers to informing government officials and persuading them to support or thwart administrative action or legislation in the interests of some client. Every organization is affected by the government, so lobbying is big business.

Speechwriting

Because company officials often have to speak at stockholder meetings, conferences, or conventions, PR practitioners often engage in **speechwriting.** They are also frequently responsible for making all the arrangements for speaking opportunities and developing answers for questions company representatives are likely to be asked. Because public relations people may sometimes represent their employers at special events, press conferences, and interviews, they too should be articulate public speakers.

Fund-raising and Membership Drives

A public relations person may be responsible for soliciting money for a nonprofit organization or for a cause the company deems worthwhile, such as the United Way or a political action committee (PAC).

Charitable organizations, labor unions, professional societies, trade associations, and other groups rely on membership fees or contributions. The PR specialist must communicate to potential contributors or members the goals of the organization and may integrate promotional tie-ins to publicize the drive or encourage participation. In the process, the company PR people may work closely with the advertising department or agency to create ads promoting the particular cause or to publicize the company's involvement with the cause in product ads.

Publications

Public relations people prepare many of a company's communications materials: news releases and media kits; booklets, leaflets, pamphlets, brochures, manuals, and books; letters, inserts, and enclosures; annual reports; posters, bulletin boards, and exhibits; audiovisual materials; and speeches and position papers. Here again, they may work with the advertising department or agency to produce these materials. The advertising people need to keep the company's overall positioning strategy in mind while trying to help accomplish the particular PR objectives.

Social Media

With the advent of social media and the rise in popularity of blogging and microblogging, staying on top of who is writing about what is a full-time job. It used to be that a PR professional would have to know a score of people for each industry; nowadays that score is exponentially bigger. However, with the bad comes the good, and the clarity that comes from social media allows PR professionals to stay on top of any trends and deal with them before they become brand epidemics. With a good social media strategy, PR professionals can help get influential people to showcase their client's products as they launch, keeping the early adopters and/or loyalists abreast of new developments before the advertising hits.

Corporate Blogs

Maintaining and managing a **corporate blog** can help address important concerns, introduce new products or services, and maintain a dialogue between a company and its publics. My IMC Campaign 18–A, "Corporate Blogging," provides some guidelines for using this public relations activity.

Special-Events Management

The sponsorship and management of special events is a rapidly growing field. In fact, it has become such an important topic that we devote the next major section of this chapter to it, following our discussion of PR tools.

My IMC Campaign 18-A

Corporate Blogging

Most corporations have guidelines for blogging. Here is a set of marketing-related guidelines that every corporation should think about if they intend to use blogging for a marketing tool.

- **Know the environment.** What are people saying about you and your products? Venture out into the web and see what happens when you type your company name into Google or visit popular blogs that deal with your company's product category.

- **Determine what you hope to accomplish.** What is your purpose? Why have you started the blog? To address rumors? Share company news? Inform customers about new products? Develop a corporate personality? Having clear objectives will make decisions about what and when to blog much easier.

- **Practice, practice, practice.** Do a trial run. Blogging is time-consuming, sometimes difficult, and a different kind of activity for many organizations. Smart companies generate initial blog posts internally until it is clear that the tactic will be useful and rewarding.

- **Remember that it's a two-way street.** Learn to share control. Blogs without comments have minimal value, but with comments comes criticism. Smart companies value input from critics at their blogs because it offers them an opportunity to respond and educate.

- **Live up to the commitment.** Attention to blogs withers if postings aren't regular.

- **Offer value.** Providing information that publics can't find elsewhere gives people a reason to visit your blog or subscribe to feeds.

- **Ask if you have readers.** Is your public suitable for blogging? Not every market contains people who read blogs. If yours doesn't, you're wasting time and resources. Search for other blogs related to your industry or product and locate secondary information on your target market's use of the web to find out whether your blog might make a difference.

- **Avoid hype and puffery.** The online community has a different personality than that of people who rely on traditional media. Web users are suspicious of hype and can be critical when they sense they are being preached to or misled.

- **Monitor the one place everyone visits**—its name is Wikipedia. If your company or product is mentioned there, it is important to monitor, and occasionally correct, what is posted.

- **Use blogging as one piece of the puzzle.** Blogging can be an effective way to reach and respond to your publics. But it is rarely a stand-alone tactic. Smart companies make it a part of their overall IMC and public relations plans.

Public Relations Tools

The communications tools at the PR person's disposal vary widely, from news releases and photos to audiovisual materials and even advertising. We'll discuss some of the more common ones briefly.

News Releases and Press Kits

A **news release** (or **press release**), the most widely used PR tool, consists of one or more typed sheets of information (usually 8½ by 11 inches) issued to generate publicity or shed light on a subject of interest. News releases cover time-sensitive hard news. Topics may include the announcement of a new product, promotion of an executive, an unusual contest, landing of a major contract, or establishment of a scholarship fund.

A **press kit** (or **media kit**) supports the publicity gained at staged events such as press conferences or open houses. It includes a basic fact sheet of information about the event, a program or schedule of activities, and a list of the participants and their biographical data. The kit also contains a news story about the event for the broadcast media, news and feature stories for the print media, and any pertinent photos and brochures.

Photos

Photos of events, products in use, new equipment, or newly promoted executives can lend credence or interest to a dull news story. In fact, a photo tells the story faster. Photos should be high quality and need little or no explanation. Typed captions should describe the photo and accurately identify the people shown.

My IMC Campaign 18-B

The Client Presentation

For most of you, the culmination of your project will be a presentation to the class or client that will be judged by the teacher, a group of peers, or local marketing and advertising executives. This presentation is by far the most important aspect of selling your ideas to the "client." It is not always the best idea that wins, and a great presentation can make a bad idea look great.

By now you have spent hours belaboring the who, what, when, and where of your campaign, and now you need to explain why. You should think of your presentation as a Cliff Notes version of your thinking. While going through the process of developing a campaign, it is likely that you did not work sequentially—in fact, most IMC processes are done in parallel—but your presentation should illustrate the linear path of thinking that netted your results.

Most presentations utilize PowerPoint, but if you have the resources and the gumption, think about different ways to illustrate your thinking and your ideas. Remember that the more creative your approach, the more (virtual) points you'll receive, assuming, of course, that the creativity doesn't get in the way of coherent thoughts. Prezi, an online software program, is more difficult than PowerPoint to master but can help you create a dazzling presentation that goes far beyond that of your competition.

Follow this basic outline and focus on how each section transitions from one to the other:

- Goals and/or objectives of the campaign—What is the campaign trying to achieve?

- Target audience analysis—Who are we planning on speaking to and why?

- SWOT analysis—What are the strengths of the brand, the weaknesses, the opportunities, and the impending threats that factor into our decision-making process?

- Strategic insight(s)—Based on everything mentioned earlier, how are you going to solve the business challenge at hand?

- Creative presentation—Ideas, ideas, ideas. And don't forget to explain why these ideas will help achieve the goals/objectives.

- Media presentation—Where will these ads be placed, and what target and strategy insights led you to choose those vehicles?

The main objective of the presentation is to communicate, in a concise and succinct manner, your ideas, both strategic and tactical. One of the biggest misconceptions is that the strategy should be an ah-ha moment. In truth, the strategy should feel more like a statement of the obvious because all of your research has led you down a certain path. If you explain the path appropriately, you will receive the proverbial head-nods on the strategy slides. Where the whiz-bang should come in is how you tactically execute the strategy in its creative and placement (media) form.

Be sure to include everyone on your team in the presentation. This will be difficult, as some people are better presenters than others, but that's okay because if the ideas and thinking are good, they will break through.

Last, if you are doing a PowerPoint, hand out copies of the presentation (in color) so the "clients" can follow along and take notes. Props and gadgets are great to use too, as long as they don't distract from the presentation. When Foote, Cone and Belding was pitching kibu.com (a teen girl site) in 2000, it turned one of its conference rooms into a girl's bedroom, setting the mood and ambience for the presentation. It helped the agency win the pitch because elements of the room were used to highlight the insights into the mindset of the site's main user, a teen girl.

Feature Articles

Many publications, especially trade journals, run **feature articles** (soft news) about companies, products, or services. They may be written by a PR person, the publication's staff, or a third party (such as a freelance business writer). As an MPR tool, feature articles can give the company or product great credibility. Editors like them because they have no immediate deadline and can be published at the editor's convenience.

Features may be case histories, how-to's (such as how to use the company's product), problem-solving scenarios (how one customer uses the company's product to increase production), or state-of-the-art technology updates. Other formats include roundups of what's happening in a specific industry and editorials (such as a speech or essay by a company executive on a current issue).

Printed Materials

Printed materials are the most popular tools used by public relations professionals.[24] They may be brochures or pamphlets about the company or its products, letters to customers, inserts or enclosures that accompany monthly statements, the *annual report* to stockholders, other reports, or house organs.

A **house organ** is a publication about happenings and policies at the company. An internal house organ is for employees only. External house publications go to company-connected people (customers, stockholders, suppliers, and dealers) or to the public. They may take the form of a newsletter, tabloid-size newspaper, magazine, or even a periodic e-zine. Their purpose is to promote goodwill, increase sales, or mold public opinion. A well-produced house organ can do a great deal to motivate employees and appeal to customers. However, writing, printing, and distributing can be expensive—and very time-consuming.

Posters, Exhibits, and Bulletin Boards

Posters can be used internally to stress safety, security, reduction of waste, and courtesy. Externally, they can impart product information, corporate philosophy, or other news of interest to consumers.

Companies use **exhibits** to describe the organization's history, present new products, show how products are made, or explain future plans. Exhibits are often prepared for local fairs, colleges and universities, and trade shows.

Internally, the public relations staff often uses *bulletin boards* to announce new equipment, new products, meetings, promotions, construction plans, and recreation news to employees. Many companies now maintain an *intranet* site where they can post their internal messages.

Audiovisual Materials

Slides, films, CDs, and DVDs are all forms of **audiovisual materials** and may be used for training, sales, or public relations. Considered a form of *corporate advertising,* nontheatrical or sponsored films (developed for public relations reasons) are often furnished without charge to movie theaters, organizations, and special groups, particularly schools and colleges. Classic examples include *Why Man Creates,* produced for Kaiser Aluminum, and Mobil Oil's *A Fable,* starring the famous French mime Marcel Marceau.

Many PR departments provide **video news releases (VNRs)**—news or feature stories prepared by a company and offered free to TV stations, which may use the whole video or just segments. Video news releases are somewhat controversial. Critics see them as subtle commercials or even propaganda and object when stations run the stories without disclosing that they came from a public relations firm, not the station's news staff.

Sponsorships and Events

LO **18-4**

In 1984, the owner of a large bicycle shop in the upper Midwest sent some of his mechanics to a local bicycle race sponsored by a national charity. At the time, his store was doing about $200,000 per year in retail sales, and the owner wanted to help out the charity while finding out what the racers thought of his and his competitors' businesses.

An unexpected benefit of the company's presence at the race was that participants started showing up in his store. Encouraged by these results, the company now supports more than a hundred bicycle events each year and sends staff members to dozens of them. It has hired a full-time representative to coordinate company involvement in special bicycle events that have the potential of increasing its exposure and business revenue.

In 20 years the company went from a low-key presence at bicycling events, donating a few water bottles embossed with the company's name, to large-scale sponsorship, participating in event registration, providing event participants with workshops on bicycle maintenance, and offering in-store discounts to event participants. Within a week of one event, 30 participants had visited the store. Even better news for the company was that nearly half of the more than 5,000 riders reported purchasing goods from it. The owner attributes much of his success to his sponsorship of bicycle events. In his words, "Support them, and they support us."[25]

The Growth of Sponsorship

Marketers are involved in sponsoring many kinds of special events. Sponsorship actually embraces two disciplines: sales promotion and public relations. Some sponsorships are designed to create publicity, others to improve public relations through personal contact and affiliation with a worthy cause, and others to immediately improve the bottom line.

A **sponsorship** is a cash or in-kind fee paid to a property (which may be a sports, entertainment, or nonprofit event or organization) in return for access to the exploitable

The continued popularity of sports makes them attractive targets for corporate sponsorship dollars. This photo shows that both the athlete and the tournament are sponsored (by Nike and Rolex respectively).

Leonard Zhukovsky/Shutterstock

commercial potential associated with that property.[26] In other words, just as advertisers pay a fee to sponsor a program on radio or TV, they may also sign on to sponsor a bike race, an art show or chamber music festival, a fair or exhibition, or the Olympics. The sponsorship fee may be paid in cash or **in kind** (i.e., through a donation of goods and services). For instance, if a local TV station signs on as a sponsor of a 10K run, it will typically pay for some part of its sponsorship with advertising time for the event.

While the sponsored event or organization may be nonprofit, sponsorship is not the same as philanthropy. **Philanthropy** is support of a cause without any commercial incentive. Sponsorship (and a related strategy, *cause marketing*) is used to achieve commercial objectives.[27] In 2007, U.S. companies spent nearly $15 billion on sponsorships. That figure rose to almost $17 billion in 2008. Part of the surge was doubtless due to the cost of global sponsorship at the Beijing Olympic games, estimated at $78 million for each of the 12 companies taking part.[28]

The reasons for this phenomenal growth relate to the economics of marketing we discussed earlier: the escalating costs of traditional advertising media, the fragmentation of media audiences, the growing diversity in leisure activities, and the ability to reach targeted groups of people efficiently. Initial growth probably came from the tobacco and alcohol companies, which many governments banned from broadcast advertising. Recent legislation in the United Kingdom, Canada, and the United States threatens to end tobacco sponsorships altogether, but their success at sponsoring sports and events has shown the way for mainstream advertisers.

Today, there is greater media coverage of sponsored events—everything from beach volleyball to grand prix horse shows to Xtreme games to cultural events. This provides a highly desirable venue for advertisers seeking young, upwardly mobile, educated consumers. Likewise, for transnational marketers, there is growing interest in global events such as World Cup soccer, the Olympics, and the America's Cup yacht race. Even traditional business-to-business marketers, such as Sweden's Ericsson Corp., are making a play for greater brand awareness in the United States by sponsoring the World Championships of Beach Volleyball, which is staged and marketed by ALDI.[29]

Benefits of Sponsorship

Today, the many benefits of sponsorship are well documented. Certainly one benefit is that the public approves of it. One study by Roper Starch Worldwide reported that 80 percent of Americans believe corporate sponsorship is an important source of money for professional sports and 74 percent believe sponsorships provide benefits to the cities where events occur.[30] In the Roper Starch study, 74 percent of the people also said government should have little or no influence on which types of companies sponsor professional sports events. This is a far higher approval rating than most companies would get for their advertising programs.

More than almost any other marketing communications tool, sponsorships and events have the ability to involve customers, prospects, and other stakeholders. Naturally, events vary in degree of participation. A person attending a seminar or workshop will have greater involvement with the sponsor than someone attending a sponsored stock-car race.[31] However, events are also highly self-selective of their target audience. Someone who actually attends a stock-car race will most likely have a higher degree of interest than the average person. So marketers that define their audiences tightly can select just those sponsorships that offer the closest fit. Of course, marketers that sponsor an event simply because it has a large audience are misusing this tool.[32]

Unlike advertising, sponsorships and events can provide face-to-face access to current and potential customers. Depending on the venue, this access can be relatively clean and uncluttered by competition. Sponsoring a seminar, for instance, creates an opportunity for both customer education and brand involvement. In some cases, it even enables product demonstrations and the opportunity to give a personal sales pitch to multiple prospects at a time when they are open to new information.[33] This is especially good for business-to-business marketers.

A significant benefit is the opportunity to enhance the company's public image or merchandise its positioning through affiliation with an appropriate event.

Also important, but often overlooked, is the effect sponsorship can have on employees. Affiliating with a dynamic event can really boost the morale and pride of the troops in the trenches. And many companies offer attendance at the event (Super Bowl, Olympics, etc.) as an incentive to their sales staff.[34]

Some marketers have discovered that sponsorships can rapidly convert fan loyalty into sales. For example, 74 percent of stock-car racing fans report that they often buy products they see promoted at the racetrack. This is also true for other sports: 58 percent for baseball, 52 percent for tennis, 47 percent for golf. One fan told Greg Penske, president/CEO of Penske Motorsports, how upset he was that NASCAR driver Rusty Wallace had switched from Pontiac to Ford: "I'm only one year into my Pontiac lease and it's costing me $3,000 to get out of it and into a Ford."[35]

Finally, sponsorships can be very cost-efficient. Volvo International believes the media exposure it gets from its $3 million sponsorship of local tennis tournaments is equivalent to $25 million worth of advertising time and space.[36]

Drawbacks of Sponsorship

Like all marketing communications tools, sponsorship has some drawbacks. First, it can be very costly, especially when the event is solely sponsored. For this reason, most companies participate in cosponsored events, which spreads the cost among several participants.

The problem with cosponsored events is clutter. Some events have so many sponsors that getting one marketer's message through is extremely difficult. Look again at stock-car racing. How many logos do those cars sport?

Finally, evaluating the effectiveness of a particular sponsorship can be tricky at best—especially because it rarely happens in a vacuum. The problem is in separating the effects of a sponsorship from the effects of other concurrent marketing activities. We'll deal with these issues shortly.

Types of Sponsorship

While there are many, many avenues and events available for sponsorship, IEG Inc. (www.sponsorship.com/), the main trade organization for sponsorships, groups most of them into six categories: sports; entertainment; causes; the arts; festivals, fairs, and annual events; and associations, organizations, and members (see Exhibit 18-2).[37]

Sports Marketing

North American corporations spent approximately $11.6 billion in 2008 on sports marketing sponsorships. The most popular of these are motorsports and golf.[38] In fact, the vast majority of all sponsorship budgets, more than 65 percent, is spent on sports events. This includes everything from the Olympics to NASCAR racing to professional athletic leagues. As we saw from the bicycle shop story, companies don't have to be big multinationals to reap rich rewards from sponsorships—if they do it properly.

By buying the rights to serve Gatorade on the sidelines of professional basketball and football games, that brand has received more credibility than any television ad could provide, at a fraction of the cost. During every game, TV cameras show pros drinking the product in big Gatorade cups. And it's clear they're doing it because they want to, not because their agent told them to.[39]

In hotly contested markets, the giants in their fields fight over sponsorship rights. Nike battles adidas, Coke spars with Pepsi, and Visa struggles against American Express. This has certainly contributed to the rising cost of sponsorships. For the 2018 Winter Olympics in South Korea, 13 companies paid in excess of $100 million each to gain exposures throughout the games, the chance to identify as an official sponsor, and the opportunity for tickets and services for employees and customers.[40]

Gatorade's sponsorship of high-profile sports leagues like the NFL have provided countless opportunities for exposure with their target audiences.

Matt York/AP Images

Exhibit 18-2
Sponsorship spending in the United States.

North American Sponsorship Spending by Property Type (billions)			
	2017 Spending	2018 Spending	Increase from 2017
Sports	$16.26	$17.05	4.9%
Entertainment	2.29	2.4	4.8
Causes	2.05	2.14	4.4
Arts	0.99	1.03	3.7
Festivals, Fairs, and Annual Events	0.90	0.94	3.7
Associations and Membership Organizations	0.62	0.64	3.1

Projected 2018 Shares of North American Sponsorship Market

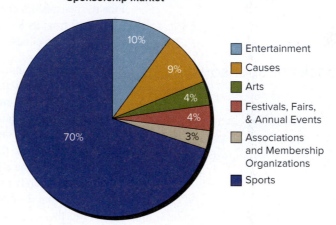

Source: "Signs Point to Healthy Sponsorship Spending in 2018," *IEG Sponsorship Report,* January 8, 2018, www.sponsorship.com/Report/2018/01/08/Signs-Point-To-Healthy-Sponsorship-Spending-In-201.aspx.

In addition to spending more than $1 million for each 30-second television spot during the 2012 London Olympics, Nike and adidas outfitted a combined 6,000 Olympic athletes. Although adidas's traditional stronghold is in soccer gear, it still supplied an estimated 1.5 million pieces of clothing, equipment, and other logo-emblazoned articles for the two-week event. Nike typically avoids Olympic sponsorship but often finds a way to blanket the host city with its "swoosh" logo anyway (see *ambush marketing* below). Because adidas is estimated to have paid in excess of $61 million to be an official sponsor of the games, it is not surprising that event hosts do everything they can to stop unauthorized associations.[41]

Many sports events are strictly local and therefore cost much less while giving the sponsor closer access to attendees and participants. Firms with modest event-marketing budgets, for example, use options ranging from local golf tournaments and tennis matches to surfing contests.

An increasingly popular promotion is the company-sponsored sports event. The event can serve as an effective focal point for an IMC campaign if it ties the company to the local community hosting the event as well as to the event's regional or national audience. But without a concerted effort to tie an event to other marketing communications activities like a currently running ad campaign, the money spent on sponsorships is generally wasted.[42]

Some companies have long associated their brands with existing events. Coca-Cola is the International Olympic Committee's longest-serving sponsor, having first participated in 1928. The South Korean winter games were the 17th Olympics for financial services giant Visa.[43]

But controversy often swirls around big sports sponsorships. The most controversial practice is **ambush marketing,** a promotional strategy nonsponsors use to capitalize on the popularity or prestige of an event or property by seeking creative ways to gain brand exposure without paying for sponsorship. The competitors of the property's official sponsor often employ ambush marketing techniques, like buying up all the billboard space around an athletic stadium. Fuji did this to Kodak in one Olympics. This often works because people are unsure who the official sponsors actually are—again, the problem is clutter. Just because a company advertises on the Olympic broadcast, for instance, does not mean it is an official sponsor. Ambush marketers take advantage of this confusion.[44] In fact, Nike executive Mark Parker reported that his company, a notorious ambush marketer, routinely posts stock-market performances 20 percent higher than the market average in Olympic years.

Sports sponsorship is now a worldwide phenomenon and growing at a faster rate than other marketing channels. And while spending in North America increased approximately 4.5 percent in 2018, it grew at a 4.9 percent clip elsewhere in the world.[45] Indeed, sports sponsorship is such a driving force in some countries that, for example, in Spain, football (soccer) sponsorship alone accounts for approximately €8 million a year, which is equivalent to 1.17 percent of that country's GDP.[46] It seems clear that companies view sponsorship as an important IMC tool. For the foreseeable future, the growth of sponsorship is likely to be higher than that of either sales promotion or traditional advertising.

Entertainment

After sports marketing, the largest area of sponsorship is **entertainment,** which includes things like concert tours, attractions, and theme parks. For instance, numerous attractions at Disneyland and Disney World are sponsored by major corporations such as GE, AT&T, ARCO, and Carnation.

Brands even sponsor entire tours. Oscar Mayer's "Wienermobile" (actually a small fleet of them) has been a part of America's roads since 1936. A 2004 contest in which winners could drive the Wienermobile for a day drew 15,000 entries. The Vans Warped Tour has a rotating lineup of 50 bands, with multiple stages and compounds sponsored by other companies, like Eastpak. Booths and tents at the festival provide ample targeted-marketing opportunities for cosponsors like Wells Fargo and Vagrant Records: The "Girlz Garage" offers fashion and makeup, and the PlayStation tent offers the latest games for the PSP.[47]

Festivals, Fairs, and Annual Events

An IEG survey of the International Association of Fairs and Expositions revealed a very healthy, growing environment. Spending in 2018 was projected to be $903 million, an increase of nearly 3 percent from the previous year.[48]

One of the largest annual events in the state of Michigan is the National Cherry Festival in Traverse City. Held every year around the Fourth of July, it boasts an impressive lineup of events and promotional activities that drives both attendance and sponsor visibility. Events include band parades, races, concerts, tournaments, an antiques show, an air show, Native American exhibits, and much more. Among the official sponsors are Pepsi, Ford, Toyota, Intel, and Sony.

Similarly, annual events such as business-to-business trade shows attract large numbers of sponsors as well as exhibitors because of the economics of being able to talk to prospects and customers in the same place at the same time (see Exhibit 18-2).

Sometimes the competition to sponsor an event even comes from within the same company. The Florida Renaissance Festival, for instance, received calls from three AT&T entities inquiring about sponsorship availabilities. Two calls were from different departments and the third was from one of AT&T's agencies. The festival ultimately signed with the phone company's Hispanic marketing department.[49]

Causes

Sponsorship of causes and educational institutions is a tried-and-true PR activity that often fits with the IMC strategy of mission marketing. A number of large corporations (including Chevrolet, AT&T, American Airlines, Pepsi, and Kodak) cosponsored the Live Aid concerts, for instance. Even politically related causes draw sponsors, at least when there is alignment between sponsor and cause. For example, the annual Women's March on Washington that takes place each January was sponsored by Planned Parenthood, NRDC, the ACLU, MoveOn.org, and the American Federation of Teachers. The March for Life event, which takes place during the same month, was sponsored by the Knights

In addition to enormous and expensive sports sponsorships like the Olympics, many smaller, charity-focused events also attract corporate support. In this ad, sponsors such as Campbell Soup Company, link to an annual food drive. IEG predicts sponsorship spending of causes will grow 4.6% in 2019.

Source: Campbell Soup Company

of Columbus and Solidarity Healthcare. In 2019, it is estimated marketers will spend $2.2 billion in cause-related sponsorships.

A vice president for corporate relations as a sponsor at one large event referred to mission marketing activities as "enlightened self-interest." People appreciate the fact that the business does not really get anything tangible out of them to put in the bank.[50]

Health care marketers such as hospitals, HMOs, and managed-care companies are increasing their sponsorship activities. Professional driver Ryan Reed and Eli Lilly have used a sponsorship deal to help increase diabetes awareness. Another driver, IndyCar Series's Charlie Kimball, promotes the NovoLog FlexPen, an insulin injection device, in partnership with Novo Nordisk.[51]

Arts and Culture

Symphony orchestras, chamber music groups, art museums, and theater companies are always in desperate need of funding. In 2011, sponsors spent an estimated $885 million to support the arts—one of the least funded of the major sponsorship categories. What this means is that this is still a relatively untapped area, and it provides outstanding sponsorship and underwriting opportunities for both national and local firms interested in audiences on the highest end of the income scale.

Unfortunately, this group is likely to be hardest hit by any legislation aimed at ending tobacco sponsorships. For instance, The Gallaher Group, Northern Ireland's largest cigarette manufacturer, regularly donates about a million pounds (U.S.$1.5M) to the Ulster Orchestra, the flagship of the arts in Northern Ireland. In the face of government plans to curtail tobacco advertising and sponsorships, the Association for Business Sponsorship for the Arts gave Gallaher its highest award for outstanding corporate citizenship, citing it for investing in the cultural life of the community in which it operates.[52]

Venue Marketing

Finally, an area not covered by IEG's report is **venue marketing,** a form of sponsorship that links a sponsor to a physical site such as a stadium, arena, auditorium, or racetrack. In 2000, for instance, the Great American Insurance Company made a good name for itself by offering the city of Cincinnati about $75 million over 30 years for the naming rights to the soon-to-be-built baseball stadium on the Ohio River. The city accepted the offer, and since 2003 the Cincinnati Reds have played at the Great American Ballpark.[53]

Likewise, Denver has Coors Field, and Charlotte, North Carolina, has Bank of America Stadium. And AT&T has put its name on San Francisco's baseball park. But what happens when sponsors with naming rights become a liability? When Enron filed for bankruptcy in 2001, the Houston Astros shelled out $2.1 million to buy back the naming rights to Enron Field. The story had a happy ending, however, when Minute Maid paid an estimated $170 million for a 28-year naming rights deal.

Venue marketing is changing the economics of professional sports. Sponsorships help pay for stadium renovations and upgrades and may assist the home team in defraying the high cost of leasing. Many teams keep the money from their stadium luxury suites, stadium advertising, naming rights, and food and beverage concessions. Under the new economic rules, big stadium revenues are essential to signing big-name players and staying competitive.[54]

Methods of Sponsorship

Companies interested in sponsorship have two choices: buy into an existing event or create their own. For most companies, it's easier to buy into an existing event, either as the sole sponsor (the Buick Invitational) or as one of many cosponsors. What's most important is to get a good fit between the sponsor and the event. For example, when food and beverage brands sponsor stadiums or arenas, they are doing more than gaining exposure for their products; they are encouraging people at the venues to consume them. Brands like Gatorade (Serena Williams), Puma (Usain Bolt), Reebok (Conor McGregor), adidas (Lionel Messi), and Under Armour (Jordan Spieth) have a natural fit with top athletes. The same fit might not be present for athletes and brands such as Tag Heuer (Christiano Ronaldo) and Lexus (Vernon Davis).[55]

Venue marketing has surged in popularity. By selling the naming rights to stadiums, arenas, and centers, cities get help paying for public venues. Advertisers get a high-profile way to see their brands mentioned thousands of times each year in sports stories.
Kirby Lee/NFL Contributor/AP Images

Kathleen Smith suggests several guidelines for brands that are selecting the right sponsorship opportunity or event.

- Look for opportunities that fit with the brand's target demographics and audience interests.
- Select events that offer value, where organizers can justify the opportunities that are created given the brand's spending.
- Find out who else is sponsoring the event to be sure it correctly targets the right audience. Even consider the events a competitor is sponsoring.
- Consider events that bring back sponsors every year. These are likely to provide value.[56]

Measuring Sponsorship Results

One of the problems with event sponsorship (as with public relations activities in general) has historically been how to evaluate results. Experts suggest there are really only three ways to do this:

1. Measure changes in awareness or image through pre- and post-sponsorship research surveys.
2. Measure spending equivalencies between free media exposure and comparable advertising space or time.
3. Measure changes in sales revenue with a tracking device such as coupons.

Unfortunately, none of these methods covers all the reasons for sponsoring. For example, how do you measure the effect on employee morale? What if the sponsorship is aimed at rewarding current customers or enhancing relationships within the trade? These are important possible objectives, but they are very difficult to measure.

Still, most companies are very concerned about the bottom line and look for a substantial return on investment for their sponsorship dollars. Delta Airlines, for example, is said to require $12 in new revenue for every dollar it spends on sponsorship—a ratio the airline claims to have achieved during its Olympic sponsorships.[57]

IEG, the sponsorship industry's leading association, suggests the following pointers for measuring the value of event sponsorships:[58]

- Have clear goals and narrowly defined objectives.
- Set a measurable goal.
- Measure against a benchmark.
- Do not change other marketing variables during the sponsorship.
- Incorporate an evaluation program into the overall sponsorship and associated marketing program.
- At the outset, establish a budget for measuring results.

Corporate Advertising

LO 18-5

When a company wants to communicate a PR message and control its content, it may use a form of *corporate advertising.* In an integrated marketing communications program, corporate advertising can set the tone for all of a company's public communications. **Corporate advertising** covers the broad area of nonproduct advertising, including public relations advertising, institutional advertising, corporate identity advertising, and recruitment advertising.

Public Relations Advertising

To direct a controlled public relations message to one of its important publics, a company uses **public relations advertising.** PR ads may be used to improve the company's relations with labor, government, customers, suppliers, and even voters.

When companies sponsor art events, programs on public television, or charitable activities, they frequently place public relations ads in other media to promote the programs and their sponsorship, enhance their community citizenship, and create public goodwill. If the public relations people don't have advertising experience, they will typically turn to the firm's advertising department or agency for help.

Corporate/Institutional Advertising

In recent years, the term *corporate advertising* has come to denote a particular type of non-product advertising aimed at increasing awareness of the company and enhancing its image. The traditional term for this is **institutional advertising.** These ad campaigns may serve a variety of purposes: to report company accomplishments, position the company competitively in the market, reflect a change in corporate personality, shore up stock prices, improve employee morale, or avoid communications problems with agents, dealers, suppliers, or customers (for some excellent examples, see the Portfolio Review).

GE's "Ideas are scary" ads are meant to support the company's reputation for having a daring, creative culture. The ads use the metaphor of an unloved creature whose value is recognized. Using tangible things as metaphors for ideas and abstract concepts is important in corporate advertising.
Source: General Electric Company

AD Lab 18–B

David Ogilvy on Corporate Advertising

David Ogilvy, the late founder and former creative director of Ogilvy & Mather, worked with Shell, Sears, IBM, International Paper, Merrill Lynch, General Dynamics, Standard Oil of New Jersey, and other successful corporations.

According to Ogilvy, big corporations are increasingly under attack from consumer groups, environmentalists, governments, and antitrust prosecutors who try their cases in the newspapers. If a corporation does not take the time to cultivate its reputation, it loses by default.

"If it were possible, it would be better for corporations to rely on public relations (that is, favorable news stories and editorials) rather than paid advertising. But the media are too niggardly about disseminating favorable information about corporations. That is why an increasing number of public relations directors have come to use paid advertising as their main channel of communication. It is the only one they can control with respect to content, with respect to timing, and with respect to noise level. And it is the only one which enables them to select their own battleground," he said.

"So I guess that corporate advertising is here to stay. Why is most of it a flop?"

First, because corporations don't define the purpose of their corporate campaigns.

Second, because they don't measure the results. In a survey conducted by The Gallagher Report, only one in four U.S. corporate advertisers said it measured changes in attitude brought about by its corporate campaigns. "The majority fly blind," said Ogilvy.

Third, because so little is known about what works and what doesn't work. The marketing departments and their agencies know what works in brand advertising, but when it comes to corporate advertising, they are amateurs.

Fourth, very few advertising agencies know much about corporate advertising. It is only a small part of their business. "Their creative people know how to write chewing-gum jingles for kids and how to sell beer to blue-collar workers. But corporate advertising requires copywriters who are at home in the world of big business. There aren't many of them," believed Ogilvy.

"I am appalled by the humbug in corporate advertising. The pomposity. The vague generalities and the fatuous platitudes. Corporate advertising should not insult the intelligence of the public," he said.

Unlike product advertising, Ogilvy said, a corporate campaign is the voice of the chief executive and his or her board of directors. It should not be delegated.

What can good corporate advertising hope to achieve? Ogilvy thought at least one of four objectives:

1. It can build awareness of the company. Opinion Research Corp. states, "The invisibility and remoteness of most companies is the main handicap. People who feel they know a company well are five times more likely to have a highly favorable opinion of the company than those who have little familiarity."

2. Corporate advertising can make a good impression on the financial community, enabling you to raise capital at lower cost—and make more acquisitions.

3. It can motivate your present employees and attract better recruits. "Good public relations begins at home," Ogilvy said. "If your employees understand your policies and feel proud of your company, they will be your best ambassadors."

4. Corporate advertising can influence public opinion on specific issues. Abraham Lincoln said, "With public opinion against it, nothing can succeed. With public opinion on its side, nothing can fail."

"Stop and go is the typical pattern of corporate advertising. What a waste of money. It takes years for corporate advertising to do a job. It doesn't work overnight. Only a few companies have kept it going long enough to achieve measurable results," Ogilvy concluded.

Courtesy of David Ogilvy.

Laboratory Application

Find and discuss a corporate ad that demonstrates what Ogilvy referred to as the humbug in corporate advertising, the pomposity, vague generalities, and fatuous platitudes.

Historically, companies and even professional ad people have questioned, or misunderstood, the effectiveness of corporate advertising. Retailers in particular cling to the idea that institutional advertising, although attractive and nice, "doesn't make the cash register ring." A series of marketing research studies, however, offered dramatic evidence to the contrary. Companies using corporate advertising registered significantly better awareness, familiarity, and overall impression than those using only product advertising. Five corporate advertisers in the study drew higher ratings in every one of 16 characteristics measured, including being known for quality products, having competent management, and paying higher dividends.[60] Ironically, the companies in the study that did no corporate advertising spent far more in total advertising for their products than the corporate advertisers did. Yet, despite the higher expenditures, they scored significantly lower across the board.

David Ogilvy, the late founder and creative head of Ogilvy & Mather, was an outspoken advocate of corporate advertising, but he was appalled by some corporate ads. For more on Ogilvy's views, see Ad Lab 18–B.

(continued on page 604)

:: Corporate Advertising

Companies use public relations activities and various forms of public relations advertising to communicate with a wide constituency. PR people refer to these groups of people as *publics*. Marketing people call them *stakeholders*.

• As you study the ads in this portfolio, see if you can determine what stakeholders the company was targeting. Then, analyze the ad to determine what objective the company was trying to achieve and if it succeeded.

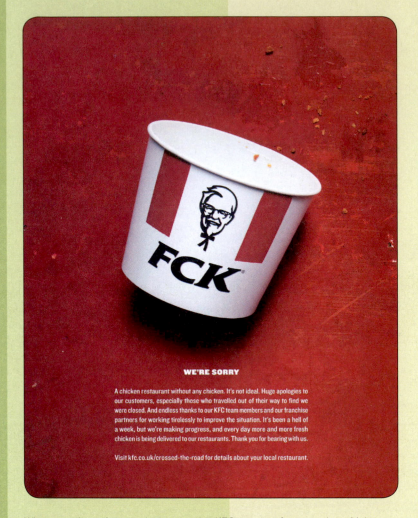

When people can't get a chicken meal at KFC, it is time for an apology. Making the apology hilarious by "making a mistake" with the logo helps reconnect with disappointed customers. "A chicken restaurant without any chicken. It's not ideal. Huge apologies to our customers, especially those who travelled out of their way to find we were closed."[59]

Source: Yum! Brands

This billboard, sponsored by Carlsberg, has an interesting way to back up its claim the being "probably the best poster in the world." It serves up visitors with a free beer.

CB2/ZOB/WENN/Newscom

The "Like a girl" campaign for Always struck a powerful cord for women's empowerment.

Source: Unilever

Procter & Gamble's Always brand sponsored one of the great corporate campaigns "Like a girl," shown previously. It hit another home run with its "Thank you, Mom" ads.

Source: Procter & Gamble

The internet is a powerful tool for corporations to keep in touch with their consumers and other key stakeholders. Even small businesses can participate in e-commerce or communicate their services to consumers or other businesses worldwide. Agencia Africa (www.africa.com.br), an advertising agency in São Paulo, Brazil, won a Bronze Lion at the International Advertising Festival in Cannes for the beautiful and exotic design of the agency's corporate website.

Source: Grupo ABC

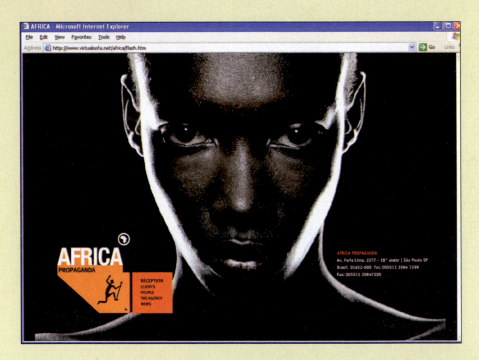

Corporate logos can reinforce the company name through a clever demonstration of qualities identified with the corporate culture or those of its consumers. Unilever's beautiful logo focuses on the brands the company manages.

Source: Unilever

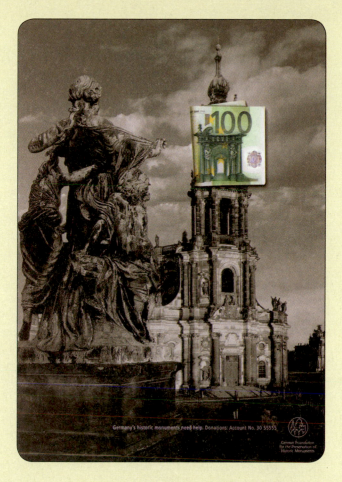

In this ad that won a Bronze Lion at Cannes, the German Foundation for the Preservation of Historic Monuments (www.denkmalschutz.de) showed how its stakeholders' euros could support its mission to preserve buildings like Dresden's Katholische Hofkirche (Catholic Cathedral).

Source: German Foundation for the Preservation of Historic Monuments

The Buenos Aires Zoo celebrated its 115th birthday with the metaphor of wrinkles. In a campaign that won a Gold Lion at Cannes, the zoo demonstrated its age with images of an orangutan's weathered hands and an elephant's crinkled eyes.

Source: The Buenos Aires Zoo

People BEHIND the Ads

Bill Imada, Chair and Chief Connectivity Officer, the IW Group

Courtesy of Bill Imada

Bill Imada is chair and chief connectivity officer at the IW Group Inc. His company describes itself as Culture Purveyors & Content Creators. They note that "Our workplace is the world around us. We uncover the most captivating stories and let the gems inspire the content we create." Its clients include Lexus, Walmart, and McDonald's.

CA: What are your current title and set of responsibilities?

BI: Chair and Chief Connectivity Officer. I am responsible for new business development, client relations, civic engagement, and partnership marketing. I also serve as the chairman of the board of directors (which meets annually).

CA: Describe the IW Group and its culture.

BI: We are a participatory company. In other words, we believe that every associate has a stake in how our agency is organized, managed, and operated. We are changing the dynamics of our company to make it more engaging, fun, and avant garde. This includes a new organizational structure that allows for greater creativity, innovation, and bottom-up engagement.

CA: Describe a "typical" day, or if none of them are typical, describe a recent day that highlights your career responsibilities.

BI: A typical day for me begins at 7:30 a.m.—the best time to reflect on the day prior and the day ahead. It is also a great time to catch up on e-mails, social media, and the latest news online.

- Coffee or tea. Heaps of coffee and tea.
- Early morning calls and conversations with clients on the East Coast and in the Midwest. Checking in to see how things are going. Conversations are usually personal and not

always business related. Offering thoughts, ideas, and suggestions on "connecting the dots" for different clients. (This occasionally includes career and professional advice.)

- About two to three hours of pro bono work. IW Group associates and I serve on more than 30 not-for-profit boards and advisory councils. Several conversations with nonprofit and civic leaders about fund-raising, sustainability, succession planning, board development, events and activities, program development, etc.
- A review of regional and national speaking opportunities. I'm on the speakers' circuit and have a problem saying no. A review of the week's speaking engagements finds me traveling to different cities in less than two weeks. Next week: Houston, New York, and Chicago. The following week I'm in Honolulu.
- A walk around the agency several times per day to see how things are going, department by department.
- Inquiries to different people in the office about lunch options. Usually I eat lunch at my desk; someone always offers to fetch lunch for me. Rarely, if ever, make lunch. Prefer salads.
- An update to the voicemail each day. I change my voicemail daily.
- A review of different presentation materials for new business opportunities. This week, there are three different new business opportunities. One meeting in the office; two outside of the office.
- End the day with a rough game of foosball with a few colleagues. The interns usually jump in.
- Usually leave the office at around 6:30 p.m. Continue working at home.

CA: What are the most important changes taking place in IMC today?

BI: Workspace environments continue to change; more communal, less structured. Office walls are coming down in favor of more communal work spaces. Cubicles are becoming a thing of the past. Office spaces look more like game rooms, playgrounds, or living spaces. Furniture is more modular (often with wheels) and can be moved quickly and efficiently. PlayStation and other video games are commonplace. Food and snacks are everywhere. Who uses traditional coffee makers these days? We have a massive machine that makes lattes and other coffee and chocolate drinks. Titles are shifting. I was once chairman and CEO. Last year, chairman and chief collaboration officer. Now, chief connectivity officer. My job is to connect the dots or to create the dots. Silos are now blurred. Advertising, planning, public relations, media, etc. are no longer divided strictly by function but by teams. All of the teams are fluid. Team members shift from team to team, as needed. Digital and social technologies now dominate the psyche of the agency; traditional public relations and advertising are no longer the norm or the expectation. It is getting harder and harder to find digital talent; salaries are sky high and the talent can now pick and choose where they wish to work. Talented individuals aren't always hung up on salaries, however. They are also concerned about work environment and perks; a creative space; fun; and active engagement (in causes and issues they believe in). The democratization of content has changed the way we work with content creators. Anyone can create content these days using their mobile devices; clients understand this but are uncertain about how to deal with user-generated content. There is lots of pressure on agencies to work with less funding. Budgets are down; however, the clients will always find money and resources for fresh ideas (regardless of what they say about their budgets). IMC agencies are also shifting their focus to teams that specialize in lifestyle and social movements (e.g., foodies and chefs; music, writers, and composers; social media evangelists; experienced creators; social inventors, et al.).

CA: How important is approaching IMC from a global perspective for you? Would you say it is increasing in importance? How can students acquire a start on becoming more globally aware?

BI: There are no borders. Everything seems porous. People are freely traveling across the country and across continents. The world no longer revolves around the U.S. There is a stronger and greater focus on what is happening in developing countries such as Brazil, India, South Africa, Russia, and China. People are also finding inspiration in other places such as Iceland and other small countries.

Students today need to be more intellectually curious. American students as a whole lack the intellectual curiosity that is needed for them to play in a more globalized world. The U.S. is one of the most diverse countries in the world, but we often fail to see the value of our diversity. Students often graduate saying they'd like to be a change-agent in the world. However, when they start their careers, their global views change. The reality of school debt sets in and they aren't quite sure where their lives will take them. Integrated marketing requires a level of open-mindedness in all aspects of our lives. Academia doesn't always teach or expose students and faculty to this need for greater open-mindedness (e.g., consumption of different foods, lifestyles, values, interests, mindsets, perspectives, etc.).

CA: What does the IW Group look for in new hires?

BI: IW Group looks for people who have the capacity and the spirit to live more worldly. We need people with a global perspective; however, they must also be able and willing to apply what they have learned at home. They need a demonstrated level of creativity. How do they present themselves in their written documents (e.g., résumés, cover letters, writing samples)? How do they use typeface, quotes, and paper to accent their knowledge, experience, and ambitions? How do they present themselves in an interview? Do they know how to act and speak beyond their elevator speech? What happens after they reach their floor?

Do they have soft skills? Can they talk about themselves in a story-telling fashion? Do they even have a story to tell? Can they relate their knowledge and experience to the needs, interests, and aspirations of the agency and our clients? Are they unafraid to offer ideas and suggestions, even in a first interview? Have they interned? Have they traveled or lived abroad? Do they speak a language other than English? Do they have questions for you during

the interview? Or ask follow-up questions? Do they have great follow-up skills? And have they sent a handwritten thank-you note?

CA: What is the most enjoyable part of your job?

BI: Connecting the dots; creating new dots; finding new ways to reach consumers. Helping people connect with others. Building new organizations. (So far, I've started two new national organizations.) Bringing clients together for conversations over drinks or dinner. Finding the opportunities that exist in every intersection you traverse. Hanging out with the interns and new staff. Discovering an ah-ha moment. New business development. Finding solutions to every challenge.

CA: What should a university student be doing to prepare to follow in your footsteps someday?

BI: They should learn how to network properly. Furthermore, they should recognize that every challenge they face often has multiple solutions. If they take on an internship (or two), they should ask if they can shadow the executives of the company or organization for a day or two. They should get to know their employer, and the people who make things happen. They should never be afraid to say, "I need help" or "I'd like to know more." They should get involved in extracurricular activities and take an active role in leading an organization. They should take time to help others. And they should always remember to give back as they advance outside of the academy.

CA: What are your pastimes, hobbies, things you enjoy doing?

BI: Mountain biking and buying old homes. (I have a fixer-upper in historic Napa, California). I am also addicted to Kickstarter and Indiegogo. I have supported more than 50 Kickstarter and Indiegogo campaigns. If I do support a crowdfunding campaign on Kickstarter, I ask the folks who are promoting the campaign to allow me to be a part of their journeys. I have met more than a dozen people I've supported on Kickstarter, and have introduced several of them to clients and staff. For instance, I invited five Kickstarter folks to Oak Brook, Illinois, to meet with leaders of McDonald's. I have also agreed to serve on the board of trustees for another organization I supported via Kickstarter: MOFAD (Museum of Food and Drink).

CA: What is your favorite place in the world?

BI: New Zealand. Clean. Mostly unspoiled. And less than five million people.

CA: Please feel free to add anything else I've not asked about.

BI: My favorite quotes:

> **"Make a customer, not a sale"**
> –Katherine Barchetti

> **"If you want to lift yourself up, lift up someone else."**
> –Booker T. Washington

> **"There is no finish line."**
> –Phil Knight

Courtesy of Bill Imada.

(continued from page 597)

Responding to such criticisms and to marketplace forces, corporations now design their corporate advertising to achieve specific objectives: develop awareness of the company and its activities, attract investors, improve a tarnished image, attract quality employees, tie together a diverse product line, and take a stand on important public issues. The primary media companies used for corporate advertising are consumer business magazines and network TV.

A variation on corporate advertising is **advocacy advertising.** Companies use it to communicate their views on issues that affect their business (to protect their position in the marketplace), to promote their philosophy, or to make a political or social statement. Such ads are frequently referred to as **advertorials** because they are basically editorials paid for by an advertiser.

Corporate advertising can also build a foundation for future sales, traditionally the realm of product advertising. Many advertisers use umbrella campaigns, called **market prep corporate advertising,** to simultaneously communicate messages about the products and the company.

While corporate advertising is an excellent vehicle for promoting the company's desired image, it cannot succeed if the image doesn't fit. If a big high-tech corporation like GE, for example, tried to project a homey, small-town image, it would not be very credible.

Corporate Identity Advertising

Companies take pride in their logos and corporate signatures. The graphic designs that identify corporate names and products are valuable assets, and companies take great pains to protect their individuality and ownership. What does a company do when it changes its name, logos, trademarks, or corporate signatures, as when it merges with another company? This is the job of **corporate identity advertising.**

When software publisher Productivity Products International changed its name to Stepstone Inc., it faced an interesting dilemma. It needed to advertise the change. But in Europe, one of its key markets, a corporate name change implies that a bankrupt business is starting over with a new identity. So rather than announcing its new name in the print media, Stepstone used direct mail targeted at customers, prospects, investors, and the press. The campaign was a success.

More familiar corporate name changes include the switch from American Harvester to Navistar International, the change from Consolidated Foods to Sara Lee Corp., and the creation of Unisys to replace the premerger identities of Burroughs and Sperry.

Recruitment Advertising

Companies use **recruitment advertising** to attract new employees. Most recruitment advertising appears in the classified help-wanted sections of daily newspapers and is placed by the human resources department rather than the advertising department. But many ad agencies now employ recruitment specialists, and some agencies even specialize in recruitment advertising.

Chapter Summary

Public relations is a process used to manage an organization's relationships with its various publics, including employees, customers, stockholders, competitors, and the general populace. The term *public relations* can describe a concept, a profession, a management function, and a practice. Many PR activities involve media communications. However, unlike product advertising, these communications are not normally sponsored or paid for.

Public relations activities include planning and research, reputation management (publicity and press agentry, crisis management, and community involvement), public affairs and lobbying, speechwriting, fundraising and membership drives, publication preparation, and special-events management.

The tools used in public relations include news releases and press kits, photos, feature articles, all sorts of printed materials, posters and exhibits, and audiovisual materials.

Sponsorship is one of the fastest-growing forms of marketing today. It actually embraces two disciplines: sales promotion and public relations. A sponsorship is a cash or in-kind fee paid to a property (which may be a sports, entertainment, or nonprofit event or organization) in return for access to the exploitable commercial potential of that property. It should not be confused with philanthropy.

Sponsorship offers many benefits. It meets with public approval. It has the ability to involve customers, prospects, and other stakeholders. Most events are highly self-selective of their target audience. Sponsorships and events can provide face-to-face access to current and potential customers. They can enhance the company's public image or reinforce its positioning through affiliation with an appropriate event. And they can boost employee morale.

However, sponsorships can be very costly, and they are also subject to clutter, which reduces their effectiveness.

Types of sponsorships include sports marketing; entertainment; festivals, fairs, and annual events; causes; the arts; and venue marketing. Sports marketing is by far the largest category, consuming over two-thirds of all sponsorship dollars.

Companies may either buy into an existing event or start their own. One problem with sponsorship is evaluating the results. Three methods include measuring changes in awareness, measuring spending equivalencies with advertising, and measuring changes in sales revenue.

To help create a favorable reputation in the marketplace, companies use various types of corporate advertising, including public relations advertising, institutional advertising, corporate identity advertising, and recruitment advertising.

Important Terms

advertorials, *604*

advocacy advertising, *604*

ambush marketing, *592*

audiovisual materials, *589*

community involvement, *584*

corporate advertising, *596*

corporate blog, *586*

corporate identity advertising, *604*

crisis management, *583*

entertainment, *593*

exhibit, *589*

feature article, *588*

house organ, *589*

in kind, *590*

institutional advertising, *596*

lobbying, *586*

marketing public relations (MPR), *581*

market prep corporate advertising, *604*

news (press) release, *587*

opinion sampling, *582*

philanthropy, *590*

poster, *589*

press agentry, *583*

press (media) kit, *587*

public affairs, *585*

publicity, *583*

public relations (PR), *578*

public relations advertising, *596*

publics, *578*

recruitment advertising, *604*

reputation management, *583*

speechwriting, *586*

sponsorship, *589*

venue marketing, *594*

video news release (VNR), *589*

Review Questions

1. How does public relations differ from advertising?

2. How is the perspective of advertising practitioners different from that of PR professionals? How is marketing public relations used?

3. What is the role of public relations in relationship marketing and integrated marketing communications?

4. What are some activities used in reputation management?

5. Why is it important to establish a crisis management plan? What types of companies are most likely to need one?

6. What types of sponsorship activities are available to marketers today?

7. Which sponsorships are likely to offer the best return on investment, and how can that be measured?

8. What are the various types of corporate advertising? Describe them.

9. What is the purpose of corporate identity advertising?

10. What is the purpose of recruitment advertising? Why is it under the domain of corporate advertising and public relations?

The Advertising Experience

1. **Advertising for Future Stakeholders**

   Every company wants the best and brightest employees. Look at five recruitment advertisements and evaluate them. Which one seems to be the most effective? What makes it superior? Then look at the one you think is the least effective. Consider what could be done to improve it: then redesign the ad to make it more attractive to the most

   qualified candidates possible. http://blog.hirerabbit .com/17-recruitment-ads-that-will-bring-a-smile-to-your-face/

2. **Public Relations Firms and Corporate Advertising**

   Chapter 17 discussed the difference between traditional advertising agencies and direct marketing or sales promotion firms. Public relations firms, too, differ substantially from ad agencies. And, in some cases, they are stealing corporate advertising duties away from traditional advertising shops. It is important to explore the function of public relations firms. Visit the websites for five of the following PR companies and answer the questions that follow.

- APCO Worldwide: www.apcoworldwide.com/
- Hill+Knowlton: www.hillandknowlton.com
- Ketchum Public Relations: www.ketchum.com
- Edleman: www.edelman.com
- Euro RSCG Magnet: www.magnet.com
- Porter Novelli: www.porternovelli.com

a. Who is the intended audience of the site?

b. What are the scope and size of the firm's business?

c. What is the focus of the firm's work (i.e., consumer, business-to-business, nonprofit)?

d. What is your overall impression of the firm and its work? Why?

3. PR Organizations

As you learned in this chapter, perhaps no other marketing communications function plays a more integrated role with advertising than public relations. Now take a moment to explore the world of PR a bit further by visiting the websites for the following public relations–related organizations and answering the following questions for each site.

- American Association for Public Opinion Research (AAPOR): www.aapor.org
- Cision PR Newswire: www.prnewswire.com
- Public Relations Society of America (PRSA): www.prsa.org
- Public Relations Student Society of America (PRSSA): www.prssa.org

a. What is the organization's purpose?

b. Who makes up the organization's membership? Its constituency?

c. What benefit does the organization provide individual members/subscribers? The overall advertising and PR communities?

d. How important is this organization to the public relations community? Why?

4. Reid Hastings had some missteps in his efforts to change the business model of Netflix. How might he have handled it differently? Create a press release announcing the change to the Netflix subscriptions that might have been better received by subscribers.

End Notes

1. Austin Carr, "Netflix: What We've Got Here Is a Failure to Communicate," *Fast Company,* September 19, 2011.

2. Austin Carr, "Netflix: What We've Got Here Is a Failure to Communicate," *Fast Company,* September 19, 2011.

3. Austin Carr, "Netflix: What We've Got Here Is a Failure to Communicate,"*Fast Company,* September 19, 2011.

4. Vishesh Raisinghani, "Netflix: 400m Subscribers by 2023?" *Seeking Alpha,* January 18, 2019, *https://seekingalpha.com/article/4234271-netflix-400m-subscribers-2023*.

5. "What Is Public Relations?" Public Relations Society of America, *www.prsa.org/aboutprsa/publicrelationsdefined/#.VcnR9flVhBc*.

6. CSPI, "Ben & Jerry's Fudging the Truth, Says CSPI: Nothing 'All-Natural' About Artificial Ingredients," news release, July 30, 2002, *www.cspinet.org/new/200207301.html*.

7. Ben & Jerry's Homemade Inc., "Ben & Jerry's Response to CSPI Concerns," press release, July 31, 2002, *www.benjerry.com*.

8. Ben & Jerry's Homemade Inc., "Ben & Jerry's Voluntarily Initiates the Recall of Pints of Karamel Sutra Ice Cream with Code 02/14/04," press release, March 28, 2003, *www.benjerry.com*.

9. Dr. Mercola, "Ben & Jerry's Sued for Misleading Customers," *Mercola,* July 24, 2018, *https://articles.mercola.com/sites/articles/archive/2018/07/24/ben-and-jerrys-environmental-lawsuit.aspx*.

10. Mitchell Friedman, "Public Relations, Integrated Marketing Communications, and Professional Development in PR," October 2012, presented to PRSSA, *http://prssa.prsa.org/events/Conference/Program/12Program/12Presentations/IMC_MitchellFriedman.pdf*.

11. Todd Defren, "Guess Who's Talking—Social Media Ethical Dilemma," *pr-squared,* 2010.

12. Gaurav Heera, "17 Sites That Pay You to Blog," August 19, 2018.

13. Rachel Strugatz and Karen Robinovitz, "To Pay or Not to Pay: A Closer Look at the Business of Blogging," *WWD,* June 5, 2012.

14. Marshall Kirkpatrick, "Forrester Is Wrong About Paying Bloggers," *ReadWrite,* March 2, 2009.

15. Clint Boulton, "Google Demotes Chrome Web Page for Violating Own Guidelines," *eWeek,* January 4, 2012.

16. "Publisher's Statement," *Inside PR,* March 1993, p. 3.

17. Thomas L. Harris, "PR Gets Personal," *Direct Marketing,* April 1994, pp. 29–32.

18. Al Ries and Laura Ries, *The 22 Immutable Laws of Branding* (New York: HarperCollins, 1998), pp. 25–31.

19. "Coke Faces Struggle in Europe Recovery, Goldman Report Says," *The Wall Street Journal,* July 28, 1999, p. B5.

20. "Coke Faces Struggle in Europe Recovery, Goldman Report Says," *The Wall Street Journal,* July 28, 1999, p. B5.

21. Bill Patterson, "Crisis Impact on Reputation Management," *Public Relations Journal,* November 1993, p. 48.

22. Ben White, "Stewart's Legal Problems Hurt Firm," *Washington Post,* August 4, 2004, p. E01, *www.washingtonpost.com/wp-dyn/articles/A38202-2004Aug3.html*.

23. Dennis L. Wilcox, *Public Relations Strategies and Tactics* (New York: HarperCollins, 1994), p. 381.

24. "What's Your Best Marketing Tool?" *Public Relations Journal,* February 1994, p. 12.

25. Adapted from Stephanie Gruner, "Event Marketing: Making the Most of Sponsorship Dollars" *Inc.,* August 1996, p. 88.

26. IEG, "FAQ: What Is Sponsorship?" IEG Network, 1998, *www.sponsorship.com*.

27. IEG, "FAQ: What Is Sponsorship?" IEG Network, 1998, *www.sponsorship.com*.

28. IEG, "Sponsorship Spending to Total $16.78 Billion in 2008," press release, January 18, 2008, *www.sponsorship.com/About-IEG/Press-Room/Sponsorship-Spending-To-Total-$16.78-Billion-in-20.aspx*; "Lenovo Ducks Out of Olympic Sponsorship, Cost a Factor," *www.marketingvex.com*.

29. *https://hamburg2019.com/*

30. "Let Sponsors Do Their Thing," *Advertising Age,* May 23, 1996, *http://adage.com*.

31. Thomas R. Duncan and Sandra E. Moriarty, *Driving Brand Value: Using Integrated Marketing to Manage Stakeholder Relationships* (New York: McGraw-Hill, 1997), p. 203.

32. Thomas R. Duncan and Sandra E. Moriarty, *Driving Brand Value: Using Integrated Marketing to Manage Stakeholder Relationships* (New York: McGraw-Hill, 1997), p. 203.

33. Thomas R. Duncan and Sandra E. Moriarty, *Driving Brand Value: Using Integrated Marketing to Manage Stakeholder Relationships* (New York: McGraw-Hill, 1997), p. 203; Terry G. Vavra, *Aftermarketing: How to Keep Customers for Life through Relationship Marketing* (Burr Ridge, IL: Irwin, 1992), p. 190.

34. Terry G. Vavra, *Aftermarketing: How to Keep Customers for Life through Relationship Marketing* (Burr Ridge, IL: Irwin, 1992), p. 192.

35. "Assertions," *IEG Sponsorship Report, www.sponsorship.com*; Ron Lemasters Jr., "Sponsorship in NASCAR Breeds Fan Loyalty," Turner Sports Interactive, July 7, 2004, *www.nascar.com/2004/news/business/07/07/sponsor_nascar*.

36. Terry G. Vavra, *Aftermarketing: How to Keep Customers for Life through Relationship Marketing* (Burr Ridge, IL: Irwin, 1992), p. 192.

37. *IEG 2005 Sponsorship Report, www.sponsorship.com*.

38. David Sweet, "Everything Is for Sale in the World of Sports," January 24, 2008, *www.msnbc.com*.

39. Francis Dumais, "Top Sponsorships—Gatorade and the NFL," *Elevent,* November 16, 2016, *https://en.elevent.co/blogs/sponsorship/top-sponsorships-gatorade-and-the-nfl*.

40. Thomas Barrabi, "Why Winter Olympics 2018 Sponsors Pay Top Dollar," *FoxBusiness,* February 7, 2018, *www.foxbusiness.com/features/why-winter-olympics-2018-sponsors-pay-top-dollar*.

41. Robert Klara, "How Nike Brilliantly Ruined Olympic Marketing Forever," *AdWeek,* August 19, 2016, *www.adweek.com/brand-marketing/how-nike-brilliantly-ruined-olympic-marketing-forever-172899/*.

42. Denise Lee Yohn, "Olympics Advertisers Are Wasting Their Sponsorship Dollars," *Forbes,* August 3, 2016, *www.forbes.com/sites/deniselyohn/2016/08/03/olympics-advertisers-are-wasting-their-sponsorship-dollars/#2649e2cb2070*.

43. Sam Carp, "The IOC's TOP Sponsors: Who Are They, and What Are They up to in PyeongChang?" *SportsPro,* February 20, 2018, *www.sportspromedia.com/analysis/iocs-top-sponsors-in-pyeongchang*.

44. John McCarthy, "The 9 Best Marketing Ambushes at the 2018 World Cup," *The Drum,* June 29, 2018, *www.thedrum.com/news/2018/06/29/the-9-best-marketing-ambushes-the-2018-world-cup*.

45. "Global Sponsorship Spending Set for Faster Rise This Year Than Last," *Marketing Charts,* February 1, 2018, *www.marketingcharts.com/cross-media-and-traditional/sponsorships-traditional-and-cross-channel-82185*.

46. "Soccer and the Winning Mentality," Banco Solidario, *www.banco-solidario.com/fondo_futbol.php*.

47. Vans Warped Tour '06, *https://vanswarpedtour.com*.

48. "Signs Point to Healthy Sponsorship Spending in 2018," *IEG Sponsorship Report,* January 8, 2018, *www.sponsorship.com/Report/2018/01/08/Signs-Point-To-Healthy-Sponsorship-Spending-In-201.aspx*.

49. Lesa Ukman, "Assertions," *IEG Sponsorship Report,* November 3, 1997, *www.sponsorship.com*.

50. Dennis L. Wilcox, *Public Relations Strategies and Tactics* (New York: HarperCollins, 1994), p. 384.

51. "Inside the Evolving Pharmaceutical Category," *IEG Sponsorship Report, www.sponsorship.com/iegsr/2016/02/08/Inside-The-Evolving-Pharmaceutical-Category.aspx*.

52. David Lister and Colin Brown, "Arts World Takes Sides with Tobacco Kings," *Independent* (UK), June 30, 1997, p. 3.

53. Cliff Peale, "Great American to Name Ballpark," *Cincinnati Enquirer,* July 1, 2000.

54. Daniel Kaplan, "NFL Revenue Reaches $14B, Fueled by Media," *Sports Business Journal,* March 6, 2017, *www.sportsbusinessdaily.com/Journal/Issues/2017/03/06/Leagues-and-Governing-Bodies/NFL-revenue.aspx*.

55. "Best Fit or Best Benefits? How to Approach Potential Sponsors," *Tandem,* October 4, 2018, *https://tandempartnerships.com/best-fit-best-benefit-sponsorship/*.

56. Kathleen Smith, "Marketers, This Is How to Choose Events to Sponsor," *SponsorMyEvent,* 2016, *www.sponsormyevent.com/blog/how-to-choose-events-to-sponsor/*.

57. Lesa Ukman, "Assertions," *IEG Sponsorship Report,* January 26, 1998, *www.sponsorship.com*.

58. Terry G. Vavra, *Aftermarketing: How to Keep Customers for Life through Relationship Marketing* (Burr Ridge, IL: Irwin, 1992), p. 191.

59. "KFC's Apology for Running out of Chicken Is Pretty Cheeky," *BBC News,* February 23, 2018.

60. "Corporate Advertising/Phase II: An Expanded Study of Corporate Advertising Effectiveness," conducted for *Time* magazine by Yankelovich, Skelly & White, undated.

Repositioning a Brand
MasterCard's "Priceless" Campaign

One of the riskiest endeavors in marketing is to relaunch a brand from scratch. It takes time—and lots of money—to develop a clear position for a brand, and major changes to the brand concept can confuse consumers and weaken brand equity. This is especially true when the brand in question is a global giant, universally recognized and used almost everywhere that people spend money.

So why, in 1997, did MasterCard issue a call to dozens of top agencies to help overhaul the venerable MasterCard brand? And what made the eventual winner, the "Priceless" campaign developed by McCann Worldwide, such a dramatic and enduring success?

In the pages that follow, you'll see how everything you've studied—from the basic truths about consumers to the most complex media strategies—can come together to make a runaway hit, in which a big idea, based on consumer insights, electrifies a brand and provides a boost for all its constituencies. You'll also see how such a campaign can be executed around the world and take the idea to the next level through IMC. You'll see how a strong brand concept, properly identified and communicated, can sustain an IMC campaign for over three decades. In short, you'll see how to translate theory into practice: from ideas to the bottom line.

A Universal Emotional Chord

The scene is immediately familiar—a father and son arriving at the ballpark for an afternoon baseball game—but the narrative device is not. As the crew-cut, all-American boy hands his ticket to the usher, a voice-over accompanied by white lettering superimposed on the screen announces, "Two tickets: $28." Next, we see the boy holding two large boxes of popcorn and the voice-over and lettering (super) continue: "Two hot dogs, two popcorns, and two sodas: $18."

The male voice-over (anonymously executed by film star Billy Crudup) is warm and comforting; the soft musical soundtrack of piano and classical guitar equally so; the production values are top quality, giving this scene as much emotional force as an Oscar-winning movie. But why the "shopping list" of costs? Within 10 seconds, the viewer is hooked, needing to know where this is going. But the mystery continues as the father and son make their way toward their seats: "One autographed baseball: $45."

Finally, the pair takes their seats, and we see the father gesturing at the field, to explain some aspect of the game that is getting under way. The voice-over and super continue: "Real conversation with 11-year-old son: Priceless."

Boom!

The emotional connection—dangled temptingly throughout the commercial—is finally made with the viewer. But a subtle message has also emerged: All of those everyday purchases—the tickets, the concessions, and the autographed ball—have added up to this enduring bonding experience between a father and son. And then, the tagline puts it all together: "There are some things money can't buy—for everything else there's MasterCard."

Source: "Creative: Inside Priceless MasterCard Moments," *Adweek,* April 12, 1999.

A Marriage of Analytic Research and Creative Execution

With the launch of the campaign, and its subsequent global rollout, McCann started the process of rebuilding a gold-standard brand in the minds of consumers everywhere.

The remarkable "Priceless" MasterCard campaign has been an enormous success because it resonates with consumers, and it's strategically dead on target. It is consistent with contemporary values and provides a positive message—something truly refreshing for a credit card company—in a format that's familiar. Every spot expresses an underlying concept that is immediately recognizable to everybody. It is eminently executable. And it translates into any culture around the world, for every nation has its own local "Priceless" stories. If you don't look too closely, it might seem easy, like a stroke of astounding good luck—one of those rare moments when a whole campaign is born from a single moment of insight that is legendary to advertising executives. But it took more than luck. A lot more.

This is the story of how McCann Worldwide and MasterCard used sophisticated proprietary techniques to reposition MasterCard within the credit card industry, giving the brand a completely new face and a meaningful, likeable point of difference in a competitive environment. It started with McCann conducting painstaking research, performing meticulous analysis, and then developing some big creative ideas, all aimed at helping MasterCard reclaim its position as the world's leading credit card. Its work shows how the commitment to research, which we discussed in Part Two, combined with the high standard in creative development and production values we presented in Part Three, helped MasterCard launch an historic, award-winning global campaign.

Since McCann Worldwide can safely assume that consumers have seen many of the "Priceless" television commercials, this print ad requires very little text to communicate the benefits of owning a MasterCard.

Source: MasterCard

business lunch: $110
(family dinner: priceless)

A Search for New Direction

When MasterCard first put its advertising account into review, the one thing everybody agreed about was that the brand—one of the most recognized in the world—needed a makeover. While successful past marketing efforts had made MasterCard a ubiquitous presence in the United States and around the world, the brand now needed a new identity and one that could endure, guiding the company into the next millennium. Nick Utton, then MasterCard's chief marketing officer, assembled a core group that represented the best minds in the global research, marketing, and advertising departments to evaluate new ideas from a variety of world-class advertising agencies.

Every agency MasterCard invited to join the pitch relished the opportunity to participate. It's not every day that a brand as well known and universally recognized as MasterCard decides to undergo such an overhaul. But what sort of overhaul? Where did the company want to go with this brand and what was the problem with where it was already?

Matt Weiss, SVP/group account director at McCann, put it this way at the time: "It was the third card in the wallet, behind Visa and American Express. Visa, the main competitor, was firmly entrenched as the top credit card with its worldly, 'Everywhere You Want to Be' campaign. Our challenge was to find a way to bring emotional aspiration back to the MasterCard brand." The current campaign, "Smart Money," developed by another agency, simply wasn't resonating with customers.

"The problem wasn't just with consumers," explained Elisa Romm, VP of U.S. advertising at MasterCard. MasterCard is an association that supports more than 30,000 member banks across the country, and these banks needed to become excited again about the brand. "The members looked to MasterCard to support them and they were very concerned about finding a consistent direction that could have a lasting impact with consumers. We needed a new, enduring campaign to energize consumers and member banks. We needed to demonstrate consistency, along with superior strategy and execution."

The company needed a big idea to bring the member banks together and lift their spirits. It was no small challenge—and the image of a major worldwide company hung in the balance.

McCann believed it could meet this challenge. "We considered it a travesty that Visa was *it* and MasterCard was just another card, even though you could use your MasterCard wherever you could use your Visa—and actually in more places around the world," explained Eric Einhorn, EVP and marketing director of McCann World Group.* To discover why this situation existed, McCann turned to its proprietary brand planning process, a comprehensive arsenal of services and tools developed over many years of experience implementing campaigns for companies like Coca-Cola, Microsoft, and L'Oréal.

*Source: "Creative: Inside Priceless MasterCard Moments," *Adweek,* April 12, 1999.

McCann's "Selling Strategy"

McCann Worldwide's Selling Strategy would provide the roadmap for developing the MasterCard campaign. The Selling Strategy is a service that is single-mindedly focused on generating brand-building ideas—ideas that attract customers, develop corporate and brand franchises, and create market dominance for McCann's clients. The McCann Selling Strategy uncovers the motivations of conceptual target audiences and results in a strategic concept that pinpoints a unique "selling idea."

According to Matt Weiss, "the Selling Strategy is a discipline to be pursued with passion—it's a way of thinking and a way of working meant to encourage greater strategic focus, consumer insight, and creative depth, resulting in advertising that sells." In the fast-paced and diversified global marketplace, a comprehensive brand campaign needs

The strength, longevity, and popularity of the MasterCard campaign help ensure that banner ads such as the one shown here are immediately recognized and understood.

Source: MasterCard

to be both consistent enough to be readily identified with the brand and flexible enough to appeal to different target consumer groups and fit into different media formats, whether they be print, electronic, or interactive.

The Selling Strategy begins with the Brand Footprint, which discovers where the brand is in the marketplace and in consumers' minds, why it is there, where it should be, and how it will get there. This process of mapping the brand footprint of MasterCard and its competitors would allow McCann to discover areas that MasterCard's brand could grow into and inhabit naturally, without a forced appearance that might alienate consumers or be confused with the brand footprints of its competitors.

Once it had identified MasterCard's current Brand Footprint and those of its competitors, McCann moved to the task of developing a new brand positioning, "the most basic of all strategic statements about the brand." This internal statement grows out of the Brand Footprint and, in turn, inspires the creative brief. The creative brief addresses several issues: what the advertising is going to do, what insights about the target consumer the advertising will connect with, and what the target consumers will think and feel about the brand. The creative brief serves as the stimulus for the selling idea—the bridge between the communications strategy and the campaign's creative execution.

The first thing the Selling Strategy calls for is information—lots of it.

Researching the Industry and a Lot More

McCann's management understood the challenge. "We knew we had to come up with a campaign that had breakthrough ability—a campaign that could endure," explains Matt Weiss. They began by teaming up with MasterCard for a comprehensive research and information-gathering program that would give them as much data as possible to help discover MasterCard's Brand Footprint.

"We started with a review of where MasterCard was," explains Weiss. They reviewed annual reports, payment industry overview/situation analyses, strategic marketing overviews, market research highlights, global issues, and Nielsen reports, the comprehensive positioning for the current advertising concept. They did content audits of MasterCard's business and consumer advertising, and they reviewed the competitive landscape in great detail.

Next, they conducted secondary data analysis: credit card usage data, and the Yankelovich Monitor and Roper Reports of credit card and financial services attitudes and behavior.

Many agencies might stop there. But McCann always relies on primary research where it talks directly to consumers. The agency conducted 28 focus groups, 24 one-on-one personal interviews, and 250 telephone interviews among credit card users. And while it

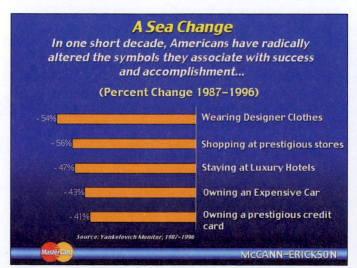

McCann-Erickson's research discovered that important changes had taken place in consumer attitudes during the previous decade.

Source: MasterCard

learned a lot about attitudes toward MasterCard and its competitors and some prelimi-
nary campaign ideas, the agency went much further. To fully understand the psychological space that MasterCard did—and could—inhabit, McCann conducted wide-ranging
sociological surveys that helped it understand the feelings and emotions behind the
brand category.

Finding the Sweet Spot

This process of mapping the brand against its available "brand-scape" was a crucial step
in the journey toward an executable and winning campaign. Studying consumer perceptions of MasterCard's principal competitors, McCann determined the Brand Footprint
for American Express included the three personality characteristics of "Membership,"
"The Business Life," and "The Charge Card." Its three descriptors were "Professional,"
"Worldly," and "Responsible." Visa's Brand Footprint was not so different. The personality characteristics were "Everywhere," "The High Life," and "The Credit Card," and its
descriptors were "Sociable," "Stylish," and "On-the-Go." MasterCard's Brand Footprint,
on the other hand, was very different. Its personality characteristics were "Everyday,"
"Ordinary Life," and "Generic"; its descriptors were "Unassuming," "Unpretentious,"
and "Practical."

MasterCard's existing Brand Footprint was, in McCann's estimation, neutral. As a
rule, this is not a good place for a brand to be. But there was an upside. MasterCard had
an opportunity to use that neutrality to create a new, more powerful and relevant brand
positioning that reflected contemporary attitudes not only about credit cards and spending, but about much more far-reaching and important themes, like success. In short, the
agency felt it had an opportunity to turn a neutral brand footprint into a powerful and
meaningful space.

"We found that consumers had some feelings about MasterCard as the card for regular
people, while Visa and American Express had a more exclusive, worldly appeal," says Joyce
King Thomas, EVP deputy creative director at McCann. In an industry based on spending
money, that might seem like a negative, but McCann saw it as a potential positive. With
American Express and Visa inhabiting dated brand spaces, MasterCard's current brand
image gave the company an opportunity to claim a fresh, new, and more contemporary
brand territory, closer to today's consumption ideals than its main competitors. "We
decided to give value to those everyday situations and emotions, the little things that add
up to the big things in life," explains Thomas.

McCann also learned that along with these new attitudes about spending, consumers
were feeling more responsible about themselves as users of credit cards. In one study,
82 percent felt their unpaid credit card balance was "necessary and justified." McCann
identified a MasterCard "sweet spot" that melded the new consumer values with the emerging credit card mind-set and dubbed it "Good Spenders."

McCann had found the Brand Footprint for MasterCard, the truth of what the
brand stood for in the minds of consumers. More important, it had found insight into
where the brand could grow: McCann could use this "sweet spot," the overlap of new
values combined with an adjustment in attitudes toward credit cards, to define a reener-
gized, repositioned, prescribed Brand Footprint for MasterCard. "Good spenders use

credit cards to acquire the things that are important to them—the things that enrich their everyday lives," explains Nat Puccio, McCann's strategic planning director. This new mind-set was in sharp contrast to that of MasterCard's competitors. With this realization—that MasterCard's core brand values were closer to credit card consumption ideals than Visa or American Express—what had been a liability was suddenly a strength. Now McCann had to figure out how to demonstrate this to MasterCard and then to leverage it with the public.

Moving from the Brand Footprint to an Executable Campaign

As the day for the pitch presentation grew closer, Puccio and his team came up with a brilliant way of differentiating MasterCard's footprint from the competitors. Alongside two identical photographs of a large-screen TV, they put an image of a Visa card under one and a MasterCard under another. Under the Visa symbol, they put the words, "The Super Bowl is going to look great on that large-screen TV"; under the MasterCard, "We really need a family entertainment center." With a single, deft touch, McCann found a way to demonstrate how different values and spending attitudes could add up to the *same* purchase.

To further the point, Puccio and his team added another page to the presentation, with two identical images of a skier and the two credit cards. Under the Visa card were the words, "I haven't been to that hot new ski resort yet"; under the MasterCard, "I should really take a moment to relax and recharge from all this stress." The message was clear: These new spending attitudes provided a new justification for the same purchases previously associated with consumption-oriented lifestyles. Consequently, that opened up a whole new space for the MasterCard brand.

Next, McCann developed the Selling Idea, "The Best Way to Pay for Everything That Matters." This wasn't the tagline, but a strategic articulation of what the agency wanted brand messages to express. With "The Best Way to Pay for Everything That Matters," McCann's planners had synthesized their painstaking research into an idea so simple that it would make what followed look effortless.

Next came the moment of inspiration. Jonathan Cranin, McCann's chief creative officer for North America, Europe, Africa, and the Middle East, was actually in the shower one morning, mulling over the fruits of the agency's research, when the line popped into his head, "There are some things money can't buy. For everything else there's MasterCard." From there, everything fell into place with amazing speed. Joyce King Thomas and creative director partner Jeroen Bours quickly came up with the shopping list approach that was expressed in the baseball spot. This would become the hallmark of the whole campaign.

McCann wasn't pitching a campaign: It was pitching an idea. And it was such a powerful idea that the agency needed to come up with a special way to present it. Bours came up with the inspiration of making giant blue velvet storybooks and a large wooden box to house them all. "We put a big cover over the box, and when we pulled the cover off, the client actually gasped," reports Thomas. MasterCard's Debra Coughlin, SVP, global brand building, remembers the moment—and the gasp—well. "One of my colleagues literally did gasp. They'd caught lightning in a bottle."

Matt Weiss remembers overhearing MasterCard officials in the halls immediately after the pitch. "They were ecstatic, talking about how we'd 'struck gold.' It was amazing."

Implementing the Campaign

The first spot, shot by Tony Kaye, a world-renowned director, was the father–son baseball story described earlier. It first aired in Game Three of the 1997 World Series. Other spots were quick to follow. Each story was different and unique, but the structure was consistent: a family prepares to pose for a photo; the voice-over (always supplied by Billy Crudup) supplies the costs of the camera and new clothes, arriving at "Five Generations in One Photograph: Priceless." In another, a young woman prepares herself meticulously for an evening out, until we're told, "Look on Old Boyfriend's Face at High School Reunion: Priceless." In still another, two golfers have a day at the course, ending with, "A Hole in One, with a Witness: Priceless."

The results of the campaign were instant and dramatic. Consumers responded immediately, with higher levels of advertising empathy and likeability toward the brand. Member banks commented on the insights embodied in the campaign and how it would improve perceptions of the brand. Importantly, neither MasterCard nor McCann lost sight of the "rational" side of the brand positioning—that MasterCard is accepted everywhere.

In 2002, MasterCard won the inaugural Gold Effie for Sustained Success—given to the most effective campaign over the course of three years. By 2004, the campaign won a total of three Effies and eight AMEs (which stands for Advertising Marketing Effectiveness).

And in what may be the surest sign of the campaign's success, it thoroughly entered the popular consciousness. People looked forward to the new spots and talked about them around the water cooler in the office. It soon became a part of the cultural vernacular. Another sign of success was when the format and line were spoofed and lampooned by top comedians, including Jay Leno (on a remarkable five separate occasions),

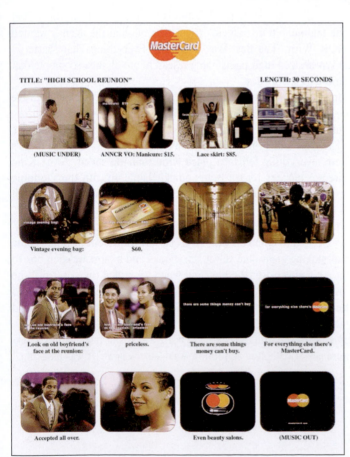

All the little purchases paid for with a MasterCard add up to one memorable moment that's so big, so important, it's priceless—in this case, the look on the old boyfriend's face.

Source: MasterCard

Every golfer knows the emotional value of a hole-in-one—priceless. The same is true for advertising people. A campaign like "Priceless" is so good and has such long legs that it can run for years. It is the advertising equivalent of a hole-in-one—with lots of witnesses.

Source: MasterCard

Consumers loved the "Priceless" campaign, and that translated into greater likeability for the brand. The advertising industry loved it, too, showering the campaign with a slew of awards.

Source: MasterCard

David Letterman, *Saturday Night Live, Talk Soup,* Gannett Newspapers, NBC's *Will and Grace,* MTV, VH1, *The Simpsons,* and many popular internet sites. Ralph Nader even used the "priceless" idea in his 2008 campaign for president. The millions of dollars' worth of free exposure that the campaign received on television and in print resulted primarily from the real appeal of the campaign. But also at work here was a parallel and deft public relations campaign by MasterCard that used publicity to build up anticipation before every major new spot. The company understood the value of high-profile spoofs and encouraged them.

The Next Step: Integrated Marketing

Now that the campaign was such a hit, there were new challenges. The first was integrating the positioning idea across all of MasterCard's different communications channels. Larry Flanagan developed an integration model that had the "Priceless" concept at the center, with all positioning and marketing activities supporting the center. While MasterCard developed sponsorships with Major League Baseball, the PGA, and the National Hockey League, McCann created new spots to promote them—and the concept applied easily to every new venture.

The MasterCard All-Century Team

In numerous ways, MasterCard integrated "Priceless" across the whole marketing mix. For example, in 1999, the company wanted to increase the efficiency and impact of its number one sponsorship property, Major League Baseball. With McCann's help, MasterCard created a fully integrated program—the MasterCard All-Century Team—that used the "Priceless" campaign to add dimension to the brand and appeal to those consumers who followed baseball.

Many of the ad concepts were adapted to fit international markets. In less than a decade, MasterCard has completely redeveloped and rejuvenated its image, and the "Priceless" campaign has become part of our popular culture. For the 2004 Oscars telecast, McCann developed the epic "Dog Trilogy" in grand Hollywood style.

Part One: "Lost Dog"

VO: film and dog food for Badger in the Redwoods: $10
Super: film and dog food: $10

VO: bandana for lost dog in Napa Valley: $3
Super: bandana: $3

VO: dog bone in Fresno: $7
Super: dog bone: $7
VO/Super: forgetting you're far from home: priceless

VO: there are some things money can't buy.
VO: for your journey there's MasterCard.

Source: MasterCard

Part Two: "On the Road"

VO: water for a lost dog in the Mojave: $2
Super: water: $2

VO: rhinestone collar in Vegas: $40
Super: rhinestone collar: $40

VO: meatloaf special in Arizona: $8
Super: meatloaf special: $8

VO/Super: Feeling at home when you're only halfway there: priceless

VO: there are some things money can't buy.
VO: for your journey there's MasterCard.

Source: MasterCard

Part Three: "Home"

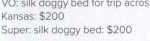

VO: chew toy for lost dog in
Colorado: $5
Super: chew toy: $5

VO: silk doggy bed for trip across
Kansas: $200
Super: silk doggy bed: $200

VO: bubble bath in Jefferson
City: $15 (dog at pet groomer)
Super: bubble bath: $15

VO: coming home after a long
trip: priceless
Super: coming home: priceless

VO: there are some things money
can't buy.
VO: for your journey there's
MasterCard

Source: MasterCard

Consumer research indicated MasterCard cardholders loved Major League Baseball. This "love of the game" ran deep and often found its way into family life. Fathers, for example, clearly remembered taking their sons to their first "big league" game—the basic premise of the very first "Priceless" spot. Moms often talked of the "good quality" times shared at the ballpark. McCann found that consumers wanted to experience the game frequently and were positively predisposed to brands that had a strong association with Major League Baseball.

For MasterCard, this presented a huge opportunity. The positioning, as demonstrated by the "Priceless" campaign, was founded on the premise of "what matters" in everyday life. To this target, Major League Baseball mattered greatly. Thus, the positioning—The Best Way to Pay for Everything That Matters—was ultimately used to form the link between the brand (MasterCard), the sponsorship partner (Major League Baseball), and the consumer (the MasterCard/Major League Baseball fan). The strategic positioning became: "MasterCard. The card at the heart of Major League Baseball," and the implementation was the wildly popular MasterCard All-Century Team, something that truly mattered to baseball fans. Without such a strong and flexible positioning to work from, it wouldn't have been such a runaway success.

By 2003, "Priceless" had gone from being an advertising campaign that lived primarily within the traditional realm of TV and print to a truly integrated global platform encompassing event sponsorship, sales promotion, and public relations activities and spanning a myriad of communication vehicles including radio, the internet, point-of-sale (POS), and direct mail.

Fastfoward to 2017. New MasterCard CMO Raja Rajamannar needed to make a big decision: keep the campaign going or chart a new course. "Dealing with an iconic campaign is both a blessing and a challenge," said Rajamannar. "How do you take it to the next level when it's doing so well? And how do you convince the system, and convince yourself, that a change is indeed needed?"

The "Priceless" campaign is ultimately about every consumer's unique dreams. In this ad, one of Justin Timberlake's biggest fans is surprised to meet her idol.

Source: MasterCard

The evolution first started in 2010 when a campaign labeled "Priceless Cities" aimed at specific audiences defined by demographics and geographics. Next came "Priceless Surprises," which moved advertising heavily into digital and social media. An example is the Justin Timberlake viral shown above.

The brand's core areas, which for now include Priceless "cities," "surprises," "causes," and "perks," expanded to nine in 2016. Rajamannar, it seems, continues nudging the brand to embrace 21st century strategies while retaining a 20th century big idea. A great example is "priceless experiences," which are available only to cardholders (see here: www.mastercard.us/en-us/consumers/offers-promotions.html) which help ensure that this phenomenal campaign continues to pay dividends into the 2020s.

One of Mastercard's new spots is "Priceless Causes," in which antagonists (like the Mets and Phillies mascots) work together to fight cancer.

Source: MasterCard

As of 2019, the campaign continues, fresh as ever, with ads like these titled "Priceless Surprises." David Ogilvy once claimed that an indicator of a Big Idea is that it could last a long time. The "Priceless" campaign has met that standard.

Source: MasterCard

A Textbook Case

Why has the campaign been so successful, not only in the United States but around the world? Larry Flanagan told *Advertising Age,* "People ask, 'How do you develop and execute a global campaign like that?' But we didn't set out with a global campaign mandate. We came up with a strong idea for the United States and, because its insights were so global and its strategic foundation so nonbiased toward any culture, we found it could resonate around the world. The core values of 'Priceless' translate well everywhere and have driven results for us globally."

As one of the most recognizable campaigns in the world, "'Priceless' has become an icon in a very short time," says former MasterCard marketer Jim Accomando. "As an ad campaign, it's as good as any I've seen."

The strategic and creative brilliance of "Priceless" has garnered lots of recognition for its creators, including over 100 creative awards worldwide. *Fortune* magazine even named the campaign's creative team as one of "Six Teams That Changed the World."

More importantly, "Priceless" has helped MasterCard achieve its marketing objectives. In 1991, a few years before the campaign began, the card was accepted at fewer than 2 million locations in the United States. Today it is accepted at more than 7 million. And since the campaign's debut, MasterCard has issued twice as many new U.S. credit cards as Visa.

Can a campaign that's run for over 30 years, involving more than 350 commercials, viewed in 108 countries and 50 languages, can keep on going. As our update shows, Master-card's new CMO and ad agency McCann plan to ensure that "Priceless" stays fresh and relevant.

After all of that success, you have to wonder if the folks at MasterCard ever think,

- Creative spots that consistently win awards—pretty good.
- A campaign that effectively conveys the essence of the MasterCard brand to the target audience—sensational.
- Over 30 years of compelling spots that continue to resonate with viewers—outstanding.
- IMC that meets and then exceeds every marketing and communications objective—Priceless!

Marketing Plan Outline

Date:
Company Name:
Brand or Service:

Encapsulation, for executive review, of entire marketing plan in no more than two or three pages.

I. Executive Summary
    A. Summary of situation analysis
    B. Summary of marketing objectives
    C. Summary of marketing strategies
    D. Budget summary

Complete statement of where the organization is today and how it got there.

II. Situation Analysis
    A. The industry
        1. Definition of industry and company business
        2. History of industry

What business the organization is in and characteristics of the industry as a whole. Information available from industry trade publications, trade association newsletters, consumer business press, Department of Commerce publications.

            a. Technological advances
            b. Trends
        3. Growth patterns within industry
            a. Demand curve
            b. Per capita consumption
            c. Growth potential
        4. Characteristics of industry
            a. Distribution patterns and traditional channels
            b. Regulation and control within industry
            c. Typical promotional activity
            d. Geographic characteristics
            e. Profit patterns

All relevant information on the company and its capabilities, opportunities, and/or problems. Information may be found in annual reports, sales records, warranty card records, customer correspondence, sales staff reports.

    B. The company
        1. Brief history
        2. Scope of business
        3. Current size, growth, profitability
        4. Reputation
        5. Competence in various areas
            a. Strengths
            b. Weaknesses

Complete description and all relevant information on the product/service mix, sales, and the strengths and weaknesses therein. See sales literature, sales reports, dealer correspondence, and so on.

    C. The product/service
        1. The product story
            a. Development and history
            b. Stage of product life cycle
                (1) Introduction

   (2) Growth

   (3) Maturity

   (4) Decline

  c. Quality factors

  d. Design considerations

  e. Goods classification

   (1) Consumer or industrial good

   (2) Durable or nondurable good or service

   (3) Convenience, shopping, or specialty good

   (4) Package good, hard good, soft good, service

  f. Packaging

  g. Price structure

  h. Uses

   (1) Primary

   (2) Secondary

   (3) Potential

  i. Image and reputation

  j. Product/service strengths

  k. Product/service weaknesses

 2. Product sales features

  a. Differentiating factors

   (1) Perceptible, imperceptible, or induced

   (2) Exclusive or nonexclusive

  b. Position in mind of customer

  c. Advantages and disadvantages (customer perception)

 3. Product research and development

  a. Technological breakthroughs

  b. Improvements planned

  c. Technical or service problems

 4. Sales history

  a. Sales and cost of sales

   (1) By product/service

   (2) By model

   (3) By territory

   (4) By market

  b. Profit history for same factors

 5. Share of market

  a. Industry sales by market

  b. Market share in dollars and units

  c. Market potential and trends

D. The market

 1. Definition and location of market

  a. Identified market segments

   (1) Past

   (2) Potential

  b. Market needs, desires

All relevant information about the people or organizations that comprise the current and prospective market for the firm's offerings. See market research reports, consumer/ business press, trade publications, Census of Manufacturers, trade association reports.

    c. Characteristics of market

       (1) Geographic

       (2) Demographic

       (3) Psychographic

       (4) Behavioral

    d. Typical buying patterns

       (1) Purchase patterns

       (2) Heavy users/light users

       (3) Frequency of purchase

    e. Buying influences on market

2. Definition of our customers

    a. Present, past, and future

    b. Characteristics

       (1) Shared characteristics with rest of market

       (2) Characteristics unique to our customers

    c. What they like about us or our product

    d. What they don't like

3. Consumer appeals

    a. Past advertising appeals

       (1) What has worked

       (2) What has not worked and why

    b. Possible future appeals

4. Results of research studies about market and customers

E. The competition

1. Identification of competitors

    a. Primary competitors

    b. Secondary competitors

    c. Product/service descriptions

    d. Growth and size of competitors

    e. Share of market held by competitors

2. Strengths of competition

    a. Product quality

    b. Sales features

    c. Price, distribution, promotion

3. Weaknesses of competition

    a. Product features

    b. Consumer attitude

    c. Price, distribution, promotion

4. Marketing activities of competition

    a. Product positioning

    b. Pricing strategies

    c. Distribution

    d. Sales force

    e. Advertising, publicity

    f. Estimated budgets

Complete information about the competition, the competitive environment, and the opportunities or challenges presented by current or prospective competitors. See SEC Form 10-Ks, consumer/business press articles, Moody's Industrial Manual, Standard & Poor's reports, Dun & Bradstreet report, Thomas Register of American Corporations.

Complete discussion of how the firm's products/services are distributed and sold, what channels are available, and characteristics of channel members. See dealer and distributor correspondence, sales staff reports, advertising reports, trade publication articles.

F. Distribution strategies
    1. Type of distribution network used
        a. History of development
        b. Trends
    2. Evaluation of how distribution is accomplished
    3. Relationships with channel members
    4. Promotional relationship with channel members
        a. Trade advertising and allowances
        b. Co-op advertising
        c. Use of promotion by dealer or middlemen
        d. Point-of-purchase displays, literature
        e. Dealer incentive programs
    5. Strengths/weaknesses of distribution systems
    6. Opportunities/threats related to distribution

Background and rationale for firm's pricing policies and strategies, discussion of alternative options. Study sales reports, channel-member correspondence, customer correspondence, competitive information.

G. Pricing policies
    1. Price history
        a. Trends
        b. Affordability
        c. Competition
    2. Price objectives and strategies in past
        a. Management attitudes
        b. Buyer attitudes
        c. Channel attitudes
    3. Opportunities/threats related to pricing

All relevant data concerning the firm's personal sales efforts and effectiveness as well as complete discussion of the firm's use of advertising, public relations, and sales promotion programs. Examine sales reports; advertising reports; articles in Advertising Age, Marketing Communications, *and so on; in-house data on advertising, sales, and training.*

H. Communication strategies
    1. Past promotion policy
        a. Personal versus nonpersonal selling
            (1) Use of sales force
            (2) Use of traditional advertising, public relations, sales promotion, sponsorship
            (3) Use of digital communications media, social media, e-mail, mobile
        b. Successes and failures of past policy
    2. Sales force
        a. Size
        b. Scope
        c. Ability/training
        d. Cost per sale
    3. Traditional advertising programs
        a. Successes and failures
        b. Strategies, themes, campaigns, media employed
        c. Appeals, positionings, and so on
        d. Expenditures
            (1) Past budgets
            (2) Method of allocation
            (3) Competitor budgets
            (4) Trends

4. Digital advertising programs
    a. Successes and failures
    b. Strategies, themes, campaigns, digital media employed
    c. Appeals, positioning
    d. Expenditures
5. Opportunities/threats related to communications

I. Environmental factors

Enumeration of environmental factors that may be beyond the firm's immediate control but affect the firm's business efforts. See government reports and announcements, consumer/business press, trade association articles.

1. Economy
    a. Current economic status
    b. Business outlook and economic forecasts
2. Political situation
3. Societal concerns
4. Technological influences

J. Corporate objectives and strategies

Recitation of relevant attitudes and directives of management as they pertain to the firm's marketing and advertising efforts. Information available from corporate business plan, management interviews, internal memos and directives.

1. Profitability
    a. Sales revenue
    b. Cost reductions
2. Return on investment
3. Stock price
4. Shareholder equity
5. Community image
6. New product development
7. Technological leadership
8. Mergers and/or acquisitions
9. Overall corporate mission

K. Potential marketing problems

Enumeration or summary of problems considered most serious to the firm's marketing success.

L. Potential marketing opportunities

Summary of those opportunities that offer the greatest potential for the firm's success. What general and specific needs the firm seeks to satisfy. Determine through study of situation analysis factors and management discussions and interviews.

III. Marketing Objectives

A. Market need objectives
    1. Market need-satisfying objectives
    2. Community need-satisfying objectives
    3. Corporate need-satisfying objectives

B. Sales target objectives

Organization sales goals defined for whole company or for individual products by target market, by geographic territory, by department, or by some other category. Must be specific and realistic based on study of company capabilities, funding, and objectives.

1. Sales volume
    a. Dollars
    b. Units
    c. Territories
    d. Markets
2. Share of market
3. Distribution expansion

The method(s) by which the organization plans to achieve the objectives enumerated above.

4. Other

IV. Marketing Strategy

A. General marketing strategy

A general description of the type of marketing strategy the organization intends to employ.

1. Positioning strategy
2. Product differentiation strategy

3. Price/quality differentiation strategy

4. Mission marketing strategy

A detailed description of the marketing mix(es) the firm intends to use to achieve its objectives.

B. Specific market strategies

1. Target market A

    a. Product

    b. Price

    c. Distribution

    d. Communication

        (1) Personal selling

        (2) Advertising

        (3) Direct marketing

        (4) Sales promotion

        (5) Public relations

        (6) Sponsorship

        (7) Digital and social media

2. Target market B

    a. Product

    b. Price

    c. Distribution

    d. Communication

        (1) Personal selling

        (2) Advertising

        (3) Direct marketing

        (4) Sales promotion

        (5) Public relations

        (6) Sponsorship

        (7) Digital and social media

The detailed tactical plans for implementing each of the elements of the firm's marketing mix.

V. Action Programs (Tactics)

A. Product plans

B. Pricing plans

C. Distribution plans

D. Communication plans

1. Sales plan

2. Advertising plan

3. Direct marketing plan

4. Sales promotion plan

5. Public relations plan

6. Digital and social media plan

E. Mission marketing plan

Description of the methods the firm will use to review, evaluate, and control its progress toward the achievement of its marketing objectives.

VI. Measurement, Review, and Control

A. Organizational structure

B. Methodology for review and evaluation

C. Interactivity monitoring

Determination of the amount of money needed to conduct the marketing effort, the rationale for that budget, and the allocation to various functions.

VII. Marketing Budget

    A. Method of allocation

    B. Enumeration of marketing costs by division

        1. New product research

        2. Marketing research

        3. Sales expenses

        4. Advertising, direct marketing, sales promotion, public relations, digital and social media

Details of information, secondary data, or research conducted to develop information discussed in the marketing plan.

VIII. Appendixes

    A. Sales reports

    B. Reports of market research studies

    C. Reprints of journal or magazine articles

    D. Other supporting documents

Advertising Plan Outline

Date:

Company (Brand/Service) Name:

Brief encapsulation, for executive review, of entire advertising plan in no more than two or three pages.

I. Executive Summary

    A. Premises—summary of information presented in marketing plan

    B. Summary of advertising objectives

    C. Summary of advertising strategy

    D. Budget summary

Condensed review of pertinent elements presented in the marketing plan.

II. Situation Analysis

    A. Company's (or product's) current marketing situation

        1. Business or industry information

        2. Description of company, product, or service

            a. Stage of product life cycle

            b. Goods classification

            c. Competitive or market positioning

        3. General description of market(s) served

        4. Sales history and share of market

        5. Description of consumer purchase process

        6. Methods of distribution

        7. Pricing strategies employed

        8. Implications of any marketing research

        9. Communications history

    B. Target market description

        1. Market segments identified

        2. Primary market

        3. Secondary markets

        4. Market characteristics

            a. Geographic

            b. Demographic

            c. Psychographic

            d. Behavioral

    C. Marketing objectives

        1. Need-satisfying objectives

        2. Long- and short-term sales target objectives

    D. Marketing mix for each target market—summarized from marketing plan

        1. Product

        2. Price

        3. Distribution

        4. Communication

E. Intended role of advertising in the communications mix

F. Miscellaneous information not included before

Analysis and statement of what the advertising is expected to accomplish—see My IMC Campaign: Developing Advertising Objectives.

III. Advertising Objectives

A. Primary or selective demand

B. Direct action or indirect action

C. Objectives stated in terms of:

1. Advertising pyramid

2. Direct response, including purchases

3. Other

D. Quantified expression of objectives

1. Specific quantities or percentages

2. Length of time for achievement of objectives

3. Other possible measurements

   a. Inquiries

   b. Increased order size

   c. Morale building

   d. Social media activity

   e. Other

Intended blend of the creative mix for the company as a whole, for each product, or for each target market.

IV. Advertising (Creative) Strategy

A. Product concept—how the advertising will present the product in terms of:

1. Product or market positioning

2. Product differentiation

3. Life cycle

4. Classification, packaging, branding

5. FCB grid purchase-decision position

   a. High/low think involvement

   b. High/low feel involvement

B. Target audience—the specific people the advertising will address

1. Detailed description of target audiences

   a. Relationship of target audience to target market

   b. Prospective buying influences

   c. Benefits sought/advertising appeals

   d. Demographics

   e. Psychographics

   f. Behavioristics

2. Prioritization of target audiences

   a. Primary

   b. Secondary

   c. Supplementary

The strategy for selecting the various media vehicles that will communicate the advertising message to the target audience—see Chapters 8, 12, 13, and 14.

C. Communications media

1. Definition of media objectives

   a. Reach

   b. Frequency

   c. Gross rating points

   d. Continuity/flighting/pulsing

2. Determination of which media reach the target audience best
    a. Traditional mass media
        (1) Radio
        (2) Television
        (3) Newspapers
        (4) Magazines
        (5) OOH
    b. Interactive media
        (1) Direct response
        (2) Digital media, including search
        (3) Social media
    c. Support media
        (1) Trade shows
        (2) Sales promotion devices
        (3) Publicity/public relations
        (4) Off-the-wall media
        (5) Sponsorship
3. Availability of media relative to purchase patterns
4. Potential for communication effectiveness
5. Cost considerations
    a. Size/mechanical considerations of message units
    b. Cost efficiency of media plan against target audiences
    c. Production costs
6. Relevance to other elements of creative mix
7. Scope of media plan
8. Exposure/attention/motivation values of intended media vehicles

What the company wants to say and how it wants to say it, verbally and nonverbally—see Chapters 10 and 11.

D. Advertising message
1. Copy elements
    a. Advertising appeals
    b. Copy platform
    c. Key consumer benefits
    d. Benefit supports or reinforcements
    e. Product personality or image
2. Art elements
    a. Visual appeals
        (1) In ads and commercials
        (2) In packaging
        (3) In point-of-purchase and sales materials
    b. Art platform
        (1) Layout
        (2) Design
        (3) Illustration style
3. Production elements
    a. Mechanical considerations in producing ads
        (1) Color
        (2) Size
        (3) Style

       b. Production values sought

         (1)   Typography

         (2)   Printing

         (3)   Color reproduction

         (4)   Photography/illustrations

         (5)   Paper

         (6)   Electronic effects

         (7)   Animation

         (8)   Film or video

         (9)   Sound effects

        (10) Music

The amount of money to be allocated to advertising and the intended method of allocation—Chapters 7, 18.

V. The Advertising Budget

   A. Impact of marketing situation on method of allocation

      1. New or old product

      2. Primary demand curve for product class

      3. Competitive situation

      4. Marketing objectives and strategy

      5. Profit or growth considerations

      6. Relationship of advertising to sales and profits

      7. Empirical experience

   B. Method of allocation

      1. Percentage of sales or profit

      2. Share of market

      3. Objective/task method

      4. Unit of sale

      5. Competitive parity

The research techniques that will be used to create the advertising and evaluate its effectiveness—see Chapter 7.

VI. Testing and Evaluation

   A. Advertising research conducted

      1. Strategy determination

      2. Concept development

   B. Pretesting and posttesting

      1. Elements tested

         a. Markets

         b. Motives

         c. Messages

         d. Media

         e. Budgeting

         f. Scheduling

      2. Methodology

         a. Central location tests

         b. Sales experiments

         c. Physiological testing

         d. Aided recall tests

         e. Unaided recall tests

         f. Attitude tests

         g. Inquiry tests

         h. Sales tests

         i. Other

      3. Cost of testing

important terms

100 showing The basic unit of sale for billboards or posters is 100 gross rating points daily. One rating point equals 1 percent of a particular market's population.

5G The fifth generation of wireless service. It will permit multi-gigabit wireless speeds. Mobile providers are introducing the technology in 2019.

AAAA See *American Association of Advertising Agencies*.

AAF See *American Advertising Federation*.

account executive (AE) The liaison between the agency and the client. The account executive is responsible for both managing all the agency's services for the benefit of the client and representing the agency's point of view to the client.

account planning A hybrid discipline that bridges the gap between traditional research, account management, and creative direction. Planners represent the view of the consumer in order to better define and plan the client's advertising program.

action advertising Advertising intended to bring about immediate action on the part of the reader or viewer; see also *direct-response advertising*.

action programs See *tactics*.

actual consumers The people in the real world who comprise an ad's target audience. They are the people to whom the sponsor's message is ultimately directed.

ad networks The internet equivalent of a media rep firm, *ad networks* act as brokers for advertisers and websites. Ad networks pool hundreds or even thousands of web pages together and facilitate advertising across these pages, thereby allowing advertisers to gain maximum exposure by covering even the small sites.

advertising The structured and composed nonpersonal communication of information, usually paid for and usually persuasive in nature, about products (goods and services) or ideas by identified sponsors through various media.

advertising agency An independent organization of creative people and businesspeople who specialize in developing and preparing advertising plans, advertisements, and other promotional tools for advertisers. The agency also arranges for or contracts for purchase of space and time in various media.

advertising allowance A fee paid to the retailer for advertising the manufacturer's product.

advertising impression A possible exposure of the advertising message to one audience member; see also *opportunity to see (OTS)*.

advertising manager An individual responsible for the planning and execution of advertising within the advertiser (client) rather than the agency.

advertising response curve Studies of this indicate that incremental response to advertising actually diminishes—rather than builds—with repeated exposure.

Advertising Self-Regulatory Council (ASRC) An organization founded by the Council of Better Business Bureaus (originally as the National Advertising Review Council) and various advertising industry groups to promote and enforce standards of truth, accuracy, taste, morality, and social responsibility in advertising.

advertising specialty A promotional product, usually imprinted with an advertiser's name, message, or logo, that is distributed free to the target audience.

advertorial An ad aimed at swaying public opinion rather than selling products.

advocacy advertising Advertising used to communicate an organization's views on issues that affect society or business.

affidavit of performance A signed and notarized form sent by a television station to an advertiser or agency indicating what spots ran and when. It is the station's legal proof that the advertiser got what was paid for.

affiliate marketing program An advertising program, often used in e-commerce, in which a seller pays a manufacturer, marketer, or other business a percentage of the sale price of an item sold. This payment is compensation for services or cooperation in making the sale. Ordinary consumers are often affiliates for online retailers like Amazon. By posting links to products at their blogs or websites, consumers can earn a percentage of Amazon's sale.

affirmative disclosure Advertisers must make known their product's limitations or deficiencies.

agricultural advertising Advertising directed to farmers as businesspeople and to others in the agricultural business. Also called *farm advertising*.

Alliance for Audited Media (AAM) Provides essential cross-media verification, digital consulting, and information services for North America's leading media brands, advertisers, ad agencies, and technology platform companies.

Amazon Echo Amazon Echo is a set of interactive technologies that respond to voice commands. Basic uses include playing music, but the devices can also make calls, operate smart homes, and place orders for products and services.

ambush marketing A promotional strategy used by nonsponsors to capitalize on the popularity or prestige of an event or property by giving the false impression that they are sponsors, such as by buying up all the billboard space around an athletic stadium. Often employed by the competitors of the property's official sponsor.

American Advertising Federation (AAF) A nationwide association of advertising people. The AAF helped establish the Federal Trade Commission, and its early "vigilance" committees were the forerunners of the Better Business Bureaus.

American Association of Advertising Agencies (AAAA) The national organization of the advertising business. It has members throughout the United States and controls agency practices by denying membership to any agency judged unethical.

ANA See *Association of National Advertisers.*

animatic A rough television commercial produced by photographing storyboard sketches on a film strip or video with the audio portion synchronized on tape. It is used primarily for testing purposes.

animation The use of cartoons, digital actions, or demonstrations of inanimate characters come to life in television commercials; often used for communicating difficult messages or for reaching specialized markets, such as children.

aperture The opening in a camera that determines the amount of light that reaches the film or videotape. To a media planner it refers to the place and time that a target audience is ready to attend to an ad message.

application protocol interface (API) A specification intended to be used as an interface to communicate between two disparate software components.

art The whole visual presentation of a commercial or advertisement—the body language of an ad. Art also refers to the style of photography or illustration employed, the way color is used, and the arrangement of elements in an ad so that they relate to one another in size and proportion.

art direction The act or process of managing the visual presentation of an ad or commercial.

art director Along with graphic designers and production artists, determines how the ad's verbal and visual symbols will fit together.

art studio Company that designs and produces artwork and illustrations for advertisements, brochures, and other communication devices.

Artist role A role in the creative process that experiments and plays with a variety of approaches, looking for an original idea.

Association of National Advertisers (ANA) An organization comprised of 370 major manufacturing and service companies that are clients of member agencies of the AAAA. These companies, which are pledged to uphold the ANA code of advertising ethics, work with the ANA through a joint Committee for Improvement of Advertising Content.

attention value A consideration in selecting media based on the degree of attention paid to ads in particular media by those exposed to them. Attention value relates to the advertising message and copy just as much as to the medium.

attitude An evaluative response—positive or negative—regarding some idea or object.

attitude test A type of posttest that usually seeks to measure the effectiveness of an advertising campaign in creating a favorable attitude or evaluation for a company, its brand, or its products.

audience The group of people exposed to a particular medium.

audience composition The distribution of an audience into demographic or other categories.

audience objectives Definitions of the specific types of people the advertiser wants to reach.

audio The sound portion of a commercial. Also, the right side of a script for a television commercial, indicating spoken copy, sound effects, and music.

audiovisual materials Slides, films, CDs, and DVDs that may be used for training, sales, or public relations activities.

author In Stern's communication model, a copywriter, an art director, or a creative group at the agency that is commissioned by the sponsor to create advertising messages.

autobiographical messages A style of advertising that utilizes the first person "I" to tell a story to the audience, "You."

avails An abbreviated term referring to the TV time slots that are *available* to an advertiser.

average quarter-hour audience (AQH persons) A radio term referring to the average number of people who are listening to a specific station for at least 5 minutes during a 15-minute period of any given daypart.

average quarter-hour rating The average quarter-hour persons estimate expressed as a percentage of the estimated population.

average quarter-hour share The radio station's audience (AQH persons) expressed as a percentage of the total radio listening audience in the area.

awareness advertising Advertising that attempts to build the image of a product or familiarity with the name and package.

Ayer No. 1 See *poster-style format.*

banner Part of a website reserved for an advertising message. Clicking a banner normally redirects an internet user to the advertiser's website.

barter syndication Marketing of first-run television programs to local stations free or for a reduced rate because some of the ad space has been presold to national advertisers.

basic bus In transit advertising, all the inside space on a group of buses, which thereby gives the advertiser complete domination.

behavioral targeting The ability for an advertiser to send an ad to someone based on his or her online activity.

behavioristic segmentation Method of determining market segments by grouping consumers based on their purchase behavior.

benefit headline Type of headline that makes a direct promise to the reader.

benefit segmentation Method of segmenting consumers based on the benefits being sought.

benefits The gratifications or relief from problems offered by a particular brand, product, or service.

Better Business Bureau (BBB) A business-monitoring organization funded by dues from more than 100,000 member companies. It operates primarily at the local level to protect consumers against fraudulent and deceptive advertising.

big idea The flash of creative insight—the bold advertising initiative—that captures the essence of the strategy in an imaginative, involving way and brings the subject to life to make the reader stop, look, and listen.

bleeds   Colors, type, or visuals that run all the way to the edge of the page.

blinking   A scheduling technique in which the advertiser floods the airwaves for one day on both cable and network channels to make it virtually impossible to miss the ads.

blog   A personal journal published on the internet consisting of posts displayed in reverse chronological order.

board   See *console*.

body copy   The text of an advertisement. It is a logical continuation of the headline and subheads and is usually set in a smaller type size than headlines or subheads.

boldface   Heavier type.

boosted post   Facebook social advertising tool for making a post more prominent in users' News Feeds.

booths   Trade show display areas. To stop traffic, they must be simple and attractive and have good lighting and a large visual.

bottom-up marketing   The opposite of standard, top-down marketing planning, bottom-up marketing focuses on one specific tactic and develops it into an overall strategy.

brainstorming   A process in which two or more people get together to generate new ideas; often a source of sudden inspiration.

brand   That combination of name, words, symbols, or design that identifies the product and its source and distinguishes it from competing products—the fundamental differentiating device for all products.

brand development index (BDI)   The percentage of a brand's total sales in an area divided by the total population in the area; it indicates the sales potential of a particular brand in a specific market area.

brand equity   The totality of what consumers, distributors, dealers, and competitors feel and think about a brand over an extended period of time; in short, it is the value of the brand's capital.

brand interest   An individual's openness or curiosity about a brand.

brand loyalty   The consumer's conscious or unconscious decision—expressed through intention or behavior—to repurchase a brand continually. This occurs because the consumer perceives that the brand has the right product features, image, quality, or relationship at the right price.

brand manager   The individual within the advertiser's company who is assigned the authority and responsibility for the successful marketing of a particular brand.

brand trains   An advertising program in which all the advertising in and on a train is from a single advertiser. This advertising concept was first used in subway trains in New York City and is being used on the Las Vegas monorail.

brand vision   An expressed description of the aspirational image for the brand; what brand managers believe the brand should stand for in the eyes of customers and other relevant groups.

branding   A marketing function that identifies products and their source and differentiates them from all other products.

broadband   A type of digital data transmission that enables a single wire to carry multiple signals simultaneously.

broadcast radio   Radio received over devices that decode messages sent over the electromagnetic broadcast spectrum. The oldest and most common form of radio.

broadcast TV   Television sent over airwaves as opposed to over cables.

broadside   A form of direct-mail advertisement, larger than a folder and sometimes used as a window display or wall poster in stores. It can be folded to a compact size and fitted into a mailer.

brochures   Sales materials printed on heavier paper and featuring color photographs, illustrations, typography. See also *folders*.

bulk discounts   Newspapers offer advertisers decreasing rates (calculated by multiplying the number of inches by the cost per inch) as they use more inches.

bulletin structure   Typically the largest outdoor advertising formats, also known as billboards.

bursting   A media scheduling method for promoting high-ticket items that require careful consideration, such as running the same commercial every half-hour on the same network in prime time.

bus-o-rama sign   In transit advertising, a jumbo roof sign, which is actually a full-color transparency backlighted by fluorescent tubes, running the length of the bus.

business advertising   Advertising directed at people who buy or specify goods and services for business use. Also called *business-to-business advertising*.

business magazines   The largest category of magazines, they target business readers and include *trade publications* for retailers, wholesalers, and other distributors; *industrial magazines* for businesspeople involved in manufacturing and services; and *professional journals* for lawyers, physicians, architects, and other professionals.

business markets   Organizations that buy natural resources, component products, and services that they resell, use to conduct their business, or use to manufacture another product.

business reply mail   A type of mail that enables the recipient of direct-mail advertising to respond without paying postage.

business-to-business (B2B) advertising   See *business advertising*.

business-to-business agency   Represents clients that market products to other businesses; also called *high-tech* agency.

buyback allowance   A manufacturer's offer to pay for an old product so that it will be taken off the shelf to make room for a new product.

cable TV   Television signals carried to households by cable and paid by subscription.

camera-ready art   A finished ad that is ready for the printer's camera to shoot—to make negatives or plates—according to the publication's specifications.

car-end posters   Transit advertisements of varying sizes, positioned in the bulkhead.

CARU   See *Children's Advertising Review Unit*.

cascading style sheets   Cascading style sheets define text styles and other aspects of web pages to ensure pages in a website have consistency in look and function.

casting brief   A detailed, written description of the characters' personalities to serve as guides in casting sessions when actors audition for the roles.

catalogs   Reference books mailed to prospective customers that list, describe, and often picture the products sold by a manufacturer, wholesaler, jobber, or retailer.

category development index (CDI)   The percentage of a product category's total U.S. sales in an area divided by the percentage of total U.S. population in the area.

cease-and-desist order   May be issued by the FTC if an advertiser won't sign a consent decree; prohibits further use of an ad.

centers of influence   Customers, prospective customers, or opinion leaders whose opinions and actions are respected by others.

central location test   A type of pretest in which videotapes of test commercials are shown to respondents on a one-to-one basis, usually in shopping center locations.

central route to persuasion   One of two ways researchers Petty, Cacioppo, and Schumann theorize that marketers can persuade consumers. When consumers have a high level of involvement with the product or the message, they are motivated to pay attention to the central, product-related information in an ad, such as product attributes and benefits, or demonstrations of positive functional or psychological consequences; see also *Elaboration Likelihood Model.*

centralized advertising department   A staff of employees, usually located at corporate headquarters, responsible for all the organization's advertising. The department is often structured by product, advertising subfunction, end user, media, or geography.

centralized network   A network of connections that form from a single point, considered the center of the system.

cents-off promotion   A short-term reduction in the price of a product designed to induce trial and usage. Cents-off promotions take various forms, including basic cents-off packages, one-cent sales, free offers, and box-top refunds.

channel   Any medium through which an encoded message is sent to a receiver, including oral communication, print media, television, and the internet.

channels of distribution   See *distribution channels.*

Children's Advertising Review Unit (CARU)   This entity, created by the Council of Better Business Bureaus, provides a general advisory service for advertisers, agencies, children, parents, and educators.

cinema advertising   Advertising in movie theaters.

cinematographer   A motion picture photographer.

circulation   A statistical measure of a print medium's audience; includes subscription and vendor sales and primary and secondary readership.

circulation audit   Thorough analysis of circulation procedures, distribution outlets, and other distribution factors by a company such as the Alliance for Audited Media.

classical conditioning   Learning through repeated association. A response that an organism has to one stimulus (salivation in anticipation of food) is transferred to a formally neutral stimulus (a bell) when the bell is repeatedly paired with food.

classified ad websites   Websites, such as Craigslist, that specialize in providing classified advertisements, often provided for free. Many classified ad websites are supported by ad banners of other advertisers.

classified ads   Newspaper, magazine, and now internet advertisements usually arranged under subheads that describe the class of goods or the need the ads seek to satisfy. Rates are based on the number of lines the ad occupies. Most employment, housing, and automotive advertising are in the form of classified advertising.

classified display ads   Ads that run in the classified section of the newspaper but have larger-size type, photos, art borders, abundant white space, and sometimes color.

clearance advertising   A type of local advertising designed to make room for new product lines or new models or to get rid of slow-moving product lines, floor samples, broken or distressed merchandise, or items that are no longer in season.

click to website   Social advertising program designed to attract Facebook users to a website.

click-through   A term used in reference to when a World Wide Web user clicks on an ad banner to visit the advertiser's site. Some web publishers charge advertisers according to the number of click-throughs on a given ad banner.

click-through rate (CTR)   The percentage of site visitors who click a display or search ad.

close   That part of an advertisement or commercial that asks customers to do something and tells them how to do it—the action step in the ad's copy.

closing date   A publication's final deadline for supplying printing material for an advertisement.

clutter tests   Method of pretesting in which commercials are grouped with noncompetitive control commercials and shown to prospective customers to measure their effectiveness in gaining attention, increasing brand awareness and comprehension, and causing attitude shifts.

cognition   The mental processes involved in perception, thinking, recognition, memory, and decision making.

cognitive dissonance   See *theory of cognitive dissonance.*

collateral material   All the accessory nonmedia advertising materials prepared by manufacturers to help dealers sell a product—booklets, catalogs, brochures, films, trade show exhibits, sales kits, and so on.

color separations   Four separate continuous-tone negatives produced by photographing artwork through color filters that eliminate all the colors but one. The negatives are used to make four printing plates—one each for yellow, magenta, cyan, and black—for reproducing the color artwork.

column inch   The basic unit by which publishers bill for advertising. It is one vertical inch of a column. Until 1984, the column width in newspapers varied greatly. In 1984, the industry introduced the standard advertising unit (SAU) system, which standardized newspaper column width, page sizes, and ad sizes. Today, most newspapers—and virtually all dailies—have converted to the SAU system. A SAU column inch is 2¹⁄₁₆ inches wide by 1 inch deep.

combination offers   A sales promotion device in which two related products are packaged together at a special price, such as a razor and a package of blades. Sometimes a combination offer may be used to introduce a new product by tying its purchase to an established product at a special price.

combination rates   Special newspaper advertising rates offered for placing a given ad in (1) morning and evening editions of the same newspaper; (2) two or more newspapers owned by the same publisher; or (3) two or more newspapers affiliated in a syndicate or newspaper group.

command headline   A type of headline that orders the reader to do something.

communication element   Includes all marketing-related communications between the seller and the buyer.

communication objectives   Outcomes that can reasonably be associated with promotional activities, such as increases in brand recognition or awareness

communications media   An element of the creative mix, comprising the various methods or vehicles that will be used to transmit the advertiser's message.

communications mix   A variety of marketing communications tools, grouped into personal and nonpersonal selling activities.

community involvement   A local public relations activity in which companies sponsor or participate in a local activity or supply a location for an event.

company conventions and dealer meetings   Events held by manufacturers to introduce new products, sales promotion programs, or advertising campaigns.

comparative advertising   Advertising that claims superiority to competitors in one or more aspects.

compiled list   A type of direct-mail list that has been compiled by another source, such as lists of automobile owners, new-home purchasers, business owners, union members, and so forth. It is the most readily available type of list but offers the lowest response expectation.

composition   The amount of a target audience that exists on a website or a TV program.

comprehensive layout (comp)   A facsimile of a finished ad with copy set in type and pasted into position along with proposed illustrations. The "comp" is prepared so the advertiser can gauge the effect of the final ad.

conceptualization   See *visualization*.

consent decree   A document advertisers sign, without admitting any wrongdoing, in which they agree to stop objectionable advertising.

console   In a sound studio control room, the board that channels sound to the appropriate recording devices and that blends both live and prerecorded sounds for immediate or delayed broadcast.

consumer advertising   Advertising directed at the ultimate consumer of the product, or at the person who will buy the product for someone else's personal use.

consumer advocates   Individuals and groups who actively work to protect consumer rights, often by investigating advertising complaints received from the public and those that grow out of their own research.

consumer behavior   The activities, actions, and influences of people who purchase and use goods and services to satisfy their personal or household needs and wants.

consumer decision process   The series of steps a consumer goes through in deciding to make a purchase.

consumer information networks   Organizations that help develop state, regional, and local consumer organizations and work with national, regional, county, and municipal consumer groups. Examples include the Consumer Federation of America (CFA), the National Council of Senior Citizens, and the National Consumer League.

consumer magazines   Information- or entertainment-oriented periodicals directed toward people who buy products for their own consumption.

consumer package goods (CPGs)   A product consumed daily by the average person. Consumers must continuously replace CPGs (such as soft drinks or paper towels), in contrast to durable goods, which can be used for long periods of time (such as dishwashers). CPG brands often advertise heavily to ensure brand loyalty.

consumer sales promotions   Marketing, advertising, and sales promotion activities aimed at inducing trial, purchase, and repurchase by the consumer. Also called *pull strategy*.

consumerism   Social action designed to dramatize the rights of the buying public.

consumers, consumer market   People who buy products and services for their own, or someone else's, personal use.

contest   A sales promotion device for creating consumer involvement in which prizes are offered based on the skill of the entrants.

continuity   The duration of an advertising message or campaign over a given period of time.

continuous schedule   A method of scheduling media in which advertising runs steadily with little variation.

contract rate   A special rate for newspaper advertising usually offered to local advertisers who sign an annual contract for frequent or bulk-space purchases.

control room   In a recording studio, the place where the producer, director, and sound engineer sit, monitoring and controlling all the sounds generated in the sound studio.

controlled circulation   A free publication mailed to a select list of individuals the publisher feels are in a unique position to influence the purchase of advertised products.

cookies   Small pieces of information that get stored in a web user's hard drive when visiting certain websites. Cookies track whether the user has ever visited a specific site and allow the site to give users different information according to whether or not they are repeat visitors.

cooperative (co-op) advertising   The sharing of advertising costs by the manufacturer and the distributor or retailer. The manufacturer may repay 50 or 100 percent of the dealer's advertising costs or some other amount based on sales. See also *horizontal cooperative advertising, vertical cooperative advertising.*

copy   The words that make up the headline and message of an advertisement or commercial.

copy points   Copywriting themes in a product's advertising.

copyright   An exclusive right granted by the Copyright Act to authors and artists to protect their original work from being plagiarized, sold, or used by another without their express consent.

copywriters   People who create the words and concepts for ads and commercials.

cord-cutters   Individuals who cancel their cable service entirely.

cord-nevers   Individuals who have never had cable subscriptions.

cord-shavers   People who continue to use cable service but cut back on the extras associated with their cable subscriptions.

corporate advertising   The broad area of nonproduct advertising aimed specifically at enhancing a company's image and increasing lagging awareness.

corporate blog   A web-based source of information about a company, its policies, products, or activities. Corporate blogs are one way companies can facilitate relationships with their consumers or other publics.

corporate identity advertising   Advertising a corporation to familiarize the public with its name, logos, trademarks, or corporate signatures, especially after any of these elements are changed.

corrective advertising   May be required by the FTC for a period of time to explain and correct offending ads.

cost efficiency   The cost of reaching the target audience through a particular medium as opposed to the cost of reaching the medium's total circulation.

cost per point (CPP)   A simple computation used by media buyers to determine which broadcast programs are the most efficient in relation to the target audience. The CPP is determined by dividing the cost of the show by the show's expected rating against the target audience.

cost per thousand (CPM)   A common term describing the cost of reaching 1,000 people in a medium's audience. It is used by media planners to compare the cost of various media vehicles.

coupon   A certificate with a stated value that is presented to a retail store for a price reduction on a specified item.

cover date   The date printed on the cover of a publication.

cover paper   Paper used on soft book covers, direct-mail pieces, and brochure covers that is thicker, tougher, and more durable than text paper.

cover position   Advertising space on the front inside, back inside, and back cover pages of a publication that is usually sold at a premium price.

CPM   See *cost per thousand.*

CPP   See *cost per point.*

creative boutique   An organization of creative specialists (such as art directors, designers, and copywriters) who work for advertisers and occasionally advertising agencies to develop creative concepts, advertising messages, and specialized art. A boutique performs only the creative work.

creative brief   A written statement that serves as the creative team's guide for writing and producing an ad. It describes the most important issues that should be considered in the development of the ad (the who, why, what, where, and when), including a definition and description of the target audience; the rational and emotional appeals to be used; the product features that will satisfy the customer's needs; the style, approach, or tone that will be used in the copy; and, generally, what the copy will say.

creative director   Heads a creative team of agency copywriters and artists that is assigned to a client's business; is ultimately responsible for the creative product—the form the final ad takes.

creative mix   Those advertising elements the company controls to achieve its advertising objectives, including the target audience, the product concept, the communications media, and the advertising message. See also *IMC strategy.*

creative process   The step-by-step procedure used to discover original ideas and reorganize existing concepts in new ways.

creative pyramid   A five-step model to help the creative team convert advertising strategy and the big idea into the actual physical ad or commercial. The five elements are attention, interest, credibility, desire, and action.

creatives   The people who work in the creative department, regardless of their specialty.

creativity   Involves combining two or more previously unconnected objects or ideas into something new.

crisis management   A company's plan for handling news and public relations during crises.

culture   A homogeneous group's whole set of beliefs, attitudes, and ways of doing things, typically handed down from generation to generation.

cume persons   The total number of different people listening to a radio station for at least one 15-minute segment over the course of a given week, day, or daypart.

cume rating   The estimated number of cume persons expressed as a percentage of the total market population.

current customers   People who have already bought something from a business and who may buy it regularly.

custom magazines   Magazine-length ads that look like regular magazines but are created by advertisers. They are sold at newsstands and produced by the same companies that publish traditional magazines.

customer lifetime value (LTV)   The total sales or profit value of a customer to a marketer over the course of that customer's lifetime.

customer retention and relationship management (CRM)   A promotional program that focuses on existing clients rather than prospecting for new clients. Due to negative reaction to spam (unsolicited e-mail), e-mail programs are often focused on CRM rather than prospecting.

DAGMAR   The acronym stands for *d*efining *a*dvertising *g*oals for *m*easured *a*dvertising *r*esults. DAGMAR is a planning tool for setting communications objectives for a campaign.

daily newspapers   Often called *dailies,* these newspapers are published at least five times a week, in either morning or evening editions.

data access   Characteristic of a database that enables marketers to manipulate, analyze, and rank all the information they possess in order to make better marketing decisions.

data management   The process of gathering, consolidating, updating, and enhancing the information about customers and prospects that resides in a company's database.

database   The corporate memory of all important customer information: name and address, telephone number, NAIC code (if a business firm), source of inquiry, cost of inquiry, history of purchases, and so on. It should record every transaction across all points of contact with both channel members and customers.

database marketing   Tracking and analyzing the purchasing patterns of specific customers in a computer database and then targeting advertising to their needs.

daypart mix   A media scheduling strategy based on the TV usage levels reported by the rating services.

decentralized system   The establishment of advertising departments by products or brands or in various divisions, subsidiaries, countries, regions, or other categories that suit the firm's needs, which operate with a major degree of independence.

deceptive advertising   According to the FTC, any ad in which there is a misrepresentation, omission, or other practice that can mislead a significant number of reasonable consumers to their detriment.

deck   The online experience provided to its customers by a mobile carrier, typically curated by the wireless carrier.

decline stage   The stage in the product life cycle when sales begin to decline due to obsolescence, new technology, or changing consumer tastes.

decode   Transform an incoming signal into something comprehensible.

demarketing   Term coined during the energy shortage of the 1970s and 1980s. It refers to advertising that is used to slow the demand for products.

demographic editions   Magazines that reach readers who share a demographic trait, such as age, income level, or professional status.

demographic segmentation   Based on a population's statistical characteristics such as sex, age, ethnicity, education, occupation, income, or other quantifiable factors.

demonstration   A type of TV commercial in which the product is shown in use.

departmental system   The organization of an ad agency into departments based on function: account services, creative services, marketing services, and administration.

design   Visual pattern or composition of artistic elements chosen and structured by the graphic artist.

designated market areas (DMAs)   The geographic areas in which TV stations attract most of their viewers.

desktop publishing   Preparing print or digital materials for commercial purposes using a computer and publishing software.

development stage   In the agency–client relationship, the honeymoon period when both agency and client are at the peak of their optimism and are most eager to quickly develop a mutually profitable mechanism for working together.

device copy   Advertising copy that relies on wordplay, humor, poetry, rhymes, great exaggeration, gags, and other tricks or gimmicks.

dialogue/monologue copy   A type of body copy in which the characters illustrated in the advertisement do the selling in their own words either through a quasi-testimonial technique or through a comic strip panel.

digital couponing   In supermarkets, the use of frequent-shopper cards that automatically credit cardholders with coupon discounts when they check out. Also, using touch-screen videos at the point of purchase, instant-print discounts, rebates, and offers to try new brands.

digital interactive media   Electronic channels of communication—including online databases, the internet, CD-ROMs, and stand-alone kiosks—with which the audience can participate actively and immediately.

direct distribution   The method of marketing in which the manufacturer sells directly to customers without the use of retailers.

direct marketing   An interactive process of addressable communication that uses one or more media to effect, at any location, a measurable sale, lead, retail purchase, or charitable donation, with this activity analyzed on a database for the development of ongoing mutually beneficial relationships between marketers and customers, prospects, or donors.

direct questioning   A method of pretesting designed to elicit a full range of responses to the advertising. It is especially effective for testing alternative advertisements in the early stages of development.

direct selling   Face-to-face selling away from a fixed retail location. Usually refers to a method of marketing consumer goods—everything from encyclopedias and insurance to cosmetics and nutritional products.

direct-mail (action) advertising   All forms of advertising sent directly to prospective customers without using one of the commercial media forms.

direct-response advertising   An advertising message that asks the reader, listener, or viewer to respond to the sender. Direct-response advertising can take the form of direct mail, or it can use a wide range of other media, from matchbook covers or magazines to radio, TV, or billboards.

direct-sales strategy   Strategy where representatives sell to customers directly at home or work rather than through a retail establishment or other intermediary.

director   The director supervises preproduction, production, and postproduction of radio and television commercials.

directories   Listings, often in booklet form, that serve as locators, buying guides, and mailing lists.

display advertising   Type of newspaper advertising that includes copy, illustrations or photographs, headlines, coupons, and other visual components.

display allowances   Fees paid to retailers to make room for and set up manufacturers' displays.

display panels   Large displays that provide text and graphic messages, similar to those found in sports stadiums.

display type   A style of typeface used in advertising that is larger and heavier than normal text type. Display type is often used in headlines, subheads, logos, and addresses, and for emphasis.

distributed network   A system of connections that does not contain a main hub or central point.

distribution channel   The network of all the firms and individuals that take title, or assist in taking title, to the product as it moves from the producer to the consumer.

distribution element   How and where customers will buy a company's product; either direct or indirect distribution.

distribution objectives   Where, when, and how often advertising should appear.

diverting   Purchasing large quantities of an item at a regional promotional discount and shipping portions to areas of the country where the discount isn't being offered.

DMAs   See *designated market areas*.

donut   When writing a jingle, a hole left for spoken copy.

drama message   One of the three literary forms of advertising messages in which the characters act out events directly in front of an imagined empathetic audience.

drive times   Radio use Monday through Friday at 6–10 a.m. and 3–7 p.m.

dummy   A dummy presents the handheld look and feel of brochures, multipage materials, or point-of-purchase displays.

e-mail advertising   Has become one of the fastest-growing and most-effective ways to provide direct mail.

early adopters   Consumers who are more willing than most others to try new products or services.

earned rate   A discount applied retroactively as the volume of advertising increases through the year.

effective frequency   The average number of times a person must see or hear a message before it becomes effective.

effective reach   Term used to describe the quality of exposure. It measures the number or percentage of the audience who receive enough exposures for the message to truly be received.

Elaboration Likelihood Model   A theory of persuasion. Psychologists Petty, Cacioppo, and Schumann theorize that the route of persuasion depends on the consumer's level of involvement with the product and the message. When consumers have high involvement with the product or the message, they will attend to product-related information, such as product attributes and benefits or demonstrations, at deeper, more elaborate levels. This can lead to product beliefs, positive brand attitudes, and purchase intention. On the other hand, people who have low involvement with the product or the message have little or no reason to pay attention to it or to comprehend the central message of the ad. As a result, direct persuasion is also low, and consumers form few if any brand beliefs, attitudes, or purchase intentions. However, these consumers might attend to some peripheral aspects of the ad or commercial—say, the pictures in the ad or the actors in a commercial—for their entertainment value. And whatever they feel or think about these peripheral, nonproduct aspects might integrate into a positive attitude toward the ad. See also *central route to persuasion* and *peripheral route to persuasion*.

electronic media   Radio and television, which may be transmitted electronically through wires or broadcast through the air.

emotional appeals   Marketing appeals that are directed at the consumer's psychological, social, or symbolic needs.

empirical research method   A method of allocating funds for advertising that uses experimentation to determine the best level of advertising expenditure. By running a series of tests in different markets with different budgets, companies determine the most efficient level of expenditure.

encode   Convert information into another form for some purpose.

endorsement   See *testimonials*.

entertainment   The second largest area of sponsorship, which includes things like concert tours, attractions, and theme parks.

environments   Surroundings that can affect the purchase decision.

equipment-based service   A service business that relies mainly on the use of specialized equipment.

ethical advertising   Doing what the advertiser and the advertiser's peers believe is morally right in a given situation.

evaluation of alternatives   Choosing among brands, sizes, styles, and colors.

evaluative criteria   The standards a consumer uses for judging the features and benefits of alternative products.

evoked set   The particular group of alternative goods or services a consumer considers when making a buying decision.

exchange   The trading of one thing of value for another thing of value.

exclusive distribution   The strategy of limiting the number of wholesalers or retailers who can sell a product in order to gain a prestige image, maintain premium prices, or protect other dealers in a geographic region.

exhibitive media   Media designed specifically to help bring customers eyeball-to-eyeball with the product. These media include product packaging and trade show booths and exhibits.

exhibits   A marketing or public relations approach that involves preparing displays that tell about an organization or its products; exhibits may be used at fairs, colleges and universities, or trade shows.

experimental method   A method of scientific investigation in which a researcher alters the stimulus received by a test group or groups and compares the results with those of a control group that did not receive the altered stimulus.

exploratory research   See *informal research*.

Explorer role   A role in the creative process that searches for new information, paying attention to unusual patterns.

exposure value The value of a medium determined by how well it exposes an ad to the target audience. In other words, how many people an ad "sees" rather than the other way around.

Eyes on Impressions (EOI) Measure of reach created by the OAAA and the Traffic Audit bureau to determine a billboard's true reach and frequency.

fact-based thinking A style of thinking that tends to fragment concepts into components and to analyze situations to discover the one best solution.

family brand The marketing of various products under the same umbrella name.

farm publications Magazines directed to farmers and their families or to companies that manufacture or sell agricultural equipment, supplies, and services.

FCC See *Federal Communications Commission*.

FDA See *Food and Drug Administration*.

feature article Soft news about companies, products, or services that may be written by a PR person, the publication's staff, or a third party.

Federal Communications Commission (FCC) Federal regulatory body with jurisdiction over radio, television, telephone, and telegraph industries. Through its licensing authority, the FCC has indirect control over broadcast advertising.

Federal Trade Commission (FTC) The major federal regulator of advertising used to promote products sold in interstate commerce.

feedback A message that acknowledges or responds to an initial message.

fee–commission combination A pricing system in which an advertising agency charges the client a basic monthly fee for its services and also retains any media commissions earned.

first-run syndication Programs produced specifically for the syndication market.

five Ms (5Ms) The elements of the media mix that include markets, money, media, mechanics, and methodology.

flat rate A standard newspaper advertising rate with no discount allowance for large or repeated space buys.

flighting An intermittent media scheduling pattern in which periods of advertising are alternated with periods of no advertising at all.

focus group A qualitative method of research in which four or more people, typical of the target market, are invited to a group session to discuss the product, the service, or the marketing situation for an hour or more.

folders Large, heavy-stock fliers, often folded and sent out as self-mailers.

font A uniquely designed set of capital, small capital, and lowercase letters, usually including numerals and punctuation marks.

Food and Drug Administration (FDA) Federal agency that has authority over the labeling, packaging, and branding of packaged foods and therapeutic devices.

foreign media The local media of each country used by advertisers for campaigns targeted to consumers or businesses within a single country.

forum Sections of websites that connect individuals around a specific topic.

forward buying A retailer's stocking up on a product when it is discounted and buying smaller amounts when it is at list price.

four Ps (4Ps) See *marketing mix*.

franchising A type of vertical marketing system in which dealers pay a fee to operate under the guidelines and direction of the parent company or manufacturer.

freestanding inserts (FSIs) Coupons distributed through inserts in newspapers.

frequency The number of times the same person or household is exposed to a vehicle in a specified time span. Across a total audience, frequency is calculated as the average number of times individuals or homes are exposed to the vehicle.

frequency discounts In newspapers, advertisers earn this discount by running an ad repeatedly in a specific time period.

FTC See *Federal Trade Commission*.

full position In newspaper advertising, the preferred position near the top of a page or on the top of a column next to reading matter. It is usually surrounded by editorial text and may cost the advertiser 25 to 50 percent more than ROP rates.

full showing A unit of purchase in transit advertising where one card will appear in each vehicle in the system.

full-service advertising agency An agency equipped to serve its clients in all areas of communication and promotion. Its advertising services include planning, creating, and producing advertisements as well as performing research and media selection services. Nonadvertising functions include producing sales promotion materials, publicity articles, annual reports, trade show exhibits, and sales training materials.

game A sales promotion activity in which prizes are offered based on chance. The big marketing advantage of games is that customers must make repeat visits to the dealer to continue playing.

gamification Employing design elements to improve user engagement.

gatefold A magazine cover or page extended and folded over to fit into the magazine. The gatefold may be a fraction of a page or two or more pages, and it is always sold at a premium.

general consumer agency An agency that represents the widest variety of accounts, but it concentrates on companies that make goods purchased chiefly by consumers.

geodemographic segmentation Combining demographics with geographic segmentation to select target markets in advertising.

geofencing Targeting consumers with relevant ads when they enter a predetermined geographical area. The ad is usually for a nearby marketer.

geographic editions   Magazines that target geographic markets and have different rates for ads.

geographic segmentation   A method of segmenting markets by geographic regions based on the shared characteristics, needs, or wants of people within the region.

global advertising   Advertising used by companies that market their products, goods, or services throughout various countries around the world with messages that remain consistent.

global marketers   Multinationals that use a standardized approach to marketing and advertising in all countries.

global positioning system (GPS)   Satellite-based system whereby outdoor advertising companies give their customers the exact latitude and longitude of particular boards. Media buyers, equipped with sophisticated software on their desktop computers, can then integrate this information with demographic market characteristics and traffic counts to determine the best locations for their boards without ever leaving the office.

goods   Tangible products such as suits, soap, and soft drinks.

government markets   Governmental bodies that buy products for the successful coordination of municipal, state, federal, or other government activities.

gross impressions   The total of all the audiences delivered by a media plan.

gross rating points (GRPs)   The total audience delivery or weight of a specific media schedule. It is computed by dividing the total number of impressions by the size of the target population and multiplying by 100, or by multiplying the reach, expressed as a percentage of the population, by the average frequency. In television, gross rating points are the total rating points achieved by a particular media schedule over a specific period. For example, a weekly schedule of five commercials with an average household rating of 20 would yield 100 GRPs. In outdoor advertising, a 100 gross rating point showing (also called a number 100 showing) covers a market fully by reaching 9 out of 10 adults daily over a 30-day period.

group system   System in which an ad agency is divided into a number of little agencies or groups, each composed of an account supervisor, account executives, copywriters, art directors, a media director, and any other specialists required to meet the needs of the particular clients being served by the group.

growth stage   The period in a product life cycle that is marked by market expansion as more and more customers make their first purchases while others are already making their second and third purchases.

GRPs   See *gross rating points*.

guaranteed circulation   The number of copies of a magazine that the publisher expects to sell. If this figure is not reached, the publisher must give a refund to advertisers.

habit   An acquired or developed behavior pattern that has become nearly or completely involuntary.

halo effect   In ad pretesting, the fact that consumers are likely to rate the one or two ads that make the best first impression as the highest in all categories.

headline   The words in the leading position of an advertisement—the words that will be read first or that are positioned to draw the most attention.

hidden differences   Imperceptible but existing differences that may greatly affect the desirability of a product.

hierarchy of needs   Maslow's theory that the lower biological or survival needs are dominant in human behavior and must be satisfied before higher, socially acquired needs become meaningful.

hook   The part of a jingle that sticks in your memory.

horizontal cooperative advertising   Joint advertising effort of related businesses (car dealers, Realtors, etc.) to create traffic for their type of business.

horizontal publications   Business publications targeted at people with particular job functions that cut across industry lines, such as *Purchasing* magazine.

house list   A company's most important and valuable direct-mail list, which may contain current, recent, and long-past customers or future prospects.

house organs   Internal and external publications produced by business organizations, including stockholder reports, newsletters, consumer magazines, and dealer publications. Most are produced by a company's advertising or public relations department or by its agency.

households using TV (HUT)   The percentage of homes in a given area that have one or more TV sets turned on at any particular time. If 1,000 TV sets are in the survey area and 500 are turned on, the HUT figure is 50 percent.

HTML   Refers to HyperText Markup Language used primarily to build websites on the internet.

icon   A pictorial image that represents an idea or thing.

ideas   Economic, political, religious, or social viewpoints that advertising may attempt to sell.

illustrators   The artists who paint, sketch, or draw the pictures we see in advertising.

image advertising   Type of advertising intended to create a particular perception of the company or personality for the brand.

imagery transfer   When advertisers run a schedule on TV and then convert the audio portion to radio commercials, fully 75 percent of consumers replay the video in their minds when they hear the radio spot.

IMC message   An element of the creative mix comprising what the company plans to say in its advertisements and how it plans to say it—verbally or nonverbally.

IMC plan   The written document that directs the company's advertising effort. A natural outgrowth of the marketing plan, it analyzes the situation, sets advertising objectives, and lays out a specific strategy from which ads and campaigns are created.

IMC research   Research activities that focus on the development and evaluation of IMC strategies and tactics.

IMC strategy   The methodology advertisers use to achieve their advertising objectives. The strategy is determined by the particular creative mix of advertising elements the advertiser selects, namely target audience, product concept, communications media, and advertising message. Also called the *creative mix*.

IMC strategy research   Used to help define the product concept or to assist in the selection of target markets, advertising messages, or media vehicles.

immersive advertising   Proprietary technique developed by Neopets.com for integrating an advertiser's products or services into the website experience.

implied consumers   The consumers who are addressed by the ad's persona. They are not real, but rather imagined by the ad's creators to be ideal consumers—acquiescing in whatever beliefs the text requires. They are, in effect, part of the drama of the ad.

in kind   The donation of goods and services as payment for some service such as a sponsorship.

in-depth interview   An intensive interview technique that uses carefully planned but loosely structured questions to probe respondents' deeper feelings.

in-house agency   Agency wholly owned by an advertiser and set up and staffed to do all the work of an independent full-service agency.

in-store sampling   The handing out of free product samples to passing shoppers.

incentive system   A form of compensation in which the agency shares in the client's success when a campaign attains specific, agreed-upon goals.

independent production house   Supplier company that specializes in film or video production or both.

independent research companies   Research firms that work outside an agency. They may come in all sizes and specialties, and they employ staff statisticians, field interviewers, and computer programmers, as well as analysts with degrees in psychology, sociology, and marketing.

independent shopping guide   Weekly local ad vehicles that may or may not contain editorial matter. They can be segmented into highly select market areas.

individual brand   Assigning a unique name to each product a manufacturer produces.

induced differences   Distinguishing characteristics of products effected through unique branding, packaging, distribution, merchandising, and advertising.

industrial age   A historical period covering approximately the first 70 years of the 20th century. This period was marked by tremendous growth and maturation of the U.S. industrial base. It saw the development of new, often inexpensive brands of the luxury and convenience goods we now classify as consumer packaged goods.

industrial markets   Individuals or companies that buy products needed for the production of other goods or services such as plant equipment and telephone systems.

influencer   A product user who shares his or her brand experiences with others.

influencer marketing   A strategic collaboration between a brand and an influencer leveraging the power of influencers with their followers.

infomercial   A long TV commercial that gives consumers detailed information about a product or service; see also *program-length advertisement*.

informal research   The second step in the research process, designed to explore a problem by reviewing secondary data and interviewing a few key people with the most information to share. Also called *exploratory research*.

informational motives   The negatively originated motives, such as problem removal or problem avoidance, that are the most common energizers of consumer behavior.

inquiry test   A form of test in which consumer responses to an ad for information or free samples are tabulated.

insert   An ad or brochure that the advertiser prints and ships to the publisher for insertion into a magazine or newspaper.

insertion order   A form submitted to a newspaper or magazine when an advertiser wants to run an advertisement. This form states the date(s) on which the ad is to run, its size, the requested position, and the rate.

inside card   A transit advertisement, normally 11 by 28 inches, placed in a wall rack above the windows of a bus.

institutional advertising   A type of advertising that attempts to obtain favorable attention for the business as a whole, not for a specific product or service the store or business sells. The effects of institutional advertising are intended to be long term rather than short range.

institutional copy   A type of body copy in which the advertiser tries to sell an idea or the merits of the organization or service rather than the sales features of a particular product.

integrated commercial   A straight radio announcement, usually delivered by one person, woven into a show or tailored to a given program to avoid any perceptible interruption.

integrated marketing communications (IMC)   The process of building and reinforcing mutually profitable relationships with employees, customers, other stakeholders, and the general public by developing and coordinating a strategic communications program that enables them to make constructive contact with the company/brand through a variety of media.

intellectual property   Something produced by the mind, such as original works of authorship including literary, dramatic, musical, artistic, and certain other "intellectual" works, which may be legally protected by copyright, patent, or trademark.

intensive distribution   A distribution strategy based on making the product available to consumers at every possible location so that consumers can buy with a minimum of effort.

intensive techniques   Qualitative research aimed at probing the deepest feelings, attitudes, and beliefs of respondents through direct questioning. Typical methods include in-depth interviews and focus groups.

Interactive Advertising Bureau (IAB)   Association of digital organizations charged with establishing standards for digital ad formats.

interactive agency   An advertising agency that specializes in the creation of ads for a digital interactive medium such as web pages, CD-ROMs, or electronic kiosks.

interactive customer relationship   Ongoing relationship between a company or brand and consumers in which both parties communicate with one another for a period of time.

interactive TV   A personal audience venue where people can personally guide TV programming through a remote control box while watching TV.

interior paragraphs   Text within the body copy of an ad where the credibility and desire steps of the message are presented.

international advertising   Advertising aimed at foreign markets.

international agency   An advertising agency that has offices or affiliates in major communication centers around the world and can help its clients market internationally or globally.

international media   Media serving several countries, usually without change, available to an international audience.

international structure   Organization of companies with foreign marketing divisions, typically decentralized and responsible for their own product lines, marketing operations, and profits.

internet   A worldwide network of computer systems that facilitates global electronic communications via e-mail, the World Wide Web, ftp, and other data protocols. Currently the fastest-growing medium for advertising.

internet publishers   Companies that generate content digital media users find interesting. The business model of publishers on the web is showing ads to people who access their content, usually as part of an ad network.

interpersonal influences   Social influences on the consumer decision-making process, including family, society, and cultural environment.

interview   See *in-depth interview*.

introductory phase   The initial phase of the product life cycle (also called the *pioneering phase*) when a new product is introduced, costs are highest, and profits are lowest.

inventory   Commercial time for advertisers.

island half   A half-page of magazine space that is surrounded on two or more sides by editorial matter. This type of ad is designed to dominate a page and is therefore sold at a premium price.

italic   A style of printing type with letters that generally slant to the right.

jingle   A musical commercial, usually sung with the sales message in the verse.

Judge role   A role in the creative process that evaluates the results of experimentation and decides which approach is more practical.

junior posters   A type of outdoor advertising offering a 5-foot by 11-foot printing area on a panel surface 6 feet tall by 12 feet wide.

junior unit   A large magazine advertisement (60% of the page) placed in the middle of a page and surrounded by editorial matter.

kerning   The measurement of the space between individual letters of text.

keyword   A single word that a user inputs into an internet search engine to request information that is similar in subject matter to that word. Advertisers may buy keywords from search engines so that their advertisements appear when a user inputs the purchased word.

landing page   A specially designed destination for those that click on online advertising.

layout   An orderly formation of all the parts of an advertisement. In print, it refers to the arrangement of the headline, subheads, visuals, copy, picture captions, trademarks, slogans, and signature. In television, it refers to the placement of characters, props, scenery, and product elements; the location and angle of the camera; and the use of lighting. See also *design*.

lead-in paragraph   In print ads, a bridge between the headlines, the subheads, and the sales ideas presented in the text. It transfers reader interest to product interest.

leading   The measurement of the space between separate lines of text (pronounced *ledding*).

learning   A relatively permanent change in thought processes or behavior that occurs as a result of reinforced experience.

letter shop   A firm that stuffs envelopes, affixes labels, calculates postage, sorts pieces into stacks or bundles, and otherwise prepares items for mailing.

licensed brands   Brand names that other companies can buy the right to use.

lifestyle technique   Type of commercial in which the user is presented rather than the product. Typically used by clothing and soft drink advertisers to affiliate their brands with the trendy lifestyles of their consumers.

lifetime customer value (LTCV)   A measurement of a consumer's economic value to a company over the course of his or her purchases over a lifetime. It can be measured by using the following formula: (Average Value of a Sale) × (Number of Repeat Transactions) × (Average Retention Time in Months or Years for a Typical Customer).

linear TV   Television content accessed in the traditional ways of cable or broadcast appointment viewing.

linkage media   In direct marketing, media that help prospects and customers link up with a company.

list broker   An intermediary who handles rental of mailing lists for list owners on a commission basis.

lobbying   Informing government officials and persuading them to support or thwart administrative action or legislation in the interests of some client.

local advertising   Advertising by businesses within a city or county directed toward customers within the same geographic area. Also called *retail advertising*.

local agency   Advertising agency that specializes in creating advertising for local businesses.

local city magazine   Most major U.S. cities have one of these publications. Typical readership is upscale, professional people interested in local arts, fashion, and business.

local time   Radio spots purchased by a local advertiser.

location   Shooting away from the studio. Location shooting adds realism but can also be a technical and logistical nightmare, often adding cost and many other potential problems.

location-based advertising   Advertising that is responsive to the location of the consumer and the advertisement.

logotype   Special design of the advertiser's name (or product name) that appears in all advertisements. Also called a signature cut, it is like a trademark because it gives the advertiser individuality and provides quick recognition at the point of purchase.

long-term macro criticisms   Criticisms of advertising that focus on the broader social or environmental impact of marketing.

lot   Acreage outside a studio that is shielded from stray, off-site sounds.

mail-response list   A type of direct-mail list, composed of people who have responded to the direct-mail solicitations of other companies, especially those whose efforts are complementary to the advertiser's.

maintenance stage   In the client–agency relationship, the day-to-day interaction that, when successful, may go on for years.

makegoods   TV spots that are aired to compensate for spots that were missed or run incorrectly.

management (account) supervisors   Managers who supervise account executives and who report to the agency's director of account services.

mandatories   The address, phone number, web address, and so on that the advertiser usually insists be included within an ad to give the consumer adequate information.

market   A group of potential customers who share a common interest, need, or desire; who can use the offered good or service to some advantage; and who can afford or are willing to pay the purchase price. Also, an element of the media mix referring to the various targets of a media plan.

market prep corporate advertising   Corporate advertising that is used to set up the company for future sales; it simultaneously communicates messages about the products and the company.

market segmentation   Strategy of identifying groups of people or organizations with certain shared needs and characteristics within the broad markets for consumer or business products and aggregating these groups into larger market segments according to their mutual interest in the product's utility.

marketer   Any person or organization that has products, services, or ideas to sell.

marketing   The activity, set of institutions, and processes for creating, communicating, delivering, and exchanging offerings that have value for customers, clients, partners, and society at large.

marketing communications   The various efforts and tools companies use to initiate and maintain communication with customers and prospects, including solicitation letters, newspaper ads, event sponsorships, publicity, telemarketing, statement stuffers, and coupons, to mention just a few.

marketing information system (MIS)   A set of procedures for generating an orderly flow of pertinent information for use in making market decisions.

marketing mix   Four elements, called the 4Ps (product, price, place, and promotion), that every company has the option of adding, subtracting, or modifying in order to create a desired marketing strategy.

marketing objectives   Goals of the marketing effort that may be expressed in terms of the needs of specific target markets and specific sales objectives.

marketing plan   The plan that directs the company's marketing effort. First, it assembles all the pertinent facts about the organization, the markets it serves, and its products, services, customers, and competition. Second, it forces the functional managers within the company to work together—product development, production, selling, advertising, credit, transportation—to focus efficiently on the customer. Third, it sets goals and objectives to be attained within specified periods of time and lays out the precise strategies that will be used to achieve them.

marketing public relations (MPR)   The use of public relations activities as a marketing tool.

marketing research   The systematic gathering, recording, and analysis of information to help managers make marketing decisions.

marketing strategy   The statement of how the company is going to accomplish its marketing objectives. The strategy is the total directional thrust of the company, that is, the how-to of the marketing plan, and is determined by the particular blend of the marketing mix elements (the 4 Ps), which the company can control.

markup   A source of agency income gained by adding some amount to a supplier's bill, usually 17.65 percent.

mass media   Print or broadcast media that reach very large audiences. Mass media include radio, television, newspapers, magazines, and billboards.

maturity stage   That point in the product life cycle when the market has become saturated with products, the number of new customers has dwindled, and competition is most intense.

mechanics   One of the five Ms of the media mix; dealing creatively with the available advertising media options.

media   A plural form of *medium,* referring to communications vehicles paid to present an advertisement to its target audience. Most often used to refer to radio and television networks, stations that have news reporters, and publications that carry news and advertising.

media buyer   Person responsible for negotiating and contracting the purchase of advertisement space and time in various media.

media classes   Broad media categories of electronic, print, outdoor, and direct mail.

media commission   Compensation paid by a medium to recognized advertising agencies, usually 15 percent (16⅔% for outdoor), for advertising placed with it.

media kit   See *press kit.*

media planning   The process that directs advertising messages to the right people in the right place at the right time.

media research   The systematic gathering and analysis of information on the reach and effectiveness of media vehicles.

media subclasses   Smaller divisions of media classes, such as radio, TV, magazines, newspapers, and so on.

media units   Specific units of advertising in each type of medium, such as half-page magazine ads, 30-second spots, and so on.

media vehicles   Particular media programs or publications.

media-buying service   An organization that specializes in purchasing and packaging radio and television time.

medium   An instrument or communications vehicle that carries or helps transfer a message from the sender to the receiver. Plural is *media*. See also *media*.

mental files   Stored memories in the consumer's mind.

merchandise   Synonymous with *product concept* when used in reference to the 5Ms of advertising testing.

message   In oral communication, the idea formulated and encoded by the source and sent to the receiver.

message strategy   The specific determination of what a company wants to say and how it wants to say it. The elements of the message strategy include verbal, nonverbal, and technical components; also called *rationale*.

message weight   The total size of the audience for a set of ads or an entire campaign.

methodology   The overall strategy of selecting and scheduling media vehicles to achieve the desired reach, frequency, and continuity objectives.

microblog   A broadcast medium in the form of blogging.

microsite   Refers to a specially designed portion of a larger domain (website) typically constructed to drive a specific action.

mission statement   A short, aspirational description of the organizations purpose

mixed-media approach   Using a combination of advertising media vehicles in a single advertising campaign.

mnemonic device   A gimmick used to dramatize the product benefit and make it memorable, such as the Imperial Margarine crown or the Avon doorbell.

mobile app installs   Facebook social advertising encouraging users to install Facebook apps.

mobile billboard   A cross between traditional billboards and transit advertising; some specially designed flatbed trucks carry long billboards up and down busy thoroughfares.

money   In media planning, one of the five elements in the media mix.

motivation   The underlying drives that stem from the conscious or unconscious needs of the consumer and contribute to the individual consumer's purchasing actions.

motivation value   A consideration in selecting media based on the medium's ability to motivate people to act. Positive factors include prestige, good-quality reproduction, timeliness, and editorial relevance.

motives   Emotions, desires, physiological needs, or similar impulses that may incite consumers to action.

multinational corporations   Corporations operating and investing throughout many countries and making decisions based on availabilities worldwide.

musical commercial   See *jingle*.

musical logo   A jingle that becomes associated with a product or company through consistent use.

NAD   See *National Advertising Division*.

NAICS   See *North American Industry Classification System*.

NARB   See *National Advertising Review Board*.

narrative copy   A type of body copy that tells a story. It sets up a problem and then creates a solution using the particular sales features of the product or service as the key to the solution.

narrative message   Advertising in which a third person tells a story about others to an imagined audience.

national advertisers   Companies that advertise in several geographic regions or throughout the country.

national advertising   Advertising used by companies that market their products, goods, or services in several geographic regions or throughout the country.

National Advertising Division (NAD)   The National Advertising Division of the Council of Better Business Bureaus. It investigates and monitors advertising industry practices.

National Advertising Review Board (NARB)   A five-member panel, composed of three advertisers, one agency representative, and one layperson, selected to review decisions of the NAD.

national agency   Advertising agency that produces and places the quality of advertising suitable for national campaigns.

national brands   Product brands that are marketed in several regions of the country.

national magazines   Magazines that are distributed throughout a country.

national rate   A newspaper advertising rate that is higher, attributed to the added costs of serving national advertisers.

native advertising   Advertising where the ad matches the form, feel, and function of the content of the media on which it appears.

needs   The basic, often instinctive, human forces that motivate us to do something.

negatively originated motives   Consumer purchase and usage based on problem removal or problem avoidance. To relieve such feelings, consumers actively seek a new or replacement product.

network   The amount of connections that are made by one individual.

network marketing   A method of direct distribution in which individuals act as independent distributors for a manufacturer or private-label marketer.

networks   Any of the national television or radio broadcasting chains or companies such as ABC, CBS, NBC, or Fox. Networks offer the large advertiser convenience and efficiency because the message can be broadcast simultaneously throughout the country.

News Media Alliance (NMA)   The promotional arm of the the nation's newspaper industry.

news release   A typewritten sheet of information (usually 8½ by 11 inches) issued to print and broadcast outlets to generate publicity or shed light on a subject of interest. Also called *press release*.

news/information headline   A type of headline that includes many of the "how-to" headlines as well as headlines that seek to gain identification for their sponsors by announcing some news or providing some promise of information.

NLEA   See *Nutritional Labeling and Education Act*.

noise   The sender's advertising message competing daily with hundreds of other commercial and noncommercial messages.

noncommercial advertising   Advertising sponsored by or for a charitable institution, civic group, religious order, political organization, or some other nonprofit group to stimulate donations, persuade people to vote one way or another, or bring attention to social causes.

nonpersonal communication   Marketing activities that use some medium as an intermediary for communication, including advertising, direct marketing, public relations, collateral materials, and sales promotion.

nonpersonal influences   Factors influencing the consumer decision-making process that are often out of the consumer's control, such as time, place, and environment.

nonprobability samples   Research samples that do not provide every unit in the population with an equal chance of being included. As a result, there is no guarantee that the sample will be representative.

nonproduct advertising   Advertising designed to sell ideas or a philosophy rather than products or services.

nonproduct facts   Product claims not about the brand but about the consumer or the social context in which the consumer uses the brand.

nonverbal   Communication other than through the use of words, normally visual.

North American Industry Classification System (NAICS) codes   Method used by the U.S. Department of Commerce to classify all businesses. The NAICS codes are based on broad industry groups, subgroups, and detailed groups of firms in similar lines of business.

Nutritional Labeling and Education Act (NLEA)   A 1994 congressional law setting stringent legal definitions for terms such as *fresh, light, low fat,* and *reduced calorie;* setting standard serving sizes; and requiring labels to show food value for one serving alongside the total recommended daily value as established by the National Research Council.

objectives   See *marketing objectives*.

objective/task method   A method of determining advertising allocations, also referred to as the *budget-buildup method,* that defines objectives and how advertising is to be used to accomplish them. It has three steps: defining the objectives, determining strategy, and estimating the cost.

observation method   A method of research used when researchers actually monitor people's actions.

off-network syndication   The availability of programs that originally appeared on networks to individual stations for rebroadcast.

on camera   Actually seen by the camera, as an announcer, a spokesperson, or actor playing out a scene.

on-sale date   The date a magazine is actually issued.

open rate   The highest rate for a one-time insertion in a newspaper.

operant conditioning   Learning that involves associating a behavior with rewards or punishments

opinion leader   Someone whose beliefs or attitudes are respected by people who share an interest in some specific activity.

opinion sampling   A form of public relations research in which consumers provide feedback via interviews, toll-free phone lines, focus groups, and similar methods.

opportunity to see (OTS)   A possible exposure of an advertising message to one audience member. Also called an *advertising impression*. Effective frequency is considered to be three or more opportunities to see over a four-week period, but no magic number works for every commercial and every product.

organic search results   Search engine listings that are unaffected by sponsorship.

organizational buyers   People who purchase products and services for use in business and government.

OTT (over-the-top) inventory   Over-the-top video content. OTT is content that people stream to watch on the internet rather than as a cable or broadcast channel.

out-of-home (OOH) advertising   Media such as outdoor advertising (billboards) and transit advertising (bus and car cards) that reach prospects outside their homes.

outdoor advertising   An out-of-home medium in the form of billboards.

outside posters   The variety of transit advertisements appearing on the outside of buses, including king size, queen size, traveling display, rear of bus, and front of bus.

packaging   The container for a product—encompassing the physical appearance of the container and including the design, color, shape, labeling, and materials used.

page likes   Facebook tool allowing brands to cultivate followers.

paid circulation   The total number of copies of an average issue of a newspaper or magazine that is distributed through subscriptions and newsstand sales.

PANTONE Matching System (PMS)   A collection of colors that are premixed according to a formula and given a specific color number. PANTONE swatch books feature over 100 colors in solid and screened blocks printed on different paper finishes.

participation basis   The basis on which most network television advertising is sold, with advertisers buying 30- or 60-second segments within the program. This allows the advertiser to spread out the budget and makes it easier to get in and out of a program without a long-term commitment.

patent   A grant made by the government that confers upon the creator of an invention the sole right to make, use, and sell that invention for a set period of time.

people-based service   A service that relies on the talents and skills of individuals rather than on highly technical or specialized equipment.

percentage of sales method   A method of advertising budget allocation based on a percentage of the previous year's sales, the anticipated sales for the next year, or a combination of the two.

perceptible differences   Differences between products that are visibly apparent to the consumer.

perception   Our personalized way of sensing and comprehending stimuli.

peripheral route to persuasion   One of two ways researchers Petty, Cacioppo, and Schumann theorize that marketers can persuade consumers. People who have low involvement with the product or message have little or no reason to pay attention to it or to comprehend the central message of the ad. However, these consumers might attend to some peripheral aspects of an ad or commercial for their entertainment value. Whatever they feel or think about these peripheral, nonproduct aspects might integrate into a positive attitude toward the ad. At some later date, these ad-related meanings could be activated to form some brand attitude or purchase intention. Typical of advertising for many everyday, low-involvement purchases such as many consumer packaged goods: soap, cereal, toothpaste, and chewing gum. See also *Elaboration Likelihood Model*.

persona   A real or imaginary spokesperson who lends some voice or tone to an advertisement or commercial.

personal communication   Marketing activities that include all person-to-person contact with customers.

personal processes   The three internal, human operations—perception, learning, and motivation—that govern the way consumers discern raw data (stimuli) and translate them into feelings, thoughts, beliefs, and actions.

personal selling   A sales method based on person-to-person contact, such as by a salesperson at a retail establishment or by a telephone solicitor.

persuasion   A change in belief, attitude, or behavioral intention caused by a message (such as advertising or personal selling).

philanthropy   Support for a cause without any commercial incentive.

photographers   The artists who use cameras to create visuals for advertisements.

physiological screens   The perceptual screens that use the five senses—sight, hearing, touch, taste, and smell—to detect incoming data and measure the dimension and intensity of the physical stimulus.

picture-caption copy   A type of body copy in which the story is told through a series of illustrations and captions rather than through the use of a copy block alone.

picture-window layout   Layout that employs a single, dominant visual that occupies between 60 and 70 percent of an advertisement's total area. Also known as *poster-style format* or *Ayer No. 1.*

podcast   Internet audio content streamed on demand.

point   In retailing, the place of business. In typography, the measurement of the size and height of a text character. There are 72 points to an inch.

point-of-purchase (P-O-P) materials   Materials set up at a retail location to build traffic, advertise the product, and promote impulse buying. Materials may include window displays, counter displays, floor and wall displays, streamers, and posters.

polybagging   Samples are delivered in plastic bags with the daily newspaper or a monthly magazine.

position   The way in which a product is ranked in the consumer's mind by the benefits it offers, by the way it is classified or differentiated from the competition, or by its relationship to certain target markets.

positioning strategy   An effective way to separate a particular brand from its competitors by associating that brand with a particular set of customer needs.

positively originated motives   Consumer's motivation to purchase and use a product based on a positive bonus that the product promises, such as sensory gratification, intellectual stimulation, or social approval.

post   An entry in a blog or internet forum.

postcards   Cards sent by advertisers to announce sales, offer discounts, or otherwise generate consumer traffic.

poster panel   See *billboards*.

poster-style format   Layout that employs a single, dominant visual that occupies between 60 and 70 percent of an advertisement's total area. Also known as *picture-window layout* and *Ayer No. 1.*

posters   For public relations purposes, signs that impart product information or other news of interest to consumers, or that are aimed at employee behavior, such as safety, courtesy, or waste reduction.

postindustrial age   Period of cataclysmic change, starting in about 1980, when people first became truly aware of the sensitivity of the environment in which we live.

postproduction phase   The finishing phase in commercial production—the period after recording and shooting when a radio or TV commercial is edited and sweetened with music and sound effects.

postpurchase dissonance   See *theory of cognitive dissonance*.

postpurchase evaluation   Determining whether a purchase has been a satisfactory or unsatisfactory one.

posttesting   Testing the effectiveness of an advertisement after it has been run.

preemption rates   Lower TV advertising rate that stations charge when the advertiser agrees to allow the station to sell its time to another advertiser willing to pay a higher rate.

preferred-position rate   A choice position for a newspaper or magazine ad for which a higher rate is charged.

preindustrial age   Period of time between the beginning of written history and roughly the start of the 19th century, during which the invention of paper and the printing press and increased literacy gave rise to the first forms of written advertising.

premium   An item offered free or at a bargain price to encourage the consumer to buy an advertised product.

preprinted inserts   Newspaper advertisements printed in advance by the advertiser and then delivered to the newspaper plant to be inserted into a specific edition. Preprints are inserted into the fold of the newspaper and look like a separate, smaller section of the paper.

preproduction phase   The period of time before the actual recording or shooting of a commercial—the planning phase in commercial production.

prerelationship stage   The initial stage in the client–agency relationship before they officially do business.

preroll   Refers to the placement of a video advertisement in front of a piece of online video content.

presenter commercial   A commercial format in which one person or character presents the product and sales message.

press agentry   The planning of activities and the staging of events to attract attention to new products or services and to generate publicity about the company or organization that will be of interest to the media.

press kit   A package of publicity materials used to give information to the press at staged events such as press conferences or open houses. Also, a package of sales material promoting a specific media vehicle. Also called a *media kit*.

press release   See *news release.*

pretesting   Testing the effectiveness of an advertisement for gaps or flaws in message content before recommending it to clients, often conducted through focus groups.

price advertising   Advertising emphasizing the value pricing of a brand or product.

price element   In the marketing mix, the amount charged for the good or service—including deals, discounts, terms, warranties, and so on. The factors affecting price are market demand, cost of production and distribution, competition, and corporate objectives.

primary circulation   The number of people who receive a publication, whether through direct purchase or subscription.

primary data   Research information gained directly from the marketplace.

primary demand   Consumer demand for a whole product category.

primary demand trend   The projection of future consumer demand for a whole product category based on past demand and other market influences.

primary motivation   The pattern of attitudes and activities that help people reinforce, sustain, or modify their social and self-image. An understanding of the primary motivation of individuals helps advertisers promote and sell goods and services.

primary research   Collecting primary data directly from the marketplace using qualitative or quantitative methods.

prime time   Highest level of TV viewing (8 p.m. to 11 p.m. EST).

print media   Any commercially published, printed medium, such as newspapers and magazines, that sells advertising space to a variety of advertisers.

print production process   The systematic process a layout for an ad or a brochure goes through from concept to final printing. The four major phases are preproduction, production, prepress, and printing and distribution.

printer   Business that employs or contracts with highly trained specialists who prepare artwork for reproduction, operate digital scanning machines to make color separations and plates, operate presses and collating machines, and run binderies.

privacy rights   Of or pertaining to an individual's right to prohibit personal information from being divulged to the public.

private labels   Personalized brands applied by distributors or dealers to products supplied by manufacturers. Private brands are typically sold at lower prices in large retail chain stores.

process   A planned series of actions or methods that take place sequentially, such as developing products, pricing them strategically, making them available to customers through a distribution network, and promoting them through sales and advertising activities.

product   The particular good or service a company sells. See also *product concept.*

product advertising   Advertising intended to promote goods and services; also a functional classification of advertising.

product concept   The consumer's perception of a product as a "bundle" of utilitarian and symbolic values that satisfy functional, social, psychological, and other wants and needs. Also, as an element of the creative mix used by advertisers to develop advertising strategy, it is the bundle of product values the advertiser presents to the consumer.

product element   The most important element of the marketing mix: the good or service being offered and the values associated with it—including the way the product is designed and classified, positioned, branded, and packaged.

product life cycle   Progressive stages in the life of a product—including introduction, growth, maturity, and decline—that affect the way a product is marketed and advertised.

product placement   Paying a fee to have a product included in a movie.

production phase   An element of creative strategy. The whole physical process of producing ads and commercials; also the particular phase in the process when the recording and shooting of commercials is done.

professional advertising   Advertising directed at individuals who are normally licensed to operate under a code of ethics or set of professional standards.

program rating   The percentage of TV households in an area that are tuned in to a specific program.

program-length advertisement (PLA)   A long-form television commercial that may run as long as an hour; also called an *infomercial.*

programmatic advertising   Advertising in which computers make decisions about what ads are inserted in what content providers. Advertisers bid for audiences based on their willingness to pay and the demographic match of audiences on content sites.

programming format   The genre of music or other programming style that characterizes and differentiates radio stations from each other (i.e., contemporary hit radio, country, rock, etc.).

projective techniques   In marketing research, asking indirect questions or otherwise involving consumers in a situation where they can express feelings about the problem or product. The purpose is to get an understanding of people's underlying or subconscious feelings, attitudes, opinions, needs, and motives.

promoted account   Twitter social advertising that appears in a user's "Who to Follow" tab. They are used to increase followers as the primary audience are not current followers of the brand.

promoted trend   Twitter social advertising allowing companies to get their hashtag near the list of trending topics on Twitter, which can be seen by all users.

promoted tweet   Social advertising on Twitter that helps to raise the prominence of a tweet to the top of follower's feeds.

proof copy   A copy of the completed advertisement that is used to check for final errors and corrections.

prospective customers   People who are about to make an exchange or are considering it.

protocols   Refers to the digital message sent between web browser and website server in an effort to communicate with each other.

provocative headline   A type of headline written to provoke the reader's curiosity so that, to learn more, the reader will read the body copy.

psychographics   The grouping of consumers into market segments on the basis of psychological makeup—values, attitudes, personality, and lifestyle.

psychological screens   The perceptual screens consumers use to evaluate, filter, and personalize information according to subjective standards, primarily emotions and personality.

public affairs   All activities related to the community citizenship of an organization, including dealing with community officials and working with regulatory bodies and legislative groups.

public notices   For a nominal fee, newspapers carry these legal changes in business, personal relationships, public governmental reports, notices by private citizens and organizations, and financial reports.

public relations (PR)   The strategic management of the relationships and communications that individuals and organizations have with other groups (called *publics*) for the purpose of creating mutual goodwill. The primary role of public relations is to manage a company's reputation and help build public consent for its enterprises.

public relations activities   Publicity, press agentry, sponsorships, special events, and public relations advertising used to create public awareness and credibility—at low cost—for the firm.

public relations advertising   Advertising that attempts to improve a company's relationship with its publics (labor, government, customers, suppliers, etc.).

public service messages   Advertising created by professionals who volunteer their services to support a valued cause or charity.

publicity   The generation of news about a person, product, or service that appears in broadcast or print media.

publics   In PR terminology, employees, customers, stockholders, competitors, suppliers, or general population of customers are all considered one of the organization's publics.

puffery   Exaggerated, subjective claims that can't be proven true or false such as "the best," "premier," or "the only way to fly."

pull strategy   Marketing, advertising, and sales promotion activities aimed at inducing trial purchase and repurchase by consumers.

pulsing   Mixing continuity and flighting strategies in media scheduling.

purchase occasion   A method of segmenting markets on the basis of *when* consumers buy and use a good or service.

push money (PM)   A monetary inducement for retail salespeople to push the sale of particular products. Also called *spiffs*.

push strategy   Marketing, advertising, and sales promotion activities aimed at getting products into the dealer pipeline and accelerating sales by offering inducements to dealers, retailers, and salespeople. Inducements might include introductory price allowances, distribution allowances, and advertising dollar allowances to stock the product and set up displays.

qualitative research   Research that tries to determine market variables according to unquantifiable criteria such as attitudes, beliefs, and lifestyle.

quantitative research   Research that tries to determine market variables according to reliable, hard statistics about specific market conditions or situations.

question headline   A type of headline that asks the reader a question.

radio or podcast personality   The host of a broadcast or podcast show.

random probability samples   A sampling method in which every unit in the population universe is given an equal chance of being selected for the research.

rate base   With magazines, the circulation figure on which the publisher bases its rates.

rate card   A document provided by a publication that communicates to advertisers relevant information about the costs of advertising, policies, requirements, and deadlines.

rating   The percentage of homes or individuals exposed to an advertising medium.

rating services   These services measure the program audiences of TV and radio stations for advertisers and broadcasters by picking a representative sample of the market and furnishing data on the size and characteristics of the viewers or listeners.

rational appeals Marketing appeals that are directed at the consumer's practical, functional need for the product or service.

rationale See *message strategy*.

reach The total number of *different* people or households exposed to an advertising schedule during a given time, usually four weeks. Reach measures the *unduplicated* extent of audience exposure to a media vehicle and may be expressed either as a percentage of the total market or as a raw number.

readers per copy (RPC) Variable used to determine the total reach of a given print medium. RPC is multiplied by the number of vendor and subscription sales to determine the total audience size.

reading notice A variation of a display ad designed to look like editorial matter. It is sometimes charged at a higher space rate than normal display advertising, and the law requires that the word *advertisement* appear at the top.

real-time bidding Programmatic advertising in which audiences for display ads are reached through an auction or bidding process where advertisers who will pay the highest amount get priority.

rebates Cash refunds on items from cars to household appliances.

recall tests Posttesting methods used to determine the extent to which an advertisement and its message have been noticed, read, or watched.

receiver In oral communication, this party decodes the message to understand it and responds by formulating a new idea, encodes it, and sends it back.

recency planning Erwin Ephron's theory that most advertising works by influencing the brand choice of consumers who are ready to buy, suggesting that continuity of advertising is most important.

recruitment advertising A special type of advertising, most frequently found in the classified sections of daily newspapers and typically the responsibility of a personnel department aimed at attracting employment applications.

reference groups People we try to emulate or whose approval concerns us.

regional advertiser Company that operates in one part of the country and markets exclusively to that region.

regional advertising Advertising used by companies that market their products, goods, or services in a limited geographic region.

regional agency Advertising agency that focuses on the production and placement of advertising suitable for regional campaigns.

regional publications Magazines targeted to a specific area of the country, such as the West or the South.

regular price-line advertising A type of retail advertising designed to inform consumers about the services available or the wide selection and quality of merchandise offered at regular prices.

relationship marketing Creating, maintaining, and enhancing long-term relationships with customers and other stakeholders that result in exchanges of information and other things of mutual value.

reliability An important characteristic of research test results. For a test to be reliable, it must be repeatable, producing the same result each time it is administered.

reputation management In public relations, the name of the long-term strategic process to manage the standing of the firm with various publics.

reseller markets Individuals or companies that buy products for the purpose of reselling them.

resellers Businesses that buy products from manufacturers or wholesalers and then resell the merchandise to consumers or other buyers; also called *middlemen*. These businesses do not change or modify the goods before they resell them. Resellers make their profits by selling the goods they buy for more than they paid. The most common examples of resellers are retail stores and catalog retailers. Internet retailers comprise a growing portion of the reseller business segment.

resources (axis) A term in the Values and Lifestyles (VALS) typology relating to the range of psychological, physical, demographic, and material capacities that consumers can draw upon. The resources axis includes education, income, self-confidence, health, eagerness to buy, and energy level.

retail advertising Advertising sponsored by retail stores and businesses.

retainer method See *straight-fee method*.

retargeting ads Display ads served to an internet user on the basis of his or her online behaviors.

RFM formula The RFM formula is a mathematical model that provides marketers with a method to determine the most reliable customers in a company's database, according to Recency, Frequency, and Monetary variables.

rich mail Technology that allows graphics, video, and audio to be included in an e-mail message.

rich-media advertising The graphical animations and ads with audio and video elements that overlay the web page or even float over the page. Most common types include animated banners, interstitials, superstitials, and rich mail.

roadblocking Buying simultaneous airtime on all four television networks.

run of paper See *ROP advertising rates*.

run of station (ROS) Leaving placement of radio spots up to the station in order to achieve a lower ad rate.

run-of-paper (ROP) advertising rates A term referring to a newspaper's normal discretionary right to place a given ad on any page or in any position it desires—in other words, where space permits. Most newspapers make an effort to place an ad in the position requested by the advertiser.

sale advertising A type of retail advertising designed to stimulate the movement of particular merchandise or generally increase store traffic by placing the emphasis on special reduced prices.

sales letters The most common form of direct mail. Sales letters may be typewritten, typeset and printed, printed with a computer insert (such as your name), or fully computer typed.

sales promotion   A direct inducement offering extra incentives all along the marketing route—from manufacturers through distribution channels to customers—to accelerate the movement of the product from the producer to the consumer.

sales promotion department   In larger agencies, staff who produce dealer ads, window posters, point-of-purchase displays, and dealer sales material.

sales test   A useful measure of advertising effectiveness when advertising is the dominant element, or the only variable, in the company's marketing plan. Sales tests are more suited for gauging the effectiveness of campaigns than of individual ads or components of ads.

sales-target objectives   Marketing objectives that relate to a company's sales. They should be specific as to product and market, quantified as to time and amount, and realistic. They may be expressed in terms of total sales volume; sales by product, market segment, or customer type; market share; growth rate of sales volume; or gross profit.

sample   A portion of the population selected by market researchers to represent the appropriate targeted population. Also, a free trial of a product.

sample unit   The actual individuals chosen to be surveyed or studied.

sampling   Offering consumers a free trial of the product, hoping to convert them to habitual use.

sans serif   A type group that is characterized by a lack of serifs.

satellite radio   An analogue or digital radio signal that is relayed through one or more satellites.

SAU   See *standard advertising unit*.

script   Format for radio and television copywriting resembling a two-column list showing dialog and/or visuals.

seal   A type of certification mark offered by such organizations as the Good Housekeeping Institute and Underwriters' Laboratories when a product meets standards established by these institutions. Seals provide an independent, valued endorsement for the advertised product.

search engines   Websites that are devoted to finding and retrieving requested information from the World Wide Web. Because search engines are the gatekeepers to information on the internet, they are extremely popular with advertisers.

search-results page   The list of potential links that are returned after a query on a search tool bar or website.

secondary (pass-along) readership   The number of people who read a publication in addition to the primary purchasers.

secondary data   Information that has previously been collected or published.

selective demand   Consumer demand for the particular advantages of one brand over another.

selective distribution   Strategy of limiting the distribution of a product to select outlets in order to reduce distribution and promotion costs.

self-mailer   Any type of direct-mail piece that can travel by mail without an envelope. Usually folded and secured by a staple or a seal, self-mailers have a special blank space for the prospect's name and address.

serif   The most popular type group that is distinguished by smaller lines or tails called serifs that finish the ends of the main character strokes and by variations in the thickness of the strokes.

services   A bundle of benefits that may or may not be physical, that are temporary in nature, and that come from the completion of a task.

session   The time when the recording and mixing of a radio commercial take place.

share   The percentage of homes with TV sets in use (HUT) tuned to a specific program.

share of market/share of voice method   A method of allocating advertising funds based on determining the firm's goals for a certain share of the market and then applying a slightly higher percentage of industry advertising dollars to the firm's budget.

short rate   The rate charged to advertisers that, during the year, fail to fulfill the amount of space for which they have contracted. This is computed by determining the difference between the standard rate for the lines run and the discount rate contracted.

short-term manipulative criticisms   Criticisms of advertising that focus on the style of advertising (e.g., that it is manipulative or deceptive).

showing   A traditional term referring to the relative number of outdoor posters used during a contract period, indicating the intensity of market coverage. For example, a 100 showing provides an even and thorough coverage of the entire market.

signature cut   See *logotype*.

situation analysis   A factual statement of the organization's current situation and how it got there. It includes relevant facts about the company's history, growth, products and services, sales volume, share of market, competitive status, market served, distribution system, past advertising programs, results of market research studies, company capabilities, and strengths and weaknesses.

slice of life   A type of commercial consisting of a dramatization of a real-life situation in which the product is tried and becomes the solution to a problem.

slogan   A standard company statement (also called a *tagline* or a *themeline*) for advertisements, salespeople, and company employees. Slogans have two basic purposes: to provide continuity for a campaign and to reduce a key theme or idea to a brief, memorable positioning statement.

slotting allowances   Fees that manufacturers pay to retailers for the privilege of obtaining shelf or floor space for a new product.

social bookmarking   A method for internet users to organize, store, manage, and search for online resources.

social classes   Traditional divisions in societies by sociologists—upper, upper-middle, lower-middle, and so on—who believed that people in the same social class tended toward similar attitudes, status symbols, and spending patterns.

social cognitive theory   Albert Bandura's theory describing how people learn from observing the rewards or punishments that accrue to others when they perform behaviors.

social listening   A way for companies to aggregate and analyze online posts about a specific key term.

social media   Electronic communication through which users create online communities.

social responsibility   Acting in accordance with what society views as best for the welfare of people in general or for a specific community of people.

software as a service (SaaS)   A software delivery model in which software and associated data are centrally hosted on the cloud or the internet.

source   In oral communication, this party formulates the idea, encodes it as a message, and sends it via some channel to the receiver.

spam   Unsolicited, mass e-mail advertising for a product or service that is sent by an unknown entity to a purchased mailing list or newsgroup.

special events   Scheduled meetings, parties, and demonstrations aimed at creating awareness and understanding for a product or company.

spectaculars   Giant electronic signs that usually incorporate movement, color, and flashy graphics to grab the attention of viewers in high-traffic areas.

speculative presentation   An agency's presentation of the advertisement it proposes using in the event it is hired. It is usually made at the request of a prospective client and is often not paid for by the client.

speechwriting   Function of a public relations practitioner to write speeches for stockholder meetings, conferences, conventions, etc.

spiff   See *push money.*

spillover media   Foreign media aimed at a national population that are inadvertently received by a substantial number of the consumers in a neighboring country.

split runs   A feature of many newspapers (and magazines) that allows advertisers to test the comparative effectiveness of two different advertising approaches by running two different ads of identical size, but different content, in the same or different press runs on the same day.

sponsor   The company or organization ultimately responsible for the message and distribution of an advertisement. Although the sponsor is often not the author, the sponsor typically pays for the creation of the ad and its distribution.

sponsored links   Paid listings in a search engine. Sponsored links are contrasted with organic listings, which reflect the search engine's best guess of what is relevant to the searcher.

sponsorial consumers   A group of decision makers at the sponsor's company or organization who decide if an ad will run or not, typically composed of executives and managers who have the responsibility for approving and funding a campaign.

sponsorship   The presentation of a radio or TV program, or an event, or even a website, by a sole advertiser. The advertiser is often responsible for the program content and the cost of production as well as the advertising. This is generally so costly that single sponsorships are usually limited to TV specials.

spot announcements   An individual commercial message run between programs but having no relationship to either. Spots may be sold nationally or locally. They must be purchased by contacting individual stations directly.

spot radio   National advertisers' purchase of airtime on individual stations. Buying spot radio affords advertisers great flexibility in their choice of markets, stations, airtime, and copy.

spots   The term "spots" refers to radio ads

stakeholders   In relationship marketing, customers, employees, centers of influence, stockholders, the financial community, and the press. Different stakeholders require different types of relationships.

standard advertising unit (SAU)   A system of standardized newspaper advertisement sizes that can be accepted by all standard-sized newspapers without consideration of their precise format or page size. This system allows advertisers to prepare one advertisement in a particular size or SAU and place it in various newspapers regardless of the format.

standard-size newspaper   The standard newspaper size, measuring approximately 22 inches deep and 13 inches wide and divided into six columns.

standardized outdoor advertising   Specialized system of outdoor advertising structures located scientifically to deliver an advertiser's message to an entire market.

statement stuffers   Advertisements enclosed in the monthly customer statements mailed by department stores, banks, utilities, or oil companies.

stimulus   Physical data that can be received through the senses.

stock posters   A type of outdoor advertising consisting of ready-made 30-sheet posters, available in any quantity and often featuring the work of first-class artists and lithographers.

storyboard   A sheet preprinted with a series of 8 to 20 blank frames in the shape of TV screens, which includes text of the commercial, sound effects, and camera views.

storyboard rough   A rough layout of a television commercial in storyboard form.

straight announcement   The oldest type of radio or television commercial, in which an announcer delivers a sales message directly into the microphone or on camera or does so off screen while a slide or film is shown on screen.

straight-fee (retainer) method   A method of compensation for ad agency services in which a straight fee, or *retainer,* is based on a cost-plus-fixed-fees formula. Under this system, the agency estimates the amount of personnel time required by the client, determines the cost of that personnel, and multiplies by some factor.

straight-sell copy   A type of body copy in which the text immediately explains or develops the headline and visual in a straightforward attempt to sell the product.

streaming radio   Radio stations that broadcast their content over the internet.

streaming video   Video content received by audiences via an internet or wireless connection, rather than through the broadcast airways or cable channels.

style sheet   Style sheets contain saved formats for typography, spacing, design, and arrangements in desktop publishing. Microsoft refers to style sheets as templates in its popular software programs.

subculture   A segment within a culture that shares a set of meanings, values, or activities that differ in certain respects from those of the overall culture.

subhead   Secondary headline in advertisements that may appear above or below the headline or in the text of the ad. Subheads are usually set in a type size smaller than the headline but larger than the body copy or text type size. They may also appear in boldface type or in a different ink color.

subliminal advertising   Advertisements with messages (often sexual) supposedly embedded in illustrations just below the threshold of perception.

substantiation   Evidence that backs up cited survey findings or scientific studies that the FTC may request from a suspected advertising violator.

Sunday supplement   A newspaper-distributed Sunday magazine. Sunday supplements are distinct from other sections of the newspaper because they are printed by rotogravure on smoother paper stock.

suppliers   People and organizations that assist both advertisers and agencies in the preparation of advertising materials, such as photography, illustration, printing, and production.

survey   A basic method of quantitative research. To get people's opinions, surveys may be conducted in person, by mail, on the telephone, or via the internet.

sweepstakes   A sales promotion activity in which prizes are offered based on a chance drawing of entrants' names. The purpose is to encourage consumption of the product by creating consumer involvement.

SWOT analysis   An acronym for internal *strengths* and *weaknesses* and external *opportunities* and *threats,* which represent the four categories used by advertising managers when reviewing a marketing plan. The SWOT analysis briefly restates the company's current situation, reviews the target market segments, itemizes the long- and short-term marketing objectives, and cites decisions regarding market positioning and the marketing mix.

synergy   An effect achieved when the sum of the parts is greater than that expected from simply adding together the individual components.

tabloid newspaper   A newspaper sized generally about half as deep as a standard-sized newspaper; it is usually about 14 inches deep and 11 inches wide.

tactics   The precise details of a company's marketing strategy that determine the specific short-term actions that will be used to achieve its marketing objectives.

tagline   See *slogan.*

take-ones   In transit advertising, pads of business reply cards or coupons, affixed to interior advertisements for an extra charge, that allow passengers to request more detailed information, send in application blanks, or receive some other product benefit.

talent   The actors in commercials.

target audience   The specific group of individuals to whom the advertising message is directed.

target market   The market segment or group within the market segment toward which all marketing activities will be directed.

target marketing process   The sequence of activities aimed at assessing various market segments, designating certain ones as the focus of marketing activities, and designing marketing mixes to communicate with and make sales to these targets.

taxicab exteriors   In transit advertising, internally illuminated, two-sided posters positioned on the roofs of taxis. Some advertising also appears on the doors or rear.

tearsheet   The printed ad cut out and sent by the publisher to the advertiser as a proof of the ad's print quality and that it was published.

technical   One of the three components of message strategy, it refers to the preferred-execution approach and mechanical outcome including budget and scheduling limitations.

telemarketing   Selling products and services by using the telephone to contact prospective customers.

telephone sales   See *telemarketing.*

teleprompter   A two-way mirror mounted on the front of a studio video camera that reflects moving text to be read by the speaker being taped.

television households (TVHH)   Households with TV sets.

terminal posters   One-sheet, two-sheet, and three-sheet posters in many bus, subway, and commuter train stations as well as in major train and airline terminals. They are usually custom designed and include such attention getters as floor displays, island showcases, illuminated signs, dioramas (three-dimensional scenes), and clocks with special lighting and moving messages.

termination stage   The ending of a client–agency relationship.

test market   An isolated geographic area used to introduce and test the effectiveness of a product, ad campaign, or promotional campaign, prior to a national rollout.

testimonials   The use of satisfied customers and celebrities to endorse a product in advertising.

text   See *body copy.*

text paper   Range of less expensive papers that are lightweight. More porous versions are used in printing newspapers, and finer, glossier versions are used for quality printed materials like magazines and brochures.

text type   The smaller type used in the body copy of an advertisement.

themeline   See *slogan.*

theory of cognitive dissonance   The theory that people try to justify their behavior by reducing the degree to which their impressions or beliefs are inconsistent with reality.

poster panel   See *billboards.*

third-party ad server   Refers to the companies that help manage online advertising for the entire online ecosystem.

thumbnail A rough, rapidly produced pencil sketch that is used for trying out ideas.

total audience The total number of homes reached by some portion of a TV program. This figure is normally broken down to determine the distribution of the audience into demographic categories.

total audience plan (TAP) A radio advertising package rate that guarantees a certain percentage of spots in the better dayparts.

total bus A special transit advertising buy that covers the entire exterior of a bus, including the front, rear, sides, and top.

trade advertising The advertising of goods and services to middlemen to stimulate wholesalers and retailers to buy goods for resale to their customers or for use in their own businesses.

trade concentration More products being sold by fewer retailers.

trade deals Short-term dealer discounts on the cost of a product or other dollar inducements to sell a product.

trade promotions See *push strategy.*

trade shows Exhibitions where manufacturers, dealers, and buyers of an industry's products can get together for demonstrations and discussion; expose new products, literature, and samples to customers; and meet potential new dealers for their products.

trademark Any word, name, symbol, device, or any combination thereof adopted and used by manufacturers or merchants to identify their goods and distinguish them from those manufactured or sold by others.

transformational motives Positively originated motives that promise to "transform" the consumer through sensory gratification, intellectual stimulation, and social approval. Also called *reward motives.*

transit advertising An out-of-home medium that actually includes three separate media forms: inside cards; outside posters; and station, platform, and terminal posters.

transit shelter advertising A newer form of out-of-home media, where advertisers can buy space on bus shelters and on the backs of bus-stop seats.

transnational (global) markets Consumer, business, and government markets located in foreign countries.

trending Refers to the topics that are currently being talked about online.

trial close In ad copy, requests for the order that are made before the close in the ad.

TV households (TVHH) The number of households in a market area that own television sets.

type families Related typefaces in which the basic design remains the same but in which variations occur in the proportion, weight, and slant of the characters. Variations commonly include light, medium, bold, extra bold, condensed, extended, and italic.

typography The art of selecting, setting, and arranging type.

U.S. Patent and Trademark Office Bureau within the U.S. Department of Commerce that registers and protects patents and trademarks.

UHF (ultrahigh frequency) Television channels 14 through 83; about half of the U.S. commercial TV stations are UHF.

unfair advertising According to the FTC, advertising that causes a consumer to be "unjustifiably injured" or that violates public policy.

Universal Product Code (UPC) An identifying series of vertical bars with a 12-digit number that adorns every consumer packaged good.

universe An entire target population.

usage rates The extent to which consumers use a product: light, medium, or heavy.

user status Six categories into which consumers can be placed, which reflect varying degrees of loyalties to certain brands and products. The categories are *sole users, semisole users, discount users, aware nontriers, trial/rejectors,* and *repertoire users.*

user-generated content (UGC) Media content that is produced by consumers, not by companies.

utility A product's ability to provide both symbolic or psychological want satisfaction and functional satisfaction. A product's problem-solving potential may include form, time, place, or possession utility.

validity An important characteristic of a research test. For a test to be valid, it must reflect the true status of the market.

value-based thinking A style of thinking where decisions are based on intuition, values, and ethical judgments.

venue marketing A form of sponsorship that links a sponsor to a physical site such as a stadium, arena, auditorium, or racetrack.

verbal Words, written or spoken.

vertical cooperative advertising Co-op advertising in which the manufacturer provides the ad and pays a percentage of the cost of placement.

vertical marketing system (VMS) A centrally programmed and managed system that supplies or otherwise serves a group of stores or other businesses.

vertical publications Business publications aimed at people within a specific industry; for example, *Restaurants & Institutions.*

VHF (very high frequency) Television channels 2 through 13; about half of the U.S. commercial TV stations are VHF.

video news release (VNR) A news or feature story prepared in video form and offered free to TV stations.

viral marketing The internet version of word-of-mouth advertising e-mail.

visualization The creative point in advertising where the search for the "big idea" takes place. It includes the task of analyzing the problem, assembling any and all pertinent information, and developing some verbal or visual concept of how to communicate what needs to be said.

visuals All of the picture elements that are placed into an advertisement.

voice-over In television advertising, the spoken copy or dialogue delivered by an announcer who is not seen but whose voice is heard.

volume discount Discount given to advertisers for purchasing print space or broadcast time in bulk quantities.

volume segmentation Defining consumers as light, medium, or heavy users of products.

wants Desires learned during a person's lifetime.

Warrior role A role in the creative process that overcomes excuses, idea killers, setbacks, and obstacles to bring a creative concept to realization.

web browser Computer program that provides computer users with a graphical interface to the World Wide Web.

web design houses Art/computer studios that employ specialists who understand the intricacies of HTML and Java programming languages and can design ads and internet web pages that are both effective and cost efficient.

web page A single page out of an online publication of the World Wide Web, known as a website. Websites are made up of one or more web pages and allow individuals or companies to provide information and services with the public through the internet.

website An internet destination designed to be read in a web browser.

weekly newspapers Newspapers that are published once a week and characteristically serve readers in small urban or suburban areas or farm communities with exclusive emphasis on local news and advertising.

wiki A website whose users can add, modify, or delete its content via a browser using a rich text editor.

word of mouth (WOM) The passing of information from one individual to another individual.

World Wide Web (WWW) A hypertext-based, distributed information system designed to be interpreted by web browsers such as Internet Explorer or Mozilla Firefox.

writing paper Form of plain, lightweight paper commonly used for printing fliers and for letterhead.

name index

n for notes

company index

subject index

A

AAAA. *see* American Association of Advertising Agencies (4A's), 98, 133, 475
ABC (Audit Bureau of Circulation), 296
Absence of externalities, 66, 72, 90
Abundance principle, 71
Account(s)
   management, 128
   planning, 129
   supervisors, 128
Account executives (AEs), 128
Account management, 128
Account planning, 129
   research and, 129
Account supervisors, 128
Accountable relationship, 14
Action, 339
   in creative pyramid, 339–340
   DAGMAR marketing objective setting system, 253
Action advertising, 8, 28; *see also* Direct-response advertising
Actual consumers, 11
Ad exposure, 310
Ad Lab
   artist, role of, 358
   audio audiences, measurement of, 450
   buying traditional local media, 286
   co-op marriage, 118
   color, psychological impact of, 329
   consumer behavior application to ad creation, 173
   corporate advertising, 597
   creative gymnasium, 343
   direct mail packages, 557
   economic effect of advertising on sales, 274
   green advertising, 585
   GRP and TV market selection, 444
   Internet ratings, 472
   legal counsel, 84
   literary form, advertising as, 12
   magazines and creative mix, 398
   market segmentation, 192
   media selection, 309
   native advertising, 403
   newspapers and creative mix, 412
   out-of-home advertising, 522
   perceived value and choice, 160
   product element, 197
   promotion element, 211
   push/pull strategies, 568
   size of agency business, 123
   Starbucks and place element, 207
   strategies of marketing warfare, 255
   TV ratings, 440
   typeface selection, 364
Ad network, 473

Added value
   Internet packages, 486
   merchandising services, 406
Addressable media, 8
AdSense, Google, 79, 315, 479, 485–486
Advertiser-supported syndication, 436
Advertisers (clients), 112–113; *see also* Advertising agencies
   client–agency relationship, 134–138
      accountability, 133
      being a better client, 137
      client obtainment, 134–135
      factors affecting, 136–138
      stages in, 135–136
   cooperative, 117–118
   expenditures on advertising (2007–2017), 140
   Hispanic media, 187
   local, 113–117
   national, 119–120
   presentation to, 588
   regional, 118–119, 404
   regulatory issues, 84–85
   self-regulation by, 101
   social responsibility, 79
   target audience, 19
   top newspaper advertisers, 410
   transnational, 121–123
   understanding, 114
Advertising, 7–8, 210; *see also* Corporate/institutional advertising; *specific topics*
   advocacy advertising, 604
   audience of, 8
   augmented reality advertising, 540
   banner ads, 491
   brands and, 3
   business cycle and, 70–71
   campaigns
      celebrity-based, 63–64
      Coca-Cola, 35–36
      creativity and "boom" in, 329–330
      IMC. *see* My IMC Campaign
      McDonald's, 111–112
      Mountain Dew, 249–250
      objectives and strategy, 308–309
      planning, 259–262
      posttesting methods, 236–238
      pretesting methods, 235–236
   children, 87, 191, 437
   cinema, 538–540
   classification, 19
   classified, 413
   color, 416
   as communication form, 8–9
   comparative, 91
   competition, 68–69

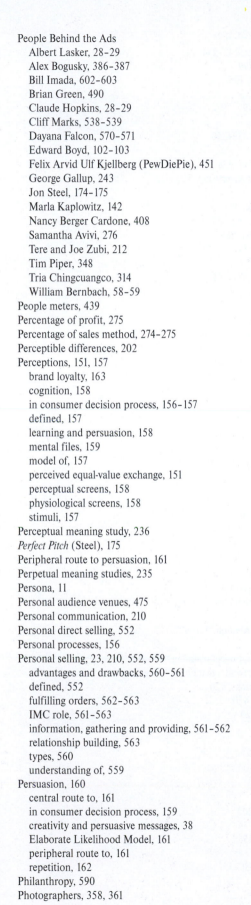